HOLT
Sociology

The Study of Human Relationships

W. LaVerne Thomas

HOLT, RINEHART AND WINSTON

A Harcourt Education Company

Austin • Orlando • Chicago • New York • Toronto • London • San Diego

Cover:
Cover art was created by Bob Commander
and illustrates three people with open arms.

Cover Photo:
main image, Bob Commander/Stock Illustration
Source; inset image, Ray Boudreau

The Author

W. LaVerne (Verne) Thomas has taught courses in the behavioral sciences at Wheat Ridge High School, Wheat Ridge, Colorado, since 1960. He received his B.A. education at Nebraska Wesleyan University and earned his M.A. in sociology at the University of Denver. Before his retirement, he was active in several professional organizations, including the Ameican Sociological Association and the National Education Association. Since his retirement, he enjoys reading, traveling, and camping in the Rocky Mountains.

Content Reviewers

Dr. Kenneth Allan
University of North Carolina
at Greensboro
*theory, culture, social
psychology, and religion*

Dr. Scott Beck
East Tennessee State University
*stratification, cross-national
economics, and gerontology*

Dr. Harold Dorton, Jr
Southwest Texas State University
*industrial sociology, theory, and
social psychology*

Dr. Bob Edwards
East Carolina University
*organizations, political sociology,
social movements, and environment*

Dr. Tracey Steele
Wright State University
*criminology, gender, and
medical sociology*

Dr. Yung-Mei Tsai
Texas Tech University
*urban sociology, globalization,
and technology and society*

Dr. Scott Phillips
University of Houston
*crime, deviance, law, and
conflict management*

Educational Reviewers

Lance L. Beehler
Mishawaka High School
Mishawaka, Indiana

Anna Bryant
Mills E. Godwin High School
Richmond, Virginia

Douglas Fralinger
Highland High School
Highland, Indiana

John Hanson
Linn-Mar High School
Marion, Iowa

Mary-Elizabeth Maynard
Leominster High School
Leominster, Massachusetts

Jennifer Matasovsky
Warren Central High School
Indianapolis, Indiana

Glenn Mechem
Union High School
Union, Missouri

Keith A. Moser
Seguin High School
Seguin, Texas

Sarah Quintin-Sheridan
Abington Heights High School
Clarks Summit, Pennsylvania

It's All About

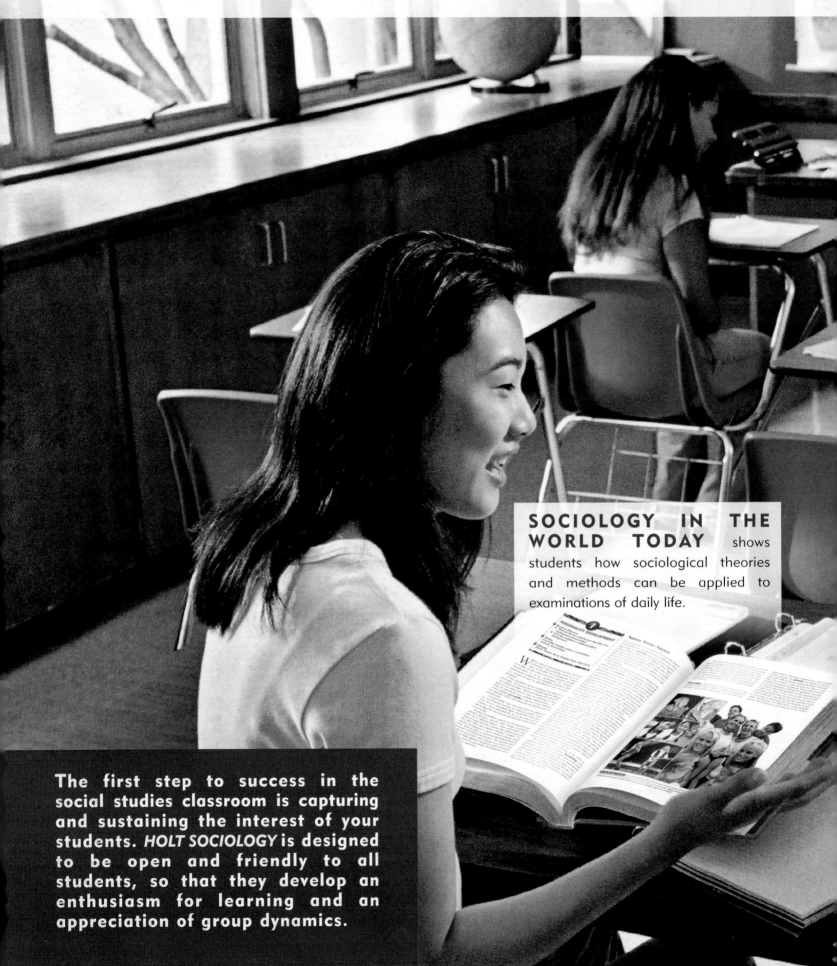

SOCIOLOGY IN THE WORLD TODAY shows students how sociological theories and methods can be applied to examinations of daily life.

The first step to success in the social studies classroom is capturing and sustaining the interest of your students. *HOLT SOCIOLOGY* is designed to be open and friendly to all students, so that they develop an enthusiasm for learning and an appreciation of group dynamics.

RELEVANCE

CNNfyi.com™ is a site designed to give students in grades 6–12 access to people, places, and environments around the globe while offering "real-world" articles, career and college resources, and online activities.

Technology that

go.hrw.com FOR STUDENTS

Your students can access interactive activities, homework help, up-to-date maps, and more when they visit **go.hrw.com** and type in the keywords they find in their text.

CHAPTER HOME PAGE

The Chapter Home Pages contain pre-screened enrichment links that extend content, teaching resources, and interactive activities that combine guided research with specific product-based projects. The Home Page is also directs students to Homework Practice Online, Holt Researcher, Holt Grapher and more!

ONLINE TEMPLATES

Your students can use these interactive templates to create newspapers, travel brochures, postcards, journals, creative works, and more. The instructional design of this tool allows students to do something with the content they have learned.

HOMEWORK PRACTICE

This helpful tool allows students to practice and review content by chapter anywhere there is a computer.

HRW ONLINE ATLAS

This helpful online tool contains over 300 well-rendered and clearly labeled country and state maps. The clean design and easy-to-use navigational tools make accessing information simple. These maps are continually updated so you can rest assured that you and your students have the latest and most accurate geographical content available. Maps are available in English and Spanish.

STATE HANDBOOKS

Visit **go.hrw.com** and find fun facts, state maps, flags, and statistics. There are also links to state-specific resources and products that are especially made for teachers and students.

Delivers Content

CNNfyi.com

At **CNNfyi.com**, students will love exploring news stories written by experienced journalists as well as student bureau reporters complete with links to homework help and lesson plans.

Named "Best Online Current Events Program" by techlearning.com!

CNN PRESENTS VIDEO LIBRARY

The **CNN PRESENTS** video collection tackles the issue of making content relevant to students head on. Real-world news stories enable students to see the connections between classroom curriculum and today's issues and events around the nation and the world.

CNN PRESENTS...

- **Sociology**
- **Psychology**
- **America: Yesterday and Today, Beginnings to 1914**
- **America: Yesterday and Today, 1850 to the Present**
- **America: Yesterday and Today, Modern Times**
- **Geography: Yesterday and Today**
- **World Cultures: Yesterday and Today**
- **American Government and Civics**
- **Economics**
- **September 11, 2001: Part 1**
- **September 11, 2001: Part 2**

Holt is proud to team up with CNN/TURNER LEARNING to provide you and your students with exceptional current and historical news videos and online resources that add depth and relevance to your daily instruction. This information collection takes your classroom to the far corners of the globe without students ever leaving their desks!

Unique Teacher's

go.hrw.com FOR TEACHERS

Throughout the *Annotated Teacher's Edition*, you'll find **Internet Connect** boxes that take you to specific chapter activities, links, current events, and more that correlate directly to the section you are teaching. Through **go.hrw.com** you'll find a wealth of teaching resources at your fingertips for fun, interactive lessons.

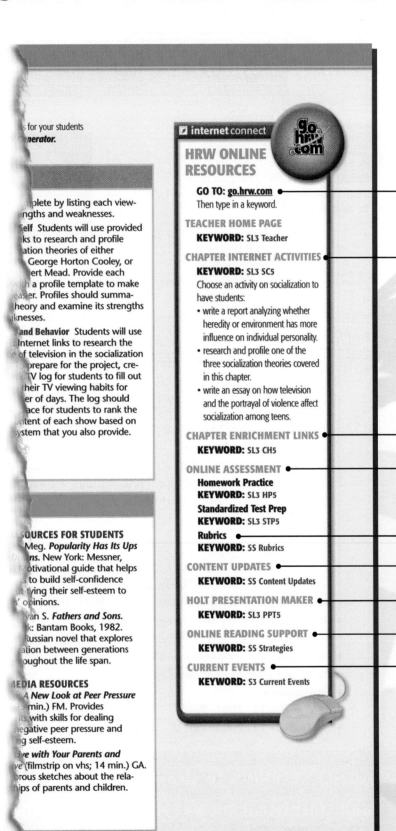

... for your students
...*nerator.*

...plete by listing each view-
...ngths and weaknesses.

...elf Students will use provided
...ks to research and profile
...ation theories of either
...George Horton Cooley, or
...ert Mead. Provide each
...h a profile template to make
...easier. Profiles should summa-
...heory and examine its strengths
...knesses.

...and Behavior Students will use
...Internet links to research the
...e of television in the socialization
...prepare for the project, cre-
...TV log for students to fill out
...heir TV viewing habits for
...er of days. The log should
...ace for students to rank the
...ntent of each show based on
...ystem that you also provide.

...OURCES FOR STUDENTS
...Meg. *Popularity Has Its Ups*
...ns. New York: Messner,
...otivational guide that helps
...s to build self-confidence
...t tying their self-esteem to
...' opinions.

...van S. *Fathers and Sons.*
...k: Bantam Books, 1982.
...Russian novel that explores
...ation between generations
...oughout the life span.

...EDIA RESOURCES
...*A New Look at Peer Pressure*
...min.) FM. Provides
...ts with skills for dealing
...negative peer pressure and
...ng self-esteem.

...*ve with Your Parents and*
...*ve* (filmstrip on vhs; 14 min.) GA.
...rous sketches about the rela-
...ips of parents and children.

internet connect

HRW ONLINE RESOURCES

GO TO: go.hrw.com
Then type in a keyword.

TEACHER HOME PAGE
KEYWORD: SL3 Teacher

CHAPTER INTERNET ACTIVITIES
KEYWORD: SL3 SC5
Choose an activity on socialization to have students:
- write a report analyzing whether heredity or environment has more influence on individual personality.
- research and profile one of the three socialization theories covered in this chapter.
- write an essay on how television and the portrayal of violence affect socialization among teens.

CHAPTER ENRICHMENT LINKS
KEYWORD: SL3 CH5

ONLINE ASSESSMENT
Homework Practice
KEYWORD: SL3 HP5
Standardized Test Prep
KEYWORD: SL3 STP5
Rubrics
KEYWORD: SS Rubrics

CONTENT UPDATES
KEYWORD: SS Content Updates

HOLT PRESENTATION MAKER
KEYWORD: SL3 PPT5

ONLINE READING SUPPORT
KEYWORD: SS Strategies

CURRENT EVENTS
KEYWORD: S3 Current Events

DIRECT LAUNCH TO CHAPTER ACTIVITIES

GUIDED ONLINE ACTIVITIES

LINKS FOR EVERY SECTION

INTERACTIVE PRACTICE AND REVIEW

RUBRICS FOR SUBJECTIVE GRADING

UP-TO-DATE INFORMATION

PRESENTATION SUPPORT

PRACTICE FOR READING SUCCESS

WEB RESOURCES FOR CURRENT ISSUES

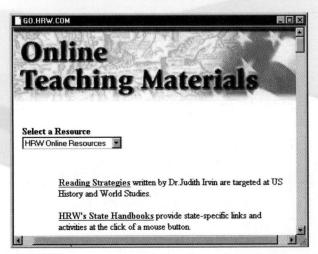

GO.HRW.COM

Online Teaching Materials

Select a Resource
HRW Online Resources ▾

Reading Strategies written by Dr. Judith Irvin are targeted at US History and World Studies.

HRW's State Handbooks provide state-specific links and activities at the click of a mouse button.

Management System

Everything you need is on one disc!

One-Stop Planner®
with Test Generator

ONE-STOP PLANNER CD-ROM WITH TEST GENERATOR

Holt brings you the most user-friendly management system in the industry with the **One-Stop Planner CD-ROM with Test Generator.** Plan and manage your lessons from this single disc containing all the teaching resources for **Holt Sociology,** valuable planning and assessment tools, and more.

- **Editable lesson plans**
- **Classroom Presentations**
- **Exam-view test generator**
- **Previews of all teaching and video resources**
- **Easy printing feature**
- **Direct launch to go.hrw.com**

Holt Sociology Program Components

Reading Support
- **Graphic Organizer Activities**
- **Reading Strategies for the Social Studies Classroom**
- **Mastering Critical Thinking Skills**

Research and Activities
- **Readings and Case Studies in Sociology**
- **Research Projects and Activities for Teaching Sociology**

Classroom Resources
- **Block Scheduling Handbook**
- **One-Stop Planner CD-ROM with Test Generator**
- **Teaching Transparencies with Teacher's Notes**

Review and Assessment
- **Alternative Assessment Handbook**
- **Chapter and Unit Tests**
- **Chapter Review Activities**
- **Social Studies Skills Review**
- **Study Skills and Writing Guide**

HOLT Sociology

The Study of Human Relationships

Contents

UNIT 1 Culture and Social Structure 1

Inuit children

U.S. sailors

American Indian mask

Students conducting a science experiment

Peer groups are important to the socialization of teenagers.

Neighborhood-watch programs
help to prevent crime.

Polo is a popular sport among some wealthier Americans.

Retired Americans are volunteering in greater numbers.

Many senior citizens exercise to remain active.

Children often learn important skills from their parents and relatives.

The Democratic and Republican Parties are the two largest political parties in the United States.

Large cities such as Singapore are centers of technology and business.

Occasionally people behave differently in large groups than they would as an individual.

New technology has changed the way people communicate.

REFERENCE SECTION

Sociology in the World

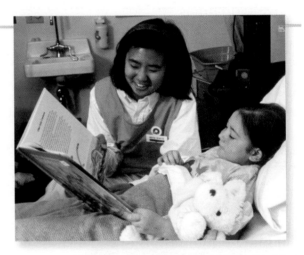
Many young Americans value volunteerism.

Long-distance phone card companies market their cards to immigrant groups.

Gerontologists work with senior citizens.

EXPLORING
Cultural Diversity

Some cultural practices in Fiji focus on food.

Case Studies

Amish family at the beach

Interdisciplinary Activities

Connecting TO

Mapping
SOCIAL FORCES

Immigration to the United States, 1900s (by region, in percentages)

Technology Activities

Skill-Building Activities

Skills Handbook

BUILDING
Social Studies Skills

Sociology in Action

Tables, Charts, and Graphs

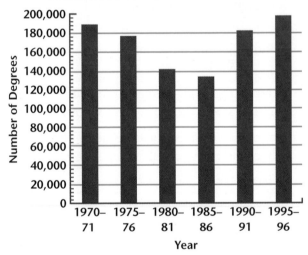

Social Science Bachelor's Degrees Awarded, 1970–71 to 1995–96*

*Note: These figures include the numbers of bachelor's degrees in history.
Source: *Digest of Educational Statistics, 2000*

Tables, Charts, and Graphs continued

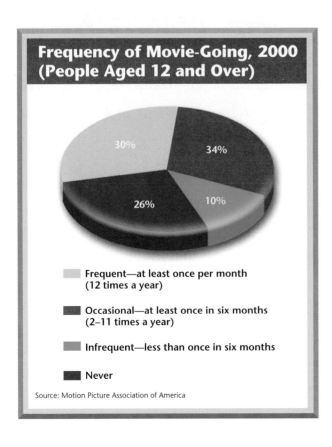

Frequency of Movie-Going, 2000 (People Aged 12 and Over)

34%
30%
26%
10%

Frequent—at least once per month (12 times a year)

Occasional—at least once in six months (2–11 times a year)

Infrequent—less than once in six months

Never

Source: Motion Picture Association of America

Tables, Charts, and Graphs continued

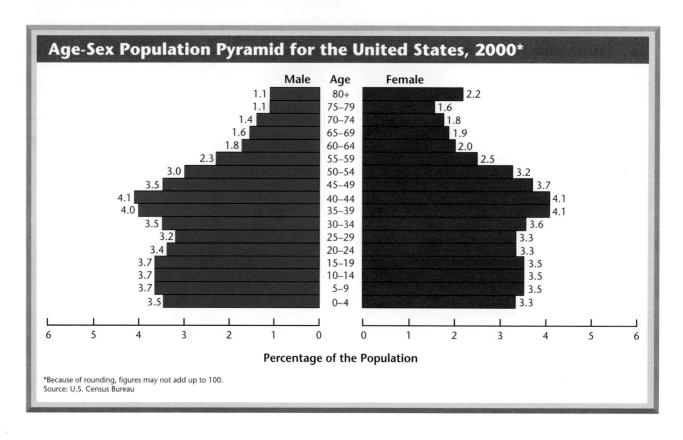

Age-Sex Population Pyramid for the United States, 2000*

Male	Age	Female
1.1	80+	2.2
1.1	75–79	1.6
1.4	70–74	1.8
1.6	65–69	1.9
1.8	60–64	2.0
2.3	55–59	2.5
3.0	50–54	3.2
3.5	45–49	3.7
4.1	40–44	4.1
4.0	35–39	4.1
3.5	30–34	3.6
3.2	25–29	3.3
3.4	20–24	3.3
3.7	15–19	3.5
3.7	10–14	3.5
3.7	5–9	3.5
3.5	0–4	3.3

Percentage of the Population

*Because of rounding, figures may not add up to 100.
Source: U.S. Census Bureau

Maps

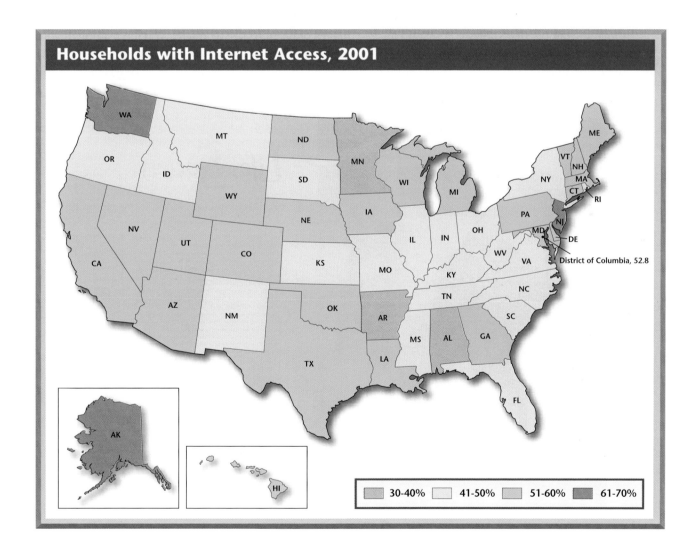

Households with Internet Access, 2001

District of Columbia, 52.8

30-40%   41-50%   51-60%   61-70%

How to Use
Your Textbook

Use the chapter opener to preview the material you are about to study.

Life in Society features an interesting topic or example that shows you that sociology is not just a collection of facts and figures, but a blend of many individual stories and adventures.

Why Sociology Matters is an exciting way for you to make connections between what you are reading in your sociology book and the world around you. Explore a topic that is relevant to our lives today by using CNNfyi.com connections.

Build on What You Know bridges the material you have studied in previous chapters with the material you are about to begin covering. As you read the Build on What you Know feature, take a few minutes to think about the topics that might apply to the chapter you are starting.

Truth or Fiction What's Your Opinion? puts you in the place of the sociologist looking at the society. In this section, you will be asked to respond to three general statements about the chapter. You should respond based on your own knowledge, and record your responses in your journal. There are no right or wrong answers, just your informed opinion.

Use these built-in tools to read for understanding.

Read to Discover questions begin each section of *Holt Sociology: The Study of Human Relationships*. These questions serve as your guide as you read through the section. Keep them in mind as you explore the section content.

Define and Identify terms are introduced at the beginning of each section. The terms will be defined in context.

Interpreting Visuals features accompany many of the book's rich images. Pictures are one of the most important primary sources sociologists can use to help them analyze societies and cultures. These features invite you to examine the images and answer questions about their content.

Interpreting Charts, Graphs, Tables, and Maps features accompany all of the graphics in the book. These features give you the opportunity to build social studies skills and support your understanding of sociology by using current statistical information.

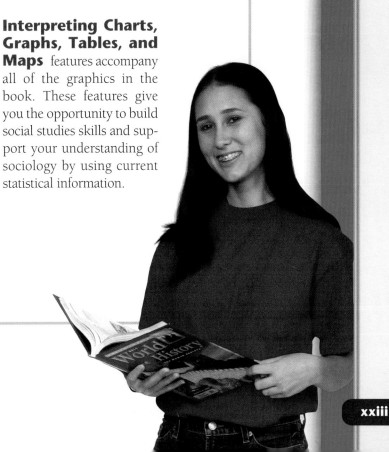

Use these review tools to pull together all the information you have learned.

Section Review:

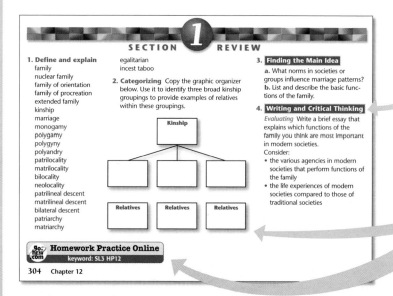

Writing and Critical Thinking activities allow you to explore a section topic in greater depth and build your skills.

Graphic Organizers will help you pull together important information from the section. You can complete the graphic organizer as a study tool to prepare for a test or writing assignment.

Homework Practice Online lets you log on to the HRW Go site to complete an interactive self-check.

Chapter Review:

Building Social Studies Skills activities will help you develop the skills you need to study sociology and to answer standardized-test questions.

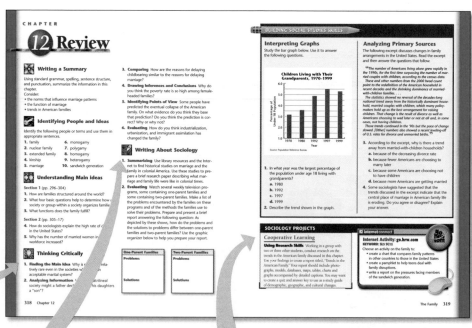

Thinking Critically activities help you develop the critical thinking skills you need to study sociology.

Writing About Sociology activities let you practice your writing skills to explore in more detail the topics you have studied in the chapter. The graphic organizers will also help you organize your ideas before you begin to write.

Sociology Projects are exciting and creative ways to explore your community and the world around you by conducting research projects. Some activities ask you to work cooperatively, and others include projects to complete on your own.

Homework Practice Online lets you log on for review anytime.

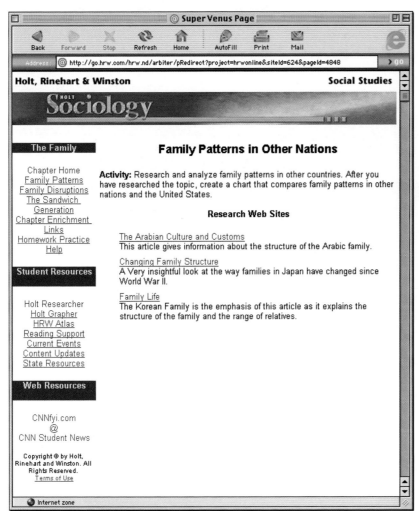

Internet Connect activities are just one part of the world of online learning experiences that awaits you on the HRW Go site. By exploring these online activities, you will take a journey through some of the richest sociological materials available on the World Wide Web. You can then use these resources to create real-world projects, such as newspapers, brochures, reports, and even your own Web site!

WHY SOCIOLOGY MATTERS

"The sociological imagination, I remind you, in considerable part consists of the capacity to shift from one perspective to another, and in the process to build up an adequate view of a total society and of its components. It is this imagination, of course, that sets off the social scientist from the mere technician."

C. Wright Mills

Sociology is the study of society. In order to understand society we must be able to see the world through the eyes of others. By using this sociological imagination you can understand the world around you.

Sociology and Your World

All you need to do is watch or read the news to see the importance of sociology. You have probably seen news stories about population growth, cultural differences, changes in family life, or social movements. How have these events affected your life? The Why Sociology Matters feature beginning every chapter of *Holt Sociology: The Study of Human Relationships* invites you to use the vast resources of CNNfyi.com or other current events sources to examine the importance of sociology. Through this feature you will be able to draw connections between what you are studying in your sociology book and the events that are taking place today.

Student reporters contribute to CNNfyi.com.

cnn_fav_ref.mov

CNNfyi.com

JANA JACOBS
CNN STUDENT BUREAU

CNN.com

Blind children share with sighted
CNN Student Bureau's Jana Jacobs reports on a program in Atlanta that brings sighted and blind children together (August 7)

00:00:00

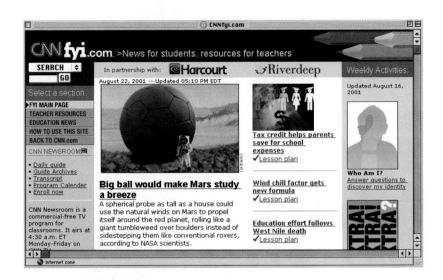

Sociology and Making Connections

When you think of sociology, what comes to mind? Perhaps you simply picture people analyzing census data. Maybe you think of people conducting surveys or interviewing people in a neighborhood to learn more about their lives. These things are important, but the study of sociology includes much more. Sociology involves asking questions and solving problems. It focuses on looking at people and their ways of life as well as studying social trends, cultural changes, human development, social institutions, and collective behavior. Studying sociology also means looking at why things are where they are and at the relationships between humans and the world around them.

The study of sociology helps us make connections between human behavior and society. It helps us understand the processes that have shaped the features we observe around us today, as well as the ways those features may be different tomorrow. In short, sociology helps us understand the processes that have created a world that is home to more than 6 billion people.

Sociologists are not only interested in social behavior but also how we see ourselves.

Sociology and You

Anyone can influence the society of our world. For example, the actions of individuals affect their local community and social networks. Some individual actions might lead to social conflict. Other actions might contribute to efforts to resolve social conflict. Various other things also influence sociology. For example, new technology, such as the Internet, can greatly affect how people communicate, conduct business, and generally interact. New technology can have both positive and negative affects. Although new technology may make communication over long distances simpler, according to some sociologists, it has limited the amount of face-to-face interaction in society. Understanding sociology helps us to evaluate the consequences of these types of changes.

Skills Handbook

Critical Thinking

Throughout *Holt Sociology: The Study of Human Relationships*, you are asked to think critically about some of the information you are studying. Critical thinking is the reasoned judgment of information and ideas. The development of critical thinking skills is essential to effective citizenship. Such skills empower you to exercise your civic rights and responsibilities as well as learn more about the world around you. Helping you develop critical thinking skills is an important goal of *Holt Sociology: The Study of Human Relationships*. The following critical thinking skills appear in the section reviews and chapter reviews of the textbook.

Papua New Guinean drum ceremony

▶ **Summarizing** involves briefly restating information gathered from a larger body of information. Much of the writing in this textbook is summarizing. The sociological data in this textbook has been collected from many sources. Summarizing all the characteristics of a society or even a social institution involves studying a large body of demographic, cultural, economic, geological, and historical information. For example, you might be asked to summarize the socioeconomic changes that the African American community has experienced in many U.S.cities.

▶ **Finding the Main Idea** is the ability to identify the main point in a set of information. This textbook is designed to help you focus on the main ideas in sociology. The Read to Discover questions in each chapter help you identify the main ideas in each section. To find the main idea in any piece of writing, first read the title and introduction. These two elements may point to the main ideas covered in the text. Also, formulate questions about the subject that you think might be

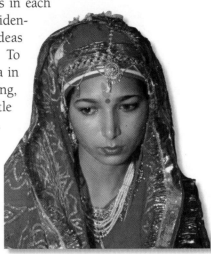

Brahman bride in India

answered in the text. Having such questions in mind will help you focus your reading. Pay attention to any headings or subheadings, which may provide a basic outline of the major ideas. Finally, as you read, note sentences that provide additional details about the general statements that those details support. For example, a trail of facts may lead to a conclusion that expresses the main idea.

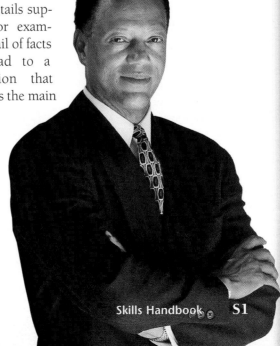

Lloyd Ward, CEO of the U.S. Olympic Committee

Working child

▶ Identifying Points of View

involves noting the factors that influence the outlook of an individual or group. A person's point of view includes beliefs and attitudes that are shaped by factors such as age, gender, race, and economic status. Identifying points of view helps us examine why people see things as they do. It also reinforces the realization that people's views may change over time or with a change in circumstances.

▶ Analyzing Information is the

process of breaking something down into parts and examining the relationships between those parts. For example, to understand the processes behind the growing religious diversity in the United States, you might study issues involving immigration, demography, geographic distribution, and religious life in America.

Religious ceremonies in America

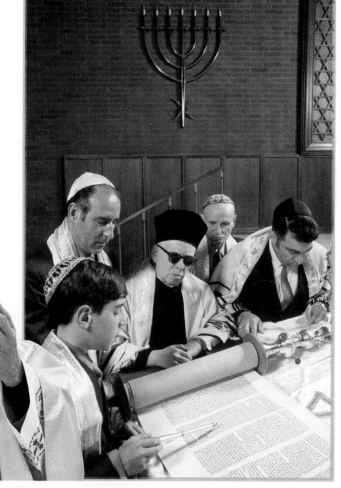

▶ Comparing and Contrasting

involve examining events, points of view, situations, or styles to identify their similarities and differences. Comparing focuses on both the similarities and the differences. Contrasting focuses only on the differences. Studying similarities and differences between people and things can give you clues about social theories, human interaction, and societies. For example, you might be asked how the lives of adolescents during the early 1900s are similar to and different from adolescents today.

▶ Supporting a Point of View

involves identifying an issue, deciding what you think about it, and persuasively expressing your position. Your stand should be based on specific information. When taking a stand, state your position clearly and give reasons that support it.

Family tree

Immigrants becoming nationalized U.S. citizens

Sequencing

is the process of placing events in correct chronological order to better understand the historical relationships among events. You can sequence events in two basic ways: according to absolute or relative chronology. Absolute chronology means that you pay close attention to the exact dates that events took place. Placing events on a time line would be an example of absolute chronology. Relative chronology refers to the way events relate to one another. To put events in relative order, you need to know which one happened first, which came next, and so forth. Sequencing can be used when studying kinship networks and determining the order of descendents.

Evaluating

involves assessing the significance or overall importance of a policy or event. For example, you might evaluate the success of certain civil rights laws or the impact of foreign trade on a society. You should base your evaluation on standards that others will understand and are likely to consider valid. For example, an evaluation of international relations after World War II might assess the political and economic tensions between the United States and the Soviet Union. Such an evaluation would also consider the ways those tensions affected other countries around the world.

Identifying Cause and Effect

is part of interpreting the relationships between sociological events. A cause is any action that leads to an event; the outcome of that action is an effect. To explain sociological developments, geographers may point out multiple causes and effects. Sociologists first begin by looking for clues that may show a cause-and-effect relationship. Then, sociologists would identify the relationships that they have evidence to support. A sociologist would also look for complex connections beyond the immediate cause-and-effect relationships. For example, sociologist studying demographic trends such as population growth might point to growing birthrates, longer life-expectancy, and increasing immigration as causes. Sociologists would then try to link the possible causes of population growth to the effects of the trend. Sociologists might point to the growing demands on American institutions and the growing diversity of the U.S. population.

Categorizing

is the process by which you group things together by the characteristics they have in common. By putting things or events into categories, it is easier to make comparisons and to see differences among them.

► Drawing Inferences and Conclusions

are two methods of critical thinking that require you to use evidence to explain events or information in a logical way. Inferences and conclusions are opinions, but they are based on facts and reasonable deductions. For example, suppose you know that people are moving in increasing numbers to cities in a particular region. You also know that poor weather has hurt farming in outlying areas while industry has been expanding in cities. You might infer from this information some of the reasons for the increased migration to cities. You could conclude that poor harvests have pushed people to leave outlying areas. You might also conclude that the possibility of finding work in new industries may be pulling people to cities.

► Making Generalizations and Predictions

are two critical thinking skills that require you to form concise ideas from a large body of information. When you are asked to generalize, you must take into account many different pieces of information. You then form a unifying concept that can be applied to all of the pieces of information. Many times making generalizations can help you see trends. Looking at trends can help you make a prediction. Making predictions, involves looking at trends in the past and present and making an educated guess about how these trends will affect the future, such as dating practices among American teens.

Dating during the mid-1900s

Family having dinner

Decision Making is the process of reviewing a situation and then making decisions or recommendations for the best possible outcome. To complete the process, first identify a situation that requires a solution. Next, gather information that will help you reach a decision. You may need to do some background research to study the history of the situation, or carefully consider the points of view of the individuals involved. Once you have done your research, identify options that might resolve the situation. For each option, predict what the possible consequences might be if that option was followed. Once you have identified the best option, take action by making a recommendation and following through on any tasks that option requires.

Conflict Resolution is the process of helping people create solutions to disputes and conflicts. There are several ways to help people resolve conflicts. You may use persuasion, compromise, debate, or negotiation to solve differences between people. Conflict resolution is an essential skill. You could even look at historic conflict situations such as the political movement for women's suffrage in the early 1900s. How might the use of persuasion, compromise, debate, or negotiation have solved differences between women's suffrage supporters and those who opposed the change.

Problem Solving is the process by which you pose workable solutions to difficult situations. The first step in the process is to identify the problem. Next you will need to gather information about the problem, such as its history and the various factors that contribute to the problem. Once you have gathered your information, you should list and consider the options for solving the problem. For each of the possible solutions, weigh its advantages and disadvantages and, based on your evaluation, choose and implement a solution. Once the solution is in place, go back and evaluate the effectiveness of the solution that you selected. The problem solving process is an important skill for everyday life. Family members may use this skill to solve problems such as who will cook dinner or do chores.

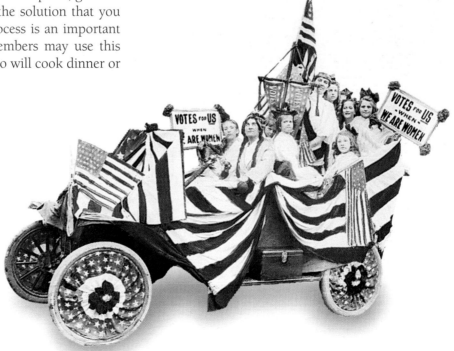

Women's suffrage supporters

Critical Thinking   **S5**

Becoming a Strategic Reader

by Dr. Judith Irvin

Everywhere you look, print is all around us. In fact, you would have a hard time stopping yourself from reading. In a normal day, you might read cereal boxes, movie posters, notes from friends, t-shirts, instructions for video games, song lyrics, catalogs, billboards, information on the Internet, magazines, the newspaper, and much, much more. Each form of print is read differently depending on your purpose for reading. You read a menu differently from poetry, and a motorcycle magazine is read differently than a letter from a friend. Good readers switch easily from one type of text to another. In fact, they probably do not even think about it, they just do it.

When you read, it is helpful to use a strategy to remember the most important ideas. You can use a strategy before you read to help connect information you already know to the new information you will encounter. You can also predict what a text will be about by using a previewing strategy. During the reading you can use a strategy to help you focus on main ideas, and after reading you can use a strategy to help you organize what you learned so that you can remember it later. *Holt Sociology: The Study of Human Relationships* was designed to help you more easily understand the ideas you read. Important reading strategies employed in *Holt Sociology: The Study of Human Relationships* include:

1 Methods to help you **anticipate** what is to come

2 Tools to help you **preview and predict** what the text will be about

3 Ways to help you **use and analyze visual information**

4 Ideas to help you **organize the information** you have learned

1. Anticipate Information

How Can I Use Information I Already Know to Help Me Understand What a New Chapter Will Be About?

Anticipating what a new chapter will be about helps you connect the upcoming information to what you already know. By drawing on your background knowledge, you can build a bridge to the new material.

1 Each chapter of *Holt Sociology: The Study of Human Relationships* asks you to explore the main themes of the chapter before you start reading by forming opinions based on your current knowledge.

TRUTH OR FICTION

What's Your Opinion?

Read the following statements about sociology. Do you think they are true or false? You will learn whether each statement is true or false as you read the chapter.

- Families are the same all over the world.

- Marriage patterns have remained unchanged in the United States since colonial times.

- Family disruptions, such as divorce, have little effect on the adults and children involved.

Create a chart like this one to help you analyze the statements.

A **Before Reading** Agree/Disagree		B **After Reading** Agree/Disagree
2	Families are the same all over the world.	**4**
	Marriage patterns have remained unchanged in the United States since colonial times.	
	Family disruptions, such as divorce, have little effect on the adults and children involved.	

3 Read the text and discuss with classmates.

Anticipating Information

▶ **Step 1** Identify the major concepts of the chapter. In *Holt Sociology: The Study of Human Relationships,* these are presented in the **What's Your Opinion?** feature at the beginning of each chapter.

▼

Step 2 Agree or disagree with each of the statements.

▼

Step 3 Read the text and discuss your responses with your classmates.

▼

Step 4 After reading the chapter, revisit the statements and respond to them again based on what you have learned.

2. Preview and Predict

How Can I Figure out What the Text Is about before I Even Start Reading a Section?

Previewing and Predicting

► **Step 1** Identify your purpose for reading. Ask yourself what will you do with this information once you have finished reading.

▼

Step 2 Ask yourself what the main idea of the text is and what key vocabulary words you need to know.

▼

Step 3 Use signal words to help identify the structure of the text.

▼

Step 4 Connect the information to what you already know.

Previewing and **predicting** are good methods to help you understand the text. If you take the time to preview and predict before you read, the text will make more sense to you during your reading.

1 Usually, your teacher will set the purpose for reading. After reading some new information, you may be asked to write a summary, take a test, or complete some other type of activity.

"After reading about family structure around the world, you will work with a partner to create an illustrated chart comparing two families..."

2 As you preview the text, use graphic signals such as headings, subheadings, and boldfaced type to help you determine what is important in the text. Each section of *Holt Sociology: The Study of Human Relationships* opens by giving you important clues to help you preview the material.

Read to Discover questions give you clues as to the section's main ideas.

Define and Identify terms let you know the key vocabulary you will encounter in the section.

Looking at the section's **main heading** and **subheadings** can give you an idea of what is to come.

3 Other tools that can help you in previewing are **signal words.** These words prepare you to think in a certain way. For example, when you see words such as *similar to, same as,* or *different from,* you know that the text will probably compare and contrast two or more ideas. Signal words indicate how the ideas in the text relate to each other. Look at the list below of some of the most common signal words grouped by the type of text structures they indicate.

Signal Words

Cause and Effect	Compare and Contrast	Description	Problem and Solution	Sequence or Chronological Order
• because	• different from	• for instance	• the question is	• not long after
• since	• same as	• for example	• a solution	• next
• consequently	• similar to	• such as	• one answer is	• then
• this led to . . . so	• as opposed to	• to illustrate		• initially
• if . . . then	• instead of	• in addition		• before
• nevertheless	• although	• most importantly		• after
• accordingly	• however	• another		• finally
• because of	• compared with	• furthermore		• preceding
• as a result of	• as well as	• first, second . . .		• following
• in order to	• either . . . or			• on (date)
• may be due to	• but			• over the years
• for this reason	• on the other hand			• today
• not only . . . but	• unless			• when

4 Learning something new requires that you connect it in some way with something you already know. This means you have to think before you read and while you read. You may want to use a chart like this one to remind yourself of the information already familiar to you and to come up with questions you want to answer in your reading. The chart will also help you organize your ideas after you have finished reading.

What I know	What I want to know	What I learned

3. Use and Analyze Visual Information

How Can All the Pictures, Maps, Graphs, and Time Lines with the Text Help Me Be a Stronger Reader?

Analyzing Information

Step 1 As you preview the text, ask yourself how the visual information relates to the text.

▼

Step 2 Generate questions based on the visual information.

▼

Step 3 After reading the text, go back and review the visual information again.

Step 4 Connect the information to what you already know.

Using visual information can help you understand and remember the information presented in *Holt Sociology: The Study of Human Relationships*. Good readers form a picture in their mind when they read. The pictures, charts, graphs, cartoons, time lines, and diagrams that occur throughout *Holt Sociology: The Study of Human Relationships* are placed strategically to increase your understanding.

1 You might ask yourself questions like:

> Why did the author include this image with text? What details about this visual are mentioned in the text?

After you have read the text, see if you can answer your own questions.

2

1. What is happening in this image?

2. How does this image illustrate the functions of family?

3. What benefits might this family receive from this type of interaction?

3 After reading, take another look at the visual information.

4 Try to make connections to what you already know.

4. Organize Information

Once I Learn New Information, How Do I Keep It All Straight So That I Will Remember It?

To help you remember what you have read, you need to find a way of **organizing information**. Two good ways of doing this are by using graphic organizers and concept maps. **Graphic organizers** help you understand important relationships—such as cause-and-effect, compare/contrast, sequence of events, and problem/solution—within the text. **Concept maps** provide a useful tool to help you focus on the text's main ideas and organize supporting details.

Identifying Relationships

Using graphic organizers will help you recall important ideas from the section. They are also study tools you can use to prepare for a quiz or test or to help with a writing assignment. Some of the most common types of graphic organizers are shown below.

▶ Cause and Effect

Events in history cause people to react in certain ways. Cause-and-effect patterns show the relationship between results and the ideas or events that made the results occur. You may want to represent cause-and effect relationships as one cause leading to multiple effects,

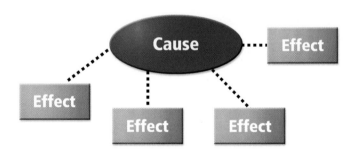

or as a chain of cause-and-effect relationships.

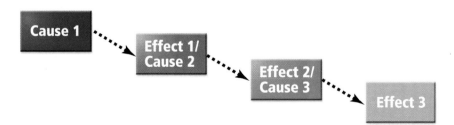

> **Constructing Graphic Organizers**
>
> ▶ **Step ❶** Preview the text, looking for signal words and the main idea.
>
> ▼
>
> **Step ❷** Form a hypothesis as to which type of graphic organizer would work best to display the information presented.
>
> ▼
>
> **Step ❸** Work individually or with your classmates to create a visual representation of what you read.

▶ Comparing and Contrasting

Graphic organizers are often useful when you are comparing or contrasting information. Compare-and-contrast diagrams point out similarities and differences between two concepts or ideas.

▶ Sequencing

Keeping track of dates and the order in which events took place is essential to understanding history. Sequence or chronological-order diagrams show events or ideas in the order in which they happened.

▶ Problem and Solution

Problem/solution patterns identify at least one problem, offer one or more solutions to the problem, and explain or predict outcomes of those solutions.

Identifying Main Ideas and Supporting Details

One special type of graphic organizer is the concept map. A concept map, sometimes called a semantic map, allows you to zero in on the most important points of the text. The map is made up of lines, boxes, circles, and/or arrows. It can be as simple or as complex as you need it to be in order to accurately represent the text.

Here are a few examples of concept maps you might use.

Constructing Concept Maps

▶ **Step** ❶ Preview the text, looking for what type of structure might be appropriate to display a concept map.
▼
Step ❷ Taking note of the headings, boldfaced type, and text structure, sketch a concept map you think could best illustrate the text.
▼
Step ❸ Using boxes, lines, arrows, circles, or any shapes you like, display the ideas of the text in the concept map.

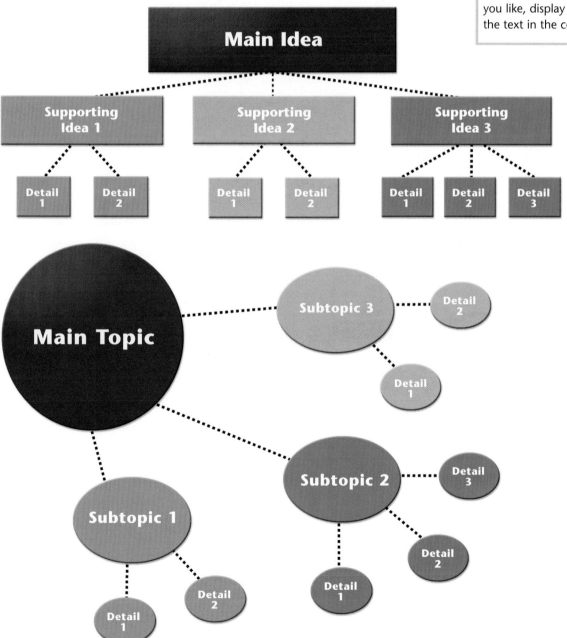

Standardized Test-Taking Strategies

A number of times throughout your school career, you may be asked to take standardized tests. These tests are designed to demonstrate the content and skills you have learned. It is important to keep in mind that in most cases the best way to prepare for these tests is to pay close attention in class and to take every opportunity to improve your general social studies, reading, writing, and mathematical skills.

Tips for Taking the Test

1. Be sure that you are well rested.
2. Be on time and be sure that you have the necessary materials.
3. Listen to the instructions of the teacher.
4. Read directions and questions carefully.
5. **DON'T STRESS!** Just remember what you have learned in class and you should do well.

▶ **Practice these Strategies at go.hrw.com**

go.hrw.com **Test Prep Online**
keyword: SL3 STP TOC

Tackling Social Studies

The social studies portions of many standardized tests are designed to test your knowledge of the content and skills that you have been studying in one or more of your social studies classes. Specific objectives for the test vary, but some of the most common include:

1. Demonstrate an understanding of issues and events in history.
2. Demonstrate an understanding of geographic influences on historical issues and events.
3. Demonstrate an understanding of economic and social influences on historical issues and events.
4. Demonstrate an understanding of political influences on historical issues and events.
5. Use critical thinking skills to analyze social studies information.

Standardized tests usually contain multiple-choice questions and may also contain open-ended questions. The multiple-choice items will often be based on maps, tables, charts, graphs, pictures, cartoons, and/or reading passages and documents.

Tips for Answering Multiple-Choice Questions

1. If there is a written or visual piece accompanying the multiple-choice question, pay careful attention to the title, author, and date.
2. Then read through or glance over the content of the piece accompanying the question to familiarize yourself with it.
3. Next, read the multiple-choice question first for its general intent. Then reread it carefully looking for words that give clues or can limit possible answers to the question. For example, words such as *most* or *best* tell you that there may be several

correct answers to a question, but you will look for the one that is the most important or had the greatest effect.

4. Read through the answer choices. Always read **all** of the possible answer choices even if the first one seems like the correct answer. There may be a better choice farther down in the list.

5. Reread the accompanying information (if any is included) carefully to determine the answer to the question. Again, note the title, author, and date of primary-source selections. The answer will rarely be stated exactly as it appears in the primary source, so you will need to use your critical thinking skills to read between the lines.

6. Think of what you already know about the time in history or person involved and use that to help limit the answer choices.

7. Finally, **reread** the question and selected answer to be sure that you have made the best choice and that you marked it correctly on the answer sheet.

Strategies for Success

There are a variety of strategies you can prepare ahead of time to help you feel more confident about answering questions on social studies standardized tests. Here are a few suggestions:

Helpful Acronyms

For a document, use **SOAPS**, which stands for

S Subject

O Occasion (or time)

A Audience

P Purpose

S Speaker/author

For a picture, cartoon, map, or other visual piece of information, use **OPTIC**, which stands for

O Overview

P Parts (labels or details of the visual)

T Title

I Interrelations (how the different parts of the visual work together)

C Conclusion (what the visual means)

---

1. Adopt an acronym—a word formed from the first letters of other words—that you will use for analyzing a document or visual that accompanies a question.

2. Form visual images of maps and try to draw them from memory. The standardized test will most likely include important maps from the time periods and subjects you have been studying. For example, in early U.S. history, be able to see in your mind's eye such things as where the New England, Middle, and Southern colonies were located, what land the Louisiana Purchase and Mexican Cession covered, and the dividing line for slave and free states. Know major physical features, such as the Mississippi River, the Appalachian and Rocky Mountains, the Great Plains, and the various regions of the United States and be able to place them on a map.

3. When you have finished studying any historical era, try to think of who or what might be important enough for the test. You may want to keep your ideas in a notebook that you can refer to when it is almost time for the test.

4. Pay particular attention to the Constitution and its development. Many standardized tests contain questions about this all-important document and the period during which it was written. Questions may include Magna Carta, the English Bill of Rights, the Declaration of Independence, and Common Sense, as well as many other important historical documents.

5. For the skills area of the tests, practice putting major events and personalities in order in your mind. Sequencing people and events by dates can become a game you play with a friend who also has to take the test. Always ask yourself "why" this event is important.

6. Follow the tips under Ready for Reading on the next page when you encounter a reading passage in social studies, but remember that what you have learned about history can help you answer reading-comprehension questions.

Ready for Reading

The main goal of the reading sections of most standardized tests is to determine your understanding of different aspects of a reading passage. Basically, if you can grasp the main idea and the author's purpose, and pay attention to the details and vocabulary so that you are able to draw inferences and conclusions, you will do well on the test.

Tips for Answering Multiple-Choice Questions

1. Read the passage as if you were not taking a test.

2. Look at the big picture. Ask yourself questions like, "What is the title?", "What do the illustrations or pictures tell me?", and "What is the author's purpose?"

3. Read the questions. This step will help you know what information to look for.

4. Reread the passage, underlining information related to the questions.

5. Go back to the questions and try to answer each one in your mind before looking at the answers.

6. Read all the answer choices and eliminate the ones that are obviously incorrect.

Types of Multiple Choice Questions

1. Main Idea The main idea is the most important point of the passage. After reading the passage, locate and underline the main idea.

2. Significant Details You will often be asked to recall details from the passage. Read the question and underline the details as you read. But remember that the correct answers do not always match the wording of the passage precisely.

3. Vocabulary You will often need to define a word within the context of the passage. Read the answer choices and plug them into the sentence to see what fits best.

4. Conclusion and Inference There are often important ideas in the passage that the author does not state directly. Sometimes you must consider multiple parts of the passage to answer the question. If answers refer to only one or two sentences or details in the passage, they are probably incorrect.

Tips for Answering Short-Answer Questions

1. Read the passage in its entirety, paying close attention to the main events and characters. Underline information you think is important.

2. If you cannot answer a question, skip it and come back later.

3. Words such as compare, contrast, interpret, discuss, and summarize appear often in short answer questions. Be sure you have a complete understanding of each of these words.

4. To help support your answer, return to the passage and skim the parts you underlined.

5. Organize your thoughts on a separate sheet of paper. Write a general statement with which to begin. This will be your topic statement.

6. When writing your answer, be precise but brief. Be sure to refer to details from the passage in your answer.

Targeting Writing

On many standardized tests, you will be asked to write an essay. In order to write a concise essay, you must learn to organize your thoughts before you begin writing the actual composition. This keeps you from straying too far from the essay's topic.

Tips for Answering Composition Questions

1. Read the question carefully.

2. Decide what kind of essay you are being asked to write. Essays usually fall into one of the following types: persuasive, classificatory, compare/contrast, or "how to." To determine the type of essay, ask yourself questions like, "Am I trying to persuade my audience?", "Am I comparing or contrasting ideas?", or "Am I trying to show the reader how to do something?"

3. Pay attention to key words, such as *compare*, *contrast*, *describe*, *advantages*, *disadvantages*, *classify*, or *speculate*. They will give you clues as to the structure that your essay should follow.

4. Organize your thoughts on a separate sheet of paper. You will want to come up with a general topic sentence that expresses your main idea. Make sure this sentence addresses the question. You should then create an outline or some type of graphic organizer to help you organize the points that support your topic sentence.

5. Write your composition using complete sentences. Also, be sure to use correct grammar, spelling, punctuation, and sentence structure.

6. Be sure to proofread your essay once you have finished writing.

Gearing up for Math

On most standardized tests you will be asked to solve a variety of mathematical problems that draw on the skills and information you have learned in class. If math problems sometimes give you difficulty, use the tips below to help you work through the problems.

Tips for Solving Math Problems

1. Determine the goal of the question. Read or study the problem carefully and decide what information must be found.

2. Locate the factual information. Decide what information represents key facts—the facts you must use to solve the problem. You may also find facts you do not need to reach your solution. In some cases, you may determine that more information is needed to solve the problem. If so, ask yourself, "What assumptions can I make about this problem?" or "Do I need a formula to help solve this problem?"

3. Decide what strategies you might use to solve the problem, how you might use these strategies, and what form your solution will be in. For example, will you need to create a graph or chart? Will you need to solve an equation? Will your answer be in words or numbers? By knowing what type of solution you should reach, you may be able to eliminate some of the choices.

4. Apply your strategy to solve the problem and compare your answer to the choices.

5. If the answer is still not clear, read the problem again. If you had to make calculations to reach your answer, use estimation to see if your answer makes sense.

Sociological Research Methods

We have defined sociology as the science that studies human society and social behavior. Because sociology is a science, it seeks answers to questions through empirical research. Empirical research is research that relies on the use of experience, observation, and experimentation to collect facts. In scientific terms, these facts are called data. Although the word data sometimes is treated as a singular noun, it actually is the plural form of datum. Thus when speaking of data, scientists generally mean "the data are . . ." If something can be seen, smelled, tasted, touched, or heard, it is considered to be empirical.

Sociologists, like most scientists, collect empirical data by using the scientific method. The scientific method is an objective, logical, and systematic way of collecting empirical data and arriving at conclusions. Researchers who use the scientific method (1) try to prevent their own notions, values, and biases from interfering in the research process; (2) use careful and correct reasoning in drawing conclusions from their data; and (3) carry out research in an organized and methodical manner.

Festival in downtown Chicago

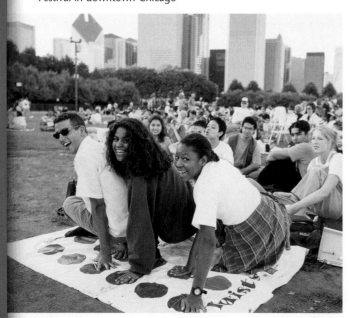

The Characteristics of Social Research

Sociological research covers a wide range of topics. This fact is evident from the topics in your textbook's table of contents. Nevertheless, most research shares certain basic characteristics. Among these characteristics are the types of research issues that are of interest to sociologists and the importance placed on determining causation and correlation.

Issues of Interest The main interest of most sociologists lies in examining the structure and function of various features of society. For example, sociologists are concerned with the structure and function of groups. This interest leads sociologists to examine how groups are organized and the consequences that group actions have for society. Sociologists are also interested in rates of behavior—how often particular behaviors occur under specific conditions. Unlike psychologists, who are interested in individual behavior, sociologists are interested in how groups of people with similar characteristics are likely to act under given circumstances. Finally, sociologists are interested in stability and change. They seek to understand how and why certain features of society change over time, while other features remain relatively stable.

Causation and Correlation Like all scientists, sociologists want to uncover the causal connections between events. Things do not just happen. There is a cause behind each occurrence. Whether we are talking about biological growth, riots, atomic fission, or wars—all events have causes.

Sociologists study cause and effect by examining the relationships among variables. A variable is a characteristic that can differ from one individual, group, or situation to another in a measurable way. Anything that can vary in amount or quality from case to case can be considered a variable. Age, race, income, level of education, and marital status are just a few of the things that can serve as sociological variables. A causal relationship exists when a change in one variable causes a change in another variable.

When examining cause and effect, sociologists distinguish between two types of variables: independent variables and dependent variables. An independent variable is a variable that causes a change in another variable. A dependent variable, on the other hand, is the variable that is changed by the independent variable. In a study of teenage drug use, for instance, the level of drug use might be the dependent variable, while the independent variables might include school grades or teenage attitudes toward drug use. In this instance, sociologists might be interested in determining if the level of drug use is influenced by grades in school or attitudes toward drug use. For example, is drug use lower among students who are on the honor roll at school?

The first step in determining cause and effect is to establish whether a correlation exists between two variables. A correlation exists when a change in one variable is regularly associated with a change in another variable. Correlations may or may not be causal. In addition, correlations may be either positive or negative. In the case of a positive correlation, both variables change in the same direction. Cigarette smoking, for example, is positively correlated with diseases such as lung cancer. The higher the rate of cigarette use, the higher the rate of lung cancer. In the case of a negative correlation, the variables change in opposite directions. For example, as individuals age they need fewer hours of sleep.

In some cases, variables appear to be correlated, but the relationship actually is spurious. A spurious correlation exists when variables appear to be related but actually are being affected by the existence of a third variable. For example, hospitalization and death appear to be highly correlated. However, this does not mean that hospitalization causes death. It is more likely that a third variable—serious illness—is responsible for the high correlation. Thus, hospitalization and death are spuriously correlated.

Sociologists determine whether variables are causally related, correlated, or spuriously correlated through the use of controls. In sociological terms, controls are ways of excluding the possibility that outside variables are affecting the relationship between the two variables under investigation. For example, suppose that a group of sociologists finds that the level of government spending on social programs and the level of voter participation are positively correlated in most nations of the world. To determine whether increased government spending causes higher rates of voter participation, the sociologists might control for the level of economic development in each nation. If the sociologists find that both the level of government spending and the level of voter participation are related to the level of economic development in a nation, they will conclude that the correlation between government spending and voter participation is spurious.

The Research Process

Sociologists generally follow a series of seven steps when conducting empirical research. These steps include defining the problem, reviewing the literature, forming a hypothesis, choosing a research design, collecting the data, analyzing the data, and presenting conclusions. Émile Durkheim's classic 1897 study of the social causes of suicide provides the earliest example of the application of these steps to a sociological problem.

Defining the Problem The first step in the research process involves selecting a topic for study and developing operational definitions of key concepts. An operational definition is a definition that is stated in terms of measurable characteristics. For example, Durkheim wished to study the effect of social integration on suicide rates among various groups of individuals. In order to do this, he had to define suicide and social integration in terms that would enable him to measure both concepts.

Reviewing the Literature Good sociological research is conducted within the context of an existing body of knowledge. In order to determine how others have approached a particular research problem and

Many older Americans remain active in their later years.

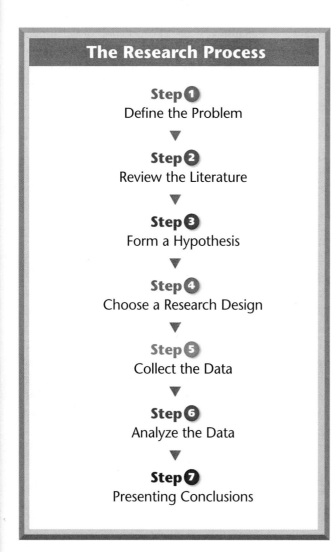

The Research Process

Step ❶
Define the Problem

▼

Step ❷
Review the Literature

▼

Step ❸
Form a Hypothesis

▼

Step ❹
Choose a Research Design

▼

Step ❺
Collect the Data

▼

Step ❻
Analyze the Data

▼

Step ❼
Presenting Conclusions

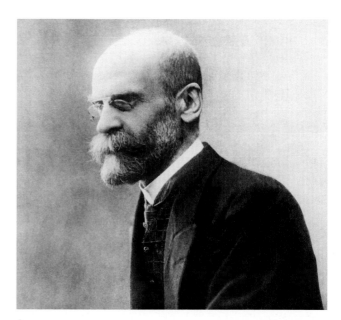

Émile Durkheim

what conclusions they have reached, sociologists review the published reports of studies that have a bearing on their research interests. This review not only provides researchers with valuable insights that help guide their work, it also prevents the unnecessary duplication of research efforts.

Thus when Durkheim began his study of suicide, he examined the existing literature to determine how other researchers explained the phenomenon. In addition, Durkheim reviewed the available statistics on suicide. What he found led him to dismiss the psychological explanations that were popular in the literature and to concentrate his attention on social factors.

Forming a Hypothesis Once the existing literature has been reviewed, sociologists develop testable hypotheses. A hypothesis is a statement that predicts the relationship between two or more variables. Durkheim, for example, hypothesized that suicide rates within groups vary inversely with the degree to

which group members are integrated into society. In other words, Durkheim predicted that the more family, religious, and community bonds group members have, the less likely they are to commit suicide.

Choosing a Research Design The next step in the research process involves selecting a research design. A research design is a plan for collecting, analyzing, and evaluating data. Not all research problems lend themselves to every data collection technique. Selecting the correct research design, therefore, is extremely important. Most of the data collection methods used by sociologists fall into four categories: surveys, experiments, observational studies, and the analysis of existing sources.

Once the data are collected, many sociologists employ some form of statistical analysis to evaluate their findings. For example, Durkheim statistically analyzed existing sources—official suicide records from various European nations—to test his hypotheses.

Collecting the Data Once they have developed a research design, sociologists must follow the design in collecting their data. Different research designs require taking different factors into consideration. However, regardless of the method being used information must be carefully recorded. Careless data collection can affect the accuracy of the research findings.

Analyzing the Data The analysis of data is a very important step. Even if the proper research design has been used and data have been carefully collected, the accuracy of findings can be affected by how the data are analyzed. Researchers must be careful to maintain their objectivity and not read more into the data than is there. Research findings are only as good as the methods used to collect and analyze the data.

The purpose of data analysis is to determine whether the data support the research hypotheses. When Durkheim analyzed his data on suicide, he found that rates varied among different groups within society. For example, he found that Catholics had lower rates of suicide than did Protestants and that married people, particularly those with children, were less likely than single people to commit suicide. He attributed these findings to the weakness of social bonds among Protestants and single individuals. Durkheim reasoned that the importance of individual actions in the religious values and practices of Protestantism would lead Protestants to rely on themselves rather than on others in times of crisis. Similarly, he reasoned that unmarried individuals generally have fewer people on whom to rely for support. These findings led Durkheim to confirm his hypothesis that suicide rates vary inversely with the degree of social integration.

Presenting Conclusions The last step in the research process involves drawing conclusions from the data and presenting the research findings to others. Sociologists generally report their findings in professional journals, in scholarly books, and at professional meetings. By reporting their research findings, sociologists add to the body of sociological knowledge. They also make it possible for other sociologists to evaluate the data and the research process. When sociologists do not supply enough information to allow their research to be repeated by other sociologists, the findings often are viewed as suspicious.

Basic Research Methods

Sociologists study how people interact with one another and with their social environment. There are four broad categories of research methods that sociologists employ to collect data, or scientific information, on society and human behavior. These categories are surveys, experiments, observational studies, and the analysis of existing sources. Under these broad headings fall a series of more specific research techniques, such as the historical method or content analysis. Sociologists also employ various techniques to analyze their data once the collection process is completed. The most common of these techniques involve some form of statistical analysis.

The Historical Method

The historical method is one of the techniques used to analyze existing sources. It involves examining any materials from the past that contain information of sociological interest. These materials can include such things as toys, clothes, pictures, tools, or furniture. However, more often they consist of written documents, such as diaries, newspapers, magazines, government records, laws and letters.

The historical method enables researchers to learn about events that happened in the recent past or long ago. It also provides a way to study trends. In the case of personal material, such as letters and diaries, the historical method allows researchers to view the private, unguarded feelings of individuals who lived at another point in time.

Content Analysis

Content analysis is another technique used to analyze existing sources. The process involves counting the number of times a particular word, phrase, idea, event, symbol, or other element appears in a given context. Content analysis can be used to analyze any form of recorded communication. Common sources of information include television, radio, sound recordings, movies, photographs, art work, newspapers, magazines, books, and personal or government documents.

Content analysis is a popular research technique because it is easy to use and is inexpensive. Researchers merely have to count the number of times the characteristics of interest appear in the source. In recent years, computer programs have further simplified the evaluation of data collected through content analysis.

The Survey Method

The survey method allows sociologists to collect data on attitudes and opinions from large numbers of people. Two techniques are commonly used to gather survey data—questionnaires and interviews.

A questionnaire, which sometimes takes the form of a public opinion poll, is a list of questions or statements to which people are asked to respond in writing. Questionnaires can be administered in person or sent through the mail. This technique has the advantage of making it possible to collect information from a large number of people in a relatively short period of time. However, questionnaires also have several disadvantages. For example, they do not enable soci-

Questionnaire being administered

ologists to know if the respondents have interpreted the questions correctly. Furthermore, researchers must rely solely on survey answers in drawing conclusions.

An interview is like a questionnaire, but respondents respond orally to questions. Interviews can be administered in person or over the telephone. This makes it easier for researchers to determine whether respondents understand the questions. It also makes it possible for researchers to ask for clarifications and to note various context clues, such as facial expressions, hesitations, or side comments. One disadvantage of using interviews is that they are much more time consuming and expensive to administer than are questionnaires.

Whether sociologists use questionnaires or interviews, they must first select the people they wish to question. Sociologists refer to the people who respond to surveys as respondents. Sometimes sociologists will study people of the same ages, or birth cohorts, to gather information about that group. Unless a population is very small, it is impractical to survey everyone in the population. Thus, sociologists generally survey a sample of a population. A sample is a small number of people drawn from a larger population.

For a sample to be useful, it must be representative of the population from which it was drawn. To help ensure representativeness, sociologists generally rely on random samples. A random sample is a sample chosen in such a way that every member of the population has an equal chance of being included in the sample.

A famous example of the consequences of not using a random sample is provided by the presidential election poll conducted by the *Literary Digest* in 1936. The *Literary Digest* wished to predict the outcome of the presidential election between Republican Alfred E. Landon and Democrat Franklin D. Roosevelt. The magazine selected its respondents from telephone directories and automobile registration lists. The results of their survey of over 2 million Americans indicated that Landon would beat Roosevelt by a margin of 15 percentage points. The magazine was quite embarrassed when Roosevelt won by a landslide.

Why was the magazine's survey so far off the mark? During the Great Depression, only members of the middle and upper classes could afford telephones and automobiles. Members of the middle and upper classes were mostly Republican in the 1930s. Thus, Republicans were vastly overrepresented in the sample. Members of the much larger working class, on the other hand, were not included in the survey. It was the working class, most of whom were Democrats, that was primarily responsible for electing Roosevelt as president.

Observation

In observational studies, researchers observe the behavior of individuals in actual social settings. Data can be collected through either detached observation or participant observation.

In detached observation, researchers observe the situation under study from a distance. Because researchers do not participate in the situation being studied, individuals often do not realize that they are being observed. This method has the advantage of making it less likely that behavior will be affected by the known presence of a researcher. However, detached observation is not always an effective technique. By remaining outside of the situation being studied, social researchers sometimes miss important details.

A more accurate picture of a situation often can be achieved through participant observation. In participant observation, researchers become directly involved in the situation under investigation. Sometimes researchers make their identities known to the people being studied. At other times, researchers remain anonymous. The latter technique has the advantage of increasing the chances that the subjects of the study will act naturally.

The Case Study

A case study is an intensive analysis of a person, group, event, or problem. Although case studies tend to rely heavily on observational techniques, researchers often use survey methods and the analysis of existing source material in their investigations. Thus it is not so much the technique that distinguishes case studies, but rather the intense focus of the investigation.

Case studies are particularly useful in analyzing infrequent or temporary events such as riots or natural disasters. Like observational studies, case studies have the advantage of providing an in-depth picture of a real-life situation. However, researchers must be careful not to generalize on the basis of one case.

Statistical Analysis

Statistical analysis involves the use of mathematical data. Provided the data can be translated into numbers, statistical analysis can be used with any of the research methods we have discussed. Statistical analysis involves analyzing data that have already been collected to determine the strength of the relationship that may exist between two or more variables. A variable is a characteristic that can differ from one individual, group, or situation to another in a measurable way. Examples of variables include income, age, and level of education.

Once data are collected, they must be analyzed. Sociologists use a wide range of statistical methods, many of them very complicated. Students of sociology, however, can interpret a great deal of sociological information if they have a basic understanding of a few statistical concepts. The most important of these concepts are the three measures of central tendency: the mode, the mean, and the median.

When sociologists speak of a measure of central tendency, they are referring to a statistical average—a single value—that describes the data under consideration. Measures of central tendency can be calculated on any set of data as long as the data can be translated into numbers.

The same data will produce different averages depending on which of the three measures of central tendency are being used. The mode is the number that occurs most often in the data. The mean, on the other hand, is the measure obtained by adding up all of the numbers in the data and dividing that number by the total number of cases. This quotient is the measure that we most often think of when we think of averages. The median is the number, or value, that divides the range of data into two equal parts.

Internet technology has greatly influenced the research and study of sociology.

We can illustrate the differences between mode, mean, and median using the following set of data on the prices of nine different makes of compact cars:

$11,500
$12,500
$ 9,000
$10,000
$15,000
$11,000
$13,000
$14,000
$13,000

To calculate the mode on the above set of figures, we simply need to look for the price that occurs most often. In this case, the price that occurs most often is $13,000. To calculate the mean, we must add up all of the prices and divide the total by nine. This procedure yields a mean of approximately $12,111. Finally, to calculate the median, we need to rank the prices from low to high and pick out the price that is in the middle. In the above set of data, the median is $12,500. As you can see, each measure of central tendency produces a different average of the data.

In the computer age, statistical analysis has become the preferred method for interpreting data. The computer allows large amounts of information to be processed in a relatively short amount of time. Many statistical packages are available to assist sociologists in analyzing their data. Sociology, like many of the social sciences, is becoming increasingly dependent on the use of statistics.

The methods described above are only some of the research methods used by sociologists to collect and evaluate data. It is important to note that sociologists often will use more than one method in the research process.

Using Statistics

Analyzing Observations

Conducting a research study is actually only a small part of the research process. Imagine that you decide to conduct a survey about the amount of television teenagers watch daily. After you have conducted interviews and received dozens of completed questionnaires you would probably feel overwhelmed by the amount of data you had collected. What is the next step?

When faced with this situation, sociologists use mathematical procedures, involving statistics to organize, analyze, and interpret the data. Sociologists then use the statistical analyses to construct charts and graphs. In short, statistics help sociologists make sense of their research findings.

Understanding Frequency

One of the most common forms of statistical analysis researchers use to organize their data is the frequency distribution. A frequency distribution is a way of arranging data to determine how often a certain piece of data—such as a score, salary, or age—occurs. In setting up a frequency distribution, researchers arrange the data from highest to lowest, and enter a mark when a piece of data occurs. The sum of each group's marks determines the frequency.

If there are too many different pieces of data to list individually, as is sometimes true for class scores, a researcher may substitute specific numerical spans, called class intervals, for individual scores. Again, the data are arranged from highest to lowest. A frequency distribution would allow a teacher to see at a glance how well a group of students did on a test, for instance, but it does not provide any information about individual performance.

Understanding Bell Curves

A useful statistical concept for sociologists is the bell curve, or normal curve. The bell curve is an ideal, a hypothetical standard against which actual categories of people or things (such as scores) can be measured and compared.

Usually, bell curves are used to categorize characteristics of people in large groups. The closer the group comes to the center of the curve, where the most "normal" traits congregate, the more validity the study appears to have.

For example, the bell curve, "Distribution of IQ Scores," shown on this page, illustrates a hypothetical standard against which actual IQ scores can be compared. This curve is a model of an ideal. It shows what would happen if the largest number of scores fell exactly in the middle of a range of scores. A comparison of the actual scores against this bell curve tells a researcher how representative the IQ test really is.

Correlations represent the relationship between two variables. When two variables show a positive correlation, one rises as the other rises. If the two variables are negatively correlated, one of the variables rises as the other falls.

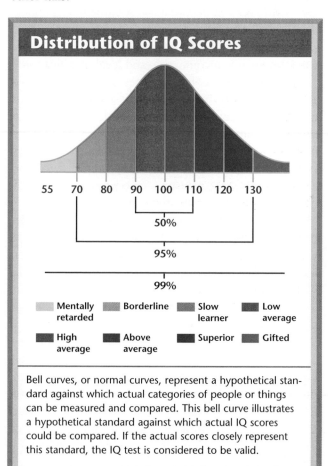

Distribution of IQ Scores

55 70 80 90 100 110 120 130

50%

95%

99%

Mentally retarded | Borderline | Slow learner | Low average
High average | Above average | Superior | Gifted

Bell curves, or normal curves, represent a hypothetical standard against which actual categories of people or things can be measured and compared. This bell curve illustrates a hypothetical standard against which actual IQ scores could be compared. If the actual scores closely represent this standard, the IQ test is considered to be valid.

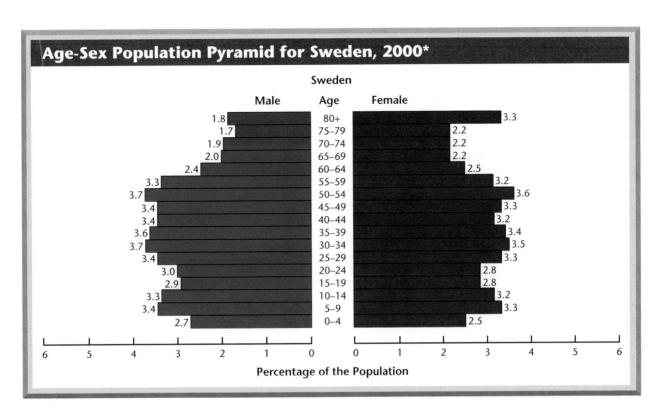

Age-Sex Population Pyramid for Sweden, 2000*

Sweden

| Male | | Age | | Female |

Male	Age	Female
1.8	80+	3.3
1.7	75–79	2.2
1.9	70–74	2.2
2.0	65–69	2.2
2.4	60–64	2.5
3.3	55–59	3.2
3.7	50–54	3.6
3.4	45–49	3.3
3.4	40–44	3.2
3.6	35–39	3.4
3.7	30–34	3.5
3.4	25–29	3.3
3.0	20–24	2.8
2.9	15–19	2.8
3.3	10–14	3.2
3.4	5–9	3.3
2.7	0–4	2.5

6 5 4 3 2 1 0   0 1 2 3 4 5 6

Percentage of the Population

A bell curve is a normal frequency distribution. This means that after counting the frequency of specific data, researchers can create an arrangement, or distribution, that is concentrated on or near the curve's center, which represents the norm. The fewest entries of data should appear at the far ends of the distribution—away from the highly concentrated norm.

It follows then that when the graphed results of an experiment come close to matching a bell curve, the results are assumed to be highly representative of that experiment. If most scores or data cluster towards the ends of the curve, however, the experiment or test is assumed to be unrepresentative of the group.

Bell curves and frequency distributions seem very complicated. However, they are simply ways to condense information and put it in a visual form. Within moments of glancing at a real plotted curve and the bell curve beside it, researchers can judge approximately how far from the norm their experimental group was, and how closely their results conform to what is "perfectly" normal.

Mode, Mean, and Median: Measures of Central Tendency

Three other measures are used to compare data that fall within the central points of a distribution: the mode, the mean, and the median.

Mode Simply, the mode is the piece of data that occurs most often in a given set of numbers. To find the mode, examine any frequency distribution and choose the number that appears most often. The mode is of limited use to researchers because "occurring most often" in a distribution may mean, for example, that this number occurred only twice among fifty different test scores.

Mean The mean is an average. The mean is found by adding all the scores or data together and then dividing that sum by the number of scores. The formula for finding the mean is:

$$\text{mean} = \frac{\text{sum of the scores}}{\text{number of scores}}$$

A significant disadvantage of using the mean is that any extreme score, whether high or low, distorts a researcher's results. For instance, if five waiters earn $300, $350, $325, $390, and $600 per week respectively, the mean—or average—weekly salary for this group would be $393. Yet four of the five waiters earn less than the average amount. In this circumstance, using the mean would not necessarily be representative of the waiters' wages.

Median The median is the score or piece of data that falls precisely in the middle of all the scores when they are arranged in descending order. Exactly half of the students score above the median, and exactly half score below it. In the previous example of waiters' salaries, the median would be $350, because two waiters earned more and two earned less.

The median, unlike the mean, is usually an actual number or score. To find the median of an even number of scores, you would find the median of the two numbers that fall in the middle, and then take the mean of those two central numbers in the distribution.

One major advantage of the median is that extreme scores, high or low, will not affect it. For example, examine the following two distributions:

Group X: 4, 10, 16, 18, 22
Group Y: 4, 10, 16, 18, 97

The median for each group is 16, because that number falls precisely in the middle of all the scores. However, the mean for Group X is 14 (4 + 10 + 16 + 18 + 22 = 70; 70 ÷ 5 = 14), while the mean for Group Y is 29 (4 + 10 + 16 + 18 + 97 = 145; 145 ÷ 5 = 29). The mean changes dramatically simply by introducing one extreme score. The median, however, remains the same.

The kind of central point that researchers choose to use in any given situation depends on what they are trying to find out. The median is not the best choice in all instances. Actually, in a bell curve—the idealized norm—the mode, the mean, and the median are identical.

Variability

Knowing what the mode, the mean, and the median are tells a researcher a great deal but not everything about the data. Researchers also need to know how much variability there is among the scores in a group of numbers. That is, researchers must discover how far apart the numbers or scores are in relation to the mean. For this purpose, sociologists use two measures: the range and the standard deviation.

Range The range is the mathematical difference between the highest and lowest scores in a frequency distribution. If the highest grade in a class is 100 and the lowest is 60, the range is 40 (100 − 60 = 40).

Two groups of numbers may have the same mean but different ranges. For example, consider the batting averages of two baseball teams:

Team A: 210 250 285 300 340
Team B: 270 270 275 285 285

The mean for each team is 277. However, the range for Team A is 130 points, whereas the range for Team

B is 15 points. This would tell a researcher that Team B is more alike in its batting abilities than is Team A.

The range tells sociologists how similar the subjects in each group are to one another in terms of what is being measured. This information could not be obtained from the mode, the mean, or the median alone, since each is just one number and not a comparison.

The disadvantage of the range, though, is that it takes only the lowest and highest scores of a frequency distribution into account. The middle numbers may be substantially different in two groups that have the same range. For example, here are two distributions:

Group A: 5, 8, 12, 14, 15
Group B: 5, 6, 7, 8, 15

Each group has the same range of 10. But the scores in Group A differ greatly from the scores in Group B. For this reason, sociologists often use the standard deviation.

Standard Deviation Sociologists sometimes want to know how much any particular score is likely to vary from the mean, or how spread out the scores are around the mean. To derive these measures, researchers calculate the standard deviation. The closer the standard deviation is to zero, the more reliable that data tends to be.

Let's say that the standard deviation of Team A's batting average is about 44.2, and the standard deviation of Team B's batting average is 6.8. From this information we know that the typical score of Team A will fall within 44.2 points of the mean, and the typical score of Team B will be within 6.8 points of the mean. This tells us that the quality of batting is more consistent on Team B than on Team A.

Two bell curves can have the same mode, mean, and median, but different standard deviations. If you were plotting two bell curves on a line graph, and one curve had a much larger standard deviation than the other, the curve with the larger standard deviation would show a more pronounced bell shape on the graph.

Correlation Correlation is a measure of the relationship between two variables. A variable is any behavior or condition that can change in quantity or quality. Examples of variables that people frequently encounter are age, hair color, weight, and height.

Correlation and causation are two types of relationships between variables that have great importance for psychologists.

When two variables are related, they are said to have a correlation. Changes in variables often occur together. Sometimes, an increase or decrease in one is accompanied by a corresponding increase or decrease in the other. For example, a decrease in someone's caloric intake is accompanied by a decrease in that person's weight. Such variables are said to be positively correlated.

Sometimes, when one variable increases, the other decreases, or vice-versa. These variables are said to be negatively correlated.

Correlation Coefficient The correlation coefficient describes the degree of relationship between variables. The concept of correlation allows researchers to predict the value of one variable if they know the value of the other and the way that the variables are correlated. A perfect positive correlation would have a coefficient of +1.00; a perfect negative correlation has a coefficient of –1.00. A correlation coefficient of zero indicates that there is no correlation between two variables.

Perfect positive correlations (+ 1.00 coefficient), when graphed, form a straight line that leans to the right; a perfect negative correlation (–1.00 coefficient), shown on a line graph, would form a straight line that leans to the left. In reality, few correlations are perfect. While one variable may increase or decrease in relation to the other, both variables probably will not change to the same degree.

The following is an example of a strong negative correlation with predictive potential: the more hours a person spends commuting to work, the less he or she enjoys driving. We can predict that if the person shortens the commute, his or her enjoyment of driving will increase.

Causation Although correlation is an important concept in statistics, it does not explain everything about relationships between variables. For one thing, correlation does not speak to the concept of causation. No correlation, of any degree, in itself proves that one variable causes another.

It is difficult to determine whether one variable actually causes another. Researchers determine causal relationships scientifically rather than relying on the intuitive sense of causality that may be implied in a correlation. They compare the differences between an experimental group—the group that displays the condition that is being studied—and a control group, in which this condition is not present. The independent variable is the variable being manipulated by the researcher.

If Group A is exposed to a virus and gets sick, and Group B is exposed to the same virus but has been vaccinated and does not become ill, there appears to be a causal relationship at work. It seems that the vaccine protected Group B from the virus, and therefore from illness. But researchers probably would want to examine how the vaccine actually worked—if it did. It may have been coincidental that Group B remained well.

Positive and Negative Correlations

Positive Correlation

Generally speaking, people who have a higher need for achievement achieve higher salaries.

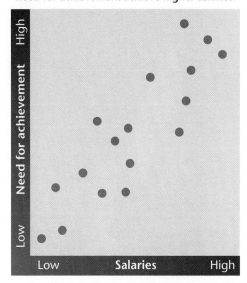

Negative Correlation

Generally speaking, the immune systems of people who are under high amounts of stress tend to function more poorly than the immune systems of people under less stress.

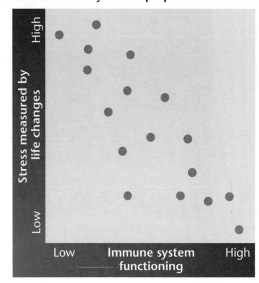

Correlations represent the relationship between two variables. When two variables show a positive correlation, one rises as the other rises. If the two variables are negatively correlated, one of the variables rises as the other falls.

UNIT 1

CHAPTER 1

The Sociological Point of View

Sociology developed in response to the social unrest caused by the Industrial Revolution. Early sociologists tried to understand the many changes that were occurring in society. Most influential among these early sociologists were Auguste Comte, Herbert Spencer, Karl Marx, Émile Durkheim, and Max Weber. Out of their work arose three broad theoretical perspectives that form the basis of modern sociology—the functionalist, conflict, and interactionist perspectives.

CHAPTER 2

Cultural Diversity

Humans adapt to and change their environment. Culture—the shared material and nonmaterial products of human groups—arises from attempts by people to deal with their environment. All cultures consist of five basic components: physical objects, symbols, language, values, and norms. However, specific examples vary from society to society and often from group to group within a society. The scope and nature of cultural variation is of particular interest to sociologists.

Internet Activity

internet connect go.hrw.com

TOPIC: Sociology in the Classroom
GO TO: go.hrw.com
KEYWORD: SL3 UNIT 1

Have students access the Internet through the HRW Go site to conduct research on the study of sociology. Then ask students to imagine that they are preparing to petition the principal and school board to introduce a sociology course into the curriculum. Have each student create a handout to pass out at a school board meeting to encourage the principal and school board to institute the course. Handouts should contain a description of what sociology is, how it has developed over the years, the major theorists and theories that might be covered in the course, and why sociology is an important course to offer to high-school students.

CHAPTER 3

Cultural Conformity and Adaptation

All societies establish norms and values and use internalization and sanctions to enforce them. Societies also change. Major sources of change are values and beliefs, technology, population, diffusion, the physical environment, and wars and conquests. Resistance to change includes ethnocentrism and vested interests.

CHAPTER 4

Social Structure

Social structure is the network of interrelated statuses and roles that guides human interactions. Among the most common forms of social interaction are exchange, competition, conflict, cooperation, and accommodation. These interactions take place within societies and groups. Societies are categorized as either preindustrial, industrial, or postindustrial. Groups include primary and secondary groups, reference groups, and ingroups and outgroups.

UNIT MOTIVATOR

Share the information in the chapter overviews with students. Ask students to suggest ways in which society shapes human behavior and beliefs and vice versa. Tell students that sociologists examine these two interactions to learn about society and social behavior.

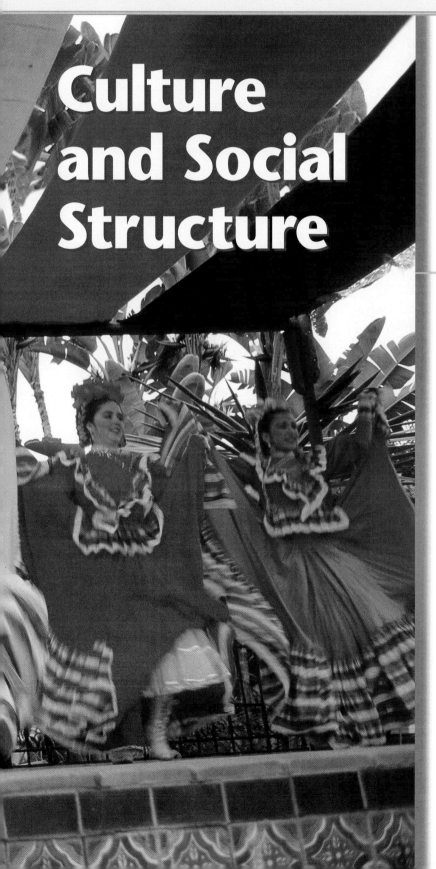

Culture and Social Structure

U N I T

1

C H A P T E R

1 The Sociological Point of View

2 Cultural Diversity

3 Cultural Conformity and Adaptation

4 Social Structure

Many sociologists are interested in the way culture influences the daily lives of people. Cultural festivals such as Cinco de Mayo celebrations are a product of these cultural influences.

Using Visual Resources

Cinco de Mayo. The Mexican cultural holiday of Cinco de Mayo is held each year on May 5. The holiday commemorates the date of the Mexican army's victory over invading French forces at the Battle of Puebla in 1862. Today people throughout Mexico and the United States celebrate Cinco de Mayo in a variety of ways, including performing dances and wearing vibrant clothing as shown in this photo.

CRITICAL THINKING

In what ways does the Cinco de Mayo celebration pictured here reflect Mexican culture? What are some holidays and celebrations that reflect your culture?

ANSWER: Students might suggest that the traditional dress and dance reflect Mexican traditions and heritage. Answers regarding holidays and celebrations will vary.

The Sociological Point of View

CHAPTER RESOURCE MANAGER

Objectives	Pacing Guide		Resources

SECTION 1:
Examining
Social Life
(pp. 4–8)

REV Section 1
Review, p. 8

- Describe what sociology is and explain what it means to have a sociological imagination.
- Explain how sociology is similar to and different from other social sciences.

Regular 1 day	**Block** **Scheduling** 0.5 day

Block Scheduling Handbook with Team Teaching Strategies, Chapter 1

Resources

📼 **CNN** Presents Sociology: Papua New Guinea Culture

RS Graphic Organizer 1

🌐 HRW Go site

SM Mastering Critical Thinking Skills 1

PS Readings and Case Studies in Sociology 1

E Research Projects and Activities for Teaching Sociology 1

SM Study Skills and Writing Guide

SECTION 2:
Sociology:
Then and
Now
(pp. 9–19)

REV Section 2
Review, p. 17

- Describe how the field of sociology developed.
- Explain how the three main theoretical perspectives in sociology differ in their focus.

Regular 2 days	**Block** **Scheduling** 1 day

Block Scheduling Handbook with Team Teaching Strategies, Chapter 1

Chapter Review And Assessment

REV Chapter 1 Review, pp. 20–21

REV Chapter Review Activities with Answer Key

💿 Global Skill Builder CD–ROM

💿 Chapter 1 Test Generator (on the One-Stop Planner)

A Chapter 1 Test (Form A or B)

A Alternative Assessment Handbook

🌐 HRW Go site

Chapter Resource Key

PS	Primary Sources	**A**	Assessment	📼	Video
RS	Reading Support	**REV**	Review	🌐	Internet
E	Enrichment		Transparencies	💻	Holt Presentation Maker Using Microsoft® PowerPoint®
SM	Skills Mastery	💿	CD–ROM		

One-Stop Planner CD–ROM

See the *One-Stop Planner* for a complete list of additional resources for students and teachers.

One-Stop Planner CD–ROM

It's easy to plan lessons, select resources, and print out materials for your students when you use the *One-Stop Planner CD–ROM with Test Generator.*

Chapter Project Preview

The following activities are included in the Chapter Review. You may want to make the suggested preparations.

CHAPTER REVIEW ACTIVITY

Using Your Observation Skills Students will attend or watch three different types of sporting events, take notes on the behavior of the spectators and the athletes, and create a table of the observations. Students will then discuss their notes in small groups in class and, based on these discussions, write an interactionist analysis of the effect that a sporting event has on group behavior. For consistency in grading, you might want to plan a class field trip to a local or school-sponsored sporting event.

LESSON ACTIVITY

Linking to Community Students will conduct a survey of five adults in their community to find out what each person thinks are some of the most pressing problems facing society today and then report on their results to the class. Before starting the project, review with students the proper ways to conduct surveys. Then help students work together to create one class survey. Provide each student with five copies of the class survey to use in the project.

INTERNET ACTIVITY

Sociology's Place in the Social Sciences Students will use provided Internet links to conduct research on how sociology relates to other disciplines. Students will then work in groups to prepare a script for a fictional television show called *Sociology Today.* The script should compare and contrast sociology to the other disciplines. In preparation, you might want to obtain some actual television scripts from a local cable access or network television studio to provide students with some examples. In addition, create a template or a series of guidelines for students to follow when creating their television scripts.

Additional Resources

PRINT RESOURCES FOR TEACHERS

Goodman, Norman. *Introduction to Sociology.* New York: HarperCollins, 1992. Concise overview of sociology presented in an outline format.

Macionis, John. *Society: The Basics.* Englewood Cliffs, NJ: Prentice-Hall, 1991. Survey of sociological concepts and issues.

Turner, Jonathan H. *The Structure of Sociological Theory,* 4th ed. Chicago: The Dorsey Press, 1986. Overview of the major theoretical perspectives in sociology.

PRINT RESOURCES FOR STUDENTS

Gilbert, Robert N. *Doing Survey Research in the Introductory Social Science Course.* Washington, D.C.: American Sociological Association. 1996. An introduction to social science research methods.

Levin, Jack. *Sociological Snapshots: Seeing Social Structure in Everyday Life.* Newbury Park, CA: Sage Publications, 1992. A solid overview of basic sociological concepts.

Mills, C. Wright. *The Sociological Imagination.* New York: Oxford University Press, 1959. Mills' classic work. Provides students with a foundation in sociological thought and analysis.

MULTIMEDIA RESOURCES

Introduction to Sociology: The Science of Groups (filmstrip, color; 34 min.) Social Studies School Service. Two-part introduction to the field of sociology.

The Social Sciences: What Is Sociology? (filmstrip on vhs; 45 min.) Guidance Associates. Asks students to assume the role of sociologists and apply what they have learned to make analyses and predictions.

The Sociological Point of View

SECTION 1
Examining Social Life

SECTION 2
Sociology: Then and Now

CHAPTER REVIEW

Ask students to answer the following questions:

How do you think the study of sociology might be similar to the study of history?

Consider:

• the goals of studying history
• the methods of studying and researching history
• how studying past events can help explain current social behaviors and attitudes

What might you already know about the study of sociology?

Consider:

• issues that affect individuals and groups in society
• issues that concern culture
• issues that concern social institutions such as the economic or political system

Internet Activity

☑ internet connect

TOPIC: Sociology's Place in the Social Sciences
GO TO: go.hrw.com
KEYWORD: SL3 SC1

Have students access the Internet through the HRW Go site to conduct research on how sociology relates to other disciplines. Then ask students to imagine that they work for a television show called *Sociology Today*. Organize students into groups and have each group write a television script for the show that compares and contrasts sociology to other disciplines. Ask one or two volunteer groups to present their television shows to the class.

CHAPTER

The Sociological Point of View

Build on What You Know

By now, you are probably familiar with the study of history. Although sociology is quite distinct from history, these two social sciences use similar methods of inquiry. In this chapter you will explore the nature of sociological inquiry and how it differs from approaches used by the other social sciences. You will also review the early years of sociology and then examine current theoretical perspectives.

To better understand human society, sociologists study how humans interact with each other.

What's Your Opinion?

To help introduce the chapter, have students discuss the Truth or Fiction statements that appear on this page. You might want to help students by reading the following **true/false** responses to the class.

True Because society is made up of individuals, sociologists must focus on individuals to understand how societies operate.

False Sociologists study human society and social behavior. Consequently, sociologists focus on the group rather than on the individual.

True Sociology, which focuses on current societies, has little in common with social sciences such as history, which focuses on the past, or psychology, which focuses on the mind.

False All social sciences overlap in their focus. Sociologists might be interested in the histories of society, the psychology of group behavior, or the effects of economic or political systems on societies.

True Over the years, the study of sociology has probably produced some standard theories about the nature of social life to which all sociologists subscribe.

False Because society can be examined from a variety of perspectives, sociologists probably disagree as to the nature of social life.

Life in Society

Did you know that you are surrounded by the subject of sociology? Your life is affected by the society and culture in your community. By skimming some recent newspaper stories you can see how sociological issues are currently affecting the world around you. Consider the following issues.

A 1999 study of the Internet's effect on society suggested that Internet use was helping to create a new form of social isolation. The study found that 13 percent of people who spent five or more hours per week online reported that they spent less time with family and friends. Eight percent noted that they attended fewer social events.

The average age at which people in the United States first marry has been rising steadily for several decades. As a result, single people are a rapidly growing segment of our population. In 2000 there were more than 26 million Americans aged 25 or older who had never been married.

Approximately 26 million Americans were victims of crime in 2000. On average, there was one violent crime every 22 seconds, one property crime every 3 seconds, and one murder every 34 minutes in the year 2000.

These familiar topics of technology use, marriage, and crime are of great interest to many sociologists. More than likely, these issues have affected people in your community. By studying and analyzing information on these and related topics, sociologists have developed theories that explain social behavior and its effect in our communities.

 What's Your Opinion?

Read the following statements about sociology. Do you think they are true or false? You will learn whether each statement is true or false as you read the chapter.

- The key focus of sociology is the individual.
- Sociology has little in common with the other social sciences.
- All sociologists are in broad agreement on the nature of social life.

▶ **WHY SOCIOLOGY MATTERS**

Sociologists look at everyday issues in a particular way—from a sociological perspective. Use **CNNfyi.com** or other current events sources to learn about sociological studies of various issues, such as drug-use among American high-school students, the effects of the Internet, or the incidence of crime. Write a short summary on the information you find.

CNNfyi.com

SCIENCE

The Natural and Social Sciences. The broad study of science can be divided into the natural and social sciences. The natural sciences examine and analyze the natural world. These sciences include biology, chemistry, geology, and physics. The social sciences examine and analyze the social world, or the world of human beings. These sciences include anthropology, economics, history, political science, psychology, and sociology.

ACTIVITY: Before beginning their study of the chapter, have students create a flowchart that categorizes and briefly defines each of the natural and social sciences listed above.

OBJECTIVES

1. *Describe what sociology is and explain what it means to have a sociological imagination.*

2. *Explain how sociology is similar to and different from other social sciences.*

REPRODUCIBLE & REVIEW

• Section 1 Review, p. 8

TECHNOLOGY

• One-Stop Planner, Lesson 1.1

• **CNN** Presents Sociology: Papua New Guinea Culture

• Homework Practice Online

Visual Answer

might result in workers being laid off or receiving smaller raises and fewer promotions

LET'S GET STARTED!

Before class, write the term *sociology* and its definition on the chalkboard. *(Sociology is the science that studies human society and social behavior. Sociologists are mainly interested in social interaction—how people relate to one another and influence each other's behavior.)* Below the definition, write this question: *Why do you think studying sociology is important?* As students enter the classroom, ask them to read the definition and to write a few sentences in response to the question. Have students briefly discuss their responses. Then tell students that Section 1 will introduce them to the sociological perspective and explain why developing such a perspective will benefit them now and in the future.

❶

EXAMINING SOCIAL LIFE

● **Read to Discover**
  1. What is sociology, and what does it mean to have a sociological imagination?
  2. How is sociology similar to and different from other social sciences?

● **Define**
  sociology, social sciences, social interaction, social phenomena, sociological perspective, sociological imagination, anthropology, psychology, social psychology, economics, political science, history

● **Identify**
  C. Wright Mills

Our daily lives shape our view of the world. The values, beliefs, lifestyles, and experiences of those around us, as well as historic events, help to mold us into unique individuals who have varied outlooks on life. The fact that we do not all view things in exactly the same way is what gives society its rich diversity. At the same time, however, most of us in society share many of the same characteristics and ideas. It is this combination of diversity and similarity that is of primary interest to sociologists.

Sociology is the social science that studies human society and social behavior. **Social sciences** are the disciplines that study human social behavior or institutions and functions of human society in a scientific manner. Sociologists are mainly interested in **social interaction**—how people relate to one another and influence each other's behavior. Consequently, sociologists tend to focus on the group rather than on the individual. Sociologists do this by examining **social phenomena**—observable facts or events that involve human society.

The Sociological Perspective

Why study sociology? Most importantly, because it can help you gain a new perspective on, or view of, yourself and the world around you. This new view involves looking at social life in a scientific systematic way, rather than depending on common-sense explanations. By adopting a **sociological perspective**, you can look beyond commonly held beliefs to the hidden meanings behind human actions.

INTERPRETING VISUALS Sociologists study human institutions, such as the stock market, and their effects on social life. *What effect might a downturn in the stock market have on workers in a large company?*

TEACH OBJECTIVE 1

Call on students to review the definition of sociology. *(See the* Let's Get Started! *activity.)* Then call on students to explain what it means to have a sociological imagination *(the ability to see the connection between the larger world and one's personal life).* To help students learn the term, copy the graphic organizer at the right onto the chalkboard, omitting the italicized answers. Have students copy the organizer and complete it by drawing an image in each box to illustrate the sociological imagination. Have volunteers share their organizers with the class. Then ask students to suggest some examples of using their sociological imaginations. Provide feedback and, if necessary, help students by providing some examples of your own. *(One example would be to consider how the issue of drinking and driving affects society at large, affects specific groups in society, and then affects each student in the class personally.)*

ENGLISH LANGUAGE LEARNERS

Illustration	**SOCIOLOGICAL IMAGINATION**	**Illustration**
Students might draw an image that represents the larger world or society, such as an image of Earth or a city skyline.	⟷	*Students might draw an image that represents an individual, such as a figure of a person or a face.*

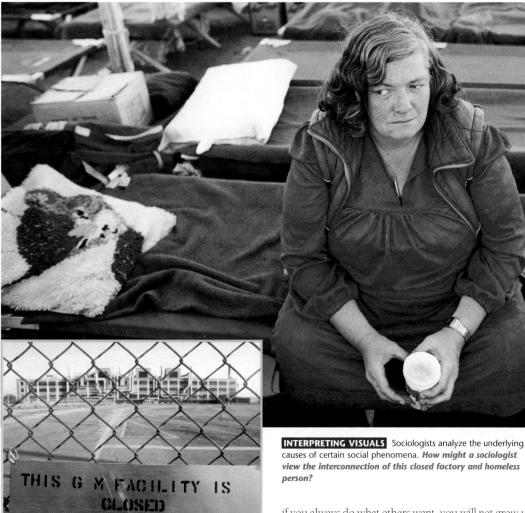

INTERPRETING VISUALS Sociologists analyze the underlying causes of certain social phenomena. *How might a sociologist view the interconnection of this closed factory and homeless person?*

The sociological perspective helps you see that all people are social beings. It tells you that your behavior is influenced by social factors and that you have learned your behavior from others. The sociological perspective can also help you broaden your view of the social world. It tells you that there are many different perceptions of social reality. Using the sociological perspective allows you to see beyond your own day-to-day life by viewing the world through others' eyes.

Further, the sociological perspective can help you find an acceptable balance between your personal desires and the demands of your social environment. If you always do what you want to do, you are likely to conflict with others a great deal of the time. On the other hand,

if you always do what others want, you will not grow very much as an individual. Applying the sociological perspective can help you decide the most acceptable point between these two extremes.

Finally, the sociological perspective can help you view your own life within a larger social and historical context. It can give you insights into how your social environment shapes you and how you, in turn, can shape your social environment. This ability to see the connection between the larger world and your personal life is what sociologist C. Wright Mills called the **sociological imagination**. Mills described the sociological imagination as "the capacity to range from the most impersonal and remote [topics] to the most intimate features of the human self—and to see the relations between the two." All good sociologists and students of society, Mills added, must possess this ability.

Case Studies and Other True Stories

▦ TEACH

Have students read the feature The American Sociological Association on this page. Then organize students into groups and have each group create a pamphlet designed to educate people about the ASA and its importance. Have each group present and explain its pamphlet to the class. As an extension to the activity, have students vote on what aspect of the ASA they would like to learn more about. Take the winning topic and write a letter to the ASA requesting information on that topic. Share any responses you receive with the class. **COOPERATIVE LEARNING**

▦ SPOTLIGHT *on the ASA Publications*

Organize the class into small groups and assign each group one of the ASA publications listed in this feature *(American Sociological Review, Sociological Theory, Journal of Health and Social Behavior, Teaching Sociology,* and *Contemporary Sociology).* Have each group create a classroom display about its assigned journal. Each display should include either copies of the journal or photocopies of representative articles, features, and columns in the journal. In addition, each group should create a handout highlighting the journal's main features. **COOPERATIVE LEARNING , BLOCK SCHEDULING**

◆ Sociology in the World Today

The International Sociological Association. To promote and advance the knowledge of sociology worldwide, the International Sociological Association (ISA) was founded in 1949. This organization provides a network for sociologists throughout the world to share research, debate ideas, and present new findings. Journals published by the ISA include *International Sociology* and *Current Sociology.*

CRITICAL THINKING

How might international research groups help advance the field of sociology?

ANSWER: Students might answer that such groups give sociologists access to more data and provide a greater awareness of the pressing social issues in other countries.

Think About It Answers

1. The ASA gave sociologists a national association through which to promote the study of sociology and its importance.

2. hosts conventions and provides a means of sharing new research and ideas in the field of sociology, publishes journals, and supports sociology education

6

Case Studies
AND OTHER TRUE STORIES

THE AMERICAN SOCIOLOGICAL ASSOCIATION

In the early 1900s sociology was still a young discipline in the United States. The first class on sociology—at the University of Kansas—had been held in 1889. A few years later the first department of sociology was established in 1892 at the University of Chicago. Not surprisingly, a professional organization serving the interests and concerns of American sociologists did not exist. Most sociologists belonged to organizations that served other disciplines, such as the American Economic Association.

In 1905 a small group of sociologists met to discuss the possibility of organizing their own association. They were unsure whether this association should exist under the umbrella of one of the established organizations or whether it should stand alone. After intense debate, they decided to form an organization that was separate and independent from all other organizations. At a later meeting the attendees established the constitution of the organization, elected the officers, and set the dues and membership requirements. Thus, the American Sociological Association (ASA) was born.

The establishment of the ASA was an important step in the development of sociology as a distinct discipline in the United States. Sociologists now had a national association that could promote their subject to the American public.

From very small beginnings—it had just 115 members in 1906—the ASA has grown into the largest professional organization of sociologists in the United States. Today the membership roll numbers about 13,000. Most ASA members are involved in education as scholars, researchers, teachers, or college students. However, some 20 percent of the membership work for the government, in businesses, or for nonprofit organizations.

The ASA serves as an important vehicle for the sharing of new research and new ideas in the field of sociology. One way in which the ASA does this is through its annual convention, which brings together sociologists from across the country and throughout the world. At each annual convention, sociologists present papers outlining their most current research and discuss the problems and issues of their discipline. Each of the many specialty areas of sociology—family sociology, criminology, theory, and medical sociology, for example—is represented at conventions. The annual meeting is an important means to extend knowledge, elaborate on new theoretical perspectives, and explore new areas of research.

Another way that the ASA helps sociologists to share their ideas and research is through the sponsoring and publishing of professional journals. The ASA's most influential journals include the *American Sociological Review, Sociological Theory, Journal of Health and Social Behavior,* and *Teaching Sociology.* The ASA also publishes *Contemporary Sociology,* a journal containing book reviews of recent publications from the many specialty areas of sociology.

In addition, the ASA is actively involved in developing materials to assist those teaching sociology. The ASA Teaching Services Program, established in 1980, operates a teaching resources center and organizes workshops for sociology teachers. The ASA also provides funds for teacher development and training and presents awards to outstanding teachers.

For additional information on the American Sociological Association, visit the ASA Web site at www.asanet.org or write to the following address:

**American Sociological Association
1307 New York Avenue, NW, Suite 700
Washington, D.C. 20005**

Think About It

1. **Finding the Main Idea** *Why was the establishment of the ASA important to the development of sociology as a discipline?*

2. **Evaluating** *The ASA states that part of its mission is to "promote the vitality, visibility, and diversity" of sociology. What does the ASA do to fulfill this task?*

SUGGESTION 1: Organize the class into five groups and assign each group one of the following disciplines: anthropology, economics, history, political science, or psychology. Instruct each group to use library and in-class resources to research its assigned discipline and then to create a poster about it. Instruct a spokesperson from each group to present its poster to the class and to explain the role of that discipline in the social sciences. Then display the posters in a row and have the class discuss the relationship between sociology and the other social sciences. *(Many sociologists borrow freely from the various social sciences to better understand the social forces that help to shape peoples' lives.)* **COOPERATIVE LEARNING**

SUGGESTION 2: Lead a class discussion about the social sciences discussed in this section and about sociology's place among them. *(See the previous activity for a list of social sciences.)* Then name a general issue, such as crime, family relationships, or labor practices. Call on volunteers to discuss how each discipline might focus on that issue. Continue the activity with two or three more examples.

HOMEWORK: Have each student create an eye-catching advertisement describing the benefits of studying sociology and gaining a sociological perspective. When students next meet, have volunteers present and explain their advertisements to the class. Then display the advertisements.

INTERPRETING VISUALS The perspective of social scientists vary depending on their field of study. *How might a sociologist's view of this Papua New Guinean drum ceremony differ from an anthropologist's perspective?*

Sociology's Place in the Social Sciences

In addition to sociology, the social sciences include anthropology, psychology, economics, and political science. History is also often included as a social science. **Anthropology**—the comparative study of past and present cultures—is most similar to sociology in its subject matter. Anthropologists have traditionally concentrated on examining past cultures and present simple—or less advanced—societies. Sociology, on the other hand, is most interested in group behavior in complex—more advanced—societies. Today, however, many anthropologists concentrate on complex societies. For example, urban anthropologists examine such things as the cultural characteristics of neighborhoods in large modern cities.

The social science that deals with the behavior and thinking of organisms is **psychology**. It differs from sociology primarily in that it focuses on individual behavior rather than on group behavior. In addition, it

■ **CLOSE**

To conclude, have students discuss what they think the following statement means based on what they have learned in this section: There are many different perceptions of social reality. Give students with differing viewpoints a chance to express and defend their opinions.

■ **REVIEW AND ASSESS**

Have students complete the **Section 1 Review** on p. 8. As **Alternative Assessment**, you may want to use the social sciences posters or the sociology advertisement in this section's lessons.

■ **RETEACH**

Have students work in pairs to create a matching quiz for this section's Define and Identify terms. Pairs should list the terms in one column and their definitions in a different order in a second column. Then have pairs exchange their quizzes, match the terms to their correct definitions, and return the quizzes to be checked.
ENGLISH LANGUAGE LEARNERS , COOPERATIVE LEARNING

■ **EXTEND**

Have each student write an essay discussing which of the benefits derived from developing a sociological perspective is most important to him or her and why. Ask volunteers to read their essays to the class. **BLOCK SCHEDULING**

Visual Answers

the personal effects of economic hardship; might focus less on social effects

SECTION ❶ REVIEW ANSWERS

1. Define:
- sociology, p. 4
- social sciences, p. 4
- social interaction, p. 4
- social phenomena, p. 4
- sociological perspective, p. 4
- sociological imagination, p. 5
- anthropology, p. 7
- psychology, p. 7
- social psychology, p. 8
- economics, p. 8
- political science, p. 8
- history, p. 8

2. Identify:
- C. Wright Mills, p. 5

3. Sociology examines the relations between society and culture, the individual, economics, politics, and past events, which are all the focus of one or more of the other social sciences.

4a. helps people view their lives within a larger social and historical context and gain insight into how the social environment shapes them and vice versa

b. studies human society and social behavior

5. Paragraphs will vary, but students should focus on how examining the relationships between oneself and the larger world can help them.

---

draws more heavily on the tools of the natural sciences. Areas of interest to psychologists include personality, perception, motivation, and learning. Despite differences in emphasis and methods of analysis, sociology and psychology are related. This is particularly true in the area of **social psychology**, the study of how the social environment affects an individual's behavior and personality.

Economics is the study of the choices people make in an effort to satisfy their needs and wants. Economists examine the processes by which goods and services are produced, distributed, and consumed. They also examine the effects of government policies on economic growth and stability. Sociologists share many areas of interest with economists. For example, the effect of economic factors on various groups in society has attracted the attention of sociologists since the earliest days of the discipline.

The examination of the organization and operation of governments is the focus of political science. The interests of sociology and **political science** often overlap. Areas of mutual interest include voting patterns, the concentration of political power, and the formation of politically based groups.

History is the study of past events. Sociologists are also interested in the past. Like many social historians, sociologists study past events in an effort to explain current social behaviors and attitudes.

Over time, the divisions between the social sciences have become less distinct. Many sociologists now borrow freely from the various social sciences in an effort to better understand the social forces that help to shape our lives.

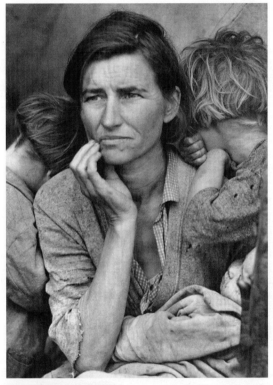

INTERPRETING VISUALS The Great Depression was a historic event that has been explored by historians, economists, political scientists, and sociologists. *What might a sociologist find interesting about this image? How might this view differ from that of other social scientists?*

SECTION ❶ REVIEW

1. Define and explain
   sociology
   social sciences
   social interaction
   social phenomena
   sociological perspective
   sociological imagination
   anthropology
   psychology
   social psychology
   economics
   political science
   history

2. Identify and explain
   C. Wright Mills

3. Comparing Copy the graphic organizer below. Use it to compare the focus of sociology with the focus of the other social sciences.

Sociology

Social Sciences

4. **Finding the Main Idea**

a. Why did C. Wright Mills think that a sociological imagination was important to sociology?

b. What does a sociologist study?

5. **Writing and Critical Thinking**

Analyzing Information Write two or three brief paragraphs explaining how a sociological imagination can assist you in your everyday life. Consider:
- seeing people as social beings
- finding balance between your personal desires and the demands of your social environment
- viewing your own life within a larger social and historical context

 Homework Practice Online
keyword: SL3 HP1

SECTION 2

OBJECTIVES

1. Describe how the field of sociology developed.

2. Explain how the three main theoretical perspectives in sociology differ in their focus.

LET'S GET STARTED!

As students enter the classroom, have them examine the Section 2 Review questions on p. 17 of their textbooks. Ask each student to list five things that they expect to learn in this section based on the review questions. After a brief period, call on volunteers to discuss their answers with the class. Instruct students to save their lists for later. Then tell students that in Section 2 they will learn about some of the early leaders in sociology and about the three main schools of thought for studying sociology.

2 SOCIOLOGY: THEN AND NOW

Read to Discover

1. How did the field of sociology develop?
2. In what ways do the three main theoretical perspectives in sociology differ in their focus?

Define

social Darwinism, function, *Verstehen*, ideal type, theory, theoretical perspective, functionalist perspective, dysfunctional, manifest function, latent function, conflict perspective, interactionist perspective, symbol, symbolic interaction

Identify

Auguste Comte, Herbert Spencer, Karl Marx, Émile Durkheim, Max Weber

SECTION 2 RESOURCES

REPRODUCIBLE & REVIEW
- Section 2 Review, p. 17

TECHNOLOGY
- One-Stop Planner, Lesson 1.2
- Homework Practice Online
- HRW Go site

Visual Answer

because societies experience major changes and upheavals during revolutionary periods

The nature of social life and human interaction has been of interest to scholars throughout history. However, a separate academic discipline dedicated to the analysis of society—sociology—did not develop until the 1800s.

Several factors led to the development of sociology as a distinct field of study. The rapid social and political changes that took place in Europe as a result of the Industrial Revolution were of primary importance. During the Industrial Revolution the rural economy, with its farms and cottage industries, gave way to an economy based on large-scale production. The factory replaced the home as the main site for manufacturing. With the growth of factories came the growth of cities, as people left their homes in the countryside in search of work.

The rapid growth of urban populations produced a multitude of social problems. The number of people seeking work outpaced available jobs. Housing shortages developed, crime increased, and pollution became a major problem. In addition, many people found it difficult to adapt to the impersonal nature of cities. Urban life was different from life in the small rural communities where most people were raised. Interactions in the country were based on personal relationships.

Over time, it became more difficult to ignore the effect of society on the individual. Individual liberty and individual rights became the focus of a wide variety of political movements. These demands for freedom and rights gave rise to the American and French Revolutions.

INTERPRETING VISUALS The ideas of individualism and the social changes created by the French Revolution encouraged European scholars to analyze society. *Why do you think a revolutionary time might encourage this type of analysis?*

SUGGESTION 1: Hang a long piece of butcher paper on one wall of the classroom. Organize students into five groups and assign each group one of the following leaders in sociology: Auguste Comte, Herbert Spencer, Karl Marx, Émile Durkheim, or Max Weber. In addition, assign each group a section of the butcher paper. Then have each group create graffiti slogans and symbols on its part of the paper that describe its assigned sociologist and his views about society and the role of sociologists. When students have completed the activity, use the graffiti wall to discuss the views of each of these early sociologists. **COOPERATIVE LEARNING**

SUGGESTION 2: As students enter class, hand them each a piece of paper with one of the following names on it: Auguste Comte, Herbert Spencer, Karl Marx, Émile Durkheim, or Max Weber. Tell students that the names indicate their secret identities and not to let anyone else know who they are. Begin with a class discussion on each of these early leaders in sociology. Give students five minutes to review this section and their discussion notes to gather information about their secret identities. Then call on students to stand up, assume the role of their secret identity, and provide a clue as to who they are. For example, a student might say, "Some people consider me to be the founder of sociology. Who am I?" *(Auguste Comte)* Other students should try to guess who each student is.

These sweeping political, social, and economic changes caused some scholars to question the traditional explanations of life. A similar situation had developed in the physical sciences in the 1700s. Many scientists rejected traditional religious explanations of the physical world. Rather, they speculated that the physical world operated according to systematic properties and laws.

They attempted to prove their beliefs through observation, controlled experiments, and careful collection and analysis of information. In the 1800s some scholars believed that the social world was based on a set of basic principles that could be studied and analyzed through the use of scientific research methods.

The Early Years

Sociology took root in the 1800s, primarily in France, Germany, and England. These countries had most strongly felt the effects of the Industrial Revolution. Auguste Comte, Herbert Spencer, Karl Marx, Émile Durkheim, and Max Weber were perhaps the most influential of the early sociologists.

French philosopher Auguste Comte attempted to apply the methods of scientific research to the study of society, which contributed to the development of sociology.

Auguste Comte Many people consider French philosopher Auguste Comte (1798–1857) the founder of sociology as a distinct subject. He was one of the first scholars to apply the methods of the physical sciences to the study of social life. He also coined the term *sociology* to describe the study of society.

Like most French scholars of his day, Comte was intrigued by the causes and consequences of the French Revolution. As a result, Comte began to focus on two basic areas of study—social order and social change. He suggested that certain processes, which he called *social statics*, hold society together. Similarly, Comte argued that society changes through definite processes, which he called *social dynamics*. The basic principles of these two social forces, Comte believed, could be uncovered through the methods of scientific research. He hoped this knowledge could be used to reform society.

In 1816 he was thrown out of school for taking part in a student protest. Comte never completed his college education. Throughout his life, Comte suffered from depression and other emotional problems. At one point he began to practice what he called "cerebral hygiene." This involved ignoring the works of other writers in order to keep his mind pure. Comte lectured for many years and published several studies that had an enormous influence on early sociology. Today, however, most of his ideas regarding society have been refuted. Even so, nearly 150 years after Comte's death, modern sociologists are still concerned with his basic issues of order and change.

Herbert Spencer Herbert Spencer (1820–1903), an English contemporary of Comte, started his working life as a civil engineer for a railway company. When he was in his thirties, he inherited a large sum of money and was freed from the need to earn a living. Thus, he began to pursue his interest in the study of society.

Spencer was strongly influenced by the views of Charles Darwin, an evolutionist from the 1800s. Spencer adopted a biological model of society. In a living organism, the biological systems work together to maintain the organism's health. Spencer attributed a similar process to society. Society, he said, is a set of interdependent parts that work together to maintain the system over time.

Spencer also used Darwin's theory of the evolution of biological organisms to describe the nature of society. Spencer considered social change and unrest to be natural occurrences during a society's evolution toward stability and perfection. Because he believed that the best aspects of society would survive over time, Spencer thought that no steps should be taken to correct social ills.

Spencer also believed that only the fittest societies would survive over time, leading to a general upgrading of the world as a whole. Although the phrase "survival of the fittest" is often credited to Charles Darwin, it was coined by Herbert Spencer to describe this process. Because of its similarities to Darwin's ideas, Spencer's view of society became known as **social Darwinism**.

Spencer's ideas gained a wide following, particularly in Britain and France. However, like Comte, Spencer refused to read the writings of scholars whose ideas differed from his own. As a result, he disregarded the rules of careful scholarship and made scientifically unfounded claims about the workings of the world. Over time, Spencer's social Darwinism fell out of favor.

Herbert Spencer (above) adapted the ideas of evolution, which Charles Darwin developed in his study *The Origin of Species*, and applied them to the functions of society.

Functionalists
see society as a set of interrelated parts that work together to produce a stable social system; focus on functions and dysfunctions

THREE SOCIOLOGICAL PERSPECTIVES

Conflict Theorists
focus of forces in society that promote competition and change; see social change as an inevitable feature of society

Interactionists
focus on how individuals interact in society and on the meanings individuals attach to their own and to others' actions

Karl Marx (above) and Émile Durkheim (right) each established the groundwork for a major sociological perspective. Marx's ideas led to conflict theory, and Durkheim's ideas helped establish the functionalist perspective.

Karl Marx Karl Marx (1818–83) was born to middle-class parents in a part of Prussia that is now Germany. He attended several universities and received a doctorate degree in 1841. Marx was unable to get a teaching position because of his political views. Instead, he worked as a writer and editor for a radical newspaper. In time the government closed the newspaper because of its revolutionary point of view. Marx moved to the more liberal atmosphere of Paris. However, the French soon expelled him at the request of the Prussian government. Marx moved on to Brussels, returned for a short time to Paris and Prussia, and finally settled in London. There, he earned a scant living from his writings. Marx died in poverty and obscurity. Nevertheless, his writings have influenced generations of scholars and social critics around the world.

Marx believed that the structure of a society is influenced by how its economy is organized. According to Marx, society is divided into two classes—the *bourgeoisie,* or capitalists, and the *proletariat,* or workers. The bourgeoisie own the means of production—the materials and methods used to produce goods and services. The proletariat, on the other hand, own nothing. They provide the labor needed to produce goods and provide services. Marx believed this imbalance in power would inevitably lead to conflict between the capitalists and the workers. This class conflict would end only when the proletariat united to overthrow those in power. After this rebellion, Marx said, the victorious workers would build a classless society in which each citizen would contribute "according to his ability" and would be rewarded "according to his needs."

Marx did not really consider himself a sociologist. Nevertheless, his belief that a society's economic system strongly influences its social structure has had a lasting influence on sociology. His emphasis on conflict as the primary cause of social change led to the development of one of the major sociological perspectives—conflict theory.

Émile Durkheim Frenchman Émile Durkheim (1858–1917) was educated in both France and Germany. In his late twenties he accepted a teaching position at the University of Bordeaux in France. There, Durkheim developed the country's first university sociology course. Durkheim was also one of the first sociologists to systematically apply the methods of science to the study of society.

Like Comte, Durkheim was concerned with the problem of social order. Like Spencer, he saw society as a set of interdependent parts that maintain the system

HOMEWORK: For each type of theoretical perspective, have each student find one article that discusses an issue in which sociologists of that type might be interested. When students next meet, have volunteers share some of their articles with the class for discussion.

SPOTLIGHT *on Manifest and Latent Functions*
Organize the class into small groups and have each group list five elements of society. Next, for each element, have group members list an example of one manifest function and one latent function. Have each group share its list with the class.
COOPERATIVE LEARNING , BLOCK SCHEDULING

CONNECTING *to Political Science*
Have students locate and read a copy of the *Communist Manifesto,* cowritten by Karl Marx and Friedrich Engels. Then have each student explain how Marx and Engels viewed society by writing a report based on the work. In addition, students should summarize the political systems of communism and socialism, which developed as a result of this book and Marx's views of society. Remind students to provide excerpts from the book to support their statements and to use standard grammar, spelling, sentence structure, and punctuation in their reports. **BLOCK SCHEDULING**

throughout time. However, Durkheim viewed the role of these interdependent parts in terms of their functions. A **function** is the consequence that an element of society produces for the maintenance of its social system. Durkheim was particularly interested in the function of religion in maintaining social order, because he believed that shared beliefs and values were the glue that held society together. Durkheim's functionalist view of society has been very influential in modern American sociology.

The basis of Durkheim's scientific analysis of society was his belief that sociologists should only study features of society that are directly observable. Ideas about observable phenomena, Durkheim noted, can be tested by applying the scientific tool of statistical analysis.

Durkheim used this approach in his 1897 study, *Suicide.* This study examined suicide rates in several European countries. The first true sociological study, *Suicide* is still used by sociology professors and students today.

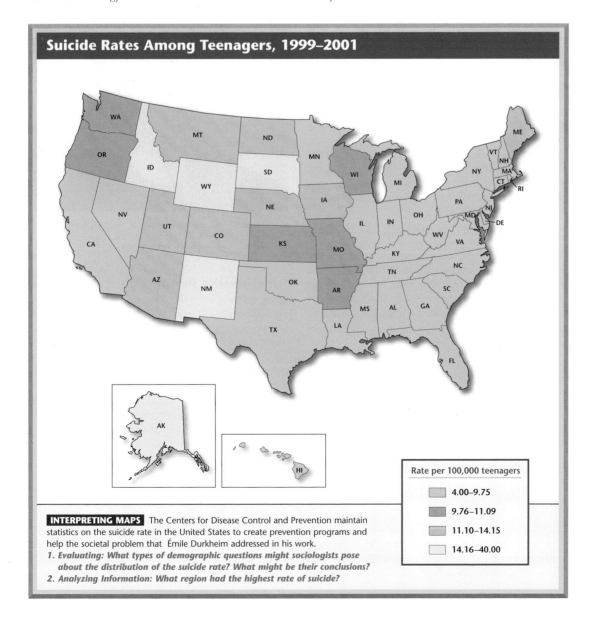

Suicide Rates Among Teenagers, 1999–2001

Rate per 100,000 teenagers
- 4.00–9.75
- 9.76–11.09
- 11.10–14.15
- 14.16–40.00

INTERPRETING MAPS The Centers for Disease Control and Prevention maintain statistics on the suicide rate in the United States to create prevention programs and help the societal problem that Émile Durkheim addressed in his work.
1. *Evaluating: What types of demographic questions might sociologists pose about the distribution of the suicide rate? What might be their conclusions?*
2. *Analyzing Information: What region had the highest rate of suicide?*

Case Study

Social Change and Suicide. Durkheim believed that change occurred so rapidly in a modern society that it led to social problems. These problems in turn led people to experience feelings of anomie, or purposelessness. In his study of suicide, Durkheim showed that the decision to commit suicide was based not only on personal factors but also on social factors, such as anomie.

RESEARCH ACTIVITY: Ask each student to conduct research on Durkheim's views of social change and anomie and then to write a short essay on the topic.

Map Answers

1. Sociologists might ask questions such as how population density or regional culture affects the distribution of the suicide rate. Conclusions will vary based on the questions students suggest.

2. the far Midwest

Max Weber Max Weber (VAY-bur) (1864–1920) was born in Prussia to wealthy parents. He received his doctoral degree from the University of Berlin in 1889 and later attained a teaching position at that same university. A few years later, he took a position as professor of economics at the University of Heidelberg. There, he produced some of his most important writings.

Unlike Comte, Spencer, Marx, and Durkheim, Weber was interested in separate groups within society rather than in society as a whole. This emphasis on groups led Weber to focus more on the effect of society on the individual. Weber also thought that sociologists should go beyond studying what can be directly observed and attempt to uncover the feelings and thoughts of individuals. Weber proposed doing this by using the principle of **Verstehen** (fehr-SHTAY-en). *Verstehen* involves an attempt to understand the meanings individuals attach to their actions. In essence, with *Verstehen* one puts oneself in the place of others and tries to see situations through their eyes.

In addition to *Verstehen*, Weber employed the concept of **ideal type** in much of his work. An ideal type is a description comprised of the essential characteristics of a feature of society. A feature of society might be public schools or attitudes about work. Sociologists construct an ideal type first by examining many different examples of the feature and then by deducing its essential characteristics. Yet any particular example of the feature might not contain all of the characteristics described in the ideal type. For example, the ideal type for a school might not be a perfect representation of your school. However, you would recognize it as a general description of an educational institution.

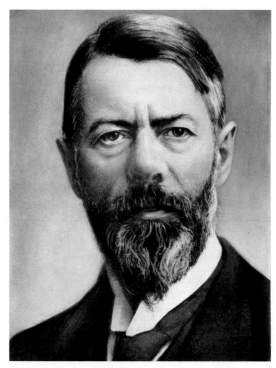

One of Max Weber's most-read works was his study of the relationship between the Protestant faith and the ideas of capitalism, *The Protestant Ethic and the Spirit of Capitalism.*

Current Perspectives

A **theory** is an explanation of the relationships among particular phenomena. Sociologists develop theories to guide their work and help interpret their findings. Sociologists not only develop theories to explain specific phenomena, they also adopt broad **theoretical perspectives** to provide a foundation for their inquiries. A theoretical perspective, or a school of thought, is a general set of assumptions about the nature of things. In the case of sociology, a theoretical perspective outlines specific ideas about the nature of social life.

Three broad theoretical perspectives form the basis of modern sociology. These are the functionalist perspective, the conflict perspective, and the interactionist perspective. Each one presents a slightly different image of society or focuses on different aspects of social life.

Functionalist Perspective The **functionalist perspective** is broadly based on the ideas of Comte, Spencer, and Durkheim. People who employ this perspective view society as a set of interrelated parts that work together to produce a stable social system. According to functionalists, society is held together through consensus. In other words, most people agree on what is best for society and work together to ensure that the social system runs smoothly. Topics of interest to functionalist sociologists include the functions that family or education serve in society.

Like Durkheim, functionalists view the various elements in society in terms of their functions, or their positive consequences for society. Recognizing that not everything in society operates smoothly, functionalists also label certain elements as **dysfunctional**. A dysfunction is the negative consequence an element has for the stability of the social system. Dysfunctional elements, such as crime, disrupt society rather than stabilize it.

In addition to being either positive or negative, functions can be either manifest or latent. A **manifest function** is the intended and recognized consequence of some element of society. For example, a manifest

Building Social Studies Skills

■ TEACH

Go through the steps in the feature on this page with students. Then organize students into groups and have each group go through the steps under Applying the Skill to reach its own decision. Each group should create a flowchart or diagram that fully illustrates all the steps in its decision-making process and why members chose one action and rejected others. Call on a spokesperson from each group to present its flowchart or diagram to the class. **COOPERATIVE LEARNING**

■ EXTEND

Have each student apply the decision-making steps detailed on this page to a real or fictional decision that they are facing in their lives. Each student should create a written or visual representation of the five-step process he or she used to reach a decision or course of action. Then have volunteers present and explain their work to the class. **BLOCK SCHEDULING**

BUILDING
Social Studies Skills

Desi Arnaz, who starred on *I Love Lucy*, was one of the first Hispanic actors to play a major role in a prime time American television show.

DECISION-MAKING SKILLS

Like you, many sociologists face difficult decisions. With the use of decision-making skills you will be better able to make a decision on important issues. The following activities will help you develop and practice these skills.

Decision making involves choosing between two or more options. Listed below are guidelines that will help you with making decisions.

1. **Identify a situation that requires a decision.** Think about your current situation. What issue are you faced with that requires you to take some sort of action?
2. **Gather information.** Think about the issue. Examine the causes of the issue or problem and consider how it affects you and others.
3. **Identify your options.** Consider possible actions. When making a decision you should consider the actions that you could take to address the issue. List these options so that you can compare them.
4. **Make predictions about consequences.** Consider possible effects of actions. Before taking action, you should predict the consequences of taking the actions listed for each of your options. Compare these possible consequences. Some options might be easier or seem more satisfying. But do they produce the results that you want?
5. **Take action to implement a decision.** After weighing options and making predictions, the next step is to take action. Choose a course of action from your available options and put it into effect.

Applying the Skill

One decision that sociologists must make is what type of theoretical perspective to follow when beginning a research project. Here is an example of the decision-making process that sociologists might use when beginning a study on the changes in media and the presence of positive minority role models.

1. **Identify a situation that requires a decision.**
   What type of theoretical perspectives should a sociologist follow when researching media and role models over time?
2. **Gather information.**
   - The research project involves studying how the media portrays minority role models and how they have changed.
   - The project is likely to focus on television.
   - The researcher will need to evaluate the positive and negative.
3. **Identify options.**
   - using a functionalist approach
   - using a conflict perspective
   - using an interactionist approach
4. **Make predictions about consequences.**
   - Using a functionalists approach would lead to a study of how the role models and media function as a part of a stable society.
   - Using a conflict perspective would lead to a study of how the role models and media promote change in society.
   - Using an interactionist approach would lead to a study on how the media role models operate as symbols and how people react to these symbols.
5. **Take action to implement a decision.**
   The sociologists decide to use a conflict perspective because it emphasizes social change.

Practicing the Skill

Study the research that Émile Durkheim conducted on suicide. Use the decision-making process to consider what type of approach you might take in a study of suicide or other social problems today. Record your responses to each of the steps in the decision-making process and summarize the actions you plan to take.

DECISION MAKING

Ask students to apply their decision-making skills to an ongoing issue or problem within their school. Students should describe their decision-making process using the five-step format shown in the feature on this page.

Practicing the Skill

As an extension to the activity, have students create a flowchart that illustrates the decision-making process they used. The chart should clearly illustrate the consequences of each possible decision and explain why students made their final decision. Have volunteers present their flowcharts to the class.

CLOSE

Have students take out the lists they made in the *Let's Get Started!* activity at the beginning of this section. Next, ask students to review their lists and determine if they learned what they thought they would. Have students discuss their results with the class. Then use students' responses as a way to summarize the section.

REVIEW AND ASSESS

Have students complete the **Section 2 Review** on p. 17. As **Alternative Assessment**, you may want to use the sociologists' dialogue or theoretical perspective chart in this section's lessons.

RETEACH

Organize the class into two groups and assign each group one of the Read to Discover questions at the beginning of this section. Within each group, pair students and have each pair create a detailed outline in answer to its assigned question. Then team up pairs from each group to create foursomes. Have the pairs in each foursome exchange outlines and review the ones they receive for accuracy and completeness. Have group members revise their outlines based on this feedback. Finally, have the class help you create two master outlines on the chalkboard.

ENGLISH LANGUAGE LEARNERS , COOPERATIVE LEARNING

Applying Sociology

Manifest and Latent Functions. Public education provides a good example of manifest and latent functions. The manifest function, or intended purpose, of public schools is to educate youth. However, schools have several latent functions. They help socialize children, teach teamwork and cooperation, and teach societal values such as being honest.

CRITICAL THINKING

What other latent functions might public schools have?

ANSWER: Answers will vary, but students should exhibit an understanding of the definition of latent function.

Visual Answer

It represents a conflict between workers and employers.

Visual Answer

(see p. 17)
The children's hands forming "camera lenses" in front of their eyes indicate a symbolic interaction.

SECTION 2 REVIEW ANSWERS

1. Define:
• social Darwinism, p. 11
• function, p. 13
• *Verstehen*, p. 14

16

---

function of the automobile is to provide speedy transportation from one location to another. A **latent function**, on the other hand, is the unintended and unrecognized consequence of an element of society. A latent function of the automobile is to gain social standing through the display of wealth.

Conflict Perspective People who employ the **conflict perspective** focus on the forces in society that promote competition and change. Following in the tradition of Karl Marx, conflict theorists are interested in how those who possess more power in society exercise control over those with less power. Conflict theorists do not limit their attention to acts of violent conflict. They are also interested in nonviolent competition between various groups in society—men and women, people of different ages, or people of different racial or national backgrounds. Some of the topics that conflict sociologists research include decision-making in the family, relationships among racial groups, and disputes between workers and employers.

According to conflict theorists, competition over scarce resources is at the basis of social conflict. Because resources such as power and wealth are in limited supply, people must compete with one another for them. Once particular groups gain control of society's resources, they tend to establish rules and procedures that protect their interests at the expense of other groups. This leads to social conflict as those with less power attempt to gain access to desired resources. Conflict, in turn, leads to social change. Thus, conflict theorists see social change as an inevitable feature of society.

INTERPRETING VISUALS Many sociologists who study labor issues use conflict theory to analyze labor disputes. *How do you think a labor strike such as this represents a conflict?*

![EXTEND icon] **EXTEND**

1. Have students conduct research on current leaders in sociology. Then have each student select one sociologist and create a one-page written report describing his or her academic background, theoretical perspective and areas of interest, and contributions to sociology. Remind students to use standard grammar, spelling, sentence structure, and punctuation in their reports. Call on volunteers to read their reports to the class.
BLOCK SCHEDULING

2. Briefly review the three main theoretical perspectives in sociology *(the functionalist, conflict, and interactionist perspectives).* Then have each student write five questions that sociologists of each type of theoretical perspective might ask when studying a classroom of high school students. For example, conflict theorists might consider differences in power between the teacher and students or among students of different genders. Call on volunteers to share some of their questions with the class. Encourage class discussion of each question. **BLOCK SCHEDULING**

Interactionist Perspective Functionalists and conflict theorists tend to focus on society in general or on groups within society. However, some sociologists adopt an **interactionist perspective**, which focuses on how individuals interact with one another in society. These sociologists are interested in the ways in which individuals respond to one another in everyday situations. They are also interested in the meanings that individuals attach to their own actions and to the actions of others. Interactionist theorists are heavily indebted to the work of Max Weber.

Interactionists are particularly interested in the role that symbols play in our daily lives. A **symbol** is anything that represents something else. In order for something to be a symbol, however, members of society must agree on the meaning that is attached to it. Such things as physical objects, gestures, words, and events can serve as symbols. The American flag, the bald eagle, Fourth of July celebrations, and Uncle Sam are examples of symbols used to represent the United States. In the case of gesture, a salute is a sign of respect for authority.

Interactionists focus on how people use symbols when interacting. This process is called **symbolic interaction**. The interactionist perspective is used to study topics such as child development, relationships within groups, and mate selection. This theoretical perspective has been particularly influential in the United States.

Which theoretical perspective should you use? Each one poses different questions and provides contrasting insights into the social world. Combining the elements each has to offer will provide you with a more complete understanding of human behavior.

INTERPRETING VISUALS A photographer visiting a village in Africa captured this playful image of Ugandan children imitating his camera. *What gesture gives clues to the type of interaction occurring in this image?*

![Section 2 emblem] **SECTION 2 REVIEW**

1. Define and explain
social Darwinism
function
Verstehen
ideal type
theory
theoretical perspective
functionalist perspective
dysfunctional
manifest function
latent function
conflict perspective
interactionist perspective
symbol
symbolic interaction

2. Identify and explain
Auguste Comte
Herbert Spencer
Karl Marx
Émile Durkheim
Max Weber

3. Categorizing Copy the graphic organizer below. Use it to categorize information regarding the early sociologists and their theoretical perspectives.

Early Sociologists	Topics of Interest	Theoretical Approach
Comte		
Spencer		
Durkheim		
Marx		
Weber		

4. **Finding the Main Idea**

a. What are the contributions of Comte, Spencer, Marx, Durkheim, and Weber to the development of sociology?
b. Trace the development of the field of sociology.

5. **Writing and Critical Thinking**

Comparing and Contrasting Select one of the news items in the Life in Society feature at this beginning of the chapter. Write a brief essay that describes how adopting each of the three theoretical perspectives might affect your view of the chosen news item.
Consider:
• what functionalists might focus on
• the interests of conflict theorists
• the interests of interactionists

![go.hrw.com logo] **Homework Practice Online**
keyword: SL3 HP1

• ideal type, p. 14
• theory, p. 14
• theoretical perspectives, p. 14
• functionalist perspective, p. 14
• dysfunctional, p. 14
• manifest function, p. 14
• latent function, p. 16
• conflict perspective, p. 16
• interactionist perspective, p. 17
• symbol, p. 17
• symbolic interaction, p. 17

2. Identify:
• Auguste Comte, p. 10
• Herbert Spencer, p. 10
• Karl Marx, p. 12
• Émile Durkheim, p. 12
• Max Weber, p. 14

3. Comte—social order and social change, functionalist; Spencer—social Darwinism, functionalist; Marx—social effects of economic power imbalances and class conflict, conflict; Durkheim—function of different elements of society in maintaining social order, functionalist; Weber—effect of society on the individual and the meanings individuals attach to their actions, interactionist

4a. They are the most influential of the early sociologists.

b. Sociology developed in the 1800s primarily in response to social problems produced by sweeping political changes and industrialization.

5. Essays will vary, but students should exhibit an understanding of each perspective.

Exploring Cultural Diversity

▨ TEACH

Have students read the feature Diversity in Early Sociology on pp. 18 and 19. Ask each student to create a chart that summarizes the contributions that Harriet Martineau and Jane Addams made to sociology and the problems that each woman faced. Then create a master chart on the chalkboard and call on volunteers to help you complete it. Finally, have each student create a plaque for each woman in honor of her contributions to sociology. As homework, assign students the Think About It question and activity at the end of the feature.

▨ EXTEND

Ask students to imagine that they are writers for the *American Journal of Sociology.* They have traveled back in time to interview one of the two women described in this feature. Have students write 10 questions that they would ask and provide the 10 answers that they think Martineau or Addams would provide. Each student should also write a one-paragraph introduction for the interview. Then select the best interview with each woman and have volunteers perform the interviews for the class.

BLOCK SCHEDULING

Interdisciplinary Connection

HISTORY

The Progressive Spirit of Social Reform. Jane Addams was one of many American women who joined the Progressive movement in the early 1900s. This movement focused on reforming social and urban problems, such as the plight of workers, poor sanitation, and corrupt political machines. Many middle-class women were attracted to the Progressive movement because reform work was considered an acceptable way for women to influence politics and society. Women were also enrolling in colleges in increasing numbers during the early 1900s yet had limited career options. Reform work provided college-educated women with a way to apply their knowledge.

CRITICAL THINKING

How did many middle-class, college-educated women contribute to social change in the early 1900s?

ANSWER: They joined the Progressive movement.

E X P L O R I N G
Cultural Diversity

DIVERSITY IN EARLY SOCIOLOGY

In its early years, sociology, like most of the social sciences, was dominated by men. In the 1800s women had a limited role in society. Most were wives and mothers or caretakers for aging or sickly parents. Very few women—mostly the daughters of the wealthy—had the opportunity to get a college education. Even fewer became college professors. However, two women who did make major contributions to the early development of sociology were Harriet Martineau and Jane Addams. Because of the people's attitudes during the late 1800s, their contributions were not recognized until well into the 1900s.

Harriet Martineau Harriet Martineau was born in Norwich, England, in 1802. Her parents valued learning, and they made sure she received a good education. After her father died, Martineau was forced to support herself. She was determined to make a living as a writer. Even though she received little help or encouragement from publishers, she succeeded. By the 1830s, she was a respected author in Britain.

In 1837—a year or so before Auguste Comte coined the term *sociology*—Martineau published *Theory and Practice of Society in America.* Based on observations she made while traveling in the United States, the book was a review of how well the United States lived up to its promise of democracy. The topics on which Martineau reported in her book—including the family, race relations, and religion—established the focus of sociological study. Her detached style of reporting also set the standard for objectivity in sociological research. Despite the pioneering nature of Martineau's study, it was largely ignored by early sociologists.

Martineau's next major sociological work, however, did make an impression on the world of sociology. In 1853 she published a translation of Comte's *Positive Philosophy.* This book introduced Comte's ideas concerning the study of society to English speakers and had a great influence on scholars in Great Britain and the United States.

SPOTLIGHT *on Women in Sociology*

Have each student conduct research on the number of women who have received graduate degrees in sociology or on the number of female members in the American Sociological Association over the past few decades. Then have students create a one-page report describing their findings. **BLOCK SCHEDULING**

SPOTLIGHT *on Social Work*

Have each student locate and interview someone who works as a social worker. Students should ask about the educational requirements for becoming a social worker and about some of the types of work that social workers do. If possible, have students record their interviews and play them for the class. Then have each student create a fact sheet describing the career of a social worker and explaining how a knowledge of sociology can help people in that profession. **BLOCK SCHEDULING**

Jane Addams Jane Addams was born into a wealthy Quaker family in Cedarville, Illinois, in 1860. Her family, like Martineau's, valued learning. Addams attended Rockford College and earned a bachelor's degree. She then went on to medical school but had to quit because of her poor health.

During the 1880s she traveled extensively in Europe. On one visit, she saw Toynbee Hall, a settlement house in London. Impressed with the services Toynbee Hall offered to poor people, Addams became determined to open a similar center in the United States. In 1889 she set up Hull House on the West Side of Chicago. There, she offered welfare, educational, and recreational services for poor residents of the neighborhood.

Addams soon realized that if she wanted to solve the problems of poor people, she needed to know the exact nature of those problems. She undertook a series of surveys of the people of Chicago's West Side and the conditions under which they lived. In 1895—three years after the University of Chicago established a sociology department—she published her results. Entitled *Hull-House Maps and Papers,* the study covered such subjects as wage levels, sweatshops, child labor, the immigrant experience, and living conditions in poverty-stricken neighborhoods. This groundbreaking work provided the first serious discussion of the effects of two major social forces—industrialization and urbanization.

Addams was an early member of the American Sociological Society. She spoke at national conferences and was a frequent contributor to the *American Journal of Sociology.* However, the vast majority of sociologists did not give her work serious consideration. Because she chose to live and work with the subjects of her studies, they considered her a social worker rather than a sociologist.

Harriet Martineau (upper left) and Jane Addams (middle left) overcame limits women faced during their time. Both published studies on American society. Addams also improved her community by establishing Hull House to aid residents and provide a community center for children such as these, who are playing table hockey.

Think About It

1. **Drawing Inferences and Conclusions**
   Why were the social sciences dominated by men in the 1800s?
2. **Summarizing** *Other American women—Emily Greene Balch, Jessie Bernard, and Florence Kelley, for example—made contributions to the early development of sociology. Research one of these female pioneers of sociology and present a brief oral report on her work.*

Think About It Answers

1. At the time, women had a limited role in society, and few women had the opportunity to attend college.

2. Oral reports will vary, but students should provide information on the woman's birth and death dates, education, and main contributions to sociology.

CHAPTER *1* REVIEW

ANSWERS

WRITING A SUMMARY
See the section subtitles for the main topics in the chapter.

IDENTIFYING PEOPLE AND IDEAS

1. the study of human society and social behavior

2. how people relate to one another and influence each other's behavior

3. an observable fact or event

4. the ability to see the connection between the larger world and one's personal life

5. sciences that include anthropology, economics, history, political science, psychology, and sociology

6. French philosopher who is considered the founder of sociology as a distinct subject

7. French sociologist interested in the functions of different elements of society in maintaining social order

CHAPTER 1

Review and Assessment Resources

- Chapter 1 Review, pp. 20–21
- Chapter Review Activities with Answer Key
- Global Skill Builder CD–ROM
- Chapter 1 Test Generator (on the One-Stop Planner)
- Chapter 1 Test (Form A or B)
- Alternative Assessment Handbook
- HRW Go site

REVIEW

Have students complete the **Chapter 1 Review** on pp. 20–21.

ASSESS

Use one of the chapter tests to assess students' understanding of the content. For **Alternative Assessment**, see the **Alternative Assessment Handbook**.

---

8. German sociologist interested in groups within society and the effect of society on the individual

9. an explanation of the relationships among particular phenomena

10. people's use of symbols when interacting

UNDERSTANDING MAIN IDEAS

1. the study of human society and social behavior

2. to be able to see the connection between the larger world and one's personal life

3. Sociology focuses on complex societies and social behavior while other social sciences focus on past cultures or events, simple societies, individuals, or political or economic systems.

4. Comte, Spencer, Marx, Durkheim, and Weber

5. functionalist—Comte, Spencer, and Durkheim; conflict—Marx; interactionist—Weber

THINKING CRITICALLY

1. psychology—how social environment affects individual behavior; economics—effect of economic factors on society; history—studying past events to explain current social behaviors

2. Industrial Revolution, rapid growth of cities, social problems related to urban growth, American and French Revolutions

3. Believing that the fittest aspects of society would survive over time, Spencer considered social unrest to be a natural part of a society's evolution.

20

CHAPTER 1 Review

 Writing a Summary

Using standard grammar, spelling, sentence structure, and punctuation, summarize the information in this chapter.
Consider:
- the development of the field of sociology as a separate discipline
- the major early sociologists and their contributions to the field

 Identifying People and Ideas

Identify the following people or terms and use them in appropriate sentences.

1. sociology
2. social interaction
3. social phenomenon
4. sociological imagination
5. social sciences
6. Auguste Comte
7. Émile Durkheim
8. Max Weber
9. theory
10. symbolic interaction

 Understanding Main ideas

Section 1 (pp. 4–8)
1. What is the main focus of sociology?
2. What does it mean to have a sociological imagination?
3. What are the differences between sociology and the other social sciences?

Section 2 (pp. 9–17)
4. Identify the major early sociologists.
5. What are the three main theoretical perspectives in sociology, and which of the founders of sociology is connected to which perspective?

Thinking Critically

1. **Analyzing Information** What ideas and approaches has sociology borrowed from the other social sciences?

2. **Identifying Cause and Effect** What social and political factors led to the emergence of sociology as a separate discipline?

3. **Identifying Points of View** How did Herbert Spencer's belief in the survival of the fittest influence his view of social unrest?

4. **Drawing Inferences and Conclusions** How might a sociologist's theoretical perspective influence his or her choice to study certain types of social issues?

5. **Supporting a Point of View** Which of the three theoretical perspectives do you think provides the fullest explanation of human behavior? Explain your answer.

Writing About Sociology

1. **Evaluating** Imagine that you are a sociologist who is a member of a panel studying homelessness. The panel also includes an economist, a psychologist, an anthropologist, and a historian. As a sociologist what issues of homelessness would most interest you? Write a brief report about how your views of the issue would differ from others on the panel.

2. **Sequencing** Complete the chart below to create an illustrated time line of the development of field sociology. Be sure to list the early contributors to the subject. Write a brief paragraph explaining how each of the events and people helped to create the field of sociology. Use the graphic organizer below to help you organize a timeline of the development of the field of sociology.

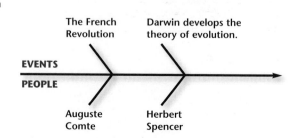

RETEACH

Have students, working either individually or in pairs, create a crossword puzzle based on the content in this chapter. Instruct students to incorporate into their puzzles as many of the chapter's key people, ideas, and terms as possible. Each student or pair should create a small completed version of the puzzle for an answer key as well as a larger unanswered version. Then have students exchange puzzles, complete the one they receive, and then compare their answers against the answer key. **ENGLISH LANGUAGE LEARNERS , COOPERATIVE LEARNING**

SOCIOLOGY PROJECTS

1. Linking to Community Have each student conduct a survey of five adults in their community to find out what each person thinks are some of the most pressing problems facing society today. Have students report on their results to the class. Then use the activity to discuss how sociological research can help solve some of these problems.

2. Connecting to History Have students conduct library research to learn what life was like in the United States during the Second Industrial Revolution. Then have each student use the research to identify and describe five social issues or problems that people faced during that time period.

BUILDING SOCIAL STUDIES SKILLS

Interpreting Graphs

Study the graph below. Then use the information to answer the questions that follow.

Social Science Bachelor's Degrees Awarded, 1970–71 to 1995–96*

*Note: These figures include the numbers of bachelor's degrees in history.
Source: *Digest of Educational Statistics, 2000*

1. The number of social science degrees awarded in 1980–81 was
   a. greater than the number awarded in 1975–76.
   b. less than 120,000.
   c. greater than 160,000.
   d. less than the number awarded in 1990–91.

2. What can you infer from the numbers of students enrolled in social science courses during the time period shown in the graph?

Analyzing Primary Sources

C. Wright Mills developed the idea of sociological imagination to apply sociology to the issues of individuals' daily lives. Read the following excerpt and answer the questions that follow.

"*No social study that does not come back to the problems of biography, of history and of their intersections within a society has completed its intellectual journey. Whatever the specific problems of the classic social analysts, however limited or however broad the features of social reality they have examined, those who have been imaginatively aware of the promise of their work have consistently asked three sorts of questions:*
   (1) What is the structure of this particular society as a whole? What are its essential components, and how are they related to one another? . . .
   (2) Where does this society stand in human history? What are the mechanics by which it is changing? What is its place within and its meaning for the development of humanity as a whole? How does any particular feature we are examining affect, and how is it affected by, the historical period in which it moves? . . .
   (3) What varieties of men and women now prevail in this society and in this period? And what varieties are coming to prevail? In what ways are they selected and formed, liberated and repressed, made sensitive and blunted?"

3. According to Mills, a social study that does not come back to the problems of biography, history, and their intersections
   a. does not qualify as sociology.
   b. has not completed its intellectual journey.
   c. will not be read by sociologists.
   d. cannot be considered for publication.

4. What are the three kinds of questions that sociologists must ask?

---

4. functionalist—topics related to the functions and dysfunctions or manifest and latent functions of society; conflict—topics related to competition and conflict within or between social groups; interactionist—topics related to how individuals interact with one another in society and the meanings they attach to their actions and to symbols

5. Answers will vary, but students should exhibit an understanding of each perspective.

WRITING ABOUT SOCIOLOGY

1. Reports will vary but should exhibit an understanding of sociology's focus on society and social behavior and how this differs from those of other social sciences.

2. Time lines should include Comte, Spencer, Marx, Durkheim, and Weber.

BUILDING SOCIAL STUDIES SKILLS

1. d

2. enrollment dropped during the 1970s and 1980s but then increased during the 1990s

3. b

4. (1) What is the unique nature of a society? (2) How has the society been changing over time, and what are the unique characteristics of the time period under study? (3) What types of people live in the society, and how does the society shape its citizens?

SOCIOLOGY PROJECTS

Cooperative Learning

Using Your Observation Skills Attend or watch two different types of sporting events and create a table that includes headings such as how many players participated, how many fans attended, and what reaction the fans had to the events. Next, in class organize into small groups to discuss your notes. Based on your group discussions, write an interactionist analysis of the effect that a sporting event has on group behavior.

internet connect

Internet Activity: go.hrw.com
KEYWORD: SL3 SC1
Choose an activity on the sociological point of view to:
• examine sociology's place in the social sciences.
• create a theoretical profile of a historical sociologist.
• create a thematic map, graph, or chart related to a sociological issue in your community such as demographic and cultural patterns.

Cultural Diversity

CHAPTER RESOURCE MANAGER

Objectives

- Define the meaning of the term *culture* and explain how material culture and nonmaterial culture differ.
- Identify and describe the basic components of culture.

Pacing Guide

Regular 1 day	**Block Scheduling** 0.5 day

Block Scheduling Handbook with Team Teaching Strategies, Chapter 2

Resources

- CNN. Presents Sociology: Disgusting Foods
- **RS** Graphic Organizer 2
- HRW Go site
- **SM** Mastering Critical Thinking Skills 2
- **PS** Readings and Case Studies in Sociology 2
- **E** Research Projects and Activities for Teaching Sociology 2
- **SM** Study Skills and Writing Guide
- Teaching Transparency: The Levels of Culture

- Describe cultural universals and explain why they exist.
- Explain what the terms *ethnocentrism* and *cultural relativism* mean.
- Identify factors that account for variations among and within cultures.

Regular 1 day	**Block Scheduling** 0.5 day

Block Scheduling Handbook with Team Teaching Strategies, Chapter 2

Chapter Review And Assessment

- **REV** Chapter 2 Review, pp. 40–41
- **REV** Chapter Review Activities with Answer Key
- Global Skill Builder CD–ROM
- Chapter 2 Test Generator (on the One-Stop Planner)
- **A** Chapter 2 Test (Form A or B)
- **A** Alternative Assessment Handbook
- HRW Go site

Chapter Resource Key

PS	Primary Sources	**A**	Assessment
RS	Reading Support	**REV**	Review
E	Enrichment		Transparencies
SM	Skills Mastery		CD-ROM

- Video
- Internet
- Holt Presentation Maker Using Microsoft® PowerPoint®

 One-Stop Planner CD–ROM

See the *One-Stop Planner* for a complete list of additional resources for students and teachers.

One-Stop Planner CD–ROM

It's easy to plan lessons, select resources, and print out materials for your students when you use the **One-Stop Planner CD–ROM with Test Generator.**

Chapter Project Preview

The following activities are included in the Chapter Review. You may want to make the suggested preparations.

CHAPTER REVIEW ACTIVITY

Using Observation Skills Students will work in pairs or small groups to review current-affairs magazines and newspapers for one week and note the symbols of American culture in them. Each pair or group will then use clippings, sketches, and other visual materials to create a collage of these symbols. In preparation, have students bring magazines and newspapers to class for several days.

LESSON ACTIVITY

Applying Sociology Students will conduct research to find a foreign cultural practice or belief that they find odd or unfamiliar and then use cultural relativism to write a short paper analyzing the practice or belief. In preparation, you might make a list of appropriate foreign cultural practices or beliefs for students to research.

INTERNET ACTIVITY

Culture in the Local Community Students will use provided Internet links to research the components of culture and then work in small groups to create Web pages on the topic. Before starting the project, prepare student instructions for creating Web pages or obtain some instructions. Then hold a training session for students. To increase uniformity, you might also create guidelines for the format and content of the Web pages.

Additional Resources

PRINT RESOURCES FOR TEACHERS

Harrison, Lawrence and Samuel Huntington, eds. *Culture Matters: How Values Shape Human Progress.* New York: Basic Books. 2000.

Henslin, James M., ed. *Down to Earth Sociology: Introductory Readings,* 9th ed. New York: The Free Press. 1997. Essays and readings covering major topics in sociology, including culture.

Masey, Garth, ed. *Readings for Sociology,* 2nd ed. New York: W. W. Norton. 1996. Essays and readings covering major topics in sociology, including culture.

PRINT RESOURCES FOR STUDENTS

Axtell, Roger E., ed. *Do's and Taboos Around the World,* 3rd ed. New York: John Wiley and SONGS, 1993. Topical presentation of cultural practices found around the world. Helps students to understand cultural diversity.

Harris, Marvin. *The Sacred Cow and the Abominable Pig: Riddles of Food and Culture.* New York: Simon & Schuster. 1985. Discussion of cultural food habits.

Hellman, Lillian. "The Children's Hour." In *Six Modern American Plays.* New York: Random House, 1966. Play focusing on a group of children who start a rumor that their teacher has broken one of society's mores. Enables students to analyze the social significance of norms.

MULTIMEDIA RESOURCES

American Tongues (vhs, color; 56 min.) Social Studies School Service. Explores the rich diversity of regional dialects found in the United States and illustrates how language can reveal much about a culture. (Contains brief strong language).

Powwow! (vhs, color; 16 min.) Social Studies School Service. Documentary that explores the symbolism underlying American Indian culture practices.

U.S. Regions: Contrasts of Land and People (vhs, color; 30 min.) Encylopaedia Britannica Educational Corporation. Identifies how climate, geography, time of settlement, and type of settlers determined cultural development in eight regions of the United States.

CHAPTER

Cultural Diversity

SECTION 1
The Meaning of Culture

SECTION 2
Cultural Variation

CHAPTER REVIEW

Internet Activity

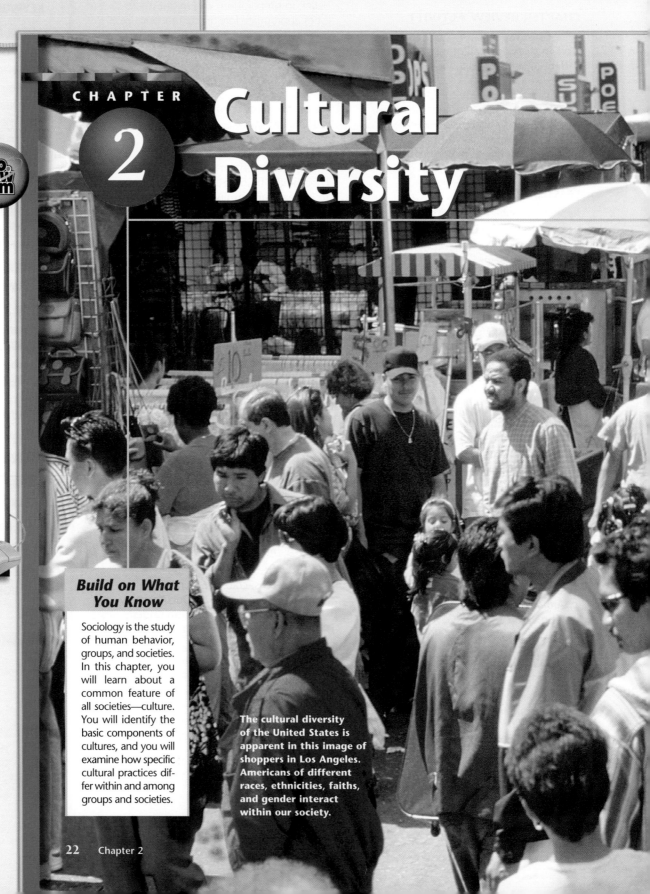

CHAPTER

Cultural Diversity

Build on What You Know

Sociology is the study of human behavior, groups, and societies. In this chapter, you will learn about a common feature of all societies—culture. You will identify the basic components of cultures, and you will examine how specific cultural practices differ within and among groups and societies.

The cultural diversity of the United States is apparent in this image of shoppers in Los Angeles. Americans of different races, ethnicities, faiths, and gender interact within our society.

Life in Society

What do you think when you hear the word *culture*? Does it conjure up images of fine art and literature? For sociologists culture has a much broader meaning. A brief description of the culture of the San, a southern African ethnic group, illustrates this point.

The San live in southern Africa. They speak a distinctive language, which is characterized by the use of verbal clicks. Although the San have begun to leave their homelands, some San still follow a traditional way of life in the harsh environment of the Kalahari Desert.

The San live in small groups of about 10 families. Each group has its own territory. After the food and water supply is exhausted in one part of the territory, the group moves on to another. Group life is based on cooperation. With the exception of the very young and the very old, all group members are expected to hunt for or to gather food. The San are also skilled rock painters. Their paintings cover the walls of the caves in which they sometimes live. These paintings probably have religious significance.

When sociologists look at culture they consider a people's language, art, ceremonies and rituals, religion, rules of behavior, social organization, ways of producing food, and work roles. Culture is a key focus of sociology because it is the feature that distinguishes one human group from another.

TRUTH OR FICTION

What's Your Opinion?

Read the following statements about sociology. Do you think they are true or false? You will learn whether each statement is true or false as you read the chapter.

• All cultures are the same.

• Cultural practices are only dictated by wealthy societies.

• Sociologists consider western culture superior to all other cultures.

> **WHY SOCIOLOGY MATTERS**
>
> Sociologists consider symbols central to a society's culture. Use CNNfyi.com or other current events sources to learn more about the symbols of American culture today. Create a visual report that illustrates the results of your research.
>
> **CNNfyi.com**

SECTION 1

OBJECTIVES

1. *Define the meaning of the term* culture *and explain how material culture and nonmaterial culture differ.*

2. *Identify and describe the basic components of culture.*

As students enter the classroom, write the following terms on the chalkboard: *technology, symbol, language, values,* and *norms.* Call on volunteers to turn to the glossary and read aloud the definitions for the terms. Then ask students to imagine that they have been sent back in time to conduct anthropological research on American culture of the early 2000s. On this basis, have students provide descriptive information that can be written under each of the five terms on the chalkboard. Then tell students that in Section 1 they will learn about the components of culture, which consist of these five terms.

SECTION 1 RESOURCES

REPRODUCIBLE & REVIEW

- Graphic Organizer 2
- Research Projects and Activities for Teaching Sociology 2
- Section 1 Review, p. 29

TECHNOLOGY

- One-Stop Planner, Lesson 2.1
- Teaching Transparency: The Levels of Culture
- Homework Practice Online
- HRW Go site

1

THE MEANING OF CULTURE

Read to Discover
1. What is the meaning of the term *culture,* and how do material culture and nonmaterial culture differ?
2. What are the basic components of culture?

Define
culture, material culture, nonmaterial culture, society, technology, language, values, norms, folkways, mores, laws, culture trait, culture complexes, culture patterns

Identify
Yanomamö, San, Napoleon Chagnon

Most sociologists believe that, unlike other animals, humans are not controlled by natural instincts. Because humans are not locked into a set of predetermined behaviors, they are able to adapt to and change their environment. The methods by which collections of people—be they small groups or entire societies—deal with their environment form the foundation of their culture.

What Is Culture?

Culture consists of all the shared products of human groups. These products include both physical objects and the beliefs, values, and behaviors shared by a group.

The physical objects that people create and use form a group's **material culture**. Examples of material culture include automobiles, books, buildings, clothing, computers, and cooking utensils. Abstract human creations form a group's **nonmaterial culture**. Examples of nonmaterial culture include beliefs, family patterns, ideas, language, political and economic systems, rules, skills, and work practices.

In everyday speech, people tend to use the terms *society* and *culture* interchangeably. However, sociologists distinguish between the two terms. A **society** is a group of interdependent people who have organized in such a way as to share a common culture and feeling of unity. Society consists of people, and culture consists of the material and nonmaterial products that people create.

The Components of Culture

Culture is both learned and shared. This idea does not mean that everyone in the United States dresses the same way, belongs to the same church, or likes the same type of music. It does mean that most people in the United States choose from among the same broad set of material and nonmaterial elements of culture in dealing with and making sense of their environment. Many languages are spoken in the United States; however, English is the most shared language.

Specific examples of the material and nonmaterial elements of culture vary from society to society, but all cultures have certain basic components. These components are technology, symbols, language, values, and norms.

Technology A society's culture consists of not only physical objects but also the rules for using those objects. Sociologists sometimes refer to this combination of objects and rules as **technology**. Using items of material culture, particularly tools, requires knowledge of various skills, which is part of the nonmaterial culture. For example, an understanding of how silicon chips work, knowledge of computer languages, and the ability to access and surf the Internet are all skills related to the computer. Sociologists are not only interested in skills but also in the rules of acceptable behavior when using material culture. For example, the practice of "hacking"—accessing Web sites or computer systems illegally—is usually considered unacceptable behavior.

Symbols The use of symbols is the very basis of human culture. It is through symbols that we create our culture and communicate it to group members and future generations. As you learned in Chapter 1, a symbol is anything that represents something else.

Artifacts such as this wooden mask are part of the material culture of the Inuit, who are commonly known as Eskimos.

SUGGESTION 1: Write the term *culture* on the chalkboard and ask a volunteer to define the term *(all the shared products of human groups, including both physical objects and the beliefs, values, and behaviors shared by a group)*. Then, to help students explain how material culture and nonmaterial culture differ, copy the graphic organizer at the right onto the chalkboard, omitting the italicized answers. Have students copy and complete the organizer. Discuss the answers with the class. Then have students list examples of material and nonmaterial culture for the United States and for any other countries with which students are familiar.
ENGLISH LANGUAGE LEARNERS

```
                    ┌─────────────────────┐
                    │      CULTURE        │
                    │ all the shared      │
                    │ products of human   │
                    │ groups              │
                    └─────────────────────┘
                       ╱              ╲
        ┌──────────────────┐   ┌──────────────────┐
        │ Material Culture │   │ Nonmaterial      │
        │ physical objects │   │ Culture          │
        │ that people      │   │ abstract human   │
        │ create and use   │   │ creations        │
        └──────────────────┘   └──────────────────┘
                 │                      │
        ┌──────────────────┐   ┌──────────────────┐
        │     Examples     │   │    Examples      │
        │ automobiles,     │   │ beliefs, family  │
        │ books, buildings,│   │ patterns, ideas, │
        │ clothing,        │   │ language,        │
        │ computers,       │   │ political and    │
        │ and cooking      │   │ economic systems,│
        │                  │   │ and rules        │
        └──────────────────┘   └──────────────────┘
```

Although English is the most commonly used language, many other languages are spoken in American communities. This street sign in Washington, D.C., is written in English and Chinese.

Language One of the most obvious aspects of any culture is its **language**. Language is the organization of written or spoken symbols into a standardized system. When organized according to accepted rules of grammar, words can be used to express any idea. In the United States most people learn to speak an American form of English and use this language as their primary means of communicating with one another. English is the principal language used in schools, in books and magazines, on radio and television, and in business dealings, even though there are members of American society who do not speak English. Have you ever visited a foreign country and been unable to speak the language? If so, you will realize how important the use of language is in daily life.

Values Language and other symbols are important partly because they allow us to communicate our **values** to one another and to future generations. Values are shared beliefs about what is good or bad, right or wrong, desirable or undesirable. The types of values held by a group help to determine the character of its people and the kinds of material and nonmaterial culture they create. A society that values war and displays of physical

In other words, a symbol has a shared meaning attached to it. Any word, gesture, image, sound, physical object, event, or element of the natural world can serve as a symbol as long as people recognize that it carries a particular meaning. A church service, a class ring, the word *hello*, the Lincoln Memorial, and a handshake are examples of common symbols in the United States. Although, specific examples vary from culture to culture, all cultures communicate symbolically.

Some people who live along the Amazon River use blowguns to hunt. People in these cultures value hunting skills.

Exploring Cultural Diversity

Lost in Translation. The diversity of world languages has created some funny mistakes as the economy has become more global. General Motors executives wondered why their Chevy Nova cars were not selling well in Spanish-speaking countries. Then the management learned that *no va* in Spanish means "it won't go."

ACTIVITY: Have students research and discuss other American product names that might translate poorly.

SUGGESTION 2: Call on students to define the meanings of the terms *culture, material culture,* and *nonmaterial culture. (See the graphic organizer from the previous activity for these definitions.)* Next, ask students to use each term in a sentence. Then ask students to imagine that they are writing a first letter to a pen pal in another country. Have each student write a letter introducing himself or herself and describing some examples of American material culture and nonmaterial culture, focusing on culture that relates to American youth. Have volunteers read their letters aloud to the class.

TEACH OBJECTIVE 2

SUGGESTION 1: Call on student volunteers to list the five components of culture and to review the definitions of each term *(technology—physical objects and the rules for using them; symbol—anything that represents something else and has a shared meaning; language—the organization of written or spoken symbols into a standardized system; values—shared beliefs about what is good or bad, right or wrong, desirable or undesirable; norms—shared rules of conduct that tell people how to act in specific situations).* Next, organize students into small groups and have each group list examples of each component of their school culture. Then have the groups share and discuss their lists. **COOPERATIVE LEARNING**

INTERPRETING VISUALS Using a seat belt in an automobile and covering one's mouth when one yawns are norms in American society. *What types of values do you think these norms are enforcing?*

strength above all else will be very different from one that places emphasis on cooperation and sharing. The Yanomamö of South America and the San provide examples of how different value systems produce different cultures.

The Yanomamö are farmers who live in small villages along the border between Brazil and Venezuela. Warfare and feats of male strength play such an important role in the Yanomamö way of life that anthropologist Napoleon Chagnon called them the Fierce People. Warfare is so common that approximately 30 percent of all deaths among Yanomamö males result from wounds received in battle.

Although farming villages normally can support between 500 to 1,000 people, Yanomamö villages rarely have as many as 200 people. Conflicts within the village usually cause groups to split off and form new settlements. Hostilities do not end with the splitting up of the village. Most instances of warfare occur between villages that were originally part of the same settlement.

In contrast, the San way of life is based on cooperation. San groups have their own territories, and they take great care not to trespass on the lands of others. Within groups, all members—except for the very young, the

very old, and the sick—take part in the search for food. The group shares the game it has hunted with all its members. If there is little game to hunt, the group breaks into smaller units to look for food. When food is more plentiful, these small units come back together.

Norms All groups create **norms** to enforce their cultural values. Norms are shared rules of conduct that tell people how to act in specific situations. For example, in the United States the value of a democratic government is reinforced through norms governing political participation, respect for the American flag, and the treatment of elected officials. It is important to keep in mind that norms are expectations for behavior, not actual behavior.

SUGGESTION 2: Write the five components of culture on the chalkboard and have students review the definition of each term. *(See the previous activity for the components and their definitions.)* To underscore the importance of culture to societies, ask students to imagine what American society would be like if there were no shared culture—for example, if everyone spoke a different language. Have students consider each component of culture in turn. Use the discussion to emphasize that no society can exist without a shared culture. Then have each student write a short story or create a comic strip that illustrates what a society might be like without one shared component of culture. Have volunteers present their stories or comic strips to the class.

SUGGESTION 3: Have students discuss the five basic components of culture. *(See the Suggestion 1 activity on p. 26 for the components and their definitions.)* Then have each student use library and in-class resources to create a fact sheet that lists information about each cultural component of another country as well as about the country's physical location.

HOMEWORK: Instruct each student to list 20 norms and to indicate whether each one is a folkway, more, or law. When the class next meets, call on volunteers to share items on their lists with the class. Correct any inaccuracies students have made in labeling their items.

The fact that a group has norms governing certain behaviors does not necessarily mean that the actions of all individuals will be in line with those norms. In the United States, there are norms concerning financial responsibility, but some people do not pay their bills.

A tremendous number of norms exists in our society ranging from the unimportant, such as cover your mouth when you yawn, to the very important, such as do not kill a human being. While some norms apply to everyone in society, others are applied selectively. For example, no one in American society is legally allowed to marry more than one person at a time. But only selected groups of people, such as children and the clergy of some religions, are forbidden from marrying at all. Norms have also been influenced by geographic factors. Restrictions against campfires have been placed in some regions of the western United States to prevent deadly and costly forest fires.

Even important norms are sometimes applied selectively. The norm against taking another person's life, for example, is applied differently to soldiers and police officers acting in the line of duty than it is to most members of society. Norms also vary in the strictness with which they are enforced. In recognition of all these variations, sociologists distinguish between two types of norms: folkways and mores (MOR–ayz).

Folkways are norms that describe socially acceptable behavior but do not have great moral significance attached to them. In essence, they outline the common customs of everyday life. All of the following are folkways: do not put food in your mouth with a knife; when lowering the American flag, do not allow it to touch the ground; shake hands when you are introduced to someone; do not jostle and push people when waiting in line; get to class on time; do your homework. Failure to abide by such rules usually results in a reprimand or a minor punishment. Some degree of nonconformity to folkways is permitted because it does not endanger the well-being or stability of society.

Mores, on the other hand, have great moral significance attached to them. This relation exists because the violation of such rules endangers society's well-being and stability. For example, dishonesty, fraud, and murder all greatly threaten society. These are deviances from cultural mores.

Societies have established punishments for violating mores in order to protect the social well-being. These serious mores are formalized as **laws**—written rules of conduct enacted and enforced by the government. Most laws enforce mores essential to social stability, such as those against arson, murder, rape, and theft. However, laws may also enforce less severe folkways, such as not parking in spaces reserved for drivers with disabilities.

Examining Culture

Although some cultural norms such as prohibiting murder have existed in almost every society over time, culture is continually changing. In sociological terms, it is *dynamic* rather than *static*. New material objects are constantly being introduced, as are new words, expressions, and ideas. If cultures are so vast and complicated and are constantly changing, how do sociologists study them? Sociologists examine a culture by breaking it down into levels and studying each level separately. The features of a culture can be divided into three levels of complexity: traits, complexes, and patterns.

Culture Traits The simplest level of culture is the **culture trait.** A culture trait is an individual tool, act, or belief that is related to a particular situation or need. Using knives, forks, and spoons when eating is a culture trait. Another trait is the specific greeting used when meeting people. If you see a good friend you probably say, "Hi." On the other hand, when greeting the human-resources manager at a job interview you probably would not be as informal. The greeting you use is related to the particular situation or need.

The Levels of Culture

CULTURE

- ⬤ Culture Pattern
- ◯ Culture Complex
- ● Culture Trait

INTERPRETING VISUALS Sociologists often break culture down into distinct levels to gain a better understanding of culture. *Copy this chart and describe specific culture traits, complexes, and patterns noted in this chapter.*

Case Studies and Other True Stories

TEACH

Have students read the feature Body Ritual Among the Nacirema on this page and then complete the Think About It section. You might want to assign the activity in this section to students as homework. Then ask students to imagine that they are space aliens who are visiting Earth for the first time. They have landed at the students' school but cannot speak the local language. Have students discuss how they, as aliens, might view various activities, items, and behaviors in the school. Use the activity to help students gain an objective view of their school culture.

SPOTLIGHT on Anthropologist Horace Miner

Have students conduct research on the career and contributions of anthropologist Horace Miner, who wrote the excerpt shown in the feature on this page. Then have each student use the research to write a biographical profile that focuses on Miner's career. Remind students to use standard grammar, spelling, sentence structure, and punctuation in their profiles. Call on one or two volunteers to read their profiles to the class.

BLOCK SCHEDULING

Think About It Answers

1. The shrine is the bathroom; the box is the medicine cabinet; Miner describes washing, brushing teeth, shaving, and hair curling.

2. Answers will vary, but each student should select a common aspect of American culture and describe it in the style that Miner used.

Visual Answer

(See p. 29)
Answers include the soccer ball, soccer shoes and pads, and the soccer uniforms.

Case Studies

AND OTHER TRUE STORIES

BODY RITUAL AMONG THE NACIREMA

Ceremonies and rituals—formal patterns of behavior that symbolically express shared beliefs—are an integral part of any culture. They provide sociologists with insight into a culture's system of values and beliefs. In the 1950s anthropologist Horace Miner examined some of the rituals of the Nacirema culture. The following is an excerpt from the article he wrote on his findings, "Body Ritual Among the Nacirema."

[The Nacirema] are a North American group living in the territory between the Canadian Cree, the Yaqui and Tarahumare of Mexico, and the Carib and Arawak of the Antilles. Little is known of their origin, although tradition states that they came from the east. . . .

Nacirema culture is characterized by a highly developed market economy which has evolved in a rich natural habitat. While much of the people's time is devoted to economic pursuits, a large part of the fruits of these labors and a considerable portion of the day are spent in ritual activity. The focus of this activity is the human body. . . .

The fundamental belief underlying the whole system appears to be that the human body is ugly and that its natural tendency is to debility and disease. Incarcerated in such a body, man's only hope is to avert these characteristics through the use of ritual and ceremony. Every household has one or more shrines devoted to this purpose. . . .

The focal point of the shrine is a box or chest which is built into the wall. In this chest are kept the many charms and magical potions without which no native believes he could live. These preparations are secured from a variety of specialized practitioners. The most powerful of these are the medicine men, whose assistance must be rewarded with substantial gifts. However, the medicine men do not provide the curative potions for their clients, but decide what the ingredients should be and then write them down in an ancient and secret language. This writing is understood only by the medicine men and by the herbalists who, for another gift, provide the required charm. . . .

According to Horace Miner, the Nacirema women bake their heads under ovens several times a month.

Beneath the charm-box is a small font. Each day every member of the family, in succession, enters the shrine room, bows his head before the charm-box, mingles different sorts of holy water in the font, and proceeds with a brief rite of ablution [bathing]. The holy waters are secured from the Water Temple of the community, where the priests conduct elaborate ceremonies to make the liquid ritually pure. . . .

The daily body ritual performed by everyone includes a mouth-rite. Despite the fact that these people are so punctilious[careful] about care of the mouth, this rite involves a practice which strikes the uninitiated stranger as revolting. . . . The ritual consists of inserting a small bundle of hog hairs into the mouth, along with certain magical powders, and then moving the bundle in a highly formalized series of gestures. . . .

A distinctive part of the daily body ritual . . . is performed only by men. This part of the rite includes scraping and lacerating the surface of the face with a sharp instrument. Special women's rites are performed only four times during each lunar month, but what they lack in frequency is made up in barbarity. As part of this ceremony, women bake their heads in small ovens for about an hour.

Can you identify the culture Miner studied? If not, read the word Nacirema *backwards.*

Think About It

1. Analyzing Information *What is the shrine that Miner refers to? What does the box or chest in the shrine represent? What are the various rites and rituals described by Miner?*

2. Evaluating *You might consider other aspects of American culture that lend themselves to being analyzed from an outside perspective. Choose some of these aspects and write an article similar to the one written by Miner.*

CLOSE

Review with students the meaning of the term *culture* and the five basic components of culture *(technology, symbols, language, values, and norms).* Then have students discuss teen slang and symbols and how they contribute to teen culture.

REVIEW AND ASSESS

Have students complete the **Section 1 Review** on p. 29. As **Alternative Assessment**, you may want to use the culture letter or the components of culture short story or comic strip in this section's lessons.

RETEACH

Organize students into pairs or groups of three. Have each pair or group make an annotated outline of this section that includes brief summaries of each subsection.

ENGLISH LANGUAGE LEARNERS , COOPERATIVE LEARNING

EXTEND

Have students use old magazines and newspapers to create collages that illustrate each of the five aspects of American culture or that show culture traits and complexes for a specific American culture pattern. Display students' collages in the classroom.

BLOCK SCHEDULING

Culture Complexes Individual culture traits combine to form the next level—**culture complexes.** A culture complex is a cluster of interrelated traits. The game of football is a culture complex that involves a variety of traits. Material traits include the football, the measuring chain, cleated shoes, helmets, pads, first-aid kits, and sideline benches. Kicking, passing, catching, running with the ball, blocking, and tackling are among the specific acts of football. Specific beliefs related to the game also exist, including the belief that certain rules should be followed and that penalties should be given for rule violations. The financing, marketing, and advertising of football games also form a large part of the sport's culture. In industrial societies, thousands of culture complexes can be identified and studied.

Culture Patterns Culture complexes combine to form larger levels called **culture patterns.** A culture pattern is the combination of a number of culture complexes into an interrelated whole. For example, the separate complexes of baseball, basketball, football, soccer, swimming, tennis, and track combine to form the American athletic pattern. Other patterns relate to such aspects of society as agriculture, education, family life, manufacturing, and religion. These patterns form important components of a society's culture.

INTERPRETING VISUALS Soccer is another culture complex within the culture pattern of American athletics. *What material culture traits can you identify in this image?*

SECTION 1 REVIEW

1. Define and explain
culture
material culture
nonmaterial culture
society
technology
language
values
norms
folkways
mores
laws
culture trait
culture complexes
culture patterns

2. Identify and explain
Yanomamö
San
Napoleon Chagnon

3. Categorizing Copy the graphic organizer below. Use it to identify the three levels of culture by creating a key for the diagram.

Culture

4. Finding the Main Idea

a. Identify and describe the basic components of a culture.

b. In what ways are material and nonmaterial culture different?

5. Writing and Critical Thinking

Comparing and Contrasting Write a brief essay comparing and contrasting the values of the Yanomamö with those of the San. Use the comparison to show how geographic factors have influenced the development of cultural values and norms.

Consider:
• farming lifestyle and geography of each group
• how each group's culture is affected by geographic factors
• other factors that influenced each groups cultural values

Homework Practice Online
keyword: SL3 HP2

SECTION 1 REVIEW ANSWERS

1. Define:
• culture, p. 24
• material culture, p. 24
• nonmaterial culture, p. 24
• society, p. 24
• technology, p. 24
• language, p. 25
• values, p. 25
• norms, p. 26
• folkways, p. 27
• mores, p. 27
• laws, p. 27
• culture trait, p. 27
• culture complexes, p. 29
• culture patterns, p. 29

2. Identify:
• Yanomanö, p. 26
• San, p. 26
• Napoleon Chagnon, p. 26

3. smallest boxes—culture trait; next larger-sized boxes—culture complex; two large boxes containing all of the smaller boxes—culture pattern

4a. technology—physical objects and rules for using them; symbols—anything that represents something else and has a shared meaning; language—the organization of written or spoken symbols into a standardized system; values—shared beliefs about what is good and bad or right or wrong; norms—shared rules of conduct

b. material culture—physical objects that people create and use; nonmaterial culture—abstract human creations

5. Responses will vary, but students should consider the harshness of the local geography.

SECTION 2

OBJECTIVES

1. *Describe cultural universals and explain why they exist.*

2. *Explain what the terms* ethnocentrism *and* cultural relativism *mean.*

3. *Identify factors that account for variations among and within cultures.*

🔊 LET'S GET STARTED!

As students enter the classroom, ask volunteers to share with the class any foreign cultural practices that they know of that differ greatly from American cultural practices. Next, explain that despite the varieties of cultures in the world, all cultures have certain things in common. Ask each student to list what he or she thinks some of these things might be. Instruct students to save their lists so that they can determine later how accurate they were. Then tell students that in Section 2 they will learn about ways in which cultures are the same and different, reasons for variations among cultures, and the approach sociologists take when studying other cultures.

SECTION 2 RESOURCES

REPRODUCIBLE & REVIEW

- Mastering Critical Thinking Skills 2
- Readings and Case Studies in Sociology 2
- Section 2 Review, p. 39

TECHNOLOGY

- One-Stop Planner, Lesson 2.2
- **CNN** Presents Sociology: Disgusting Foods
- Homework Practice Online
- HRW Go site

2 CULTURAL VARIATION

● **Read to Discover**
1. What are cultural universals, and why do they exist?
2. What do the terms *ethnocentrism* and *cultural relativism* mean?
3. What factors account for variations among and within cultures?

● **Define**
cultural universals, ethnocentrism, cultural relativism, subculture, counterculture

● **Identify**
George Murdock, Margaret Mead, Arapesh, Mundugumor, Marvin Harris, Edwin Sutherland

Suppose you take a trip to Tokyo. Japanese friends invite you to dinner. They tell you that they will be dining in traditional Japanese style. Would you know what to expect? Here are some guidelines.

Bring a small gift to your friends in order to show your appreciation for their hospitality. On entering the house, take off your shoes and put on the slippers they offer you. They will probably suggest that you take the place of honor at the table. Decline a couple of times before accepting. The table will be very low to the floor. Because the Japanese do not use chairs, you will have to kneel or sit on the floor. Do not stretch your legs out under the table. It is considered bad manners to point the soles of your feet at someone. During the meal, lift your bowl to your chest; then grip a bite-sized piece of food with your chopsticks and move it from the bowl to your mouth. Slurping while eating soup or noodles is acceptable. Never pour a drink for yourself. Pour drinks for others. Someone else at the table will fill your glass. After the meal, do not leave a mess. Place chopsticks on your plate and fold your napkin neatly.

This everyday activity—dinner with friends—shows that cultures can differ widely. To get an idea of how diverse world cultures are, you might consider languages. If you count only the languages that have more than 2 million speakers, there are more than 220 different languages in the world today. If you include all the local languages, the number is enormous. In addition, because there may be dialects of the same basic language, even people who speak the same language may have difficulty understanding one another. In the English language, for example, British English, American English, Canadian English, and Australian English are just a few of the possible variations.

When eating a traditional Japanese meal, certain cultural traditions are expected to be followed such as sitting on the floor, using chopsticks, and serving your company.

TEACH OBJECTIVE 1

Call on volunteers to define the term *cultural universals* *(general traits common to all cultures)* and explain why they exist *(because some needs are so basic that all societies must develop certain features to ensure their fulfillment)*. Then organize students into small groups and ask them to imagine that they are new product developers for a large multinational company. Each group is to use its knowledge of cultural universals to come up with an idea for a new product that could be marketed to many other countries. Ask each group to write a paragraph describing its product and explaining why it has wide global appeal. Finally, have each group present its idea to the class. **COOPERATIVE LEARNING**

SPOTLIGHT *on Rites of Passage*

Have students work in small groups to conduct research on how five cultures differ in their practices of a major rite of passage, such as birth, attaining womanhood or manhood, marriage, divorce, or death. You should approve each group's research topic. Then have each group use its research to create a covered booklet that describes and illustrates some different cultural practices related to the rite of passage. **COOPERATIVE LEARNING**, **BLOCK SCHEDULING**

INTERPRETING VISUALS Marriage rituals are another cultural universal. However, these rituals will vary from culture to culture. *In what ways is this Indian wedding different from a traditional American wedding?*

What Do We Have in Common?

You may be wondering how cultures can be so different when all humans have the same basic needs. The answer is that humans have the ability to meet their needs in a vast number of ways. Only biological makeup and the physical environment limit this ability. Nevertheless, some needs are so basic that all societies must develop certain features to ensure their fulfillment. These features, common to all cultures, are called **cultural universals**.

In the 1940s anthropologist George Murdock examined hundreds of different cultures in an attempt to determine what general traits are common to all cultures. Murdock used his research to compile a list of more than 65 cultural universals. Among these universals are body adornment, cooking, dancing, family, feasting, forms of greeting, funeral ceremonies, gift giving, housing, language, medicine, music, myths and folklore, religion, sports, and toolmaking.

Murdock also found that although survival may dictate the need for cultural universals, the specific nature of these traits can vary widely. One factor that gives rise to families is the need to care for young children. He argued that in all cultures, the purpose of the family is the same. The family ensures that new members will be added to society and cared for until old enough to fend for themselves. In addition, the family introduces children to the components of their culture.

The makeup of a family, however, varies from culture to culture. In most of the Western world, a family consists of one or both parents and their children. In the case of three-generation families, grandparents may be included in the definition.

In some parts of the world a family may include a man, his several wives, and their children. While the structure of family may be different, Murdock argued that the existence and purpose of families compose a cultural universal.

TEACH OBJECTIVE 2

SUGGESTION 1: To help students explain what the terms *ethnocentrism* and *cultural relativism* mean, copy the graphic organizer at the right onto the chalkboard, omitting the italicized answers. Have students copy and complete the organizer. Discuss the answers with the class. Then have students list some positive and negative consequences of both ethnocentrism and cultural relativism. Encourage group discussion and provide students with differing opinions a chance to express and defend their views. As an extension, you might have the class debate the two cultural viewpoints. **ENGLISH LANGUAGE LEARNERS**

Ethnocentrism	Cultural Relativism
the tendency to view one's own culture and group as superior to other different cultures	*belief that a culture should be judged by its own standards rather than by those of another culture*

Example	Example
Examples will vary but might include labeling another culture as inferior based on its technology.	*Examples will vary but might include examining how another society views its dress or diet.*

Religion in Canada and the United States. The cultures of Canada and the United States may seem similar on the surface. Both countries speak English, have democratic governments, and are located in North America. However, a 1996 poll of Canadian and U.S. cities found some striking differences regarding religion and politics in the two countries. Significantly more Americans said that they go to church and pray than Canadians did. In addition, more than twice as many Americans as Canadians said that religion influences their political opinions. Although a large majority of Canadians said they would be willing to vote for an atheist candidate, fewer than half of Americans would be willing to do so.

CRITICAL THINKING

What might be the reason for some cultural differences between Canada and the United States?

ANSWER: Answers will vary, but students might note the significant role of religion in early U.S. history.

Variation Among Societies

In the 1930s anthropologist Margaret Mead conducted a now classic study of cultural variation. Her purpose in the study was to determine whether differences in basic temperament—the fundamental emotional disposition of a person—result mainly from inherited characteristics or from cultural influences. To find out, she made first-hand observations of the shared, learned behaviors of several small societies in New Guinea. The desire for an in-depth understanding of cultural variation led Mead to live among the people of New Guinea and to participate in their activities.

Two of the societies that Mead examined were the Arapesh and the Mundugumor. Both groups lived in the northern part of what today is Papua New Guinea. Mead found that although the two societies lived only about 100 miles apart and shared many social traits, their cultures were vastly different. While reading the following descriptions, make comparisons between the Arapesh and Mundugumor cultures. Keep in mind, however, that the two cultures have changed greatly since the time of the study. The use of the present tense to describe past cultures is simply a method employed by some anthropologists to improve the clarity of their findings.

The Arapesh The Arapesh are contented, gentle, nonaggressive, receptive, trusting, and warm people. Their society is based on complete cooperation. They live in close-knit villages consisting of clans—families with a common ancestor. The women bring in the firewood and water, prepare the daily meals and carry goods from place to place. The men clear and fence the land, build and repair the houses, carry heavier loads, hunt, plant and care for certain crops, and cook and carve ceremonial food. Both men and women make ornaments and take care of the children. The fathers are very much involved in child care. If the mother's work is more pressing—if there is no water or firewood, for example—the father minds the children while the mother completes her tasks.

The children grow up in a very loving and friendly social environment. Babies always are tended to when they cry, and they spend much of their time being held by someone.

Children are often "lent out" to relatives, thereby increasing the number of people the children trust. The young are also encouraged to join in their elders' activities.

Children are discouraged from displaying any aggression toward others. When they feel aggressive, they are taught to express it in a way that will not harm others, such as by throwing stones on the ground or by hitting a palm tree with a stick.

When an Arapesh girl is about seven or eight years old, she is promised to a boy who is approximately six years her senior. The boy's father makes the match. In choosing a wife for his son, the father considers several factors. For convenience, he might choose a girl close to home. Or he might prefer to widen his circle of relatives by selecting a girl from far away. If the group is in need of specific skills, such as pottery making, the father might choose a girl with the desired skills. The father probably wants a responsible girl with the right kind of relatives. The Arapesh view marriage as an opportunity to increase the warm family circle in which one's descendants may live.

After the selection is made, the girl lives with the boy's family and works with her mother-in-law. She relates to her husband and his brothers and sisters as if she were a sister in the family. After five years or so, with no pressure and in their own time, the girl and her husband begin to live as a true married couple.

Most Arapesh marriages consist of one husband and one wife. Sometimes, however, a man has two wives. When a woman's husband dies, she usually marries a man who already has a wife.

The Mundugumor Unlike the Arapesh, the Mundugumor are aggressive. Mead found the men and women alike to be competitive, jealous, and violent. They are ready to recognize and avenge any insult. In addition, they delight in showing off and fighting. Until the government banned such activities, the Mundugumor were headhunters. Open hostility among all members of the same sex force the Mundugumor to scatter their residences throughout the bush. Brothers do not speak to one another and are ashamed to sit together. There is great hostility between fathers and sons. Similarly, hostility exists between sisters and between mothers and daughters.

Margaret Mead was interested in the temperament and child-rearing practices of the people of Papua New Guinea.

In the New Guinea Highlands dancers wear ceremonial wigs made from the feathers of local birds.

Although some of Margaret Mead's findings have been questioned, her initial research explored the cultural variations of many isolated groups of people.

The only ties between members of the same sex are through members of the opposite sex. These occur through a form of social organization called the rope. One rope consists of the father, his daughters, his daughters' sons, his daughters' sons' daughters, and so on. Another rope consists of the mother, her sons, her sons' daughters, and so forth. When a person dies, his or her property passes down the rope. For example, daughters inherit their father's property, and sons inherit their mother's property.

For a Mundugumor man, wealth and power come mainly from having a large number of wives. The more wives a man has, the more help he can get doing everyday tasks. Not only does he get the assistance of his wives, but can also demand help from his wives' brothers. Many Mundugumor men have as many as 8 to 10 wives. Wives are obtained by trading sisters.

Children tend to push parents apart rather than unite them. The father wants a daughter to trade for another wife. The mother, on the other hand, wants a son to work with her and be her heir.

The child-rearing practices of the Mundugumor are very different from those of the Arapesh. The Mundugumor infant is carried in a rigid basket that gives no contact with the mother. When the mother works outdoors, she leaves the child hanging in the basket in the house. The mother feeds the child when she is ready. Children are not picked up or comforted. The child faces a world full of rules: Do not wander out of sight, do not cling to your mother, and do not go to the houses of your father's other wives. Children receive slaps and other physical punishment for violating these rules.

Comparing the Two Societies What factors might account for the vast cultural differences between these two societies? At the time of Mead's study, the Arapesh lived in the mountains while the Mundugumor lived in a river valley. The Arapesh planted gardens while the Mundugumor were primarily food gatherers. For the Arapesh, food was usually scarce. The Mundugumor, on the other hand, had an abundance of food, and life was relatively easy.

Based on her research, Mead concluded that temperament is mainly the result of culture rather than biology. She noted that differences in temperament were much greater between the two societies than between males and females in the same society. Among the Arapesh, men and women alike were gentle and cooperative. Similarly, among the Mundugumor, everyone was hostile and competitive. In recent years, Mead's research methods and observations have been criticized. Nonetheless, her study vividly illustrates the wide variance among cultures.

Sociology in the World Today

TEACH

Instruct students to read the feature Language and Culture on this page and to answer the questions in the Think About It section. Then ask students to suggest concepts or objects for which there are many words in English. *(For example, English has several words for different types of businesses and automobiles.)* List students' suggestions on the chalkboard. Then have the class discuss whether the examples support the linguistic-relativity hypothesis. Finally, have each student write a few paragraphs explaining whether he or she agrees with this hypothesis. Have volunteers read their papers aloud to the class.

EXTEND

Have students, working either individually or in pairs, create two cause-and-effect charts—one that illustrates the linguistic-relativity hypothesis and one chart that illustrates the theory that language is a product of experience. Beneath the two charts, have students write a caption summarizing the information. Ask a volunteer to share his or her charts with the class. Then have students discuss their points of view regarding the connection between language and culture. **COOPERATIVE LEARNING**, **BLOCK SCHEDULING**

Exploring Cultural Diversity

Language and the Penan. The Penan people, who live in Borneo, have one word for *he* and one word for *she* in their language. However, they have six words for *we*.

CRITICAL THINKING

What might the number of words that the Penan have for the term *we* indicate about their culture and society?

ANSWER: Answers will vary, but students might suggest that the Penan may value group cooperation highly and may put the goals of the group before that of the individual.

Think About It Answers

1. that language shapes the way people perceive the real world and what is significant in it

2. Linguistic-relativity posits that to understand a culture, one must consider how its language has shaped it. Similarly, cultural relativism states that one should study and judge a culture by its own value system.

SOCIOLOGY IN THE
World Today

LANGUAGE AND CULTURE

Language, as you know, is a major component of any culture. First, language is the means by which people express all the abstract elements of culture. Second, language is the chief method through which culture is conveyed to new members of society. However, those social scientists who support the linguistic-relativity hypothesis think that language plays a far more important role. They suggest that language actually determines the content of culture. Initially advanced by anthropologist Edward Sapir and extended by his student linguist Benjamin Whorf, the linguistic-relativity hypothesis consists of two basic principles. The first principle states that language shapes the way people think. The second asserts that people who speak different languages perceive the world in different ways.

In his writings, Whorf suggested that people are conditioned by their language to notice some features of the real world and to ignore others. If a language has no word to describe an object, for example, that object has no significance for the people who speak the language. On the other hand, when a language contains many terms to describe an object, that object has great significance. When many words are provided to describe a single object or condition, people are forced to think about the object or condition in a complex way.

To illustrate that point, Whorf cited the Inuit of North America. The continuous presence of snow has great significance in the lives of the Inuit, and this significance is reflected in their language. The Inuit language contains many terms describing different types and conditions of snow. For example, Inuit use different words to describe falling snow, hard-packed snow, and drifting snow. This wide variety of terms for snow, Whorf wrote, allows the Inuit to think about it in a complex way. The English language, on the other hand, has a limited number of terms to describe snow. Hence, English-speakers do not think about snow with the same degree of complexity as the Inuit. Language paints the picture of reality. But what is considered reality, Whorf suggested, varies from language to language.

At an early age Inuit children learn their culture's different words for snow.

The linguistic-relativity hypothesis has been the subject of debate ever since it was first put forward. Recent studies have questioned the accuracy of Whorf's evidence. The observation that the Inuit have many words to describe snow is not exactly true. In the Inuit language many words may be combined into a single word. Other languages use a phrase or a sentence to achieve a similar meaning. Some studies have suggested that the debate over the number of words the Inuit use for snow is of little importance. People who have extensive experience of a particular subject—the Inuit and snow, for example—will have a large vocabulary about that subject. English-speaking skiers—who also have extensive experience of snow—use at least a dozen words for snow. Far from determining culture, then, language may simply be a product of experience.

Think About It

1. Finding the Main Idea *What is Whorf's main point about language?*

2. Drawing Inferences and Conclusions *Some social scientists think that the linguistic-relativity hypothesis contributed to the development of cultural relativism. Explain how the linguistic-relativity hypothesis and cultural relativism are related.*

On the chalkboard, write the term *cultural universals,* leave a space below it, and then write the term *cultural variation.* Ask each student to copy the terms and to link them by using the space to list some factors that account for variations among and within cultures. Then call on volunteers to share with the class some of the factors that they listed. Make a master list on the chalkboard. Finally, review the terms *subculture* and *counterculture* with the class and have students discuss ways in which each type of group might benefit and harm a society.

Have each student interview a member of a subgroup to which the student does not belong. Before conducting the interview, students should list any historical or current stereotypes of the subgroup of which they are aware. Then instruct students to ask questions about these stereotypes and about the subgroups' cultures. Have each student create a written report of his or her interview.
BLOCK SCHEDULING

Studying Variation

The study of variations in cultures presents challenges for social scientists. Cultural variations are what make different societies interesting to study. However, social scientists must be careful to remain critical of biases in their observations and conclusions.

Ethnocentrism Turn back to the beginning of this section and reread the description of Japanese cultural traits. Do some of them seem odd? It is not unusual for people to have a negative response to cultural traits that differ drastically from their own. This tendency to view one's own culture and group as superior is called **ethnocentrism**. People in all societies are, at times, ethnocentric. The belief that the characteristics of one's group or society are right and good helps to build group unity. At times, belief of the superiority of a society results from technological advances that make one group see others as inferior. However, when ethnocentrism becomes extreme in this way, culture can stagnate. By limiting the pool of acceptable members, groups and societies run the risk of excluding new influences that might prove beneficial.

Even anthropologists and sociologists struggle with ethnocentrism. Napoleon Chagnon's first impression of the Yanomamö was filtered through the

INTERPRETING VISUALS Different cultures have distinct cultural traditions that may seem odd to people outside their culture. Many people in India believe cows are sacred and refuse to eat them, while Jewish people have specific rules for preparing meat. *How might these cultural traditions be visible in everyday life?*

GOVERNMENT

Democracy and Ethnocentrism. Most Americans are proud to live in a democracy and believe that all countries should have a democratic and free society. Is this an ethnocentric view? Sociologist Robert Kaplan writes that it is wrong to assume that every culture in the world can become a democracy. He suggests that democracy works in countries such as the United States, where citizens value egalitarianism and respect institutions and elected officials. In societies that lack these cultural values, Kaplan suggests, democracy will not take hold.

RESEARCH ACTIVITY: Instruct each student to identify a country that has become a democracy in the past 15 years and to examine how successful the democratic system is or was.

Visual Answer

by the foods that different people choose to eat and how people prepare those foods

Sociology in the World Today

American Kids Abroad. American children and youth whose parents find work in other countries may spend many years living abroad. Known as third-culture kids (TCKs), such children and teens often grow up experiencing and learning two or more cultures. As a result, some TCKs experience a form of culture shock when they return to the United States after many years away. They may feel lost and different and not completely American. Seminars and organizations exist to help TCKs cope with the confusion of coming home.

ACTIVITY: Have students contact the Foreign Service Youth Foundation, which is part of the U.S. State Department, to find out what services the foundation provides for TCKs.

Visual Answer

Cultural relativism helps explain that the family wearing black are dressed differently from the other beachgoers because the family is Amish and has different cultural beliefs about proper dress for the beach.

INTERPRETING VISUALS Cultural relativism can help sociologists understand the behavior of smaller groups of people within the American society. For example, the Amish have a traditional way of dressing and try to avoid using modern technology. *How might cultural relativism help you explain this image?*

standards of his own culture. Everything about the Yanomamö culture contradicted Chagnon's expectations of how people should look and act. Chagnon admits that when he began to study the Yanomamö of Venezuela and Brazil, their appearance and behavior initially horrified him.

Cultural Relativism Social scientists attempt to keep an open mind toward cultural variations. To do so, many adopt an attitude of **cultural relativism**, which is the belief that cultures should be judged by their own standards rather than by applying the standards of another culture. In other words, researchers who practice cultural relativism attempt to understand cultural practices from the points of view of the members of the society being studied.

Cultural relativism helps sociologists and anthropologists understand practices that seem strange or different from those of their own culture. In *Cannibals and Kings*, anthropologist Marvin Harris explored the religious prohibition in India against killing cows even when food shortages exist. He suggested that the prohibition was related to the development of Indian agriculture. Cows played a vital role in feeding the Indian people, even though cows themselves were not eaten. Cattle provided the power for plowing, which prepared the land for planting. Therefore, a large number of cows were needed to ensure good harvests. In addition, cows provided milk, a traditionally important part of the Indian diet. When viewed from this perspective, it is possible to see that the prohibition against killing cows has practical benefits.

TEACH

Have students read the feature Cultural Discontinuity and the American Indian Dropout Rate on this page and discuss as a class the questions in the Think About It section. Then ask students to suggest some positive and negative results of the educational changes listed in the feature. Allow students with different views a chance to express and defend their opinions. Then ask students to suggest other ways in which schools could deal with issues related to cultural discontinuity.

SPOTLIGHT
on Case Studies of Cultural Discontinuity

Have each student conduct research to find another example of a cultural discontinuity case study. Then have each student write a short report describing the study, the ways in which the problems stemming from the cultural discontinuity were addressed, and the situation's outcome (if applicable). Each student should adopt an attitude of cultural relativism and should suggest some actions for resolving the culture clash. Have one or two volunteers share their case studies with the class. **BLOCK SCHEDULING**

Case Studies
AND OTHER TRUE STORIES

CULTURAL DISCONTINUITY AND THE AMERICAN INDIAN DROPOUT RATE

For the most part, members of subgroups have little problem living within the predominant culture of society. However, some subgroup members find that the values, beliefs, and practices of the larger culture are at odds with those of their subculture. This clash of cultures results in a situation that sociologists call cultural discontinuity. Subgroup members are forced to choose between their subculture and the predominant culture.

Several studies of dropout rates among American Indian high-school students have focused on the effect of cultural discontinuity. Many factors such as poverty, segregation, and poor schools have also contributed to the dropout rate. The studies on cultural discontinuity point out that there are fundamental differences in the culture traits valued by the school system (the predominant culture) and those valued by traditional American Indians (the subculture). In her study of Ute high-school students, Betty J. Kramer notes that school systems generally view competition as a positive feature of American society. One of the goals of education is seen as providing students with the tools necessary to compete in a market economy. In keeping with the competitive model, achievement is measured on the basis of grades and scores on standardized tests.

Ute society, Kramer points out, is not based on a competitive model. Rather, the Ute culture is basically cooperative. Thus, the Ute prefer to measure achievement on the basis of effort, commitment, and the degree of satisfaction people receive from the creative process. Most jobs in the Ute community are interchangeable, and people transfer from one job to another with ease. Formal education does not play an important role among the Ute because jobs are not assigned on the basis of whether or not a person has a high-school diploma. Success in school among Ute and other American Indian peoples, then, is not necessarily a valued trait. In some respects, failure is seen as a reinforcement of traditional culture.

Because of many factors, American Indians face challenges in the American education system.

The continuing high level of failure among American Indian high-school students worries many American Indian leaders. The American Indian dropout rate stands at about 35 percent—more than twice the national average. The lack of a high-school diploma, these leaders know, places young American Indians at a disadvantage in today's economy. These leaders have suggested several changes to address cultural discontinuity and reverse the high failure rate. These changes include the following:

- hiring more American Indian teachers and training teachers to be more sensitive to American Indian culture
- using teaching and testing methods that are culturally appropriate
- developing a curriculum that is culturally relevant to American Indian students
- encouraging greater parental involvement in schools

Such changes, American Indian leaders believe, will help preserve students' traditional cultures yet still provide them with the skills to succeed in the wider world.

Think About It

1. **Analyzing Information** *What is cultural discontinuity? Why might it be a particular problem for students who belong to racial and ethnic minority groups?*
2. **Making Generalizations and Predictions** *Do you think the educational changes noted above will enable more American Indian students to succeed in high school? Why or why not?*

internet connect

TOPIC: Cultural Adaptation in the United States
GO TO: go.hrw.com
KEYWORD: SL3 SC2

Have students access the Internet through the HRW Go site to conduct research on and analyze the effects of immigrant and American Indian groups on the components of American culture. Then have students work in small groups to create a chart or database that contains information on the changes to the majority culture that have resulted.

Think About It Answers

1. when members of a subculture find their beliefs, values, or practices at odds with those of the larger or predominant culture; because public schools promote and value the culture traits of the predominant culture

2. Answers will vary. Students who agree might respond that a greater sensitivity to American Indian culture will help more Indian students to remain interested and to see the value of staying in school. Students who disagree might respond that the changes will not affect American Indian students' preference not to compete for success.

■ CLOSE

Ask each student to imagine that he or she is writing an advice column on interacting with people of different cultures. Ask students to use what they have learned in this section to describe some suggestions that they might make. Use the activity to review the section's main ideas and key terms.

■ REVIEW AND ASSESS

Have students complete the **Section 2 Review** on p. 39. As **Alternative Assessment**, you may want to use the culturally universal product activity or the ethnocentrism–cultural relativism essay in this section's lessons.

■ RETEACH

Review the section's Define and Identify terms with students. Then have each student write one or two paragraphs summarizing this section's main ideas. In addition, the paragraphs must incorporate each of the section's Define and Identify terms. Call on volunteers to share their paragraphs with the class. As they do, review this section's main ideas. Finally, have the class work together to create a master paragraph summarizing these main ideas. **ENGLISH LANGUAGE LEARNERS**

Map Answers

1. CA, FL, NY, TX

2. Answers will vary, but students might suggest questions such as how cultural patterns might differ in states with higher immigrant populations.

SECTION 2 REVIEW ANSWERS

1. Define:
- cultural universals, p. 31
- ethnocentrism, p. 35
- cultural relativism, p. 36
- subculture, p. 38
- counterculture, p. 39

2. Identify:
- George Murdock, p. 31
- Margaret Mead, p. 32
- Arapesh, p. 32
- Mundugumor, p. 32
- Marvin Harris, p. 36
- Edwin Sutherland, p. 38

3. negatives—can lead to cultural stagnation, excludes new ideas; positives—helps build unity, helps enforce cultural mores

4a. some needs are so basic that all societies must develop certain features to meet them

b. ethnocentrism—the tendency to view one's own culture as superior; cultural relativism—belief that cultures should be judged by their own standards

c. The farming culture of the Arapesh promoted cooperation. The hunting culture of the Mundugumor promoted competition and fierceness.

Variation Within Societies

Cultural variations exist not only among societies but also within societies. Among the major sources of variation within a society are the unique cultural practices of various subgroups.

As an American, you share a common culture with all other Americans. American culture is a collection of traits, complexes, and patterns that, by and large, are distinct from those of other societies. In addition to these broad cultural features some groups in society share values, norms, and behaviors that are not shared by the entire population. The unique cultural characteristics of these groups form a **subculture**. Criminologist Edwin Sutherland developed the idea of subcultures in the 1920s, through his work on crime and juvenile delinquency. In addition to deviant subcultures, sociologists today recognize age, gender, ethnic, religious, political, geographic, social-class, and occupational subcultures.

Most subcultures do not reject all of the values and practices of the larger society. For example, residents of San Francisco's Chinatown have many broad American cultural traits, such as going to public schools, playing with toys, and working at similar jobs. The culture of the Chinatown residents also includes the Chinese language and specific foods and celebrations that are not shared by most Americans. Chinese New Year is one such cultural celebration. The residents of Little Havana in Miami and the

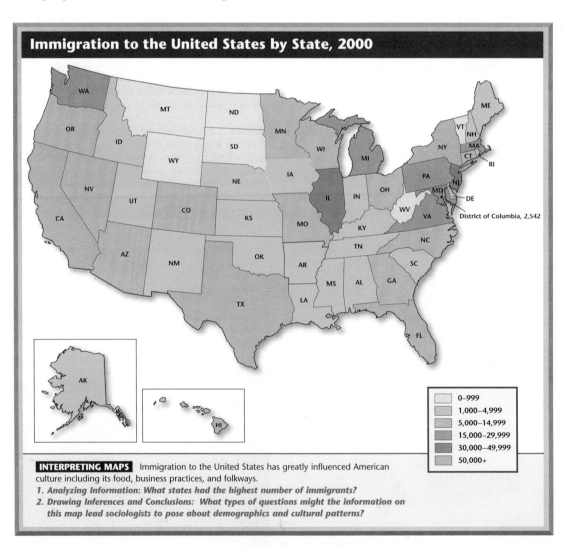

Immigration to the United States by State, 2000

District of Columbia, 2,542	

0–999
1,000–4,999
5,000–14,999
15,000–29,999
30,000–49,999
50,000+

INTERPRETING MAPS Immigration to the United States has greatly influenced American culture including its food, business practices, and folkways.
1. Analyzing Information: What states had the highest number of immigrants?
2. Drawing Inferences and Conclusions: What types of questions might the information on this map lead sociologists to pose about demographics and cultural patterns?

1. Review with the class the works of Margaret Mead and George Murdock. Then have each student write a reaction paper describing what he or she thinks is the most significant contribution each person made to the understanding of culture.
BLOCK SCHEDULING

2. Have each student prepare a short research paper on one of the following counterculture groups or on another counterculture group of his or her choosing: hippies, ravers, skinheads, or terrorists.
BLOCK SCHEDULING

3. Have selected groups of students visit shops in the local community that specialize in foods from other nations. Ask each group to compile two lists of foods available in the shops: those that are generally common in the United States and those that are generally unfamiliar in the United States. Groups should write short descriptions of each food on the latter lists. Then have the groups quiz their classmates on their familiarity with the variety of foods available worldwide. **COOPERATIVE LEARNING , BLOCK SCHEDULING**

Navajo of the Southwest also have their own languages and other cultural traits that are not shared by the larger American society. Subcultures have also developed around age groups. Youth subcultures have existed in the United States throughout the 1900s. Characteristics of these youth cultures have included owning fast cars, listening to rock or hip hop music, and wearing certain clothes.

Most subcultures do not present a threat to society. Modern society is dependent on various subcultures—such as the military, the police, lawyers, physicians, teachers, and religious leaders—to provide many important functions. Furthermore, subcultures, particularly those based on race and ethnicity, add diversity and may make society more open to change.

In some instances, however, subcultural practices are consciously intended to challenge the values of the larger society. Sometimes a group rejects the major values, norms, and practices of the larger society and replaces them with a new set of cultural patterns. Sociologists call the resulting subculture a **counterculture**. The cyberpunk movement, anarchists, organized crime families, and the hippie movement of the 1960s are examples of countercultures in the United States. For example, some organized crime families reject societal norms such as obeying laws.

As is true in the case of cultural variation among societies, cultural variation within a society may give rise to ethnocentric feelings. Sociologists try to maintain the same attitude of cultural relativism when studying subcultures and countercultures.

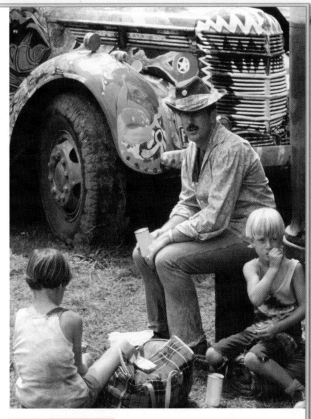

INTERPRETING VISUALS The hippie counterculture movement of the 1960s rejected cultural norms and values concerning dress, hairstyle, work, and raising children. *What clues does this photo offer about the values and norms of the hippie counterculture?*

5. Paragraphs will vary, but students should exhibit an understanding of subculture groups.

Visual Answer

might include an appreciation of the outdoors and relaxed living

CHAPTER 2 REVIEW
ANSWERS

WRITING A SUMMARY
See the section subtitles for the main topics in this chapter.

IDENTIFYING PEOPLE AND IDEAS

1. all the shared products of human groups

2. a group of mutually interdependent people who share a common culture and feeling of unity

3. shared beliefs about what is good or bad, or right or wrong

4. shared rules of conduct for specific situations

5. norms that do not have great moral significance

6. norms with great moral significance because violating them endangers society

7. general traits that are common to all cultures

8. anthropologist who in the 1940s compiled a list of cultural universals

9. anthropologist whose 1930s study of New Guinea peoples examined how culture influences temperament

---

SECTION 2 REVIEW

1. Define and explain
cultural universals
ethnocentrism
cultural relativism
subculture
counterculture

2. Identify and explain
George Murdock
Margaret Mead
Arapesh
Mundugumor
Marvin Harris
Edwin Sutherland

3. Categorizing Copy the graphic organizer below. Use it to identify the negative and positive consequences of ethnocentrism.

Ethnocentrism
Positives   Negatives

4. **Finding the Main Idea**
a. Why do cultural universals exist?
b. How does ethnocentrism differ from cultural relativism?
c. How did geographic factors influence the culture of the Arapesh and Mundugumor people that Mead studied?

5. **Writing and Critical Thinking**
Analyzing Information Write two brief paragraphs comparing the cultural norms and practices of American subculture groups, such as the residents of Chinatown and Little Havana as well as the Navajo.
Consider:
• cultural traits of each group
• how ethnocentrism and cultural relativism might influence the study of these subcultures

Homework Practice Online
keyword: SL3 HP2

Review and Assessment
Resources
• Chapter 2 Review, pp. 40–41
• Chapter Review Activities with Answer Key
• Global Skill Builder CD–ROM
• Chapter 2 Test Generator
  (on the One-Stop Planner)
• Chapter 2 Test (Form A or B)
• Alternative Assessment Handbook
• HRW Go site

 REVIEW
Have students complete the
Chapter 2 Review on pp. 40–41.

 ASSESS
Use one of the chapter tests to assess students' understanding of the content.
For **Alternative Assessment**, see the
Alternative Assessment Handbook.

10. belief that cultures should be judged by their own standards

UNDERSTANDING MAIN IDEAS

1. material—includes automobiles, books, buildings, clothing, and computers; nonmaterial—includes beliefs, language, work practices, political systems, and economic systems

2. a standardized system of written or spoken symbols; enables societies to communicate their values

3. folkways—acceptable behaviors with little moral significance; mores—acceptable behaviors with great moral significance; laws—written rules of conduct; examples will vary

4. trait—individual tool, act, or belief that is related to a specific situation; complex—a cluster of interrelated cultural traits; pattern—combination of several culture complexes into an interrelated whole

5. She helped show how cultures can vary despite geographical proximity.

6. Ethnocentrism is the tendency to view one's own culture as superior, whereas cultural relativism is the belief that cultures should be judged by their own standards.

7. A subculture shares some values, norms, and behaviors that are not shared by the larger culture. When subcultural practices consciously challenge the values of the larger society, the subculture is a counterculture.

CHAPTER

2 Review

 Writing a Summary

Using standard grammar, spelling, sentence structure, and punctuation, summarize the information in this chapter.
Consider:
• the basic components of culture
• cultural universals
• factors that account for differences within and between cultures

Identifying People and Ideas

Identify the following people and terms and use them in appropriate sentences.

1. culture
2. society
3. values
4. norms
5. folkways
6. mores
7. cultural universals
8. George Murdock
9. Margaret Mead
10. cultural relativism

 Understanding Main ideas

Section 1 (pp. 24–29)

1. List five examples of material culture and five examples of nonmaterial culture.

2. What is language, and why is it such an important part of culture?

3. How do folkways, mores, and laws differ? List three examples of each type of norm.

4. How do cultural traits, cultural complexes, and cultural patterns differ?

Section 2 (pp. 30–39)

5. How did Margaret Mead contribute to the study of cultures?

6. What is ethnocentrism? How does it differ from cultural relativism?

7. How are subcultures and countercultures related?

Thinking Critically

1. Comparing and Contrasting How are the norms of different subcultures similar and different? What cultural universals can you find within these groups?

2. Finding the Main Idea What types of things can serve as symbols? What determines whether something can serve as a symbol?

3. Identifying Cause and Effect How might you explain the cultural differences between the Arapesh and Mundugumor in terms of geographic factors?

4. Identifying Points of View Is Miner's description of the Nacirema an example of cultural relativism? Explain your answer.

5. Evaluating How do you think stereotypes about different American subcultures are related to ethnocentrism?

 Writing About Sociology

1. Summarizing Imagine that you have invited friends from a foreign country to dinner. Write a description of the dinner that focuses on typical American dining and entertaining practices that your guests might find odd or unfamiliar.

2. Analyzing Information Conduct research on several American subcultures that may be distinct because of ethnicity, national origin, age, socioeconomic strata, or gender traits. Copy the graphic organizer below and use it to collect and examine data on cultural norms and stereotypes of subcultures. Write a report on your findings.

	Stereotypes	Actual Norms
Subculture		
Subculture		
Subculture		
Subculture		

RETEACH

Organize students into pairs or small groups. Have each pair or group create a diagram or flowchart that illustrates, organizes, and relates the main ideas covered in this chapter. Call on volunteers to share their diagrams or flowcharts with the class. Use the volunteers' work as samples to review the chapter's main concepts and how they relate to each other. Finally, have each student write one paragraph summarizing the chapter.
ENGLISH LANGUAGE LEARNERS

SOCIOLOGY PROJECTS

1. Applying Sociology Have students conduct research to find a foreign cultural practice or belief that they find odd or unfamiliar. Then ask each student to use cultural relativism to analyze the practice or belief and to write a short paper describing his or her results.

2. Using Observation Skills Instruct students to spend several hours observing people in a public place and to note the variety of gestures that people use to communicate. Have students report their findings to the class. Then lead a discussion on the topic.

BUILDING SOCIAL STUDIES SKILLS

Interpreting Charts

Study the chart below. Then use the information to answer the questions that follow.

Norms of Culture

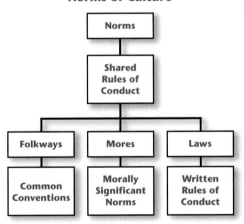

1. Which of the following is the most complete definition of the term *norms*?
   a. common conventions
   b. morally significant rules
   c. shared rules of conduct
   d. written rules of conduct
2. Which types of norms—folkways, mores, or laws—do you think are more readily internalized? Why?

Analyzing Primary Sources

McKenzie Wark, a communications professor, has written extensively on culture and technology. Read the following excerpt and answer the questions that follow.

"In a sense, subcultures are always a product of the media technology of the age. . . . Cyberpunk is a product of the huge array of technical and scientific universities created in the U.S. to service the military industrial complex. Your typical cyberpunk is white, suburban, middle class, and technically skilled. . . . They don't drop out, they jack in. They are a fabulous example of how each generation, growing up with a given level of media technology, has to discover the limits and potentials of that technology by experimenting with everyday life itself.

Subcultures are an art form. They can have their delinquent edge, its true. . . . Cyberpunks sometimes have a romantic fascination with hacking into other peoples' computers. All this is a testing of limits, a pushing to the limit of the social norm. The enduring product of any subculture is a rapid innovation in popular style. Subcultures pioneer styles of life for the mainstream. In the case of cyberpunk, the networked world of cyberspace, the interactive world of multimedia and the new sensoria of virtual reality will all owe a little to [the cyberpunks'] willingness to be the test pigs for these emergent technologies."

3. According to Wark, subcultures are always a product of which one of the following?
   a. the media technology of the age
   b. middle-class, suburban discontent
   c. the military-industrial complex
   d. experimentation with drugs
4. What purposes do subcultures perform?

SOCIOLOGY PROJECTS

Cooperative Learning

Using Your Observation Skills With two or three other students, review several current-affairs magazines and newspapers over a period of a week. Note and list the symbols of American culture that you and other group members observe during your reading. Using photocopies, clippings, sketches, and other visual materials, create an annotated collage of these symbols. You may want to display and discuss your collage.

internet connect

Internet Activity: go.hrw.com
KEYWORD: SL3 SC2
Choose a topic on cultural diversity to:
- create a Web page on cultural universals and the material and nonmaterial aspects of your community's culture.
- research the influence of immigrant and American Indian groups on American culture.
- create an illustrated pamphlet on the effect of global communication technology on cultural universals.

THINKING CRITICALLY

1. Some subcultures will share the larger cultures' norms, such as family structures. Norms that differ may include religious beliefs. Cultural universals may include traits related to family, religion, and housing.

2. anything; people must recognize its shared meaning

3. Arapesh—farm, live in clans in close-knit villages, and cooperate; Mundugumor—hunt, live scattered in small groups, and relations are competitive

4. No, it is a satiric look at ethnocentrism, as shown by the use of terms such as *revolting* and *barbaric*.

5. Such stereotypes are often based on ethnocentric beliefs.

WRITING ABOUT SOCIOLOGY

1. Descriptions will vary, but students might mention table manners, utensils, and how food is served.

2. Reports will vary, but students should include a description and stereotype of each subculture.

BUILDING SOCIAL STUDIES SKILLS

1. c

2. Answers will vary, but students should give reasons to support their positions.

3. a

4. Subcultures test the limits of social norms and provide innovation in styles of life.

CHAPTER 3

Cultural Conformity and Adaptation

CHAPTER RESOURCE MANAGER

Objectives	Pacing Guide	Resources

SECTION 1:
The American Value System
(pp. 44–49)

REV Section 1
Review, p. 48

- Identify the basic values that form the foundation of American culture.
- Describe new values that have developed in the United States since the 1970s.

Regular 1 day	Block Scheduling 0.5 day

Block Scheduling Handbook with Team Teaching Strategies, Chapter 3

Resources

- 📼 **CNN** Presents Sociology: American Values: Patriotism
- **RS** Graphic Organizer 3
- 🌐 HRW Go site
- **SM** Mastering Critical Thinking Skills 3
- **PS** Readings and Case Studies in Sociology 3
- **E** Research Projects and Activities for Teaching Sociology 3
- **SM** Study Skills and Writing Guide

SECTION 2:
Social Control
(pp. 50–53)

REV Section 2
Review, p. 53

- Identify how the norms of society are enforced.
- Describe the differences between positive and negative sanctions and between formal and informal sanctions.

Regular 0.5 day	Block Scheduling 0.25 day

Block Scheduling Handbook with Team Teaching Strategies, Chapter 3

Chapter Review And Assessment

- **REV** Chapter 3 Review, pp. 62–63
- **REV** Chapter Review Activities with Answer Key
- 💿 Global Skill Builder CD–ROM
- 💿 Chapter 3 Test Generator (on the One-Stop Planner)
- **A** Chapter 3 Test (Form A or B)
- **A** Alternative Assessment Handbook
- 🌐 HRW Go site

SECTION 3:
Social Change
(pp. 54–61)

REV Section 3
Review, p. 61

- Identify and describe the main sources of social change.
- Describe the factors that lead people to resist social change.

Regular 1 day	Block Scheduling 0.5 day

Block Scheduling Handbook with Team Teaching Strategies, Chapter 3

Chapter Resource Key

PS Primary Sources	**A** Assessment	📼 Video
RS Reading Support	**REV** Review	🌐 Internet
E Enrichment	🖥 Transparencies	💻 Holt Presentation Maker Using Microsoft® PowerPoint®
SM Skills Mastery	💿 CD-ROM	

 One-Stop Planner CD–ROM

See the *One-Stop Planner* for a complete list of additional resources for students and teachers.

One-Stop Planner CD–ROM

It's easy to plan lessons, select resources, and print out materials for your students when you use the **One-Stop Planner CD–ROM with Test Generator.**

Chapter Project Preview

The following activities are included in the Chapter Review. You may want to make the suggested preparations.

CHAPTER REVIEW ACTIVITY

Linking to Community Student groups will develop, administer, and analyze surveys of what the community considers to be the core values of American society. To help students, provide samples of surveys or of survey questions. You might also create guidelines to ensure the uniformity of the surveys.

LESSON ACTIVITY

Applying Sociology Student groups will develop a propaganda campaign to urge fellow students to uphold one or more of the core American values. Before starting the project, make certain that students understand the term *propaganda.* You might also describe some forms of propaganda and provide some examples of its use.

INTERNET ACTIVITIES

American Value System Students will use provided Internet links to research American values and then create a pamphlet evaluating how these values influence the attitudes, behaviors, and perceptions of persons and groups. In preparation, create a paper or computer template for students' pamphlets and provide some sample pamphlets for students to examine.

Norms and Social Control Students will use provided Internet links to conduct research on the ways in which norms can be enforced through social control. Students will then work in small groups to design a system of social control to enforce the norm of students bringing all necessary materials to class. To promote uniformity, create a table or other type of graphic organizer to help groups include the required elements in their systems of social control.

Additional Resources

PRINT RESOURCES FOR TEACHERS

Maybury-Lewis, David, and Roy Richard Grinker, contributors. *Peoples of the World: Their Cultures, Traditions and Ways of Life.* Washington, D.C.: National Geographic Society, 2001. Leading experts explore the multitude of diverse cultures on Earth.

Yankelovich, Daniel. *New Rules: Searching for Self-Fulfillment in a World Turned Upside Down.* New York: Random House, 1981. Examines the importance of self-fulfillment in American society.

PRINT RESOURCES FOR STUDENTS

Bradbury, Ray. *Fahrenheit 451.* New York: Ballantine Books. 1987. Futuristic novel in which the government controls the people through censorship.

Orwell, George. *1984.* New York: New American Library, 1983. Pessimistic prediction of society's future.

MULTIMEDIA RESOURCES

All the Troubles of the World (vhs; 23 min.) Encyclopaedia Britannica Educational Corporation. Isaac Asimov describes a futuristic world in which a computer controls the earth's economy, science, and people.

The Klan: A Legacy of Hate in America (vhs, color; 29 min.) Films Incorporated Video. Illustrates the concept of ethnocentrism through an examination of the history, ideas, and activities of the Ku Klux Klan.

Tradition and Change (filmstrip on vhs; color; 10 min.) Social Studies School Service. Uses a global, cross-cultural approach to analyze the conflict between traditional practices and forces for change.

Values (vhs; 30 min.) Cambridge Educational. Helps students to focus on values and priorities and illustrates how values may change over the course of a lifetime.

HRW ONLINE RESOURCES

internet connect · go.hrw.com

GO TO: go.hrw.com
Then type in a keyword.

TEACHER HOME PAGE
KEYWORD: SL3 Teacher

CHAPTER INTERNET ACTIVITIES
KEYWORD: SL3 SC3
Choose an activity to have students:
• create a pamphlet that evaluates how American values influence perceptions, attitudes, and behaviors.
• design a system of social control in which a specific norm is enforced.
• create a thematic flowchart that outlines the sources of and resistance to social change.

CHAPTER ENRICHMENT LINKS
KEYWORD: SL3 CH3

ONLINE ASSESSMENT
Homework Practice
KEYWORD: SL3 HP3
Standardized Test Prep
KEYWORD: SL3 STP3
Rubrics
KEYWORD: SS Rubrics

CONTENT UPDATES
KEYWORD: SS Content Updates

HOLT PRESENTATION MAKER
KEYWORD: SL3 PPT3

ONLINE READING SUPPORT
KEYWORD: SS Strategies

CURRENT EVENTS
KEYWORD: S3 Current Events

CHAPTER

3

Cultural Conformity and Adaptation

SECTION 1
The American Value System

SECTION 2
Social Control

SECTION 3
Social Change

CHAPTER REVIEW

Build on What You Know

Ask students to answer the following questions:

What are some general American values?

Consider:

- the U.S. political and economic systems
- the nation's history
- the life goals of many Americans

Why might a society's values change over time?

Consider:

- changes in technology
- governmental or economic changes
- social movements and warfare

Internet Activity

Have students access the Internet through the HRW Go site to conduct research on American values and the ways in which messages regarding values are reflected in the media or through social institutions. Then have each student create a pamphlet that evaluates the ways in which the American value system is used to influence attitudes, behaviors, and perceptions of persons and groups.

CHAPTER

3

Cultural Conformity and Adaptation

Build on What You Know

Values and norms are two basic components of culture. Values and norms are expressed in cultural folkways, mores, and laws. In this chapter you will explore the American value system and examine how American society attempts to ensure that its values and norms are upheld. You will also review the sources of change and the reasons that some people resist change.

Although culture is always changing, many values and norms are formulated and enforced in informal social situations.

*L*ife *in* *S*ociety

The American culture is dynamic, meaning that it has changed over time. However, some values have endured since the earliest days of the country. In the late 1700s Benjamin Franklin listed 13 virtues that he considered important.

"1. Temperance: Eat not to dullness; drink not to elevation.

2. Silence: Speak not but what may benefit others or yourself. . . .

3. Order: Let all your things have their places. . . .

4. Resolution: Resolve to perform what you ought; perform without fail what you resolve.

5. Frugality: Make no expense but to do good to others or yourself; i.e., waste nothing.

6. Industry: Lose no time; be always employ'd in something useful; cut off all unnecessary action.

7. Sincerity: Use no hurtful deceit; think innocently and justly. . . .

8. Justice: Wrong none by doing injuries. . . .

9. Moderation: Avoid extremes; forbear resenting injuries so much as you think they deserve.

10. Cleanliness: Tolerate no uncleanliness. . . .

11. Tranquility: Be not disturbed at trifles or at accidents. . . .

12. Chastity: Rarely use venery but for health . . . or offspring.

13. Humility: Imitate Jesus and Socrates."

TRUTH OR FICTION

What's Your Opinion?

Read the following statements about sociology. Do you think they are true or false? You will learn whether each statement is true or false as you read this chapter.

• There are no values that are central to the American way of life.

• The only reason people comply with the norms of society is to avoid being punished.

• Cultures change at the same rate and for the same reasons.

► **WHY SOCIOLOGY MATTERS**

Sociologists are interested in the development of new American values. Use **CNN fyi.com** or other current events sources to learn more about the emerging values of self-fulfillment in America. Write a short report on your findings.

CNN fyi.com

LET'S GET STARTED!

As students enter the classroom, discuss with them how many politicians in recent years have urged a return to traditional American values as part of their campaigns. Then conduct a brainstorming session in which students consider what values might be considered traditionally American. List students' suggestions on the chalkboard. When no new ideas are forthcoming, tell students that in Section 1 they will learn about some traditional American values and ways in which American values are changing.

SECTION 1 RESOURCES

REPRODUCIBLE & REVIEW

- Graphic Organizer 3
- Research Projects and Activities for Teaching Sociology 3
- Section 1 Review, p. 48

TECHNOLOGY

- One-Stop Planner, Lesson 3.1
- **CNN** Presents Sociology: American Values: Patriotism
- Homework Practice Online

Visual Answer

Most students will answer yes, because athletes must work hard to improve their abilities and often are willing to do so because they have a strong desire for personal achievement.

---

1 THE AMERICAN VALUE SYSTEM

Read to Discover
1. What are the basic values that form the foundation of American culture?
2. What new values have developed in the United States since the 1970s?

Define
self-fulfillment, narcissism

Identify
Robin M. Williams, James M. Henslin, Christopher Lasch, Daniel Bell, Daniel Yankelovich

Ethnic, racial, religious, social-status, and geographical variations in American society make for a diverse culture. Nevertheless, the vast majority of Americans share certain values. Sociologists are referring to these values when they speak of traditional American culture.

Traditional American Values

In his study *American Society* sociologist Robin M. Williams analyzed American values. He identified a set of 15 values that are central to the American way of life. Among these basic values are personal achievement, individualism, work, morality, humanitarianism, efficiency and practicality, progress and material comfort, equality, democracy, and freedom.

Personal Achievement Most Americans value personal achievement. This value is not a surprise considering that the United States was built primarily by people who believed in individualism and competition. This belief in the importance of personal achievement is most evident in the area of employment, where achievement often is measured in terms of power and wealth.

Individualism For most Americans, individual effort is the key to personal achievement. They strongly believe that success comes through hard work and initiative. This emphasis on individualism has a negative side, however. Most Americans feel that if a person does not succeed, that person is to blame.

Work Most Americans value work, regardless of the rewards involved. Americans view discipline, dedication,

and hard work as signs of virtue. They often view those who choose not to work as lazy or even immoral.

Morality and Humanitarianism The United States was founded on strong religious faith, on a belief in justice and equality, and on charity toward the less fortunate. Most Americans place a high value on morality and tend to view the world in terms of right and wrong. At the same time, they are quick to help those who are less fortunate than themselves.

Efficiency and Practicality Americans tend to be practical and inventive people. They believe that every problem has a solution. Problem solving involves discovering the most efficient technique for dealing with a situation or involves determining the most practical response to the issue at hand. As a result, Americans tend to judge objects such as new technology on their usefulness and judge people on their ability to get things done.

Progress and Material Comfort Americans have always looked to the future with optimism. They believe that through hard work and determination, living standards will continue to improve. This belief in progress is paired with a belief in the ability of science and technology to make the world a better and more comfortable place. Both views are important because most Americans also place a high value on material comfort.

INTERPRETING VISUALS Many American athletes such as Venus Williams have a strong sense of personal achievement. *Do you think the values of hard work and individualism are also important to these athletes? Why?*

Equality and Democracy The United States was founded on the principle of human equality. The U.S. Declaration of Independence proclaims, "We hold these truths to be self-evident, that all men are created equal." Many Americans believe that to have human equality, there must be an equality of opportunity and an equal chance at success. Although Americans value equality of opportunity, they do not necessarily believe that everyone will be equally successful. The values of hard work and personal achievement lead most Americans to view success as a reward that must be earned.

The belief in equality extends to the form of government that Americans value—democracy. Americans believe that citizens have the right to express their opinions and to participate freely in choosing their representatives in government.

Freedom Freedom is an important value for most Americans. Americans particularly value personal freedoms of choice such as the freedom of religion, speech, and press, which are guaranteed in the U.S. Constitution. Americans steadfastly protect these freedoms from direct government interference in their daily lives and in business dealings.

INTERPRETING VISUALS American students are taught the values of humanity, democracy, and freedom in school. *What values do visiting the Jefferson Monument and raising funds for needy Afghan children reflect?*

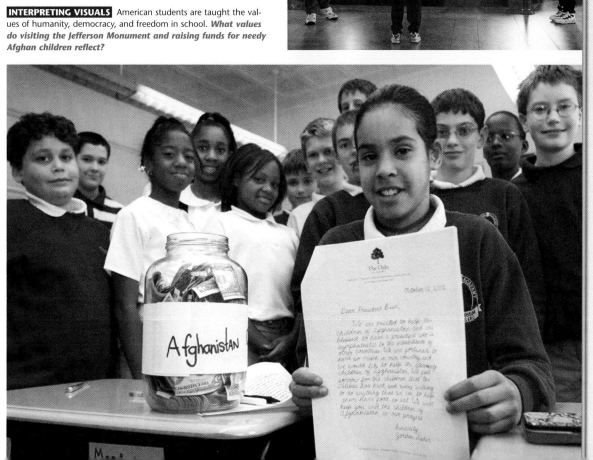

45

◼ TEACH OBJECTIVE 2

SUGGESTION 1: Organize students into small groups and have each group write a short skit that describes one of the new values that have developed in the United States since the 1970s *(values related to self-fulfillment and concern for the environment)*. Then have each group present its skit to the class. Encourage student feedback. **COOPERATIVE LEARNING**

SUGGESTION 2: Lead a class discussion on the new values that have developed in the United States since the 1970s *(as listed in the previous activity)*. Then have each student write an essay expressing whether he or she thinks the value of self-fulfillment has hurt or benefited American society.

INTERPRETING VISUALS Many Americans consider participation in our democratic system of government to be an important civic duty. *Why might some Americans consider attending a city council meeting an act of good citizenship?*

Other Core Values These values are not the only values that help define American culture. Williams also included nationalism and patriotism, science and rationality, and racial and group superiority in his list of core values. Another sociologist, James M. Henslin, suggested that additional values such as education might be included. Many Americans think that everyone should achieve the highest level of education that his or her abilities will allow. Americans tend to unfavorably view those who deliberately choose not to fulfill their educational potential. Henslin also pointed out that religious values are important in American culture. While Americans do not expect people to belong to a church, temple, or mosque, they do expect them to live according to basic religious principles. Finally, Henslin suggested romantic love was another core American value. Americans strongly believe that people should marry primarily because they fall in love with each other.

Even though values are vital to the stability of society, they may sometimes produce conflict. Not everyone agrees on what are acceptable American values. Even when people agree on the importance of a certain set of values, individuals do not uphold all of these values to the same degree. Strongly upholding the values of personal achievement and material comfort, for example, may weaken an individual's commitment to such values as morality and equality.

Our Changing Values

The problem of conflicting values is complicated by the fact that values, like all aspects of society, are dynamic. Over time, some values change and new ones emerge. In the years since Williams's and Henslin's studies, sociologists have traced the development of several related new values in the United States. These values, which include leisure, physical fitness, and youthfulness, might be grouped under the term **self-fulfillment**.

Self-fulfillment is a commitment to the full development of one's personality, talents, and potential. The emergence of this value can be seen in the self-help industry and the human-potential movement. Seminars, television programs, and books offer people ideas on how to improve their personal and professional lives. Health clubs and diet centers promise to transform people's health and looks. Advertisements challenge people to "be all you can be," to "grab the gusto," and to "experience the good life."

This growing emphasis on personal fulfillment created debate among social scientists. In his book *The Culture of Narcissism*, social historian Christopher Lasch went so far as to consider this emphasis on personal fulfillment a personality disorder. He termed this disorder

Sociology in the World Today

TEACH

Have students read the feature Young Americans and Values on this page. Ask volunteers to discuss their responses to each of the Think About It questions. Then conduct a class poll of the issues that students find most important and whether students think their values differ from their parents' values. Have students discuss the results. As an extension, have the class expand the poll by asking young people not in the class the same questions. Have students tally and rank their findings at the next class and discuss the results.

SPOTLIGHT on American Family Values

Ask students to watch several episodes of television situation comedies that focus on family life. Half of the episodes should be reruns from the 1950s, 1960s, or 1970s. The other half should be current shows. Have students identify and list the main values depicted in the programs. When students have completed the activity, call on volunteers to share their findings with the class. Then use the activity as the basis for a class discussion on how American values change over time. **BLOCK SCHEDULING**

SOCIOLOGY IN THE
World Today

YOUNG AMERICANS AND VALUES

Did the social changes in the late 1950s through the 1990s affect the core values of American culture? Do young Americans still uphold the traditional American values? *Generation 2001*, a survey conducted by Harris Interactive, Inc., attempts to answer these questions. Carried out in 2001, the poll asked the opinions of students who were graduating college that year. A majority—some 56 percent—of those polled stated that their values differed some or a lot from those of their parents. However, their responses to other questions seemed to suggest a strong adherence to traditional American values.

Several questions asked students their views on personal achievement and work. In response to inquiries concerning their future plans, nearly 90 percent of the students said that they had set specific goals for the next five years. Further, more than 80 percent said that they were very sure that they would achieve those goals. A large majority also stated that hard work was the principal means to achieving success.

Personal achievement, then, was important to students—but not necessarily for high wages or job prestige. Rather, their definition of success included a strong humanitarian element. For example, a majority stated that, for them, the most important feature of a job was doing work that had a positive effect on the world. Also, nearly 75 percent of students had done volunteer work in the past year.

Not surprisingly, education was important to students that were polled. Practically all respondents said that they were concerned about the future of education in the United States. They ranked education as the most important issue for government or society to address.

Religion seemed to be another basic value for most students. Some 86 percent said that they believed in God, and nearly 75 percent said that they believed in an afterlife. However, less than half reported that they attended religious services regularly.

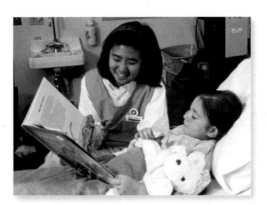

According to the *Generation 2001* survey, many young Americans valued volunteer work.

There seemed to be some support among students for newly emerging values too. Most students expressed concern for the environment, ranking it second among the most important issues for government or society to address.

The poll indicated some ambivalence among students concerning the importance of the family. More than three quarters strongly agreed with the statement that close family relationships are the key to happiness. Yet only a little more than a third strongly agreed that marriage is a cornerstone of social values. Overall, however, *Generation 2001*'s findings suggest that young Americans—like their parents—support the core values of American culture.

Think About It

1. **Supporting a Point of View** *The respondents in the Generation 2001 survey ranked education and the environment as the most important issues for government or society to address. Which issues concern you most? Why?*

2. **Evaluating** *A majority of those surveyed thought that their values differed from the values of their parents. Do your values differ from your parents' values? In what ways?*

Case Study

Character Education. Should morality be taught? Concerns that a growing number of American youth no longer place a high value on morality has led many public schools to embrace character education. This movement involves the use of various techniques to teach students values such as honesty, respect for others, and responsibility.

CRITICAL THINKING

Do you think that public schools should teach students social values such as morality?

ANSWER: Answers will vary, but students should consider the social effects if citizens fail to uphold core cultural values.

Think About It Answers

1. Answers will vary, but students should list one or more values and explain why they consider them to be important.

2. Answers will vary, but students should provide examples of how their values either do or do not differ from their parents' values.

narcissism, which means extreme self-centeredness. Sociologist Daniel Bell also saw dangers in the focus on the self. He felt that it weakened the established values of hard work and moderation and that it threatened the stability of the capitalist system. Psychologist and survey researcher Daniel Yankelovich took a different view. He admitted that this new value probably indicated that Americans believed less in hard work than did earlier generations. However, he viewed this shift toward self-fulfillment as a beneficial change. It marked a movement away from satisfaction based on material gain, he suggested.

Studies during the 1990s noted the emergence of other new American values, such as concern for the environment. Public opinion polls during that time then reflected a growing support among Americans for environmental protection. Throughout much of the 1990s, for example, more than 60 percent of Americans said that they favored protecting the environment, even if it limited economic growth. However, according to a 2001 poll, these numbers may be dropping.

The emergence of environmentalism illustrates how values often change. For long periods in American history, the desire for progress led people to alter the natural world. Americans cleared forests, diverted rivers, and built factories and roads in an effort to improve life in the United States. After a time, however, it became clear that some of these actions had damaged the environment. This damage had an adverse effect on quality of life. Americans then began to realize that they value the environment as well as industrial progress.

INTERPRETING VISUALS In recent years, more and more American women have taken jobs in untraditional occupations such as construction work and telephone-line repair. *How might this change reflect the value of self-fulfillment?*

SECTION 1 REVIEW

1. Define and explain
self-fulfillment
narcissism

2. Identify and explain
Robin M. Williams
James M. Henslin
Christopher Lasch
Daniel Bell
Daniel Yankelovich

3. Drawing Inferences and Conclusions Copy the graphic organizer below. Use it to identify how American values affect economic decisions and government policies.

```
        American
         Values
       /        \
      ↓          ↓
  Economic    Government
  Decisions    Policies
```

4. Finding the Main Idea

a. List and describe the values that form the foundation of traditional American culture.
b. How have American values changed?

5. Writing and Critical Thinking

Making Generalizations and Predictions New values have brought changes to American culture, economic decisions, and government policies. Write a short essay describing how you think the new values of your generation will affect these aspects of American life.
Consider:
• the effect of American values on economic decisions, motivations, and aspirations
• the effect of American values on government policies and social institutions

go. hrw .com **Homework Practice Online**
keyword: SL3 HP3

Applying Sociology

▪ TEACH

Have students read the feature Advertising and Culture on this page. Then organize students into groups and assign each group one of the American values discussed in Section 1. Provide art supplies and instruct each group to create a large print advertisement that uses the assigned value to influence Americans to buy a specific product. Have each group present its work to the class and encourage other students to provide feedback. Then have students discuss whether they think advertisers should use American values to try to influence people's buying decisions. **COOPERATIVE LEARNING**

▪ EXTEND

Bring in some old magazines with advertisements suitable for students to examine. Then have students cut out several of the magazines' advertisements and hang the ads around the classroom. Have students slowly tour and examine the ads. Then ask students to discuss the values that they see illustrated in different ads and how various ads might influence Americans' perceptions, attitudes, and behaviors. You might also have students discuss which ads they like and dislike, explain why, and see how their preferences relate to the discussion of how ads shape culture. **BLOCK SCHEDULING**

APPLYING
Sociology

ADVERTISING AND CULTURE

While American values have affected business practices in the United States, companies have also influenced American values through advertising. Advertisers have attempted to sell their products to American consumers by explaining how their products will enhance consumers' material comfort and lead to self-fulfillment. Advertisers have tapped into American values to influence people's perceptions, attitudes, and behaviors.

The advertising industry has grown significantly since the first American advertising agency opened in 1841. In 1998, U.S. businesses spent more that $200 billion in advertising. This amount reflects a 55 percent increase since 1990.

American advertisers often spread their messages through mass media such as newspapers, magazines, television, radio, and the Internet. In recent years, advertisers have also sought to advertise in unused public spaces. Companies have placed television monitors airing commercials at gas stations, in coffee shops, in elevators, and on train platforms. It is estimated that the average American sees between 1,500 and 3,000 commercials a day.

If you look around, you can find advertisements just about anywhere. Fruits at the supermarket have stickers promoting their brands. Dry cleaners place advertisements on their plastic bags. Even restroom walls are now used to advertise products.

Most ads not only reinforce American values by encouraging material comfort and self-fulfillment but also influence peoples views and actions. During the last several decades, a culture of exercise and physical health has grown in the United States. Fitness and health magazines have flourished. Health food stores and restaurants have multiplied. Healthy living has grown into a major component of American culture. Advertisers of sporting goods such as Nike have encouraged this growth through advertising. Commercials for running shoes and apparel attempt to show that their products can help Americans achieve a sense of self-fulfillment through physical fitness. Thus, these commercials helped to create a new American cultural value by influencing peoples perceptions, attitudes, and behavior.

Using Observation Skills

By watching commercials on television with a critical eye, you can determine the American values to which ads are trying to appeal while selling their products. Copy the chart below. Use it to log your observations while watching several commercials.

	Ad 1	Ad 2	Ad 3
Product			
Values to Which It Appeals			
Perceptions, Attitude, and Behaviors It Influences			

Think About It

1. **Analyzing Information** *How do the commercials you analyzed reflect and influence the perceptions, attitudes, and behaviors of people or groups of people?*
2. **Evaluating** *How do you think commercials use American values to influence individuals' economic decisions?*

Case Study

Patriotic Ads in the Wake of September 11. Advertisers use of American values to sell products can backfire. After the September 11 terrorist attacks in 2001, many ads appeared with strong patriotic themes. However, a number of consumers did not respond positively to these ads. These Americans disliked companies using patriotism to sell their products in the wake of a national tragedy.

RESEARCH ACTIVITY: Have students conduct research on the use of patriotic themes in American ads during World War II and then discuss their findings.

Think About It Answers

1. Answers will vary, but students should provide at least two specific examples based on what they learned in the feature.

2. Students might respond that commercials present their products as promoting or helping people achieve one or more American values to convince consumers to buy the products.

SECTION 2

OBJECTIVES

1. *Identify how the norms of society are enforced.*

2. *Describe the differences between positive and negative sanctions and between formal and informal sanctions.*

SECTION 2 RESOURCES

REPRODUCIBLE & REVIEW
- Mastering Critical Thinking Skills 3
- Section 2 Review, p. 53

TECHNOLOGY
- One-Stop Planner, Lesson 3.2
- Homework Practice Online
- HRW Go site

Visual Answer

It makes them feel proud of their accomplishments and encourages them to continue working hard to succeed.

LET'S GET STARTED!

Write the term *norms* on the chalkboard and review its definition with students *(shared rules of conduct that tell people how to act in specific situations)*. Then ask students to discuss some of the norms within their friendship groups. As students call out norms, have a volunteer list them on the chalkboard. Then for each norm listed, have students explain how their friendship groups ensure that members follow that norm. Explain to students that society, like friendship groups, cannot run smoothly unless norms are enforced. Tell students that in Section 2 they will learn about the ways in which society enforces norms.

2 SOCIAL CONTROL

Read to Discover
1. How are the norms of society enforced?
2. What are the differences between positive and negative sanctions and between formal and informal sanctions?

Define
internalization, sanctions, positive sanction, negative sanction, formal sanction, informal sanction, social control

Every society develops norms that reflect the cultural values its members consider important. For a society to run smoothly, these norms must be upheld. There are two basic means through which norms are enforced—internalization and sanctions.

Internalization of Norms

When people come to believe that a particular norm is good, useful, and appropriate, they generally follow it and expect others to do the same. They do this because they have internalized the norm. **Internalization** is the process by which a norm becomes a part of an individual's personality, thus conditioning that individual to conform to society's expectations. For example, when you sit down to eat, you automatically pick up your knife and fork. When the traffic signal ahead shows red, you stop without thinking. You do not take these actions because you fear being punished. Rather, you have internalized society's norms concerning eating and driving.

Sanctions

Most members of society follow norms without conscious thought. However, not everyone internalizes all of society's norms. Some people must be motivated by **sanctions**. These are rewards or punishments used to enforce conformity to norms.

Positive Sanctions An action that rewards a particular kind of behavior is a **positive sanction**. People are introduced to positive sanctions early in life through interaction in the family. Most parents praise their children for good behavior. Positive sanctions are also a common form of control outside of the family. Teachers react favorably to students who turn in good work, giving them good grades. Positive sanctions continue into adulthood. Employers often give pay raises to workers who show initiative and dedication. Cheers from teammates and the crowd are used to push athletes to try even harder. In all areas of life, ceremonies, ribbons, badges, and awards are used to reward and encourage conformity to society's norms.

INTERPRETING VISUALS Ceremonies such as the awarding of medals to Olympic winners are a form of positive sanction. *What affects do you think this type of award has on these athletes?*

To help students identify how the norms of society are enforced and describe the four types of sanctions, copy the graphic organizer at right onto the chalkboard, omitting the italicized answers. Have students work in pairs to copy and complete the organizer. Discuss the answers with the class. Then have students provide examples of each type of norm enforcement.

ENGLISH LANGUAGE LEARNERS , COOPERATIVE LEARNING

HOMEWORK: Have each student write an essay or short story describing what life might be like in a society free of norms. Remind students to use standard grammar, spelling, sentence structure, and punctuation in their writing. Select the best essay or story to read to the class.

ENFORCEMENT OF SOCIAL NORMS

Internalization: *how a norm becomes part of a person's personality, thus conditioning the person to conform to society's expectations*	**Sanctions:** *rewards or punishments used to enforce conformity to norms*

Positive: *action that rewards a particular kind of behavior*	**Negative:** *punishment or the threat of punishment to enforce conformity*	**Formal:** *reward or punishment by a formal organization or regulatory agency, such as the government*	**Informal:** *spontaneous expression of approval or disapproval by an individual or group*

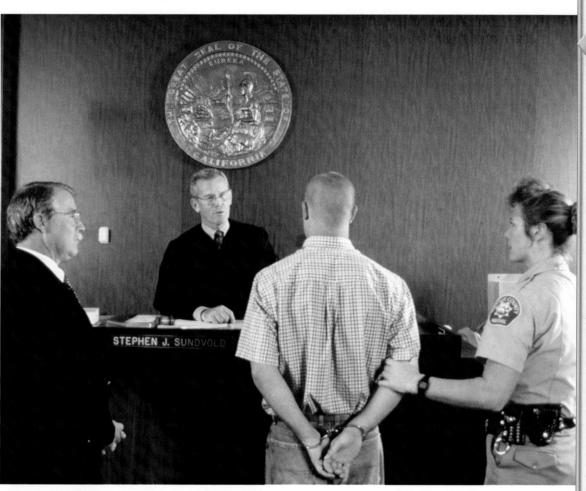

INTERPRETING VISUALS Facing a criminal charge in a court of law is one type of negative sanction. *How might this experience reaffirm a social norm or law?*

Negative Sanctions Positive sanctions are not always enough to ensure conformity. Society also employs negative sanctions to discourage undesired behavior. A **negative sanction** is a punishment or the threat of punishment used to enforce conformity. The threat of punishment is often enough to ensure acceptable behavior. The possibility of having your car towed is usually enough to persuade you not to park in a "no parking" zone. However, if the threat of punishment is not enough, the actual punishment is there to remind you that conformity to the "no parking" rule is expected. Negative sanctions can range from frowns, ridicule, and rejection to fines, imprisonment, and even death. In general, the more important the norm is to social stability, the more serious the negative sanction.

Neither positive nor negative sanctions work if people are not sure that rewards or punishment will follow particular behavior. If you are rarely or never rewarded for good behavior nor punished for bad behavior, then sanctions quickly become meaningless to you. In other words, they lose their power to encourage or enforce conformity.

Formal Sanctions In addition to being positive or negative, sanctions also can be either formal or informal. A **formal sanction** is a reward or punishment given by a formal organization or regulatory agency, such as a school, business, or government. Negative formal sanctions include low grades, suspension from school, termination from a job, fines, and imprisonment. Graduation certificates, pay raises, promotions, awards, and medals are examples of positive formal sanctions.

Mapping Social Forces

◼ TEACH

Have students read the feature Capital Punishment on this page. Then organize students into small groups and have each group create a list of five to eight questions that sociologists might ask about the information on the map (such as reasons for any regional patterns in the use of capital punishment). After a specified period of time, have each group share some of the questions on its list with the class and encourage students to suggest possible answers. Then have each student complete the activity and questions in the Interpreting Maps section. **COOPERATIVE LEARNING**

✳ CONNECTING *to History*

Have each student conduct research on some of the widely held norms in colonial America and on the formal and informal sanctions used to enforce them. Then have students use their research to create a series of fictional colonial news briefs that illustrate these norms and sanctions. Finally, have students collect modern news articles that illustrate current norms and sanctions. Place some of the better articles from both time periods on a bulletin board for students to examine and discuss.
BLOCK SCHEDULING

Map Answers

1. Answers will vary, but students might respond that many people consider executions to be a violation of the norm against killing other human beings.

2. Florida, Missouri, Texas, and Virginia

Mapping
SOCIAL FORCES

CAPITAL PUNISHMENT

The sanctions that are imposed for the violation of norms vary. Generally, the more central the norm is to society's well being and stability, the more severe the sanction. The severest sanction, death, is reserved for violations of the most significant norm. As of the year 2000, the federal government and 37 states had capital statutes—laws whose violation are punishable by death. The actual implementation of the death penalty, however, has varied from state to state.

Capital Punishment in the United States

Executions Carried Out 1990–2000
(actual number shown in parentheses)

- (None)
- (10 or Fewer)
- (11 to 25)
- (26 to 50)
- (Over 50)
- (States with No Capital Statute)

*District of Columbia also has no capital statute

Interpreting Maps

Some states with capital punishment laws have implemented—or are thinking of implementing—a moratorium on executions. Use the Internet or library resources to research the capital punishment moratorium movement.

1. **Analyzing Information** *Why do people think a moratorium is needed?*
2. **Evaluating** *What states had the largest number of executions?*

CLOSE

Have students discuss the importance of enforcing conformity to social norms and cultural values through the use of internalization and sanctions. Then have students discuss whether they think that positive or negative sanctions are more effective in controlling the behavior of teenagers.

REVIEW AND ASSESS

Have students complete the **Section 2 Review** on p. 53. As **Alternative Assessment**, you may want to use the social norms graphic organizer or the homework essay or short story in this section's lessons.

RETEACH

Have each student write a one- or two-sentence summary for each part of this section. Ask volunteers to read their summaries to the class. Correct students where needed. Then review any topics with which students still need help. **ENGLISH LANGUAGE LEARNERS**

EXTEND

Have students interview school administrators and faculty about formal and informal sanctions used to control student behavior. Then have each student create a table that lists the formal positive, informal positive, formal negative, and informal negative sanctions used in their school. **BLOCK SCHEDULING**

Informal Sanctions Formal sanctions play a major role in maintaining social stability. However, the majority of norms are enforced informally. An **informal sanction** is a spontaneous expression of approval or disapproval given by an individual or a group. Positive informal sanctions include standing ovations, compliments, smiles, pats on the back, and gifts. Negative informal sanctions include frowns, gossip, rebukes, insults, ridicule, and ostracism—exclusion from a particular group. Informal sanctions are particularly effective among teenagers, who consider group acceptance highly important. Few teenagers want to be told that their clothes are out of style.

Social Control

The enforcing of norms through either internal or external means is called **social control**. The principal means of social control in all societies is self-control, which is learned through the internalization of norms. Various agents of social control perform external enforcement through the use of sanctions. These agents include authority figures, the police, the courts, religion, the family, and public opinion.

Individuals must follow certain rules of behavior if society is to function smoothly. If people ignore society's basic norms, then the social order is in jeopardy. When a society's methods for ensuring conformity break down, social stability is lost. No society can survive for long without an effective system of social control.

If police officers were unable to enforce laws, the social order of our society would be jeopardized by criminals.

SECTION 2 REVIEW ANSWERS

1. Define:
   • internalization, p. 50
   • sanctions, p. 50
   • positive sanction, p. 50
   • negative sanction, p. 51
   • formal sanction, p. 51
   • informal sanction, p. 53
   • social control, p. 53

2. formal/positive—graduation certificates, pay raises, promotions, awards; formal/negative—low grades, being suspended or fired, fines, imprisonment; informal/positive—smiles, compliments, clapping; informal/negative—frowns, ridicule, ostracism

3a. through internalization and sanctions

b. Positive sanctions are rewards, such as smiles, to reinforce desired behavior. Negative sanctions are punishments, such as detention hall, to discourage undesired behavior.

4. Paragraphs will vary, but students should address the importance of following and enforcing certain rules of behavior to ensure social order and stability.

SECTION 2 REVIEW

1. **Define and explain**
   internalization
   sanctions
   positive sanction
   negative sanction
   formal sanction
   informal sanction
   social control

2. **Categorizing** Copy the graphic organizer below. Use it to identify examples of the various kinds of sanctions.

Types of Sanctions	Positive	Negative
Formal		
Informal		

3. **Finding the Main Idea**
   a. What are the two basic ways in which the norms of society are enforced?
   b. Briefly compare positive and negative sanctions.

4. **Writing and Critical Thinking**
   Analyzing Information Write two paragraphs describing the relationship between the enforcement of values, norms, and government policies.
   Consider:
   • the role of norms in society and the effect on social order when norms are violated
   • the role of the government in social control

Homework Practice Online
keyword: SL3 HP3

SECTION 3

OBJECTIVES

1. *Identify and describe the main sources of social change.*
2. *Describe the factors that lead people to resist social change.*

SECTION 3 RESOURCES

REPRODUCIBLE & REVIEW

- Readings and Case Studies in Sociology 3
- Study Skills and Writing Guide
- Section 3 Review, p. 61

TECHNOLOGY

- One-Stop Planner, Lesson 3.3
- Homework Practice Online
- HRW Go site

LET'S GET STARTED!

Ask students to identify ways in which the society of their high school has changed over the past few years. *(Students might mention physical changes to the school, changes to school policies or rules, changes in the performance of school teams, changes to the student body, or changes in fads or trends popular among students.)* Explain to students that all societies change over time. Next, ask students to use the earlier activity to suggest possible causes of social change. List students' suggestions on the chalkboard. Then tell students that in Section 3 they will learn about the main reasons for social change and about various forms of resistance to such change.

3
SOCIAL CHANGE

● **Read to Discover**
1. What are the main sources of social change?
2. What factors lead people to resist social change?

● **Define**
ideology, social movement, technology, diffusion, reformulation, cultural lag

All cultures change over time. Yet some cultures change much faster than others. The pace of change is closely related to the total number of culture traits that a culture has at a particular time. The more culture traits a culture has, the faster the culture can change since more possibilities for change exist. The rate of change can also accelerate because each change brings about other changes. For example, the invention of the automobile did more than furnish Americans with a new form of transportation. It also provided employment and affected the way people shopped, where they lived, and what they did with their leisure time.

Sources of Social Change

The modern world changes rapidly. Each week brings new material goods, new styles of dress, new ways of doing things, and new ideas. What causes all of these changes? There are many factors that stimulate change. This section addresses six factors: values and beliefs, technology, population, diffusion, the physical environment, and wars and conquests.

Values and Beliefs As functionalist sociologists have noted, society is a system of interrelated parts. A change in one aspect of society produces change throughout the system. Changes in values and beliefs, therefore, can have far-reaching consequences for society. These consequences are particularly noticeable when new values and beliefs are part of a larger ideology.

An **ideology** is a system of beliefs or ideas that justifies the social, moral, religious, political, or economic interests held by a group or by society. Ideologies often are spread through social movements. A **social movement** is a long-term conscious effort to promote or prevent social change. Social movements usually involve large numbers of

The civil rights movement of the 1960s was one important social movement that sought to ensure equal rights for African Americans and other minority groups.

Applying Sociology

■ TEACH

Have students read the feature The Adaptive American Culture on this page and then discuss each of the Think About It questions that follow. Then ask students to suggest examples not mentioned in the text of ways in which American practices have changed as a result of immigration or the infusion of traits from other cultures. In addition, have students consider the reasons for the changes. *(For example, the handover of Hong Kong from British to Chinese control in 1997 led many people in the Hong Kong movie industry to go to Hollywood. As a result, movies with Chinese themes have increased in number and popularity in the United States.)*

SPOTLIGHT
on the Adaptive American Language

Point out to students that American English reflects the infusion of many other cultures. Have students try to identify the cultures from which the following terms originated: *crepe* (France), *fiesta* (Spain and Latin America), *frankfurter* (Germany), *judo* (Japan), *samba* (Brazil), and *taco* (Mexico). Then have students work in pairs to find 10 other terms that have been adapted into American English and to identify the cultures from which these terms originated.
COOPERATIVE LEARNING, **BLOCK SCHEDULING**

APPLYING
Sociology

THE ADAPTIVE AMERICAN CULTURE

The long history of immigration has influenced the American culture. Each group of immigrants brings new cultural traditions from their country of origin. Many of these new cultural traditions have been incorporated into American culture and have influenced American food, business practices, and advertising.

Travel writer and social commentator Pico Iyer has noticed this trend in American culture.

"This is the typical day of a relatively typical soul in today's diversified world. I wake up to the sound of my Japanese clock radio, put on a T shirt sent [to] me by an uncle in Nigeria and walk out into the street, past German cars, to my office. Around me are English-language students from Korea, Switzerland and Argentina— all on the Spanish-named road in the Mediterranean-style town. On TV, I find, the news is in Mandarin; today's baseball game is being broadcast in Korean. For lunch I can walk to a sushi bar, a tandoori palace, a Thai café or the newest burrito joint (run by an old Japanese lady). Who am I, I sometimes wonder, the son of Indian parents and a British citizen who spends much of his time in Japan? . . . And where am I?

I am, as it happens, in Southern California, in a quiet, relatively un-international town, but I could as easily be in Vancouver or Sydney or London or Hong Kong."

In the past few decades the large number of immigrants from Mexico and other Latin American countries have greatly influenced American culture. Foods such as tortillas and salsa are an important part of Mexican cuisine. These foods have also become common in American kitchens. Some sources report that salsa is now more popular than ketchup and that the sale of tortillas in the United States has reached $4 billion.

Maintaining close communication with their family and loved ones in their country of origin provided a growing market. Some long-distance telephone

Calling cards such as this one have been created by American businesses to market to recent Mexican immigrants.

service providers have changed their business and advertising practices to adapt to Spanish-speaking immigrants. Calling card companies advertise in Spanish and sell their cards at convenient locations in immigrant neighborhoods. They also offer special rates for calls to Mexico and other Latin American countries.

The growth in popularity of Spanish language television, such as Telemundo, has also changed the way large corporations such as General Motors and Ford advertise. Spanish-language ads for new automobiles have been made specifically to reach the more than 2.8 million viewers in the United States.

Linking to Community

If you study the community in which you live, you are bound to find examples of how immigrant groups have influenced American culture—particularly food and business practices. Create a list of cultural traits that have been adapted from an immigrant group in your community.

Think About It

1. **Evaluating** *How have immigrant groups influenced American culture in your community?*
2. **Analyzing Information** *What are some examples of how food, business practices, and advertising have changed because of immigration?*

Sociology in the World Today

The Adaptive American Workplace. American companies have had to adapt to an increasingly culturally diverse workforce. Some companies now provide more flexible holiday schedules to allow for a variety of religious and cultural traditions. Some businesses with large numbers of Muslim employees have changed cafeteria menus and dress codes to address workers' religious beliefs and practices. In addition, more companies now provide cultural and religious sensitivity training.

CRITICAL THINKING

How have changing demographics affected the American workplace?

ANSWER: Increasing cultural diversity has forced companies to address workers' varied beliefs and practices.

Think About It Answers

1. Answers will vary, but students should provide some examples similar to those cited in the feature.

2. Examples include a variety of ethnic restaurants and more advertisements in languages other than English.

SUGGESTION 1: To help students identify and describe the main sources of social change, copy the graphic organizer at right onto the chalkboard, omitting the italicized answers. Have students copy the organizer and complete it by listing each of the six factors that promote social change. Then have students provide specific examples of each of the sources of social change and suggest some of the social consequences of each example. *(For technology, an example might be cell phones, with the consequences of changing how and where people communicate, creating new norms for public behavior, and affecting road safety.)* Discuss students' answers as a class. **ENGLISH LANGUAGE LEARNERS**

Source of Social Change	Example	Social Consequence
values and beliefs		
technology		
population		
diffusion		
physical environment		
wars and conquests		

Did You Know?

According to the 2000 U.S. census, nearly 40 percent of Americans under the age of 18 belonged to a minority population group. In addition, close to half of the people who reported that they belonged to more than one race were also under the age of 18.

Visual Answer

Answers will vary, but students should recognize the length of these movements, the organization of each movement, and the dedication of the participants.

people. Examples of social movements include the prohibition movement, the women's rights movement, the peace movement, the gay rights movement, the civil rights movement, and the environmental movement.

The consequences of shifts in ideology can be seen by examining how the civil rights movement changed politics in the United States. As recently as the 1950s, African Americans were forced to live as second-class citizens throughout the United States, particularly in the South. Laws limited where they could live, go to school, sit on buses, and eat lunch. Through legal and illegal means, African Americans were denied the right to vote or to hold public office. Civil rights supporters staged boycotts, marches, and demonstrations to publicize this situation. A surge of support for change among U.S. citizens soon developed. Responding to public pressure, Congress passed a number of civil rights laws, including the Voting Rights Act of 1965. This act outlawed the various methods that had been used to deny African Americans the vote.

The changes brought about by the civil rights movement transformed the American political landscape. Today African Americans are a powerful group of voters. The number of African American elected officials has jumped from fewer than 1,500 in 1970 to nearly 9,000 by the end of the 1990s. More than half of these officials hold offices in southern states.

Technology Social change also occurs when people find new ways to manipulate their environment. The knowledge and tools that people use to manipulate their environment are called **technology**. Two ways that new technologies arise are through discovery and invention.

Discovery occurs when people recognize new uses for existing elements in the world or begin to understand them in new ways. Examples of discoveries include atomic fission, chewing gum, and oil shale. Oil shale was discovered by accident. Many stones along the banks of the Colorado River contain rock shale saturated with oil. According to one story, a man used these stones to construct a fireplace. When he lit a fire in the fireplace, the fireplace itself burst into flames! Nevertheless, a new use of oil shale as fuel provided new resources for America's growing industrial society.

Invention occurs when people use existing knowledge to create something that did not previously exist. Inventions can take the form of material objects, ideas, or patterns of behavior. New tools, such as a gadget to take the pits out of cherries or a computer small enough to hold in your hand, are examples of material inventions. Examples of nonmaterial inventions include political movements, religious movements, new hobbies, and business organizations.

INTERPRETING VISUALS Earth Day celebrations such as the one shown below play a significant role in the environmental movement. The suffragette pictured on the right won her battle for a woman's right to vote. *Contrast the impact of the civil rights movement, the women's movement, and the environmental movement in the United States.*

SUGGESTION 2: Call on students to identify and describe the main sources of social change. *(See the graphic organizer on p. 56 for a list.)* Next, organize students into six groups and assign each group one of these sources of social change. Remind students of the *Let's Get Started* activity, in which they discussed recent social changes at their school. Ask each group to provide examples for its assigned category of real and possible social changes at the high-school level. Then have each group share some of the changes it listed with the class. Encourage discussion. Finally, have each group select one of its listed social changes and create a mock TV news report about the change and its consequences. Have each group present its news report to the class. **COOPERATIVE LEARNING**

CONNECTING *to History*

Have students conduct research on the social changes that occurred in the United States as a result of one of the following events: World War I, World War II, the Cold War, the Vietnam War, the Persian Gulf War, or the September 11 terrorist attacks. Have each student use the research to write a medium-length feature to appear in a fictional magazine on an anniversary related to the event. The feature should include visuals, such as charts, maps, drawings, or photographs. Encourage students to use computer software to create their features, if possible. **BLOCK SCHEDULING**

© Bill Keane, Inc. Reprinted with special permission of King Features Syndicate.

INTERPRETING VISUALS Sociologists have raised concerns about some trends of increasing population and the social changes this growth might produce. *How does this cartoon illustrate these concerns?*

Population A change in the size of the population may bring about changes in the culture. For example, the population of the United States has increased rapidly since the early 1900s. The arrival of new groups of people with their own unique cultural traits and values has influenced American culture. For example, food brought to this country by immigrant groups—such as Mexican, Chinese, and Italian food—have become common in American kitchens.

Population increases and decreases affect the economy. By increasing the demand for goods and services, a growing population may increase employment and stimulate the economy. On the other hand, a community with a declining population may need fewer goods and services. As a result, there may be limited employment opportunities for the people who remain.

An increase in the general population also means that there are more people occupying the same amount of space, which creates more crowded conditions. In addition, the larger population brings increased demand for energy, food, housing, schools, stores, and transportation.

People bring about changes simply by moving from one place to another. When a family moves to a new community, change is stimulated both in the community it leaves and in the new community it enters. Migrations of people within a country can cause social changes, such as the loss of regional distinction within the country.

Social and cultural changes also result from changes in the average age of a population. When fewer people are having babies, for example, there is less need for

schools, recreation centers, and other services geared toward children. The need for specialized services geared toward elderly people, on the other hand, increases as more people live longer.

Diffusion People often borrow ideas, beliefs, and material objects from other societies. This process of spreading culture traits from one society to another is called **diffusion**. The more contact a society has with other societies, the more culture traits it will borrow. Today, with mass transportation and instant communication through radio, television, the telephone, and the Internet, diffusion takes place constantly.

Some culture traits spread more rapidly than others. Generally, societies adopt material culture and technology more freely than ideas and beliefs. For example, most societies readily accept tools and weapons that are superior to their own. Societies often adapt the culture traits they borrow to suit their own particular needs. For example, many of the societies in Africa, Asia, and South America that have adopted Christianity have blended Christian beliefs with elements of their traditional religions. Sociologists refer to this process of adapting borrowed cultural traits as **reformulation**.

Diffusion is a two-way process. As a result of contact with other cultures, Americans eat foods such as pasta from Italy, sushi from Japan, Mongolian barbecue, and baklava from Greece. At the same time, American movies, music, cars and farm machinery, soft drinks, and fast foods can be found in countries throughout the world.

Exploring Cultural Diversity

Reformulating *Sesame Street.* The childrens' television show *Sesame Street* centers around humans and Muppets along a city neighborhood street. As the show has gone global, this format has been adapted to fit other cultures. The South African version incorporates all of the country's 11 official languages and replaces the brownstone buildings of the American set with round mud huts. The Chinese version of *Sesame Street* is set in an urban Chinese neighborhood with a bicycle and noodle shop. Instead of Bert and Ernie, Muppets such as Puffing Pig and Little Plum entertain children and teach Chinese values and traditions.

ACTIVITY: Have students discuss examples of cultural diffusion and reformulation in their area or in the United States as a whole.

Visual Answer

The cartoon shows in a humorous fashion how a growing population can lead to overcrowding and a shortage of available resources.

The Physical Environment The environment provides conditions that may encourage or discourage cultural change. People in some societies wholly rely on foods that they can grow locally. Other societies must import much of their food or adapt new crops to grow in their area. The introduction of new foods or the scarcity of a familiar food can bring about cultural change.

Natural disasters such as droughts, floods, earthquakes, tornadoes, and tidal waves can also produce social and cultural change. These disasters can destroy whole communities. Afterward, people often take precautions for the future. Dams may be built to lessen the effects of floods and droughts. People may also adopt new construction methods to enable buildings to better withstand earthquakes or tornadoes.

A change in the supply of natural resources may bring about cultural change. For example, in the 1970s high fuel prices and fuel shortages caused long lines at American gasoline stations. This shortage encouraged Americans to seek alternative sources of energy and to develop smaller, more fuel-efficient cars. The search for alternative forms of energy slowed in the 1980s in part because the fuel shortages eased. In addition, the production of less-fuel-efficient cars, such as high-performance sports cars, increased once again.

Wars and Conquests Wars and conquests are not as common as other sources of social change. However, they probably bring about the greatest change in the least amount of time. War causes the loss of many lives. It brings about the destruction of property and leads to the rise of new cities and towns that must be built to replace those destroyed. In addition, war causes changes in the economy as industry focuses on producing war materials rather than consumer goods. For example, after September 11, 2001, some industries contributed to the war on terrorism by providing military supplies and services. War can also promote advances in technology and medicine that can have civilian applications. War may also result in changes in government as new rulers come to power. These changes may contribute to new economic policies and political rights.

Resistance to Change

Cultural change, regardless of its source, rarely occurs without some opposition. For each change introduced in society, there are usually people who strongly oppose it. Social changes often result from a compromise between opposing forces. This is true both on an interpersonal level and on a societal level. Many people, after time, may accept a new idea that they strongly resisted at first. Other people may never accept the new idea but may simply adapt. Changes in the role of women in the workplace first met with some resistance that has waned in recent years. Ethnocentrism, cultural lag, and vested interests are among the reasons that people resist cultural change.

Ethnocentrism Change that comes from outside a society often meets with particularly strong resistance. People tend to believe that their own ideas and ways of doing things are best. This tendency to view one's own culture or group as superior to others is called ethnocentrism. Extreme ethnocentrism can make cultural borrowing difficult or even impossible.

The "Buy American" campaign of the 1970s and 1980s provides an example of how ethnocentrism can affect one

In 2001 Houston suffered severe flooding. Natural disasters can create social changes such as the movement of people or new construction practices.

Case Studies and Other True Stories

◼ TEACH

Call on students to read aloud the feature The 100-Percent American? on this page and complete the Think About It section that follows. Then provide each student with a blank outline map of the world. Have students label the various regions of the world, such as Africa, Asia, and Europe. Then have each student, using the feature and classroom resources for information, indicate on the map where various common culture traits originated. Students might use text labels or symbols to indicate traits.

◼ EXTEND

Have students work in pairs to list 10 culture traits not mentioned in the feature that they believe originated outside of the United States. Have the pairs conduct library research to determine where and when these culture traits originated. When the class next meets, have volunteer pairs share some of the information that they learned with the class. Then use the activity as the basis of a class discussion about the role of culture diffusion and reformulation in social change. **COOPERATIVE LEARNING**, **BLOCK SCHEDULING**

Case Studies
AND OTHER TRUE STORIES

THE 100-PERCENT AMERICAN?

Have you ever thought about how much of American culture was borrowed from other cultures, both past and present? Anthropologist Ralph Linton explored this question in a humorous way in the 1930s. Following is an excerpt from his classic essay on how much Americans owe to other cultures. The essay first appeared in the 1936 edition of his book The Study of Man: An Introduction.

The origin of the popular American dish spaghetti is diverse. Noodles were developed in ancient China, tomatoes were discovered in the Americas by Spanish explorers, and marinara sauce was a popular dish among Italian immigrants to America.

Our solid American citizen awakens in a bed built on a pattern which originated in the Near East but which was modified in northern Europe before it was transmitted to America. He throws back covers made from cotton, domesticated in India, or linen, domesticated in the Near East, or wool from sheep, also domesticated in the Near East, or silk, the use of which was discovered in China. All of these materials have been spun and woven by processes invented in the Near East. He slips into his moccasins, invented by the [American] Indians of the Eastern woodlands, and goes to the bathroom, whose fixtures are a mixture of European and American inventions, both of recent date. He takes off his pajamas, a garment invented in India, and washes with soap invented by the ancient Gauls. . . .

Returning to the bedroom, he removes his clothes from a chair of southern European type and proceeds to dress. He puts on garments whose form originally derived from the skin of the nomads of the Asiatic steppes, puts on shoes made from skins tanned by a process invented in ancient Egypt and cut to a pattern derived from the classical civilizations of the Mediterranean. . . . Before going out to breakfast he glances through the window made of glass invented in Egypt, and if it is raining, puts on overshoes made of rubber discovered by the Central American Indians and takes an umbrella, invented in southeastern Asia. . . .

On his way to breakfast he stops to buy a paper, paying for it with coins, an ancient Lydian invention. At the restaurant a whole new series of borrowed elements confronts him. His plate is made of a form of pottery invented in China. His knife is of steel, an alloy first made in southern India, his fork,

a medieval Italian invention, and his spoon a derivative of a Roman original. He begins breakfast with an orange, from the eastern Mediterranean, a cantaloupe from Persia, or perhaps a piece of African watermelon. With this he has coffee, an Abyssinian plant. . . . After his fruit and first coffee he goes on to waffles, cakes made by a Scandinavian technique from wheat domesticated in Asia Minor. Over these he pours maple syrup, invented by the Indians of the Eastern woodlands. As a side dish he may have the egg of a species of bird domesticated in Indo-China, or thin strips of the flesh of an animal domesticated in Eastern Asia, which have been salted and smoked by a process developed in northern Europe.

When our friend has finished eating, . . . he reads the news of the day, imprinted in characters invented by the ancient Semites upon a material invented in China by a process invented in Germany. As he absorbs the accounts of foreign troubles he will, if he is a good conservative citizen, thank a Hebrew deity in an Indo-European language that he is 100 percent American.

Think About It

1. **Categorizing** *Using Africa, the Americas, Asia, and Europe as categories, list the traits mentioned in the article according to their origin. How have American Indians and immigrant groups influenced American culture?*

2. **Drawing Inferences and Conclusions** *Based on your reading of Linton's essay, what can you conclude about the extent of cultural diffusion that has taken place in the United States?*

Pitching an American Pastime. Baseball may be as American as apple pie, but fans around the world are evidence of its wide diffusion. The game traces back to an English game called rounders, which emerged as baseball in the United States during the late 1700s and early 1800s. As American baseball gained popularity, it spread to countries such as Cuba, Japan, Mexico, Puerto Rico, and Venezuela. In the late 1990s more than 30 percent of U.S. professional baseball players were born outside of the United States. Today fans in more than 100 countries can watch a local baseball game.

RESEARCH ACTIVITY: Have students conduct research on the spread of American music, such as jazz or rock, or of American blue jeans and then present their findings in an oral report.

Think About It Answers

1. Students should correctly attribute the cultural traits listed in the feature at left. Students should provide several examples from the feature to illustrate how these groups have enriched American culture.

2. An immense amount of cultural diffusion has occurred.

CLOSE

Review with students the six sources of social change *(values and beliefs, technology, population, diffusion, physical environment, wars and conquests)* and the three factors that lead people to resist change *(ethnocentrism, cultural lag, and vested interests)*. Ask students to discuss how the last three factors can have negative consequences for society. Then ask students to discuss what they consider to be some recent positive and negative changes in American society.

REVIEW AND ASSESS

Have students complete the **Section 3 Review** on p. 61. As **Alternative Assessment**, you may want to use the social change TV news report or the resistance to change illustrations in this section's lessons.

RETEACH

Make certain that students know what a rebus is *(a riddle made up of pictures and symbols that each represent a word or phrase)*. Have students work in pairs to create a rebus for each of six key terms or concepts in this section. Then have students exchange their puzzles and try to solve the ones they receive.

ENGLISH LANGUAGE LEARNERS , COOPERATIVE LEARNING

Map Answers

1. mainly the South and Midwest; perhaps between 33 and 50 percent

2. perhaps questions such as how large or dense populations relate to Internet use

SECTION 3 REVIEW ANSWERS

1. Define:
- ideology, p. 54
- social movement, p. 54
- technology, p. 56
- diffusion, p. 57
- reformulation, p. 57
- cultural lag, p. 60

2. Students should provide examples for each factor.

3a. Students should provide examples for the following and explain how they affect society: values and beliefs, technology, population, diffusion, the physical environment, and wars and conquests.

b. ethnocentrism—might lead to segregation; cultural lag—might lead to continued summer breaks or to a lag in the use of computers; vested interests—might lead to a focus on maintaining budgets over a focus on providing a quality education and instruction

4. Paragraphs will vary, but students should mention some of the examples provided in the text of how the civil rights movement led to social change.

culture's acceptance of another culture's material objects and ideas. One target of the campaign was the importation of Japanese automobiles. Allowing these cars into the United States, campaign supporters said, would put Americans out of work. Some Americans agreed with this view and refused to buy Japanese cars, stating that this refusal was the patriotic thing to do. Some American autoworkers went further. They demonstrated their feelings by publicly demolishing Japanese cars. Nevertheless, Japanese cars were eventually accepted in the United States. Today it can be difficult to differentiate between Japanese and American cars. Some Japanese cars are now made by American workers at factories in the United States. At the same time, some American automobiles are assembled at factories in foreign countries. Ethnocentrism and other economic factors led to the anti-Japanese-car bias, which has decreased in recent years.

Cultural Lag Not all cultural traits change at the same rate. Some traits change rapidly, and the transformation of others may take considerable time. This situation is called **cultural lag**. Material culture usually changes faster and nonmaterial culture lags behind. Often, technological change results in cultural lag.

Sociologist James M. Henslin identified the traditional school year as an example of cultural lag. In the 1800s the United States was a largely rural agricultural country. At that time, farming was a very labor-intensive activity. A long summer break from school was needed so that children could work on the farms. Over time, technological developments transformed the United States into a mostly urban and industrial country. Today, therefore, a long summer break is not needed. Even so, the traditional school year persists. Efforts to introduce year-round schooling have met with significant opposition.

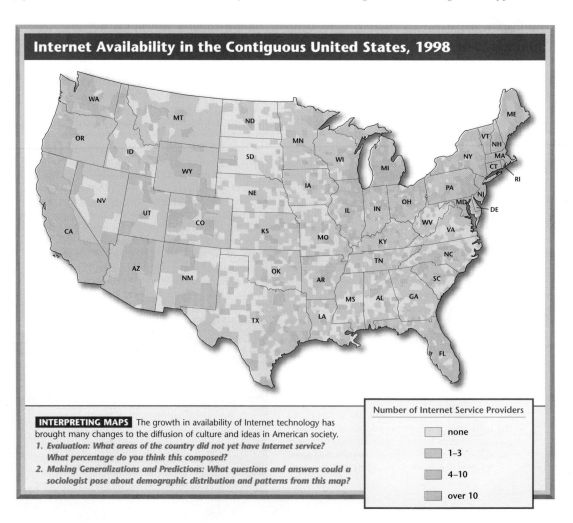

Internet Availability in the Contiguous United States, 1998

Number of Internet Service Providers
- none
- 1–3
- 4–10
- over 10

INTERPRETING MAPS The growth in availability of Internet technology has brought many changes to the diffusion of culture and ideas in American society.
1. *Evaluation: What areas of the country did not yet have Internet service? What percentage do you think this composed?*
2. *Making Generalizations and Predictions: What questions and answers could a sociologist pose about demographic distribution and patterns from this map?*

1. Have students conduct research to find examples of current scientific or technological innovations in the United States. Then have each student select one innovation and write a science article that describes the innovation, explains how it might be or is being used, and discusses some positive and negative consequences of the innovation. Call on volunteers to present their articles to the class. Encourage student discussion and feedback. Finally, use the activity as the basis for a class discussion about innovation as a source of social change. **BLOCK SCHEDULING**

2. Have each student conduct research on current movements for social change occurring in foreign nations. Instruct students to select one social movement and write a synopsis describing the changes being sought and any resistance to the movement. In addition, students should provide a map showing the location of the social movement. Have volunteers present their synopses and maps to the class. Then have students discuss some of the possible consequences of the social changes being sought. **BLOCK SCHEDULING**

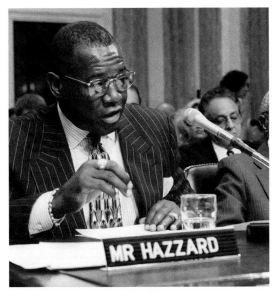

Representatives and lobbyists for businesses and interest groups often appear before the U.S. Congress to explain their vested interests.

The development of computers and the growth of the Internet in the 1990s led to a cultural lag. Computers and the Internet offer many educational opportunities. However, because of costs and other factors, some school districts have yet to put this new technology to effective use in the classroom. In addition, some elements of Internet technology—notably the "trapping" and storing of information about users—have created questions concerning privacy that the U.S. legal system is struggling to address.

Vested Interests A person who is satisfied with the way things are now is likely to resist change. Some individuals feel that the present, even if somewhat imperfect, is better than an unknown future. They will resist any change that threatens their security or standard of living. In other words, they have a vested interest to protect. For example, workers may oppose the introduction of new technology because they fear the technology may replace them and cost them their jobs.

Entire industries also have vested interests to protect. Consider the American oil industries, for example. During the energy crisis of the 1970s, oil prices rose dramatically. While many people around the country called for a new energy policy, the oil industry benefited from the rising prices. It was not until 1992, under President George Bush, that the Energy Policy Act was passed. However, critics charged that the new policy did not focus enough on conservation or on the use of renewable fuels.

One reason it was difficult to implement an energy policy to permanently solve the energy problems of the 1970s and 1980s was that many people in the oil industry benefited from the high prices of petroleum products. To protect their vested interests, oil companies and workers in the oil industry have lobbied the government to protect their industry and interests in the energy issue.

SECTION ③ REVIEW

1. Define and explain
ideology
social movement
technology
diffusion
reformulation
cultural lag

2. Summarizing Copy the graphic organizer below. Use it to explain how different factors lead to social change and are affected by changing values.

Social Institutions

Social Change

Government Policies

New Technology

go. hrw .com **Homework Practice Online**
keyword: SL3 HP3

3. **Finding the Main Idea**
a. Briefly describe how each of the six sources of social change can affect society.
b. How do ethnocentrism, cultural lag, and vested interests produce resistance to social change in an educational setting?

4. **Writing and Critical Thinking**
Identifying Cause and Effect Using the civil rights movement as an example, write two short paragraphs demonstrating how changes in values and beliefs can bring about changes in government policy.
Consider:
• the laws passed as a result of the civil rights movement
• the resulting changes in the American political landscape

CHAPTER 3 REVIEW

ANSWERS

WRITING A SUMMARY
See the section subtitles for the main topics in the chapter.

IDENTIFYING PEOPLE AND IDEAS

1. a commitment to the full development of one's personality, talents, and potential

2. sociologist whose study identified a set of 15 core American values

3. rewards or punishments used to enforce conformity to norms

4. a system of beliefs or ideas that justifies the social, moral, religious, political, or economic interests held by a group or by society

5. the process of adapting borrowed cultural traits to one's own cultural traits

6. extreme self-centeredness

7. the process by which a norm becomes part of an individual's personality

8. the enforcing of norms through either internal or external means

9. the process of spreading culture traits from one society to another

10. a variation in the speed of cultural change or adaptation

CHAPTER 3

Review and Assessment Resources

- Chapter 3 Review, pp. 62–63
- Chapter Review Activities with Answer Key
- Global Skill Builder CD–ROM
- Chapter 3 Test Generator (on the One-Stop Planner)
- Chapter 3 Test (Form A or B)
- Alternative Assessment Handbook
- HRW Go site

 REVIEW

Have students complete the **Chapter 3 Review** on pp. 62–63.

ASSESS

Use one of the chapter tests to assess students' understanding of the content. For **Alternative Assessment**, see the **Alternative Assessment Handbook**.

UNDERSTANDING MAIN IDEAS

1. personal achievement, individualism, work, morality and humanitarianism, efficiency and practicality, progress and material comfort, equality and democracy, freedom, nationalism and patriotism, science and rationality, racial and group superiority, education, religion, romantic love

2. self-fulfillment and concern for the environment

3. internalization and sanctions

4. Positive sanctions are rewards, such as smiles, to reinforce desired behavior. Negative sanctions are punishments, such as imprisonment, to discourage undesired behavior.

5. provide formal sanctions, such as laws, to enforce values and norms

6. These movements produced changes in ideologies, laws and policies, and politics.

7. made more culturally diverse foods and dishes available and popular

8. ethnocentrism, cultural lag, and vested interests

THINKING CRITICALLY

1. These values might lead people to make decisions so as to increase their individual wealth and success.

2. Policies might include sanctions such as laws, fines, and imprisonment. Values affect what norms these policies enforce.

CHAPTER

 3 Review

 Writing a Summary

Using standard grammar, spelling, sentence structure, and punctuation, summarize the information in this chapter.
Consider:
- the values that form the foundation of American culture
- how norms are enforced
- the main sources of social change

 Identifying People and Ideas

Identify the following people or terms and use them in appropriate sentences.

1. self-fulfillment
2. Robin M. Williams
3. sanctions
4. ideology
5. reformulation
6. narcissism
7. internalization
8. social control
9. diffusion
10. cultural lag

Understanding Main Ideas

Section 1 (pp. 44–48)

1. What are the core American values outlined by Robin M. Williams and James M. Henslin?

2. What new American values have emerged in recent years?

Section 2 (pp. 50–53)

3. Identify the two methods through which society enforces norms.

4. Explain the difference between positive sanctions and negative sanctions by giving an example of each.

5. What role do government policies play in enforcing cultural values and social norms?

Section 3 (pp. 54–61)

6. How are the civil rights movement and the women's rights movement examples of social change?

7. How has cultural diffusion changed eating habits in the United States?

8. For what reasons do people resist change?

 Thinking Critically

1. Analyzing Information How might a strong commitment to such values as personal achievement and individualism affect an individual's economic decisions?

2. Finding the Main Idea Identify government policies that establish social control. How do American values affect these government policies?

3. Identifying Cause and Effect List some of the cultural changes caused by communication and transportation technology, such as the Internet, the airplane, and the automobile.

4. Evaluating Identify a historical or current social movement in the United States, such as the civil rights movement. Describe the changes the movement has made or is attempting to make in American society.

5. Drawing Inferences and Conclusions How do you think geographic factors might influence American values?

Writing About Sociology

1. Evaluating During the civil rights movement, African Americans were attempting to end discrimination and other social problems; however, some local governments created policies to resist the social change. Write a paragraph describing how social problems, resistance to social change, and cultural values can affect government policies and social controls.

2. Comparing and Contrasting The people of the United States share a set of values that defines the American culture. The people of various regions of the country, too, are members of particular cultures with distinctive regional characteristics. Research the distinctive values and norms held by people in two different regions of the country. Compare and contrast the two regional cultures in a short essay. Use the graphic organizer below to help you write the essay.

	Values	Norms	Distinct Characteristics
Region			
Region			

Have students work in pairs or small groups to create a crossword puzzle of key terms and concepts in this chapter. Clues should be in definition form, and the key terms and concepts used as the answers. Each pair or group should create a small version of the completed crossword puzzle as an answer key and then a larger unanswered version of the puzzle. Collect students' puzzles and then redistribute them. Have the pairs or groups complete the puzzles they receive and then check their responses against the answer keys.

ENGLISH LANGUAGE LEARNERS , COOPERATIVE LEARNING

SOCIOLOGY PROJECTS

1. Applying Sociology Organize students into small groups and have each one develop a propaganda campaign to urge fellow students to uphold one or more of the core American values. Campaigns should include at least three of the following: banners, buttons, posters, slogans, songs, or t-shirts.

2. Using Sociological Imagination Organize students into groups and have each group establish the values, norms, and sanctions for a new society. The groups should prepare multimedia presentations of their societies' values, norms, and formal sanctions.

BUILDING SOCIAL STUDIES SKILLS

Interpreting Graphs

Study the graph below. Use the information to answer the questions that follow.

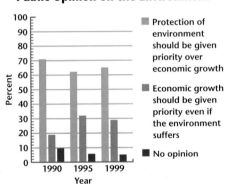

Public Opinion on the Environment

Legend:
- Protection of environment should be given priority over economic growth
- Economic growth should be given priority even if the environment suffers
- No opinion

Source: The Gallup Organization, 2000.

1. In which year was concern for protecting the environment the highest?
   a. 1990
   b. 1995
   c. 1999
   d. Concern remained level throughout the 1990s.

2. Why do you think sociologists use these results to support their claim that concern for the environment has emerged as a core value?

Analyzing Primary Sources

In the following excerpt examines the social factors that led to beef becoming the most popular meat in the United States. Read the excerpt and then answer the questions that follow.

❝First came the growth of suburban homeownership and the use of outdoor living space for cooking and entertaining. To the suburban refugees from the central cities, charcoal broiling represented the fulfillment of pent-up recreational and gustatory aspirations. . . . Charcoal-broiled steaks were the favorites, made all the more delectable no doubt, because they had once been unaffordable. . . .
The move to suburbia was shortly followed by other social changes that contributed to the beefing of America: the entrance of women into the work force, the formation of families in which both parents work, the rising tide of feminism, and the growing resentment of women against pots, pans, sinks, and stoves. These changes set the stage for an orgy of beef eating outside the home and for the rise of America's most distinctive culinary contribution to world cuisine, the fast-food hamburger. For the new post-war, two-wage-earner families, the fast-food hamburger restaurant provides an opportunity to eat out, to be free of the drudgery of the kitchen—even without homeownership and backyard barbecues—at a cost that is comparable to a medium-budget home-cooked meal.❞

3. What social changes led to the emergence of beef as America's favorite meat?
   a. the move to suburbia
   b. the entrance of women into the workforce
   c. the rise of feminism
   d. the overpopulation of cattle

4. How has the fast-food industry played an important role in the increased consumption of beef in the United States?

SOCIOLOGY PROJECTS

Linking to Community

Using Surveys Working with a group, develop a survey to discover what your community considers to be the core values of American society. Administer the survey to fellow students and to older members of the community. Collate and analyze your survey results. Create a data base or table that shows changing demographic and cultural patterns in your community. Create a quiz and answer key based on your data base that you can give to your class.

🖪 **internet** connect

Internet Activity: go.hrw.com
KEYWORD: SL3 SC3
Choose a topic on a cultural conformity and adaptation to:
- create a pamphlet that evaluates how American values influence perceptions, attitudes, and behaviors.
- design a system of social control in which a specific norm is enforced.
- create a thematic flow chart that outlines the sources of and resistance to social change.

---

3. Students might mention increased cultural diffusion and reformulation.

4. Answers will vary, but students should examine how the movement has affected government policies and cultural values and norms.

5. Students might mention that the size of the country's open territory led to the historical importance of the values of freedom, individualism, and personal achievement.

WRITING ABOUT SOCIOLOGY

1. Paragraphs will vary, but students should exhibit an understanding of values, social change, ideologies, and social movements.

2. Essays will vary, but students should identify and then compare and contrast the values and norms of two separate regions of the country.

BUILDING SOCIAL STUDIES SKILLS

1. a

2. A majority of Americans throughout the 1990s considered protection of the environment a priority over economic growth.

3. a

4. Fast-food restaurants often sell beef hamburgers and provide an easy and affordable way to eat out.

Social Structure

CHAPTER RESOURCE MANAGER

| Objectives | Pacing Guide | Resources |

SECTION 1:
Building Blocks of Social Structure
(pp. 66–68)

REV Section 1 Review, p. 68

- Identify and describe the two major components of social structure.
- Analyze how these two components of social structure affect human interaction.

| **Regular** 0.5 day | **Block Scheduling** 0.25 day |

Block Scheduling Handbook with Team Teaching Strategies, Chapter 4

SECTION 2:
Types of Social Interaction
(pp. 69–72)

REV Section 2 Review, p. 72

- Identify the most common types of social interaction.
- Distinguish between types of interactions that stabilize social structure and those that can disrupt it.

| **Regular** 0.5 day | **Block Scheduling** 0.25 day |

Block Scheduling Handbook with Team Teaching Strategies, Chapter 4

SECTION 3:
Types of Societies
(pp. 73–77)

REV Section 3 Review, p. 77

- Identify and describe the types of societies that exist in the world today.
- Explain the roles individuals play in these models of group systems.

| **Regular** 0.5 day | **Block Scheduling** 0.25 day |

Block Scheduling Handbook with Team Teaching Strategies, Chapter 4

SECTION 4:
Groups Within Society
(pp. 78–82)

REV Section 4 Review, p. 81

- Summarize the major features of primary and secondary groups.
- Identify the purposes that groups fulfill.

| **Regular** 0.5 day | **Block Scheduling** 0.25 day |

Block Scheduling Handbook with Team Teaching Strategies, Chapter 4

SECTION 5:
The Structure of Formal Organizations
(pp. 83–89)

REV Section 5 Review, p. 89

- Explain how bureaucracies are structured.
- Evaluate the effectiveness of bureaucracies.

| **Regular** 0.5 day | **Block Scheduling** 0.25 day |

Block Scheduling Handbook with Team Teaching Strategies, Chapter 4

Resources

- **CNN** Presents Sociology: Daycare and Socialization
- **RS** Graphic Organizer 4
- **HRW** Go site
- **SM** Mastering Critical Thinking Skills 4
- **PS** Readings and Case Studies in Sociology 4
- **E** Research Projects and Activities for Teaching Sociology 4
- **SM** Study Skills and Writing Guide
- Teaching Transparency: Organization of One Public School System

Chapter Review And Assessment

- **REV** Chapter 4 Review, pp. 90–91
- **REV** Chapter Review Activities with Answer Key
- Global Skill Builder CD–ROM
- Chapter 4 Test Generator (on the One-Stop Planner)
- **A** Chapter 4 Test (Form A or B)
- **A** Alternative Assessment Handbook
- **HRW** Go site

Chapter Resource Key

PS Primary Sources	**A** Assessment	Video
RS Reading Support	**REV** Review	Internet
E Enrichment	Transparencies	Holt Presentation Maker Using Microsoft® PowerPoint®
SM Skills Mastery	CD–ROM	

One-Stop Planner CD–ROM

See the *One-Stop Planner* for a complete list of additional resources for students and teachers.

It's easy to plan lessons, select resources, and print out materials for your students when you use the **One-Stop Planner CD–ROM with Test Generator.**

Chapter Project Preview

The following activities are included in the Chapter Review. You may want to make the suggested preparations.

CHAPTER REVIEW ACTIVITY

Using Observation Skills Students will work in groups of two or three to collect photographs from magazines and newspapers and create a photo essay contrasting achieved and ascribed statuses. Before starting the project, you might bring several old magazines and newspapers to class. You might also provide each group with a posterboard on which to create its photo essay.

INTERNET ACTIVITIES

Types of Societies Students will use provided Internet links to conduct research on different types of societies and then write one or more journal entries from the point of view of someone living in one of the societies. You might prepare a sample journal entry as a model for students before starting the activity.

Conflict Resolution in the Workplace Students will use provided Internet links to conduct research on the use of mediation and arbitration to resolve conflicts in the workplace. Students will then work in groups to create a skit about resolving a hypothetical workplace conflict. Before starting, create a list of appropriate hypothetical conflicts to provide as examples or to assign to the groups.

Bureaucracies Students will use provided Internet links to conduct research on the structure, relationships, and effectiveness of bureaucracies and then create a flowchart of a bureaucratic system. For uniformity or to help structure students' research, you might want to preview the activity Web sites and then create a blank flowchart for students to complete.

Additional Resources

PRINT RESOURCES FOR TEACHERS

Deal, Terrence E., and Allan A. Kennedy. *Corporate Cultures: the Rites and Rituals of Corporate Life.* Reading, MA: Addison-Wesley, 1982. Examines the types of cultures that develop within companies and the effect they have.

Peter, Laurence J., and Raymond Hull. *The Peter Principle.* New York: William Morrow, 1969. Humorous analysis of problems that occur in society and why they happen.

PRINT RESOURCES FOR STUDENTS

De Mente, Boye. *Japanese Etiquette and Ethics in Business,* 5th ed. Lincolnwood, IL: NTC Business Books, 1987. Examines business methods in Japan. Enables students to see how culture and social structure affect Japanese corporations.

Nordhoff, Charles, and James Hall. *Mutiny on the Bounty.* Boston; Little, Brown & Co., 1932. The classic novel about a ship's crew that mutinies against a tyrannical captain. Enables students to analyze patterns of social interaction that involve military hierarchy and conflict.

Steinbeck, John. *The Grapes of Wrath.* New York: Penguin Books, 1976. Chronicles the journey of a poverty-stricken family during the Dust Bowl years of the 1930s. Enables students to study roles, in-groups, and out-groups.

MULTIMEDIA RESOURCES

Boys and Girls (film; vhs; 26 min.) Beacon Films. A young girl fights against the stereotyped role imposed on her by her parents because of her sex. Based on the story by Alice Munro.

The Turkana (vhs; 60 min.) Films Incorporated Video. Explores life among the East African Turkana cattle herders, pastoralists who live in the Rift Valley of northern Kenya.

internet connect

HRW ONLINE RESOURCES

GO TO: go.hrw.com
Then type in a keyword.

TEACHER HOME PAGE
KEYWORD: SL3 Teacher

CHAPTER INTERNET ACTIVITIES
KEYWORD: SL3 SC4
Choose an activity to have students:
• write journal entries on daily life in the six types of societies discussed in this chapter.
• create a skit showing how mediation and arbitration are used to resolve conflicts.
• create a flowchart of a bureaucratic system and write a summary of its effectiveness.

CHAPTER ENRICHMENT LINKS
KEYWORD: SL3 CH4

ONLINE ASSESSMENT
Homework Practice
KEYWORD: SL3 HP4
Standardized Test Prep
KEYWORD: SL3 STP4
Rubrics
KEYWORD: SS Rubrics

CONTENT UPDATES
KEYWORD: SS Content Updates

HOLT PRESENTATION MAKER
KEYWORD: SL3 PPT4

ONLINE READING SUPPORT
KEYWORD: SS Strategies

CURRENT EVENTS
KEYWORD: S3 Current Events

Build on What You Know

Ask students to answer the following questions:

How might factors such as the mass media and popular entertainment influence American norms and values?

Consider:

• the rapid spread of information and ideas
• the influence of famous people as role models

What factors might help determine how a person functions in society?

Consider:

• the groups to which the person belongs
• the jobs or roles the person fulfills

Internet Activity

internet connect

go.
hrw
.com

TOPIC: Types of Societies
GO TO: go.hrw.com
KEYWORD: SL3 SC4

Have students access the Internet through the HRW Go site to conduct research on different types of societies. Then ask each student to write one or more journal entries from the point of view of someone living in one of these types of societies. Remind students that journal entries should accurately reflect their research. As a reinforcement activity, ask volunteers to read their journal entries aloud and have the rest of the class try to identify what type of society is being described and explain how they knew.

CHAPTER
4 Social Structure

Build on What You Know

Within American society, norms and values help establish social control. In this chapter you will explore the factors that create social structure. You will examine the two major components of social structure—statuses and roles. You will also look at the structure of groups and societies.

In order to gain an understanding of the structure of societies, sociologists study groups of people.

Life in Society

Humans are social beings—we live and work in groups and interact in predictable ways. As scholars Lionel Tiger and Robin Fox have noted, "We are none of us truly isolated; we are connected to one another by a web of regularities and by a host of shared, deep-seated certainties." In other words, every society has a structure that guides human interaction.

This structure helps people know what is expected of them in most social situations and what they can expect from others. It also ensures that the general nature of the society remains relatively stable from one generation to the next, even though the actual members of that society change.

In most situations, sociologists studying social behavior are looking at group behavior. Many sociologists focus their research on the actions of groups and the roles of individuals within groups. Sociologists study both formally organized groups and informally organized groups.

WHY SOCIOLOGY MATTERS

Sociologists have recently become interested in media-generated primary groups. Use CNN**fyi**.com or other current events sources to learn more about e-communities. Write a report summarizing the information you find.

CNN**fyi**.com

TRUTH OR FICTION

What's Your Opinion?

Read the following statements about sociology. Do you think they are true or false? You will learn whether each statement is true or false as you read the chapter.

- An individual's statuses and roles are limited and unchanging.
- Sociologists have little interest in groups and group activities.
- Informal interaction has little effect on the functioning of formal organizations.

SECTION 1

OBJECTIVES

1. *Identify and describe the two major components of social structure.*

2. *Analyze how these two components of social structure affect human interaction.*

 LET'S GET STARTED!

As students enter the classroom, ask them to consider the meaning of the term *status*. Call on volunteers to state what this word means to them. *(Students might say social standing determined by wealth, symbols, or behaviors, such as wearing a certain brand of clothing.)* Tell students that sociologists define status as a socially determined position in a group or in a society, such as a farmer, a wife, or a student. Based on this definition, have volunteers list some of their statuses. Then tell students that in Section 1 they will learn about how statuses and roles define social structure and affect human interaction.

SECTION *1* RESOURCES

REPRODUCIBLE & REVIEW

- Research Projects and Activities for Teaching Sociology 4
- Section 1 Review, p. 68

TECHNOLOGY

- One-Stop Planner, Lesson 4.1
- Homework Practice Online

1

BUILDING BLOCKS OF SOCIAL STRUCTURE

Read to Discover

1. What are the two major components of social structure?

2. How do these two components of social structure affect human interaction?

Define

social structure, status, role, ascribed status, achieved status, master status, reciprocal roles, role expectations, role performance, role set, role conflict, role strain, social institution

---

Social structure gives a society its enduring characteristics and makes patterns of human interaction predictable. Sociologists have viewed society as a system of interrelated parts—as a structure—since the time of Auguste Comte. However, social structure as a concept has often been very loosely defined. Throughout this textbook, the term **social structure** will mean the network of interrelated statuses and roles that guide human interaction. A **status** is a socially defined position in a group or in a society. Each status has attached to it one or more roles. A **role** is the behavior—the rights and obligations—expected of someone occupying a particular status.

Status

To understand social structure, one must be familiar with the concept of status. Each individual in society occupies several statuses. For example, an individual can be a teacher, a father, a husband, an African American, and a church deacon all at the same time. Statuses are ways of defining where individuals fit in society and how they relate to others in society.

Ascribed and Achieved Statuses While some statuses are assigned, others are gained through effort. An **ascribed status** is assigned according to qualities beyond a person's control. Ascribed statuses are not based on an individual's abilities, efforts, or accomplishments. Rather, they are based on a person's inherited traits or are assigned automatically when a person reaches a certain age. You hold the status of teenager or young adult, for example, because of your age. You did nothing to earn this status. Neither can you change it.

Other examples of ascribed statuses include your sex, family heritage, and race.

Individuals acquire an **achieved status** through their own direct efforts. These efforts include special skills, knowledge, or abilities. For example, a person achieves the status of basketball player because of his or her physical skills and knowledge of the game. Similarly, someone achieves the status of actor because of his or her acting abilities.

Unlike their ascribed statuses, people have some control over their achieved statuses. In a complex society such as the United States, the list of achieved statuses is almost endless. For example, all occupations are achieved statuses. Other achieved statuses include husband or wife, parent, high school or college graduate, and athlete.

Master Status All individuals hold many statuses. For most people, one status tends to take rank above all others. This status plays the greatest role in shaping a person's life and determining his or her social identity and is called a **master status**. A master status can be either achieved or ascribed. In the United States, an adult's master status is usually achieved. For example, occupation, wealth, marital status, or parenthood can serve as a master status.

A person's master status changes over the course of his or her life. During the teenage years, being a student or athlete often serves as a master status. During much of adulthood, on the other hand, master status is often based on one's occupation. Finally, in late adulthood—generally after a person retires from his or her primary occupation—volunteer work, hobbies, grandparenthood, or past accomplishments serve as a person's master status.

A person's master status can be achieved such as being a doctor or be ascribed such as being a woman or child.

TEACH OBJECTIVES 1 AND 2

Call on students to identify and describe the two major components of social structure (*statuses and roles*) and to explain how they affect human interaction. Then, to help students understand statuses and roles, copy the graphic organizer at right onto the chalkboard and include the sample answers. Have students copy the organizer but instead of the sample answers enter information either about someone they know or a fictional person.

ENGLISH LANGUAGE LEARNERS , COOPERATIVE LEARNING

HOMEWORK: Have each student select a fictional character from a book, television show, or movie and draw a cartoon of this character wearing at least five stacked hats labeled with his or her various statuses.

Status	Examples of Roles	Examples of Conflict/Strain
fire fighter	putting out fires, saving lives, wearing a uniform	voluntarily puts self in danger but has loved ones who need him or her
mother	providing food and shelter, nurturing family, disciplining children	work fatigue and long shifts make household tasks and interactions difficult
P.T.A. president	running meetings, recruiting new members, planning activities	has trouble getting members to attend and follow through on promises

INTERPRETING VISUALS The role of coaches and athletes are reciprocal in that they rely upon each other, since if athletes did not exist then there would be no need for coaches. *What types of behaviors does society expect from coaches?*

Roles

Statuses serve simply as social categories. Roles are the component of social structure that bring statuses to life. As Ralph Linton noted, you *occupy* a status, but you *play* a role. You play many different roles every day. At home you probably play the role associated with the status of son or daughter. At school you play the role associated with the status of student. You may also perform the roles that go along with the status of a reporter on the school newspaper or of a member of the gymnastics team.

Most of the roles you perform have reciprocal roles. **Reciprocal roles** are corresponding roles that define the patterns of interaction between related statuses. For example, one cannot fulfill the role associated with the status of husband without having someone else perform the role that goes along with the status of wife. Other statuses that require reciprocal roles include doctor-patient, athlete-coach, friend-friend, employee-employer, leader-follower, and sales clerk-customer.

Role Expectations and Role Performance

Ideally, when people interact with one another their behavior corresponds to the particular roles they are playing. The socially determined behaviors expected of a person performing a role are called **role expectations**. For example, doctors are expected to treat their patients with skill and care. Parents are expected to provide emotional and physical security for their children. Police officers are expected to uphold the law.

In reality, people's **role performance**—their actual role behavior—does not always match the behavior expected by society. Some doctors do not give their patients the best possible care. Some parents mistreat their children. Occasionally, this problem arises because role behaviors considered appropriate by a certain segment of society are seen as inappropriate by society as a whole. Even when someone tries to fulfill a role in the manner expected by society, actual performance may fall short of expectations. This problem occurs, in part, because each of us is asked to perform many roles, some of which are contradictory.

Applying Sociology

Role Models. One way that people form their role expectations is by observing role models. Many people of all ages work to imitate others whom they admire, either for their beauty, character traits, fame, or success. Role models can provide positive guidance. However, they must be chosen with care. Success in one role does not mean that someone's performance in other roles is appropriate and meets society's expectations.

ACTIVITY: Have each student list one or two people whom they consider role models. Then have students list how these people help define students' role expectations. Have students discuss their responses.

Visual Answer

Society expects coaches to be knowledgeable about their sport and to help athletes improve their performance and achieve their best.

Social Structure **67**

67

CLOSE

Tell students to imagine that they are exchange students to a foreign country of their choice. Have each student write a list of role expectations that he or she thinks might differ in this other country from the student's current role expectations. Then have students share and discuss some of their responses with the class.

REVIEW AND ASSESS

Have students complete the **Section 1 Review** on p. 68. As **Alternative Assessment**, you may want to use the status/role graphic organizer or the "many hats" cartoon that are described in this section's lessons.

RETEACH

Pair students and have each pair create flash cards for this section's Define terms. Then have partners use their flash cards to quiz each other on the section content.
ENGLISH LANGUAGE LEARNERS , COOPERATIVE LEARNING

EXTEND

Have students interview two to four adults about the various roles that they play. Then have students use the interviews to make a list of at least 10 examples of role conflict or role strain in the lives of these adults. **BLOCK SCHEDULING**

Visual Answer

because she may feel that to be a good mother she should stay with her child, but to be a good breadwinner and employee she must go to work

---

SECTION 1 REVIEW ANSWERS

1. **Define:**
   - social structure, p. 66
   - status, p. 66
   - role, p. 66
   - ascribed status, p. 66
   - achieved status, p. 66
   - master status, p. 66
   - reciprocal roles, p. 67
   - role expectations, p. 67
   - role performance, p. 67
   - role set, p. 68
   - role conflict, p. 68
   - role strain, p. 68
   - social institution, p. 68

2. Answers will vary. Most students will enter *student* for his or her master status, and students should be careful not to confuse role with status.

3a. status—a socially defined position in a group or in a society, has attached to it one or more roles; role—the behavior expected of someone occupying a particular status

b. Answers will vary, but students should exhibit an understanding of the terms *status* and *role,* as defined in the previous answer.

4. Paragraphs will vary, but students should suggest possible solutions such as contacting a close friend or family member to take care of the sick child or obtaining permission to work at home.

Role Conflict and Role Strain Even within a single status, there are many interrelated roles to perform. Sociologists call the different roles attached to a single status a **role set**. Each of us, because we hold more than one status, must deal with many role sets in our daily lives. The often contradictory expectations within and between our role sets can lead to role conflict and role strain.

Role conflict occurs when fulfilling the role expectations of one status makes it difficult to fulfill the role expectations of another status. In other words, role conflict occurs between statuses. For example, to be a good employee an individual needs to go to work. However, to be a good parent, that individual needs to stay home and take care of a sick child. **Role strain**, on the other hand, occurs when a person has difficulty meeting the role expectations of a single status. The boss who must maintain the morale of workers while getting them to work long periods of overtime is likely to experience role strain.

Social Institutions

Statuses and their related roles determine the structure of the various groups in society. When these statuses and roles are organized to satisfy one or more of the basic needs of society, the group is called a **social institution**. The basic needs of a society include providing physical and emotional support for its members, transmitting knowledge, producing goods and services, and maintaining social control.

INTERPRETING VISUALS Many working parents face role conflict because the needs of their family and the requirements of work demand a great deal of time. *Why might a mother dropping her child off at day care experience role conflict?*

Although sociologists have recognized many significant social institutions, some scholars have focused on the major institutions of family, the economy, politics, education, and religion. Sociologists have also studied the social institutions of the media, medicine, and science. You will take a closer look at these social institutions in later chapters.

SECTION 1 REVIEW

1. **Define and explain**
   social structure
   status
   role
   ascribed status
   achieved status
   master status
   reciprocal roles
   role expectations
   role performance
   role set
   role conflict
   role strain
   social institution

2. **Categorizing** Copy the graphic organizer below. Use it to identify your master status and other statuses.

Master Status

3. **Finding the Main Idea**

   a. What are the two major building blocks of social structure?

   b. Describe the interactive roles and statuses of individuals and groups in your community.

4. **Writing and Critical Thinking**

   Identifying Points of View Study the example of role conflict in this chapter's text. Write one or two short paragraphs suggesting how this conflict might be resolved.

   Consider:

   - the reasons for the conflict

   - individual and group resolutions to the conflict

Homework Practice Online
keyword: SL3 HP4

2

TYPES OF SOCIAL INTERACTION

● **Read to Discover**
1. What are the most common types of social interaction?
2. Which types of interactions stabilize social structure and which can disrupt it?

● **Define**
exchange, reciprocity, exchange theory, competition, conflict, cooperation, accommodation

● **Identify**
Georg Simmel

When you play a role, most of the time you have to interact with others. This interaction can take many forms. Some kinds of interaction help stabilize the social structure. Others promote change. Among the most common forms of social interaction are exchange, competition, conflict, cooperation, and accommodation. These five types of interaction take place in societies throughout the world.

Exchange

Whenever people interact in an effort to receive a reward or a return for their actions, an **exchange** has taken place. Almost all daily interaction involves exchange. In fact, scholar Peter Blau suggested that exchange is the most basic and common form of interaction. Dating, family life, friendship, and politics all involve exchanges. **Reciprocity**—the idea that if you do something for someone, that person owes you something in return—is the basis of exchange. The reward might be nonmaterial. For example, a simple "thank you" from your parents

might be a reward for washing the dishes. The reward could also be material, such as the wage you might receive for working at a supermarket.

The volume of exchange in daily interactions has led to the emergence of an **exchange theory**. Exchange theorists believe that people are motivated by self-interest in their interactions with other people. In other words, people do things primarily for rewards. Behavior that is rewarded tends to be repeated. However, when the costs of an interaction outweigh the rewards, individuals are likely to end the relationship. According to exchange theorists, most of social life can be explained as the attempt to maximize rewards while minimizing costs.

Competition

Imagine that you have applied for an after-school job at a local store. When you arrive for your interview, you find that you are competing with several other applicants for the job. **Competition** occurs when two or more people or groups oppose each other to achieve a goal that only one can attain.

Competition is a common feature of Western societies. Some scholars consider it to be the cornerstone of the capitalist economic system and the democratic form of government. Advancement in business, school, and sports is achieved through competition. As long as competition follows accepted rules of conduct, most sociologists view it as a positive means of motivating people to perform the roles society asks of them. On the negative side, competition can also lead to psychological stress, a lack of cooperation in social relationships, inequality, and even conflict.

Visual Answer

Couples provide each other with love and companionship in the hope of getting those things in return.

INTERPRETING VISUALS Couples in a relationship often have interactions based on exchange. *What part do you think reciprocity plays in a couple's relationship?*

Sociology in the World Today

TEACH

Have students read the feature The Argument Culture? on this page and complete the Think About It section. Then have each student write a one- to two-page essay agreeing or disagreeing with Tannen's assertions. Remind students to support their points of view with facts and examples. You may want students to peer-edit each other's essays.

CONNECTING to Literature

Organize the class into small groups. Have each group examine American and world literature anthologies to find two pieces in each that include examples of accommodation, cooperation, or confrontation in solving problems. *(Examples include Franz Kafka's* Metamorphosis *[European] and Arthur Miller's* Death of a Salesman *[American].)* Then have groups share their examples with the class and discuss whether they support Tannen's assertion that the United States is an argument culture. **COOPERATIVE LEARNING**, **BLOCK SCHEDULING**

Sociology in the World Today

Conflict as Popular Entertainment. A woman screams and attacks her husband, as the audience howls and yells out encouragement. Just another episode of one of the many confrontation-oriented talk shows that have become popular in America. Whether staged or real, such shows have a large following of people who enjoy watching as others discuss controversial issues, bicker, and fight. The trend is not limited to television. Talk-radio shows where the host and callers argue and complain also have large followings.

CRITICAL THINKING

What might be some reasons for the popularity of conflict-oriented talk shows?

ANSWERS: Students might suggest that such shows provide people with a chance to air their viewpoints or to feel superior to others.

Think About It Answers

1. cooperation and agreement

2. Conclusions will vary, but students should provide specific examples to support their positions.

SOCIOLOGY IN THE
World Today

THE ARGUMENT CULTURE?

Does one form of interaction dominate American culture? Deborah Tannen, a professor of linguistics, thinks it may be competition or conflict. In her book *The Argument Culture*, Tannen suggests that, through their culture, Americans learn to approach human interaction as a duel of wills in which all issues have only two sides. This approach is based on the assumption that contention is the best way to get things done. In the media, the best way to present the news objectively is to find people with extreme views and cast them as the two sides of the issue. In politics, the best way to make a point is to attack the views or character of a political opponent. In the courts, the best way to settle disputes is to set up an adversarial situation that pits one party against the other. In colleges and universities, the best way to do valid work is to challenge the ideas of others.

This argument culture, Tannen says, presupposes that there will be winners and losers. Even everyday phrases such as "the war on drugs," "the fight against cancer," "to join the fray," and "the battle is half won" frame life in terms of a contest in which winning or losing is the major concern. It is as if human relationships are modeled on a gunfight in a western movie, Tannen suggests. Interaction is "a shoot-out between two gunslingers, which one must lose while the other wins."

A Valid Approach?

Tannen challenges the argument culture on two points. First, the assumption that every issue has two sides is flawed. Most issues are a complex mix of many views. Focusing on the extremes of these views does not necessarily reveal the truth behind the issue. Second, Tannen questions the usefulness of arguments. During an argument, she says, you are not trying to understand another's point of view. Rather,

you are looking for weaknesses, misstatements, and anything else you can use to win the argument. When winning is the goal, you are sometimes driven to reject the facts that support your opponent's view and use only those that support yours. Worse still, if you fear losing you may even resort to lying.

A Better Way?

Tannen does not believe that arguing is always wrong. She says, "There are times when we need to disagree, criticize, oppose, and attack—to hold debates and view issues as polarized battles." To stand up for right against wrong or to argue against dangerous ideas, then, is perfectly acceptable—even needed. However, conflict and opposition seem to be overly favored as ways to settle all issues or problems. Cooperation and agreement, Tannen suggests, are valid approaches too. In addition, she states that cooperation does not mean the absence of conflict. Rather, it means that people have reached some kind of accommodation among conflicting views.

According to Tannen the argument culture can be found in a variety of social interactions and is learned at an early age.

STONE SOUP © 1998 Jan Eliot. Reprinted with permission of UNIVERSAL PRESS SYNDICATE. All rights reserved.

Think About It

1. **Summarizing** *What alternatives does Tannen offer to the argument culture?*
2. **Supporting a Point of View** *Do you agree with Tannen that Americans live in an argument culture in which conflict and opposition dominate social interaction? Explain your answer.*

TEACH OBJECTIVES 1 AND 2

To help students identify common types of social interaction, copy the graphic organizer at right onto the chalkboard, omitting the italicized answers. Have students work in pairs to copy and complete the organizer by entering the common types of social interactions into the inner circles and three examples of each type into the outer circles. Tell students to underline the stabilizing interactions. **ENGLISH LANGUAGE LEARNERS , COOPERATIVE LEARNING**

HOMEWORK: Have students choose one type of social interaction and look for examples of it over the course of two or three days. Have students list any examples they observe and report their results back to the class.

Conflict

The main emphasis in competition is on achieving the goal. With conflict the emphasis is on defeating the opponent. **Conflict** is the deliberate attempt to control a person by force, to oppose someone, or to harm another person. Unlike competition, conflict has few rules of conduct, and even these often are ignored. Conflict may range from the deliberate snubbing of a classmate to the killing of an enemy.

Sociologist Georg Simmel identified four sources of conflict: wars, disagreements within groups, legal disputes, and clashes over ideology, such as religion or politics. Sometimes conflicts begin as competition. Rival businesses may first engage in intense competition for customers.

However, as the competition increases, the emphasis shifts from attracting customers to undermining the other business. One business may sell merchandise well below cost to try to force the other business into bankruptcy.

Although we tend to think of conflict as negative, some sociologists have pointed out that conflict serves some useful purposes. For example, conflict reinforces group boundaries and strengthens group loyalty by focusing attention on an outside threat. Focusing on an outside threat also draws attention away from internal problems. In addition, conflict can also lead to social change by bringing problems to the forefront and forcing opposing sides to seek solutions.

Cooperation

The members of a football team work together to win a game. The pep club, school band, and student body also contribute to this effort by encouraging the team. If, in the end, the team takes a trophy, it will be through the shared efforts of the entire school. Similarly, the employees of a corporation work together to increase sales for the organization. If their efforts are successful, everyone benefits. In both of these examples, the people involved are cooperating to achieve a desired goal. **Cooperation** occurs when two or more people or groups work together to achieve a goal that will benefit more than one person.

Cooperation is a social process that gets things done. No group can complete its tasks or achieve its goals without cooperation from its members. Cooperation is often used along with other forms of interaction. Competition may be used along with cooperation to motivate members to work harder for the group. For example, individuals who go out for a team sport often compete with one another to make the varsity team.

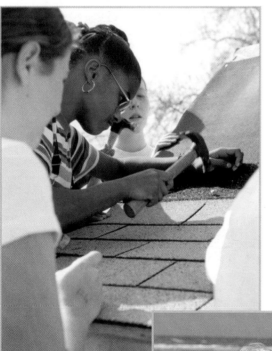

INTERPRETING VISUALS By using cooperation, members of a group can work together to complete a goal that might have been unobtainable by an individual. *How do you think these student volunteers and children are completing their goals using cooperation?*

CLOSE

To conclude, write the following statement on the chalk-board: *Cooperation and accommodation are good; competition and conflict are bad.* Have each student write a paragraph explaining whether he or she agrees and why. Then have students discuss their opinions.

REVIEW AND ASSESS

Have students complete the **Section 2 Review** on p. 72. As **Alternative Assessment**, you may want to use the social inter-action graphic organizer or observations in this section's lessons.

RETEACH

Have each student write a one-paragraph summary of the main points in this section and then give an example of each type of social interaction covered. Finally, lead a class review of the section's main ideas. **ENGLISH LANGUAGE LEARNERS**

EXTEND

Organize students into pairs or triads. Have them write and perform skits in which they role-play one of the types of social inter-actions described in this section. **COOPERATIVE LEARNING**, **BLOCK SCHEDULING**

SECTION 2 REVIEW ANSWERS

1. Define:
- exchange, p. 69
- reciprocity, p. 69
- exchange theory, p. 69
- competition, p. 69
- conflict, p. 71
- cooperation, p. 71
- accommodation, p. 72

2. Identify:
- Georg Simmel, p. 71

3. from difficult to easily achieved: truce, compromise, mediation, and arbitration; examples will vary

4a. exchange—interacting in an effort to receive a reward or a return for one's actions; competition—two or more people or groups in opposition to achieve a goal that only one can attain; conflict—the deliberate attempt to control a person by force, to oppose someone, or to harm another person; cooperation—two or more people or groups working together to achieve a goal that will benefit more than one of them

b. competition and conflict

5. Essays will vary, but students should describe a plausible scenario that involves more than one form of interaction.

Accommodation

In many of your interactions, you neither cooperate nor engage in conflict. You simply accommodate the other party in the interaction. In other words, you give a little, and you take a little. **Accommodation** is a state of balance between cooperation and conflict. One way to remember this type of interaction is by thinking about staying at a motel. The owner of the motel is accommodating you by letting you stay for the night in exchange for $60. If the owner were cooperating with you, you would be able to stay for free. On the other hand, if the owner refused to let you stay under any condition, you would be in a conflict situation.

Accommodation can take a number of different forms. One of these forms is compromise. A compromise occurs when two parties both give up something to come to a mutual agreement. For example, you and a friend want to see different movies. To compromise, you might choose a third movie that you both would like to see. Another form of accommodation is the truce, which brings a halt to the conflict until a compromise can be reached. Sometimes, when two parties cannot agree on a compromise, they will use mediation. This form of accommodation involves calling in a third party who acts as adviser and counselor to help the two parties reach an agreement. However, they may use arbitration. In arbitration, a third party makes a decision that is binding on both parties. These types of interaction help to ensure social stability.

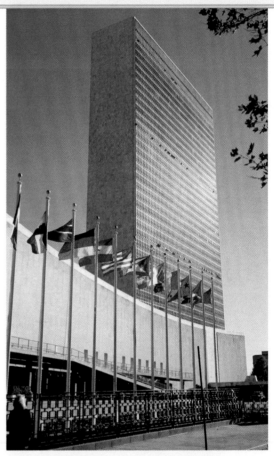

The United Nations is a global organization that tries to solve world problems through cooperation and compromise.

SECTION 2 REVIEW

1. Define and explain
exchange
reciprocity
exchange theory
competition
conflict
cooperation
accommodation

2. Identify and explain
Georg Simmel

3. Sequencing Copy the graphic organizer below. Use it to sequence the four forms of accommodation. Then describe a case in which each could be used.

Difficult to Achieve

Easily Achieved

4. Finding the Main Idea
a. Briefly describe the five most common forms of social interaction.
b. Which types of interaction can lead to a disruption of social stability?

5. Writing and Critical Thinking
Analyzing Information Write a brief essay showing how you might employ several forms of interaction in one situation involving another person or group.
Consider:
- examples of exchange, competition, cooperation, and conflict you have used in your relationships with friends
- examples of the various forms of accommodation you have used in your relationships with friends

go. hrw .com **Homework Practice Online**
keyword: SL3 HP4

SECTION 3

OBJECTIVES

1. *Identify and describe the types of societies that exist in the world today.*
2. *Explain the roles individuals play in these models of group systems.*

 LET'S GET STARTED!

Before class, write the following quotation on the chalkboard: *"It is easy to understand that any condensation of the social mass, especially if it is accompanied by an increase in population, necessarily stimulates an advance in the division of labor."* As students enter the classroom, have a volunteer look up *division of labor* and define it for the class. Ask students to think about Durkheim's statement and discuss whether it is true. Then ask students what other factors might influence increased division of labor (*such as new technology, increased knowledge, or better educational systems*). Then tell students that in Section 3 they will learn about types of societies that exist in the world today.

3 TYPES OF SOCIETIES

Read to Discover
1. What types of societies exist in the world today?
2. What roles do individuals play in these models of group systems?

Define
group, subsistence strategies, preindustrial society, hunting and gathering societies, pastoral society, division of labor, horticultural society, agricultural society, barter, industrial societies, urbanization, postindustrial society, mechanical solidarity, organic solidarity, *Gemeinschaft, Gesellschaft*

SECTION 3 RESOURCES

REPRODUCIBLE & REVIEW
- Graphic Organizer 4
- Section 3 Review, p. 77

TECHNOLOGY
- One-Stop Planner, Lesson 4.3
- Homework Practice Online

Role behavior often takes place in groups. In sociological terms, a **group** is a set of people who interact on the basis of shared expectations and who possess some degree of common identity. The largest and most complex groups that sociologists study are societies. Sociologists tend to classify societies according to **subsistence strategies**. A subsistence strategy is the way a society uses technology to provide for the needs of its members. Sociologists place societies in three broad categories—preindustrial, industrial, or postindustrial.

Preindustrial Societies

In a **preindustrial society,** food production—which is carried out through the use of human and animal labor—is the main economic activity. Preindustrial societies can be subdivided according to their level of technology and their method of producing food. These subdivisions are hunting and gathering, pastoral, horticultural, and agricultural.

Hunting and Gathering Societies The main form of food production in **hunting and gathering societies** is the daily collection of wild plants and the hunting of wild animals. Hunter-gatherers move around constantly in search of food. As a result, they do not build permanent villages or create a wide variety of artifacts. The need for mobility also limits the size of hunting and gathering societies. Such societies generally consist of fewer than 60 people and rarely exceed 100 people. Statuses within the group are relatively equal, and decisions are reached through general agreement. The family forms the main social unit, with most societal members being related by birth or by marriage. This type of organization requires the family to carry out most social functions—including production and education.

Pastoral Societies Pastoralism is a slightly more efficient form of subsistence. Rather than searching for food on a daily basis, members of a **pastoral society** rely on domesticated herd animals to meet their food needs. Pastoralists live a nomadic life, moving their herds from pasture to pasture. Because their food supply is far more reliable, pastoral societies can support larger populations. Since there are food surpluses, fewer people are needed to produce food. As a result, the **division of labor**—the specialization by individuals or groups in the performance of specific economic activities—becomes more complex. For example, some people become craftworkers, producing tools, weapons, and jewelry.

Pastoral societies exist in countries such as Kenya where community members tend to animals such as goats.

73

Call on students to identify the three main types of societies discussed in this chapter (*preindustrial, industrial, and postindustrial*). Write the three terms on the chalkboard as the first level of a flow-chart. Next, draw a line from preindustrial that leads to four boxes and ask students to identify the four types of preindustrial societies (*hunting and gathering, pastoral, horticultural, and agricultural*). Then, to help students describe the characteristics of these different types of societies, copy the following graphic organizer onto the chalkboard, omitting the italicized answers. Have each student copy and complete the organizer. Discuss the answers with the class. **ENGLISH LANGUAGE LEARNERS**

Preindustrial
hunting and gathering; pastoral; horticultural; mechanical solidarity

agricultural

TYPES OF SOCIETIES

Industrial
manufacturing

urban; technology; organic solidarity

Postindustrial
information; provision of services

HISTORY

The Industrial Revolution. Modern industrialization began in Great Britain in the mid-1700s. This period, known as the Industrial Revolution, was marked by major advances in science and technology. New machines, such as the spinning jenny, and new sources of energy, such as the use of steam, improved production. In time, this wave of industrialization spread to other countries, including the United States.

RESEARCH ACTIVITY: Have each student conduct research on the Industrial Revolution and create a time line of its major events.

Did You Know?

Although pastoral peoples herd livestock, most of them eat very little meat. Pastoralists must ensure the survival of their herds because they cannot easily obtain new animals. If pastoral societies regularly ate their animals, they would soon use up their herds. Instead, pastoralists eat dairy products made from milking their animals. When herders do eat meat, they choose a male animal because it cannot produce milk or young.

The production of goods encourages trade. This trade, in turn, helps to create inequality, as some families acquire more goods than others do. These families often acquire power through their increased wealth. The passing on of property from generation to generation helps to centralize wealth and power. In time, hereditary chieftainships—the typical form of government in pastoral societies—emerge.

Horticultural Societies Fruits and vegetables grown in garden plots that have been cleared from the jungle or forest provide the main source of food in a **horticultural society**. Horticultural societies have a level of technology and complexity similar to pastoral societies. Some horticultural groups use the slash-and-burn method to raise crops. The wild vegetation is cut and burned, and the ashes are used as fertilizer. Horti-culturists use human labor and simple tools to cultivate the land for one or more seasons.

When the land becomes barren, horticulturists clear a new plot and leave the old plot to revert to its natural state. They may return to the original plot several years later and begin the process again. By rotating their garden plots, hor-ticulturists can stay in one area for a fairly long period of time. This allows them to build semipermanent or perma-nent villages. The size of a village's population depends on the amount of land available for farming. Villages can range from as few as 30 people to as many as 2,000.

As with pastoral societies, surplus food leads to a more complex division of labor. Specialized roles that are part of horticultural life, include those of craftspeople, shamans—or religious leaders—and traders. This role specialization allows horticulturists to create a wide variety of artifacts. As in pastoral soci-eties, surplus food can lead to inequalities in wealth and power within horticultural societies, and as a result, hereditary chieftainships are prevalent. Eco-nomic and political systems may be better developed in horticultural societies than in pastoral societies because of the more set-tled nature of horticultural life.

Agricultural Societies In an **agricultural society**, animals are used to pull plows to till the fields. This technological innovation allows agriculturists to plant more crops than is possible when only human labor is used. Irrigation—another innovation—further increases crop yields, as does terracing, which is the practice of cutting fields into the sides of hills.

Higher crop yields allow agricultural societies to sup-port very large populations. Most people must still work in food production, but many people are able to engage in specialized roles. In turn, specialization leads to the devel-opment of cities, as individuals engaged in specialized roles come together in central areas. As the number of cities within a society increase, power often becomes con-centrated in the hands of a single individual. This power was transferred from generation to generation, usually in the form of a hereditary monarchy.

Leaders of agricultural societies build powerful armies to provide protection from outside attack. The leaders also construct roads. Efficient transportation sys-tems help increase trade in agricultural societies. Increased trade leads to a number of significant cultural advances. For example, many agricultural societies abandon **barter**—the exchange of a good or service—to facilitate trade. In place of bartering, they use money as the medium of exchange. Many agricultural societies also develop a system of writing to assist the government, landowners, and traders in keeping records.

It is with agricultural societies that sharp status differ-ences first arise. Most people in an agricultural society belong to one of two groups: landowners or peasants. The small group of landowners controls the wealth and power in society. The large peasant group provides the labor on which the landowners' wealth and power depend.

Industrial Societies

In **industrial societies** the emphasis shifts from the pro-duction of food to the production of manufactured goods. This shift is made possible by changes in production meth-ods. In preindustrial societies, food and goods are pro-duced using human and animal labor. Production is slow, and the small number of available workers limits the amount that can be produced. In industrial societies the bulk of production is carried out through the use of machines. Thus, production can be increased by adding more machines or by developing new technologies.

Industrialization also affects population size by increasing the amount of food that can be produced. The more food that is produced, the more people the society can support. Industrialization also changes the nature of the economy by reducing the demand for agricultural laborers. These workers are free to transfer their labor to the production of goods. The size of the industrial

Industrial societies use machines to increase productivity, which leads to a larger society and a greater division of labor.

Connecting to Economics

CONNECTING TO
Economics

Internet technology has made bartering easier by connecting potential barterers.

THE NEW BARTER

One of the major cultural developments of agricultural societies was the creation of a money system. In some postindustrial societies, the method of trade that money replaced—barter—has made something of a comeback in recent years. It has certainly found favor with American businesses. Estimates suggest that in the late 1990s, more than 400,000 North American companies were involved in the commercial barter industry. The barter transactions these companies made averaged more than $9 billion a year.

How the New Barter Works

The commercial barter of today differs greatly from barter of the past. Companies do not trade directly with one another, swapping one product or service for another. Rather, they work through a barter exchange. There are about 700 of these exchanges in North America, with a total membership of more than 460,000 businesses. A member company sells its products or services to the exchange for "barter dollars" or "trade credits." These "dollars" or "credits" are entered into the company's account with the exchange. The company then draws on the account to pay for goods or services that it wants to buy. In essence, a barter exchange acts as a marketplace for its members to buy and sell products and services among themselves.

Barter exchanges handle every type of trade. Most member companies are looking to sell products and buy advertising. For example, one fruit-juice company partially financed an advertising campaign by bartering 2 million pounds of guava jelly!

Of course, barter exchanges do not offer their services for free. Companies pay a membership fee, usually between $200 and $500, to join an exchange group. The exchange also charges a commission of 10 to 15 percent on every barter transaction and has other monthly fees.

Reasons for Growth

The commercial barter industry grew rapidly during the 1990s. The value of barter transactions, for example, has been increasing by more than 8 percent per year. One reason for this rapid growth is the development of new computer technology. Computers make the recording and tracking of trades—many of which involve several companies—much easier. The Internet also allows exchanges to locate potential trade partners in distant markets.

There are many advantages to barter trade. To begin with, it provides a way to dispose of outdated inventory or excess capacity. For example, a hotel can reduce the number of empty rooms during the off-season by trading hotel stays for barter credits. Another company might use its credits to buy the hotel stays, which it could use for sales meetings or promotional giveaways. Barter also allows companies to conserve cash for absolutely essential services. In addition, barter provides a way for companies to buy services that, under normal circumstances, might be beyond their means.

If commercial barter continues at its present rate of growth, it could soon change the face of business in the United States. Barter exchanges have grown to include foreign companies, creating worldwide trade networks. As a result, the way we use money could change significantly. Obviously, such changes would have a major effect on society—an effect that sociologists will seek to analyze and explain.

Think About It

1. **Analyzing Information** *Why has barter grown, and how does it differ from barter in the past?*
2. **Making Generalizations and Predictions** *What effect do you think the expansion of commercial barter will have on society in the United States? Explain your answer.*

TEACH OBJECTIVE 2

Organize students into six groups. Assign each group one of the following types of societies: hunting and gathering, pastoral, horticultural, agricultural, industrial, or postindustrial. Tell group members to work together to write a series of five to six creative journal entries that illustrate how a teenager in their assigned type of society might spend his or her days. Have each group read one or more of its journal entries to the class. **COOPERATIVE LEARNING**

HOMEWORK: Have each student sketch three maps that show the progression of a society from a preindustrial to an industrial to a postindustrial society. Tell students to provide clear legends that indicate scale (the scale will shrink as the civilization grows), population, human activities and movement, industries, and modifications to the land. Display students' completed maps in the classroom and discuss outstanding examples with the class.

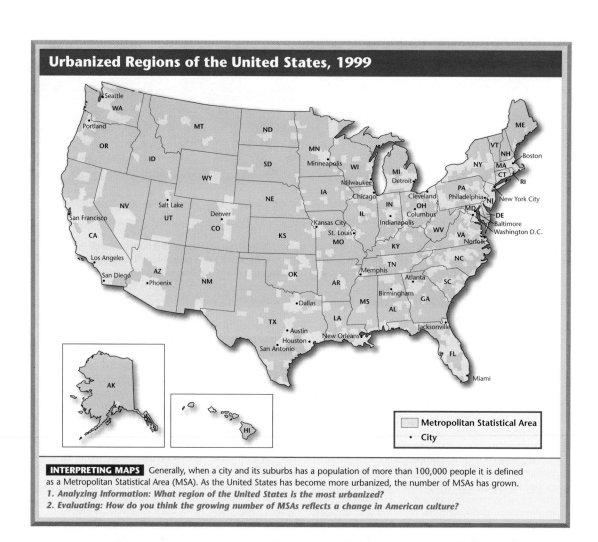

Urbanized Regions of the United States, 1999

Metropolitan Statistical Area
· City

INTERPRETING MAPS Generally, when a city and its suburbs has a population of more than 100,000 people it is defined as a Metropolitan Statistical Area (MSA). As the United States has become more urbanized, the number of MSAs has grown.
1. *Analyzing Information: What region of the United States is the most urbanized?*
2. *Evaluating: How do you think the growing number of MSAs reflects a change in American culture?*

workforce also increases as new technologies make it possible to manufacture a wider variety of goods.

Industrialization also changes the location of work. In preindustrial societies most economic activities are carried out within the home setting. With the development of machines, production moves from the home to factories. As factories are built in cities, many people move to these areas. This trend leads to **urbanization**—the concentration of the population in cities.

Industrialization also changes the nature of work. In preindustrial societies, craftspeople are responsible for manufacturing an entire product. With the use of machines, the production process is divided into a series of specific tasks, with each task being assigned to a different person. This process greatly increases productivity. However, it serves to reduce the level of skill required of most workers and tends to create boredom on the job.

Industrialization also changes the role of various institutions in society. In preindustrial societies the family is the primary social institution. For example, production and education are the responsibility of the family. However, in industrial societies production and education take place outside the bounds of the family. The need for mass literacy leads industrial societies to establish programs of compulsory education. The role of religion in society is also changed by industrialization. In advanced industrial societies, scientific ideas often challenge religious beliefs.

One positive effect of industrialization is that it brings people more freedom to compete for social position. In preindustrial societies most social statuses are ascribed. Thus, it is difficult for individuals to work their way up the social ladder. In industrial societies most statuses are achieved. As a result, individuals have more control over their position in the social structure.

CLOSE

Ask students to imagine that they are adults living in any of the societies described in this section. Then have each student create a résumé that shows the type of work experiences an individual in that society might have. Have volunteers share their résumés with the class.

REVIEW AND ASSESS

Have students complete the **Section 3 Review** on p. 77. As **Alternative Assessment**, you may want to use the society types graphic organizer or the progression map in this section's lessons.

RETEACH

Have each student list all the types and subtypes of societies discussed in this section and write a sentence or two describing each one. Then have each student list a few verbs that define the primary tasks of individuals in each society. Have volunteers share their work with the class. **ENGLISH LANGUAGE LEARNERS**

EXTEND

Have students examine art books to find and photocopy examples of appropriate art that portray people in preindustrial, industrial, and postindustrial working roles. Display the better examples on a bulletin board. **BLOCK SCHEDULING**

Postindustrial Societies

It may be a surprise, but the United States is not an industrial society. The United States—like many Western countries—is a postindustrial society. In a **postindustrial society** much of the economy is involved in providing information and services. In the United States about 73 percent of the workforce is involved in those activities. In contrast, a little more than 2 percent of workers are employed in agriculture and nearly 25 percent are employed in the production of goods.

Many significant social changes result from the transition from an industrial society to a postindustrial society. For example, the standard of living and the quality of life improve as wages increase for much of the population. In general, postindustrial societies place strong emphasis on roles of science and education in society. Technological advances are viewed as the key to future prosperity. The rights of individuals and the search for personal fulfillment also take on added importance. Belief in these rights leads to a strong emphasis on social equality and democracy.

Contrasting Societies

Sociologists have long been interested in how the social structures of preindustrial and industrial societies differ. Émile Durkheim used the concepts of mechanical and organic solidarity to describe the types of social relationships found in preindustrial and industrial societies. According to Durkheim, preindustrial societies are held together by **mechanical solidarity**. By this Durkheim

meant that when people share the same values and perform the same tasks, they become united in a common whole.

As the division of labor within societies becomes more complex, mechanical solidarity gives way to **organic solidarity**. This term refers to the impersonal social relationships that arise with increased job specialization, in which individuals can no longer provide for all of their own needs. They become dependent on others for aspects of their survival. Thus, many societal relationships are based on need rather than on values.

The German sociologist Ferdinand Tönnies (TUHRN-yuhs) was also interested in the ways in which simple and complex societies differ. He distinguished two ideal types of societies based on the structure of social relationships and the degree of shared values among societal members. He called these two types of societies **Gemeinschaft** (guh-MYN-shahft), the German word meaning "community," and **Gesellschaft** (guh-ZEL-shahft), the German word meaning "society."

Gemeinschaft refers to societies in which most members know one another. Relationships in such societies are close, and activities center on the family and the community. In a *Gemeinschaft*, people share a strong sense of group solidarity. A preindustrial society or a rural village in a more complex society are examples of a *Gemeinschaft*.

In a *Gesellschaft* most social relationships are based on need rather than on emotion. Thus, relationships in a *Gesellschaft* are impersonal and often temporary. Traditional values are generally weak in such societies, and individual goals are more important than group goals. A modern urban society such as the United States is an example of a *Gesellschaft*.

SECTION 3 REVIEW

1. **Define and explain**
   group
   subsistence strategies
   preindustrial society
   hunting and gathering societies
   pastoral society
   division of labor
   horticultural society
   agricultural society
   barter
   industrial societies
   urbanization
   postindustrial society
   mechanical solidarity

   organic solidarity
   Gemeinschaft
   Gesellschaft

2. **Sequencing** Copy the graphic organizer below. Use it to arrange the six types of societies in order of complexity.

3. **Finding the Main Idea**
   a. Identify the feature that sociologists tend to use to classify societies and then list the three broad categories of societies that they recognize.
   b. What roles and statuses can individuals in each type of society hold and achieve?

4. **Writing and Critical Thinking**
   Contrasting Write a brief essay contrasting the social structures of simple and complex societies. Consider:
   • Émile Durkheim's concepts of mechanical and organic solidarity
   • Ferdinand Tönnies's concepts of *Gemeinschaft* and *Gesellschaft*

Homework Practice Online
keyword: SL3 HP4

SECTION 3 REVIEW ANSWERS

1. **Define:**
   • group, p. 73
   • subsistence strategies, p. 73
   • preindustrial society, p. 73
   • hunting and gathering societies, p. 73
   • pastoral society, p. 73
   • division of labor, p. 73
   • horticultural society, p. 74
   • agricultural society, p. 74
   • barter, p. 74
   • industrial societies, p. 74
   • urbanization, p. 76
   • postindustrial society, p. 77
   • mechanical solidarity, p. 77
   • organic solidarity, p. 77
   • *Gemeinschaft*, p. 77
   • *Gesellschaft*, p. 77

2. from least to most complex: hunting and gathering, pastoral, horticultural, agricultural, industrial, and postindustrial

3a. based on subsistence strategy, or the way a society uses technology to provide for its members' needs; preindustrial, industrial, and postindustrial

b. roles related to leadership, family, and work

4. Essays will vary, but students should recognize that simple societies are held together by common values and close relationships, while complex societies are bound by need rather than familiarity or emotion.

SECTION 4

OBJECTIVES

1. *Summarize the major features of primary and secondary groups.*
2. *Identify the purposes that groups fulfill.*

LET'S GET STARTED!

As students enter the classroom, ask them to make a list of what types of groups they belong to *(such as families, circles of friends, sports teams, clubs, or e-communities)*. Next, ask students how their lives might be different if they did not belong to any groups. Students might find it difficult to imagine such an existence. Point out that this situation would mean that they would be responsible for meeting all their own needs because people in such a world would operate independently of each other. Tell students that in Section 4 they will learn about different types of groups and their social functions.

SECTION 4 RESOURCES

REPRODUCIBLE & REVIEW
- Section 4 Review, p. 81

TECHNOLOGY
- One-Stop Planner, Lesson 4.4
- **CNN.** Presents Sociology: Daycare and Socialization
- Homework Practice Online

Visual Answer

their matching uniforms, common use of the salute, and ordered configuration

GROUPS WITHIN SOCIETY

Read to Discover
1. What are the major features of primary and secondary groups?
2. What purposes do groups fulfill?

Define
aggregate, social category, dyad, triad, small group, formal group, informal group, primary group, secondary group, reference group, in-group, out-group, e-community, social network, leaders, instrumental leaders, expressive leaders

A society is not only a group; it is a group made up of other smaller groups. Every individual in society participates in groups. In fact, sociologists such as David Orenstein consider "groups and group activities . . . the very foundation upon which social life is structured." A group can be very small—two people on a date, for example. Or it can be very large—500 soldiers at boot camp. A group can be very intimate, as in the case of the family. It can also be very formal, as in the case of people attending a conference.

What Is a Group?

In sociological terms, a group has four major features. First, it must consist of two or more people. Second, there must be interaction among members. If you exchange greetings with a friend in the hall at school, for example, interaction has taken place. Interaction occurs whenever the actions of one person cause another person

or persons to act. Third, the members of the group must have shared expectations. Fourth, the members must possess some sense of common identity.

The last three features—interaction, shared expectations, and a common identity—distinguish a group from an aggregate or a social category. When people gather in the same place at the same time but lack organization or lasting patterns of interaction, they form an **aggregate**. Passengers on an airplane or people standing in a ticket line at the movies are examples of aggregates. In the case of social categories, it is not necessary for the people to interact in any way. A **social category** is simply a means of classifying people according to a shared trait or a common status. Students, women, teenagers, and left-handed people are examples of social categories.

All groups are not the same. Obviously, they can differ in size. They also differ in the length of time they remain together and in their organizational structure.

Size While some groups are very small, other groups are enormous. The smallest group possible, a group with two members, is called a **dyad**. In a dyad each member of the group has direct control over the group's existence. If one member leaves the group, the group ends. Consequently, decision making in a dyad can be difficult. If the two members fail to agree, one member must convince the other to change his or her position or the group may cease to exist.

According to sociologist Georg Simmel, a major change occurs in groups when group size increases from two members to three members. With a three-person group, called a **triad**, the group takes on a life of its own, independent of any individual member. No one person can disband the group. In addition, decision making in a triad is often easier than in a dyad, since two-against-one alliances can form in cases of disagreement.

How large can a small group be? Sociologists consider a **small group** one with few enough members that everyone is able to interact on a face-to-face basis. The more members, the greater the number of face-to-face relationships. For example, in a group of just 10 members the possible number of face-to-face relationships is 45. Sociologists have found that 15 is the largest number of people that can work well in one group. When the group is larger than that, members have a tendency to sort themselves into smaller groups.

INTERPRETING VISUALS This group of sailors has a shared identity as part of a military unit. *What other factors make this a group?*

Types of Groups

We all are members of different types of groups. The most common types of groups recognized by sociologists include primary groups, secondary groups, reference groups, in-groups, and out-groups. Since the development of the Internet, sociologists have noted the emergence of a new kind of group, called e-communities.

Primary and Secondary Groups One of the easiest ways to classify groups is according to the degree of intimacy that occurs among group members. Charles Horton Cooley used the term *primary group* to describe those involving the most intimate relationships. "By primary groups," Cooley said, "I mean those characterized by intimate face-to-face association and cooperation. They are primary in several senses, but chiefly in that they are fundamental in forming the social nature and ideals of the individual."

A **primary group** is a small group of people who interact over a relatively long period of time on a direct and personal basis. In primary-group relationships the entire self of the individual is taken into account. The relationships are intimate and often face-to-face. Communication is deep and intense, and the structure is informal. Family relationships are probably the most common primary relationships.

Against this, Cooley contrasted secondary groups. A **secondary group** is a group in which interaction is impersonal and temporary in nature. Secondary-group relationships involve a reaction to only a part of the individual's self. Secondary-group relationships also tend to be casual and limited in personal involvement. The person's importance to the group lies in the function that he or she performs in the group. An individual can be replaced easily by anyone who can carry out the specific tasks needed to achieve the group's goals. This characteristic is particularly important because secondary groups

Formal groups such as the Shriners have established goals and activities that give structure to the group.

Time Some groups you may participate in meet once and never meet again. Other groups you are part of—such as your family—exist for many years. Most groups fall somewhere in between these two extremes. However, regardless of the type of group, interaction is not continuous. Few people spend 24 hours a day with their families, for example. Instead, family members meet as a group during different periods of the day, such as at breakfast or dinner.

Organization The organization of groups can be either formal or informal. In a **formal group**, the structure, goals, and activities of the group are clearly defined. In an **informal group** there is no official structure or established rules of conduct. The student government in your school is a formal group. All meetings are conducted according to specific rules. The goals of the group are stated in the constitution, and norms for all occasions are listed in the bylaws. Your circle of friends would be an example of an informal group, because you likely do not have rules or structure for meetings.

The Continuum of Primary-Secondary Group Relationships

Primary Group Relationships			Secondary Group Relationships	
family	groups of friends	school club	classroom	job

INTERPRETING CHARTS Most people participate in primary and secondary groups. *Based on this chart what type of groups are families and friends?*

To help students identify the purposes and functions of groups, copy the graphic organizer at right onto the chalkboard, omitting the italicized answers. Have students copy and complete the organizer. Discuss the answers with the class. Then ask volunteers to give examples of how these functions apply to the groups to which students belong and to analyze how different types of groups might suffer if one or more of these functions was not adequately fulfilled. Finally, have each student write an essay summarizing the purposes that groups fulfill in society.

ENGLISH LANGUAGE LEARNERS

define boundaries · select leaders · set goals · **GROUP FUNCTIONS** · assign tasks · make decisions · control members' behavior

---

Sociology in the World Today

The Ins and Outs of High School. School cliques provide a good example of in-groups and out-groups. Cliques are usually highly visible, with members often dressing alike, acting alike, and participating in the same activities. For students who belong to them, cliques can provide positive benefits such as a sense of identity and friendship. But for students who do not belong to a clique, life on the outside can be lonely and painful.

CRITICAL THINKING
How can you work to decrease the negative aspects and increase the positive aspects of cliques?

ANSWER: Students might suggest being less judgmental and more accepting of others.

Did You Know?

Groups can spring up from unlikely sources and have tremendous longevity. For example, devoted fans of the science-fiction television series *Star Trek,* which originally aired from 1966 to 1969, became known as Trekkies. Although the show has been in syndication for more than 30 years, Trekkie fan clubs still exist, and members remain as devoted as ever.

---

are generally organized around specific goals. Examples of secondary groups include a classroom, a factory, and a political party.

Suppose you work at a cement factory, loading cement into sacks. The factory management has little interest in your personality. Whether you attend religious services regularly and what you do with your leisure time is of little concern to them. They are interested only in your ability to load cement into the sacks. If you cannot handle the responsibilities of the job adequately, you will likely be replaced by someone else who can.

It is also possible for primary and secondary relationships to exist in the same group. Within most secondary groups to which you may belong, you might develop some primary relationships. Look again at the example of the cement factory. Within that secondary group you might form primary relationships with other workers on the line. These relationships provide you with the regular interaction and friendship lacking in the secondary group.

Reference Groups People usually perform their social roles and judge their own behaviors according to standards set by a particular group. They do not have to belong to this group. When people identify with the group's standards and attitudes, the group influences their behavior. Any group with whom individuals identify and whose attitudes and values they adopt is called a **reference group**.

Groups of friends or school clubs serve as reference groups for many students. Members of a particular occupation often serve as reference groups for adults. As children grow up or as adults adjust to changing social conditions, they often change their reference groups. The choice of reference groups is particularly important because groups can have both positive and negative effects on behavior.

In-Groups and Out-Groups
All groups have boundaries—methods of distinguishing between members and nonmembers. When a group's boundaries are clearly marked, group members tend to think in terms of in-groups and out-groups. Some sociologists refer to these as a third-group phenomenon. The group that a person belongs to and identifies with is called an **in-group**. Any group that the person does not belong to or identify with is called an **out-group**. Both primary and secondary groups can serve as in-groups

and out-groups.

Most in-groups exhibit three characteristics. First, group members tend to separate themselves from other groups through the use of symbols. For example, groups often use badges, clothing, names, or slogans as forms of identification. Second, members view themselves positively and they often view out-groups in negative terms. Finally, in-groups generally compete with out-groups, even to the point of engaging in conflict.

E-communities Some sociologists have suggested that computer technology—most notably the Internet—has given rise to a new type of group. In an **e-community**, people interact with one another regularly on the Internet. Most of these communities are based on Usenet, a system of Internet discussion groups called newsgroups. At present, there are some 90,000 newsgroups covering an almost endless array of subjects. Most newsgroups are little more than sites for members to discuss issues of common interest. However, some seem like primary groups. Members exhibit behaviors similar to those of primary-group members in the "real world." They argue, engage in intellectual discussions, exchange knowledge, share intimate details of their lives, gossip, argue, play games, and even flirt. The only difference is that they do it online rather than face-to-face.

Social Networks We all belong to more than one group and interact with more than one set of people, whether on the Internet or in the "real world." The web of relationships that is formed by the sum total of a person's interactions with other people is termed a **social network**. Social networks include both direct and indirect relationships. We have direct relationships with those whom we interact with in our primary and secondary group relationships. We have indirect relationships with people we know or who know us but with whom we have little or no interaction, such as friends of a friend.

Unlike groups, social networks do not have clear boundaries and do not give rise to a common sense of identity. Yet they do provide us with a feeling of community and with opportunities for social interaction and career advancement. In some instances, knowing the "right" person can mean the difference between getting or not getting a job. Social networks also provide a support system that can help us through stressful periods.

Sports fans who support a specific team or player such as Michael Jordan often form in-groups. They view fans of other teams as out-groups.

■ CLOSE

On the chalkboard, write a list of at least 10 groups that relate to students' social functions. Have each student copy the list and label each group with the key terms from the section that apply to it *(for example, chess club—formal, secondary, reference, and in-group).*

■ REVIEW AND ASSESS

Have students complete the **Section 4 Review** on p. 81. As **Alternative Assessment**, you may want to use the group types collage or poster, or the group functions essay in this section's lessons.

■ RETEACH

Have students work in pairs to write five fill-in-the-blank sentences that can be completed by one of the section's Define terms. Have pairs exchange their sentences, complete the ones they receive, and then return them for grading.
ENGLISH LANGUAGE LEARNERS , COOPERATIVE LEARNING

■ EXTEND

Have students create diagrams or flowcharts of their own social networks, showing how their various groups, acquaintances, and activities interrelate. Then have volunteers share their work with the class for discussion. **BLOCK SCHEDULING**

Group Functions

In order to exist, all groups must fulfill several basic functions. Groups must define their boundaries so that members can tell who belongs and who does not. To do this, groups use an array of methods, including symbols, such as uniforms or other styles of dress; gestures, such as hand signals or handshakes; and language.

Groups must also select **leaders**—people who influence the attitudes and opinions of others. In some cases leadership roles are assigned. For example, the board of directors of a large corporation selects the company's chief executive officer. With other groups, individuals achieve leadership because of some ability, such as soccer skills or expertise at chess. Still other groups use elections to choose leaders. Members of many professional associations cast ballots to select their presidents.

Studies suggest that, regardless of how they are selected, leaders fall into two categories. **Instrumental leaders** are task-oriented. They find specific means that will help the group reach its goals. **Expressive leaders**, on the other hand, are emotion-oriented. They find ways to keep the group together and to maintain morale. Groups need both kinds of leadership to be successful. An instrumental leader might develop a game plan for the football team to win a championship. At the same time, an expressive leader might use fight songs and chants to keep team spirits high in the days before the big game.

Groups also need to perform the related functions of setting goals, assigning tasks, and making decisions. If groups have no purpose, then there is no reason for them to exist. Therefore, groups set goals. The nature and scope of these goals varies from group to group. The goals for an informal group may be as simple as maintaining the group. Formal groups may have very large goals. For example, the American Sociological Association has a very broad goal—advancing sociology as a science and profession. In contrast, the goal of a National Football League team is fairly narrow in scope—to win the Super Bowl.

To achieve their goals, groups need to assign tasks to their members. Knowing what is being done, and who is doing it, helps strengthen members' support for the group. Setting goals and assigning tasks involves making decisions. Whatever a group's decisions, the methods of making them must be acceptable to members.

Finally, groups need to control their members' behavior. If members constantly violate group norms, the group cannot long survive. The group, therefore, needs to employ effective sanctions to ensure conformity to norms. Primary groups generally allow a greater level of nonconformity than do secondary groups. Interestingly, people tend to show a greater commitment to primary group norms. This is because they place a high value on primary-group membership. In turn, members tend to belong to primary groups longer than secondary groups. Conformity is linked to the importance that people attach to a particular group.

SECTION 4 REVIEW

1. Define and explain
aggregate
social category
dyad
triad
small group
formal group
informal group
primary group
secondary group
reference group
in-group
out-group
e-community
social network
leaders

instrumental leaders
expressive leaders

2. Categorizing Copy the graphic organizer below. Use it to describe the main characteristics of the six types or models of groups discussed in this section.

Type of Group	Main Characteristic

3. Finding the Main Idea
a. What are the features of primary and secondary groups? Based on the examples in this section, what roles do group members play in primary and secondary groups?
b. Compare the roles of group members in formal and informal groups.

4. Writing and Critical Thinking
Comparing Select a formal and an informal group to which you belong. Compare the different ways leaders might help you to fulfill the group's goals.
Consider:
• the methods that instrumental leaders might use
• the methods that expressive leaders might use

Homework Practice Online
keyword: SL3 HP4

SECTION 4 REVIEW ANSWERS

1. Define:
• aggregate, p. 78
• social category, p. 78
• dyad, p. 78
• triad, p. 78
• small group, p. 78
• formal group, p. 79
• informal group, p. 79
• primary group, p. 79
• secondary group, p. 79
• reference group, p. 80
• in-group, p. 80
• out-group, p. 80
• e-community, p. 80
• social network, p. 80
• leaders, p. 81
• instrumental leaders, p. 81
• expressive leaders, p. 81

2. primary—interact on a personal basis over a long period of time; secondary—marked by interaction that is impersonal and temporary; reference—groups whose attitudes and values individuals adopt; in- and out-groups—groups that a person identifies with, or does not belong to; e-communities—interact on the Internet

3a. See previous answer for the features. Members fulfill group functions, such as providing friendship or doing a specific job.

b. Members of formal groups fill specific roles. Members of informal groups do not have to fit into established roles.

4. Comparisons will vary but should discuss how instrumental leaders are task oriented, while expressive leaders are emotion oriented.

Case Studies and Other True Stories

◼ TEACH

Have students read the feature A Small World on this page and complete the Think About it section. Then ask students to conduct a social networks experiment of their own but on a smaller scale. Provide students with the name of a high school teacher (who has agreed to participate in the experiment) in a neighboring town or city. Next, have students try to contact this person by following the same procedures as in the experiment described in the feature. Then have students report the results back to the class for evaluation and discussion.

◼ EXTEND

Organize students into groups and have them play a few rounds of *Six Degrees of Kevin Bacon.* (Students might use another actor or actress of their choice.) To play the game, students need to select an actor or actress and see how many co-starring associations it takes to link that person to Kevin Bacon (or to whomever the group selected as its end-point). **COOPERATIVE LEARNING**, **BLOCK SCHEDULING**

Did You Know?

Actor and rap star Will Smith starred in the movie version of John Guare's play *Six Degrees of Separation.* Guare wrote the screenplay for the movie, which was released under the same title in 1993. Besides Smith, the movie starred Stockard Channing, Anthony Michael Hall, Mary Beth Hurt, and Donald Sutherland. Can you connect Will Smith to Kevin Bacon in six movies or less? *(Kevin Bacon starred in* JFK *with Tommy Lee Jones, and Tommy Lee Jones starred in* Men in Black *with Will Smith.)*

Think About It Answers

1. Milgram's experiment established that people are more closely interconnected than they might believe.

2. Students' lists and conclusions will vary but should reflect an understanding of the results of Milgram's experiment.

Case Studies

AND OTHER TRUE STORIES

A SMALL WORLD

Imagine that you are on vacation in France. At a café, you share a table with another American whom you have never met before. Much to your surprise, you discover that even though you live more than 1,000 miles apart, you have a mutual friend. "Small world!" you both remark.

Such events intrigued social psychologist Stanley Milgram. He wondered if it would be possible to randomly select two people and connect them through their social networks. Milgram created a rather inventive experiment to test his hypothesis. He asked people from varied backgrounds in Kansas and Nebraska to get letters to a "target"—a named person in Massachusetts.

The Experiment

The letter senders had to follow certain rules. First, unless they knew the target personally, they could not directly contact him or her. Instead, they had to send the letter to a personal acquaintance— someone they knew on a first-name basis—who might know the target. The sender included information about the target to help the acquaintance locate him or her. If the acquaintance did not know the target personally they sent a letter to another acquaintance. Senders could dispatch the letter to only one friend—not to several at the same time. This process continued until the letter reached its destination.

Milgram found the results of his experiment intriguing. The number of intermediary acquaintances needed to connect the original sender to the target varied from 2 to 10. The median number of acquaintances was five. In other words, on average a letter had to be moved just six times to reach the target. Milgram found this quite impressive, because the distance between sender and target stretched more than 1,300 miles. However, he also realized that the median number gave a misleading picture of closeness between the two. They were not five people apart. Rather, they were five groups of acquaintances—or social networks—apart.

Six Degrees of Separation

Milgram's experiment entered popular culture shortly after playwright John Guare published *Six Degrees of Separation.* In 1993, three students took the premise of the play—that anyone in the world is separated by at most six connections from anyone else—and turned it into a trivia game. Called *Six Degrees of Kevin Bacon,* the game challenged players to link actor Kevin Bacon to other actors through costarring roles. Today there are versions of the game focusing on practically every major Hollywood actor.

Interestingly enough, this popular culture version of Milgram's idea was used to illustrate a mathematical concept known as the small-world effect. In mathematical terms, movies are small worlds. The cast of each movie constitutes a distinct population cluster. However, there are many interconnections among the clusters, because most actors appear in several movies. Even so, only a few connections among distant clusters are needed to achieve the degree of interconnectedness found in Milgram's original experiment. For example, there are just three degrees of separation between Kevin Bacon and Charlie Chaplin—who died around the time that Bacon began his movie career. Chaplin appeared in a movie with Marlon Brando. Brando acted with Laurence Fishburne in another movie. And a third movie starred Fishburne and Bacon.

Playing a movie trivia game may seem to have little scientific significance. However, the small-world effect is of great importance to sociology. For example, it may help to explain how and why disease, rumors, and even fashions and fads spread through social networks.

Think About It

1. **Finding the Main Idea** *What did Milgram's experiment establish about the interconnectedness of people?*
2. **Evaluating** *How far does your social network stretch? Make a list of five friends and note their addresses. Then ask these friends to make their own lists of five friends. Collect the lists and mark the location of the various addresses on a sketch map. Are these locations clustered tightly together or do they stretch out across the map? How might this network change if each person listed 50 or 100 friends?*

5
THE STRUCTURE OF FORMAL ORGANIZATIONS

Read to Discover
1. How are bureaucracies structured?
2. How effective are bureaucracies?

Define
formal organization, bureaucracy, rationality, voluntary association, iron law of oligarchy

Sociologists use the term **formal organization** to describe a large, complex secondary group that has been established to achieve specific goals. Formal organizations include a variety of groups such as schools, businesses, government agencies, religious organizations, youth organizations, political organizations, volunteer associations, labor unions, and professional associations.

Most formal organizations are structured in a form that is known as a **bureaucracy**. A bureaucracy is a ranked authority structure that operates according to specific rules and procedures. Bureaucracies existed in ancient times in Egypt, China, and Rome. However, they rose to prominence during the Industrial Revolution.

Industrialization was part of the process called the rationalization of society. **Rationality** involves subjecting every feature of human behavior to calculation, measurement, and control.

Bureaucracies were created to rationally organize groups to complete a set of goals. Today we use the word *bureaucracy* to refer to any organization that has many departments, or bureaus. If you have ever applied for a driver's license or been admitted to a large hospital, you have dealt with a bureaucracy.

Weber's Model of Bureaucracies

The German sociologist Max Weber developed a theoretical model of bureaucracies that is still widely used by sociologists today. According to Weber's model, bureaucracies have the following characteristics:

- *division of labor* Work is divided among specialists in various positions. Each specialist is expected to perform specific duties.
- *ranking of authority* There are clear-cut lines of responsibility, and each individual is responsible to a supervisor at a higher level.

- *employment based on formal qualifications* Specific qualifications are required for each job, and individuals are hired on the basis of tests, education, or previous experience. Also, in a bureaucracy, the job—not the job-holder—is important. Therefore, everyone is replaceable.
- *rules and regulations* There are objective rules, regulations, and routine procedures that identify the exact responsibilities and authority of each person on the staff.
- *specific lines of promotion and advancement* It is assumed that employees expect a career with the organization. Thus, there are clear-cut lines of promotion and advancement. Among the rewards for remaining with the organization are job security and seniority.

The chart on page 86 shows the bureaucratic organization of a large school system. Notice how the job titles represent specific duties. Also, notice that lines of authority and responsibility are clearly indicated. All members of the organization, then, know what they should be doing and to whom they should report.

Remember that Weber's model of bureaucracy is an ideal type. In other words, it describes the essential characteristics of bureaucracies. The structures of formal organizations conform to the model to varying degrees. Many governmental agencies and large business corporations fit these characteristics very rigidly. Other organizations—such as voluntary associations—may be much less bureaucratic. A **voluntary association** is typically a nonprofit organization formed to pursue some common interest. As the name suggests, membership is voluntary. Many office-holders and workers are unpaid volunteers. Examples of voluntary associations include amateur sports teams, professional associations, service clubs, charities, and political interest groups.

INTERPRETING VISUALS Bureaucracies serve important functions such as establishing proper rules and regulations. *Why might it be important to have a bureaucracy in a hospital?*

Exploring Cultural Diversity

▮ TEACH

Have students read the feature on this page and complete the Think About It section. Then ask students to imagine that they are new Ringo Bank employees. Have them write a series of brief journal entries in which they describe their experiences as trainees and express their feelings about life at Ringo. Students may choose to write their entries from the perspective of a Japanese businessperson or an American businessperson who has been transferred to the Japanese branch of the company. Students should make it clear in their journals which perspective they have chosen. Have volunteers read some of their journal entries to the class.

▮ EXTEND

Have students conduct research on the formal structures of Japanese schools in comparison to American schools. Then have students report their findings to the class in a round-robin discussion. Point out to students how the more rigid structures present in Japanese schools correspond to the rigid corporate life that many Japanese students will experience after graduation.

BLOCK SCHEDULING

Exploring Cultural Diversity

The Japanese Work Ethic. Many Japanese companies expect employees to work long hours. Often, lower-level employees feel obligated to remain at work until their co-workers and bosses leave, no matter how late. During busy periods, it is not unusual for workers to sleep at the office. As a result, Japanese courts now recognize the existence of *karoshi,* meaning "death from overwork." In proven cases of *karoshi,* family members can receive compensation from the deceased's employer.

ACTIVITY: Have students discuss how the formal Japanese business structure may contribute to employees feeling pressured to work long hours.

EXPLORING
Cultural Diversity

CORPORATE LIFE IN JAPAN

Formal structures play a central role in the day-to-day life of Japanese businesspeople. Noboru Yoshimura, a Japanese executive, and Philip Anderson, a business professor, provide vivid evidence of this in their study Inside the Kaisha: Demystifying Japanese Business Behavior. *Using hundreds of hours of interviews with Japanese middle managers, they create a picture of the operation of a typical Japanese corporation, or kaisha. In the excerpt below, they describe the initiation of a new salaryman, or business executive, into the ways of the corporations. Both the salaryman—"Hiro"—and the corporation—"Ringo Bank"—are composite portraits, drawn from the many managers and businesses that Yoshimura and Anderson studied.*

In the beginning, new salaryman trainees are never quite sure how to dress or behave. An easy solution would be to imitate one's senpai's [mentor's] haircut and dress, but a senpai is, by definition, several years senior—the men in Hiro's doki (year group of salarymen entering the bank) had to learn how to dress like first-year trainees, not veteran Ringo men. Hiro's first lesson in the Ringo way: get a new haircut. His senpai had warned him beforehand that a Ringo trainee's hair should be "really, really short," so, like the others in his doki, he showed up for the training program prepared. Later in his career, after he had been posted to a branch bank in the Ringo system, Hiro came to understand the symbolic purpose of Ringo's code.

"You are insulting our customers with that long hair!" spluttered a senior officer there, who sported a crew cut. Ringo men had to wear their hair short as a sign of respect for the bank's customers.

A new haircut was just the beginning. The company directed each trainee to master a seventy-page guide to business manners. Hiro and the others in his year group had to learn how to sit on a chair, where to place their hands while talking with others, how to bow, what posture to assume when standing, how to exchange name cards, how to get on an elevator, where to sit in a car, and where to sit in a train. . . . New trainees were expected to make mistakes and learn by having them corrected. For example, if a junior employee exited an elevator before a senior one, his mistake was pointed out immediately, and he was expected to feel shame. The purpose of all these rules was basically to keep the new salaryman from looking like an idiot, which would reflect badly on both him and his trainers. For example, someone who did not know where to sit when accompanying a branch manager on a business call would feel intensely embarrassed, so Ringo's minutely prescribed etiquette served to protect trainees from humiliating themselves.

Hiro later discovered that some of these rules seemed common to all kaisha, whereas others were peculiar to Ringo. Yet it never occurred to him or his peers to ask why they should observe rules whose violation would have gone unnoticed outside Ringo. Anyone who asked that kind

Tell students that beginning with the rise of high-tech companies led by young entrepreneurs during the 1980s, a new kind of corporate culture began to develop in the United States. These companies and many others since have adopted more informal structures than traditional American corporations. For example, employees may wear casual clothing such as jeans and T-shirts rather than suits and ties, be flexible in their work hours, decorate their offices and cubicles to reflect their personalities and interests, and in some cases telecommute, or work from home. Lead students in a class discussion in which you encourage them to make educated guesses about whether these relaxed structures have had a positive or negative effect on the productivity of employees, company morale, and customer relations. Then have each student write a one-page essay on the topic. Remind students to use standard grammar, spelling, sentence structure, and punctuation when writing their essays. **BLOCK SCHEDULING**

of question wouldn't last long in a Japanese company. Through sharing the same rules, the employees of a kaisha strengthen the ties that bind them to each other. Those who do not follow the rules are outsiders, and only an insider can meet the expectations of other people, allowing him to function within the organization.

Many Japanese businesses have a strict formal structure that may include rules for dining (left) and special training sessions for new employees (below). However, some business practices have been changing in Japan, including the rise in number of women in professional fields of business.

Think About It

1. **Sociology and Culture** *Ringo Bank instills culture through a rigid system of formal social controls. How might the bank's culture be imparted through informal structures?*

2. **Sociology and You** *You spend much of your day in a formal organization—your school. Describe some of the formal structures that guide day-to-day life in the school.*

Japanese Company Life. Many Japanese corporations blur the line between employees' work and private lives. For example, employees from the lowest-level worker to the president might all wear company uniforms. Employees might start each day by singing the company song and spend their leisure time at company-sponsored events. In the evening, Japanese employees may go home to company houses.

CRITICAL THINKING

Why do you think some Japanese corporations provide workers with benefits such as uniforms and housing?

ANSWER: Students might suggest that such benefits increase employees' loyalty and dedication to the firm.

Think About It Answers

1. Students might suggest through observing and emulating superiors and through communication among employees and friends.

2. Answers will vary, but students might mention class bells, class schedules, seating assignments, and rules governing students' appearance and behavior.

To help students understand how bureaucracies are structured, copy the graphic organizer at right onto the chalkboard, omitting the italicized answers. Pair students and have each pair copy the organizer and then expand and complete it by entering information about a bureaucratic organization of their choice. Next, guide students in a class discussion evaluating the effectiveness of bureaucracies in general, and analyzing what functions they serve in society. Finally, have each student pair create a one- or multipanel cartoon that uses humor to point out common flaws in bureaucratic systems. **ENGLISH LANGUAGE LEARNERS ,**
COOPERATIVE LEARNING

SAMPLE BUREAUCRATIC HIERARCHY

Head of the Bureaucracy
(CEO, Superintendent, president, etc.)

Department Head/VP   Department Head/VP

(subordinates)

---

internet connect

TOPIC: Bureaucracies
GO TO: go.hrw.com
KEYWORD: SL3 SC4

Have students access the Internet through the HRW Go site to conduct research on the structure, relationships, and effectiveness of bureaucracies. Then have each student create a flowchart of a bureaucratic system and write a summary of its effectiveness. Call on volunteers to present their flowcharts and summaries to the class.

Chart Answer

the board of education

Technology Resources

Teaching Transparency: Organization of One Public School System

---

Relationships in Formal Organizations

According to Weber's model, bureaucracies are formal impersonal structures. However, informal structures based on strong primary relationships may exist within the most rigid bureaucracies. For example, the director of sales in a large corporation may play golf every weekend with the director of purchasing. Or, they may have gone to the same college and now attend the same religious services.

The importance of primary group relationships within formal organizations was first noted in a research project at the Hawthorne, Illinois, plant of the Western Electric Company. The intended purpose of the study, conducted between 1927 and 1932, was to determine how various factors affected worker productivity.

As part of the research, the sociologists studied the interaction between members of a group of employees assigned the task of wiring complex telephone circuits.

Three worker roles were involved—wirer, solderer, and inspector. The wirers connected the proper wires together. The solderers then soldered them. The inspectors examined the completed circuits to make sure they met specifications. The company paid workers according to the number of circuits, or units, they completed. Management assumed that each worker would try to complete as many units as possible in order to make more money.

However, this was not the case. An informal structure developed among the workers. Together, they decided what the norms would be for a day's production. Workers who produced more were called ratebusters. Those who produced less were called chiselers. Workers who gave any information to a supervisor were called squealers. Conformity to the norms was enforced through a system of negative sanctions, such as ridicule and exclusion. This informal structure operated independently of the formal structure of the organization and was far more important to the individual workers.

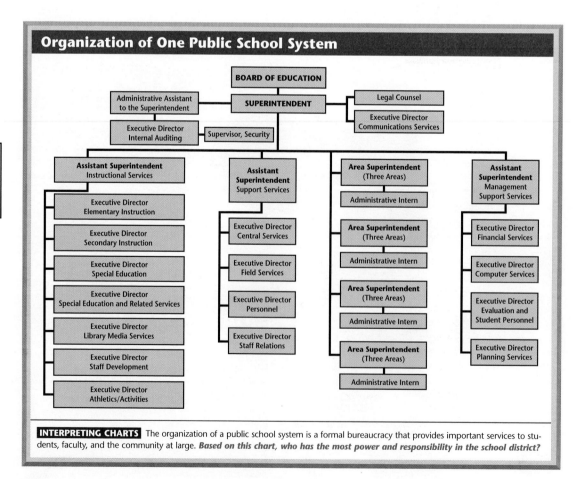

Organization of One Public School System

INTERPRETING CHARTS The organization of a public school system is a formal bureaucracy that provides important services to students, faculty, and the community at large. *Based on this chart, who has the most power and responsibility in the school district?*

HOMEWORK: Ask students to imagine that they are business consultants. Have each student review the criticisms of bureaucracies discussed on pp. 87 and 89 and then write a memo making suggestions for addressing these criticisms and improving the effectiveness of bureaucracies.

SPOTLIGHT *on Weber's Model of Bureaucracies*

Have students conduct research on a real bureaucratic organization of their choosing to identify how closely it meets the five characteristics outlined in Weber's model on p. 83. Then have each student write a one-page report describing the results of his or her research. **BLOCK SCHEDULING**

SPOTLIGHT *on Voluntary Associations*

Invite a member of a local voluntary association to make a presentation to the class about the goals and activities of his or her group. Have each student draw up a list of questions beforehand to ask the speaker. After the main presentation, hold a short question-and-answer session. Later, have the class use the information they learned to compare the bureaucratic structure of voluntary associations with that of more formal organizations. **BLOCK SCHEDULING**

Bureaucracies help to organize large processes like the manufacturing of electronics at this factory.

How Effective Are Bureaucracies?

Some scholars have suggested that Weber's theoretical model views bureaucracies in a positive light, as the best method of coordinating large numbers of people to achieve large-scale goals. Weber also suggested that bureaucracies create order by clearly defining job tasks and rewards. Further, they also provide stability, since individuals come and go but the organization continues. However, this view is a rather broad overstatement of the effectiveness of bureaucracies. In reality, they have several important weaknesses.

One reason why actual bureaucracies are less effective is that they lose sight of their original goals. Sometimes, bureaucracies seem to abandon their original purpose in favor of self-continuation. For example, certain government agencies emphasize their need to exist, regardless of whether or not they continue to provide useful services. A study of the Environmental Protection Agency provides a striking illustration of this. The study found that officials' actions often favored survival of the agency over enforcement of environmental standards.

Sociologists have suggested that the effectiveness of bureaucracies is weakened because they tend to encourage the development of a bureaucratic personality. The formal structure of a bureaucracy requires officials to closely follow rules and regulations. However, some officials focus too intently on the rules and ignore the goals of the bureaucracy. This often leads to a related weakness—the proliferation of "red tape," or bureaucratic delay. Individual officials play a limited role in the overall operation of a bureaucracy. As a result, their knowledge and power is often limited as well. This may cause people to become entangled in red tape. Consequently, they spend hours filling out forms, standing in seemingly endless lines, or being shuffled from one department to another before they accomplish their goals. You probably know stories or have had experiences about how frustrating it can be to deal with the red tape of a government agency or large corporation.

Another weakness of bureaucracies involves their tendency to result in oligarchies. An oligarchy is a situation in which few people rule the many. In bureaucracies, power tends to concentrate in the hands of a few people at the top. These people then use their position to promote their own interests over the interests of the organization. Sociologist Robert Michels called this tendency of organizations to become increasingly dominated by small groups of people the **iron law of oligarchy**.

Some critiques of bureaucratic effectiveness have made their point through humor. In his book *The Peter Principle*, Laurence J. Peter suggested that employees in a bureaucracy often are promoted to positions for which they may have little ability. Bureaucracies are able to function, he

Interdisciplinary Connection

LITERATURE

Catch-22. As a bombardier during World War II, writer Joseph Heller saw the Peter Principle in action. He felt that bureaucracies, in particular the U.S. military, tend to have contradictory rules that can create insoluble dilemmas. Heller coined the term *Catch-22* to refer to such a situation. In his novel of the same name, Heller describes a Catch-22. A person had to be crazy to fly dangerous bombing missions. Crazy people were considered unfit for military service and did not have to fly. Yet as soon as someone asked permission not to fly, that person proved his sanity.

ACTIVITY: Have students describe bureaucratic examples of the Peter Principle or a Catch-22 in action. Ask students: *Why do such problems arise? What are some possible solutions?*

Applying Sociology

TEACH

Have students read the feature The Peter Principle on this page and complete the Think About it section. Then have each student write a scenario similar to the J. S. Minion example that illustrates the Peter Principle at work. Students' examples may be drawn from real life or be entirely fictional (although they should be believable). If drawn from real life, tell students to replace the players' real names with fake ones to protect the identities of the individuals described. Call on volunteers to share their scenarios with the class for discussion.

EXTEND

Tell students that cartoons are a common way for people to comment on the humorous or exasperating aspects of bureaucratic decision-making, such as the Peter Principle. Have students use the library and other available resources to find examples of such cartoons. Good examples are political cartoons commenting on government regulations and red tape, or cartoon strips such as *Dilbert* that focus on corporate culture. Have students share some of their cartoons with the class and discuss how the jokes are based on real problems that are difficult or impossible to solve within a rigid bureaucratic framework. **BLOCK SCHEDULING**

APPLYING Sociology

THE PETER PRINCIPLE

Have you ever been told to stand in the wrong line by a person who you thought understood your problem? Then after an hour or so, did you find yourself waiting in another seemingly endless line to correct the situation caused by that person's mistake?

Professor Laurence J. Peter describes incidents like these in his book *The Peter Principle.* To what does he attribute such occurrences? Quite simply, Peter notes, "In a hierarchy every employee tends to rise to his level of incompetence." In other words, in all organizations in which members are arranged in order of rank, grade, or class, people are promoted into jobs that they are not truly qualified to perform. The following is an example of the Peter Principle at work.

J. S. Minion

"J. S. Minion was a maintenance supervisor in the public works department of Excelsior City. He was a favorite of the senior officials at City Hall. They all praised his constant friendliness. 'I like Minion,' said the superintendent of works. 'He has good judgment and is always pleasant and agreeable.'

This behavior was appropriate for Minion's position. As supervisor, he was not supposed to make policy, so he had no need to disagree with his supervisors.

When the superintendent of works retired, Minion succeeded him. Minion continued to agree with everyone. He passed to his supervisor every suggestion that came from above. The resulting conflicts in policy, and the continual changing of plans, soon demoralized the department. Complaints poured in from the Mayor and other officials, from taxpayers, and from the maintenance-workers' union. Minion still says "Yes" to everyone, and carries messages briskly back and forth between his superiors and his subordinates. Though his title is superintendent, he actually does the work of a messenger. The maintenance department regularly goes above its budget, yet fails to fulfill its program of work. In short, Minion, a competent supervisor, became an incompetent superintendent of works."

After analyzing hundreds of other similar cases of occupational incompetence, Peter formulated his own famous principle. He also noted that if there are enough ranks in the bureaucracy, "In time, every post tends to be occupied by an employee who is incompetent to carry out its duties." If this is the case, how, then, does any work get accomplished? If all of the employees in a bureaucratic organization eventually reach their level of incompetence, why does the structure not collapse? Peter answers that in most systems there are always some employees who have not yet been promoted beyond their capabilities. "Work is accomplished by those employees who have not yet reached their level of incompetence."

As an example of the Peter Principle, Dilbert treats his boss with a lack of respect and assumes that he is incompetent.

DILBERT reprinted by permission of United Feature Syndicate, Inc.

Think About It

1. **Supporting a Point of View** *Based on your experiences with different formal organizations, do you agree that in a bureaucracy every employee tends to rise to his or her level of incompetence? Why or why not?*

2. **Drawing Inferences and Conclusions** *If the Peter Principle is correct, what factors should companies consider when promoting workers to positions of responsibility? Explain your answer.*

CLOSE

Ask students to consider how large, complex formal organizations such as governments and corporations might be structured if not as bureaucracies. Then have the class discuss the viability of students' suggestions.

REVIEW AND ASSESS

Have students complete the **Section 5 Review** on p. 89. As **Alternative Assessment**, you may want to use the bureaucracy graphic organizer or cartoon in this section's lessons.

RETEACH

Pair students and have them take turns teaching each other the material in this section by going back over their notes and examples from their own graphic organizers and cartoons.
ENGLISH LANGUAGE LEARNERS , COOPERATIVE LEARNING

EXTEND

Have each student interview someone who works in a bureaucratic organization about what they like and dislike about working in a bureaucracy. Then have students present short oral reports of their interviews. **BLOCK SCHEDULING**

---

added, only because not all officials have been promoted to their "level of incompetence." Another humorous criticism of bureaucracies has become known as Parkinson's Law. C. Northcote Parkinson argued that "work expands to fill the time available for its completion."

For example, assume that a civil servant is overworked. The person can solve the problem in one of three ways: (1) The person can resign. (2) The person can cut the work in half by sharing it with a new colleague. (3) The person can demand the assistance of two subordinates. Parkinson's Law says that the individual will always choose the third alternative. The first alternative is unacceptable because resigning will mean losing pension, medical, and other benefits. The second alternative is unacceptable because people who gain a new colleague then have a rival for promotion. If, however, people have two subordinates, then their job looks more important because they have control over two individuals. There must be *two* subordinates so that each is kept in line by fear of the other person's promotion.

Eventually one of the subordinates will complain about being overworked. Then that subordinate will need two subordinates. Naturally, if one subordinate gets two subordinates, the other subordinate must have two subordinates. Our civil servant soon has six subordinates. This should ensure a promotion. But now our civil servant is more overworked than ever before, because all six of the subordinates are sending work to be approved. The civil servant has to work overtime to get all the work done but concludes that late hours are a penalty of success.

INTERPRETING VISUALS One of the weaknesses of bureaucracies is red tape. *How do you think government bureaucracies like the Immigration and Naturalization Service can reduce red tape?*

SECTION 5 REVIEW

1. **Define and explain**
   formal organization
   bureaucracy
   rationality
   voluntary association
   iron law of oligarchy

2. **Categorizing** Copy the graphic organizer below. Use it to identify the characteristics of bureaucracies identified by Max Weber.

   Bureaucracy

3. **Finding the Main Idea**
   a. Describe the structure of Max Weber's understanding of bureaucracies.
   b. How effective are bureaucracies?

4. **Writing and Critical Thinking**
   Drawing Inferences and Conclusions Write a short essay on whether you think the formal structure or the informal structure has a greater effect on the operations of bureaucracies. Consider:
   • the primary group relationships that may develop in bureaucracies
   • the weaknesses created by the formal structure of bureaucracies

Homework Practice Online
keyword: SL3 HP4

CHAPTER 4 REVIEW

ANSWERS

WRITING A SUMMARY
See the section subtitles for the main topics in this chapter.

IDENTIFYING PEOPLE AND IDEAS

1. network of interrelated statuses and roles that guide human interaction

2. a socially defined position in a group or society

3. the behavior expected of someone of a particular status

4. interacting in an effort to receive a reward or a return

5. two or more people who interact with each other, have shared expectations, and possess a common identity

6. a small group of people who interact over a relatively long period of time on a direct and personal basis

7. a group in which interaction is impersonal and temporary in nature

8. the web of relationships formed by the sum total of a person's interactions

9. a large, complex secondary group created to achieve certain goals

10. a ranked authority structure that operates according to specific roles and procedures

Review and Assessment Resources

- Chapter 4 Review, pp. 90–91
- Chapter Review Activities with Answer Key
- Global Skill Builder CD–ROM
- Chapter 4 Test Generator (on the One-Stop Planner)
- Chapter 4 Test (Form A or B)
- Alternative Assessment Handbook
- HRW Go site

REVIEW

Have students complete the **Chapter 4 Review** on pp. 90–91.

ASSESS

Use one of the chapter tests to assess students' understanding of the content. For **Alternative Assessment**, see the **Alternative Assessment Handbook**.

UNDERSTANDING MAIN IDEAS

1. A status is a socially defined position. A role is the behavior expected for that status.

2. Role conflict occurs when fulfilling the role expectations of one status makes it difficult to fulfill those of another. People can choose to fulfill only one status or compromise and try to fulfill the expected roles of both statuses in a limited fashion.

3. exchange, competition, conflict, cooperation, and accommodation

4. preindustrial—food production is the main economic activity; industrial—production of manufactured goods is the main economic activity; postindustrial—providing information and services is the main economic activity

5. primary—intimate, often face-to-face, and informal; secondary—impersonal, temporary, casual, limited in personal involvement, based on function within the group

6. division of labor, ranking of authority, employment based on formal qualifications, rules and regulations, and specific lines of promotion and advancement

7. They can overlook goals in favor of self-continuation, create red tape, lead to oligarchies, reward incompetence, and expand uncontrollably.

 Review

Writing a Summary

Using standard grammar, spelling, sentence structure, and punctuation, summarize the information in this chapter. Consider:
- the importance of roles, status, and social institutions
- types of social interaction and societies
- the organization of groups

Identifying People and Ideas

Identify the following terms and use them in appropriate sentences.

1. social structure
2. status
3. role
4. exchange
5. group
6. primary group
7. secondary group
8. social network
9. formal organization
10. bureaucracy

Understanding Main Ideas

Section 1 (pp. 66–68)

1. How can a person's status differ from his or her role?
2. How does role conflict affect groups and individuals? How can it be resolved?

Section 2 (pp. 69–72)

3. What are the five most common forms of interaction recognized by sociologists?

Section 3 (pp. 73–77)

4. Identify and describe the three broad categories of societies used by sociologists.

Section 4 (pp. 78–81)

5. How do the roles of group members differ between primary and secondary groups?

Section 5 (pp. 83–89)

6. What, according to Max Weber's model, are the major characteristics of a bureaucracy?

7. What weaknesses influence the effectiveness of bureaucracies?

Thinking Critically

1. **Analyzing Information** Identify five sets of reciprocal roles not mentioned in the chapter. Explain how the roles in each set are reciprocal.

2. **Identifying Points of View** List several examples of interactions you have had with other people. Briefly explain how an exchange theorist might interpret these interactions.

3. **Comparing and Contrasting** How do the six types of societies discussed in the chapter differ from each other in social structure?

4. **Drawing Inferences and Conclusions** Compile a list of your current group memberships by type of group. Next, compile a list of the groups you belonged to while at elementary school. How and why have your group memberships changed as you have grown older?

5. **Supporting a Point of View** Which of the five criticisms of bureaucracies outlined in the chapter has the greatest effect on bureaucratic effectiveness? Give reasons for your answer.

Writing About Sociology

1. **Analyzing Information** Select a group, such as a branch of the military or a religious order. Conduct research on your selected group to find the methods that group members use to separate themselves from members of out-groups. Describe the interactive roles of individuals, groups, and communities.

2. **Making Generalizations and Predictions** Imagine that you are going to interview someone who works in a large bureaucracy. Develop a set of questions to ask the interviewee. These questions should get the interviewee to describe the types of formal and informal structures that may exist within the bureaucracy. Also consider questions that focus on roles of employees in primary and secondary groups at work. Use the graphic organizer below to help you write a transcript of the types of answers you believe an interviewee would give to your questions.

Interviewee: Roles at work			
Formal	Informal	Primary	Secondary

Organize students into pairs or groups of three and have partners or group members review the chapter together while taking notes on important terms, theories, and examples. Then have each pair or group discuss the material and make a list of what members think are the 10 most important points in the chapter. Have pairs or groups share their lists with the class as you create a master list on the chalkboard. Finally, have students work to come up with a class list. **ENGLISH LANGUAGE LEARNERS ,**
COOPERATIVE LEARNING

SOCIOLOGY PROJECTS

1. Linking to Community Encourage students to join a volunteer organization in their community and write a short report on how the sociology concepts in this chapter apply to their experiences with the organization.

2. Using Observation Skills Have students keep a journal in which they record observed examples of exceptions to sociological "rules" presented in this chapter (such as an example of a very competent person who was promoted within a bureaucracy).

BUILDING SOCIAL STUDIES SKILLS

Interpreting Cartoons

Study the cartoon below. Use the information in the cartoon to answer the questions that follow.

"I'm surprised, Marty. I thought you were one of us."

© The New Yorker Collection 1983, Jack Ziegler, from cartoonbank.com. All rights reserved.

1. What sociological concept does the cartoon address?
   a. in-groups and out-groups
   b. primary groups and secondary groups
   c. reference groups
   d. social networks

2. What are the negative outcomes of dividing society into "us" and "them"?

Analyzing Primary Sources

In the following excerpt Terrence Deal and Allan Kennedy describe the cultural network. Read the excerpt and then answer the questions that follow.

❝*Everyone in a strong culture has a job—but he also has another job. This 'other job' won't get stamped on a business card, but that doesn't matter. In many ways this work is far more important than budgets, memos, policies, and five-year plans. Spies, storytellers, priests, whisperers, cabals—these people form the* hidden hierarchy *which looks considerably different from the organization chart. In the hidden hierarchy, a lowly junior employee doubles as a highly influential spy. Or an 'unproductive' senior manager gets the best office in the building, precisely because he does little but tells good stories—an ability that makes him tremendously valuable to the corporation as an interpreter of events. As consultants, we've found that these 'other jobs' are critical to the effective management of any successful organization. They make up what we call the cultural network.*
  This network is actually the primary means of communication within the organization; it ties together all parts of the company without respect to positions or titles. The network is important because it not only transmits information but also interprets the significance of the information for employees. . . . The real business goes on in the cultural network.❞

3. What function does a cultural network serve?
   a. a means by which workers find other jobs
   b. the means of communication in an organization
   c. the means of advancement in an organization
   d. a means by which workers find out about social events

4. Do the authors think formal structure or informal structure is more important to the functioning of the organization? Support your answer with statements from the excerpt.

THINKING CRITICALLY

1. Possible reciprocal roles include teacher–student, conductor–musician, and parent–child.

2. Answers will vary, but students should identify the rewards or returns gained through each interaction.

3. They exhibit an increasing economic, political, and technological complexity; and increasing urbanization.

4. Answers will vary, but students should exhibit an understanding of the different functions and types of groups discussed.

5. Conclusions will vary, but students should select one of the weaknesses listed in the answer to Question 7 on p. 90 and defend their choice.

WRITING ABOUT SOCIOLOGY

1. Students should include in their essays at least two ways in which group members define themselves, such as by wearing uniforms or using certain equipment.

2. Questions will vary but should address each type of group listed in the chart.

BUILDING SOCIAL STUDIES SKILLS

1. a

2. can lead to one group feeling superior to the other, discrimination of "them," and social conflict

3. b

4. informal structure, based on the use of terms such as "hidden hierarchy," "spies," and "whisperers"

SOCIOLOGY PROJECTS

Cooperative Learning

Using Your Observation Skills Work in a group with two or three other students to collect 10 magazine or newspaper pictures showing achieved statuses and 10 pictures showing ascribed statuses. Use the pictures to create a photo essay showing how the two types of statuses differ. You may want to include a caption to explain your group's essay to the class.

🖅 **internet** connect

Internet Activity: go.hrw.com
KEYWORD: SL3 SC4
Choose an activity on social structure to:
• write journal entries on daily life in the six types of societies discussed in this chapter.
• create a skit showing how mediation and arbitration are used to resolve conflicts.
• create a flowchart of a bureaucratic system and write a summary of its effectiveness.

Across Space and Time

Across Space and Time

Have students read the feature The Israeli Kibbutz and answer the questions that follow. Discuss the answers with the class. Then ask students to imagine that they are writers for a sociology journal in 1975, when A. I. Rabin and his associates did their follow-up study. Have each student write a sociology news brief summarizing the results of Rabin's follow-up study. In addition, students should create an accompanying chart that details Rabin's initial findings in 1955 and his later findings in 1975.

🎬 SPOTLIGHT *on the Israeli Kibbutz*

Have students conduct research on the Israeli kibbutzim. Students should examine why they were established, the philosophy behind them, their effectiveness, life in them, and how and why they have evolved over time. Students should present their findings in the form of an entry for a fictional Sociology Encyclopedia.

BLOCK SCHEDULING

Think About It Answers

1. as a method of establishing Jewish settlements in the Palestinian area of the Middle East and to promote among members a strong commitment to group goals

2. Adults who were raised in kibbutzim as children evidenced slightly more anxiety and psychological distress, were less productive and less satisfied with their marriages, and were less attached to parents and friends than adults with similar backgrounds but who were not raised in kibbutzim. However, kibbutz-raised adults were equally as satisfied with their jobs, ranked higher in the military, and were more athletic.

The Israeli Kibbutz

In an effort to explain how culture influences personality development, much sociological attention has been paid to the kibbutz movement. Kibbutzim—the plural form of *kibbutz*—are of special interest to sociologists because they provide a natural laboratory in which to study the relationship between culture and the psychological and social characteristics of individuals.

A kibbutz is a collective farm or settlement in Israel. Kibbutzim originated in early 1900s as a method of establishing Jewish settlements in the Palestinian area of the Middle East. The first kibbutzim were agricultural settlements and were founded on the principles of complete equality among group members and a strong commitment to group goals.

As a result of the collective nature of these settlements, individualism—the belief that the individual is more important than the group—was considered an undesirable quality. To reduce individualism, the founders of the kibbutzim adopted group child-rearing practices. Rather than living with their parents, children lived in separate houses from birth through adolescence. Each house was occupied by children of the same age group. Contact with parents and brothers and sisters was primarily limited to nightly visits, weekends, and holidays.

Kibbutz founders thought that the family promoted individualism by reducing the influences of the group over the individual. Thus, the founders reasoned that less contact between parents and children would strengthen commitment to group goals. In addition, they believed that housing children according to age would result in close bonds between members of the same age group, thereby strengthening group unity.

Since the 1960s the role of the family in child rearing has increased dramatically in many kibbutzim. It now is common for children, particularly young children, to live with their parents. However, from a sociological perspective the group-based child-rearing arrangements of the past remain of particular interest.

In an effort to determine the long-term consequences of group-based child-rearing practices, A. I. Rabin and his associates compared a group of 92 kibbutz members with 79 individuals from traditional families. The individuals were first studied as children and then were reexamined 20 years later when they reached adulthood. Both groups were rural,

A group of children within a kibbutz interact with each other.

agricultural, and of the same income level. They differed only in how they were raised (group versus family) and in whether farming was done on a collective (kibbutz) or individual (nonkibbutz) basis.

The first comparison was conducted in 1955 when the subjects of the study ranged in age from 8 months to 17 years. Among the findings was that kibbutz infants developed more slowly than nonkibbutz infants but caught up by early childhood. In addition, the researchers found kibbutz children to be less attached to their parents and friends, less aggressive, slightly more anxious, and less clear on career goals.

When Rabin and his associates looked at the two groups 20 years later (1975), they found that the kibbutz-raised group evidenced slightly more anxiety and psychological distress, were less productive and less satisfied with their marriages, and remained less attached to their parents and friends. On the positive side, kibbutz-raised adults were equally as satisfied with their jobs, ranked higher in the military, and were more athletic.

Although the differences between the two groups were not great, Rabin's research of others would seem to support the idea that personality development is influenced by cultural factors.

Think About It

1. Evaluating *Why did Jewish settlers establish kibbutzim?*

2. Summarizing *What did Rabin learn from studying kibbutzim in the mid 1900s?*

Sociology in Action

TEACH

Have students read the Sociology in Action feature and then work in small groups to perform the simulation activity. Before starting the activity, work with the school librarian to obtain additional sources that students can use to gather information. Then, after groups make their presentations, have the class discuss each group's decision. **COOPERATIVE LEARNING**

EXTEND

Have students work in pairs or in groups of three to write one-act plays about a fictional state where children are removed from their families at an early age and raised in group settings by political officials. Groups' plays should focus on a specific group of children and may take either a positive or negative view of group-based child rearing. Then select the best play and have its authors or other volunteers perform it for the class.

COOPERATIVE LEARNING , BLOCK SCHEDULING

Sociology in Action

UNIT 1 SIMULATION

You Make the Decision

Should you raise your in children in a group-based child-rearing arrangement or as a member of a family?

Complete the following activity in small cooperative groups. Imagine that you live on a collective farm with a growing family. You have a decision to make about how your children will be raised. Do you want your children to live with children of their own age group ? Or do you want them to live with you as a family unit? You must consider how your children's living arrangement will affect their future personality and well-being. Follow the steps below to reach your decision.

1 Gather Information

Use your textbook and other sources to find information that might influence you to raise your children as members of a group or as a family.

- What advantages could be gained by group-based child rearing?

- What is gained with family-based child rearing?

Be sure to use what you learned from the Building Social Studies Skills feature on Decision Making in Chapter 1 to help you make an informed choice. You may want to divide up different parts of the research among group members.

2 Identify Options

After reviewing the information you have gathered, consider the options you have for raising your children. Your final decision may be easier to reach if you consider as many options as possible. Be sure to record your possible options for your presentation.

3 Predict Consequences

Now take each option that your group came up with and consider what might be the outcome of each course of action. Ask yourselves questions like the following:

- Are my children going to be negatively affected by group-based rearing?

- What will the children and I gain from group-based child rearing?

Once you have predicted the consequences, record them as notes for your presentation.

4 Take Action to Implement Your Decision

After you have considered your options, you should create your presentation. Be sure to make your decision about how to raise your children very clear. You will need to support your decision by including the information that you gathered and by explaining why you rejected other options. You may want to create cluster diagrams, maps, or charts to support your decision. When you are ready, decide who in your group will make which part of the presentation. Good luck!

Have students interview professionals who work with families and children as part of their job, such as child therapists and social workers. Students should ask about the importance of cultural influences, such as parental involvement, to a child's personality development and well-being. Students might also explain the example of kibbutz group-based child rearing and ask the interviewee his or her opinion of the practice. Then have students write summaries of their interviews and what they learned from them.

CHAPTER 5
Socializing the Individual

Humans become functioning members of society through socialization. Socialization is an interactive process through which individuals learn the skills, values, beliefs, and behavior patterns of their society. Chapter 5 examines the factors that shape personality development and the social forces that mold people into functioning members of society.

CHAPTER 6
The Adolescent in Society

In industrialized societies, adolescence is a distinct stage of the life cycle. In recent years social scientists have devoted considerable attention to adolescence. The topics Chapter 6 examines include dating, peer pressure, the influences on and the consequences of drug and alcohol use, and factors contributing to teen suicide.

Internet Activity

☑ internet connect ≡

TOPIC: Conformity, the Individual, and Society
GO TO: go.hrw.com
KEYWORD: SL3 UNIT 2

Have students access the Internet through the HRW Go site to conduct research on social norms and conformity. Then ask each student to create a pamphlet explaining why people conform, how social norms are involved, and the importance of groups for the individual and society.

CHAPTER 7

The Adult in Society

Sociologists are interested in how people adapt to the changing roles and statuses that accompany each stage of adult development. Chapter 7 examines how male development is different from and is similar to female development during early and middle adulthood, in the world of work, and during the later years of life.

CHAPTER 8

Deviance and Social Control

Deviance and crime are everyday events in modern society. Chapter 8 examines how high levels of deviance and crime can disrupt society and how low levels can serve positive functions. Societies usually work to control or minimize deviance and crime.

UNIT MOTIVATOR

Share the chapter overviews with students. Then ask each student to write a paragraph about ways in which people experience socialization throughout their lives. Ask volunteers to share their responses with the class. Tell students to keep the responses in mind as they study Unit 2.

The Individual in Society

UNIT 2

CHAPTER

5 **Socializing the Individual**

6 **The Adolescent in Society**

7 **The Adult in Society**

8 **Deviance and Social Control**

Sociologists study how individuals learn about norms and proper behavior in society. These expected behaviors change as the individual ages.

Using Visual Resources

Social Organizations. Social groups and school organizations, such as the marching band shown in this photo, are important to the socialization process of young people. Such groups teach adolescents to respect and conform to accepted social standards of behavior and to learn to work with others to accomplish common goals.

CRITICAL THINKING
What are some of the student organizations in your school? How do you think such groups help teach young adults to become functioning members of society?

ANSWER: Students might mention groups such as sports teams, political and academic organizations, student pride groups, drama and other arts groups, and agricultural and vocational groups. Such groups teach cooperative and collaborative skills and help young adults learn how to fit in with others.

Socializing the Individual

CHAPTER RESOURCE MANAGER

Objectives	Pacing Guide		Resources

SECTION 1:
Personality
Development
(pp. 98–106)

REV Section 1
Review, p. 106

- Identify the four main factors that affect the development of personality.
- Explain how isolation in childhood affects development.

Regular 2 days	**Block** **Scheduling** 1 day

Block Scheduling Handbook with Team Teaching Strategies, Chapter 5

 CNN. Presents Sociology: School Dress Codes

RS Graphic Organizer 5

HRW Go site

SM Mastering Critical Thinking Skills 5

PS Readings and Case Studies in Sociology 5

E Research Projects and Activities for Teaching Sociology 5

SM Study Skills and Writing Guide

SECTION 2:
The Social
Self
(pp. 107–11)

REV Section 2
Review, p. 109

- Explain how a person's sense of self emerges.
- Identify and describe the theories that have been put forth to explain the process of socialization.

Regular 1 day	**Block** **Scheduling** 0.5 day

Block Scheduling Handbook with Team Teaching Strategies, Chapter 5

Chapter Review And Assessment

REV Chapter 5 Review, pp. 116–17

REV Chapter Review Activities with Answer Key

Global Skill Builder CD–ROM

Chapter 5 Test Generator (on the One-Stop Planner)

A Chapter 5 Test (Form A or B)

A Alternative Assessment Handbook

HRW Go site

SECTION 3:
Agents of
Socialization
(pp. 112–15)

REV Section 3
Review, p. 115

- Identify the most important agents of socialization in the United States.
- Explain why family and education are important social institutions.

Regular 2 days	**Block** **Scheduling** 1 day

Block Scheduling Handbook with Team Teaching Strategies, Chapter 5

Chapter Resource Key

PS	Primary Sources	**A**	Assessment		Video
RS	Reading Support	**REV**	Review		Internet
E	Enrichment		Transparencies		Holt Presentation Maker Using Microsoft® PowerPoint®
SM	Skills Mastery		CD–ROM		

One-Stop Planner CD–ROM

See the *One-Stop Planner* for a complete list of additional resources for students and teachers.

One-Stop Planner CD–ROM

It's easy to plan lessons, select resources, and print out materials for your students when you use the **One-Stop Planner CD–ROM with Test Generator.**

Chapter Project Preview

The following activities are included in the Chapter Review. You may want to make the suggested preparations.

CHAPTER REVIEW ACTIVITY

Using Observation Skills Students will work in groups to locate and collect magazine pictures to create an annotated visual essay on George Herbert Mead's theory of the self. Before beginning the project, have students bring old magazines to class for several days. You might also provide each group with a posterboard for its project.

INTERNET ACTIVITIES

Nature v. Nurture Students will use provided Internet links to research the influence of heredity and environment on individual personality and then write a report on which factor they consider more influential. To guide students in their research, create a worksheet for

them to complete by listing each viewpoint's strengths and weaknesses.

The Social Self Students will use provided Internet links to research and profile the socialization theories of either John Locke, Charles Horton Cooley, or George Herbert Mead. Provide each student with a profile template to make grading easier. Profiles should summarize the theory and examine its strengths and weaknesses.

Television and Behavior Students will use provided Internet links to research the influence of television in the socialization process. In addition, students will conduct "field research" by interviewing their peers regarding the influence of television. Students will then use both sets of research to write an essay on television's influence on behavior. To increase the uniformity of students' essays, after the Internet research have students create a class set of questions to use in their field research.

Additional Resources

PRINT RESOURCES FOR TEACHERS

Bettelheim, Bruno. *The Uses of Enchantment: The Meaning and Importance of Fairy Tales.* New York: Vintage Books, 1989. Examines the history of fairy tales and folklore and their effects on the socialization of children.

Burkitt, Ian. *Social Selves: Theories of the Social Formation of Personality.* Newbury Park, CA: Sage Publications, 1992. Good introduction to the theories of personality development.

Curtiss, Susan. *Genie: A Psycholinguistic Study of a Modern-Day "Wild Child."* New York: Academic Press, 1977. Examines language development and speech disorders in children based on the author's experiences with Genie.

Lee, Nick. *Childhood and Society: Growing Up in an Age of Uncertainty.* Philadelphia, PA: Open University Press, 2001. Examines socialization and its effects on child development.

PRINT RESOURCES FOR STUDENTS

Schneider, Meg. *Popularity Has Its Ups and Downs.* New York: Messner, 1991. Motivational guide that helps students to build self-confidence without tying their self-esteem to others' opinions.

Turgenev, Ivan S. *Fathers and Sons.* New York: Bantam Books, 1982. A classic Russian novel that explores socialization between generations and throughout the life span.

MULTIMEDIA RESOURCES

Fitting In: A New Look at Peer Pressure (vhs; 25 min.) Focus Media, Inc. Provides students with skills for dealing with negative peer pressure and building self-esteem.

How to Live with Your Parents and Survive (filmstrip on vhs; 14 min.) Guidance Associates. Humorous sketches about the relationships of parents and children.

🔗 **internet** connect

HRW ONLINE RESOURCES

GO TO: go.hrw.com
Then type in a keyword.

TEACHER HOME PAGE
KEYWORD: SL3 Teacher

CHAPTER INTERNET ACTIVITIES
KEYWORD: SL3 SC5
Choose an activity to have students:
• create a theoretical profile on theorists presented in this chapter.
• write a report on the influences of nature and nurture on personality development.
• conduct field research on the influence of television in their peer group.

CHAPTER ENRICHMENT LINKS
KEYWORD: SL3 CH5

ONLINE ASSESSMENT
Homework Practice
KEYWORD: SL3 HP5
Standardized Test Prep
KEYWORD: SL3 STP5
Rubrics
KEYWORD: SS Rubrics

CONTENT UPDATES
KEYWORD: SS Content Updates

HOLT PRESENTATION MAKER
KEYWORD: SL3 PPT5

ONLINE READING SUPPORT
KEYWORD: SS Strategies

CURRENT EVENTS
KEYWORD: S3 Current Events

CHAPTER

5

Socializing the Individual

SECTION 1
Personality Development

SECTION 2
The Social Self

SECTION 3
Agents of Socialization

CHAPTER REVIEW

Build on What You Know

Ask students to answer the following questions:

How might culture shape an individual's personality?

Consider:

• cultural values and beliefs
• the internalization of cultural norms

How might status and role expectations shape personality?

Consider:

• economic and educational status
• parental status and personal status

Internet Activity

Have students access the Internet through the HRW Go site to conduct research on the influence of heredity and environment on individual personality. Then have each student prepare a report on which factor he or she considers more influential. Remind students to use standard grammar, spelling, sentence structure, and punctuation in their reports.

CHAPTER

5 Socializing the Individual

Build on What You Know

How would you describe your personality? Each individual has a unique personality, shaped by different factors. In this chapter you will explore how personalities and a sense of self are developed and how isolation affects social behavior. You will also read about the major socialization agents in American society.

Matryoshka dolls are Russian artifacts that reflect the idea of an individual as a unique person while also part of a whole.

TRUTH OR FICTION

What's Your Opinion?

To help introduce the chapter, have students discuss the Truth or Fiction statements that appear on this page. You might want to help students by reading the following **true/false** responses to the class.

True An individual's personality is based on his or her genetic makeup.

False An individual's personality is the result of both his or her genetic makeup and experiences.

True Children develop basic skills as a natural part of physical development.

False Children need contact with other people to learn to model and develop basic skills.

True People's personalities are shaped by their genetic makeup, intelligence, and knowledge.

False People's families, experiences, and interactions with others play a large role in shaping personality.

*L*ife *in* Society

In some respects, we are all alike. We all have physical bodies that operate in very similar ways. We all eat and sleep. Each of us is born, ages, and eventually dies.

In other respects, we are only similar to some specific groups of people. We speak a language shared by many but by no means all people. We wear the same kinds of clothes as many people, yet our clothes are different from those of many others. We hold beliefs that are accepted by some people but not by others. We create and use cultural artifacts that fit easily into our own society but might seem alien in other societies.

In other ways each of us is unique. No one else has your exact personality. No one else has your particular personal history.

It is the task of sociologists to look at the factors that bring about the similarities and differences among people. In this chapter we will examine the process of personality development. You will learn how the factors that shape individual personality make each of us unique. Then you will examine how various social forces mold us into functioning members of society in spite of our individual differences.

> ▶ **WHY SOCIOLOGY MATTERS**
>
> Sociologists debate what factors are most significant in the development and socialization of an individual. Use **CNN fyi**.com or other current events sources to learn more about how the family, peer groups, school, and mass media shape our lives today. Create a cartoon illustrating your findings.
>
> **CNN fyi**.com

TRUTH OR FICTION

What's Your Opinion?

Read the following statements about sociology. Do you think they are true or false? You will learn whether each statement is true or false as you read the chapter.

- It has been proven that people's personalities are not shaped by their environment.

- As long as a child's basic physical requirements, such as food and clothing, are being met, he or she has no need of human contact to develop basic skills.

- People's personalities are rarely shaped by their families and environments.

◆ **Sociology Then and Now**

Personality by Body Type? In 1921 German psychiatrist Ernst Kretschmer, in his book *Physique and Character*, theorized that people's body types reflected their personalities. For example, Kretschmer argued that frail and slim people tended to be introverts, while people with heavier, shorter bodies tended to be happier and more extroverted. Kretschmer's theories have long since lost support, but his work raises interesting questions: What is personality? How is a person's personality formed? How can personality be measured or characterized?

ACTIVITY: Organize students into small groups and have each group briefly discuss the above questions. Then have the groups report on their discussions to the class.

OBJECTIVES

1. *Identify the four main factors that affect the development of personality.*

2. *Explain how isolation in childhood affects development.*

LET'S GET STARTED!

As students enter the classroom, ask them to consider the meaning of the term *personality*. Have one student look up the term in a dictionary and read aloud the definitions provided. Tell students that sociologists define personality as the sum total of behaviors, attitudes, beliefs, and values that are characteristic of an individual. Based on this definition, have students write some nouns and adjectives that describe their personalities. Tell students that the lists will remain private. Then tell students that in Section 1 they will learn about the main factors that affect personality development and about the effects of isolation in childhood on development.

SECTION *1* RESOURCES

REPRODUCIBLE & REVIEW

- Readings and Case Studies in Sociology 5
- Research Projects and Activities for Teaching Sociology 5
- Section 1 Review, p. 106

TECHNOLOGY

- One-Stop Planner, Lesson 5.1
- Homework Practice Online

PERSONALITY DEVELOPMENT

Read to Discover
1. What are the four main factors that affect the development of personality?
2. How does isolation in childhood affect development?

Define
personality, heredity, instinct, sociobiology, aptitude, feral children

Identify
John B. Watson, the Ik, Kingsley Davis, Rene Spitz

What comes to mind when you hear the term *personality*? You probably think of someone's social skills or social appeal. People often use the term to describe someone's specific characteristics or as an explanation for achievements or failures. For example, a woman's skill as a salesperson may be attributed to her assertive personality.

A man's popularity may be credited to his humorous personality. Or a person's lack of friends may be blamed on a selfish personality. When sociologists and psychologists use the term, however, they are referring to more than an individual's most striking characteristics. To social scientists, **personality** is the sum total of behaviors, attitudes, beliefs, and values that are characteristic of an individual.

Our personality traits determine how we adjust to our environment and how we react in specific situations. No two individuals have exactly the same personalities. Each individual has his or her own way of interacting with other people and with his or her social environment. Each individual also has his or her own temperament, or emotional nature.

People's personalities continue to develop throughout their lifetimes. Specific traits change at different rates and to different degrees. Some personality traits seem to remain basically constant throughout a person's life, while other traits undergo dramatic changes. Personality development is more obvious during childhood, when people are experiencing rapid physical, emotional, and intellectual growth. Once people reach adulthood, personality traits change at a slower rate. Thus, most adults appear to maintain stable personalities over time. However, personality development varies from individual to individual.

Nature Versus Nurture

For many years, social scientists have heatedly debated what determines personality and social behavior. Some argue that it is **heredity**—the transmission of genetic characteristics from parents to children. Others suggest that the social environment—contact with other people—determines personality. This debate is usually referred to in terms of nature versus nurture, or inherited genetic characteristics versus environment and social learning.

The nature viewpoint that held sway throughout the 1800s states that much of human behavior is instinctual in origin. An **instinct** is an unchanging, biologically inherited behavior pattern. Instinct is most often applied to animal behavior. For example, birds possess the instinct to build certain types of nests and to migrate at particular times of the year. Supporters of the nature argument extended this notion of the biological basis of behavior to humans. They claimed that instinctual drives were responsible for practically everything—laughing, motherhood, warfare, religion, capitalism, and even the creation of society itself. At the height of the debate in the early 1900s, social scientists claimed to have identified more than 10,000 human instincts.

From the nurture point of view a person's behavior and personality are the result of his or her social environment and learning. The work of Russian scientist Ivan Pavlov helped this viewpoint gain acceptance. Pavlov found that supposedly instinctual behavior could be taught. To find the relationship between the nervous system and digestion, Pavlov conducted experiments with dogs. He knew that dogs would salivate when they were fed because saliva aids digestion of the food. Pavlov rang a bell every time he fed the dogs. Eventually, he rang the bell but did not feed them. Even so, the dogs still salivated. They had learned to salivate at the sound of the bell. American psychologist John B. Watson suggested that what applies to dogs can also be applied to humans. He claimed that he could take a dozen healthy infants and train them to become anything he wanted—doctors, lawyers, artists, beggars, or thieves.

The emergence of sociobiology in the 1970s reemphasized the nature viewpoint. **Sociobiology** is the systematic study of the biological basis of all social behavior. Sociobiologists argue that such varied cultural characteristics and behavioral traits as religion, cooperation, competition, slavery, territoriality, and envy are rooted in the genetic makeup of humans. In general sociobiologists argue that most of human social life is determined by biological factors.

TEACH OBJECTIVE 1

SUGGESTION 1: To help students identify the four main factors that affect the development of personality, copy the graphic organizer at right onto the chalkboard, omitting the italicized answers. Have students copy the organizer and complete it by listing and briefly describing each of the four main factors. Discuss the answers. Then have each student create a "recipe" for personality development. Students should list the four "ingredients" from the graphic organizer, provide amounts for each ingredient based on how much students think each factor plays a part, and provide cooking and preparation instructions. Encourage students to be creative.

ENGLISH LANGUAGE LEARNERS

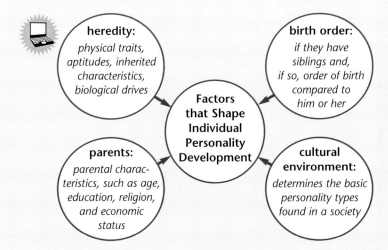

heredity: *physical traits, aptitudes, inherited characteristics, biological drives*

birth order: *if they have siblings and, if so, order of birth compared to him or her*

Factors that Shape Individual Personality Development

parents: *parental characteristics, such as age, education, religion, and economic status*

cultural environment: *determines the basic personality types found in a society*

However, few social scientists accept the sociobiologists' argument. Instead, most social scientists assume that personality and social behavior result from a blending of hereditary and social environmental influences. They believe that environmental factors have the greatest influence. Heredity, birth order, parents, and the cultural environment are among the principal factors that social scientists see influencing personality and behavior.

Heredity Everyone has certain characteristics that are present at birth. These hereditary characteristics include body build, hair type, eye color, and skin pigmentation. Hereditary characteristics also include certain aptitudes. An **aptitude** is a capacity to learn a particular skill or acquire a particular body of knowledge. For example, a natural talent for music or art would be considered an aptitude. Most social scientists do not limit aptitudes to inherited capabilities. Instead, they believe that some aptitudes can be learned as well as inherited. Some social scientists also believe that inherited aptitudes often develop only because of environmental factors. Specifically, parents' responses tend to encourage or discourage the development of aptitudes. For example, if a child shows verbal aptitude, parents often respond by praising his or her ability.

Interdisciplinary Connection

SCIENCE

Genetics. Gregor Mendel (1822–84), an Austrian botanist and monk, is generally credited with being the father of the modern science of genetics. Mendel conducted experiments at his monastery. One experiment on garden peas led to the discovery of genes and to some of the theories that now form the foundation of modern genetics. Mendel died virtually unknown to the scientific community. The groundbreaking value of his work was not recognized until some 34 years after his death.

RESEARCH ACTIVITY: Have each student conduct research on the science of genetics and then write a few paragraphs describing the science and some of its findings about heredity.

Visual Answers

similarities—physical appearance and in several cases, dress and hairstyle; differences—in a few cases, dress and some slight physical differences

INTERPRETING VISUALS Even though identical twins share the same genetic makeup, environmental factors contribute a great deal to their personalities and social behavior. *What do these twins have in common? What differences can you identify in these sets of twins?*

SUGGESTION 2: Call on students to describe the nature and nurture viewpoints of personality development *(nature—holds that much of human behavior is instinctual in origin; nurture—holds that behavior and personality are the result of the social environment and learning).* Explain that most social scientists today believe that personality and social behavior result from a blending of hereditary and social environmental influences, with environmental factors having the most influence. Discuss with students the four main factors that affect personality development. *(See the graphic organizer on p. 99.)* Then have students, working individually or in pairs, create rap lyrics that describe those factors. **COOPERATIVE LEARNING**

HOMEWORK: Have each student ask three people the following question: Which do you believe has a greater influence on personality development—heredity or environment? Tell students to write down each person's response and some reasons why he or she holds that opinion. When the class next meets, tally the poll responses and list the results on the chalkboard. Then have students compare the results with current sociological thinking and research.

INTERPRETING VISUALS Many people have argued that Mozart was a musical genius. With his father's reinforcement, Mozart was composing music at the age of five. *How might parental reinforcement cause problems for developing children such as Mozart?*

They may also spend extra time reading to the child. These actions tend to encourage the development of the child's innate talent. Positive or negative parental reinforcement may also affect the development of such personality traits as shyness, sociability, and aggression.

Humans also inherit certain basic needs and capacities. For example, like all animals, human beings have biological drives. The hunger drive makes you want to eat. However, drives do not determine your specific behavior. The hunger drive does not tell you when to eat, what to eat, or how to eat. You learn such things through interaction with other human beings. Heredity provides you with certain biological needs, but culture determines how you meet those needs.

Heredity also plays an important role in shaping human personalities by setting limits on individuals. If you have little aptitude for music, you will probably not become a great musician. If your biological inheritance endowed you with a five-foot-tall frame, you are not likely to become a professional basketball player. On the other hand, you may not become one even if you are seven feet tall. Inherited characteristics place

limits on what is possible, but they do not determine what a person will do. No one factor alone determines what kind of personality someone will have.

Birth Order Our personalities are also influenced by whether we have brothers, sisters, both, or neither. Children with siblings have a different view of the world than do children who have no brothers or sisters. The order in which we are born into our families also influences our personalities. People born first or last in a family have a different perspective than people born in the middle. For example, research has indicated that firstborn children are more likely to be achievement-oriented and responsible than are later-born children. Later-born children, on the other hand, tend to be better in social relationships and to be more affectionate and friendly. Other studies suggest that first-borns are conservative in their thinking and are defenders of the status quo. Later-borns, in contrast, are often risk-takers and social and intellectual rebels.

Parental Characteristics Personality development in children is also influenced by the characteristics of their parents. For example, the age of parents can have a bearing on their children's development. Parents who are in their early twenties when their children are born are likely to relate differently to their offspring than parents

Personality and social development are often influenced by the order in which you are born into a family.

CONNECTING *to Literature*

Have each student locate and read one of the following plays: *A Doll's House,* by Henrik Ibsen, *Hamlet,* by William Shakespeare, or *The Glass Menagerie,* by Tennessee Williams. As students read, tell them to consider the characters' personalities and the factors that might have affected the development of each personality. Then have each student select one character in the play he or she read and write an essay describing that character's personality and explaining some of the possible factors that affected its development. Tell students to provide specific examples from the play or story to support their positions. Have volunteers read their essays to the class. **BLOCK SCHEDULING**

TEACH OBJECTIVE 2

Ask students to explain why sociologists are interested in case studies of feral and isolated children. *(Such cases reveal how children develop with little or no human contact and social guidance.)* Next, ask students to write the names *Anna, Isabelle,* and *Genie* across the top or side of a piece of paper. Under each name, have each student list four or five main points about that case study. Then have students write one sentence below each list summarizing the case study. When students have finished with the activity, discuss their results. Then ask the class to summarize what sociologists have learned about development from case studies of isolated children *(that people's personality and humanity are based in large part on their social and cultural environments).*

who are in their mid- to late thirties. Other differences between sets of parents are also likely to affect their child's personality development. Some parental characteristics that can influence a child's personality are level of education, religious orientation, economic status, cultural heritage, and occupational background.

The Cultural Environment Culture has a strong influence on personality development. Generally, the cultural environment determines the basic types of personalities that will be found in a society. Each culture gives rise to a series of personality traits—model

personalities—that are typical of members of that society. For example, in the United States competitiveness, assertiveness, and individualism are common personality traits.

The Ik [eek] of northern Uganda provide a powerful example of the effects of cultural environment on personality development. Prior to World War II, the Ik were hunters and gatherers who lived in a mountainous region of northern Uganda. Ik villagers were like one large family. Children viewed every adult in the village as a parent and all other children as brothers and sisters. However, after World War II the Ugandan government turned

INTERPRETING VISUALS A person's cultural environment can greatly influence his or her personality and social behavior. *How do you think these kids learn about the value of work in their community?*

Interdisciplinary Connection

HISTORY
Cultural Diversity over Time. Customs differ from culture to culture, but ideas and practices in a single culture may also change over time. For example, the concept of childhood is relatively new in Western culture. Until the 1700s, children were given little time or attention and by the age of seven were often sent to live elsewhere to work or attend school.

CRITICAL THINKING
How do you think that cultural changes in the treatment of children may have affected personality development?

ANSWER: Students might suggest that children's personalities are shaped more by parental characteristics now than in the past.

Visual Answer

by observing how much their parents and other adults in the community value work

Have students conduct research on the studies that Dr. Harry Harlow did with baby monkeys raised in isolation in the 1950s and 1960s. Have each student create either a written or visual description of the experiments and their results. Have one or two volunteers present their work to the class. Then have students discuss how the baby monkeys' behavior compares and contrasts to the behavior of human children based on the case studies provided on pp. 102–03 of the textbook. **BLOCK SCHEDULING**

Teacher to Teacher

Keith A. Moser of Seguin, Texas, suggested the following activity: Organize students into three groups and tell them that they are going to hold a debate on the nature versus nurture issue. Assign one group the nature viewpoint and a second group the nurture viewpoint. Tell the third group that they will serve as the media panel in the debate and present questions to each side. You might want to specify a number of questions. Have each group conduct research to prepare. During the debate, serve as the moderator and give each side a set amount of time for answers and rebuttal. **BLOCK SCHEDULING**

Case Study

Isolation's Effects on Rhesus Monkeys. Dr. Harry Harlow's experiments on rhesus monkeys demonstrated that being raised in isolation produces a kind of psychosis. Such monkeys exhibited fear, hostility, unsociability, and a lack of feeling. Harlow also offered young rhesus monkeys the choice of two substitute mothers—one made of soft materials with no bottle and one made of wire with a bottle. The monkeys invariably clung to the soft, cuddly dummy and went to the colder, wire dummy only for the bottle attached to it.

CRITICAL THINKING

Can Harlow's conclusions about rhesus monkeys be applied to humans? Why or why not?

ANSWER: Students who agree may respond that humans also depend on social interaction. Students who disagree may respond that humans are more complex intellectually than rhesus monkeys.

Visual Answer

because the doll is soft and has similar facial characteristics to the monkey's true mother

much of the Ik's land into a national park. The government then resettled the Ik on barren land. Faced with insufficient food sources, the Ik's social structure soon collapsed. In frustration, the Ik turned on each other.

Today Ik children are generally thrown out of their homes at the age of three. They survive by forming age bands—groups of children of the same general age. These bands, which serve as protection against older children, are short-lived. By the time a child reaches the age of 12 or 13, he or she has formed and broken several protective alliances and has decided that in most instances acting alone is better. Parents do not help their children, and adult children do not assist their aged parents. Only the strongest and most clever Ik survive. The culture of the Ik influences the personality of Ik children.

How we experience our culture also influences our personalities. For example, our experiences may differ depending on whether we are born male or female. Boys and girls are treated differently almost from the moment of birth. As they grow, male and female children are often nudged in different directions. Areas of difference include fields of interest, clothing, types of activities, speech habits, and ideas. All of these cultural differences in attitudes, expectations, and behavior affect the personalities of male and female adults.

Regardless of gender, subcultural differences also affect personality development. Growing up in an Italian American family provides an experience different from that found in a Polish American family. Both of these differ from the experience of growing up in an American family in which there is no clear ethnic pattern. Similarly, the region of the country or the type of neighborhood in which an individual is raised also affects personality.

Isolation in Childhood

Remarkably, several recorded instances exist in which children have been raised without the influence of a cultural environment. In a few cases, these **feral children**—wild or untamed children—were found living with animals. In other instances, the children were isolated in their homes by parents or family members so that no one would know of their existence. Regardless of the circumstances, these children had few human characteristics other than appearance. They had acquired no reasoning ability, no manners, and no ability to control their bodily functions or move about like other human beings. Sociological studies of feral children point strongly to the conclusion that our personality comes from our cultural environment.

INTERPRETING VISUALS Research conducted in the 1950s and 1960s by Dr. Harry Harlow found that even baby monkeys need social and physical contact in order to thrive. *Why might this monkey believe that the doll is its mother?*

Anna and Isabelle Kingsley Davis's studies of Anna and Isabelle provide evidence of the devastating effect of isolation during childhood. Anna was born to an unmarried woman, a fact that enraged the woman's father. At first forbidden to bring the child into the house, Anna's mother attempted to place her in a children's home. When this plan proved too expensive, Anna was moved to a series of foster homes. Finally, at the age of six months, the child was returned to her mother. Because of the grandfather's hostility, Anna was confined to an attic room where she was given only a minimum of care. She was undernourished and emaciated and received almost no human contact. She was not spoken to, held, bathed, or loved.

Anna was finally discovered by a social worker in 1938. At six years of age, Anna was little more than a skeleton. She could not walk, talk, or feed herself. Her face was expressionless, and she showed no interest in other people. Over time, though, Anna made some progress. She learned to walk, feed herself, and brush her teeth. She could also talk in phrases and follow simple directions. However, Anna died at the age of 10, probably as a result of her earlier isolation.

The story of Isabelle has a somewhat happier ending. Isabelle, whose mother was also unmarried, was found at about the same time as Anna. The child's grandfather kept her and her deaf mother confined to a dark room. Although deprived of a normal cultural environment,

CLOSE

Write the four main factors that affect personality development on the chalkboard (*heredity, birth order, parental characteristics, and cultural environment*). Next, have students discuss which of the four factors they think have more influence on personality development and which have less. Provide students with differing viewpoints a chance to express and defend their opinions. Try to get students to come to a class consensus. If they cannot, have students discuss why they may disagree on how much each factor matters (*most likely because the four factors have differing levels of importance for different students*).

REVIEW AND ASSESS

Have students complete the **Section 1 Review** on p. 106. As **Alternative Assessment**, you may want to use the personality-factors essay or the case-study summary in this section's lessons.

RETEACH

Have each student, working either with a partner or a small group, create an outline of the section. Students should use the headings of the subsections as the main points in their outlines. Have students save their outlines for review purposes.

ENGLISH LANGUAGE LEARNERS , COOPERATIVE LEARNING

Isabelle did have the advantage of her mother's company. But because she and her mother communicated only through gestures, Isabelle did not learn to speak. When she was found at the age of six, Isabelle crawled around on her hands and knees and made grunting, animal-like sounds. She ate with her hands and behaved in many ways like an infant.

Isabelle was at first thought to be mentally disabled and incapable of speech. However, after several months of intensive training she began to speak. She eventually developed a considerable vocabulary. After two years, Isabelle had reached a level of social and mental development consistent with her age group. Davis concluded that Isabelle's constant contact with her mother and skillful training by specialists allowed her to overcome her early social deprivation.

Genie Sometimes it is impossible to reverse the effects of prolonged isolation, even with the help of dedicated specialists. This situation proved true in the case of Genie, who was discovered in 1970 when she was 13 years old. Genie's father, a man who hated children, had confined her from the age of 20 months to a small bedroom. She spent her days tied to an infant's potty-chair and her nights wrapped in a sleeping bag enclosed in a mesh-covered crib. Her world was almost totally silent, and she was beaten if she made noise. Whenever Genie's father interacted with her, he behaved like an angry dog, barking, growling, and baring his teeth. Consequently, Genie did not learn to talk.

The room in which Genie spent all of her time was bare except for the potty-chair and the crib. It had two partially covered windows and was occasionally lit by a bare light bulb. Genie's only toys were two plastic raincoats that sometimes hung in a closet, empty spools of thread, and an empty cottage-cheese container.

When Genie was found, she could not stand straight and had the social and psychological skills of a one-year-old child. Even after eight years of training, Genie had not progressed past the level of a third-grade student. Although she had mastered some language and had learned to conform to basic social norms, Genie was unable to truly function as a social being. At the age of 21, she was placed in a facility for people with developmental disabilities.

INTERPRETING VISUALS The "Wild Child of France" was found living in the woods in the 1700s, unable to speak. This photo was taken from a film based on his life. *How do you think growing up in isolation from cultural influences can affect a child's social behavior?*

Sociology Then and Now

Children in Isolation. In the 1200s Emperor Frederick II conducted an experiment in which he isolated a number of very young children from communication and physical contact with their foster mothers and nurses. The emperor was curious to see what language the children would speak if they were never exposed to one. When the children all died, the emperor found out instead the importance of close, emotional contact for young children.

CRITICAL THINKING

How does this experiment compare to the case studies of feral children presented in this chapter?

ANSWER: Genie was irrevocably damaged by her isolation during early childhood. Anna, like the emperor's test subjects, died as a result of her isolation.

Visual Answer

The child will not learn cultural views of acceptable behavior or important values.

Exploring Cultural Diversity

◼ TEACH

Before class, write on the chalkboard the five-question test in the Exploring Cultural Diversity feature on pp. 104–05. At the start of class, have students take the test without referring to their textbooks. Make certain that you tell students that they will not be graded on this test. When students have completed the test, have them check it against the answers provided on p. 104. Then go through the feature with students to help them understand why most of them probably did not do very well on the test. Ask students if they think a Tibetan teenager would have found the test difficult *(probably not, because he or she is regularly exposed to Tibetan culture)*. Next, organize students into pairs or groups of three and have each pair or group list elements of American culture that are familiar to most Americans but perhaps not to many people in other parts of the world *(such as the traditional Thanksgiving dishes and the identity of Abraham Lincoln)*. After a few minutes, call on each pair or group to share some of its items with the class. Discuss them and have students consider how American culture has shaped their personalities and social behavior. Finally, have each student answer the questions that follow the feature.

COOPERATIVE LEARNING

Interdisciplinary Connection

GEOGRAPHY AND HISTORY

Tibet. Often called "the roof of the world," Tibet is located in a mountainous region of Central Asia. Natural geographic barriers long helped to keep Tibet isolated from the rest of the world. Although the Chinese influenced Tibet's government, style of dress, and food, Tibetan culture remains unique.

In the 1800s Great Britain failed in an attempt to gain control of Tibet. With British permission, China then moved to take over Tibet in 1906. Five years later, however, Tibetans expelled all Chinese and declared independence. China again invaded and assumed control of Tibet in 1950. The present Dalai Lama, the spiritual leader of Tibet, fled to India in 1959. From his base there, the Dalai Lama today works to educate the world about Tibet and its culture.

RESEARCH ACTIVITY: Have each student create a list of 5 to 10 interesting facts about Tibet not mentioned in the textbook feature on pp. 104–05.

EXPLORING
Cultural Diversity

ARE YOU A PRODUCT OF YOUR CULTURAL ENVIRONMENT?

Have you ever stopped to think about just how much your cultural environment influences what you experience and learn? A simple experiment might shed some light on just how influential the cultural environment can be. This experiment involves taking a brief test similar to many tests you have taken in school. However, it is different in one respect—you will not be graded on it! On a blank sheet of notebook paper, write answers to the questions below. Remember that this is a test, so do not look up any answers.

Test

1. Does the term *Dalai Lama* best describe a spiritual leader or an Eastern religion?
2. If someone gave you some Lapsang souchong, would you spread it on bread or drink it?
3. Is Lhasa a type of dog or a capital city?
4. In which country do you think yak butter is an important part of the people's diet—India, Russia, or Tibet?
5. The English translation of the word *Chomolungma* is "Goddess Mother of the World." What do you think Chomolungma is?

Answers

Here are the answers so that you can check your score.
1. The Dalai Lama is the spiritual leader of the people of Tibet, a region in the southwest of China.
2. Since Lapsang souchong is a type of tea—and a favorite beverage of the people of Tibet—you would drink it.
3. Lhasa is the capital city of Tibet.
4. Because Tibet is mountainous, the climate is severe. The yak is one of the few animals that can survive in this harsh setting. Consequently, the Tibetans rely on the yak for food, clothing, and shelter. Yak butter, then, forms a major part of the Tibetan diet.
5. Chomolungma is a mountain—it is the Tibetan name for Mount Everest.

How many questions did you answer correctly? Chances are that you and your classmates did not know the answers to most of these questions. The test focused on aspects of Tibetan culture. Therefore, in order to know the correct answers, you would need to know about life in Tibet. If you had grown up in Tibet, the answers would seem more obvious.

If you relate the test to American culture, you will understand this point. For example, suppose that Question 1 asked you to identify George Washington. You would probably answer "the first president of the United States." What if, in Question 4, "peanut butter" was substituted for

The region of Tibet has a complex culture. Tibetan Buddhist monks wear traditional skeleton costumes in celebration of the Chinese Tibetan New year. The Norbulinka was a home for the Dalai Lama.

EXTEND

Have students interview someone who moved to the United States from another country. Students should ask the interviewee about aspects of American culture that differ from his or her native culture. In addition, students might ask if living in America has changed the person and, if so, how. Encourage students to record their interviews, if possible. Then call on volunteers to summarize their interviews for the class. Follow up the presentations with a brief class discussion. **BLOCK SCHEDULING**

SPOTLIGHT *on Tibet*

Have students use atlases, encyclopedias, and other sources to conduct research on Tibet. Ask each student to use the research to create a poster or brochure providing basic information about the location, size, terrain, people, political system, economy, and culture of Tibet. Have volunteers present their work to the class. Then have the class discuss ways in which Tibetan life and culture shape the development of the people who live there. **BLOCK SCHEDULING**

"yak butter" and "United States" for "Tibet"? You would probably say that many people in the United States eat peanut butter. With both questions, you would not have to think very hard before the answer came to you. You would almost take it for granted that *everyone* knows that George Washington was our first president and that peanut butter is a popular food in the United States. Of course, you know this information because you live in the United States. These facts are part of the American cultural environment.

Think About It Answers

1. Answers will vary, but students should exhibit an understanding of the importance of the cultural environment in socialization.

2. Answers will vary, but students may suggest that they might wear different types of clothes, eat different types of foods, participate in different types of sports, or practice different religions.

Think About It

1. **Sociology and Culture** *Based on this experiment, what role do you think the cultural environment plays in socialization?*
2. **Sociology and You** *How might your life be different if you had grown up in a cultural environment other than that of the United States?*

105

1. Organize the class into four groups and have each group conduct research and compile lists of 5 to 10 personality traits characteristic of first-born, middle-born, last-born, and only-children. Then have each group create a presentation on their findings. Group members may want to divide up the work by taking on separate roles, such as researcher, designer, writer, editor, and presenter. Have each group deliver its presentation to the class. Then have students discuss whether they agree with each group's findings. **COOPERATIVE LEARNING, BLOCK SCHEDULING**

2. Have students interview health-care workers who are assigned to neonatal intensive-care units to determine the workers' views on the importance of human contact during the first months of life. Ask the students to present an oral report of their findings to the class. **BLOCK SCHEDULING**

3. Have students write an imaginative short story about a world in which all newborn children are raised by robots in a separate newborn facility. Ask volunteers to read their stories to the class. Follow up the stories with a brief class discussion. **BLOCK SCHEDULING**

SECTION ① REVIEW ANSWERS

1. Define:
- personality, p. 98
- heredity, p. 98
- instinct, p. 98
- sociobiology, p. 98
- aptitude, p. 99
- feral children, p. 102

2. Identify:
- John B. Watson, p. 98
- the Ik, p. 101
- Kingsley Davis, p. 102
- Rene Spitz, p. 106

3. nature—Argument is that much of human behavior is inherited; evidence includes an enumeration of human instincts; conclusion is that there are more than 10,000 human instincts; nurture—Argument is that behavior and personality are the result of the social environment and learning; evidence includes research such as Pavlov's; conclusion is that humans can be environmentally shaped to become anything.

4a. Students should describe the following factors: heredity, birth order, parental characteristics, and cultural environment.

b. It can lead to severe effects such as causing children to waste away and die or to have stunted development.

5. Paragraphs will vary, but students should recognize that the more severe and the longer the isolation, the less the child was able to recover.

106

Institutionalization Sociologists have also studied the human development of children living in institutions such as orphanages and hospitals. These children may show some of the characteristics of isolated children. In 1945 psychologist Rene Spitz studied the effects of institutionalization on a group of infants living in an orphanage. The children were given food and proper medical care but otherwise had little or no human contact. The nurses, although well-trained and efficient, had little time to hold, hug, and talk to the children. Within two years, about a third of the children in the study had died. They seemed to have simply wasted away from a lack of love and attention. Of the children who survived, fewer than 25 percent could walk by themselves, dress themselves, or use a spoon. Only one child could speak in complete sentences.

The cases of Anna, Isabelle, Genie, and the institutionalized infants illustrate how important human interaction is for social and psychological development. Recent research continues to support these earlier findings. Although foster care and orphanages are not seen as harmful today, studies of Romanian orphanages show that most young residents have learning delays and problems forming attachments to others. It is clear, then, that children who lack a caring environment in general develop their mental, physical, and emotional skills at a much slower pace.

Knowing the importance of human touch for development, doctors and nurses devote much time to holding and caring for hospitalized babies.

SECTION ① REVIEW

1. Define and explain
personality
heredity
instinct
sociobiology
aptitude
feral children

2. Identify and explain
John B. Watson
the Ik
Kingsley Davis
Rene Spitz

3. Categorizing Copy the graphic organizer below. Use it to describe the nature versus nurture debate.

Nature		Nurture
Argument	vs.	Argument
Evidence		Evidence
Conclusion		Conclusion

4. **Finding the Main Idea**

a. List and describe the four principal factors that most contemporary social scientists see as influencing personality development and social behavior.
b. According to research by Rene Spitz, what effect does the lack of close human contact have on institutionalized children?

5. **Writing and Critical Thinking**

Identifying Cause and Effect Write two short paragraphs describing what factors might have led to the different levels of success in the efforts to teach Anna, Isabelle, and Genie to function normally in society. Consider:
- the amount of human contact each child had
- the age at which each child was found

 Homework Practice Online
keyword: SL3 HP5

SECTION 2

OBJECTIVES

1. *Explain how a person's sense of self emerges.*
2. *Identify and describe the theories that have been put forth to explain the process of socialization.*

🔊 **LET'S GET STARTED!**

Before class, draw a Venn diagram on the chalkboard. Label the right circle *How I View Myself,* label the middle section *Both,* and label the left circle *How Others See Me.* As students enter the classroom, have them copy the Venn diagram and complete it. Tell students that their answers will remain private. When students have completed the activity, ask for volunteers to discuss reasons for similarities and differences in how people view themselves and how others view them. Then tell students that in Section 2 they will learn about three sociological theories to explain how individuals develop a sense of self and become socialized.

2 THE SOCIAL SELF

Read to Discover
1. How does a person's sense of self emerge?
2. What theories have been put forth to explain the process of socialization?

Define
socialization, self, looking-glass self, role-taking, significant others, generalized other, I, me

Identify
John Locke, Charles Horton Cooley, George Herbert Mead

At birth, human beings cannot talk, walk, feed themselves, or protect themselves from harm. They know nothing about the norms of society. Through interaction with their social and cultural environments, people are transformed into participating members of their society. This interactive process through which people learn the basic skills, values, beliefs, and behavior patterns of a society is called **socialization**.

A number of theories exist to explain how people become socialized and develop a sense of self. Your **self** is your conscious awareness of possessing a distinct identity that separates you and your environment from other members of society. This section examines three theories of socialization—those of John Locke, Charles Horton Cooley, and George Herbert Mead.

Locke: The Tabula Rasa

John Locke, an English philosopher from the 1600s, insisted that each newly born human being is a tabula rasa, or clean slate, on which just about anything can be written. Locke claimed that each of us is born without a personality. We acquire our personalities as a result of our social experiences. Locke believed that human beings could be molded into any type of character. He further believed that, if given a newborn infant, he could shape that child's personality, giving the child whatever characteristic he chose. As you recall, more than 200 hundred years later, psychologist John B. Watson made a similar claim.

Today few people would take such an extreme view. Nevertheless, many of our basic assumptions about socialization are related to Locke's views. Most sociologists think of socialization as a process by which individuals absorb the aspects of their culture with which they come into contact. Through the socialization process, they develop the sense of being distinct members of society.

Cooley: The Looking-Glass Self

Social psychologist Charles Horton Cooley was one of the founders of the interactionist perspective in sociology. He is most noted for developing the idea of the primary group and for his theory explaining how individuals develop a sense of self. The concept of the looking-glass self is central to that theory. The **looking-glass self** refers to the interactive process by which we develop an image of ourselves based on how we imagine we appear to others. Other people act as a mirror, reflecting back the image we project through their reactions to our behavior.

According to Cooley, the development of the looking-glass self is a three-step process. First, we imagine how we appear to others. Second, based on their reactions to us, we attempt to determine whether others view us as we view ourselves. Finally, we use our perceptions of how others judge us to develop feelings about ourselves.

According the Cooley, our understanding of how others see us influences how we view ourselves and forms part of our identity.

SECTION 2 RESOURCES

REPRODUCIBLE & REVIEW
- Graphic Organizer 5
- Mastering Critical Thinking Skills 5
- Section 2 Review, p. 109

TECHNOLOGY
- One-Stop Planner, Lesson 5.2
- Homework Practice Online
- HRW Go site

Ask students to describe how a person's sense of self emerges. Then, to help students identify the three theories that have been put forth to explain the process of socialization and how people develop a sense of self, copy the graphic organizer at right onto the chalkboard, omitting the italicized answers. Have students copy and complete the organizer. **ENGLISH LANGUAGE LEARNERS**

HOMEWORK: Have each student create a cartoon strip that illustrates either the theory of Locke, Cooley, or Mead to explain the process of socialization and how people develop a sense of self. Cartoon strips should include both illustrations and dialogue bubbles or captions.

Name	Process of Socialization Theory
John Locke	*The Tabula Rasa: Each person is a blank slate at birth, with no personality. People develop personality as a result of their social experiences. Moreover, infants can be molded into any type of person.*
Charles Horton Cooley	*The Looking-Glass Self: Infants have no sense of person or place. Children develop an image of themselves based on how others see them. Other people act as a mirror, reflecting back the image a child projects through their reactions to the child's behavior.*
George Herbert Mead	*Role-Taking: People not only come to see themselves as others see them but also take on or pretend to take on the roles of others through imitation, play, and games. This process enables people to anticipate what others expect of them.*

internet connect

go.
hrw.
.com

TOPIC: The Social Self
GO TO: go.hrw.com
KEYWORD: SL3 SC5

Have students access the Internet through the HRW Go site to conduct research on the socialization process. Then have each student create a theoretical profile of one of the three theories presented in this section. The profile should identify the theorist who suggested the theory, summarize the theory, and explain the theory's strengths and weaknesses.

Visual Answer

That the team not at bat will make an active effort to tag the other team's players out to prevent them from scoring.

INTERPRETING VISUALS School-age children participate in organized games to help further the socialization process. During these games children play specific roles and anticipate others' actions. *What types of actions might you anticipate in this game?*

The process of identity development begins very early in childhood. According to Cooley, a newborn baby has no sense of person or place. The entire world appears as one mass. Then various members of the child's primary group—parents, brothers, sisters, other family members, and friends—interact with the growing infant. They pick up the child. They talk to him or her. They reward or punish the child's behavior. They provide the child with a mirror that reflects his or her image. From this interactive process, the child develops a sense of self.

This theory puts a great deal of responsibility on parents and other primary-group members who have contact with children. Parents who think little of a child's ability, or children who perceive this attitude from their parents, will likely give rise to feelings of inferiority in the child. On the other hand, parents who treat their children as capable and competent are likely to produce capable and competent children.

Cooley was quick to note that although this process starts early in childhood, it continues throughout life. Individuals continually redefine their self-images as they alter their interpretations of the way they think others view them.

Mead: Role-Taking

American philosopher George Herbert Mead, another founder of the interactionist perspective, developed ideas related to Cooley's theories. According to Mead, seeing ourselves as others see us is only the beginning. Eventually we not only see ourselves as others see us but actually take on or pretend to take the roles of others. This act of **role-taking** forms the basis of the socialization process by allowing us to anticipate what others expect of us. We thus learn to see ourselves through the eyes of others.

According to Mead, we first internalize the expectations of the people closest to us. These people include parents, siblings, relatives, and others who have a direct influence on our socialization. Although Mead may not have used the term, sociologists now refer to such people as **significant others**. As we grow older, significant others become less important. Instead, the expectations and attitudes of society take on added importance in guiding our behavior and reinforcing our sense of self. Mead called the internalized attitudes, expectations, and viewpoints of society the **generalized other**. We internalize the generalized other through the process of role-taking.

CLOSE

Review with students the three theories discussed in the section. *(See the graphic organizer on the previous page for a description of each theory.)* Then have students discuss which theory they most agree with and why. Provide students with differing viewpoints a chance to express and defend their opinions.

REVIEW AND ASSESS

Have students complete the **Section 2 Review** on p. 109. As **Alternative Assessment**, you may want to use the theories of socialization chart or the cartoon strip in this section's lessons.

RETEACH

Have each student create a 10-item, true-false quiz for this section. Students should also create separate answer keys for their quizzes. Then have students exchange their quizzes, answer the ones they receive, and lastly return them to have the answers checked. **ENGLISH LANGUAGE LEARNERS**

EXTEND

Have pairs or groups of students write short skits illustrating the concepts of the "I" and the "me" and their integration in adulthood. Have each pair or group present its skit to the class. Follow up the skits with a class discussion. **COOPERATIVE LEARNING** , **BLOCK SCHEDULING**

Children are not automatically capable of role-taking. They must develop the necessary skills through social interaction. Mead visualized role-taking as a three-step process involving imitation, play, and games.

Under about three years of age, children lack a sense of self. Consequently, they can only imitate the actions of others. Young children most often imitate the gestures and actions of family members and others in their immediate environment. Such mimicking is not role-taking, but rather preparation for learning expectations associated with roles.

At about the age of three, children begin to play and act out the roles of specific people. They may dress up in their parents' clothes, play house, or pretend to be doctors and nurses. For the first time, the children are attempting to see the world through someone else's eyes.

By the time children reach school age, they begin to take part in organized games. Organized games require children not only to take on roles of their own but also to anticipate the actions and expectations of others. Because it requires internalizing the generalized other, the game stage of role-taking most closely resembles real life.

Through role-taking, individuals develop a sense of self. According to Mead, the self consists of two related parts—the "I" and the "me." The **I** is the unsocialized, spontaneous, self-interested component of personality and self-identity. The **me**, on the other hand, is the part of ourselves that is aware of the expectations and attitudes of society—the socialized self.

The earliest influences on the self-image of a child come from interaction within the family setting. Children often imitate their parents, seeing the world through their eyes.

In childhood, the I component of personality is stronger than the me component. Through the process of socialization, however, the me gains power by acting together with the I and bringing actions in line with the expectations of society. The me never totally dominates the I. To develop into a well-rounded member of society, a person needs both aspects of the self.

SECTION 2 REVIEW

1. Define and explain
socialization
self
looking-glass self
role-taking
significant others
generalized other
I
me

2. Identify and explain
John Locke
Charles Horton Cooley
George Herbert Mead

3. Sequencing Copy the graphic organizer below. Use it to list and describe the three steps involved in the development of the looking-glass self.

Step 3
Step 2
Step 1

4. **Finding the Main Idea**
a. What is role-taking, and what three stages do children go through when developing the skills needed for role-taking?
b. According to Mead, what are the two components of the self, and how are they related?

5. **Writing and Critical Thinking**
Analyzing Information Write a short essay exploring the common thread that runs through all three theories of socialization discussed in this section.
Consider:
• identity and early childhood
• a person's image of self
• the role of others in a person's sense of self

Homework Practice Online
keyword: SL3 HP5

SECTION 2 REVIEW ANSWERS

1. Define:
• socialization, p. 107
• self, p. 107
• looking-glass self, p. 107
• role-taking, p. 108
• significant others, p. 108
• generalized other, p. 108
• I, p. 109
• me, p. 109

2. Identify:
• John Locke, p. 107
• Charles Horton Cooley, p. 107
• George Herbert Mead, p. 108

3. Step 1—we imagine how we appear to others; Step 2—we determine whether others view us as we view ourselves; Step 3—we use our perceptions of how others judge us to develop feelings about ourselves.

4a. role-taking—to take or pretend to take on roles of others, to anticipate what others expect of us; imitation, play, and games

b. I—the spontaneous, unsocialized, self-interested component of personality; the me—the socialized self; combine to form a well-rounded personality

5. Essays will vary, but students should note that in all three theories, the formation of personality is dependent upon interaction with others during early childhood.

Building Social Studies Skills

TEACH

Read aloud the beginning of the Building Social Studies Skills feature on pp. 110–11. Next, ask volunteers to read aloud the two excerpts in the feature to the class. After each one, have students discuss the excerpt's meaning and examine the chart's analysis of the perspective. Then have the class use the chart to compare and contrast the two perspectives. After a brief period of discussion, have each student write two paragraphs comparing and contrasting the two perspectives. Finally, assign students the Practicing the Skill activity on p. 111 as homework.

EXTEND

As an extension to the Practicing the Skill activity on p. 111, have each student write an essay comparing and contrasting the two sociological perspectives that they detailed in their chart and then express which perspective they agree with and explain why. Remind students to provide reasons to support their positions and to use standard grammar, spelling, sentence structure, and punctuation in their essays. Ask volunteers to present their excerpts, charts, and essays to the class. Encourage student feedback.

BLOCK SCHEDULING

IDENTIFYING AND COMPARING POINTS OF VIEW

Select two newspaper editorials that give different perspectives on a current event, preferably one related to sociology. Give each student a copy of the editorials. As students read them, draw a blank chart on the chalkboard similar to the one in the textbook on p. 111. Have students apply their skills at identifying and comparing points of view by helping you complete the chart for the two editorials. Students should use the two-step process provided on this page to identify and compare the points of view.

BUILDING Social Studies Skills

READING ABOUT SOCIOLOGY: IDENTIFYING AND COMPARING POINTS OF VIEW

A sociological perspective is a way of viewing the social world. Not all sociologists view the social world in exactly the same way. One reason for differences in sociological perspectives is that there are several theoretical orientations in sociology. Different theoretical orientations often give rise to different interpretations of the same phenomena. Thus, it is important to be able to identify and compare points of view. Comparing sociological perspectives involves analyzing the similarities and differences among various approaches.

How to Identify and Compare Points of View

To identify and compare two or more sociological perspectives, follow the steps below:
1. **Determine the nature of the source.** Note whether the reading is from a primary or a secondary source.
2. **Read each source carefully.** Identify the main idea as well as all of the supporting details contained in each source. As you read, note the similarities and differences between the sources. Identify any theoretical bias in either account.

Applying the Skill

Read Excerpts A and B. Following the guidelines listed above, compare the two sources. The chart on page 111 is an effective way of organizing information for comparison. You will note from the chart that Lionel Tiger and Robin Fox contend that human behavior is determined primarily by genetic characteristics (the position of the sociobiology perspective). Albert Bandura, on the other hand, argues that social learning—socialization—plays the key role in determining human behavior.

Excerpt A: From *The Imperial Animal*

"The human organism is "wired" in a certain way so that it can process and emit information about certain facts of social life such as language and rules about sex, and that, furthermore, it can process this information only at certain times and only in certain ways. The wiring is geared to the life cycle so that at any one moment in a population of *Homo sapiens* there will be individuals with a certain "store" of behavior giving out information at another stage to others who are wired to treat this information in a particular way. The outcome of the interaction of these individuals will be certain "typical" relationships.

There is nothing specific in the genetic code about initiation ceremonies for young males. . . . But neither are male initiation ceremonies pure cultural inventions—results of the free activity of intellect. They occur because we are biologically wired the way we are. We can predict how older and younger males in a community will relate to one another because of the way their wiring allows them to be programmed and to program them in turn. In post adolescent males the genetic message is one of sinister and often undirected rebelliousness; this threatening information is received by older males, whose steadier hormonal systems go into a reaction and insist on containment. So all societies find ways of taming and using the young men and of forcing them to identify with the system."

Lionel Tiger and Robin Fox

110

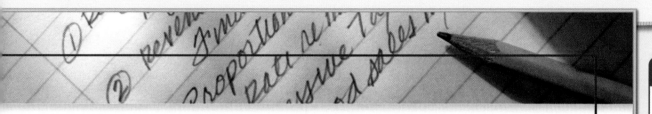

SPOTLIGHT on Cooley and Mead

Have students, working in pairs or small groups, conduct research on the Cooley and Mead theories of socialization presented on pp. 107–09 of the textbook. Instruct each group to describe each theory by creating a chart similar to the one on this page. Then draw a blank master chart on the chalkboard and have students use their charts to help you complete it. Conclude the activity with a class discussion of the two theories. **COOPERATIVE LEARNING ,**
BLOCK SCHEDULING

SPOTLIGHT on Violence in Video Games

Locate two magazine articles that present differing views on the effects of violent video games on children or youth. Distribute copies of the articles to each student. Next, call on volunteers to read the articles aloud to the class. Draw a chart on the chalkboard similar to the one on p. 111. After each article is read aloud, have the class discuss the article and complete the appropriate column in the chart. Then have students discuss the two perspectives.
COOPERATIVE LEARNING , BLOCK SCHEDULING

	Sociobiology Perspective	**Social-Learning Perspective**
Main Theme	Behavior is primarily determined by genetic factors.	Most behavior is learned through observation.
Supporting Evidence	All societies find ways of taming young men and forcing them to identify with the system.	Societies do not teach important skills by trial and error.
Conclusions	Biological wiring is geared to the life cycle and allows us to predict typical relationships, such as those between younger and older men.	Psychological functioning is explained in terms of continuous reciprocal interaction of personal and environmental determinants.
Assumptions	The human organism is wired in a certain way to process and emit information at certain times and in certain ways.	The capacity to learn through observation enables people to quickly acquire large integrated patterns of behavior.

Practicing the Skill

Students' charts should match the model on this page and clearly compare and contrast the relevant points of the two perspectives examined. Students' statements should summarize the information provided in the charts.

Excerpt B: From *Social Learning Theory*

"In the social learning view, people are neither driven by inner forces nor buffeted by environmental stimuli. Rather, psychological functioning is explained in terms of continuous reciprocal interaction of personal and environmental determinants. Within this approach, symbolic, vicarious, and self-regulatory processes assume a prominent role.

Psychological theories have traditionally assumed that learning can occur only by performing responses and experiencing their effects. In actuality, virtually all learning phenomena resulting from direct experience occur on a vicarious basis by observing other people's behavior and its consequences for them. The capacity to learn by observation enables people to acquire large, integrated patterns of behavior without having to form them gradually by tedious trial and error.

The abbreviation of the acquisition process through observational learning is vital for both development and survival. Because mistakes can produce costly, or even fatal consequences, the prospects for survival would be slim indeed if one could learn only by suffering consequences of trial and error. For this reason, one does not teach children to swim, adolescents to drive automobiles, and novice medical students to perform surgery by having them discover the appropriate behavior through the consequences of their successes and failures. The more costly and hazardous the possible mistakes, the heavier is the reliance on observational learning from competent examples. Apart from the question of survival, it is difficult to imagine a social transmission process in which the language, lifestyles, and institutional practices of a culture are taught to each new member by selective reinforcement of fortuitous behaviors, without the benefit of models who exemplify the cultural patterns."

Albert Bandura

Practicing the Skill

Locate two commentaries on a sociological issue, each written from a different perspective. Then on a separate sheet of paper, construct a chart similar to the one shown on this page. Write a brief statement identifying and comparing the views of the two perspectives.

OBJECTIVES

1. *Identify the most important agents of socialization in the United States.*

2. *Explain why family and education are important social institutions.*

SECTION **3** RESOURCES

REPRODUCIBLE & REVIEW

• Study Skills and Writing Guide

• Section 3 Review, p. 115

TECHNOLOGY

• One-Stop Planner, Lesson 5.3

• **CNN** Presents Sociology: School Dress Codes

• Homework Practice Online

• HRW Go site

3

AGENTS OF SOCIALIZATION

● **Read to Discover**

1. What are the most important agents of socialization in the United States?

2. Why are family and education important social institutions?

● **Define**

agents of socialization, peer group, mass media, total institution, resocialization

The views of Locke, Cooley, and Mead provide theoretical explanations of the socialization process. This section examines some specific forces and situations that shape socialization. Sociologists use the term **agents of socialization** to describe the specific individuals, groups, and institutions that enable socialization to take place. In the United States, the primary agents of socialization include the family, the peer group, the school, and the mass media.

The Family

The family is the most important agent of socialization in almost every society. Its primary importance rests in its role as the principal socializer of young children. Children first interact with others and first learn the values, norms, and beliefs of society through their families.

Socialization in a family setting can be both deliberate and unintended. A father may teach his children about the importance of telling the truth or being considerate of others. A mother may instruct her children on how to spend and save money. These are deliberate, or intended, socialization activities.

There also are unintended socialization activities. Many times these activities have an even greater effect on children than do deliberate attempts at socialization. For example, suppose a father carefully explains to his child the importance of being polite. However, the child sees several situations in which the father is impolite. Is the child likely to follow what the father says or what the father actually does? Unintended

socialization is very common. Parents may take deliberate action to try to influence a child in one direction. However, on numerous occasions they send out unintended messages that push the child in another direction.

Whether deliberate or unconscious, the socialization process differs from family to family, for all families are not the same. The number of children and the number of parents vary from family to family. In addition, one-parent families may be headed by a father or a mother. Also, relationships with other family members—grandparents, uncles, and aunts—may vary. Further, families differ according to the combination of subgroups to which they belong. These subgroups include racial or ethnic group, social class, religious group, and geographic region. For example, one family may be African American, middle class, Baptist, and live in the South. Another may be Italian American, working class, Catholic, and live in the Midwest. All these differences affect the way a family socializes its children. Thus, socialization produces a society of individuals who share in the patterns of the larger culture but who retain certain unique personality and behavior characteristics.

The Peer Group

The family provides many, if not most, of the socialization experiences of early childhood. Infants and very young children are particularly likely to spend almost all of their time in a family setting. As children grow older, forces outside of the family increasingly influence them. In particular, children begin to relate more and more to their peer groups. A **peer group** is a primary group composed of individuals of roughly equal age and similar social characteristics.

Peer groups are particularly influential during the pre-teenage and early teenage years. Indeed, winning peer acceptance is a powerful force in the lives of young people of this age group. Without peer acceptance, they are labeled as misfits, outsiders, or a similar disparaging term. To win this acceptance, young people willingly adopt the values and standards of the peer group. In essence, they shape themselves into the kind of person they think the group wants them to be.

With an increase in both parents working outside the home, families turn to day-care facilities to care for their children. These day cares provide socialization experiences of our young children more than in the past.

TEACH OBJECTIVES 1 AND 2

List on the chalkboard the most important agents of socialization in the United States *(family, peer groups, the school, and the mass media)*. To help students describe the role of the mass media as an agent of socialization, copy the following graphic organizer onto the chalkboard, omitting the italicized answers. Have students copy and complete the organizer. Then have students work in pairs to create similar graphic organizers for the other main agents of socialization *(family—principal socializer of young children; peer groups—most influential during preteenage and early teenage years; education—school plays a major role between ages 5 and 18)*.

ENGLISH LANGUAGE LEARNERS , COOPERATIVE LEARNING

Mass Media as a Socialization Agent

- *Mass media include books, films, the Internet, magazines, newspapers, radio, and television.*
- *Television probably has the most influence on children.*
- *The effect of television on children is an ongoing debate.*

HOMEWORK: Provide each student with a small posterboard. Have each student use it to create a collage that illustrates the four most important agents of socialization in the United States. *(See the previous activity for a list.)*

Between the ages of 5 and 18, students spend some 30 weeks a year in school. Teachers may become role models that influence students through regular academics as well as extracurricular activities.

Peer-group socialization is different from socialization within the family. The norms and values imparted by the family usually focus on the larger culture. However, in peer groups the focus is the subculture of the group. Peer-group goals are sometimes at odds with the goals of the larger society. Parents in particular become alarmed if they come to believe that the norms and values of the peer group are more important to their children than those of society as a whole.

The School

For most young people, school occupies large amounts of time and attention. Between the ages of 5 and 18, young people spend some 30 weeks a year in school. Thus, the school plays a major role in socializing individuals. Much of this socialization is deliberate. Class activities are planned for the deliberate purpose of teaching reading, writing, arithmetic, and other skills. Extracurricular activities, such as school dances, clubs, and athletic events, are intended to prepare the student for life in the larger society. Schools also attempt to transmit cultural values, such as patriotism, responsibility, and good citizenship.

A large amount of unintentional socialization also occurs within the school. Teachers may become models for students in such unintended areas as manners of speech or styles of dress. In addition, every school contains many peer groups that influence the habits of their members.

Sociologists who study the mass media have raised concerns about the influence of violent programming on the behavior of children and adolescents.

The Mass Media

Socialization in the family, the peer group, and the school involves personal contact. Another influential agent of socialization, the mass media, involves no face-to-face interaction. The **mass media** are instruments of communication that reach large audiences with no personal contact between those sending the information and those receiving it. The major forms of mass media are books, films, the Internet, magazines, newspapers, radio, and television.

Of these various forms of mass media, television probably has the most influence on the socialization of children. Some 98 percent of the homes in the United States have television sets, with an average of more than two sets per home. More importantly, research shows that most children watch an average of about 28 hours each week. Further, watching television is the primary after-school activity for 6- to 17-year-olds. Indeed, most children spend almost twice as much time watching television as they spend in school.

⊡ internet connect ≣

TOPIC: Television and Behavior
GO TO: go.hrw.com
KEYWORD: SL3 SC5

Have students access the Internet through the HRW Go site to research the influence of television in the socialization process. Next, have students conduct "field research" by interviewing members of their peer group regarding the influence of television. Then have students use both sets of research to write an essay on television's influence on behavior. Remind students to provide information from their research to support their statements and to use standard grammar, spelling, sentence structure, and punctuation in their essays.

Technology Resources

 CNN Presents Sociology: School Dress Codes

Case Studies and Other True Stories

▩ TEACH

Have students read the feature The Function of Fairy Tales on this page. Discuss the feature with students. Then organize the class into small groups and provide each group with a short, well-known fairy tale, such as *The Three Bears* or *Little Red Riding Hood.* Have each group read and analyze its fairy tale and discuss how the tale might help children and contribute to their socialization. Then have a spokesperson from each group present its conclusions to the class. Encourage other students to provide feedback.

COOPERATIVE LEARNING

▨ SPOTLIGHT *on Urban Legends*

Have interested students conduct research on studies that have been done on the purpose and role of urban legends as agents of socialization. Students might examine studies done in several disciplines such as literature, psychology, and sociology. Then have each student write a short report similar to the feature on this page that describes how urban legends serve as agents of socialization. Students should include examples from specific urban legends to support the statements in their reports. **BLOCK SCHEDULING**

Think About It Answers

1. They help children master the problems of growing up by stimulating their imaginations and enabling them to deal with their fears.

2. Answers will vary. Students might respond that science fiction and fantasy literature offer a modern parallel to fairy tales or that other folklore, such as jokes and urban legends, also help to mold social behavior.

SECTION ③ REVIEW ANSWERS

1. Define:
- agents of socialization, p. 112
- peer group, p. 112
- mass media, p. 113
- total institution, p. 115
- resocialization, p. 115

2. family—most important agent; peer group—primary group composed of individuals of roughly equal age and social characteristics, particularly influential during pre-teenage and early teenage years; school—plays a major role; and mass media—books, films, the Internet, magazines, newspapers, radio, and television, not face-to-face

3a. Total institutions are concerned with resocialization rather than socialization.

b. They teach children important life skills as well as values, norms, and beliefs.

Case Studies
AND OTHER TRUE STORIES

THE FUNCTION OF FAIRY TALES

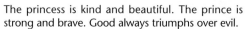

P arents and teachers have many tools at their disposal to assist in the socialization of young children. One of the most effective tools is literature. Of the various forms of literature written for children, the fairy tale has had the longest run of popularity. What is it about fairy tales that makes them such an enduring agent of socialization? Child psychologist Bruno Bettelheim explored this question in his book *The Uses of Enchantment: The Meaning and Importance of Fairy Tales.* According to Bettelheim, fairy tales are valuable because they help children master the problems of growing up. Fairy tales stimulate children's imaginations and allow them to deal with their subconscious fears.

"Little Red Riding Hood" is another fairy tale that explores death and violence, helping children come to terms with their fears.

Introduction to the Real World

Fairy tales provide children with an introduction to the real world. Their message is that evil and virtue, good and bad exist in everything. Fairy tales also teach children that difficulties in life are unavoidable and must be met head on. Children see the fairy-tale hero confront evil and, through cleverness or bravery, find a way to triumph. The lessons contained in fairy tales can be indirect, however. According to Bettelheim, children do not identify with the "good" or "bad" act. Rather, they identify with the hero, who happens to be good. The hero serves as a role model for the young child. Children do not ask, "Do I want to be good?" Instead they ask, "Whom do I want to be like?" This distinction is important. It enables children to learn socially acceptable behaviors before they are old enough to grasp the moral issues involved.

Structure and Content

The structure of the fairy tale is ideally suited to the way young children think. Children cannot understand the complexities of the adult world. Situations and people are right or wrong, good or bad. Fairy tales mimic this simplified view of the world. Fundamental issues are presented in an either/or format that children can easily grasp. The witch is bad and ugly.

The princess is kind and beautiful. The prince is strong and brave. Good always triumphs over evil.

More important than the structure of fairy tales is the subject matter. Love, fear, death, isolation, and abandonment are prominent themes. Addressing such subjects allows young children to confront fears that they might not be able to express in their own words. Fairy tales have the added advantage of taking on new meanings as a child grows. In the case of *Cinderella,* for example, very young children can understand the message of good Cinderella winning out over her bad step-sister. Older children also might grasp the notion of sibling rivalry contained in the story.

In short, the important function of fairy tales rests not in telling a literal story or in providing simple moral truths. Instead, it rests in allowing children to grasp the contradictions that exist in human nature and social life. Fairy tales do this in a way that is particularly suited to the developmental skills of growing children. By capturing children's imaginations and allowing them to explore their unspoken fears, fairy tales help to mold social behavior.

Think About It

1. Analyzing Information *How do fairy tales affect the development of children? How do they accomplish this?*

2. Evaluating *What other stories or traditions might have a function similar to that of fairy tales, and what effects do they have on psychological development?*

The effect of television on children is a topic of ongoing debate. On the negative side, research indicates that by age 18, most children will have witnessed 200,000 fictional acts of violence, including 16,000 murders. Several studies have found a connection between television violence and aggressive behavior among young people. These studies say that television violence encourages viewers to act in aggressive ways and to see aggression as a valid way to solve problems. The studies also argue that because television violence often appears painless or not harmful, it invites viewers to be less sensitive to the suffering of others. The studies conclude that television violence appears to make viewers fearful of the world around them.

Another long-standing criticism of television is that it presents an image of a society limited to white middle-class values. The life experiences of many racial, religious, and economic groups are often either ignored or portrayed in a negative light.

On the positive side, television expands the viewers' world. It can be a powerful educational tool. For example, television brings far-off places into viewers' homes, makes world events immediate, and introduces viewers to subjects they otherwise might never encounter.

Resocialization

The total institution is a rather unique agent of socialization. A **total institution** is a setting in which people are isolated from the rest of society for a set period of time and are subject to tight control. Prisons, military boot camps, monasteries, and psychiatric hospitals are examples of total institutions.

Prisons attempt to resocialize individuals by removing all semblance of a personal identity. Prisoners wear the same uniform and have to give up many freedoms.

Socialization in a total institution differs from the process found in most other settings. Total institutions are primarily concerned with resocializing their members. **Resocialization** involves a break with past experiences and the learning of new values and norms. In the case of most total institutions, resocialization is directed toward changing an individual's personality and social behavior. These modifications are accomplished by stripping away all semblance of individual identity and replacing it with an institutional identity—uniforms, standard haircuts, and so on. The individual is also denied the freedoms of the outside world. Once the person's sense of self has been weakened, it is easier for those in power to convince that person to conform to new patterns of behavior.

SECTION 3 REVIEW

1. Define and explain
agents of socialization
peer group
mass media
total institution
resocialization

2. Summarizing
Copy the graphic organizer below. Use it to list and describe the four main agents of socialization in American society.

Agent → Socialization ← Agent
Agent → Socialization ← Agent

Homework Practice Online
keyword: SL3 HP5

3. ■ Finding the Main Idea

a. In what ways are total institutions different from other agents of socialization?
b. How are institutions such as family and school important?

4. ■ Writing and Critical Thinking

Evaluating Write a short report evaluating how effective a mass medium—such as the Internet—is as an agent of socialization.
Consider:
• the variety of mass media
• people's access to the medium
• the positive and negative effects of the medium

Review and Assessment Resources

- Chapter 5 Review, pp. 116–17
- Chapter Review Activities with Answer Key
- Global Skill Builder CD–ROM
- Chapter 5 Test Generator (on the One-Stop Planner)
- Chapter 5 Test (Form A or B)
- Alternative Assessment Handbook
- HRW Go site

REVIEW

Have students complete the **Chapter 5 Review** on pp. 116–17.

ASSESS

Use one of the chapter tests to assess students' understanding of the content. For **Alternative Assessment**, see the **Alternative Assessment Handbook**.

---

10. the specific individuals, groups, and institutions that enable socialization to occur

UNDERSTANDING MAIN IDEAS

1. Most social scientists today believe that both environment and heredity affect personality.

2. heredity, birth order, parental characteristics, and cultural environment

3. A healthy cultural environment is essential for a child's full development.

4. A sense of self helps a person see himself or herself as others do and internalize societal expectations and attitudes.

5. by interacting with others, imagining how they appear to others, perceiving how others view them, and using those perceptions to refine self views; at death

6. the family, peer group, school, and mass media

THINKING CRITICALLY

1. Locke, Cooley, and Mead agree that the self emerges through interaction with others. Locke believed every aspect of personality comes from one's environment. Cooley introduced the concept of the looking-glass self. Mead built upon Cooley's theory with the concept of role-taking.

2. Answers will vary, but students should select either heredity, birth order, parental characteristics, or cultural environment and provide support for the chosen factor.

116

---

5 Review

Writing a Summary

Using standard grammar, spelling, sentence structure, and punctuation, summarize the information in this chapter.
Consider:
- the main factors that influence personality development
- the theories that explain socialization
- the most important agents of socialization

Identifying People and Ideas

Identify the following people and terms and use them in appropriate sentences.

1. personality
2. heredity
3. instinct
4. socialization
5. looking-glass self
6. role-taking
7. significant others
8. I
9. me
10. agents of socialization

Understanding Main ideas

Section 1 (pp. 98–106)

1. How has the nature-versus-nurture debate evolved?
2. What do social scientists believe are the principal factors that influence personality development?
3. What does research on children reared in isolation indicate about the effects of the cultural environment on social and psychological development?

Section 2 (pp. 107–109)

4. What is the role of self in the socialization process?
5. According to Cooley, how does a person's sense of self develop in early childhood and when does this process end?

Section 3 (pp. 112–115)

6. Identify the primary agents of socialization in the United States.

Thinking Critically

1. **Comparing and Contrasting** How are the theories of Locke, Cooley, and Mead on the emergence of the self similar, and how are they different?
2. **Supporting a Point of View** What do you think is the most important influence on a person's personality and social behavior? Explain your answer.
3. **Drawing Inferences and Conclusions** Why do you think sociologists study people who were isolated during childhood?
4. **Making Generalizations and Predictions** How do you think agents of socialization in another country may be similar or different? What do you think explains these similarities and differences?
5. **Analyzing Information** In what ways might the mass media, particularly television, reinforce and counteract the effects of the other agents of socialization?

Writing About Sociology

1. **Making Generalizations and Predictions** Culture has a strong influence on personality, but culture can change over time. Write a story that explores how future changes in the United States could affect the personality traits of Americans.
2. **Evaluating** Review the research findings on the effects of birth order on personality development. Next, watch a television program or read a story that centers on a family with several children. How do the characteristics of the fictional children compare to the birth-order traits predicted in the scientific research? Present your findings in a brief written report. Use the graphic organizer below to help you present your findings.

	Show 1	Show 2
Traits of the Firstborn		
Traits of the Laterborn		
Traits Predicted		

RETEACH

Write the chapter's key terms on notecards. Then organize the class into teams and host a game of Sociology Draw. Give a team member a card. The student has two minutes to draw images to help his or her team guess the term on the card. The student drawing may not speak, gesture, or use any numbers or words. If the team does not guess the word in the allotted time, give the next team a chance. Award one point for a correct guess. At the end of the game, the team with the most points wins. After the game, review any terms with which students were having trouble.

ENGLISH LANGUAGE LEARNERS , COOPERATIVE LEARNING

SOCIOLOGY PROJECTS

1. Connecting to History Have interested students conduct research to locate historical quotations that focus on the socialization of children. Ask students to share some of their quotations with the class. Then have the class evaluate how valid the quotations are in today's society.

2. Applying Sociology Have students visit a toy store and examine five games or toys for preschoolers. Ask each student to list some games and toys that show only boys on the package, some that show only girls, and some that show a gender mix. Have volunteers share their results with the class. Then have the class analyze the results to determine any differences in socialization patterns for boys and girls.

BUILDING SOCIAL STUDIES SKILLS

Interpreting Graphs

Study the graph below. Use it to answer the following questions.

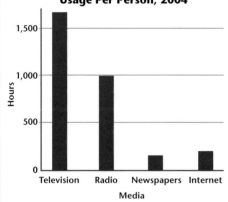

Projected Annual Hours of Media Usage Per Person, 2004

Source: *Statistical Abstract of the United States*

1. How many more hours a year do Americans spend watching television than reading newspapers?
   a. 1,528
   b. 153
   c. 1,705
   d. 1,398
2. What conclusion can you draw about how the mass media influences the socialization of Americans?

Analyzing Primary Sources

Read the following excerpt from Susan Curtiss's study on the development of Genie, who was discovered after her father kept her confined to her room for most of her first 13 years of life. Then answer the questions that follow.

> *It was her lack of socialization that was most difficult to deal with, especially in public. . . . If anyone she encountered in the street or in a store or other public place had something she liked, she was uncontrollably drawn to him or her, and without obeying any rules of psychological distance or social mores, she would go right up the person and put her hands on the desired item. . . . When the object of attention was an article of clothing, and Genie would simply attach herself to the person wearing that clothing and refuse to let go, the situations were extremely trying.*
>
> *Even when Genie did not attach herself in quite such an embarrassing manner, she still went right up to strangers, stood directly in front of them, without any accepted distance between them, and peered into their faces with her face directly in front of theirs, pointing (without looking) at whatever possession of theirs held her interest.*

3. Why does the author find Genie embarrassing in public?
   a. She will not speak to people.
   b. She walks funny.
   c. She runs away if approached.
   d. She does not observe social distance.
4. Based on the author's comments, how do you think Genie's lack of socialization affected her life?

SOCIOLOGY PROJECTS

Cooperative Learning

Using Your Observation Skills Working in a group with two or three other students, locate and collect magazine pictures showing children engaged in each of the three steps of the role-taking process described by George Herbert Mead. Use these materials to create an annotated visual essay on Mead's theory of the self. Create a model of the role-taking process using your examples. Create a quiz and answer key based on the information in your model for members of your class to use.

---

internet connect

Internet Activity: go.hrw.com
KEYWORD: SL3 SC5
Choose an activity on socializing the individual to:
- create a theoretical profile on theorists presented in this chapter.
- write a report on the influences of nature and nurture on personality development.
- conduct field research on the influence of television in your peer group and write two paragraphs summarizing your findings.

---

3. They provide a way to study the role of environment on personality development and socialization.

4. Answers will vary, but students might mention that school or mass media may not be as important in a less-developed country.

5. Answers will vary, but students might address how media messages, such as television violence, might contradict the messages of other agents of socialization, such as family.

WRITING ABOUT SOCIOLOGY

1. Students' stories will vary but should present plausible cultural changes and clearly address how these changes affect personality traits.

2. Students' reports should describe the traits of firstborns and laterborns and then explain how well those traits compare to the traits of at least one first-born and one later-born fictional character.

BUILDING SOCIAL STUDIES SKILLS

1. a

2. Answers will vary, but students might suggest that television has by far the most influence of all forms of media on socialization.

3. d

4. Students might mention that she might struggle to make friends or hold a job.

The Adolescent in Society

CHAPTER RESOURCE MANAGER

Objectives	Pacing Guide	Resources

SECTION 1:
Adolescence in Our Society
(pp. 120–26)

REV Section 1 Review, p. 126

- Explain how adolescence developed as a distinct stage of the life cycle in the United States.
- Identify the five general characteristics of adolescence.

Regular 3 days	Block Scheduling 1.5 days

Block Scheduling Handbook with Team Teaching Strategies, Chapter 6

SECTION 2:
Teenagers and Dating
(pp. 127–34)

REV Section 2 Review, p. 134

- Summarize how dating developed as a form of social interaction.
- Describe the functions that dating fulfills.

Regular 3 days	Block Scheduling 1.5 days

Block Scheduling Handbook with Team Teaching Strategies, Chapter 6

SECTION 3:
Challenges of Adolescence
(pp. 135–45)

REV Section 3 Review, p. 143

- Identify some of the social problems facing contemporary teenagers.
- Trace the causes and consequences of these problems.

Regular 4 days	Block Scheduling 2 days

Block Scheduling Handbook with Team Teaching Strategies, Chapter 6

Resources

- **CNN.** Presents Sociology: Eating Disorders
- **RS** Graphic Organizer 6
- HRW Go site
- **SM** Mastering Critical Thinking Skills 6
- **PS** Readings and Case Studies in Sociology 6
- **E** Research Projects and Activities for Teaching Sociology 6
- **SM** Study Skills and Writing Guide
- Teaching Transparency: Participation in Extracurricular Activities by Categories of 12th Graders (in percent)
- Teaching Transparency: Trends in Drug Use Among High-School Seniors, 1990–2001

Chapter Review And Assessment

- **REV** Chapter 6 Review, pp. 146–47
- **REV** Chapter Review Activities with Answer Key
- Global Skill Builder CD–ROM
- Chapter 6 Test Generator (on the One-Stop Planner)
- **A** Chapter 6 Test (Form A or B)
- **A** Alternative Assessment Handbook
- HRW Go site

Chapter Resource Key

PS Primary Sources	**A** Assessment	Video
RS Reading Support	**REV** Review	Internet
E Enrichment	Transparencies	Holt Presentation Maker Using Microsoft® PowerPoint®
SM Skills Mastery	CD–ROM	

One-Stop Planner CD–ROM

See the *One-Stop Planner* for a complete list of additional resources for students and teachers.

One-Stop Planner CD–ROM

It's easy to plan lessons, select resources, and print out materials for your students when you use the **One-Stop Planner CD–ROM with Test Generator.**

Chapter Project Preview

The following activities are included in the Chapter Review. You may want to make the suggested preparations.

CHAPTER REVIEW ACTIVITY

Cooperative Learning Students will work in groups to read short stories that have adolescents as main characters and then write a report describing how these characters deal with different character-istics of adolescence. Before starting the project, select five to seven appropriate short stories. You might also provide a set format for students' reports to make grading easier.

LESSON ACTIVITY

Applying Sociology Students will work in groups to create a Teen Years board game covering the concepts in this chapter. You will need to provide art supplies and materials for making game boards and playing pieces. In addition, you might want to bring several different types of board games to class to provide students with ideas.

INTERNET ACTIVITY

Influencing the Perceptions of Teenagers Students will use provided Internet links to research methods used by advertisers to target teens and then work in groups to create a series of anti-smoking ads directed at teens. In preparation, in the classroom display several print advertise-ments directed at teens. In addition, you might provide some anti-smoking ads. Then have students discuss some of these ads after doing their research and before starting their projects.

Additional Resources

PRINT RESOURCES FOR TEACHERS

Alsaker, Francoise D. and August Flammer, eds. *The Adolescent Experience: European and American Adolescents in the 1990s.* Mahwah, New Jersey: Lawrence Erlbaum Associates, 1999. Research monographs in adolescence.

Gallo, Donald R., ed. *Time Capsule: Short Stories About Teenagers Throughout the Twentieth Century.* Delacorte, 1999. Collection of short stories focusing on teenagers in each decade of the 1900s.

Montemayor, Raymond, et al, eds. *Adolescent Diversity in Ethnic, Economic, and Cultural Contexts.* (Advances in Adolescent Development series, vol. 10) Sage Publications, 2000. Essays examining the variety of adolescent experiences.

PRINT RESOURCES FOR STUDENTS

Bell, Ruth. *Changing Bodies, Changing Lives: A Book for Teens on Sex and Relationships.* Random House, 1998. Explores the physical and emotional changes associated with adolescence.

Hyde, Margaret O. and John F. Setard. *Alcohol 101: An Overview for Teens.* Twenty-First Century, 1999. Comprehensive, objective study of alcohol and social problems designed for young adults.

Vollstadt, Elizabeth Weiss. *Teen Eating Disorders (Overview Series: Teen Issues).* Lucent, 1999. Addresses top-ics ranging from the causes of eating disorders to prevention techniques.

MULTIMEDIA RESOURCES

The Date (vhs; 20 min.) EVEC. Uses comedy to explore what men and women expect from one another in dating situations.

Hooked: The Addiction Trap. (vhs; 3 tapes, each 25–31 min.) ACG/United Learning, 1999. Three-part series examining addictions, consequences, and alternatives presented through interviews.

Teen Suicide: A Permanent Solution to a Temporary Problem. (vhs; 26 min.) AGC/United Learning, 1998. Examines teenage suicide through teens' stories and statistics.

☑ **internet** connect

HRW ONLINE RESOURCES

GO TO: go.hrw.com
Then type in a keyword.

TEACHER HOME PAGE
KEYWORD: SL3 Teacher

CHAPTER INTERNET ACTIVITIES
KEYWORD: SL3 SC6
Choose an activity to have students:
• research methods used by advertisers to target teenagers and create an anti-smoking campaign.
• write a report on recent studies on dating.
• design an adolescent-suicide prevention program.

CHAPTER ENRICHMENT LINKS
KEYWORD: SL3 CH6

ONLINE ASSESSMENT
Homework Practice
KEYWORD: SL3 HP6
Standardized Test Prep
KEYWORD: SL3 STP6
Rubrics
KEYWORD: SS Rubrics

CONTENT UPDATES
KEYWORD: SS Content Updates

HOLT PRESENTATION MAKER
KEYWORD: SL3 PPT6

ONLINE READING SUPPORT
KEYWORD: SS Strategies

CURRENT EVENTS
KEYWORD: S3 Current Events

CHAPTER

6 The Adolescent in Society

SECTION 1
Adolescence in Our Society

SECTION 2
Teenagers and Dating

SECTION 3
Challenges of Adolescence

CHAPTER REVIEW

Build on What You Know

Ask students to answer the following questions:

How does adolescence differ from childhood?

Consider:

• social skills
• expectations and roles
• biological differences

What are some challenges facing today's teenagers?

Consider:

• school and adult expectations
• peer pressure
• media messages and advertising

Internet Activity

☑ internet connect

TOPIC: Influencing the Perceptions of Teenagers
GO TO: go.hrw.com
KEYWORD: SL3 SC6

Have students access the Internet through the HRW Go site to conduct research on propaganda techniques designed to influence the perceptions, attitudes, and behaviors of teenagers. Then have students work in small groups to create a series of advertisements to encourage teenagers to stop smoking. Each group should write a brief explanation explaining which propaganda techniques each advertisement uses and why group members think those techniques will be effective.

CHAPTER

6 The Adolescent in Society

Build on What You Know

Most values and social norms are learned during the early childhood years. In this chapter, you will explore adolescence, the life stage between childhood and adulthood. You will look at the development of the American concept of adolescence and review the characteristics of adolescence, adolescent dating practices, and the serious challenges that face teenagers today.

Peer groups are an important influence on adolescents. During their teenage years people in our society often develop their values and personal identity.

Life in Society

A reader of a teenage magazine asked the question, "Are there some areas of the body that shouldn't be pierced?" The columnist for the teenage magazine might respond by directing teenagers to scientific reports and opinions about the effects of body piercing. The columnist might point to the risks of infection and allergic reactions that can lead to serious health issues. Piercing parts of the body such as the tongue or nose can lead to the development of scars called keloids in the pierced area. The columnist might suggest to teenagers that the ear lobes are the safest part of the body to pierce.

Responding to the special problems of adolescents is an important feature of American society. For example, the magazine *Seventeen* has a paid circulation of about 2.4 million copies and reaches 87 percent of all American female teenagers.

Because adolescence is so much a part of American culture, it may surprise you that adolescence is not a universal phenomenon. As a distinct stage of the life cycle, adolescence is an invention of modern industrial society. In some parts of the world, it simply does not exist.

What's Your Opinion?

Read the following statements about sociology. Do you think they are true or false? You will learn whether each statement is true or false as you read the chapter.

- All societies recognize adolescence as a distinct stage in the life cycle.

- Dating patterns in the United States have remained unchanged for more than 100 years.

- Social forces have no effect on such issues as teenage sexual activity, teenage drug use, and teenage suicide.

SECTION 1

OBJECTIVES

1. *Explain how adolescence developed as a distinct stage of the life cycle in the United States.*

2. *Identify the five general characteristics of adolescence.*

🎧 LET'S GET STARTED!

As students enter the classroom, write the term *adolescence* on the chalkboard and ask students to define it *(the period between the normal onset of puberty and the beginning of adulthood; in general, from about ages 12 to 19 in the United States)*. Next, ask students to imagine what their lives would be like if adolescence was not considered a separate life stage. Ask students how their lives would be different if all Americans were considered adults at the age of 13. Call on volunteers to share their responses with the class. Then tell students that the concept of adolescence is a relatively recent creation and that in Section 1 they will learn about when and why the concept of adolescence developed and about the characteristics of adolescence.

SECTION *1* RESOURCES

REPRODUCIBLE & REVIEW

- Readings and Case Studies in Sociology 6
- Research Projects and Activities for Teaching Sociology 6
- Section 1 Review, p. 126

TECHNOLOGY

- One-Stop Planner, Lesson 6.1
- Teaching Transparency: Participation in Extracurricular Activities by Categories of 12th Graders (in percent)
- Homework Practice Online

1 ADOLESCENCE IN OUR SOCIETY

Read to Discover
1. How did adolescence develop as a distinct stage of the life cycle in the United States?
2. What are the five general characteristics of adolescence?

Define
adolescence, puberty, anticipatory socialization

Adolescence is a unique stage in a person's life. Adolescents are caught between two worlds. They are no longer children, yet they are not adults in the eyes of society. **Adolescence** can be defined as the period between the normal onset of puberty and the beginning of adulthood. **Puberty** is the physical maturing that makes an individual capable of sexual reproduction. Adolescence as a distinct life stage is the creation of modern industrial society. It is not a universal phenomenon. Adolescence simply does not exist as a concept in many parts of the world. However, puberty occurs in all human societies.

In American society, adolescence is generally considered to run from the ages of 12 to 19. However, puberty and acceptance into the adult world occur at different times for different people. Therefore, the beginning and end dates of adolescence are somewhat blurred.

Tattooing is an important part of puberty rites for some groups of people whose society does not have a distinct period of adolescence.

The Concept of Adolescence

Adolescence is not universal. In many preindustrial societies, young people go directly from childhood to adulthood once they have taken part in formal ceremonies known as puberty rites. These rites, which usually take place around age 13 or 14, differ from society to society. Common rites include demonstrations of strength or endurance, filing of the teeth, and tattooing or scarring of the skin. Young people who successfully complete these puberty rites immediately become accepted members of adult society. Even though they are in their early teenage years, they can take on all adult roles. For these people, adolescence is an unknown concept.

Adolescence as a life stage is a relatively recent phenomenon. In the United States, this stage did not exist prior to the Civil War. Before that time, young people were treated simply as small adults. The adolescent experience has become an acknowledged stage of development in industrialized countries in only the past century.

Three factors have been particularly important in the development of adolescence as a distinct life stage in the United States. The first factor is education. State laws make education mandatory up to the age of 16, and most young people stay in school until they are 18. Those who attend college usually are in their early 20s when they graduate. For those people who pursue graduate degrees, educational requirements lengthen the time spent in school even more. Education extends the period of adolescence because many students are dependent on others for their financial support. While in school,

TEACH OBJECTIVE 1

To help students explain the development of adolescence as a distinct stage of the life cycle in the United States, copy the graphic organizer at the right onto the chalkboard, omitting the italicized answers. Instruct students to copy the organizer and to complete it by describing each stage or development. Discuss the answers with the class. Then have students discuss how American society might be different today if adolescence had not developed as a distinct life stage. Finally, have each student create a poster that illustrates the historical development of adolescence in the United States.

ENGLISH LANGUAGE LEARNERS

Prior to 1860s
Adolescence did not exist as a separate life stage. Children treated as small adults.

Education
Children stay in school longer; extended period of dependence

Work
Laws restricted child labor, also increasing length of dependency

Courts
Juvenile-justice system legally distinguished between youth and adults.

Effect
Development of adolescence as a distinct life stage between childhood and adulthood

INTERPRETING VISUALS During the 1900s, after years of political pressure, states began to pass laws banning child labor. *How do you think labor like this prevented these children from having an adolescent period of life?*

Interdisciplinary Connection

HISTORY

The Fair Labor Standards Act. Child labor was common in the United States throughout the 1800s. The Fair Labor Standards Act, which went into effect in 1938, brought an end to child labor in most of the country's major industries. The act set the minimum age at 14 for nonmanufacturing jobs outside of school hours. It banned children under age 16 from working during school hours in industries engaged in interstate commerce. In addition, youth had to be at least 18 years of age to hold jobs that the U.S. secretary of labor defined as hazardous.

RESEARCH ACTIVITY: Have students conduct research on either current U.S. federal, state, and local laws regarding child labor or on child labor in other parts of the world, such as Asia.

Visual Answer

The work kept children too busy to have time for leisure activities common among teenagers today and forced children to take on adult responsibilities and pressures.

most students do not take on the other roles of adulthood, such as spouse, parent, and provider.

The second factor that distinguishes young people as a separate group is the exclusion of youth from the labor force. In most states, child-labor laws prevent people from working until age 16. When they do start working, most young people lack the training to compete for all but the most routine jobs. Working adolescents do not typically have full-time jobs. Most work part-time while continuing to go to school.

The third important factor in the rise of adolescence as a distinct stage of the life cycle is the development of

the juvenile-justice system. By distinguishing between juvenile and adult offenders, American society has created a separate legal status for young people.

Characteristics of Adolescence

The experiences of adolescence are not the same for everyone. However, five characteristics generally apply to all adolescents. These five characteristics are biological growth and development, an undefined status, increased decision making, increased pressures, and the search for self.

The Adolescent in Society **121**

Case Studies and Other True Stories

◧ TEACH

Before class, draw on the chalkboard a two-column chart and label the columns *Adults* and *Adolescents*. Down the left side of the chart list the terms *Clothes, Music, Recreation,* and *Other*. After class starts, have students state their views on how adults and teens behave for each topic as you fill in the chart. Students should consider similarities and differences. Then ask students to read the feature on this page, The Blurring of Adolescence, and answer the questions that follow. Afterward, have students discuss how the information in the feature compared to the chart they created. Have students discuss any differences between the two.

◧ EXTEND

Have the class work together to develop a hypothesis about teen and adult clothing styles. Next, have students decide how many people they would need to survey to test their hypothesis. Then organize students into small groups and have each group create a questionnaire about the topic. The questionnaire should include at least 10 statements or questions and should be easy to mark and tally. (You might provide a template to ensure consistency.) Have each group survey the chosen number of people and then report its findings to the class. Based on the results, have students re-evaluate their hypothesis. **COOPERATIVE LEARNING**, **BLOCK SCHEDULING**

◆ Case Study

Baby Boomers. About 76 million Americans were born between 1946 and 1964. These baby boomers have helped blur the distinction between adults and teenagers in the United States. During the late 1960s baby boomers defined themselves by rebelling against the status quo. Although most baby boomers now have children and some even grandchildren, many have not accepted that *they* are now the older generation.

ACTIVITY: Have students observe adults for two or three days and note any "youthful" behaviors or characteristics that the adults exhibit.

Case Studies
AND OTHER TRUE STORIES

THE BLURRING OF ADOLESCENCE

In recent years, a striking change has taken place in the images and roles of children and adults in industrialized countries. Children have become more adult-like, and adults have taken on more of the characteristics of children. It is becoming increasingly difficult to tell where one life stage ends and the next begins. This blurring of differences has occurred most notably in the areas of dress, behavior, and language.

Adults or Children?

Until relatively recently, one of the best indicators of age and role differences was clothing. Young people dressed in jeans and T-shirts. Adults wore suits, designer clothes, and other sophisticated fashions. Today, many adults—dressed in shorts, sneakers, and cartoon-character T-shirts—look like big kids. Some children, on the other hand, look like miniature adults in their three-piece suits and designer dresses. And people of all ages—from infants to grandparents—wear blue jeans.

Many child and adult behaviors are becoming similar as well. For example, the gestures, ways of sitting, and general posture of both groups are remarkably alike. Adults and children also play many of the same sports and even share an interest in certain toys. Video and computer games are popular with all ages. Unfortunately, many adults and children also share some of the same difficulties. In the last few years, alcoholism and suicide—once considered adult problems—have become much more common among young people.

Language has also spread across the generation gap. Adults have adopted many of the slang expressions and special vocabularies commonly used by adolescents. Even more significantly, children and adolescents now freely and openly discuss topics once discussed only by adults.

Television and the Internet

Television and the Internet have played major roles in the creation of adult-like children. Prior to the electronic age, children received much of their

One aspect of the phenomenon of the blurring of adolescence is the growing numbers of adults participating in youth-focused activities.

social information from the books that they read. These books contained information appropriate to a child's level of understanding. Adult information was contained in adult books, which children did not read. Today many children have access to adult information through television and the Internet. They are exposed to adult situations and adult views of life. Many social scientists believe that the removal of the barriers between child information and adult information has thrust children prematurely into the adult world.

Teenagers may be the biggest losers in this merging of adolescence and adulthood. Many childhood specialists fear that the shortening or blurring of adolescence may force young people to grow up too quickly. Social scientists argue that by rushing through adolescence, young people are missing many of the special features that the period has to offer. The adult-like child is denied the opportunity to experiment and to try on new roles without being judged by adult standards. According to child psychologist David Elkind, one of the results of hurrying through childhood is increased stress during adolescence and young adulthood.

Think About It

1. Summarizing *How does the blurring of adolescence and adulthood occur in dress, behavior, and language?*

2. Evaluating *Some social scientists suggest that the blurring of adolescence may make life for young people even more confusing. What confusion may the blurring of life stages bring?*

SUGGESTION 1: Call on students to identify the five general characteristics of adolescence *(biological growth and development, undefined status, increased decision making, increased pressure, and the search for self)*. List the stages across the chalkboard. Have students discuss and suggest examples of each characteristic. List the examples under the appropriate characteristic on the chalkboard. Then have each student rank the characteristics based on how difficult or stressful each one is for teens in general. Finally, have volunteers share their rankings with the class and explain them. Give other students a chance to provide feedback.

SUGGESTION 2: Have students help you create a chart on the chalkboard that identifies and describes the five general characteristics of adolescence *(listed in the Suggestion 1 activity)*. Then ask students to imagine that they write advice columns for a teen magazine. Organize students into pairs or groups of three and have each group create fictional letters from teens describing problems and write fictional responses providing advice. The teens' problems should relate to one or more of the five characteristics of adolescence, and the column as a whole should hit all five characteristics. Then call on volunteers to read their letters and responses to the class. Have other students try to identify the characteristics of adolescence being illustrated. **COOPERATIVE LEARNING**

Biological Growth and Development

Puberty is the one aspect of adolescence that is found in every society. Puberty is universal because it is biological rather than cultural in origin. The brain and the endocrine system—a group of glands that produce various hormones—control biological development.

During early adolescence, individuals often undergo spurts of growth in height and weight as well as changes in body proportions. In addition, they experience the development of primary and secondary sexual characteristics. Many also suffer complexion problems. According to the American Academy of Dermatology (AAD), almost all young people develop some form of acne. More than 40 percent of adolescents have cases of acne so severe that they seek medical advice and treatment. These various biological changes sometimes cause anxiety or embarrassment, which is particularly true when the individual is physically way ahead or way behind others of the same age.

INTERPRETING VISUALS During adolescence, teenagers not only develop biologically, but also experience increased decision-making oportunities. *How is deciding what to wear and what to spend money on an important part of adolescence?*

SUGGESTION 3: Organize students into small groups and ask each group to create a large five-panel comic strip, in which each panel illustrates one of the five general characteristics of adolescence *(listed in the Suggestion 1 activity)*. Have each group present its comic strip to the class and then display the comic strips around the classroom. **COOPERATIVE LEARNING**

HOMEWORK: Have each student create either a drawing, poem, or song lyrics that illustrate the five general characteristics of adolescence *(listed in the Suggestion 1 activity)*. When students next meet, have volunteers share their work with the class.

CONNECTING *to the Arts*

Have students examine art books or visit local art museums to find appropriate artistic depictions of youth at different points in history. Next, ask students to select five pieces of art and photograph or photocopy them. Then, for each piece, have students write a few paragraphs describing the selection, identifying the historical period in which it is set, and analyzing how it depicts youth at that time. Have volunteers present some of their selections to the class. Encourage other students to provide feedback.

BLOCK SCHEDULING

Case Study

Hazing. One specific form of peer pressure that many adolescents face is hazing. This activity requires people to do embarrassing, difficult, or dangerous acts to become part of a group. Some people consider hazing a harmless rite of passage that promotes team or group unity. However, hazing can also be humiliating, unsafe, and even deadly. Vermont high schooler Lizzie Murtie took action after undergoing hazing as a new member of the gymnastics team. Murtie's efforts helped lead to an antihazing law in Vermont. Most states ban at least some forms of hazing.

CRITICAL THINKING
Do you support the use of some forms of hazing? Explain your answer.

ANSWER: Answers will vary, but students should consider the issues on each side.

Table Answer

45.3 percent

Technology Resources

Teaching Transparency: Participation in Extracurricular Activities by Categories of 12th Graders (in percent)

Undefined Status Our society's expectations for children are quite clear. The expectations for adults are also known. The adolescent expectations are often vague, however. While some adults treat adolescents as children, others treat them as adults. It is often difficult for adolescents to determine their status. For example, many U.S. states allow young people to marry—with parental consent—at age 16. However, they must be 18 before they can legally vote.

Different people have different attitudes about adolescents. Some people are youth-oriented and have adopted some of the values and styles of dress that are popular among teenagers. On the other hand, adults are often critical of the way some adolescents dress, the music they listen to, and the way they behave.

Increased Decision Making Young children have most of their decisions made for them by adults. When children reach adolescence, they must make many of their own decisions. What courses should they take in school? What sports should they participate in? What school clubs should they join? Should they consider a college education? What career should they follow?

There seems to be no end to the decisions that must be made. Some of these decisions are of little long-term importance. Other decisions, such as choosing a career, have far-reaching consequences.

Increased Pressure Adolescents are faced with pressure from many sources. For example, parents generally make rules on what time their children must be home, whom they can see, and where they can go. Yet parents also want their children to have an active social life and to develop strong friendships. Thus, young people are under pressure to strike a balance between parental wishes and peer pressures. Adolescents also have pressures placed on them in school. They are required to attend classes, complete assignments, pass tests, and participate in activities.

Perhaps the greatest pressures come from peers. Teenagers want to be accepted by their peers and to be a part of the "in" group. If their friends have cars, most teenagers will feel some pressure to have cars of their own. Teenagers are also pressured to go along with the latest fads and fashions. Each year, billions of dollars are spent designing and marketing clothes, cosmetics,

Participation in Extracurricular Activities by Categories of 12th Graders (in percent)

Extracurricular Activity	White	African American	Hispanic	Asian American	American Indian
Team sport (interscholastic)	30.8	32.3	25.8	28.3	30.4
Individual sport (interscholastic)	20.9	21.2	14.9	21.6	20.7
Cheerleading	7.4	10.6	6.7	5.1	11.9
School band/orchestra	19.6	24.4	16.9	17.7	16.8
School play/musical	16.1	15.9	10.6	13.7	14.0
Student government	15.4	16.7	14.7	14.6	14.3
Honor Society	19.6	14.0	12.5	27.2	13.6
Yearbook/newspaper	19.7	14.3	16.8	18.9	21.2
Service clubs	13.6	13.6	14.4	19.3	11.6
Academic clubs	25.8	20.7	22.6	32.3	17.7
Hobby clubs	7.4	6.6	9.1	11.3	10.8
FTA/FHA/FFA*	17.6	22.5	16.4	8.8	22.1

(*Future Teachers of America, Future Homemakers of America, and Future Farmers of America)
Source: U.S. Department of Education, National Center for Education Statistics

INTERPRETING TABLES Extracurricular activities are an important part of the socialization process for teenagers in America. *How much greater of a percent of American Indians participated in athletic activities than in academic clubs?*

Have each student read one of the following books which focus on child labor in the United States: *Growing Up in Coal Country* by Susan Campbell Bartoletti, *We Have Marched Together* by Stephen Currie, *Child Labor: Then and Now* by Laura Offenhartz Greene, or *Cheap Raw Material* by Milton Meltzer. Have each student prepare a book report about the selected book. Then have volunteers or students that you choose present their reports orally to the class. Finally, have the class discuss the effects of child labor laws on American society. **BLOCK SCHEDULING**

CLOSE

Review with students the three major changes that led to the development of adolescence as a distinct life stage in the United States *(mandatory education, child labor laws, and the juvenile justice system)* and the five general characteristics of adolescence *(biological growth and development, undefined status, increased decision making, increased pressure, and the search for self)*. Then have students discuss which one event or characteristic in each category they feel is the most important and why.

INTERPRETING VISUALS Teenagers often face many challenges when dealing with the many roles they have to play and when developing a sense of self. *How can communicating with parents help teenagers deal with these challenges?*

Applying Sociology

Working Teens. Experts disagree about whether working benefits students. In 2000 some 44 percent of teens 16 to 17 years old worked at least part-time. Some experts believe working helps teens learn responsibility, how to manage money, and other skills that help prepare them for the future. Other experts cite that teens who work more than 20 hours a week are less likely to get enough sleep and are more likely to have lower grades and to take drugs.

ACTIVITY: Have students briefly debate the potential benefits and risks of working while attending high school.

Did You Know?

Adolescents require about 9 hours and 15 minutes of sleep a night—even more than children. One reason may be because most physical and sexual development at this life stage occurs during sleep.

Visual Answer

Parents can share what they learned through their own experiences and provide guidance and wisdom.

sports equipment, magazines, movies, and compact discs to teenage consumers. In most cases, the advertisements for these products attempt to utilize peer pressure.

Adolescents also face pressure to establish relationships. Acceptance and popularity are central concerns. What does it take to be popular? How can a meaningful relationship be established? What should be done to maintain it? Such questions are of great importance to adolescents.

Some adolescents also face job-related pressures. The first pressure is that of finding a part-time or summer job. Then there is the pressure of having enough time for family life, a job, schoolwork, and social activities. Adolescents

often find themselves in situations where their various roles of son or daughter, employee, student, athlete, club member, and friend conflict with one another.

The Search for Self Adolescents are mature enough to think about themselves and about what they want out of life. Most teens can sort through their values

REVIEW AND ASSESS

Have students complete the **Section 1 Review** on p. 126. As **Alternative Assessment**, you may want to use the development of adolescence poster or the characteristics of adolescence comic strip in this section's lessons.

RETEACH

Using the key terms and concepts in this section, create cards for a game of charades. Then organize the class into two or more teams and have them compete to silently demonstrate and correctly identify each term or concept.
ENGLISH LANGUAGE LEARNERS , COOPERATIVE LEARNING

EXTEND

Have each student write a short essay in response to the following question: Which of the characteristics of adolescence presents the most problems for today's teenagers? Remind students to provide reasons or examples to support their positions and to use standard grammar, spelling, sentence structure, and punctuation. Then select the two or three best essays and have their authors read them to the class. Encourage discussion and feedback from other students. **BLOCK SCHEDULING**

SECTION 1 REVIEW ANSWERS

1. Define:
• adolescence, p. 120
• puberty, p. 120
• anticipatory socialization, p. 126

2. the mandatory education of children through age 16, child labor laws, the development of the juvenile-justice system

3a. because in some societies, children immediately take on adult roles at a certain time

b. Students should describe the following characteristics: biological growth and development, an undefined status, increased decision making, increased pressure, and the search for self.

4. Paragraphs will vary, but students should address how different circumstances may affect each of the five general characteristics of adolescence.

and decide what things are really important to them. They can establish personal norms that will guide their behavior. They can also set priorities for their lives. Such abilities are extremely important. When people know who they are, what they want out of life, and which values will serve them best, they are in a better position to make the most of adulthood.

Preparing for future roles is one aspect of finding oneself. Thus, anticipatory socialization is quite an important part of adolescent development. **Anticipatory socialization** involves learning the rights, obligations, and expectations of a role to prepare for assuming that role in the future. For example, playing house as a child is a form of anticipatory socialization for adult family roles. During adolescence, the time for taking on adult roles is much closer at hand. Therefore, anticipatory socialization becomes much more important. A part-time job, club membership, and dating are three common forms of anticipatory socialization during adolescence.

These five characteristics of adolescence are quite general, and individual experiences may differ widely. Adolescents do not live solely in an adolescent subculture. For example, economic status, family composition, and place of residence can affect life during adolescence. Similarly, race, ethnicity, religion, and cultural heritage can make a difference in the kinds of adolescent experiences a person has.

A part-time job is one form of anticipatory socialization for an adult role. Many teenagers find part-time work in retail stores.

SECTION 1 REVIEW

1. Define and explain
adolescence
puberty
anticipatory socialization

2. Identifying Cause and Effect
Copy the graphic organizer below. Use it to identify the factors in American society that have led to the development of a separate stage of life called adolescence.

```
┌─────────────────────┐
│      Factors        │
│                     │
│                     │
│                     │
│                     │
└─────────────────────┘
        │         │
        ▼         ▼
   Adolescence as a Concept
```

3. Finding the Main Idea
a. Why do sociologists not consider adolescence to be a universal concept?
b. Describe the five general characteristics of adolescence?

4. Writing and Critical Thinking
Making Generalizations and Predictions
Write two paragraphs explaining how the experience of adolescence might differ from teenager to teenager because of individual circumstances.
Consider:
• economic status
• cultural background
• family structure
• region of residence

Homework Practice Online
keyword: SL3 HP6

126

SECTION 2

OBJECTIVES

1. *Summarize how dating developed as a form of social interaction.*

2. *Describe the functions that dating fulfills.*

 LET'S GET STARTED!

Before class, write the following questions on the chalkboard: *What is the societal purpose of dating? How do you think dating today differs from dating 25 or 30 years ago?* As students enter the classroom, have them answer the questions. Next, give students time to discuss each of the questions as a class. Then tell students that in Section 2 they will learn about dating in the United States, how it developed and has changed over time, and the social functions that it serves.

2 TEENAGERS AND DATING

● **Read to Discover**
1. How did dating develop as a form of social interaction?
2. What functions does dating fulfill?

● **Define**
dating, courtship, homogamy, courting buggy

● **Identify**
Willard Waller

Dating is a social behavior that is familiar to the vast majority of Americans—particularly teenagers. However, like adolescence, dating is not a universal phenomenon. **Dating**, or the meeting of people as a romantic engagement, is most commonly found in societies that allow individuals to choose their own marriage partners. In some societies marriages are arranged by parents or a go-between who negotiates a formal marriage contract between families. In some cases, the future spouses do not even see each other until their wedding day.

Because dating is so widespread in America today, it might seem as though it has been around forever. Actually, dating is a relatively recent phenomenon. It did not emerge as a form of social interaction between the sexes until just after World War I. Moreover, only in the past 60 years have sociologists taken an interest in dating as a topic of study.

Courtship and Dating

Prior to the rise of dating in the United States, interaction between young unmarried men and women was restricted to **courtship**. Courtship differs from dating in that courtship's express purpose is eventual marriage. Dating, on the other hand, may eventually lead to marriage. Its main purpose is entertainment and amusement, at least in the casual stages.

Dating is the means through which most individuals eventually do select their marriage mates in modern American society. Therefore, it might be helpful to view the process as a continuum. The continuum begins with casual dating, progresses to steady dating, and then moves on to engagement and, eventually, to marriage. As individuals move along the continuum, the degree of commitment given to the relationship increases. In the modern relationship system the interaction may stop at any point along the continuum. Some stages may be bypassed. Therefore, this relationship system is a very flexible one.

The courtship system that existed prior to dating was not this flexible. To understand courtship in modern terms, you might think of it as a point somewhere between steady dating and engagement on the continuum. Courtship was not casual, and roles were very strictly defined. To court a woman, a young man was expected first to meet her parents and ask their permission. It was also expected that the man's intentions would be honorable and, above all, marriage-minded.

Courtship was usually conducted in the parlor of the woman's home under close supervision or in a social situation among a group of people. Rarely was a couple left alone. If the relationship continued for any length of time, marriage was the expected outcome. Young people did have fun together during courtship, but its main purpose was to find a spouse. It was from this strictly structured base that the modern-day system of dating emerged.

INTERPRETING VISUALS At the beginning of the 1900s, courtship was the common means by which couples met and interacted. *Based on this image, how do you think courtship differs from dating today?*

SECTION 2 RESOURCES

REPRODUCIBLE & REVIEW
- Mastering Critical Thinking Skills 6
- Section 2 Review, p. 134

TECHNOLOGY
- One-Stop Planner, Lesson 6.2
- Homework Practice Online
- HRW Go site

Visual Answer

Courtship was more formal, and men took the initiative.

The Adolescent in Society **127**

SUGGESTION 1: To help students summarize how dating developed as a form of social interaction, copy the graphic organizer at the right onto the chalkboard, omitting the italicized answers. Have students copy and complete the organizer. Discuss the answers and ask students how these social changes combined to lead to dating. *(They made dating more acceptable and more practical as a form of interaction than formal courtship.)* Next, organize the class into groups and assign each group a period in the development of dating, such as before the Industrial Revolution, the 1920s, the 1950s, and today. Have each group write and perform a skit illustrating a typical date of that period.

ENGLISH LANGUAGE LEARNERS , COOPERATIVE LEARNING

Cause	Effect
Industrial Revolution	*People moved from the farms to the cities, where young adults could gain more economic freedom and their own homes. As a result, parental control over young adults and courtship decreased.*
Public Education	*By the 1900s most secondary-school students attended coeducational public schools, which increased interaction between boys and girls.*
Automobile	*Young adults had more freedom of movement away from parents.*
Telephone	*Young adults could more easily talk to members of the opposite sex.*
Equality of Women	*More women entered the workforce and took on more active community roles, which increased the interaction between single adult men and women.*

Dating in Colonial America. Courtship during the American colonial period involved some customs that would be considered strange today. For example, courting couples sometimes engaged in a custom called bundling. In this activity, parents allowed a man and woman to sleep in the same bed while clothed and separated by a board.

RESEARCH ACTIVITY: Have each student conduct research on the dating customs of another culture or time and share the results with the class.

Visual Answer

Answers might include telephones, movies, and computers and the Internet.

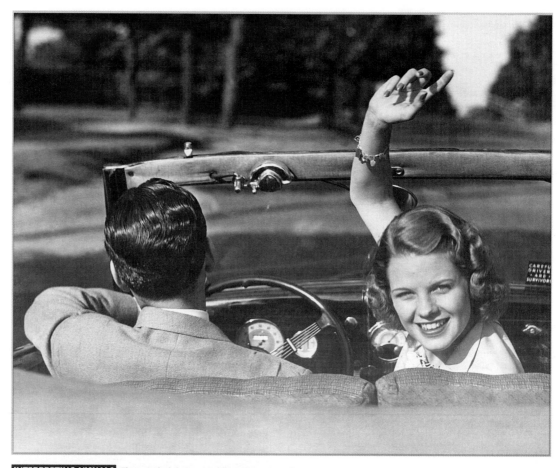

INTERPRETING VISUALS The arrival of the automobile in the early 1900s greatly transformed dating by allowing young couples more independence. *What other technologies have influenced dating?*

The Emergence of Dating

The rise of industrialization contributed greatly to the development of dating in the United States. Prior to the Industrial Revolution, the economy of the United States was based primarily on agriculture. The timing of marriage was determined by the age at which a man acquired the property necessary to support a family. This requirement generally meant that marriage was delayed until a young man's father was willing to transfer a portion of the family land to the son. Because family property was involved, parents exercised considerable control over the marriage choices of their children.

During the Industrial Revolution many people moved away from farms and into the cities. As a result, young adults became less dependent on their parents for economic security. They could seek employment away from the family farm and establish their own households independent of their parents' assistance. This economic freedom reduced parental control over courtship and set the stage for the development of dating.

Free public secondary education also helped to pave the way for dating. By the beginning of the 1900s, the majority of secondary-school students were enrolled in public schools. Unlike many private schools, public schools were coeducational, which meant that young men and women spent a good portion of their day with one another.

The trend toward dating accelerated in the years after World War I. During this time more and more Americans acquired telephones and automobiles. These two technological developments gave young people added freedom of movement. The 1920s also was a period of increased social and political equality for women. More women entered the workforce and took active roles in the community. As a result, the interaction between single adult men and single adult women increased. Under these changed social conditions, dating was a much more practical form of interaction than was the formal courtship system of earlier times.

Willard Waller conducted one of the earliest sociological analyses of American dating patterns. During the late 1920s and early 1930s, Waller studied the dating habits of students at Pennsylvania State University. Based on his findings, he concluded that casual dating was a form of entertainment that had little to do with mate selection. Status attainment and excitement were at the center of the dating process. Partners were selected on the basis of status characteristics, such as good looks, nice clothes, and popularity. Thus, dating contrasted sharply with the courtship process, in which the traits of dependability and honesty were most valuable.

Waller also found that dating on the Pennsylvania State campus was almost entirely limited to members of sororities and fraternities. Individuals dated people of similar social rank—members of the "best" fraternities dated members of the "best" sororities. Women ranked potential dates according to status characteristics such as fraternity membership, looks, money, clothes, cars, and dancing ability. The object was to be seen with the "right" people. To be seen with a person of lower status could damage an individual's social standing on campus.

INTERPRETING VISUALS During the 1920s Willard Waller found that sorority and fraternity life and dating were linked. Later studies challenged Waller's conclusions about the importance of status in dating. *How do you think dating today differs from dating in the 1920s?*

Later research challenged Waller's picture of the "rating and dating" game. Status attainment and entertainment are certainly major factors that attract people to casual dating. However, character and personality factors are also important. Many similarities exist between the qualities that an individual looks for in a casual date and what he or she looks for in a marriage partner. For example, status attainment is important both in casual dating and in spouse selection. In fact, status attainment is a function of **homogamy**—the tendency of individuals to marry people who have social characteristics similar to their own.

Connecting to Literature

■ TEACH

Have students read the feature Middletown on this page. Create on the chalkboard a two-column chart and label the columns *Positive Effects* and *Negative Effects*. Down the left side of the chart, write the terms *Automobiles* and *Movies*. Have students read the first Think About It question and then help you complete the chart to answer the question. Then organize students into groups and have each group create a similar chart but without any terms to the left. Have each group use its chart to answer the second Think About It question. **COOPERATIVE LEARNING**

■ EXTEND

Have students compare and contrast the themes of popular prime-time television shows over time. Determine how far back students' research should go based on the available resources. Students might contact local television networks or use old newspapers or magazines as resources. Students' should chart the shows and their main themes. Then have each student write an essay based on the research and the following questions: Have the themes of popular television shows changed over time, and if so, how? Do the themes reflect the time period? Do you think the shows' themes caused concern among parents at the time? **BLOCK SCHEDULING**

◆ People in Sociology

The Lynds. Robert and Helen Merrell Lynd are credited with being the first social scientists to apply methods of cultural anthropology to a modern Western city. Robert Lynd (1892–1970) taught sociology at Columbia University. Helen Merrell Lynd (1896–1982) taught at Sarah Lawrence College. The Lynds' follow-up study to *Middletown* was *Middletown in Transition* in 1937. In this study, the Lynds examined the social changes in Middletown as a result of the Great Depression.

CRITICAL THINKING

How do studies such as *Middletown* contribute to sociology today?

ANSWER: Students might mention that such studies help sociologists see how various factors have affected society in the past and the ways in which society is changing.

Think About It Answers

1. Both initially seemed to bring families together but then developed into sources of disagreement and separation.

2. Answers will vary, but students might mention the Internet, cell phones, instant messaging, and new developments in the recording of music and video.

CONNECTING TO
Literature

MIDDLETOWN

The Industrial Revolution of the late 1800s brought enormous change to the United States. Social scientists Robert S. and Helen Merrell Lynd wondered what effects this change had on American culture. They thought the best way to find out was to look at how industrial and technological innovations had affected everyday life in a typical small American town. Their 1929 study of Muncie, Indiana, Middletown: A Study in Modern American Culture, *has long been considered a classic of sociological literature. In the following excerpts, the Lynds discuss how two innovations—the automobile and the movies—affected the behavior of young people in Middletown.*

"Many families feel that an automobile is justified as an agency holding the family group together. 'I never feel as close to my family as when we are all together in the car,' said one . . . mother. . . . Sixty-one per cent of 337 boys and 60 per cent of 423 girls in the three upper years of the high school say that they motor more often with their parents than without them.

But this centralizing tendency may be only a passing phase; sets in the other direction are almost equally prominent. 'Our daughters [eighteen and sixteen] don't use our car much because they are always with somebody else in their car when we go out motoring,' lamented one . . . mother. And another said, 'The two older children [eighteen and sixteen] never go out when the family motors. They always have something else on.' . . . 'What on earth do you want me to do? Just sit around home all evening?' retorted a popular high school girl of today when her father discouraged her going out motoring for the evening with a young blade in a rakish car waiting at the curb. The fact that 348 boys and 382 girls in the three upper years of the high school placed 'use of the automobile' fifth and fourth respectively in a list of twelve possible sources of disagreement between them and their parents suggests that this may be an increasing decentralizing agent. . . .

How is life being quickened by the movies for the youngsters who bulk so large in the audiences . . . ?

Actual changes of habits resulting from the week-after-week witnessing of . . . films can only be inferred.

Robert S. and Helen Merrell Lynd found in their 1929 study on Muncie that the automobile played an important role in dating and teen life.

Young Middletown is finding discussion of problems of mating in this new agency that boast in large illustrated advertisements, 'Girls! You will learn how to handle 'em!' and 'Is it true that marriage kills love? If you want to know what love really means, its exquisite torture, its overwhelming raptures, see — —.'

'Sheiks and their shebas,' according to the press account of the Sunday opening of one film, '. . . sat without a movement or a whisper through the presentation. . . . It was a real exhibition of love-making and the youths and maidens of [Middletown] who thought that they knew something about the art found that they still had a great deal to learn.'

Some high school teachers are convinced that the movies are a powerful factor in bringing about the 'early sophistication' of the young and the relaxing of social taboos. One . . . mother frankly welcomes the movies as an aid in child rearing, saying, 'I send my daughter because a girl has to learn the ways of the world somehow and the movies are a good safe way.' The judge of the juvenile court lists the movies as one of the 'big four' causes of juvenile delinquency, believing that the disregard of group mores by the young is definitely related to the witnessing week after week of fictitious behavior sequences that habitually link the taking of long chances and the happy ending."

Think About It

1. **Evaluating** *According to the excerpt, what positive and negative effects did the automobile and movies have on the lives of young people in Middletown?*

2. **Making Generalizations and Predictions** *What technological innovations are bringing changes to the lives of young Americans today? Are these changes positive or negative? Why?*

SUGGESTION 1: Organize the class into small groups and have each group write answers to the following questions:

- Why do people they know date?
- What are some benefits and drawbacks of teen dating?
- What can be learned from dating—if anything?
- Do boys and girls view dating differently? If s~~o how?~~

Compile the answers of each group on an overh~~ead~~ the chalkboard. Next, have students identify an~~d~~ tions of dating described in this section (entertai~~nment,~~ fulfillment of psychological needs, status, and sp~~ouse~~ have students relate these functions to their list

COOPERATIVE LEARNING

SUGGESTION 2: Organize the class into five groups and assign each group one of the following functions of dating: entertainment, socialization, fulfillment of psychological needs, status, or spouse selection. Tell students that their group is to write a summary of its assigned function and then prepare a strong argument explaining why this function of dating is the most important. Have each group present its summary and arguments to the class. Then have the class vote on which argument was most persuasive. Finally, have students ~~rank the functions of dating~~ based on how important each one is to ~~them. Have volunte~~ers to share their rankings with the class

~~COO~~PERATIVE LEARNING

Handwritten note:
- Entertain./fun
- Socialization
- psych. needs
- Status
- Spouse selection

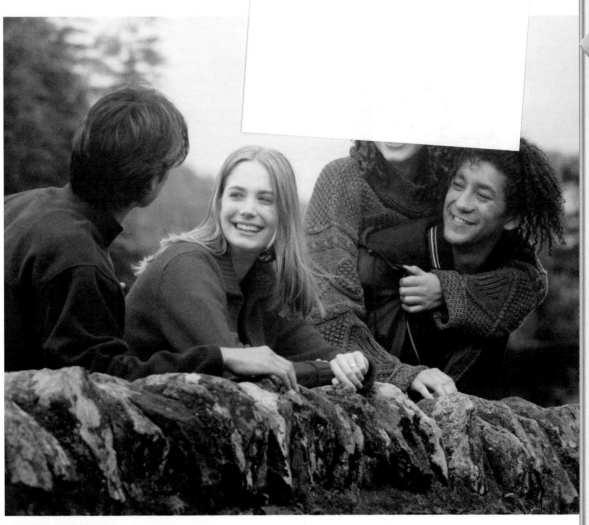

INTERPRETING VISUALS Today dating serves many social functions such as entertainment, socialization, companionship, and status obtainment. *How might double-dating provide these functions?*

Why Date?

Dating serves several important functions in adolescence. First, dating is a form of entertainment. Dating allows **1** young people to get together to simply have fun. This goal is particularly true in the case of casual dating. Second, **2** dating is a mechanism for socialization. It teaches individuals about members of the opposite sex and how to behave in social situations. It also helps individuals to learn appropriate role behaviors and to define their self-concepts. Third, dating fulfills certain basic psychological **3** needs such as conversation, companionship, and understanding. Fourth, dating helps individuals attain status. In **4**

societies where individuals choose their own marriage partners, people are judged in part by whom they date. Dating a person who is valued by others as a potential date can raise one's own status. Finally, in the later stages of **5** dating, spouse selection becomes an important issue.

All of these functions are not necessarily present at each stage of the dating continuum. If they are present, they may not carry the same weight. For example, in the case of casual dating, entertainment and status attainment may be, as Waller suggested, the most important functions. However, as the level of commitment in a relationship increases, socialization and companionship may be of primary concern.

Sociology in the World Today

Speed Dating. Have you ever been on a date so bad you felt it would never end? A new trend in dating works to end this problem. Groups and clubs are now hosting events where singles have several short dates in one evening. First, organizers pair men and women into couples. Each couple has 5 to 10 minutes to chat. A buzzer or bell then sounds, and people form new couples. No last names or phone numbers are exchanged. At the end of the night, each person submits a form indicating anyone he or she would like to see again. If two people indicate each other, organizers contact them.

ACTIVITY: Have small groups brainstorm other new dating approaches. Then have students discuss the ways in which trends such as this one might affect society.

Visual Answer

Answers will vary, but students might say that double dates might ease some of the nervousness or pressure to make conversation, thus increasing the fun of a date.

Dating Patterns

Dating patterns, like dating relationships, can be viewed as a continuum. On one end are traditional dating patterns. These are the ones most closely associated with dating behavior prior to the 1960s. On the other end of the continuum are the informal patterns that are characteristic of dating today.

Traditional Dating Patterns Traditional dating patterns can still be found in small towns and rural areas of the United States. However, they are most characteristic of dating during the 1940s and 1950s. Under the traditional dating system, responsibility for arranging a date fell to the man. He was expected to contact his intended dating partner, suggest a time and place for the date, select the activity, and pay for any expenses that arose.

Dating behavior was quite ritualized. Both parties knew what was expected of them because the rules of conduct were well defined by the group to which they belonged. Pressure to conform to expected behavior was strong. Behavior that was not in line with group expectations met with sharp disapproval. In most cases, an established weekly timetable for setting up a date existed. If Wednesday was the designated day for arranging Saturday night dates, attempts made later in the week often met with rejection. Accepting a date late in the week was often seen as an acknowledgment by a young woman that she was not a young man's first choice. Dating was so expected and so tied to social status that individuals who did not have dates on prime dating nights were known to hide in their rooms in shame.

Particularly in the early stages of a relationship, dates revolved around set activities such as going to movies or sporting events. This type of activity often helped to lessen the stress felt by dating partners. For example, if interaction between them proved awkward, they could focus their attention on the activity.

If a couple continued to date casually over a period of time, the relationship often developed into one of steady dating. This type of dating carried with it a formal set of expectations and commitments. As a visible symbol of commitment, the young man often gave the young woman his class ring, identification bracelet, or letterman's jacket. Because of the level of commitment involved, steady dating acted as a form of anticipatory socialization for marriage. Even so, steady partners were not necessarily expected to get married. Individuals commonly had several "steadies" at different times before settling on a marriage partner.

Contemporary Dating Patterns Since the 1960s, dating has not followed such formal patterns. Today there is greater opportunity for young men and women to interact with each other informally. There are no set stages of dating. In addition, there is now greater equality in dating. Both men and women now actively initiate dates. Similarly, it is acceptable for either partner to pay for the date or for each person to pay his or her own way.

This tendency toward flexibility reveals some important differences between traditional and contemporary dating patterns. Under the traditional dating system,

In traditional dating patterns a man often gave an identification bracelet as a sign of commitment. Today—with contemporary dating practices—there is greater equality in dating, and it is common for both women and men to initiate dates.

Sociology in the World Today

TEACH

Have students read the feature Themes in Popular Songs on this page. Then have students work in pairs or in small groups to conduct the activity described in the feature. Before students start their research, you might want to create the checklist chart for the activity and make copies for each group or each student. Then have each group discuss its findings and write one or two paragraphs summarizing them. Call on each group to present its summary to the class. Help students examine how the current culture and political, economic, and social events can influence popular music.

COOPERATIVE LEARNING

SPOTLIGHT *on Themes in Advertising for Youth*

Have each student locate and collect at least 10 advertisements geared toward teenagers. Students might collect print advertisements, record advertisements off television, or write down detailed descriptions of televised advertisements. Then have each student create a chart showing the main methods or themes that the ads use to attract teenagers' attention and get them to buy the advertised products. Have students share their findings with the class and discuss how themes in advertisements directed at teens relate to common themes found in popular teen music.

BLOCK SCHEDULING

SOCIOLOGY IN THE
World Today

THEMES IN POPULAR SONGS

Music is a basic part of adolescence. Many adolescents consider it very important to own the latest compact discs. They also spend many hours listening to their favorite songs on the radio. What themes are stressed in these popular songs? How do these themes relate to the lives of adolescents? A little research in the form of content analysis can help you answer such questions.

Themes of recent popular music hits—such as love, relationships, and commitment—have appealed to many teenagers.

Issues in Adolescence

Before focusing on these questions, reread this chapter's sections on the characteristics of adolescence and on the dating relationship. Based on this information, compile a list of issues that are important in adolescence. The list might include:

A. the effects of, or problems with, physical maturity
B. the effects of, or ways of dealing with, the undefined status of adolescents in modern society
C. the problems associated with, or benefits of, increased decision-making power during adolescence
D. the increased pressures of adolescence
E. the problems involved in establishing meaningful relationships
F. the search for self-identity during adolescence
G. the forms of anticipatory socialization common in adolescence
H. the learning of correct ways to behave in social and other situations
I. the importance of establishing friendships with members of the opposite sex
J. the need to be flexible in relationships
K. the expectations and commitments involved in relationships

Reviewing the Songs

Now you are ready to tackle the questions. First, you will need to obtain a list of the top 40 or 50 songs currently on the charts. Music stores and radio stations that play popular music have such lists. Next, listen to as many of the songs as you can. It might be easier to use songbooks or other sources of printed lyrics, when available. As you examine each song, jot down information that will enable you to answer the following questions:

1. What is the name of the song?
2. What is the main theme of the song?
3. Are there any secondary themes?
4. What are the key words or phrases in the song that give a clue to the main theme or secondary theme?

After you have gathered this information for a sufficient number of songs, compare the song themes with the issues raised in the chapter. To help you tabulate your findings, it might be helpful to construct a chart. The letters refer to the issues in the list you compiled, and the numbers refer to the songs you reviewed. Each song can have an entry in as many lettered categories as applicable. Each time a song deals with an issue, place a mark in the appropriate square of the chart. Once you have analyzed all of the material, count the number of marks in each square to get an idea of which themes appear to be the most common in popular songs.

Think About It

1. **Drawing Inferences and Conclusions** *Which song theme appears most often in the songs you reviewed? Why do you think this is so?*
2. **Analyzing Information** *Conduct a similar study of the books that are most popular with adolescents. Which themes appear most often in these books?*

---

interaction was formal and the relationship centered on the couple. In order to obtain a date, some men thought they needed to have a good "line"—a method of selling themselves to an intended date. Today relationships are based more on friendship and the group—than on the couple. Consequently, it is less often necessary to use a "line" to create a false but favorable first impression.

The traditional dating practices of the Amish of Lancaster County, Pennsylvania, offer an interesting counterpoint to contemporary dating patterns. The Amish have lived in the United States for several hundred years but choose to have little to do with society outside of their own community. The Amish devote themselves to farming and live without electricity, telephones, automobiles, appliances, or any other mark of the modern world.

The dating activities that many of today's high school students take for granted are practically unknown to Amish youth. Amish communities have no movie theaters, beaches, football stadiums, or cars. Yet practically all Amish youth date, court, and eventually marry.

The Amish begin dating around the age of 16. At this age Amish men customarily receive their own **courting buggy**, or horse-drawn carriage. Most opportunities for young Amish men and women to spend time together occur at formal events. These opportunities include picnics, weddings, cornhuskings, and barn raisings. However, the best time for arranging dates comes at Sunday evening "singings." At these, women and men sit across from each other, sing hymns, and talk. After the singing, they mingle socially. At the end of the evening, some men and women pair off. The men then escort the women

home, either by buggy or on foot. If the two begin to go steady, they usually see each other on dates once every one or two weeks. They are usually very discreet about dating and only make a public announcement of their relationship when they decide to marry.

Dating is a serious business for Amish youth because it is done with marriage in mind. They must be very careful in their selection of a spouse, because the Amish faith does not recognize divorce.

Young Amish men begin dating after they receive their first courting buggy.

SECTION 2 REVIEW

1. Define and explain
dating
courtship
homogamy
courting buggy

2. Identify and explain
Willard Waller

3. Sequencing Copy the continuum below. Use it to sequence the stages of commitment in the dating process.

Least Commitment ◄——┬———┬———┬———► Most Commitment

4. Finding the Main Idea

a. How did the rise of industrialization contribute to the development of dating in the United States?

b. What are the five functions served by dating?

5. Writing and Critical Thinking

Comparing and Contrasting Write two paragraphs comparing traditional dating patterns with dating patterns common today. Consider:
- the ritualized nature of traditional dating patterns
- the informal nature of modern dating patterns

Homework Practice Online
keyword: SL3 HP6

SECTION 3

OBJECTIVES

1. *Identify some of the social problems facing contemporary teenagers.*
2. *Trace the causes and consequences of these problems.*

3

CHALLENGES OF ADOLESCENCE

● **Read to Discover**
1. What are some of the social problems facing contemporary teenagers?
2. What are the causes and consequences of these problems?

● **Define**
drug, social integration

Adolescence can be a turbulent and perplexing time of life. The characteristics of adolescence that mark it as a distinct life stage give rise to pressures and problems not generally found in childhood. Caught between the relative safety of childhood and the supposed independence of adulthood, teenagers face important developmental tasks. These tasks include carving out an identity, planning for the future, becoming more independent, and developing close relationships. Most teenagers accomplish these tasks with minimal trauma. However, others do not. For these teenagers, life at times can seem overwhelming.

The 1980s and 1990s saw a boom in scientific research on the adolescent stage of development. Much of this research focused on the problems that teenagers face. Some of the more serious issues addressed in this research include sexual behavior, drug abuse, and suicide.

Teenage Sexual Behavior

As with so many other social phenomena, the norms governing sexual behavior vary widely from society to society. Some small preindustrial societies permit adolescents to engage in sexual behavior before marriage. In some of these societies—such as the Trobrianders of the South Pacific Ocean—sexual experimentation is even encouraged. Such experimentation is viewed as preparation for marriage. In Western countries, on the other hand, traditional sexual values include strict norms against premarital sexuality. Traditional sexual values in the United States are an outgrowth of Puritan and Victorian views of sexual morality. According to these views, sexual activity should be confined to marriage.

Until the 1960s, traditional sexual values had the support of the vast majority of Americans—at least in principle, if not always in practice. However, in the 1960s and 1970s the development of the birth control pill, a youth counterculture, and the feminist movement led to what has been called the "sexual revolution."

During this revolution, the norms governing sexual behavior began to change. For many people, human sexuality became a topic that was openly discussed and explored. As a consequence, sexuality is a familiar feature of American culture today. For example, sexual references are common in the programs seen in the 98 percent of American households that own television sets. Similarly, varying degrees of physical intimacy are found in almost every film that does not carry a "G" rating. In addition, advertisers have for years been using the lure of sexuality to sell their products.

One of the unanticipated consequences of the changing norms concerning sexuality has been a dramatic increase in adolescent sexual behavior. As a result, social scientists now devote considerable time to measuring the rate of teenage sexual activity and to analyzing the factors that influence teenage sexuality.

The Rate of Teenage Sexual Activity Survey data from the Centers for Disease Control and Prevention (CDC) indicate that 29 percent of unmarried American females between the ages of 15 and 19 were sexually active in 1970. By 1995 the rate of sexual activity had increased to 50 percent for the same category of teenagers. Teenage childbearing showed a similar pattern. In 1970 there were 22 births per 1,000 unmarried teenage females. By 1996 the birthrate for unmarried teenage females had risen to 43. However, these recent numbers represent a drop since the early 1990s.

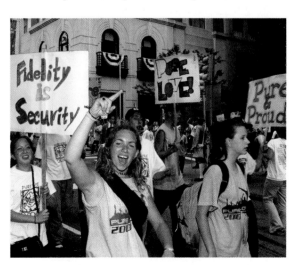

The recent drop in teenage sexual activity has come with the growth of pro-abstinence groups such as the Pure Love Alliance.

SECTION 3 RESOURCES

REPRODUCIBLE & REVIEW
- Graphic Organizer 6
- Study Skills and Writing Guide
- Section 3 Review, p. 143

TECHNOLOGY
- One-Stop Planner, Lesson 6.3
- **CNN**. Presents Sociology: Eating Disorders
- Homework Practice Online
- Teaching Transparency: Trends in Drug Use Among High-School Seniors, 1990–2001
- HRW Go site

SUGGESTION 1: To help students identify some of the social problems facing contemporary teenagers and trace the causes and consequences of these problems, copy the following graphic organizer onto the chalkboard, omitting the italicized answers. Have students copy and complete the organizer. Discuss the answers with the class. Then have each student create a poster designed to educate youth about one of these social problems and its negative consequences. Display students' posters around the classroom. **ENGLISH LANGUAGE LEARNERS**

Problem	Causes	Consequences
Teenage Sexual Behavior	loosening of norms concerning sexuality; low-income, one-parent families	teenage pregnancy; exposure to or acquiring STDs such as syphilis or AIDS
Teenage Drug Use	dropping out of school; having friends who use drugs; social and academic adjustment problems; hostile and rejecting family settings	increase in the use of some drugs among teens; increase in drug-related violence
Teenage Suicide	alcohol or drug use; triggering events such as a family crisis or other trials of adolescence; being female; social isolation; living in an underpopulated area; bad family environment; cluster effect from publicized suicides	death; possible cluster effects leading to other teenage suicides; rise in U.S. teenage suicide rate; teen suicide rate now exceeds that for adults

Case Study

Sex and the Media.
One study estimated that during the 1987–88 television season, young people in the United States viewed nearly 14,000 sexual acts on television. Of these acts, only about 165 of them addressed birth control, pregnancy, or sexually transmitted diseases.

RESEARCH ACTIVITY: Have students conduct research on school programs to help teenage mothers remain in school. Then have students discuss their findings with the class.

Did You Know?

According to a University of Michigan study, a woman's total earnings by age 29 were on average about $72,000 more if she had not borne a child while single and in her teens than if she had.

Graph Answer

The birthrate increased by about 18 million. Students might suggest questions such as the following: How has the increase in the number of births to unmarried women affected society overall?

The birthrate among American teenagers is considerably higher than it is among teenagers of other industrialized countries. During the 1990s the CDC established national health objectives to address this issue. CDC programs encouraged American teenagers to abstain from sexual activity. For those unwilling to abstain, the CDC has encouraged the use of effective methods of birth control. Surveys conducted in the late 1990s indicate that CDC programs have had some success. Sexual activity among teenagers declined during the decade, teenagers' use of birth control increased, and the teen-pregnancy rate fell.

Influences on Early Sexual Activity Social scientists have developed a number of explanations for why adolescents engage in sexual activity. Most often, these explanations focus on social and economic factors or on subcultural factors.

Among the social and economic factors found to influence early sexual activity are family-income level, parents' marital status, and religious participation. In general, teenagers from higher-income two-parent families have lower rates of sexual activity than teenagers from low-income one-parent families. Similarly, some teenagers who actively practice their religion tend to hold less-permissive attitudes and are less experienced sexually than some nonreligious teenagers.

Explanations that focus on subcultures suggest that teenage sexual activity is influenced by subgroup norms concerning sexual behavior. Generally, teenagers whose friends engage in premarital sex are more likely to be sexually active than those whose friends are not sexually active. Early sexual behavior is also associated with other risk-taking behaviors such as drug use and delinquency.

Consequences of Early Sexual Activity Sexual activity has consequences. For teenagers, these consequences are often negative. Some social scientists who study teenage sexuality focus on the social and health consequences of early sexual activity.

According to CDC statistics, less than one third of American teenage women who are sexually active use birth-control methods on a regular basis. Thus, it is not surprising that each year about 1 million teenage women become pregnant.

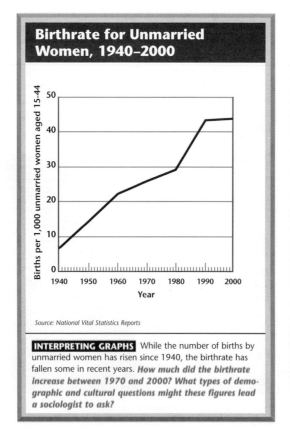

Birthrate for Unmarried Women, 1940–2000

Births per 1,000 unmarried women aged 15–44 (y-axis: 0, 10, 20, 30, 40, 50)
(x-axis: Year — 1940, 1950, 1960, 1970, 1980, 1990, 2000)

Source: National Vital Statistics Reports

INTERPRETING GRAPHS While the number of births by unmarried women has risen since 1940, the birthrate has fallen some in recent years. *How much did the birthrate increase between 1970 and 2000? What types of demographic and cultural questions might these figures lead a sociologist to ask?*

One negative affect of teenage pregnancy is the stress young mothers face as they try to balance raising a child and getting an education.

SUGGESTION 2: Have students take out a piece of paper and list a serious social problem that they think adolescents face today. Give students about 30 seconds to do the activity. When time is up, instruct each student to exchange his or her list with another student. Repeat the activity for several rounds. Then call on students to share with the class some of the items on their lists as you make a master list on the chalkboard. Have students discuss which issues they think are the most serious. Then call on students to identify the three adolescent social problems described in this section and trace the causes and consequences of these problems. *(See the graphic organizer on the previous page.)* Finally, organize students into six groups and assign each group one of the three problems. Have each group use the information in this section to design a television public service announcement related to the issue. Students might sketch out a storyboard for the spot or write a script. Then have each group present its public service announcement to the class.
COOPERATIVE LEARNING

 HOMEWORK: Have each student collect and summarize three current articles related to one or more of the following problems: teenage sexual behavior, teenage drug use, or teenage suicide. When students next meet, ask volunteers to read their summaries to the class. Encourage discussion.

Teenage pregnancy has been found to have a number of negative consequences. Chief among them are the following:

- Babies born to teenage mothers have lower birth weights and are more likely to die within the first year of life than are babies born to women older than 20.
- Teenagers who become mothers and fathers are less likely to finish high school and college than teenagers who do not become parents. This outcome is particularly true for teenage mothers.
- Due in large part to lower levels of education, individuals who become parents during adolescence have lower lifetime earnings than individuals who delay parenthood until later in life.
- Children of teenage parents are more likely to experience learning difficulties than children of older parents.
- Children of teenage parents have an increased risk of becoming teenage parents themselves.
- Teenage mothers often face significant emotional stress.

Even when pregnancy does not occur, early sexual activity can have negative health effects. Sexual contact exposes teenagers to sexually transmitted diseases (STDs), such as syphilis, gonorrhea, chlamydia, and acquired immune deficiency syndrome (AIDS). Studies indicate that some 4 million American teenagers contract a sexually transmitted disease each year. And about a quarter of all new cases of STDs occur among 15- to 19-year-olds. For example, in 2000 this age group accounted for 8 percent of all syphilis cases, about 28 percent of all gonorrhea cases, and nearly 40 percent of all chlamydia cases.

AIDS is a fatal disease caused by a virus that attacks the human immune system, leaving the person vulnerable to a host of deadly infections. This fatal disease is becoming an increasingly serious threat among the teenage population. High rates of sexual activity combined with low rates of condom use put teenagers at risk of contracting the disease through sexual contact with infected partners.

Studies show that teenagers are aware of the dangers of AIDS. Some 44 percent of 15- to 17-year-olds surveyed in 1998 said that AIDS is one of the most important health issues facing teenagers. Yet, at the same time, few teenagers say they think they are personally at risk of contracting AIDS or any other STD. However, according to the CDC, at least 50 percent of new HIV infections occur among people younger than 25. HIV is the virus that causes AIDS. More significantly, in the late 1990s AIDS ranked as the seventh leading cause of death among young people aged 15 to 24.

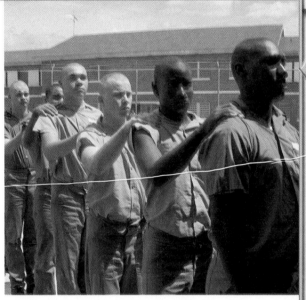
Drug use can have many negative consequences for teenagers, including jail time.

Teenage Drug Use

A **drug** is any substance that changes mood, behavior, or consciousness. Drugs exist in many forms, including medicines, alcohol, cigarettes, marijuana, cocaine, and heroin. Drug use has a long history. The Greeks smoked opium more than 3,000 years ago, and the Aztecs commonly used hallucinogens. In the United States the use of heroin and cocaine for nonmedical purposes was common until the early 1900s. In fact, even during the late 1800s cocaine could be found as an ingredient in a wide variety of products, including soft drinks, cough medicines, and nasal sprays.

Drug Violence In recent years, the public has become increasingly alarmed over the social consequences of drug abuse. This alarm is primarily a result of the dramatic increase in drug-related crime, during the 1980s and 1990s. Muggings, robberies, and burglaries committed by addicts in search of drug money have become a common occurrence. Even more frightening is the growth in violence associated with drug trafficking. During the mid-1990s about 1,000 drug-related murders occurred each year in the United States. This violence was largely the result of turf wars between rival gangs engaged in drug trafficking. Adult criminal gangs control the drug trade in the United States. However, the foot soldiers are often children and teenagers. Children as young as 9 or 10 are hired first as lookouts. In time, they rise in the gang hierarchy to become runners and eventually drug dealers.

Exploring Cultural Diversity

Mapping Teen Pregnancy. The five U.S. states with the highest rates of teenage pregnancy in 1997 were Mississippi, Arkansas, Louisiana, New Mexico, and Alabama. The five states with the lowest rates were Massachusetts, New Hampshire, New Jersey, Vermont, and Connecticut.

RESEARCH ACTIVITY: Have each student conduct research to find the most current rates of teenage pregnancy by state and then create a map illustrating the findings.

Did You Know?

Raising a child is not cheap. In 2000, the U.S. Department of Agriculture estimated the basic costs of raising an American child born that year to the age of 17 at about $233,000, after adjusting for inflation. One of the major costs is child care, which in 2000 ranged from an average of $4,000 to $6,000 a year.

SUGGESTION 3: Lead a class discussion on the social problems facing contemporary teenagers, with a focus on the causes and consequences of teenage sexual behavior, teenage drug use, and teenage suicide. Then have each student create three political cartoons that illustrate some of the negative consequences of teenage sexual behavior, teenage drug use, or teenage suicide. Tell students that the visual and textual content of their political cartoons must be appropriate for a mainstream daily newspaper. Students should provide a caption for each cartoon. Then ask volunteers to present their political cartoons to the class.

SPOTLIGHT *on Community Social Services*
Have students, working individually or in small groups, conduct research on the social services available for youth in their community, such as shelters for abused teenagers or suicide hot lines. Then have each group create a brochure or pamphlet designed to educate local youth about the social services available to them. Students' brochures or pamphlets may focus on one local social service or on several. Suggest that students who are covering several social services categorize them by issue or topic.

COOPERATIVE LEARNING, BLOCK SCHEDULING

Sociology in the World Today

Alcohol: The Forgotten Drug. Many people do not think of alcohol when they consider drug use. Yet alcohol abuse has serious consequences. For example, in the United States, deaths related to alcohol outnumber those related to illegal drugs four to one. Moreover, researchers estimate that crime, health problems, and missed work due to alcohol abuse cost the U.S. economy about $167 billion a year.

CRITICAL THINKING

What social factors do you think contribute to teenage alcohol abuse?

ANSWER: Answers will vary, but students might cite peer pressure, family environment, and the stresses of adolescence.

Table Answer

17 percent

Technology Resources

Teaching Transparency: Trends in Drug Use Among High-School Seniors, 1990–2001

Crack cocaine is the principal cause of the dramatic rise in drug-related violence. Crack is a highly addictive smokable form of cocaine. With the introduction of crack in the early to mid-1980s, drug-related juvenile arrests skyrocketed. Although these numbers dropped in 1998, more than 200,000 juveniles were arrested in the United States for drug-abuse violations. This number represents an 86 percent increase over 1990 figures.

The Rate of Teenage Drug Use Since 1975, the University of Michigan's Institute for Social Research has conducted an annual survey of high-school seniors. The table on this page shows changes in the rates of use for various drugs from 1990 through 2001.

As the table shows, usage patterns vary by type of drug. Although marijuana use declined in the early 1990s, it has risen in the last few years. Marijuana also remains the most widely used illegal drug among high-school seniors. Cocaine use has followed a similar pattern, but the use of hallucinogens such as LSD peaked in the mid-1990s. Use of new drugs such as MDMA, or ecstasy, has increased in the late 1990s and early 2000s. Cigarette smoking has dropped only slightly during the 1990s—despite repeated health warnings about the negative effects of smoking. Significantly, the survey indicates that 19 percent of high-school seniors smoke on a daily basis.

Alcohol use among teenagers has declined in recent years, but it remains a widespread problem. In 2000 some 73 percent of the high-school seniors surveyed reported having used alcohol at some point. In addition, 50 percent reported having had a drink as recently as a month before the survey was taken. Nearly 33 percent of the seniors surveyed said that they had five or more drinks on a single occasion within two weeks of the survey. These findings are particularly significant in light of the fact that it is illegal for virtually all high-school students to buy alcohol.

Any downward trend in drug use, however slight, is encouraging. Nevertheless, two factors should be kept in mind when analyzing the University of Michigan data. First, even with the recent declines, the United States has the highest rate of drug use among adolescents of any industrialized country. Second, the survey does not measure drug use among the approximately 11 percent of young Americans who do not graduate from high school. Research has indicated that high-school dropouts have much higher rates of drug use than do high-school seniors. Thus, it is likely that the survey underestimates the scope of the drug problem among teenagers.

Trends in Drug Use Among High-School Seniors, 1990–2001

	Percentage of Seniors Ever Having Used Drugs											
Drug	**1990**	**1991**	**1992**	**1993**	**1994**	**1995**	**1996**	**1997**	**1998**	**1999**	**2000**	**2001**
Marijuana/hashish	41	37	33	35	38	42	45	50	49	50	49	49
Inhalants	18	18	17	17	18	17	17	16	15	15	14	14
Hallucinogens	9	10	9	11	11	13	14	15	14	14	13	13
Cocaine	9	8	6	6	6	6	7	9	9	10	9	8
Heroin	1	1	1	1	1	2	2	2	2	2	2	2
Other narcotics	8	7	6	6	7	7	8	10	10	10	11	10
Amphetamines	18	15	14	15	16	15	15	17	16	16	16	16
Sedatives	8	7	6	6	7	8	8	8	9	10	9	9
Tranquilizers	7	7	6	6	7	7	7	8	9	9	9	9
Alcohol	90	88	88	80	80	81	79	82	81	80	80	80
Cigarettes	64	63	62	62	62	64	64	65	65	65	63	61

Source: *The Monitoring the Future Study, 2001*

INTERPRETING TABLES While the use of marijuana has dropped since 1987, the number of high-school seniors who have used the drug has risen in recent years. *Use the information in this table to create a line graph showing the changes in marijuana usage. How much did the use of marijuana grow between 1992 and 1999?*

Sociology in the World Today

◼ TEACH

Poll students about the amount of violence they are exposed to on average each week through computers, television, movies, music, video games, and other forms of media. Next, poll students about whether they think exposure to media violence leads to violent behavior and crime among youth. Write the results of the vote on the board and save them. Then ask students to read the feature Teen Violence on this page. Have the class discuss each Think About It question in turn. Finally, have students vote again on whether a link exists between media violence and teen violence. Discuss any changes in how students voted.

◼ EXTEND

Have each student conduct research on juvenile crime in their community, city, or state. Students might also examine methods being used in an attempt to reduce teen violence, such as curfews, youth centers, or anti-gang programs. Have students produce a poster or fact sheet providing information on incidents of juvenile crime by major categories such as homicides, assaults, burglary and robbery, vandalism, and minor misdemeanors. Have one or two volunteers present their findings to the class in the form of an oral report with visual aids. **BLOCK SCHEDULING**

SOCIOLOGY IN THE
World Today

TEEN VIOLENCE

Violence appears to be a growing problem among young people in the United States. In 2000, more than 20 percent of the people arrested for violent crimes were between 13 and 19 years of age. Teenagers were also victims of violent crime at higher rates than any other age group. With a growing number of incidences of school violence, sociologists have been searching for clues to the causes of teen violence. What accounts for the prevalence of violence among teenagers? Some studies suggest that the answer lies in American youth culture, particularly media-related aspects of the culture.

Violence and the Media

In a 2001 review of studies on the media and violence, the American Academy of Pediatrics (AAP) noted that television shows and movies—particularly those made for young people—are filled with violence. Much of this violence is presented in an entertaining and glamorous fashion. Because young people, on average, spend six hours or more a day using the media, they will likely be influenced by this view of violence. Some young people imitate the behavior they have seen others exhibit. The AAP suggests that if young people see their heroes resorting to violence to solve problems, they will do the same. In time, some young people accept violence as a legitimate form of behavior.

Citing several studies, the AAP argues that exposure to media violence is related to several problems among the young. Media violence may encourage aggressive behavior. For example, after playing violent video games, many young people show more aggression and exhibit violent behavior. Further, the AAP asserts that the media's heavy emphasis on violence makes the world look like a much more dangerous place than it is. As a result, some young people act more aggressively as a way to protect themselves from becoming victims of violence. Sociologists argue that the "violence as entertainment" presented by the media clouds young people's understanding of the consequences of violence—that it causes real harm to its victims.

To help keep schools safe and to halt teen violence, many schools have implemented strict security measures.

A Different View

Historian James Gilbert disagrees with that explanation of teen violence. Gilbert notes that in the 1950s, youth-oriented media—most notably crime and horror comic books—were blamed for the rise in juvenile delinquency. Congressional hearings were held on the issue, and the publishing industry agreed to control the excesses of these comic books. Over time, the comics did change. But the rate of juvenile crime did not fall. Similarly, Gilbert suggests, placing controls on the media will have little effect on teen violence.

Gilbert goes on to argue that the drive to control the media, both in the 1950s and today, may have little to do with teen violence or juvenile delinquency. The 1950s were a time of rebellion for many young Americans. They developed their own youth cultures that challenged their parents' demands for conformity. This independence was a truly disturbing development for most American adults, Gilbert wrote. Similarly, some older Americans today are disturbed by the development of the Internet, which has introduced the young to a new world of influences. Gilbert concludes that blaming the media for social problems may simply be an effort by adults to control what they do not like or understand.

Think About It

1. **Summarizing** *According to the AAP, what effects does media violence have on young people?*
2. **Supporting a Point of View** *Which theory about teen violence do you believe? Explain the reasons for your answer.*

◆ Applying Sociology

Teen Violence. Some experts argue that a media focus on teen violence has led to a wave of "Teenaphobia" across the United States. In response, many American cities have instituted youth curfews. In addition, the federal government passed the Violent Crime Control and Law Enforcement Act in 1994. This act contains special provisions for the prosecution of juveniles as adults.

RESEARCH ACTIVITY: Have students work in small groups to conduct research on various government programs aimed at decreasing youth violence. Have each group present an oral report to the class about one program and how effective it has or has not been.

Think About It Answers

1. The AAP argues that witnessing numerous violent incidents on television causes young people to act more violently.

2. Answers will vary, but students should address the arguments on each side as presented in the feature and provide reasons to support their positions.

140

CONNECTING to Science

Have each student use the library and other resources to conduct research on a popular recreational drug, such as alcohol, tobacco, marijuana, or cocaine. Students should create a poster or visual exhibit providing scientific information about the drug and its physical and behavioral effects in humans. Instruct students to provide the information in a way so that the average person can easily understand it. Then display students' work around the classroom.

BLOCK SCHEDULING

SPOTLIGHT
on Teens' Attitudes About Drug Use

Have the class work together to create a questionnaire about teenagers' attitudes about the use of alcohol, cigarettes, and illegal drugs. Then type the questionnaire and make five copies for each student. Instruct students to have five teens complete the questionnaire. Students should let the teens know that their responses will remain anonymous and that they should be as honest as possible. Then have the class tally the results and compare them to those in the chart on p. 138. Conclude with a class discussion about ways to reduce teen drug use. **COOPERATIVE LEARNING,**
BLOCK SCHEDULING

Sociology in the World Today

Steroids: The Quest to Be the Best. Recreational drugs such as alcohol, marijuana, and cocaine are not the only illegal drugs teenagers are abusing. The use of illegal steroids is also a growing problem among teenagers. A 2001 government survey of high-school seniors found that 3.7 percent reported having used steroids, up from 2.5 percent the year before. In addition, the number of high-school seniors who disapproved of steroid use dropped from 88.8 percent to 68.4 percent over the same time period.

CRITICAL THINKING

What social factors might be contributing to the increase in steroid abuse among teens?

ANSWER: Students might suggest the accessibility of illegal steroids over the Internet, an increased depiction in the media of muscular men as the ideal, and American society's focus on being the best.

Visual Answer

Such programs might help teach teenagers the dangers of drug use, ways to handle peer pressure to use drugs, and where to seek help with an existing drug abuse problem.

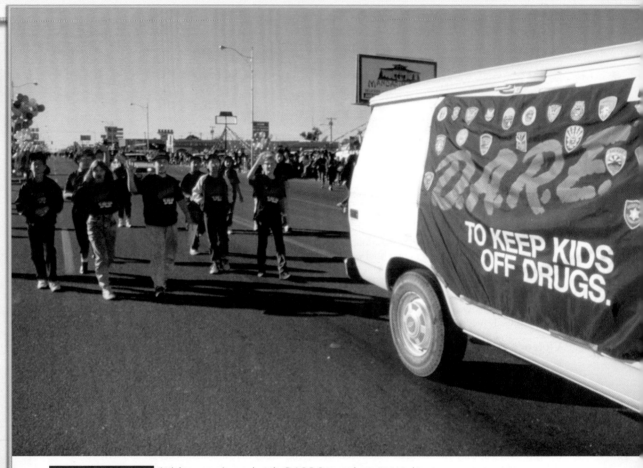

INTERPRETING VISUALS Anti-drug campaigns such as the D.A.R.E. Program have attempted to reduce teen drug use through education. *How might public activism such as this influence teenagers?*

Influences on Teenage Drug Use Why do teenagers use drugs? Social scientists have found a number of factors associated with the regular use of drugs by teenagers. Chief among these factors are

• having friends who regularly engage in drug use,
• having social and academic adjustment problems, and
• living in a hostile and rejecting family setting.

Teenage Attitudes Toward Drug Use The University of Michigan surveys also monitor changes in the attitudes of teenagers toward drug use. At the peak of marijuana use in 1979, only 42 percent of the seniors surveyed believed that regular marijuana use was harmful to one's health. By 2000 that figure stood at about 58 percent. Similarly, in the late 1970s approximately 69 percent of the seniors surveyed thought that regular cocaine use was harmful. By 2000 more than 85 percent of those surveyed reported that regular cocaine use was harmful to one's health.

The view that cigarette smoking is harmful has also gained supporters over the years of the survey. In 1975 slightly more than 51 percent of the seniors believed that smoking one or more packs of cigarettes a day was harmful to one's health. By 2000 that figure had increased to about 73 percent. However, attitudes toward the health dangers presented by alcohol have remained fairly constant—and low—over the course of the surveys. Over the years, less than 30 percent of seniors have thought that taking one or two drinks nearly every day was harmful.

In recent years, the disapproval ratings for regular use of marijuana and cigarettes have increased. For example, in 1977 slightly more than 65 percent of the seniors surveyed disapproved of regular marijuana use. By 2000 nearly 80 percent of those surveyed disapproved. However, the increase in the disapproval rate has been much smaller in the case of cigarette smoking. In 1977 about 66 percent of high-school seniors disapproved of smoking one or more packs of cigarettes a day. By 2000 that figure had increased to 70 percent.

Negative attitudes toward regular use of drugs—such as LSD, cocaine, heroin, amphetamines, and barbiturates—have remained fairly constant over the course of the surveys. Depending on the drug, disapproval ratings have ranged from 90 percent to 98 percent. Heavy daily use of alcohol received about a 90 percent negative response through the years of the survey.

Teenage Suicide

The social problems of teenage drug and alcohol abuse are contributing factors to another serious adolescent problem. The rate of suicide among young people in the United States has more than doubled in the past three decades. In 1997 Surgeon General David Satcher put the problem in perspective when he noted that "a youth suicide occurs once every 2 hours in our country, 12 times a day, 84 times a week . . . well over 4,000 times a year." As the chart on this page shows, the suicide rate for young people now exceeds the rate for the general population. Suicide is third only to accidents and homicides as the leading cause of death among people aged 15 to 24. It is the fourth leading cause of death among 10- to 14-year-olds.

Studies suggest that the actual number of suicides is higher than official statistics indicate. Many suicides are misreported as accidents. Deaths recorded as resulting from undetermined cause may actually be suicides. Researchers argue that suicide rates among the young would be much higher if certain accidental drownings, drug overdoses, and other similar deaths were taken into consideration.

In 1999 the CDC questioned high-school students on the topic of suicide. Some 8 percent of the students reported they had attempted suicide. Almost 20 percent said that they had seriously considered suicide. Some 14 percent of them had even made a suicide plan. While these findings are startling, it is important to keep in mind that suicide is a much more serious problem among elderly people. The rate of suicide for people aged 75 to 84 is almost twice as high as it is among the young.

The Sociological View of Suicide

When you think of the causes and consequences of suicide, you probably think in terms of individuals. You most likely see suicide as a personal act that results from psychological factors such as depression.

Sociologists acknowledge that suicide is an act committed by individuals, but they are more interested in the social factors that affect suicide rates. According to the sociological perspective, variations in suicide rates can be understood by studying the structure of society and the experiences of people.

Émile Durkheim's classic study *Suicide* is still the most comprehensive sociological analysis of suicide to date. Durkheim was interested in why some societies or groups within a society have higher rates of suicide than others. According to Durkheim, variations in suicide rates can be explained by the level of social integration in a group or society.

Social integration is the degree of attachment people have to social groups or to society as a whole. Durkheim predicted that groups or societies with particularly high or particularly low levels of social integration will have high rates of suicide.

In Durkheim's view, high levels of social integration can lead to increased rates of suicide because group members place the needs of the group above their own personal needs. For example, in the traditional Inuit society of Arctic North America, elderly people walked into the snowy wild to die once they became a burden on the group. Strong community bonds made the elderly value the welfare of the group over their own welfare.

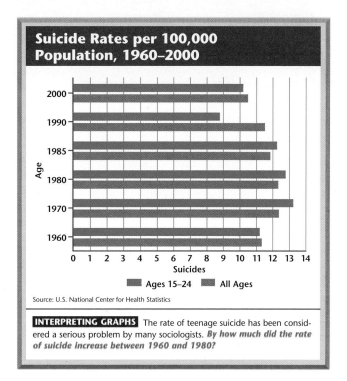

Suicide Rates per 100,000 Population, 1960–2000

Age

2000
1990
1985
1980
1970
1960

0 1 2 3 4 5 6 7 8 9 10 11 12 13 14
Suicides

■ Ages 15–24   ▨ All Ages

Source: U.S. National Center for Health Statistics

INTERPRETING GRAPHS The rate of teenage suicide has been considered a serious problem by many sociologists. *By how much did the rate of suicide increase between 1960 and 1980?*

Anna Bryant of Richmond, Virginia, suggested the following activity: Organize students into groups and have each group develop a state-wide campaign to decrease teenage drug use or teenage pregnancy in their state. The campaign should include a slogan and at least two types of publicity items, such as a poster, flyer, or script for a television ad. These items should provide related statistics and explain some of the consequences of the target behavior. Each group should conduct research to find state-specific information.

COOPERATIVE LEARNING, BLOCK SCHEDULING

CLOSE

Review with students the various social problems facing teenagers today and some of the causes and consequences of these problems. Then have students brainstorm ways to reduce these problems in their community or school.

REVIEW AND ASSESS

Have students complete the **Section 3 Review** on p. 143. As **Alternative Assessment**, you may want to use the teenage social-issues poster or public service announcement in this section's lessons.

Visual Answer

Such services provide places for teenagers to turn to when experiencing suicidal thoughts or feeling depressed. Such services can also help teach teens how to cope with the stresses of adolescence.

INTERPRETING VISUALS
Many schools and communities have initiated counseling services and suicide hotlines to reduce the number of suicides. *How might these services help teens?*

Suicides resulting from low levels of social integration are much more common than those resulting from high levels of integration. Low levels of integration occur in periods of social disorganization, which can result from many factors. Some common factors are rapid social change, increased geographic mobility, war or natural disasters, and sudden changes in economic conditions.

Suicide rates increase during periods of social disorganization because the norms that govern behavior weaken or become less clear. In addition, the social bonds that give individuals a sense of group solidarity—such as family ties and religion—tend to weaken during periods of social disorganization. Deprived of clear behavioral guidelines and adequate social support, some people turn to suicide as a last resort. Suicide caused by low levels of social integration is the form most commonly found in modern industrialized societies.

Predictors of Teenage Suicide As teenagers move from the role of child to that of adult, they are faced with new freedoms as well as new restrictions. Many of the norms that governed proper behavior during childhood no longer apply. Yet many adult behaviors are still considered inappropriate. At the same time, friends and the larger society have more and more influence over teenagers' beliefs and actions. As the control of the family lessens, teenagers begin to take increasing responsibility for their own actions.

Most teenagers adapt to these changing expectations. For some, however, the confusion and self-doubt common in adolescence are often blown out of proportion. Because teenagers tend to focus so much on the present, they often do not realize that most problems can be solved with time and patience. In some cases, social isolation and self-doubt lead to frustrations that may push adolescents toward suicidal behavior.

RETEACH

Have students work in pairs to create a 10-question, true-false quiz covering the content in this section. Student pairs should create an answer key on a separate piece of paper. When all pairs have completed their quizzes, ask students to exchange them, to answer the ones they receive, and then to return the quizzes to their authors to be checked for accuracy. Finally, have each pair review the results of its checked quiz. Review any topics with which students are still having difficulty. **ENGLISH LANGUAGE LEARNERS , COOPERATIVE LEARNING**

EXTEND

Invite one of the following types of professionals to speak to the class about trends in their field related to adolescents: health-care professionals, school nurses, psychologists or psychiatrists, social workers, police or probation officers, or school-resource officers. Afterward, have each student write one or two paragraphs summarizing what they learned. If having guest speakers is not a possibility, have students interview someone in one of these fields and present a short oral report about what they learn to the class.

BLOCK SCHEDULING

Suicide cuts across all social categories. There are cases of teenage suicide among both sexes; every economic level; and all races, religions, and nationalities. Nevertheless, certain social factors appear to affect the rates of teenage suicide. According to Brad L. Neiger and Rodney W. Hopkins, the following social factors are important:

- *Alcohol or drug use* The risk of suicide increases along with an adolescent's use of alcohol and drugs. Social scientists offer three explanations for this correlation. First, teenagers who are heavy users of alcohol and drugs typically have low levels of self-control and are easily frustrated. Second, teenagers under the influence of drugs or alcohol are more likely to act on impulse. Third, teenagers often use drugs and alcohol as the method by which to commit suicide.
- *Triggering events* In most teenage suicides, a specific event or the anticipation of a specific event triggers the suicide attempt. Common triggers include fear of punishment, loss of or rejection by an important person, unwanted pregnancy, family crisis, poor school performance, and a fight with a friend or parent.
- *Age* The risk of suicide increases with age. Although children under the age of 13 do commit suicide, rates are much higher for older teenagers and young adults.
- *Sex* Females are three times more likely than males to attempt suicide. However, males are much more likely to succeed. This outcome is partially a result of the fact that teenage men often choose guns and other weapons as the means by which to commit suicide.
- *Population density* Recent studies indicate that underpopulated areas have higher rates of teenage suicide than do heavily populated areas. Researchers believe that the higher rate may be a result of social isolation,

which is more likely in underpopulated areas. In addition, teenagers in underpopulated areas generally have access to fewer social services.

- *Family relations* As Durkheim noted, the weakening of social bonds increases the likelihood of suicide. Thus, it is not surprising that suicide rates are higher for teenagers from families in which violence, intense marital conflict, or the recent loss of a parent through divorce or death is evident. In addition, suicide is more common in those families in which parents show hostility or rejection toward their children.
- *Cluster effect* A teenage suicide sometimes results in other suicide attempts among adolescents in a community. This phenomenon is more likely to occur when a popular member of the community takes his or her life. In some instances, a well-publicized suicide can trigger "copycat" attempts in other communities as well. Mental-health officials suggest that the cluster effect occurs because the news of suicide acts as a fuse that ignites self-destructive behaviors in already unstable adolescents. Studies suggest that as many as 200 teen suicides a year are the result of the cluster effect.

As this list of factors indicates, teenage-suicide rates are influenced by the same sociological factors that affect rates of suicide in the adult population. Chief among these factors are social isolation and the weakening of social bonds. Most communities have programs and services geared toward helping teenagers over the rough spots common in adolescence. Perhaps what is most important for teenagers to learn is that they are not alone with their problems. Thus, teenagers suffering from feelings of isolation or frustration should be encouraged to seek help and guidance.

SECTION 3 REVIEW

1. Define and explain
drug
social integration

2. Categorizing
Copy the word web below. Use it to identify the chief predictors of teenage suicide.

Teen Suicide

Homework Practice Online
keyword: SL3 HP6

3. **Finding the Main Idea**
  a. According to social scientists, what are some of the causes and consequences of early sexual activity?
  b. According to social scientists, what are some of the causes of teen suicide?

4. **Writing and Critical Thinking**
  Analyzing Information Write a brief essay on the social and economic problems created by teen drug abuse.
  Consider:
  • teenage drug use
  • teenage perceptions of the dangers of drugs
  • teenage attitudes toward drug use

SECTION 3 REVIEW ANSWERS

1. Define:
  • drug, p. 137
  • social integration, p. 141

2. alcohol or drug use, triggering events, age, sex, population density, family relations, and cluster effect

3a. causes—one-parent families; low family income level, and lack of religious participation; consequences—teenage pregnancy and STDs

b. Causes of teen suicide include confusion and self-doubt, problems that seem overwhelming, and social isolation.

4. Essays will vary, but students should address the rise in some drug use among teenagers, as well as teens' increasing negative attitudes toward the use of various drugs. Students should also include the cost of drugs, both to teens and to society as a whole.

Exploring Cultural Diversity

■ TEACH

Have each student read the feature Body Image and Eating Habits in Fiji on this page and answer the questions that follow. Ask volunteers to share their answers with the class and encourage student discussion. Then organize students into groups and have each group discuss some of the social effects of the ideal body images presented in American ads, magazines, movies, and television. Have groups consider the effects on teenage boys, teenage girls, and on boy-girl relations. Groups should then discuss ways to counteract some of the negative social consequences, such as eating disorders. **COOPERATIVE LEARNING**

■ EXTEND

Have students visit their local grocery or drug store, locate the section where the diet products are, and then make a list of the types and number of different products available. Next, have students choose two different types of products and record the various side effects or cautions provided on the packaging. When the class next meets, have students share and discuss their findings and what they reveal about some of the effects of American societal pressure to be thin. **BLOCK SCHEDULING**

Interdisciplinary Connection

HEALTH

Anorexia Nervosa. A distorted perception of one's body as fat is one of the central conditions of anorexia nervosa. This eating disorder involves the use of extreme methods to maintain a weight well below what is healthy. Anorexia is predominantly found in Western societies. Bulimia, a related disorder, involves a pattern of bingeing and purging to maintain a slim body. In the 1980s and 1990s eating disorders became an important health issue in the United States.

RESEARCH ACTIVITY: Have students conduct research on eating disorders among American teenagers and on the social factors that contribute to this problem.

Technology Resources

 CNN. Presents Sociology: Eating Disorders

Think About It Answers

(see page 145)

1. Most students will probably agree with the statement and note the recent problems faced by Fijian girls as evidence.

2. Answers will vary, but students should provide at least one factor and explain why it influences them.

EXPLORING
Cultural Diversity

BODY IMAGE AND EATING HABITS IN FIJI

Body image—the view a person has about his or her body—plays an important role in adolescent development. Young people who are satisfied with the way their bodies look tend to be happier and better adjusted. Weight is a significant aspect of body image, particularly for adolescent girls. Many young American women express dissatisfaction with their weight, wishing that they could be thinner. Studies suggest that the idea that thinner is better derives from the media. In magazines, television, and the movies, attractiveness in women is equated with slimness. Young women sometimes drastically adjust their eating habits to achieve this "ideal" body image.

Not all cultures regard thinness as attractive. The people of the Pacific Island nation of Fiji have traditionally considered a sturdy rounded figure as ideal. Fijians often compliment each other by saying, "You've gained weight." Too, they look upon losing a large amount of weight as a sign of poor health. However, after the introduction of television to the island, Fijian ideas on body image have changed. This change was particularly notable among adolescent girls, as this excerpt from a news story by reporter Alexis Chiu shows.

"The year TV was widely introduced in Fiji in 1995, only three per cent of girls reported they vomited to control their weight, according to the study by Harvard researcher Anne Becker. Three years later, 15 percent reported the behavior.

'They look to television characters as role models,' said Becker. . . . 'While it's an everyday concept to Americans, reshaping the body is a new concept to Fijians,' she said.

Although Becker cautioned that the study does not establish a definitive link between television and eating disorders, she said the increases were dramatic in a culture that traditionally has focused on the importance of eating well and looking robust.

Other warning signs were high in the follow-up study in 1998, with 74 percent of the Fijian girls reporting feeling 'too big or fat' at least sometimes and 62 percent reporting dieting in the past month. . . .

Fiji has only one TV channel, which shows mostly American, Australian and British programs. Favorites include Melrose Place, ER and Xena: Warrior Princess.

One girl in the study said the teenagers on television are 'slim and very tall' and that, 'We want our bodies to become like that . . . so we try to lose a lot of weight.'

The body image and eating habits of the people of Fiji have changed greatly in recent years. Fishing, cultural festivals, and traditional foods are important parts of traditional life in Fiji.

SPOTLIGHT on Fiji

Have students conduct research on the country of Fiji. Students should compare and contrast its media and cultural differences prior to 1995, when television was introduced, to current times. Have each student create an atlas entry on Fiji providing basic demographic, economic, and government information. Then have each student write a one-page report on the culture of Fiji before and after the introduction of television and whether students think this change is responsible for the changes in eating habits of teenage Fijian girls. **BLOCK SCHEDULING**

SPOTLIGHT on Eating Habits Around the World

Organize the class into four groups. Assign one of the groups a Western country to research and the other groups countries in other parts of the world, such as Asia. (Countries to consider are Australia, Brazil, China, Egypt, France, Japan, and Russia.) Instruct each group to conduct research on the eating habits of the assigned country, such as popular foods, the ideal body, the rates of various types of eating disorders, and the number of people over- or underweight in different segments of the population. Have each group prepare a multimedia presentation or a PowerPoint® presentation of its findings. **COOPERATIVE LEARNING**, **BLOCK SCHEDULING**

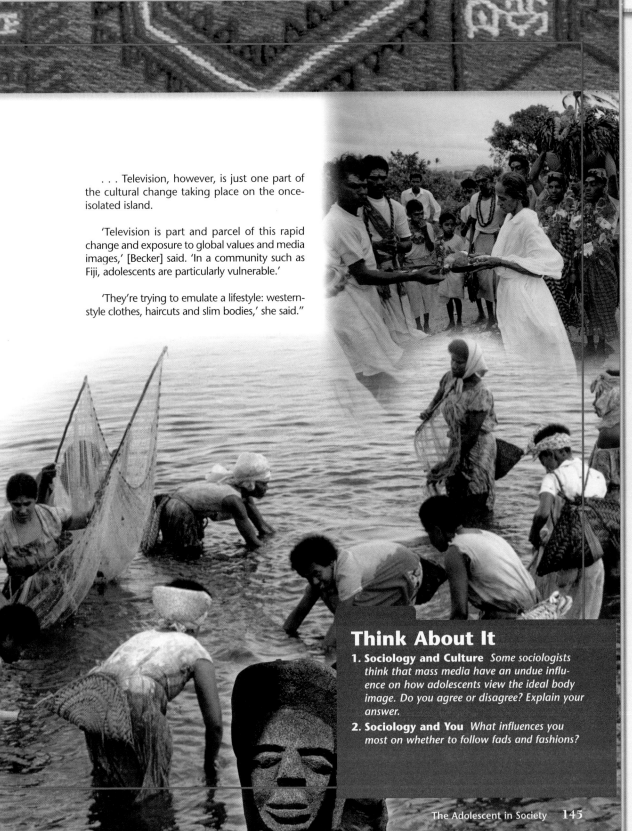

. . . Television, however, is just one part of the cultural change taking place on the once-isolated island.

'Television is part and parcel of this rapid change and exposure to global values and media images,' [Becker] said. 'In a community such as Fiji, adolescents are particularly vulnerable.'

'They're trying to emulate a lifestyle: western-style clothes, haircuts and slim bodies,' she said."

Think About It

1. **Sociology and Culture** *Some sociologists think that mass media have an undue influence on how adolescents view the ideal body image. Do you agree or disagree? Explain your answer.*

2. **Sociology and You** *What influences you most on whether to follow fads and fashions?*

CHAPTER 6 REVIEW

ANSWERS

WRITING A SUMMARY
See the section subtitles for the main topics in this chapter.

IDENTIFYING PEOPLE AND IDEAS

1. period between puberty's onset and adulthood's start

2. the physical maturation that makes an individual capable of sexual reproduction

3. learning the rights, obligations, and expectations of a future life role

4. a type of social interaction between single people

5. a form of rigid interaction between young unmarried men and women with the expected goal of marriage

6. a sociologist who conducted one of the first analyses of American dating patterns

7. the tendency to marry people who have social characteristics similar to one's own

8. a young Amish man's horse-drawn carriage, customarily used for courting

9. any substance that alters mood, behavior, or consciousness

10. the degree of attachment people have to social groups or to society as a whole

Review and Assessment Resources
- Chapter 6 Review, pp. 146–47
- Chapter Review Activities with Answer Key
- Global Skill Builder CD–ROM
- Chapter 6 Test Generator (on the One-Stop Planner)
- Chapter 6 Test (Form A or B)
- Alternative Assessment Handbook
- HRW Go site

 REVIEW

Have students complete the **Chapter 6 Review** on pp. 146–47.

ASSESS

Use one of the chapter tests to assess students' understanding of the content. For **Alternative Assessment**, see the **Alternative Assessment Handbook**.

UNDERSTANDING MAIN IDEAS

1. the mandatory education of children through age 16, the exclusion of youth from the labor force, the development of the juvenile-justice system

2. biological growth and development, an undefined status, increased decision making, increased pressure, and the search for self

3. The Industrial Revolution caused many people to move from farms to cities, where they established homes independent of their parents. This freedom, along with the development of the automobile and the telephone, reduced parental control over courtship and led to dating.

4. entertainment, socialization, fulfillment of psychological needs, status, and spouse selection

5. risks from early sexual behavior, drug use and drug violence, and suicide

THINKING CRITICALLY

1. Other societies often lack compulsory public education for youth or child labor laws, both of which helped lead to the creation of adolescence.

2. Advertisers imply that everyone else is buying their products and that someone who does not have them will appear out of place.

3. His study took place on a college campus and failed to take other situations into consideration.

CHAPTER

 6 Review

 Writing a Summary

Using standard grammar, spelling, sentence structure, and punctuation, summarize the information in this chapter.
Consider:
- the characteristics and development of adolescence
- how dating developed and the functions it serves
- the problems of adolescent life

 Identifying People and Ideas

Identify the following people or terms and use them in appropriate sentences.

1. adolescence
2. puberty
3. anticipatory socialization
4. dating
5. courtship
6. Willard Waller
7. homogamy
8. courting buggy
9. drug
10. social integration

Understanding Main ideas

Section 1 (pp. 120–26)

1. Describe the factors that led to the development of the concept of adolescence in the United States.

2. Identify and describe the five major features of adolescence.

Section 2 (pp. 127–34)

3. How did the practice of dating develop in the United States?

4. What functions does the dating process perform today?

Section 3 (pp. 135–43)

5. What major social problems face American teenagers today?

 Thinking Critically

1. Drawing Inferences and Conclusions Why do you think that adolescence, by and large, is found only in modern industrialized societies?

2. Identifying Cause and Effect How do advertisers use peer pressure to encourage you to buy various goods and services?

3. Analyzing Information Consider Willard Waller's work on dating patterns. Why might his study have produced a skewed view of dating in the United States?

4. Identifying Points of View Why do you think most teenagers see less danger in regular drinking than in the regular use of drugs and cigarettes?

5. Evaluating Émile Durkheim described certain suicides as altruistic. Do such suicides result from low levels of social integration or high levels of social integration? Explain your answer.

 Writing About Sociology

1. Evaluating Use the Internet and library resources to research the laws relating to juveniles in your state. Write a brief essay that explains how these laws mandate that courts and prison systems handle juveniles differently from adults.

2. Analyzing Information Reread the Case Studies and Other True Stories feature on page 122. Then watch several television programs that focus on the daily life of families with one or more adolescents. Note if and how each program addresses the issue of the blurring of adolescence. Use the graphic organizer to help you analyze the portrayal of adolescents and adults. Share your findings with the rest of the class in a brief written report.

Adolescent Traits — Blurred Traits — Adult Traits

RETEACH

Have students create a wordseek puzzle or a crossword puzzle by using key terms and concepts in this chapter. Clues should be in definition form, and the key terms and concepts used as the answers. Each student should create a small version of the completed puzzle as an answer key and then a larger unanswered version of the puzzle. Collect students' puzzles and then redistribute them. Have each student complete the puzzle he or she receives and then meet with the person who created the puzzle to check the answers. Finally, review with students any concepts with which they are still having difficulty. **ENGLISH LANGUAGE LEARNERS**

SOCIOLOGY PROJECTS

1. Applying Sociology Organize students into groups of four or five and have each group create a Teen Years board game. The game should address the concepts covered in this chapter but also be fun to play. Each group should provide written directions and rules for playing, scoring, and winning as well as a game board and all playing pieces.

2. Connecting to Language Arts Have students work in pairs or small groups to create a booklet entitled Surviving Adolescence: The Teenage Instruction Manual. The booklet should be based on the information students learned in this chapter. Encourage students to have fun and be creative.

BUILDING SOCIAL STUDIES SKILLS

Interpreting Graphs

Study the graph below. Use it to answer the questions that follow.

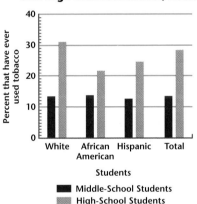

Tobacco Use by Middle-School and High-School Students, 2002

Source: Centers for Disease Control and Prevention

1. In which group of students is tobacco use the highest?
   a. White high schoolers
   b. African American middle schoolers
   c. Hispanic high schoolers
   d. Middle schoolers of all races
2. What are the similarities and differences in tobacco use between middle-school students and high-school students?

Analyzing Primary Sources

The following excerpt outlines the problems students with part-time jobs face. Read the excerpt, then answer the questions that follow.

"For decades, the conventional wisdom has been that it is great for teenagers . . . to hold after-school jobs because they teach responsibility, provide pocket money and keep the teenagers out of trouble.

But in a nation where more than five million teenagers under 18 work, a growing body of research is challenging the conventional wisdom and concluding that working long hours often undermines teenagers' education and overall development.

In the most important study, two arms of the National Academy of Sciences—the National Research Council and the Institute of Medicine—found that when teenagers work more than 20 hours a week, the work often leads to lower grades, higher alcohol use and too little time with their parents and families.

Influenced by such studies, lawmakers in Connecticut, Massachusetts, Alabama and other states have pushed in recent years to tighten laws regulating how many hours teenagers can work. . . .

While there are myriad reasons for poor school performance, legislators seeking tougher restrictions say American students would certainly do better if they placed more emphasis on work inside school and less emphasis on working outside school."

3. The National Academy of Sciences found that teenagers who work more than 20 hours a week
   a. often get higher grades.
   b. have a lower level of alcohol use.
   c. spend too little time with their families.
   d. earn needed money.
4. Do you think that legislating the amount of time students may work will improve educational achievement? Why or why not?

SOCIOLOGY PROJECTS

Cooperative Learning

Content Analysis Work in a group with two or three other students to select several short stories that have adolescents as main characters. Review the short stories and note the general characteristics of adolescence that each addresses, including demograhic, geographic, or cultural differences. Create a database or chart outlining the characteristics your group finds. Then create a quiz and answer key to use as a study guide.

internet connect

Internet Activity: go.hrw.com
KEYWORD: SL3 SC6
Choose an activity on the adolescent in society to:
- create a series of advertisements that would influence the perceptions, attitudes, and behaviors of teenagers.
- write a report on recent studies on dating.
- design an adolescent-suicide prevention program.

---

4. Societal pressures on adolescents to refrain from drinking are not as strong as societal pressures on teens to refrain from smoking cigarettes or using drugs.

5. Altruistic suicides result from high levels of social integration, because the person committing suicide is putting the needs of the group above his or her own needs.

WRITING ABOUT SOCIOLOGY

1. Essays will vary, but students should include specific documented information on the juvenile-justice system in their state.

2. Findings and conclusions will vary, but students should have completed a copy of the graphic organizer and then used the information in it as the basis for their report.

BUILDING SOCIAL STUDIES SKILLS

1. a

2. Use among high schoolers is higher than that among middle schoolers across all groups, but use in both groups varies by race and ethnicity.

3. c

4. Students who agree may say that such legislation will help because students would have more time to study and sleep. Students who disagree might argue that educational achievement is based more on students' natural abilities than on how much teens work.

7

The Adult in Society

CHAPTER RESOURCE MANAGER

Objectives	Pacing Guide		Resources

SECTION 1:
Early and Middle Adulthood
(pp. 150–56)

REV Section 1 Review, p. 156

- Summarize Daniel Levinson's theory of adult male development.
- Identify and describe the stages of adult female development.

Regular 1 day	Block Scheduling 0.5 day

Block Scheduling Handbook with Team Teaching Strategies, Chapter 7

- CNN. Presents Sociology: Midlife Crisis
- **RS** Graphic Organizer 7
- HRW Go site
- **SM** Mastering Critical Thinking Skills 7
- **PS** Readings and Case Studies in Sociology 7
- **E** Research Projects and Activities for Teaching Sociology 7
- **SM** Study Skills and Writing Guide
- Teaching Transparency: Adapting Patterns in Later Adulthood Used by Different Personality Types

SECTION 2:
The World of Work
(pp. 157–63)

REV Section 2 Review, p. 161

- Describe how the nature of work in the United States has changed.
- Explain how the composition of the labor force in the United States has changed.

Regular 1 day	Block Scheduling 0.5 day

Block Scheduling Handbook with Team Teaching Strategies, Chapter 7

Chapter Review And Assessment

- **REV** Chapter 7 Review, pp. 172–73
- **REV** Chapter Review Activities with Answer Key
- Global Skill Builder CD–ROM
- Chapter 7 Test Generator (on the One-Stop Planner)
- **A** Chapter 7 Test (Form A or B)
- **A** Alternative Assessment Handbook
- HRW Go site

SECTION 3:
The Later Years
(pp. 164–71)

REV Section 3 Review, p. 171

- Describe the characteristics of life during late adulthood.
- Identify the new challenges that older Americans face.

Regular 1 day	Block Scheduling 0.5 day

Block Scheduling Handbook with Team Teaching Strategies, Chapter 7

Chapter Resource Key

PS	Primary Sources	**A**	Assessment		Video
RS	Reading Support	**REV**	Review		Internet
E	Enrichment		Transparencies		Holt Presentation Maker Using Microsoft® PowerPoint®
SM	Skills Mastery		CD–ROM		

 One-Stop Planner CD–ROM

See the *One-Stop Planner* for a complete list of additional resources for students and teachers.

One-Stop Planner CD–ROM

It's easy to plan lessons, select resources, and print out materials for your students when you use the **One-Stop Planner CD–ROM with Test Generator.**

Chapter Project Preview

The following activities are included in the Chapter Review. You may want to make the suggested preparations.

CHAPTER REVIEW ACTIVITY

Using Statistics Students will conduct research into changes in the labor force and in the nature of work in their community and create a brief report. In preparation, you might want to select several print and online resources that students can use in their research and reserve time for students to use school computers, if available.

LESSON ACTIVITY

Linking to Community Students will perform volunteer work at a local nursing home, retirement community, or assisted-living facility. In preparation, line up volunteer jobs with several facilities. Then provide students with a list of the facilities' names, addresses, phone numbers, and available jobs.

INTERNET ACTIVITIES

Advocates for Older Americans Students will use provided Internet links to research groups that lobby for older Americans and then design a table or chart outlining the goals of one of the groups. In preparation, you might examine the provided Web sites in advance and determine what exact information you want students to include in their table or chart.

Theories of Development Students will use provided Internet links to research theories of adult development and then create a theoretical profile of one of the theorists discussed. In preparation, create a handout listing the information that students should provide in their theoretical profile. You might also provide students with a sample profile.

Additional Resources

PRINT RESOURCES FOR TEACHERS

Levinson, Daniel J. *The Seasons of a Man's Life.* New York: Ballantine Books, 1979. The classic study of the stages of adult male adulthood.

Levinson, Daniel J., Judy D. Levinson (contributor). *The Seasons of a Woman's Life.* New York: Knopf, 1996. Based on interviews with 45 women in the early 1980s, Levinson examines the stages of adult female development and the differences in the ways women and men experience adulthood.

Sheehy, Gail. *New Passages: Mapping Your Life Across Time.* New York: Random House, 1995. Discusses the opportunities and challenges of middle adulthood from the ages of 45 through 65.

Shenk, David. *The Forgetting: Alzheimer's, Portrait of an Epidemic.* New York: Doubleday, 2001. Provides a primer on memory and dementia and explores Alzheimer's effects on patients, families, and societies.

PRINT RESOURCES FOR STUDENTS

Moody, Harry R. *Aging: Concepts and Controversies,* 3rd ed., Thousand Oaks, CA: Pine Forge Press, 2000. Examines the major issues of the aging process from a personal, academic, professional, and policy perspectives.

Pavalko, Ronald M. *Sociology of Occupations and Professions.* Itasca, IL: F.E. Peacock, 1988. A sociological examination of the world of work.

MULTIMEDIA RESOURCES

Grandparents (vhs; 29 min.) Guidance Associates. Teenagers, adults, and young children share stories about their grandparents, illustrating the bond between the generations.

Women at Work: Change, Choice, Challenge (vhs; 19 min.) Encyclopaedia Brittanica Educational Corporation. Seven women discuss their attitudes toward work, their reasons for their career choices, and their views of their work-family relationships.

internet connect

go.hrw.com

HRW ONLINE RESOURCES

GO TO: go.hrw.com
Then type in a keyword.

TEACHER HOME PAGE
KEYWORD: SL3 Teacher

CHAPTER INTERNET ACTIVITIES
KEYWORD: SL3 SC7
Choose an activity to have students:
- research theories of adult development and create a theoretical profile of one of the theorists.
- create a classified ad based on statistics related to the workforce.
- design a table or chart outlining the goals of groups that lobby for older Americans.

CHAPTER ENRICHMENT LINKS
KEYWORD: SL3 CH7

ONLINE ASSESSMENT
Homework Practice
KEYWORD: SL3 HP7
Standardized Test Prep
KEYWORD: SL3 STP7
Rubrics
KEYWORD: SS Rubrics

CONTENT UPDATES
KEYWORD: SS Content Updates

HOLT PRESENTATION MAKER
KEYWORD: SL3 PPT7

ONLINE READING SUPPORT
KEYWORD: SS Strategies

CURRENT EVENTS
KEYWORD: S3 Current Events

CHAPTER

7

The Adult in Society

SECTION 1
Early and Middle Adulthood

SECTION 2
The World of Work

SECTION 3
The Later Years

CHAPTER REVIEW

Build on What You Know

Ask students to answer the following questions:

How might adulthood compare and contrast to adolescence?

Consider:

• transitions and adjustments to new experiences

• work responsibilities

• relationships and commitments

How might men and women experience adulthood differently?

Consider:

• role expectations

• education and jobs

• relationships, marriage, and child rearing

Internet Activity

Have students access the Internet through the HRW Go site to conduct research on theories of adult development. Then have each student use his or her research to create a theoretical profile of one of the theorists discussed. Remind students to use standard grammar, spelling, sentence structure, and punctuation in their profiles.

CHAPTER

7

The Adult in Society

Build on What You Know

Adolescents develop in specific stages and have common experiences as they age. In this chapter, you will look at the social characteristics of adulthood. First, you will look at male and female development during the adult years. Then you will explore the world of work. Finally, you will look at the characteristics of late adulthood.

A large part of adult life centers around work. Sociologists study the development of adults and how they form relationships in the world of work.

Life in Society

Socialization does not end with adolescence. It continues throughout the life span. At every age, we are faced with new experiences and new demands that affect the ways that we view ourselves and the society in which we live. Our first job, marriage, the birth of a first child, our first home, triumphs and disappointments at work, retirement, and approaching death in old age are all events that add new dimensions to our sense of self and our relationships with others.

Sociologists and social psychologists are interested in the ways in which people adapt to the changing statuses and roles that accompany each stage of adult development. Topics of special importance in this area include the world of work and the transition to retirement.

However, these processes of development differ somewhat for men and women. By studying the way men and women develop as adults, sociologists can draw conclusions about the important stages through which most adults pass.

What's Your Opinion?

Read the following statements about sociology. Do you think they are true or false? You will learn whether each statement is true or false as you read the chapter.

- Most sociologists agree that men and women go through the same stages of development in adulthood.

- The composition of the labor force and the nature of work in the United States have remained largely unchanged over the last 100 years.

- The process of social development ceases in old age.

> **WHY SOCIOLOGY MATTERS**
>
> Sociologists are interested in the ways older people adapt to new situations such as retirement. Use **CNNfyi.com** or other current events sources to learn more about programs, such as Elderhostel, designed for retired people. Create a pamphlet for one of these programs.
>
> **CNNfyi.com**

SECTION 1

OBJECTIVES

1. *Summarize Daniel Levinson's theory of adult male development.*

2. *Identify and describe the stages of adult female development.*

SECTION 1 RESOURCES

REPRODUCIBLE & REVIEW

- Graphic Organizer 7
- Research Projects and Activities for Teaching Sociology 7
- Study Skills and Writing Guide
- Section 1 Review, p. 156

TECHNOLOGY

- One-Stop Planner, Lesson 7.1
- CNN. Presents Sociology: Midlife Crisis
- Homework Practice Online

EARLY AND MIDDLE ADULTHOOD

Read to Discover

1. What is Daniel Levinson's theory of adult male development?
2. What are the stages of adult female development?

Define

life structure, early adulthood, middle adulthood, late adulthood, novice phase, mentor

Identify

Daniel Levinson, Irene Frieze, Esther Sales

The life patterns of adult males and females in American society are somewhat different. For example, almost 69 percent of women with children under the age of 18 work at least part-time. However, their work histories tend not to parallel those of men. For many women, a typical pattern is to enter the labor force, take time out to have children, and then go back to work once the children are grown. Men, on the other hand, generally remain in the labor force for most of adulthood.

The split employment pattern of women may be changing as more women choose to combine full-time careers with parenting. Nevertheless, the traditional pattern is still prevalent enough to merit looking at male and female adult development as two separate processes.

Adult Male Development

Psychologist Daniel Levinson and his colleagues at Yale University undertook an intensive long-term study to determine the adult male developmental stages. The research team, which included psychologists, sociologists, and psychiatrists, conducted in-depth interviews with 40 men who were between the ages of 35 and 45 at the beginning of the study. Levinson and his colleagues selected participants for the study from four broad occupational categories. Of those selected, 10 were business executives, 10 were hourly workers, 10 were biology professors, and 10 were writers of varying degrees of fame.

The researchers interviewed each subject for 10 to 20 hours during two or three months to determine how each had experienced personal development as an adult. The interviews focused on such issues as education, work, leisure, politics, and relationships with family and friends. From these interviews, Levinson and his colleagues determined each man's life structure. A **life structure** is the combination of statuses, roles, activities, goals, values, beliefs, and life circumstances that characterize an individual. Through the analysis of these life structures, the research team was able to distinguish patterns that appear to be characteristic of all men.

After analyzing the patterns, Levinson and his colleagues concluded that there are three basic eras of adulthood. They named these eras **early adulthood**, **middle adulthood**, and **late adulthood**. The diagram on page 151 shows how each era is divided into several distinct periods. Each era begins with a transitional period, which is followed by alternating stable and transitional periods.

Raising a family is an important part of life for many adults. However, many sociologists argue that the family plays a different role in the development of men than it does in the development of women.

TEACH OBJECTIVE 1

SUGGESTION 1: Have students examine the chart on p. 151 and identify the three major eras in Daniel Levinson's theory of adult male development *(early adulthood, middle adulthood, and late adulthood)*. Then organize the class into five groups and assign each group one of the first five stages of male development: early adult transition, entering the adult world, the age 30 transition, the settling down period, and the midlife transition. Each group is to become an authority on and prepare a presentation about its assigned stage. Groups should identify the stage's age range, main characteristics, and any challenges associated with it. Then have each group present its work to the class. **COOPERATIVE LEARNING**

SPOTLIGHT
on Levinson and Adult Male Development

To extend the previous activity, ask each of the five groups to interview several men whose ages fall within the group's assigned stage of male development. Based on the interviews, have group members construct a life structure for each subject and determine whether this life structure supports or contradicts Levinson's theory. Remind students to keep the identity of the men they interview anonymous. Have students share their interviews and conclusions with the class.

COOPERATIVE LEARNING, BLOCK SCHEDULING

Transitional periods last from four to five years, and stable periods last from six to eight years. Levinson placed the greatest stress on the first five periods of adulthood. These periods are the early adult transition, entering the adult world, the age 30 transition, the settling down period, and the midlife transition.

The Early Adult Transition Early adulthood begins with the early adult transition period—ages 17 through 22. This period represents the bridge between adolescence and adulthood. According to Levinson, the most important task of the period is leaving home, both physically and psychologically. The process begins when young adults go away to college or take full-time employment and move out of their parents' homes. However, the break with parents is not abrupt or total. For example, college students often receive financial support from their parents. Other young adults achieve economic independence when they enter the work world. However, they may continue to live at home in what amounts to a boarder status.

Entering the Adult World The next stage in early adulthood is called entering the adult world—ages 23 through 27. The chief tasks of this period involve two slightly contradictory objectives. On one hand, the individual is expected to explore a variety of relationships and career opportunities. This expectation means that he must avoid strong commitments that will make it difficult for him to take advantage of new opportunities. On the other hand, the young adult is expected to become a responsible member of society and to form a stable life structure.

This period is also characterized by the development of a dream of adult accomplishment. The dream is almost always phrased in terms of occupational goals. For many, the dreams are very specific, such as becoming a Nobel Prize winner, a great athlete, or a famous writer. Although these dreams often prove to be unrealistic, they do provide a sense of direction and purpose.

The Age 30 Transition For many people, the age 30 transition—ages 28 through 32—is a difficult period. It is a time to look back on the choices that have been made up to this point. Divorces are common during this period as individuals re-evaluate their current commitments. Levinson considered the age 30 transition to be crucial to future development because it is often characterized by shifts in direction. Sound choices provide a firm foundation for future development. Bad choices can have far-reaching consequences.

Levinson referred to the first three periods of the early adulthood era as the **novice phase**. It is the time

Levinson's Developmental Stages of Adulthood

Age	Stage	Phase	Era
17			
18			
19	Early Adult Transition		
20			
21		The Novice Phase	
22			
23			
24			
25	Entering the Adult World		
26			
27			EARLY ADULTHOOD ERA
28			
29			
30	Age 30 Transition		
31			
32			
33			
34			
35			
36	Settling Down Period		
37			
38			
39			
40			
41			
42	Midlife Transition		
43			
44			
45			
46			
47	Entering Middle Adulthood		
48			
49			MIDDLE ADULTHOOD ERA
50			
51			
52	Age 50 Transition		
53			
54			
55			
56			
57	Culmination of Middle Adulthood		
58			
59			
60			
61			
62	Late Adult Transition		
63			
64			
65			
66			
67			LATE ADULTHOOD ERA
68			
69			
70	Late Adult Transition		
71			
72			
73			
74			
75+			

INTERPRETING CHARTS Levinson's stages describe a general trend to the life experiences many men pass through. *According to Levinson, at what age do men often leave the novice phase?*

Sociology in the World Today

Staying at Home.
In 2000, about 25 percent of all young adults in the United States between the ages of 18 and 34 lived with one or more of their parents. At the same time, about 41 percent of Americans under the age of 35 owned their own homes.

CRITICAL THINKING
What might these statistics illustrate about the process of becoming an adult?

ANSWER: The process of becoming a financially independent adult can be difficult and take time, but many people do it by age 35.

Chart Answer

at about age 32

During the age 30 transition and settling down periods, young men often seek older role models for advice and guidance.

when men prepare for entry into the adult world. Their major task during this phase is to make a place for themselves in the adult world and to construct a life structure that fits them and works in the adult world.

The Settling Down Period The last stage of early adulthood is the settling down period—ages 33 through 39. The major task of this period is what Levinson called "making it" in the adult world. Individuals try to establish themselves in society, usually by advancing in their chosen occupations. During this period, individuals form true commitments to things such as work, family, leisure, friendship, community, or whatever is most important in their lives. They also work to fulfill the dreams they established in the previous period.

Near the end of the settling down period, men come to realize how much they are relying on others as role models for guidance. Feeling constrained by these influences, they begin a conscious effort to establish their own identities. Levinson referred to this process as Becoming One's Own Man (B.O.O.M.).

The first step in this process often involves separating oneself from a mentor. A **mentor** is someone who fosters an individual's development by believing in the person, sharing the person's dreams, and helping the person achieve those dreams. Usually the mentor is an older experienced person in the world of work. The mentor acts as a role model and helps the individual get started in adult life. Although the break with a mentor is often painful, it is important because it allows individuals to stop viewing themselves as "apprentice adults."

The Midlife Transition The first stage in the middle adulthood era is the midlife transition—ages 40 through 44. This period serves as a bridge between early and middle adulthood. The midlife transition, like the age 30 transition, is characterized by self-examination. Individuals once again question their life structures. They also take stock of their likelihood of achieving the dreams they formed during their early adulthood. In most instances, they come to realize that their earlier dreams are beyond fulfillment. The majority of people are able to reformulate their dreams along more realistic lines. Escaping from the pressure of unattainable dreams is one of the major tasks of the midlife transition.

For about 80 percent of the subjects in Levinson's study, the midlife transition was a period of moderate to severe crisis. These men experienced both internal conflict and conflict with those around them. The possibility of death became more real to them. One of the ways in

INTERPRETING VISUALS The midlife transition for men is often characterized by personal crisis.
Why might it be humorous that a 25-year-old thinks he or she is having a midlife crisis?

Case Studies and Other True Stories

◼ TEACH

Have students read the feature Differing Views of Early Adulthood on this page and answer the questions that follow. Next, have students share and discuss their answers as a class. Then have each student write a dialogue in which an adult man and woman on a first date are having a conversation in which they are telling each other about their lives. The dialogue should include several exchanges in who is speaking and illustrate the differences that Gail Sheehy's study found in how men and women view their early adult years. Have volunteers present their dialogues to the class.

◼ EXTEND

Have each student interview two adults—one man and one woman—between the ages of 25 and 50. Students are to ask each adult to describe the main events in his or her life up to the present. Instruct students to record the responses on tape or to write them down in as much detail as possible, noting the order in which subjects were mentioned. Then ask volunteers to share their results with the class and to discuss how they compare with the results of Gail Sheehy's study of adulthood, described on this page.

BLOCK SCHEDULING

Case Studies
AND OTHER TRUE STORIES

DIFFERING VIEWS OF EARLY ADULTHOOD

During adulthood, men have traditionally concentrated on their work, while women have devoted themselves to their families. This pattern is reflected in Gail Sheehy's study of adulthood, Passages: Predictable Crises of Adult Life. *In the following excerpt, Sheehy explores how men and women describe their early adult years.*

"Somehow, the source of our identity moves from outside to inside, and it is this psychological movement in sense of self that is the key to the mystery. It causes many men and women to switch from the opposite poles of their twenties to a different set of opposites by their forties.

This switch is strikingly revealed by the way in which men and women tell their life stories. The differences were particularly distinct in the way all of them spilled out the histories of the first half of their lives. The men talked about the actions they had initiated. The women talked about the people they had responded to.

That is, the men reconstructed their tracks according to the career line they had followed. They measured themselves at each step against the timetable approved for their particular occupational dream. Love partners were filled in as adjuncts to their real love affair: courting the dream of success and seeking their identity through their work. The men talked about their wives and children largely in terms of how they helped or hindered the dream, but they rarely spoke, without prompting, about the needs or nourishing of the human beings closest to them. These human connections seldom converged with what a man saw as his main track of development until he had reached his 40s.

Women, by contrast, spun out their stories around their attachments to, and detachments from, others: parents, lovers, husbands, children. The central thread running through their young lives was the state of these human connections. The pursuit of an individual dream was most often a stitch that was picked up, dropped, perhaps picked up again. It was what they did before they married, between babies, or after the divorce. Women whose lives incorporated a vital career line generally described that line as the either/or choice they had to make, the profession they doggedly pursued instead of marrying Peter or the exit route they took from Paul or the detour they made from family commitments and for which at some point they would be charged a toll. Loaned time. It was rare to find a woman under 35, even a talented and successful one, who felt complete without a man.

Until very recently in our culture, most men and women spent a good part of their 20s and 30s living one of two illusions: that career success would make them immortal, or that a mate would complete them. (Even now, these illusions die very hard.) Men and women were on separate tracks. The career as an all-encompassing end to life turned out to be a flawed vision, an emotional cul-de-sac. But did attaching oneself to a man and children prove to be any less incomplete as life's ultimate fulfillment?"

Gail Sheehy's study found that women who focused on a career spoke of the experience as a choice that involved forgoing a commitment to family.

Think About It

1. **Analyzing Information** *How do many men and women differ in the ways in which they discuss their early adulthood years?*
2. **Identifying Points of View** *Sheehy's book was written in the 1970s. Do you think that male and female young adults today still view the early adult years differently? Explain your answer.*

Case Study

Gender Differences in Conversation. Not only do men and women differ in what they say about their early adulthood years, but they also differ in how they talk. Sociologists who study conversational patterns have found that men tend to speak and interrupt more than women. On the other hand, women tend to smile, laugh, and ask more questions during conversation.

CRITICAL THINKING
What might explain gender differences in conversation?

ANSWER: Students might suggest that differences in the socialization of boys and girls may be responsible as well as physical differences.

Think About It Answers

1. Men tend to define their lives according to their occupational history. Women tend to define themselves through their relationships with others.

2. Answers will vary, but some students may argue that many women stop working to raise children, so that differences continue. Other students may note that more women work while raising children, so differences may be disappearing.

TEACH OBJECTIVE 2

To help students identify and describe the stages of adult female development, copy the following graphic organizer onto the chalkboard, omitting the italicized answers. Have students copy and complete the organizer. Then discuss the answers with the class. Next, organize the class into three groups—one group for each phase of adult female development. Instruct each group to discuss the possible effects of changing work patterns, delayed marriage, delayed parenthood, and single parenthood on that phase. Then have each group report its ideas to the class. Encourage other students to provide feedback and discussion.

ENGLISH LANGUAGE LEARNERS , COOPERATIVE LEARNING

PHASES OF ADULT FEMALE DEVELOPMENT

> **Phase 1:** *Leaving the Family*
> **Characteristics:** *Young women leave home, break from their parents, and form a life plan, with an emphasis on marriage over establishing a career.*

> **Phase 2:** *Entering the Adult World*
> **Characteristics:** *Many women, often in their twenties, marry and have children. More than half combine work and motherhood. Others leave work, which limits later job opportunities.*

> **Phase 3:** *Entering the Adult World Again*
> **Characteristics:** *Many women, often in their early thirties, return to work after their children start school. They then pursue their career goals, similar to men in their twenties.*

which many of the men worked through the crisis was by becoming a mentor. For those who successfully completed the transition, middle adulthood proved to be a fulfilling and creative period.

Support for Levinson's theory can be found in the fact that all of the subjects in the study went through the various periods in order and at relatively the same age. The research findings also indicate that the degree of difficulty that an individual experiences in a period depends on his success in mastering the previous period.

An important step in development for both men and women is leaving home and beginning an independent life. Marriage can be a part of this step.

Adult Female Development

Levinson suggested that his findings were equally valid for women. Later, he repeated his life-structure study using women to test his thesis. Employing the same interview method, he studied 45 women drawn from three broad categories—homemakers, college professors, and corporate executives. Comparing his findings to those of his earlier study, he concluded that men and women go through the same stages of adult development. However, he noted that men and women differ in terms of their social roles and identities. Therefore, Levinson said, men and women deal with the developmental tasks in each stage differently.

Levinson's ideas on the similarity of male and female adult development have been a subject of some debate since he first made the suggestion in the 1970s. Some people argue that the differences he noted exist because the developmental processes for men and women are different. Irene Frieze and Esther Sales have both done work that lends support to this argument. The research led to a suggestion of three phases in adult female development. These are leaving the family, entering the adult world, and entering the adult world again.

Phase I: Leaving the Family Women's entry into the adult world begins much the same way as that of men. It involves leaving home, making a psychological break from parents, and developing a life plan. However, for many women the emphasis is less on a career than on marriage. Even when women plan to combine marriage with a career, marriage is often considered the more important step. In these instances, the specifics of the life plan are likely to be determined by marriage. This likelihood is particularly seen in relationships in which the husband's career plans take priority. This emphasis on marriage over career is one factor that distinguishes female development from male development during adulthood.

Organize students into groups and assign each group a European country. Have each group conduct research on laws regarding maternity leave in the assigned country and in the United States. Groups should consider issues such as the amount of leave, pay, and job security. Then instruct each group to create a chart that compares and contrasts U.S. laws for maternity leave with such laws in the assigned country. Each group should also write a few paragraphs expressing and defending its opinion on which system most benefits families, the economy, and society. Have each group present its work to the class. **COOPERATIVE LEARNING**, **BLOCK SCHEDULING**

CLOSE

Write the section's Define and Identify terms *(listed on p. 156)* on the chalkboard. In a round-robin format, ask students questions about each term until each member of the class has had an opportunity to answer a question or you have covered all the information in the section.

REVIEW AND ASSESS

Have students complete the **Section 1 Review** on p. 156. As **Alternative Assessment**, you may want to use the adult male development drawings or the adult female development graphic organizer in this section's lessons.

Phase II: Entering the Adult World Age at first marriage in the United States has been rising since the 1960s. Today it is an average of 25.1 years for women and 26.8 years for men. Nevertheless, most women still marry and become mothers during their twenties. Although many women find motherhood and a career to be a workable combination, dual roles tend to put an added strain on women. Consequently, only about 59 percent of new mothers who were in the labor force return to work before their children reach one year of age.

According to Sales, women's job advancement possibilities become limited when they remain out of the labor force while their children are young. This break in employment is another factor that distinguishes female development from male development during adulthood.

INTERPRETING VISUALS In recent decades many women in the second phase of adulthood find that they have to balance work with raising children. Increasing numbers of women have also found occupations in nontraditional fields such as architecture and automobile maintenance. *How do the images above reflect these trends?*

Did You Know?

According to a Rand Corporation study, having one child lowers the lifetime wages a woman can earn by approximately 13 percent. Having two children drops a woman's lifetime earning potential by 19 percent. Despite this fact, many women choose to put their careers on hold or work part-time after having a child.

Visual Answer

They show a woman dressed for work holding a child and two women working in the nontraditional fields of architecture or engineering and auto repair.

Technology Resources

  CNN. Presents Sociology: Midlife Crisis

Divide the class into two teams for a game of Baseball Review. Draw a baseball infield on the chalkboard and flip a coin to decide which team is at bat first. Then ask the first member of that team a question about the section. If the student answers the question correctly, his or her team moves forward one base. *(You might provide more difficult questions that count as doubles, triples, or home runs.)* Continue asking each member a question in turn. Each missed question counts as an out. After three outs, the other team comes to bat. Award one point each time a team reaches home plate. The team with the most points at the end wins.

ENGLISH LANGUAGE LEARNERS , COOPERATIVE LEARNING

EXTEND

1. Have each student conduct research on the average salaries for the top 10 professions for men and women and create a graph of the information. Then have students discuss their findings, what they reveal about society, and their opinions of any differences. **BLOCK SCHEDULING**

2. Have each student create a time line that goes from the student's current age to age 40. Instruct students to indicate on the time line some of the activities, events, or goals that they hope to participate in or achieve at different ages. Students might indicate attending college, getting married, getting a job, buying a house, and other major life events. **BLOCK SCHEDULING**

Chart Answer

more than half of all working women are married

SECTION ❶ REVIEW ANSWERS

1. Define:
- life structure, p. 150
- early adulthood, p. 150
- middle adulthood, p. 150
- late adulthood, p. 150
- novice phase, p. 151
- mentor, p. 152

2. Identify:
- Daniel Levinson, p. 150
- Irene Frieze, p. 154
- Esther Sales, p. 154

3. males—early, middle, and late adulthood; females—leaving the family, entering the adult world, and entering the adult world again

4a. early—ages 17 to 39, involves entering the adult world, choosing a career, establishing oneself in society, and making and re-evaluating commitments; middle—ages 40 to 59, involves self-examination, reformulation of life goals, perhaps a midlife crisis, realization of one's own mortality; late—ages 60 to 75+, involves transitions

b. an emphasis on marriage over career, a break in employment for child rearing, and a later re-entrance into the labor force

5. Essays will vary, but students should discuss how the goals of men and women differ at different life stages.

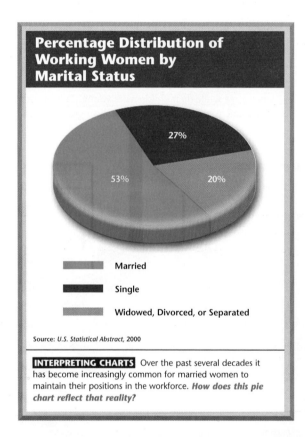

Percentage Distribution of Working Women by Marital Status

- 27%
- 53%
- 20%

■ Married
■ Single
■ Widowed, Divorced, or Separated

Source: *U.S. Statistical Abstract, 2000*

INTERPRETING CHARTS Over the past several decades it has become increasingly common for married women to maintain their positions in the workforce. *How does this pie chart reflect that reality?*

Phase III: Entering the Adult World Again Once their children reach school age, many mothers who left the labor force again seek employment. According to Sales, these women—most of whom are in their early thirties—find themselves in a situation similar to that of men in their twenties. Fewer obligations at home make it possible for them to actively pursue their career goals. Sales notes that it is somewhat ironic that these women develop a commitment to their careers at a time when their husbands are beginning to have serious doubts about their own careers.

American attitudes on marriage and gender roles seem to be changing. As you have read, Americans are delaying marriage. More and more Americans simply are not getting married. The marriage rate has dropped by more than 30 percent since the 1960s. Women are delaying parenting, as well. The age of mothers at the birth of their first child has risen slowly but steadily since the 1970s. Furthermore, the number of women in full-time executive, administrative, and managerial positions—typical career positions—is increasing. In nearly one third of all working couples, the wife earns more than the husband does. Such changes may signal that the developmental patterns of working-age men and women are merging.

SECTION ❶ REVIEW

1. Define and explain
life structure
early adulthood
middle adulthood
late adulthood
novice phase
mentor

2. Identify and explain
Daniel Levinson
Irene Frieze
Esther Sales

3. Comparing and Contrasting
Copy the graphic organizer below. Use it to compare and contrast adult male development and adult female development.

	Stages of Adult Development
Men	
Women	

4. **Finding the Main Idea**

a. What, according to Daniel Levinson, are the three basic eras of male adulthood? Identify their major characteristics.

b. According to Irene Frieze and Esther Sales, what factors distinguish female development from male development during adulthood?

5. **Writing and Critical Thinking**

Supporting a Point of View Write a short essay explaining whether you agree or disagree that there is little difference between adult female development and adult male development. Consider:
- attitude changes toward marriage
- changing views about gender roles

Homework Practice Online
keyword: SL3 HP7

SECTION 2

OBJECTIVES

1. *Describe how the nature of work in the United States has changed.*

2. *Explain how the composition of the labor force in the United States has changed.*

LET'S GET STARTED!

Before class, write the phrase *What I expect from my future career:* on the chalkboard. As students enter the classroom, have them list several things that they hope to obtain or achieve in their future careers. After a few minutes, call on volunteers to share their responses with the class. As they do so, create a master list on the chalkboard and organize the responses into general categories. Save the list for later. Tell students that in Section 2 they will learn about how the nature of work and the composition of the labor force in the United States have changed and what to expect in their future careers.

THE WORLD OF WORK

Read to Discover

1. How has the nature of work in the United States changed?

2. How has the composition of the labor force in the United States changed?

Define

labor force, profession, unemployment, unemployment rate

W ork is an important aspect of adult life. If you begin working at age 18 and retire at 65, you will have spent 47 years in the labor force. Even if you go to college and graduate school or spend several years at home raising children, you still will be in the labor force for a long time. What will your years in the labor force be like? An examination of the labor force, the types of jobs workers hold, and the degree of job satisfaction among workers can provide answers to this question.

The Labor Force

By definition, the **labor force** consists of all individuals age 16 and older who are employed in paid positions or who are seeking paid employment. People who are not paid for their services, such as homemakers, are not considered to be part of the labor force. In 2000 approximately 67 percent of the United States population over the age of 16 was in the labor force. Who are these workers and what types of jobs do they hold?

Composition The composition of the American labor force is changing. One of the biggest changes involves the number of working women and the types of jobs they hold. In 1970, women made up 38 percent of the labor force. In 2000, women made up more than 47 percent. Projections indicate that between 2000 and 2010, women will account for approximately 58 percent of the growth in the labor force. Women now hold about half of the professional jobs in the United States. A **profession** is a high-status occupation that requires specialized skills obtained through formal education. Professional-level work includes occupations such as engineer, lawyer, teacher, dentist, and writer.

Another changing aspect of labor-force composition is the rise of minority workers as a percentage of the total labor force. This trend is particularly true of Hispanics, who

now are the fastest growing population group among American workers. Currently, Hispanics make up close to 11 percent of the country's labor force. This figure is expected to increase to more than 13 percent by the year 2010.

In addition, American workers now have a higher level of education. In 1940 most workers barely had more than an eighth-grade education. Today approximately 90 percent of labor-force workers aged 25 to 64 have graduated from high school. And almost one third of the labor force has a college degree.

Unemployment One way to gain an understanding of the employment patterns in society is to look at unemployment. **Unemployment** is the situation that occurs when a person does not have a job but is actively seeking employment. The **unemployment rate** is the percentage of the civilian labor force that is unemployed but actively seeking employment. The unemployment rate varies according to such factors as age, gender, race, and cultural background. The graph on this page shows the unemployment rate for various groups in American society.

It is nearly impossible to employ every adult member of society. There are always some people who are in the process of seeking employment. Other people cannot or do not want to work. Consequently, society sets a level of unemployment that is generally considered acceptable. In the United States, that level hovers around 5 percent. Thus, the U.S. economy is considered to have achieved full employment when about 95 percent of the labor force is employed.

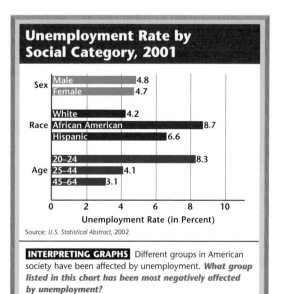

Unemployment Rate by Social Category, 2001

		Unemployment Rate (in Percent)
Sex	Male	4.8
	Female	4.7
Race	White	4.2
	African American	8.7
	Hispanic	6.6
Age	20–24	8.3
	25–44	4.1
	45–64	3.1

Source: *U.S. Statistical Abstract*, 2002

INTERPRETING GRAPHS Different groups in American society have been affected by unemployment. *What group listed in this chart has been most negatively affected by unemployment?*

SECTION 2 RESOURCES

REPRODUCIBLE & REVIEW

- Mastering Critical Thinking Skills 7
- Section 2 Review, p. 161

TECHNOLOGY

- One-Stop Planner, Lesson 7.2
- Homework Practice Online
- HRW Go site

Graph Answer

African Americans

TEACH OBJECTIVES 1 AND 2

To help students describe how the nature of work and the composition of the labor force have changed in the United States, copy the graphic organizer at right onto the chalkboard, omitting the italicized answers. Have students copy and complete it. Then have students work in pairs to create a poster entitled The World of Work: Then and Now. The poster should contrast the workforce in 1900 and in 2000. **ENGLISH LANGUAGE LEARNERS , COOPERATIVE LEARNING**

HOMEWORK: Have students examine the classified ads in a local newspaper and list the main job categories. Then have each student choose two specific jobs and list the skills and qualifications for each of them.

Farming and Manufacturing
fell from 85 percent of U.S. labor force in 1900 to 27 percent in 2000; most work now is in professions, office work, sales, and service jobs

Education
workers' education level has increased; about 90 percent of workers aged 25 to 64 have high school diplomas; about one third have college degrees

Changes in the Nature of Work and the Labor Force

Women
have increased as a percentage of the total labor force; now hold about half of all professional jobs

Minorities
have increased as a percentage of the total labor force; in particular Hispanics, who are the fastest growing group of American workers

---

internet connect

TOPIC: Workforce Patterns
GO TO: go.hrw.com
KEYWORD: SL3 SC7

Have students access the Internet through the HRW Go site to conduct research on job growth patterns and job satisfaction in the workforce. Ask students to gather facts and statistics related to job growth, salary, satisfaction, and skills. Then have each student use the research to create a classified advertisement for a job that he or she would like to have in the future.

Chart Answer

20.8 percent

Women have a growing role in the American labor force, including professional specialty fields such as science and research.

Occupations What types of jobs do American workers hold? The chart on this page gives a breakdown of the United States labor force by occupational category. The following are some examples of jobs that fall into each category listed in the chart.

- *executive, administrative, and managerial:* business executives, office managers, sales managers, credit managers, personnel managers, public relations supervisors, and store managers
- *professional specialty:* doctors, lawyers, dentists, pharmacists, librarians, nurses, engineers, artists, veterinarians, psychiatrists, social workers, teachers, and accountants
- *technical occupations:* laboratory technicians, dental hygienists, medical assistants, licensed practical nurses, and X-ray technicians
- *sales workers:* manufacturers' representatives, retail salespeople, insurance salespeople, and real-estate agents
- *administrative support occupations:* business machine operators, bookkeepers, office clerks, secretaries, receptionists, cashiers, telephone operators, postal workers, and bank workers
- *service occupations:* private household workers—maids, cooks, butlers, and nursemaids; protective service workers—police officers and fire fighters; other service workers—waitpersons, cooks, dental and nursing assistants, janitors, hairdressers, airline attendants, and child-care workers
- *precision production, craft, and repair workers:* mechanics, television repairers, shoemakers, dressmakers, tailors, printers, carpenters, plumbers, electricians, concrete workers, and skilled precision production workers
- *operators, fabricators, and laborers:* packagers, assemblers, welders, heavy equipment operators, freight handlers, warehouse workers, and laborers
- *farming, forestry, and fishing:* farm owners and operators, farm laborers, lumberjacks, fishers, hunters, and trappers
- *transportation and material moving:* truck and bus drivers

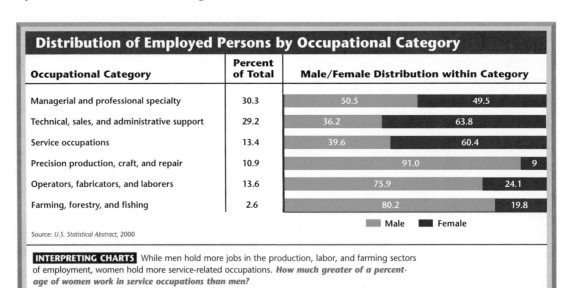

Distribution of Employed Persons by Occupational Category

Occupational Category	Percent of Total	Male/Female Distribution within Category	
Managerial and professional specialty	30.3	50.5	49.5
Technical, sales, and administrative support	29.2	36.2	63.8
Service occupations	13.4	39.6	60.4
Precision production, craft, and repair	10.9	91.0	9
Operators, fabricators, and laborers	13.6	75.9	24.1
Farming, forestry, and fishing	2.6	80.2	19.8

■ Male ■ Female

Source: *U.S. Statistical Abstract, 2000*

INTERPRETING CHARTS While men hold more jobs in the production, labor, and farming sectors of employment, women hold more service-related occupations. *How much greater of a percentage of women work in service occupations than men?*

158

Applying Sociology

▦ TEACH

Have students read the feature A New Labor Pool on this page and answer the questions that follow. Discuss the answers as a class. Then provide students with recent labor and unemployment statistics for your state or the nation. Ask students to analyze the data and to find the number of part-time workers, the number of workers with two or more jobs, and the number of retired workers who have re-entered the labor force. Once students have found the information, have them discuss the effects of these different groups on the labor pool, the job market, and the economy.

▦ SPOTLIGHT on Sweatshops

Have students conduct research on sweatshops being operated in the United States or on American businesses who operate sweatshops abroad. Students should examine who, what, when, where, and why when doing their research as well as describe efforts by the government and others to deal with sweatshops. Have each student use the research to write a letter to a U.S. congressperson, expressing his or her viewpoint on sweatshops and describing actions the student would like to see taken in regard to them.

BLOCK SCHEDULING

A P P L Y I N G
Sociology

A NEW LABOR POOL

During the 1990s, the United States enjoyed one of the longest and strongest economic booms in its history. This boom brought changes to the American labor force. In the boom years, employment rates soared to about 96 percent—above the generally accepted level of full employment. Such high employment rates, economists point out, reduced the pool of people available for work. Available workers are those who are unemployed and seeking work and those who, while not seeking work, would accept any suitable jobs they were offered.

However, some economists doubt that there was a shortage of workers. They agree that the traditional pool of available workers had been reduced. But they suggest that businesses simply found new resources of labor to tap. These new resources, for the most part, consist of women and illegal immigrants.

From Part Time to Full Time

Women already make up about 47 percent of the American labor force. But about half of all working women held part-time jobs, working a few hours a day or a few days a week. Yet during the 1990s more and more women—as many as 1 million a year—moved from part-time to full-time work. This change added millions of working hours to the economy. However, it did not affect the size of the labor force or the employment rate because these measures include both part-time and full-time workers.

A Floating Labor Pool

There are about 5 million illegal immigrants working or available for work in the United States. Economists count these people in the pool of available workers. However, there are vast numbers of illegal immigrants that are not counted. These people live in Canada, Mexico, and the countries of Central and South America. When work is available, they cross the border into the United States. After a few months, they go back to their home countries, waiting to return once again when work is available.

These workers are, according to one observer, "a floating labor pool that kind of floats back and forth across the border."

Other groups help to swell this pool of labor resources. Some older Americans are delaying retirement or returning to the labor force after they have retired. Increasing numbers of students are joining the part-time labor force. More and more people—about 8 million in the late 1990s—are working at two or more jobs.

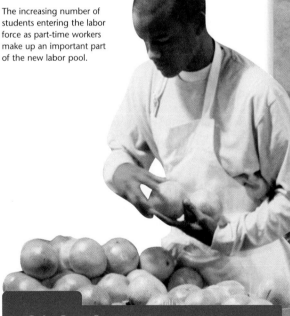

The increasing number of students entering the labor force as part-time workers make up an important part of the new labor pool.

Think About It

1. **Finding the Main Idea** *Who makes up the new labor pool?*
2. **Making Generalizations and Predictions** *The economic boom of the 1990s led businesses to look for these new sources of labor. What do you think happened to the new labor pool when the economy went into a recession? Explain your answer.*

◆ Sociology in the World Today

Part-Time and Temporary Employment. Part-time jobs differ from full-time jobs. Part-time jobs often pay less. In addition, many do not provide benefits such as health insurance or paid vacation. Although many people work part-time to earn extra money, some part-time employees are the sole breadwinners for their families. For these people an unexpected crisis such as an illness can quickly plunge them and their families into poverty. When examining the effects of employment upon society, some sociologists consider how many workers hold only part-time jobs.

RESEARCH ACTIVITY: Have students access the Current Population Survey on the Bureau of Labor Statistics Web site (http://www.bls.gov/cps/) and identify the current top five reasons that Americans gave for working part-time.

Think About It Answers

1. mainly women, illegal immigrants, older Americans

2. The new labor pool probably shrank as many people lost their jobs and other employees moved from full-time to part-time work.

SPOTLIGHT *on Occupational Categories*

Organize students into 10 groups and give each group a slip of paper on which one of the 10 occupational categories listed on p. 158 is written. Tell the groups to not let the other groups see their categories. Then ask each group to write two to three riddles describing the type of work done by people in their occupational category. For example: "I cut down trees used to make paper and furniture. Who am I, and what is my occupational category?" *(lumberjack—farming, forestry, and fishing).* Have the groups alternate in reading their riddles aloud for other students to try and solve.

COOPERATIVE LEARNING , BLOCK SCHEDULING

CLOSE

Remind students of the list that they made in the *Let's Get Started* activity in which they described what they expected from their future careers. Have students discuss how they might change their responses based on the information in this section.

REVIEW AND ASSESS

Have students complete the **Section 2 Review** on p. 161. As **Alternative Assessment**, you may want to use the world of work graphic organizer or poster in this section's lessons.

◆ Applying Sociology

Gender and Job Preference. How does gender affect job choice? A 1984 survey of high schoolers examined this issue and found significant differences in what young men and women hope for in a job. Women were more likely to want jobs where they could work with and help others. Men were more interested in jobs where they could make money and obtain leadership.

Percent Answering YES

Very interested in a career with opportunities to help others:
   Men: 47   Women: 72

Very interested in working with people:
   Men: 40   Women: 68

Very interested in leading:
   Men: 22   Women: 11

Very interested in making money:
   Men: 22   Women: 13

ACTIVITY: Ask students the questions above to see if their views match those of high schoolers in 1984. Use the results of the survey as the basis for a class discussion. For example, you might ask students about some reasons for any gender differences in their class's survey results.

The Changing Nature of Work

As in the case of labor-force composition, there have also been changes in the nature of work in the United States. In 1900 about 35 percent of the labor force worked in farming. About 45 percent were employed in manufacturing and other jobs that required physical labor, such as construction. Only about 20 percent of the labor force worked in jobs that focused on mental effort and interaction with people, such as the professions, management, office work, and sales.

By midcentury, manufacturing jobs dominated the labor force. Today the situation is dramatically different. Farming and manufacturing together now account for 27 percent of the jobs in the United States. Considerable growth, on the other hand, has occurred in the number of people with professional, office work, sales, and service jobs. People holding such jobs make up almost 73 percent of the labor force.

Much of this increase can be attributed to the growth of bureaucracies and professional occupations. Managerial, professional, and administrative support positions account for more than 44 percent of the labor force. Technological developments, particularly the computer, have also contributed to this growth in the service-producing sector. The table on page 161 lists the 10 occupations that are expected to experience the fastest growth in the early years of the 2000s. Note that 5 of the top 10 occupations are directly related to computers.

Job satisfaction is an important factor of work that sociologists study. Americans have found satisfaction in jobs involving botanical sciences, film, and the law.

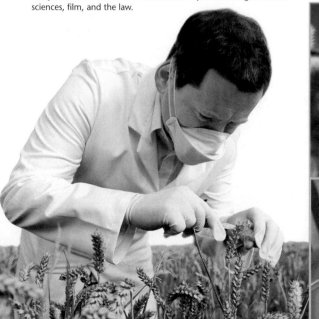

Job Satisfaction

Opinion polls and social-science research indicate that the vast majority of workers in the United States, regardless of what they do, are satisfied with their jobs. For example, in a 1999 Harris poll, 54 percent of the respondents said that they were "very satisfied" with their jobs. Another 37 percent said that they were "somewhat satisfied." However, the level of satisfaction varied according to such factors as income and age. For example, workers with higher incomes reported greater satisfaction with their work than people with lower incomes. Similarly, older workers were more satisfied with their jobs than younger workers.

What factors contribute to job satisfaction? Another Harris poll conducted in 2000 found that the most-satisfied workers were those who had a lot of control over their work, those who got to use their skills and talents, and those who received a lot of recognition and appreciation. A Gallup poll conducted the following year received somewhat different responses. It found that workers expressed the greatest satisfaction with such job characteristics as workplace safety conditions, relations with co-workers, flexibility of hours, the opportunity to do what they do best, and job security.

The conditions that workers are unhappy with provide a better measure of what drives job satisfaction. In the Gallup poll, workers expressed dissatisfaction with the amount of on-the-job stress, their income, and their chances of promotion. They also displayed unhappiness with the benefits they received, such as health insurance and retirement plans.

RETEACH

Organize the class into two groups and assign each group one of the Read to Discover questions at the beginning of this section. Within each group, pair students and have each pair create a detailed outline in answer to its assigned question. Then team up pairs from each group to create foursomes. Have the pairs in each foursome exchange outlines and review the ones they receive for accuracy and completeness. Have group members revise their outlines based on this peer feedback. Finally, have the class help you create two master outlines on the chalkboard.

ENGLISH LANGUAGE LEARNERS , COOPERATIVE LEARNING

EXTEND

Ask students to consider which current jobs did not exist 25 years ago *(such as cell phone manufacturers or Web page designers)*. Then have each student write a few paragraphs describing a job that does not currently exist but that he or she thinks will exist 25 years from now. Remind students to use standard grammar, spelling, sentence structure, and punctuation when writing their paragraphs. Ask volunteers to read their paragraphs to the class.

BLOCK SCHEDULING

One solution for dissatisfied workers is to look for new jobs. Even people who express high levels of satisfaction with their jobs do not stay in those jobs for their entire working lives. For example, one third of the people surveyed in the 1999 Harris poll said that it was very likely that they would change jobs in the next five years. Statistics suggest that moving from job to job is a well-established practice among American workers. A long-term study conducted by the U.S. Bureau of Labor Statistics (BLS) found that, on average, American workers hold about nine jobs between the ages of 18 and 34. Another BLS study found that employee tenure—the median number of years that workers have been with their current employer—is 3.5 years.

Career changes are also becoming a common occurrence among American workers. Changing careers means that workers go into a new field for which their previous experience does not directly qualify them. Statistics indicate that the average worker will change careers from five to six times in a lifetime.

Projected Growth in Employment Opportunities in Selected Occupations, 1998–2008

Occupation	Percentage Increase
Computer engineers	108
Computer support specialists	102
Systems analysts	94
Database administrators	77
Desktop publishing specialists	73
Paralegals and legal assistants	62
Personal care and home health aides	58
Medical assistants	58
Social and human service assistants	53
Physician assistants	48

Source: U.S. Bureau of Labor Statistics

INTERPRETING TABLES While jobs in the service industry are projected to grow, high-tech jobs seem to have the largest growth possibilities. *How do you think future scientific and technological developments will affect society?*

SECTION 2 REVIEW

1. Define and explain
labor force
profession
unemployment
unemployment rate

2. Sequencing
Copy the graphic organizer below. Use it to demonstrate how the nature of work changed during the 1900s.

1900	Mid-1900s	2000

Homework Practice Online
keyword: SL3 HP7

3. Finding the Main Idea
a. Give three examples of how the composition of the labor force has changed over time.
b. What effect have technological developments, such as the computer, had on work in the United States?

4. Writing and Critical Thinking
Evaluating Write two paragraphs discussing workers' satisfaction with their jobs.
Consider:
• the reasons that workers are satisfied with their jobs
• the reasons workers give for dissatisfaction with their jobs
• courses of action for dissatisfied workers

Building Social Studies Skills

TEACH

Draw a two-column chart on the chalkboard and label the columns *School* and *Food*. Have each student copy the chart and provide the following information under each heading:

- School—all the types of activities the student does at school and the percentage of the school day spent doing each type
- Food—all the types of foods the student eats at school and how often on average he or she eats them a week

After going through the feature with students, have them use the information they listed in their chart to make at least one table and one graph.

EXTEND

Have each student select a fun or interesting topic for a fictional or real bar, line, or circle graph. For example, students might create graphs providing data about sports, their family characteristics (age, height, weight, hair color, eye color), or the amount of money they spend on various types of music or entertainment. Have each student create a graph and write a caption explaining it. Then call on volunteers to present their graphs to the class.

BLOCK SCHEDULING

CREATING CHARTS AND GRAPHS

Ask students to apply their skills at creating graphs to one of the tables of data in this textbook. Students should select the best type of graph to present the data and then follow the instructions provided on p. 163 for creating graphs. Have students present their work to the class along with a copy of the table that they graphed.

BUILDING
Social Studies Skills

CREATING CHARTS AND GRAPHS

Charts and graphs display information in visual form. The exact form depends on the type of chart or graph being used and the subject matter conveyed.

Charts This textbook uses several types of charts. Flowcharts, for example, show a sequence of events or the steps involved in a process. Organizational charts show the structure of an organization. The most common type of chart you will see in this textbook is the table. This type of chart presents information in columns and rows.

Graphs Three basic types of graphs are used in this textbook—line graphs, bar graphs, and pie graphs. A line graph usually plots changes in quantities over time. A bar graph can also be used to display changes in quantities over time. However, most often bar graphs compare quantities within categories. Both line and bar graphs have two axes—a vertical axis that usually shows quantities and a horizontal axis that usually shows time or categories. A pie graph, or circle graph, displays the relationship among the parts of a whole by showing sections of a circular image totaling 100 percent. Each section looks like a slice of a pie.

Applying the Skill

To create a table, follow the steps below.
1. **Gather information.** Pull together the information you want to present in your table. The information that you want to present visually might be in text form. Or you might conduct research to locate data that illustrate points in the text. The information in the table below was drawn from U.S. Census Bureau publications on the older population in the United States.
2. **Select a title.** Compose a title that identifies the purpose of your table. The purpose of the table below is to provide information on the older population by age group.
3. **Design the chart.** Decide on column and row headings that identify the categories you intend

Older Population by Age, 1980–2000 (in Thousands)				
Year	65–74	75–84	85+	Total, 65+
1980	15,581	7,729	2,240	25,550
1990	18,045	10,012	3,022	31,079
2000	18,199	12,335	4,312	34,835

Source: U.S. Census Bureau

Have students conduct research on the population of senior citizens in Canada. Students should find statistics on the number of Canadians who were 55 to 64 years of age, 65 to 74 years of age, 75 to 84 years of age, and 85+ years of age for 1980, 1990, and 2000. Have students use the data to create a table similar to the one titled Older Population by Age, 1980–2000 (in Thousands) at the bottom of p. 162. Then have students compare and contrast the Canadian and U.S. data in the two tables. **BLOCK SCHEDULING**

SPOTLIGHT *on Birthrates and Death Rates*

Organize students into small groups and have each group choose one of the following pairs of countries: Australia and Kenya, Canada and Mexico, India and England, Pakistan and Russia, and the Sudan and Norway. Each group should conduct research on the birthrates and death rates in its pair of countries over several years or decades. Groups should then use the data to create at least one table and one graph. Have each group present its work to the class. Then have students discuss their findings.

COOPERATIVE LEARNING, BLOCK SCHEDULING

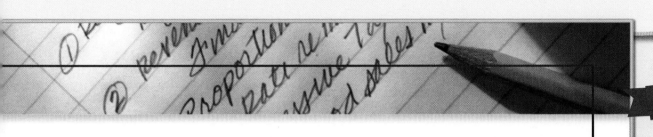

Interdisciplinary Connection

to use. In the table on the previous page, the row headings indicate the years covered and the column headings indicate the age groups.

4. **Complete the table.** Organize your information and enter it in your table. Remember to note the source of the information.

To create a graph using information in the table, follow the steps below.

1. **Select the type of graph.** Decide on the type of graph most suitable to present the information shown in the table. A line graph or pie graph could be used here, but a bar graph is a better choice to show changes in the older population over time.

2. **Compose a title.** Choose a title that describes what you are showing in the graph. When you are creating a graph from a table, it is customary to use the title of the table.

3. **Label the graph axes.** If you are creating a line or bar graph, select labels for the vertical axis and the horizontal axis. As noted before, the vertical axis usually shows quantities and the horizontal axis usually shows time or categories.

4. **Plot the graph.** Calibrate the axes, then plot the information on the graph. Complete the graph by joining the plotted points with a line or by drawing the appropriate bars. Once again, remember to include a source line.

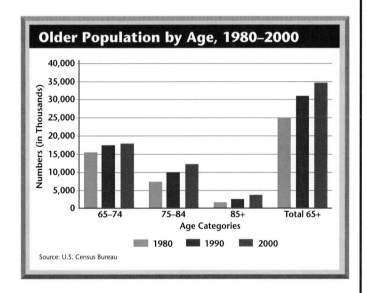

Older Population by Age, 1980–2000

Source: U.S. Census Bureau

MATH

Linear and Curvilinear Relationships. The relationships among variables or quantities in a line graph may be linear (a straight line) or curvilinear (a curved line). For example, the relationship between education and income is linear—that is, the more education people have, the higher their income usually is. The relationship between age and income, however, is curvilinear—that is, income usually rises until retirement and then drops.

CRITICAL THINKING

Do you think that the relationship between age and birth rate is linear or curvilinear?

ANSWER: curvilinear, because birth rate increases as women get older up to a certain age, past which the birth rate begins to decline

Practicing the Skill

Consult the most recent edition of the Statistical Abstract of the United States. *Locate the various tables that include information on the older population in the United States. Select a topic addressed in these tables—older population by region, for example. Using the guidelines listed above, gather data on your selected topic and present the data in a table. Use the table to construct a graph. Remember to use the type of graph that best presents the information.*

Practicing the Skill

As an extension to the activity, have each student write a paragraph explaining why the type of graph they chose was the best one for presenting the data in the table. Then have students mount their table, graph, and paragraph on a posterboard.

SECTION 3

OBJECTIVES

1. *Describe the characteristics of life during late adulthood.*

2. *Identify the new challenges that older Americans face.*

SECTION 3 RESOURCES

REPRODUCIBLE & REVIEW

- Readings and Case Studies in Sociology 7
- Section 3 Review, p. 171

TECHNOLOGY

- One-Stop Planner, Lesson 7.3
- Teaching Transparency: Adapting Patterns in Later Adulthood Used by Different Personality Types
- Homework Practice Online
- HRW Go site

LET'S GET STARTED!

Before class, write the following statements on the chalkboard:

- *I look forward to being 65 years old because . . .*
- *I do not look forward to being 65 years old because . . .*

As students enter the classroom, have them copy and complete the statements. Next, call on volunteers to share their completed statements with the class. Encourage student discussion. Then tell students that in Section 3 they will learn about social gerontology, the study of the nonphysical aspects of the aging process, and what social gerontologists have learned about the characteristics of late adulthood.

3

THE LATER YEARS

Read to Discover

1. What are the characteristics of life during late adulthood?

2. What new challenges do older Americans face?

Define

gerontology, social gerontology, young-old, middle-old, old-old, Alzheimer's disease, dependency

Improved health care has enabled more and more people around the world to live longer than ever before. People age 65 and older are the fastest-growing segment of the world's population. In the United States, people age 65 and older made up just over 11 percent of the population in 1980. This figure was more than 12 percent in 2000. Some estimates indicate that by the year 2030, 20 percent of the population will be age 65 and older.

What is the period of late adulthood like? The field of **gerontology**—the scientific study of the processes and phenomena of aging—provides answers to this question. Sociologists are most interested in **social gerontology**, the study of the nonphysical aspects of the aging process. This section examines what social gerontologists have discovered about the characteristics of late adulthood.

Change Continues

People are now living longer. Thus, it has become impossible to view the late adulthood era as a single period of development. Life at age 65 is very different from life at 85. In recognition of this fact, gerontologists place individuals aged 65 and older into three groups. These groups are the young-old, the middle-old, and the old-old.

It is misleading to think that Americans over the age of 65 are a single group with common life experiences. Men and women have different experiences in each of the stages of later adulthood.

TEACH OBJECTIVE 1

Write the terms *gerontology* and *social gerontology* on the chalkboard and call on volunteers to define them *(gerontology—the scientific study of the processes and phenomena of aging; social gerontology—the study of the nonphysical aspects of the aging process).* Explain to students that late adulthood, like early and middle adulthood, includes different stages of development. To help students describe the characteristics of each stage of late adulthood, copy the graphic organizer at right onto the chalkboard, omitting the italicized answers. Have students copy and complete the organizer and then discuss the answers with the class. Next, organize students into groups and have each group create the front page of a monthly newsletter for senior citizens. The paper should include a masthead and several short articles that reflect the issues that are important to seniors and the characteristics of late adulthood. Have each group present its work to the class. **ENGLISH LANGUAGE LEARNERS , COOPERATIVE LEARNING**

THE THREE PHASES OF LATE ADULTHOOD

Young-Old	Middle-Old	Old-Old
ages 65 to 74; issues related to the adjustment to retirement	*ages 75 to 84; issues related to declining physical and mental functioning, dependency, and death*	*ages 85+; issues related to declining physical and mental functioning, dependency, and death*

INTERPRETING VISUALS Many Americans over the age of 65 have managed to stay physically fit and mentally engaged. *How might this older American feel about his physical accomplishments?*

The topics of interest to gerontologists differ depending on the age group they are studying. Among the **young-old**—ages 65 through 74—adjustment to retirement is one of the most important developmental issues. When the **middle-old**—ages 75 through 84—and the **old-old**—ages 85 and older—are considered, issues surrounding physical and mental decline and death take on added importance. This shift in emphasis is related to health and physical well-being. The young-old generally are in good health and are capable of caring for themselves. However, the body begins to wear out eventually. For most senior citizens, physical and mental functioning declines with advancing years, although the level of decline varies widely. Therefore, health and death issues become major areas of concern for the middle-old and the old-old.

Adjustment to Retirement In American society we tend to identify individuals by their jobs. When two people meet for the first time, the question of what each does for a living is likely to arise. In light of the importance placed on an individual's role in the labor force, it is reasonable to assume that people have difficulty adjusting to retirement. But is this actually the case?

For some people, the loss of the work role is a great shock. This shock is particularly evident in those who strongly identify with their jobs or who do not want to retire. However, research indicates that work-role loss affects a much smaller number of retired people than generally is assumed. In fact, one study found that elderly people consider retirement among the least stressful events that they have experienced. Most gerontologists feel that the level of adjustment to retirement reflects a person's earlier attitudes and behavior. People who were happy and well adjusted in their working lives will generally enjoy retirement. Conversely, people who were unhappy or unfulfilled in their work rarely find retirement satisfying.

Studies have found that such factors as income, health, social networks, and identity affect adjustment to retirement. Retirees need enough income to live comfortably. If they constantly struggle to make economic ends meet, retirees will have little time to enjoy retirement. Similarly, retirees need to have good health. Sickness makes adjustment to any stage of life—not just retirement—difficult. Income and health are related to one of the strongest desires of senior citizens—to remain independent. Retirees quickly lose this feeling of independence if their comfort, both economic and physical, depends on the help and generosity of others.

Retirees also adjust better to their new situation if they remain linked to the larger social world to which they belong. Maintaining social networks—both with friends and with family—greatly contributes to retirees' quality of life. Remaining active in the community helps retirees' adjust because it bolsters their sense of identity within society. For example, contributing to the community through volunteering can help retirees develop a new identity to replace the identity they lost when they left work.

◆ **Applying Sociology**

The Aging of America. The population of the United States continues to age. In 1850 the median age of Americans was 18.9 years of age. By 1999 the median age had increased to 35.5 years. By 2025 the median age of Americans is expected to rise to 38.5 years.

CRITICAL THINKING
How do you think that the aging of the U.S. population influences the perception of age in American society?

ANSWER: Students might respond that the idea of what constitutes "young" and "old" may gradually change along with the aging of the population, with "old" referring to an increasingly older age class.

Visual Answer

proud that he has remained physically fit enough to participate in sports

The Adult in Society **165**

165

TEACH OBJECTIVE 2

Lead a class discussion on the new challenges that older Americans face. As you go through the discussion, have students identify some of these challenges *(for example, challenges related to living longer, the adjustment to retirement and the loss of one's work identity, depression and suicide, declining mental and physical functioning such as dementia, loss of independence, and the fear of death and other death-related issues such as the death of friends).* Then ask students to imagine that they are 70 to 85 years old. Have each student write a poem expressing the opportunities, challenges, concerns, and joys of late adulthood. Call on volunteers to present their poems to the class.

HOMEWORK: Have students list the following headings on a piece of paper: *17 to 39, 40 to 59, 60 to 74,* and *75+.* Instruct each student to list five goals that he or she hopes to achieve during each age range and a brief statement as to how he or she plans to go about achieving each goal. When students next meet, have volunteers share some of their goals and plans with the class. Then have the class consider and discuss the following questions: Do the goals of men and women differ at various life stages, and if so, how? Do most students in the class share the same goals? Why or why not? How do students' goals for later adulthood differ from those of other stages of adulthood?

Chart Answer

the armored and unintegrated personalities

Technology Resources

Teaching Transparency: Adapting Patterns in Later Adulthood Used by Different Personality Types

---

Adapting Patterns in Later Adulthood Used by Different Personality Types

Personality Type

Adapting Patterns

Integrated Personalities: mature, flexible, happy people with rich inner lives who are open to new things and not afraid of their emotions

The *reorganizers* substitute new activities for lost ones. They give time to community or church affairs and keep active.

The *focused* select only one or two areas of activity and concentrate on them.

The *disengaged* abandon their commitments and are content to do so. They take a "rocking chair" approach to old age.

Armored Personalities: striving ambitious people who keep a tight control over their anxieties and impulses

The *holders* are threatened by aging and find satisfaction in holding on to the patterns used during middle age.

The *constrictors* reduce their number of social interactions and close themselves off to experience. They are moderately satisfied with this low level of activity.

Passive-Dependent Personalities: passive people who are dependent on others

The *succourance-seeking* get along with medium activity and medium satisfaction as long as they have someone on which to lean.

The *apathetic* are kept from doing anything by long-standing patterns of passivity and apathy.

Unintegrated Personalities: people with disorganized patterns of aging

The *disorganized* exhibit low levels of activity and satisfaction. They can neither control their emotions nor think clearly.

Source: "Personality and Patterns of Aging" by Bernice L. Neugarten, Robert J. Havighurst, and Sheldon S. Tobin from *Journal of Gerontology,* 1965.

INTERPRETING CHARTS The transition to later adulthood affects people differently. Personality types can help determine how people will be affected. *What personality types do you think will have the most difficulty adapting to later adulthood?*

SPOTLIGHT *on Dependency*

Write the term *dependency* on the chalkboard and call on a volunteer to define it *(the shift from being an independent adult to being dependent on others for physical or financial assistance)*. Then create a chart on the chalkboard with the following headings: *Young Children, Adolescents, Young Adults, Middle-Aged Adults,* and *Older Adults*. Ask students to suggest ways in which each age group is dependent on others. Discuss with students how independence changes with age, increasing and then decreasing. In conclusion, have students explore the effects of the loss of independence on older Americans and possible societal measures for preserving independence for elderly people. **BLOCK SCHEDULING**

INTERPRETING VISUALS Although many older Americans face health problems, a great number continue to remain active like this nurse. *How does this image reflect the reality that many older Americans retain their intellectual abilities throughout life?*

Sociology in the World Today

Ageism. An issue facing many older people today is ageism, or discrimination against older Americans based upon assumptions about their physical and mental abilities. Although U.S. federal law prohibits employers from discriminating on the basis of age, the issue remains a problem for many older workers. For example, many older television writers have trouble finding work in the youth-oriented television industry.

CRITICAL THINKING

What effects might ageism have on American society?

ANSWER: Students might respond that as Americans live longer, ageism could limit individuals' years of financial independence and that many employers will lose the benefit of experienced workers.

Visual Answer

The older nurse in the image is performing a highly skilled job that requires a high degree of skill and mental ability.

Failure to adapt to retirement can have negative consequences. Suicide rates are high among people over the age of 65, particularly among white men. Some sociologists suggest that suicide is more prevalent among white male retirees because their identity is more directly tied to their work.

Physical and Mental Functioning As an individual ages, body cells begin to die. As a result, muscles and tissues shrink. The skin develops wrinkles. The entire body slowly loses weight. The weakened muscles lessen the individual's strength and endurance. The nervous system functions more slowly and less accurately. Hair gradually turns to gray or white as the cells in the roots produce less and less pigment. All the organs and functions of the body slow down. As a result, elderly individuals do everything more slowly than they did when they were younger.

Although people tend to slow down as they age, most remain mentally alert. Recent research has shown that most elderly people retain their intellectual abilities throughout life. This finding runs counter to the earlier assumption that loss of intellectual ability is an unavoidable part of aging. The earlier assumption was based on the results of intelligence tests given to people of different ages. Young people always achieved better scores. Researchers took this as an indication that intellectual ability declines with old age.

Psychologists now believe that two factors influenced the test results. First, the items on the tests related mainly to the youth and young-adult cultures. Second, young people tend to have more formal education than people age 65 and older. New testing techniques and revised test items have produced new results. These results indicate that there is a less-marked decline in intellectual ability among elderly people.

Now psychologists are also looking at changes in an individual's test scores over time rather than comparing test results of people of different ages. For example, a person's score at age 70 might be compared with his or her score at age 50. This approach reveals that intelligence may be more stable than had been previously thought. Studies have found that intelligence, learning, and memory do decline with aging. However, the extent of loss is not so great as originally believed and varies greatly from individual to individual. Some aspects of intelligence and learning improve. Vocabulary, for example, increases until people are in their 70s. Certain kinds of intelligence can be improved with training in thinking skills and strategies.

Nonetheless, for some people aging is accompanied by marked mental decline, or dementia. The most common form of dementia among elderly people is **Alzheimer's disease**—an organic condition that results in the progressive deterioration of brain cells. The progress of this disease is slow but steady, usually lasting

INTERPRETING VISUALS Recognizing the possiblity of mental decline in the later years of life, many senior citizens work to maintain their mental sharpness by volunteering and participating in art programs. *What types of activities would you consider if you were over the age of 65?*

Mapping Social Forces

TEACH

Provide each student with an outline map of the United States. With their textbooks closed, have students select the five states that they think have the highest percentage of older Americans. Call on volunteers to share some of their selections with the class and explain why they chose them. Then have the class turn to the feature Elderly Population Growth in the United States on this page, read the introduction, and examine the map. In conclusion, have students answer the questions following the feature and then discuss the answers as a class.

SPOTLIGHT *on Retirement Communities*

Have students conduct research on the types of housing, communities, and assisted-living facilities available to senior citizens. Students might want to look at the entire country in their research or limit themselves to one region, state, or community. Then have each student use the research to create a brochure or pamphlet to inform senior citizens of their housing options. The brochure or pamphlet should identify and describe each option and then rank each one based on various characteristics, such as affordability, quality of life, and social activities. **BLOCK SCHEDULING**

Mapping
SOCIAL FORCES

ELDERLY POPULATION GROWTH IN THE UNITED STATES

Traditionally, older Americans moved to the Sunbelt states of Florida and Arizona for their retirement years. During the 1990s, however, new trends in elderly population movement developed. The "New Sunbelt"—southwestern states such as Nevada, New Mexico, Utah, Texas, and Colorado, and the Atlantic states of North Carolina, South Carolina, and Georgia—showed the greatest growth in elderly residents. Some distinctly non-Sunbelt states made gains, as well. The elderly population of Alaska, for example, grew by nearly 50 percent in the 1990s. These developments, most observers feel, signal where the elderly population will be concentrated in the 2000s.

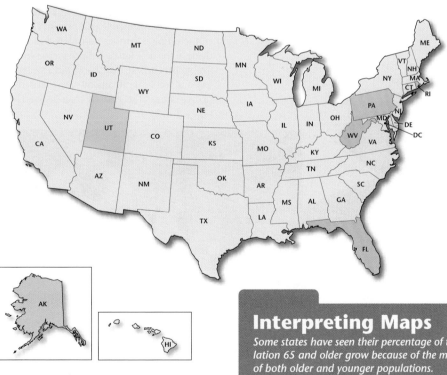

Aging in the United States, 2001

Percent of Population 65 Years and Older
- 5–9
- 10–14
- 15–20

Interpreting Maps

Some states have seen their percentage of the population 65 and older grow because of the migration of both older and younger populations.

1. **Analyzing Information** *What states had the highest percentage of population 65 years and older?*
2. **Drawing Inferences and Conclusions** *What conclusions might a sociologist draw about the demographic patterns and distribution of older Americans?*

Sociology in the World Today

Seniors on the Move. Many older Americans are joining a new subculture called work campers. These retired senior citizens live in their RVs and travel to find work. Work campers most often find jobs at campgrounds, traveling fairs, theme parks, and guest ranches. A network of magazines, RV associations, and Internet sites helps work campers find jobs. Some employers prefer work campers for certain jobs because they find that older employees combine experience with a strong work ethic. Estimates in 2001 put the number of American work campers at 750,000.

CRITICAL THINKING

What might be some consequences of many Americans continuing to work past retirement?

ANSWER: Older workers might increase health care costs for employers, raise productivity, and decrease the number of elderly people living in poverty.

Map Answers

1. Florida, Pennsylvania, and West Virginia

2. except for in a few states, the distribution of older Americans as a percentage of the population is fairly even

▣ CLOSE

Remind students of the statements that they completed in the *Let's Get Started* activity. As a reminder, write the two statements on the chalkboard:

- *I look forward to being 65 years old because . . .*
- *I do not look forward to being 65 years old because . . .*

Then have each student complete each statement again but this time do so based on the information in this section. Finally, call on volunteers to discuss their statements, note if the statements are different from the original ones, and, if so, explain why. Encourage student discussion.

▣ REVIEW AND ASSESS

Have students complete the **Section 3 Review** on p. 171. As **Alternative Assessment**, you may want to use the senior citizen newsletter or bulletin and the senior citizen poem in this section's lessons.

▣ RETEACH

Have students work in pairs to write 10 true/false questions based on the content in this section. Then have the pairs exchange their quizzes, complete the ones they receive, and return them to their authors to be checked for accuracy.

ENGLISH LANGUAGE LEARNERS , COOPERATIVE LEARNING

Visual Answer

Such activities can provide senior citizens with income and make them feel like productive members of society.

SECTION ③ REVIEW ANSWERS

1. Define:
- gerontology, p. 164
- social gerontology, p. 164
- young-old, p. 165
- middle-old, p. 165
- old-old, p. 165
- Alzheimer's disease, p. 168
- dependency, p. 170

2. young-old—ages 65 through 74; middle-old—ages 75 though 84; old-old—ages 85 and older

3a. young-old, middle-old, and old-old. For the young-old, adjusting to retirement is one of the most important issues. For the middle-old and old-old, declining physical health and concerns regarding death are of primary concern. For some people, aging is accompanied by dementia, such as Alzheimer's disease.

b. Challenges faced by aging Americans include the adjustment to retirement, declining physical and mental functioning, and dealing with dependency and death.

4. Paragraphs will vary, but students should use evidence from the text to exhibit an understanding of the factors that influence senior citizens' ability to adjust to retirement.

about 8 to 10 years from first symptoms to death. One of the early symptoms of Alzheimer's disease is the inability to remember current events even though memories from the past can be recalled quite clearly. As the disease progresses, Alzheimer's sufferers may also have trouble performing simple tasks even though they are physically able to do them. For example, they may be unable to perform their work duties or to drive a car. In time, Alzheimer's sufferers often become hostile and disoriented. Eventually, their eyesight, speech, and muscle coordination begin to fail. In the final stages of the disease, they often regress to a childlike state and are no longer able to control their bodily functions.

Only about 8 to 15 percent of the population over age 65 suffers from Alzheimer's disease. However, after age 60 the incidence of dementia nearly doubles with every five years of age. Dementia will become a greater challenge in the future because the American population is aging and people are living longer.

Dealing with Dependency and Death For the middle-old and the old-old, the issues of **dependency** and death take on increasing significance. In this context, dependency is the shift from being an independent adult to being dependent on others for physical or financial assistance. As you have already read, remaining independent is one of the greatest desires of elderly people.

Dependency changes an individual's status in society and necessitates new role behaviors. For example, when an aged parent is forced to live with a grown child because of dependency, the parent-child relationship often becomes reversed. The child takes over the role of the caregiver and authority figure. The aged parent is expected to be grateful for the assistance and to follow the wishes of the child. This change in roles can be very difficult for a person who has become accustomed to making his or her own decisions. Consequently, dependency often strains the parent-child relationship.

Although elderly people do fear dependency, they do not appear to fear death. In fact, fear of death is much more common among middle-aged people. This middle-age fear is interesting when one considers that the likelihood of dying in the near future is much greater for elderly people. Researchers believe that several factors contribute to lower levels of fear of death among senior citizens. First, elderly people are at the end of their lives. They see fewer

INTERPRETING VISUALS Another trend among older Americans is to take on a new career or to do volunteer work after retirement. *How can these activities limit the feeling of dependency that senior citizens might feel?*

1. Ask each student to create a piece of art, such as a painting, drawing, statue, or montage, that illustrates or symbolizes the characteristics of late adulthood. In addition, have each student write a paragraph explaining the artwork. Display students' work in the classroom. **BLOCK SCHEDULING**

2. Have students work in small groups to create a nonprofit television ad that promotes the value of senior citizens to society. Groups might create a storyboard for the ad or videotape the ad. Have each group present its ad to the class.
COOPERATIVE LEARNING , BLOCK SCHEDULING

3. Have students interested in learning more about late adulthood read a nonfiction work on the subject. Some books you might suggest are *The Ageless Spirit* edited by Phillip L. Berman and Connie Goldman or *Old Age Is Not for Sissies* by Art Linkletter. Have each student write a one- to two-page book report about the book.
BLOCK SCHEDULING

---

prospects for the future; thus, they feel they have less to lose. Second, many elderly people, having lived longer than they expected, feel they are "living on borrowed time." Finally, facing the deaths of friends and family members who are close to them in age helps prepare older Americans for their own deaths.

New Opportunities

For many older Americans—particularly those who are financially secure—retirement is accompanied by a feeling of freedom. In retirement, they have the time to do many of the things they always wanted to do. They also have the chance to try new things. Many people use part of the time in late adulthood to travel. Others take college courses. Still others pursue activities—such as crafts, golf, photography, or gardening—that they may have been interested in for many years. Some may become active in politics. For example, they may participate in such lobbying groups as the Gray Panthers or the American Association of Retired Persons (AARP).

Some elderly Americans begin a second career, either for pay or as volunteers. In recent years, part-time employment opportunities have increased for senior citizens. Many businesses, particularly those in the service sector, have attempted to draw from this growing pool of experienced workers. Many volunteer programs provide opportunities for older people to get involved in the community. The Retired Senior Volunteer Program (RSVP) finds positions for people aged 60 and older in libraries, museums, and various social-service agencies. Former managers and administrators may work with Service Corps of Retired

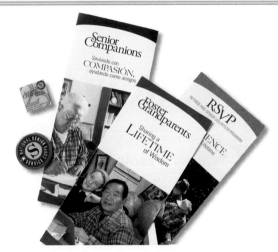

The growth of community-service organizations have provided new opportunities for senior citizens eager to volunteer their time and expertise.

Executives (SCORE). SCORE volunteers offer management assistance to small businesses and community organizations. In the Foster Grandparent Program, older adults spend 20 hours per week caring for youngsters in hospitals, correctional institutions, and day-care centers.

Research has shown that individuals who have planned ahead for retirement are in a better position to take advantage of the opportunities in this period of life. This preparation involves financial planning. It also involves broadening one's interests and perhaps developing some hobbies during middle adulthood. Similarly, it involves taking care of one's health. Probably most important of all, it involves cultivating patterns of living that make the most of life in every growth period.

---

③ SECTION REVIEW

1. Define and explain
gerontology
social gerontology
young-old
middle-old
old-old
Alzheimer's disease
dependency

2. Sequencing Copy the time line below. Use it to place the three groups described in this section according to their year spans.

65 70 75 80 85 90 95 100

3. Finding the Main Idea
a. Into what three groups do gerontologists organize the aged population? How do the issues confronting people in these groups differ?
b. List some of the challenges that face aging Americans.

4. Writing and Critical Thinking
Analyzing Information Write a paragraph that discusses the factors that influence one's adjustment to retirement.
Consider:
• the loss of work
• economic independence
• health
• social networks

Homework Practice Online
keyword: SL3 HP7

ANSWERS

WRITING A SUMMARY
See the section subtitles for the main topics in this chapter.

IDENTIFYING PEOPLE AND IDEAS

1. Yale psychologist who determined three main stages of adult male development

2. the combination of statuses, roles, activities, goals, values, beliefs, and life circumstances that characterize a person

3. usually someone older who fosters a person's development by believing in that person, sharing that person's dreams, and helping that person achieve those dreams

4. with Irene Frieze, conducted research that indicated three distinct phases of adult female development

5. all individuals 16 and older who are employed in paid positions or who are seeking paid employment

6. a high-status occupation that requires specialized skills obtained through formal education

7. situation that occurs when people do not have jobs but are seeking employment

8. scientific study of the processes and phenomena of aging

9. organic condition that results in the progressive

Review and Assessment Resources

- Chapter 7 Review, pp. 172–73
- Chapter Review Activities with Answer Key
- Global Skill Builder CD–ROM
- Chapter 7 Test Generator (on the One-Stop Planner)
- Chapter 7 Test (Form A or B)
- Alternative Assessment Handbook
- HRW Go site

REVIEW

Have students complete the **Chapter 7 Review** on pp. 172–73.

 ASSESS

Use one of the chapter tests to assess students' understanding of the content. For **Alternative Assessment**, see the **Alternative Assessment Handbook**.

---

destruction of brain cells

10. the shift from being an independent adult to being dependent on others for physical or financial aid

UNDERSTANDING MAIN IDEAS

1. Levinson identified three main eras of adult male development—early, middle, and late adulthood. Each era begins with a transitional period followed by alternating stable and transitional periods.

2. Adult female development emphasizes marriage and family over career, and child rearing often interrupts or halts career advancement.

3. Changes include increases in the number of women and minority workers, a better-educated workforce, changes in the type of work people do, and a rise in career changes.

4. During the 1900s, the majority of jobs shifted from being in farming, manufacturing, and physical labor to being in professions and service industries.

5. challenges—adjusting to retirement, coping with changes in physical and mental functioning, and dealing with issues of dependency and death; opportunities— freedom to pursue dreams, and start a new career

6. young-old—adjusting to retirement; middle-old and old-old—concerns include declining physical health and dependency and death

 Writing a Summary

Using standard grammar, spelling, sentence structure, and punctuation, summarize the information in this chapter.
Consider:

- theories of adult development among men and women
- the changing nature of work and the labor force
- the characteristics of late adulthood

 Identifying People and Ideas

Identify the following people or terms and use them in appropriate sentences.

1. Daniel Levinson
2. life structure
3. mentor
4. Esther Sales
5. labor force
6. profession
7. unemployment
8. gerontology
9. Alzheimer's disease
10. dependency

 Understanding Main ideas

Section 1 (pp. 150–56)

1. Briefly describe Daniel Levinson's views on adult male development.

2. How does adult female development differ from adult male development?

Section 2 (pp. 157–63)

3. How has the composition of the American labor force changed?

4. In what ways has the nature of work in the United States changed during the 1900s?

Section 3 (pp. 164–71)

5. What challenges and opportunities are associated with the later stages of life?

6. What are the main characteristics of each stage of life during the later years of adulthood?

 Thinking Critically

1. Supporting a Point of View Some sociologists suggest that adult female development and adult male development are similar—only the ways that men and women handle the various stages are different. Do you agree or disagree? Explain your answer.

2. Making Generalizations and Predictions How do you think the nature of work and the composition of the labor force in the United States will change over the next 25 years? Explain your answer.

3. Drawing Inferences and Conclusions What job characteristics do you think contribute most to job satisfaction? How do different motivations and aspirations affect economic decisions?

4. Evaluating How and why are social networks important when adjusting to retirement?

5. Analyzing Information Why have views concerning intellectual ability in older adults changed in recent years?

 Writing About Sociology

1. Summarizing Locate and read Daniel Levinson's study, *The Seasons of a Woman's Life*. Write a brief summary of Levinson's main arguments. Conclude your summary with a brief explanation of why you agree or disagree with Levinson's point of view.

2. Evaluating Work in a group with two or three other students to review ads in several newspapers and current events magazines. Note the number of ads that target older Americans. Also, review the techniques used in these ads and compare them to techniques used in other ads. Present your findings in a brief written report. Use the graphic organizer below to help you write the report.

	Number of ads aimed at older Americans	Techniques used to reach older Americans
Media Source 1		
Media Source 2		
Media Source 3		

RETEACH

Write the chapter's Define and Identify terms on note cards. Then organize the class into two or more teams and host a game of Sociology Draw. Give a team member a card. The student has one minute to draw images to help his or her team guess the term on the card. The student drawing may not speak, gesture, or use any numbers or words. If the team does not guess the word in the allotted time, give the next team a chance. Award one point for a correct guess. The team with the most points at the end of the game wins.

ENGLISH LANGUAGE LEARNERS , COOPERATIVE LEARNING

SOCIOLOGY PROJECTS

1. Connecting to Science Have students conduct research on Alzheimer's disease. Students should create a magazine article describing the disease in layman's terms and presenting the latest advances and research in treating, understanding, and preventing the disease.

2. Linking to Community Have interested students volunteer at a local nursing home, retirement community, or assisted-living facility. Have volunteers keep a running journal of their experiences and then present a short oral report about the work and what they learned about older adults.

BUILDING SOCIAL STUDIES SKILLS

Interpreting Graphs

Study the graph below. Use it to answer the following questions.

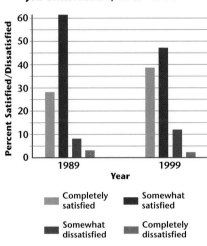

Job Satisfaction, 1989–1999

Source: The Gallup Organization

Legend:
- Completely satisfied
- Somewhat satisfied
- Somewhat dissatisfied
- Completely dissatisfied

1. Which category showed the greatest change from 1989 to 1999?
   a. completely satisfied
   b. somewhat satisfied
   c. completely dissatisfied
   d. somewhat dissatisfied
2. Was there an increase or decrease in overall job satisfaction from 1989 to 1999?

Analyzing Primary Sources

In the following excerpt explores a new study on older Americans and independence. Read the excerpt and then answer the questions that follow.

"*Americans are not only living longer, but they are living more robust lives, according to a new study that tracked chronic disability rates from 1982 to 1999. . . .*
Chronic disability, defined in the study as impairments for three months or longer that impede daily activities, has been slowly falling since 1982. But the pace quickened in the 1990s. . . .
[T]he report's authors found that eight in 10 people over age 65 said they were able to care for themselves in 1999, the last year for which data is available. That figure represents an increase of nearly 8 percent from 1982. . . .
Some of the reasons are straightforward: better diet, fewer smokers and widely available treatments for arthritis and cataracts, two of the most common causes of disability in the elderly. Preventive medicine for illnesses such as heart disease and less physically demanding jobs were also credited with keeping Americans healthy longer.
Most striking was the relationship between education and health. . . . [T]here is increasing evidence that additional schooling (or increased brain activity) reduces the risk of Alzheimer's disease."

3. What could be the most striking results of the study?
   a. the link between better diet and health
   b. the widely available treatments for the common causes of disability
   c. preventive medicine for illnesses such as heart disease
   d. the link between better education and the reduction of risk of Alzheimer's
4. What effect do you think this trend will have on life in general for older Americans?

SOCIOLOGY PROJECTS

Linking to Community

Using Statistics Conduct research and create a report on changes in the labor force and in the nature of work in your community over the last 50 years. Be sure to include a list of possible questions and answers people might have about your report. Illustrate your report with drawings, charts, graphs, and other appropriate visual materials.

internet connect

Internet Activity: go.hrw.com
KEYWORD: SL3 SC7
Choose an activity on the adult in society to:
- create a classified ad based on statistics related to the workforce.
- design a table or chart outlining the goals of groups that lobby for older Americans.
- create a theoretical profile of one theorist of adult life.

THINKING CRITICALLY

1. Answers will vary, but students should discuss how the tension between family and career roles affects adult female development.

2. Students might predict that the professions and service sectors will continue to expand as a result of rapid technological development.

3. Students might mention doing enjoyable or interesting work, working with people they like, and having a friendly and flexible work environment.

4. They contribute to retirees' quality of life by bolstering older people's sense of identity.

5. Recent research has shown that most older adults retain their intellectual abilities throughout life.

WRITING ABOUT SOCIOLOGY

1. Summaries will vary, but students should explain why they agree or disagree with Levinson's arguments, and then defend their viewpoints.

2. Reports will vary, but students should exhibit an understanding of how advertising addresses the issues facing older Americans.

BUILDING SOCIAL STUDIES SKILLS

1. b

2. increase

3. d

4. This trend will enable older Americans to live longer and more robust lives and to remain productive.

Deviance and Social Control

CHAPTER RESOURCE MANAGER

Objectives	Pacing Guide	Resources

SECTION 1:
Deviance
(pp. 176–86)

REV Section 1
Review, p. 185

- Explain the nature and social functions of deviance.
- Compare the theories that have been proposed to explain deviance.

Regular	Block
2 days	Scheduling
	1 day

Block Scheduling Handbook with Team Teaching Strategies, Chapter 8

Resources

- 📼 **CNN.** Presents Sociology: School Violence Prevention Programs
- **RS** Graphic Organizer 8
- 🌐 HRW Go site
- **SM** Mastering Critical Thinking Skills 8
- **PS** Readings and Case Studies in Sociology 8
- **E** Research Projects and Activities for Teaching Sociology 8
- **SM** Study Skills and Writing Guide
- 📀 Teaching Transparency: Merton's Structural Strain Theory of Deviance
- 📀 Teaching Transparency: Percentage of Total Arrests by Type of Crime

SECTION 2:
Crime
(pp. 187–97)

REV Section 2
Review, p. 197

- Identify the principal types of crime in the United States.
- Explain the characteristics of the American criminal-justice system.

Regular	Block
3 days	Scheduling
	1.5 days

Block Scheduling Handbook with Team Teaching Strategies, Chapter 8

Chapter Review And Assessment

- **REV** Chapter 8 Review, pp. 198–99
- **REV** Chapter Review Activities with Answer Key
- 💿 Global Skill Builder CD–ROM
- 💿 Chapter 8 Test Generator (on the One-Stop Planner)
- **A** Chapter 8 Test (Form A or B)
- **A** Alternative Assessment Handbook
- 🌐 HRW Go site

Chapter Resource Key

PS Primary Sources	**A** Assessment	📼 Video	
RS Reading Support	**REV** Review	🌐 Internet	
E Enrichment	📀 Transparencies	💻 Holt Presentation Maker Using Microsoft® PowerPoint®	
SM Skills Mastery	💿 CD–ROM		

💿 **One-Stop** Planner CD–ROM

See the *One-Stop Planner* for a complete list of additional resources for students and teachers.

One-Stop Planner CD-ROM

It's easy to plan lessons, select resources, and print out materials for your students when you use the *One-Stop Planner CD–ROM with Test Generator.*

Chapter Project Preview

The following activities are included in the Chapter Review. You may want to make the suggested preparations.

CHAPTER REVIEW ACTIVITY

Interviewing Skills Students will work in pairs or groups of three to interview members of the local police department about how the tools and techniques of crime reporting have changed. Before the activity, contact the local police department and line up several officials who are willing to be interviewed or to speak to the class.

LESSON ACTIVITY

Connecting to Government Students will read the U.S. Constitution and locate and discuss sections that focus on the rights of crime victims and of individuals accused of crime. Before starting the activity, identify and summarize these sections yourself. You might also refer to a government book for additional information or have a government teacher cross-teach the lesson with you.

INTERNET ACTIVITIES

Crime Statistics Students will use provided Internet links to research and create a database of state crime statistics. Students will need either access to software for creating databases or guidelines for creating a database manually.

Private Prisons: Pros and Cons Students will use provided Internet links to conduct research on the growth in the trend of prison privatization. Students will then work in small groups to create a brochure either supporting or opposing a new private prison in their community. In preparation, provide sample brochures for students to examine and a template for students to use when they create their brochures.

Additional Resources

PRINT RESOURCES FOR TEACHERS

Juvenile Offenders and Victims: 1999 National Report. Washington, D.C.: U.S. Department of Justice, 2000. Provides data and information on juvenile statistics, victims, and offenders and on the juvenile-justice system.

Pontell, Henry N. *Social Deviance: Readings in Theory and Research.* Englewood Cliffs, NJ: Prentice-Hall, 1993. Scholarly anthology of readings on deviance.

Sourcebook of Criminal Justice Statistics, 2000. Washington, D.C.: U.S. Department of Justice, 2000. Presents a wide range of criminal justice data from more than 100 sources.

PRINT RESOURCES FOR STUDENTS

Brown, Gene. *Violence on America's Streets: Headliner Series.* Brookfield, CT: Millbrook Press, 1992. Draws upon newspaper headlines to examine crime and the criminal-justice system.

Dolan, Edward, and Scariano, Margaret. *The Police in American Society.* New York: Franklin Watts, 1988. Examines the role of the police in society from a historical and contemporary perspective. Gives students a broad picture of police work.

Jankowski, Martin Sanchez. *Islands in the Street: Gangs and American Urban Society.* Berkeley, CA: University of California Press, 1991. Presents results of interviews with gang members from around the country.

MULTIMEDIA RESOURCES

Gangs: Decisions and Options (vhs; 17 min.) Nystrom. Presents three young people from different backgrounds who wrestle with their decision to join a youth gang.

Juvenile Law (vhs; 24 min.) Guidance Associates. Illustrates the differences between criminal procedures and juvenile law.

internet connect

HRW ONLINE RESOURCES

GO TO: go.hrw.com
Then type in a keyword.

TEACHER HOME PAGE
KEYWORD: SL3 Teacher

CHAPTER INTERNET ACTIVITIES
KEYWORD: SL3 SC8
Choose an activity to have students:
• create a thematic graph or chart on crime statistics in your state.
• analyze gangs from the four theoretical perspectives explained in this chapter.
• create a pamphlet on criminal justice and the corrections system.

CHAPTER ENRICHMENT LINKS
KEYWORD: SL3 CH8

ONLINE ASSESSMENT
Homework Practice
KEYWORD: SL3 HP8
Standardized Test Prep
KEYWORD: SL3 STP8
Rubrics
KEYWORD: SS Rubrics

CONTENT UPDATES
KEYWORD: SS Content Updates

HOLT PRESENTATION MAKER
KEYWORD: SL3 PPT8

ONLINE READING SUPPORT
KEYWORD: SS Strategies

CURRENT EVENTS
KEYWORD: S3 Current Events

CHAPTER

8

Deviance and
Social Control

SECTION 1
Deviance

SECTION 2
Crime

CHAPTER REVIEW

Build on What You Know

Ask students to answer the
following questions:

**In what developmental stage
of adulthood might people be
most likely to commit a crime?**

Consider:

- age
- economic and educational
  status
- responsibilities and
  commitments

**Why might people decide to
break society's rules?**

Consider:

- inherited characteristics and
  socialization
- family or other primary
  relationships
- economic and educational
  status

Internet Activity

☑ internet connect

TOPIC: Crime Statistics
GO TO: go.hrw.com
KEYWORD: SL3 SC8

Have students access the
Internet through the HRW
Go site to conduct research
on crime statistics and the
frequency of criminal activity
in their state. Then have
students work in groups to
create databases of state
crime statistics. The groups
should use their databases
to determine the top five
crimes most likely to be
committed in their state.
Then ask group members
to discuss and list possible
sociological reasons to
explain the frequency of
these crimes.

CHAPTER

8

Deviance and Social Control

Build on What You Know

Adults pass through
multiple stages of
development as they
age. In this chapter,
you will learn what
happens when a per-
son ignores the rules
of society—engag-
ing in deviance and
crime. You will exam-
ine five influential
theories of deviance.
Finally, you will
explore the charac-
teristics of crime and
the criminal-justice
system.

Hoping to limit crime, Americans
have formed groups such as the
Fraud Fighters to raise public consciousness about particular crimes
and crime-prevention techniques.

Life in Society

Deviant and criminal acts are everyday events in modern society. Most communities have at least one "character"—someone known for his or her strange behavior. People living on the streets and in abandoned buildings are an increasingly common sight. While this behavior is not necessarily illegal, unusual behavior often makes many Americans uncomfortable. Americans are also wary of crime. Neighborhood Crime Watch signs are common. Intricate locks and dead bolts can be found on the doors of homes throughout the United States. Some Americans have installed security systems and bars on their windows to prevent crime.

Television programs and movies based on the activities of fictional criminals, detectives, and lawyers have become favorites among the viewing public. Despite the popularity of these crime shows and movies, violent crime rates have actually dropped in recent years. Yet fear of violent crime remains one of the most pressing concerns for many Americans. In this chapter we will explore the reasons for these changes in crime rates as well as other issues related to deviance and crime in the United States.

WHY SOCIOLOGY MATTERS

Sociologists are interested in the ways the justice system handles young offenders. Use **CNNfyi.com** or other current events sources to learn more about the juvenile justice system. Write a report about the effectiveness of the system. Be sure to include graphs, charts, and maps where appropriate.

CNNfyi.com

TRUTH OR FICTION

What's Your Opinion?

Read the following statements about sociology. Do you think they are true or false? You will learn whether each statement is true or false as you read the chapter.

• Deviance fulfills no positive functions for society.

• Being labeled as deviant has little influence on a person's life.

• Criminal sentences have one purpose—to punish the offender.

175

🔊 *LET'S GET STARTED!*

Before class, write the following statement on the chalkboard: *A deviant is . . . .* As students enter the classroom, have each of them without using their textbooks jot down two or three examples of a deviant or of deviant behavior. Next, call on volunteers to read their definitions and examples to the class. Then call on a student to read aloud the definition of the term *deviance* in the Glossary *(behavior that violates significant social norms)*. Tell students that in Section 1 they will learn about the nature and social functions of deviance and about sociological theories that have been proposed to explain deviant behavior.

Visual Answer

because some businesspeople prefer employees to have a professional, conservative appearance and manner and consider tattoos to be a sign of rebellious youthful behavior

① DEVIANCE

- **Read to Discover**
  1. What are the nature and social functions of deviance?
  2. How do the theories that have been proposed to explain deviance compare?

- **Define**
  deviance, stigma, criminologists, strain theory, anomie, control theory, cultural transmission theory, differential association, techniques of neutralization, labeling theory, primary deviance, secondary deviance, degradation ceremony

- **Identify**
  Robert K. Merton, Richard Quinney, Travis Hirschi, Edwin Sutherland, Edwin Lemert, Howard Becker, Harold Garfinkel

Read through and consider the following list of five behaviors. What do you think they have in common?

- continuously talking to oneself in public
- drag racing on a public street or highway
- regularly using illegal drugs
- a man wearing women's clothing
- attacking another person with a weapon

As you recall from Chapter 3, most people internalize the majority of the norms in their society. However, individuals do not internalize every norm. Even sanctions—the rewards and punishments used to enforce conformity to norms—cannot bring about complete social control. There are always individuals who break the rules of their society or the group. Behavior that violates significant social norms is called **deviance**. Look again at the behaviors listed above. They are examples of deviant behavior in American society.

The Nature of Deviance

Every society has countless norms that govern behavior. Some norms deal with fairly insignificant behaviors, such as personal cleanliness or table manners. Other norms are vital to the smooth operation of a society and the safety of its members. For example, norms governing the taking of another person's life or property are essential in any society.

Because there are so many norms governing behavior, occasional violations are unavoidable. Not all norm violations are considered deviant acts. An act that is considered deviant in one situation may be considered acceptable in another, even within the same society. For example, to kill someone is generally illegal. However, if a member of the military or a police officer kills someone in the line of duty, the action is usually judged quite differently.

What is considered deviant also varies from society to society. For example, divorce is legal in the United States. However, it is prohibited in the Philippines. Similarly, an act might be considered deviant during one period of time but not in another. Throughout much of the 1900s it was illegal for stores to do business on Sunday. However, today most stores open for at least a few hours each Sunday.

How do people come to be considered deviant? Suppose a person gets a speeding ticket. That person would not be considered deviant on the basis of this one event. However, if that person was continually caught driving at high speeds, such reckless behavior would be considered deviant. Repeating an offense is not the only way a person comes to be labeled a deviant. A person who commits an act that has serious

INTERPRETING VISUALS Although many Americans consider tattoos deviant, the norm against tattoos in the world of business has become less strict in recent years. *Why do you think American businesspersons consider tattoos deviant?*

◼◻ TEACH OBJECTIVE 1

SUGGESTION 1: Write the definition of deviance on the chalkboard *(behavior that violates significant social norms).* Next, ask students to identify some deviant acts. On the chalkboard, list criminal acts in one column and noncriminal acts in another column. After students have listed several ideas, point out that crime is just one form of deviance and that not all deviant acts are negative. Then call on volunteers to identify the social functions of deviance *(to clarify norms, unify the group, diffuse tension, promote social change, and provide jobs)* and apply the functions to some of the acts listed. Finally, have each student create a large visual diagram illustrating the five social functions of deviance. The diagram should include images representing each function.

SUGGESTION 2: Lead a class discussion on the nature and social functions of deviance. *(See the previous lesson suggestion.)* As you do, list the five social functions on the chalkboard. Then organize students into small groups. Instruct each group to select one or more of the social functions of deviance and prepare a short skit that illustrates the selected functions. Each group member should participate in the skit in some way. Then have each group present its skit to the class and have other students try to identify the social functions being depicted. Finally, have each student write a paragraph describing how deviant behaviors can have both positive and negative consequences. **COOPERATIVE LEARNING**

negative consequences for society—such as murder, sexual assault, or robbery—is likely to be labeled as deviant because of his or her single act.

The labeling of someone as deviant involves two components. To be considered deviant by society, an individual must first be detected committing a deviant act. A person will not be labeled as deviant unless his or her deviant behavior is in some way known to other people. Next, the individual must be stigmatized by society. A **stigma** is a mark of social disgrace that sets the deviant apart from the rest of society. Stigmas have been used as a form of social control throughout history. For example, the ancient Greeks cut or burned signs into the bodies of criminals to warn others that these deviants were to be avoided.

The power of the outward sign as a form of social control is still used today. For example, prison inmates in the United States are forced to wear special clothing and are assigned numbers as a visual sign of stigma. Some people have suggested that the cars of people convicted of driving while drunk should be marked in some way, such as with a decal. This visual sign would serve both as a warning to others and as a form of public humiliation.

When sociologists speak of the stigma resulting from the label of deviance, they usually do not mean outward signs. Rather, they are referring to the negative social reactions that result from being labeled deviant. According to sociologist Erving Goffman, a person labeled as deviant has a "spoiled social identity." He or she is no longer seen as being normal or whole.

The Social Functions of Deviance

In *The Rules of Sociological Method,* Émile Durkheim observed that deviance has some uses in social life. Deviance, Durkheim suggested, helps to clarify norms, unify the group, diffuse tension, and promote social change. Deviance also serves another positive function not mentioned by Durkheim—it provides jobs such as law enforcement.

Clarifying Norms Deviance serves to define the boundaries of acceptable behavior. When rules are broken and the guilty parties are caught, members of society are reminded of the norms that guide social life. The punishment of norm violators serves as a warning to others that certain behaviors will not be tolerated by society. For example, harsh prison sentences are intended to discourage crime. People may choose not to commit deviant acts if they are aware of how severe the consequences of those acts will be.

INTERPRETING VISUALS Homeless persons are often labeled deviant. *What visual signs act as stigmas of deviance for homeless persons?*

Case Studies and Other True Stories

■ TEACH

Have students read the feature American Youth Gangs on this page. Then call on volunteers to answer the questions that follow without referring to their textbooks. As students respond, summarize their answers on the chalkboard. Then ask students to discuss the differences and similarities between gangs and other groups that young people join. Use students' responses as the basis of a class discussion on how youth gangs are deviant. You might also have students apply each of the five theories of deviance (explained on pp. 180–82 and 184–85) to youth gangs.

SPOTLIGHT on Youth Gang Prevention

Have students conduct research on the programs and services available in the local community to prevent young people from joining gangs or to help youth leave gangs. Then have students work in small groups to create a televised public service announcement designed either to promote local gang prevention efforts, to encourage youth not to join gangs, or to provide youth who want to leave gangs with information about where to go for help. Have each group present its public service announcement to the class.
COOPERATIVE LEARNING , BLOCK SCHEDULING

Think About It Answers

1. because of threats and force or to escape poverty-stricken neighborhoods, rebel, or gain friendship and protection

2. Suggestions will vary, but students should consider the reasons that young people join gangs and the difficulty of leaving gangs.

Case Studies
AND OTHER TRUE STORIES

AMERICAN YOUTH GANGS

The number of youth gang members has grown considerably over the last 40 years. According to sociologist Malcolm W. Klein, only 23 U.S. cities had serious gang problems in 1961. Today youth gangs are a presence in every city that has a population of 250,000 or greater. However, it is false to assume that gangs are a problem in only major urban areas. In 1998, one third of cities with populations of 25,000 or smaller and 18 percent of the rural counties in the United States reported having active youth gangs. The U.S. Department of Justice estimates that there are some 28,700 youth gangs with a total membership of about 780,200 nationwide.

Increasing Violence

Not only has the number of youth gang membership grown over the years, but the level of violence associated with such gangs has also increased. Many of today's youth gangs—whose members usually range in age from 12 to 24—are illegally armed with guns. Research shows that gangs are more likely to recruit young people who own guns. Gang members are more likely to have guns for protection. The availability of weapons has led to an increase in gang-related homicides. In 1997 there were more than 3,340 member-based homicides—murders in which either the perpetrator or the victim was a gang member. The risk of being killed is 60 times greater for youth gang members than it is for the general public.

Why Young People Join Gangs

Central to the problem of youth gangs is the question of why young people choose to join them. According to Léon Bing, gangs often offer the only escape for young people from neighborhoods characterized by poverty and limited economic opportunities. Yet poverty alone cannot explain the rise in gang membership, because gangs are increasingly found in middle-class areas. Sociologist Jack Katz suggests that the elaborate subculture of the gang, which includes the wearing of certain colors or

Motorcycle gangs could be found throughout the United States during the 1950s and 1960s. Even then, these gang members were characterized as lawless deviants.

articles of clothing, may be attractive to some young people who feel the need to rebel. Others appear to be willing to risk imprisonment or death for the companionship and protection provided by the gang. However, some young people are forced into joining gangs by threats from gang members.

Members of youth gangs who want to leave their gang often find that there are few ways out. Some who want to leave are forced to undergo a ceremony that consists of being beaten by fellow gang members. Often this leaves the individual badly injured. Sometimes it results in death.

Think About It

1. **Summarizing** *Why do young people join gangs?*

2. **Supporting a Point of View** *Many programs have been designed to prevent young people from joining gangs. Some of these programs provide remedial education, skills training, or jobs. Others provide crisis intervention and counseling for young people and their families. What methods do you think should be used to keep young people out of gangs?*

CONNECTING *to Literature*
Have students read or reread Nathaniel Hawthorne's novel *The Scarlet Letter* and write a brief essay on the effect the stigma of the scarlet letter has on one of the characters' lives. Although many students might choose to focus on Hester Prynne, encourage students to consider other characters, such as Arthur Dimmesdale, Roger Chillingworth, or Pearl. Students should provide specific examples from the novel that support their positions. Ask volunteers to read their essays to the class. **BLOCK SCHEDULING**

SPOTLIGHT *on Festivals and Deviance*
Numerous cultures have holidays or celebrations in which social norms are routinely violated without consequences to the participants. Mardi Gras and other pre-Lenten festivals are one example. Ask students to conduct research on one such holiday and then prepare a short oral report analyzing the social functions that the holiday serves. For example, students might consider whether the holiday and its relaxing of certain norms reinforces societal norms, unifies the society, or helps relieve tension.
BLOCK SCHEDULING

Unifying the Group Deviance also serves to draw the line between conforming members of society and "outsiders"—the nonconforming members. This "us against them" attitude reinforces the sense of community and the belief in shared values. Durkheim suggested that deviance is so important to the maintenance of group unity, it would have to be invented if it did not exist naturally.

Diffusing Tension When people are unhappy with their lives or social conditions, they may want to strike out at society. In such situations, minor acts of deviance serve as a safety valve. These acts allow individuals to relieve tension without disrupting the basic fabric of society. For example, participating in unauthorized demonstrations allows people to express political or social discontent without destroying the social order.

Promoting Social Change Deviance can help prompt social change by identifying problem areas. When large numbers of people violate a particular norm, it is often an indication that something in society needs to be changed. Once alerted to the problem, individuals in positions of authority can take steps to correct the situation.

Providing Jobs Deviance also provides legitimate jobs for a wide range of people. Judges, lawyers, police officers, prison personnel, and parole officers have jobs related to one aspect of deviance—crime. So too do crime reporters and **criminologists**—the social scientists who study criminal behavior. In addition, there are many other jobs that are based in part on the existence of deviance. For example, workers at clothing manufacturers might make prison uniforms as well as other types of clothes.

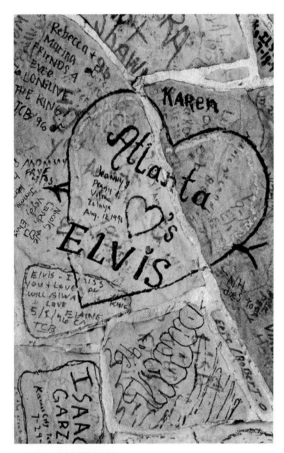

INTERPRETING VISUALS One function of deviance is to help foster an "us against them" attitude. *How might deviant acts like spraying graffitti unify groups?*

Case Study

Deviant Subcultures: Hackers. People who commit deviant acts sometimes form deviant subcultures, or groups whose members share their deviance, view it as normal, and encourage it. Deviant subcultures, in turn, have their own norms. For example, hackers are people who illegally gain access to private computer systems. Among the subculture of hackers, accessing private computer data is acceptable, but only if the action does not damage important data or involve a further crime. Hackers consider people who perform such acts to be crackers, or criminal hackers, and often stigmatize and ostracize them.

CRITICAL THINKING
What might be some other deviant subcultures?

ANSWER: Students might mention youth gangs or cults.

Visual Answer

(top) Such acts can unite neighbors and communities in an effort to prevent the acts or to catch those responsible.

Visual Answer

(bottom) It shows how actions considered normal by one group can be considered deviant by another.

© Zits Partnership. Reprinted with special permission of King Features Syndicate.

INTERPRETING VISUALS What one person or group considers deviant, another person or group may not. *How does this cartoon capture the ways in which interpretation of an event can vary between groups?*

SUGGESTION 1: To help students compare the theories that have been proposed to explain deviance, copy the graphic organizer at the right onto the chalkboard, omitting the italicized answers. Have each student copy the organizer and complete it by identifying each theory and then providing one or more questions that characterize the theory. *(Example questions are provided in italics.)* Ask volunteers to share some of the questions that they listed with the class. Then use the questions as the basis for a class discussion on each of the five theories. During the discussion, have students extend their organizers by adding a fourth column that lists the main characteristics of each theory.

ENGLISH LANGUAGE LEARNERS

Perspective	Theory	Questions
Functionalist	*Strain*	*How do individuals respond to culturally approved goals and the legitimate means of achieving them? (conformity, innovation, ritualism, retreatism, rebellion)*
Conflict	*Conflict*	*What is the result of competition and social inequality? (deviance) Who decides what is deviant? (ruling classes)*
Interactionist	*Control*	*Why do people conform to norms? (The strength of social ties determines conformity.)*
	Cultural Transmission	*How do people learn conformity or deviance? (through socialization, or interaction with others) Where does this learning mainly occur? (primary groups)*
	Labeling	*How do people become identified as deviant? (through secondary deviance, or being labeled as deviant)*

People in Sociology

Robert K. Merton.
Robert King Merton (1910–) is a sociologist of diverse interests. His most important work was done at Harvard University. Working with professors from other disciplines, Merton helped to advance the importance of historical research in sociology and to improve the standards of training for the social sciences.

CRITICAL THINKING
How can historical research contribute to sociology?

ANSWER: Students should recognize that by studying history, sociologists can better understand present societies.

Visual Answer

They have all conformed to naval standards of dress and behavior.

Table Answer

Answers should accurately reflect the information provided in the table.

Technology Resources
Teaching Transparency: Merton's Structural Strain Theory of Deviance

Explaining Deviance

Why do people commit deviant acts? You can better understand the answers to this question by considering how the three sociological perspectives explain deviance. The functionalist perspective views deviance as a natural part of society. The conflict perspective explains deviance in terms of power and inequality. The interactionist perspective looks at how interaction among individuals influences deviance.

Functionalist Perspective The major functionalist explanation, strain theory, was developed by sociologist Robert K. Merton. **Strain theory** views deviance as the natural outgrowth of the values, norms, and structure of society. According to Merton, American society places a high value on certain goals, such as economic success. However, not everyone in society has access to the legitimate means to achieve these goals. For example, individuals may be prevented from finding a job because of social conditions or because they lack an adequate education. Nevertheless, they are expected to meet this goal, and society judges them according to how well they do so.

Under the strain of incompatible goals and means, these individuals fall victim to anomie. **Anomie** is the situation that arises when the norms of society are unclear or are no longer applicable. It leaves individuals without sufficient guidelines for behavior, thus causing confusion both for individuals and for society. The concept was originally proposed by Émile Durkheim to explain high rates of suicide in countries undergoing industrialization.

Merton suggested that individuals respond to the culturally approved goals and the legitimate means of achieving these goals in five ways. The chart on this page lists these ways, which Merton called modes of adaptation.

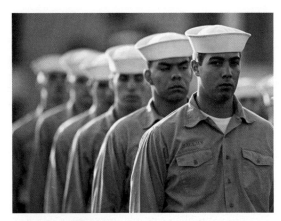

INTERPRETING VISUALS According to Merton, the most common response to cultural goals and the means of achieving them is conformity. *How do you think this group of sailors has adapted the response of conformity?*

The first and most common response is conformity. Many individuals in a society accept both the culturally approved goals and the means for achieving these goals. Whether they succeed or fail in reaching these goals, their efforts always involve legitimate means. The other four modes of adaptation—innovation, ritualism, retreatism, and rebellion—employ deviant behavior.

People who use innovation accept the cultural goals of their society but do not accept the approved means for reaching these goals. For example, they want to be successful in acquiring wealth but reject the acceptable means to obtain the wealth. Therefore they innovate, or devise new means for achieving the goals, and consequently violate accepted norms. Thus, they become deviants. Criminals such as drug dealers and burglars fit into this category.

Ritualists also find it impossible to achieve cultural goals by acceptable means. Instead of violating the norms for achievement, they abandon the goals while continuing to observe the expected rules of behavior. For example, a worker may pass up opportunities for promotion rather than face possible failure. A bureaucrat may make a ritual of upholding the rules and procedures of the organization while abandoning personal goals. The ritual of upholding the norms becomes an end in itself.

Merton's Structural Strain Theory of Deviance

	Mode of Adaptation	Cultural Goals	Cultural Norms
Deviant Responses	Conformity	Accept	Accept
	Innovation	Accept	Reject
	Ritualism	Reject	Accept
	Retreatism	Reject	Reject
	Rebellion	Reject and Replace	Reject and Replace

Source: *Social Theory and Social Structure* by Robert K. Merton

INTERPRETING TABLES Merton believed that deviance grew out of individual responses to the values, norms, and structure of society. *Copy this table and use it to describe a deviant behavior's mode of adaptation, reaction to cultural goals, and cultural norms.*

SUGGESTION 2: On the chalkboard, write a deviant act or behavior, such as burglary. Below the deviant act, list the five theories that have been proposed to explain deviance. *(See the graphic organizer on p. 180.)* Call on volunteers to explain each theory. Then call on other volunteers to explain how each theory would explain the specific deviant act that you listed. Next, write another deviant behavior on the chalkboard. Have each student create a chart that explains how each theory would explain that behavior. Finally, perform the same activity as a class to help students review the accuracy of their charts.

SUGGESTION 3: Organize students into five groups and assign each group one of the five theories that have been proposed to explain deviance. *(See the graphic organizer on p. 180.)* Next, ask students to imagine the following scenario: *You live in Norm Town, where all houses are painted either shocking pink, electric yellow, or bright purple. A new neighbor moves to town and paints his house white. Outraged by this violation of local norms, residents gather for a town meeting. As the only sociologist, you decide to speak up.* Instruct each group to use its assigned theory to prepare a short speech to help explain the new resident's deviance. Then have one member of each group present the speech to the "town meeting" (the rest of the class). **COOPERATIVE LEARNING**

INTERPRETING VISUALS Conflict theorists argue that people commit deviant acts, such as begging for money and protesting, to challenge those who have power or to gain economic rewards. **Why do you think these groups are committing deviant acts?**

Some individuals, whom Merton called retreatists, reject both the cultural goals and the socially acceptable means of attaining them. Unlike innovators and ritualists, they make no effort to appear to share their society's goals and norms. Instead, they may simply drop out of society. Examples of retreatists may include drug addicts, beggars, and hermits.

Not all individuals who reject the cultural goals and the socially acceptable means to attain them follow the path of retreatism. Some people rebel. Rebels want to substitute a new set of goals and means for the currently approved set. Members of any revolutionary movement fall into this category of deviant adaptation.

The four categories of deviant behavior are not considered equally deviant. Innovators and rebels obviously pose a threat to society. Retreatists also are perceived as a serious problem because they lead what society considers to be an unproductive life. However, ritualists are generally not regarded as a serious threat.

Conflict Perspective Conflict theorists believe that competition and social inequality lead to deviance. They see social life as a struggle between those who possess power—the ruling classes—and those who do not—the lower classes. People with power commit deviant acts in an effort to maintain their position. People without power, on the other hand, commit deviant acts for one of two reasons. They turn to deviance either to obtain economic rewards or because they have low self-esteem and feelings of powerlessness.

According to conflict theorist Richard Quinney, the ruling classes label any behavior that threatens their power base as deviant. Because the lower classes have only limited opportunities in life, they are often forced to commit acts defined as deviant. To protect their power, the ruling classes then establish ideologies—belief systems—that explain deviance as a problem found primarily among the lower classes. Thus, law enforcement efforts are most often directed toward the types of crimes committed by the lower classes. As a result, these groups have higher rates of arrest and conviction. People without power do not necessarily commit more crimes than do other people. Rather, they commit the types of crimes that are most likely to be detected and punished.

Exploring Cultural Diversity

Japan's *Hikikomori*.
In Japan, the term *hikikomori* refers to people who choose to stay secluded in their rooms. This form of social withdrawal is most often found among young men. Japan's strong cultural emphasis on conformity and academic success lead many *hikikomori* to withdraw from society. Young Japanese who do not fit in or perform well at school can feel great shame. They may begin to hide in their rooms, sometimes staying in them for many years. In 2000, some experts estimated that Japan may have had as many as 50,000 *hikikomori*.

CRITICAL THINKING
How would strain theory explain the behavior of *hikikomori*?

ANSWER: These people do not feel that they can conform or be successful, goals on which Japanese society places a high value, and as a result they become retreatists.

Visual Answer

Answers will vary, but students should base their responses on the information in this section.

HOMEWORK: Have each student write a position paper stating which of the five theories that have been proposed to explain deviance he or she thinks offers the best explanation. Remind students to provide specific reasons and examples that support their positions and to use standard grammar, spelling, sentence structure, and punctuation. When students next meet, have one or two volunteers read their papers to the class. Encourage student feedback and discussion.

 SPOTLIGHT *on Deviance and the Media*
Organize the class into small groups and have each group for one week collect news reports that mention deviant behaviors. Groups should collect printed articles where possible or, in cases of televised or other types of news reports, note the subject and the time or space devoted to the coverage of the deviant activity. Then have each group analyze the reports and write a few paragraphs summarizing the members' views about the nature and extent of media coverage of deviant behavior. Ask each group to present its conclusions to the class. Use the activity as the basis for a class discussion. **COOPERATIVE LEARNING**, **BLOCK SCHEDULING**

Case Study

The Power of Social Control. In a famous study on conformity in the 1950s, sociologist Solomon Asch asked test subjects in a classroom to judge the length of different lines. The test subjects did not know that some of their "classmates" were actually cooperating with Asch. Answers had to be spoken aloud and in the order by which people were sitting. The fake students were to give inaccurate responses. Swayed by these responses, about one third of the test subjects also gave wrong answers. However, when just one of the fake students opposed the majority answer, the rate of conformity among the test subjects dropped to 6 percent.

CRITICAL THINKING

What conclusions might you draw from this study about the effects of social pressure on conformity?

ANSWER: Many people will conform rather than go against the majority. However, one person taking a stand can make a difference.

 Visual Answer

by using family and community pressure to make people conform and by ostracizing those who do not

Interactionist Perspective Interactionists have offered three major explanations of deviance—control theory, cultural transmission theory, and labeling theory. Like strain theory, **control theory** explains deviance as a natural occurrence. However, the focus of control theory is somewhat different. Control theorists are interested in why people conform rather than the causes of deviance. Social ties among individuals, control theorists propose, determine conformity. Control theorists suggest that individuals who are integrated into the community are likely to conform. Conversely, those who have weak ties to the community are likely to commit deviant acts. Communities in which most members have strong social bonds will have lower rates of deviance because community members are able to exert stronger social control over those who deviate.

According to Travis Hirschi, a leading control theorist, people develop strong social bonds in four ways. First, they form attachments with others—parents, teachers, and friends—who accept the norms of society. Second, they have a strong belief in the moral codes of society, accepting that some behavior is simply wrong. Third, they show commitment to traditional societal values and goals, such as getting a good education or job. Finally, they are fully involved in nondeviant activities—leaving no time for deviant behavior. People who display strong attachment and commitment to, belief in, and involvement with their community are likely to conform. On the other hand, people who lack these qualities are more likely to engage in deviant acts.

INTERPRETING VISUALS Many people who live in small communities in the United States develop strong ties with their neighbors. *How do you think these communities might encourage conformity?*

182

Applying Sociology

■■ TEACH

Go through the feature Observing Norms in Social Interaction on this page with students. As you do, either videotape the class or have a visitor observe and take notes on students' social interactions. After discussing the feature, share the video or observations with students. Ask students what they can tell from their facial expressions, gestures, and postures? Were they engaged in the discussion or focused elsewhere? (*Emphasize that the observations will not form the basis for any assessment.*) Then assign students the Using Observation Skills activity as homework.

■■ EXTEND

Organize the class into groups of four. In each group, one member should interview a second member, while a third member listens and observes. The fourth member should observe the interview from a distance close enough to see but not hear it. Provide each group with a set of 5 to 10 interview questions. During the interview, the two observers should complete charts similar to the one on this page. Group members should then rotate roles until each member has played each role. Afterward, call on volunteers to share their observations with the class. **COOPERATIVE LEARNING** , **BLOCK SCHEDULING**

APPLYING
Sociology

OBSERVING NORMS IN SOCIAL INTERACTION

Have you ever thought about the norms you obey when carrying on an ordinary conversation or when engaging in some common form of social interaction? Most of us probably have not given it much thought. Yet when talking to other people, we all follow certain guidelines regarding how close to stand to the other person, hand gestures, eye contact, and facial expressions.

Social Distance

Suppose you and a friend decide to complete a homework assignment together. You sit down to begin work on the project. Where do you sit? You probably sit close enough to one another to be able to work together yet far enough away to be comfortable.

Hand Gestures

Norms concerning hand gestures are equally important guidelines for conversation. Have you ever had discussions with people who "talked with their hands"? Did those hand gestures help you better understand the speakers point? Or, did the hand gestures distract you? Or have you ever spoken with someone who emphasized every point by tapping your arm, or who rested his or her hand on your shoulder while talking? What was your reaction to this situation?

Eye Contact

Eye contact is another aspect of interaction in which you are expected to follow certain norms. You are expected to keep your eyes on your teachers when they give their lessons. You usually make a better impression when you look directly at an interviewer during a job interview. You are told by your parents to look at them when they speak to you. How important is eye contact to you? Do you think people who avoid looking directly at you are less sincere or less trustworthy? Do your think people who look you straight in the eye are more honest? How important do you think eye contact is to your friends?

Facial Expressions

Facial expressions are another part of everyday interaction. How many times have people been able to "read your face"? How often do you suddenly realize that you are scowling? Many times we are unaware of the appearance we are conveying to others. Sometimes we intentionally try to put on a certain face. We smile to please job interviewers. As with the other components of interaction, certain norms guide our facial expressions. For example, it would be a bad idea to stick out your tongue at a police officer or at a judge!

Using Observation Skills

To try to determine what some of these norms are, observe your friends, family, and other people during conversation. Copy the table below. Fill in the table with your observations about the norms people follow in social interaction.

Whom are you observing?	Social Distance	Hand Gestures	Eye Contact	Facial Expressions

Think About It

1. **Evaluating** *What conclusions can you draw about the social norms followed by the people you observed?*
2. **Categorizing** *Did any of the people you observed violate social norms? How did other people react to the violation?*

CLOSE

Write the names of the five theories of deviance on the chalkboard *(functionalist perspective—strain theory; conflict perspective—conflict theory; interactionist perspective—control, cultural transmission, and labeling theories)*. Call on volunteers to summarize each theory without referring to their textbooks or notes. List the main characteristics of each theory on the chalkboard. Then have students discuss which of the theories they think best explains deviance. Allow students with differing viewpoints an opportunity to express and defend their positions.

REVIEW AND ASSESS

Have students complete the **Section 1 Review** on p. 185. As **Alternative Assessment**, you may want to use the functions of deviance visual diagram or the theories of deviance position paper in this section's lessons.

RETEACH

Pair students and give each pair note cards. Have the pairs use the cards to create flash cards for the section's Define and Identify terms. Then have partners use their flash cards to quiz each other. **ENGLISH LANGUAGE LEARNERS , COOPERATIVE LEARNING**

◆ Applying Sociology

The Self-Fulfilling Prophecy of Labeling. Labeling can have both negative and positive results. A study of junior-high students found that being labeled as a deviant led to feelings of self-rejection. Those feelings in turn contributed to students being more likely to view deviant acts as positive and to associate with others who performed deviant acts. Such associations in turn often led to increased acts of deviance.

CRITICAL THINKING

Do you agree that labeling is self-fulfilling? Why or why not?

ANSWER: Answers will vary, but students should exhibit an understanding of the labeling theory.

Visual Answer

Many of the people labeled as communists experienced discrimination, such as losing their jobs and social standing.

SECTION REVIEW ANSWERS

1. **Define:**
   • deviance, p. 176
   • stigma, p. 177
   • criminologists, p. 179
   • strain theory, p. 180

INTERPRETING VISUALS During the 1950s, U.S. senator Joseph McCarthy accused many of his enemies and other Americans of being communists. McCarthy held hearings to publicly denouce people he considered deviants. *How do you think these public hearings and the labeling affected the lives of those accused?*

In a recent study, Travis Hirschi and Michael Gottfredson have suggested that conformity is the result of self-control. People with strong self-control conform, and those with weak self-control do not. Socialization—particularly during childhood—determines a person's level of self-control. In the sociologist's view, children develop high levels of self-control if their parents punish them for deviant behavior and reward them for conformity. Children who grow up without such parental interest in their behavior develop low self-control and are more prone to deviance.

Socialization is also central to the **cultural transmission theory**. This theory explains deviance as a learned behavior. Deviant behavior is learned in much the same way that nondeviant behavior is learned—through interaction with others. However, in the case of deviant behavior, the interaction is primarily among individuals who are engaging in deviant acts. Thus, the norms and values being transmitted are deviant. As a result, the individual is socialized into deviant behavior rather than into socially acceptable behavior.

The concept of **differential association** is at the heart of the cultural transmission theory. This concept refers to the frequency and closeness of associations a person has with deviant and nondeviant individuals. If the majority of a person's interactions are with deviant individuals, the person is likely to be socialized into patterns of deviant behavior. On the other hand, if the person's associations are primarily with individuals who conform to society's norms, that person is more likely to conform.

American sociologist and criminologist Edwin Sutherland first proposed the concept of differential association. He suggested that the learning of deviant behavior occurs in primary groups. People become deviant or conformist in the same way that they become fluent in a particular language. They have personal relationships with people who do those things.

Cultural transmission theory views all individuals as conformists. The difference between deviants and the rest of society lies in the norms to which each chooses to conform. The deviant individual conforms to norms that are not accepted by the larger community. The nondeviant conforms to socially accepted norms.

Gresham Sykes and David Matza offered an extension to Sutherland's concept of differential association. They

1. To help students understand the significance of stigma, have volunteers debate the following statement: *All cars belonging to people convicted of driving under the influence of alcohol should carry a special bumper sticker that reads "WARNING: This driver has received a DWI."* **COOPERATIVE LEARNING , BLOCK SCHEDULING**

2. To reinforce the point that some types of deviance have positive social functions, have each student write a creative short story about a society in which norm violations never occur. When students next meet, ask volunteers to read their stories to the class. **BLOCK SCHEDULING**

3. Have students conduct library research to find examples of cultural practices that are considered normal elsewhere but that most Americans would consider deviant. Have each student write a one-page report about one practice. Remind students to maintain cultural relativism and to use standard grammar, spelling, sentence structure, and punctuation in their reports. Select the two best reports and have their authors read them to the class. **BLOCK SCHEDULING**

---

noted that some people show strong commitment to society's norms yet still engage in deviance. Through **techniques of neutralization**, people suspend their moral beliefs to commit deviant acts. These techniques, which are learned through the process of social interaction, act as a block on the controls that discourage deviant behavior. Sykes and Matza identified five techniques—denying responsibility, denying injury, denying the victim, condemning the authorities, and appealing to higher loyalties.

When accused of a deviant act, some people deny responsibility. A person might claim that the act was an accident or that it was the result of a force beyond his or her control—such as a lack of parental supervision. Other people accept responsibility for their behavior, but they deny that it caused any harm. Such a person may ask "If no one was hurt, has a crime really been committed?" Similarly, people sometimes accept responsibility but deny the victim. A person may claim that "he had it coming," or "she got what she deserved." On occasions, people condemn the authorities to justify their actions. "The police and the courts are corrupt," he or she may claim, "so they have no right to accuse others." Finally, some people claim that their loyalties to a particular group are more important than loyalty to society. He or she committed the act "to protect my family" or "to help my friend."

Instead of focusing on why people perform deviant acts, **labeling theory** focuses on how individuals come to be identified as deviant. Labeling theory is heavily influenced by the work of sociologists Edwin Lemert and Howard Becker. Labeling theorists note that all people commit deviant acts during their lives. These acts range from the minor to the serious. Yet not everyone is labeled as a deviant. Labeling theorists suggest that this is because deviance is of two types: primary and secondary. **Primary deviance** is nonconformity that goes undetected by those in authority. The occasional deviant act and acts that are well concealed both fall into this category. Individuals who commit acts of primary deviance do not consider themselves to be deviant and neither does society. **Secondary deviance**, on the other hand, results in the individual being labeled as deviant and accepting the label as true.

The process of labeling an individual as deviant is usually accompanied by what sociologist Harold Garfinkel called a **degradation ceremony**. In some kind of public setting—such as a trial—the individual is denounced, found guilty, and given the new identity of deviant. For the individual, this is a life-changing event. People begin to judge practically all of his or her actions in light of the deviant label. For all intents and purposes, being a deviant becomes the person's master status. In many instances the label of deviant restricts an individual's options in the larger society and forces him or her into a deviant life style. The label of deviant is a self-fulfilling prophecy. Labeling people as deviants and treating them as such, may encourage them to commit more deviant acts.

SECTION 1 REVIEW

1. Define and explain
deviance
stigma
criminologists
strain theory
anomie
control theory
cultural transmission theory
differential association
techniques of neutralization
labeling theory
primary deviance
secondary deviance
degradation ceremony

2. Identify and explain
Robert K. Merton
Richard Quinney
Travis Hirschi
Edwin Sutherland
Edwin Lemert
Howard Becker
Harold Garfinkel

3. Categorizing Copy the word web below. Use it to identify the functions of deviance.

Deviance

4. **Finding the Main Idea**
a. Explain how someone comes to be considered deviant.
b. Briefly discuss how the three sociological perspectives view deviance.

5. **Writing and Critical Thinking**
Comparing and Contrasting Write a brief essay describing an act of deviance and how the three sociological perspectives would explain that act.
Consider:
• functionalist theories
• conflict theories
• interactionist theories

Homework Practice Online
keyword: SL3 HP8

Sidebar:

• anomie, p. 180
• control theory, p. 182
• cultural transmission theory, p. 184
• differential association, p. 184
• techniques of neutralization, p. 185
• labeling theory, p. 185
• primary deviance, p. 185
• secondary deviance, p. 185
• degradation ceremony, p. 185

2. Identify:
• Robert K. Merton, p. 180
• Richard Quinney, p. 181
• Travis Hirschi, p. 182
• Edwin Sutherland, p. 184
• Edwin Lemert, p. 185
• Howard Becker, p. 185
• Harold Garfinkel, p. 185

3. clarifying norms, unifying the group, diffusing tension, promoting social change, and providing jobs

4a. A person is caught committing a deviant act and then stigmatized by society.

b. functionalists—as the natural outgrowth of the values, norms, and structures of society; conflict theorists—as the result of competition and social inequality; interactionists—as either natural in people with weak ties to the community (control theory), as a learned behavior (cultural transmission theory), or as a label (labeling theory)

5. Essays will vary, but students should exhibit an understanding of how each perspective views deviance.

Building Social Studies Skills

![] TEACH

Have students read the feature Conflict Resolution on this page. Then ask for volunteers to play the various roles described in the scenario under Applying the Skill. Without looking at their textbooks, the volunteers should try to work out the conflict by using the persuasion approach to conflict resolution. Afterward, have other students provide feedback. Repeat the role-playing activity with different volunteers for each of the other approaches to conflict resolution. Finally, have the class discuss each approach.

COOPERATIVE LEARNING

![] SPOTLIGHT *on International Diplomacy*

Have students conduct research on some past or present diplomatic efforts to resolve an international conflict. Students might want to conduct additional research on the history of the conflict, previous efforts to resolve it, and the background of the diplomatic negotiators. Then have each student write a one-page feature for a news magazine describing the conflict and the diplomatic efforts being used to resolve it. Finally, have students discuss how the approaches described on this page apply to international diplomacy. **BLOCK SCHEDULING**

CONFLICT RESOLUTION

Ask students to apply the conflict resolution skills to their daily lives. Have each student try to apply one or more of the four approaches described on this page in at least one real-life situation. Then have each student write a paragraph describing the results. To maintain privacy, tell students they do not need to describe the details of their conflicts in their paragraphs.

Practicing the Skill

To extend the activity, have each student create a chart to supplement the written explanation. The chart should list the four approaches discussed on this page and then rate each one based on various factors. Have volunteers present their charts and papers to the class.

BUILDING
Social Studies Skills

CONFLICT RESOLUTION

Conflict—one of the five major forms of social interaction—is of great interest to sociologists. Examining the causes and consequences of the conflicts that arise between individuals or groups is central to an understanding of social interaction.

Conflict resolution is a problem-solving process in which individuals or groups who disagree on an issue voice their points of view and seek mutually acceptable solutions. Listed below are several approaches that could help you resolve conflicts.

1. **Persuasion** Sometimes conflicting parties need to be persuaded that finding a resolution is in their best interests. Explaining to each party the benefits that might result from a swift and reasonable resolution is a powerful method of persuasion.
2. **Compromise** Often both conflicting parties want things their way. Demonstrating that the parties are partners in the resolution process and that they may well have interests in common will help them move toward a compromise that is acceptable to both.
3. **Debate** Allowing conflicting parties to express their points of view through debate often leads to a successful resolution. Encourage the two parties to present their solutions to the conflict. Have them debate these solutions. Guide the debate toward solutions that seem to be acceptable to both parties.
4. **Negotiation** Having conflicting parties present and discuss their views in a formal negotiation process is sometimes the only way to achieve a resolution. Ask both sides to present their views in writing. Encourage the two sides to look for compromise positions on those that are unacceptable. Guide the negotiation by focusing on those points that seem to address the issues of both parties.

Applying the Skill

Imagine that the following situation has developed in your neighborhood. A group of young people has taken to gathering on one of the street corners. People who live nearby have complained about the noise made by the young people. However, the young people continue to meet on the corner. Here are examples of how you might use the four approaches to conflict resolution to resolve the situation.

1. **Persuasion** The two parties need to be persuaded to move toward a resolution. You might suggest to the young people that the constant "harassment" from neighbors is a high price to pay for hanging out. At the same time, you might point out to the neighbors that they are expending a great deal of energy on this problem. If it was resolved, that energy could be used on more productive ways of improving the neighborhood.
2. **Compromise** You might point out to the two parties that they have a common interest—they both want to feel comfortable in their own neighborhood. Encourage them to look for a possible compromise.
3. **Debate** You might invite representatives of the two groups to present their points of view in a debate. Remind the participants that debate involves clearly presenting one's own ideas and listening carefully to the views of others. Encourage them to look for common ground.
4. **Negotiation** You might ask the two groups to make a formal presentation of their points of view. Encourage them to negotiate in these areas by suggesting that they might be able to give ground on particular points. Use the negotiations to move both parties toward a compromise.

Practicing the Skill

Identify a conflict taking place at your school or in your community. Write an explanation of how you might use the four approaches discussed above to bring the situation to a satisfactory resolution. Conclude by discussing which approach is the most effective and why.

SECTION 2

OBJECTIVES

1. *Identify the principal types of crime in the United States.*

2. *Explain the characteristics of the American criminal-justice system.*

LET'S GET STARTED!

Write the following incomplete statement on the chalkboard: *There ought to be a law against. . . .* As students enter the classroom, ask them to take a few minutes to complete the statement on a piece of paper. Instruct students to take the assignment seriously and tell them not to put their names on their papers. Collect the papers and read some of the statements to the class. Provide a few minutes for discussion. Then tell students that in Section 2 they will learn about crime—any act that is labeled a crime by people in authority, is prohibited by law, and is punishable by the government.

2

CRIME

Read to Discover

1. What are the principal types of crime in the United States?
2. What are the characteristics of the American criminal-justice system?

Define

crime, terrorism, white-collar crime, crime syndicate, criminal-justice system, police discretion, racial profiling, plea bargaining, corrections, recidivism

Crime affects everyone in the United States. Some people are victims. Some people are criminals. Some people are both. However, the majority of Americans are affected by crime as bystanders. Newspapers, radio, television, and movies bombard us every day with information about and images of crime. As a result of our own experiences and exposure through the mass media, most of us consider crime a serious social problem.

A **crime** is any act that is labeled as such by those in authority, is prohibited by law, and is punishable by the government. For example, a person who robs a bank—an act that is labeled criminal, is prohibited by law, and is punishable by the government—has committed a crime. On the other hand, a champion swimmer who stands by and watches a friend drown instead of attempting a rescue has not necessarily committed a crime. The swimmer may have violated a moral code but not necessarily a law.

Who commits crimes? The table and chart on this page shows a breakdown of arrests by the offenders' sex, race, and age. Note that men are much more likely than women to be arrested. In terms of race, more than two thirds of all people arrested are white. However, African Americans, who make up approximately 12 percent of the population, account for nearly 30 percent of the arrests. Even so, many factors lead an individual to commit a crime, and there is no causal link between race and crime. The percentages for age are particularly dramatic. Almost half of all arrests involve people under the age of 25. Moreover, people younger than 35 account for nearly three quarters of all arrests.

Crime Statistics

The statistics in the chart and table are taken from the *Uniform Crime Reports* (UCR). Published annually by the Federal Bureau of Investigation (FBI), the UCR is one of the major sources of information concerning crime in the United States. The FBI uses data provided by local police departments to compile nationwide statistics. However, these statistics

SECTION 2 RESOURCES

REPRODUCIBLE & REVIEW

- Graphic Organizer 8
- Research Projects and Activities for Teaching Sociology 8
- Study Skills and Writing Guide
- Section 2 Review, p. 197

TECHNOLOGY

- One-Stop Planner, Lesson 8.2
- **CNN**. Presents Sociology: School Violence Prevention Programs
- Teaching Transparency: Percentage of Total Arrests by Type of Crime
- Homework Practice Online
- HRW Go site

Chart Answer

12.1 percent; Younger people tend to commit more crimes.

Persons Arrested by Sex, Race, and Age

67.1%

2.5%

White   African American   Other

Characteristic	Percentage Total
Sex	
Male	78
Female	22
Age	
Under 18	18.5
18–24	28.8
25–34	23.4
35–44	19.5
45–54	7.4
55 and over	2.4

Source: Federal Bureau of Investigation, *Uniform Crime Reports, 2000*

INTERPRETING CHARTS All types of people find themselves on the wrong side of the law. However, certain trends have developed in the characteristics of people who are arrested. *How much lower was the percentage of people age 45 to 54 arrested than that of those age 35 to 44? What factors contributed to this difference?*

TEACH OBJECTIVE 1

SUGGESTION 1: Have each student create a flowchart of American crime. The first level of the flowchart should read *Types of Crime in the United States.* The next level should list the five principal types of crime *(violent crime, crime against property, victimless crime, white-collar crime, and organized crime).* The third level should provide general definitions of each type, and the fourth level should provide specific examples of each type of crime. In addition, students should write a caption summarizing the information in the flowchart. Call on volunteers to present their flowcharts to the class, or display on an overhead projector a transparency of a completed flowchart that you prepared in advance.

SUGGESTION 2: Lead a class discussion on the five principal types of crime in the United States. *(See the Suggestion 1 activity on this page for a list.)* Then ask students to imagine that they are crime reporters for a local newspaper or radio station. Have each student write one or two short news bulletins for each of the five types of crime. News bulletins might be about a specific crime, such as a murder (violent crime); about changing crime rates, such as the drop in the number of burglaries (crime against property); or about the mayor's pledge to crack down on illegal gambling (victimless crimes). Encourage students to be creative. Then ask volunteers to read some of their news bulletins to the class.

Did You Know?

Based on the 2000 U.S. Census data on crime rates, the safest cities in the United States are located in the Southwest and along the Pacific Coast. The top three cities with the lowest homicide rates are El Paso, Texas; Austin, Texas; and San Jose, California. The top three cities with the lowest robbery rates are San Jose, El Paso, and San Antonio, Texas.

Table Answer

felonies such as murder, nonnegligent manslaughter, forcible rape, and robbery

Technology Resources

 CNN Presents Sociology: School Violence Prevention Programs

Types of Crimes

The Federal Bureau of Investigation (FBI) classifies crime into 29 categories:

Part 1 Offenses (More Serious)

1. **Murder and Nonnegligent Manslaughter**–The willful killing of one human being by another

2. **Forcible Rape**–Sexual violation of a person by force and against the person's will

3. **Robbery**–Taking anything of value from a person by using force or threat of force

4. **Aggravated Assault**–An unlawful attack by one person on another for the purpose of causing great bodily injury

5. **Burglary (breaking and entering)**–An attempt at or unlawful entry of a structure to commit a felony or theft

6. **Larceny (theft, except auto)**–The unlawful taking or stealing of property or articles without the use of force, violence, or fraud. Examples include shoplifting, pocket picking, and purse snatching

7. **Motor Vehicle Theft**–The unlawful stealing or driving away and abandoning of a motor vehicle

8. **Arson**–Willful or spiteful burning, including attempts at such acts

Part 2 Offenses (Less Serious)

9. **Other Assaults**–Attacks of a less serious nature than aggravated assault

10. **Forgery and Counterfeiting**–Attempting to or making, altering, or possessing anything false that is intentionally made to appear true in order to deceive

11. **Fraud**–Deceitful obtaining of money or property by false pretenses

12. **Embezzlement**–Misappropriation or misapplication of money or property entrusted to the individual's care, custody, or control

13. **Stolen Property**–Attempting to or buying, receiving, and possessing stolen property

14. **Vandalism**–Willful or vicious destruction, injury, disfigurement, or defacement of property

15. **Weapons**–All violations of regulations relating to manufacturing, carrying, possessing, or using firearms

16. **Prostitution and Commercialized Vice**–Sex offenses of a commercialized nature

17. **Sex Offenses**–Charges such as statutory rape (in which the girl consents but is under age) and offenses against common decency, morals, and chastity, or attempts at these offenses

18. **Drug Abuse Violations**–The unlawful possession, sale, or use of narcotics

19. **Gambling**–Promoting, permitting, or engaging in gambling

20. **Offenses Against Family and Children**–Nonsupport, neglect, desertion, or abuse of family and children

21. **Driving Under the Influence**–Driving or operating any motor vehicle while under the influence of liquor or narcotics

22. **Liquor Laws**–Violations of state or local liquor laws

23. **Drunkenness**–Intoxication

24. **Disorderly Conduct**–Breach of the peace

25. **Vagrancy**–Includes vagabondage, begging, and loitering

26. **Suspicion**–Arrests for no specific offense, followed by release without placing charges

27. **Curfew and Loitering Laws (juveniles)**–Violations of local curfew and loitering laws, where such laws exist

28. **Runaways (juveniles)**–Limited to juveniles taken into custody under local statutes as runaways

29. **All Other Offenses**–All violations of state and local laws except traffic laws and those listed here

Note: The dividing line between serious and less serious crimes varies somewhat from state to state.
Source: Federal Bureau of Investigation

INTERPRETING TABLES Generally, more serious crimes carry a sentence of a year or more and are called felonies. The less serious crimes are called misdemeanors. *What are the most serious types of crimes?*

SUGGESTION 3: Organize students into five groups and assign each group one of the five principal types of crime in the United States. *(See the Suggestion 1 activity on p. 188 for a list.)* Then have each group use the textbook and in-class and library resources to create a multimedia presentation on the assigned type of crime. Group members might provide definitions of different types of crime within that category, charts and graphs providing a variety of crime statistics, photographs, news articles, and other related items. Have each group set up its presentation in the classroom.

COOPERATIVE LEARNING

HOMEWORK: Have each student write a short essay in response to the following questions: *Is crime a more significant social problem now than when your parents were teenagers? Why or why not?* Remind students to provide logical reasons that support their positions and to use standard grammar, spelling, sentence structure, and punctuation. When students next meet, have volunteers read their essays to the class. Encourage student feedback and discussion.

---

have certain limitations. Sociologist Donald Black identified the following characteristics that limit the filing of formal crime reports.

- Not all of the complaints that citizens make to the police find their way into the official statistics. The responding officer decides whether or not to file a formal report. Officers are more likely to file reports in the cases of serious offenses.
- Individuals are less likely to report a crime if family or friends are involved.
- The police are more likely to file formal reports on serious crimes when the injured parties are members of the higher social classes.
- Whether an officer files a formal complaint is influenced by the attitude of the individual making the

complaint. An officer is more likely to file a formal complaint when the person making the complaint shows courtesy and respect toward the officer.

In addition, certain types of crime—such as sexual assault—are more likely to go unreported by the victims. Crime figures can also be affected by changes in the way that statistics are reported or by incorrect reporting.

Types of Crime

The FBI organizes the crimes reported in the UCR into 29 offense classifications. The chart on page 188 provides descriptions of these classifications, while the graph on page 189 shows the percentage of total arrests for each offense. In this discussion, crimes are grouped into five broad

Percentage of Total Arrests by Type of Crime

Type of Crime	Percentage
murder and manslaughter	.12%
forcible rape	.21%
robbery	.94%
aggravated assault	3.4%
burglary	2.2%
larceny	8.8%
motor vehicle theft	1%
arson	.11%
other assaults	8.9%
forgery and counterfeiting	.78%
fraud	2.8%
embezzlement	.11%
stolen property	.93%
vandalism	2%
weapons	1.3%
prostitution and commercialized vice	.71%
sex offenses	.64%
drug abuse violations	11.3%
gambling	.14%
offenses against family and children	.91%
driving under the influence	8.7%
liquor laws	5.1%
drunkenness	4.6%
disorderly conduct	4.9%
vagrancy	.24%
suspicion	.03%
curfew and loitering laws	1.2%
runaways	1.1%
all other offenses (except traffic)	27%

Percentage of Total Arrests

■ Part 1 Offenses (more serious crimes)   ■ Part 2 Offenses (less serious crimes)

Source: *U.S. Statistical Abstract, 2000*

INTERPRETING GRAPHS Data provided by the Federal Bureau of Investigation shows that larceny is the most common serious crime for which people are arrested. **What is the difference in the percentage of total arrests for murder compared to larceny?**

SPOTLIGHT *on Local Crime Statistics*

SPOTLIGHT *on Local Crime Statistics*

Contact the headquarters of the local police department and obtain the most current local crime statistics for the last three to four years. Next, have students examine the statistics to analyze local trends in crime rates and other characteristics of crime, such as the number of people who commit certain types of crimes for various age ranges. Then have students compare local crime statistics to recent national crime statistics. *(You might do this activity in conjunction with the Internet activity on p. 174, in which students examine state crime statistics.)* **BLOCK SCHEDULING**

SPOTLIGHT *on Neighborhood Crime Watch Programs*

Have students conduct research on neighborhood crime watch programs in their area or state. Students should find out how to set up a crime watch program and what agencies can assist in the effort, what such a program entails, and the effectiveness of these programs. Have students present their information in a brochure designed to educate local residents about neighborhood crime watch programs. You might have students perform the activity individually or in small groups. Display the two or three best brochures. **COOPERATIVE LEARNING** , **BLOCK SCHEDULING**

Sociology in the World Today

Sports, Violence, and Crime. In most areas of American society, violence is not considered appropriate. In many sports, however, some level of violence is not only permitted but is praised and admired. Some people believe that physical sports such as football provide a safe outlet for aggression that might otherwise become destructive. Many sociological studies fail to support this theory, however. Such studies show that watching a violent sport increases spectators' levels of hostility. According to one study, the homicide rate increased by about 13 percent immediately after a televised heavyweight boxing match.

RESEARCH ACTIVITY: Have students conduct research on the number of athletes in one professional sport who were convicted of crimes during one recent year. Then have students report and discuss their findings.

Visual Answer

by helping neighbors spot suspicious strangers and know when houses are empty

Graph Answer

a decrease in its rate

categories: violent crimes, crimes against property, victimless crimes, white-collar crime, and organized crime.

Violent Crime Violent crimes—murder, forcible rape, robbery, and aggravated assault—make up a very small percentage of all crimes committed. Nonetheless, violent crime statistics are quite alarming. According to UCR statistics, a violent crime occurs every 22 seconds in the United States. An aggravated assault occurs every 35 seconds, a robbery every 1 minute and 18 seconds, a forcible rape every 5 minutes and 48 seconds, and a murder every 33 minutes and 54 seconds. The graph on this page shows variations in the rate of violent crimes. Note that the four kinds of violent crime have followed a similar pattern in recent years. All experienced a period of increase in the early 1990s. Since then, they have steadily declined.

Most victims of violence are African Americans. In the case of murder, young African American men are much more likely to be victims. African American men between the ages of 18 and 24 have a victimization rate that is 8 times that of African American women, 8 times that of white men, and more than 30 times that of white women in the same age group.

The majority of murders are committed with guns and other weapons. Guns are used in about 65 percent of all murders, with handguns being the weapon used in

INTERPRETING VISUALS Americans have formed neighborhood watch organizations to reduce incidences of violent crime and crime against property. *How can neighborhood involvement help decrease crime?*

about 51 percent of the cases. Another 13 percent of murders are committed with knives. The rate of handgun use in homicides is higher in the United States than it is in any other industrialized country in the world.

Crime Against Property Crimes against property—burglary, larceny (theft other than auto), motor vehicle theft, and arson—are much more common than

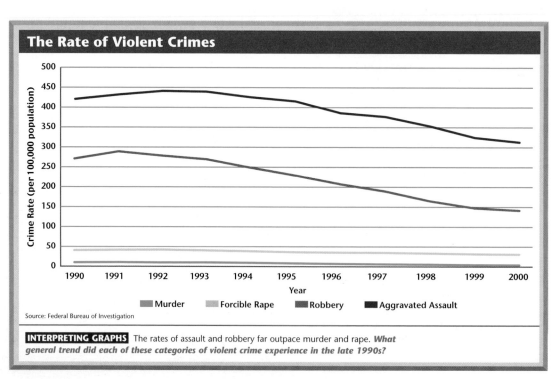

The Rate of Violent Crimes

Crime Rate (per 100,000 population)

Year: 1990 1991 1992 1993 1994 1995 1996 1997 1998 1999 2000

■ Murder ■ Forcible Rape ■ Robbery ■ Aggravated Assault

Source: Federal Bureau of Investigation

INTERPRETING GRAPHS The rates of assault and robbery far outpace murder and rape. *What general trend did each of these categories of violent crime experience in the late 1990s?*

TEACH

Have students read the feature Terrorism on this page and answer the questions that follow it. Ask students to consider the two acts of terrorism described in the feature and to compare and contrast the two events. Next, ask students what they think the purpose of each terrorist act was. Then ask students whether the general goals of domestic and international terrorism are the same or not. Finally, have students discuss what they believe to be some of the social causes and consequences of terrorism.

SPOTLIGHT
on Government Anti-Terrorism Efforts

Have students conduct research on the current anti-terrorism efforts and policies of the U.S. government and military. For example, students might examine actions that different government agencies, such as the U.S. Postal Service, are taking to prevent terrorism and prepare for possible terrorist attacks. Students should present their findings in a short written or oral report. **BLOCK SCHEDULING**

Case Studies
AND OTHER TRUE STORIES

TERRORISM

In recent years, **terrorism**, the threat or actual use of violence to achieve political goals, has become a major threat to the safety and well-being of Americans. In the last 20 years, there have been in excess of 325 terrorist acts or suspected terrorist acts in the United States. Prior to the events of September 11, 2001, these incidents claimed the lives of more than 200 and injured thousands more.

The FBI and Terrorism

Many government agencies such as the Federal Bureau of Investigation (FBI) work to prevent terrorist acts in America. The FBI investigates terrorist incidents. The FBI is also involved in terrorism prevention. Terrorism prevention occurs when FBI investigators uncover and stop a terrorist incident before it takes place. In 1999 the FBI took action in 10 terrorist incidents, 2 suspected terrorist incidents, and 7 terrorism preventions.

The FBI places incidents, suspected incidents, and preventions of terrorism in two broad categories. Domestic terrorism involves actions taken by individual terrorists or terrorist groups based and operating only in the United States. International terrorism, on the other hand, involves acts committed by groups or individuals based outside the United States or directed by organizations outside the United States. Acts of international terrorism may take place on American soil or may be directed against American interests or U.S. citizens in foreign countries.

Two Terrorist Acts

The worst incident of domestic terrorism took place in April 1995 when a huge bomb destroyed the Alfred P. Murrah Federal Building in Oklahoma City. The explosion took the lives of 168 people and injured hundreds of others. Timothy McVeigh and Terry Nichols, who both held strong antigovernment views, were found guilty of the attack. McVeigh was sentenced to death, and Nichols received a life sentence. McVeigh was executed in June 2001.

The events of September 11, 2001, mark the worst international terrorist attack on the United States. Within minutes of each other, two

After the events of September 11, 2001, president George Bush appointed Tom Ridge as the director of the new Office of Homeland Security.

hijacked passenger jets crashed into the towers of the World Trade Center in New York City. Less than an hour later, another hijacked jet smashed into the Pentagon, the headquarters of the U.S. military leadership, near Washington, D.C. A fourth hijacked airplane, which many people believe was also headed for the U.S. capital, crashed in the Pennsylvania countryside a short time later. Less than two hours after the first plane hit, both towers of the World Trade Center collapsed. The death toll from these terrorist actions was nearly 3,000.

Immediately after the attack, the FBI launched the largest criminal investigation in U.S. history, placing more than 4,000 special agents on the case. These agents quickly arrested hundreds of people suspected of having ties to the hijackers or with terrorist groups. They also began to piece together a case against the group suspected of planning the attacks—al Qaeda. Al Qaeda was one of the few organizations with the membership and funds to carry out such a devastating attack. U.S. investigators were already pursuing al Qaeda, which was suspected of having a role in terrorist attacks against U.S. forces overseas. The U.S. investigation of al Qaeda and the countries that have supported the group and their terrorist acts continues.

Think About It

1. **Analyzing Information** How does domestic terrorism differ from international terrorism?
2. **Supporting a Point of View** What do you think is the best way to combat terrorism? Explain your answer.

Think About It Answers

1. Domestic terrorism involves actions taken by individual terrorists or terrorist groups based and operating in the United States. International terrorism involves acts committed by groups or individuals based outside the United States or directed by organizations outside the United States.

2. Opinions will vary, but students might discuss actions being taken in the United States, such as forming the Office of Homeland Security, increasing security procedures at airports, and tracking people suspected of having terrorist ties.

CONNECTING *to Government*
Have students discuss what they think the penalties and punishments should be for political officials accused of wrongdoing in the course of their jobs, such as officials who use campaign funds for personal purchases. Guide students in identifying some of the main offenses that politicians commit. Then have students conduct research on the actual types of repercussions that officials accused of different crimes face. Finally, have students discuss if the current system is just, in their opinions, and why or why not.
BLOCK SCHEDULING

SPOTLIGHT *on the Mafia*
Most people have heard of the Mafia, but how accurate are people's perceptions of this organization? Have students work individually or in small groups to conduct research on the Mafia, its history, and its current status. Then have students create storyboards for a documentary on the topic. Storyboards should use images and text to provide a rough outline or sketch of the documentary. In addition, students should write summaries of their findings.
COOPERATIVE LEARNING , BLOCK SCHEDULING

◆ **Applying Sociology**

Killer Summers. Based on a study of crime in the United States from 1950 to 1995, more violent crimes occurred during the summer months than during other seasons. Laboratory experiments have also shown a direct link between hot temperatures and aggressive thoughts and behavior. Sociologist Jack Levin suggests another reason, however, for higher summer crime rates. Levin states that during summer, people tend more often to congregate in large groups. More gatherings provide a greater chance for arguments to occur and for more potential victims to be located in one place.

CRITICAL THINKING
What other sociological factors might lead to higher rates of violent crime during summer months?

ANSWER: Students might suggest an increase in the number of tourists in some areas or that people tend to go out more and do more—including committing violent acts—when the weather is warmer.

Graph Answer

about 1,800 cases per 100,000 people

crimes of violence. All property crimes involve either stealing someone else's property or intentionally damaging it. FBI estimates suggest that a property crime is committed every three seconds in the United States. The graph on this page shows the crime rates for larceny and burglary in recent years. Note that the rates have declined since the early 1990s.

Sociologists generally tie variations in the crime rate to changes in the population. As you read earlier, people under the age of 25 commit a large percentage of crimes. As the size of this segment of the population changes, the crime rate varies in the same direction. Therefore, as the younger population decreases, the crime rate should decrease as well. However, in the 1980s and 1990s increases in the crime rate appeared to be partially the result of illegal drug use. Expensive drug habits are often financed through crime. In addition, many serious crimes are committed while people are under the influence of drugs.

Victimless Crime Crimes such as prostitution, illegal gambling, illegal drug use, and vagrancy are classified as victimless crimes. Such offenses are termed victimless because they supposedly harm no one but the person committing the act. This classification may be somewhat misleading in some of these crimes, however.

While people other than the offenders may not suffer directly, the consequences for society of crimes such as drug abuse can be significant.

White-Collar Crime Edwin Sutherland coined the term **white-collar crime** to describe offenses committed by individuals of high social status in the course of their professional lives. Politicians, employees of corporations, and corporations themselves sometimes commit crimes of this type. Misrepresentation, fraud, tax evasion, embezzlement, price fixing, toxic pollution, insider trading, and political corruption are examples of white-collar crime. Traditionally, the public and the press have played down white-collar crime even though it is a serious social problem. Yet in recent years crimes such as insider trading on Wall Street, political corruption, corporate crimes, and computer-related crimes have received much attention.

It may seem odd that a corporation can be charged with a white-collar crime when people within the corporation actually commit the offense. However, corporations can be charged with offenses because, under the laws of incorporation, they are considered "legal persons." Once incorporated, a business becomes subject to the same laws as any individual in the United States.

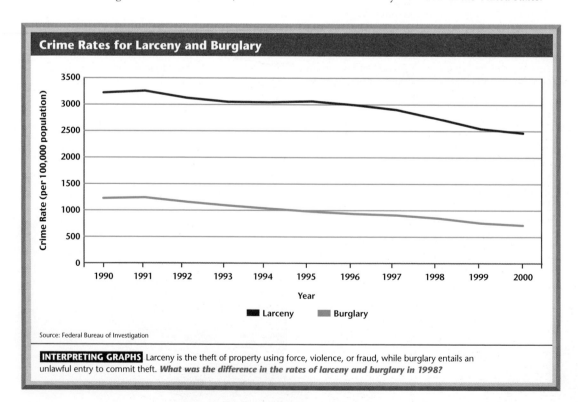

Crime Rates for Larceny and Burglary

Source: Federal Bureau of Investigation

■ Larceny   ■ Burglary

INTERPRETING GRAPHS Larceny is the theft of property using force, violence, or fraud, while burglary entails an unlawful entry to commit theft. *What was the difference in the rates of larceny and burglary in 1998?*

To help students explain the characteristics of the American criminal-justice system, copy the graphic organizer at the right onto the chalkboard, omitting the italicized answers. Have each student copy the organizer and complete it by describing the four main components of the criminal-justice system. Discuss the answers with the class. Then have each student create a poster promoting one of the four components of the criminal-justice system. Ask volunteers to present and explain their posters to the class. Display students' posters in the classroom. **ENGLISH LANGUAGE LEARNERS**

AMERICAN CRIMINAL-JUSTICE SYSTEM

Police	Courts
have the most control over who is arrested for crimes; use police discretion, which has raised the controversial issue of racial profiling	*determines the accused's guilt or innocence in a court trial and then assigns a punishment; actually settles 90 percent of cases through plea bargaining*
Corrections	**Juvenile-Justice System**
includes probation, imprisonment, parole; serves four functions—retribution, deterrence, rehabilitation, and social protection	*applies to offenders younger than 18; guarantees juvenile defendants the same legal rights and privileges as adults; often provides more services*

Conservative estimates suggest that white-collar crimes cost the United States more than $300 billion each year. Some people feel that the nonfinancial costs of such crimes are far greater. When political and corporate leaders engage in activities that fall outside the law, they abuse the trust and confidence of the American people. This abuse threatens the very structure of American society.

Organized Crime   For many criminals, crime is an individual enterprise. However, some criminals are part of organized crime syndicates. A **crime syndicate** is a large-scale organization of professional criminals that controls some vice or business through violence or the threat of violence. These organizations pursue crime as a big business.

Such syndicates operate in many areas of business, many of them legal. They often use legitimate businesses as "fronts" for their criminal activities. This enables the syndicates to reinvest their money through legal channels. By using such methods as drug trafficking, illegal gambling, unfair labor practices, hijacking of merchandise, and loan-sharking—lending money at very high interest rates—organized crime syndicates make huge profits.

The Criminal-Justice System

Once a crime has been committed and reported, it falls under the jurisdiction of the **criminal-justice system**. The most important components of the criminal-justice system are police, courts,

Recent scandals and reports of white-collar crime have received increasing media atttention. The court cases of Michael Milken (top) and Jonathan Strawder (right) were widely covered. Milken was accused of insider trading, and Strawder was accused of securities fraud.

Interdisciplinary Connection

HISTORY

Prohibition and Organized Crime. In 1919 the Eighteenth Amendment was ratified, banning the sale, manufacture, and transportation of alcoholic beverages in the United States. Called prohibition, this ban led to the growth of organized crime through the smuggling and selling of alcohol. As millions of dollars shifted from legal businesses to criminal organizations, crime became big business. After the Twenty-first Amendment repealed prohibition in 1933, organized crime "families" turned to other criminal activities.

CRITICAL THINKING

How did prohibition lead to the growth of organized crime in the United States?

ANSWER: By banning alcohol, which was a popular consumer product, prohibition opened the way for criminal organizations to take over the big business of distributing and selling alcohol.

TEACH OBJECTIVES 1 AND 2

Lead a class discussion on the principal types of crime in the United States *(violent crime, crime against property, victimless crime, white-collar crime, and organized crime)* and the characteristics of the criminal-justice system *(includes the police, courts, corrections, and the juvenile-justice system)*. Then organize students into groups of four to five and have each member select one of the following roles: a police officer, a judge, a parole officer, a prison warden, or a concerned citizen. Ask the groups to imagine that they are the members of a panel discussing crime at a local meeting. Have each group prepare and present its panel discussion to the class or create a written script. **COOPERATIVE LEARNING**

SPOTLIGHT *on the Criminal-Justice System*

Have students conduct research on the criminal-justice system in their state. Then have each student create a diagram to illustrate the many steps and options in the criminal-justice system, starting with the commission of a crime and ending with the return of the offender to society. Students' diagrams should show the various routes the system may take, such as plea bargaining, probation, and parole. In addition, each student should write a caption summarizing the diagram. Have volunteers present their diagrams to the class. **BLOCK SCHEDULING**

The United States Prison Population, 1995–2000

Population (in thousands)

Year	Population
'95	1079
'96	1128
'97	1177
'98	1224
'99	1287
'00	1312

Source: U.S. Bureau of Justice Statistics

INTERPRETING GRAPHS Mandatory sentencing and other factors have led to a rising prison population in the United States. *How much did the prison population increase between 1995 and 2000?*

and corrections. In most states, a special section of the criminal-justice system—the juvenile-justice system—deals with young offenders.

Police The police hold the most immediate control over who is arrested for a criminal act. It might seem reasonable to assume that the police arrest everyone who is accused of committing a crime. In reality the police have considerable power to decide who is actually arrested. This power is referred to as **police discretion**. The size of the U.S. population, the number of criminal offenses, and the number of full-time police officers make it necessary for the police to employ discretion in their decisions involving arrest.

Research has indicated that several factors are considered by a police officer when deciding whether to make an arrest. First, the seriousness of the offense is considered. Less-serious offenses are more likely to be ignored. Second, the wishes of the victim are taken into consideration. If the offense is serious or if the suspect is a male, victims generally

Although most criminal cases do not go to trial, Americans have a right to a trial by a jury of their peers.

Graph Answer

by 233,000

194

Douglas Fralinger of Highland, Indiana, suggested the following activity: Organize students into groups of five and provide each group with the following statements: *(1) The rate and seriousness of the deviant acts that a person commits will increase if the person is imprisoned. (2) After being released from prison, more than 60 percent of ex-convicts will be charged with new crimes, and more than 40 percent will return to prison within three years.* Have each group member select one of the theories of deviance covered in Section 1. Group members should then write one paragraph summarizing the selected

theory and a second paragraph explaining how the theory applies to each statement. Once students have completed their paragraphs, they should exchange them with another group member to evaluate the work for accuracy and completeness. Each student should use this peer review to revise his or her work. Finally, group members should combine the paragraphs into one report. Each group will receive one final grade. After the activity, you might want to have students conduct research on the current accuracy of the two statements, or you might provide students with this information.
COOPERATIVE LEARNING, BLOCK SCHEDULING

Careers
IN SOCIOLOGY

CRIMINOLOGIST

Criminologists investigate the causes of crime and methods of crime prevention. Some criminologists focus on an area of criminology called penology, which deals with the investigation of punishments for crime, the management of prisons, and the rehabilitation of criminal offenders.

Criminologists have many career options in the criminal-justice system. Some work as consultants or advisers to police departments, while others work in administrative positions in the courts. Criminologists work as parole and probation officers and as counselors in substance-abuse and rehabilitation programs. They also work in the corrections system, assessing problems and setting policies.

Criminologists not only conduct research on crime and punishment, but may also work as consultants for police departments.

press for an arrest. Third, the attitude of the suspect is considered. An uncooperative suspect is more likely to be arrested than one who is polite or apologetic. Fourth, if bystanders are present, the police are more likely to make an arrest. In doing so, the police reinforce the point that they are in control of the situation. Finally, police are more likely to arrest—and use force against—African Americans than white Americans. Many people charge that the high rate of arrests among African Americans is a result of police use of **racial profiling**. This is the practice of assuming that nonwhite Americans are more likely to commit crime than white Americans. The issue of racial profiling has become an important political topic, particularly in the aftermath of the terrorist attacks on America in September 2001.

Courts Once a person is arrested, the responsibility shifts to the courts. The courts' role is a twofold process. First, a court determines the guilt or innocence of an accused person by means of a trial. Second, if there is a guilty finding, the court assigns some form of punishment. In reality, however, more than 90 percent of all criminal cases are settled through plea bargaining before going to trial.

Plea bargaining is the process of legal negotiation that allows an accused person to plead guilty to a lesser charge in return for a lighter sentence. This process allows

courts to reduce their huge volume of caseloads while avoiding many expensive and time-consuming jury trials.

Corrections People who are found guilty of crimes are punished. The sanctions such as imprisonment, parole, probation, and community service used to punish criminals are called **corrections**. These sanctions serve four basic functions.

• *Retribution.* The punishing of a criminal serves as an act of revenge for the victim and society.
• *Deterrence.* Corrections are intended to discourage offenders from committing future crimes and to make the rest of society think twice before breaking laws.
• *Rehabilitation.* During the 1800s, prisons emerged as places in which to reform criminals so that they could return to society as law-abiding citizens.
• *Social protection.* By limiting the freedom of offenders, society prevents them from committing additional crimes. In the case of the death penalty, the threat of an offender committing future criminal acts is eliminated.

The effectiveness of corrections is a topic of heated debate. One indication that corrections are not always effective is the rate of recidivism among convicted criminals. **Recidivism** is the term for repeated criminal behavior. According to a U.S. Department of Justice study, 62 percent of released prisoners will be charged with new

Sociology Then and Now

The Science of Criminology. Criminology, or the scientific study of criminals, criminal behavior, and the criminal justice system, emerged in Italy during the 1700s. The publication of *On Crimes and Punishments* by Italian Cesare Bonesana, Marchese di Beccaria, helped found the classical school of criminology. This school protested the harsh punishments in place at the time. Its members held that punishment should serve only to prevent future crime and that everyone convicted of the same crime should receive the same punishment, regardless of status. These beliefs provide the foundation for many of the principles in modern U.S. criminal law.

CRITICAL THINKING
What do you think the goals of criminal punishment should be?

ANSWER: Answers will vary, but students might mention to prevent further crime, protect society, rehabilitate prisoners, or punish criminals.

CONNECTING *to Government*

How are judges in your state selected? Are they elected by the voters? Appointed by the governor and then subject to later approval by the voters? Ask students to conduct research on their state's court system and judicial selection process. Then have each student use the research to create a poster illustrating this information. Have volunteers share their posters with the class. Finally, have students discuss the advantages and disadvantages of the current court system and judicial selection process. **BLOCK SCHEDULING**

CLOSE

Review with students the principal types of crime described in this section and the main components and characteristics of the criminal-justice system. Then have students discuss the ways in which crime affects society, from negative effects such as loss of human life, to positive effects, such as providing jobs.

REVIEW AND ASSESS

Have students complete the **Section 2 Review** on p. 197. As **Alternative Assessment**, you may want to use the news bulletins or criminal-justice system poster in this section's lessons.

Map Answers

1. Louisiana, Maryland, Mississippi, Oklahoma, and Texas

2. a rate of 300 to 499

SECTION 2 REVIEW ANSWERS

1. Define:
- crime, p. 187
- terrorism, p. 191
- white-collar crime, p. 192
- crime syndicate, p. 193
- criminal-justice system, p. 193
- police discretion, p. 194
- racial profiling, p. 195
- plea bargaining, p. 195
- corrections, p. 195
- recidivism, p. 195

2. violent crime—includes murder, forcible rape, robbery; most victims are African American; crime against property—includes burglary, larceny, vehicle theft; more common than violent crimes; victimless crime—includes prostitution, gambling, illegal drug use; offender is the only victim; white-collar crime—committed by high-status individuals in the course of their professions; includes fraud, tax evasion, embezzlement; organized crime—the pursuit of crime as a big business

3a. Both have declined.

b. police, courts, corrections, juvenile-justice system

4. Paragraphs will vary, but students should support their answers with facts, statistics, and examples from the text.

196

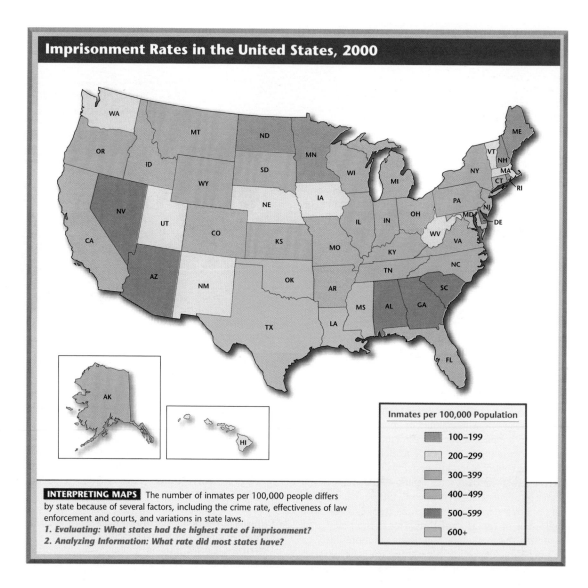

Imprisonment Rates in the United States, 2000

Inmates per 100,000 Population
- 100–199
- 200–299
- 300–399
- 400–499
- 500–599
- 600+

INTERPRETING MAPS The number of inmates per 100,000 people differs by state because of several factors, including the crime rate, effectiveness of law enforcement and courts, and variations in state laws.
1. Evaluating: What states had the highest rate of imprisonment?
2. Analyzing Information: What rate did most states have?

crimes and 41 percent will return to prison within three years of release.

Courts can assign punishments ranging from fines to probation to imprisonment. The majority of convicted criminals are punished through fines and probation. However, in the case of serious crimes—particularly murder, rape, and robbery—prison sentences are common. As can be seen in the graph on page 194, the size of the prison population has increased dramatically in recent years.

Juvenile-Justice System The third largest category of criminals in the United States consists of juvenile offenders—offenders younger than 18. Until the 1960s,

juveniles charged with crimes had few rights and were not protected by the same legal safeguards provided for adult offenders. Laws that pertain to adult offenders refer to well-defined offenses, carry specific punishments, and apply more or less equally to all offenders. However, the laws for juvenile offenses were much less specific. For example, they contained vague provisions about "incorrigible, ungovernable" children who associate with "immoral or vicious persons." A juvenile offender could, and sometimes did, remain in custody for a longer period of time than an adult convicted of the same offense.

The reasoning behind having separate regulations was that juvenile offenders, because of their age, could

◼ RETEACH

Have students work in pairs to create a 10-item, fill-in-the-blank quiz, in which each of the answers is one of the Define terms or key concepts in this section. Each pair should also create an answer key on a separate piece of paper. Have the pairs exchange their quizzes, complete the ones they receive, and then return the quizzes to their authors to be checked. Use the quizzes to pinpoint any concepts with which students are having trouble.
ENGLISH LANGUAGE LEARNERS , COOPERATIVE LEARNING

◼ EXTEND

1. Have students ask five people (friends, family members, neighbors, or acquaintances) the following question: *What do you think is the primary cause of teenage crime?* Have students report their results in class, and ask a volunteer to list and tally the results on the chalkboard. Then have students speculate about the causes that were given most often. **BLOCK SCHEDULING**

2. Have volunteers debate the following statement: *Juvenile offenders who commit serious crimes should be tried as adults.* Allow students with differing points of view a chance to express and defend their opinions. **COOPERATIVE LEARNING , BLOCK SCHEDULING**

not be expected to be as responsible as adults. Thus, it was thought that they needed a special, more considerate kind of treatment. Sometimes the result was that juveniles were denied equal protection under the law, however. Consequently, they were not usually granted any special care or attention.

To guard against such abuses, the courts now must guarantee juvenile defendants the same legal rights and privileges as adult defendants. At the same time, juvenile delinquents are still regarded as a special kind of offender. Juvenile courts try, in principle at least, to provide many more services for offenders than do adult criminal courts. Yet in some areas of the country, particularly in large cities, tougher juvenile laws are being established. For example, in some places juveniles—even very young suspects—can be tried as adults for certain serious offenses, such as murder.

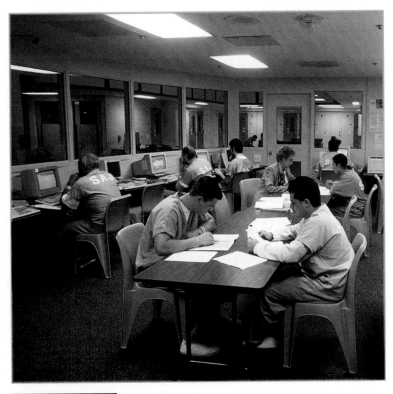

INTERPRETING VISUALS Many juvenile and adult prisoners are encouraged to participate in education programs. *How might gaining an education help rehabilitate convicted criminals?*

② SECTION REVIEW

1. Define and explain
crime
terrorism
white-collar crime
crime syndicate
criminal-justice system
police discretion
racial profiling
plea bargaining
corrections
recidivism

2. Summarizing Copy the graphic organizer below. Use it to identify and describe the characteristics of the five categories of crime discussed in this section.

Type of Crime	Characteristics

3. Finding the Main Idea

a. Describe the trends in the incidence of violent crimes and property crimes over the last few years in the United States.
b. What are the four major components of the U.S. justice system?

4. Writing and Critical Thinking

Drawing Inferences and Conclusions Write two paragraphs explaining why the effectiveness of corrections is a subject of considerable debate.
Consider:
• the functions of corrections
• recidivism rates

go. Homework Practice Online
keyword: SL3 HP8

CHAPTER 8 REVIEW

ANSWERS

WRITING A SUMMARY
See the section subtitles for the main topics in this chapter.

IDENTIFYING PEOPLE AND IDEAS

1. behavior that violates significant social norms

2. a mark of social disgrace that sets the deviant apart from the rest of society

3. social scientists who study criminal behavior

4. sociologist who developed the strain theory of deviance

5. sociologist and criminologist who proposed the concept of differential association

6. any act that is labeled as such by those in authority, is prohibited by law, and is punishable by the government

CHAPTER

Review and Assessment Resources

- Chapter 8 Review, pp. 198–99
- Chapter Review Activities with Answer Key
- Global Skill Builder CD–ROM
- Chapter 8 Test Generator (on the One-Stop Planner)
- Chapter 8 Test (Form A or B)
- Alternative Assessment Handbook
- HRW Go site

REVIEW
Have students complete the **Chapter 8 Review** on pp. 198–99.

ASSESS
Use one of the chapter tests to assess students' understanding of the content. For **Alternative Assessment**, see the **Alternative Assessment Handbook**.

---

7. the power to decide who is arrested

8. the practice of assuming nonwhites are more likely to commit crime than whites

9. the process of legal negotiation that allows an accused person to plead guilty to a lesser charge in return for a lighter sentence

10. repeated criminal behavior

UNDERSTANDING MAIN IDEAS

1. to clarify norms, unify the group, diffuse tension, promote social change, and provide jobs

2. It focuses on how individuals come to be labeled as deviant rather than why they perform deviant acts.

3. violent crime—includes murder, robbery; crime against property—includes burglary, vehicle theft; victimless crime—includes prostitution, gambling, illegal drug use; white-collar crime—crime committed in the course of a high-status profession, such as fraud or insider trading; organized crime—the pursuit of crime as a big business

4. retribution, deterrence, rehabilitation, social protection; by applying similar correctional practices to juveniles

---

CHAPTER

8 Review

Writing a Summary

Using standard grammar, spelling, sentence structure, and punctuation, summarize the information in this chapter.
Consider:
- the functions and theories of deviance
- the types of crime in the United States
- the structure and function of the criminal-justice system

Identifying People and Ideas

Identify the following people or terms and use them in appropriate sentences.

1. deviance
2. stigma
3. criminologists
4. Robert K. Merton
5. Edwin Sutherland
6. crime
7. police discretion
8. racial profiling
9. plea bargaining
10. recidivism

Understanding Main ideas

Section 1 (pp. 176–85)

1. What are the functions of deviance?
2. How does labeling theory differ from other theories of deviance?

Section 2 (pp. 187–97)

3. Describe the five general categories of crime. Be sure to list the types of crime in each category.
4. What purposes does the corrections system fulfill? How does the juvenile-justice system meet these same purposes?

Thinking Critically

1. **Supporting a Point of View** Do you agree that minor acts of deviance serve as a safety valve for society? Why or why not?
2. **Analyzing Information** How might the label of deviance act as a self-fulfilling prophecy?

3. **Identifying Cause and Effect** What factors cause fluctuations in the crime rate? Describe the recent trends in crime statistics.
4. **Identifying Points of View** Why do some people question the validity of the term *victimless crime*?
5. **Drawing Inferences and Conclusions** In recent years, the crime rate has fallen, yet the prison population has increased. Why do you think this is so?

Writing About Sociology

1. **Identifying Points of View** Some labeling-theory studies combine the interactionist and conflict perspectives. Locate and read the article "The Saints and the Roughnecks" by William Chambliss. Write a brief essay discussing how Chambliss used the control perspective to explain why the Roughnecks were labeled as deviant but the Saints were not.
2. **Evaluating** Locate a written account of the life of someone who has been convicted of a crime. The description can be from a book, magazine, or newspaper. In a brief written report, describe how being stigmatized as a criminal affected the person's daily life and future goals. How has court punishment affected his or her life? Use the graphic organizer below to help you write your report.

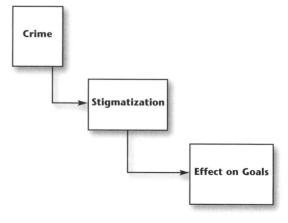

BUILDING SOCIAL STUDIES SKILLS

Interpreting Graphs

Study the bar graph below. Use it to answer the following questions.

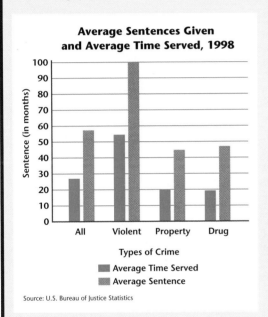

Average Sentences Given and Average Time Served, 1998

Sentence (in months)

All — Violent — Property — Drug

Types of Crime

■ Average Time Served
■ Average Sentence

Source: U.S. Bureau of Justice Statistics

1. Which category of crime received the longest sentence?
   a. drug offenses
   b. property offenses
   c. violent offenses
   d. weapons offenses

2. On average, prisoners serve only a little over half of their sentence. Why do you think this is so?

Analyzing Primary Sources

The following excerpt from an article published in The *New York Times* discusses recent trends in the numbers of crimes reported to the police. Read the excerpt, and then answer the questions that follow.

"*Serious crimes reported to the police dropped in 1999 for an eighth consecutive year, down 7 percent from the year before and by far the longest-running crime decline on record, the Federal Bureau of Investigation reported today.*

The bureau's preliminary figures for 1999 extended a trend that began in 1992 and that is now almost three times longer than the previous record decline, the three years from 1982 to 1984. The F.B.I.'s crime records go back to 1960. . . .

The F.B.I. figures, reported by 17,000 police agencies across the country, showed that all seven major types of crime were down in suburbs, rural areas and cities of all sizes. . . .

The F.B.I. report said homicide was down 2 percent in cities over 500,000, 7 percent to 14 percent in smaller cities, 12 percent in suburbs and 17 percent in rural areas. . . .

Crime was down 7 percent in rural areas, 8 percent in suburbs, 7 to 8 percent in cities under 500,000 and 6 percent in cities over 500,000."

3. In which location did the incidence of homicide show the greatest decrease?
   a. Cities over 500,000
   b. Smaller cities
   c. Suburbs
   d. Rural areas

4. Why do you think there was an extended decline in serious crime during the 1990s?

☑ internet connect

Internet Activity: go.hrw.com
KEYWORD: SL3 SC8

Choose an activity on deviance and social control to
• analyze gangs from the four theoretical perspectives explained in this chapter.
• create a thematic graph or chart on crime statistics in your state.
• create a pamphlet on criminal justice and the corrections system.

Across Space and Time

TEACH

Have students read the feature Tiananmen Square and Protests and answer the questions that follow it. Then have each student create a political cartoon that might have appeared during or following the Tiananmen Square protest. Students' political cartoons should be from the perspective of either a state-controlled Chinese newspaper that is sympathetic to the Chinese government or a student newspaper that is sympathetic to the protesters. Have volunteers present their political cartoons to the class.

SPOTLIGHT *on Political Protest*

Organize the class into three groups and assign each group one of the following roles in the Tiananmen Square protest—the protesters, the Chinese government, or other world government leaders. Have the groups conduct library research to determine the goals, objectives, points of view, and methods of their assigned group regarding the protest. Then host a mock debate between the protesters, the Chinese government, and the other world government leaders. **COOPERATIVE LEARNING** , **BLOCK SCHEDULING**

Think About It Answers

1. The protesters' goals were to reform China's communist government in order to establish a democratic pro-capitalist government, to express discontentment with the lack of individual rights, and to demand democratic reforms and a better standard of living.

2. Students might suggest that the Chinese government was nervous that protests and political struggles throughout the country might get out of hand. Students might also point out that totalitarian regimes tend to keep the peace through force and do not often tolerate antigovernment protests.

Across Space and Time

Tiananmen Square and Protests

In May and June 1989, the world watched as dramatic protests in China threatened to bring down the Chinese government. The students and workers wanted to reform or change the country's communist government. The protesters wanted China to establish a democratic pro-capitalist government. The student movement was an expression of years of discontent brought on by the problems and lack of rights under the communist government.

The protests worried the Chinese government. During the 1980s former communist countries such as the Soviet Union had been adapting pro-capitalist reform measures to stop protests and to shore up their faltering economies. After Deng Xiaoping took control of the Communist Party in China in 1978, a series of free-market reforms were implemented in China. These changes resulted in increased production of goods, particularly of agricultural products. Deng also oversaw several market reforms in transnational corporations and other private firms in Special Economic Zones. By 1989 about 50 million rural workers had migrated to urban areas and to the Special Economic Zones for work. However, these reforms eventually led to economic problems including inflation, unemployment, and shortages of agricultural goods.

To try to solve these economic problems, the Chinese government imposed emergency austerity measures in 1988. These policies cut government spending, workers' wages, and jobs. These reforms seemed to end the free market reforms. Workers and students began to strike. Students began to call for greater democratic reforms such as freedom of the press and assembly and an end to the government's dominance over the market economy.

The students carried banners and distributed leaflets that pointed to the "steady decline of the people's living standards " and the "long term control of a dictatorial bureaucracy." Students and workers held large daily rallies in the symbolic center of China, Tiananmen Square. The square holds several monuments and is surrounded by government buildings. The student protests drew tens of thousands of supporters to the square, and the Chinese government banned the protests.

The large protests led to a conflict within the Chinese government. Some officials wanted to send troops into the square to restore order. Other officials

Tiananmen Square was the location of the student protests and military response.

wanted to offer concessions to the students and workers. The government offered some concessions, meeting with the students and promising to increase the budgets of the universities. However, the government refused to recognize the student movement as a legitimate independent organization.

In defiance, the students continued their protest in Tiananmen Square and began a hunger strike. The movement began to grow even larger, becoming a general anti-government protest. More than a half a million students and workers had gathered in the square by mid-May 1989. As the protest continued, the Chinese government became more nervous about political struggles brewing in various regions of the country. On June 4 Deng Xiaoping sent soldiers and tanks to remove the peaceful protesters gathered in Tiananmen Square. Estimates of the number of protesters killed range from a few hundred to more than a thousand. The military suppression of the protest seemed to represent a movement of the Chinese government away from democratic and economic reforms.

Think About It

1. Evaluating *What were the goals of the protesters?*

2. Analyzing Information *Why do you think the Chinese government sent troops into Tiananmen Square?*

Sociology in Action

Sociology in Action

UNIT 2 SIMULATION

You Resolve the Conflict . . .

How can people settle a disagreement among members of an after-school organization about how to spend the club's money?

Complete the following activity in small groups. Imagine that you are a member of an organization whose members are arguing about how to spend money. Prepare a presentation outlining ways to resolve the conflict.

1 Consider Persuasion.
Encourage your quarreling friends to try to persuade one another to come around to the other's point of view. To help club members come up with persuasive arguments for their side, have them list the reasons why they hold the positions that they do. Then rank each reason in order of persuasiveness. Finally, urge each of your friends to present the most persuasive reasons to one another in an effort to sway the other to his or her point of view.

2 Compromise.
Explain to the club members that sometimes compromise is necessary to resolve a conflict. Tell them that each will have to give up something to reach an agreement. Have them consider what they would be willing to give up to resolve their disagreement. Then encourage the club members to meet and discuss ways in which they would be willing to compromise.

3 Debate the Issue.
Suggest to your friends that they hold a debate. Gather information about the advantages and disadvantages of each side of their disagreement. Ask them questions like the following:

• What reasons do club members have for spending the money?

• Has one of the club members developed extensive plans for what benefits will be returned?

Then consider having the club members prepare flash cards outlining the best arguments

they can come up with in support of their side. Finally, recommend that the club members debate their disagreement. They might want to include charts and graphs to better demonstrate their positions.

4 Consider Negotiation.
Urge the club members to begin negotiations about the conflict. Suggest that they meet to discuss their positions and what they would be willing to agree upon. Tell them that perhaps by working together to resolve the conflict, they will arrive at a solution that neither had considered before. When you are ready, decide who in your group will make which part of the presentation. Then make your presentation to the class. Good luck!

CHAPTER 9

Social Stratification

Social stratification is the ranking of individuals or categories of individuals on the basis of unequal access to scarce resources and social rewards. Stratification, by definition, implies social inequality. There are two basic types of stratification systems—caste systems and class systems. Two theoretical approaches have been used to explain stratification: functionalist theory and conflict theory. Chapter 9 examines social stratification and its impact on society.

CHAPTER 10

Racial and Ethnic Relations

The resources and rewards in any given society are limited. Consequently, the privileged position of a society's dominant group is often gained at the expense of the life chances of minority groups. A minority group is a category of people who are singled out and treated unfairly because of their physical characteristics or cultural practices. Minority groups frequently face discrimination and prejudice. Thus, not all groups in the United States have been equally successful in carving out a secure place in society.

Internet Activity

internet connect

go.hrw.com

TOPIC: Inequality in America
GO TO: go.hrw.com
KEYWORD: SL3 UNIT 3

Have students access the Internet through the HRW Go site to locate statistics on poverty and social inequality. Then have each student create a thematic graph or chart that illustrates a current trend related to social inequality. Students should write brief captions explaining the trends shown in their graphs or charts.

CHAPTER 11

Gender, Age, and Health
Race and ethnicity are not the only factors that affect a person's standing in society. An individual's position in the social structure is also influenced by whether he or she is male or female, young or old, or disabled or not disabled. Oftentimes, to be female, old, or a person with a disability is to experience inequality in society. Chapter 11 examines the degree of that power difference and how it varies from society to society.

UNIT MOTIVATOR
Share the chapter overviews with students. Then pair students and have each pair discuss examples of ways in which different groups are treated differently or unfairly in American society. Have students consider real-life examples from a variety of sources. Next, ask pairs to share with the class some of the examples they discussed. Tell students to keep these examples in mind as they study Unit 3.

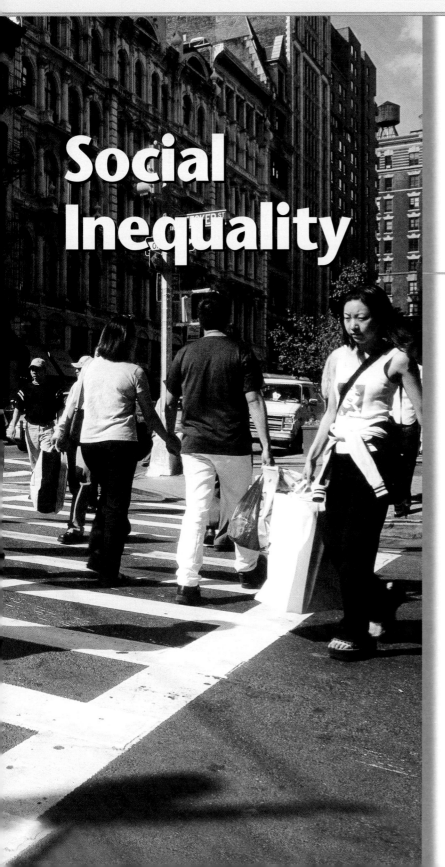

Social Inequality

UNIT 3

CHAPTER

9 Social Stratification

10 Racial and Ethnic Relations

11 Gender, Age, and Health

Almost every society is stratified, or divided, according to specific categories. In American society, stratification categories might include economics, race, and ethnicity, gender, age, and health.

Using Visual Resources

Social Class and Society.
Social stratification divides people in a society according to certain factors and is a source of social inequality. In the United States, social classes contribute to social stratification. Despite such stratification, people from many different groups and social classes come together in places such as a busy street corner, as shown by the photo.

CRITICAL THINKING
What might the people in this photo be doing? How might these activities reflect social inequalities and stratification?

ANSWER: Answers will vary. Students might suggest that the people are shopping, going to and from work, or taking a walk. Students might suggest that the type of job a person has, how people spend their money, and how a person spends his or her leisure time can be some of the many indicators of social inequality.

Social Stratification

CHAPTER RESOURCE MANAGER

Objectives	Pacing Guide		Resources

SECTION 1:
Systems of Stratification
(pp. 206–13)

REV Section 1 Review, p. 212

- Identify the characteristics of caste systems and class systems.
- Contrast the major theories of social stratification.

Regular 2 days	**Block Scheduling** 1 day

Block Scheduling Handbook with Team Teaching Strategies, Chapter 9

📼 **CNN.** Presents Sociology: Indian Caste System

RS Graphic Organizer 9

🌐 HRW Go site

SM Mastering Critical Thinking Skills 9

PS Readings and Case Studies in Sociology 9

E Research Projects and Activities for Teaching Sociology 9

SM Study Skills and Writing Guide

🖥 Teaching Transparency: The Distribution of Income and Assets in the United States

---

SECTION 2:
The American Class System
(pp. 214–20)

REV Section 2 Review, p. 220

- Identify the characteristics of the American class system.
- Explain how different motivations and cultural values influence the American class system.

Regular 2 days	**Block Scheduling** 1 day

Block Scheduling Handbook with Team Teaching Strategies, Chapter 9

Chapter Review And Assessment

REV Chapter 9 Review, pp. 228–29

REV Chapter Review Activities with Answer Key

💿 Global Skill Builder CD–ROM

💿 Chapter 9 Test Generator (on the One-Stop Planner)

A Chapter 9 Test (Form A or B)

A Alternative Assessment Handbook

🌐 HRW Go site

SECTION 3:
Poverty
(pp. 221–27)

REV Section 3 Review, p. 227

- Identify the groups of Americans that are affected by poverty.
- Describe the steps that have been taken by the federal government to lessen the effects of poverty.

Regular 2 days	**Block Scheduling** 1 day

Block Scheduling Handbook with Team Teaching Strategies, Chapter 9

Chapter Resource Key

PS	Primary Sources	**A**	Assessment	📼 Video
RS	Reading Support	**REV**	Review	🌐 Internet
E	Enrichment	🖥	Transparencies	🖥 Holt Presentation Maker Using Microsoft® PowerPoint®
SM	Skills Mastery	💿	CD-ROM	

 One-Stop Planner CD–ROM

See the *One-Stop Planner* for a complete list of additional resources for students and teachers.

One-Stop Planner CD–ROM

It's easy to plan lessons, select resources, and print out materials for your students when you use the *One-Stop Planner CD–ROM with Test Generator.*

Chapter Project Preview

The following activities are included in the Chapter Review. You may want to make the suggested preparations.

CHAPTER REVIEW ACTIVITY

Using Surveys Students will work in groups to interview a sample of their peers at school to discover how they rank occupations according to prestige. The groups will then collate the results and compare them with the chart on p. 209. Before starting the project, you will want to complete your coverage of Section 1 and lead a class discussion on occupational prestige as it relates to social class.

LESSON ACTIVITY

Linking to Community Interested students will volunteer to work in a local food bank and then write a report describing its operation. In preparation, line up local food banks willing to participate in the project.

INTERNET ACTIVITIES

The Great Debate Students will use provided Internet links to conduct research on the conflict and functionalist points of view regarding social stratification. Students will then work in pairs to write a dialogue or to role-play a debate in which a conflict theorist and a functionalist discuss power, prestige, and stratification. Before starting the project, you will want to cover Section 1, pp. 211–12.

Income and Social Class Students will use provided Internet links to locate census data regarding income differences among groups in American society. Students will then use the data to create charts, graphs, and databases. For uniformity, examine the Web sites in advance and determine the charts and graphs students should create. You might then have students work in groups to create their databases.

Additional Resources

PRINT RESOURCES FOR TEACHERS

Fussell, Paul. *Class: A Guide Through the American Status System.* Touchstone Books, 1992. Entertaining observations of how individuals' classes are revealed in the United States.

Grusky, David B., ed. *Social Stratification: Class, Race, and Gender in Sociological Perspective.* Boulder, CO: Westview Press, 2000. A collection of essays on issues related to social stratification.

PRINT RESOURCES FOR STUDENTS

Chute, Carolyn. *The Beans of Egypt.* New York: Ticknor & Fields, 1985. Tale of a poverty-stricken extended family in rural Maine.

Moon, Vasant. *Growing Up Untouchable in India.* Gail Omvedt, trans. Rowman & Littlefield Publishing, 2000. The first Dalit autobiography published in English.

Orwell, George. *1984.* New York: New American Library, 1983. Pessimistic prediction about the future of society. Enables students to examine the effects of enforced stratification.

MULTIMEDIA RESOURCES

School for the Homeless (vhs; 30 min.) CBS Television Network, 2001. This episode of the *60 Minutes* news program examines the issues surrounding education for homeless children.

I'm a Fool (vhs; 38 min.) Zenger Media. Dramatization of a short story by Sherwood Anderson. A poor boy pretends to be rich to impress a girl.

India Unveiled: Modern India (vhs; 28 min.) Encyclopaedia Britannica Educational Corporation. Examines the effects of industrialization and modern technology on Indian society.

South Africa: After Apartheid (filmstrip on vhs, color; 25 min.) National Geographic Society. Examines the policy of apartheid in South Africa, including its origins and effects.

Young, Rich, and Black in the U.S.A. (vhs, color, 28 min.) Films for the Humanities and Sciences. Specially adapted Phil Donahue program that focuses on the lives of young affluent African Americans.

☑ internet connect

go.hrw.com

HRW ONLINE RESOURCES

GO TO: go.hrw.com
Then type in a keyword.

TEACHER HOME PAGE
KEYWORD: SL3 Teacher

CHAPTER INTERNET ACTIVITIES
KEYWORD: SL3 SC9

Choose an activity to have students:
• write a dialogue between a conflict theorist and a functionalist that explains power, prestige, and stratification.
• use census data to analyze the American class system and then create charts, graphs, and databases to illustrate their findings.
• evaluate the effects of the Great Society and other historic poverty programs.

CHAPTER ENRICHMENT LINKS
KEYWORD: SL3 CH9

ONLINE ASSESSMENT
Homework Practice
KEYWORD: SL3 HP9

Standardized Test Prep
KEYWORD: SL3 STP9

Rubrics
KEYWORD: SS Rubrics

CONTENT UPDATES
KEYWORD: SS Content Updates

HOLT PRESENTATION MAKER
KEYWORD: SL3 PPT9

ONLINE READING SUPPORT
KEYWORD: SS Strategies

CURRENT EVENTS
KEYWORD: S3 Current Events

CHAPTER

Social Stratification

SECTION 1
Systems of Stratification

SECTION 2
The American Class System

SECTION 3
Poverty

CHAPTER REVIEW

Build on What You Know

Ask students to answer the following questions:

How might a person's ascribed and achieved statuses affect his or her social position?

Consider:

- ascribed statuses such as age, race, and gender
- achieved statuses such as educational attainment and occupation

How might deviance and crime be related to social inequality?

Consider:

- values, beliefs, and expectations of different social classes
- the relationship between crime and social class

Internet Activity

internet connect

TOPIC: The Great Debate
GO TO: go.hrw.com
KEYWORD: SL3 SC9

Have students access the Internet through the HRW Go site to conduct research on the conflict and functionalist perspectives regarding social stratification. Then have students work in pairs to write a dialogue or to role-play a debate in which a conflict theorist and a functionalist discuss their points of view on power, prestige, and stratification. Make certain that students address the major arguments of both sides.

CHAPTER 9 Social Stratification

Build on What You Know

Deviance and crime represent abnormalities and breaks in the norms and functions of social order. In this chapter, you will look at another aspect of social life in the United States— social inequality. You will explore social stratification by looking at caste and class, and you will examine several theories of stratification. You will also look at social class and poverty in the United States.

Sociologists have found evidence of social stratification in many everyday experiences in the United States. For example, it might be difficult for this service employee to afford to stay in the hotel in which she works.

Life in Society

All societies distinguish among their members on the basis of certain characteristics. The distinguishing characteristics used and the degree to which distinctions are made vary from society to society. For example, until the mid-1900s India had class distinctions based on caste and the family into which a person was born. Indian laws and customs reinforced the rigid caste system. With the passage of a new constitution in 1950, restrictions on the lower castes were outlawed. In many other countries, such as Great Britain and the United States, people are considered equal under the law. Nevertheless, class distinctions are still a recognized feature of the social structure in these countries.

Social inequality can exist even in those countries that claim not to have a class structure. For example, the former Soviet Union denied that it made class distinctions. However, in reality, access to scarce resources and social rewards in this formerly communist country were affected by such factors as party ranking and national origin.

> ### WHY SOCIOLOGY MATTERS
>
> Sociologists are interested in how people view social problems such as poverty. Use CNNfyi.com or other current events sources to learn more about American attitudes toward poverty. Create a storyboard for a documentary on poverty and class in America.
>
> **CNNfyi.com**

TRUTH OR FICTION

What's Your Opinion?

Read the following statements about sociology. Do you think they are true or false? You will learn whether each statement is true or false as you read the chapter.

- Stratification systems differ little from society to society.

- The United States has a closed class system in which there is no movement between or within social classes.

- Whether rich or poor, Americans live remarkably similar lives.

SECTION 1

OBJECTIVES

1. *Identify the characteristics of caste systems and class systems.*

2. *Contrast the major theories of social stratification.*

1
SYSTEMS OF STRATIFICATION

Read to Discover
1. What are the characteristics of caste systems and class systems?
2. How do the major theories of social stratification differ?

Define
social stratification, social inequality, caste system, exogamy, endogamy, class system, bourgeoisie, proletariat, social class, wealth, power, prestige, socioeconomic status

Identify
Ralf Dahrendorf, Gerhard Lenski

Almost every society in the course of human history has separated its members on the basis of certain characteristics. Sociologists call this division of society into categories, ranks, or classes **social stratification**. The levels of stratification and the types of characteristics used have varied from society to society. Such ascribed statuses as ancestry, race, age, physical appearance, and gender are among the most common distinguishing characteristics. Achieved statuses—such as educational attainment and occupation—can also be used to determine social standing. Other factors that play a part in determining rank or position in society include talent and effort. Divisions based on such individual characteristics, abilities, and behaviors lead to **social inequality**—the unequal sharing of scarce resources and social rewards.

Types of Stratification Systems

The level of social inequality in a society varies according to the degree to which that society's stratification system is open or closed. In a closed system, movement between the strata, or status levels, is impossible. A person is assigned a status at birth and remains at that level throughout life. In an open system, movement between strata is possible. The ease of movement depends on the degree of openness in the system.

Sociologists recognize two basic types of stratification systems in today's societies—caste systems and class systems. Picture a stratification continuum with closed systems to the left and open systems to the right. Caste systems would fall at the far left of the continuum. In a caste system, a person's status is assigned at birth. In all but the rarest cases, the individual remains in that status throughout life. Class systems, on the other hand, would fall somewhere on the right of the continuum. The actual location depends on the society under consideration, because class systems range from slightly open to very open.

Caste Systems In a **caste system**, scarce resources and social rewards are distributed on the basis of ascribed statuses. A newborn child's lifelong status—or caste—is determined by the status of his or her parents. While effort and talent may affect someone's position within a caste, they cannot help the person move to a higher status.

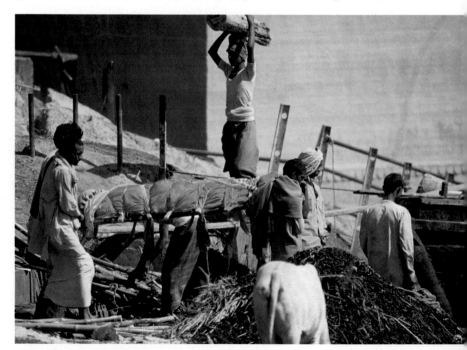

INTERPRETING VISUALS
Historically India had a rigid caste system that included the Harijans, the lowest caste. Harijans in this image are carrying a body to a cremation ceremony. *How do you think life has changed for the Harijans in recent years?*

TEACH OBJECTIVE 1

SUGGESTION 1: Write the terms *caste system* and *class system* on the chalkboard and ask volunteers to identify, in one or two words, an attribute of either system. As students answer, write each response under the appropriate term on the chalkboard. *(Possible responses for caste system include closed, lifelong, immobility, inherited, restricted occupation, ascribed status. For class system, responses include open, mobility, control, achieved status.)* Now ask students whether caste is easier to characterize than class, and, if so, why. *(Caste systems are near one extreme on the continuum from closed to open systems of social stratification. Class systems can be based on many factors. An individual's class is harder to fix or define.)*

SPOTLIGHT *on India's Caste System*

Organize the class into five groups and have each group research one of the main divisions of the Indian castes before 1950. Ask students to find out the occupations available for caste members as well as the norms governing members' daily lives in areas such as diet, dress and personal appearance, housing, and transportation. Have each group use its research to create a multimedia exhibit about its assigned caste. Then have students examine the groups' exhibits. **COOPERATIVE LEARNING**, **BLOCK SCHEDULING**

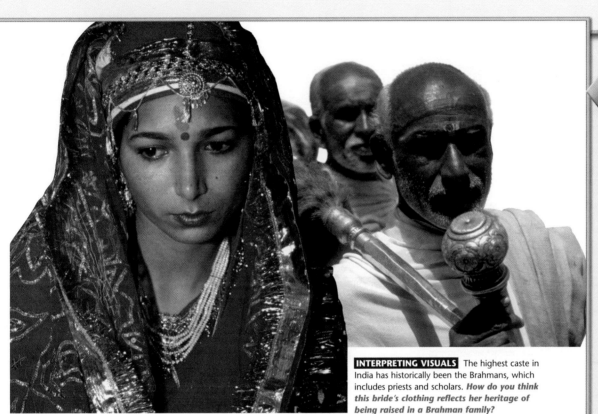

INTERPRETING VISUALS The highest caste in India has historically been the Brahmans, which includes priests and scholars. *How do you think this bride's clothing reflects her heritage of being raised in a Brahman family?*

Because status is inherited, a caste system has elaborate norms governing interaction among the different castes. For example, marriage between members of different castes would make it difficult to assign a status to children. Which parent's status would be used? To avoid this problem, caste systems have traditionally forbidden the practice of **exogamy**, marriage outside one's own social category. Instead, caste systems generally have practiced **endogamy**. Endogamy is marriage within one's own social category.

Caste systems were once a very common form of social organization in South Asia. India provides one of the best examples of this system of stratification. Developed more than 3,000 years ago, the Indian caste system assigned individuals to one of four castes: Brahmans, Kshatriyas (kuh-SHA-tree-uhz), Vaisyas (VISH-yuhz), and Sudras. These castes were subdivided into thousands of subcastes based on specific occupations. Below these four castes was a class of outcastes, Harijans—or Dalits, as they now call themselves. Harijans were considered unclean and were given only the most undesirable tasks to perform. Other castes avoided all contact with them because being touched by a Harijan made a higher-caste person unclean. The only way to remove this "stain" of uncleanness was to go through special cleansing rituals.

The Indian constitution, which was adopted in 1950, outlawed the discrimination against the Harijans. It also declared that all Indians, regardless of background, were equal. In addition, government programs set aside places in schools and government jobs for lower caste members and Harijans. But dismantling the caste system has proved extremely difficult. Some blurring of distinctions among the castes has taken place in the cities. There, modern transportation systems and work arrangements force mixing among the castes. However, in the rural areas—where most Indians live—caste still plays a major role in organizing everyday life.

The Caste System in India

Caste	Occupations
Brahmans	Priests, scholars
Kshatriyas	Rulers, nobles, soldiers
Vaisyas	Merchants, bankers, businesspeople
Sudras	Laborers, artisans
Harijans	Outcastes, limited to the most undesirable tasks

INTERPRETING TABLES For centuries India had a rigid caste system that included the categories listed above. *What group is highest in the caste system? What group is lowest?*

Exploring Cultural Diversity

Hinduism and Caste in India. In the late 1990s Hindus made up more than 900 million of the population in India. According to the Hindu religion, people are reincarnated, or reborn, after their deaths. The faith teaches that a person's actions during past lives determine the caste into which the person will be born in the next life. Since the passage of the Indian Constitution, Hinduism in India has slowly moved away from its association with the caste system, particularly in more urban areas. However, in rural areas caste still pervades society.

CRITICAL THINKING
How do you think Hinduism contributes to the perpetuation of caste in India?

ANSWER: Students might mention that because caste is deeply embedded in Hinduism it may be hard to overcome.

Visual Answer

Her clothing appears to be elaborate and expensive, as would befit the highest caste.

Table Answer

highest—Brahmans; lowest—Harijans (or Dalits)

SUGGESTION 2: Lead a class discussion on the characteristics of caste systems and class systems. Then pair students and ask the students in each pair to imagine that they are teenage pen pals, one living in India and one living in the United States. Each student is to write a letter to his or her pen pal that describes either the caste system in India and how it has changed over time or the class system in the United States. Partners should then review each other's letters for accuracy, completion, and correct grammar, spelling, sentence structure, and punctuation. Finally, have students revise their letters based on their partners' feedback. Call on volunteers to read their letters aloud to the class. **COOPERATIVE LEARNING**

SUGGESTION 3: Have each student create a flowchart or diagram that illustrates the characteristics of caste systems and class systems and the dimensions of social stratification *(wealth, power, and prestige)*. Students should also provide a caption that summarizes the information in the chart.

HOMEWORK: Ask students to examine magazines, newspapers, or other sources to find images illustrating social class in the United States or one of the dimensions of social stratification *(wealth, power, and prestige)*. When the class next meets, have volunteers share some of their images with the class for discussion.

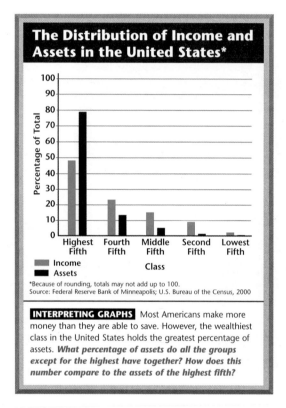

The Distribution of Income and Assets in the United States*

Percentage of Total (y-axis: 0, 10, 20, 30, 40, 50, 60, 70, 80, 90, 100)

Classes (x-axis): Highest Fifth, Fourth Fifth, Middle Fifth, Second Fifth, Lowest Fifth

■ Income
■ Assets

*Because of rounding, totals may not add up to 100.
Source: Federal Reserve Bank of Minneapolis; U.S. Bureau of the Census, 2000

INTERPRETING GRAPHS Most Americans make more money than they are able to save. However, the wealthiest class in the United States holds the greatest percentage of assets. *What percentage of assets do all the groups except for the highest have together? How does this number compare to the assets of the highest fifth?*

Class Systems In a **class system** the distribution of scarce resources and rewards is determined on the basis of achieved statuses. This linking means that individuals have some control over their place in the stratification system. Given talent, effort, and opportunity, individuals can move up the social-class ladder. However, the reverse is also true. Circumstances can reduce an individual's standing in the stratification system.

Sociologists have defined social class in various ways. Those who base their work on the theories of Karl Marx define social class in terms of who owns the means of production. The means of production are the materials and methods used to produce goods and services. In this view of social class, society is divided into two basic groups—those who own the means of production and those who own only their labor. According to the followers of Marx, the owners of the means of production in a capitalist society are called the **bourgeoisie**. The workers who sell their labor in exchange for wages are called the **proletariat**. The bourgeoisie reaps all of the profits, even though the proletariat does the work. According to Marx, the only determining feature of class is the ownership of property.

Max Weber expanded Marx's ideas. Weber believed that class consists of three factors—property, prestige, and power. Weber accepted that property plays a significant role in determining people's places in society. However, he suggested that prestige and power also greatly affect social standing. For example, inheritance taxes and the costs of maintaining their estates have greatly reduced the wealth of many English nobles. However, they still may hold a position of power in the community. On the other hand, the wealthy individual who made his or her money through illegal means may be shunned by the established upper class.

The Dimensions of Social Stratification

Today many sociologists adopt Weber's view of social stratification. They define **social class** as a grouping of people with similar levels of wealth, power, and prestige. For sociologists, these three terms mean very specific things.

Wealth An individual's **wealth** is made up of his or her *assets*—the value of everything the person owns—and *income*—money earned through salaries, investment returns, or other capital gains. In the United States, wealth is concentrated overwhelmingly in the hands of a small

Sociologists identify several classes in American society. The wealthiest class of Americans is small but can afford many luxury items such as yachts, fine clothes, and jewelry. Bill Gates, the founder of Microsoft, is a member of this class.

SPOTLIGHT on the Dimensions of Social Stratification

Have each student ask five people the following questions: Which would you rather have—wealth, power, or prestige? Why? (Students should be prepared to explain the definition of each term.) Instruct students to take notes of each respondent's answer and explanation. When the class next meets, tally the responses students collected. Then use them as the basis of a class discussion on the dimensions of social stratification and social class. As a further extension, you might have each student write a paragraph giving his or her own answer to the question. **BLOCK SCHEDULING**

SPOTLIGHT on Power and Prestige

Have each student write an essay on a person who, in the student's opinion, has or had substantial power or prestige but not wealth. Students should consider the source of the person's power or prestige (for example, prestige based on individual achievement or on a role traditionally accorded great respect). If the person is no longer living, students might also consider whether the individual had power or prestige in his or her lifetime or only in retrospect. Students might need to conduct research to complete the activity. Ask volunteers to read their essays to the class. **BLOCK SCHEDULING**

Prestige Ratings for Selected Occupations in the United States

Occupation	Rating	Occupation	Rating	Occupation	Rating
Physician	86	Police Officer	60	Carpenter	39
Lawyer	75	Actor	60	Brick/stone mason	36
College Professor	74	Radio/TV announcer	55	Child-care worker	36
Architect	73	Librarian	54	File clerk	36
Chemist	73	Aircraft mechanic	53	Hairdresser	36
Physicist/astronomer	73	Firefighter	53	Baker	35
Aerospace engineer	72	Dental hygienist	52	Bulldozer operator	34
Dentist	72	Painter/sculptor	52	Auto body repairperson	31
Member of the clergy	69	Social worker	52	Retail apparel salesperson	30
Psychologist	69	Electrician	51	Truck driver	30
Pharmacist	68	Computer operator	50	Cashier	29
Optometrist	67	Funeral director	49	Elevator operator	28
Registered Nurse	66	Realtor	49	Garbage collector	28
Secondary-school teacher	66	Bookkeeper	47	Taxi driver	28
Accountant	65	Machinist	47	Waiter/waitress	28
Athlete	65	Mail carrier	47	Bellhop	27
Electrical engineer	64	Musician/composer	47	Bartender	25
Elementary-school teacher	64	Secretary	46	Farm laborer	23
Economist	63	Photographer	45	Household laborer	23
Veterinarian	62	Bank teller	43	Door-to-door salesperson	22
Airline pilot	61	Tailor	42	Janitor	22
Computer programmer	61	Welder	42	Shoe shiner	9
Sociologist	61	Farmer	40		
Editor/reporter	60	Telephone operator	40		

Source: *General Social Survey Cumulative File* by James A. Davis and Tom W. Smith

INTERPRETING TABLES Occupations are an important factor in determining prestige. James A. Davis and Tom W. Smith developed a rating system for occupational prestige. *How prestigious is being an athlete compared to being a police officer or a lawyer?*

minority of the population. The richest 1 percent of the population controls more than one third of the country's wealth. As you can see in the graph on page 208, about four fifths of the country's assets are in the hands of the richest one fifth.

Income is also distributed unequally in the United States, although not as strikingly as total wealth. The top one fifth of income earners receives approximately 50 percent of the total national income. Recent studies suggest that this income gap is growing. One study estimates that the average corporate executive makes 419 times as much money as the average production worker. This ratio stood at 326 to 1 in 1997 and just 42 to 1 in 1980.

Power People with substantial wealth also usually possess considerable power. **Power** is the ability to control the behavior of others, with or without their consent. Power can be based on force, the possession of a special skill or type of knowledge, a particular social status, personal characteristics, or custom and tradition.

Prestige Individuals can be ranked according to prestige as well as by the wealth and power they possess. **Prestige** is the respect, honor, recognition, or courtesy an individual receives from other members of society. Prestige can be based on any characteristics a society or group considers important. Income, occupation, education, family background, area of residence, possessions, and club memberships are among some of the most common factors that determine prestige.

In the United States, occupation tends to be the most important determinant of prestige. When asked to rate occupations according to levels of prestige, Americans consistently place jobs that require higher levels of education at the top of the list. The table on this page shows the prestige ratings for selected occupations. The ratings are based on a scale ranging from a low of 1 to a high of 100. Generally, jobs with higher prestige ratings produce higher incomes. The Applying Sociology feature on page 210 explores the relationship between income and occupational prestige.

Applying Sociology

TEACH

Ask students to read the feature Occupational Prestige and Salaries and to answer the questions that follow it. Then discuss the feature with students. Point out that the salary figures shown in the table are *median* annual salaries, not averages. Next, ask students to discuss if they agree or disagree with the prestige ratings in the tables on this page and on the preceding page (p. 209). Then ask students to suggest occupations not shown in the two tables and to rank those occupations based on prestige. Students might consider political, military, or film and music industry occupations.

EXTEND

To expand upon the second Think About It item, ask students to conduct research on the educational requirements for three of the occupations listed in the table on p. 210. Then call on volunteers to share their findings with the class. Have students use the information as the basis for a discussion on the relationship between educational requirements and occupational prestige and wealth. Students might also discuss factors other than expected financial return that might influence a person to pursue an advanced education or advanced training. **BLOCK SCHEDULING**

Applying Sociology

The U.S. President.
Many Americans consider the office of the president of the United States to be the most powerful and prestigious job in the country. However, the president's salary of $400,000 a year, although high, is not the highest in the country.

CRITICAL THINKING

How would you rate the prestige of the job of being president of the United States? Why?

ANSWER: Answers will vary, but students should explain their rating in reference to ratings of other occupations.

Think About It Answers

1. In general, as prestige increases, salary increases.

2. no; prestige level—factors such as the power, level of media attention, or cultural importance of the occupation; salary level—factors such as changes in the economy, the occupation's number of job openings and people seeking to fill them, the talent or skill needed to hold the job, and the occupation's profitability

APPLYING Sociology

OCCUPATIONAL PRESTIGE AND SALARIES

Prestige can be assigned on the basis of any characteristic that a group or society considers important. However, in industrial societies occupation is generally the most common source of prestige. Consequently, sociologists periodically conduct research to determine the prestige rankings of various occupations.

Occupational Prestige Studies

Some of the largest studies of occupational prestige have been conducted by the National Opinion Research Center (NORC) of the University of Chicago. NORC first carried out the study in 1947. Researchers asked a sample of Americans to rank 90 occupations as either "excellent," "good," "average," "somewhat below average," or "poor." Based on these rankings, NORC researchers assigned a prestige score to each occupation. The scores ranged from a low of 1 to a high or 100. The highest prestige scores went to those occupations that require a high level of training or skill. At the head of the list were such occupations as physician, college professor, and architect. At the bottom of the list were garbage collector, street sweeper, and shoe shiner.

NORC conducted the study in the 1960s and again in the 1990s to determine if the rankings had changed over the years. The similarities in rankings among the studies were striking. With the exception of some slight changes, the scores were almost identical. Studies conducted by other researchers produced similar results. The relative order of occupational prestige in the United States remained basically the same over the second half of the 1900s.

Prestige and Wealth

Prestige is only one dimension of social stratification, however. Wealth and power also are important dimensions. For example, what is the connection between occupational prestige and wealth? A review of the salaries for some occupations might provide an answer.

Prestige Ratings and Salaries

Occupation	Prestige Rating	Median Annual Salary
Physician	86	$160,000
College professor	74	$46,330
Architect	73	$52,510
Dentist	72	$129,030
Teacher	66	$39,845
Registered nurse	66	$44,840
Veterinarian	62	$60,910
Airline pilot	61	$110,940
Electrician	51	$40,123
Realtor	49	$27,640
Machinist	47	$30,742
Mail carrier	47	$38,420
Secretary	46	$31,090
Bank teller	43	$19,156
Telephone operator	40	$20,196
Child-care worker	36	$18,075
Truck driver	30	$28,579
Cashier	29	$10,712
Waiter/waitress	28	$13,353

Source: *General Social Survey Cumulative File* by James A. Davis and Tom W. Smith

The table on page 209 lists the latest prestige ratings for selected occupations in the United States. The ratings for several occupations have been reproduced in the table on this page. The median annual salaries for these occupations are also listed.

Think About It

1. **Analyzing Information** By studying the table on this page, what can you conclude about the relationship between prestige and salary?

2. **Evaluating** Are prestige and salary necessarily connected? What other factors besides salary might influence an occupation's prestige level? What factors other than prestige might affect an occupation's salary level?

TEACH OBJECTIVE 2

To help students compare and contrast the major theories of social stratification, copy the graphic organizer at the right onto the chalkboard, omitting the italicized answers. Have students copy and complete the organizer. Discuss the answers with the class. Then ask students to explain how Ralf Dahrendorf and Gerhard Lenski have blended the two theories. *(Dahrendorf—Functionalism explains why people are willing to spend years becoming doctors or lawyers, and conflict theory explains why children of the wealthy tend to go to the best colleges. Lenski—Functionalism explains simple societies, in which survival depends on cooperation. Conflict theory better explains complex societies, in which groups struggle for power.)*

ENGLISH LANGUAGE LEARNERS

Theory	Cause of Stratification	Criticisms of Theory
Functionalist	*Stratification is needed to help society function smoothly by ensuring that specific roles are performed. Higher rewards guarantee that important roles that require more skill are filled.*	• *Society does not provide equal access to education and jobs.* • *Rewards do not always reflect the social values of roles.*
Conflict: • Marxists • American Theorists	• *The bourgeoisie exploit and control the proletariat to maintain wealth and power.* • *Groups compete for scarce resources. Those with power use it to maintain their position.*	*It fails to recognize that unequal rewards are based in part on differences in talents, skills, and desires among people.*

INTERPRETING VISUALS One criticism of the functionalist view of stratification points to its limited explanation of why pop stars receive such high incomes compared to the average American worker. ***How might a functional sociologist respond to this criticism?***

To make the ranking of people according to wealth, power, and prestige possible, sociologists often calculate people's **socioeconomic status** (SES). This is a rating that combines social factors such as educational level, occupational prestige, and place of residence with the economic factor of income. These combined factors are then used to determine an individual's relative position in the stratification system.

Explaining Stratification

Sociologists are interested not only in the nature of social stratification, but also in its causes and consequences. Functionalists and conflict theorists have offered explanations. Other sociologists, seeing weaknesses in both approaches, have tried to blend the two.

Functionalist Theory Functionalists view stratification as a necessary feature of the social structure. The functionalist explanation assumes that certain roles in society must be performed if the system is to be maintained. Higher rewards for the performance of these roles ensure their fulfillment—the more important the role and the more skill needed to perform the role, the higher the reward. Functionalists claim that without varying rewards, many jobs would not be filled, and society could not function smoothly. For example, why would someone take the time and

expense to become a physician if the reward for being a salesclerk were the same?

Critics have suggested that the functionalist explanation has weaknesses. The theory fails to consider that not everyone in society has equal access to such resources as education. Without this access, people are unlikely to obtain high-status occupations. The functionalist approach also ignores the likelihood that there may be many talented people in the lower classes. Because of stratification, these people may be prevented from making a contribution to society. Finally, it cannot explain why rewards sometimes do not reflect the social value of the role. Why should movie stars and professional athletes—whose importance to society is limited—command such high incomes?

Conflict Theory Conflict theorists see competition over scarce resources as the cause of social inequality. Conflict theorists who base their work on Marxist theory say that stratification comes from class exploitation. The owners of the means of production control the working class in order to make profits and maintain their power in society.

Many American conflict theorists—such as C. Wright Mills, Irving Louis Horowitz, and G. William Domhoff—take a broader view of inequality. According to their view, various groups within society compete with one another for scarce resources. Once a group

CLOSE

Review with students the functionalist theory and the conflict theory of social stratification. Then ask students to discuss which theory or blending of theories they agree with and why. Give students with differing viewpoints a chance to express and defend their opinions.

REVIEW AND ASSESS

Have students complete the **Section 1 Review** on p. 212. As **Alternative Assessment**, you may want to use the pen pal letters or the flowchart or diagram in this section's lessons.

RETEACH

Have each student create a 10-item, true-false quiz using the section's Define and Identify terms. Students should create answer keys as well. Then have students exchange quizzes, answer the ones they receive, and return them to be checked.
ENGLISH LANGUAGE LEARNERS , COOPERATIVE LEARNING

EXTEND

Have students informally debate the following statement: *There should be a limit on the amount of money that corporate executives can earn.* Have students consider both theories of social stratification. **COOPERATIVE LEARNING , BLOCK SCHEDULING**

Visual Answer

benefits such as a high salary, prestige, and the satisfaction of helping others

SECTION 1 REVIEW ANSWERS

1. **Define:**
   • social stratification, p. 206
   • social inequality, p. 206
   • caste system, p. 206
   • exogamy, p. 207
   • endogamy, p. 207
   • class system, p. 208
   • bourgeoisie, p. 208
   • proletariat, p. 208
   • social class, p. 208
   • wealth, p. 208
   • power, p. 209
   • prestige, p. 209
   • socioeconomic status, p. 211

2. **Identify:**
   • Ralf Dahrendorf, p. 212
   • Gerhard Lenski, p. 212

3. Students should describe wealth, power, and prestige.

4a. Caste systems are closed; class systems are open.

b. functionalists—view stratification as a necessary feature of the social structure and argue that the more important a role and the more skill needed to perform it, the higher the reward; conflict theorists—view stratification as a result of conflict over scarce resources and argue that groups who gain power use it to maintain power.

5. Essays will vary, but students should exhibit an understanding of the theories of Dahrendorf and Lenski.

212

gains power, it is able to shape public policy and public opinion to its own advantage. In that way, it maintains its position of power.

Critics have found shortcomings in conflict theory as well. One of its major weaknesses is that it fails to recognize that unequal rewards are based, in part, on differences in talent, skill, and desire. Not everyone is suited for every position in the social structure. Consequently, society must have some way to urge the proper individuals into positions that are vital to its operation. One way to do this is through the offer of different rewards.

Efforts at Synthesis

Some sociologists, noting that neither approach fully explains stratification, have tried to synthesize, or blend, the two. Ralf Dahrendorf suggests that each approach might be used to explain specific aspects of stratification. For example, functionalist theory helps explain why people are willing to spend years training to become doctors or lawyers. Conflict theory helps to explain why the children of the wealthy tend to go to the best colleges.

Gerhard Lenski takes a similar approach. However, he asserts that the usefulness of the theory depends on the society under study. He notes that functionalists state that a stratification system functions because

INTERPRETING VISUALS Critics of conflict theory argue that if the rewards for being a doctor were the same as less skilled occupations, few people would work so hard to get through medical school. *What do you think the rewards of being a doctor might be?*

members of society accept it. Such a view would apply to simple societies—such as hunter-gatherer societies. In simple societies, survival depends on cooperation. Lenski suggests that the conflict theory would apply to more complex societies, in which people struggle to control wealth and power. A ruling group emerges from the struggle, and social inequality develops as this group takes steps to maintain its position.

SECTION 1 REVIEW

1. **Define and explain**
   social stratification
   social inequality
   caste system
   exogamy
   endogamy
   class system
   bourgeoisie
   proletariat
   social class
   wealth
   power
   prestige
   socioeconomic status

2. **Identify and explain**
   Ralf Dahrendorf
   Gerhard Lenski

3. **Summarizing** Copy the graphic organizer below. Use it to identify and describe the three dimensions of social stratification discussed in the section.

   Social Stratification

4. **Finding the Main Idea**
   a. Compare and contrast the two major systems of stratification.
   b. Briefly discuss how the functionalist and conflict perspectives explain social stratification.

5. **Writing and Critical Thinking**
   Identifying Points of View Some sociologists believe that the functionalist and conflict theories of stratification are complementary rather than contradictory. Write two paragraphs describing how you think such sociologists explain the complementary relationship between the two theories. Consider:
   • the ideas of Ralf Dahrendorf
   • the ideas of Gerhard Lenski

Homework Practice Online
keyword: SL3 HP9

Building Social Studies Skills

TEACH

Have students read the feature Identifying Assumptions. To help students identify and evaluate assumptions, go over the excerpt under Applying the Skill as a class. Have students address each of the three steps when analyzing the excerpt. Call on students to write on the chalkboard the conclusion and the assumptions of the excerpt. Then ask students to evaluate the conclusion and discuss whether they agree with it and the author's assumptions. Assign students the activity under Practicing the Skill as homework.

EXTEND

Have each student select another excerpt provided in their textbooks. Students should then create a flowchart or another type of graphic organizer that shows the excerpt's conclusions and the assumptions and facts that support it. Then have each student write a paragraph evaluating the assumptions. Call on volunteers to indicate which excerpt they selected and to share their results with the class. Correct students' work as necessary.

BLOCK SCHEDULING

BUILDING
Social Studies Skills

IDENTIFYING ASSUMPTIONS

Actions and beliefs are heavily influenced by assumptions. An assumption is a statement that is taken for granted as being true.

Science could not proceed if scientists did not hold assumptions about phenomena under study. However, for assumptions to be valid, they must be consistent with existing knowledge and with the conclusion they are meant to support. Although assumptions are sometimes stated outright, they are most often implied. Thus, sociologists must be able to identify and evaluate the basic assumptions that underlie an argument.

How to Identify an Assumption

To identify an assumption, follow these guidelines.
1. **Identify the conclusion.** As you read or listen to the argument, look for clues that point to a concluding statement. Some examples are *in summary, thus, so, therefore,* and *however.*
2. **Identify which statements are assumptions.** Make a list of the statements about the phenomenon. Determine which statements of fact are not supported by direct evidence. Label these statements as assumptions.
3. **Evaluate the assumptions.** Examine the assumptions and determine whether they appear consistent with the conclusion and with the existing body of knowledge.

Applying the Skill

Read the following excerpt on diversity and the workplace by Allan G. Johnson. The excerpt is taken from Johnson's book *The Forest and the Trees: Sociology as Life, Practice and Promise.* Johnson's conclusion is that discrimination has negative effects on an organization. In the excerpt, Johnson makes a number of assumptions about diversity, noting that it is used to benefit some while penalizing others. No direct evidence is offered in support of these assumptions. But, as you will read in this and other chapters in Unit 3 of this textbook, there is ample evidence of the existence of social inequality. The assumptions do tend to support the conclusion.

"As most people know, however, in the world as it is, difference amounts to more than just variety. It's also used as a basis for including some and excluding others, for rewarding some more and others less, for treating some with respect and dignity and some as if they were less than fully human or not even there. Difference is used as a basis for privilege, for reserving for some the simple human dignities that everyone should have, to the extreme of deciding who lives and who dies. Since the workplace is part of the world, patterns of inequality and oppression that permeate the world also show up at work, even though people may like to think of themselves as 'colleagues' or part of 'the team.' And just as these patterns shape people's lives in often damaging ways, they can eat away at the core of a community or an organization, weakening it with internal division and resentment bred and fed by injustice and suffering."

In the following excerpt, also from *The Forest and the Trees,* Johnson discusses people's reaction to privilege in the workplace.

"Because members of privileged groups often react negatively to looking at privilege, women, blacks, Latinos, gays, lesbians, workers, and other groups may not bring it up. They know how easily privilege can be used to retaliate against them for challenging the status quo and making people feel uncomfortable. So, rather than look at the reality of what's going on, the typical pattern in organizations—and just about everywhere else—is to choose between two equally futile alternatives: to be stuck in cycles of guilt, blame, and defensiveness; or to avoid talking about issues of privilege at all."

Practicing the Skill

Using the steps outlined above, identify the assumptions in Allan G. Johnson's excerpt on privilege. What makes these statements assumptions? Do you think that these assumptions are valid?

IDENTIFYING ASSUMPTIONS

Have students apply their skills of identifying assumptions to a newspaper editorial. You might either select an editorial for the class to examine or let students choose their own editorials. Have students follow the three steps provided on this page for identifying assumptions. Then have the class discuss the assumptions found in the editorial that you chose or in one of the editorials that the students chose.

Practicing the Skill

To extend the activity, have students discuss where they might find factual support for the assumptions in Johnson's two excerpts. Remind students to question assumptions when reading.

SECTION 2

OBJECTIVES

1. *Identify the characteristics of the American class system.*

2. *Explain how different motivations and cultural values influence the American class system.*

Table Answer

because education helps a person get a better job, earn more money, and obtain many of the status symbols of a higher class

---

LET'S GET STARTED!

As students enter the classroom, ask them to consider social stratification in their school. Is there an upper class or a lower class, and, if so, on what characteristics are these classes based? Do some groups of students seem to be classless? Ask each student to list on a piece of paper the social classes found in the school and to describe some of the characteristics used to distinguish them. Tell students that their lists will remain private. Then tell students that in Section 2 they will learn about the American class system and about the characteristics of the various social classes in it.

2

THE AMERICAN CLASS SYSTEM

Read to Discover

1. What are the characteristics of the American class system?

2. How do different motivations and cultural values influence the American class system?

Define

reputational method, subjective method, objective method, social mobility, horizontal mobility, vertical mobility, intergenerational mobility

By definition, social inequality exists in all class systems. What form inequality takes varies from society to society—the fewer the number of ascribed characteristics used to determine access to rewards, the more open the class system. The United States has a fairly open system. The law forbids discrimination based on ascribed characteristics such as race, religion, ancestry, or sex.

In theory, all Americans have equal access to the resources needed for social advancement. However, the United States has a wide range of social classes, and the rate of social mobility is not equal for every segment of American society. To understand why such conditions exist, one needs to look at the characteristics of social class and the patterns of social mobility in the United States.

Determining Social Class

Sociologists do not agree on the number of class divisions that exist in the United States. Some researchers identify three social classes: upper class, middle class, and lower class. Other researchers divide each of these three broad classes into upper and lower divisions. Still others use a five-category classification system of upper class, upper middle class, lower middle class, working class, and lower class. Today most sociologists use a six-class system. As you can see from the chart on this page, the divisions in this system are upper class, upper middle class, lower middle class, working class, working poor, and underclass.

Sociologists rely on three basic techniques to rank individuals according to social class—the reputational, subjective, and objective methods. In the **reputational method**, individuals in the community are asked to rank other community members based on what they know of their characters and lifestyles. This method is suitable only when studying small communities in which almost everyone knows almost everyone else. The findings from these studies cannot be used to make conclusions about other communities.

Social Classes in the United States

Social Class	Level of Education	Occupations	Percentage of Population
Upper class	Prestigious universities	Owners of large businesses, investors, heirs to family fortunes, some top business executives	1
Upper middle class	College or university	Business executives, professionals	14
Lower middle class	High school, some college	Lower-level managers, skilled craftworkers, supervisors	30
Working class	High school	Factory workers, clerical workers, lower-level salespeople, some craftworkers	30
Working poor	Some high school	Laborers, service workers—gardeners, house cleaners, etc.	22
Underclass	Some high school	Undesirable, low-paying jobs, unemployed, on welfare	3

*Note: Because of rounding these numbers may not add up to 100 percent.
Source: *The American Class Structure: A New Synthesis* by Dennis Gilbert and Joseph A. Kahl

INTERPRETING TABLES Many factors are used to define the social class to which a person belongs. However, certain factors such as education and occupation tend to be most important in determining class divisions. ***Based on this table, why do you think education might be important to someone motivated to move to a higher class?***

TEACH OBJECTIVE 1

SUGGESTION 1: To help students identify the characteristics of the American class system, copy the graphic organizer at the right onto the chalkboard, omitting the italicized answers. Have students copy and complete the organizer. Discuss the answers with the class. Then write on the chalkboard a list of several levels of occupations, such as bank president, factory worker, nurse, office manager, police officer, and sales clerk. Ask students to indicate into which social class they would place each occupation and to give reasons for the choices they have made. **ENGLISH LANGUAGE LEARNERS**

AMERICAN CLASS SYSTEM

Upper Class:
1 percent; prestigious schools; heirs, investors, large business owners and top executives

Upper Middle Class:
14 percent; college or university; business executives and professionals

Lower Middle Class:
30 percent; high school or college; lower-level managers, skilled craftworkers, supervisors

Working Class:
30 percent; high school; factory and clerical workers, lower level salespeople, some craftworkers

Working Poor:
22 percent; some high school; laborers, service workers— gardeners, house cleaners, etc.

Underclass:
3 percent; some high school; undesirable low-paying jobs, unemployed, or on welfare for some time

---

In the second technique, the **subjective method**, individuals are asked to determine their own social rank. When the choices are limited to upper, middle, and lower class, most people say they are middle class. Researchers have found that people do not like to place themselves in the upper or lower classes. This problem can be partially eliminated by including the upper middle class and working class in the list of choices.

The third classification technique is the **objective method**. In this approach, sociologists define social class by income, occupation, and education. The statistical basis of this method makes it the least biased determination of class. However, it is not without its shortcomings. This technique's major problem involves the selection and measurement of social factors. Each combination of factors produces a slightly different picture of social-class membership.

Social Classes in the United States

Regardless of the method used to identify class membership, sociologists generally agree on the basic characteristics of the American social-class system. Many of them also agree on the relative distribution of the population within the system. Estimates suggest that about 1 percent of the population of the United States belongs to the upper class. Another 14 percent of Americans are part of the upper middle class, while the lower middle class makes up about 30 percent of the population. Another 30 percent comprise the working-class category. Of the remaining 25 percent of Americans, 22 percent are members of the working poor, and 3 percent are members of the underclass. However, recent figures suggest that the underclass may be shrinking.

One major difference between the classes is income. Classes also differ in terms of lifestyle and beliefs. A brief look at the general characteristics of each class will help you understand how social class affects life patterns.

The Upper Class Although the upper class makes up just 1 percent of the population, it controls a sizable proportion of the country's wealth. Generally, the upper class can be divided into two groups—"old money" and "new money."

America's old money includes such families as the Rockefellers, Vanderbilts, Du Ponts, and Kennedys. The term *old money* refers to the fact that these families have been wealthy for generations. The great bulk of their wealth comes from inheritance. Yet in terms of social rank, the family name and the accomplishments of previous generations are as important as the size of the family fortune. Members of this class are born into an atmosphere of wealth and power. They are able to attend prestigious schools, eat at the best restaurants, and vacation at the most exclusive resorts. Most have some of the world's richest and most famous people among their friends.

Interdisciplinary Connection

HISTORY

The Upper Class of the Gilded Age. The lifestyles of America's superrich of the late 1800s helped define the period called the Gilded Age. The wealthy of the day had extensive social calendars. They spent the spring in Europe, the summer back in the states at their country homes or on their yachts, and the fall in New York attending lavish parties. For example, Alva Vanderbilt hosted one ball on which she spent about $125,000 (equal to about $4.25 million today). The social season usually climaxed with Caroline Astor's annual ball, one of the most prestigious events of the year. Astor always invited 400 guests, and not being among the chosen was tantamount to social disgrace.

CRITICAL THINKING
How do the superrich of the Gilded Age reflect the three aspects of class— wealth, power, and prestige?

ANSWER: Each aspect helped define who the upper class were at the time as well as to stratify people within the upper class.

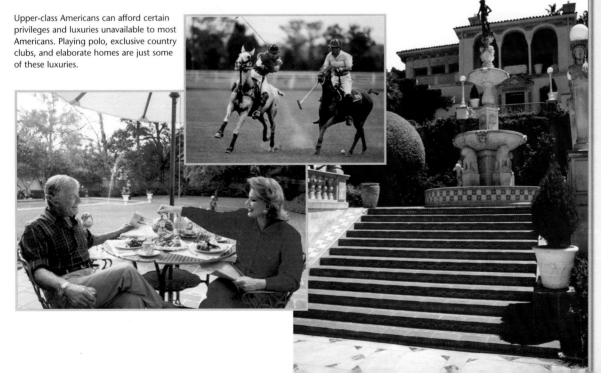

Upper-class Americans can afford certain privileges and luxuries unavailable to most Americans. Playing polo, exclusive country clubs, and elaborate homes are just some of these luxuries.

The term new money refers to the newly rich. They generally have acquired wealth through their own efforts rather than through inheritance. New money is not as prestigious as old money because it is not backed by a long family heritage. However, it does purchase most of the privileges of upper-class membership. These privileges include luxurious homes, expensive cars, and fine art collections. Some of those with old money look down on the newly rich for their conspicuous consumption. This term was coined by economist Thorstein Veblen in 1899 to describe the purchase of goods for the status they bring rather than for their usefulness.

Not surprisingly, membership in the upper class sometimes carries with it great power and influence. Members often fill top positions in government and private enterprise. Upper-class members also use their wealth to support charities. Some—particularly old-money families—consider helping those less fortunate than themselves an obligation of their social rank. Many members of this class hold traditional views and are politically conservative.

The Upper Middle Class Members of the upper-middle class are primarily high-income businesspeople and professionals. Most have a college education, and many have advanced degrees. Their money buys them large houses and expensive cars, yearly vacations, a college education for their children, and many added luxuries. Class membership is generally based on income rather than on assets. Consequently, many in the upper

middle class are career oriented. Many people in this class are politically and socially active. However, their power and influence are limited to the community level and do not extend to the national level.

The Lower Middle Class Most individuals in the lower middle class also hold white-collar jobs—work that does not involve manual labor. Many of their jobs require less education and provide a lower income than the jobs held by the upper middle class. Lower middle class jobs include nursing, middle management, and sales. Owners of small businesses also belong to the lower middle class. Members of this class live a comfortable life but must work hard to keep what they have achieved. Many of them also hold traditional values and are politically conservative.

The Working Class Many members of the working class hold jobs that require manual labor. Factory workers, tradespeople, less skilled workers, and some service workers fall into this category. Such jobs have traditionally been labeled blue-collar jobs. Some of these jobs pay as much or more than many of the positions held by members of the lower middle class. However, these jobs do not carry as much prestige. Other working-class people hold clerical, lower-level sales, and various

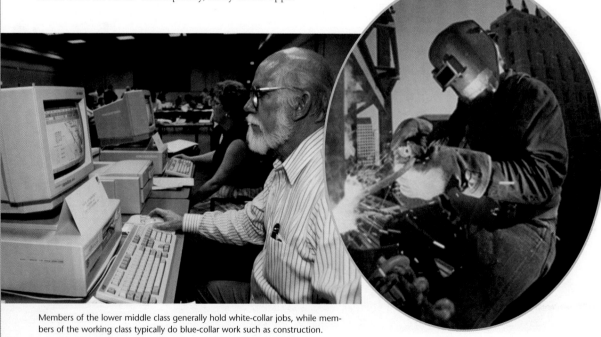

Members of the lower middle class generally hold white-collar jobs, while members of the working class typically do blue-collar work such as construction.

Pair students and have each pair make a list of American cultural values and motivations that influence the class system (*such as, the belief that all Americans have equal access to social advancement, the values of hard work and economic success, and the motivations to better one's life and one's children*). To help students get started, remind them of related sayings (*such as, America—the land of opportunity; every child can grow up to be president; you can be anything if you just work hard enough*). Ask volunteer pairs to share some of the items on their lists with the class. Have students discuss them. Point out that many of the values and motivations hold the individual responsible for his or her social class. **COOPERATIVE LEARNING**

CONNECTING *to Literature*

Horatio Alger Jr. (1832–1899) was a prolific writer of popular inspirational fiction for young people. His formulaic stories of poor boys who rose to wealth and success influenced generations of Americans. True rags-to-riches stories came to be referred to as Horatio Alger tales. Ask students to read one of Alger's books and to conduct research on his life. Then have each student write a book report that summarizes and evaluates the book and that includes an introduction summarizing Alger's life and career.

BLOCK SCHEDULING

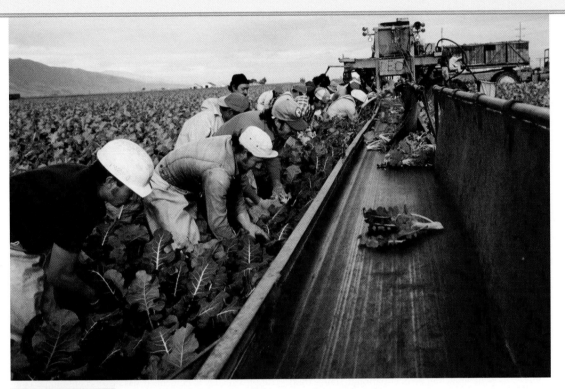

INTERPRETING VISUALS Migrant farmworkers are often categorized as working poor because of the seasonal nature of their work. *Why do you think seasonal work would make it hard to earn a living wage?*

service jobs that do not require manual labor. These types of jobs are sometimes called pink-collar jobs because women have traditionally held them. Many members of the working class have few financial reserves. Consequently, unexpected crises—such as medical emergencies or the loss of a job—can push working-class individuals into lower class levels.

The Working Poor Members of the working poor work at the lowest-paying jobs. These jobs are often temporary or seasonal—such as housecleaning, migrant farmwork, and day laboring. Even though the working poor work hard, they rarely make a living wage. Many depend on government-support programs to make ends meet. Most are high-school dropouts and, because of their lack of education and skills, their future prospects are often bleak. Most are not involved politically. They believe their situation will remain the same regardless of which party is in power.

The Underclass Families that have experienced unemployment and poverty over several generations are considered part of the underclass. Some members of the underclass do work, but usually only at undesirable, low-paying jobs. Their chief source of income is often public

assistance. Life for people in the underclass is a day-to-day struggle for survival. Typically, only 50 percent of children in the underclass make it into a higher class.

Social Mobility

The United States has an open class system. **Social mobility**—the movement between or within social classes or strata—is an important feature of the open class system. Sociologists generally study three types of social mobility: horizontal mobility, vertical mobility, and intergenerational mobility.

The term **horizontal mobility** refers to movement within a social class or stratum. When an individual moves from one job to another of equal social ranking, that individual experiences horizontal mobility. An accountant may consider a move from one firm to another an important step up his or her career ladder. However, if the move does not involve any major change in the accountant's wealth, power, or prestige, sociologists view it as horizontal mobility.

Vertical mobility, on the other hand, is the movement between social classes or strata. This type of mobility can be either upward or downward, depending on whether an individual moves to a higher or lower position in the stratification system. The monetary and social rewards of promotion from a secretarial to a management position may move an individual from the working class to the lower middle class.

Sociologists consider **intergenerational mobility**—status differences between generations in the same family—a special form of vertical mobility. When sociologists examine patterns of vertical mobility, they generally focus on changes during adulthood. With intergenerational mobility, the focus is on differences between people's class of origin—their parents' social class—and their current social position. For example, the son or daughter of an automobile mechanic who becomes a doctor experiences intergenerational mobility.

Most Americans believe that all people in the United States are free to reach their own particular level of achievement. They believe that people who possess enough ability and motivation will rise to the top. Others, they believe, will rise or fall to various levels according to their efforts and abilities. Although this theory appears to be true, the reality is somewhat different. Research indicates that even though the majority of Americans achieve a higher occupational status than their parents, most remain within the same social class. When individuals do experience vertical mobility, they rarely move more than one social class above or below their class of origin.

Structural Causes of Upward Mobility

Individual effort often plays a major role in a person's movement up the social-class ladder. However, sociologists are more interested in the structural factors that influence social mobility. The structural factors that affect upward mobility include advances in technology, changes in merchandising patterns, and increases in the population's general level of education.

When technologies change, the jobs available to workers also change, which can result in downward mobility for individuals caught in the shift. However, it often means upward mobility for the next generation of workers.

For example, advances in farming technology have made it possible to grow more food with fewer people. Consequently, the percentage of the workforce engaged in agriculture has declined from 40 percent in 1900 to less than 3 percent today. Similarly, mechanization has drastically reduced the need for less skilled

labor. The result has been intergenerational upward mobility as the sons and daughters of farmers and laborers have sought employment in higher-status occupations. The same process is now at work in the manufacturing sector of the economy. The disappearance of millions of factory jobs over the past three decades has forced some new workers into higher-status jobs, primarily in the service industry.

Changes in merchandising patterns in the United States have also affected social mobility. Recent changes include an explosion in the credit industry, a greater emphasis on insurance, increased real-estate transactions, and an extraordinary growth in personal services. These changes have created a larger white-collar workforce. In 1940 approximately 31 percent of all workers held white-collar jobs. Today nearly 73 percent of the labor force is engaged in traditional white-collar and service-industry jobs.

Another structural factor that has promoted upward mobility is an increase in the general level of education. In 1940 more than 75 percent of the population aged 25 and older had not completed high school. Today that figure is approximately 9 percent. It has also become more common for Americans to have a college education. In 1940 less than 5 percent of the population aged 25 and older had graduated from college. Today 26 percent of people aged 25 or older have completed a bachelor's degree or higher. Research has shown that upward mobility increases with level of education.

Education is one of the most important means to achieve upward mobility.

SOCIOLOGY IN THE
World Today

THE OVERCLASS

One of the great social developments of the late 1800s and early 1900s was the rise of the middle class in the United States. Some observers feel that as the new century begins, a similar major development is underway—the rise of the first mass affluent class. Writer Dinesh D'Souza calls this group of superrich people the overclass.

Who Are the Overclass?

D'Souza admits that there has always been a class of superrich people. The overclass, he suggests, is different in terms of its size and its membership. In general, someone is superrich if he or she has a net worth—assets minus liabilities—of $1 million or more. D'Souza points out that in the 1990s the number of American families with a net worth of at least $1 million grew from 1.3 million to 5 million. This rapid growth is expected to continue, D'Souza notes. Demographers predict that there will be 20 million American millionaires by 2010. The number of American billionaires is growing too. In the early 1980s there were just 13. Today there are nearly 270.

The origin of the overclass's wealth is different, D'Souza suggests. Most of the overclass did not inherit their fortunes. For example, more than 60 percent of the 1999 Forbes 400—a list of the 400 richest people in the United States—got rich through their own efforts. D'Souza points out that the rich have traditionally been white, male, and older. While the overclass is still primarily white and male, he notes, more and more of its members are quite young. A surprisingly large number are between the ages of 20 and 35.

A Different View of Wealth

Perhaps the greatest difference between the overclass and the superrich of the past, D'Souza thinks, is their attitude toward wealth. According to Thorstein Veblen, the mark of the superrich was wasteful excess. However, the overclass try to avoid extravagance, D'Souza suggests. While the overclass certainly live comfortable lives, "conspicuous consumption is usually less conspicuous . . . than it used to be." What excess there is, he continues, usually takes place out of public view. Why are the overclass reluctant to flaunt their wealth? D'Souza argues that it is the result of their background. Many grew up middle class, and they cling to such middle-class values as hard work and self-discipline. Despite their great wealth, D'Souza says, they want to maintain a middle-class image.

Steve Jobs, a founder of Apple Computers, is one of the new members of the overclass who did not inherit money.

Think About It

1. Evaluating *Who, according to D'Souza, makes up the overclass?*

2. Contrasting *In what ways, if any, is D'Souza's overclass different from the upper class described on pages 215–16? Explain your answer.*

CLOSE

Review with students the general characteristics of the six American social classes. Ask students what three classes include the majority of Americans *(the lower middle class, the working class, and the working poor)*. Then ask which class includes the fewest Americans *(the upper class)*. Conclude by having students discuss the realities of social mobility in the United States.

REVIEW AND ASSESS

Have students complete the **Section 2 Review** on p. 220. As **Alternative Assessment**, you may want to use the social class collage or essay in this section's lessons.

RETEACH

Have students work in pairs to create detailed outlines of this section. Students should use the subsection headings as the main points in their outlines and should be sure to include any boldfaced terms. Then review students' outlines as a class. **ENGLISH LANGUAGE LEARNERS , COOPERATIVE LEARNING**

EXTEND

Have students read Barbara Ehrenreich's book *Nickel and Dimed: On (Not) Getting By in America* (New York: Metropolitan Books, 2001), in which Ehrenreich describes her experiences working in several low-paying jobs in the United States. Then have each student write a short review of the book. **BLOCK SCHEDULING**

Structural Causes of Downward Mobility Although upward mobility is more common, movement down the social-class ladder also occurs. Downward mobility can result from such personal factors as illness, divorce, widowhood, and retirement. Once again, sociologists are more interested in the structural causes of this movement.

Changes in the economy are the primary structural causes of downward mobility. As you just read, breakthroughs in technology can alter the demand for labor. Workers may suddenly find themselves without jobs and with skills that are no longer marketable. If these workers are unable to find new jobs that produce incomes comparable to what they were earning, they may experience downward mobility. For younger workers, the drop in social status is often temporary. However, for older workers the shift may be permanent.

Economic changes also can affect intergenerational mobility. In times of economic growth and low unemployment, individuals just entering the job market have less difficulty finding desirable employment. However, in times of economic recession good jobs are not as plentiful. As a result, even highly qualified recent college graduates sometimes cannot find jobs in their chosen fields.

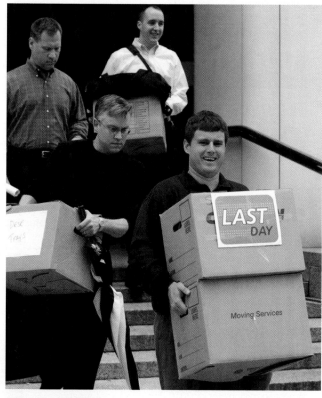

INTERPRETING VISUALS Changes in the economy, such as a recession or corporate bankruptcy, might lead to downward mobility of some workers. *What options do you think these laid-off workers have to fight downward mobility?*

SECTION 2 REVIEW

1. Define and explain
reputational method
subjective method
objective method
social mobility
horizontal mobility
vertical mobility
intergenerational mobility

2. Identifying Cause and Effect Copy the graphic organizer below. Use it to identify and describe the structural factors that affect social mobility.

Upward Mobility

Downward Mobility

3. Finding the Main Idea

a. What are the general characteristics of the six social classes in the United States?

b. How do American cultural values and economic aspiration and motivation influence the American class system and social mobility?

4. Writing and Critical Thinking

Evaluating Write three short paragraphs evaluating the methods of measuring social class.
Consider:
- applicability of results
- personal feelings of respondents
- social factors selected for measurement

Homework Practice Online
keyword: SL3 HP9

OBJECTIVES

1. *Identify the groups of Americans that are affected by poverty.*

2. *Describe the steps that have been taken by the federal government to lessen the effects of poverty.*

LET'S GET STARTED!

As students enter the classroom, ask them to consider the term *poverty*. Have students write a list of words that come to mind when they think of poverty. Explain to students that the U.S. government defines poverty as a standard of living that is below the minimum level considered adequate by society. The government calculates the poverty level by determining the cost of an adequate diet and multiplying that figure by three because research has shown that poor people spend a third of their income on food. Tell students that in Section 3 they will learn about poverty in the United States and about government efforts to decrease poverty.

3 POVERTY

Read to Discover

1. What groups of Americans are affected by poverty?
2. What steps have been taken by the federal government to lessen the effects of poverty?

Define

poverty, poverty level, life chances, life expectancy, transfer payments

The United States is one of the richest countries in the world. However, not everyone in American society shares equally in this prosperity. More than 31 million people—about 11 percent of the population—live below the poverty level. Many millions more make incomes that are too low to meet their basic needs. However, they make too much money to qualify for public assistance. For all of these people, daily life is often a struggle.

Who is classified as poor depends on how poverty is defined. In general, **poverty** is seen as a standard of living that is below the minimum level considered adequate by society. Thus, poverty is a relative measure. What is considered poverty in one society might be regarded as an adequate standard of living in another. For example, many poor Americans live more comfortable lives than the majority of people in some industrializing nations. This fact does not mean there are no poor people in the United States. Rather, it means that the standard of living in the United States is particularly high.

What does it mean to be poor in the United States? To answer this question, you need to look at the characteristics of poverty in the United States and at the effects that poverty has on people's lives. You also need to examine some of the ways that government responds to the problem of poverty.

Defining Poverty in the United States

The U.S. Bureau of the Census defines poverty in terms of the minimum annual income needed by a family to survive. This minimum income is called the **poverty level**. The government considers families with income levels below this amount to be poor.

The poverty level is determined by calculating the cost of providing an adequate diet, based on the U.S. Department of Agriculture's minimum nutritional standards. This figure is then multiplied by three because research has indicated that poor people spend a third of their income on food. Each year, the government adjusts the poverty level to reflect increases in the cost of living. The poverty level most often quoted in news stories is for a family of four. The government actually establishes a series of poverty levels that takes into account the number of people in a family. The table on this page lists the poverty levels for various family sizes.

Recently, poverty researchers have questioned the usefulness of the government's poverty levels. They point out that the method for calculating poverty was developed in the 1960s. Since then, eating and spending habits have changed greatly. In response to this criticism, the Census Bureau has begun to experiment with different definitions of poverty. One definition bases the poverty level on spending for the basic necessities, which include food, clothing, housing, and "a little bit more"—other personal expenses. Using this definition would raise the poverty level for a family of four by a few thousand dollars. As a result, several million more Americans would be added to the ranks of those in poverty.

Poverty Level by Family Size, 2000

Family Size	Poverty Level (in dollars)
1 person	8,794
Under 65 years	8,959
Over 65 years	8,259
2 persons	11,239
Householder under 65	11,590
Householder over 65	10,419
3 persons	13,738
4 persons	17,603
5 persons	20,819
6 persons	23,528
7 persons	26,754
8 persons	29,701

Source: U.S. Bureau of the Census

INTERPRETING CHARTS The poverty level is determined by multiplying what it costs to feed a family. *Why do you think the issue of affordability would be important to someone living at the poverty level?*

SECTION 3 RESOURCES

REPRODUCIBLE & REVIEW

- Research Projects and Activities for Teaching Sociology 9
- Study Skills and Writing Guide
- Section 3 Review, p. 227

TECHNOLOGY

- One-Stop Planner, Lesson 9.3
- Homework Practice Online
- HRW Go site

Chart Answer

because such a person would be able to afford very little

SUGGESTION 1: To help students identify the groups of Americans that are affected by poverty, copy the graphic organizer at the right onto the chalkboard, omitting the italicized answers. Have students copy and complete the organizer. Discuss the answers with the class. Then organize students into pairs and ask each pair to discuss reasons why the groups listed in the graphic organizer are more likely than other groups to be impoverished. Ask the pairs to think of two or three possible causes of poverty for each group. Have a volunteer from each pair report the pair's conclusions to the class. **ENGLISH LANGUAGE LEARNERS , COOPERATIVE LEARNING**

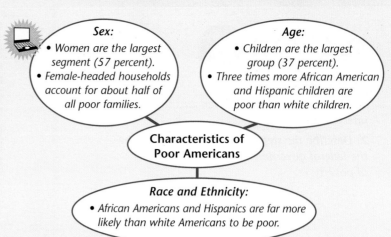

Sex:
• *Women are the largest segment (57 percent).*
• *Female-headed households account for about half of all poor families.*

Age:
• *Children are the largest group (37 percent).*
• *Three times more African American and Hispanic children are poor than white children.*

Characteristics of Poor Americans

Race and Ethnicity:
• *African Americans and Hispanics are far more likely than white Americans to be poor.*

Applying Sociology

The Causes of Poverty. Sociologists disagree about the causes of poverty. Some sociologists argue that poverty is a by-product of social change. For example, the expansion of the service sector and the decrease in manufacturing jobs has impoverished many of the people who once worked in manufacturing. Other sociologists argue that poverty is an inherent feature of capitalism. Therefore, even when the economy is strong the number of available jobs will never be enough for everyone looking for work. In short, these sociologists argue that for some to be rich, others must be poor. At the same time, most capitalist countries have lower levels of poverty than other countries.

CRITICAL THINKING
Which viewpoint do you agree with? Why?

ANSWER: Answers will vary, but students should address the arguments on each side.

Visual Answers

1. the Southwest and the Lower South

2. Questions might include the following: What societal factors contribute to high levels of poverty in certain regions? What social programs do different states provide to help decrease poverty?

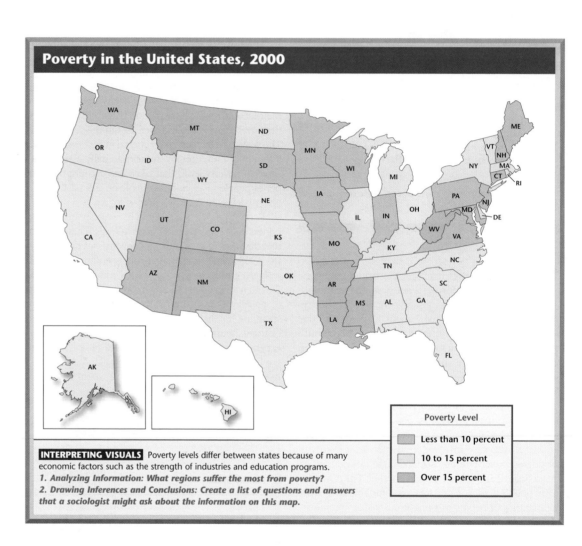

Poverty in the United States, 2000

Poverty Level
■ Less than 10 percent
□ 10 to 15 percent
■ Over 15 percent

INTERPRETING VISUALS Poverty levels differ between states because of many economic factors such as the strength of industries and education programs.
1. Analyzing Information: What regions suffer the most from poverty?
2. Drawing Inferences and Conclusions: Create a list of questions and answers that a sociologist might ask about the information on this map.

American Poverty

Not every person in society runs an equal risk of being poor. Among the characteristics that affect poverty are age, sex, race, and ethnicity, or cultural background.

Age As an age group, children have the largest percentage in poverty. Children under the age of 18 make up 25 percent of the population, but they represent 35 percent of the people who live in poverty. Not all children have an equal likelihood of being poor. The level of poverty among African American and Hispanic children is three times the level among white children.

Sex About 57 percent of the poor are women. Also, women head about one half of all poor families. As in the case of children, not all households headed by women

are at equal risk. Of the households headed by African American and Hispanic women, about 34 percent are poor. This compares to a rate of nearly 20 percent for families headed by white women.

Race and Ethnicity As is obvious from the statistics above, poverty varies by race and cultural background. Regardless of age or sex, African Americans and Hispanics in the United States are more likely than whites to live in poverty. The poverty rate for whites averages 2 percentage points lower than the rate for the overall population. African Americans and Hispanics, on the other hand, have poverty rates that are about twice that of the United States as a whole. The table on page 223 gives the poverty rates for select categories of people.

Lead a class discussion on the groups of Americans who are most affected by poverty *(listed in the graphic organizer on p. 222)* and on the effects of poverty *(decreased life chances, higher rates of disease, poor nutrition, less access to medical care and education, unsafe housing and working conditions, and more exposure to environmental hazards).* Then have each student create a poster designed to raise Americans' awareness of the problems associated with poverty. Encourage students to make their posters eye-catching and informative. Display students' posters in the classroom.

Teacher to Teacher

John Hanson of Marion, Indiana, suggested the following activity: Bring to class a selection of food containers and attach a large price tag to each item. In addition, create or provide fake money. Then organize students into six groups and randomly assign each group one of the six social classes in the United States. Give each group a certain amount of money based on the group's social class. Ask each group to imagine that it is a family and to use its money to buy food. Afterward, have different groups discuss how much they could buy with their money. **COOPERATIVE LEARNING , BLOCK SCHEDULING**

Percentage of the Population Below the Poverty Level Based on Selected Characteristics, 2000

Characteristic	All Races	White	African American	Hispanic American
Total Population	11.3	9.4	22.0	21.2
Under 18 years old	16.7	12.9	30.6	28.0
18–24 years old	14.4	12.6	23.6	21.5
25–34 years old	10.4	9.2	17.1	19.1
35–44 years old	8.2	7.0	15.6	15.5
45–54 years old	6.4	5.2	13.6	12.3
55–59 years old	8.8	7.5	18.9	12.8
60–64 years old	10.2	9.2	18.6	22.1
65 years old and older	10.4	8.9	22.4	18.8

Source: U.S. Bureau of the Census

INTERPRETING TABLES Poverty affects people of all races, ethnicities, and age groups. However, because of a history of discrimination and many other factors, specific communities have faced greater percentages of poverty. *What age group has the highest percentage of members below the poverty level?*

The Effects of Poverty

The lives of poor Americans differ markedly from the lives of the wealthier members of society. Poor and wealthy members of society differ in the range of their life chances and in their behavior patterns.

Life Chances By **life chances**, sociologists mean the likelihood that individuals have of sharing in the opportunities and benefits of society. Life chances include such things as health, length of life, housing, and education. Research has shown that life chances vary by social class. The lower their social class, the less opportunity individuals have to share in the benefits of society.

Among the most important life chances are health and length of life. Poor Americans are at a serious disadvantage in both. For example, rates of heart disease, diabetes, cancer, arthritis, pneumonia, and tuberculosis are highest among those living in poverty. In light of this fact, it is not surprising that poor people have shorter life expectancies than do other members of society. **Life expectancy** refers to the average number of years a person born in a particular year can expect to live. The differences in life expectancy are particularly dramatic in

the case of infants. One study found that poor children are 60 percent more likely to die in the first year of life than are children not born into poverty.

Two reasons for ill health and a shorter life expectancy among poor Americans are inadequate nutrition and less access to medical care. Poor people have less money to spend on food and are often less informed about good nutrition. A lack of money also limits the amount of health care that poor people receive. A significant number of poor Americans do not have health insurance because it is too expensive. Uninsured people are less likely than those with insurance to get routine physical checkups and other kinds of preventive care. In addition, the uninsured are more likely not to fill prescriptions. They are also more likely to postpone medical treatment—even for serious conditions.

The environment that poor Americans work and live in has negative effects on health. The working poor often have jobs that involve considerable health and safety risks. The housing

INTERPRETING VISUALS Poverty can severely limit the life chances that an individual has. *How might homelessness limit one's life chances?*

Social Stratification 223

Sociology in the World Today

The Feminization of Poverty. The expansion of the high-tech industry provided upward social mobility for some American workers. However, high-tech growth also eliminated many entry-level and clerical positions, jobs that were often held by women.

ACTIVITY: Have students discuss the effects related to poverty of the decrease in entry-level and clerical positions. *(The decrease in these types of jobs meant that many women lost their jobs. Some of these women might not have the skills to get new jobs that pay as well, which probably contributed to the number of American families, and more specifically women and children, living in poverty.)*

Table Answer

under 18 years old

Visual Answer

It would likely mean poorer health and a shorter life span as a result of exposure, poor nutrition, and other factors.

TEACH

Have students read the feature Rural Poverty on this page and lead a discussion on the first item under Think About It. Then have students brainstorm for responses to the second item. Write students' ideas on the chalkboard and encourage other students to provide feedback on the practicality, cost, and effectiveness of the ideas. If students have already read the text about government responses to poverty, have the class consider those responses during the brainstorming session. Then assign the essay under Think About It as homework.

CONNECTING to Government

Ask students to conduct research on the history of the Tennessee Valley Authority or the history of the Rural Electrification Administration. If you live in an area served by a rural electric cooperative, you may want to have students conduct research on that cooperative instead. Students should prepare brief written reports or short oral presentations on the topics that they researched. **BLOCK SCHEDULING**

Sociology in the World Today

Global Rural Poverty.
Rural poverty is a worldwide problem. Globally, about 1.2 billion people live in extreme poverty. Of these people, some three quarters live in rural areas.

RESEARCH ACTIVITY: Ask students to conduct research and to report on the urban and rural poverty levels of a country of their choosing.

Think About It Answers

1. The poverty rate of rural areas (13.4 percent) is greater than that of urban areas (10.8 percent), but the same groups suffer from poverty in about the same proportions in both rural and urban areas.

2. Essays will vary, but students should exhibit an understanding of the reasons that rural poverty is less visible than urban poverty, such as the increased media coverage of social conditions that contribute to and arise from urban poverty.

Case Studies

AND OTHER TRUE STORIES

RURAL POVERTY

For most Americans, poverty statistics bring to mind images of urban areas. They picture single mothers and their children living in dark and dingy tenements. Or people might see images of crime-infested city streets controlled by drug dealers and street gangs. For others, images of the homeless come to mind.

Characteristics of Rural Poverty

Urban poverty, however, is only part of a larger picture. About 22 percent of poor Americans—nearly 7 million people—live in rural areas. In recent years, the level of poverty in rural areas has exceeded the level found in big cities. According to government statistics, 13.4 percent of rural Americans are poor. In contrast, the poverty rate for urban areas stands at 10.8 percent. However, the characteristics of poverty are much the same in rural areas as elsewhere. Poverty rates are much higher among rural minorities than among rural whites. African American, Hispanic, and American Indian families are more than twice as likely as white families to be poor. Rural young people are also more likely to be poor than are members of other age groups. In fact, one out of every five rural Americans under the age of 17 is poor. Families headed by single women are more likely to be poor than are married-couple families.

Special Challenges

The poor people living in rural areas face special challenges. They seldom have easy access to government services. Social-welfare offices, public health clinics, job-training programs, and federally funded day-care centers are rare in rural areas. Poor people in rural areas are at particular risk in terms of health care. Many rural hospitals have closed, and registered nurses are in short supply at those that remain open. In addition, the ratio of physicians to residents in small communities is less than one third the national average. Many rural communities in the United States do not have any primary-care physicians at all.

Changes in the economy have worsened the already difficult employment situation of

Local communities have tried to ease some of the burdens of rural poverty by providing health services and job training to those living in poverty in rural areas.

poor people in rural areas. Many of the industries that traditionally supported the rural economy, such as farming, mining, timber, and manufacturing, suffered declines during the 1980s and 1990s. Some businesses relocated factories to other countries to take advantage of cheap labor. This relocation has led to a general economic decline. Many rural jobs have also been lost to automation.

A Hidden Problem?

Urban poverty is visible. The social conditions it helps produce—crime, drug abuse, and violence—make the news practically every day. Rural poverty, however, is less visible and, therefore, easier for many Americans to ignore. The reality of rural poverty is largely hidden.

Think About It

1. **Comparing and Contrasting** How are the characteristics of rural poverty similar to and different from poverty characteristics nationwide?

2. **Drawing Inferences and Conclusions** The "invisibility" of rural poverty intensifies the problem. What steps would you take to bring this issue to the public's attention? Explain your ideas in a brief essay.

that poor people are able to afford is often inadequate and unsafe. As a result, poor children are more likely to be exposed to environmental hazards such as lead paint.

The educational life chances of poor Americans are also limited. School funding is based in part on local property taxes. As a result, schools in low-income areas are often inadequately funded because of low tax revenues. Limitations in education are particularly serious because of their negative effect on future life chances.

Patterns of Behavior Certain behaviors also vary depending on social class. For example, divorce rates are higher among low-income families than among other segments of the population. Poor Americans are also more likely to be arrested, convicted, and sent to prison for crimes than are Americans from higher social classes. This situation results, in part, from the fact that people living in poverty are more likely to commit crimes that the police pursue more agressively. Among them are violent crime and crimes against property, such as burglary and auto theft. Because criminals usually commit offenses in or near their own communities, poor people are more likely to be the victims of crime.

Government Responses to Poverty

In 1964 President Lyndon B. Johnson declared a "war on poverty" to improve the lives of the poorest Americans. Since then, the federal government has taken an active role in attempting to reduce inequality in America. The results have been mixed.

There are still more than 31 million people in the United States who live in poverty. In addition, the poverty rate is about the same as it was in the early 1970s. Nevertheless, the situation has improved. For example, poverty among elderly Americans was almost two times as high as it was among the general population in 1960. Today the poverty rate for people 65 and older is lower than the rate for the country as a whole. This improvement is primarily a result of increases in Social Security benefits and the introduction of Medicare, the government-sponsored health-insurance program for people 65 and older.

INTERPRETING VISUALS The U.S. government has taken some steps to reduce the effects of poverty. President Lyndon B. Johnson initiated antipoverty programs during the 1960s. *How do you think programs like free school lunches help limit the effects of poverty in the United States?*

The government attempts to reduce inequality through various social-welfare programs. These programs use one of two approaches—either transfer payments or government subsidies. The government uses **transfer payments** to redistribute money among various segments of society. This redistribution involves taking a percentage of the money collected through taxes and then funneling it to groups that need public assistance. These groups include people who are poor, unemployed, elderly, or disabled. The major transfer-payment programs include Supplemental Security Income (SSI) and Temporary Assistance for Needy Families (TANF). SSI provides income support for people 65 years of age and older and for blind and disabled adults and children. TANF, which until 1996 was called Aid to Families with Dependent Children (AFDC), gives cash payments to poor families with children.

The second approach used by the government to assist poor Americans is subsidies, which transfer goods and services rather than cash. The Food Stamp program is, perhaps, the best-known government subsidy. Under this program, poor people receive coupons or cards that can be used to buy food. Other subsidies include those for housing, school lunches, and Medicaid—a health-insurance program for the poor.

As part of an effort to reduce the effects of poverty, state governments have issued benefit cards that can be used to help purchase food, housing, and other necessities.

From the 1980s onward, calls for reform of the social-welfare system grew louder. Critics charged that the system had created a permanent "welfare class" who choose to live off government assistance rather than to work. The welfare class had to be moved off the welfare roles and into the working world, these critics said. In 1996 the federal government responded by passing the Personal Responsibility and Work Opportunity Reconciliation Act. This act turned the administration of some welfare programs over to the states. It

Careers
IN SOCIOLOGY

SOCIAL-WELFARE RESEARCHER

Social-welfare researchers investigate such social problems as poverty, homelessness, substance abuse, child abuse, and violence. They collect and analyze statistics on these issues and write reports based on their findings. These reports are then used to plan and carry out social-welfare programs. Some social-welfare researchers specialize in the task of raising funds or writing grants to support these programs.

Many social-welfare researchers are employed in governmental welfare agencies. Others work for community welfare organizations. Still others work in the research departments of schools of social work. Recently, social-welfare researchers have studied new methods of helping families to avoid the problems that have hampered welfare programs in the past. Among the new programs being studied are the welfare-to-work initiatives.

Many social-welfare researchers work with children who live in poverty.

226

CLOSE

Write the terms *Age, Sex,* and *Race or Ethnicity* on the chalkboard and ask students to use the terms to describe the characteristics of poverty in the United States. Then ask students to identify the federal government's main poverty assistance programs. *(See the Suggestion 1 activity on p. 225.)* Finally, ask students to discuss whether they believe poverty can ever be eliminated and why or why not.

REVIEW AND ASSESS

Have students complete the **Section 3 Review** on p. 227. As **Alternative Assessment**, you may want to use the poverty poster or the poverty flyer in this section's lessons.

RETEACH

Have students work in pairs to create a graphic organizer that will help them understand the characteristics of poverty and the federal government's transfer and subsidy programs.
ENGLISH LANGUAGE LEARNERS , COOPERATIVE LEARNING

EXTEND

Have students work in small groups to conduct research on different aspects of the school lunch program. Groups might interview cafeteria managers or school district officials, research eligibility requirements, or research the history of the program. Have each group report its findings to the class. **COOPERATIVE LEARNING , BLOCK SCHEDULING**

also replaced AFDC with TANF, which changed the rules for payment of assistance. Under AFDC, people could receive payments indefinitely. However, with TANF most people receive payments for no more than a total of five years. Further, most TANF recipients are required to work after two years in the program.

Some observers have hailed welfare reform as a success, pointing out that it has greatly reduced the number of people on welfare. For example, in 1993 AFDC recipients numbered more than 14.1 million. By 1999 only 6.3 million people received TANF payments. How well the people who have moved from welfare to work are doing is less clear.

One study found that nearly a third of those who had left welfare were back on the rolls within two years. Those who remained off welfare reported facing considerable economic problems. About half said they sometimes ran out of food and did not have money to buy more. More than a third reported that at least once during the year they could not pay their rent or utility bills. Some observers suggest that such statistics show that the success of welfare reform should be judged as much on "income and poverty outcomes" as on welfare-roll reductions.

Many Americans attend colleges and other vocational schools hoping to escape poverty by gaining a better job.

SECTION 3 REVIEW

1. Define and explain
poverty
poverty level
life chances
life expectancy
transfer payments

2. Summarizing
Copy the graphic organizer below. Use it to describe the effect that poverty has on people's life chances and behavioral characteristics.

The Effects of Poverty	
Life Chances	**Behavior**

3. Finding the Main Idea
a. How do age, sex, race, and ethnicity affect the likelihood of being poor in the United States?
b. What programs has the federal government established to address poverty and its effects?

4. Writing and Critical Thinking
Making Generalizations and Predictions
Welfare reforms passed in 1996 led to many changes for Americans with the most economic needs. Write a short essay on what effects you think welfare reform will have on poverty in the United States.
Consider:
• the jobs open to former welfare recipients
• the effects of economic recession on welfare reform

Homework Practice Online
keyword: SL3 HP9

Social Stratification **227**

CHAPTER 9 REVIEW

ANSWERS

WRITING A SUMMARY
See the section subtitles for the main topics in this chapter.

IDENTIFYING PEOPLE AND IDEAS
1. the division of society into categories, ranks, or classes based on certain characteristics

2. the unequal sharing of scarce resources and social rewards

3. a grouping of people with similar levels of wealth, power, and prestige

4. a person's assets (the value of everything the person owns) and income (money earned through salaries, investment returns, or other capital gains)

5. the ability to control the behavior of others, with or without their consent

6. the respect, honor, recognition, or courtesy an individual receives from other members of society

7. the movement between or within social classes or strata

8. a standard of living below the minimum level considered adequate by society

9. the likelihood a person has of sharing in the opportunities and benefits of society

10. government methods to redistribute money among various segments of society

Review and Assessment Resources

- Chapter 9 Review, pp. 228–29
- Chapter Review Activities with Answer Key
- Global Skill Builder CD–ROM
- Chapter 9 Test Generator (on the One-Stop Planner)
- Chapter 9 Test (Form A or B)
- Alternative Assessment Handbook
- HRW Go site

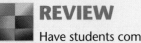

REVIEW

Have students complete the **Chapter 9 Review** on pp. 228–29.

ASSESS

Use one of the chapter tests to assess students' understanding of the content. For **Alternative Assessment**, see the **Alternative Assessment Handbook**.

UNDERSTANDING MAIN IDEAS

1. Caste systems are closed; class systems are open.

2. functionalists—view stratification as a necessary feature of the social structure and argue that the more important a role and the more skill needed to perform it, the higher the reward; conflict theorists—view stratification as a result of conflict over scarce resources and argue that groups who gain power then use that power to maintain it

3. upper class, upper middle class, lower middle class, working class, working poor, and underclass

4. The poverty level is the minimum annual income needed by a family to survive. It is determined by calculating the cost of providing an adequate diet, based on the U.S. Department of Agriculture's minimum nutritional standard, and then multiplying that figure by three.

5. Poverty can lead to a decrease in life expectancy, increased health risks, and limitations in education.

6. Welfare reform has turned over the management of some welfare programs to the states and replaced AFDC with TANF, which changed the rules for payment of assistance.

THINKING CRITICALLY

1. In 1950 the Indian constitution outlawed discrimination based upon caste. In modern urban areas there has been some blurring among the castes. However, in rural areas,

---

C H A P T E R

9 Review

 Writing a Summary

Using standard grammar, spelling, sentence structure, and punctuation, summarize the information in this chapter.
Consider:

- the theories of social stratification
- the characteristics of the American class system
- the nature of poverty in America

 Identifying People and Ideas

Identify the following people or terms and use them in appropriate sentences.

1. social stratification
2. social inequality
3. social class
4. wealth
5. power
6. prestige
7. social mobility
8. poverty
9. life chances
10. transfer payments

 Understanding Main ideas

Section 1 (pp. 206–12)

1. How do caste systems and class systems differ?
2. How do the functionalist and conflict explanations of stratification differ?

Section 2 (pp. 214–20)

3. What are the six social classes recognized by most American sociologists?

Section 3 (pp. 221–27)

4. What is the poverty level, and how is it calculated?
5. How can poverty affect the life chances of Americans?
6. How have government programs to assist poor Americans changed in recent years?

 Thinking Critically

1. **Analyzing Information** How has the caste system in India changed since the 1800s? What factors have contributed to these changes?
2. **Drawing Inferences and Conclusions** What does a person's socioeconomic status tell sociologists about that individual?
3. **Supporting a Point of View** What factors do you think should be used to measure social class? Why?
4. **Identifying Cause and Effect** Why do poor people have a higher incidence of illness and a shorter life expectancy than wealthier people?
5. **Finding the Main Idea** Why might the welfare reform programs introduced in 1996 be called welfare-to-work?

 Writing About Sociology

1. **Drawing Inferences and Conclusions** Research recent welfare-reform programs and their effect on the recipients' self-esteem. Write a short essay analyzing the relationship between socioeconomic stratification and human motivation.
2. **Evaluating** For a set time period, check newspapers, magazines, and television news programs for items on poverty in the United States. Note the content and tone of the items. Then use your findings to write a brief essay that answers the following questions: How does the media characterize poverty—as improving or worsening? What information is provided to support the characterization? Use the graphic organizer below to help you prepare your essay.

News Item	Tone on Poverty	Characteristics of Poverty	Improving Worsening

RETEACH

Select students with a solid grasp of the material presented in the chapter to act as a panel of "experts" to answer other students' questions about the chapter. Have students prepare questions based on key concepts in the chapter, gaps in their notes, or topics they do not understand. Then have students ask the expert panel their questions. During the question-and-answer session, encourage all students to take notes. Expand upon or correct panelists' answers as necessary. **ENGLISH LANGUAGE LEARNERS**, **COOPERATIVE LEARNING**

SOCIOLOGY PROJECTS

1. Applying Sociology Have students work in groups to investigate the basic costs of living for a family of four people in your area. Students should consider only basic needs: housing, food, transportation, clothing, and minimal medical care. Then ask each group to prepare a written report and to present its findings to the class.

2. Linking to Community If your area has a food bank, have interested students volunteer to work in it. Students should also prepare a brief written report describing the food bank operation and its services (such as who it serves, how many people it serves, and where the food bank obtains its food).

BUILDING SOCIAL STUDIES SKILLS

Interpreting Graphs

Study the line graph below. Use it to answer the following questions.

SSI, TANF, and Food Stamp Recipients: 1990 to 1998

Source: *Statistical Abstract of the United States;* Social Security Administration; Department of Agriculture

1. Which of the following best describes the trends shown on the line graph?

  a. The number of recipients for all three programs grew steadily throughout the 1990s.

  b. The number of recipients for all three programs fell markedly during the 1990s.

  c. The number of recipients of TANF and Food Stamps fell, but SSI recipients rose slightly.

  d. The number of recipients of TANF and Food Stamps rose, but SSI recipients fell slightly.

2. What might explain the marked drop in recipients of Food Stamps and TANF after 1996?

Analyzing Primary Sources

The following excerpt discusses poverty in the rural areas of the United States. Read the excerpt, and then answer the questions that follow.

> "While the nation overall benefited from the prosperous 1990s, the booming economy still left large pockets of poverty. A third or more of the residents in dozens of mostly rural counties in the South and Midwest still lived below the poverty level in 1998.
>
> New Census Bureau figures . . . show counties along the U.S.-Mexico border remained among the worse off nationally. . . . Various factors contribute to the range of poverty and income estimates across the country, said Eva Deluna, a budget analyst for the Center for Public Policy Priorities in Austin, Texas. For instance, states like Texas have a higher percentage of minorities and bigger family sizes—characteristics of households that tend to be worse off financially.
>
> In the Texas counties that border Mexico, Deluna described the situation as a 'continuing treadmill' of poverty. . . . 'Educating the workforce is what most local officials think is the most important thing to have to fight poverty,' Deluna said."

3. In which areas of the country were large pockets of poverty found?

  a. South and Midwest

  b. North and Southwest

  c. Northeast and Midwest

  d. South and Northeast

4. Why do you think that many people see education as the best weapon to fight poverty?

caste still plays an important role in daily life.

2. It provides sociologists with an understanding of a person's relative position in the stratification system.

3. Answers will vary, but students should exhibit an understanding of how sociologists measure class based on wealth, power, and prestige.

4. Poor people often experience inadequate nutrition and have less access to health care.

5. because TANF recipients must work after two years in the program and can stay in the program only five years

WRITING ABOUT SOCIOLOGY

1. Essays will vary, but students should exhibit an understanding of the reforms that have been made to welfare and the effects of these reforms on recipients.

2. Essays will vary, but students should provide specific examples and facts from the articles and news items they examined that support their conclusions.

BUILDING SOCIAL STUDIES SKILLS

1. c

2. welfare reform, such as the Personal Responsibility and Work Opportunity Reconciliation Act

3. a

4. Education provides the skills and knowledge necessary to get a better job.

SOCIOLOGY PROJECTS

Cooperative Learning

Using Surveys Working with one or two other students, interview a sample of students in the school to discover how they rank occupations according to prestige. List the top 10 occupations from the chart on page 209 in alphabetical order. Then ask each student in the sample to list the occupations according to the prestige he or she attaches to them. Collate the results and list the occupations according to their rank. Then compare your top 10 with the top 10 in the chart. How might you explain the similarities or differences?

internet connect

Internet Activity: go.hrw.com
KEYWORD: SL3 SC9

Choose an activity on social stratification to
- write a dialogue between a conflict theorist and a functionalist explaining power, prestige, and stratification.
- use census data to analyze the American class system. Create charts, graphs, and databases to illustrate your findings.
- evaluate effects of the Great Society and other historic poverty programs.

Racial and Ethnic Relations

CHAPTER RESOURCE MANAGER

Objectives	Pacing Guide		Resources

SECTION 1:
Race, Ethnicity, and the Social Structure
(pp. 232–37)

REV Section 1 Review, p. 235

- Summarize how sociologists define the terms *race, ethnicity,* and *minority group.*
- Identify the characteristics that distinguish minority groups from one another.

Regular 2 days

Block Scheduling 1 day

Block Scheduling Handbook with Team Teaching Strategies, Chapter 10

Resources

📼 **CNN.** Presents Sociology: Inequality and Internet Access

RS Graphic Organizer 10

🌐 HRW Go site

SM Mastering Critical Thinking Skills 10

PS Readings and Case Studies in Sociology 10

E Research Projects and Activities for Teaching Sociology 10

SM Study Skills and Writing Guide

💾 Teaching Transparency: Merton's Patterns of Prejudice and Discrimination

---

SECTION 2:
Patterns of Intergroup Relations
(pp. 238–46)

REV Section 2 Review, p. 246

- Distinguish between discrimination and prejudice.
- Describe the most common patterns of minority-group treatment.

Regular 2 days

Block Scheduling 1 day

Block Scheduling Handbook with Team Teaching Strategies, Chapter 10

Chapter Review And Assessment

REV Chapter 10 Review, pp. 258–59

REV Chapter Review Activities with Answer Key

💿 Global Skill Builder CD–ROM

💿 Chapter 10 Test Generator (on the One-Stop Planner)

A Chapter 10 Test (Form A or B)

A Alternative Assessment Handbook

🌐 HRW Go site

SECTION 3:
Minority Groups in the United States
(pp. 247–57)

REV Section 3 Review, p. 257

- Describe the conditions under which minority groups in the United States live.
- Explain how government policies have affected the lives of minority groups in the United States.

Regular 2 days

Block Scheduling 1 day

Block Scheduling Handbook with Team Teaching Strategies, Chapter 10

Chapter Resource Key

PS Primary Sources	**A** Assessment	📼 Video
RS Reading Support	**REV** Review	🌐 Internet
E Enrichment	💾 Transparencies	💻 Holt Presentation Maker Using Microsoft® PowerPoint®
SM Skills Mastery	💿 CD-ROM	

 One-Stop Planner CD–ROM

See the *One-Stop Planner* for a complete list of additional resources for students and teachers.

One-Stop Planner CD–ROM

It's easy to plan lessons, select resources, and print out materials for your students when you use the **One-Stop Planner CD–ROM with Test Generator.**

Chapter Project Preview

The following activities are included in the Chapter Review. You may want to make the suggested preparations.

CHAPTER REVIEW ACTIVITY

Case Study: Patterns of Minority Group Treatment Students will work in groups to research actual societies that have used the patterns of minority group treatment covered in the chapter. Each group will create a table of its findings. To help students with their research, before starting the project locate at least one society that has used each pattern of minority group treatment.

LESSON ACTIVITY

Applying Sociology Students will imagine that they are sociologists who are advising local leaders on how best to deal with a race-related issue in the local community. In preparation, select one or two issues appropriate for the activity. Or instead create a handout describing a fictional scenario for students to consider.

INTERNET ACTIVITY

Minorities in the United States Students will use provided Internet links to conduct research on changes in demographics for minorities and then create one or more charts or graphs. To provide students with extra guidance, examine the provided Web sites in advance and choose the charts or graphs that you want students to create. Then prepare a handout providing detailed project guidelines.

Additional Resources

PRINT RESOURCES FOR TEACHERS

Asante, Molefi K., and Mark T. Mattson. *Historical and Cultural Atlas of African Americans.* New York: Macmillan, 1992. Resource book that combines demographic maps and graphics with text to chronicle African American history.

Duckitt, John. *The Social Psychology of Prejudice.* Westport, CT: Greenwood Press, 1992. Good introductory text on the social and psychological causes and consequences of prejudice.

Jones, Maldwyn Allen. *American Immigration.* Chicago: University of Chicago Press, 1992. Traces how immigration to the United States has influenced the nation's ethnic mosaic.

PRINT RESOURCES FOR STUDENTS

Brown, Dee. *Bury My Heart at Wounded Knee: An Indian History of the American West.* New York: Henry Holt, 1991. Provides a detailed account of American Indians during the second half of the 1800s from an American Indian point of view.

Kranz, Rachel. *Straight Talk About Prejudice.* New York: Facts on File, 1992. Discusses prejudice and stereotypes as they apply to a number of American minority groups.

Takaki, Ronald. *Strangers from a Different Shore; A History of Asian Americans.* New York: Penguin Books, 1989. Details 150 years of Asian immigration to the United States.

MULTIMEDIA RESOURCES

Eye of the Storm: A Look at Racial Prejudice (vhs, c; 25 min.) Focus Media. ABC news documentary of a startling classroom experiment on prejudice conducted by a third-grade teacher.

Heritage in Black (vhs; 27 min.) Encyclopaedia Brittanica Educational Corporation. Focuses on the struggle of African Americans to achieve freedom and examines African American contributions in science, industry, education, music, labor, and sports.

Immigration: Maintaining the Open Door (sim, sw; 30 student booklets) Zenger Media. Simulation that puts students in the role of a U.S. president faced with the decision of what to do with a group of refugees seeking asylum in the United States.

internet connect

go.hrw.com

HRW ONLINE RESOURCES

GO TO: go.hrw.com
Then type in a keyword.

TEACHER HOME PAGE
KEYWORD: SL3 Teacher

CHAPTER INTERNET ACTIVITIES
KEYWORD: SL3 SC10
Choose an activity to have students:
• research the latest U.S. census data for minority groups.
• analyze the debate over possible institutional discrimination in the SAT test.
• research immigrant patterns and create charts and graphs to illustrate any changes.

CHAPTER ENRICHMENT LINKS
KEYWORD: SL3 CH10

ONLINE ASSESSMENT
Homework Practice
KEYWORD: SL3 HP10
Standardized Test Prep
KEYWORD: SL3 STP10
Rubrics
KEYWORD: SS Rubrics

CONTENT UPDATES
KEYWORD: SS Content Updates

HOLT PRESENTATION MAKER
KEYWORD: SL3 PPT10

ONLINE READING SUPPORT
KEYWORD: SS Strategies

CURRENT EVENTS
KEYWORD: S3 Current Events

Racial and Ethnic Relations

Build on What You Know

Ask students to answer the following questions:

How might race stratify society?

Consider:

• the ways in which social class stratifies society

• variations in wealth, power, and prestige

• how different groups are viewed by society

How might discrimination relate to poverty?

Consider:

• how each one affects a person's life chances

• how each one relates to crime and victimization

• how each one affects society

Internet Activity

internet connect

go. hrw. com

TOPIC: Minorities in the United States
GO TO: go.hrw.com
KEYWORD: SL3 SC10

Have students access the Internet through the HRW Go site to conduct research on changes in demographics for minorities in the United States. Have each student use the census data available on the Web sites to create one or more charts or graphs. As an extension to the activity, have each student create a one-page report on the topic. The report should include the student's charts or graphs.

CHAPTER

10 **Racial and Ethnic Relations**

Build on What You Know

Social stratification is one of many factors that has greatly influenced the structure of American society. In this chapter you will study another factor that is sometimes used to stratify society—race. You will first explore the concepts of race, ethnicity, and minority groups. Next, you will examine the sources of prejudice and discrimination and the patterns of minority group treatment. Finally, you will review minority group experiences in the United States.

Sociologists consider race and ethnic relations an important factor that influences the daily lives of Americans.

Life in Society

Until recently in South Africa, economic, social, and political power rested in the hands of the country's approximately 6 million white citizens. Although this group made up only about 15 percent of the population, it controlled the government and the lives of South Africa's more than 34 million black Africans, Asians, and people of mixed race. The white South Africans who controlled the government enacted a system of laws called apartheid that limited the access of other racial groups to housing, education, employment, health care, legal protection, and public facilities. This legal system also limited the personal freedoms of members of these groups. Attempting to exercise the right to free speech, the right to travel, and the right to public assembly often drew a violent response from white authorities.

In the early 1990s South Africa began to dismantle this legal system of discrimination. Today the country is a democracy where power is shared among the races. Yet the attitudes that the various races have toward one another are proving hard to change. South Africa remains a society stratified according to race in spite of efforts to make reforms.

What's Your Opinion?

Read the following statements about sociology. Do you think they are true or false? You will learn whether each statement is true or false as you read the chapter.

- Race as a biological classification is of great use to sociologists.

- There is no connection between prejudice and discrimination.

- The life experiences of all minority groups in the United States are essentially the same.

> ### ▶ WHY SOCIOLOGY MATTERS
>
> Sociologists are interested in the way people view race and racial issues. Use **CNNfyi.com** or other current events sources to learn more about American attitudes toward race relations. Create a script for a radio or television broadcast on race in America.
>
> **CNNfyi.com**

SECTION ①

OBJECTIVES

1. *Summarize how sociologists define the terms* race, ethnicity, *and* minority group.

2. *Identify the characteristics that distinguish minority groups from one another.*

SECTION *1* RESOURCES

REPRODUCIBLE & REVIEW

• Mastering Critical Thinking Skills 10

• Research Projects and Activities for Teaching Sociology 10

• Section 1 Review, p. 235

TECHNOLOGY

• One-Stop Planner, Lesson 10.1

• Homework Practice Online

①

RACE, ETHNICITY, AND THE SOCIAL STRUCTURE

● **Read to Discover**
1. How do sociologists define the terms *race*, *ethnicity*, and *minority group*?
2. What characteristics distinguish minority groups from one another?

● **Define**
race, ethnicity, ethnic group, minority group

You read in Chapter 9 that societies use a variety of characteristics to determine social standing. Race and ethnicity are two of the most prominently ascribed statuses that societies use to distinguish one group of people from another.

Race

Since ancient times, people have attempted to group human beings into racial categories based on physical characteristics, such as skin color, hair texture, and body structure. These attempts have produced a number of classification systems ranging in size from 2 to nearly 200 racial categories.

Historically scholars have placed people into three racial groups—Caucasoids, Mongoloids, and Negroids. According to this system, Caucasoids—or whites—are characterized by fair skin and straight or wavy hair. Mongoloids—or Asians—are identified by yellowish or brownish skin and by distinctive folds on the eyelids. Negroids—or blacks—are distinguished by dark skin and tightly curled hair. However, in reality people who are recognized as belonging to each of these racial categories exhibit a wide range of skin colors and hair textures.

However, this well-known classification system has difficulty describing the complexity of race. For example, how should the people of southern India, with their Caucasoid-like facial features, dark skin color, and straight hair be classified? In what group should the Ainu people of Japan, who have Mongoloid-like features but have light skin, be placed? How should Australian Aborigines, many of whom have dark skin and blond tightly curled hair, be categorized?

As these examples indicate, it is difficult to classify people into clear-cut racial categories because people often possess the traits of more than one race. There are no biologically "pure" races. For this reason, race as a biological classification is of little use to sociologists.

Almost every sociologist looks at race from a social perspective. In sociological terms, a **race** is a category of people who share inherited physical characteristics and whom others see as being a distinct group. For sociologists, the important issue is not that a person has a specific color of skin or hair of a certain texture. Rather, sociologists are concerned with how people react to these physical characteristics and how these reactions affect individuals in society.

For most sociologists, race is not determined by a set of physical features but is based on people's reactions to physical characteristics.

Discuss with students the sociological definitions of the terms *race (see p. 232)*, *ethnicity (see p. 233)*, and *minority group (see p. 235)*. Then to help students review the terms, copy the graphic organizer at the right onto the chalkboard. Have students work in pairs to copy and complete the organizer.

ENGLISH LANGUAGE LEARNERS , COOPERATIVE LEARNING

HOMEWORK: Have students write short position papers that either support or refute the following statement: *Everyone in the United States is a member of some minority group.* Tell students to use the definitions of the key terms in Section 1 to help them support their positions.

INTERPRETING VISUALS The diversity of American life is apparent in the cultural activities such as Chinese New Year parades, Cinco de Mayo celebrations, German folk festivals, and Kwanzaa ceremonies. *How do you think the diversity of race and ethnicity in the United States affects your community?*

Ethnicity

Like most other societies, American society consists of people of different cultural backgrounds. The set of cultural characteristics that distinguishes one group from another group is called **ethnicity**. People who share a common cultural background and a common sense of identity are known as an **ethnic group**. Ethnicity is generally based on such cultural characteristics as national origin, religion, language, customs, and values.

If an ethnic group is to survive over time, its cultural beliefs and practices must be passed from generation to generation. Some ethnic groups in the United States have been more successful than others in keeping their heritage alive. For example, Asian Americans and Hispanics tend to have strong ethnic roots. Unlike recent immigrants, many generations of German Americans who were raised in the United States no longer feel deep ties to their ancestral homeland or its cultural traditions. Consequently, they share few cultural characteristics with people in Germany.

In some cases, ethnic identity over steps racial or national boundaries. Jewish people worldwide are thought to form an ethnic group. Their ethnic-group status is based on their religious and cultural heritage. Even Jewish people who no longer firmly hold to the religious beliefs of Judaism are linked by factors such as a common history.

Ethnicity and race refer to two separate sets of characteristics. Ethnicity is based on cultural considerations. On the other hand, race is based on physical considerations. Nevertheless, some ethnic groups are also racially distinct. For example, African Americans are viewed as a racially distinct group in the United States. Many African Americans also share a common ethnic heritage that includes particular foods, types of music, forms of speech, and cultural traits. Similarly, groups such as Japanese Americans, Chinese Americans, and Korean Americans can be classified both ethnically and racially.

Minority Groups

No particular skin color, physical feature, or ethnic background is superior or inferior by nature. However, many sociologists recognize that those who hold power in a society may place an arbitrary value on specific characteristics. By establishing the values and norms of society, dominant-group members consciously and unconsciously

Case Studies and Other True Stories

■ TEACH

Have students read the feature A Blue- (or Brown-) Eyed Minority on this page. Then have the class discuss the questions that follow the feature. Next, have each student write an essay discussing the various dominant and minority groups, based on racial or other characteristics, that exist in their school and how relations between these groups affect group members and their school. Call on volunteers to read their essays to the class. Give other students a chance to provide feedback.

✴ CONNECTING to Literature

Obtain a copy of the children's book *The Sneetches* by Dr. Seuss and read the story to the class. Ask students to state the theme of the story as it relates to the experiment described in this feature. *(The Sneetches felt alternately superior and miserable as the arbitrary designation of dominance based on the presence or absence of belly stars rapidly changed, until they finally realized that all Sneetches were in fact the same, with or without stars.)* Then have students work in small groups to write and illustrate similar stories to teach young children about prejudice and discrimination.

COOPERATIVE LEARNING, BLOCK SCHEDULING

◆ Applying Sociology

The Ethics of Research. While Jane Elliot's experiment provides insight into the power of discrimination, most researchers today would consider it unethical. Sociologists, like all researchers, must follow strict guidelines for experiments that involve humans. For example, an experiment cannot hurt a human subject in any way. Because Elliot's experiment has the potential for severe psychological consequences, it would not be allowed today under most research ethics guidelines.

ACTIVITY: Have students discuss the pros and cons of ethical guidelines in research.

Think About It Answers

1. first day—The brown-eyed children seemed happy and alert, their work improved, and they acted as if they felt superior. The blue-eyed children seemed miserable, and their work declined; second day—The brown-eyed children behaved just as the blue-eyed children had. However, the blue-eyed children were far less unpleasant to the brown-eyed group than the latter had been to them.

2. Learned attitudes and behaviors strongly affect relations between dominant and minority groups.

234

Case Studies

AND OTHER TRUE STORIES

A BLUE- (OR BROWN-) EYED MINORITY

What if you lived in a society where blue-eyed people were considered inferior? How do you think blue-eyed people would feel and behave? What about brown-eyed people? Third-grade teacher Jane Elliot conducted a unique experiment to find the answers to these questions.

The Experiment

Elliot assigned her 28 students to one of two groups, depending on whether their eyes were blue or brown. Blue-eyed students, she told the class, were inferior. Elliot made up a list of rules that both groups would have to follow.

Brown-eyed children would be given five extra minutes of recess. They could go to lunch first and could go back for second helpings. In addition, they could use the drinking fountain in the room. In contrast, the blue-eyed children would get a shorter recess period, would have to wait to go to lunch, and would have to use paper cups.

With the rules in place, Elliot took every opportunity to praise the brown-eyed students and to criticize those with blue eyes. For example, when a brown-eyed student missed a word while reading, she helped him or her. When a blue-eyed child did likewise, she shook her head in disapproval. Then she asked a brown-eyed student to read the passage correctly. Elliot made sure to treat each group differently for the sake of her research.

How did the students react to the experiment? Elliot noted that by lunchtime it was easy to tell if a child was blue- or brown-eyed. The brown-eyed children were happy and alert. Their work was much better than before. The blue-eyed children, on the other hand, looked miserable and defeated. Their work had deteriorated. More frightening, Elliot said, was the way the brown-eyed children behaved. Everything they said and did suggested that they truly believed they were superior.

Jane Elliot's study showed that discrimination and prejudice can quickly affect young students.

The Roles Reversed

On the second day of the experiment, the roles were reversed. The blue-eyed students were now told that they were superior and that brown-eyed students were inferior. How did the students react this time? Elliot expected that since they knew this was a one-day experiment, the brown-eyed students would not react so intensely. Surprisingly, they behaved exactly as the blue-eyed children had. In a very short time they began to look miserable, resentful, and defeated. Interestingly, however, the blue-eyed children—now the dominant group—were far less unpleasant to the brown-eyed group than the latter had been to them.

Think About It

1. Summarize *What were students' reactions on the first day of the experiment? What were their reactions on the second day?*

2. Drawing Inferences and Conclusions *What can you learn from Jane Elliot's experiment about the relations between dominant groups and minority groups?*

CLOSE

Have students contrast the biological and sociological definitions of race and then contrast the terms *race* and *ethnicity*. Finally, have students review the five characteristics of a minority group *(as listed on p. 235)*.

REVIEW AND ASSESS

Have students complete the **Section 1 Review** on p. 235. As **Alternative Assessment**, you may want to use the graphic organizer or the position paper in this section's lessons.

RETEACH

Have students use the Glossary to review the definitions of the section's Define terms—*race, ethnicity, ethnic group,* and *minority group*. Next, ask students to provide examples of each term. Finally, have each student use all four terms in a paragraph summarizing this section. **ENGLISH LANGUAGE LEARNERS**

EXTEND

Ask students to think of a minority group in the United States that is difficult to classify racially or ethnically. Have students write a paragraph or two explaining why it is difficult to classify this group based on the five characteristics of minority groups.
BLOCK SCHEDULING

create a social structure that operates in their favor. Speaking the language most common in a society is one position of power held by the dominant group. Using a conflict theory perspective, many sociologists have concluded that a dominant group's position of power allows them to enjoy certain privileges, such as better housing, better schools, and higher incomes.

The resources and rewards found in society are limited. Consequently, the privileged position of the dominant group is often gained at the expense of minority groups within the society. Sociologist Louis Wirth identified a **minority group** as a group of people who—because of their physical characteristics or cultural practices—are singled out and unequally treated. As a result, group members view themselves as objects of collective discrimination. You should be aware that the term *minority* has nothing to do with group size. For example, in South Africa white people made up about 15 percent of the population during the second half of the 1900s. Yet, for much of that time, they dominated the lives of the other racial groups in the country. Minority status, then, is not related to group size but to the group's unequal standing in their society.

Certain characteristics distinguish minority groups from other groups in society.

- The group possesses identifiable physical or cultural characteristics that differ from those of the dominant group.
- Group members are the victims of unequal treatment at the hands of the dominant group.

Aborigines of Australia are a minority group that have been treated differently than other Australians because of their racial background.

- Membership in the group is an ascribed status.
- Group members share a strong bond and a sense of group loyalty.
- Members tend to practice endogamy—marriage within the group.

To be considered a minority group, a group must exhibit all of the above characteristics. Exhibiting only one or two of the characteristics is not enough. For example, blue eyes are an identifiable physical characteristic, and having blue eyes is an ascribed status. However, blue-eyed people do not face challenges because of their eye color. Consequently, they are not considered a minority group. Haitians in the United States or Aborigines in Australia, on the other hand, are often treated differently because of their ethnic and racial backgrounds. Therefore, they are considered to be minority groups.

SECTION 1 REVIEW

1. Define and explain
race
ethnicity
ethnic group
minority group

2. Summarizing Copy the concept web below. Use it to identify and describe the characteristics that distinguish minority groups from other groups.

Minority Group

3. Finding the Main Idea

a. How does the sociological view of race differ from the biological view?

b. Identify a minority group and explain what characteristics distinguish the group as such.

4. Writing and Critical Thinking

Analyzing Information Write a paragraph explaining why, when sociologists discuss minority groups, they do not use the term *majority* to describe the dominant group. Consider:

- the role that group size plays in minority status
- the role that a group's unequal standing plays in its minority status

Homework Practice Online
keyword: SL3 HP10

SECTION 1 REVIEW ANSWERS

1. Define:
- race, p. 232
- ethnicity, p. 233
- ethnic group, p. 233
- minority group, p. 235

2. identifiable physical or cultural characteristics, victims of unequal treatment, group membership is an ascribed status, members share strong bonds and a sense of loyalty, and members tend to practice endogamy

3a. biological—grouping people as either Caucasoids, Mongoloids, or Negroids, based on physical characteristics; sociological—a category of people who share inherited physical characteristics and whom are seen as a distinct group

b. Answers will vary, but students should exhibit an understanding of the characteristics that distinguish minority groups, as described in the text.

4. Paragraphs will vary, but students should note that the dominant group is not always a numerical majority. Instead, the dominant group is a group that has power over others.

Building Social Studies Skills

◼ TEACH

Have students read the feature Problem Solving. Next, call on volunteers to review the steps in the problem-solving process. Then ask students to discuss how they can use this problem-solving process in their daily lives. *(Students might reply that they can use this skill in their classes, to help resolve conflicts with friends and others, to make a difference in their community, and so on.)* Finally, have students work individually or in groups to complete the Practicing the Skill activity. **COOPERATIVE LEARNING**

✳ CONNECTING *to History*

Pair students and have each pair take on the roles of two historical civil rights activists who proposed different solutions to the problems of race relations in the United States. For example, one pair might choose to role-play Dr. Martin Luther King Jr. and Malcolm X. After conducting research to find out how these leaders' strategies differed, each pair should write a dialogue in which each activist uses the problem-solving process to explain why his or her solution is best. Have volunteer pairs role-play their dialogues for the class. **COOPERATIVE LEARNING**, **BLOCK SCHEDULING**

PROBLEM SOLVING

Have each student create a poster designed to teach other students the six-step problem-solving process outlined on this page. Students' posters should use simple text and strong colorful visuals to present the information. Have volunteers explain their posters to the class. Then display students' posters in the classroom. In addition, you might select the two or three best posters and display them in public areas of your school.

BUILDING
Social Studies Skills

PROBLEM SOLVING

Sociologists involved in the making and implementation of social policy—the programs that governments use to guard the welfare and social well-being of their citizens—spend much of their time identifying and seeking solutions to social problems. The problem-solving skills that sociologists employ can help you adapt and adjust to new situations as you learn more about the world around you. The following activities will help you develop and practice these skills.

Problem solving, like decision making, involves choosing between two or more options. Listed below are guidelines that may help you solve future problems.

1. **Identify the problem.** Identify the problem that you are facing. Sometimes you may face a difficult situation made up of several different problems.

2. **Gather information.** Conduct research on any important issues related to the problem. Try to find the answers to questions like the following: What is causing the problem? Whom or what does it affect?

3. **List and consider options.** Look at the problem and the answers to the questions you asked in Step 2. List and then think about your options—all the possible ways in which the problem can be solved.

4. **Examine advantages and disadvantages.** Consider the advantages of all the options that you have listed. Make sure that you consider the possible long-term effects of each solution. You should also determine what steps you will need to take to achieve each possible solution.

5. **Choose and implement a solution.** Select the best solution from your list and take the necessary steps to achieve it.

6. **Evaluate the effectiveness of the solution.** After putting your plan into action, evaluate its effectiveness. Is the problem solved? Were the results worth your effort? Has the solution created any other problems?

Students can work together to resolve problems that they and our society face.

SPOTLIGHT *on Racial Profiling*

Have students work in small groups to conduct research on racial profiling in law enforcement in the United States. Then have each group use the problem-solving process outlined in the feature to consider, discuss, and suggest possible solutions to racial profiling in law enforcement. Groups should consider both the needs of law enforcement and the rights of minority groups. Each group should record its responses to each of the steps in the problem-solving process and then summarize the actions it suggests. Finally, have the class evaluate the effectiveness of each group's solutions.
COOPERATIVE LEARNING, **BLOCK SCHEDULING**

CONNECTING *to Drama*

Have interested students or groups of students write one-act plays about a group of extraterrestrials who land in the United States. The scripts should concentrate on how U.S. and other world leaders work to prevent the aliens from becoming either a new dominant group or a new minority group. Leaders should use the problem-solving process to decide what actions to take. Then choose the one or two best plays and have volunteers act them out for the class. **COOPERATIVE LEARNING**, **BLOCK SCHEDULING**

Applying the Skill

Sociological studies concerning the patterns of interaction among dominant and minority groups have uncovered several societal issues. Here is an example of the problem-solving process that sociologists might use when looking at population distribution and housing.

1. **Identify the problem.** When looking at population studies of rental units in a neighborhood, sociologists might notice that certain minority groups are underrepresented.
2. **Gather information.** To collect information on this issue, the sociologists might look at previous population studies of the neighborhood. They might also study all available census information for the neighborhood. In addition, they might look at the economic factors that may affect where minority groups live. As a comparison, the sociologists might also interview minority and dominant group members living in rental units at the present time. To add further to their understanding of the situation, the sociologists might interview local real estate agents. The sociologists will want to determine the factors that influence the neighborhood such as housing costs, transportation, and the age and avaliablity of units.
3. **List and consider options.** After some consideration, the sociologists may decide that they have the following options:
   • to present their findings to the local housing authority, urging officials to draft legislation to solve the problem of a lack of availability of low-cost housing
   • to present their findings to the various real estate agencies involved in renting in the neighborhood, urging them to work with low-income mortgage programs and to show available units to minority-group members
   • to present their findings to local minority-group community organizations, urging them

Sociologists often address problems such as what policies might help solve an urban problem like underrepresentation of minority groups in specific neighborhoods.

to work with government officials and real-estate managers to find ways to increase minority-group renters in the neighborhood
4. **Examine advantages and disadvantages.**
   • The issue would be solved by a government agency.
   • The issue would be resolved by businesses that may or may not have ties to the community.
   • The issue would be resolved by local neighborhood groups.
5. **Choose and implement a solution.** Feeling that this is an issue that should be settled in the neighborhood by the parties involved, the sociologists may decide to implement the third option.
6. **Evaluate the effectiveness of the solution.** The sociologists might continue to monitor the situation, and if diversity among renters is not achieved, they might choose to implement one of the other two options.

Practicing the Skill

Use the problem-solving process to consider possible solutions to the issue of equal political representation of minority groups. Research the issues surrounding political representation of minority-group members. Record your responses to each of the steps in the problem-solving process and summarize the actions you might take.

Sociology Then and Now

Housing and Discrimination. The effects of discrimination can be long-lasting. For example, many American housing developments once included restrictive covenants to maintain segregation. Such covenants excluded people of certain racial or religious groups, such as African Americans or Jews. In 1948 the U.S. Supreme Court declared such covenants to be unenforceable. Despite this decision and later fair-housing laws, housing discrimination still exists.

CRITICAL THINKING

Why do you think housing discrimination continues despite laws against it?

ANSWER: Students might note that such discrimination is institutionalized in certain segments of American society.

Practicing the Skill

To extend the activity, have students share some of their suggested actions with the class. Then have the class discuss and evaluate each suggestion. Students should consider the practicality of implementing each action and its potential effectiveness.

SECTION ❷

OBJECTIVES

1. *Distinguish between discrimination and prejudice.*
2. *Describe the most common patterns of minority-group treatment.*

🔊 LET'S GET STARTED!

Before class, write the definitions of the terms *discrimination* and *prejudice* on the chalkboard *(discrimination—the denial of equal treatment to individuals based on their group membership—refers to behaviors; prejudice—an unsupported generalization about a category of people—refers to attitudes).* As students enter the classroom, ask them to study the definitions. Next, ask volunteers to share with the class examples of discrimination or prejudice that they have seen or heard about recently, including examples from local and national news sources. Discuss the examples with students and point out sociological factors influencing each incident. Then tell students that in Section 2 they will learn about discrimination and prejudice and how these factors affect minority-group treatment.

SECTION ❷ RESOURCES

REPRODUCIBLE & REVIEW
- Graphic Organizer 10
- Section 2 Review, p. 246

TECHNOLOGY
- One-Stop Planner, Lesson 10.2
- **CNN**. Presents Sociology: Inequality and Internet Access
- Teaching Transparency: Merton's Patterns of Prejudice and Discrimination
- Homework Practice Online
- HRW Go site

Visual Answer

Many white southerners were prejudiced against African Americans and used these prejudices to justify discrimination, such as the segregation of schools.

❷ PATTERNS OF INTERGROUP RELATIONS

Read to Discover
1. How do discrimination and prejudice differ?
2. What are the most common patterns of minority-group treatment?

Define
discrimination, prejudice, legal discrimination, institutionalized discrimination, stereotype, self-fulfilling prophecy, racism, scapegoating, cultural pluralism, assimilation, segregation, de jure segregation, de facto segregation, subjugation, slavery, genocide, ethnic cleansing

As you read in Section 1, no particular skin color, physical feature, or ethnic background is superior or inferior by nature. Minority status exists because of the attitudes and actions of the dominant members of a society. In this section, you will learn more about these attitudes and actions—the interaction patterns among dominant and minority groups.

Discrimination and Prejudice

Discrimination and **prejudice** are common features of the minority-group experience. Although the words are often used interchangeably, discrimination and prejudice are two separate but related conditions. Discrimination is the denial of equal treatment to individuals based on their group membership. By definition, discrimination involves *behaviors*. Prejudice is an unsupported generalization about a category of people. Prejudice refers to *attitudes*. In daily conversation, you might say that you are prejudiced *for* or *against* someone or something. Sociologists generally focus on negative forms of prejudice.

Discrimination Discrimination can be found either on an individual level or on a societal level. Discriminatory acts by individuals range from name-calling and rudeness to acts of violence. In their most extreme forms, such acts can lead to physical harm or even death. For example, between 1882 and 1970, more than 1,170 African Americans were lynched by white mobs in the United States. In many cases, those lynched had not committed a crime. Rather, they were attempting to vote, use the same public facilities as white Americans, or had become too successful.

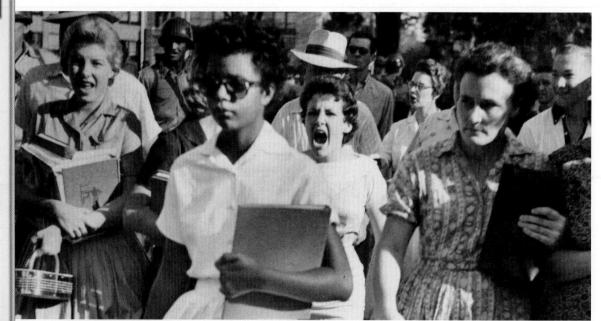

INTERPRETING VISUALS During the 1950s the U.S. Supreme Court issued the *Brown v. Board of Education of Topeka* decision that declared racial segregation of public schools illegal. Like many other communites, some Little Rock residents protested the integration of the public high school. *How do you think discrimination and prejudice were factors in the opposition to desegregation?*

To help students distinguish between discrimination and prejudice, copy the Venn diagram to the right onto the chalkboard, omitting the italicized answers. Have students copy and complete the organizer. Discuss the answers with the class. Then present several scenarios that are examples of either prejudice, discrimination, both, or neither. Call on students to identify which of the four categories each scenario fits. For example, you might describe a situation in which a dominant-group member silently dislikes members of a minority group but does not openly do anything to show it (*prejudice only*). **ENGLISH LANGUAGE LEARNERS**

Prejudice

- *unsupported generalization about a category of people*
- *involves attitudes*
- *can be in favor of a group*

- *can be individual or societal*
- *sociological, psychological*

Discrimination

- *denial of equal treatment based on group membership*
- *involves behaviors*

Societal discrimination can appear in one of two forms—legal discrimination or institutionalized discrimination. **Legal discrimination** is upheld by law. **Institutionalized discrimination**, on the other hand, is an outgrowth of the structure of a society.

The apartheid (uh-PAHR-tayt) system in South Africa is an example of legal discrimination. South Africa had an elaborate system of laws that defined the political, economic, and legal rights of white and nonwhite South Africans within the country. Many other countries, including the United States, have had systems of legal discrimination. Women in the United States did not gain the right to vote until 1920, with the passage of the Nineteenth Amendment. Until the 1940s, some states did not allow women to enter into legal contracts. African Americans faced even more widespread legal discrimination. For example, the Jim Crow laws passed in southern states during the late 1800s required African American and white Americans to use separate public facilities and to attend separate schools. This so-called separate-but-equal doctrine was upheld as constitutional by the U.S. Supreme Court in the 1896 case of *Plessy v. Ferguson*. Almost 60 years passed before the Court reversed its decision in 1954 with the *Brown v. Board of Education of Topeka* decision. Because legal discrimination is based on laws, it can be stopped by changing the offending laws.

Institutionalized discrimination is far more resistant to change. Over time, unequal access to the resources of society pushes some minority groups into less-powerful positions. Once this occurs, it is not necessary for the dominant group to consciously discriminate against these groups to maintain a system of inequality. Discrimination thus becomes a part of the social structure. Therefore, institutional discrimination is self-perpetuating and can occur even when the society takes legal steps to end discriminatory practices.

For example, consider what can happen when minority groups are denied access to jobs and housing because of a prejudiced employer or landlord. Over time, group members may become concentrated in low-income communities. If schools in these communities are poorly funded, minority group members may not acquire the skills needed to compete effectively in the labor market. Thus, even when housing and employment restrictions are lifted, many group members cannot qualify for higher-paying jobs. Without these jobs, members of this group are unable to move to better neighborhoods. As a result, their children will have few opportunities for advancement. Therefore, the cycle of inequality is maintained even when there is no intentional discrimination.

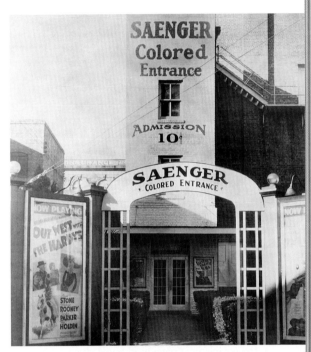

Until the Civil Rights Act of 1964, many institutions and businesses in the United States discriminated against African Americans by creating separate facilities and entrances. Civil rights legislation banned such practices.

Prejudice Negative forms of prejudice often involve stereotypes. A **stereotype** is an oversimplified, exaggerated, or unfavorable generalization about a group of people. When stereotyping, an individual forms an image of a particular group and then applies that image to all members of the group. For example, a stereotype held by some Americans was that all Irish people were hot-tempered. If individuals are found to differ from the stereotyped group image, they are thought to be exceptions to the rule, rather than proof that the stereotype is wrong.

Stereotyping can have grave consequences for society. If people are told often enough and long enough that they or others are socially, mentally, or physically inferior, they may come to believe it. It does not matter whether the accusations are true. American sociologist W. I. Thomas recognized this phenomenon in his famous theorem: "If [people] define situations as real, they are real in their consequences." In other words, individuals see reality based on what they *believe* to be true, not necessarily on what *is* true.

Robert K. Merton further expanded on Thomas's theorem by suggesting that a false definition of a situation can become a **self-fulfilling prophecy**. A self-fulfilling prophecy is a prediction that results in behavior that

☑ **internet** connect

TOPIC: College Admissions and Discrimination
GO TO: go.hrw.com
KEYWORD: SL3 SC10

Have students access the Internet through the HRW Go site to conduct research on possible institutional discrimination or cultural bias in the SAT and the college admissions process. Then have each student write a letter to the president of a fictional university either supporting or opposing the use of the SAT in the college admissions process. Students should use their research to provide support for their positions. In addition, students who oppose the SAT should suggest one or more alternate methods for determining college admissions.

Did You Know?

According to a study by social psychologist Philip Zimbardo, 8 out of every 10 people hold some sort of prejudice.

SPOTLIGHT on Stereotypes

Ask students to suggest various groups that are stereo-typed. Encourage students to be creative, such as the stereotype that all rock musicians lead a certain type of lifestyle. Have students discuss how these groups are stereotyped, why the stereotypes exist, and how inaccurate the stereotypes are. Then organize students into small groups and have each group discuss actions that members could take to teach the student body to avoid stereo-typing. Have a spokesperson from each group share its ideas with the class. Encourage student feedback. **COOPERATIVE LEARNING ,** **BLOCK SCHEDULING**

CONNECTING to Government

Have students use the library and other available resources to conduct research on U.S. Supreme Court cases dealing with discrimination—either legalizing discriminatory practices or abol-ishing them. Have each student select one case and create a writ-ten summary of the case, the Court's decision, and its effects on American society. Call on volunteers to orally summarize their cases for the class. **BLOCK SCHEDULING**

makes the prediction come true. If members of a minority group are considered incapable of understanding technical information, they will not be given technical training. As a result, they will lack the skills needed to gain employment in highly technical occupations. This lack of employment in technical fields will then be taken as proof of the group's inability to understand technical information.

For the dominant group in society, prejudice serves as a justification for discriminatory actions. Once individuals come to believe negative claims made against members of a minority group, they may find it easier to accept open acts of discrimination. Prejudicial beliefs that serve as justifica-tions for open discrimination often take the form of **racism**—the belief that one's own race or ethnic group is naturally superior to other races or ethnic groups. Throughout history, racism has been used as a justifica-tion for atrocities such as slavery and genocide.

While prejudice and discrimination are related, they do not always go hand-in-hand. According to Merton, individuals can combine discrimination and prejudice in four possible ways.

- The *active bigot* is prejudiced and openly discriminatory.
- The *timid bigot* is prejudiced but is afraid to discrimi-nate because of societal pressures.
- The *fair-weather liberal* is not prejudiced but discrimi-nates anyway because of societal pressure.
- The *all-weather liberal* is not prejudiced and does not discriminate.

Merton's Patterns of Prejudice and Discrimination

	Prejudice	
	Yes	**No**
Discrimination **No**	**Timid Bigot** Prejudiced person who does not discriminate	**All-Weather Liberal** Nonprejudiced person who does not discriminate
Discrimination **Yes**	**Active Bigot** Prejudiced person who discriminates	**Fair-Weather Liberal** Nonprejudiced person who discriminates

Source: *Sociological Ambivalence and Other Essays* by Robert K. Merton.

INTERPRETING CHARTS Robert K. Merton's chart shows the differences between prejudice and discrimination. *How might some sociologists consider this chart too simplified?*

Sources of Discrimination and Prejudice

Various explanations have been offered for the develop-ment of discrimination and prejudice. Sociologists often organize these explanations into three broad categories: sociological, psychological, and economic.

Sociological Explanations Most sociological explanations of discrimination and prejudice focus on the social environment. This environment includes the accepted social norms of society and the process through which these norms are learned—socialization. In some societies, prejudices are embedded in the social norms. Such norms describe the ways in which members of the society are expected to relate to members of certain out-groups. People become prejudiced simply by internaliz-ing these norms.

Even if prejudice is not a part of the culture of society at large, it may be a norm of groups within society. Peo-ple often become prejudiced to maintain their group membership. They may also become prejudiced through their identification with a reference group that encour-ages and supports such behavior.

Psychological Explanations Individual behav-ior provides the focus for psychological explanations of prejudice and discrimination. One such explanation sug-gests that people are prejudiced because they have a par-ticular kind of personality. In a survey of a broad sample of American society, a team of psychologists lead by Theodor Adorno found that prejudiced people share cer-tain characteristics. These characteristics made up what Adorno called the authoritarian personality. Authoritari-ans are strongly conformist, have a great respect for authority, and are highly likely to follow the orders of those in authority. They also exhibit a great deal of anger and are likely to blame others for their problems.

Another psychological explanation suggests that prej-udice may be the product of frustration and anger. When individuals have problems but cannot confront the real causes of those problems, they often turn their frustration and anger on innocent groups. The practice of placing the blame for one's troubles on an innocent individual or group is called **scapegoating**. By focusing on scapegoats, people sometimes gain a sense of superiority at a time when they are feeling powerless.

Minority groups often become scapegoats for a variety of reasons. First, they are easy to recognize because of their physical features, language, style of dress, or religious prac-tices. Second, they lack power in society and may be unlikely to fight back. Third, they are often concentrated

Case Studies and Other True Stories

TEACH

Have students read the feature Ethnic Relations in Great Britain and then discuss the questions that follow. Next, have students conduct case studies of the racial and ethnic relations at their school. Tell students to keep observation journals over the course of a few days and record how different groups interact with each other. Instruct students to make special note of any groups that lead "parallel lives." Have volunteers summarize their observations for the class.

EXTEND

Have each student write a newspaper editorial expressing and defending his or her point of view about the idea of a British oath of allegiance and the chances of such an oath uniting the different ethnic and racial groups of Great Britain. Instruct students to take a position on the issue and to support this position with facts, examples, and educated guesses about the probable effectiveness of a British oath. Students may write from the point of view of an American observer or of a British citizen. Have volunteers read their essays to the class for discussion. **BLOCK SCHEDULING**

Case Studies

AND OTHER TRUE STORIES

ETHNIC RELATIONS IN GREAT BRITAIN

Great Britain, like most other countries, is concerned with ethnic relations. However, it has only been in the last 40 to 50 years that large numbers of non-European people have immigrated to the country. Today racial and ethnic minorities make up 7.1 percent of Britain's population—a total of about 4 million people. The majority of Britain's racial and ethnic minorities are South Asians originally from India and Pakistan and black people originally from the Caribbean and Africa.

The issue of ethnic relations in Britain became headline news during the summer of 2001, when riots broke out in Bradford, Oldham, and Burnley—three cities with large South Asian populations. Violent clashes between groups of white people and South Asians left hundreds injured and caused damage estimated in the millions of dollars. The government ordered an inquiry into the riots. The resulting report, titled *Community Cohesion*, painted a depressing picture of ethnic relations in Britain.

"Parallel Lives"

The authors of the report noted that while they were not surprised by the physical segregation in ethnically diverse communities, they were shocked at how deep the divide between the ethnicities ran. The physical divisions, they wrote, "were compounded by so many aspects of our daily lives. . . . These lives often do not seem to touch at any point, let alone overlap and promote any meaningful interchanges."

Because the ethnic groups had little contact, the authors continued, they were completely ignorant of each other's lives. This ignorance led to fear and mistrust. This suspicion was a root cause of the riots. Another contributing factor, they added, was the lack of economic opportunity for both ethnic minorities and poor white people.

The authors noted that the fear and mistrust between white Britons and minority groups were made worse by the reluctance of all groups to confront the issues and to seek solutions. If future ethnic violence was to be avoided, they concluded, an honest and open debate on issues of ethnicity had to take place.

A large percenage of Great Britain's minority population is composed of South Asian immigrants.

Recommendations for the Future

The authors also offered several other recommendations. They encouraged cross-cultural contact between the different communities to foster understanding and respect. They also recommended that all agencies that came into contact with a diverse population should establish diversity-training programs for staff members. They urged public agencies and private enterprises to recruit ethnic minorities more aggressively.

Perhaps the most controversial recommendation focused on what it meant to be a citizen of a modern multicultural country. The authors proposed establishing a dialogue to develop a clear and meaningful concept of the rights and responsibilities of British citizenship, based on common values accepted by all sectors of society. They also suggested that this might be formalized into an oath of allegiance, enabling people to demonstrate a "clear primary loyalty" to Britain. This generated considerable debate among Britons. What, some asked, would be these "common values"? And would all Britons—or just those from racial and ethnic minorities—be required to take this oath of allegiance?

Think About It

1. **Summarizing** *Why, according to the authors of* Community Cohesion, *do white people and nonwhite people in Britain live "parallel lives"?*
2. **Evaluating** *Why do you think the recommendation to establish a clear definition of British citizenship and to tie it to an oath of allegiance caused controversy?*

Interdisciplinary Connection

MATH

Calculating Great Britain's Minority Political Representation. In 2000, black and Asian minorities in Great Britain made up between 5 and 6 percent of the voting population. At the same time, just 9 of the 659 members of the British Parliament's House of Commons were minorities.

CRITICAL THINKING

What percentage of the House of Commons were minorities in 2000? How does this figure relate to the percentage of minority voters at the time?

ANSWER: about 1 percent; underrepresented the minority population in 2000

Think About It Answers

1. because they often have little contact and are ignorant of each other's lives

2. because some Britons wondered who would have to take the oath and who would decide what common values all Britons should uphold

Have students examine the chart on p. 242 and then discuss with students each of the seven patterns of minority group treatment. Next, stretch a large piece of butcher paper along one wall of the classroom to create a graffiti wall. Organize students into seven groups and assign each group one of the patterns of minority group treatment. Have each group label its pattern on the wall in the same order as in the chart. Then have each group provide symbols, phrases, slogans, and other "graffiti" to describe its assigned pattern of minority group treatment. Finally, have each group explain its work to the class. **COOPERATIVE LEARNING**

HOMEWORK: Have each student create a crossword puzzle that uses most or all of the key terms in Section 2. Tell students to provide clear but challenging clues and to supply an answer key on a separate page. As an extension, pair students and have them trade crossword puzzles to complete.

SPOTLIGHT on *Current Events*

Have students follow the news for a few days and summarize any reports on racial and/or ethnic relations in the United States. Instruct each student to select one issue and to write a few paragraphs explaining his or her opinion of it. Then have students take turns sharing their summaries and opinions with the class.
BLOCK SCHEDULING

Case Study

Canada's Cultural Pluralism. Canada's province of Quebec provides another example of cultural pluralism. Quebec has a strong French heritage, and more than three fourths of its population speaks French. The Canadian government recognizes both English and French as official languages in Quebec, New Brunswick, and at the level of the federal government. In addition, the government has allowed Quebec to maintain a Roman Catholic school system and a French system of civil law. However, Canada has not achieved the level of cultural pluralism found in Switzerland. Quebec's French Canadians have experienced discrimination at the hands of the province's small English-speaking population. Such inequalities have led to some failed movements to separate Quebec from Canada.

RESEARCH ACTIVITY: Have interested students conduct research on Quebec and then informally share their findings with the class.

Chart Answer

questions such as why various societies fall in different places along the continuum and how a society's place on the continuum affects different racial and ethnic groups

During the late 1800s, many Americans discriminated against new immigrants. Dennis Kearny headed the Workingmen's Party of California, which cited economic reasons for opposing Chinese immigration.

the second half of the 1800s large numbers of Chinese workers immigrated to the West Coast of the United States. In the beginning, they were welcomed as an inexpensive source of labor. However, when jobs became scarce many white workers began to view the Chinese immigrants as economic competitors. Many white Americans reacted to this competition with open violence. This discrimination was legalized with the passage of laws restricting Chinese immigration.

Conflict theorists suggest that the dominant group, to protect its position, encourages competition for resources among minority groups. This competition creates a split labor market, in which workers are set against each other along racial and ethnic lines. In the struggle for jobs, the various minority groups come to fear, distrust, and hate one another.

Patterns of Minority Group Treatment

Official policies toward minority groups within a society vary widely. The most common patterns of minority treatment include cultural pluralism, assimilation, legal protection, segregation, subjugation, population transfer, and extermination. Look at the chart on this page and note that these patterns may be placed on a continuum that runs from acceptance to rejection.

Cultural Pluralism One response to ethnic and racial diversity is **cultural pluralism**. This policy allows each group within society to keep its unique cultural identity. Switzerland provides an example of cultural

in one geographic area and therefore are easily accessible and an easy target. Fourth, they often have been the target of scapegoating in the past, so a certain amount of hostility toward them already exists. Finally, they often represent something—such as an idea, attitude, or way of life—that the scapegoater does not like.

Economic Explanations According to economic explanations, prejudice and discrimination arise out of competition for scarce resources. For example, during

---

A Continuum of Intergroup Relations

Acceptance   Rejection

Cultural Pluralism	Assimilation	Legal Protection	Segregation	Subjugation	Population Transfer	Extermination
Ethnic and racial variety encouraged	Culturally distinct groups blended into a single group with common culture	Minority rights protected by law	Minority group physically separated from the dominant group	Dominant group controls every aspect of minority group life through force	Dominant group moves minority group to new locations within or outside the country	Dominant group attempts to destroy minority group

INTERPRETING CHARTS Intergroup relations can be seen as a range from acceptance to rejection. *What types of questions on cultural patterns might this chart lead a sociologist to pose?*

CONNECTING to History

Organize students into small groups and have each group conduct research on the civil rights movement in the United States. Have each group use its research to create an illustrated time line of some of the major events in the history of U.S. civil rights. Students might highlight major protests and marches, Supreme Court cases, specific movements, important leaders, and so on. Display the groups' time lines in the classroom. **COOPERATIVE LEARNING**, **BLOCK SCHEDULING**

SPOTLIGHT on Reverse Discrimination

Explain to students that in recent years, criticism has grown over affirmative action policies, charging that they are a form of reverse discrimination. Have students conduct research on this topic to learn more about both sides of the controversy. Then select two teams of volunteers to conduct an informal debate in class on the issue of reverse discrimination. Encourage other students to prepare questions to ask the students in the debate.

COOPERATIVE LEARNING, **BLOCK SCHEDULING**

Switzerland is an example of a society based on cultural pluralism. This sign on a Swiss bank includes four languages—German, French, Italian, and English.

pluralism in action. Switzerland has three official languages—French, German, and Italian—one language for each of its three major ethnic groups. These groups live together peacefully and are extremely loyal to Switzerland. Furthermore, none of the groups has taken on a dominant or minority role in Swiss society.

Assimilation In many societies, racial and ethnic minorities attempt to hold onto some of their unique cultural features. However, official policies do not always favor such efforts. For example, at one time in the United States it was hoped that the various groups that make up American society could be blended into a single people with a common, homogeneous culture. This hope formed the basis of the image of America as a "melting pot." The blending of culturally distinct groups into a single group with a common culture and identity is called **assimilation**.

In most societies, some assimilation occurs voluntarily. Over time, the various groups within society exchange many cultural traits as a natural outcome of daily interaction. On the other hand, attempts to force assimilation often lead to conflict. For example, in the 1980s the Bulgarian government waged a long campaign to forcibly assimilate the country's large Turkish minority. This campaign involved forbidding the Turks from practicing their religion, from using their language, and from celebrating their culture. Thousands of Turks were reportedly killed or tortured in conflicts over these assimilation policies.

One indication of cultural pluralism and assimilation is the variety of ethnic food enjoyed by Americans.

Legal Protection Many countries have taken legal steps to ensure that the rights of minority groups are protected. The Civil Rights Act of 1964 and the Voting Rights Act of 1965 are examples of such legislation in the United States. Great Britain adopted similar legislation in 1965 with the passage of the Race Relations Act.

Affirmative action programs in the United States are another example of legal efforts to achieve equal rights. These programs are designed to correct past imbalances in the educational and employment opportunities given to minority groups. Affirmative action programs generally give preference to racial and ethnic minorities and women for jobs and school admission. In recent years, criticism has grown over affirmative action policies, charging that they are a form of "reverse discrimination." Recent legal challenges have been made against affirmative action, and government institutions have been reconsidering their policies.

Segregation Policies that physically separate a minority group from the dominant group are referred to as **segregation**. Under segregation, the minority group is forbidden to live in the same areas as the dominant group and cannot use the same public facilities. Sociologists recognize two types of segregation. **De jure segregation** is based on laws. Segregation based on informal norms is called **de facto segregation**.

History provides many examples of segregation. For example, Jews in Europe during the Middle Ages were forced to live in walled-off communities called ghettos. Segregation was practiced openly and legally in the United States until the 1960s. As a result of earlier segregation policies, many American minority groups are still concentrated in specific areas of cities.

Applying Sociology

American Residential Patterns. According to the Lewis Mumford Center for Comparative Urban and Regional Research, urban residential patterns in the United States remain fairly segregated. For example, the average white American lives in a neighborhood that is 80 percent white. Similarly, the average black American lives in a neighborhood that is 51 percent black. Residential integration is slightly higher for other minority ethnic and racial groups.

CRITICAL THINKING

What might be some social effects of the current racial and ethnic urban residential patterns in the United States?

ANSWER: Answers will vary, but students might note that different groups will not learn to understand each other well unless neighborhoods become more integrated. Also, current residential patterns can lead to continued ethnic and racial prejudice and discrimination.

SPOTLIGHT *on Eliminating Discrimination*

Ask students to imagine that all prejudice and discrimination in the world have been magically eliminated overnight. How is the world different? How is life in the United States and in their community better than before? Have students take on the roles of news reporters and interviewees and take turns reporting on this amazing turn of events and its effects on society. To conclude, ask students to discuss if they think it is possible to eliminate prejudice and discrimination completely. **COOPERATIVE LEARNING, BLOCK SCHEDULING**

SPOTLIGHT *on Global Race Relations*

Have each student select a country other than the United States and use the library and other resources to find out about current or past racial and ethnic relations there. Each student should use the research to create charts and/or graphs that illustrate issues or events related to race relations and discrimination in that country. In addition, students should write a few paragraphs summarizing how organizations and governments there have attempted or are attempting to deal with racial issues. **BLOCK SCHEDULING**

◆ Applying Sociology

Differences in the Treatment of Indigenous People. The treatment of indigenous minority groups often varies according to economic circumstance. In North America, for example, the goal of early European settlers was to gain control of the land. Therefore, this dominant group engaged in the extermination and resettlement of American Indians. In contrast, in South Africa, European settlers depended upon the labor of indigenous groups. As a result, the dominant group used segregation and subjugation to control the indigenous minority groups.

ACTIVITY: Have students contrast the patterns in the treatment of African Americans and American Indians in U.S. history.

Technology Resources

CNN. Presents Sociology: Inequality and Internet Access

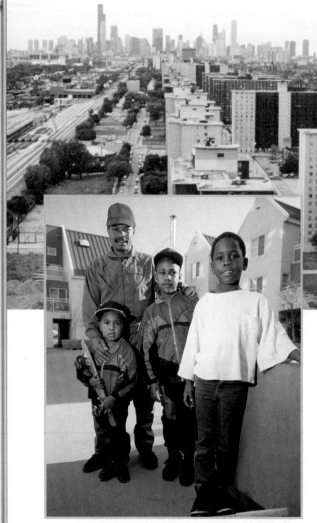

Sociologists and other critics have suggested that public housing is a de facto segregation that keeps minorities in lower-income neighborhoods. New housing initiatives, such as Section 8 housing, have attempted to integrate public housing and encourage diverse neighborhoods.

Subjugation Some countries engage in **subjugation**—the maintaining of control over a group through force. **Slavery**—the ownership of one person by another—is the most extreme form of subjugation. Examples of slavery can be found throughout history.

South Africa's system of apartheid is a recent example of subjugation. Apartheid, which literally means "apartness," called for the legal segregation of all groups within the country. Political and economic power rested in the hands of the white few and was rigidly maintained through force. International opposition eventually brought about the dismantling of the system in the mid-1990s.

Population Transfer Sometimes the dominant group in a society separates itself from a minority group by transferring the minority population to a new territory. This policy can be carried out indirectly or directly. With indirect transfer, the dominant group makes life for minorities so miserable that they simply leave. Direct transfer, on the other hand, involves the use of force. In some cases, people are forcibly moved to new locations within the country. An example of direct transfer in the United States is the resettlement of American Indians on reservations during the 1800s.

Direct population transfers may also involve expelling the group from the country. For example, in the 1750s the British authorities in Canada expelled the Acadians, a French-speaking minority, from Nova Scotia. A more recent example is the forceful removal of the Asian population from Uganda in 1972.

Extermination The most extreme response to the existence of minority groups within a country is extermination. When the goal of extermination is the intentional destruction of the entire targeted population, it is referred to as **genocide**. This kind of extermination has been attempted many times, and sometimes achieved, throughout history.

Anti-Semitism, or hatred of Jews, has led to several attempts at Jewish extermination. After the assassination of Czar Alexander II in 1881, Jews in Russia came under attack. During that year, some 200 pogroms were carried out against Jewish residents. A *pogrom*—a Russian word meaning "devastation"—usually involved mob attacks on

Connecting to History

■ TEACH

Call on students to take turns reading aloud the feature Japanese American Internment. After a brief discussion, have each student write an essay expressing and defending his or her opinion on whether the United States has a right to intern certain groups during wartime.

■ EXTEND

Have students use the library and other resources to find personal accounts of Japanese Americans who were interned during World War II. Instruct each student to summarize one account while maintaining the first-person perspective. Then have volunteers perform their summaries for the class as if they were the older Japanese Americans dramatically recalling for an audience their experiences in World War II internment camps. **BLOCK SCHEDULING**

CONNECTING TO
History

JAPANESE AMERICAN INTERNMENT

On December 7, 1941, Japan bombed Pearl Harbor, bringing the United States into World War II. At the time, there were more than 125,000 Japanese Americans and resident aliens of Japanese ancestry living in the United States—mostly in California and Hawaii. Following the bombing, these people became the victims of a wave of racial prejudice and discrimination.

In February 1942 President Franklin D. Roosevelt signed Executive Order 9066. The order led to the forced removal of more than 110,000 Japanese Americans from the West Coast to internment camps in the interior of the United States. This order was not the first time Japanese Americans had experienced prejudice and discrimination.

A History of Prejudice

Japanese immigrants were originally recruited as a source of cheap agricultural labor in California. Some prospered and soon owned large areas of farmland. Many Californian farmers resented this competition and sought ways to stop the growth of Japanese American's farms. In 1913 the California state legislature passed the Alien Land Law. This law restricted land ownership by foreigners. Other laws enacted over the years limited Japanese immigration and denied citizenship to those Japanese immigrants already in the United States.

Barred from owning land, many Japanese immigrants moved to the cities. There, they built successful small businesses. Other workers not only envied the successes of these Japanese Americans but also feared losing jobs to them. Some became increasingly hostile and attempted to damage Japanese American businesses through boycotts. Despite such prejudice and discrimination, Japanese American immigrants worked hard to build a life for themselves. Their children born in the United States automatically gained a prized possession—U.S. citizenship.

After Pearl Harbor, many Americans questioned the loyalty of Japanese Americans, including those who were U.S. citizens. General John L. Dewitt, head of the West Coast Defense Command, agreed. "The Japanese race is an enemy race," he said. "It

Japanese Americans who were interned established schools and other social institutions.

makes no difference whether he is an American citizen or not."

Internment

Branded as disloyal without trial or due process of law, Japanese Americans were moved to internment camps in the desolate barren interior of the United States. Life in the camps was generally harsh. Inmates were crowded into barely furnished barracks. Food and medical care were often in short supply. "These camps were all barbed wire, guard towers, searchlights," one internee recalled. "They were concentration camps. There's no question about it." Despite the internment policy, many Japanese Americans volunteered for military service. Some served as combat troops, interpreters, and translators.

At the end of 1944, most internees were released from the camps. The majority returned to their old homes only to find that others had appropriated their property. Nevertheless, they began to rebuild their lives. Many Japanese Americans sought redress for the ordeal. In 1989 the U.S. government issued an apology and small payments to surviving internees.

Interdisciplinary Connection

HISTORY
Japanese Americans and World War II. Some 25,000 Japanese Americans—including residents of internment camps—served in World War II. Of this group, many of the volunteers served with the 100th Infantry Battalion and 442nd Regimental Combat Team, one of the most highly decorated units in the history of the U.S. armed forces.

RESEARCH ACTIVITY: Have students conduct research on the treatment of German Americans during World War II and share their findings with the class.

Think About It Answers

1. Some resented the economic success of some Japanese Americans, while others feared losing jobs to Japanese immigrants.

2. Answers will vary, but students should exhibit an understanding of the discrimination that Japanese Americans experienced and what it was like to lose their property and businesses and be forced to stay in internment camps.

Think About It

1. Identifying Points of View *Why did many Californians feel resentment toward Japanese Americans?*

2. Drawing Inferences and Conclusions *Put yourself in the place of the Japanese American internees. How would you feel about your treatment? What would your feelings toward other Americans and the U.S. government be? Give reasons for your answers.*

CLOSE

Have students identify in writing the three sources of discrimination and prejudice *(the sociological, psychological, and economic explanations)* and the seven patterns of minority-group treatment *(cultural pluralism, assimilation, legal protection, segregation, subjugation, population transfer, and extermination)*.

REVIEW AND ASSESS

Have students complete the **Section 2 Review** on p. 246. As **Alternative Assessment**, you may want to use the Venn diagram or crossword puzzle in this section's lessons.

RETEACH

Have each student write 10 true-false statements based on the material in Section 2. Then pair students and have partners trade their statements, identify which ones are true, and correct any false statements by rewriting them.
ENGLISH LANGUAGE LEARNERS , COOPERATIVE LEARNING

EXTEND

Pair students and have each pair brainstorm ways in which young people can work to reduce or eliminate discrimination in their school or community. Then have each pair design a poster that presents an anti-discrimination message.
COOPERATIVE LEARNING , BLOCK SCHEDULING

SECTION 2 REVIEW ANSWERS

1. Define:
- discrimination, p. 238
- prejudice, p. 238
- legal discrimination, p. 239
- institutionalized discrimination, p. 239
- stereotype, p. 239
- self-fulfilling prophecy, p. 239
- racism, p. 240
- scapegoating, p. 240
- cultural pluralism, p. 242
- assimilation, p. 243
- segregation, p. 243
- de jure segregation, p. 243
- de facto segregation, p. 243
- subjugation, p. 244
- slavery, p. 244
- genocide, p. 244
- ethnic cleansing, p. 246

2. legal discrimination—upheld by law, apartheid; institutionalized discrimination—outgrowth of society, inequality of income and education

3a. Discrimination is a behavior; prejudice is an attitude. Examples will vary.

b. cultural pluralism, assimilation, legal protection, segregation, subjugation, population transfer, and extermination

4. Essays will vary, but students should exhibit an understanding of the sources of prejudice as described in the text.

Jews and their businesses or homes. Thousands of Jews were killed, badly injured, or left homeless. Russian Jews faced several more pogroms during the late 1800s and early 1900s.

Millions of European Jews were killed in the Holocaust during World War II. This mass extermination, carried out by Adolf Hitler's Nazi forces, resulted in the deaths of some 6 million Jews. This figure represented nearly two thirds of Europe's Jewish population and more than one third of the world's Jews. The Holocaust also claimed the lives of many Slavs, Roma (Gypsies), Jehovah's Witnesses, Communists, and other groups the Nazis hated.

Other examples of genocide include the British extermination of the Tasmanians and the South African destruction of the Khoikhoi during the 1800s. More recent examples include the massacre of about 1.5 million Armenians by Turks and the mutual slaughter of Muslims and Hindus in India during the first half of the 1900s. Many people have also been killed in genocides in Rwanda and Cambodia.

In the last years of the 1900s, some dominant groups have combined population transfer and extermination in a practice called **ethnic cleansing**. This practice involves removing a group from a particular area through terror,

Concentration camps such as Auschwitz were the site of the mass extermination of Jews during the Holocaust. An estimated 1 to 2.5 million prisoners died at this camp during World War II.

expulsion, and mass murder. For example, in early 1998 the Serbian government began a campaign that sought to drive out or kill about 1.7 million ethnic Albanians in the province of Kosovo. Within a year, more than 1.5 million ethnic Albanians had been expelled from their homes. As many as 10,000 had been killed. Only armed intervention by forces of the North Atlantic Treaty Organization (NATO) prevented the Serbs from achieving their goal.

SECTION 2 REVIEW

1. Define and explain
discrimination
prejudice
legal discrimination
institutionalized discrimination
stereotype
self-fulfilling prophecy
racism
scapegoating
cultural pluralism
assimilation
segregation
de jure segregation
de facto segregation

subjugation
slavery
genocide
ethnic cleansing

2. Contrasting Copy the graphic organizer below. Use it to illustrate the differences between legal discrimination and institutionalized discrimination.

Type of Discrimination	Description	Example

3. Finding the Main Idea

a. What is the difference between discrimination and prejudice? Give an example to illustrate the difference.
b. List the common patterns of minority group treatment.

4. Writing and Critical Thinking

Drawing Inferences and Conclusions
Write a brief essay explaining why some groups of people experience prejudice.
Consider:
- sociological reasons
- psychological reasons
- economic reasons

Homework Practice Online
keyword: SL3 HP10

SECTION 3

OBJECTIVES

1. *Describe the conditions under which minority groups in the United States live.*

2. *Explain how government policies have affected the lives of minority groups in the United States.*

 LET'S GET STARTED!

Before class, write the following questions on the chalkboard: *(1) What are some of the minority groups found in the United States? (2) What kinds of problems have minority groups faced? (3) For what kinds of rights have members of minority groups struggled? (4) What strides have members of minority groups made over the years? (5) What problems remain?* As students enter the classroom, have them copy the questions into their notebooks. Then tell students that in Section 3 they will learn the answers to these questions. Students should add the answers as they study the section. (Have students save their answers for the Close activity.)

3

MINORITY GROUPS IN THE UNITED STATES

Read to Discover
1. What are the conditions under which minority groups in the United States live?
2. How have government policies affected the lives of minority groups in the United States?

Define
white ethnics

In 1944 Swedish sociologist Gunnar Myrdal examined the issue of race relations in the United States. He came to the conclusion that the American people faced a great psychological and cultural conflict. He called this conflict "an American dilemma." A gap existed, he said, between what Americans claim to believe and how they actually behave. Although Americans express support for equality, freedom, dignity of the individual, and inalienable rights, they have not always lived up to these ideals. The enslavement and segregation of African Americans, the establishment of American Indian reservations, and the internment of Japanese Americans during World War II are but a few examples of the denial of these ideals.

The conflict between ideals and actions has been part of the American experience since the arrival of white settlers on the North American continent in the late 1500s. When the original English colonists came to this land, they brought with them the cultural values of English society. As these colonists established dominance in the new land, their values became the standards for the entire society.

These early settlers also provided the image of what many people think of as the typical American—white, of Anglo-Saxon (northern European) descent, and Protestant. This white Anglo-Saxon Protestant (WASP) image does not do justice to the country's great multicultural reality. Yet the image has been the yardstick against which other groups within the United States have been compared.

For the most part, minority groups have prospered in relation to how closely they adapt to the WASP image. Those who can more easily adapt are accepted into mainstream American society relatively quickly. Immigrants from heavily Protestant countries such as Sweden, the Netherlands, and Germany generally gained dominant status within one generation. Other groups—such as African Americans, Hispanics, American Indians, Asian Americans, and white ethnics—have had more difficulty gaining acceptance. This section focuses on the current conditions under which various minority groups live in the United States.

African Americans

Comprising more than 12 percent of the population, African Americans are one of the largest minority groups in the country. With the possible exceptions of American Indians and women, no other American minority group has suffered such a long history of prejudice and discrimination. First brought to this country as slaves in the early 1600s, African Americans have only recently gained an economic and political foothold in American society.

The civil rights movement of the 1950s and 1960s brought significant gains for African Americans. For example, the percentage of the population completing

A growing number of African Americans, such as Lloyd Ward–the former CEO of Maytag and current CEO of the U.S. Olympic Committee–are in business leadership positions.

SECTION 3 RESOURCES

REPRODUCIBLE & REVIEW
- Readings and Case Studies in Sociology 10
- Study Skills and Writing Guide
- Section 3 Review, p. 257

TECHNOLOGY
- One-Stop Planner, Lesson 10.3
- Homework Practice Online
- HRW Go site

To help students describe the conditions under which minority groups in the United States live, copy the graphic organizer at the right onto the chalkboard, omitting the italicized answers. Have students copy and complete the organizer. Discuss the answers with the class. Then organize students into five groups and assign each group one of the five minority groups. Have each group create a collage that illustrates its assigned minority group and its history, conditions, and challenges. Groups might use magazine and newspaper clippings, cartoons, words, and drawings to convey their message. Display the collages in the classroom.

ENGLISH LANGUAGE LEARNERS , COOPERATIVE LEARNING

Minority Group	Conditions/Concerns
African Americans	*making gains toward equality, but statistics still show members are lagging in education, employment, and income; becoming more politically active*
Hispanics	*rapidly growing population; trailing in income and education; diverse population*
Asian Americans	*contrast between first-generation immigrants, who are often poor, and second-generation, many of whom succeed educationally and financially; viewed as a "model minority," although this term is resented*
American Indians	*often live on reservations; high poverty and poor education; encouraged to assimilate; taking steps to establish sources of income and better schools*
White Ethnics	*includes some who assimilate quickly and others who remain victims of prejudice and discrimination; making gains in religious tolerance; good education level*

Applying Sociology

Black Wealth, White Wealth. In the book *Black Wealth, White Wealth* (1995), Melvin Oliver and Thomas Shapiro analyze economic inequality between African and white Americans. According to Oliver and Shapiro, economic inequalities between the two groups have improved, with African Americans making gains in average income, education, and occupational prestige. However, at the same time, the gap between the average wealth of African and white Americans has grown.

RESEARCH ACTIVITY: Have students conduct research on the average income of African Americans and white Americans over the past few decades and then create a graph of the results.

Did You Know?

According to a 2001 online survey by the magazine *Black Enterprise*, Houston is the best U.S. city for African Americans, based on factors such as economic opportunity. Rounding out the top three cities were Washington, D.C., and Atlanta, Georgia.

Chart Answer

58.3 percent

---

high school is now only a few points lower for African Americans than for white Americans. About 24 percent of employed African Americans now hold managerial or professional jobs. In comparison, 35 percent of employed white Americans hold such jobs. The rise in the number of African Americans holding professional jobs marks a considerable increase over the past two decades. Statistics show that some 41 percent of African American households have middle-class incomes.

However, other statistics are not as promising:

- The percentage of African Americans completing four or more years of college is just more than half that of white Americans.
- African American family income averages about 64 percent of white family income.
- The percentage of African American families living below the poverty level is almost three times that of white families.
- Approximately 31 percent of African Americans 18 years old or younger live below the poverty level.
- The unemployment rate among African Americans is more than twice as high as the unemployment rate among white workers.

These statistics represent a serious social problem, and solutions are being sought. The process is being

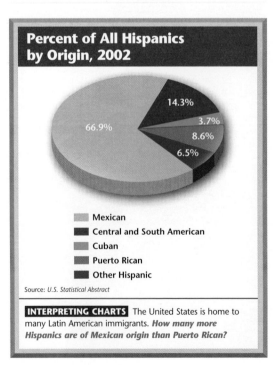

Percent of All Hispanics by Origin, 2002

66.9%
14.3%
3.7%
8.6%
6.5%

- Mexican
- Central and South American
- Cuban
- Puerto Rican
- Other Hispanic

Source: U.S. Statistical Abstract

INTERPRETING CHARTS The United States is home to many Latin American immigrants. *How many more Hispanics are of Mexican origin than Puerto Rican?*

aided by the active role that African Americans are taking in the political process. Since the passage of the Voting Rights Act in 1965, the number of elected African American officials has jumped from 200 to nearly 9,000. In addition, in 2000 President George W. Bush appointed several African Americans to high-level positions, including Rod Paige as secretary of education, Colin Powell as secretary of state, and Condoleezza Rice as national security advisor.

Hispanics

The 2000 census shows that the United States is home to more than 35 million Hispanics. This figure represents a 58 percent increase in the size of the Hispanic population since 1990. During the same time period, the size of the general population grew only by about 13 percent. The Hispanic population is growing so fast that Hispanics have replaced African Americans as the country's largest minority group.

Until the 1960s the Hispanic population in the United States consisted primarily of people of Mexican, Puerto Rican, and Cuban ancestry. Then in the 1960s immigrants from Central and South America and the Caribbean began to swell the number of Hispanics living in the United States. The graph on this page shows a percentage breakdown of the Hispanic population by area of origin.

Many of the immigrants who began arriving in the United States in the 1960s entered through legal means. Others arrived illegally, searching for political freedom and economic opportunities. The United States government estimates that there are more than 5 million illegal immigrants in the United States, at least 70 percent of whom are Hispanic. It is likely that the actual number of illegal immigrants—both Hispanic and non-Hispanic—is considerably higher.

Hispanics have gained increasing political power in recent years and currently hold more than 6,000 elected and appointed offices. Hispanics also control large voting blocks in several states, particularly California, New York, Texas, Illinois, and Florida.

Despite these gains, Hispanics still lag behind non-Hispanics in areas such as education and employment. For example, the poverty rate among Hispanics is about twice that of white Americans. However, it is somewhat misleading to make generalizations about Hispanics. With the exception of a shared language and a shared religion—the majority are Roman Catholic—Hispanics are a diverse people. The tables on page 249 indicate how different Hispanic groups vary on selected social characteristics and how Hispanics compare with non-Hispanics on occupational distribution.

Organize students into five groups and assign each group one of the five minority groups covered in this section *(listed in the graphic organizer on the previous page)*. Then have group members use this chapter and library resources to learn how government policies have affected that minority group. Have each group create a two-page magazine spread on the topic that is to appear in a fictional magazine running a series on minority experiences in the United States. Groups' magazine spreads should include one or more articles and two or more visuals, such as charts and graphs, illustrations, or photographs. Have each group present and explain its work to the class. **COOPERATIVE LEARNING**

HOMEWORK: Have each student create an artistic representation of the struggles for equality of one of the five minority groups mentioned in this section *(listed in the graphic organizer on the previous page)*. Art might take the form of a drawing, painting, song, poem, dance, or any other creative media. Encourage students to use symbolism, figurative language, or other appropriate devices to convey their messages clearly and creatively. Call on volunteers to share their artistic representations with the class.

Hispanic Characteristics and Occupations, 1999

Characteristic	Country or Place of Origin				
	Mexico	Puerto Rico	Cuba	Central and South America	Other
Median Age in Years	24.2	27.5	41.3	29.9	28.3
Percent Completed High School	49.7	63.9	70.3	64.0	71.1
Median Family Income	$27,883	$28,953	$39,530	$32,676	$35,264
Percent Unemployed	4.5	5.1	2.9	4.1	4.0
Percent of Families Below the Poverty Level	24.4	26.7	11.0	18.5	18.2
Percent of Female-Headed Households	21.3	37.2	17.0	23.7	30.6

Source: *U.S. Statistical Abstract*

Occupation	Percent of Hispanics		Percent of White Non-Hispanics	
	Male	Female	Male	Female
Managerial and Professional	11.3	17.8	27.3	31.1
Technical, Sales, and Administrative Support	15.2	37.6	20.8	38.8
Service Occupations	15.8	27.6	11.4	19.9
Farming, Forestry, and Fishing	8.1	1.5	2.5	0.7
Precision Production, Craft, and Repair	20.6	2.8	16.4	2.2
Operators, Fabricators, and Laborers	28.4	12.7	21.8	7.4

Because of rounding, totals may not add up to 100.
Source: U.S. Census Bureau

INTERPRETING TABLES Sociologists have studied the relationship of education, income, and occupations among Hispanics and other ethnic and racial groups. *What Hispanic group had the highest percent of high school completion? What was the median family income for that group? What occupation do the greatest number of Hispanic women hold?*

Exploring Cultural Diversity

Hispanic Immigrant Settlement Patterns. Most Hispanic immigrants to the United States have settled in large urban areas such as Los Angeles or New York City. Two factors have contributed to this settlement pattern. First, regardless of their work experience and qualifications, most Hispanic immigrants are forced to take entry-level jobs, whether of a professional or less-skilled nature. Large cities often have greater opportunities for entry-level workers. Second, established ethnic communities act as a magnet for newly arrived immigrants. For example, many Hispanic immigrants settle in New York City because of its many thriving Hispanic communities.

CRITICAL THINKING

Where do you think that many Mexican immigrants might settle and why?

ANSWER: in the Southwest, because of the region's proximity to Mexico

Table Answer

group—Other (71.1 percent); median income—$35,264; occupation—technical, sales, and administrative support

Teacher Mary-Elizabeth Maynard of Leominster, Massachusetts, suggested the following activity: Compile a list of books relating to race relations in the United States that are appropriate for students. Have each student select and read one book on the list and then write a two-page book report. Next, organize students into small groups and have each member share three important lessons he or she learned from the selected book. Finally, have students discuss the books as a class. **COOPERATIVE LEARNING**, **BLOCK SCHEDULING**

SPOTLIGHT *on Sociological Research*

Remind students that one of a sociologist's most powerful research strategies is interviewing people about their experiences. Have each student interview an older member of one of the minority groups described in this section to find out how the treatment of the group has changed over the past few decades. Have students share their interview findings with the class. **BLOCK SCHEDULING**

Interdisciplinary Connection

HISTORY

The Immigration Act of 1965. Prior to 1965, immigrants entering the United States from a specific country could not exceed 2 percent of that country's total population. The Immigration Act of 1965 repealed these quotas and eliminated national origin, race, and ancestry as a basis for U.S. immigration. Priority for immigration is now given to refugees, relatives of U.S. citizens, and people with special occupational skills.

CRITICAL THINKING

Should the United States restrict the number of immigrants entering the country? Why or why not?

ANSWER: Answers will vary, but students should consider the social and economic effects of large numbers of incoming immigrants on the existing U.S. population.

The growing number of Asian American communities has influenced American society. Parades and celebrations such as this Vietnamese drumming ceremony have become regular events in many cities. Asian Americans such as Transportation Secretary Norman Mineta, have attained high positions.

Asian Americans

Like Hispanics, Asian Americans come from a variety of national backgrounds. Immigrants from almost every Asian country have come to the United States during the past 100 years. The six largest groups of Asian Americans are of Chinese, Filipino, Indian, Korean, Vietnamese, and Japanese ancestry.

Representing close to 4 percent of the total U.S. population, Asian Americans are the country's third-largest ethnic minority group. The 1990 census placed the size of the Asian American population at more than 7 million. By the 2000 census, that figure had grown to more than 10 million. Based on current growth rates, the U.S. Census Bureau projects that Asian Americans will make up 9 percent of the U.S. population by the year 2050.

The relatively small size of the Asian American population and its current high growth rate are a reflection of changes in the United States immigration policies over the years. The first wave of Asian immigration began in the 1850s when Chinese workers were brought to the West Coast to work in the gold mines and to help build railroads.

When the economy slowed and white workers had to compete with Chinese workers for jobs, physical violence and discrimination against the Chinese became widespread. Some Americans formed anti-immigrant political organizations to push for legislation limiting the number of Asian immigrants. In response, Congress passed the Chinese Exclusion Act in 1882. This act ended Chinese immigration. It was not until the 1940s, when labor was once again in short supply, that the ban on Chinese immigration was lifted.

The second wave of Asian immigration began in 1890 when Japanese workers came to Hawaii and California in search of work. The majority of these early immigrants were employed as agricultural laborers. However, as in the case of Chinese workers, labor competition soon resulted in discrimination. In 1905 the *San Francisco Chronicle*, with the support of local labor unions, encouraged the growth of an anti-Japanese movement. A series of anti-Japanese laws were passed in California over the next two decades. Then Congress passed the Immigration Act of 1924. This act set Asian immigration quotas at nearly zero, virtually stopping the flow of Asian immigrants into the United States.

Filipinos were the only Asians excluded from the Immigration Act of 1924. The annexation of the Philippines as a U.S. possession in 1898 meant that Filipinos could freely enter the United States. They soon replaced Chinese Americans as the largest Asian American group. In 1934 the Tydings-McDuffie Act limited Filipino immigration to 50 people per year. Not surprisingly, this resulted in a decline in the number of Filipinos in the country.

The third wave of Asian immigration was ushered in with the passage of the McCarran-Walter Act of 1952. This act allowed Asians to enter the United States on the basis of national quotas and eligibility for citizenship. Immigration policy was further expanded in 1965, causing a jump in Asian immigration. Between 1971 and 1998, people from Asia accounted for more than 35 percent of all immigrants entering the United States. The Vietnam War was also a factor that led to the rise of Asian immigration in the 1970s. In addition, immigration laws passed in the early 1990s favored Asian immigration. About one third of the immigrants who entered the United States during the 1990s came from Asia.

Much has been written about the commitment to education exhibited by Asian Americans. For example, Asian American students consistently achieve high scores on both the verbal and mathematical sections of the Scholastic Aptitude Test (SAT). Moreover, 1999 figures show that 44 percent of Asian Americans over the age of 25 have a bachelor's or more advanced degree. This level compares to a figure of 26 percent for white Americans in the same age group. Asian Americans have used education as a vehicle for moving up the economic ladder. For example, the median household income for Asian Americans is about $13,000 higher than the median household income for all Americans.

The success of Asian Americans in achieving economic security and social acceptance has led some to call them a "model minority." Many Asian Americans resent this label. It hides the fact that the group has faced severe hardships in its quest for acceptance. The road to economic success has been littered with anti-Asian laws, open violence, and discrimination. Perhaps the most notable of these incidents was the internment of more than 110,000 Japanese Americans during World War II.

The label "model minority" also serves to blur differences among the various national groups that make up the Asian American population. Although the group as a whole tends to hold high-status jobs and be better educated than the general population, not all Asian American groups are equally successful.

For example—like most recent immigrants—most southeast Asian immigrants who arrived in the 1980s and 1990s faced language barriers. Therefore, they tended to be concentrated in low-paying jobs. In general, when compared with the Asian American population as a whole, recent Asian immigrants have lower incomes, and a higher percentage are classified as poor.

Sociology in the World Today

Ranking Above the Average. As a group, Asian Americans rank above the national average in median household income. In 1998 the median household income of Asian Americans was $46,637, compared with $40,912 for white Americans, $25,351 for African Americans, and $28,330 for Hispanics. The national median household income in the United States that year was $38,885.

ACTIVITY: Have each student use the data above to create a bar or line graph. In addition, each student should write a caption summarizing the information in the graph.

The growing education opportunities and economic successes of some Asian American groups have led many Asian Americans to more prominent and lucrative occupations such as journalists and news broadcasters.

Mapping Social Forces

■ TEACH

Tell students that immigration has often been a controversial issue in the United States. While some Americans want to limit immigration to protect jobs and slow population growth, other Americans think the United States should encourage immigration to increase diversity and gain the contributions of immigrants. Discuss these and related concerns. Then have each student write a short position paper in support of either limiting or expanding immigration.

■ EXTEND

Invite a first-generation immigrant from your community to visit your sociology classes and talk about his or her reasons for coming to the United States and his or her experiences since arriving. Encourage students to ask the speaker questions and to take notes on what he or she says. After the visitor leaves, ask students if anything about the person's story surprised them and why. Briefly discuss how immigrants might feel during their first days or weeks in a new country. **BLOCK SCHEDULING**

Map Answers

1. In the first decade of the 1900s, southern and eastern Europe were the areas of origin of most immigrants. In the last decade the chief sources of immigration were Latin America and Asia.

2. Answers will vary, but students should use examples from the text to support their responses.

Mapping
SOCIAL FORCES

IMMIGRATION IN THE 1900s

Immigration is one of the most dynamic aspects of the U.S. population. Immigration created the ethnic and racial diversity of the population. The first great wave of immigrants came from northwestern Europe. By the beginning of the 1900s, southern and eastern Europe were the areas of origin of most immigrants. Today the chief sources of immigration are Latin America and Asia. Each group has added to the cultural diversity of American communities. In addition, about one third of the U.S. population growth in the last five years of the 1990s resulted from immigration.

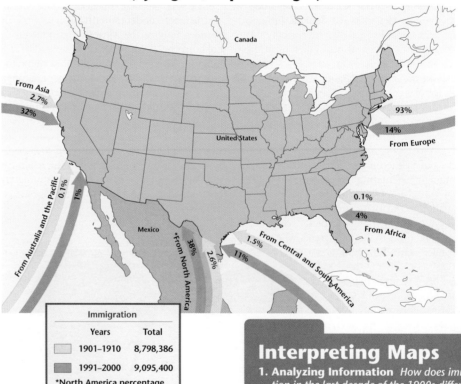

Immigration to the United States, 1900s (by region, in percentages)

Immigration		
Years	**Total**	
1901–1910	8,798,386	
1991–2000	9,095,400	

*North America percentage combines data for Canada, Mexico, and Caribbean.

Interpreting Maps

1. **Analyzing Information** *How does immigration in the last decade of the 1900s differ from immigration in the first decade?*

2. **Making Generalizations and Predictions** *How do you think such changes will affect the U.S. population in the future?*

SPOTLIGHT *on Minority Accomplishments*

Ask students to conduct research to find examples of exceptional accomplishments by members of minority groups in the United States. Examples can be historical or recent and can come from fields such as the arts, business, science and technology, sports, or politics. Have each student select one inspirational example and create a poster that highlights the minority individual and his or her major accomplishment(s). Display students' posters around the classroom. **BLOCK SCHEDULING**

CONNECTING *to the Arts*

Organize students into small groups and have each group conduct research to learn about the arts associated with one of the minority groups covered in this section and the influence of one of these types of art on American culture. For example, students might examine African American or Hispanic contributions to American music. Have each group create a multimedia display to share its findings with the class. Then have the groups set up their displays in the classroom and tour them. **COOPERATIVE LEARNING , BLOCK SCHEDULING**

American Indians

Estimates indicate that when Europeans first set foot on the shores of what is now the United States, the American Indian population numbered in the millions. These people, the ancestors of contemporary American Indians, were divided into hundreds of tribes. Each of these tribes had its own rich history and culture. Early American Indians developed important trade practices and food crops such as corn and potatoes, which greatly altered the life of those Europeans who later settled in the Americas. However, disease, warfare, and the destruction of traditional ways of life reduced the American Indian population to about 228,000 in 1890. During the 1900s, American Indian numbers steadily increased. Figures from the 2000 census put the American Indian population at 2.5 million. Even so, of all the country's minority groups, American Indians face the greatest challenges. The following statistics speak for themselves.

- Approximately 50 percent of the American Indian workforce on or near the reservations is unemployed.
- Some 31 percent of all American Indians live below the poverty level. About 30 percent of those employed have incomes below the poverty level.

- The rate of alcohol-related deaths among American Indians is about 7 times higher than among the general population. The suicide rate is about 1.5 times higher among American Indians as it is among all other Americans. It is the second leading cause of death among American Indians aged 15 to 24 years old.
- Only about 66 percent of American Indians aged 25 and over have graduated from high school, and less than 10 percent have graduated from college.

American Indian problems, in large part, are the result of a history of changing governmental policies. During the early years of contact, the government took American Indian lands by force and through treaties. In the late 1800s a new policy was adopted. American Indians were made wards of the U.S. government, and most were moved to reservations.

The government also created policies aimed at assimilating American Indians into white society. The men were encouraged to become farmers, even though many were traditionally hunters or herders. Tribal land was redistributed to male heads of households, thus disrupting the communal nature typical of American Indian societies. Children were separated from their parents and sent to boarding schools. American Indians who lived away from the reservations and adopted the ways of white society

Interdisciplinary Connection

GOVERNMENT

Nations-Within-a-Nation. The U.S. government now recognizes most American Indian groups within the U.S. boundaries as separate sovereign nations. Each American Indian group governs its own affairs as a "nation-within-a-nation." However, the U.S. Congress maintains oversight power.

CRITICAL THINKING

Why do you think the U.S. Congress maintains this oversight power?

ANSWER: because of the unique "nations-within-a-nation" status of sovereign American Indian groups

Many American Indians today celebrate their cultural heritage. Some groups hold powwows with traditional dancing and music.

Exploring Cultural Diversity

◆ Sociology in the World Today

Working in the United States. Once in the United States, immigrants adapt in a variety of ways. Many take jobs that involve manual labor. On the other hand, immigrants who arrive on professional visas often come for a specific job. Such jobs are generally career-track positions. A significant percentage of immigrants also start their own businesses.

CRITICAL THINKING

What types of immigrants would be most likely to start their own business?

ANSWER: Answers will vary, but students might suggest immigrants with specific skills or immigrants in a newly settled community that has specific needs.

EXPLORING
Cultural Diversity

THE EFFECTS OF IMMIGRATION ON AMERICAN CULTURE

During the 1990s about 1 million immigrants came to the United States each year. Most of these newcomers emigrated from Latin America and Asian countries. These immigrants have had a tremendous influence on the social and economic life of the United States.

Social Life

Recent immigrants, like the millions who came before them, have brought some features of their culture to the United States. Reminders of home—such as favorite foods—provided comfort as they adjusted to their new life. Many of these foods soon became popular with Americans. While long familiar with the foods of Mexico and Cuba, Americans were introduced to new dishes from the countries of Central America. The influx of Asian immigrants, particularly from South Asia, helped bring the spicy curry dishes of India and Pakistan to America.

The effects of U.S. immigration went far beyond the dinner table. During the 1990s the foreign-born population of the United States increased to more than 28 million. About 10 percent of this number are children of school age. For the most part, these children do not speak English as a first language. The education system has had to make changes to ensure that foreign-born students are proficient enough in English to understand what is going on in the classroom. This task has been a particular challenge for cities that have very diverse school districts. In such districts the student body may speak as many as 150 different languages. Schools have adopted several programs to help immigrant students, including bilingual education and English as a Second Language (ESL) programs.

Post-secondary education has also felt the effects of recent immigration patterns. Close to 45 percent of Asian immigrants are college-educated. Many of these immigrants came to the United States not only to attend colleges but also to teach in American schools.

New immigrants have also brought changes to organized religion in the United States. Although the United States remains a predominantly Christian country, the new immigration has made it much more religiously diverse. Largely because of the increase in immigration from Asia, such religions as Buddhism, Hinduism, and Islam are becoming more prevalent. Some estimates suggest that Islam is the fastest-growing religion in the United States.

American culture has become more diverse because of the influence of immigrant groups. This influence can be seen in the popular food of America that includes Mexican, Cajun, and Chinese dishes.

Some churches serve several congregations of differing ethnic backgrounds, with each congregation holding services in its own language. For example, in some churches today, services are as likely to be held in Spanish as in English.

Economic Life

Many recent immigrants have embraced American free enterprise, and by doing so they have begun to change aspects of economic life in the United States. Many immigrants have become entrepreneurs and have opened their own businesses. Most of these businesses serve the needs of the newly settled immigrant communities—such as grocery stores and restaurants that sell traditional foods. The success of many of these businesses has caught the attention of the larger business world.

Some large corporations have begun to develop plans to market to new immigrant communities. These plans include advertising in the communities' own languages and placing advertisements with the small media outlets—newspapers and television and radio stations—that serve immigrant groups. In addition, some companies have begun to adjust their products to suit the tastes of various immigrant groups. If the new immigrants continue to grow in number and economic strength, experts agree that more and more mainstream businesses will adopt similar marketing plans.

Think About It

1. **Sociology and Culture** *How has the immigration of the 1990s affected the social and economic life of the United States?*
2. **Sociology and You** *One of the aspects of American culture affected by immigration is food. Use local telephone directories, restaurant guides, and other sources to find the various ethnic restaurants in your community. List these restaurants and note if you think they are linked to the immigration of the 1990s or an earlier period of immigration.*

Think About It Answers

1. Schools have adopted several programs to help immigrant students, such as bilingual education and English as a Second Language (ESL) programs. Religious diversity has increased. Many immigrants have become entrepreneurs and opened their own businesses. Some companies have targeted their advertising and products to specific immigrant groups.

2. Results and conclusions will vary, but students should use the text of this section to support their conclusions.

Racial and Ethnic Relations **255**

CONNECTING to Government

Organize students into pairs or groups of three and have each pair or group list some methods through which American minority groups can make their voices heard in federal, state, and local government (such as forming political action committees, electing minorities to political positions, speaking through the media, and staging marches and protests). Have students in each pair or group select one method and write a brief plan for how a minority group might use that method as a vehicle to influence the government on an issue important to that particular minority group. Have each student pair or group share its plan with the class. Encourage student feedback. **COOPERATIVE LEARNING , BLOCK SCHEDULING**

SPOTLIGHT on Civil Rights Legislation

Have interested students conduct research on the number and kinds of laws meant to protect American minority groups' civil rights passed between 1960 and 1990. Have each student use this research to create a large annotated and illustrated time line of civil rights legislation. Display the best time line in the classroom.
BLOCK SCHEDULING

Table Answer

163,709

SECTION 3 REVIEW ANSWERS

1. Define:
• white ethnics, p. 256

2. African Americans—gains: civil rights; challenges: education, income, poverty, unemployment; Hispanics—gains: political power; challenges: education, employment; American Indians—gains: Native American Graves Protection and Repatriation Act; challenges: unemployment, poverty, alcohol and suicide-related deaths, education

3a. Conditions vary by group, but minority groups face the various challenges described in the previous answer.

b. Government policies have both helped and hindered minorities. For example, in the past, de jure segregation hurt African Americans, but the Civil Rights Act of 1964 forbade racial discrimination.

4. Essays will vary, but students should exhibit an understanding of the definition of minorities as groups of people who are singled out for unequal treatment because of their physical characteristics or cultural practices.

Current Immigration to the United States, 2000

Country of Birth	Total Immigrants	Country of Birth	Total Immigrants
Mexico	179,919	Russia	17,110
China, People's Republic of	45,652	Canada	16,210
Philippines	42,474	Jamaica	16,000
India	42,046	Korea	15,830
Vietnam	26,747	Ukraine	15,810
Nicaragua	24,029	Pakistan	14,535
El Salvador	22,578	Colombia	14,498
Haiti	22,364	United Kingdom	13,385
Cuba	20,831	Bosnia and Herzegovina	11,828
Dominican Republic	17,536	Poland	10,114

Source: U.S. Immigration and Naturalization Service

INTERPRETING TABLES The long history of the United States as a destination for immigrants has contributed to the number of minority groups in the country. In 2000 the total immigration to the United States was 849,807. *How many more immigrants come to the United States from Mexico than from Canada?*

were rewarded with U.S. citizenship. However, the rest of the American Indian population—about one third of the total—did not gain citizenship until 1924. In that year, Congress passed the Indian Citizenship Act, which made all American Indians living in the United States citizens.

Today American Indians, both individually and collectively, are celebrating their past and looking toward the future. Legislation passed in 1989 established a museum of American Indian history and culture as part of the Smithsonian Institution in Washington, D.C. A year later, Congress passed the Native American Graves Protection and Repatriation Act. This act gives American Indians the right to deny or allow archaeological excavations on Indian sites and the right to decide how Indian artifacts and remains should be displayed. The act also requires museums to allow American Indians to retrieve human remains and sacred

artifacts. The drive to get this legislation passed was accompanied by a renewed interest in traditional languages, religions, and arts and crafts.

Some American Indians are focusing their efforts on business development. Gambling operations provide considerable income and employment for many American Indian groups. Others have set up manufacturing and other industries on their reservations. American Indian arts, businesses, and cultural traditions have influenced American culture.

White Ethnics

You read before that the early settlers in America provided the image of what many people think of as the typical American—European and Protestant. However, not all European immigrants were quickly accepted into mainstream society. During the 1800s and early 1900s, white ethnics—immigrants from the mainly Catholic countries of Ireland, Italy, France, Poland, and Greece—entered the United States in great numbers. These immigrants—who are known collectively as **white ethnics**—often faced open discrimination at the hands of the American-born Protestant majority.

Although most immigrants from Ireland have assimilated into American society, some Irish cultural traditions such as celebrating St. Patrick's day have been assimilated into the larger American culture.

◼ CLOSE

Ask students to retrieve the notes they made in answer to the questions presented in the *Let's Get Started* activity. Then, one at a time, read the questions aloud to the class and call on volunteers to supply the answers. Instruct other students to fill in any gaps in their own notes at this time.

◼ REVIEW AND ASSESS

Have students complete the **Section 3 Review** on p. 257. As **Alternative Assessment**, you may want to use the magazine spread or artwork in this section's lessons.

◼ RETEACH

Pair students and have partners take turns teaching each other the material in Section 3. **ENGLISH LANGUAGE LEARNERS**

◼ EXTEND

Have each student write a short story set in a world in which every being looks exactly the same. Have students address issues of prejudice, discrimination, and minority groups. For example, might minority groups still form in such a world? Select the best story and have the author read it to the class. **BLOCK SCHEDULING**

The discrimination faced by white ethnics was based on cultural and economic concerns. Unlike earlier European immigrants, most white ethnics came to the United States with little money and few skills. They often spoke little or no English, and most of them were Catholic. Opposition by the American-born white majority was vocal and often violent. Anti-Catholic riots were common, and lynchings occurred in several states. When white ethnics looked for work, they often were told that "only Americans need apply." If they did find work, it was generally in the lowest-paying and least prestigious jobs.

Many white ethnics responded to discrimination by assimilating rapidly into mainstream society. Some adopted American-sounding names and required their children to speak English at home as well as in public. Other white ethnics chose the opposite response. They banded together in ethnic neighborhoods in an attempt to hold on to their ethnic identities.

Today many white ethnics have been accepted into mainstream society. However, other white ethnics still are struggling against mainstream prejudice. White ethnics are often stereotyped as poorly educated. In reality half of all white ethnics have attended college—about the same percentage as white non-ethnics.

Some white-ethnic immigrants have passed their cultural traditions on to their children raised in America. These slavic girls wear traditional clothing during a Polish Day parade in New York City.

SECTION 3 REVIEW

1. **Define and explain**
   white ethnics

2. **Summarizing** Copy the graphic organizer below. Use it to identify some of the gains made by and challenges still facing African Americans, Hispanics, or American Indians.

Minority Group — Gains — Challenges

3. **Finding the Main Idea**

   a. Describe the conditions under which minority groups in the United States live.

   b. In what ways have the lives of minority groups in the United States been affected by government policies?

4. **Writing and Critical Thinking**

   Supporting a Point of View Write a brief essay explaining why you think white ethnics should be or should not be considered a minority group.
   Consider:
   • the characteristics of minority groups
   • the life experiences of other minority groups in the United States

Homework Practice Online
keyword: SL3 HP10

CHAPTER 10 REVIEW

ANSWERS

WRITING A SUMMARY
See the section subtitles for the main topics in this chapter.

IDENTIFYING PEOPLE AND IDEAS

1. a category of people who share inherited physical characteristics and who are seen as being a distinct group

2. the set of cultural characteristics that distinguishes one group from another

3. people who share a common cultural background and sense of identity

4. a group of people who are singled out for unequal treatment because of their physical characteristics or cultural practices

5. the denial of equal treatment to individuals based on their group membership

6. an unsupported generalization about a category of people

7. an oversimplified, exaggerated, or unfavorable generalization about a group of people

8. the belief that one's own race or ethnic group is naturally superior to other races or ethnic groups

9. the practice of blaming one's troubles on an innocent individual or group

10. the intentional destruction of an entire population

CHAPTER

Review and Assessment Resources

- Chapter 10 Review, pp. 258–59
- Chapter Review Activities with Answer Key
- Global Skill Builder CD–ROM
- Chapter 10 Test Generator
  (on the One-Stop Planner)
- Chapter 10 Test (Form A or B)
- Alternative Assessment Handbook
- HRW Go site

 REVIEW

Have students complete the **Chapter 10 Review** on pp. 258–59.

 ASSESS

Use one of the chapter tests to assess students' understanding of the content. For **Alternative Assessment**, see the **Alternative Assessment Handbook**.

UNDERSTANDING MAIN IDEAS

1. race—inherited physical characteristics; ethnicity—cultural characteristics; minority group—physical or cultural

2. They are separate but related features of the minority group experience.

3. cultural pluralism—allows each minority group to keep its cultural identity; assimilation—blends culturally distinct groups into a single group with a common culture and identity; legal protection—legally protects minority groups' rights; segregation—physically separates a minority group from the dominant group; subjugation—controls a minority group through force; population transfer—moves a minority group to a new location; extermination—destroys a minority group

4. similar—are all minority groups; different—face different challenges and levels of discrimination and prejudice

5. because white ethnics have also faced open discrimination

6. American Indian food crops greatly altered the life of European settlers. More recently, gambling operations and industries have been set up on Indian reservations.

THINKING CRITICALLY

1. People often possess the physical characteristics of more than one race.

2. Such unequal access pushes minority groups into less powerful positions. Thus,

258

CHAPTER

10 Review

 Writing a Summary

Using standard grammar, spelling, sentence structure, and punctuation, summarize the information in this chapter.
Consider:
- the characteristics that define race, ethnicity, and minority groups
- the differences between discrimination and prejudice
- the conditions of life for minority groups in America

 Identifying People and Ideas

Identify the following people or terms and use them in appropriate sentences.

1. race	**6.** prejudice
2. ethnicity	**7.** stereotype
3. ethnic group	**8.** racism
4. minority group	**9.** scapegoating
5. discrimination	**10.** genocide

 Understanding Main ideas

Section 1 (pp. 232–35)

1. What characteristics are used to define *race, ethnicity,* and *minority group*?

Section 2 (pp. 238–46)

2. How are discrimination and prejudice related?

3. List and describe the seven most common patterns of minority treatment.

Section 3 (pp. 247–57)

4. How are the experiences of African Americans, Hispanics, Asian Americans, and American Indians similar? How are they different?

5. Why have sociologists studied the experiences of white ethnics?

6. Analyze changes such as food and business in the majority American culture resulting from adaptations to various American Indian cultures.

 Thinking Critically

1. Finding the Main Idea Why is it difficult to classify people racially?

2. Analyzing Information How can unequal access to social rewards and resources lead to institutionalized discrimination?

3. Drawing Inferences and Conclusions What is scapegoating, and what functions does it serve? Illustrate your answer with examples.

4. Summarizing What function does prejudice serve for members of the dominant group in a society?

5. Supporting a Point of View What did Gunnar Myrdal mean by the term *American dilemma*? Do you think that this dilemma still exists today? Why or why not?

6. Evaluating Why have Asian Americans been called a "model minority," and why do many resent the label?

Writing About Sociology

1. Evaluating Select and watch a television program that depicts the life of a person or persons from a racial or ethnic minority. Write a brief report that answers the following questions: What stereotypes are supported by the program? What stereotypes does the program break?

2. Categorizing Write an essay describing the ways in which African Americans, Hispanics, Asian Americans, American Indians, and white ethnics exhibit the five characteristics of minority groups listed on page 235. Draw your examples from the information presented in this chapter and from outside research. Use the graphic organizer below to help you write your essay.

	1st	2nd	3rd	4th	5th
African Americans					
Hispanics					
Asian Americans					
American Indians					
White Ethnics					

RETEACH

Have each student create five note cards. On the front of the cards, students should write questions pertaining to the chapter material, and on the back of the cards students should write the answers. Then collect the note cards, organize students into two or three teams, and conduct a high-speed quiz game to review the material covered in the chapter. **ENGLISH LANGUAGE LEARNERS ,
COOPERATIVE LEARNING**

SOCIOLOGY PROJECTS

1. Applying Sociology Ask students to imagine that they are sociologists who advise local leaders on how best to deal with racial tensions. Have students use the problem-solving skills they learned in this chapter to propose some solutions to race-related issues in their local community.

2. Connecting to the Arts Have students, working individually or in groups, create a photo essay illustrating gains that different minority groups in the United States have made. Encourage students to be creative in their choice. Then display the photo essays in the classroom.

BUILDING SOCIAL STUDIES SKILLS

Interpreting Charts

Study the pie charts below. Use them to answer the following questions.

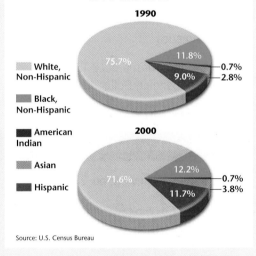

Population by Race and Hispanic Origin, 1990 and 2000

1990
75.7% 11.8% 0.7% 9.0% 2.8%

White, Non-Hispanic

Black, Non-Hispanic

American Indian

Asian

Hispanic

2000
71.6% 12.2% 0.7% 11.7% 3.8%

Source: U.S. Census Bureau

1. Which group's percentage of the population fell from 1990 to 2000?

  a. African American, non-Hispanic

  b. Hispanic

  c. Native American

  d. White, non-Hispanic

2. Which group seems to be growing at the fastest rate? What effects do you think this will have on American society?

Analyzing Primary Sources

The following excerpt discusses a drive to end the collection of racial data by governments. Read the excerpt and then answer the questions that follow.

" *Saying that the country is ready to move past the age-old practice of labeling people by their color or origin, supporters of a proposed ballot initiative are seeking to stop governments in California from collecting racial data and classifying people into racial categories.*

'My worry is that when you stop collecting the data, it becomes possible to sweep certain issues under the rug,' said Hugh Price, president and chief executive officer of the National Urban League, . . .

'Without data, it would be difficult to keep track of how minority children are doing academically, to keep track of discrimination in employment, criminal justice and many other areas,' he said. . . .

The proposal . . . is striking a chord with the growing biracial community in California, whose members increasingly are dismissing traditional definitions of race and resisting government attempts to categorize them.

'We don't ask people what religion they are, what their party affiliation is or what their sexual orientation is. So why is it critical to ask about race?' said Connerly, who is African-American. "

3. Which of the following statements expresses the views of supporters of the Racial Privacy Initiative?

  a. It is important to accept the traditional definitions of race.

  b. People are more interested in shared traits.

  c. We will not be able to keep track of discrimination in employment.

  d. With the Racial Privacy Initiative, important issues might get swept under the rug.

4. If you were a California voter, would you support the collection of racial data? Why or why not?

discrimination becomes part of the social structure and is self-perpetuating.

3. Scapegoating is the practice of placing the blame for one's troubles on an innocent person or group to gain a sense of superiority. Examples will vary.

4. It serves as a justification for discriminatory actions.

5. He was referring to the conflict between what Americans claimed to believe about equality and freedom and how Americans actually behaved. Answers will vary, but students should provide reasons and examples that support their opinions.

6. model minority—because of their economic and social success; resent—because it denies that the group has faced severe hardships

WRITING ABOUT SOCIOLOGY

1. Reports will vary, but students should exhibit an understanding of stereotypes and provide examples that support their conclusions.

2. Essays will vary, but students should apply each of the five characteristics to each of the minority groups listed.

BUILDING SOCIAL STUDIES SKILLS

1. d

2. Hispanics; answers will vary.

3. b

4. Answers will vary, but students should consider the issues of tracking and preventing discrimination.

SOCIOLOGY PROJECTS

Cooperative Learning

Case Study Working in a group with two or three other students, research the ways in which the patterns of minority-group treatment discussed in the chapter have been used by actual societies. Your research may focus on contemporary and historical societies. Use your findings to construct a table titled "Patterns of Minority Group Treatment." Create a list of steps to resolve conflicts between individuals and groups.

🔲 **internet** connect

Internet Activity: go.hrw.com
KEYWORD: SL3 SC10

Choose an activity on racial and ethnic relations to:
- research the latest U.S. census data for minority groups.
- analyze the debate over possible institutional discrimination in the SAT test.
- research immigrant patterns and create charts and graphs to illustrate any changes.

go.hrw.com

Gender, Age, and Health

CHAPTER RESOURCE MANAGER

	Objectives	Pacing Guide		Resources
SECTION 1: Gender (pp. 262–71) **REV** Section 1 Review, p. 271	• Analyze how gender roles affect the opportunities available to men and women in society. • Explain how gender roles are affected by socialization.	**Regular** 2 days *Block Scheduling Handbook with Team Teaching Strategies, Chapter 11*	**Block Scheduling** 1 day	CNN. Presents Sociology: ADA Anniversary **RS** Graphic Organizer 11 HRW Go site **SM** Mastering Critical Thinking Skills 11 **PS** Readings and Case Studies in Sociology 11
SECTION 2: Age and Disability (pp. 272–79) **REV** Section 2 Review, p. 277	• Discuss the effect that the aging of the population is having on society. • Explain how the aging of the population is affecting the life chances of older Americans.	**Regular** 1 day *Block Scheduling Handbook with Team Teaching Strategies, Chapter 11*	**Block Scheduling** 0.5 day	**E** Research Projects and Activities for Teaching Sociology 11 **SM** Study Skills and Writing Guide Teaching Transparency: The Graying of America Teaching Transparency: The Health-Care Spending Dollar, 1999
SECTION 3: Health (pp. 280–87) **REV** Section 3 Review, p. 287	• Describe the state of health care in the United States. • Identify some of the special health-care concerns of various segments of American society.	**Regular** 2 days *Block Scheduling Handbook with Team Teaching Strategies, Chapter 11*	**Block Scheduling** 1 day	**Chapter Review And Assessment** **REV** Chapter 11 Review, pp. 288–89 **REV** Chapter Review Activities with Answer Key Global Skill Builder CD–ROM Chapter 11 Test Generator (on the One-Stop Planner) **A** Chapter 11 Test (Form A or B) **A** Alternative Assessment Handbook HRW Go site

Chapter Resource Key

PS	Primary Sources	A	Assessment		Video
RS	Reading Support	REV	Review		Internet
E	Enrichment		Transparencies		Holt Presentation Maker Using Microsoft® PowerPoint®
SM	Skills Mastery		CD-ROM		

 One-Stop Planner CD–ROM

See the *One-Stop Planner* for a complete list of additional resources for students and teachers.

One-Stop Planner CD–ROM

It's easy to plan lessons, select resources, and print out materials for your students when you use the **One-Stop Planner CD–ROM with Test Generator.**

Chapter Project Preview

The following activities are included in the Chapter Review. You may want to make the suggested preparations.

CHAPTER REVIEW ACTIVITY

Using Statistical Analysis Students will work in groups to find statistics on gender, age, and health inequalities and then create a data bank entitled Gender, Age, and Health Inequality: By the Numbers. To enhance consistency in grading, create project guidelines explaining what data banks are and what students' data banks should include.

LESSON ACTIVITY

Linking to Community Students will volunteer at a local hospital or retirement community as "candy stripers" or visit a training facility for guide dogs or therapy pets. Contact local facilities to line up several that are willing to participate in the project. Then create a list of the facilities for students. You might have students keep journals during the project.

INTERNET ACTIVITY

AIDS Research and Treatment Students will use provided Internet links to conduct research on recent developments in AIDS research and treatment methods. Students will then create a pamphlet to inform others about recent developments in this area. To help students and increase project uniformity, create a pamphlet template for students to use. You might also provide several sample pamphlets for students to examine.

Additional Resources

PRINT RESOURCES FOR TEACHERS

Kurtz, Richard A., and Chalfant, Paul. *Sociology of Medicine and Illness.* Needham Heights, MA: Allyn & Bacon, 1991. Examines the issues of health and illness from a sociological perspective.

The Young and the Old: A Source Book on Aging. Portland, ME: J. Weston Walch, 1988. Collection of lessons with accompanying reproducible activities that focus on various aspects of aging and on social issues important to elderly people.

PRINT RESOURCES FOR STUDENTS

Bowe, Frank. *Equal Rights for Americans with Disabilities.* New York: Franklin Watts, 1992. Describes what it is like to grow up as a person with a disability and discusses the civil rights issues that inspired the disability rights movement.

Stefoff, Rebecca. *Women of the World: Women Travelers and Explorers.* New York: Oxford University Press, 1992. Traces the adventures of nine courageous women throughout history.

Walker, Alice. *The Color Purple.* New York: Washington Square Press, 1983. Novel about a young African American woman in the South that enables students to examine the issue of women's rights. (This book may not be suitable for all students.)

MULTIMEDIA RESOURCES

The Aging of America: CNN Special Report (vhs, color; 30 min.) Social Studies School Service. Focuses on some of the problems faced by today's elderly population.

Main Street: He's My Brother (vhs; 8 min.) Films Incorporated Video. Explores the challenges and rewards of having a sibling who has a disability by sharing the story of a teenage girl whose younger brother is autistic. Enables students to see what life is like for families who have members with disabilities.

Who You Are and What You Are: Understanding Sex Roles (filmstrip on vhs; 40 min.) Guidance Associates. Explores gender-role related issues involving careers, marriage, romance, and relationships.

internet connect

HRW ONLINE RESOURCES

GO TO: go.hrw.com
Then type in a keyword.

TEACHER HOME PAGE
KEYWORD: SL3 Teacher

CHAPTER INTERNET ACTIVITIES
KEYWORD: SL3 SC11
Choose an activity to have students:
• create a thematic graph or chart on gender inequality in education, in the workplace, or in politics.
• write a report on new technologies and products that have been developed to help disabled people.
• create a pamphlet on recent developments related to AIDS treatment.

CHAPTER ENRICHMENT LINKS
KEYWORD: SL3 CH11

ONLINE ASSESSMENT
Homework Practice
KEYWORD: SL3 HP11
Standardized Test Prep
KEYWORD: SL3 STP11
Rubrics
KEYWORD: SS Rubrics

CONTENT UPDATES
KEYWORD: SS Content Updates

HOLT PRESENTATION MAKER
KEYWORD: SL3 PPT11

ONLINE READING SUPPORT
KEYWORD: SS Strategies

CURRENT EVENTS
KEYWORD: S3 Current Events

11 Gender, Age, and Health

Build on What You Know

Ask students to answer the following questions:

How might discrimination affect a woman's ability to achieve her goals?

Consider:
• career and earnings potential
• balancing work and family
• perceptions of traditional women's roles

How might a person's social class relate to the health care available to him or her?

Consider:
• income level
• ability to work
• level of dependence on others

Internet Activity

Have students access the Internet through the HRW Go site to conduct research on gender inequality in either education, employment, or politics. Then have students, working in small groups, use computer software to prepare a multimedia presentation on one of these topics. Groups' presentations should include one or more thematic charts and graphs illustrating gains that women have made and gender inequalities that persist today. Presentations should also provide explanations for existing gender inequalities and suggestions for how to decrease or eliminate them.

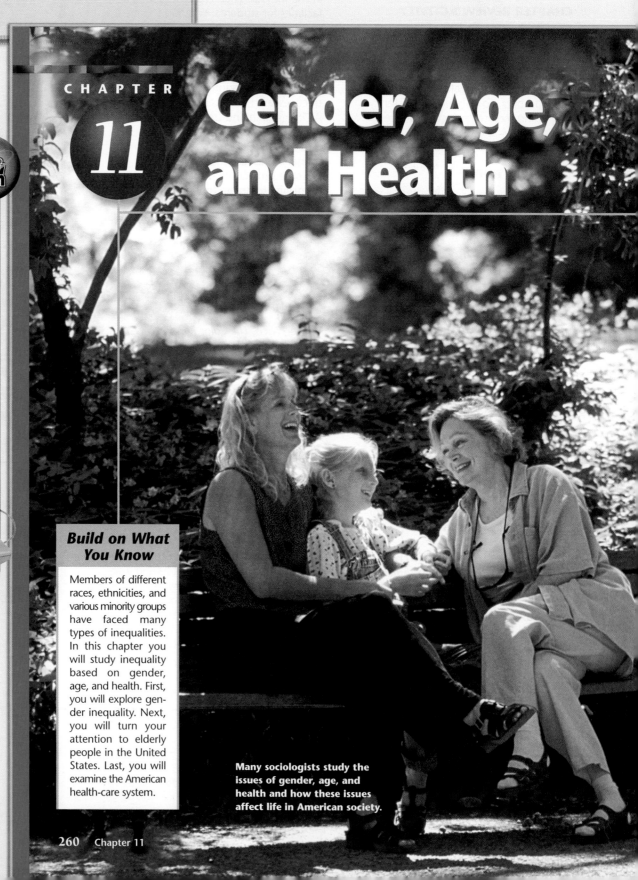

CHAPTER

11 Gender, Age, and Health

Build on What You Know

Members of different races, ethnicities, and various minority groups have faced many types of inequalities. In this chapter you will study inequality based on gender, age, and health. First, you will explore gender inequality. Next, you will turn your attention to elderly people in the United States. Last, you will examine the American health-care system.

Many sociologists study the issues of gender, age, and health and how these issues affect life in American society.

TRUTH OR FICTION **What's Your Opinion?**

To help introduce the chapter, have students discuss the Truth or Fiction statements that appear on this page. You might want to help students by reading the following **true/false** responses to the class.

True In modern American society, men and women have equal roles.

False Most societies have strong gender-role expectations, which dictate the behaviors of men and women and the opportunities available to each gender.

True The median age has fallen because people are not living as long and because birthrates have risen.

False The median age has risen because people are living longer and because birthrates have dropped.

True Everyone in the United States has an equal opportunity to receive adequate health care.

False Some people cannot afford adequate health care, and their health suffers as a result.

Life in Society

Race and ethnicity are not the only factors that affect a person's position in the social structure. A person's standing in society is also influenced by whether he or she is male or female, young or old, able-bodied or disabled. In general, to be female, old, or disabled is to be in a position of lesser power in society. Even in the United States, a country founded on the ideal of equality, inequalities based on gender, age, and health do exist. This fact is illustrated by the following statistics:

- Only 11 percent of American engineers, about 25 percent of American doctors, and some 29 percent of the country's lawyers and judges are women.

- Elderly Americans age 75 and older have a higher poverty rate than the general population. Almost one in six women age 75 or older live in poverty.

- Although most Americans with disabilities want to work, only 50 percent are employed. The employment rate for those with severe disabilities is even lower—31 percent.

- About 14 percent of the U.S. population is not covered by medical insurance. Among the working poor, some 45 percent are uninsured.

WHY SOCIOLOGY MATTERS

Sociologists are interested in how different age groups view the same issues. Use **CNNfyi.com** or other current events sources to learn more about how young Americans and Americans of the baby-boom generation view the Social Security debate. Write a short essay describing those views.

CNNfyi.com

TRUTH OR FICTION **What's Your Opinion?**

Read the following statements about sociology. Do you think they are true or false? You will learn whether each statement is true or false as you read the chapter.

- Gender has little effect on the roles that men and women play in society.

- The median age of the U.S. population has fallen in the last few decades.

- Social status does not influence a person's health or the health care he or she receives.

Interdisciplinary Connection

HISTORY

Social Movements for Equal Rights. The civil rights movement of the 1960s launched similar movements among other minority groups, such as women, elderly people, and people with disabilities. These groups used many of the same protest methods, such as marches and boycotts, to fight for equal rights and end discrimination. Although each movement did make gains, many women, disabled people, and elderly people today still face prejudice and discrimination in American society.

CRITICAL THINKING

What types of discrimination do you think these groups face?

ANSWER: Students might mention discrimination in hiring and in the workplace, and for the latter two groups, discrimination in obtaining health coverage.

SECTION ❶

OBJECTIVES

1. *Analyze how gender roles affect the opportunities available to men and women in society.*

2. *Explain how gender roles are affected by socialization.*

SECTION *1* RESOURCES

REPRODUCIBLE & REVIEW

- Mastering Critical Thinking Skills 11
- Readings and Case Studies in Sociology 11
- Section 1 Review, p. 271

TECHNOLOGY

- One-Stop Planner, Lesson 11.1
- Homework Practice Online

 LET'S GET STARTED!

Write the following list of paired words on the chalkboard: *pink/blue, dog/cat, salt/pepper, vanilla/chocolate, home/office, beach/mountain,* and *sedan/sports car.* As students enter the classroom, have them copy the pairs of words and indicate which item in each pair seems more masculine and which item seems more feminine to them. Tally students' responses on the chalkboard. *(Many students might say that* blue, dog, pepper, chocolate, office, mountain, *and* sports car *seem more masculine.)* Note the pairs that most students agreed upon and discuss what the identifications reveal about students' perceptions about men and women and their roles in society. Then tell students that in Section 1 they will learn about gender roles and gender inequalities.

GENDER

Read to Discover

1. How do gender roles affect the opportunities available to men and women in society?

2. How are gender roles affected by socialization?

Define

gender, gender roles, gender identity, patriarchy, sexism, women's movement, suffrage, wage gap, glass ceiling, second shift

How would you answer the following question? In what ways do men and women differ? Some of the ways you might mention would be based on biological characteristics. Certainly, men and women do differ in such physical traits as average height and weight, amount of body hair, and muscle-to-fat ratio. However, most of the ways you might mention would refer to gender differences. **Gender** comprises the behavioral and psychological traits considered appropriate for men and women. A person's sex refers to the biological identity of that person. The variety of biological characteristics are the same in all societies. In contrast, gender traits are socially created and may vary from culture to culture.

The consequences of gender differences are far-reaching. It is gender, not biology, that determines the majority of the roles men and women play in society. Equally as important, it is primarily beliefs about gender that determine the distribution of power between the sexes. In this section, you will examine the social significance of gender.

Gender Roles and Identity

What do people mean when they say that a man is being masculine or a woman is being feminine? These labels simply mean that the person exhibits behaviors and attitudes considered appropriate for his or her gender. All societies have norms governing how men and women should act. The specific behaviors and attitudes that a society establishes for men and women are called **gender roles**. In most societies, men and women do specific kinds of work. In a division of labor based on gender, women are generally assigned child-care and domestic duties. Men are often charged with providing economic support and physical safety for the family.

Traditionally gender roles for women have included child care and domestic duties. However, these roles have been challenged over the past several decades.

TEACH OBJECTIVE 1

Call on a volunteer to write the definition of the term *gender roles* on the chalkboard *(the specific behaviors and attitudes that a society establishes for men and women).* Use the definition to lead into a class discussion on how gender roles affect the opportunities available to men and women in society. Then to help students analyze how gender roles and the self-fulfilling prophecy (see the last paragraph on p. 265) affect women, copy the graphic organizer at the right onto the chalkboard, omitting the italicized answers. Have students copy the organizer and complete it by entering an example from their textbook (as shown) or one of their own. Discuss students' answers. **ENGLISH LANGUAGE LEARNERS**

The Self-Fulfilling Prophecy of Sexism

People who see women as incapable of holding positions of power make choices based on this belief.

Men who see women as inferior oppose women entering powerful positions.

Women who accept an inferior role do not pursue traditionally male roles.

Thus, not enough women are in positions of power to push for greater access.

The fact that few women hold positions of power is used to justify the opinion that women must be incapable of holding such positions.

What does it mean to be a boy or a girl, and how does this knowledge affect behavior? Sociologists are concerned with how **gender identity** is formed and how this identity influences social behavior. Gender identity is the awareness of being masculine or feminine as those traits are defined by culture. However, the cultural values that influence gender identity and roles are not static and have changed in recent decades. The degree to which a person takes on a gender identity affects his or her response to the gender roles established in society.

Between Cultures Most societies follow a division of labor similar to the one mentioned previously. However, as Margaret Mead's study of three New Guinea societies indicates, there are some exceptions. In one of these societies, the Tchambuli, men and women care for the children. Women provide food for the family. Even in societies in which men are the principal breadwinners, gender-based duties can vary widely. For example, in most preindustrial societies cooking, carrying water, or grinding grain are considered women's work. However, in some societies these tasks fall to men.

Even more variation exists in the psychological characteristics considered appropriate for men and women. For example, Mead found that among the Tchambuli, the women were bossy and efficient, while the men were gossipy and artistic. In addition, the men wore cosmetics and curled their hair.

In contrast, the women wore few adornments. The other two societies Mead studied showed similarly interesting gender-role variations. Among the Mundugumor, the traditionally masculine trait of aggressiveness was the norm for men and women alike. However, both men and women of the Arapesh were expected to be passive and emotionally warm. Such traits are considered feminine in most cultures. Studies of other Pacific Island societies have found more gender-role variations. For example, in

INTERPRETING VISUALS In some New Guinea societies it is common for men to wear make-up. *How does this offer evidence that gender roles are socially created rather than biological instilled?*

Tahiti both men and women are expected to be passive, yielding, and forgiving. The Tahitians do not use given names that are easily identifiable as male or female.

Sociologists interpret cross-cultural variations as evidence that gender roles are socially created rather than biologically based. They argue that if gender roles were based primarily on biology, there would be little variation in gender behavior from society to society.

Gender Identity and Socialization Individuals learn appropriate gender-role behavior through socialization. As you read in Chapter 5, socialization is the interactive process through which people learn the basic skills, values, beliefs, and behavior patterns of their society. In virtually all societies, gender socialization begins at birth and continues throughout life.

Visual Answer

This practice varies from the gender roles followed in many other societies. If gender roles were based mainly on biology, there would be little societal variation in gender behavior.

Organize the class into four groups—two groups of female students and two groups of male students. Have one female and one male group each prepare a description of female socialization in the United States. Have the other female and male groups each prepare a description of male socialization. Once the groups have presented their descriptions to the class, have students use the activity as the basis of a discussion about how gender roles are affected by socialization, how male and female perceptions of each other's socialization differ, and the effects of these differing perceptions. *(Gender socialization starts at birth and influences what traits and behaviors a person considers either feminine or masculine.)*

COOPERATIVE LEARNING

SPOTLIGHT

on Television's Portrayal of Gender Roles

Have students view one or two syndicated family television programs from the 1950s or 1960s (such as *Father Knows Best, I Love Lucy, Leave It to Beaver,* or *Ozzie and Harriet*) and one or two similar types of current television shows. Instruct students to write a short essay that compares the gender-role expectations evident in these programs with the gender-role expectations portrayed in modern television shows. Have volunteers read their essays aloud to the class and invite other students to discuss their observations.

BLOCK SCHEDULING

Gender Roles in Children. Studies show that by the time children are about five years old, their gender roles are set. Most boys tend to play with traditionally male toys such as trucks, while most girls tend to play with traditionally female toys such as dolls. Little crossing of gender lines occurs. However, those children who do cross gender lines are usually girls.

CRITICAL THINKING

Why do you think it is more common for girls to cross gender lines than for boys?

ANSWER: Many parents may discourage boys from playing with traditionally female toys or from dressing in traditionally female clothing.

Visual Answer

Women and girls who play sports challenge the gender expectations that they should be gentle and passive.

In the United States a person's gender role is often reinforced at birth. The newborn is usually given sex-specific clothes, toys, and nursery furnishings. Traditionally, girl babies are dressed in pink, and boy babies are dressed in blue. Infant girls are given dolls while infant boys are given stuffed animals. Nursery furnishings include delicate pastels and frills for girl babies. Boys' nurseries, on the other hand, often use strong primary colors and clean lines.

Such gender-typing is not as widespread as it was 20 or 30 years ago. Change is more evident in the treatment of girls. Girls' clothes now come in a wide range of colors,

INTERPRETING VISUALS Although boys and girls learn many of the traditional gender roles and identities at an early age, these roles have been changing. *How do you think girls and women playing sports challenges some of the gender expectations of the 1800s?*

fabrics, and styles. Most people no longer discourage girls from playing with traditionally male toys, such as model cars, trucks, and airplanes. Although girls have taken up many traditionally male activities, boys are rarely dressed in pink or in clothing that has ribbons, lace, or other frills on it. Few boys are encouraged to play with dolls or other traditionally feminine toys.

Even more important than the physical trappings of gender are the different expectations that most people hold for girls and boys. Have you ever heard the following nursery rhyme?

What are little boys made of?
What are little boys made of?
Frogs and snails,
And puppy-dogs' tails,
That's what little boys are made of.

What are little girls made of?
What are little girls made of?
Sugar and spice
And all that is nice,
That's what little girls are made of.

This nursery rhyme dates from the 1800s. However, for most of the 1900s these gender expectations have held true. Nevertheless, the traditional understanding of the proper roles and behaviors of boys and girls has begun to change. Traditionally, little boys were expected to be

CONNECTING *to Language Arts*

Pair students and have each pair come up with a profile for the main character of a short story. After each pair agrees on a description and short personality sketch for a character, instruct the pairs to write two different life stories starring this character. One partner in each pair should write a story set in a patriarchal society, while the other partner should write a story set in a matriarchal society. Have volunteer pairs read their stories aloud to the class for comparison. **COOPERATIVE LEARNING** , **BLOCK SCHEDULING**

SPOTLIGHT *on Successful Women*

Invite several women from your community to participate in a panel discussion for your classes. Select women who have found success and fulfillment in their chosen roles, such as educators, politicians, businesspeople, or homemakers. Have students prepare questions for the speakers beforehand. Ask guests to introduce themselves, describe their primary roles, and explain how they have found success in those roles. Encourage students to ask the women questions about any opposition or barriers they encountered in seeking to fulfill their goals. **BLOCK SCHEDULING**

Traditional notions of masculinity have also changed. Gender expectations that have historically limited men's domestic roles have shifted in recent years as men take on more domestic roles, including child care.

adventuresome, aggressive, and physically active. Little girls were expected to be polite, gentle, and passive. Parents and teachers often expressed concern over little girls who were too aggressive or too adventuresome. Passivity in boys generated similar concerns among adults.

Differing gender expectations have extended to school as well. Boys were expected to be good at math and science and mechanically inclined. Girls were expected to excel in reading and the social sciences and to be creative in the arts. During the school years, boys were encouraged to prepare for a career. However, girls were generally encouraged to look to marriage and a family as their future. These gender expectations have begun to change. More and more young women are being encouraged to pursue careers. Today marriage is not the sole goal for most women.

The family is the most powerful agent of gender socialization. Parents, siblings, and other relatives all act as role models for young children. Through family members' conscious and unconscious actions, children quickly learn what gender behaviors are expected of them. Schools, peer groups, and the media all reinforce these gender expectations. During adulthood, peer groups and the media take on increasingly important roles in the gender-socialization process.

Gender Roles and Social Inequality Gender roles are both different and unequal. In practically every society, gender is the primary factor used to determine a person's social standing. In general, to be female is to be in a position of lesser power in society. Sociologists are interested in how this inequality between men and women arose.

One widely held view is that gender inequality is related to the nature of human reproduction. The growth of primitive societies depended on the birth and survival of children. Women spent many of their adult years in pregnancy or nursing young children. As a result, they took on roles that allowed them to stay close to home. However, men took on the roles that required strength and travel away from the home base. They became hunters, traders, and warriors. They provided the group with meat and trade goods. They protected the group by fighting wars. In essence, men risked their lives for the group, and they gained much prestige as a result. This prestige and the ownership of weapons provided men with a source of power within the group. In time, the power relationship between men and women developed into a **patriarchy**. This system is one in which men are dominant over women.

Families in industrial societies are generally small, and most people live well into their seventies. As a result, women in industrial societies spend much of adulthood free from the responsibilities of child care. However, women are still generally seen as more responsible than men. In addition, few jobs in industrial societies require such physical strength that they preclude women from performing them. Yet women still occupy a secondary position in many industrial societies.

The conflict perspective provides an explanation for this situation. According to conflict theory, gender roles are a reflection of male dominance. Through their control of the economic and political spheres of society, men have established laws and customs that protect their dominant position. In so doing, men have blocked women's access to power.

Another explanation for the persistence of gender roles is institutionalized discrimination. Over the generations, certain discriminatory customs based on gender have become part of the social structure. **Sexism**—the belief that one sex is by nature superior to the other—is at the heart of gender-based discrimination. The long history of male economic and political dominance has led many people in society to adopt the view that men possess natural qualities that make them superior to women. This view has been used as a justification for continued male dominance.

As with racism, sexism becomes a self-fulfilling prophecy. People who believe that women are in some way incapable of occupying positions of power make

Case Study

Gender Expectations and Socialization.
Gender expectations influence how adults treat and perceive children. In one experiment, a group of young mothers were observed with a six-month-old child introduced as Beth. The women gave the infant dolls to play with and described her as being sweet. Next, a second group of mothers was observed with a six-month-old child introduced as Adam. The women treated this child differently than the first group had treated Beth. For example, the second group of women offered Adam traditional male toys. What the two groups of women did not know was that the same child—a girl—was used for both observations.

ACTIVITY: Ask students to identify examples of gender socialization by families, the mass media, schools, and peers. Then have students discuss the effects of this socialization.

Exploring Cultural Diversity

■ TEACH

Call on students to read the feature Women in the World Today aloud to the class. Lead students in a brief discussion that addresses the first item under Think About It. Next, have students work independently or in pairs to create a series of charts or graphs illustrating some of the statistics cited in the feature. Finally, have students work independently to complete the assignment described in the second item under Think About It.

COOPERATIVE LEARNING

■ EXTEND

Organize the class into three groups and assign each group one of the following topics: women and education, women and work, or women and politics. Then within each group, organize students into pairs or small groups. Instruct students to use available resources to find out more about global trends in their assigned area and to make predictions about future trends based on the information they find. Have students present their predictions in short reports. Ask volunteers to share their findings with the class.

COOPERATIVE LEARNING , BLOCK SCHEDULING

Interdisciplinary Connection

GOVERNMENT

Margaret Thatcher.
British politician Margaret Thatcher was the first woman in Europe to serve as a prime minister. Thatcher held the office of prime minister of Great Britain from 1979 to 1990, making her also the first British politician during the 1900s to hold the office for three consecutive terms.

Born Margaret Hilda Roberts in 1925, Thatcher went on to study chemistry and law. She entered politics in 1959 as a member of the British Conservative Party and rose to become party leader by the mid-1970s. During her terms as prime minister, Thatcher earned the nickname Iron Lady for her strong policies and leadership. In 1992 she was made a baroness in appreciation of her years of political service.

RESEARCH ACTIVITY: Have students conduct research on a prominent or successful woman in politics or business. Ask each student to write a short biographical profile about the selected woman's life, career, and accomplishments.

E X P L O R I N G
Cultural Diversity

WOMEN IN THE WORLD TODAY

What is the status of the world's women at the beginning of the new millennium? The United Nations attempted to answer that question in *The World's Women 2000: Trends and Statistics*. The report concluded that while women have made notable gains recently, gender inequalities still exist. A review of three areas—education, work, and politics—will illustrate this.

Education

The report found that the gender gap in elementary and secondary schooling is closing. In South America, the Caribbean, and some countries in East Asia there are more girls than boys enrolled in school. However, girls still lag behind boys in parts of Africa and South Asia. There, girls' access to schooling is limited. Girls are also more likely to drop out of school than boys are. The gap in school enrollment is reflected in illiteracy statistics. Of the 876 million people in the world who cannot read and write, two thirds are women. The regions where school enrollment and literacy rates for women are the lowest—some countries of Africa and South Asia—have high population-growth rates. The rising population strains educational institutions leaving many children without educational opportunities. As a result, the gender gap in literacy is not likely to close in the near future.

The report found that women have made the most significant gains in college enrollment. In countries of North America, South America, the Caribbean, Europe, and parts of Asia, women's enrollment equals or is higher than that of men. However, women's enrollment markedly trails that of men in sub-Saharan Africa.

Work

According to the report, the number of women in the world's labor force is growing. Women now make up at least one third of the labor force in all regions except northern Africa and western Asia. The report found that this growth results, in large part, from women's self-employment and part-time work. Women are also heavily involved in the underground economy—in some Latin American countries more than 50 percent of the female nonfarm labor force work in the informal sector. However, self-employment, part-time jobs, and work in the underground economy offer little job security, provide few benefits, and usually are not well paid.

The report also found that more women now occupy administrative and managerial jobs. However, the actual number of women in these positions is still very low. In the most industrially developed regions outside of Europe, women hold only 35 percent of managerial and administrative jobs. The majority of women, the report noted, remain in the lowest-paying jobs.

One reason gender inequalities in employment exist, the report suggests, is the way that work in the home is divided between the sexes. Women continue to do most of the household work—such as cleaning, preparing meals, and caring for children.

In spite of the inequalities that women face, many women have achieved success in education, work, and politics. Women have reached high-level positions in government, such as U.S. Supreme Court Justice Sandra Day O'Connor (right).

CONNECTING to Government

Have each student choose a current American female government official and design a mock Web page for her. Students may choose female leaders or officials at the local, state, or national level. Instruct students to write about the official's life, her decision to run for office, her campaign(s), her platform, and her experiences while in office. Ask volunteers to present their Web-page designs to the class. **BLOCK SCHEDULING**

SPOTLIGHT on Women in the United States

Remind students that the gains that American women have made have not affected all women in the United States. Some disparities still exist. For example, a woman brought up in poverty is unlikely to have the same opportunities as a middle- or upper-class woman. Organize students into small groups and have each group use problem-solving skills (described on p. 236) to come up with ways to help close the opportunity gap that exists among different groups of American women. **COOPERATIVE LEARNING,** **BLOCK SCHEDULING**

Politics

Even though women play a greater role in government today, they are underrepresented, the report found. Women make up just 11 percent of those elected to legislative bodies. Women's representation in legislatures is highest in Western Europe at 21 percent. In the Scandinavian countries—Denmark, Finland, Norway, Iceland, and Sweden—and the Netherlands, women occupy at least one third of the legislative seats. In addition, just 8 percent of the world's cabinet ministers are women. However, women have made more progress in appointments to lower-level government offices. Again, the highest rates of representation are found in the countries of Western Europe.

Think About It

1. **Sociology and Culture** *The regions where women have made the least progress are among the world's poorest. What do you think is the connection between poverty and lack of progress for women?*
2. **Sociology and You** *Write three paragraphs comparing the standing of women in the fields of education, work, and politics in the United States with the standing of women in these fields worldwide.*

Sociology in the World Today

Violence Against Women. Although women have made great strides toward equality, women in some countries are treated as second-class citizens, facing discrimination and violence. The killing of female babies, the buying and selling of women, and harsh restrictions on women's freedoms and rights still occur in some places. Many groups today work to improve life for all women.

CRITICAL THINKING

What might be some reasons for the harsh treatment of women in some countries?

ANSWER: Reasons might include cultural attitudes.

Think About It Answers

1. Answers will vary, but students might note that poverty forces women to focus on daily survival and limits their chances to obtain the education necessary for better paying jobs.

2. Paragraphs will vary, but students should note that in general the standing of women worldwide has improved in all three fields, but American women have accomplished more in these fields than women in parts of Africa and Asia.

SPOTLIGHT *on Stay-at-Home Moms*

Remind students that many women choose to stay at home to raise their children rather than pursue careers, political office, or other positions of power. Like women who work, these women face many challenges. For example, such women must find ways to get by on just their husband's income or ways to work from home while taking care of children. Have each student interview a stay-at-home mother in the community to find out more about why some women choose this path and what challenges and rewards they experience. Ask students to share what they learned from their interviews with the class. **BLOCK SCHEDULING**

Interdisciplinary Connection

HISTORY

Susan B. Anthony. An early leader in the women's movement in the United States was Susan B. Anthony (1820–1906). After the Civil War, Anthony and Elizabeth Cady Stanton founded the National Woman Suffrage Association to work toward voting rights for women. In 1872 Anthony was fined $100 for illegally voting in the U.S. presidential election, although she never paid the fine. She died 14 years before the passage of the Nineteenth Amendment in 1920, which granted American women full voting rights.

CRITICAL THINKING

How might denying a minority group the right to vote help maintain its minority status?

ANSWER: Without political power, minority groups have limited means by which to fight discrimination and to gain legal protection of their rights.

Visual Answer

by making society more aware of the inequalities that women faced and by attracting other women to the cause

choices based on this belief. Men who see women as inferior often oppose the entrance of women into powerful positions in business, politics, and the professions. Women who accept this stereotype do not attempt to pursue careers in traditionally male fields. Consequently, there are not enough women in positions of power to push for greater access.

Gender Inequality in the United States

Less than 150 years ago, women in the United States were very much second-class citizens. They had few rights. They could not vote, sign contracts, or sit on juries. Their opportunities in life were much more limited than were those of men. Very few women had the opportunity to get anything more than the most basic education. Many jobs were closed to them. Women who did work received lower wages than men. When women married, their wages and their possessions became their husbands' property. Many Americans accepted this situation as the natural relationship between men and women. However, some American women took steps to end gender discrimination. These women were the founders of the American **women's movement**, which held that the sexes were socially, politically, and economically equal.

The Women's Movement In July 1848, delegates at a women's rights convention in Seneca Falls, New York, issued a Declaration of Sentiments and Resolutions. Based on the Declaration of Independence, this document called for reforms to strengthen women's standing in society. These reforms included allowing married women to control their own property and earnings independently of their husbands. However, the most important reform was **suffrage**—the right to vote.

Although some states did pass laws giving women greater rights, suffrage was not so easily won. Women leaders undertook a program of civil disobedience to bring their cause to the public's attention. They chained themselves to public buildings, harassed public officials, and,

when imprisoned, went on hunger strikes. At one point, they picketed the White House for six months. Eventually, their efforts proved successful. The Nineteenth Amendment to the U.S. Constitution, adopted in 1920, gave women the vote.

For the most part, the women's movement was inactive for the next 40 years. However, the publication of Betty Friedan's book *The Feminine Mystique* sparked the movement into action once more. Friedan rejected the popular notion that women were content with the roles of wife and mother. She argued that the "feminine mystique"—the glorification of these roles—was simply a ploy to keep women in a secondary position in society. Friedan's ideas struck a chord with many women. They soon began to demand greater educational opportunities and fairer treatment at work.

Many feminists argued that the only way to ensure such changes was a constitutional amendment ending discrimination based on sex. Congress approved the Equal Rights Amendment (ERA) in 1972. To become part of the Constitution, the ERA had to be ratified by 38 states. However, it fell three states short in the ratification process. Despite this failure, women made important gains in other areas during the last few decades of the 1900s. For example, Congress passed several acts outlawing gender discrimination in education and in the workplace.

Progress toward gender equality has been made in almost every area of American social life. However, equality has not yet been achieved. A review of women's standing relative to men in education, work, and politics will illustrate this point.

The Granger Collection, New York

INTERPRETING VISUALS The women's movement in the United States began more than 150 years ago. During the early 1900s the women's movement achieved some success in gaining women the right to vote. *How do you think parades and protests might have helped the cause of women's suffrage?*

Education Prior to 1979, women were underrepresented among the ranks of college students. Since that time, women have outnumbered men on college campuses. Today women make up about 57 percent of the total college population. They earn 56 percent of all the bachelor's degrees awarded. However, there are strong gender distinctions in degree majors. Men tend to pursue degrees in engineering, physical science, and architecture. Women tend to concentrate on education, the humanities, and library science. How marked are these gender distinctions? Women earn only about 17 percent of the engineering bachelor's degrees awarded. However, 88 percent of library-science bachelor's degrees go to women.

More and more women are attending graduate school. Women make up more than 57 percent of those enrolled in graduate courses. They earn 58 percent of the master's degrees awarded each year. However, women are less likely than men to pursue doctoral or professional degrees. Only about 41 percent of the doctorates awarded go to women. Women earn slightly more—about 43 percent—of the professional degrees awarded. Yet, as the bar graph on this page shows, these percentages are a marked improvement over the past.

A similar situation exists in college and high-school athletics. In the early 1970s funding for women's athletics was practically nonexistent at most coeducational colleges and universities. Only 16 percent of college athletes were women. In high school, girls accounted for just 8 percent of students participating in athletic programs. This situation began to change after the passage of the Education Amendment Act of 1972. Title IX of the act bars discrimination on the basis of gender in any program—including athletics—at any educational institution receiving federal funds. Over the years, Title IX has been loosely enforced at best. It has faced considerable opposition, particularly from those involved in men's college sports. They expressed the fear that it would limit athletic opportunities for men. Despite such problems, female participation in collegiate sports has increased markedly. Today roughly 40 percent of all college athletes are women. Female participation in high-school sports has made similar gains. Yet even with this progress, disparities still exist. Less than one quarter of the funding for college sports goes to women's athletics. Female athletes receive less than one third of available scholarship money.

The World of Work In Chapter 7, you read that the world of work has changed considerably since the 1960s. Most notably, more women have entered the workforce. One thing that has changed little is the **wage gap**—the level of women's income relative to that of men. During the 1960s, female workers earned between 58 and 61 cents for every dollar earned by male workers. Today the wage gap is about 75 cents to the dollar. The difference in the yearly median earnings of female and male full-time workers is nearly $10,000. Even when the incomes of men and women working in the same occupations are examined, women consistently earn less money. A wage gap exists in all age groups and at every level of education.

You also read in Chapter 7 that the number of women in full-time executive, administrative, and managerial positions is increasing. These increases indicate to some that the "glass ceiling" is beginning to crack. The **glass ceiling** is the invisible barrier that prevents women from gaining upper-level positions in business. Yearly studies conducted by Catalyst, an organization that works to advance women in

Doctorates and Professional Degrees Awarded to Men and Women, 1980–2000

Source: U.S. Statistical Abstract, 2002

INTERPRETING GRAPHS Many women have sought new opportunities in profession careers. *What field saw the largest growth in women?*

SPOTLIGHT on Women in Sports

Have each student create a collage that illustrates the role of women in professional sports. Students might clip images of female athletes from magazines and newspapers, create their own illustrations, or include graphic organizers and text elements in their collages to convey the variety and intensity of women's participation in sports of all kinds. Encourage students to include images of young women participating in sports at their high school. Display students' collages in the classroom. **BLOCK SCHEDULING**

CONNECTING to the Arts

Have each student create a comic strip that illustrates an issue related to gender roles or gender inequality. For example, a comic strip might take a humorous look at working women and the second shift to illustrate inequalities between genders in the area of household duties and chores. Have each student draw the comic strip on a medium-sized posterboard. Call on volunteers to present their comic strips to the class and have students discuss the gender issues that the comic strips address. **BLOCK SCHEDULING**

Applying Sociology

Analyzing the Second Shift. Some sociologists cite the wage gap as one reason many married working women also perform most household duties—and are in effect, working a second shift. The reasoning is that most working wives earn less than their husbands. As a result, such women handle most of the duties at home to make up for the wage gap. Examinations of couples where the wives earned more than the husbands did not support this view, however. Even when they earned more than their husbands, the wives still performed most of the household duties.

ACTIVITY: Have students discuss both the effects of the wage and leisure gaps on women and society and possible ways to narrow or close these gaps.

Graph Answer

prejudice and institutionalized discrimination against women in the workplace and particularly at executive levels; the outdated view that men are usually the sole breadwinners in households and thus need larger salaries than women

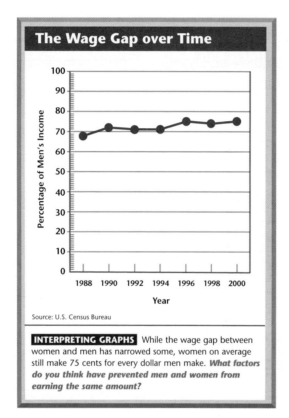

The Wage Gap over Time

Source: U.S. Census Bureau

INTERPRETING GRAPHS While the wage gap between women and men has narrowed some, women on average still make 75 cents for every dollar men make. *What factors do you think have prevented men and women from earning the same amount?*

Despite the challenges women still face in the workforce, some women have earned leadership positions, such as the president and COO of BET, Debra Lee, (bottom left) and the president and CEO of PBS, Pat Mitchell (bottom center).

business, suggest that small cracks are beginning to appear in the ceiling. In 2001 Catalyst found that women accounted for nearly 12 percent of corporate officers in America's 500 largest companies. This number represents a nearly 37 percent increase since 1995. However, the study also showed that women occupy few "line officer" positions—the jobs that have the most responsibility. Interestingly, men in traditionally female occupations—such as nursing, social work, and library administration—do not face a glass ceiling. Rather, they often quickly rise to high-level positions with top salaries.

Married women who work face a particular kind of gender inequality. Sociologist Arlie Hochschild noted that working wives work a **second shift**. After their day at work, they also have household duties to complete—such as cooking, cleaning, and child care. Most wives feel that their husbands should share in these tasks. However, Hochschild observed that most husbands adopt "strategies of resistance" to avoid them. For example, they do not volunteer, hoping that their wives will not ask them to help. According to Hochschild's observations, if husbands do undertake a task, some may make a mess of it in the hope that they will not be asked again. Where husbands do share in the second shift, wives still do the most work. Women in the United States have on average at least 10 hours per week less leisure time than men. Wives face not only a wage gap at work, but also a "leisure gap" at home.

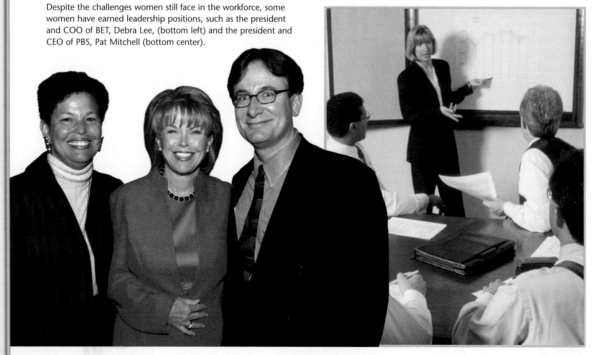

CLOSE

In a closing discussion, ask students to consider how their own gender-role socialization has affected their gender expectations of adult life. Ask volunteers to share some of their thoughts on this topic with the class.

REVIEW AND ASSESS

Have students complete the **Section 1 Review** on p. 271. As **Alternative Assessment**, you may want to use the self-fulfilling prophecy graphic organizer or the women's movement time line in this section's lessons.

RETEACH

Pair students and have partners review their notes from this section and compare them to the text of Section 1. Tell each pair to add to their notes if necessary and then to highlight the most important points in each part of the section.
ENGLISH LANGUAGE LEARNERS , COOPERATIVE LEARNING

EXTEND

Have students consider and list 5 to 10 gender stereotypes. Ask volunteers to share some of their stereotypes with the class for discussion. Then have students discuss ways in which they can avoid gender stereotyping. **BLOCK SCHEDULING**

The Political Arena There is also a political gender gap in the United States. Women make up 52 percent of the voting-age population, outnumbering men by some 7 million. They are more likely than men to vote in elections. Yet men dominate the political arena. For example, in 2000, women made up nearly 14 percent of the U.S. Congress—13 percent of senators and close to 14 percent of representatives. Women held 29 percent of statewide elective offices and 23 percent of state legislative seats. These figures represent large increases over previous years. In 1981 women made up 4 percent of the U.S. Congress, 11 percent of statewide elected officials, and 12 percent of state legislators. Even so, women still are underrepresented in government.

One development on the political scene is that many Americans seem open to women occupying public office—even the presidency. In a 1999 Gallup poll, 92 percent of the respondents said that they would be willing to vote for a woman as president. In a Roper poll taken in the same year, some 60 percent of respondents said that they expected a woman to be elected president in their lifetime. A more perceptible change is that women are being appointed to high office in growing numbers. In recent years, several women have held leadership roles in Congress. On taking office as president, George W. Bush appointed a number of women to positions of great responsibility. They included Elaine Chao as Secretary of Labor, Gale Norton as Secretary of the Interior, Condoleezza Rice as National Security Advisor, and Christine Todd Whitman as head of the Environmental Protection Agency.

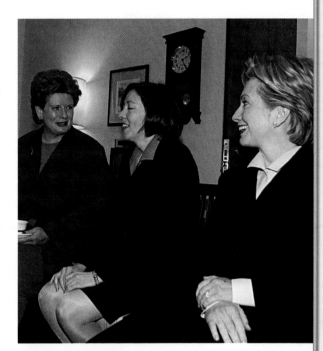

INTERPRETING VISUALS The number of women who serve in the federal government has risen in recent years. Americans have elected women to serve in the U.S. House of Representatives and Senate. Senators Hillary Rodham Clinton, Maria Cantwell, and Debbie Stabenow were each elected in the 2000 election. *How do you think the growing number of female representatives and senators might change government policies?*

Visual Answer

Government policies might increasingly address issues related to gender inequality and discrimination as well as issues traditionally important to women, such as child care.

SECTION 1 REVIEW ANSWERS

1. **Define:**
   - gender, p. 262
   - gender roles, p. 262
   - gender identity, p. 263
   - patriarchy, p. 265
   - sexism, p. 265
   - women's movement, p. 268
   - suffrage, p. 268
   - wage gap, p. 269
   - glass ceiling, p. 269
   - second shift, p. 270

2. education—still gender distinctions in degree majors, fewer women pursuing doctoral or professional degrees, and less funding for women's college athletics; employment—still a wage gap and a glass ceiling for women; politics—underrepresented in political office

3a. Men are expected to be more adventuresome, aggressive, physically active, and career-oriented; women are expected to be more passive and more involved in the home and child care.

b. Children learn American gender-role behaviors through socialization, such as in the family or at school.

4. Essays will vary, but students should support their conclusions with specific facts, statistics, and examples.

SECTION 1 REVIEW

1. **Define and explain**
   gender
   gender roles
   gender identity
   patriarchy
   sexism
   women's movement
   suffrage
   wage gap
   glass ceiling
   second shift

2. **Categorizing** Copy the graphic organizer below. Use it to identify examples of gender inequality in education, employment, and politics.

Area	Example of Gender Inequality
Education	
Employment	
Politics	

3. **Finding the Main Idea**
   a. How do gender expectations differ for men and women in the United States?
   b. How are gender roles affected by socialization in America?

4. **Writing and Critical Thinking**
   Supporting a Point of View Write a brief essay agreeing or disagreeing with the view that as more women enter—and stay in—the workforce, differences in gender roles will fade.
   Consider:
   - explanations for why gender inequality exists
   - progress made by women toward gender equality

Homework Practice Online
keyword: SL3 HP11

🎵 LET'S GET STARTED!

As students enter the classroom, ask them to flip through the pages of Section 2 to get a feeling for what they will learn. Then instruct students to write a list of 5 to 10 things that they expect to learn from the section based on their examination and to save the list for future reference. Tell students that in Section 2 they will learn about the aging of the population and its effects on American society and on the lives of aging individuals.

SECTION 2 RESOURCES

REPRODUCIBLE & REVIEW

- Study Skills and Writing Guide
- Section 2 Review, p. 277

TECHNOLOGY

- One-Stop Planner, Lesson 11.2
- **CNN** Presents Sociology: ADA Anniversary
- Teaching Transparency: The Graying of America
- Homework Practice Online
- HRW Go site

Visual Answer

Glenn's experience shows that senior citizens can be active and productive members of society.

2
AGE AND DISABILITY

● Read to Discover

1. What effect is the aging of the population having on society?

2. How is the aging of the population affecting the life chances of older Americans?

● Define

ageism, graying of America, baby-boom generation, dependency ratio, Medicare, Medicaid

---

Different societies place different values on age. In preindustrial societies, the social standing of individuals increased with age. The older members of society were viewed as sources of knowledge and as the enforcers of social customs. In industrial societies, middle-aged people hold the greatest social power. Employment is one of the major indicators of social status in industrial societies, and employment opportunities decline with age. The closer people get to retirement age, the more difficult it is for them to find re-employment in the event of job loss. Job-retraining programs are seldom geared toward older workers.

Ageism

Ageism—the belief that one age category is by nature superior to another age category—is at the heart of age-based role loss. Although ageism can apply to any age group, it is most often directed toward elderly people in industrial societies. One way in which ageism can be seen is in the stereotypes used to portray elderly citizens. They are often shown as unproductive, cranky, and physically or mentally impaired. In reality, the vast majority of people aged 65 and older are self-sufficient, active members of society.

In American society, the media reinforces ageism. For example, in television commercials elderly people are seldom used to sell household products, cosmetics, clothing, or automobiles. Instead, they endorse products such as over-the-counter medications, health-related devices, denture preparations, or insurance and burial plans. Moreover, news coverage of senior citizens often focuses on the negative aspects of aging, such as poor health, poverty, and loneliness.

Efforts are now being made to change the image Americans have of people aged 65 and older. In the United States, television programs, movies, and children's books that present older adults as positive role models are beginning to appear. Nevertheless, much age discrimination still exists. This ageism is particularly significant in light of current world population trends.

INTERPRETING VISUALS In 1998 astronaut John Glenn, at the age of 77, became the oldest person to travel in space. *How do you think Glenn's experience provides a positive example of life as a senior citizen?*

To help students understand how the aging of the population is affecting American society, copy the graphic organizer at the right onto the chalkboard, omitting the italicized answers. Have students copy and complete the organizer. Discuss the answers with the class. Then because several of the answers are negative effects, ask students for some positive effects of an aging population. *(Students might note some of the following: People are healthier and live longer lives. More young people get to enjoy spending time with their grandparents and vice versa. A more powerful elderly voting bloc means an increased focus on and reduction of problems for elderly people.)*

ENGLISH LANGUAGE LEARNERS

Effects of an Aging Population on American Society

Economic Effects
rising cost of health care; cost of Social Security; burden to family and younger workers; living longer in retirement

Political Effects
becoming a stronger political force; organized voting bloc (AARP, etc.) focusing on health care, retirement, and Social Security

The Aging World

The world's population is aging. Today there are approximately 606 million people aged 60 and older worldwide. It is estimated that by the year 2050, this number will have grown to almost 2 billion. Europe—with a population median age of 37.7—is the oldest region of the world. In contrast, Africa is the world's youngest region, with a median population age of 18.4. Projections suggest that over the first half of the 2000s, the European population will continue to age. By 2050, the median age will be 49.5 and close to 40 percent of Europeans will be age 60 and older. While Africa's population will also age, it will remain the world's youngest region. By 2050, people age 60 and older will outnumber children under the age of 15 by nearly three to one in Europe. The chart on this page shows the age composition of various world regions.

Population trends in the United States reflect what is happening worldwide. In 2000 about 12 percent of the population in the United States was aged 65 or older. This figure is expected to hold steady through the year 2010 and then rise to nearly 19 percent by the year 2025. Moreover, by the year 2050, one in every five Americans will be elderly. Sociologists refer to this phenomenon as the "**graying of America.**" The chart on page 274 presents selected statistics on the graying of America.

There are two primary reasons for the graying of America. First, advances in health care and better living conditions have resulted in more people surviving into old age. Second, variations in birthrates have changed the age structure of the United States. Birthrates in the United States rose sharply in 1946 and stayed about the same until the 1960s when they noticeably declined. The approximately 76 million children born during this

Applying Sociology

Myths About Old Age. The lives of many older Americans do not support stereotypes about senior citizens. Studies show that the productivity and attendance of workers above age 65 actually exceeds that of younger age groups. In addition, 95 percent of people above age 65 live in private dwellings, and only 7 percent show symptoms of senility.

CRITICAL THINKING
How do stereotypes about seniors contribute to ageism?

ANSWER: Such stereotypes justify people's beliefs that elderly people are less able than younger adults to hold jobs or be self-sufficient.

Table Answer

Europe, North America, and Oceania

Age Composition of the Population in Major Regions and Areas

Major Area and Region	Percentage of Population Under 15	Percentage of Population Aged 15 to 64	Percentage of Population 65 and Over
Africa	43	54	3
East Africa	46	51	3
Middle Africa	47	50	3
North Africa	38	58	4
Southern Africa	35	60	5
West Africa	45	52	3
Asia	32	62	6
East Asia	25	67	8
South-Central Asia	37	59	4
Southeast Asia	34	62	4
Western Asia	37	59	4
Europe	19	66	15
Eastern Europe	20	67	13
Northern Europe	19	66	15
Southern Europe	17	67	16
Western Europe	17	68	15
Latin America and the Caribbean	33	62	5
Caribbean	31	62	7
Central America (includes Mexico)	36	60	4
South America	32	62	6
North America (Canada and the United States)	21	66	13
Oceania	26	64	10
Australia/New Zealand	22	66	12
Micronesia/Melanesia/Polynesia	39	58	3

Source: Population Reference Bureau, *2001 World Population Data Sheet*

INTERPRETING TABLES Highly industrialized nations often have advanced health-care systems that help people live longer. Such systems affect the age composition of these countries. *Which continents have the highest percentage of population over 65?*

SPOTLIGHT on Social Security

Organize students into two groups and assign the groups opposing positions for a formal debate on Social Security. One side should argue for methods of preserving the present system. The other side should argue for either abolishing the current system or changing it drastically. Tell students that they must support their points with statistics, facts, and statements from authorities on the subject. Allow students time to conduct research to prepare their arguments. Then serve as the moderator during the debate and provide each side with specific amounts of time to present its points and to make rebuttals. **COOPERATIVE LEARNING ,**
BLOCK SCHEDULING

SPOTLIGHT on the Elderly in the Media

Have students watch a night or two of television while making notes about positive, negative, and neutral portrayals of elderly people in television shows, movies, and news programs. In addition, have students note any differences in how older and newer shows portray elderly people. In class, call on students to report on their observations. Then use the results as the basis for a class discussion about how the popular media in the United States portrays senior citizens and some reasons for this portrayal. *(Negative portrayals may be the result of ageism, while more positive portrayals might be evidence of the baby-boom generation's growing influence.)*
BLOCK SCHEDULING

Sociology in the World Today

Widowhood. According to the 2000 U.S. Census, almost half of American women age 65 and older are widows. About 70 percent of widowed women live alone, and two fifths are living below the poverty level within five years of their husbands' deaths. In addition, older widowed women are far less likely to remarry than older widowed men. One reason is that men tend to choose younger mates, while women tend to choose older mates.

ACTIVITY: Have students discuss the societal effects of a growing population of elderly widows.

Table Answer

the aging baby-boom generation and the decline in the birthrate following this generation, increasing life expectancy rates as a result of advances in health care and better living conditions

Technology Resources

Teaching Transparency: The Graying of America

The Graying of America

Characteristic	1970	1990	2010
2010 Population			
Aged 65–84 (in millions)	18.7	28.2	33.7
85 and over (in millions)	1.4	3.1	5.7
65+ as percentage of population	10%	12%	13%
Life Expectancy			
Total	70.8	75.4	77.4
Male	67.1	72.0	74.1
Female	74.7	78.8	80.6
White	71.7	76.0	78.3
African American	64.1	70.3	70.4

Source: U.S. Census Bureau

INTERPRETING TABLES Based on population projections, demographers have predicted that the U.S. population will have many more older citizens. *What factors have contributed to these projections?*

period are known as the **baby-boom generation**. After the early 1960s the birthrate began to drop and has remained relatively low ever since. This rise in the birthrate, followed by a decline, made the baby-boom generation the largest segment of the American population. Today baby boomers are in their late thirties to mid-fifties. By the year 2030, all of the baby boomers will have reached at least 65 years of age, thereby swelling the ranks of the elderly population to nearly 70 million.

The Politics of Aging

The changing age structure of the United States has thrust elderly people into the center of American politics. In short order, they have become both a political force and a topic of debate. Recently, the image of the elderly population has changed from one of an underprivileged and forgotten segment of society to one of a powerful and effective voting bloc. Exactly how organized a voting bloc senior citizens represent is unclear. However, what is clear is that few politicians today are willing to run the risk of

One political issue important to older Americans is how they are portrayed in the media. They are concerned that senior citizens be shown in active roles. More retired Americans are finding enjoyment in physical excerise such as Tai Chi.

ignoring the needs of older Americans. The influence of elderly people on the political process is likely to continue to grow as the ranks of older Americans swell with the aging of the baby boomers.

Several groups work to bring the special needs of the elderly to national attention. Among the largest are the American Association of Retired Persons (AARP), the National Council of Senior Citizens, the National Council on Aging, and the Gray Panthers. The AARP is one of the most successful of these organizations. With more than 34 million members, the AARP is the largest special-interest group in the United States. In addition to its political lobbying efforts, the AARP provides many services for its members. These services include financial advice, health-insurance plans, and travel and prescription-drug discounts. In addition, the AARP publishes the magazine *Modern Maturity,* produces weekly radio programs, and operates a Web site.

One of the major issues of concern for older Americans is the Social Security system. Some people have expressed fears that the system is not up to the task of caring for future generations of elderly people. The Social Security system is funded by payroll or income taxes on workers, employers, and the self-employed. Current payroll taxes fund the benefits paid to current retirees. However, declining birthrates and longer life expectancies mean that there are fewer workers available to support growing numbers of retirees. In 1960 the **dependency ratio**—the number of workers for each person receiving Social Security benefits—stood at 5 to 1. By 1998 the ratio had declined to just more than three workers for every retiree. In 2030 when all the baby boomers reach retirement age, the ratio will have dropped to 2 to 1.

Longer life expectancies have created another challenge for the Social Security system. Because of increasing life expectancies, the fastest growth in the elderly population is among the old-old—individuals aged 85 and older. For example, in 1970 there were approximately 1.4 million Americans aged 85 or older. By 1990 the number had reached 3 million. Projections show that by 2010 there will be nearly 5.8 million old-old—about 15 percent of the elderly population. Therefore, not only is the number of people receiving Social Security benefits increasing, but so is the length of time people receive those benefits.

The old-old present another challenge, because they are most likely to be in poorest health. This challenge places an added strain on government transfer-payments programs, particularly Medicare and Medicaid. **Medicare** is the government-sponsored health-insurance plan for elderly Americans and Americans with disabilities. **Medicaid** is the state and federally funded health-insurance program for low-income individuals. These programs are the sole sources of health insurance for close to one quarter of elderly Americans.

Ways to ensure the future of Social Security have stirred much heated debate. Some people have suggested raising the retirement age, cutting benefits, or increasing

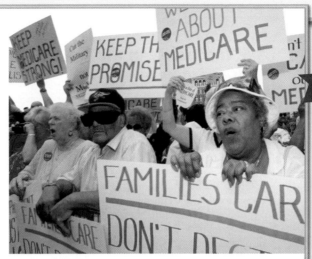

Many senior citizens are politically active, particularly on the issues of Social Security and Medicare.

Social Security payroll taxes. Others have pointed out that including state and local government workers have raised contributions markedly. Still others have suggested that individuals or Social Security administrators should have the freedom to invest funds in the stock market. However, none of these solutions has received the enthusiastic backing of a majority of Americans.

Careers
IN SOCIOLOGY

GERONTOLOGIST

Gerontologists study the processes and phenomena of aging. Most sociologists who specialize in gerontology focus on the social aspects of aging. Because the U.S. population is aging, gerontology is a rapidly growing area of specialization in the field of sociology.

Gerontologists assist in setting policies for senior citizens and in assessing the needs of an aging population. Related to the field of gerontology are the health fields and service industries geared toward the needs of the elderly. Geriatrics is the branch of medicine that deals with the diseases and health problems of the elderly. Like gerontology, geriatrics is a rapidly expanding field.

Gerontologists are concerned with the effects of aging on the social life of Americans.

TEACH OBJECTIVE 2

SUGGESTION 1: Lead a class discussion about how the graying of America is affecting American society and the life chances of elderly people. During the discussion, have students take notes. Then instruct students to use their notes to compose five-minute speeches about the aging of the American population and the various effects of this phenomenon. Students may write their speeches from the point of view of educators who want to inform the public or from the point of view of political activists seeking change. Have students present their speeches to the class.

SUGGESTION 2: Organize students into groups of three and have each group write three contrasting descriptions of typical elderly people's lives. For example, group members might write about one person who is among the old-old and living in poverty, one elderly person who has just reached retirement age and has saved enough to live comfortably for 20 years, and one elderly person who is dependent upon Social Security and Medicare. Students should write two to three paragraphs about each person, taking care to describe a realistic lifestyle for the elderly person in each case. Invite groups to share their descriptions with the class. Then have students summarize how the aging of the population is affecting the life chances of older Americans.
COOPERATIVE LEARNING

■ internet connect ≡

TOPIC: Technology for People with Disabilities
GO TO: go.hrw.com
KEYWORD: SL3 SC11

Have students access the Internet through the HRW Go site to conduct research on the ways in which technology is being employed to help people with disabilities. Then have each student write a short report describing some of the products he or she learned about in the research.

Did You Know?

Many famous people throughout history have overcome disabilities to accomplish great things. The German composer Ludwig van Beethoven wrote many of his masterpieces after becoming deaf. American inventor Thomas Edison was also deaf for much of his life. U.S. president Franklin D. Roosevelt was partially paralyzed as a result of polio.

Technology Resources

CNN. Presents Sociology: ADA Anniversary

Age Inequality in the United States

Some people claim that government transfer payments like Social Security have made older Americans financially secure at the expense of younger generations. They base this claim on the falling poverty rate among Americans aged 65 and older. In 1959, 35 percent of older Americans lived in poverty. Today the poverty rate for the elderly is 10.2 percent. In comparison, the poverty rate is 11.3 percent for the general population and about 16.2 percent for children under the age of 18.

On the surface, these statistics paint a positive picture for older Americans. However, they mask a great deal of variation in living conditions among the different segments of the elderly population. When viewed from the perspective of race and gender, poverty among older Americans looks very different. For example, more than 22 percent of elderly African Americans live in poverty. For older Hispanics, the figure is about 19 percent. Poverty among elderly white Americans, on the other hand, is more than 8 percent. Women are harder hit by poverty than are men. About 12 percent of women aged 65 and older are poor, compared to 7 percent of elderly men. Among elderly African American and Hispanic women, the figures are about 26 percent and 25 percent, respectively. Poverty levels are also higher among the old-old.

The poverty level for a single person aged 85 or older is more than $8,250 a year. For elderly couples, the poverty level is about $10,400. Social Security benefits and other government transfer payments have managed to pull most elderly individuals above that level, but often by only a few hundred dollars. Thus, many elderly people are living their lives in conditions of near-poverty.

Americans with Disabilities

Disabilities also affect many older Americans. There are 53 million people with disabilities in the United States. The term disability covers a wide variety of conditions. These include physical disabilities; chronic health impairments; mental retardation; mental illness; and visual, hearing, or speech impairments. Disabilities vary in level of severity, as well. The severest forms of disability include blindness, deafness, and paralysis. About 33 million Americans have severe disabilities.

Prejudice and Discrimination In addition to dealing with their health problems, Americans with disabilities have to deal with prejudice and discrimination. A particular problem for people with disabilities is the stereotypical belief that their disabilities make them incapable of doing productive work. As a consequence, people with disabilities often have difficulty finding meaningful employment. Unemployment rates are high, particularly among those with severe disabilities. Those who do work usually receive lower-than-average wages. Not surprisingly, many Americans with disabilities receive some form of government assistance but still struggle to make ends meet. For example, some 28 percent of Americans with severe disabilities live below the poverty line.

Disability rights activists have struggled for decades to gain the civil rights afforded to other groups in society. Over the years, they have had some success. For

Sociologists have studied the social interactions and norms developed by Americans with disabilities.

CLOSE

Have students refer back to the lists of things they expected to learn in this section, which they made in the *Let's Get Started!* activity. Then discuss with students any topics they listed that were not addressed in the section.

REVIEW AND ASSESS

Have students complete the **Section 2 Review** on p. 277. As **Alternative Assessment**, you may want to use the interviews or speeches in this section's lessons.

RETEACH

Have each student create an outline of the material in this section and highlight the most important points. Then have the class help you create a master outline on the chalkboard. As you create the outline, have students point out the main ideas that they highlighted. **ENGLISH LANGUAGE LEARNERS**

EXTEND

Have students conduct research to locate statistical information about how many elderly Americans lived in poverty in each decade between 1950 and the present. Instruct students to create line or bar graphs to represent the information. **BLOCK SCHEDULING**

example, the Education for All Handicapped Children Act of 1975 guaranteed children with disabilities a public education geared toward their needs and abilities. In 1988 the Fair Housing Amendments Act gave persons with disabilities protection from discrimination in housing.

The ADA The Americans with Disabilities Act (ADA) of 1990 has the potential to bring the most sweeping changes in the lives of people with disabilities. The ADA addresses four main areas: employment, public services, public accommodations, and telecommunications. In employment, the ADA makes it illegal to discriminate against people with disabilities in hiring, promotion, and pay. In addition, to improve opportunities for people with disabilities, the ADA requires companies to provide job training and aids, such as readers or interpreters. However, companies do not have to comply if they can show that doing so would cause undue economic hardship.

The ADA also makes it illegal to deny Americans with disabilities the benefit of public services, including transportation. This provision means that all new public buses and trains must be made accessible to citizens with disabilities. The ADA also requires changes in public accommodations. Hotels, restaurants, theaters, and other businesses that serve the public must make their facilities accessible to people with disabilities. In telecommunications, the ADA requires that telephone companies provide telecommunications-relay services (TRS). TRS allows communication between regular telephones and the text telephones used by the hearing-impaired and speech-impaired. These services must be available 24 hours a day. Rates for relay calls can be no higher than rates for calls on regular telephones.

The ADA has brought some improvement to the lives of Americans with disabilities but much remains to be done. One of the main goals of the ADA was to increase employment opportunities for people with disabilities. However, since its passage, employment rates among Americans with disabilities have risen only slightly. Finding meaningful employment remains a major problem for those with disabilities. As one observer noted, "The A.D.A. unlocked the door, but didn't push it open."

INTERPRETING VISUALS Many Americans with disabilities enjoy physical activities similar to those enjoyed by Americans without disabilities. *How might this skier be a role model to Americans with disabilities?*

SECTION 2 REVIEW

1. **Define and explain**
   ageism
   graying of America
   baby-boom generation
   dependency ratio
   Medicare
   Medicaid

2. **Identifying Cause and Effect** Copy the graphic organizer below. Use it to identify and describe the factors that led to the graying of America.

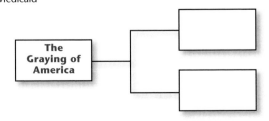

3. **Finding the Main Idea**
   a. How has the aging of the population affected American society?
   b. How does social inequality affect Americans 65 years of age or older?

4. **Writing and Critical Thinking**
   Making Generalizations and Predictions Write two or three paragraphs detailing the steps you would take to ensure the future of the Social Security system. Consider:
   • the problems facing the Social Security system, such as the growing number of recipients and the changes in the dependency ratio
   • solutions already offered
   • the possible effects of these solutions

Homework Practice Online
keyword: SL3 HP11

Visual Answer

by proving that disabled Americans can remain physically active and have fun

SECTION 2 REVIEW ANSWERS

1. **Define:**
   • ageism, p. 272
   • graying of America, p. 273
   • baby-boom generation, p. 274
   • dependency ratio, p. 274
   • Medicare, p. 275
   • Medicaid, p. 275

2. the aging baby-boom generation and the decline in the birthrate following that generation, increasing life expectancies because of advances in health care and better living conditions

3a. Elderly people have become a political force and a topic of debate, bringing greater attention to issues such as Social Security and Medicare.

b. Many elderly Americans face discrimination because of ageism or live in poverty, particularly minorities.

4. Paragraphs will vary, but students should consider in detail both the causes of the problems facing the Social Security system and the potential effects of their proposed solutions.

Building Social Studies Skills

◼ TEACH

Have students read the feature Interpreting Statistics and Using Census Data on pp. 278–79 and answer the questions under Applying the Skill. Discuss the answers with the class. Then have students use almanacs and other sources of statistical information to find and copy one or two charts and graphs about sociological topics that interest them. Instruct students to go through the steps described in the feature to interpret the data and then to summarize the charts and graphs in paragraph form. Finally, have students complete the assignment under Practicing the Skill as homework.

◼ EXTEND

Have students present the information in one of the tables in this feature in another form, such as in a graph. For example, students might choose to show the information in the table Percentage of Adults Engaging in Leisure-Time Physical Activity, 1998 in the form of a bar graph. Display students' completed graphs in the classroom. **BLOCK SCHEDULING**

INTERPRETING STATISTICS AND USING CENSUS DATA

Have students flip through their textbooks to locate other charts and graphs providing statistical data. Then have each student select one chart or graph, examine it, and write responses to each of the five steps listed on p. 278 for interpreting statistics and using census data. Ask volunteers to indicate the charts or graphs they selected. Then have the class examine them together.

BUILDING

Social Studies Skills

INTERPRETING STATISTICS AND USING CENSUS DATA

Many studies have established that regular physical activity contributes to good health and mental well-being. But how many Americans and what section of the American population exercise regularly? To find an answer to this question, sociologists would start by examining statistical reports. The data collected and recorded by the U.S. Bureau of the Census is particularly useful in answering sociologists' many questions.

The Census Bureau provides statistical information on all manner of topics, including population, health, education, income and wealth, employment, and trade. This information is organized into charts, graphs, and tables. By analyzing such data, sociologists are able to note trends and draw conclusions about various social, economic, and political issues.

How to Interpret Statistics and Use Census Data

To interpret statistics published by the Census Bureau, use the following guidelines.

1. **Identify the type of data.** Note the title of the chart, table, or graph. Also, study any headings, subheadings, and labels.

2. **Examine the components.** Note the specific statistics given under each heading or subheading. Check to see if any information about the statistics is given in the title. Also, look at the source of the data to see how current it is.

3. **Identify relationships among the data.** Note trends in the data. Determine comparisons as well as any cause-and-effect relationships.

4. **Read footnotes.** Pay attention to asterisks or other symbols that refer to footnotes.

5. **Make generalizations and draw conclusions.** Make a general statement based on the information. Also, try to draw conclusions from the statistics. If the chart, table, or graph is part of a text discussion, you can formulate generalizations and conclusions by looking for key words and phrases in the accompanying text.

Study the table on this page. The title indicates that the subject is the percentage of adults who engaged in leisure-time physical activity during 1998. The table is divided into different population characteristics, and percentages are given for different levels of physical activity.

Notice that participation rates differ from one population characteristic to another. For example,

Percentage of Adults Engaging in Leisure-Time Physical Activity, 1998			
Characteristic	No Participation	Participation in Regular, Sustained Activity*	Participation in Regular, Vigorous Activity#
Total	28.7	20.8	13.6
Male	26.2	21.9	13.3
Female	31.0	19.7	13.8
White, non-Hispanic	26.7	21.6	14.0
Black, non-Hispanic	33.8	17.8	12.3
Hispanic	38.4	17.4	11.4
Other	28.8	21.8	14.3

* Any type or intensity of activity 5 or more times per week and 30 minutes or more per session.
\# Rhythmic contraction of large muscle groups at 50 percent or more of capacity, 3 times per week or more for at least 20 minutes per session.
Source: *Statistical Abstract of the United States*

CONNECTING *to Government*

Tell students that some Americans object to the number and types of personal questions asked on the U.S. Census questionnaire. These people believe that some of the questions are an intrusion on their privacy. However, sociologists, politicians, and others rely heavily on census data in drawing conclusions about the U.S. population. Ask students to find out more about this debate and to examine a sample Census form for reference. Then have each student write a position paper expressing and defending his or her point of view on the topic. **BLOCK SCHEDULING**

SPOTLIGHT *on Statisticians*

Have students look up the job description of a statistician. Then instruct each student to use the information to write a bulleted list of the types of skills and education a person needs to become a statistician *(strong math, logic, and reasoning skills; attention to detail; interest in facts and trends; and so on)*. Finally, have students examine the types of jobs available to statisticians. Ask students to share their findings in an informal class discussion. **BLOCK SCHEDULING**

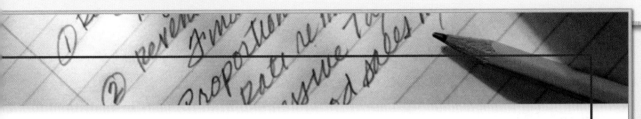

APPLYING THE SKILL ANSWERS

1. percentage of adults who engage in leisure-time physical activity by level of education and household income; provides data on the same general topic but by different factors

2. The second table is grouped by level of education and household income as well as by level of physical activity.

3. college (16 or more years)

4. less than $10,000

5. Answers will vary, but students should recognize the connection between higher education and income levels and greater participation in leisure-time physical activity.

Percentage of Adults Engaging in Leisure-Time Physical Activity by Level of Education and Household Income, 1998

Characteristic	No Participation	Participation in Regular, Sustained Activity*	Participation in Regular, Vigorous Activity#
School Years Completed			
Less than 12 years	49.7	14.3	8.2
12 years	33.9	18.2	10.7
Some College (12–15 years)	23.9	22.3	13.9
College (16 or more years)	16.3	25.7	19.7
Household Income			
Less than $10,000	42.4	17.8	10.7
$10,000 to $19,999	39.8	16.9	10.5
$20,000 to $34,999	31.3	19.4	12.1
$35,000 to $49,999	24.4	21.4	14.0
$50,000 and over	16.9	25.5	17.6

* Any type or intensity of activity 5 or more times per week and 30 minutes or more per session.
# Rhythmic contraction of large muscle groups at 50 percent or more of capacity, 3 times per week or more for at least 20 minutes per session.
Source: *Statistical Abstract of the United States*

21.9 percent of men engaged in regular, sustained activity, while 19.7 percent of women did so. For participation in regular, vigorous activity, the results were reversed—13.3 percent for men, and 13.8 percent for women. Also, white nonparticipation stood at 26.7 percent, while 33.8 percent of African Americans and 38.4 percent of Hispanics did not participate in physical activity.

Several generalizations can be made from this information. First, women are more likely than men not to participate in physical activity. Second, white Americans are more likely to participate in both regular, sustained and regular, vigorous physical activity than African Americans and Hispanics. Finally, of those who participate in some form of physical activity, more are likely to do regular, sustained activity than regular, vigorous activity.

Applying the Skill

Study the table on this page. Then answer the following questions.

1. **Finding the Main Idea** What is the subject of the table? How does this table relate to the one on the previous page?

2. **Analyzing Information** How is the information presented in the table?
3. **Comparing** At which level of education is there the greatest participation in physical activity?
4. **Evaluating** At which income level is there the least participation in physical activity?
5. **Drawing Inferences and Conclusions** What generalizations can you make about the information in this table?

Practicing the Skill

Use U.S. Census Bureau information found in the **Statistical Abstract of the United States** *to find data on changes in the life expectancy of the U.S. population. Use the information in the census table to create a chart or graph.*

Practicing the Skill

To extend the activity, have students create additional charts or graphs that show life expectancy by characteristics such as education, income level, or race and ethnicity.

OBJECTIVES

1. *Describe the state of health care in the United States.*

2. *Identify some of the special health-care concerns of various segments of American society.*

SECTION 3 RESOURCES

REPRODUCIBLE & REVIEW

- Graphic Organizer 11
- Research Projects and Activities for Teaching Sociology 11
- Section 3 Review, p. 287

TECHNOLOGY

- One-Stop Planner, Lesson 11.3
- Teaching Transparency: The Health-Care Spending Dollar, 1999
- Homework Practice Online
- HRW Go site

Visual Answer

costs of hospital care, increased number and use of diagnostic tests, increased spending on prescription drugs

---

🎙 *LET'S GET STARTED!*

Before class, research the cost of the following medical services in your area: a private hospital room, a semiprivate hospital room, a visit to the doctor's office, a school physical examination, the setting of a broken arm, a blood test, and the delivery of a baby without complications. Write these items on the chalkboard, without their associated costs. As students enter the classroom, ask them to write down estimates for the cost of each of these services. Then write some of the students' responses on the chalkboard and compare them to the actual costs. Tell students that in Section 3 they will learn about health care in the United States.

---

③ HEALTH

● Read to Discover

1. What is the state of health care in the United States?

2. What are some of the special health-care concerns of various segments of American society?

● Define

managed care, alternative medicine, acquired immune deficiency syndrome (AIDS)

In a 1995 nationwide Gallup poll, respondents rated the quality and cost of health care as one of the most important problems facing the country. Four years later, a poll conducted by the Discovery Channel and *Newsweek* found that 61 percent of respondents were frustrated or angry with the country's health-care system. An examination of the state of health care in the United States will help you understand the American public's concerns.

Health Care in the United States

As you might guess from the Gallup poll results, people's worries about the American health-care system focus on two major issues. These are health-care costs and the quality of the health care that people receive. People also express concern about a third issue—access to health care.

Cost of Health Care The United States spends a higher percentage of its gross domestic product (GDP) on health care than any other country in the world. In 2000 health-care expenditures in the United States exceeded $1.3 trillion, an increase of 88 percent over 1990 expenditures. Estimates suggest that health-care costs will top $2 trillion by 2006. Everything from the cost of a stay in the hospital to health-insurance premiums has increased steadily in recent years. For example, American health-insurance companies paid approximately $61 billion for health care in 1980. By 2000 this figure had increased to almost $387 billion. Similarly, Medicare payments increased from about $107 billion in 1990 to nearly $219 billion in 2000. Group health-insurance plans also have shown marked cost increases. Between 1992 and 2000 health-insurance costs for large American companies rose at an annual rate of about 7 percent. Most employers expect costs to rise at an even faster rate over the first years of the 2000s.

Many factors have contributed to the rapid rise in health-care costs. At the top of the list is hospital care, which accounts for nearly 32 percent of all medical expenditures. In recent years, hospitals have been attempting to contain costs through shorter hospital stays and increased treatment on an outpatient basis. Even with those efforts, hospital care cost the country nearly $416 billion in 2000.

Advances in medical technology have also affected health-care costs. Doctors now have at their disposal more than 1,000 diagnostic tests, ranging from simple blood tests to high-technology techniques. Some of these tests, such as magnetic resonance imaging (MRI) and computerized axial tomography (CAT) scanning, are very

INTERPRETING VISUALS Although new technologies are used to advance the quality of health care available to Americans, the costs of health care have also increased. *What factors have contributed to the rise in health-care costs?*

TEACH OBJECTIVE 1

Organize students into seven groups and assign each group one of the following topics: health care costs, quality of health care, access to health care, inequality and health, health insurance, alternative medicine, or AIDS. Have group members refer to their textbooks and other available resources to prepare 8- to 10-minute lessons on their assigned topics. Then have groups take turns teaching their topics to the rest of the class. Encourage students to take notes on each other's presentations. Fill in or correct any missing or incorrect information in students' lessons. **COOPERATIVE LEARNING**

HOMEWORK: Have students create posters that call the public's attention to issues related to health care. Students might choose to convey messages about improving access to health care, address a specific problem such as AIDS, praise advances in medical research or technology, encourage people to enter the health-care industry, or address another relevant topic. Display students' completed posters in the classroom.

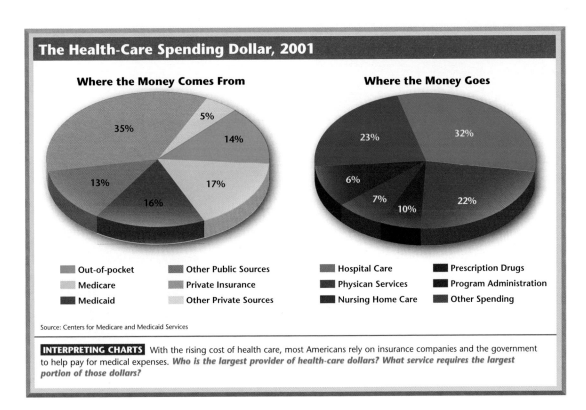

The Health-Care Spending Dollar, 2001

Where the Money Comes From

- 5%
- 14%
- 35%
- 13%
- 16%
- 17%

Legend:
- Out-of-pocket
- Medicare
- Medicaid
- Other Public Sources
- Private Insurance
- Other Private Sources

Where the Money Goes

- 23%
- 32%
- 6%
- 7%
- 10%
- 22%

Legend:
- Hospital Care
- Physican Services
- Nursing Home Care
- Prescription Drugs
- Program Administration
- Other Spending

Source: Centers for Medicare and Medicaid Services

INTERPRETING CHARTS With the rising cost of health care, most Americans rely on insurance companies and the government to help pay for medical expenses. *Who is the largest provider of health-care dollars? What service requires the largest portion of those dollars?*

expensive to administer. Nevertheless, many doctors rely heavily on such testing in their efforts to provide the best health care possible. Fears of malpractice lawsuits have also played a part in the increased use of these expensive diagnostic techniques. Doctors—particularly those in high-risk specialty areas—often order batteries of tests simply as a precaution against possible lawsuits. As a result, many of the diagnostic tests involved in defensive medicine, as it is called, may be unnecessary. Estimates suggest that somewhere between 5 and 9 percent of health-care spending goes toward defensive medicine.

Another reason for rising health-care costs is increased spending on prescription drugs. Prescription-drug costs have been rising at double-digit rates recently. Prescription drugs are the fastest-rising cost item for many group health-insurance plans. Drug costs have risen for several reasons. First, drug companies have increased their spending on advertising and marketing their products, thus driving up prices. Second, drugs are becoming the preferred form of treatment for many illnesses. Third, the number of elderly Americans—the leading consumers of prescription drugs—is rapidly increasing.

Escalating medical costs affect all sectors of society. Medicare and Medicaid account for 33 percent of the country's medical expenditures. Medical costs account for

a sizable chunk of the federal budget. A share of medical expenditures comes from business in the form of health-insurance premiums. Businesses can ask their employees to share increased health-insurance costs, or they can cover the costs themselves by accepting lower profits or raising prices. American consumers also share the burden of increasing medical costs. About 14 percent of annual health-care spending—about $200 billion—comes directly out of consumer's pockets. The effects of such expenditures can be seen in the fact that many personal bankruptcies are caused by huge medical bills.

Quality of Health Care One popular method of controlling health expenditures is the use of alternative health-insurance plans called **managed care**. Although there are several types of managed-care plans, they generally follow the same pattern. In return for a set monthly or annual charge, plan members receive health-care services. The plan limits costs by requiring patients to choose approved doctors who have agreed to reduced rates, requiring approval for treatments, and setting limits on drugs that can be prescribed. According to estimates, 75 percent of Americans with private health insurance—some 160 million—are members of managed-care plans.

Connecting to Science and Technology

▧ TEACH

Have students read the feature Doctors Online and answer the questions under Think About It. Then ask students if they or anyone they know has ever referred to health-related Web sites for information about medical conditions, treatments, or support groups. Ask students why they think such online medical sites are so popular. *(People can find out if their symptoms warrant a doctor's visit, they can find others dealing with the same conditions and get support and advice, and they can research available treatments and facilities.)*

▧ EXTEND

If possible, download a few sample pages from two different health-related Web sites. You might want to select a specific medical condition, such as Hodgkin's Disease, as the subject of some of the pages you download from both sites. Distribute copies of the pages to students and have them work in small groups to compare and contrast the types of information and services that each Web site provides. Then ask each group to orally evaluate the sites and to select the one the group thinks would be more useful.

COOPERATIVE LEARNING , BLOCK SCHEDULING

Think About It Answers

1. information on common and not so common ailments, sales of prescription drugs and other health-related products, chat groups on various medical topics, advice from doctors

2. advantages—can help inform people about their illnesses and treatments, can help people better evaluate their doctors or treatments, can provide people with health-related support groups, can make it easier for housebound people to obtain medications; problems—may prescribe drugs without proper diagnoses, might provide information that is inaccurate, might lead some people to engage in self-diagnosis without adequate medical training

CONNECTING TO
Science and Technology

DOCTORS ONLINE

Today more and more Americans are seeking medical advice not in face-to-face visits with doctors but on the Internet. A recent survey found that nearly 30 percent of Americans have sought health information online. They certainly have plenty of information from which to search. Estimates suggest that there are somewhere between 15,000 and 20,000 health-related Web sites.

Health-Sites Services

With so many sites, there are a wide variety of services available to consumers. However, most sites offer one or more of the following services.

- *Information on common and not-so-common ailments, including symptoms and various treatments available* Some sites carry regular articles on health issues of the day.
- *Sales of prescription drugs, over-the-counter medicines, vitamins, nutritional substitutes, and other health-related products* Many of the larger health sites have forged partnerships with online drug stores. Many health sites also get most of their income from advertising and the sale of health-related products.
- *Chat groups where people with the same medical problems can meet and compare information* Many sites also provide access to support groups for sick people and their families.
- *Advice from doctors* Some sites provide an e-mail advice service. Consumers mail in their questions and receive a response from a doctor a short time later. Other sites offer real-time, one-on-one discussions with doctors. Such "ask the doctor" sites are very popular, receiving as many as 3,000 hits, or visits, a day.

The Future

One thing most health sites do not do is diagnose, treat, or prescribe drugs over the Internet. Most

Doctors often use teleconferencing and the Internet to communicate with other doctors and patients.

sites carry warnings that they do not offer diagnoses or treatment. Such actions, the sites point out, require face-to-face meetings with doctors. However, many experts in the Internet health-care field predict that as video conferencing techniques, video quality, and screen technology improve, distance diagnosis and treatment will be possible. Another development these experts foresee is the merging of patient records with medical information and treatment guidelines in one central online databank.

Think About It

1. Summarize *What basic services do health-related Web sites offer?*

2. Making Generalizations and Predictions *What advantages do you see in the development of online health care? What problems do you think online health-care sites might create?*

TEACH OBJECTIVE 2

To help students identify some of the special health-care concerns of various segments of American society, copy the graphic organizer at the right onto the chalkboard, omitting the italicized answers. Have students copy and complete the organizer. Discuss the answers with the class. Then organize students into groups and have group members use their graphic organizers to discuss solutions to some of the health-care challenges that different groups of Americans face. Finally, have group members share some of their ideas with the class for discussion and evaluation.

ENGLISH LANGUAGE LEARNERS , COOPERATIVE LEARNING

Segment of Society	Special Health-Care Concerns
poor people	*often not insured; have difficulty accessing and paying for care; cannot afford prescription drugs; have few doctors in poor communities*
elderly individuals	*need more care than general population; often poor or on strict budgets; sometimes refused insurance coverage due to pre-existing conditions*
AIDS sufferers	*need constant care in advanced stages; sometimes refused care by caregivers because of fear of infection; often not covered by insurance*
people suffering from chronic illnesses	*often refused insurance coverage due to pre-existing conditions; life-long care of illness is often extremely expensive*

Managed care has brought down costs. However, a growing number of Americans feel that the savings have come at a price—a decline in the quality of care. Polls conducted in the late 1990s by the Kaiser Family Foundation and in 2000 by the Harvard School of Public Health found that more than half of the respondents said that managed care had decreased the quality of health care for the sick. More than 60 percent of respondents said that managed care had cut the time doctors spend with patients and made it harder for the sick to see specialists. Perhaps most alarmingly, close to 60 percent said that they were worried that if they became sick, their health plans would be more concerned about saving money than about providing them with the best treatment.

In response to public discontent with managed care, Congress began to develop a "patients' bill of rights" in 1999. This bill would allow patients to use hospital facilities and doctors not included in their plans and to have easier access to specialists. The bill of rights would also enable patients to gain more information on treatments available and to appeal any denials of treatment or coverage.

Access to Health Care Studies of the American medical workforce estimate that there is a surplus of somewhere between 100,000 and 150,000 doctors. In spite of this oversupply of doctors, access to health care is a problem for many Americans. One of the major factors affecting

access to health care is the distribution of physicians, both geographically and within the medical profession.

Geographically, most physicians concentrate in wealthy urban and suburban areas. In such areas, doctor-to-population ratios are low. In poor inner-city and rural areas, on the other hand, ratios are high. For example, in the exclusive Beverly Hills area of Los Angeles there is one doctor for every 254 people. In some poverty-stricken areas of south-central Los Angeles, however, there is approximately one doctor for every 24,500 people. This shortage of doctors is particularly problematic because underserved areas usually have a greater number of people with chronic diseases. These areas are also usually home to many elderly people, who have an array of health-care needs.

Professionally, many physicians concentrate in specialty fields such as cardiology, internal medicine, and obstetrics. It is among specialists, not general practitioners, that surpluses are developing. Of the more than 700,000 government and private physicians in the United States, only about 65,000 are in general and family practice. This shortage of general practitioners is partially a result of doctors' pay structures. For example, the average yearly income for all specialists is about $230,000. General practitioners earn about $144,000 a year. These factors have contributed to the shortage in general-practice doctors.

Interdisciplinary Connection

HISTORY

The Development of Private Health Care. During World War II, the U.S. government enacted controls on prices and wages. As a result, many American businesses were unable to offer workers raises. To attract and keep employees, companies began offering benefits as a form of indirect pay. Health insurance was one of the most popular benefits provided, and many companies continued the practice after the war ended. Today many companies pay either all or a portion of employees' private health insurance costs.

CRITICAL THINKING
Do you think that all businesses in the United States should be required to provide employees with health coverage? Why or why not?

ANSWER: Answers will vary, but students should consider issues such as the number of employees businesses have, effects on business profits, and the high cost of health care in the United States.

Visual Answer

Doctors may not have time to examine patients adequately, which may lead doctors to diagnose patients incorrectly or to miss serious medical conditions.

INTERPRETING VISUALS One issue in the American health-care system is the limited access to doctors that many patients face. *How can doctors spending less time with patients lead to medical problems?*

John Hanson of Marion, Indiana, suggested the following activity: Before starting Section 3, have students discuss what they think are the top-five concerns in high school students' lives. Create a class list. Next, have each student interview one adult over the age of 40 about his or her top-five concerns in life. Have students' share their results and create a class tally. Likely many adults will include concerns related to health or health care. Ask students to discuss reasons why adults might be so concerned with health care. Then use the activity to introduce students' study of Section 3.

BLOCK SCHEDULING

SPOTLIGHT *on Poor Neighborhoods*

After discussing the factors that affect access to health care in the United States, have students speculate on what can be done to encourage more doctors to become general practitioners and to serve in poor inner-city and rural areas of the country. Then have students work independently or in pairs to make brochures that could be passed out to medical students and interns to encourage them to participate in programs that would increase the number of doctors serving poor areas. **COOPERATIVE LEARNING**,

BLOCK SCHEDULING

Case Study

Race and Health-Care Inequalities. Social class is not the only factor that reveals inequalities in health care. Race is also a factor. In 1999 the U.S. infant mortality rate for African Americans was 14.6 percent, compared to 5.8 percent for white Americans. That same year, the life expectancy at birth of African Americans was 71.4, compared to 77.3 for white Americans.

ACTIVITY: Have students discuss some possible sociological reasons that African Americans have higher infant mortality and lower life expectancies than white Americans and some ways that the government might address this inequality.

Map Answers

1. Students should list the states shown in orange.

2. Students should list the states shown in blue; questions such as how low rates of health-insurance coverage in those states relate to poverty statistics for the region

Inequality and Health

Access to health care is just one way in which health is directly related to social status. Poor people are less likely than wealthy Americans to receive adequate medical care. The effects of poverty—such as malnutrition, lack of health insurance, and lack of access to health services—lead to greater health problems for many Americans.

- Children born to poor families are 60 percent more likely to die within the first year of life than children born to wealthier families.
- Children born to poor families are three times more likely than children born to wealthy families to have only fair or poor health.

- Some 34 million Americans face hunger and cannot afford to buy the food needed for a healthy diet. Children who are hungry are four times more likely than children who are not hungry to have trouble concentrating at school.
- More than 23 percent of poor children have no health insurance.
- About one third of the non-elderly low-income population does not have health insurance. Uninsured people are less likely than those with insurance to get routine physical checkups and other kinds of preventive care. In addition, the uninsured are more likely to delay or postpone medical treatment—even for serious conditions.
- People with lower incomes are more likely to characterize their health as fair or poor than people with higher incomes.

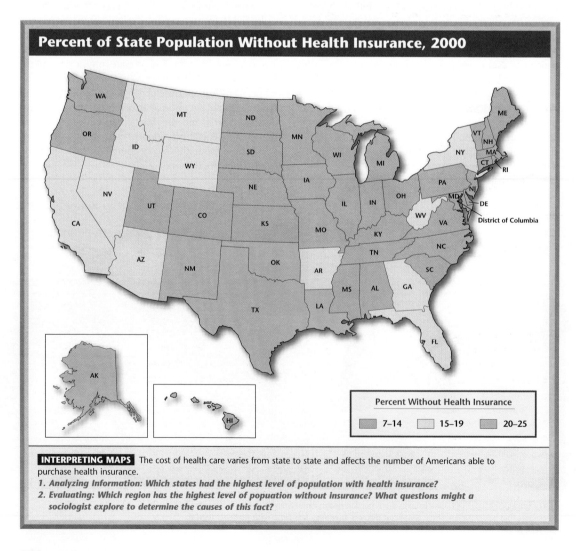

Percent of State Population Without Health Insurance, 2000

Percent Without Health Insurance

◼ 7–14   ◻ 15–19   ◼ 20–25

INTERPRETING MAPS The cost of health care varies from state to state and affects the number of Americans able to purchase health insurance.
1. *Analyzing Information: Which states had the highest level of population with health insurance?*
2. *Evaluating: Which region has the highest level of population without insurance? What questions might a sociologist explore to determine the causes of this fact?*

Have students interview public health officials, hospital administrators, or social workers about the health-care needs of the poor in the local community. Instruct students to ask interviewees for statistical information and overviews of programs and organizations that are in place to help poor people get adequate health care. Students might also ask interviewees for their opinions about what, if anything, ought to be done to help improve poor people's access to health care. Have students share their findings with the class in brief oral reports. **BLOCK SCHEDULING**

Have each student conduct research on one of the following types of alternative medicine: acupuncture, acupressure, biofeedback, chiropractic care, massage, meditation, yoga, herbal remedies, or relaxation techniques. Have students examine the views of medical practitioners who support and oppose the use of the selected type of alternative medicine. Then have each student write a newspaper editorial about whether health-insurance plans should cover that type of alternative medicine and why. Students should support their positions with facts, statistics, and examples.

BLOCK SCHEDULING

The poor also suffer disproportionately from diseases such as influenza, pneumonia, tuberculosis, alcoholism, and heart disease. Thus, it is not surprising that poor Americans have a much lower life expectancy than wealthy Americans.

Health-Care Issues for Today

In the early 2000s, health-care issues—costs, quality, and access—are major concerns for the United States. Several other health-care issues are also at the center of political debates. These issues include health insurance, the search for alternative treatments, and the AIDS epidemic.

Health Insurance The majority of medical costs in the United States—more than 80 percent—are covered by private or public insurance. With private insurance, people pay set periodic fees. When they are sick, the insurance companies pay the medical bills. Most people obtain private insurance through group plans offered by their employers. Public insurance includes government programs such as Medicare and Medicaid, which provide coverage for elderly, disabled, and poor people.

Critics note that the Medicare-Medicaid system has created very uneven health-care delivery. The kinds of procedures and treatments covered and the levels to which they are covered, vary among private health-insurance plans. Some doctors and hospitals will not accept Medicare and Medicaid patients. Many private health-insurance companies are reluctant to offer coverage to people with pre-existing medical conditions. The working poor also find it difficult to get coverage. The companies they work for often do not offer group plans, and they do not earn enough to pay for their own coverage. About 16 percent of the population—more than 44 million people—are uninsured.

Some people have suggested that such problems could be overcome by the creation of a national health system—a centrally planned health-care delivery system. In many industrialized nations, the government actually owns and operates the health-care system. Medical care is provided free or nearly free of charge to all citizens, regardless of their incomes. For example, in Great Britain all citizens have access to the National Health Service (NHS). Hospitals in the NHS system are controlled and funded by the government, and NHS physicians are government employees. People in Great Britain are also free to seek health care from private physicians and from private hospitals. However, the government will not assist people with the costs for such services. Moreover, critics of the NHS have argued that the quality of health care in Great Britain has been negatively affected by the program.

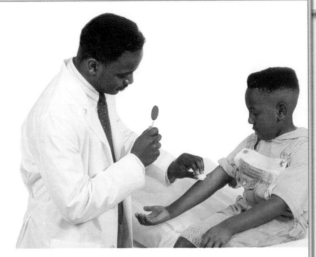

INTERPRETING VISUALS One important benefit of health insurance is that it helps pay for preventative medicine such as immunization shots for children. *How might preventative medicine help keep health-care costs down?*

In other industrialized nations—such as Canada—the government finances health care through national health insurance. Under such a system, the government pays for health services, but physicians are not government employees. Critics have also challenged the quality of the Canadian health-care system. Early in his first term, President Bill Clinton suggested setting up a system similar to that of Canada. However, strong opposition from the American Medical Association (AMA) and the public led Clinton to abandon the plan.

Alternative Medicine Many Americans have become interested in **alternative medicine** in recent years. Alternative medicine includes treating illness with unconventional methods such as acupuncture, acupressure, biofeedback, massage, meditation, yoga, herbal remedies, and relaxation techniques. Between the years 1990 and 1997, visits to alternative practitioners increased by 47 percent. During the same period, visits to general-practice physicians fell slightly. Today about 40 percent of Americans say that they have used some kind of alternative treatment. Estimates set yearly spending on alternative medicine at about $20 billion. Most of that amount is out-of-pocket spending because very few health-insurance plans cover these treatments.

The medical profession has expressed considerable concern about alternative medicine. Doctors point out that there are few scientific studies on the effectiveness of alternative treatments. Unlike new drugs, herbal remedies and diet supplements do not have to be tested or approved by the Food and Drug Administration (FDA). The result, some doctors suggest, may be harmful to patients. Indeed, recent studies have linked some herbal

internet connect

TOPIC: AIDS Research and Treatment
GO TO: go.hrw.com
KEYWORD: SL3 SC11

Have students access the Internet through the HRW Go site to conduct research on recent developments in AIDS research and treatment methods. Then have students work in pairs or in small groups to create a pamphlet designed to inform fellow students and teachers about recent developments in AIDS treatments both in the United States and around the world. Students' pamphlets should include a list of online resources that people can access to get additional information.

Visual Answer

by preventing some illnesses and thereby decreasing the amount of health care, diagnostic tests, and prescription drugs that people may need later in life

AIDS: A Global Challenge (Regional Statistics, 2003)

Region	Adults and Children Living with HIV/AIDS	Adults and Children Newly Infected with HIV
Sub-Saharan Africa	25.0-28.2 million	3.0-3.4 million
North Africa & Middle East	470,000-730,000	43,000-67,000
South & Southeast Asia	4.6-8.2 million	610,000-1.1 million
East Asia & Pacific Islands	700,000-1.3 million	150,000-270,000
Latin America	1.9 million	120,000-180,000
Caribbean	360,000-590,000	45,000-80,000
Eastern Europe & Central Asia	1.2-1.8 million	180,000-280,000
Western Europe	520,000-680,000	30,000-40,000
North America	790,000-1.2 million	36,000-54,000
Australia & New Zealand	12,000-18,000	700-1,000
Total	34-46 million	4.2-5.8 million

Source: United Nations/World Health Organization

INTERPRETING TABLES AIDS is a global health problem that has affected every country around the world. *Which regions have experienced the greatest challenges from the AIDS crisis? Which regions have experienced the least?*

remedies to kidney diseases and cancer. Many doctors have urged that, for the safety of patients, herbs and supplements should undergo the same FDA testing-and-approval process required for other drugs.

AIDS—A Pressing Health Problem

In 1981 when the first few cases of a strange new ailment were reported in the United States, no one imagined the potential effects on society. However, in just two decades the ailment has developed into one of the most serious public-health problems in the United States and around the world.

Acquired immune deficiency syndrome (AIDS) is a disease that attacks the immune system, leaving a person vulnerable to a host of deadly infections. The number of cases of AIDS in the United States has grown from a few hundred in 1981 to more than 753,000 in 2000. Another 127,000 Americans are living with human immuno deficiency virus (HIV), the virus that causes AIDS. About 40,000 become infected with HIV each year. Researchers believe that virtually all people who test positive for HIV eventually will develop AIDS if a cure is not found. They almost certainly will die from the disease. Of the people who have contracted AIDS since 1981, 448,060—some 58 percent—are known to have died.

HIV is transmitted through sexual contact, contaminated blood and tissue, and the use of contaminated hypodermic needles, but it does not threaten every segment of society equally. The groups at highest risk of becoming infected with HIV are homosexual and bisexual men, intravenous drug abusers, the sexual partners of high-risk persons, persons receiving blood transfusions, and the babies of high-risk mothers. Homosexual and bisexual men account for the largest percentage of AIDS sufferers (46 percent). The next largest category is that of intravenous drug abusers (25 percent). However, patterns of HIV transmission have changed somewhat in recent years. The number of new AIDS cases among homosexual and bisexual men has dropped. In contrast, the proportion of AIDS cases contracted through heterosexual sex has risen. Among young women under the age of 25, heterosexual contact is the main method of HIV infection.

Many AIDS activists claim that the United States government has not responded adequately to the AIDS crisis. However, in recent years the U.S. government has made major efforts to combat this deadly disease. It has enacted several laws establishing programs in the areas of AIDS research, education and prevention, and treatment. Over the years, the government has increased its spending on these programs. In 2000 government spending on AIDS exceeded $10 billion. The majority of the money—about 70 percent—went toward care and assistance. AIDS treatments are very expensive, and health-care costs for an individual AIDS patient may run as high as $7,800 a month.

Medical treatments and government programs finally seem to be having an effect. The numbers of new AIDS cases have begun to decline. Also, since the mid-1990s powerful new drugs that slow the progress of HIV have

CLOSE

In an open class discussion, ask students if they think the U.S. government should be involved in health care and how. For example, should it provide a national health system like Great Britain, or national health insurance like Canada?

REVIEW AND ASSESS

Have students complete the **Section 3 Review** on p. 287. As **Alternative Assessment**, you may want to use the health-care poster or graphic organizer in this section's lessons.

RETEACH

Call on students to take turns orally summarizing each of the subsections in this section. Correct and expand upon students' summaries, as needed. **ENGLISH LANGUAGE LEARNERS**

EXTEND

Acquire several current informational packets about popular health-insurance plans and distribute them to groups of students. Have students compare and contrast the costs and benefits of two or more plans and decide which to buy. Ask students to explain their decisions to the class. **COOPERATIVE LEARNING**, **BLOCK SCHEDULING**

been used in AIDS treatment. As a result, AIDS deaths have decreased, and the numbers of people living with AIDS have increased. However, AIDS is the fifth-leading cause of death among Americans between the ages of 25 and 44. Among African Americans in the same age group, it is the second-leading cause of death.

AIDS is not simply an American problem. The disease has become a global epidemic. Since the outbreak of the epidemic in the late 1970s, more than 21 million people have died of AIDS worldwide. In 2001 alone, the death toll was 3 million. In that year, some 5 million new HIV infections were reported. This brought the worldwide total of people living with HIV or AIDS to 40 million. Such figures, experts say, indicate that the death toll is bound to rise in the next few years.

Sub-Saharan Africa, where some 70 percent of HIV and AIDS sufferers live, is the hardest hit of the world's regions. Approximately 6,300 people die of AIDS each day in Africa. Experts expect that number to rise to 13,000 by 2005. Because of AIDS-related increases in death rates, the life expectancy in sub-Saharan Africa has fallen to 47 years. Without AIDS, the life expectancy would be 62 years. AIDS is also having devastating effects on the economy of Africa. The disease is rapidly reducing the number of available workers. At the same time, the cost of caring for AIDS patients is rising. As a result, economic growth is slowing at an alarming rate across the continent. Economists fear that as AIDS takes hold in Asia, its economy could share the same fate.

New developments in the treatment of AIDS have extended the lives of patients in technologically advanced countries.

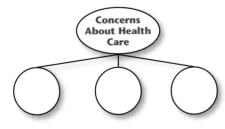

SECTION 3 REVIEW

1. Define and explain
managed care
alternative medicine
acquired immune deficiency syndrome (AIDS)

2. Summarizing Copy the graphic organizer below. Use it to identify and describe the issues that are at the center of Americans' concern about health care.

Concerns About Health Care

3. Finding the Main Idea
a. Why do you think many Americans have faced challenges using the health-care system in the United States?
b. What health-care issues have been at the center of public debate recently?

4. Writing and Critical Thinking
Drawing Inferences and Conclusions Write a brief essay illustrating how and why social status helps to determine health.
Consider:
• the cost of health care
• access to health care
• the relative health of wealthy and poor people

Homework Practice Online
keyword: SL3 HP11

CHAPTER 11 REVIEW

ANSWERS

WRITING A SUMMARY
See the section subtitles for the main topics in this chapter.

IDENTIFYING PEOPLE AND IDEAS

1. the specific behaviors and attitudes that a society establishes for men and women

2. a system in which men are dominant over women

3. the belief that one sex is by nature superior to the other

4. the level of women's income relative to that of men

5. the invisible barrier that prevents women from gaining upper-level positions in business

6. the belief that one age category is by nature superior to another age category

7. the steady increase in the population of elderly Americans

8. the number of workers for every person receiving Social Security benefits

9. health-insurance plans in which members pay a set monthly or annual charge for health-care services

10. treating illness with unconventional methods

CHAPTER

Review and Assessment Resources

- Chapter 11 Review, pp. 288–89
- Chapter Review Activities with Answer Key
- Global Skill Builder CD–ROM
- Chapter 11 Test Generator (on the One-Stop Planner)
- Chapter 11 Test (Form A or B)
- Alternative Assessment Handbook
- HRW Go site

 REVIEW

Have students complete the **Chapter 11 Review** on pp. 288–89.

ASSESS

Use one of the chapter tests to assess students' understanding of the content. For **Alternative Assessment**, see the **Alternative Assessment Handbook**.

UNDERSTANDING MAIN IDEAS

1. Men earn more than women for the same jobs and are much more likely to be promoted to higher positions.

2. Married working men have more free time on average than married working women because the latter are often responsible for most household duties in addition to their careers.

3. Gender roles and gender identity influence how boys and girls are treated while growing up, how they behave, and what expectations adults have of children.

4. Older Americans have become a more powerful voice in politics and society, but the graying of America has also put a strain on the economy and government as more people collect Social Security benefits.

5. The aging of the population has increased political power for elderly people and led to less age discrimination, although many elderly people still face ageism and poverty.

6. cost of health care, quality of health care, and access to health care

7. AIDS is an epidemic that has spread throughout the world since 1981, causing many deaths. No cure has been found, and the cost of treating the disease continues to rise.

THINKING CRITICALLY

1. Because they bear the children, women often end up staying closer to the home than men, and child care takes a lot of work and time.

288

CHAPTER

 11 Review

 Writing a Summary

Using standard grammar, spelling, sentence structure, and punctuation, summarize the information in this chapter.
Consider:
- how gender roles affect opportunities in life for men and women in America
- the effects of aging on society
- the state of health care in America

Identifying People and Ideas

Identify the following people or terms and use them in appropriate sentences.

1. gender roles
2. patriarchy
3. sexism
4. wage gap
5. glass ceiling
6. ageism
7. graying of America
8. dependency ratio
9. managed care
10. alternative medicine

Understanding Main ideas

Section 1 (pp. 262–71)

1. Explain how the wage gap and the glass ceiling can be used to illustrate gender inequality.

2. How has the second shift helped to create a "leisure gap" between men and women?

3. How are gender roles and gender identity related to the experiences of boys and girls?

Section 2 (pp. 272–77)

4. How has the aging of the population affected American society?

5. What effects have the aging of the population had on the opportunities in life available to eldery people?

Section 3 (pp. 280–87)

6. What health-care issues are causing concern among Americans?

7. What is AIDS, and why is it considered such a pressing medical issue?

 Thinking Critically

1. **Analyzing Information** Explain how gender inequality may be related to the nature of human reproduction.

2. **Identifying Bias** How might the stereotypical image of elderly people affect their life chances?

3. **Drawing Inferences and Conclusions** One of the major goals of the Americans with Disabilities Act (ADA) was to help Americans with disabilities find and keep meaningful employment. Why do you think the act has not been more successful in fulfilling this goal?

4. **Summarizing** Why are poor people more likely than wealthier people to experience serious health problems?

5. **Evaluating** How have individual, societal behavior, and cultural norms changed because of scientific discoveries and technological innovations in health care?

 Writing About Sociology

1. **Analyzing Information** Observe at least 10 television commercials or magazine advertisements that use one or more elderly characters. Write a brief report describing the images of elderly people reflected in these commercials. In your report, analyze health as a social institution in relationship to other major societal institutions.

2. **Drawing Inferences and Conclusions** Choose a television program that has a female lead and a male lead. Compile lists of the gender behaviors exhibited by each of the two characters. Imagine that you are from another country. Write one or two paragraphs discussing the conclusions on proper gender behavior that you have drawn from analyzing the lists. Use the graphic organizer below to help you organize your lists.

Behaviors of Female Character	Behaviors of Male Character

Organize the class into three groups and assign each group one of the sections in this chapter. Instruct each group to create a bulletin-board display that incorporates images, text, and graphics to illustrate the main ideas and key concepts in its assigned section. Then have each group use its bulletin board to review the main ideas in its section for the class. Finally, display the bulletin boards in the classroom. **ENGLISH LANGUAGE LEARNERS**, **COOPERATIVE LEARNING**

1. Using Sociological Imagination Ask students to make predictions about the future of gender- and age-based movements for equal treatment. Then have each student write a paragraph providing his or her predictions. Students should support their predictions with facts, trends, and educated guesses.

2. Linking to Community Encourage students to volunteer at a local hospital or retirement community as "candy stripers" or to visit a training facility for guide dogs or therapy pets. Then have students report back to the class on their experiences and observations.

BUILDING SOCIAL STUDIES SKILLS

Interpreting Cartoons

Study the cartoon below. Use it to answer the following questions.

© 2000, The Washington Post Writers Group. Reprinted with permission.

1. Many sociologists and other Americans are concerned about the future needs of the aging population of baby boomers. The large population of older baby boomers will affect ideas about aging, health care, and many other aspects of American life. Which of the following government programs do you think is the focus of this cartoon?

a. Food Stamps

b. Social Security

c. Supplemental Security Income

d. Temporary Assistance for Needy Families

2. Why will the retirement of the baby-boom generation present challenges to this program?

Analyzing Primary Sources

The following excerpt discusses young women's attitudes toward computers. Read the excerpt and answer the questions that follow.

"*Despite the rapid proliferation of the so-called e-culture, young American women exhibit a marked distaste for computer technology, an antipathy that may threaten their future professional and economic success, according to a [recent] report. . . .*

Girls are not afraid of computers. They simply don't like them or what they perceive as the competitive and solitary environment surrounding their use. Unless it is corrected, this will leave women at a disadvantage competing in a market where one out of four new jobs will be technically oriented by 2010, according to the [report]. . . .

Lack of interest [among young women] in [technical] subjects . . . appears in high school, where girls generally are well-out-numbered by boys taking courses in computer science. The only area where more girls enroll than boys is in clerical and data-entry computer courses, which the report calls 'the 1990s version of typing.'"

3. Why, according to the excerpt, do young women shun computers?

a. because computers can't help them with their careers

b. because they are afraid of computers

c. because they dislike what they perceive as the environment surrounding the use of computers

d. because the courses in computer science offered at high school and college are of no interest to them

4. How might a sociologist use the information in the excerpt to illustrate gender inequality in the United States?

SOCIOLOGY PROJECTS

Cooperative Learning

Using Statistical Analysis Working in a group with two or three other students, use library and Internet sources to find statistics on gender, age, and health inequalities. Use your findings to create a data bank titled "Gender, Age, and Health Inequality: By the Numbers." Use the statistics you find to create maps, charts, graphs, models, or databases to illustrate your report. You may want to present your report to the class.

internet connect

Internet Activity: go.hrw.com
KEYWORD: SL3 SC11

Choose an activity on gender, age, and health to:

• create a thematic graph or chart on gender inequality in education, in the workplace, or in politics.

• write a report on new technologies and products that have been developed to help disabled people.

• create a pamphlet on recent developments related to AIDS treatment.

go.hrw.com

---

2. Stereotypes about elderly people promote ageism, which can limit the job opportunities available to senior citizens.

3. People with disabilities face discrimination in finding and keeping employment as well as transportation problems and other hurdles related to working.

4. Poor people have less access to doctors, to important tests, and to good nutrition and often lack health insurance.

5. People are obtaining more medical information and care online, and doctors are administering more diagnostic tests as a form of defensive medication.

WRITING ABOUT SOCIOLOGY

1. Students should analyze the images to determine if they reflect the reality or the stereotypes of elderly people. Students should recognize the significance of health as a social institution.

2. Paragraphs will vary, but students should summarize the gender roles for American men and women based on their observations.

BUILDING SOCIAL STUDIES SKILLS

1. b

2. because more people will be receiving benefits, decreasing Social Security's dependency ratio

3. c

4. by noting that men have an advantage in achieving professional and economic success.

Across Space and Time

TEACH

Have the students read the feature The Women's Movement in the 1800s and answer the questions that follow it. Then lead a class discussion about the right to vote. Challenge students to explain why women and African Americans fought for the right to vote. Then write the following statistics on the board: *American citizens age 18 and older in 2000: 186 million; Voters in the November 2000 election: 111 million (60 percent).* Ask students to discuss why 40 percent of Americans eligible to vote in the November 2000 presidential election opted not to do so.

CONNECTING *to Government and History*

Read to the class the Nineteenth Amendment to the Constitution of the United States: "The right of citizens of the United States to vote shall not be denied or abridged by the United States or by any state on account of sex. Congress shall have power to enforce this article by appropriate legislation." Then have the class construct a time line of women's suffrage, starting with the American Women's Rights Convention and ending with the ratification of the Nineteenth Amendment. **COOPERATIVE LEARNING**, **BLOCK SCHEDULING**

Think About It Answers

1. to forward the cause of women's rights—specifically, to gain the right for women to vote, to end legal discrimination against women, and to gain equal treatment under the law for women

2. Today women have the right to vote, own property, sign contracts, have custody of their children in the event of divorce, and many other rights. Additionally, women have gained greater opportunities in public life, as well as in the areas of education, employment, and treatment under law.

Across Space and Time

The Women's Movement in the 1800s

In the early 1800s enormous changes were taking place in the United States. As industrialization began women began leaving home to work in the factories. Although women were leaving home to enter the workforce, women faced inequalities in income and the type of jobs they received. However during this time, new opportunities became available for some women. Women's colleges such as Oberlin College began to open in the United States during the 1830s. These schools offered opportunities for wealthier women to pursue a higher education.

The abolitionist movement of the 1830s helped provide a strong push toward women's rights. Although slavery was an accepted practice in some states during this time, many people considered it to be inhumane and tried to abolish it. Involvement in the abolitionist movement taught many women how to be effective public speakers. However, some women found that they were barred from abolitionist meetings and from public speaking because of their sex.

Abolitionists Elizabeth Cady Stanton and Lucretia Mott were barred from participating in the London World's Anti-Slavery Convention in 1840. Although they protested, Stanton and Mott were told that only men could participate. Incidents such as this soon led some women to realize that they had to fight not only for the rights of enslaved African Americans, but also for their own rights. Stanton, Mott, and others continued their efforts for the abolitionist cause, but they also began to speak out on behalf of women's issues.

In 1848 Stanton and Mott decided to hold the first American Women's Rights Convention in Seneca Falls, New York. They placed advertisements in the newspaper announcing the meeting, but they expected little response. To their surprise, more than 300 men and women arrived, prepared to discuss the social, legal, and economic position of women. Two days of meetings and speeches produced the Declaration of Sentiments, based on the Declaration of Independence. The Declaration of Sentiments stated that "all men and women are created equal." The declaration also contained a number of resolutions, among which were women's suffrage and the elimination of legal discrimination against women. The right of women to vote was considered the most radical issue, and much heated debate occurred before the resolution was passed.

Abolitionists such as Elizabeth Cady Stanton pushed for an expansion of rights for women.

Although great effort was made to secure legislative enactment of these resolutions, most people of the day did not believe in women's rights. Thus, little change was made in the years following the convention. When the Civil War began in 1861, women's rights activists were urged to give up their cause and join the war effort. Following the war, activists once again took up their cause. However, this time almost all of their efforts were concentrated on a single issue—gaining suffrage for women.

A number of groups, including the Women's Trade Union League and the Woman's Christian Temperance Union, joined forces to work for women's suffrage. The goal took years to accomplish. Many women were ridiculed and jailed for speaking out. Finally, in 1920 the Nineteenth Amendment to the U.S. Constitution became effective, and women gained the right to vote.

Think About It

1. **Identifying Points of View** *Why do you think Elizabeth Cady Stanton and Lucretia Mott organized a women's rights convention?*

2. **Evaluating** *What effects do you think the women's rights movement had on women today?*

Sociology in Action

■ TEACH

Have students read the Sociology in Action feature and then work in small groups to perform the simulation activity. Have each group start by preparing an action plan (such as what resources they plan to consult, how long they expect each step to take, what members will perform what roles, and so on). When students have planned their approach to the activity, have them follow the steps as described in the text and submit their reports to the class. Close with a brief discussion about the viability of students' proposed solutions.
COOPERATIVE LEARNING

■ EXTEND

Organize the class into small groups and have each group prepare a community survey to determine how domestic chores are accomplished within two-parent households where both parents work. Surveys should focus on who does what chores, when chores are performed, and whether chores are generally accomplished to the satisfaction of the members of the household. Have groups survey 15 to 20 families apiece and prepare reports providing the raw data gathered, relevant charts to illustrate the data, and a summary of the results. **COOPERATIVE LEARNING , BLOCK SCHEDULING**

Sociology in Action

UNIT 3 SIMULATION

You Solve the Problem . . .

How can a sociologist help solve the problem of women having to work a "second shift" of domestic chores in addition to their other jobs?

Complete the following activity in small groups. Imagine that a sociologist has asked your group for advice on helping create a solution to the "second shift" problem many women face. The sociologist has asked for a report outlining the proposal your group formulates.

1 Gather Information.
Use your textbook and other resources to find information that might influence your plan of action for preparing the report. Remember that your report must include information to convince the sociologist that your suggested method should be used. This information might include charts and graphs to show the sociologist how your solutions might help women and families deal with the second shift problem. You may want to divide different parts of the research among group members.

2 List and Consider Options.
After reviewing the information you have gathered, list and consider the options you might use to help the sociologist choose how to solve the problem. Your final solution to the problem may be easier to reach if you consider as many options as possible. Be sure to record all of your possible options for the preparation of your report.

3 Consider Advantages and Disadvantages.
Now consider the advantages and disadvantages of choosing each option. Ask yourselves questions such as the following:

• What seems to be causing the second shift problem?

• Could someone outside the family provide services to relieve the second shift for a family of average income?

• Are there any other time management solutions that could help a family?

Once you have considered the advantages and disadvantages, record them as notes for use in preparing your report.

4 Choose and Implement a Solution.
After considering the advantages and disadvantages of each probable solution, you should choose a solution. Next, plan and create your report. Be sure to make the solution you have chosen very clear.

5 Evaluate the Effectiveness of the Solution.
Once you have prepared your report, write a paragraph evaluating how effective your recommendation will be for the sociologist. Explain why you believe your solution will be the most effective. When you are ready, decide which group members will present which parts of the report. Then take your report to the sociologist (the rest of the class). Good luck!

SOCIOLOGY IN ACTION

Ask students to review Unit 3 and to make a list of 10 major issues to which they could apply their problem-solving skills. Then have students share some of the issues they listed with the class. Finally, encourage students to remember their problem-solving skills and use them to evaluate the sociological issues that they study.

CHAPTER 12

The Family

The family is a universal phenomenon. In all societies, no matter how small, the family serves as the basic social unit. The form that the family takes, however, can vary widely from society to society and even within a single society over time. These variations include differences among societies in marriage-partner, residential, descent, and authority patterns.

CHAPTER 13

The Economy and Politics

Economic and political institutions ensure that the economic activities of individuals are controlled and that order is maintained in society. Forms of economic and political institutions can vary widely from society to society. In some societies these institutions are influenced by a belief in human freedom. In other societies these same institutions greatly limit human freedom.

Internet Activity

internet connect

go.hrw.com

TOPIC: Science and Student Life
GO TO: go.hrw.com
KEYWORD: SL3 UNIT 4

Have students access the Internet through the HRW Go site to conduct research on scientific discoveries that have changed the world. Then ask each student to select one scientist that he or she feels has had a major influence and to write a short report on that scientist and some of his or her discoveries. Students should also explain in their reports why they chose the scientists that they did.

CHAPTER 14

Education and Religion

Education and religion, like all social institutions, arose in response to basic human needs. If societies are to survive over time, children must be provided with the knowledge they need to maintain the world they inherit from their elders, and all members must be afforded the emotional strength they need to face the challenges of life. Consequently, all societies develop educational and religious social institutions.

CHAPTER 15

Science and the Mass Media

Two social institutions that have gained increasing importance in many societies are science and mass media. Science grows in importance as a society industrializes and becomes more advanced. Mass media are necessary to aid communication among a large population.

UNIT MOTIVATOR

Share the chapter overviews with students. Then ask students to identify and discuss major institutions that help societies function (*family, economy, politics, education, religion, science, mass media*). Tell students to keep this discussion in mind as they study Unit 4.

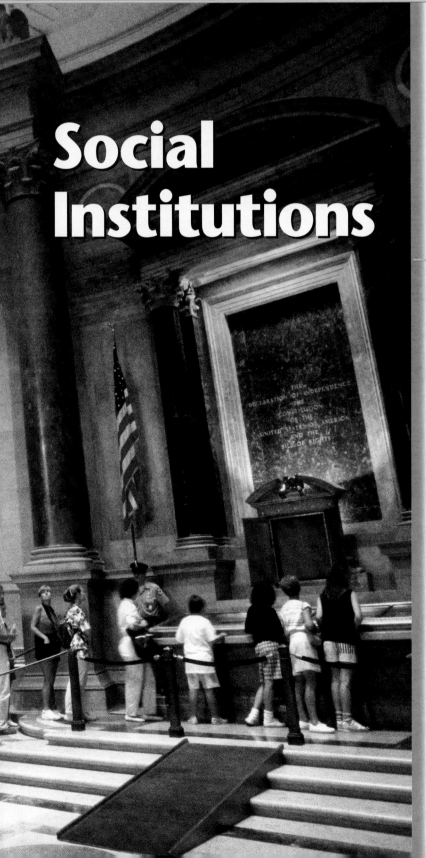

Social Institutions

UNIT 4

CHAPTER

12 The Family

13 The Economy and Politics

14 Education and Religion

15 Science and the Mass Media

Many sociologists focus their research on the role of social institutions in American society. Many Americans value their freedoms and democratic government. The U.S. Constitution in Washington, D.C., is a popular tourist attraction.

Using Visual Resources

Historical Documents. Many social institutions are based on historical documents. For example, the political system of the United States is based on the U.S. Constitution, which was in turn based on other documents that predated it. Some religions are based in part on writings that contain historical content, such as the Bible or the Qur'an. In addition, economics, science, and education are fields built on bodies of works written by generations of theorists and practitioners.

CRITICAL THINKING

Why do you think that social institutions are so often based on documents and writings that have been preserved and passed down through generations?

ANSWER: because such documents help to define, codify, and preserve the theories, practices, and beliefs espoused by social institutions

The Family

CHAPTER RESOURCE MANAGER

Objectives	Pacing Guide		Resources

SECTION 1:
The Family in Cross-Cultural Perspective
(pp. 296–304)

REV Section 1 Review, p. 304

Objectives

- Describe the norms that influence the ways in which marriage patterns are organized around the world.
- Identify the basic societal needs that the institution of the family satisfies.

Pacing Guide

Regular 2 days	Block Scheduling 1 day

Block Scheduling Handbook with Team Teaching Strategies, Chapter 12

Resources

- CNN. Presents Sociology: Parents Help Keep Kids Off Drugs
- **RS** Graphic Organizer 12
- HRW Go site
- **SM** Mastering Critical Thinking Skills 12
- **PS** Readings and Case Studies in Sociology 12
- **E** Research Projects and Activities for Teaching Sociology 12
- **SM** Study Skills and Writing Guide
- Teaching Transparency: Median Age at Marriage in the United States, 1890–1998

SECTION 2:
The American Family
(pp. 305–17)

REV Section 2 Review, p. 317

Objectives

- Explain how American families begin and describe some of the disruptions they might face.
- Analyze some of the trends in American family life currently being examined by sociologists.

Pacing Guide

Regular 3 days	Block Scheduling 1.5 days

Block Scheduling Handbook with Team Teaching Strategies, Chapter 12

Chapter Review And Assessment

- **REV** Chapter 12 Review, pp. 318–19
- **REV** Chapter Review Activities with Answer Key
- Global Skill Builder CD–ROM
- Chapter 12 Test Generator (on the One-Stop Planner)
- **A** Chapter 12 Test (Form A or B)
- **A** Alternative Assessment Handbook
- HRW Go site

Chapter Resource Key

PS	Primary Sources	**A**	Assessment		Video
RS	Reading Support	**REV**	Review		Internet
E	Enrichment		Transparencies		Holt Presentation Maker Using Microsoft® PowerPoint®
SM	Skills Mastery		CD–ROM		

One-Stop Planner CD–ROM

See the *One-Stop Planner* for a complete list of additional resources for students and teachers.

One-Stop Planner CD–ROM

It's easy to plan lessons, select resources, and print out materials for your students when you use the **One-Stop Planner CD–ROM with Test Generator.**

Chapter Project Preview

The following activities are included in the Chapter Review. You may want to make the suggested preparations.

CHAPTER REVIEW ACTIVITY

Using Research Skills Students will work in groups to conduct research on the trends in the American family discussed in this chapter and then create a wall chart titled Trends in the American Family. Wall charts should include photographs, tables, charts, and graphs accompanied by detailed captions. Before starting the project, you might want to have the school librarian help you select several appropriate sources for students to use in their research. In addition, have students collect newspapers and magazines and bring them to class to use in the project.

LESSON ACTIVITY

Applying Sociology Students will interview local marriage counselors or social workers to find out about some of the problems that American families face today and how people in those jobs help families overcome challenges. Before starting the project, locate several marriage counselors and social workers who are willing to be interviewed. Then provide students with a list of willing participants and their contact information. Remind students of confidentiality issues.

INTERNET ACTIVITY

Family Disruption and Teens Students will use provided Internet links to conduct research on the effects of family disruption on children, schools, and society and then create a pamphlet to help teens deal with family disruptions. To enhance project uniformity, you might want to create or obtain a template for students' pamphlets. In addition, you might ask the school counselor if he or she knows if any of the students in your class(es) are dealing with family violence, in which case you might not want to do this project.

Additional Resources

PRINT RESOURCES FOR TEACHERS

Farrell, Betty G. *Family: The Making of an Idea, an Institution, and a Controversy in American Culture.* Boulder, CO: Westview Press, 1999. Examines the public debate over family values and contemporary family-related issues from a historical perspective.

Garey, Anita Ilta. *Weaving Work and Motherhood.* Philadelphia, PA: Temple University Press, 1999. Analyzes what it means to be a working mother through interviews and sociological perspectives. Winner of the 2000 William J. Goode Book Award from the Family Section of the American Sociological Association.

PRINT RESOURCES FOR STUDENTS

The American Family Album Series. Oxford University Press, 1995, 1996. This cross-cultural series includes *The Cuban American Family Album, The German American Family Album,* and *The Japanese American Family Album.*

Tan, Amy. *The Joy Luck Club.* New York: Putnam's, 1989. Highlights the experiences of women in China who later immigrated to the United States and the experiences of their American-born daughters.

Taylor, Maureen. *Through the Eyes of Your Ancestors: A Step-by-Step Guide to Uncovering Your Family's History.* Houghton Mifflin Company, 1999. A resource book for students interested in exploring their genealogy.

MULTIMEDIA RESOURCES

Coping with Family Crisis: Violence, Abuse, Separation, Divorce (vhs; 57 min.) Guidance Associates. Presents interviews with people who have experienced family abuse, separation, or divorce.

Families: Will They Survive? (vhs; 20 min.) Encyclopaedia Britannica Educational Corporation. Examines various family forms, including nuclear families and extended families throughout history.

internet connect

go. hrw .com

HRW ONLINE RESOURCES

GO TO: go.hrw.com
Then type in a keyword.

TEACHER HOME PAGE
KEYWORD: SL3 Teacher

CHAPTER INTERNET ACTIVITIES
KEYWORD: SL3 SC12
Choose an activity to have students:
- create a chart that compares family patterns in other countries to those in the United States.
- create a pamphlet to help teens deal with family disruptions.
- write a report on the pressures facing members of the sandwich generation.

CHAPTER ENRICHMENT LINKS
KEYWORD: SL3 CH12

ONLINE ASSESSMENT
Homework Practice
KEYWORD: SL3 HP12
Standardized Test Prep
KEYWORD: SL3 STP12
Rubrics
KEYWORD: SS Rubrics

CONTENT UPDATES
KEYWORD: SS Content Updates

HOLT PRESENTATION MAKER
KEYWORD: SL3 PPT12

ONLINE READING SUPPORT
KEYWORD: SS Strategies

CURRENT EVENTS
KEYWORD: S3 Current Events

CHAPTER

12

The Family

SECTION 1
The Family in Cross-Cultural Perspective

SECTION 2
The American Family

CHAPTER REVIEW

Build on What You Know

Ask students to answer the following questions:

What might be some universal characteristics of families around the world?

Consider:

- biological factors
- cultural norms
- gender roles

How might family patterns in a society change over time?

Consider:

- economic changes
- shifts in gender roles
- acceptance of diversity

Internet Activity

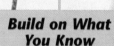

TOPIC: Charting Family Patterns
GO TO: go.hrw.com
KEYWORD: SL3 SC12

Have students access the Internet through the HRW Go site to conduct research on and analyze family patterns in other countries. Next, have each student use the research to create a chart comparing family patterns in the United States with those in other countries. Students should write captions summarizing the information in their charts. Then have volunteers present their charts to the class.

CHAPTER

12

The Family

Build on What You Know

Gender and aging play important roles in the family—one of the most important social institutions. First, you will examine the general characteristics of the family. Then you will turn your attention to the American family while investigating marriage patterns, family disruptions, and recent trends in family patterns.

Sociologists study families because they are a social institution that influences the behavior of people as well as the transfer of values and norms between people.

*L*ife *in* Society

In an article published several years ago, writer William Sayres asked the question, "What is a family, anyway?" How would you answer this question? The answer that many older adults might give would probably be deeply influenced by images of family life shown in 1950s and 1960s television programs, such as *Father Knows Best* and *Leave It to Beaver*.

The families depicted in those programs were strong and child-centered. Duties within the family were rigidly defined—the father was the breadwinner and the mother was the homemaker. For some children the most serious problems they faced were what to spend their allowances on or how to deal with having two dates on the same night. Some critics challenged these presentations of family life because the images did not accurately represent the reality of family life.

In the 2000s many more television shows depict the variety found in family life. Today the vast majority of children live in families with two working parents or with only one parent in the household. While allowances and dating are still important factors in the lives of young people, other far more serious issues have been added to the list of youthful concerns.

TRUTH OR FICTION

What's Your Opinion?

Read the following statements about sociology. Do you think they are true or false? You will learn whether each statement is true or false as you read the chapter.

- Families are the same all over the world.

- Marriage patterns have remained unchanged in the United States since colonial times.

- Family disruptions, such as divorce, have little effect on the adults and children involved.

WHY SOCIOLOGY MATTERS

Sociologists are interested in such family patterns as dual-earner families, one-parent families, childless couples, and stepfamilies. Use CNNfyi.com or other current events sources to learn more about these family patterns. Create a plot for a television show about family life in America.

CNNfyi.com

Sociology Then and Now

The Universal Family. In 1937 sociologist Robert M. MacIver suggested that the institution of the family has several features that are universal. These features include a mating relationship, a creation through some sort of ritual such as marriage, a system of naming (such as father, mother), an economic unity, a common habitation, a mechanism of socialization for children, a system of roles and positions, and a management of conflict resolution among its members.

CRITICAL THINKING

Do you think that the institution of the family has some features that are universal, and if so, do you think these features are the same today? Explain your answer.

ANSWER: Students might note that many families around the world do exhibit many of these features but that variations exist. Have students keep these features in mind as they read the chapter and learn about the institution of the family today.

OBJECTIVES

1. *Describe the norms that influence the ways in which marriage patterns are organized around the world.*

2. *Identify the basic societal needs that the institution of the family satisfies.*

Write the following statement on the chalkboard: *The social institution of the American family is undergoing so much change that the institution might eventually cease.* When students enter the classroom, ask them to write a few sentences either agreeing or disagreeing with this statement. Ask volunteers to share their responses with the class. Then explain to students that the family is the most universal social institution in the world. Every society organizes its members into families. However, what constitutes a family varies widely from culture to culture. Tell students that in Section 1 they will learn about family systems, patterns, and functions around the world.

Visual Answer

Extended family members may provide additional support, such as emotional and childrearing support. In addition, extended families may be able to live together for less expense than the different nuclear-family units could live separately.

① THE FAMILY IN CROSS-CULTURAL PERSPECTIVE

Read to Discover

1. What are the norms that influence the ways in which marriage patterns are organized around the world?
2. What are the basic societal needs that the institution of the family satisfies?

Define

family, nuclear family, family of orientation, family of procreation, extended family, kinship, marriage, monogamy, polygamy, polygyny, polyandry, patrilocality, matrilocality, bilocality, neolocality, patrilineal descent, matrilineal descent, bilateral descent, patriarchy, matriarchy, egalitarian, incest taboo

As you read in Chapter 4, a social institution is a system of statuses, roles, values, and norms organized to satisfy one or more of the society's basic needs. The most universal social institution is the family—every society organizes its members into families. However, what constitutes a family varies widely from culture to culture. Despite this variety, families throughout the world follow similar organizational patterns and fulfill common functions.

Family Systems

A **family** is a group of people who are related by marriage, blood, or adoption and who often live together and share economic resources. How would you answer the question, What is a typical family? You would probably describe what sociologists call the nuclear family. A **nuclear family** consists of one or both parents and their children. The nuclear family is the family form most recognizable to Americans.

During his or her lifetime, a person often is a member of two different overlapping nuclear families. An individual's **family of orientation** is the nuclear family into which the person is born or adopted. This family is composed of the individual and his or her siblings—brothers and sisters—and parents. When an individual marries, a new nuclear family is formed. The new nuclear family is now a **family of procreation**, consisting of the individual, his or her spouse, and their children.

In many societies the nuclear family is embedded in a larger family group. Sociologists refer to this family unit as the **extended family**. An extended family consists of two or more generations. In an extended family, grandparents, parents, children, uncles, aunts, and cousins may all live in one house or grouping of houses or even in different countries.

Nuclear families and extended families are often part of a much larger kinship system. **Kinship** refers to a network of people who are related by marriage, birth,

INTERPRETING VISUALS Extended families include multiple generations of family members. *What sociological needs do you think an extended family may fulfill?*

SUGGESTION 1: Write the term *marriage* on the chalkboard and call on a volunteer to read aloud the term's definition in the Glossary *(the set of norms that establishes and characterizes the relationship between married individuals)*. Next, ask students to identify what these sets of norms are *(norms related to marriage-partner patterns, residential patterns, descent patterns, and authority patterns)*. Then to help students describe these sets of norms, copy the graphic organizer at the right onto the chalkboard, omitting the italicized answers. Have students copy the organizer and complete it by entering the norms found in each pattern and then providing a definition of each norm. Discuss the answers with the class.
ENGLISH LANGUAGE LEARNERS

Marriage-Partner Patterns
- *monogamy*
- *polygamy*
  - *—polygyny*
  - *—polyandry*

Descent Patterns
- *patrilineal descent*
- *matrilineal descent*
- *bilateral descent*

Residential Patterns
- *patrilocality*
- *matrilocality*
- *bilocality*
- *neolocality*

Authority Patterns
- *patriarchy*
- *matriarchy*
- *egalitarian*

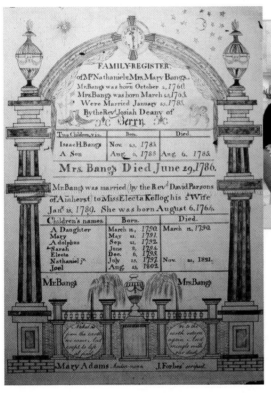

INTERPRETING VISUALS Nuclear families are comprised of one or both parents and children. Many nuclear families use family trees to map their relationships with members of their extended families. *How does a family tree portray kinship systems?*

or adoption. Kinship systems can be quite large. In fact, in some kinship systems there are close to 200 possible categories of relatives. These categories can be organized into three broad groupings—primary, secondary, and tertiary—depending on relationships among individual family members.

An individual's closest relatives are called primary relatives. They are the members of an individual's families of orientation and procreation. The seven possible categories of primary relatives are mother, father, sister, brother, spouse, daughter, and son. An individual's next closest relatives are called secondary relatives. Secondary relatives are the primary relatives of an individual's primary relatives. Secondary relatives consist of more than 30 additional categories of people, including grandparents, grandchildren, in-laws, aunts, uncles, nephews, and nieces. When the primary relatives of an individual's secondary relatives are considered, some 150 other categories of people are added to the kinship system. Individuals at this level are called tertiary relatives, and include great-grandparents, great-grandchildren, great-aunts, great-uncles, and cousins. These nearly 200 categories can translate into literally hundreds of relatives because several people can occupy each category.

Marriage and Kinship Patterns

Some form of family organization exists in all societies. However, the exact nature of the family varies from society to society and even within societies. Family organization is determined by how a society or group within a society answers four questions: (1) How many marriage partners may a person have? (2) Who will live with whom? (3) How will family membership be determined? (4) Who will make the decisions in the family?

Before examining the ways in which societies around the world answer those questions, you should know what is meant by the term **marriage**. Sociologists use the term to refer not to the married couple but to the set of norms that establishes and characterizes the relationship between married individuals. Because marriage often marks the beginning of a family, this set of norms influences the ways in which societies answer the questions of family organization.

Marriage Partners No universal norm limits the number of marriage partners an individual may have. In most industrialized nations, however, an individual is allowed to be married to only one person at a time. The marriage of one man to one woman is called **monogamy**. However, in the majority of pre-industrial societies around the world individuals are permitted to have multiple marriage partners. Marriage with multiple partners is called **polygamy**.

Exploring Cultural Diversity

◼ TEACH

Have students read the feature Changing Family Life on pp. 298–99. Use the first question under Think About It to guide a class discussion about the feature. Then have each student create a chart comparing and contrasting American marriage patterns with those of the past and present in Egypt, based on the feature. Assign the second activity under Think About It as homework. When the class next meets, call on volunteers to share with the class what they learned from the people they interviewed about their experiences of family life.

◼ EXTEND

1: Organize students into pairs and ask them to use their sociological imaginations to rewrite the two narratives in the feature as if they had been written by different generations of American women. One partner in each pair should write a narrative from the point of view of an American woman about Hamida's age. The other partner should write a narrative from the point of view of the older woman's granddaughter. Students should address the four types of marriage patterns. Call on pairs to share their narratives with the class. Encourage student feedback.

COOPERATIVE LEARNING, BLOCK SCHEDULING

◆ Exploring
Cultural Diversity

Families Around the World. Family structure and family life differ around the world. Hunter-gatherer societies in Africa, Australia, South America, and the Arctic still live in large bands of about 20 to 200 people. Until the Communist takeover in 1949, the Chinese had a strict patriarchal clan system. Among the Hopi of the Southwest United States, the oldest woman is considered the head of the family, although her brother or maternal uncle usually holds the greater authority.

ACTIVITY: Have students discuss the advantages and disadvantages of living with a large extended family and of living in a nuclear family.

EXPLORING
Cultural Diversity

CHANGING FAMILY LIFE

In the mid-1990s, writer Perdita Huston traveled to 11 countries and conducted interviews with dozens of families. Huston hoped to gain a greater understanding of the world's families and the forces that were changing them. She tried to talk to at least three generations in a family to better understand social changes. The excerpts below are taken from interviews Huston conducted with members of an Egyptian family.

Hamida

Hamida, the matriarch of the family, is 63 years old.

"I was twelve when I married. My husband didn't know me. His father saw me at the market where he sold his crops. He admired me and asked, 'Who is this girl? Who is her father?' He brought his son to my father and we became engaged. I left my parents and came to live with his large, extended family. Every day I cried and pleaded to go back to my mother. I cried to my husband, his father, his mother, begging to go home to my family. My mother and father came and told me, 'You are now locked in this family. You must stay here. This is your place.' I was homesick but they just said, 'You must stay here.'

My in-laws treated me like a daughter because their family didn't have any girls. . . . [My mother-in-law] didn't leave me on my own. We did everything together. I do the same with my daughters-in-law. . . .

When I was young, women stayed in their homes, but now when they finish their education, if they have a chance for a job, it's allowed.

The negative change that I see is that some wives push their husbands to live apart from the large family, away from the village. When

Family structure, marriage, and family life have changed greatly in Egypt over the past few generations. However, many traditions remain intact. Some Egyptian women wear burkas. A burka is a veil similar to the one worn by the woman at the top right. Although much of Egypt remains a rural society, growing educational opportunities for Egyptians have led to changes.

my eldest son married the teacher, her mother didn't want them to live with us. She insisted they live outside this village, in a separate apartment. But when we built this house my son wanted to be with us. When my daughter-in-law saw that there was no hope of living separately, she finally agreed. . . .

In this house each couple has their own apartment and manages their budget. Sometimes they come here for lunch or dinner but usually everyone eats in their own homes. . . . We are separate but we are also together. And the grandchildren are with us. They come to see me every day after school."

My Sayeed

Seventeen-year-old My Sayeed is Hamida's granddaughter.

"Women used to be isolated from society. Men had all the authority. Women lived in a world of their own, inside, and didn't even see people. There was no role for the woman outside the house, no chance to voice an opinion in the family. My generation insists on our opinions. Women are half of our society. We are trying to expand our roles so that we can do everything like men. . . .

I'd like to marry after finishing university, between age twenty-two and twenty-five. I want

---

2: Ask students to make predictions about the next generation or two of Egyptian marriage and family customs based on the trends illustrated in the feature's narratives. Have students take turns orally summarizing their predictions for the class. Encourage students to consider a range of future possibilities, from a gradual return to traditional customs to a continued trend toward westernized marriage and family norms. **BLOCK SCHEDULING**

3: Have each student write a poem or short story based on the marriage and family experiences of either of the two women whose narratives are provided in the feature. Students might write the poem or story from the direct perspective of one of the women or from a third-person perspective. Remind students to employ cultural relativism when writing their poems or stories. Then call on volunteers to read their work aloud to the class. **BLOCK SCHEDULING**

to choose my husband, but my parents will have to agree. It's my choice, but also the choice of the parents. Boys and girls are now together in the university, in clubs, and all activities. This was not possible before. The man I marry must be understanding, one who shares my opinions as well as all responsibilities. I don't like traditional men who say that a woman must stay at home. And I don't want a large family. The population is increasing too much, and if we are to improve our lives, two children are enough. . . . Some girls say that when they finish their education they'll stay at home if their husbands have money. They say, 'Why not?' But money is not everything. I want to be self-sufficient. . . .

At school we get together to discuss the problems of our society. We learn about women in other countries; we ask about women working outside the home, what their opinions are. We don't accept things as they are."

Interdisciplinary Connection

LITERATURE

Three Generations of Inuit Women. In *Saqiyuq: Stories from the Lives of Three Inuit Women,* anthropologist Nancy Wachowich documents three generations of Inuit women in Canada's eastern High Arctic. The book examines the changing Inuit experience through the lives of Apphia, her daughter Rhoda, and Rhoda's daughter Sandra. The word *Saqiyuq* is an Inuit word meaning "a strong wind that suddenly shifts direction but still maintains its force." The word provides the book's theme—how despite many changes, Inuit women and the Inuit people have maintained their spirit and sense of community.

ACTIVITY: Have each student read *Saqiyuq: Stories from the Lives of Three Inuit Women* (McGill-Queen's University Press, 2001) and write a book report on it.

Think About It

1. **Sociology and Culture** *How has marriage and family life changed in Egypt since Hamida was young? Do you think the interviewed women are happy with these changes? Explain your answer.*
2. **Sociology and You** *Interview older relatives or neighbors to discover their experiences of family life. Have there been changes in family life in your community similar to the changes in Egypt?*

Think About It Answers

1. Arranged marriages are rarer, and women have taken on more authority and gained greater freedom. Older women, such as Hamida, may view these changes more negatively.

2. Results will vary.

SUGGESTION 2: Organize students into small groups and have each group create a mock Web page about the types of norms found in each of the four marriage patterns covered in this section (listed in the graphic organizer on p.297). Each Web page should include a title, at least one image or graphic element, descriptions of the marriage patterns categorized by type, and links to other related pages on the same Web site. Have each group present its Web site design to the class. If possible, have each group actually create its Web page after you make corrections and revisions to the group's design. **COOPERATIVE LEARNING**

HOMEWORK: To help students understand the basic concepts of family systems, have each student create a large flowchart showing the relationships among the nuclear family, the family of orientation, the family of procreation, and the kinship system of primary, secondary, and tertiary relatives. In addition, ask any volunteers whose families have extensive genealogical information, or family trees, to bring some of this information to class to show the other students. You might need to have parents sign a permission slip authorizing their children to bring this information to school.

Exploring Cultural Diversity

Fraternal Polyandry in Tibet. Among some Tibetan farming people, fraternal polyandry is still practiced. In such families, the eldest brother has authority over the household, although all the brothers share responsibilities equally. The wife, in turn, treats each of her husbands equally. The brothers consider all of the children in the family as their own. As a result, the children call all the men *Father*, differentiating among them by birth order, such as eldest father.

The basis of the tradition is economic. By remaining a family unit, the brothers' keep their family inheritance intact instead of dividing it. Tibetan women have several men to support them. If one brother dies, his wife and children are not left alone.

CRITICAL THINKING

Why do some Tibetans practice fraternal polyandry?

ANSWER: economic reasons

Visual Answer

If only the father works, then he must make enough money to support two wives and several children. If all three parents work, then they will make more money than a dual-earner family.

Polygamy can take either of two forms. The most common form of polygamy is **polygyny**, in which a man is permitted to marry more than one woman at a time. The practice of polygyny in preindustrial societies generally occurs when there are large areas of land available for cultivation. A husband who has two or more wives gains additional workers for the land. With multiple wives, the husband is likely to produce more children. These factors add to the man's prestige and economic wealth.

Polyandry—in which a woman is permitted to marry more than one man at a time—is a much rarer form of polygamy. Polyandry, which is found primarily in parts of Asia, appears to arise in response to extreme poverty and a shortage of women. For example, the Toda of India practiced female infanticide—the killing of female babies. As a result, there were not enough women to provide monogamous partners for all of the men in the society. Because of this shortage the Toda developed a system of polyandry. When a woman married a man, she became a wife to all of his brothers. This practice also served to keep the birthrate down, which is important in a poverty-stricken society that cannot afford to support a large population.

Polygamy is the more common marital system in the majority of preindustrial societies around the world. Nevertheless, most people in polygamous societies take only one spouse. There are two reasons for this practice. First, it is very expensive to have more than one marriage partner. In all polygamous societies, individuals are expected to marry only the number of spouses that they can support. Few people can support two or more spouses and their children. For the most part, polygamy is limited to the wealthy few in a society and serves to increase their status and prestige. Second, most societies tend to produce roughly equal numbers of men and women. If a substantial number of people in a society took multiple spouses, there simply would not be enough eligible partners to enable everyone to marry. This situation would prove to be very disruptive to the functioning of the society.

Residential Patterns Once individuals are married, they must decide where to live. Rules of residence vary from society to society. In some societies the newly married couple is expected to live with or near the husband's parents. This residential pattern is called **patrilocality**—*patri* means "father" in Latin, *locality* means "location." Patrilocality is the rule of residence found most commonly around the world. In some societies the couple is expected to live with or near the wife's parents. This pattern is called **matrilocality**—*matri* means "mother." One residential pattern, called **bilocality**—*bi* means "two"—allows the newly married

INTERPRETING VISUALS Polygyny occurs in some societies including Muslim groups in the rural regions of China. This man has two wives and six children. *How might this family arrangement affect the economic life of the family?*

SPOTLIGHT
on Gathering Statistical Information

Have each student survey three to five other students to find out their peers' expectations and goals for marriage and family life. Before starting the activity, have the class work together to create a list of survey questions, such as: *Do you plan to marry someday? How old do you think you will be when you marry? Do you expect to live with or near extended family members?* Then have each student make a copy of the final list of survey questions. When students have finished the survey, have the class tally the results and discuss what they say about possible future trends in American marriage patterns. Remind students to maintain the confidentiality of the students they surveyed. **BLOCK SCHEDULING**

CONNECTING *to Science and Technology*

Ask students to examine how advances in technology have affected family life in the United States over the last century. For example, the introduction of new technologies—such as affordable automobiles, central air and heating, television, computers, the Internet, and cellular phones—have each had a profound effect on family interactions and activities. Have students list three to five such technological advances in chronological order and write two or three paragraphs explaining in their opinions how each new technology has affected American family life. Call on volunteers to share some of their ideas with the class. **BLOCK SCHEDULING**

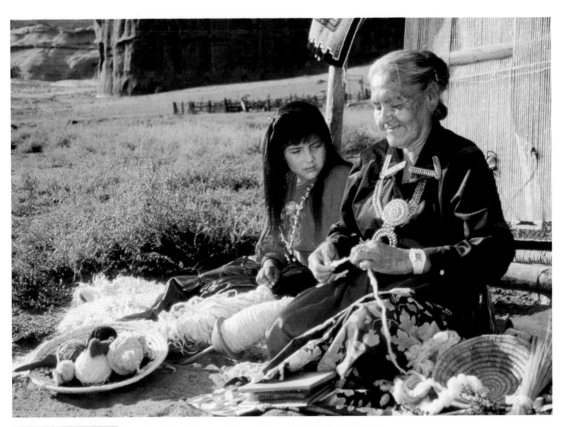

INTERPRETING VISUALS Some American Indian societies practice matrilineal descent, in which kinship is traced through the mother's family. *How might matrilineal descent affect the organization of these societies?*

couple to choose whether they will live near the husband's or the wife's parents. Patrilocal, matrilocal, and bilocal rules of residence encourage the development of extended-family living.

In most industrial societies the newly married couple is free to set up a residence apart from both sets of parents. This residential pattern is called **neolocality**—*neo* means "new." Neolocal residence is most commonly associated with nuclear-family living.

Descent Patterns In some societies, people trace their kinship through the father's side of the family. In other societies, kinship is traced through the mother's side of the family. In still other societies, kinship is traced through both parents.

Societies that trace kinship through the father's family follow the rule of **patrilineal descent**. Patrilineal descent is common in preindustrial societies in which men produce the most valued resources. In a patrilineal society, property is passed from father to son.

Matrilineal descent—the tracing of kinship through the mother's family—is much less common. In matrilineal descent, property is passed from mother to daughter. Most industrial societies practice bilateral descent. In **bilateral descent**, kinship is traced through both parents, and property can be inherited from either side of the family.

Rules for descent are important for the smooth operation of society because they establish who is eligible to inherit property from whom. However, the need to maintain lines of descent can lead to interesting practices. For example, in a few patrilineal societies a father can declare one of his daughters a "son" if he does not have male heirs. This "son" takes a bride who then bears children by various men. These children are considered members of the "son's" kinship group. The marriage between the two women is in name only, however. The women never live together. In fact, the "son" may already be married to a man from another village. The only purpose of the marriage is to produce

TEACH OBJECTIVE 2

SUGGESTION 1: Lead a class discussion on the four basic societal needs that the institution of the family satisfies, as discussed in the section: regulation of sexual activity, reproduction, socialization, and economic and emotional security. Then ask students to imagine that they are going to be foreign exchange students in the United States. Have each student create a print advertisement seeking a family to live with while abroad. The advertisement should address the four functions of the family. Encourage students to be creative. Then ask volunteers to share their advertisements with the class.

SUGGESTION 2: Ask students to imagine that they have been appointed to a new U.S. government department called American Family Affairs. Instruct each group to create an instruction manual entitled Family 101, designed to educate newly married American couples about the social institution of the family. The manual should describe the four main functions of the family as well as the norms influencing American marriage patterns. In addition, each group should create a cover and a table of contents for its manual. Have each group present its manual to the class.
COOPERATIVE LEARNING

Applying Sociology

Marriage Taboos in South Korea. In South Korea, marriages among people with the same surname and whose descendants are from the same place were not only taboo but also illegal. Because South Korea has a relatively small number of surnames, this taboo led to difficulties. For example, in the late 1990s more than 2 million South Koreans with the surname Lee traced their descendants back to one place—Chŏnju. Under law, none of these people could marry each other. A growing number of couples began breaking the law and the taboo by marrying. As a result, in 1997 South Korea overturned the restriction.

ACTIVITY: Have students discuss the reasons why this taboo may have developed.

Visual Answer

These images show both parents equally involved in household chores or sharing chores and child care.

Technology Resources

CNN. Presents Sociology: Parents Help Keep Kids Off Drugs

children who will qualify as legitimate members of the "husband's" kinship group, thereby ensuring that the group will continue.

Authority Patterns In theory there are three possible patterns of authority in families. A family may be a **patriarchy**, in which the father holds most of the authority. It may be a **matriarchy**, in which the mother holds most of the authority. Or it may be **egalitarian**, meaning that the mother and the father share authority.

The vast majority of societies around the world are patriarchal. Matriarchal societies are rare. Even in societies that practice matrilineal descent, true authority rests with the mother's brothers. Although many industrialized societies—such as the United States—are moving toward more egalitarian authority patterns, patriarchal authority is still the cultural norm for many. These egalitarian authority patterns have greatly altered domestic life in many American families. American couples are increasingly sharing the demands of domestic chores, earning income, and raising children.

The Functions of the Family

All families perform similar functions even though the ways these functions are fulfilled may differ from culture to culture. Among the family's most important functions are the regulation of sexual activity, reproduction, socialization, and the provision of economic and emotional security.

INTERPRETING VISUALS Authority patterns in many American families have been changing in recent decades. Today, in many families, men are expected to share in family chores, and women have an equal say in family budgets. *How do these images reflect this egalitarian authority trend?*

Regulation of Sexual Activity All societies regulate the sexual activities of their members to some degree. At the very least, they enforce some type of **incest taboo**. An incest taboo is a norm forbidding sexual relations or marriage between certain relatives. The incest taboo is found universally, but the relatives that are included in this taboo vary from society to society.

For example, in the United States a person cannot marry his or her parents, siblings, grandparents, aunts, uncles, nieces, or nephews. However, 26 states allow marriages between first cousins. Marriages between first cousins are also allowed among the patrilineal Yanomamö of South America. These marriages are restricted to cross cousins—the children of an individual's paternal aunt or maternal uncle. The Yanomamö consider marriages between parallel cousins—the children of an individual's maternal aunt or paternal uncle—incestuous.

The labeling of biologically related individuals as nonrelatives is common in patrilineal and matrilineal societies because ancestry is traced only through one side of the family. For example, among the Lakher of Southeast Asia individuals can marry their maternal half-siblings but not their paternal half-siblings. Because the Lakher are a patrilineal group, they do not consider their maternal half-siblings to be relatives.

Reproduction To survive, societies must replace members who die or move away. In every society the family is the approved social unit for the performance of this function. Consequently, societies establish norms governing childbearing and child rearing. These norms determine such things as who is eligible to marry and to bear children, the number of children that is considered appropriate, and the rights and responsibilities of parents.

Explain to students that there is no such thing as a "perfect" family but that research by psychologists, sociologists, and others has shown the effects of various family organizations and marriage patterns on individuals' happiness and success in life. Organize students into groups and have each group conduct research to find the results of several studies that have been done on families. Groups should investigate issues such as how children of single-parent families do compared to children of dual-parent families, or the effects of blended families, or stepfamilies, on adults and children. Groups might also examine how the number of siblings affects an individual's happiness and success in later life. Encourage students to consider as many family types as possible and to analyze how these dynamics affect individuals. Each group should create a written report that presents the results of the studies researched and includes charts and graphs. Then have each group summarize its findings for the class. **COOPERATIVE LEARNING , BLOCK SCHEDULING**

One function of the family is to socialize children and to teach them how to survive in the society around them.

Sociology in the World Today

Substitute Families.
In the past, Chinese children often lived their entire lives with their parents in extended families. In modern China, young adults increasingly live apart from their parents to seek better job opportunities and a different lifestyle in the cities. The result is that a growing number of older Chinese live alone, without any family to provide emotional support and companionship. To fill this social need, a new type of service has developed. A number of businesses now enable Chinese adult children to pay a fee to have someone visit with their parents.

CRITICAL THINKING
What might be the pros and cons of such a service?

ANSWER: The pros might be that parents receive the companionship they desire. The cons might be that children are losing contact with their parents.

Socialization Children must be taught the ways of the society into which they were born. The family is the first agent of socialization that most children encounter. As a result, most children first learn about the values and norms of society from the family. Parents, siblings, and other relatives usually serve as the earliest role models for children.

Economic and Emotional Security The family acts as the basic economic unit in society. In most societies, labor is divided on the basis of gender—some tasks in the family fall to males while others fall to females. Most societies also have a division of labor based on age. Tasks are divided within the family depending on the ages of the family members. Through this division of labor, the family ensures that its members are fed, clothed, and housed. However, not every family meets these needs.

Although most societies divide labor within the family, specific roles vary from society to society. For example, in some societies that rely on horticulture—simple gardening—for food production, the men tend plants. In other societies, the same task often falls to women. The division of labor also varies among industrialized nations. For example, in Russia many physicians and sanitation workers are women. In the United States, on the other hand, men hold those jobs more often. These roles also change within a society over time. For example, American women now work as lawyers and doctors, which was rare in the 1800s.

In addition to economic support, the family also provides emotional support for its members throughout their lives. As the basic and most intimate primary group in society, the family is expected to guide the individual's psychological development and to provide him or her with a loving and caring environment. In practice, not all families provide such an environment.

In industrialized societies, many of the traditional functions of the family have been taken over, in part, by other social institutions. For example, the educational system plays a major role in socializing young people. Similarly, the government fulfills many of the economic functions that would be the task of families in traditional societies. You will examine the functions of these other social institutions in the remaining chapters of this unit.

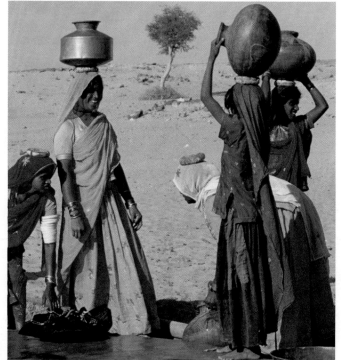

Women play an essential role in the economic survival of families living in regions of India.

SECTION 1 REVIEW

1. Define and explain
family
nuclear family
family of orientation
family of procreation
extended family
kinship
marriage
monogamy
polygamy
polygyny
polyandry
patrilocality
matrilocality
bilocality
neolocality
patrilineal descent
matrilineal descent
bilateral descent
patriarchy
matriarchy
egalitarian
incest taboo

2. Categorizing Copy the graphic organizer below. Use it to identify three broad kinship groupings and to provide examples of relatives within these groupings.

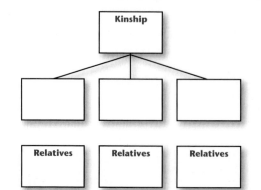

Kinship

Relatives   Relatives   Relatives

3. **Finding the Main Idea**

a. What norms in societies or groups influence marriage patterns?
b. List and describe the basic functions of the family.

4. **Writing and Critical Thinking**

Evaluating Write a brief essay that explains which functions of the family you think are most important in modern societies.
Consider:
- the various agencies in modern societies that perform functions of the family
- the life experiences of modern societies compared to those of traditional societies

Homework Practice Online
keyword: SL3 HP12

SECTION 2

OBJECTIVES

1. *Explain how American families begin and describe some of the disruptions they might face.*

2. *Analyze some of the trends in American family life currently being examined by sociologists.*

2 THE AMERICAN FAMILY

Read to Discover

1. How do American families begin and what disruptions might they face?
2. What are trends in American family life currently being examined by sociologists?

Define

homogamy, heterogamy, dual-earner families, sandwich generation, voluntary childlessness

Traditionally the popular image of the "typical" American family includes a working father, a stay-at-home mother, and two or three children. However, American families are much more diverse. Some families consist of just a married couple who have decided not to have children. Other families have just one parent present. In still other families, no parents are present—the children live with their grandparents or other relatives. Since the 1970s the percentage of married women with children and careers has grown.

INTERPRETING VISUALS The traditional American family of a working father, stay-at-home mom, and two children does not reflect the diversity of the American family structure today. *How common do you think this type of family was in the 1950s?*

Courtship and Marriage

However American families are arranged, most begin in the same way—with marriage. The majority of American adults marry at least once during their lifetimes. In 2000 about 56 percent of American men and 52 percent of American women over 15 years of age were married. However, marriage rates are declining, particularly among younger Americans. For example, about 28 percent of Americans over the age of 15 have never been married. Among Americans between the ages of 25 and 34—the prime years for marriage—this figure is about 35 percent.

Why do people marry? In the United States romantic love is often the basis of marriage. People marry because they are emotionally and physically attracted to one another. Yet love is neither blind nor random. Americans overwhelmingly marry individuals who have social characteristics similar to their own. This kind of marriage is called **homogamy**. Homogamy is based on characteristics such as age, socioeconomic status, religion, and race.

In general, Americans marry individuals who are close to them in age, with the husband slightly older than the wife. Americans also marry within their own socioeconomic class. When differences between a couple do exist, it is most often the woman who is of a lower socioeconomic standing. In the case of religion, marriages between individuals from different Protestant

SUGGESTION 1: Ask students to list several different types of family situations based on the information in this section *(such as, homogamous/heterogamous; married/divorced/single/widowed; several children/one or two children/no children; single/dual earner)*. List the different types on the chalkboard. Next, organize students into small groups and assign each group a different family scenario *(such as heterogamous, married, no children, dual earner)*. You might also want to assign characteristics such as age of parents or grown versus young children. Then instruct each group to create a fictitious history for its assigned family. Histories should describe how the family began, the events that led to its current state, and any family disruptions encountered along the way. Tell

students to refer to the statistical information in the section to come up with believable family histories. Then have each group share its history with the class. **COOPERATIVE LEARNING**

SUGGESTION 2: Ask volunteers to explain how most American families begin *(with courtship and marriage between either homogamous or heterogamous couples)* and describe some of the disruptions they might face *(family violence, divorce, empty nest, return of adult children, and death of a spouse)*. Then ask students to imagine that they are newspaper reporters. Have each student write a short article on one of these topics. The article should include at least one chart or graph.

◆ Applying Sociology

Interfaith Marriages. According to *The Journal of Marriage & Family*, about half of Jews now marry non-Jews and about half of Catholics now marry non-Catholics. Such interfaith marriages are on the rise in the United States, although divorce rates among interfaith marriages are higher than the national rate.

ACTIVITY: Have students discuss what effects a growing number of interfaith marriages could have on American society.

Did You Know?

The practice of using rings as symbols of marital commitment probably originated with the ancient Romans. The custom of adding gems to engagement rings began in the 1200s. During the 1600s, it was popular for romantic partners to exchange poesy rings, or rings engraved with a short poem.

Chart Answer

Hispanic and other non-Hispanic

Most Americans marry individuals with characteristics similar to their own. For example, Americans often marry people with a similar religious faith. However, some Americans marry people with different racial, age, and religious characteristics.

Intergroup Couples, 1999

10.4%
55.5%
33.2%
.9%

■ African American/White Non-Hispanic
■ White Non-Hispanic/Other Non-Hispanic
■ African American/Other Non-Hispanic
■ Hispanic/Other Non-Hispanic

Source: U.S. Census Bureau

INTERPRETING CHARTS Heterogamy has become more common and accepted in many parts of American society. *What is the most common type of heterogamous marriage?*

denominations are relatively common. However, it is much less common for Protestants to marry non-Protestants. The same is true for Catholics, Jews, and people of other faiths. When individuals from different religious backgrounds do marry, one partner sometimes adopts the other partner's religion.

Homogamy is even stronger when it comes to race. Only 2.4 percent of all marriages are between individuals who are black and white. Nevertheless, the number of interracial marriages in the United States has grown by almost 10 times since the late 1960s. Before that time, at least a dozen states had laws that made interracial marriages illegal. In 1967 a Supreme Court ruling struck down those laws.

Although homogamy is still typical in the United States, an increasing number of marriages are heterogamous. **Heterogamy** is marriage between individuals who have different social characteristics. This increase in heterogamy is a function of changing social conditions. As contact between people of differing social backgrounds increases, the likelihood of heterogamous marriages also increases. Some of the factors that have contributed to heterogamy are higher college enrollments, more geographical mobility, and the increased participation of women in the workforce.

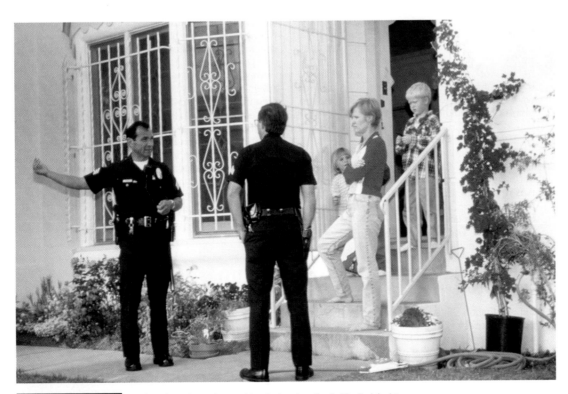

SPOTLIGHT *on Family Violence*

Have students interview people working in the area of family violence. Interviewees might include police officers, social workers, attorneys, alcohol-abuse counselors, and personnel who work at shelters for abused women and children. Encourage students to ask for statistical information about family-abuse cases in the local community as well as information about programs to help reduce family violence and aid victims. Have the students report their findings to the class orally. **BLOCK SCHEDULING**

CONNECTING *to History*

Organize students into small groups. Have half of the groups conduct research on family life in colonial America and the other half conduct research on family life during the Industrial Revolution. Then have each group write and present a short skit depicting family life during its assigned time period. Use the activity as the basis for a brief class discussion on changing trends in American family life over time. **COOPERATIVE LEARNING,**
BLOCK SCHEDULING

Family Disruption

Most families experience disruption in one form or another. Some disruptions are very serious—threatening or even destroying family stability. Others are simply a part of the family life cycle.

Family Violence Some sociologists argue that family violence is the most-devastating family disruption. Until relatively recently, family violence was considered a fairly rare phenomenon. However, sociologists now know that family violence is a serious problem among all social classes and racial and ethnic groups.

One reason family violence was at first considered a problem of the lower classes was the way in which statistics were collected. Most early research was based on police and hospital reports. Because the police and hospitals were more likely to be involved in cases of domestic violence involving lower-income families, these families were over-represented in the statistics. Cases of violence among middle- and upper-income families generally went unreported.

The widespread nature of family violence was confirmed in a 1975 nationwide study. The researchers found that nearly one third of the people they interviewed had experienced some form of family violence in the course of their marriages. Moreover, almost three fourths of the people interviewed reported hitting their children, usually more than once. The study also revealed that wives were as likely to commit violent acts within the family. However, the acts committed by wives were less violent in nature and less damaging to spouses and children.

A repeat of this study some 10 years later found that family violence had decreased somewhat. There is some support for this conclusion in studies done by various government and private agencies. Statistics collected by the U.S. Department of Justice suggest that female victims of abuse and of murder have dropped while the number of male victims have stayed the same. Surveys by child-advocacy groups suggest that child abuse is also increasing. The following statistics give an indication of the seriousness of the problem of family violence.

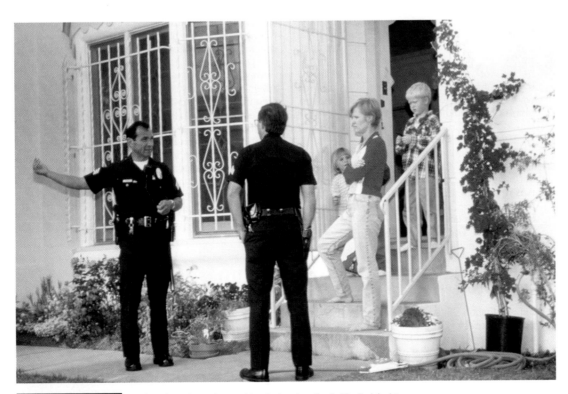

INTERPRETING VISUALS Family violence is a serious problem in American family life. Sociologists have studied some of the factors that influence family violence. *How does this image illustrate the effects of family violence on children?*

Case Studies and Other True Stories

■ TEACH

Have students read the feature Industrialization and the Family and then discuss how industrialization has affected the American family—past, present, and future. Then have each student create an annotated time line that illustrates some of these effects of industrialization. To help students with the activity, bring to class several sources that list the dates of major industrial advances or periods.

■ EXTEND

The growing practice of telecommuting is allowing more full-time employees to work from home. Have students write help-wanted ads for telecommuters that might appear in newspapers and on the Internet 5 to 10 years from now. Ads should focus on potential employees' office equipment as well as on needed skills and experience. Then in a class discussion, ask students to consider how such technology-driven trends might affect marriages, families, and related societal issues such as child care, gender roles, and traffic. **BLOCK SCHEDULING**

Did You Know?

In the past, American families tended to be quite large, but high mortality rates among all age groups also limited family size. From the early 1600s to the late 1800s, the average household size in the United States was about five people. In the late 1990s the average household size was about three people.

Think About It Answers

1. It shifted economic activity from the home to the factory, limited the functions of the family, and changed roles within the family. Men became breadwinners, and women became homemakers. Women's status within the family diminished, and adolescence emerged as a life stage.

2. Answers will vary, but students might note that telecommuting might increase the amount of time that parents can spend with children and lead to more equality of gender roles within the family.

Case Studies

AND OTHER TRUE STORIES

INDUSTRIALIZATION AND THE FAMILY

The family, like other social institutions, is subject to the forces of change. Great societal changes bring equally great changes to society's institutions. For example, industrialization profoundly altered the nature and roles of the family.

The Preindustrial Family

In preindustrial times, the family was the center of economic activity. Family members provided for their own needs by growing their own food, making their own clothes, and building their own houses. What goods and services families could not produce, they acquired through barter.

Family life and economic life were essentially one and the same in preindustrial times because the home was where work was done. Even skilled artisans who lived in urban areas usually plied their trades from workshops located next to or in the home. Work was a family activity, and all family members had a role to play. Even young children were expected to contribute by doing simple work tasks or household chores. Because children were considered important to the economic survival of the family, families tended to be large.

Family authority patterns in preindustrial times were patriarchal. The father made all of the major decisions for the family and told other family members what to do. However, mothers played a major role in the family. Women undertook many important productive tasks of the family—such as making food, clothes, and candles. They also assured the continuation of the family through their leading role in child rearing.

Effects of Industrialization

Industrialization shifted economic activity from the home to the factory. The family no longer needed to be self-sufficient because the goods manufactured in the factories could meet most of its needs. Over time, many of the services the family performed were taken over by charitable organizations and government agencies.

The shift of work from the home to the factory brought changes to roles within the family, too. Because they now worked outside the home, men and women could no longer watch over their children during the workday. In time, men began to push for a "living" wage that would support the whole family. Then women could stay at home and take care of the children.

The change of role from worker to homemaker had an enormous effect on the social and economic status of women. Domestic tasks, such as cooking, cleaning, making and repairing clothes, and child rearing, which had been an integral part of the economic activity of the preindustrial family, was now considered a chore. Comparing the contributions of wives to those of their "breadwinning" husbands greatly diminished women's status within the family and in society as a whole. Married women regularly received lower wages than men because employers saw women's pay as an "add-on" to the living wage that their husbands already earned.

Industrialization also brought changes to the family roles of children. In preindustrial times, children were productive members of the family economic unit. In the early years of industrialization, many children continued to fulfill this role by taking factory jobs. However, laws that restricted child labor and the advent of compulsory education largely removed children from the world of work. This severing of ties between children and the world of adult work helped give rise to adolescence as a life stage.

Many sociologists predict that the technological revolution brought about by the computer will bring new changes to the family. The growing practice of telecommuting—working at home using a computer—may make the home a major center of economic activity once again.

Think About It

1. **Evaluating** *How did industrialization change the institution of the family?*

2. **Making Generalizations and Predictions** *How do you think the technological advances of the last few years will change the family? Give reasons for your answer.*

SPOTLIGHT on Divorce

A growing number of children witness the breakup of their parents' marriages every year. Have students work in small groups to design and develop public service materials (such as posters, television commercials, and magazine ads) to raise awareness of the effects of divorce on children. Materials might target children (such as how to cope with divorce), married couples (such as how to avoid divorce), divorced couples (such as how to help children cope with divorce), and single adults (such as things to look for in a mate). Have students present their public service materials to the class.

COOPERATIVE LEARNING , BLOCK SCHEDULING

Teacher to Teacher

Anna Bryant of Richmond, Virginia, suggested the following activity: Have the class debate the following statement: *Divorce is too easy to obtain today.* Organize the class into three groups and have one group argue in favor of the statement, one group argue against it, and the third group serve as a media panel, which will ask questions during the debate. Provide students with time to prepare for the debate. Then serve as the moderator during the debate and provide each side a set amount of time for arguments and rebuttal.

COOPERATIVE LEARNING , BLOCK SCHEDULING

- In 1998 about 1 million crimes of violence were committed against people by intimate partners. About 85 percent of the victims were women.
- About 11 percent of all murders committed in 1998 were the result of intimate-partner violence. Some 75 percent of the victims of intimate-partner murder were women.
- Nearly 3.2 million cases of neglect or physical abuse against children were reported in 1999. Just over 1 million children were confirmed by child protective services to be victims of maltreatment.
- Child abuse resulted in the deaths of almost 1,400 children in 1999. However, experts estimate that the true figure was considerably higher because abuse-related deaths are often attributed to other causes.

Divorce One type of family disruption that has received a great deal of media attention is divorce. The statistic the media most often cites is that in the United States one out of every two marriages eventually ends in divorce. There are more than 19.8 million Americans over the age of 19 who are divorced. The United States divorce rate—the number of divorces per 1,000 population—is the highest in the world at 4.2.

The rate of divorce varies among different segments of the population. For example, couples who marry during their teenage years have a greater likelihood of divorce than couples who marry after the age of 20. Education also influences the rate of divorce. Couples with college educations are less likely to divorce than couples who have not attended college. However, women who have attended graduate school are more likely to divorce than less-educated women.

Divorce also varies by race and ethnicity. African American women are more likely than white women to be separated or divorced. Hispanic women, on the other hand, are slightly less likely than white women to experience divorce. The higher rate of divorce among African American women is partially explained by the fact that a higher percentage of African American women are young and have low incomes when they marry.

Divorce has major consequences for former partners. In economic terms, divorce has greater effects on women than on men. One study found that after divorce, women's incomes fell by 30 percent. In contrast, men's incomes showed a 10 percent reduction. Conversely, women seem to make better emotional adjustments to divorce. Rates of suicide, alcoholism, drug abuse,

INTERPRETING VISUALS Some American couples seek counseling to resolve the conflicts that arise in marriage. *How might therapy help prevent divorce?*

TEACH OBJECTIVE 2

SUGGESTION 1: To help students analyze some of the trends in American family life currently being examined by sociologists, copy the graphic organizer at the right onto the chalkboard, omitting the italicized answers. Have students copy and complete the organizer. Discuss the answers with the class. Then have students use their organizers to help them create collages that illustrate one or more of the trends identified in the graphic organizer. Display students' completed collages in the classroom.

ENGLISH LANGUAGE LEARNERS

delayed marriage *delayed childbearing*

Trends in American Family Life

childlessness *remarriage*

dual-earner marriages *one-parent families*

Sociology Then and Now

The Good Old Days?

Some Americans believe that family life was stronger and more stable in the past. Others see this nostalgia for the past as misguided, pointing out that the ideal family has never existed and that every time period has posed its own unique challenges. For example, in the 1950s, more children went hungry and poverty rates were higher than today. Housewives were more likely to suffer anxiety and depression. In addition, many incidents of family violence and abuse were either covered up, overlooked, or not believed.

Today American fathers spend more time with their families than in the last 100 years. Men do a larger share of the housework than they did in the 1950s. In addition, women have more economic independence and are freer to leave an unhappy marriage.

RESEARCH ACTIVITY: Have each student conduct research on marriage- and family-related statistics for 1900, 1950, and 2000, and then create charts and graphs to present the findings.

Visual Answer

by humorously suggesting complex stepfamilies for both children

depression, and anxiety are all higher among divorced men than among divorced women.

Adults are not the only ones affected by divorce. Each year, more than 1 million children under the age of 18 witness the breakup of their parents' marriages. Like their parents, children of divorce often struggle to adjust to their new situations. Studies suggest that children of divorced parents have more emotional problems and are lower achievers than children of parents who have not divorced. Some 40 percent of these children are still struggling to adjust 10 years after their parents divorced.

Sociologists suggest several reasons for the high divorce rate. First, the laws governing the divorce process have become less complicated, and the cost of obtaining a divorce has decreased. Most states now have some form of no-fault divorce law. In no-fault divorces, neither party has to state a specific reason for seeking the divorce. Second, the increase in the number of **dual-earner families**—families in which both husband and wife have jobs—and the growth of day care facilities has decreased the economic dependence of women. It now is financially possible for more women to remove themselves from unhappy marriages. Third, society in general has become more tolerant of divorce. It no longer carries the same social stigma it did 20 or 30 years ago. Finally, many people expect more of marriage and are less ready to accept marital problems. When these problems become overwhelming, people often see divorce as an acceptable alternative to staying in an unsatisfactory marriage.

Family Disruptions in Later Life

Most parents spend a good part of their lives raising their children. When the children grow up and leave home, parents are left with what sociologists call an empty nest. Most people assume that parents, particularly mothers, have difficulty adjusting to this disruption. However, studies suggest that mothers feel a sense of increased satisfaction after their children have left home.

In recent years, the empty-nest stage has been delayed for many families. Children, for the most part, are leaving home later than in the past. Close to 50 percent of Americans between the ages of 18 and 24 still live at home. Some children are returning to their parents' homes after living independently for several years. About 8 percent of 25- to 44-year-olds now live with their parents.

The final disruption that families face is family dissolution that follows the death of a spouse. Because women statistically have a longer life expectancy than men, they are more likely to experience this disruption. About 16 percent of men aged 65 and older are widowers. However, close to 40 percent of all women over the age of 65 are widows.

Widowhood creates identity problems, particularly for women who have defined themselves primarily in terms of being a wife. Such women often continue to judge their own actions and life choices against the values of their dead husbands. In essence, these women continue to use the wife role as a guide to behavior long after they become widows. Widowed women also frequently face economic problems. The loss of employment income or the decrease in Social Security benefits that accompanies the death of a husband may push some widows into poverty. Less money means that it is more difficult for these women to enjoy activities outside of the home. This change in circumstances translates into increased levels of loneliness for many widowed women.

Trends in American Family Life

Over the past few decades, the traditional family—with the father as the sole breadwinner and the mother as the homemaker—has become the exception rather than the rule in the United States. Dual-earner families, one-parent families, childless couples, and stepfamilies now are common features of American family life. Sociologists are particularly interested in these and other developments, such as delayed marriage, delayed childbearing, and remarriage.

JEFF STAHLER reprinted by permission of United Feature Syndicate, Inc., and Newspaper Enterprise Association, Inc.

INTERPRETING VISUALS Divorce and remarriage have led to complex family structures in many American families. *How does this cartoon illustrate the complexity and growth of stepfamilies?*

Mapping Social Forces

Mapping
SOCIAL FORCES

THE CHANGING AMERICAN FAMILY

In the face of all the changes that are sweeping our society, the family is also changing. It is taking many forms that were uncommon in the past. Of course, the traditional American family—a wage-earner husband, a homemaker wife, and their two children—can still be found. However, such families are now a minority in our society. What are some of the new forms that the American family is taking? The pie charts and bar graph below offer some clues.

Marital Status of the Population 15 Years of Age and Older

1970
71.7%
8.9%
16.2%
3.2%

2000
59.5%
6.7%
9.9%
23.9%

■ Married ■ Never Married ■ Separated/Divorced ■ Widowed

Source: U.S. Census Bureau

Married Women in the Workforce (in thousands)

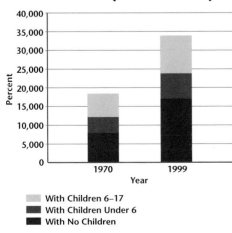

With Children 6–17
With Children Under 6
With No Children

Source: U.S. Census Bureau

Interpreting Charts

1. Drawing Inferences and Conclusions *Describe the trends shown in the various graphs. What do you think helped to bring about these trends?*

2. Analyzing Information *Consult the Statistical Abstract of the United States, and other sources to find other information on changes in the American family. Use your findings to create a chart and graph booklet titled "Statistics on Changes in the American Family."*

Sociology in the World Today

The Changing Family. Recent sociological studies show that the social institution of the family is changing in many parts of the world. Six general trends are apparent—a decline in influence of the clan and other kinship groups, the ability to choose one's spouse, a greater recognition of the rights of women, a decline in kin marriages, higher levels of sexual freedom in formerly restrictive countries, and a growing awareness of children's rights.

CRITICAL THINKING
What might be some of the causes of these changes?

ANSWER: Students might mention that some of these changes are the result of Western ideas of the family being spread around the world through television, the Internet, and satellite communications.

Chart Answers

1. Fewer Americans are married, more are divorced, and more married women—both with and without children—are part of the workforce. Causes might include industrialization, the women's movement, a rise in the average age at marriage, and fewer social taboos against divorce.

2. Booklets will vary.

SUGGESTION 2: Lead a class discussion on the trends in American family life discussed in this section *(listed in the graphic organizer on p. 310)*. Organize students into pairs and have each pair discuss trends in American family life and make predictions about how American families might continue to change over the next few decades. Then instruct each pair to create a poster that illustrates how family life has changed over the last century or so and the different ways in which families might evolve in the future. Have volunteer pairs present their work to the class and explain their predictions. **COOPERATIVE LEARNING**

SUGGESTION 3: Call on volunteers to summarize the trends in American family life discussed in this section *(listed in the graphic organizer on p. 310)*. Then organize students into groups and ask the groups to imagine that they are designing a new family theme or amusement park called Familyland. The park's rides, shows, exhibitions, restaurants, and shops should all reflect past, current, and future trends in the American family. Instruct each group to create either a brochure or a large tourist map naming and describing several of the park's planned attractions. The brochure or map should be designed to show to potential financial investors. Have each group present and explain its work to the class. **COOPERATIVE LEARNING**

Applying Sociology

The Family of the Future? Combine the "graying of America" with increases in childlessness and in the median age at first marriage, and the result could be a future in which the typical American family is an elderly childless couple. Sociologists call such a couple the gerontic family.

ACTIVITY: Have each student write his or her own prediction of the future American family, based on the information in this section.

Graph Answer

a little less than five years

Technology Resources

Teaching Transparency: Median Age at Marriage in the United States, 1890–1998

Delayed Marriage In 1890 the median age at first marriage in the United States was 22.0 years for women and 26.1 years for men. By 1960 the median age at first marriage had dropped to 20.3 years for women and 22.8 years for men. However, in recent years this trend toward earlier marriages has reversed itself. In 2000 the median age at first marriage was 25.1 years for women and 26.8 years for men. As you can see in the table on this page, these ages are among the highest recorded since the Bureau of the Census first began collecting this information in 1890.

Some sociologists view this tendency toward later marriage as an indication that being single has once again become an acceptable alternative to being married. Relatively common in the early part of the last century, being single lost ground in the marriage-minded years following World War II. By 1970 only 6.2 percent of American women between the ages of 30 and 34 had never been married. This number was down from 16.6 percent in 1900. Then in the 1970s and 1980s, the marriage rate began to slow. By 2000 the proportion of women between the ages of 30 and 34 who had never been married had increased to about 22 percent. If this trend continues, demographers estimate that more than 15 percent of today's young adults will never marry.

Sociologists note that most young people today are delaying marriage in order to finish their education and to launch their careers. This trend is particularly notable among women. Sociologists also note that the increase in

the number of unmarried people may partially be the result of more couples living together outside of marriage. Sociologists refer to this practice as cohabitation. In 2000 there were more than 3.8 million cohabiting couples in the United States. This number is up from 523,000 couples in 1970. Cohabitation is particularly common among the young. Estimates suggest that about 25 percent of unmarried women between the ages of 25 and 39 are currently cohabiting and an additional 25 percent have cohabited at some time in the past. Cohabitation now precedes more than half of all first marriages. Although most individuals who cohabit eventually marry someone—not necessarily their current partner—the practice usually delays marriage.

Delayed Childbearing Another trend in family life in the United States that sociologists have noted in recent years is delayed childbearing. In the 1960s the average length of time between marriage and the birth of the first child was 15 months. By the 1970s that interval had increased to 27 months. Today it is not at all uncommon for women to have their first child after the age of 30. Women between the ages of 30 and 34 accounted for 23 percent of all births in 1998. An additional 12 percent of the births in 1998 were to women between the ages of 35 and 39. The reasons for delaying childbearing are similar to the reasons for delaying marriage—to allow time to complete education and to establish a career.

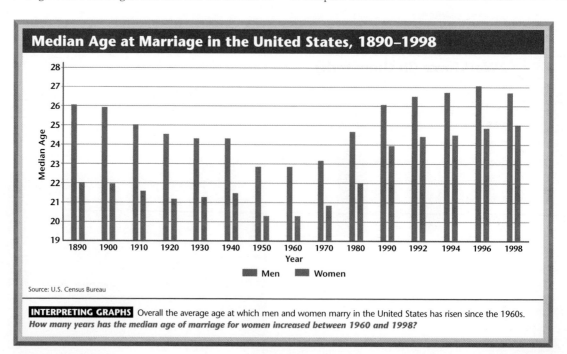

Median Age at Marriage in the United States, 1890–1998

Median Age (y-axis: 19–28)

Year (x-axis): 1890, 1900, 1910, 1920, 1930, 1940, 1950, 1960, 1970, 1980, 1990, 1992, 1994, 1996, 1998

■ Men ■ Women

Source: U.S. Census Bureau

INTERPRETING GRAPHS Overall the average age at which men and women marry in the United States has risen since the 1960s. *How many years has the median age of marriage for women increased between 1960 and 1998?*

HOMEWORK: Instruct students to write short essays explaining which of the trends in American family life has had the largest effect, in their opinions, and why. In addition, students should discuss what effects the trend has had and may continue to have in the future. Remind students to provide facts, statistics, and examples that support their positions and to use standard grammar, spelling, sentence structure, and punctuation in their essays. When the class next meets, ask one or two volunteers to read their essays aloud to the class.

CONNECTING *to Government*

Tell students that the concept of family values has become a controversial and important point of debate in American politics. Ask students to write their own definitions of the term *family values* and what it means in the political arena. Call on a few volunteers to share their definitions with the class. Guide students in understanding how different American political groups define and view family values. **BLOCK SCHEDULING**

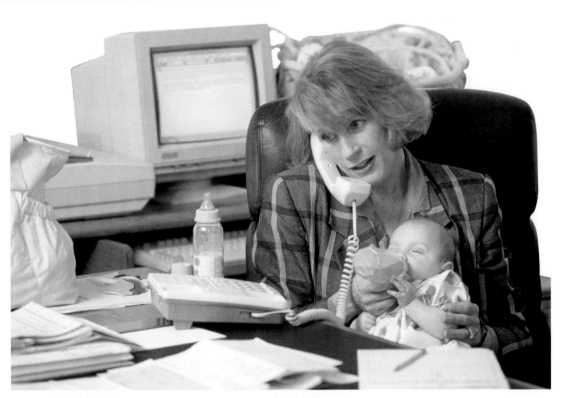

INTERPRETING VISUALS Many changes in family life—such as delayed childbirth, dual-earner marriages, and single-parent families—have led to a growing number of working mothers. *What types of challenges might working mothers face?*

Some couples who delayed having children until their thirties are now facing a particularly challenging situation. They have young children to raise at the same time that they have aging parents who need care and assistance. These couples have been labeled the **sandwich generation** because they are caught between the needs of their children and those of their parents. Worn down by family duties and the demands of work, members of the sandwich generation often feel overwhelmed.

Childlessness There has also been an increase in the number of married couples who never have children. Some couples who at first plan to delay parenting find later that they have waited too long. Other married couples discover that they cannot have children because of infertility. Still others consciously choose never to have children. Sociologists call the conscious choice to remain childless **voluntary childlessness**. The number of voluntarily childless couples has increased markedly in recent years. In 2000, 22 percent of married women between the ages of 30 and 44 had no children. Among childless married women in their early thirties, a little more than 40 percent had no plans to have children in the future.

Studies have found that married couples who choose to remain childless often have high levels of education and income. Career success is a priority for many voluntarily childless women. Many voluntarily childless couples place great value on women achieving success. These couples also value the freedom, financial security, and the opportunity to spend time together that childlessness allows.

Dual-Earner Marriages Another trend in American family life is an increase in the number of dual-earner marriages because of the increased numbers of married women entering the labor force. The percentage of married women who work outside the home increased steadily for more than 50 years until the mid 1990s. In 1940 about 17 percent of married women were employed outside the home. This figure rose to 22 percent after World War II in 1948. By 1960 the number of married women in the labor force had grown to 31 percent. Today about 61 percent of all married women work outside the home at least part-time.

Married women work for the same basic reason that married men work—economic necessity. Few families today can survive or live as comfortably as they want on

Connecting to Economics

■ TEACH

Have students read the feature Dual-Earner Families aloud in class. Then use the questions under Think About It to launch a class discussion about dual-earner families and gender roles. Challenge students to brainstorm ways of determining how to divide family responsibilities fairly among family members. Tell students to focus on communication and planning strategies. Then have students discuss their ideas. Encourage student feedback.

■ EXTEND

Tell students that technology has dramatically reduced the amount of time spent on household chores over the last century. Ask students to name various household chores. As they do, list the chores on the chalkboard. Then help students estimate the time it might have taken to complete each chore 100 years ago and how long on average it takes to complete each chore today. If possible, you might also have students watch a video of the PBS television series *The 1900 House*, in which a modern family lives for three months in an authentic Victorian home with no modern amenities.

BLOCK SCHEDULING

◆ Case Study

Quality Time at Home.
A 1997 study found that American parents spent an average of four to six more hours a week with their children than the previous generation of parents did. In addition, the study found that working mothers spent about the same amount of time with their children as stay-at-home mothers did in the early 1980s—about 26 hours a week. How are modern parents finding the extra time to spend with their children? According to the study, parents are either doing less housework or paying someone to do it.

ACTIVITY: Have students conduct research on other case studies related to dual-earner families and share their findings with the class.

Think About It Answers

1. In many dual-earner families, the wife earns more than the husband does, and the amount of time women spend on housekeeping is on the decline.

2. Answers will vary, but students might mention more flexible work schedules or telecommuting.

CONNECTING TO
Economics

DUAL-EARNER FAMILIES

Dual-earner families are a permanent fixture of the American labor landscape. Recent figures show that there are close to 32 million dual-earner families in the United States. This number is nearly three times that of traditional families in which one spouse is the wage earner and the other stays at home. Sociologists have begun to investigate what effects, if any, dual-earner status has on family roles.

Changing Roles?

In a 1998 study Anne E. Winkler suggests that there is some evidence that gender roles within marriages may be changing. In past dual-earner families, the husband usually earned more than the wife. As a result, it was assumed that the husband's job was always more important than the wife's and that advancement in his career took precedence over advancement in hers. However, in recent years more women have entered high-paying executive and professional positions. In a growing number of dual-earner families, the wife earns more than the husband does. Close to 10 percent of these wives earn as much as 50 percent more than their husbands. While these figures do not necessarily mean that these wives' careers take precedence over those of their husbands, they may be an indication that the way economic decisions are made in dual-earner households is changing.

Another study, this one by Francine D. Blau, uses the amount of time spent on housework as an indication that there may be a change in gender roles in dual-earner families. This study found that the amount of housework done by women had declined since the 1970s even though women still spent much more time on household chores than men did. Even so, because housework has traditionally been seen as "woman's work," any change might indicate an adjustment in family roles.

Dual-earner families have to find ways to balance the tasks of raising children and the demands of work.

Do Traditional Roles Still Hold?

A study that looked directly at these two points—career precedence and workload in the home—suggests that there may be less gender-role change than at first appears. This study noted that to accommodate the stresses and strains of running two jobs and a home, dual earners assign greater importance to one spouse's job. The study's findings showed that, typically, it is the husband's job that is assigned this position. Only 15 percent of the men interviewed said that their wives' jobs are given higher priority.

Another of the study's findings illustrated the higher priority given to men's careers. Family-related matters that required missing work—such as parent-teacher conferences and children's medical appointments—were usually handled by women.

On the subject of household chores, the survey found that, on average, women spent over 30 minutes more on housework each workday than men. The survey also found that more women than men felt that their spouses should do more around the house.

All these studies show that the dual-earner family is growing in importance in American society. Whether it is helping to forge new gender roles within the family, however, still seems open to question.

Think About It

1. Analyzing Information *What two types of evidence do the studies use to suggest that gender roles in dual-earner families may be changing?*

2. Supporting a Point of View *What changes in the way people work do you think need to be made to make life easier for dual-earner families? Explain your answer.*

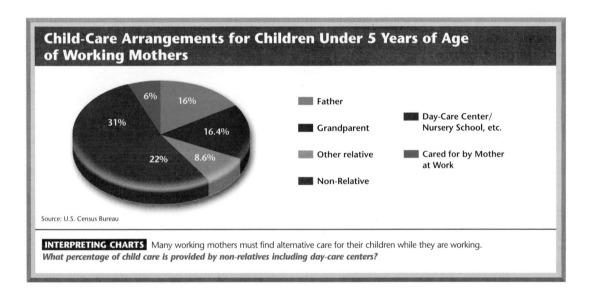

SPOTLIGHT on Widowhood

Tell students that widowhood can create identity problems for men and women who define themselves primarily in terms of being married. Widows and widowers may face single parenthood, aging alone, and the sometimes frightening prospect of dating again. Then have students discuss the affects of trends such as delayed childbearing, childlessness, dual-earner incomes, and remarriage on widowhood. Finally, have each student write one or two paragraphs summarizing some of the challenges faced by widows and widowers. **BLOCK SCHEDULING**

CONNECTING to Economics

Tell students that one economic factor that single parents and dual-earner parents may have to consider is the cost of child care. Have students contact a variety of day-care centers, preschools, and home-based caregivers in their state or local community to find out the average monthly cost of different types of child care. Have students report their findings to the class. Then use the activity as the basis for a class discussion on some of the issues facing working parents in American society. (Other issues might include latchkey kids and child-care-related stress.) **BLOCK SCHEDULING**

Child-Care Arrangements for Children Under 5 Years of Age of Working Mothers

6% · 16% · 31% · 16.4% · 22% · 8.6%

Father
Grandparent
Other relative
Non-Relative
Day-Care Center/Nursery School, etc.
Cared for by Mother at Work

Source: U.S. Census Bureau

INTERPRETING CHARTS Many working mothers must find alternative care for their children while they are working. *What percentage of child care is provided by non-relatives including day-care centers?*

a single salary. Also, in the past few years, more and more women have been entering colleges and universities. Education enables women to pursue more-attractive better-paying positions in the labor market. In nearly one third of all dual-earner couples, the wife earns more than the husband does. The growing number of married working women in the labor force has helped to lessen the stigma once attached to working wives and mothers. This favorable climate has encouraged more women to seek work outside of the home.

The labor market itself has been a factor in the increase of dual-earner families. Since World War II, there has been a tremendous rise in the number of available jobs in service and other industries that traditionally employ large numbers of women. Many women are also entering nontraditional occupations at a rate never before seen in the United States. Women today make up nearly 25 percent of the doctors, 31 percent of the computer scientists, and 43 percent of the college and university teachers in this country.

Women's participation in the labor force is influenced by the ages of their children. In 1998 about 62 percent of married women with children under the age of 6 were employed outside the home, compared to about 77 percent of married women with children between the ages of 6 and 17. Many women with newborn children in the home leave the labor force for a period of time. However, in 1993 Congress passed the Family and Medical Leave Act to help parents care for their newborn children without having to drop out of the labor force. The law requires companies with more than 50 workers to give up to 12 weeks of unpaid leave to parents of newborns.

The law also covers workers who need to take time to arrange for the adoption of a child or to care for a sick spouse, child, or parent. Federal government officials estimate that about 20 million people have taken advantage of the Family and Medical Leave Act since 1993.

Some people have expressed concern that the increased participation of married women in the labor force may have negative consequences for their children. However, research has failed to establish any meaningful negative effect. On the other hand, studies suggest that daughters of working women may benefit. Daughters of working mothers often have a better self-image, are more independent, and are higher achievers than daughters of nonworking mothers.

One-Parent Families Another trend in American family life that has gained the attention of social scientists in recent years is the increase in one-parent families. One-parent families are formed through separation, divorce, death of a spouse, births to unwed mothers, or adoption by unmarried individuals. However, in the United States most one-parent families are the result of divorce or of births to unwed mothers.

One-parent families account for about 25 percent of the families in the United States with children under the age of 18. Women head about 8 out of every 10 of these one-parent families. As can be seen from the pie charts on page 316, one-parent family statistics vary by race.

Although all families experience problems, single parents are subject to a special set of stresses and strains. Sociologist Robert S. Weiss identified three problems common to the single-parent experience. Weiss labeled one source

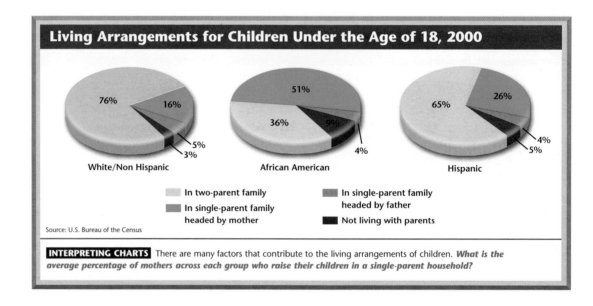

Living Arrangements for Children Under the Age of 18, 2000

White/Non Hispanic: 76%, 16%, 5%, 3%

African American: 51%, 36%, 9%, 4%

Hispanic: 65%, 26%, 4%, 5%

- In two-parent family
- In single-parent family headed by mother
- In single-parent family headed by father
- Not living with parents

Source: U.S. Bureau of the Census

INTERPRETING CHARTS There are many factors that contribute to the living arrangements of children. *What is the average percentage of mothers across each group who raise their children in a single-parent household?*

of stress found among single parents as responsibility overload. In two-parent households, husbands and wives share the responsibility of making plans and decisions. Single parents, on the other hand, often make their plans and decisions alone. They are also generally alone in providing the care needed by their families.

Weiss called a second source of stress among single parents task overload. Single parents must handle all of the tasks usually divided between two people—such as maintaining the home, caring for children, and earning a living. They spend so much time handling those tasks that they often have little or no time for themselves.

Single parents also experience emotional overload, Weiss noted. Single parents must often cope with the emotional needs of their children by themselves. Handling this task, along with everything else they must do, generally means that their own emotional needs go unmet.

The major source of stress for most single parents, particularly single mothers, is the lack of money. In 2000, families led by women accounted for more than half of all poor families. Many of the women who lead poor families are young unwed mothers or divorced mothers who did not work when they

Single parents face many challenges while raising children, working, and providing for the needs of family members.

were married. For the most part, the only positions open to these women are low-skilled low-paying jobs. As a result, they find it very difficult to climb out of poverty.

Single parenthood affects not only adults but also children. In 1998 about 19.8 million children under the age of 18 lived in single-parent families. Studies suggest that these children are two to three times more likely than children who live in two-parent families to experience negative life outcomes. School drop-out rates, teen-pregnancy rates, and arrest rates all are higher for children of single-parent families. In addition, children of single-parent families are more likely to suffer emotional problems.

Remarriage Another trend in American family life that is of interest to sociologists is the increase in the rate of remarriage. In some 43 percent of the marriages occurring today, one or both of the partners have previously been married. The majority of the people who get divorced—about 75 percent— eventually remarry.

The high rates of divorce and remarriage in the United States have led to a large increase in the number of stepfamilies. Stepfamilies, also called blended families, arise when one or both of the marriage partners

316

316   Chapter 12

bring children from their previous marriages into their new family. Some 65 percent of families created by remarriage involve children from prior marriages. About 30 percent of children under the age of 18 now live in stepfamilies. Estimates suggest that more than 50 percent of Americans have been, are now, or will be members of stepfamilies.

Becoming part of a stepfamily may involve a period of adjustment. The marital partners take on the parenting roles formerly held by biological parents. This process is sometimes a source of conflict in the family. Children may resent stepparents who appear to be trying to take the place of a biological mother or father. Similarly, stepparents may resent not being treated with the love and respect usually given to parents. Studies have shown that it takes approximately four years for children to accept a stepparent in the same way that they accept a biological mother or father.

Learning to accept new stepparents is not the only adjustment that children in a stepfamily have to make. They may also have to adjust to having new stepbrothers or stepsisters living in the home with them. This adjustment often involves learning how to share a parent's affections with their new siblings.

Adjusting to life in a stepfamily takes patience, understanding, and a willingness to work together. The reward can be a strong family unit. However, the pressures of family life sometimes prove too much for these marriages as well. About 60 percent of all remarriages eventually end in divorce.

Remarriage is another growing trend in American family life. Remarriage often leads to stepfamilies with children from previous marriages.

SECTION 2 REVIEW

1. Define and explain
homogamy
heterogamy
dual-earner families
sandwich generation
voluntary childlessness

2. Summarizing Copy the graphic organizer below. Use it to identify and describe the types of disruptions that American families might face.

Family Disruption	Description

3. Finding the Main Idea
a. Whom, in general, do Americans marry?
b. What trends in American family patterns have sociologists been studying in recent years?

4. Writing and Critical Thinking
Supporting a Point of View Write a brief essay explaining whether you think there is such a thing as a typical American family. Consider:
• whom Americans marry
• the disruptions that American families face
• recent developments in American family patterns

Homework Practice Online
keyword: SL3 HP12

CHAPTER 12

Review and Assessment Resources

- Chapter 12 Review, pp. 318–19
- Chapter Review Activities with Answer Key
- Global Skill Builder CD–ROM
- Chapter 12 Test Generator (on the One-Stop Planner)
- Chapter 12 Test (Form A or B)
- Alternative Assessment Handbook
- HRW Go site

REVIEW

Have students complete the **Chapter 12 Review** on pp. 318–19.

ASSESS

Use one of the chapter tests to assess students' understanding of the content. For **Alternative Assessment**, see the **Alternative Assessment Handbook**.

UNDERSTANDING MAIN IDEAS

1. by marriage, blood, or adoption

2. How many marriage partners may a person have? Who will live with whom? How will family membership be determined? Who will make the decisions in the family?

3. regulation of sexual activity, reproduction, socialization, and economic and emotional security

4. The laws governing the divorce process have become less complicated, the number of dual-earner families and the growth of day-care facilities have increased the economic independence of women, society is more tolerant of divorce, and people expect more of marriage and are less willing to accept marital problems.

5. Few families today can survive on just one salary.

THINKING CRITICALLY

1. because such a household is expensive to support, and not many people can afford to support multiple spouses and numerous offspring

2. to carry on the bloodline in situations where the father does not have any sons

3. Both often result because people want to spend more time focusing on their educations and careers.

4. because women still face discrimination in the workplace, such as making less money than men for the same work, or may lack the education needed to obtain higher-paying jobs

318

---

12 Review

Writing a Summary

Using standard grammar, spelling, sentence structure, and punctuation, summarize the information in this chapter.
Consider:
- the norms that influence marriage patterns
- the function of marriage
- trends in American families

Identifying People and Ideas

Identify the following people or terms and use them in appropriate sentences.

1. family
2. nuclear family
3. extended family
4. kinship
5. marriage
6. monogamy
7. polygamy
8. homogamy
9. heterogamy
10. sandwich generation

Understanding Main ideas

Section 1 (pp. 296–304)

1. How are families structured around the world?
2. What four basic questions help to determine how a society or group within a society organizes families?
3. What functions does the family fulfill?

Section 2 (pp. 305–17)

4. How do sociologists explain the high rate of divorce in the United States?
5. Why has the number of married women in the workforce increased?

Thinking Critically

1. **Finding the Main Idea** Why is polygamy relatively rare even in the societies where it is an acceptable marital system?
2. **Analyzing Information** Why in a patrilineal society might a father declare one of his daughters a "son"?

---

3. **Comparing** How are the reasons for delaying childbearing similar to the reasons for delaying marriage?
4. **Drawing Inferences and Conclusions** Why do you think the poverty rate is so high among female-headed families?
5. **Identifying Points of View** Some people have predicted the eventual collapse of the American family. On what evidence do you think they base that prediction? Do you think the prediction is correct? Why or why not?
6. **Evaluating** How do you think industrialization, urbanization, and immigrant assimilation has changed the family?

Writing About Sociology

1. **Summarizing** Use library resources and the Internet to find historical studies on marriage and the family in colonial America. Use these studies to prepare a brief research paper describing what marriage and family life were like in colonial times.
2. **Evaluating** Watch several weekly television programs, some containing one-parent families and some containing two-parent families. Make a list of the problems encountered by the families on these programs and of the methods the families use to solve their problems. Prepare and present a brief report answering the following question: As depicted by these shows, how do the problems and the solutions to problems differ between one-parent families and two-parent families? Use the graphic organizer below to help you prepare your report.

One-Parent Families	Two-Parent Families
Problems	**Problems**
Solutions	**Solutions**

■ RETEACH

Have students work in pairs to create mock course descriptions for several college-level classes that focus on sociological topics covered in this chapter. For example, students might write course descriptions for classes such as Courtship and Marriage Practices, Family Disruption, and Trends in American Family Life. Then have volunteers share some of their course descriptions with the class. Review any topics that students have not yet mastered.

ENGLISH LANGUAGE LEARNERS , COOPERATIVE LEARNING

■ SOCIOLOGY PROJECTS

1. Applying Sociology Have students interview local marriage counselors or social workers to find out about some of the problems that American families face today and how people in those jobs help families overcome challenges. Have students summarize their findings.

2. Using Sociological Imagination Have students write science-fiction short stories with the premise of an alien species with three sexes rather than two. Tell students to write their stories in the context of alien families that have up to three parents. The stories should address some of the main topics discussed in this chapter.

BUILDING SOCIAL STUDIES SKILLS

Interpreting Graphs

Study the bar graph below. Use it to answer the following questions.

Children Living with Their Grandparents, 1970–1999

Percentage of Under-18 Population (y-axis: 1.0 to 6.0)

Year (x-axis): 1970, 1980, 1992, 1997, 1999

Source: Population Reference Bureau

1. In what year was the largest percentage of the population under age 18 living with grandparents?
   a. 1980
   b. 1992
   c. 1997
   d. 1999
2. Describe the trend shown in the graph.

Analyzing Primary Sources

The following excerpt discusses changes in family arrangements in the United States. Read the excerpt and then answer the questions that follow.

❝*The number of Americans living alone grew rapidly in the 1990s, for the first time surpassing the number of married couples with children, according to the census data.*
   These and other numbers from the 2000 head count point to the redefinition of the American household in recent decades and the shrinking dominance of married-with-children families. . . .
   The statistics showed no reversal of the decades-long national trend away from the historically dominant household, married couples with children, which many policymakers hold up as the best arrangement for raising children. That change is the result of divorce as well as Americans choosing to wed later or not at all and, in some cases, not having children.
   Those trends continued in the '90s but the pace of change slowed. [Other] numbers also showed a recent leveling-off of U.S. rates for divorce and unmarried births.❞

3. According to the excerpt, why is there a trend away from married-with-children households?
   a. because of the decreasing divorce rate
   b. because fewer Americans are choosing to marry later
   c. because some Americans are choosing not to have children
   d. because more Americans are getting married
4. Some sociologists have suggested that the trends discussed in the excerpt indicate that the central place of marriage in American family life is eroding. Do you agree or disagree? Explain your answer.

5. These people base that prediction on the rising rates of divorce, single-parent families, and cohabitation. Students' opinions will vary, but students should provide support for their positions.

6. Industrialization and urbanization have led to the increased development of the nuclear family, as children left their homes to work in cities. Immigrant assimilation has probably led to more heterogamous marriages.

WRITING ABOUT SOCIOLOGY

1. Research papers should include information such as the average family size and the roles of different members and genders within families.

2. Reports will vary, but students should include concrete examples from the shows and compare the problem-solving process in each type of household.

BUILDING SOCIAL STUDIES SKILLS

1. c

2. The percentage of children under the age of 18 who live with their grandparents rose between 1970 and 1997 and then declined slightly.

3. c

4. Answers will vary, but students should provide support for their positions.

SOCIOLOGY PROJECTS

Cooperative Learning

Using Research Skills Working in a group with two or three other students, conduct research on the trends in the American family discussed in this chapter. Use your findings to create a report titled, "Trends in the American Family." Your report should include photographs, models, databases, maps, tables, charts and graphs accompanied by detailed captions. You may want to create a quiz and answer key to use as a study guide of demographic, geographic, and cultural changes.

✎ **internet** connect

Internet Activity: go.hrw.com
KEYWORD: SL3 SC12
Choose an activity on the family to:
• create a chart that compares family patterns in other countries to those in the United States.
• create a pamphlet to help teens deal with family disruptions.
• write a report on the pressures facing members of the sandwich generation.

The Economy and Politics

CHAPTER RESOURCE MANAGER

Objectives	Pacing Guide		Resources

SECTION 1:
The Economic Institution
(pp. 322–33)

REV Section 1 Review, p. 333

- Compare and contrast the characteristics of the capitalist and the socialist economic systems.
- Discuss developments that have transformed the American economic system.

Regular
2 days

Block Scheduling
1 day

Block Scheduling Handbook with Team Teaching Strategies, Chapter 13

Resources

- **CNN** Presents Sociology: Mongolian Capitalists
- **RS** Graphic Organizer 13
- **go.hrw.com** HRW Go site
- **SM** Mastering Critical Thinking Skills 13
- **PS** Readings and Case Studies in Sociology 13
- **E** Research Projects and Activities for Teaching Sociology 13
- **SM** Study Skills and Writing Guide
- Teaching Transparency: Voter Participation by Selected Characteristics, 1996–2000

SECTION 2:
The Political Institution
(pp. 334–45)

REV Section 2 Review, p. 345

- Explain how the exercise of power varies by type of government.
- Describe the major characteristics of the U.S. political system.

Regular
2 days

Block Scheduling
1 day

Block Scheduling Handbook with Team Teaching Strategies, Chapter 13

Chapter Review And Assessment

- **REV** Chapter 13 Review, pp. 346–47
- **REV** Chapter Review Activities with Answer Key
- Global Skill Builder CD–ROM
- Chapter 13 Test Generator (on the One-Stop Planner)
- **A** Chapter 13 Test (Form A or B)
- **A** Alternative Assessment Handbook
- **go.hrw.com** HRW Go site

Chapter Resource Key

PS Primary Sources	**A** Assessment	Video
RS Reading Support	**REV** Review	Internet
E Enrichment	Transparencies	Holt Presentation Maker Using Microsoft® PowerPoint®
SM Skills Mastery	CD–ROM	

 One-Stop Planner CD–ROM

See the *One-Stop Planner* for a complete list of additional resources for students and teachers.

One-Stop Planner CD–ROM

It's easy to plan lessons, select resources, and print out materials for your students when you use the *One-Stop Planner CD–ROM with Test Generator.*

Chapter Project Preview

The following activities are included in the Chapter Review. You may want to make the suggested preparations.

CHAPTER REVIEW ACTIVITY

Using Your Observation Skills Students will work in small groups to locate political cartoons on two or three issues discussed in this chapter. Ask groups to make copies of the cartoons and then to accompany each cartoon with a brief written report that explains the issue that the cartoon is addressing, the cartoon's message, and the cartoonist's point of view. Before starting the activity, you might want to review with students how to analyze political cartoons. In addition, you might want to have students collect and bring several newspapers and news magazines to class.

LESSON ACTIVITY

Linking to Community Students will attend a city council meeting or town hall and take notes detailing their observations.

Each student will then write a newspaper article covering the meeting and any decisions made. Before starting the chapter, obtain information on the upcoming, scheduled city council or town hall meetings and find out any information available about the meetings' agendas. Then create a handout of this information for students.

INTERNET ACTIVITY

Globalization Students will use provided Internet links to conduct research on the sociological implications of globalization and free trade. Students will then work individually or in pairs to create a pamphlet illustrating the effects of globalization on social institutions. Before starting the project, provide a pamphlet template for students to use and several sample pamphlets. In addition, for consistency, you might want to examine the Web sites beforehand to create a specific list of topics that students should address in their pamphlets.

Additional Resources

PRINT RESOURCES FOR TEACHERS

Hutton, Will and Anthony Giddens, eds. *On the Edge: Living With Global Capitalism.* London: Jonathan Cape, 2000. A collection of essays covering issues related to the global economy.

Weber, Max. *Essays in Economic Sociology,* edited by Richard Swedberg. Princeton, N.J.: Princeton University Press, 1999. A collection of Max Weber's work on economic sociology.

PRINT RESOURCES FOR STUDENTS

Craft, Donna, ed. *Company Profiles for Students.* 2 vol. The Gale Group Inc., 1999. Detailed profiles of 280 top companies.

Morin, Isobel V. *Politics, American Style: Political Parties in American History.* Twenty-First Century, 1999. Traces the events and issues that led to the modern U.S. political system.

Special Interest Group Profiles for Students. The Gale Group Inc., 1999.

Includes information on organizations representing economic, social-action, and single-issue interest groups.

Stein, Herbert, and Foss, Murray. *An Illustrated Guide to the American Economy.* Washington, D.C.: AEI Press, 1992. Helps students visualize more than 100 key economic topics.

MULTIMEDIA RESOURCES

The Almost Painless Guide to the Election Process (vhs; 20 min.) Altschul Group Corporation. Provides a broad introduction to the U.S. election process.

Communism and the Cold War (lvd) Coronet/MTI Film & Video. Examines the events that led to the collapse of communism in Eastern Europe and to the end of the Cold War.

What is Capitalism? (filmstrip on vhs; 36 min.) Guidance Associates. Presents a historical perspective on capitalism, from the theories of Adam Smith to modern times.

⏸ internet connect

go hrw .com

HRW ONLINE RESOURCES

GO TO: go.hrw.com
Then type in a keyword.

TEACHER HOME PAGE
KEYWORD: SL3 Teacher

CHAPTER INTERNET ACTIVITIES
KEYWORD: SL3 SC13
Choose an activity to have students:
- create a pamphlet on the sociological implications of globalization and the growth of multinational corporations.
- create a multimedia display on power and authority in political institutions.
- write a theoretical profile of Max Weber and his ideas on authority.

CHAPTER ENRICHMENT LINKS
KEYWORD: SL3 CH13

ONLINE ASSESSMENT
Homework Practice
KEYWORD: SL3 HP13
Standardized Test Prep
KEYWORD: SL3 STP13
Rubrics
KEYWORD: SS Rubrics

CONTENT UPDATES
KEYWORD: SS Content Updates

HOLT PRESENTATION MAKER
KEYWORD: SL3 PPT13

ONLINE READING SUPPORT
KEYWORD: SS Strategies

CURRENT EVENTS
KEYWORD: S3 Current Events

CHAPTER

13

The Economy
and Politics

SECTION 1
The Economic Institution

SECTION 2
The Political Institution

CHAPTER REVIEW

Build on What You Know

Ask students to answer the following questions:

Why might a sociologist be interested in the economy?

Consider:

- methods of gathering or producing food
- distribution of limited resources
- ways people earn and spend money

How might political systems reflect the ideals of a society?

Consider:

- methods of election
- distribution of power
- historical factors

Internet Activity

Have students access the Internet through the HRW Go site to conduct research on the ways in which power and authority are exercised and held by political institutions. Then have students work in small groups to create a multimedia exhibit to illustrate their research. As an extension to the activity, ask students to apply their knowledge to explain the ways in which a local political institution holds and exercises power.

CHAPTER

13

The Economy and Politics

Build on What You Know

Both economic and political forces have the power to influence the social institution of the family. In this chapter you will study economic and political institutions. First, you will examine the characteristics of economic systems, including the U.S. economic system. Then you will move on to explore politics, focusing on the exercise of power, types of governments, and the U.S. political system.

Many sociologists are interested in the role economic and political institutions play in the daily lives of people and groups.

Life in Society

When the world was populated by small bands of people, the family was the main authority in society. The family institution coordinated all economic activities and established society's rules. Today events in one country can dramatically affect events in other countries, and powerful countries compete with one another for influence. Thus, ultimate power no longer rests with the family.

In place of the family other institutions that attempt to coordinate economic and social life have gained prominence. The economy and politics are two of the most important of these institutions. The economic and political institutions can help to control the economic activities of individuals and help to maintain order in society.

The forms taken by economic and political institutions vary widely from society to society. In some societies, these institutions are influenced by a belief in human freedom. In other societies these same institutions greatly limit personal freedoms. Economic and political systems also influence the other institutions within a society.

TRUTH OR FICTION

What's Your Opinion?

Read the following statements about sociology. Do you think they are true or false? You will learn whether each statement is true or false as you read the chapter.

- Capitalism is the only economic system found in the world today.
- Computer technology has had little effect on the U.S. economy.
- Democratic and authoritarian governments differ little in the way they wield power.

► **WHY SOCIOLOGY MATTERS**

Sociologists are interested in the issues raised during political campaigns. Use **CNNfyi.com** or other current events sources to learn more about the issues that dominated the most recent presidential or congressional elections. Write a news report and create visuals that illustrate recent election issues.

CNNfyi.com

◆ **Applying Sociology**

Freedom Around the World. Freedom is a concept easily taken for granted in the United States, but what exactly does freedom mean? Freedom House, a nonprofit organization, rates the freedom of countries and territories based on the level of political rights and civil liberties that citizens enjoy. The organization looks at issues such as the right to vote and hold public office and the freedom to voice political opinions. Freedom House then categorizes countries and territories as either Free, Partly Free, or Not Free. In 2000 the organization rated 44 percent of the world's 192 countries as free, 31 percent as partly free, and 24 percent as not free. The United States rated as one of the world's freest countries.

CRITICAL THINKING

What do you think makes a society free?

ANSWER: Answers will vary, but students should consider factors such as having a free-enterprise economic system and a democratic form of government that protects citizens' rights and liberties.

SECTION 1

OBJECTIVES

1. *Compare and contrast the characteristics of the capitalist and the socialist economic systems.*

2. *Discuss developments that have transformed the American economic system.*

LET'S GET STARTED!

Before class, write the following hypothetical scenario on the chalkboard: *Imagine that you have a $20 bill. You have to buy lunch, and you have plans to go to a movie after school. You would also like to have enough money left over to buy a new CD and a gift for your sister's birthday tomorrow.* As students enter the classroom, ask them how they would handle this situation. After listening to a few responses, tell the class that they have just encountered the problem of limited economic resources. Tell students that in Section 1 they will learn about how societies use economic institutions to address the issue of limited resources.

SECTION 1 RESOURCES

REPRODUCIBLE & REVIEW

- Research Projects and Activities for Teaching Sociology 13
- Study Skills and Writing Guide
- Section 1 Review, p. 333

TECHNOLOGY

- One-Stop Planner, Lesson 13.1
- **CNN.** Presents Sociology: Mongolian Capitalists
- Homework Practice Online
- HRW Go site

1

THE ECONOMIC INSTITUTION

Read to Discover

1. What are the characteristics of the capitalist and the socialist economic systems?

2. What developments have transformed the American economic system?

Define

economic institution, factors of production, primary sector, secondary sector, tertiary sector, capitalism, socialism, law of supply, law of demand, laissez-faire capitalism, free-enterprise systems, communism, totalitarianism, corporations, oligopoly, protectionism, free trade, multinational, e-commerce

Identify

Adam Smith

In every society people have certain needs and wants that must be met if their health and happiness are to be maintained. Needs—such as food, clothing, and shelter—are basic to survival. Wants—such as new cars, stereo systems, and personal digital assistants—are not necessary for survival, but they often add to the quality of life. To satisfy people's needs and wants, every society develops a system of roles and norms that governs the production, distribution, and consumption of goods and services. This system is called the **economic institution**.

The need for economic institutions is rooted in the problem of scarcity. People's needs and wants are unlimited. However, the resources available to satisfy these needs and wants are limited. Consequently, societies must decide how best to use their limited resources to satisfy the most needs and wants. Societies do that by answering three basic questions: (1) What goods and services should be produced? (2) How should these goods and services be produced? (3) For whom should these goods and services be produced?

How a society answers these questions is determined in large part by the society's available factors of production and its level of technology. The **factors of production**—resources needed to produce goods and services—include land, labor, capital, and entrepreneurship. Land refers to natural resources such as soil, water, minerals, plants, animals, sunlight, and wind. Labor, also called human resources, involves anyone who works to produce goods and services. Capital refers to all the manufactured goods used in the production process—such as tools, machinery, and factories. Capital also refers to resources available and the means to purchase goods, stock, or other items. Entrepreneurship includes the organizational skills and the risk-taking attitude required to start a new business or develop a new product. In economic terms, technology is the use of science to produce new products or to make the production process more efficient. A society's ability to use technology to exploit the factors of production shapes that society's economic system.

Entrepreneurship is one of the essential factors of production. Many entrepreneurs open new businesses or develop new products.

TEACH OBJECTIVE 1

SUGGESTION 1: To help students compare and contrast the characteristics of the capitalist and the socialist economic systems, copy the graphic organizer at the right onto the chalkboard, omitting the italicized answers. Have students copy and complete the organizer. Discuss the answers with the class. Then have each student create either a political cartoon or a comic strip that contrasts capitalism and socialism. Students should write captions that explain their cartoons. **ENGLISH LANGUAGE LEARNERS**

ECONOMIC MODELS

Capitalism
- *factors of production owned by individuals*
- *forces of profit and competition regulate economic activity*
- *minimum government interference*

(overlap)
- *industrial and postindustrial societies*
- *"pure" forms are ideal types*

Socialism
- *factors of production owned by the government*
- *economic activity regulated by the government*
- *pure form is communism*

INTERPRETING VISUALS Natural resources, human labor, and capital are all factors of production that help determine the economic institution of a society. Natural resources include soil, water, and plants. Human labor is used to turn these resources into products. Capital is the manufactured goods used in the process. *Which factor of production do each of these images represent? Explain your answer.*

Sociology Then and Now

Changing American Economic Sectors.
In 1900 the jobs available in the United States were almost evenly divided among the three economic sectors, with the primary sector forming the largest portion. By the 1950s, however, the United States had become the first country in the world to have more than half of its labor force engaged in the tertiary sector. At the same time, the nation's primary sector had decreased significantly. For example, in 1900 farmers made up 40 percent of American workers. In 2000, farmers comprised about 3 percent.

CRITICAL THINKING
How did the American economy change during the 1900s?

ANSWER: The majority of jobs changed from being in the primary sector to being in the tertiary sector.

Visual Answer

left—capital and human labor; top right—natural resources; bottom right—human labor

Economic Systems

All economic systems comprise three basic sectors—the primary sector, the secondary sector, and the tertiary sector. The **primary sector** deals with the extraction of raw materials from the environment. Examples of activities in the primary sector include fishing, hunting, mining, and farming. The **secondary sector**, on the other hand, concentrates on the use of raw materials to manufacture goods. Activities in the secondary sector can range from turning a log into a primitive canoe to manufacturing a rocket that can travel deep into space. In the **tertiary sector** the emphasis shifts to providing services. The degree to which any one of the sectors is emphasized over the others depends on a society's subsistence strategy. As you read in

Chapter 4, a subsistence strategy is the way in which a society uses technology to provide for the needs of its members.

Preindustrial Economic Systems In preindustrial societies, there is very little technological development. All economic activity is carried out using human labor and animal power. One major consequence of this low level of technology is an inefficient system of food production that requires the majority of the population to engage in producing food.

In all preindustrial societies, labor is heavily concentrated in the primary sector. However, the degree of concentration varies by type of society. As you read in Chapter 4, there are four types of preindustrial societies—hunting

The Economy and Politics **323**

323

People in Sociology

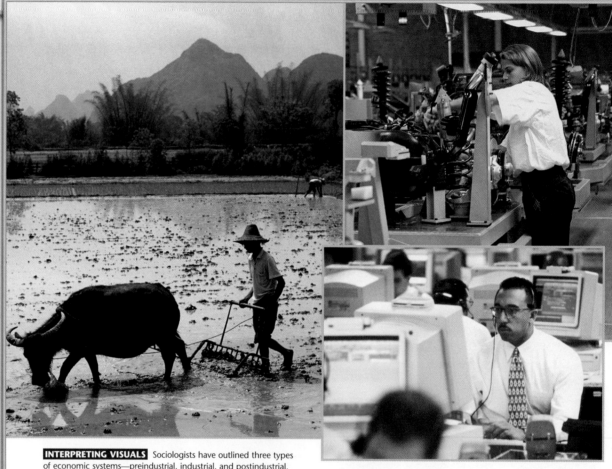

INTERPRETING VISUALS Sociologists have outlined three types of economic systems—preindustrial, industrial, and postindustrial. Preindustrial societies generally have an agricultural based economy, while industrialized societies are characterized by an emphasis on the use of machinery to produce goods. Postindustrial societies place a greater emphasis on the collection and distribution of information. *How do each of these images represent a different form of economic system?*

and gathering, pastoral, horticultural, and agricultural. As the subsistence strategy progresses from hunting and gathering to agriculture, the economic system becomes more complex.

In the simplest preindustrial societies, providing sufficient food to feed the population demands the efforts of the entire population. Consequently, the secondary and tertiary sectors of the economy are very small. People are involved in these sectors on just a part-time basis. Even essential secondary-sector activities, such as the production of tools, take second place to food production.

As technology improves, food production becomes more efficient, which allows more people to transfer their labor to the secondary and tertiary sectors without affecting food supplies. Even so, the number of people holding secondary and tertiary positions is still relatively small.

Industrial Economic Systems In industrial societies, the main emphasis in the economy shifts from the primary sector to the secondary sector. Advances in technology—machines and new sources of energy—make this shift possible. These technological advances have a tremendous effect on society. To begin with, agricultural productivity increases. This income means that industrial societies can support larger populations. Higher agricultural productivity also causes fewer workers to be needed in the primary sector. Consequently, the labor pool for the secondary and tertiary sectors swells.

Technological advances also change the nature of work—jobs become specialized. The Scottish economist Adam Smith first suggested job specialization in his 1776 book *The Wealth of Nations.* Smith argued that production could be greatly increased by dividing the manufacturing process into a series of tasks and by assigning each task to a different individual. Each person would become more efficient at completing his or her task. Job specialization would cut the time needed to make each product, therefore increasing productivity.

Job specialization also increases the variety of jobs found in the secondary and tertiary sectors. In industrial economies people no longer make the goods and services they need for their own daily lives. Instead, they perform their jobs in return for wages. They then use these wages to buy goods and services created by other workers.

Postindustrial Societies In postindustrial societies the tertiary sector becomes the most important area of the economy. Several factors lead to this shift. First, technological innovations such as automation lead to more-efficient production techniques. As a result, the number of jobs available in the secondary sector begins to decline. Second, in postindustrial economies greater emphasis is placed on knowledge and on the collection and distribution of information. These emphases create a demand for administrative, managerial, professional, technical, and service personnel. Finally, the higher standard of living that is characteristic of postindustrial societies increases the demand for services.

Economic Models

Industrial and postindustrial societies are categorized by the type of economic model they follow. Sociologists recognize two basic economic models: capitalism and socialism. However, in reality most countries have characteristics of each of these models. The differences between the two models hinge on who owns the factors of production and on how economic activity is regulated. In **capitalism** the factors of production are owned by individuals rather than by the government. The forces of profit and competition regulate economic activity. In **socialism** on the other hand, the factors of production are owned by the government, which regulates economic activity.

Keep in mind that the descriptions of capitalism and socialism are ideal types—that is, they are descriptions of the essential characteristics of the systems in their purest forms. In reality, no society has a purely capitalist or purely socialist system, but some societies lean heavily toward one or the other. For example, the United States follows the capitalist model. The People's Republic of China and Cuba, on the other hand, follow the socialist model. Between those extremes are a host of countries that combine the elements of capitalism and socialism to various degrees. France and Sweden, for example, fall in the middle of the spectrum. In those countries the government controls certain essential services and industries, such as health care, energy production, and the manufacture of industrial goods. However, individuals own a wide range of businesses in both countries.

Capitalism In a purely capitalist system, the economy is regulated by self-interest and market competition. Self-interest regulates the economy by guiding the actions of consumers and producers. It leads consumers to try to purchase the goods and services they desire at the lowest prices possible. Self-interest also guides producers to undertake only those business ventures that have the potential for profit.

Market competition regulates the economy by ensuring that businesses produce goods or services wanted by consumers at prices consumers are willing to pay. Businesses that do this will be successful. Businesses that do not will soon fail. For competition to be effective, however, it must operate with limited government interference.

Prices in a purely capitalist system are regulated not by the government but by the laws of supply and demand. The **law of supply** states that producers will supply more products when they can charge higher prices and fewer products when they must charge lower prices. The **law of demand** states that consumers will demand more of a product as the price of the product decreases. On the other hand, consumer demand for a product decreases as the price increases.

Adam Smith called this interplay between the forces of supply and demand the "invisible hand." According to Smith, if government interference is kept to a minimum and if competition is not restricted, the invisible hand of market forces will keep the economy in balance. This pure form of capitalism is sometimes referred to as

In 1776 economist Adam Smith suggested that specialization could greatly increase productivity. His ideas form the foundation of modern capitalism.

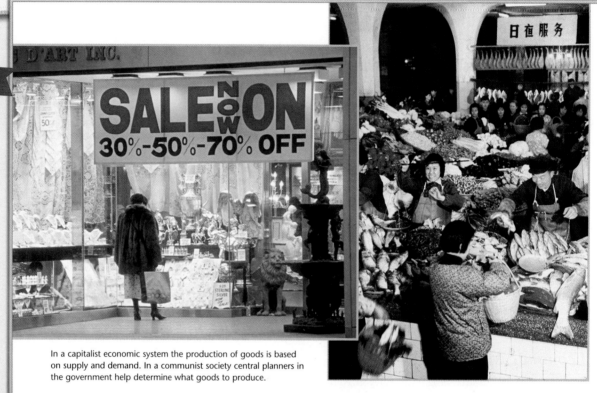

CONNECTING *to Economics and Geography*

Draw a continuum on the chalkboard and label one end *Pure Capitalism* and the other end *Pure Socialism*. Assign each student a country other than the United States and instruct students to conduct research on that country to determine where its economic system falls along the continuum. Each student should write one to two paragraphs indicating his or her conclusion and providing examples and facts that support it. Then have students share their findings with the class as you fill in the continuum on the chalkboard. **BLOCK SCHEDULING**

SPOTLIGHT *on Entrepreneurship*

Organize students into small groups. Have groups come up with ideas for new businesses that they think would be profitable. Then have each group select one business idea and write a mock business plan that first summarizes the idea and then lists its potential strengths and weaknesses. The strengths and weaknesses should address each of the factors of production: land, labor, capital, and entrepreneurship. Have students write their plans from the point of view of new business owners seeking investors.

COOPERATIVE LEARNING , BLOCK SCHEDULING

Interdisciplinary Connection

ECONOMICS
Command Economies.
A system in which government officials answer the three basic economic questions is called a command system. Although pure command economies no longer exist, several have existed in the past. For example, during the Old Kingdom period of Egyptian history (2700–2200 B.C.), the pharaoh, or monarch, ruled both the economy and the government of Egypt. The pharaoh owned the land, controlled all trade, collected taxes, and supervised all public construction. This control enabled the pharaoh to make all decisions concerning what, how, and for whom to produce.

CRITICAL THINKING
Why might a society have a command economy?

ANSWER: Answers will vary, but perhaps to ensure that necessary goods are produced, because of societal tradition, or because a powerful individual or group forced the system on a society's citizens.

Technology Resources
CNN. Presents Sociology: Mongolian Capitalists

In a capitalist economic system the production of goods is based on supply and demand. In a communist society central planners in the government help determine what goods to produce.

laissez-faire capitalism. Laissez-faire is a French term that is best translated as "let people do as they choose."

In practice, all capitalist systems have government regulations that protect the consumer and ensure fair business competition. These regulations do not prevent individuals from setting up and running their own businesses with limited government interference. This commitment to limited government control of business operations has resulted in the labeling of capitalist economies as **free-enterprise systems**.

Socialism In a pure socialist system, economic activity is controlled by social need and by the government through central planning. Thus, the three basic economic questions are answered quite differently under pure socialism than they are under pure capitalism.

What to produce is determined by the needs of society. If the members of society need a good or service, it is provided regardless of whether it can be produced profitably. However, need is not determined by consumer demand. Rather, economic planners in the central government determine it.

Central planners also determine how to produce goods. These central planners decide which factories will produce which items and in what quantities. Rather than a range of similar products from which to choose, government planners provide consumers with

one type of each good. Thus, market competition is not a factor in regulating supply and demand in a purely socialist economy.

For whom to produce is determined by need rather than by the ability to pay. It is for this reason that the government owns the means of production in a socialist system. Supporters of the socialist system claim that equal access to goods and services cannot be guaranteed if the means of production are owned by individuals.

For some socialists the ultimate goal of socialism is communism. Ideally **communism** is a political and economic system in which property is communally owned. In such a system, social classes cease to exist, and the role of the government declines as individuals learn to work together peacefully and willingly for the good of all. As you read in Chapter 1, Karl Marx argued that the imbalance of economic power between workers (the proletariat) and capitalists (the bourgeoisie) would lead to conflict. This class conflict would end only when the proletariat united to overthrow the bourgeoisie. After the revolution, a dictatorship of the proletariat would be established to assist in the transformation to communism.

The goal of communism has never been achieved in practice. In theory, on the way to establishing communism, the government should "wither away." However, in practice countries that adopted strong socialist economic models have also adopted totalitarian forms of government.

TEACH OBJECTIVE 2

SUGGESTION 1: Pair students and have each partner select two of the four developments that have transformed the American economic system: the rise of corporate capitalism, economic globalization, the changing nature of work, and e-commerce. Each partner should then write two newspaper articles, each describing a fictional example of one of the developments and the example's effects on the economy. Then have partners exchange their articles and edit them for accuracy, completion, and correct grammar, spelling, sentence structure, and punctuation. Have partners revise their articles based on this feedback. **COOPERATIVE LEARNING**

SUGGESTION 2: Have each student create a large then-and-now chart explaining how the American economy has changed between 1900 and today. Students charts should address the four main changes described in this section: the rise of corporate capitalism, economic globalization, the changing nature of work, and e-commerce. Then have each student write a short essay describing which change was in his or her opinion most important and why. Remind students to provide reasons or examples that support their positions and to use standard grammar, spelling, sentence structure, and punctuation. Have volunteers read their essays to the class. Encourage student feedback and discussion.

Under **totalitarianism** those in power exercise complete authority over the lives of individual citizens. Public opposition to government policies is rarely allowed, and most personal freedoms are greatly restricted. Even though they do not meet the communist ideal outlined by Karl Marx, societies that combine socialism with totalitarianism are referred to as communist.

Changes in Capitalism and Socialism Over time, both the capitalist and socialist economic systems have undergone changes. The United States, a capitalist country, has adopted economic programs and practices that are socialist in nature. For example, the government actively promotes economic well-being through the redistribution of wealth. Tax revenues collected from the working population fund programs that benefit people with low incomes, such as Medicare, Medicaid, and Social Security.

The socialist economic system did not so much change as collapse. In the late 1980s and early 1990s, the Soviet Union and other communist-bloc countries abandoned the socialist economic model. They replaced the system of central planning, which was riddled with corruption and inefficiency, with a market system. Even countries that retained socialism introduced elements of free enterprise. In the People's Republic of China the government allowed local managers of state-owned factories to make more decisions on how business should be run. Further, it began to privatize—sell off to private businesses—some large state-owned industries. Reflecting these changes, China adjusted its constitution in 1999 to note that private business was an important part of the economy.

For some people, these changes support the theory of economic convergence. According to this theory, the two systems are converging and, in time, will merge to create a new economic system that is a mix of capitalism and socialism. Other people disagree. They suggest that the collapse of communism in the late 1980s and early 1990s indicates that capitalism is the only viable economic system.

The American Economy

At the beginning of the 1900s, the United States was one of several large economies in the world. Today it is the world's most powerful economy. It is also one of the most distinctive. Several developments helped bring about that transformation. These developments include the rise of corporate capitalism, the globalization of the economy, and the change in the nature of work in postindustrial America. The most recent development, e-commerce, has brought an even greater transformation in the 2000s.

Careers
IN SOCIOLOGY

INDUSTRIAL SOCIOLOGIST

Industrial sociologists specialize in the study of work and professions. They are particularly interested in analyzing the social relationships within an industry or institution.

Businesses and corporations typically employ these specialists to analyze and assess the needs and problems of workers and management. Industrial sociologists may also work for government agencies in the areas of industrial relations and economic, social, and organizational planning. Some industrial sociologists are concerned with the relationship between workers and their work environment. Some industrial sociologists focus on unions and other organizations formed by workers.

Industrial sociologists study social relationships in work environments.

SUGGESTION 3: Organize the class into four groups, each focusing on a different aspect of the recent transformations in the American economy: the rise of corporate capitalism, economic globalization, the changing nature of work, and e-commerce. Have group members use their textbooks and the library to find examples to support the premise that their assigned topic is most responsible for the United States becoming the world's most powerful economy. Then hold a four-way informal debate in which each group presents arguments that support its assigned viewpoint.
COOPERATIVE LEARNING

SPOTLIGHT *on Big Business*

Have each student select a major corporation in the United States to investigate. Ask students to find out information such as the company's products, profits, market value, and stockholders. Instruct students to use their findings to design overhead transparencies that might be used in presentations to major stockholders about the company's activities. **BLOCK SCHEDULING**

Applying Sociology

Oligopolies and Competition. Companies in an oligopoly often compete for market share by producing several products under different brand names. For example, the number of different breakfast cereals might make it seem that dozens of cereal makers are battling for market share. However, just three companies—General Mills, Kellogg's, and Post—account for 80 percent of breakfast cereal sales.

CRITICAL THINKING

Why do you think that companies in oligopolies compete in this way?

ANSWER: because they want Americans to think that they have a large selection of choice in a given market

---

The Rise of Corporate Capitalism In Adam Smith's time, economic activities were controlled by the efforts of individual capitalists. However, by the late 1800s **corporations** had become the moving forces behind the economy. A corporation is a business organization that is owned by stockholders and is treated by law as if it were an individual person. Because it has the same legal rights as a person, a corporation can enter into contracts, negotiate bank loans, issue stocks and bonds, and buy and sell goods and services.

The rise of corporate capitalism has changed the relationship between business ownership and control. Like the owners of most small businesses and privately held companies today, early stockholders managed the day-to-day affairs of their businesses. Today management by stockholders is praticed only by the smallest corporations. Few stockholders participate in daily business operations. In many cases, stockholders are not even individuals. Other corporations, Wall Street financial firms, foreign governments, and pension and mutual funds own the stocks of most large corporations in the United States.

Corporations account for only about 20 percent of the businesses in the United States, yet they dominate the economy. They generate approximately 88 percent of business sales. More significantly, the country's top 25 corporations produce the vast majority of these sales. A few big companies exercise tremendous economic power.

One of the chief consequences of corporate capitalism is the growth of oligopolies. An **oligopoly** is the market situation in which a few large companies control an industry. The American automobile, oil, and breakfast-cereal industries are examples of oligopolies. The many mergers among companies in recent years have resulted in these and other American industries becoming more oligopolistic.

Corporate capitalism is an important part of the American economic system. Many American corporations sell stock on the New York Stock Exchange. These corporations regularly give reports on the state of their businesses to stockholders.

Connecting to Economics

▪ TEACH

Have students read the feature Entrepreneurs and the Profit Motive. Use the questions under Think About It to guide a class discussion about entrepreneurship. Then have each student create a print advertisement designed to encourage Americans to start their own businesses. Advertisements should explain the importance of entrepreneurship and its role in the American free-market economy. Display students' advertisements in the classroom.

▪ EXTEND

Many motivations can determine personal career choices: fame, power, desire to help others, self-expression, and of course profit. Create a varied list of occupations on the chalkboard (for example, entrepreneur, reporter, CEO, ambassador, artist, professional athlete, politician, mechanic, chef, and private detective). Next, ask students to provide motivations for pursuing each occupation. Challenge students to consider how strong a role the profit motive might play in each choice. Then have students think of one or two careers they might pursue and write a few sentences explaining their motivations. **BLOCK SCHEDULING**

CONNECTING TO
Economics

ENTREPRENEURS AND THE PROFIT MOTIVE

Entrepreneurs are one of the most essential forces in a free-enterprise economy such as that of the United States. Entrepreneurs open new businesses or come up with ideas for new products. Sometimes they develop new ways to produce or distribute existing products. They also provide start-up money, advice, and ideas for other people opening new businesses. Entrepreneurs often risk everything in the attempt to make their new ventures successful. Entrepreneurs must often invest time and money and take risks to achieve their goals. They are willing to do this because of the chance that they might make a profit. The profit motive—the driving force that guides people to improve their material well-being—is one of the major characteristics of free enterprise.

This drive to make a profit may reap tremendous benefits for individual entrepreneurs—they may become very wealthy. For example, Texan Michael Dell began refurbishing and selling used computers to make money to cover his college expenses. Dell quickly saw that there was an opening in the market for this kind of company, so he went into business full-time. As time went on, Dell introduced new business approaches—such as building computers to consumer specifications and selling directly to consumers rather than through retail stores. Dell's entrepreneurial spirit and his desire to maximize profits helped to build one of the world's largest computer companies. It also made him one of the wealthiest people in the United States.

The desire of entrepreneurs to make a profit also has a major influence on the economy as a whole. In their effort to maximize profits, many entrepreneurs develop new resources or find ways to use existing ones more efficiently. Through their willingness to take risks with new ideas, entrepreneurs often develop new technology. Much of the computer-related technology that was developed in recent years is the product of entrepreneurial innovation.

Profit-driven entrepreneurs affect the economy in a much broader sense as well. In many cases they introduce a host of new and better products to the market. The entrepreneurs' success then

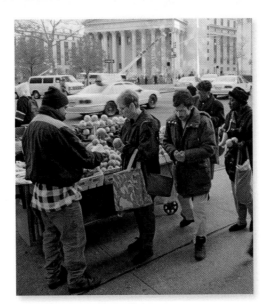

Entrepreneurs are an essential force in the free-market economy of the United States. Entrepreneurial spirit is the hope of success that is held by businesspeople ranging from company presidents to fruit-stand operators.

draws more companies into their particular market, which increases competition. More competition usually results in lower prices for consumers and more job opportunities for workers. The overall increase in economic activity provides greater tax revenues for government. Thus, the basic economic desire of an entrepreneur to make a profit may greatly contribute to the country's economic growth.

Think About It

1. **Analyzing Information** *What is the profit motive?*
2. **Evaluating** *How does entrepreneurship affect the economy as a whole?*

Case Study

Franchises. Some entrepreneurs opt to open franchises. In this business arrangement, a parent company agrees for a fee to let a person or group set up a franchise, an enterprise that uses the parent company's same name. Common franchises include hotel and motel chains, fast-food chains, and real estate agencies. Franchise agreements generally require franchise owners to maintain quality standards and to provide particular goods or services. In return, the parent company may pay for national advertising. Because of these advantages and due to the parent company's name recognition, a franchise can lower the costs associated with starting a new business.

RESEARCH ACTIVITY: Have students conduct research on some of the most profitable franchises in the United States and on how much it costs to start each of them.

Think About It Answers

1. the driving force that guides people to improve their material well-being

2. Entrepreneurs' new ideas, methods, or products may benefit society, lower prices, create new industries and jobs, employ people, and increase tax revenues.

Because of its hold on an industry, an oligopoly can control the pricing and quality of products. In addition, it can protect its hold on the industry by making it difficult for competing companies to enter the market. An oligopoly can also limit competition by using pressure tactics in the political arena. Because of their wealth and power, oligopolistic companies are often able to push through legislation that maintains or increases their share of the market.

In the 1980s and 1990s, for example, American automobile companies faced stiff competition from Japanese carmakers. They urged the government to impose protectionist policies. **Protectionism** is the use of trade barriers to protect domestic manufacturers from foreign competition. Common trade barriers include quotas—limits on the amount of goods that may be imported—and tariffs—surcharges on goods entering the country. American automakers faced opposition from supporters of **free trade**—trade that is not restricted by trade barriers between countries.

The Globalization of Corporate Capitalism

In recent years, the debate between protectionists and supporters of free trade has been complicated by the globalization of corporate capitalism. Many of the larger corporations are also multinationals. A **multinational** is any corporation that has factories and offices in several countries. Generally, a multinational has its head office in one country and operates subsidiaries in one or more other countries. For example, an American multinational might make products in its factories in Mexico

with materials from its subsidiaries in several European countries. The finished products might then be shipped for sale in countries throughout the Americas. Similarly, a foreign multinational might make products in its American factories, use American labor and materials, and sell the product in the United States.

Some American multinationals are huge. Several have economies that are bigger than many national economies. Wal-Mart, for example, has a bigger economy than some 160 countries! The graphs on page 331 compare the economies of several American multinationals with certain national economies.

Great power comes with such wealth. Boardmembers of one corporation often serve on other boards or in political organizations, which adds to the power of the original corporation. Indeed the world's largest multinationals, many of which are American, help to set the economic, social, and political policies of many countries. Multinationals have led the drive to reduce trade barriers around the world. For some people, the growing power of multinational corporations signals the end of the old world order of nation-states. They suggest that in the future, international affairs will be driven less by national loyalties than by market forces.

The Changing Nature of Work
You read in Chapter 7 that work in the United States has steadily shifted from an industrial base to a service base. This shift is due in part to advances in technology. Automation and increased efficiency have reduced the number

INTERPRETING VISUALS Multinational corporations have subsidiaries in many different countries. *Do you think this business is a multinational? Explain your answer.*

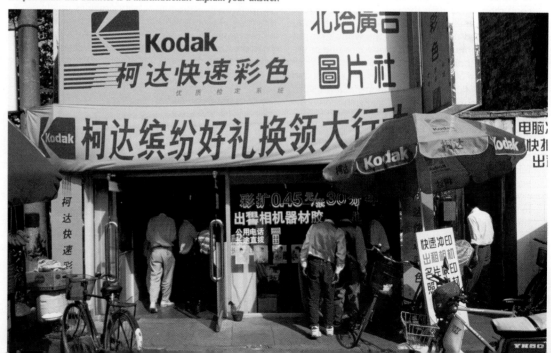

SPOTLIGHT *on E-commerce and Privacy*

Have students conduct research on the issue of privacy on the Internet and then ask them to give short speeches about issues related to this topic. Speeches might describe typical e-commerce transactions and address topics such as credit card fraud, "cookies" and personalization, techniques for consumers to protect themselves, and methods for e-commerce businesses to secure personal information. Have each student present his or her speech to the class. **BLOCK SCHEDULING**

CONNECTING *to Economics*

Review with students the economic systems of pure capitalism and pure socialism and the ways in which the American economy has changed. Then organize students into small groups and have each group create a fictional country. Groups should name their country and then design its economic system. Remind students to consider the effects of their economic decisions and encourage groups to be creative and to have fun. Have each group create a poster that uses charts, graphics, and text to describe the fictional country's economic system. **COOPERATIVE LEARNING,**

BLOCK SCHEDULING

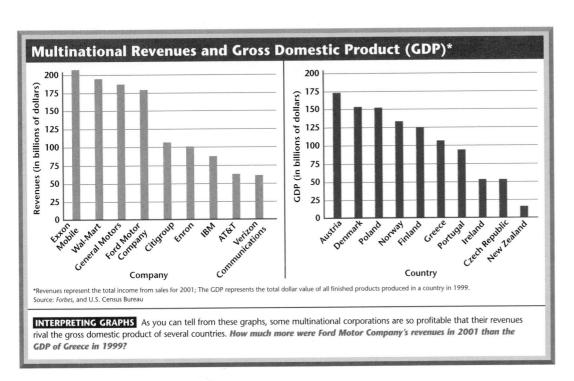

Multinational Revenues and Gross Domestic Product (GDP)*

*Revenues represent the total income from sales for 2001; The GDP represents the total dollar value of all finished products produced in a country in 1999.
Source: *Forbes*, and U.S. Census Bureau

INTERPRETING GRAPHS As you can tell from these graphs, some multinational corporations are so profitable that their revenues rival the gross domestic product of several countries. *How much more were Ford Motor Company's revenues in 2001 than the GDP of Greece in 1999?*

Interdisciplinary Connection

ECONOMICS AND MATH

The New Economy?
During the 1990s the term *the new economy* came to refer to the rapid economic growth based on computers, software, telecommunications, and Internet dot-com companies. However, the new economy hit a major slump in 2000. Between January 2000 and December 2001, some 760 Internet firms went bankrupt, and some 135,000 Internet workers were laid off. Nonetheless, in early 2002 more than 5 million Americans still worked in high-tech industries. E-commerce sales for 2001 totaled about $33 billion, up about 19 percent from 2000, according to the U.S. Department of Commerce.

ACTIVITY: Have students calculate total e-commerce sales for 2000.
(33 x 0.19 = $6.2 billion; 33 − 6.2 = 26.8 billion)

Graph Answer

about $70 billion more

of workers needed to meet the demand for manufactured goods. The globalization of the economy has played an equally important role in the shift. In recent years American workers have faced competition from workers in the newly industrializing countries (NICs), particularly in Latin America and Asia. Some American multinationals, attracted by tax breaks and lower wage rates, have moved their manufacturing operations to NICs. Other American companies, to combat competition from foreign countries, have cut their costs by reducing their workforces. This downsizing resulted in 300,000 to 400,000 American workers losing their jobs each year through most of the 1990s. Many of these displaced workers quickly found new employment, mostly in service jobs, while others retired.

Recent developments suggest that the service sector will not be able to continue to absorb large numbers of displaced workers. Technological advances are eliminating many less-skilled service jobs. Further, the majority of new service jobs require a relatively high level of education but do not always pay high wages. Many of the manufacturing jobs that remain require higher-level skills. Yet studies indicate that about 40 percent of American workers have limited reading-and-writing skills. To ensure that workers can handle the jobs of the future, government and business leaders have called for a strong commitment to quality education in the United States.

E-commerce The most recent development in the American economy—e-commerce—may bring the greatest changes. The computer completely transformed the way people store and access information. The Internet, a global network that links millions of computers, revolutionized the way people communicate. **E-commerce**—business conducted over the Internet—is not based on the traditional factors of production but instead is based on information.

The most widely used service provided by the Internet is the World Wide Web (WWW). The Web is a set of computer programs that makes multimedia presentations—combinations of text, sound, pictures, animation, and video—possible on the Internet. The Web makes it easier for businesses to directly reach both consumers and suppliers.

Businesses can draw consumers' attention to products by advertising on the Web. American companies spent some $7.3 billion on Internet advertising in 2001. This figure is expected to increase in the years to come. Also, businesses can sell their products directly to consumers through company Web sites. In 2000 more than 17 million American households spent about $33 billion on Web purchases. Projections suggest that in 2003 the consumer base will reach 40 million and spending will be about $108 billion. The largest sector of e-commerce is business-to-business activity. In 1999, businesses

Case Studies and Other True Stories

◼ TEACH

Have students read the feature Economics and Immigration and answer the questions under Think About It. Then ask students to imagine that they are recent immigrants from countries of their choice and are considering starting businesses in the United States. Have each student write a series of brief journal entries outlining his or her business ideas and talking about the steps needed to make this dream a reality. Encourage students to address socioeconomic elements as well as personal thoughts about the risk factors.

◼ EXTEND

Ask each student to conduct research or interviews to gather information about immigrant entrepreneurs (local or elsewhere) and then to prepare an oral report profiling one businessperson. Students' oral reports should include the immigrant's country of origin, reasons for coming to the United States, area of residence, business or occupation, whether or not the person feels successful and why, and how the person's life would have been different had he or she not immigrated to the United States.

BLOCK SCHEDULING

Case Studies

AND OTHER TRUE STORIES

ECONOMICS AND IMMIGRATION

O ver the last 200 years, millions of immigrants have moved to the United States in search of a better life. The immigrants who have arrived in the last 10 years or so are no exception. Like those who came before them, these new immigrants were drawn by the hope that the open social and economic life in the United States would provide opportunities for advancement and prosperity.

A Hope Unfulfilled?

A recent report on the foreign-born population of the United States seems to suggest that this hope is yet to be fulfilled for many immigrants. The report found that about one third of foreign-born residents have not graduated from high school. These immigrants may not have the skills or knowledge to compete in today's high-tech job market. Not surprisingly, then, the report found that foreign-born residents, particularly foreign-born women, are more likely to be unemployed than the rest of the population.

The report also found that immigrants are more likely to work in traditionally lower-paid service jobs. Indeed, statistics showed that foreign-born residents earn less than the native population. Foreign-born full-time workers are less likely to earn more than $50,000 a year than are American-born workers. Further, more than one third of foreign-born workers make less than $20,000 a year. In contrast, only about one fifth of the American-born population earns less than that total. As a consequence of lower earning power, poverty rates are much higher among the foreign-born population than among the rest of the population—nearly 17 percent as compared to about 11 percent. Because immigrants are not a homogenous group, the actual economic experiences of immigrants may differ from individual to individual or among groups.

The Promise of Entrepreneurship

Whatever level of economic success they achieve, many immigrants get their start in the American

Many immigrants find work in service occupations or lower-skill jobs, such as those found in the meat-packing industry.

economy in the same way—as entrepreneurs. Statistics show that immigrants are more likely to be self-employed than other Americans. In fact, some economists believe that immigrants have been a major force in a revival of the spirit of entrepreneurship in the United States.

Some immigrant entrepreneurs have used their special skills or education to earn great wealth. According to some estimates, about 25 percent of the companies in Silicon Valley—California's high-tech industrial area—were started by immigrants. A study of 10 of these firms found that in the mid-1990s they had total revenues of $28 billion and employed some 70,000 workers.

However, most immigrant business owners run small stores, restaurants, or other similar businesses—usually in neighborhoods where their ethnic group predominates. These businesses require hard work and long hours, and the monetary return is often limited. Nevertheless, they offer immigrants and their families a chance at economic success.

Think About It

1. **Analyzing Information** *According to statistics, how economically successful are immigrants?*

2. **Drawing Inferences and Conclusions** *Why is entrepreneurship a promising economic alternative for immigrants?*

CLOSE
In a closing discussion, ask students to explain why sociologists study economic systems *(to discover how societies use their limited resources to meet the needs and wants of individuals and groups).*

REVIEW AND ASSESS
Have students complete the **Section 1 Review** on p. 333. As **Alternative Assessment**, you may want to use the capitalism-versus-socialism cartoon or the American economy then-and-now chart in this section's lessons.

RETEACH
Have students prepare 10-question quizzes and answer keys that cover the information in this section. Then pair students and have partners exchange quizzes and complete the ones they receive. **ENGLISH LANGUAGE LEARNERS , COOPERATIVE LEARNING**

EXTEND
Have students locate and summarize two newspaper or magazine articles that examine economic issues in a country other than the United States. Then call on volunteers to report their findings to the class. **BLOCK SCHEDULING**

exchanged about $43 billion in goods and services. By 2003, business-to-business online sales are expected to top $1 trillion.

The Internet represents not so much a new location to do business as a new way of doing business. Computer links between businesses and suppliers streamline communication and other activities between the two. For example, tasks such as resupplying and billing can be handled automatically. Businesses can track, store, and analyze consumers' buying practices. Using this information, businesses can quickly respond to changes in buying trends. They can also "package" goods and services to meet the exact requirements of individual consumers.

While consumers appreciate the level of service available through e-commerce, they worry about the loss of privacy it creates. Many express concern about what businesses might do with all the personal information they collect. Others worry that businesses will not be able to keep sensitive information—such as credit card numbers—secure. Such fears seem to be well founded. More than 60 percent of American companies reported breaches of their computer systems in 1999. Realizing the importance of e-commerce, many businesses have begun to search for ways to make it more secure.

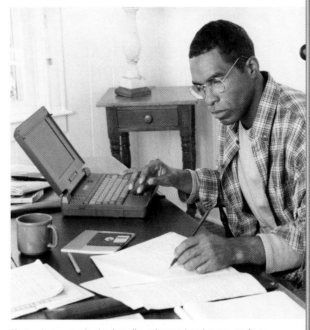

Electronic communication has allowed some Americans to work at home and enjoy more flexible work schedules.

SECTION 1 REVIEW

1. Define and explain
economic institution
factors of production
primary sector
secondary sector
tertiary sector
capitalism
socialism
law of supply
law of demand
laissez-faire capitalism
free-enterprise systems
communism
totalitarianism
corporations
oligopoly
protectionism
free trade
multinational
e-commerce

2. Identify and explain
Adam Smith

3. Comparing and Contrasting Copy the graphic organizer below. Use it to identify how preindustrial, industrial, and postindustrial economic systems differ in terms of the economic sectors that each emphasizes.

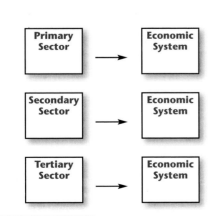

4. Finding the Main Idea
a. What are the characteristics of the ideal capitalist model and the ideal socialist model of economic systems?
b. How do you think different motivations and aspirations influence economic decisions?

5. Writing and Critical Thinking
Analyzing Information Write two or three paragraphs on how globalization of the economy and technology have affected the nature of work in the United States.
Consider:
• competition from workers in foreign countries
• postitive and negative effects on workers

Homework Practice Online
keyword: SL3 HP13

SECTION 1 REVIEW ANSWERS

1. Define:
• economic institution, p. 322
• factors of production, p. 322
• primary sector, p. 323
• secondary sector, p. 323
• tertiary sector, p. 323
• capitalism, p. 325
• socialism, p. 325
• law of supply, p. 325
• law of demand, p. 325
• laissez-faire capitalism, p. 326
• free-enterprise systems, p. 326
• communism, p. 326
• totalitarianism, p. 327
• corporations, p. 328
• oligopoly, p. 328
• protectionism, p. 330
• free trade, p. 330
• multinational, p. 330
• e-commerce, p. 331

2. Identify:
• Adam Smith, p. 324

3. primary—preindustrial; secondary—industrial; tertiary—postindustrial

4a. See the graphic organizer on p. 323.

b. by shaping how people and groups answer the three basic economic questions

5. Paragraphs will vary, but students should recognize that globalization and technology have led to many primary- and secondary-sector jobs moving outside the country and to some downsizing.

SECTION 2

OBJECTIVES

1. *Explain how the exercise of power varies by type of government.*
2. *Describe the major characteristics of the U.S. political system.*

2

THE POLITICAL INSTITUTION

Read to Discover
1. How does the exercise of power vary by type of government?
2. What are the major characteristics of the U.S. political system?

Define
power, state, political institution, legitimacy, authority, traditional authority, rational-legal authority, charismatic authority, coercion, democracy, monarchy, constitutional monarchy, democratic socialism, authoritarianism, absolute monarchy, dictatorship, junta, political party, proportional representation, interest group, power-elite model, pluralist model

No society can survive for long if each person in the society does exactly as he or she pleases. For society to run smoothly, people must often act together for the common good. Thus, all societies exercise some degree of power over societal members. **Power** is the ability to control the behavior of others with or without their consent. The family holds power in very simple societies. In more complex societies power is exercised by the **state**—the primary political authority in society. The nature of a state's power is shaped by its **political institution**—the system of roles and norms that governs the distribution and exercise of power in society.

The different sociological perspectives view the political institution differently. Functionalists analyze the political institution in terms of the functions of the state. These functions include the creation and enforcement of laws, the settling of conflicts between individuals, the provision of services, the establishment of economic and social policies, and the maintenance of relations with other countries. All of these functions center on the task of maintaining order in society.

Conflict theorists, on the other hand, focus on how the political institution brings about social change. According to this view, different groups in society compete with one another for power. Although the political institution generally favors the wealthier segments of society, ongoing conflict causes the distribution of power to shift enough to result in varying degrees of social change.

The Legitimacy of Power

All sociologists, regardless of the perspective they take, are interested in the legitimacy of power. **Legitimacy** refers to whether those in power are viewed as having the right to control, or govern, others. When power is exercised with the consent of the people being governed, it is considered legitimate. Power is considered illegitimate when it is exercised against the will or without the approval of the people.

Authority Max Weber referred to legitimate power as **authority**. Weber was particularly interested in why people accepted the idea that leaders had the legitimate right to exercise power over others. According to Weber, this right to govern is based on one of three types of authority: traditional, rational-legal, or charismatic.

Traditional authority is power that is based on long-standing custom. In other words, people accept the exercise of power as legitimate because people in the past considered it so. Traditional authority is usually hereditary and is passed down from one generation to the next. Kings, queens, and tribal chieftains are examples of leaders who rely on traditional authority for their right to rule. Until the rise of the modern political state, traditional authority was the most common form of legitimate power.

INTERPRETING VISUALS Charismatic leaders, such as Communist Chinese ruler Mao Zedong, often exercise authority by promising a better life to their followers. *Why might these Chinese citizens have supported Mao Zedong?*

SUGGESTION 1: Lead a class discussion on the features of democratic and authoritarian systems of government and how power is exercised in each type *(democratic systems—place power in the people, who exercise it by participating in the decision-making process, require well-informed voters and shared values, place limits on power; authoritarian systems—place power in the state, which exercises it by controlling the people, giving citizens little or no say in the decision-making process, and often not allowing leaders to be legally removed).* Then challenge students to speculate aloud about how their lives and American society would be different if the United States had an authoritarian system of government.

SUGGESTION 2: Create a two-column chart on the chalkboard and label the columns *Democratic Systems* and *Authoritarian Systems.* Call on students to help you complete the chart by contrasting the features of democratic and authoritarian governments and the exercise of power in each. *(See the Suggestion 1 activity to the left.)* Then organize students into four groups and assign each group to be either a pure democracy, a constitutional monarchy, a dictatorship, or a totalitarian government. Have each group prepare a mural to portray its assigned form of rule. Have each group present its mural to the class. **COOPERATIVE LEARNING**

🖳 internet connect ≣ **go hrw .com**

TOPIC: Max Weber
GO TO: go.hrw.com
KEYWORD: SL3 SC13

Have students access the Internet through the HRW Go site to conduct research on Max Weber's contributions to sociology. Then have each student create a theoretical profile explaining Weber's theories and contributions to the field of sociology. Students should also explain which theories of Weber's remain valid today.

INTERPRETING VISUALS Coercion is occasionally used by governments to maintain power. In Cuba, Fidel Castro exercises strong control over the country and its people (above). In Turkey police officers search people during a demonstration (left). *How might these acts be seen as coercion?*

Visual Answer

The action of the Turkish police illustrates an example of the use of military force and fear to maintain order. Fidel Castro, a dictator, rules through force and fear.

Formal rules and regulations provide the basis for **rational-legal authority**. These rules and regulations clearly outline the rights and obligations of those in power. Frequently, they are part of a written constitution or a set of laws. Rational-legal authority rests not with a particular individual but in the office or position that he or she holds. Thus, the authority to govern is lost when an individual leaves or is removed from office. For example, the president of the United States has the right to govern only while in office. Rational-legal authority is the most common form of authority in modern societies.

Charismatic authority is based on the personal characteristics of the individual exercising the power. People accept the authority of a charismatic leader because they believe that he or she possesses special qualities that merit devotion and obedience. Charismatic leaders often emerge during periods of social unrest. At such times people are searching for leaders who promise a better life.

Examples of charismatic leaders include Adolf Hitler, Mohandas Gandhi, Mao Zedong, the Reverend Martin Luther King Jr., Ayatollah Khomeini, and Saddam Hussein. As this list shows, charismatic leaders are not always people whom you would consider "good". Charismatic leadership, then, can have positive or negative consequences for society.

Coercion The opposite of authority is **coercion**, power that is considered illegitimate by the people being governed. Coercion is exercised through force or the threat of force and is based on fear. The use of armed troops to maintain order is one example of coercion. Leaders who have seized power through a military takeover or a revolution often use troops to maintain their hold on power. However, coercion is not limited to the use or threat of physical violence. Placing restrictions on the press or denying citizens the right to hold public meetings are also examples of coercion.

All political systems use force to some degree to maintain order. For example, the threat of being sent to prison for breaking a law is a form of coercion. Yet in a legitimate political system, coercion is used as a last resort. In an illegitimate system, on the other hand, coercion is the main method of maintaining order.

Types of Government

Although people often use the words interchangeably, the terms *state* and *government* are not the same thing. The combined political structures of a society, such as the presidency, Congress, and Supreme Court in the United States, form the state. The government on the other hand, consists of the people who direct the power of the state. In the United States, the federal government

Case Studies and Other True Stories

▪ TEACH

Have students read the feature Propaganda and World War II. Use the questions under Think About It to guide a class discussion about World War II propaganda movies. Then, if possible, show students one or more cartoons that contain World War II propaganda. An example of a video collection featuring war propaganda cartoons is *Cartoon Crazys Goes to War* by WinStar Entertainment (1998). Discuss the cartoons and what messages they were promoting.

✳ CONNECTING *to History and the Arts*

Tell students that World War II propaganda posters often featured catchphrases meant to rally civilians to the war effort, such as "We're in the fight too," "Be careful what you say or write," and "We can do it!" Organize the class into several groups and have students create similar World War II–era propaganda posters. Ask each group to present its poster to the class and describe the target audience, the intended propaganda message, and the hoped-for response. Display the posters in the classroom.

COOPERATIVE LEARNING , BLOCK SCHEDULING

Interdisciplinary Connection

HISTORY

Nazi Propaganda. Before and during World War II, the government of Nazi Germany used a variety of propaganda techniques to spread its ideology. Adolf Hitler had German textbooks revised to present his view that Communists and Jewish bankers were responsible for Germany's defeat in World War I. Nazi officials removed educators who did not support the party line and publicly burned books considered controversial. In addition, the Nazi government often portrayed Jews as dirty and animal-like, while portraying Germans as tall, clean, and intelligent.

CRITICAL THINKING

Why was rewriting textbooks an important part of the Nazi propaganda?

ANSWER: because it revised history to match the Nazi version

Think About It Answers

1. to promote unified support among the American people for the war effort

2. Students might answer that some audiences probably responded with feelings of patriotism and an increased desire to support the U.S. war effort.

Case Studies
AND OTHER TRUE STORIES

PROPAGANDA AND WORLD WAR II

Propaganda is the organized and deliberate effort to shape the opinions of the public toward some specific conclusion. In times of war, governments often use propaganda to get the public to support the war effort. For example, during World War II the U.S. government established the Office of War Information (OWI). Hundreds of writers and artists employed by the OWI created pamphlets, posters, and other media designed to explain the U.S. role in the war, to encourage national pride, and to raise morale. The OWI even co-opted Hollywood to help in its attempt to get the American public behind the war effort.

Barbarizing the Enemy

During World War II, most of Hollywood's war movies followed a similar pattern. American and other Allied soldiers were portrayed as decent honorable men who were fighting for freedom and democracy. In contrast, enemy soldiers were shown as immoral murderers. To get this message across, the moviemakers used broad stereotypes of the enemy forces. They depicted Italians as bumbling fools who cared more about wine and food than fighting. The Germans were shown as unthinking "robots," fanatically committed to spreading Nazism across the world. The Japanese were shown as dishonest, sneaky, and cunning.

Stereotyping involves a propaganda technique known as *name-calling*. This term refers to the use of negative labels or images designed to make the enemy appear in an unfavorable light. Moviemakers used a variety of names to refer to Italian, German, and Japanese soldiers. Some of these slurs were intended to imply that the enemy lacked intelligence. More commonly, the moviemakers chose terms that characterized the enemy as brutal and uncivilized. The most vicious names were reserved for the Japanese. Moviemakers often used animal names to refer to Japanese soldiers, thus implying that they were less than human.

During World War II Germany developed an extensive propaganda campaign to build support for its war efforts.

The Effects of Movie Propaganda

Hollywood-movie propaganda helped to develop a unity among the American people in support of the war effort. Hollywood's portrayal of the adversary as either bumbling or savage generated a hatred for the enemy, particularly the Japanese. Hollywood's role in the war effort was short-lived, however. As the war dragged on, the American public began to demand an escape from the constant reminders of the conflict. Hollywood responded by cutting back on propaganda and by focusing more on romance and adventure movies.

Think About It

1. **Summarizing** *What was the purpose of the Hollywood propaganda movies of World War II?*
2. **Drawing Inferences and Conclusions** *What do you think was the response of audiences to these propaganda movies? Explain your answer.*

SUGGESTION 3: Have each student write a short essay comparing and contrasting democratic and authoritarian systems of government and the way in which power is exercised in each one. *(See the Suggestion 1 activity on p. 335.)* Remind students to use standard grammar, spelling, sentence structure, and punctuation. Ask volunteers to read their essays aloud to the class.

SUGGESTION 4: Organize students into small groups and have each group create six mock artifacts for an exhibit contrasting how power is exercised in democratic and authoritarian systems of government. Three of the artifacts should represent democratic systems and three should represent authoritarian systems. Have each group label its artifacts and set up its exhibit in the classroom. **COOPERATIVE LEARNING**

SPOTLIGHT *on Constitutional Monarchy*

Review with students the definition of a constitutional monarchy *(monarchies in which ultimate power rests with elected officials and in which the monarch is the symbolic head of state).* Then organize the class into small groups and have each group conduct research to learn more about the constitutional monarchy of Great Britain. Instruct each group to use its findings to write and illustrate a children's book designed to teach elementary-age children about Britain's government. Groups' children's books should combine images with simple text to make concepts easy for young children to understand. Display the books in the classroom.
COOPERATIVE LEARNING , BLOCK SCHEDULING

The founders of the United States created a representational democracy because they were unhappy with the experiences they had under the control of Great Britain's monarchy.

Sociology in the World Today

Monarchies. Today about 30 countries have monarchies. Of these countries, monarchs have substantial power in only a handful, such as in Kuwait and Saudi Arabia. The others are constitutional monarchies, including Denmark, Japan, the Netherlands, Norway, Sweden, and the United Kingdom.

RESEARCH ACTIVITY: Have each student conduct research to determine which countries currently have monarchies and which have constitutional monarchies and then create a chart listing the results. Each student should write a caption to summarize the information in his or her chart.

includes the president, the members of Congress, and the Supreme Court justices. The individuals who make up the government come and go, but the state gives a society's political system continuity by providing an underlying structure.

How power is exercised by a state varies by its type of government. Sociologists recognize two basic types of government: democratic systems and authoritarian systems. As in the case of economic models, these systems are ideal types. Actual governments vary widely in their characteristics. However, all governments can be roughly categorized as one of those types.

Democratic Systems In a **democracy**, power is exercised through the people. The central feature of a democracy is the right of the governed to participate in the political decision-making process. In practice modern democratic systems are representational democracies. Voters elect representatives who undertake the task of making political decisions. If these elected officials do not perform to the people's liking, they can be voted out of office.

For much of history, democracies were rare. It was much more common for states to establish monarchies. A **monarchy** is a type of government in which one person rules. The ruler—known as the monarch—inherits power. However, most of the few remaining monarchs have limited power. True political power rests primarily with elected officials. In many instances, the monarch is nothing more than the symbolic head of state, which is a system called a **constitutional monarchy**. Constitutional monarchies are considered democratic because ultimate power rests with elected officials. The United Kingdom is an example of a constitutional monarchy.

Today democracies are much more common because more and more societies possess the conditions needed for a democracy to thrive. These conditions include the following:

• *Industrialization* Although industrialization does not necessarily lead to democracy, most democratic societies are industrialized. According to sociologist Gerhard Lenski, one reason for this relationship is that the

CONNECTING *to History*

Have each student create an annotated time line of major U.S. conflicts since 1900, including World War I, World War II, the Korean War, the Vietnam War, the Cold War, the Gulf War, and the start of the War on Terror. For each conflict, ask students to list U.S. allies and enemies and to label each country as either democratic or authoritarian. When students have completed the activity, ask them to speculate about why the United States often finds itself in conflict with absolute monarchies, dictatorships, and totalitarian states. **BLOCK SCHEDULING**

SPOTLIGHT *on Democracy*

Ask students to identify and describe the conditions for a democracy to thrive, described on pp. 337–38 *(industrialization, access to information, limits on power, and shared values)*. Write the four conditions on the chalkboard. Then have each student use these conditions and other features of democratic societies to create a "recipe" for a democracy. Recipes should include lists of "ingredients" as well as preparation instructions. Encourage students to be creative. Call on volunteers to share their recipes with the class. **BLOCK SCHEDULING**

Interdisciplinary Connection

GOVERNMENT
Power Among Levels of Government.

Governments also differ in how power is distributed among national, regional, and local levels. Ways of sharing power fall into three systems: unitary, federal, and confederal. In a unitary system, all legal power is held by the national, or central, government. Local governments do not have any independent powers and simply represent the national government. Japan and the United Kingdom are examples. In a federal system, powers are divided between national, state, and local governments. In this system, each level of government has certain powers while sharing others. The United States has a federal system of government. In a confederal system, independent countries join together to accomplish common goals. Confederations usually set up an organization to carry out agreed-upon policies. The European Union (EU) is an example of a confederation.

CRITICAL THINKING

How does a federal system set limits on power?

ANSWER: by dividing powers among three levels of government: federal, state, and local

According to the representational democracy of the United States, voters elect representatives to make political decisions for them. Representatives hold hearings and propose new laws to help better run the country.

educated urban populations found in industrial societies expect to have a voice in the political process.

- *Access to information* Democracy requires well-informed voters. Thus, democracies are strongest in those societies where the public and the media have open access to information.
- *Limits on power* All governments exercise power. However, in democracies clear limits are placed on the scope of government power. One way to limit power is to spread the power among many different groups. When power is divided among the branches of government and among nongovernmental organizations, such as labor unions and businesses, it cannot be concentrated in the hands of a few people.
- *Shared values* Although the right to hold opposing views is a cornerstone of democracy, a shared set of basic values is essential. Without some agreement among voters on basic values, it would be difficult to reach the compromises necessary in a functioning democratic system.

Democratic governments can be distinguished by the type of economic model they adopt. Many democracies have capitalist economies. The United States is an example of a democratic country with a capitalist economy. Some other democracies have socialist economies. The combination of a democratic government and a socialist economy is called **democratic socialism**. Under democratic socialism, the government owns some of the

factors of production. However, individuals maintain control over economic planning through the election of government officials. The Scandinavian countries of Sweden, Denmark, and Norway are examples of democratic-socialist states.

Authoritarian Systems In a government based on **authoritarianism**, power rests firmly with the state. Members of society have little or no say in the political decision-making process. In most cases, government leaders cannot be removed from office through legal means.

Authoritarian governments exist in a variety of forms. An **absolute monarchy** is an authoritarian system in which the hereditary ruler holds absolute power. Absolute monarchs rule several states in the Persian Gulf. An authoritarian system in which power is in the hands of a single individual is called a **dictatorship**. Many Latin American countries, at one time or another, have been ruled by dictators. A **junta** is an authoritarian system in which a small group has seized power from the previous government by force. Juntas have been more common in Africa and Latin America.

The most extreme form of authoritarianism is totalitarianism. As you read earlier, under totalitarianism, government leaders accept few limits on their authority. Because totalitarian governments allow little opposition to their policies, individuals in totalitarian states have little freedom. Nazi Germany under Adolf Hitler,

TEACH OBJECTIVE 2

SUGGESTION 1: To help students identify and describe the major characteristics of the U.S. political system, copy the graphic organizer at the right onto the chalkboard, omitting the italicized answers. Have students copy and complete the organizer. Then use the activity as the basis of a class discussion about the U.S. political system. Ask students to evaluate the system's fairness and effectiveness in responding to the will of the people, including both majority and minority views. **ENGLISH LANGUAGE LEARNERS**

Major Characteristics of the U.S. Political System

dominated by two major political parties—Democrats and Republicans

includes interest groups and PACs, which help groups with minority views influence government decisions

has proportional representation, but debate exists over who holds power

consists of three branches of government—the executive, legislative, and judicial

includes public participation, although voter participation varies and is relatively low overall

INTERPRETING VISUALS For authoritarian governments, such as the former Soviet Union, shows of military strength are an important reminder of the government's power. *How might this parade reflect military authority?*

the Soviet Union under Joseph Stalin, and Cambodia under the Khmer Rouge present some striking examples of totalitarianism. However, the world does not lack current examples. Countries that are totalitarian or nearly totalitarian today include Iraq and Libya.

The question of why individuals submit to totalitarian rule is of greater interest to sociologists than which countries are totalitarian. Psychoanalyst Erich Fromm attempted to provide an answer in *Escape from Freedom*, his classic study on totalitarianism in Germany under Adolf Hitler. Fromm was interested in why the German people supported the Nazi government.

According to Fromm, people succumb to totalitarianism because they want to escape feelings of isolation and powerlessness. By submitting to the will of those more powerful or by dominating those less powerful, people achieve a sense of security. Fromm labeled the personality structure that gives rise to this response as the "authoritarian character." (Turn to page 347 to read an excerpt from Fromm's *Escape from Freedom*.)

The American Political System

Since the time of Max Weber, sociologists have devoted considerable attention to the analysis of political systems. The topics of special interest to sociologists who study the American political system include the role of political parties, the effects of special-interest groups on politics, variations in voter participation, and the question of who actually rules America.

Political Parties A **political party** is an organization that seeks to gain power through legitimate means. Political parties distinguish themselves from one another in two basic ways. First, they adopt specific points of view on issues of interest to voters. Second, they formulate programs for legislative action based on these points of view.

By supporting candidates from the party that most closely represents their views, voters directly influence government decision making. A party that cannot get enough of its candidates elected to office will not be able to put its programs into effect. These programs may need

Connecting to Government

■ TEACH

Have students read the feature Aiding Democracy. Then pair students and have partners take opposing sides on the debate about the role of the United States in aiding democracy around the world. Partners should debate the merits and drawbacks of both an active and a more isolationist role, and they should consider related economic, political, and humanitarian considerations. Then call on pairs to share with the class some of the points that they discussed.
COOPERATIVE LEARNING

■ EXTEND

Have students conduct research and write position papers on the U.S. aid of democracy abroad. Students' papers should address the following questions: How has the United States helped spread democracy around the world? What methods are being used? What is the monetary cost of such programs? To what extent have the programs been successful? Are the programs worth the cost? How important is the task of aiding democracy relative to other national priorities? Should the United States continue in this role? **BLOCK SCHEDULING**

Think About It Answers

1. diplomatic measures, economic rewards and punishments, military means, and democratic aid

2. Answers will vary. Students who think the United States should support democracy in other countries might respond that the government has the moral obligation to promote human rights around the world and that democracies are most likely to protect human rights. Students might also respond that an increase in global democracy will benefit the United States politically and economically. Students who think the United States should not support democracy in other countries might respond that other countries are independent societies, which have the right to form their own governments.

CONNECTING TO
Government

AIDING DEMOCRACY

During the 1990s, after the collapse of communism in the Soviet Union and Eastern Europe, many countries began to move away from authoritarianism and toward democracy. The United States assisted in this process by offering aid to countries undergoing democratization. In this excerpt from his book Aiding Democracy Abroad, *lawyer and political scientist Thomas Carothers discusses the policy tools available to support the growth of democracy worldwide.*

"When policy makers decide they are going to try to promote democracy in another country, they typically reach for various tools. The officials may use diplomatic measures, as either carrots or sticks: criticizing a government that is backtracking from democracy, praising a prodemocracy leader, granting or withdrawing high-level diplomatic contacts in response to positive or negative developments, and so on. Or they may apply economic tools, again as carrots or sticks: economic pressure, such as sanctions, on governments that crush democracy movements; or economic rewards, such as trade benefits or balance-of-payments support for governments taking steps toward democracy. In extreme circumstances, the United States may even employ military means to promote democracy, intervening to overthrow a dictatorship and install or re-install an elected government—although U.S. military interventions that politicians justify on democratic grounds are usually motivated by other interests as well.

The most common and often most significant tool for promoting democracy is democracy aid: aid specifically designed to foster a democratic opening in a nondemocratic country or to further a democratic transition in a country that has experienced a democratic opening. Donors typically direct such aid at one or more institutions or political processes from what has become a relatively set list: elections, political parties, constitutions, judiciaries, police, legislatures, local government, militaries, nongovernmental civic advocacy groups, civic education organizations, trade unions, media organizations. Unlike the other tools of the trade, democracy assistance is neither a carrot nor a stick. It is not awarded for particular political behavior, nor is it meted out as punishment for democratic slippage (though people in recipient countries may sometimes view it as such).

Prior to the 1980s, the United States did not pursue democracy aid on a wide basis. In the past two decades, such aid has mushroomed, as part of the increased role of democracy promotion in American foreign policy. It started slowly in the 1980s then expanded sharply after 1989 with the quickening of the global democratic trend. By the mid-1990s, U.S. annual spending on such programs reached approximately $600 million and now exceeds $700 million. . . .

The reach of such assistance is broad. In 1998 the United States carried out democracy programs in more than 100 countries, including most countries in Eastern Europe, the former Soviet Union, sub-Saharan Africa, and Latin America, as well as many in Asia and the Middle East. The current wave of democracy aid is by no means the first for the United States. . . . The democracy programs of the 1980s and 1990s, however, are by far the most systematic, sustained, and wide-reaching that America has undertaken."

Think About It

1. Finding the Main Idea *What are the typical tools used by U.S. policy makers to support democracy abroad?*

2. Supporting a Point of View *Do you think that the United States should be involved in supporting the democratic process in foreign countries? Why or why not?*

to be adjusted to attract more voters. Political parties thus form a bridge between the will of the people and their government's actions. Political parties also provide a check on the concentration of power.

In the United States, voters have a choice between candidates from the Democratic Party, the Republican Party, or one of several third parties. These third parties regularly run candidates for local, state, and national office. However, nearly all elected officials since the Civil War have been members of either the Democratic Party or the Republican Party. The United States is considered to have a two-party system.

A two party system is relatively rare in a democracy. Most democracies have multiparty systems. The parties in such a system generally hold clearly differentiated views on the major issues. Therefore, they tend to appeal to specific groups of voters. Appealing to limited numbers of voters is workable in multiparty systems because of the way in which legislative seats are assigned. For example, if a party receives 10 percent of the popular vote on the national level, it will receive 10 percent of the seats in the national legislature. This system is called **proportional representation**. Proportional representation ensures that minority parties—and thus minority viewpoints—receive a voice in the government.

Except for the president, in the United States candidates are elected to office on the basis of a simple plurality, meaning that whichever candidate receives the most votes wins. Critics charge that minority-party candidates have little hope of winning a majority of votes. Therefore, this winner-takes-all rule discourages the formation of minority parties. Further, it prevents citizens who hold minority views from having a voice in the government.

Political cartoonists have represented the Republican Party with an elephant and the Democratic Party with a donkey. These symbols have become widely used in the United States.

Critics also argue that the winner-takes-all rule discourages sharp differences between the policy positions of the Republican and Democratic Parties. According to this view, the two parties fear that adopting "extreme" positions on issues might cost them votes. Therefore, to avoid alienating voters, the parties adopt positions that are only slightly different from each other.

In the 1992 presidential election voter disenchantment with the "sameness" of Democratic and Republican policy positions helped a third-party candidate make an unusually strong showing. In that election, independent H. Ross Perot vied with Democrat Bill Clinton and

Third-Party Candidates in Presidential Elections, 1968–2000

Election	Candidate	Party	Share of Popular Vote
1968	George Wallace	American Independent	13%
1972	John Schmitz	American	1%
1976	Eugene McCarthy	Independent	1%
1980	John Anderson	Independent	7%
1984	David Bergland	Libertarian	Less than 1%
1988	Ron Paul	Libertarian	Less than 1%
1992	H. Ross Perot	Independent	19%
1996	H. Ross Perot	Reform	8%
2000	Ralph Nader	Green	3%

Source: *Statistical Abstract of the United States*

INTERPRETING CHARTS While American politics has been dominated by two parties, these smaller-party candidates have influenced politics by guiding political debates and by drawing votes away from other candidates. *How much support did Ross Perot lose between 1992 and 1996?*

SPOTLIGHT *on the Two-Party System*

Organize the class into two groups and assign one group the Democratic Party and the other the Republican Party. Tell each team to build its party's platform—a list of issues and positions—based on current newspaper articles, televised debates, and campaign advertisements. Ask each group to designate a "party leader" and have each party leader present his or her party's platform to the class. Then lead a discussion noting similarities and differences between the two platforms. Challenge students to spot opportunities for third-party candidates to present opposing viewpoints.

COOPERATIVE LEARNING, BLOCK SCHEDULING

CONNECTING *to Civics*

Ask students to think of ways that they can participate in the political system even if they are not yet old enough to vote. *(Students might suggest volunteering for political campaigns, participating in "Get Out the Vote" drives, donating to or working for PACs, or joining peaceful demonstrations.)* Then have each student design a poster or bumper sticker encouraging young people to become involved in the political process. **BLOCK SCHEDULING**

Applying Sociology

Voter Turnout. The low voter turnout in the United States contrasts with that of many other democracies. According to the International Institute for Democracy and Electoral Assistance, average voter turnouts in parliamentary or presidential elections during the 1990s was 85.5 percent in Italy, 79.9 percent in Germany, 74.7 percent in the United Kingdom, 68.7 percent in Canada, and 61.8 percent in the United States.

ACTIVITY: Have each student ask three adults of voting age if they voted in the last election, and if not, why? Have students share their findings with the class.

Chart Answer

Voter participation is highest among women, white Americans and African Americans, older people, more educated people, people in the Midwest and Northeast, and employed people. Higher participation among these groups means that they have more power and representation in politics.

Technology Resources

Teaching Transparency: Voter Participation by Selected Characteristics, 1996–2000

Voter Participation by Selected Characteristics, 1996–2000

Characteristic	Percentage Voting 1996	Percentage Voting 1998	Percentage Voting 2000
Sex			
Male	52.8	41.4	53.1
Female	55.5	42.4	56.2
Race			
White	56.0	43.3	56.4
African American	50.6	39.6	53.5
Hispanic	26.7	20.0	27.5
Age			
18–20 years old	31.2	13.5	28.4
21–24 years old	24.2	16.2	24.2
25–34 years old	43.1	28.0	43.7
35–44 years old	54.9	40.7	55.0
45–64 years old	67.8	53.6	64.1
65 and over	70.1	59.5	67.6
Education			
Less than eight years of school	28.1	24.6	26.8
High school graduate	49.1	37.1	49.4
College graduate	73.0	57.2	72.0
Region			
Northeast	54.5	41.2	55.2
Midwest	59.3	47.3	60.9
South	52.2	38.6	53.5
West	51.8	42.3	49.9
Employment Status			
Unemployed	37.2	28.4	35.1
Employed	55.2	41.2	55.5

Source: U.S. Census Bureau

INTERPRETING CHARTS Despite the strong value of democracy most Americans hold, the percentage of voter participation remains low for many sectors of the American population. *Which groups have the highest voter turn out? How do you think this affects U.S. politics?*

Republican George Bush. Perot's share of the popular vote—some 19 percent—was the highest of any third-party candidate since Theodore Roosevelt took 27 percent in 1912. Turn to the chart on page 341 to see how minority-party candidates fared in other recent presidential elections.

Interest Groups People with minority views can get their voices heard through interest groups. An **interest group** is an organization that attempts to influence the political decision-making process. There are thousands of such groups in the United States. They represent a variety of interests—such as business, labor, medical practitioners, patients, environmentalists, and senior citizens.

These groups use a variety of techniques to win political and public support for the issues of interest to their

members. Contributing money to the campaigns of political candidates is one of the most common pressure techniques used by interest groups. Most interest groups use political action committees (PACs) to collect and distribute political-campaign contributions. Currently, more than 3,800 PACs operate in the United States. In the 2000 elections, PACs contributed more than $245 million to congressional candidates, which was about a quarter of all the campaign funds raised. The power of PAC contributions becomes apparent when you consider that candidates for the House of Representatives spend an average of $275,000 each on their election campaigns. Candidates for the Senate spend $1.3 million.

Other methods that interest groups use to apply political pressure include collecting petitions, organizing

Applying Sociology

TEACH

Have students read the feature Public Opinion and the 2000 Presidential Election and discuss the main points. Give students time to write answers to the questions under Think About It. Then tell students that public opinion is most often measured with polls of a sampling or cross-section of the American public. Although most major polling companies strive to be unbiased and honest in their methods and reporting, some Americans are skeptical about the fairness and accuracy of polls. Other Americans are concerned about public officials making decisions based on polls taken from a small segment of the population. In addition, journalists and others who report the outcomes of polls may present the results inaccurately or out of context to better support a particular point of view. Tell students that although polls are useful to sociologists, politicians, the media, and the public in determining public opinion, it can be difficult to formulate completely unbiased survey questions or to poll a perfect cross-section of the American public. In a class discussion, ask students to express their opinions about the practice of polling in the American political process and the effects of this practice on American society. As an extension, have each student write a short essay on the topic.

APPLYING
Sociology

PUBLIC OPINION AND THE 2000 PRESIDENTIAL ELECTION

The 2000 presidential election, which pitted Democrat Al Gore against Republican George W. Bush, was one of the most dramatic in American history. The election was close, and both the Republican and Democratic Parties claimed victory. In the end, the election generated deep concern about the electoral process among many Americans.

A Delayed Election

As results began to come in after the polls closed, it became clear that the presidential race would be close. It also became clear that winning Florida would be crucial in the drive to get the necessary 270 electoral votes. Initially, all major television networks predicted that Florida would be won by Gore. However, a few hours later the networks changed their position and called the Florida vote too close to name a winner. About 2:00 A.M. the next morning, most networks announced that Bush would win Florida. Yet as results from Florida continued to trickle in, Bush's lead began to narrow. Once again, the networks changed their position and said that Florida was too close to call.

The margin of victory in Florida was so small that state law required an automatic machine recount. Gore asked for a manual recount in four counties. Each candidate sent advisers to Florida to oversee the process. Disputes soon arose, and citizens and officials from both parties took their cases to the courts. In the five weeks following the election, state and then federal courts debated the merits of machine counts, hand counts, and absentee ballots.

On December 12, the U.S. Supreme Court—by a 7–2 vote—ruled in *Bush* v. *Gore* that hand recounts in several Florida counties were not valid. As a result, with a lead of 537 popular votes, Bush was awarded Florida's 25 electoral votes. This result gave him 271 electoral votes—one more than needed for victory. Gore, however, had won the national popular vote with more than 48 percent of the vote. Thus, Bush became the first president in more than 100 years to win the electoral vote but not the popular vote.

Public Reaction

In the days after the U.S. Supreme Court decision, several public-opinion organizations and media outlets conducted polls to gauge the reaction of the American people. These polls produced some interesting results.

A little more than half the people believed that the Supreme Court made the right decision and acted fairly. However, about a third of the respondents said that as a result of the decision, they had a lower opinion of the Supreme Court. The polls found that the public held similar feelings about the Florida court's involvement in the recount process.

On the recount process, a majority of those polled felt that the Florida votes had not been fairly counted. Also, many harbored the feeling that if the recount process had been allowed to proceed, Al Gore would have won. Nearly half said that the whole chain of events had seriously shaken their confidence in the U.S. electoral system. A huge majority, some 86 percent, said that there are major problems with the way votes are cast and counted and that these need to be fixed.

Since the election, some ideas on how to fix the electoral system have been offered. One is to establish federal standards for elections—at present the rules for running elections are set by the individual states.

Despite the controversy of the 2000 election, many Americans joined together in support of President Bush after the events of September 11. Bush's approval rating soared, and he received bipartisan support for many of his antiterrorist measures.

Think About It

1. **Identifying Points of View** *What concerns about the electoral system were expressed in the public-opinion polls taken after the 2000 presidential election?*
2. **Supporting a Point of View** *What steps would you take to reform the electoral system? Give reasons for your answer.*

Did You Know?

The U.S. presidential election of 1876 was also controversial. The winner, Republican Rutherford B. Hayes, lost the popular vote by more than 250,000. Moreover, the vote totals for Florida, Louisiana, Oregon, and South Carolina were called into question. An electoral commission of 15 people was established and decided by one vote not to investigate the disputed vote counts. Finally, after lengthy negotiations, Southern Democrats agreed to honor Hayes as president in return for Republican promises that a southerner would be appointed to the cabinet, that federal troops would be removed from the South, that Reconstruction would be ended, and that the South would receive financial aid.

Think About It Answers

1. Nearly half of those polled said that their confidence in the U.S. electoral system had been seriously shaken, and some 86 percent said there were major problems with the way votes are cast and counted.

2. Answers will vary, but students' suggested actions should address the concerns that Americans expressed about the electoral system.

SPOTLIGHT *on Bush Versus Gore, 2000*

Have students conduct research on the controversial 2000 presidential election. Then ask students to take on the roles of attorneys representing either George W. Bush or Al Gore during the U.S. Supreme Court arguments. Have each student prepare a brief statement defending his or her client's position. Select volunteers to read their statements to the class. Then in a class discussion challenge students to decide if election rules and the electoral system need reform. **BLOCK SCHEDULING**

SPOTLIGHT
on the Pluralist Model and Interest Groups

Tell students that interest groups provide a collective voice for voters who individually lack the resources to interface directly with government officials. Ask each student to research two interest groups: one they might support and one they would not support. Have students study, compare, and contrast the mission, messages, strategies, and relative success of the two interest groups. Then have each student present the information in a report that includes charts and graphs and concludes by either defending or opposing the pluralist model. **BLOCK SCHEDULING**

Table Answer

Answers will vary.

SECTION 2 REVIEW ANSWERS

1. Define:
- power, p. 334
- state, p. 334
- political institution, p. 334
- legitimacy, p. 334
- authority, p. 334
- traditional authority, p. 334
- rational-legal authority, p. 335
- charismatic authority, p. 335
- coercion, p. 335
- democracy, p. 337
- monarchy, p. 337
- constitutional monarchy, p. 337
- democratic socialism, p. 338
- authoritarianism, p. 338
- absolute monarchy, p. 338
- dictatorship, p. 338
- junta, p. 338
- political party, p. 339
- proportional representation, p. 341
- interest group, p. 342
- power-elite model, p. 345
- pluralist model, p. 345

2. democratic—exercise power through the people, give the governed the right to participate in the political system, require well-informed voters, place limits on power, and have shared values; authoritarian—place power in the state, give citizens little or no say in the political

344

Getting People to the Polls—Some Ideas

Political scientists have suggested several ways to increase voter participation in elections. These include the following:

1. Make Election Day a national holiday or move elections to the weekend, when most people will not be working.

2. Use a cumulative voting system, in which each voter gets several votes to be shared among the candidates as the voter sees fit.

3. Use the proportional representation system rather than the winner-take-all system.

4. Hold a run-off election between the top two vote-getters if no candidate gains more than 50 percent of the vote.

5. Dispense with the traditional polling centers and go to all mail-in elections.

6. Vote via the Internet.

INTERPRETING TABLES These proposals were created in order to attract more registered voters to the polls. *Which ideas do you think will work the best?*

letter-writing campaigns, and promising to have their members vote for candidates sympathetic to their causes. Many large interest groups—such as the National Rifle Association (NRA), the National Education Association (NEA), and the National Organization for Women (NOW)—also launch expensive media campaigns to sway public opinion. In addition, most groups employ lobbyists to meet directly with government officials in order to win their support. Federal reports suggest that there are more than 12,000 political lobbyists registered to work in Washington, D.C. In the late 1990s special-interest groups spent nearly $1.4 billion a year on lobbying the federal government.

Political Participation

Public participation is at the heart of the democratic process. Yet the United States has one of the lowest rates of voter participation among the democratic countries of the world. Some 38 percent of voting-age Americans are not registered to vote. Among registered voters, only about 54 percent voted in the 1996 presidential election. As you can see from the chart on page 342, the percentage of registered voters who cast ballots in nonpresidential

elections is even lower. Winning candidates often speak of landslide victories and of having the mandate of the people. However, they are generally basing those claims on having received the support of about one third of potential voters.

As you can see from the chart on page 342, voter participation varies among different groups of Americans. For example, white Americans and African Americans are much more likely to vote than are Hispanics. Similarly, employed people are far more likely to vote than are people who are unemployed. Voter participation also varies by level of education—people with college educations have a higher voter-participation rate than do people who have never attended college.

Age is also associated with voter participation. Generally, voter participation increases with age. People under the age of 25 are the least likely to vote, and people aged 45 to 64 have the highest voter-participation rate. In recent elections, people aged 65 and older have been the group most likely to vote. Since the 1980s voter participation among senior Americans has shown an overall increase in presidential-election years and has held steady in congressional-election years. However, participation among all other age groups has shown a decline. Voter apathy, or disinterestedness, particularly among the young, poses a threat to American democracy.

Who Rules America? Low voter turnout, among other features of the American political system, has led sociologists to question who actually rules America. Sociologists who examine this question generally adopt one of two models: the power-elite model or the pluralist model.

ETTA HULME reprinted by permission of Newspaper Enterprise Association, Inc.

Some sociologists have been critical of interest groups and political action committees in U.S. politics.

CLOSE

In a round-robin discussion, ask each student to express a well-thought-out opinion about American politics based on what students have learned in this section.

REVIEW AND ASSESS

Have students complete the **Section 2 Review** on p. 345. As **Alternative Assessment**, you may want to use the democratic and authoritarian systems essay or the U.S. political system theme song in this section's lessons.

RETEACH

Have each student prepare a riddle and answer for each of the section's Define terms. An example might be: "I am the primary political authority in society. What am I?" *(the state)* Collect students' riddles and use them to host a fast-paced quiz game with the class. **ENGLISH LANGUAGE LEARNERS**

EXTEND

Have each student look up information about five current and historical world leaders and classify each leader and his or her government using the information in the section *(for example, Queen Elizabeth II of England—traditional authority, constitutional monarchy).* **BLOCK SCHEDULING**

The **power-elite model**, first presented by sociologist C. Wright Mills, states that political power is exercised by and for the privileged few in society. According to Mills, the top ranks in America's political, economic, and military organizations are controlled by people who are linked by ties of family, friendship, and social background. In his studies on the ruling class, G. William Domhoff came to a similar conclusion. Domhoff found that while they make up just 1 percent of the American population, members of the ruling class are heavily represented in the top levels of business, politics, and the military.

The **pluralist model**, on the other hand, states that the political process is controlled by interest groups that compete with one another for power. Pluralists do admit that power is distributed unequally in society and that this asymmetry has led to such social problems as poverty, unemployment, and racial inequality. However, they argue that competition among interest groups prevents power from becoming concentrated in the hands of a few people.

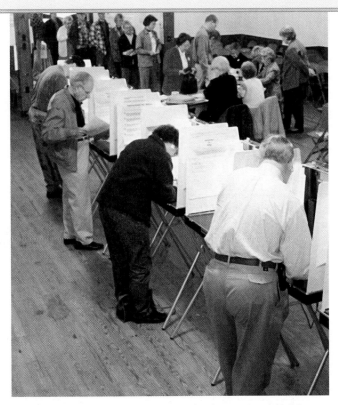

Political participation, such as voting, is essential to the operation of the U.S. political system.

SECTION 2 REVIEW

1. Define and explain
power
state
political institution
legitimacy
authority
traditional authority
rational-legal authority
charismatic authority
coercion
democracy
monarchy
constitutional monarchy
democratic socialism
authoritarianism
absolute monarchy
dictatorship
junta
political party

proportional representation
interest group
power-elite model
pluralist model

2. Comparing and Contrasting
Copy the graphic organizer below. Use it to compare and contrast the characteristics of democratic and authoritarian political systems.

Democratic Systems	Authoritarian Systems

3. Finding the Main Idea

a. Describe the three forms of legitimate power of authority outlined by Max Weber.

b. What are the major characteristics of the American political system?

4. Writing and Critical Thinking

Drawing Inferences and Conclusions
Write two paragraphs that outline the reasons for low voter-participation rates in the United States and that identifies the steps that could be taken to encourage different groups to vote.
Consider:
• recent changes in voter-participation characteristics
• why participation rates are low
• ways to encourage people to vote

Homework Practice Online
keyword: SL3 HP13

Review and Assessment Resources

- Chapter 13 Review, pp. 346–47
- Chapter Review Activities with Answer Key
- Global Skill Builder CD–ROM
- Chapter 13 Test Generator (on the One-Stop Planner)
- Chapter 13 Test (Form A or B)
- Alternative Assessment Handbook
- HRW Go site

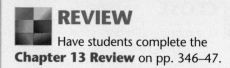

REVIEW
Have students complete the **Chapter 13 Review** on pp. 346–47.

ASSESS
Use one of the chapter tests to assess students' understanding of the content. For **Alternative Assessment**, see the **Alternative Assessment Handbook**.

---

8. legitimate power

9. a government system in which power is exercised through the people

10. an organization that works to influence the political decision-making process

UNDERSTANDING MAIN IDEAS

1. capitalism—factors of production owned by individuals, with limited government control of economic activity; socialism—factors of production owned by government, which regulates economic activity

2. changed the way business is done and the way businesses advertise and access consumers and suppliers

3. democracy—place power in the people, who exercise it by participating in the decision-making process; authoritarian—place power in the state, which uses it to control the people and to remain in power

4. contribute money to political campaigns, collect petitions, organize letter-writing campaigns, vote in blocs, and employ lobbyists

THINKING CRITICALLY

1. The interplay between the laws of supply and demand helps keep a capitalist economy in balance when government interference is kept to a minimum and competition is not restricted.

2. Oligopolies can control the pricing and quality of products and use political pressure tactics to promote legislation that maintains or increases their market share.

346

CHAPTER

13 Review

 ### Writing a Summary

Using standard grammar, spelling, sentence structure, and punctuation, summarize the information in this chapter.
Consider:
- the different types of economic systems
- the features of the U.S. economic system
- the role of power in different political systems
- the characteristics of the U.S. political system

 ### Identifying People and Ideas

Identify the following people or terms and use them in appropriate sentences.

1. Adam Smith
2. capitalism
3. socialism
4. free-enterprise systems
5. communism
6. e-commerce
7. power
8. authority
9. democracy
10. interest group

Understanding Main ideas

Section 1 (pp. 322–33)

1. How do capitalism and socialism differ in terms of ownership of the factors of production and in terms of regulation of economic activity?

2. How has e-commerce changed the American economy?

Section 2 (pp. 334–45)

3. How do democratic and authoritarian governments differ in the ways they use power?

4. What methods do interest groups and political action committees use to win political and public support for their issues?

 ### Thinking Critically

1. Identifying Cause and Effect How do the laws of supply and demand help regulate a capitalist economy?

---

2. Making Generalizations and Predictions How might oligopolies undermine the self-regulatory features of the free-enterprise system?

3. Identifying Points of View Why do some sociologists think that capitalism and socialism are converging?

4. Drawing Inferences and Conclusions Why do you think countries that adopted strong socialist economic models also adopted authoritarian forms of government?

5. Analyzing Information Why do you think voter participation varies according to race, age, and education?

6. Evaluate What do you think the relationships are between American cultural values and the purposes and policies of the U.S. government?

 ### Writing About Sociology

1. Summarizing Prepare a brief report on either (a) multiparty versus two-party political systems or (b) the role of political action committees (PACs) in campaign financing.

2. Analyzing Information Conduct research to find actual examples of governments that practice each of the three kinds of authority. Use your findings to write a brief report titled: "Weber's Three Types of Authority: A Comparison." Use the graphic organizer below to help you complete the report.

Types of Authority	The Ideal Type Description	Real Example
Traditional		
Rational-Legal		
Charismatic		

RETEACH

Organize the class into four groups and assign each group one of the Read to Discover questions in either Section 1 or Section 2 of this chapter. Instruct each group to write a lesson plan to teach the class the answer to its assigned question. Then have each group teach its lesson to the class. Encourage students in the audience to take notes. Fill in or correct any missing or incorrect information during students' lessons, as needed.

ENGLISH LANGUAGE LEARNERS , COOPERATIVE LEARNING

SOCIOLOGY PROJECTS

1. Connecting to Economics and Government Have students conduct research on events from the late 1980s to today that influenced the economic and political systems of either the former Soviet Union or the People's Republic of China. Have each student present his or her findings in a written report.

2. Linking to Community Have students attend a city council meeting or town hall and take notes detailing their observations. Notes should describe in particular any local economic and/or political issues discussed at the meeting. Then have each student write a newspaper article covering the meeting, its agenda, and any decisions made.

BUILDING SOCIAL STUDIES SKILLS

Interpreting Cartoons

Study the cartoon below. Use it to answer the following questions.

STILL WALKING THE EARTH

© 1991 Jeff Koterba, Omaha World Herald. Reprinted by permission.

1. After the fall of the Soviet Union, many political analysts thought that Cuba and China would have to reform their communist governments or collapse as well. Why did the cartoonist choose to draw the rulers of these countries as dinosaurs?

   a. Their form of governments are almost extinct.

   b. Dinosaurs are scary.

   c. The governments have been around a long time.

   d. Dinosaurs are powerful.

2. Do you think the cartoonist views these governments of China and Cuba favorably?

Analyzing Primary Sources

The following excerpt is taken from Erich Fromm's study of Nazi Germany, *Escape from Freedom*. Read the excerpt and then answer the questions that follow.

"*The feature common to all authoritarian thinking is the conviction that life is determined by forces outside of man's own self, his interest, his wishes. The only possible happiness lies in the submission to these forces. . . . The authoritarian character does not lack activity, courage, or belief. But these qualities for him mean something entirely different from what they mean for the person who does not long for submission. For the authoritarian character activity is rooted in a basic feeling of powerlessness which it tends to overcome. Activity in this sense means to act in the name of something higher than one's own self. . . . The authoritarian character wins his strength to act through his leaning on superior power. . . .*
He has belief in authority as long as it is strong and commanding. . . . For him the world is composed of people with power and those without it, of superior ones and inferior ones. . . . He experiences only domination or submission. Differences, whether of sex or race, to him are necessarily signs of superiority or inferiority. A difference which does not have this connotation is unthinkable to him."

3. According to Fromm, the authoritarian character believes in authority as long as it is

   a. executed with ruthlessness.

   b. strong and commanding.

   c. courageous and active.

   d. executed with kindness.

4. Why do you think Germany under Hitler is a good example of the authoritarian character?

---

3. because many capitalist systems have adopted elements of socialism, while many socialist systems have either collapsed or adopted elements of capitalism

4. because such societies favored total government control of state and economy

5. As people age and increase their education, they become more aware of the importance of voting, and racial differences in voter participation might reflect feelings of political power.

6. American cultural values such as freedom have shaped the U.S. government's purposes and policies.

WRITING ABOUT SOCIOLOGY

1. Reports will vary, but students should exhibit an understanding either of how multiparty and two-party systems differ or of how PACs affect campaign financing.

2. Reports will vary, but students should exhibit an understanding of Weber's three types of authority.

BUILDING SOCIAL STUDIES SKILLS

1. a

2. No, because he depicts their leaders as "extinct" dinosaurs.

3. b

4. Students might note that at the time of Hitler's rise to power the German people might have felt powerless because of a severe economic depression and Germany's defeat in World War I.

SOCIOLOGY PROJECTS

Cooperative Learning

Using Your Observation Skills An editorial cartoon is a drawing that presents a point of view on an economic, political, or social issue or topic. Working in a group with two or three students, locate cartoons on two or three issues discussed in this chapter. Make copies of the cartoons. Accompany each cartoon with a brief written report that answers the following questions: What issue is being examined in the cartoon? What is the message of the cartoon? What is the cartoonist's point of view?

internet connect

Internet Activity: go.hrw.com
KEYWORD: SL3 S13
Choose an activity on the economy and politics to:
- create a pamphlet on the sociological implications of globalization and the growth of multinational corporations.
- create a multimedia display on power and authority in political institutions.
- write a theoretical profile of Max Weber and his ideas on authority.

go.hrw.com

Education and Religion

CHAPTER RESOURCE MANAGER

Objectives	Pacing Guide		Resources

**SECTION 1:
The Sociology of Education**
(pp. 350–61)

REV Section 1 Review, p. 361

- Explain how the views of functionalist, conflict, and interactionist sociologists differ concerning education.
- Identify some of the current issues in American education.

| **Regular**
3 days | **Block Scheduling**
1.5 days |
|---|---|

Block Scheduling Handbook with Team Teaching Strategies, Chapter 14

Resources

- 📼 **CNN.** Presents Sociology: American Indians and New Approaches to Teaching Science
- **RS** Graphic Organizer 14
- 🌐 HRW Go site
- **SM** Mastering Critical Thinking Skills 14
- **PS** Readings and Case Studies in Sociology 14
- **E** Research Projects and Activities for Teaching Sociology 14
- **SM** Study Skills and Writing Guide
- 💻 Teaching Transparency: Average Income by Educational Attainment
- 💻 Teaching Transparency: Percentage of Population with a Bachelor's Degree by State, 1999

**SECTION 2:
The Sociology of Religion**
(pp. 362–71)

REV Section 2 Review, p. 371

- Identify the basic societal needs that religion serves.
- Describe the distinctive features of religion in American society.

| **Regular**
3 days | **Block Scheduling**
1.5 days |
|---|---|

Block Scheduling Handbook with Team Teaching Strategies, Chapter 14

Chapter Review And Assessment

- **REV** Chapter 14 Review, pp. 372–73
- **REV** Chapter Review Activities with Answer Key
- 💿 Global Skill Builder CD–ROM
- 💿 Chapter 14 Test Generator (on the One-Stop Planner)
- **A** Chapter 14 Test (Form A or B)
- **A** Alternative Assessment Handbook
- 🌐 HRW Go site

Chapter Resource Key

PS	Primary Sources	**A**	Assessment	📼	Video
RS	Reading Support	**REV**	Review	🌐	Internet
E	Enrichment	💻	Transparencies	💻	Holt Presentation Maker Using Microsoft® PowerPoint®
SM	Skills Mastery	💿	CD–ROM		

 One-Stop Planner CD–ROM

See the *One-Stop Planner* for a complete list of additional resources for students and teachers.

One-Stop Planner CD–ROM

It's easy to plan lessons, select resources, and print out materials for your students when you use the **One-Stop Planner CD–ROM with Test Generator.**

Chapter Project Preview

CHAPTER PROJECT PREVIEW

The following activities are included in the Chapter Review. You may want to make the suggested preparations.

CHAPTER REVIEW ACTIVITY

Linking to Community Students will work in groups to conduct research on how such religious rituals as baptisms, weddings, and funerals are performed in the various religions practiced in their community. Groups will use their research to write an illustrated report comparing and contrasting the religious rituals. Before starting the project, make a list of local religious groups to give students a head start on their research. In addition, you might invite members of various religious groups to speak to your class.

LESSON ACTIVITY

Using Observation Skills Students will visit a preschool or elementary classroom and observe the teacher-student interactions.

Students will then analyze their observations from an interactionist perspective. Before starting the project, you will need to arrange for students to visit a specific classroom and obtain permission notes from students as well as suitable transportation. You will also want to complete your coverage of the theoretical perspectives on education, discussed in Section 1 on pp. 350–55.

INTERNET ACTIVITY

Functionalist Versus Conflict Perspective on Education Students will use provided Internet links to conduct research on the functionalist and conflict perspectives on education and then develop a three-dimensional model of education based on one of the theories. In preparation, obtain art supplies or arrange for access to computers with software for creating 3-D models. You might also suggest that students sketch their models on paper before creating them.

Additional Resources

PRINT RESOURCES FOR TEACHERS

Kozol, Jonathan. *Savage Inequalities: Children in America's Schools.* New York: Random House, 1991. Argues that the nation's poor will be condemned to inferior schools as long as the quality of education is tied to community affluence.

Religion in America: Opposing Viewpoints. San Diego, CA: Greenhaven Press, 1989. Anthology of divergent views on the role and influence of religion in American society.

Sherrow, Victoria. *Separation of Church and State.* New York: Franklin Watts, 1992. Discusses how the separation of church and state emerged in American society and how it has been challenged in the courts through the years.

PRINT RESOURCES FOR STUDENTS

Michener, James. *The Source.* New York: Fawcett, 1988. Archaeological dig in Israel is used as a vehicle to explore the evolution of Judeo-Christian religion.

Provides students with insights into the nature and functions of religion.

Potok, Chaim. *The Promise.* New York: Fawcett, 1985. Story of two Jewish boys coming to terms with their faith in the modern world. Enables students to examine the influence of religion on social relations.

MULTIMEDIA RESOURCES

Faith and Belief: Five Major World Religions (vhs, color; 21 min.) Zenger Media. Introduction to Judaism, Christianity, Islam, Hinduism, and Buddhism.

Inner City vs. Suburban Schools (vhs, color; 28 min.) Films for the Humanities & Sciences. Examines and compares inner-city and suburban schools.

Look Before You Leap: The Dropping-Out Crisis (vhs; 30 min.) Cambridge Educational. Emphasizes the importance of staying in school by focusing on the diminished opportunities available to people who drop out.

☑ **internet** connect

go.hrw.com

HRW ONLINE RESOURCES

GO TO: go.hrw.com
Then type in a keyword.

TEACHER HOME PAGE
KEYWORD: SL3 Teacher

CHAPTER INTERNET ACTIVITIES
KEYWORD: SL3 SC14
Choose an activity to have students:
- create a pamphlet on contemporary issues in public education.
- make a 3-D model of education from either the functionalist or conflict perspective.
- write a profile of a religious group's beliefs and organizational structure.

CHAPTER ENRICHMENT LINKS
KEYWORD: SL3 CH14

ONLINE ASSESSMENT
Homework Practice
KEYWORD: SL3 HP14
Standardized Test Prep
KEYWORD: SL3 STP14
Rubrics
KEYWORD: SS Rubrics

CONTENT UPDATES
KEYWORD: SS Content Updates

HOLT PRESENTATION MAKER
KEYWORD: SL3 PPT14

ONLINE READING SUPPORT
KEYWORD: SS Strategies

CURRENT EVENTS
KEYWORD: S3 Current Events

CHAPTER

14

Education and Religion

SECTION 1
The Sociology of Education

SECTION 2
The Sociology of Religion

CHAPTER REVIEW

Build on What You Know

Ask students to answer the following questions:

How might the educational institution reflect a society's goals and core values?

Consider:

* the adult working world
* technological innovation and economic productivity
* the transmission of culture and socialization

How might the institution of religion help unite a society?

Consider:

* religious values and beliefs
* religious festivals and other practices
* religious figures of authority

Internet Activity

internet connect

TOPIC: Issues in Education
GO TO: go.hrw.com
KEYWORD: SL3 SC14

Have students access the Internet through the HRW Go site to conduct research on current issues in education. Then pair students and have each pair create a pamphlet about one or more of the issues. Pairs' pamphlets should outline the issues, list the pros and cons on each side, and explain where someone might go to obtain more information about the issues.

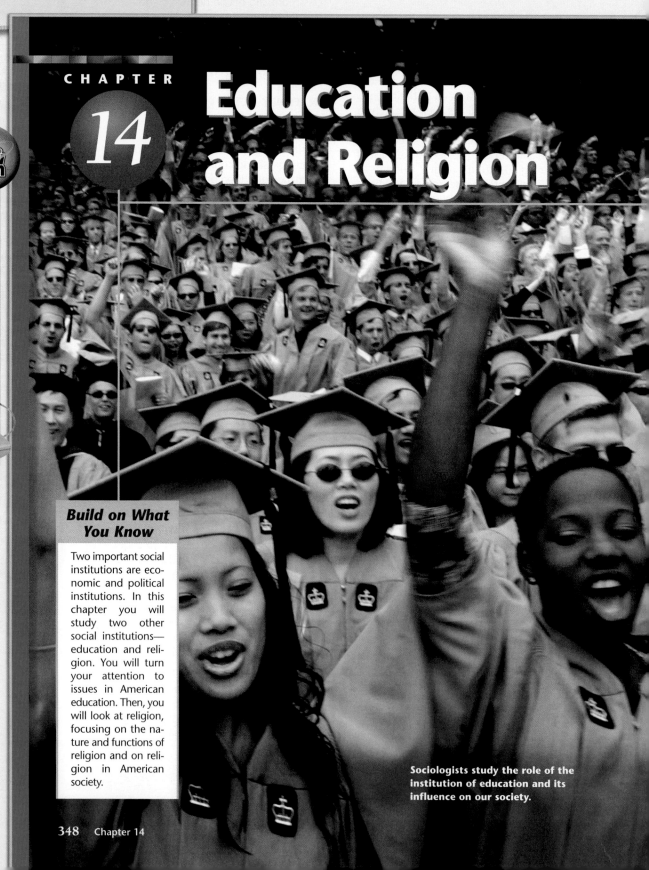

CHAPTER

14

Education and Religion

Build on What You Know

Two important social institutions are economic and political institutions. In this chapter you will study two other social institutions—education and religion. You will turn your attention to issues in American education. Then, you will look at religion, focusing on the nature and functions of religion and on religion in American society.

Sociologists study the role of the institution of education and its influence on our society.

What's Your Opinion?

To help introduce the chapter, have students discuss the Truth or Fiction statements that appear on this page. You might want to help students by reading the following **true/false** responses to the class.

True All societies formally organize schools because that is the most effective way to pass on norms, values, and skills.

False Education in small preindustrial societies takes place within the family, and children learn by participating in adult activities.

True With rare exceptions, American public schools are generally safe institutions of learning for students.

False School safety is a growing issue of concern in the United States today as a result of several well-publicized incidents of school violence.

True Human efforts to understand life's mysteries have always focused on worshiping one or more supreme beings.

False Religions around the world vary in their forms of worship, beliefs, and practices.

Life in Society

E ducation and religion, like all social institutions, arose in response to basic human needs. Providing children with the knowledge they need to inherit the world of their elders and the emotional strength to face that world are among the goals that bind groups of people together as social beings.

How people choose to educate their children varies widely from society to society. The educational process may be as simple as a few tribal elders passing on their ancient lore to the youth of the tribe. Or it may be as complex as a bureaucratic educational system found in most modern societies.

The institution of religion exists in various forms as well, depending on how a society attempts to provide answers to life's mysteries. In some societies, these answers are sought in nature or through the worship of ancestors. In many societies, people believe in a supreme being. No society exists without some form of religion. Each form of religion has its own set of beliefs, sacred objects, and moral lessons.

> ### ▶ WHY SOCIOLOGY MATTERS
>
> Sociologists are interested in how people view such institutions as education. Use **CNNfyi.com** or other current events sources to learn more about public opinion on the American educational system. Create and present an oral report on one aspect of education in the United States.
>
> **CNNfyi.com**

TRUTH OR FICTION

What's Your Opinion?

Read the following statements about sociology. Do you think they are true or false? You will learn whether each statement is true or false as you read the chapter.

• All societies have school systems.

• Violence and other criminal activity are not a problem for schools in the United States.

• Belief systems vary little from religion to religion.

SECTION 1

OBJECTIVES

1. *Explain how the views of functionalist, conflict, and interactionist sociologists differ concerning education.*

2. *Identify some of the current issues in American education.*

LET'S GET STARTED!

After students enter the classroom, remind them that all social institutions exist to meet basic human needs in society. Then ask students to suggest some of the basic needs met by the institution of education. *(Students might mention socialization, the teaching of cultural norms and values, the transmission of knowledge needed for adulthood, and teaching youth the skills they will need to get jobs and support themselves.)* List students' responses on the chalkboard. When students begin running out of ideas, tell them that in Section 1 they will learn about sociological perspectives of education and about some current issues in American education.

1 THE SOCIOLOGY OF EDUCATION

Read to Discover

1. How do the views of functionalist, conflict, and interactionist sociologists differ concerning education?

2. What are some of the current issues in American education?

Define

education, schooling, hidden curriculum, tracking, charter schools, school choice, homeschooling, zero tolerance, bilingual education

A society's future largely depends on the successful socialization of new members. Young members must be taught their society's norms and values and the skills necessary to continue the work of the older generation. In other words, children must acquire the knowledge, skills, behavior patterns, and values necessary to become functioning members of their society. To accomplish this goal, every society has developed a system of **education**. Education consists of the roles and norms that ensure the transmission of knowledge, values, and patterns of behavior from one generation to the next.

In some small preindustrial societies, education is largely informal and occurs mainly through a process of socialization that occurs within the family. Family members teach children the norms and values of their society as well as certain basic skills. Parents may teach young sons and daughters the skills of cooking, pottery making, food gathering, hunting, and fishing. In this way children learn the ways of society, mainly by participating in adult activities. As societies become more complex, the family shares the process of educating the young with more formally established organizations. Formal education, which involves instruction by specially trained teachers who follow officially recognized policies, is called **schooling**. Sociologists who study the institution of education typically focus more on schooling than on the informal education that takes place within the family.

As with many topics in sociology, functionalist, conflict, and interactionist sociologists approach the study of educational institutions differently. The functionalist sociologist studies the ways in which education contributes to the smooth operation of society. The conflict sociologist looks at how education serves to limit certain individuals and groups access to power. The interactionist sociologist is interested in the face-to-face relationships in the classroom. Each sociological perspective provides valuable insight into education. Yet no one perspective gives a complete explanation of this institution.

The Functionalist Perspective on Education

Functionalist sociologists believe that the functions performed by education work to maintain the stability and smooth operation of society. The most important of these functions include the teaching of knowledge and skills, the transmission of culture, social integration, and occupational placement.

Teaching Knowledge and Skills The basic function of education is to teach children the knowledge and skills they will need in the adult world. Schools fulfill this function through a core curriculum—or a set of courses—that includes such subjects as language and literature, history, geography, mathematics, science, and foreign languages.

In addition to transmitting existing knowledge and skills to the students, education also serves to generate new knowledge. All societies must be able to adapt to changing conditions. Education provides the means through which individuals can develop approaches and solutions to new problems, making this adaptation possible. Schools develop the intellectual and critical-thinking skills that are necessary to serve students' needs in the future.

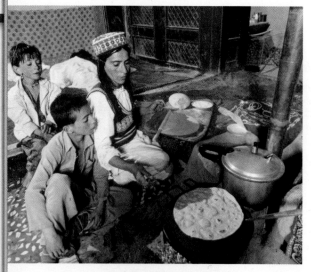

In almost every society children receive some education in their homes as family members teach them necessary skills.

SUGGESTION 1: Before students read Section 1, ask them to use what they have learned so far about theoretical perspectives to suggest what the functionalist, conflict, and interactionist perspectives on education might be. (If needed, quickly review the three perspectives with students.) Write students' suggestions on the chalkboard and encourage students to provide reasons for their suggestions. Next, have students read pp. 350–55 in Section 1. Then call on volunteers to summarize and contrast the three perspectives on education. *(functionalist—schools help maintain the stability and smooth operation of society through the teaching of knowledge and skills, the transmission of culture, social integration, and occupational placement; conflict—the educational system serves to limit the potential of certain individuals and groups to gain power and social rewards; interactionist—students' educational achievements and success are shaped in part by teacher-student interactions.)*

HOMEWORK: Have each student create a poster about the institution of education in the United States from the point of view of either the functionalist, conflict, or interactionist perspective. The posters should be designed to persuade others to support that view of education.

The acquisition of new knowledge and technology is central to the development of society. As a result, much of the research conducted in colleges and universities worldwide is funded by governmental agencies. In many societies, the funds for research also come from private corporations eager for innovations and inventions that can be used to increase their profits.

Transmission of Culture For societies to survive over time, they must pass on the core values of their culture to following generations. After families, schools are perhaps the most important and obvious means through which children learn social norms, values, and beliefs. Within the core curriculum, schools also teach students patriotism, loyalty, and socially acceptable forms of behavior.

Schoolchildren learn about patriotism through songs, rituals, plays, and stories. For example, in the United States young children are taught to salute the flag, recite the Pledge of Allegiance, and stand when the national anthem is played. Children may not understand the words of the pledge or the national anthem. However, they learn very early that these are important rituals that produce feelings of pride. Their sense of pride in the country is strengthened through studying subjects such as U.S. history and civics. American schools also emphasize the benefits of the free-enterprise system, individualism, and democracy—values on which the United States is based.

Other societies also use education to socialize their young to support their communities' own social and political systems. For example, Japanese education emphasizes conformity, cooperation, group loyalty, and respect for elders—qualities that are highly valued in Japan. Before the former Soviet Union collapsed, schoolchildren there were taught the principles of socialism.

Socializing the young to accept the superiority of their own political and social systems is sometimes accomplished by teaching them that other such systems are inferior. This approach serves to create a bond of unity and loyalty among members of a society. Loyalty to one's nation is reinforced by emphasizing that country's accomplishments in history books while downplaying or ignoring the less positive aspects of the country's history.

Schools also help to teach socially acceptable forms of behavior. Children are taught to be punctual, to obey rules, and to respect authority by encountering a series of rewards and punishments designed to encourage these behaviors. Teachers may award gold stars, certificates, and badges to students not only for good academic performance but also for good behavior. Because teachers and other school officials are such visible authority figures, the school is a powerful agent of social control. However, schools do not rely on the strength of sanctions alone to enforce acceptable behavior. Their ultimate goal is to produce citizens who have internalized cultural norms and thus have learned to control their own behavior in the social world.

Social Integration Functionalist sociologists also believe that education serves to produce a society of individuals who share a common national identity. Modern societies very often consist of a number of different religious, ethnic, and racial groups. This is the situation in

INTERPRETING VISUALS Education serves many functions such as transmitting culture and encouraging social integration. *How do these images reflect these functions of education?*

Interdisciplinary Connection

HISTORY
The Expansion of Formal Schooling. The word *school* has its origins in the Greek word for "leisure." Although school might not feel like a leisure activity, the word's origins reveal the early history of education. Before industrialization, only the wealthy and some members of the clergy were formally educated. These groups had enough leisure time to devote to study. Modern formal education began to develop after industrialization led to the need to train people for specific jobs and after child labor laws freed children from having to work.

CRITICAL THINKING
What two major events helped contribute to the development of modern education?

ANSWER: industrialization and child labor laws

Visual Answer

Students might mention that the images portray diverse groups of children learning both patriotic rituals and how to work together in groups.

SUGGESTION 2: Organize students into groups of four or five. Ask the groups to imagine that they are to appear on a televised panel talk show discussing the social functions of education. Three group members should adopt the roles of sociologists who support either the functionalist, conflict, or interactionist perspective on education. One member should support each perspective. The other group members should adopt the role of the show's anchors. Have each group write a script for the show, in which the anchor(s) ask each panel member at least three questions, rotating the questions among panel members. The complete script should fully contrast the views of each perspective on education. Have one group present its show to the class. **COOPERATIVE LEARNING**

SPOTLIGHT *on the Functionalist Perspective*

Ask students to identify and describe the four main functions of education, according to the functionalist perspective. *(See the Suggestion 1 activity on p. 351.)* List the functions on the chalkboard. Next, have students write down an example of each function. Call on volunteers to share their examples with the class for discussion. *(Examples might include saying the Pledge of Allegiance to the American flag each morning, which transmits cultural values and promotes national unity. Another example might be vocational courses, which teach the knowledge and skills needed for certain future occupations.)* **BLOCK SCHEDULING**

Sociology in the World Today

Falling Behind in Math and Science. The United States needs an educated workforce to remain globally competitive. However, American students often perform worse than students in other countries on tests in math and science, two important subjects in today's high-tech world. A study by the American Federation of Teachers in the mid-1990s found that only 4 percent of American 18-year-olds could pass advance college placement tests in subjects such as biology and math. In addition, just 7 percent of American high-school students had completed a course in calculus, whereas in countries such as Japan most high-school students take such advanced math courses.

ACTIVITY: Conduct an informal poll of students to find out how many are currently taking or plan to take upper-level courses in math and science, such as calculus and physics. Have students discuss their responses in light of the information above.

Did You Know?

There are currently at least 11 countries in which half the children are no longer in school by age 11.

the United States, which admits large numbers of immigrants from all around the world each year. American schools are expected to provide a common, homogeneous set of cultural values and skills to all members of society, regardless of their national origin.

This expectation formed the basis of the "melting pot" view of American society. In the past in this "melting pot," immigrant identities were to be melted down to form a new, American identity. During the first two decades of the 1900s, immigrants poured into the United States at a rate of about 725,000 a year. The schools were expected to "Americanize" immigrant students by eliminating all traces of their cultural backgrounds.

Today most people view American society as a mosaic—a picture formed by putting together many small pieces of tile. Each tile is separate and distinct from the others. Yet together the tiles create a larger picture. In keeping with this view of society, many schools around the country teach a curriculum designed to help students understand how their racial and ethnic heritages contribute to a richer American culture. However, at the same time schools continue to foster social integration and a national unity by teaching a core set of skills and values common to the American way of life.

Occupational Placement

All societies must have some system for identifying and training the young people who will do the important work of society in the future. Education often serves to screen and select the members of society for the work they will do as adults. Some societies assign adult positions on the basis of ascribed statuses, such as family background or wealth. Others assign these positions on the basis of achieved statuses.

Acceptance into one of Japan's competitive universities requires years of intense study and challenging placement tests. Some Japanese students celebrate after their test.

According to the functionalist perspective, schools in industrialized countries such as the United States identify students who show special talents and abilities at an early age. The schools then train these students to occupy the important positions in society. Beginning in elementary school and continuing throughout their educational lives, children are tested and evaluated. Based on these tests and evaluations, some students are steered toward college-preparatory courses while others are steered toward vocational courses or other non-college programs.

The occupational selection function of education is particularly prominent in Japanese society. In Japan, students are admitted into universities only if they pass the entrance examinations. These examinations are very demanding and require students to undertake an incredible amount of studying. Parents often hire tutors to supplement the classroom instruction their children receive. They also send their children to "cram schools" that prepare students for the examinations. Most high-school students spend much of their free time preparing for what the Japanese call the "examination war."

The college entrance examinations are a national event in Japan, and they gain wide media coverage. A student's high score results in his or her admission to one of the top universities. Future employment greatly depends on the university that a student attends. On the day that the results are released, families, friends, and observers wait for hours for university officials to post the names of successful students. However, the effects of the "examination war" have come into question. Many Japanese worry about the pressure it places on students. They also wonder whether it identifies the best students. In response, the Japanese Ministry of Education has proposed that other methods of evaluation—such as interviews, essays, and grade point averages—might be used along with examinations. However, few parents or students are willing to give up the "examination war."

The Conflict Perspective on Education

While the functionalists believe that the educational system functions to maintain the stability and smooth operation of society, conflict sociologists believe that the educational system serves to limit the potential of certain individuals and groups to gain power and social rewards. Conflict sociologists typically point to two factors as evidence that education helps to maintain inequality: social control and tracking. Additionally, conflict sociologists note that a student's achievement or failure in school tends to reflect existing inequalities in society.

SUGGESTION 3: Lead a class discussion contrasting the views of functionalist, conflict, and interactionist sociologists on education. As you go through the discussion, list the main points of each perspective in a three-column chart on the chalkboard. Then organize students into pairs or triads and have each group write three news headlines that reflect the views of each perspective on education, for a total of nine headlines per pair or group. *(Examples might be "Local High School to Hold Annual Career Day" for functionalist, "Study: Minority Students Less Likely to Receive Career Counseling" for conflict, and "Award-Winning Teacher Believes All Students are Winners" for interactionist.)* Have volunteers share their headlines with the class.
COOPERATIVE LEARNING

SPOTLIGHT *on the Conflict Perspective*

Review conflict sociologists' use of the term *hidden curriculum* to describe schools' transmission of cultural goals that are not openly acknowledged. Then, to contrast the functionalist and conflict perspectives on education, have students list examples of the main functions of education, according to functionalist sociologists (or use students' examples from the previous Spotlight activity). Then have students work in pairs to consider each example from the conflict perspective. In which examples might a conflict sociologist detect a hidden curriculum? Ask groups to share their analyses with the class. **COOPERATIVE LEARNING , BLOCK SCHEDULING**

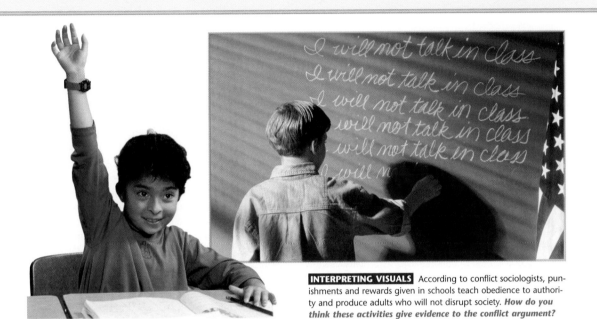

INTERPRETING VISUALS According to conflict sociologists, punishments and rewards given in schools teach obedience to authority and produce adults who will not disrupt society. *How do you think these activities give evidence to the conflict argument?*

internet connect

TOPIC: The Functionalist Versus the Conflict Perspective of Education
GO TO: go.hrw.com
KEYWORD: SL3 SC14

Have students access the Internet through the HRW Go site to conduct research on the functionalist and conflict perspectives on education. Then have students work in small groups to create three-dimensional models of education, based on one of the two perspectives. Groups should label the various parts of their models and be prepared to explain how their models represent one of the theories.

Visual Answer

Answers will vary, but students might compare the first student, who is observing class rules, to the other student, who is being punished for disobeying class rules.

Social Control Both functionalist and conflict sociologists view the school as an agent of social control. However, they disagree on the purpose of this control. Functionalists propose that the purpose of social control is to produce citizens who share a common set of values. Conflict sociologists, on the other hand, believe that this control serves to produce unquestioning citizens who accept the basic inequalities of the social system. Conflict sociologists further propose that most individuals are unaware of this process.

Sociologists use the term **hidden curriculum** to describe schools' transmission of cultural goals that are not openly acknowledged. The hidden curriculum involves teaching a conservative set of values that center on obedience to authority. According to conflict sociologists, this activity serves the dominant groups in society by helping them maintain their position of power.

From the time of their earliest experiences in school, children are taught to be punctual, to stand in line, to be quiet, and to obey. Students who do not meet these expectations often have difficulties in school, no matter how well they perform academically. Once students are identified and labeled as those with behavioral problems, teachers and administrators often watch them closely. Conflict sociologists believe that the goal of the hidden curriculum, and the tight social control associated with it, is to produce cooperative adult workers who will willingly accept the demands of those in power.

Tracking According to conflict sociologists, tracking is another way that the educational system maintains inequality. **Tracking** involves the assignment of students to different types of educational programs, such as general studies, vocational training, and college-preparatory studies. Students are assigned to tracks on the basis of intelligence and aptitude test scores, classroom grades, and teacher evaluations. The stated educational goal of tracking is to allow students to progress at their own pace by grouping them with other students of similar ability.

Functionalist sociologists view tracking as a way of fulfilling the occupational placement function of education. Conflict sociologists, on the other hand, view tracking as a means by which the wealthy and powerful maintain their position in society. Conflict sociologists point out that members of the lower social classes and minority groups are typically assigned to the lower, or less demanding and less advantageous, tracks. These tracks are geared toward blue-collar or vocational jobs in which salaries and prestige are low. Middle-class students, on the other hand, are more likely to be assigned to college tracks. This assignment gives them access to prestigious, high-paying occupations.

Conflict theorists further suggest that the methods of classroom instruction used in the different tracks serve to maintain the status quo. Educational sociologist Jeannie Oakes maintained this view in her study of 300 high-school English and Mathematics classes of various tracks in the United States. She found that higher-track classes, which generally contained large numbers of higher-income students, encouraged the development of skills related to critical thinking, problem solving, and creative writing. Lower-track classes, which generally contained large numbers of low-income and minority students, focused instead on classroom drills and memorization. Lower-track classes also tended to emphasize conforming behavior, cooperation, and getting along with other people.

Conflict sociologists believe that the type of instruction students receive in the different tracks is designed to mold their behavior to fit their future occupations. For example, students in the higher tracks learn creativity, independence, and self-motivation. Such qualities are desirable in managerial and professional jobs. Students in the lower tracks, on the other hand, learn to work under supervision, follow a routine, and obey instructions. These traits are typically called for in lower-paying, or vocational-level, jobs.

Education and Socioeconomic Status

Most Americans have long believed that education is the key to social mobility. For example, in a recent survey the vast majority of respondents said that a college education is the key to a good job and a comfortable lifestyle. Statistics show that there is a strong relationship between education and income. As you can see in the graph on page 355, income increases as education increases. Functionalist sociologists view education as a system that gives all people the chance to succeed according to their own abilities and talents. Conflict sociologists, in contrast, argue that the opportunities for educational success and social mobility are distributed unequally. In this way, achievement in school reflects existing inequalities in society.

Educational achievement appears to be tied strongly to socioeconomic status. Generally, higher-status students are more likely to attend and graduate from college. Sociologist Samuel Bowles found that among the highest-achieving high-school students, 90 percent of those from wealthy families attended college. In contrast, college attendance among high-achieving students from low-income families was only 50 percent. Bowles noted that this inequality was even more marked among students who did not perform well in high school. Among low-achieving students, those from wealthy families were four times more likely to attend college than those from poor families.

Because socioeconomic status and race overlap to a great extent, minority groups tend to have less educational success. For example, African American and Hispanic students are more likely to drop out of high school than are white students. Hispanic and African American students are also less likely than white students to go on to college and to earn a degree.

Conflict theorists propose that socioeconomic status affects the distribution of educational achievement in a number of ways. First, conflict theorists hold that the expectations families have for their children's achievement differ by socioeconomic class. Higher-status families tend to assume that their children will succeed at school and therefore tend to motivate them toward this end. Conflict theorists believe that lower-status families, on the other hand, hope that their children will be successful, but do not necessarily believe that education is the key to this success. Thus, they may stress the value of getting a good job over higher education, even though education is tied to economic success.

Second, conflict theorists suggest that higher-status families are better able than are lower-status families to provide a home environment well-suited to enrich learning. For example, the homes of middle- and upper-class students are more likely to contain books and toys that stimulate thought and creativity. Higher-status children are also more likely to be exposed to cultural events that

INTERPRETING VISUALS Conflict sociologists argue that socioeconomic status can affect the degree to which students are prepared to face the challenges of education. *How might a community's wealth or poverty affect opportunities in local schools, such as the availability of computers?*

SPOTLIGHT *on the Interactionist Perspective*

Briefly review with students the interactionist perspective on education *(summarized in the Suggestion 1 activity on p. 351)*. Next, ask students to list ways in which a teacher in a classroom setting might convey his or her expectations for individual or groups of students. Have students consider issues such as physical arrangements of classrooms, project assignments, cooperative groups, and the frequency of calling on certain students. Ask volunteers to share their lists with the class. Then have students discuss ways in which they convey their expectations for themselves in different classroom settings. **BLOCK SCHEDULING**

SPOTLIGHT *on ADD and ADHD*

Explain to students that in recent years controversy has surrounded the rising number of diagnoses of Attention Deficit Disorder and Attention Deficit Hyperactivity Disorder in children and the use of medications, such as Ritalin, to treat these disorders. Some researchers claim that schools play a large role in the controversy. Others claim that minorities are underdiagnosed and thus often do not receive the treatments that would help them succeed in school. Have students work in groups to conduct research on the controversy and then present oral reports giving a balanced view of the issues. **COOPERATIVE LEARNING , BLOCK SCHEDULING**

broaden their horizons and to values that emphasize long-term goal setting. Lower-status families, on the other hand, are unable to provide their children with as many opportunities. The incomes of lower-status families are often barely enough to provide the basic necessities of life.

Finally, the expense involved in keeping a child in school is high. Higher-status families are better able to pay the expenses involved in putting their children through college. Conflict theorists hold that this opportunity perpetuates the access of higher-status people to well-paying and prestigious jobs.

The Interactionist Perspective on Education

Interactionist sociologists seek to explain social phenomena in terms of the interaction among the individuals involved. To explain educational achievement they look at the interaction that takes place among students and teachers.

In a study of educational achievement and tracking, sociologist Ray Rist looked at student-teacher interaction at a grade school. Rist noted that early in the school year, the kindergarten teacher assigned her students to three work groups—fast learners, average learners, and slow learners. This tracking was not based on ability, for the teacher had not given the students any tests. Rather, the teacher assigned students to work groups based on social class. Those labeled fast learners were mostly middle class, and those labeled average or slow learners were mostly children of working class or working poor parents. Those labeled fast learners received most of the teacher's attention and praise. In contrast, those labeled slow learners received little attention. The teacher put physical distance between herself and those labeled slow learners. The table at which they worked was the farthest from her desk. Not surprisingly, at the end of the school year those labeled fast learners were performing at a high level while those labeled slow learners were making little progress. This tracking pattern, amount of teacher involvement, and level of achievement affected the students throughout their education.

In a study of educational achievement among disadvantaged high-school students, Eigil Pedersen and Terese Annette Faucher noted the power of teacher expectations. They found that most of the highest achievers in their study had been taught by the same first grade teacher. Intrigued, they looked at this teacher's classroom methods. They found that she stressed the value of education and the importance of hard work. She gave as much or more time to slow learners than she did to better students. She also expected much of her students. She assumed that all would succeed, regardless of their backgrounds or abilities.

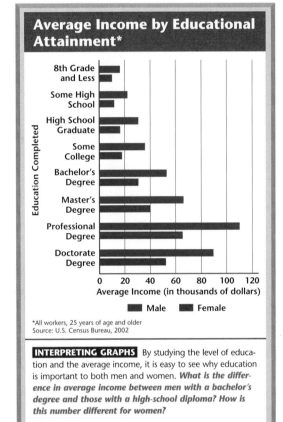

Average Income by Educational Attainment*

Education Completed (y-axis):
8th Grade and Less; Some High School; High School Graduate; Some College; Bachelor's Degree; Master's Degree; Professional Degree; Doctorate Degree

Average Income (in thousands of dollars) (x-axis): 0 20 40 60 80 100 120

■ Male   ■ Female

*All workers, 25 years of age and older
Source: U.S. Census Bureau, 2002

INTERPRETING GRAPHS By studying the level of education and the average income, it is easy to see why education is important to both men and women. *What is the difference in average income between men with a bachelor's degree and those with a high-school diploma? How is this number different for women?*

Social psychologists Robert Rosenthal and Lenore Jacobson took a different approach to the study of the relationship between educational achievement and teacher expectations. They administered a test to grade-school students and identified some students as likely to succeed. But in actuality Rosenthal and Jacobson had selected the students at random. Nevertheless, these students did perform better than other members of the class.

All three of these studies provide examples of the self-fulfilling prophecy—a prediction that leads to behavior that makes the prediction come true. Teachers, through words and actions, let students know what is expected of them, and the students perform according to these expectations. Students who are expected to achieve come to think of themselves as bright and capable because they have been, and continue to be, treated as bright and capable people. Students not expected to achieve, on the other hand, may come to think of themselves as inferior. Once students believe that they are intellectually superior or inferior, they behave in such a way as to confirm that belief. Thus, they fulfill the prophecy of their teachers' expectations.

SUGGESTION 1: To help students identify some of the current issues in American education, copy the graphic organizer at the right onto the chalkboard, omitting the italicized answers. Have students copy and complete the organizer. Discuss the answers with the class. Then have each student create a political cartoon illustrating one of these issues. Students might express and defend one point of view in their cartoons or provide an overall description of the chosen issue. Have students include captions explaining their political cartoons. Ask volunteers to share their political cartoons with the class. **ENGLISH LANGUAGE LEARNERS**

Current Issues in American Education

- *educational reform* — to address a decline in the level of the quality of education; has led to some improvements
- *educational alternatives* — provides school choice through vouchers, charter schools, and options such as homeschooling
- *violence in the schools* — has led to the use of security measures, zero tolerance policies, and conflict-resolution programs
- *bilingual education* — controversial, particularly in states with many Hispanics; has led to "English Only" movement

Sociology in the World Today

American Education in Crisis? According to a study by the Harvard Graduate School of Education, about one in four American students fails to graduate from high school. In addition, according to another study, about 3 percent of American adults were functionally illiterate in the mid-1990s.

RESEARCH ACTIVITY: Have students conduct research on how American students compare with students in other countries in their knowledge of various subjects, such as math and science. Then have the class discuss its findings.

Map Answers

1. Colorado, Connecticut, Maryland, Massachusetts, Minnesota, New Hampshire, and Virginia

2. Questions and answers will vary but may focus on why certain regions of the country share similar percentages.

Technology Resources

 Teaching Transparency: Percentage of Population with a Bachelor's Degree by State, 2000

Issues in American Education

Americans have always had a great deal of faith in the institution of education. There is a strong belief among Americans that education can cure social ills. Many Americans also believe that it can serve as a major tool in encouraging and upholding democracy and free enterprise around the world.

Because Americans believe so strongly in the value of education, educational issues have often been the focus of public concern. In the early part of the 1900s concerns about American education centered on the assimilation of the steady stream of immigrants coming from around the world. In the mid-1900s Americans believed that superior education could produce a country able to beat the Soviet Union in the space race. The educational issues facing the United States during the early 2000s include educational reform, educational alternatives, violence in schools, and English as a second language.

Educational Reform In 1983 the National Commission on Excellence in Education published a report entitled *A Nation at Risk.* This report detailed a sharp decline in the level of quality of American education. This decline, the commission warned, "threatens our very future as a nation and as a people." The commission charged that the United States had fallen behind other industrialized countries in math, science, and literacy skills. A continuation of this trend, the commission predicted, would hurt U.S. efforts to compete in world markets. The commission also noted that the skills of American youth were not keeping pace with technological change.

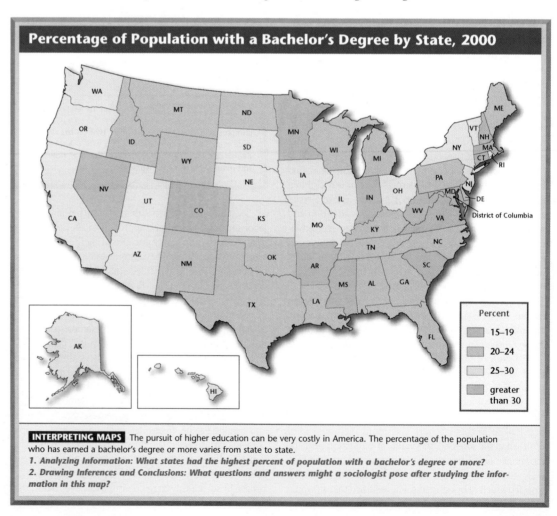

Percentage of Population with a Bachelor's Degree by State, 2000

Percent
- 15–19
- 20–24
- 25–30
- greater than 30

INTERPRETING MAPS The pursuit of higher education can be very costly in America. The percentage of the population who has earned a bachelor's degree or more varies from state to state.

1. Analyzing Information: What states had the highest percent of population with a bachelor's degree or more?

2. Drawing Inferences and Conclusions: What questions and answers might a sociologist pose after studying the information in this map?

Case Studies and Other True Stories

■ TEACH

Have students read the feature Alternative Education and answer the questions that follow it. Discuss the answers as a class. Then ask students to list what they would consider to be 10 attributes of a perfect school. Tell students that their schools need to meet some of the social functions of education. Students might consider the role of teachers, how learning would occur, locations and hours, how discipline would be handled, and how to assess students' progress. Call on volunteers to describe their perfect schools to the class.

■ SPOTLIGHT on Maria Montessori

The educational methods developed and promoted by Maria Montessori (1870–1952), an Italian educator and doctor, have been influential in the United States, particularly in early childhood education. Ask interested students to conduct research on Maria Montessori and the Montessori method of schooling. Then have each student write a profile covering both topics. Students may also want to compare and contrast their own elementary school experience with descriptions of the Montessori classroom and approaches. **BLOCK SCHEDULING**

Case Studies

AND OTHER TRUE STORIES

ALTERNATIVE EDUCATION

The alternative education movement, which promotes alternate approaches to traditional schooling methods, took root in the United States in the 1890s. Its chief proponents were Francis W. Parker, who felt that play and creative activities were essential to learning, and John Dewey, who advocated the "learning by doing" approach. However, the movement did not gain significant support until the 1960s.

Three Approaches

Since the 1960s, three distinctive styles of alternative education have developed in the United States. The first, which arose in the mid-1960s, was driven by the view that traditional schools were suppressing children's natural urge to learn. Proponents of this style said that schools should encourage creativity by allowing students to learn through exploration and experimentation. Various types of schools were set up with this aim in mind. Some of these schools maintained aspects of the traditional school setting but had open classrooms where grade levels and subjects were completely integrated. Others took a far more radical approach. In these "democratic schools," faculty, staff, and students had an equal say in the running of the school, and classes were optional.

The second style, which emerged in the mid- to late 1960s, hoped to give parents and students greater choice. Supporters of this style felt that students learned better in situations where they felt comfortable. Therefore, they said, a wide variety of choices in school settings and teaching styles should be available to students.

The third style, which developed in the 1970s, was very different from the other two styles. It focused on students who were considered at risk—those who seem destined to fail because they were dropouts or truant, or because they had behavior problems. For advocates of this style, the problem was not the traditional school approach, but was the students themselves. For the most part, programs developed for at-risk students—back-to-basics curriculum, teacher-directed instruction, and strict discipline—were chiefly designed to

YOUR GUIDE TO HOME SCHOOLING

THIS IS THE THIRD TIME TOBY'S TEACHER HAS SENT US THIS ARTICLE..

THE BUCKETS reprinted by permission of United Feature Syndicate, Inc.

For some, the debate around alternative education centers on how to educate kids with social problems.

prepare them for their return to mainstream schools. This third style was designed as a substitute for traditional schooling, not as a way to change it. Programs that separate students who are seen as troublesome from other students have come to symbolize alternative education.

A Broader View

Advocates of alternative education are concerned that people view it as little more than classes for bad kids. For them, alternative education has a much broader meaning. It is, according to long-time supporter Dr. Robert Fizzell

"a perspective, not a procedure or program. It is the belief that there are many ways to become educated, many possible environments and structures within which this may occur. Further, it is the belief that all people can be educated, and that it is in society's interest to ensure that all are educated to at least something like an ideal, general high school education at the mastery level. . . . To accomplish this requires that we provide a variety of structures and environments such that each person can find one that is sufficiently comfortable to facilitate progress."

Think About It

1. Comparing and Contrasting *What three movements in alternative schooling developed in the 1960s and 1970s? How were they similar? How were they different?*

2. Supporting a Point of View *Do you think alternative education as defined by Dr. Robert Fizzell is needed in the United States? Explain your answer.*

SUGGESTION 2: Organize students into four groups and assign each group one of the current issues in American education (*educational reform, educational alternatives, violence in the schools, and bilingual education*). Have each group discuss the various concerns or viewpoints related to its assigned issue. Then instruct group members to propose, discuss, and decide on some possible courses of action or solutions related to the issue. Have each group create a one-page report summarizing its suggestions. Then have a spokesperson from each group explain some of its suggestions to the class. Encourage student feedback. **COOPERATIVE LEARNING**

SUGGESTION 3: Lead a class discussion on the current issues in American education covered in this section (*educational reform, educational alternatives, violence in the schools, and bilingual education*). During the discussion, encourage students to share their opinions about each issue. Then have each student write an essay explaining which specific educational issue he or she thinks is most serious and why. Remind students to provide logical reasons that support their positions and to use standard grammar, spelling, sentence structure, and punctuation. Have one or two volunteers read their essays aloud to the class. Encourage student discussion.

In addition to addressing the deficits found in the public schools, the commission made specific recommendations to reform the country's educational system. These recommendations included a more demanding curriculum, an emphasis on achievement, and stricter requirements for graduation. The commission also urged more homework, more discipline, better attendance, and a longer school year in American schools.

During the 1980s many states and school districts overhauled their educational systems, and most raised their requirements for graduation. To attract and keep better teachers, most school districts raised teacher salaries. In addition, many states required new teachers to pass strict competency exams.

Most observers noted that, despite these reforms, little progress was made in the 10 to 12 years after *A Nation at Risk* was published. For example, students' scores on the nationwide Scholastic Aptitude Test (SAT) showed little or no increase during that period. Further, the 1995 SAT scores were considerably below the students' scores during the late 1960s and early 1970s. Moreover, American students continued to lag behind students of other industrialized countries regarding their knowledge of math and science.

In 1994 Congress passed Goals 2000: Educate America Act to improve the quality of education in the United States. This legislation provided grants to states so that they could develop plans to reform their schools. It also established a series of educational goals for schools to meet by the year 2000. These goals included:

- All children in America will start school ready to learn.
- The number of high-school graduates will rise to 90 percent or more.
- All students will show a command of challenging subject matter in English, math, science, foreign languages, civics, economics, the arts, history, and geography.
- American students will be first in the world in math and science.
- Every American adult will be literate.
- All schools will be free of drugs, violence, firearms, and alcohol and will offer a safe environment that encourages learning.
- Teachers will have the opportunity to acquire and improve instructional knowledge and skills.
- All schools will promote parents' participation in their children's education.

This act set up the National Education Goals Panel (NEGP), which consisted of educators and leaders from business, labor, and government to oversee schools' progress toward meeting these goals.

In 1999 the NEGP admitted that American schools would not meet the set goals by the 2000 deadline. However, the panel noted that considerable progress had been made—the goals had focused the public's attention on the issue of higher student achievement and had encouraged educational reform.

Educational Alternatives Some Americans think that reforming the public schools is not enough. They believe that alternative approaches to education should also be adopted. One popular alternative to the public school system is the charter school. **Charter schools** are funded with public money but are privately operated and run. A charter school receives a charter of operation from the state education department or the local school board. The charter establishes the school's educational philosophy, budget, staffing plans, and student goals. In addition, the charter establishes the amount of public funding the school will receive and the duration the school will receive it. The charter gives the school considerable freedom in the way it operates. It also frees the school from many regulations that public schools must follow. However, the state or school board can cancel the charter if the school violates charter conditions or fails to meet its goals.

The first charter school in the United States was established in Minnesota in 1991. By late 2000, there were about 2,300 charter schools serving more than 575,000 students in 34 states and Washington, D.C. About 100,000 other students attended some 200 contract schools. These schools are similar to charter schools, but they are run by private, for-profit businesses.

Charter schools are a part of a broader educational alternative known as school choice. With **school choice**, parents may receive a voucher equal to the amount their state spends on education for their child. Parents are then

INTERPRETING VISUALS Year-round schooling is an educational reform that has received a lot of public attention. *What reasons does this cartoonist offer for and against year-round schooling?*

Sociology in the World Today

SOCIOLOGY IN THE
World Today

SCHOOL CHOICE

The issue of school choice has generated considerable debate among politicians, educators, and parents. The areas of greatest controversy involve charter schools and voucher programs. Charter schools are privately operated schools that are funded with public money, and the voucher program is a system that allows parents to use vouchers provided by state governments to pay tuition at the school of their choice.

Charter Schools

Supporters of charter schools stress that charter schools offer innovative approaches to curriculum and teaching. They also note that charter schools allow students to learn in a small-school setting. Average enrollment at charter schools is fewer than 200 students, and nearly one third of the schools have enrollments of fewer than 100 students. Supporters point out that test scores and graduation rates are rising among charter school students. In addition, they observe that existing charter schools are oversubscribed—some 70 percent of the schools have waiting lists.

Critics of charter schools suggest that these statistics do not necessarily indicate success. First, they assert that charter schools have been operating for too short a time for test scores and graduation rates to be used as a measure of progress. Second, charter schools serve a minute part—less than 1 percent—of the total student population. Critics also note that charter schools can be selective in the students they take, whereas public schools must take all students. A major criticism of charter schools is that they offer little more than the basic curriculum. The most often voiced criticism is that charter schools take money from the already hard-pressed public school system.

Vouchers

Proponents of vouchers argue that the system allows all parents—regardless of income—to send their children to private schools. Escaping from failing public schools, proponents continue, ensures that children receive a decent education. They add that the competition for students will force public schools to improve. Opponents of vouchers charge that private

Florida governor Jeb Bush leads a rally supporting school vouchers.

schools do not necessarily provide a better education. As evidence, they cite studies that show little difference between test scores for students in public schools and students attending private schools under the voucher system. Opponents add that public schools will find it increasingly difficult to compete for students as the voucher system consumes more public funds.

The debate on vouchers has taken a new turn since the courts struck down two voucher programs. In late 1999 a federal judge declared the voucher program in Cleveland, Ohio, unconstitutional. Because most parents used the vouchers to send their children to parochial schools, the judge said, the program violated the Constitution's separation of church and state. A few months later in Florida, a state judge struck down that state's voucher system. His ruling said that the system sent students to private schools that provided the same programs as by public schools, it superseded "the system of free public schools mandated by the [Florida] constitution." Observers predict that, in all likelihood, the U.S. Supreme Court will settle the issue of school vouchers at some future date.

Think About It

1. **Identifying a Point of View** *What are the arguments in support of charter schools? What are the arguments against them?*
2. **Supporting a Point of View** *Critics of school choice often note that charter schools and private schools are not subject to the same kinds of regulations that public schools are. Do you think that all schools should have to operate under the same rules and regulations? Explain your answer.*

Write on the chalkboard the three perspectives on education *(functionalist, conflict, interactionist)* and the four current issues in American education *(educational reform, educational alternatives, violence in the schools, and bilingual education)* covered in this section. Then ask volunteers to suggest how sociologists for each perspective might view each current education issue. For example, what position might conflict sociologists take on bilingual education and how might they explain the controversy over it. Guide students in their analyses.

Have students complete the **Section 1 Review** on p. 361. As **Alternative Assessment**, you may want to use the perspectives on education panel talk show or the issues in education essay in this section's lessons.

Have students work in pairs to write nine fill-in-the-blank sentences to be completed by one of the Define terms. Then have pairs exchange quizzes and complete the ones they receive.

ENGLISH LANGUAGE LEARNERS , COOPERATIVE LEARNING

Case Study

Homeschooling. A 1999 study by the Department of Education asked families who homeschool to identify their reasons for making the choice. Families were able to mark more than one reason.

- Can give child a better education at home 48.9%
- Religious reasons 38.4%
- Poor learning environment at school 25.6%
- Family reasons 16.8%
- To develop character/morality 15.1%
- Object to what school teaches 12.1%
- School does not challenge child 11.6%
- Other problems with available schools 11.5%
- Student behavior problems at school 9.0%
- Child has special needs/disability 8.2%

ACTIVITY: Have students discuss some advantages and disadvantages to homeschooling.

Visual Answer

Students might suggest that metal detectors keep weapons out of schools and after-school programs provide students with positive ways in which to spend their free time.

INTERPRETING VISUALS Many school districts have taken measures to prevent school violence including using metal detectors and creating after-school community programs to reduce violence. *How do you think these efforts might prevent violence?*

free to use the voucher to pay tuition at the school of their choice—charter, private, religious, or public. Turn to the Sociology in the World Today feature on page 359 to read more about charter schools and the voucher system.

Homeschooling, a system in which a child's main education is undertaken by parents at home, is rapidly growing as an alternative to public schools. Between 1.5 and 2 million students—about 3 to 4 percent of the total student population—are presently being homeschooled. Estimates suggest that this number is growing by between 15 and 20 percent each year.

Some parents homeschool their children because they are dissatisfied with the quality of education offered by the public schools. Others homeschool because they feel that public-school education does not meet the needs or interests of their children. However, other parents choose homeschooling for ideological or religious reasons.

Critics of homeschooling argue that it often does not provide a broad enough curriculum. In addition, they argue that most parents do not have the strong teaching skills necessary to provide children with an education. Nevertheless, most homeschooled students score as well or better than do public school students on standardized tests like the SAT. Also, homeschooled students are just as likely to attend college as are public-school students.

Violence in the Schools Many Americans worry that the country's schools are unsafe. A Gallup poll conducted in September 1999 found that 47 percent of parents fear for their children's safety at school. In a poll conducted two months later by the *Washington Post*, 60 percent of respondents said they worried that "children in America are no longer safe at their own schools." Indeed, those respondents who had children in school said that school safety was their most pressing worry.

Such fears are generated by violent incidents such as the Columbine High School shootings. In April 1999,

2 students at this school in Littleton, Colorado, shot and killed 1 teacher and 12 students and wounded more than 20 others before killing themselves. Such deadly rampages are rare. However, violence in American schools is a real problem. Some 10 percent of American schools reported at least one serious violent incident in one school year in the mid-1990s. Another 47 percent of schools reported a less serious violent incident or some other type of crime. Teachers are often the victims of violent incidents. About 133,600 violent crimes were committed against teachers each year between 1994–1998. Violent incidents in schools frequently involve some kind of weapon. According to the 1999 Youth Risk Behavior Survey, conducted by the Centers for Disease Control, 17 percent of high-school students reported carrying a weapon in the last month. Nearly 5 percent reported carrying a gun.

However, the occurence of all types of crime in schools has shown a steady decline in recent years. In terms of violent crime, schools may be some of the safest places for children. For example, students are twice as likely to be victims of violent crime off-campus as they are at school. The chance that a school-age child will die at school is about 1 in 2 million. Further, students appear not to feel threatened in their schools. In a 1999 poll of teenagers between 12 and 18 years of age, only 4 percent reported a fear of being attacked or harmed.

To combat on-campus violence, a growing number of schools are taking security measures such as requiring visitors to sign in before entering. Other measures include metal detectors, school guards or other law enforcement officers, closed campuses, and controlled access to school

1. Have students conduct library research on one of the following topics: the history of education in the United States, the use of computers in education, or the system of education in a country other than the United States. Have students present their findings in a written report. **BLOCK SCHEDULING**

2. Throughout the study of this section, have students examine current news sources and magazines and collect any articles related to education. Use the articles to create a bulletin board and take a few minutes to discuss some of the articles each class period. **BLOCK SCHEDULING**

3. Have each student create a chart listing the arguments for and against bilingual education. Then have students discuss the arguments and express and defend their own opinions on the issue. Do students agree with one side or the other, or do they support alternative solutions or approaches? Ask students to discuss the issue as if they are at a local school board meeting on bilingual education. **BLOCK SCHEDULING**

---

grounds. Most schools have also adopted **zero tolerance** policies. These involve set punishments—often expulsion—for serious offenses such as carrying a weapon, committing a violent act, or possessing drugs or alcohol.

Some educators believe that the best approach to curbing violence in schools is the implementation of educational programs that teach young people how to resolve their disputes peacefully. The philosophy behind such programs is that young people who learn cooperation, concern for others, and problem-solving skills will be less likely to resort to violence. More than 75 percent of American public schools offer some kind of school-violence prevention program.

English as a Second Language One of the most controversial issues in American education is over **bilingual education**, which is a system in which non-English-speaking students are taught in their native languages until they are proficient enough in English to attend regular classes. Congress passed several laws concerning bilingual education in the 1960s and 1970s. However, bilingual education did not become established in the United States until the Supreme Court decision in *Lau* v. *Nichols*. This decision required schools to provide language programs for students with limited proficiency in English.

Supporters of bilingual education believe this system is the best way to ensure that non-native-speaking students can progress in school while they become familiar with the English language. Opponents of bilingual education believe that this system interferes with the assimilation of students. Critics argue that it may take four to five years

Bilingual education attempts to meet the needs of students whose first language is not English.

under the bilingual program for students to learn English. During this time, students may lose critical language development skills. Alternative programs have been developed to assist students facing language challenges.

According to the U.S. Department of Education, about 3.2 million students are currently classified as having limited English proficiency. Spanish is the first language of more than 70 percent of these students. Thus, the debate over bilingual education tends to be most intense in states that have large Hispanic populations, such as California, Florida, Texas, New York, and Illinois. In 1998, California voters passed Proposition 227, which ended bilingual education in that state. In other states, an "English Only" movement has tried to end bilingual education by having English declared as the official recognized language. More than 20 states around the country have already passed laws making English their official language.

SECTION 1 REVIEW

1. Define and explain
education
schooling
hidden curriculum
tracking
charter schools
school choice
homeschooling
zero tolerance
bilingual education

2. Comparing and Contrasting
Copy the graphic organizer below and use it to compare and contrast the conflict, functionalist, and interactionist perspectives of education.

Sociological Perspective	View of Education
Functionalist	
Conflict	
Interactionist	

3. **Finding the Main Idea**
a. How do the functionalist, conflict, and interactionist views of tracking and other educational programs differ?
b. What are some of the educational alternatives that have grown in popularity in the last few years?

4. **Writing and Critical Thinking**
Analyzing Information Write two paragraphs discussing the issue of violence in schools and noting what measures could be taken to prevent violence.
Consider:
• statistics on violence in schools
• approaches to curbing violence within schools

go. **Homework Practice Online**
hrw. keyword: SL3 HP14
.com

---

1. Define:
• education, p. 350
• schooling, p. 350
• hidden curriculum, p. 353
• tracking, p. 353
• charter schools, p. 358
• school choice, p. 358
• homeschooling, p. 360
• zero tolerance, p. 361
• bilingual education, p. 361

2. functionalist—schools help maintain the stability and smooth operation of society; conflict—the educational system serves to limit the potential of certain people and groups to gain power and social rewards; interactionist—students' educational achievements and success are shaped in part by teacher-student interactions.

3a. Functionalists view tracking as a practical way to determine who will do the important work in society. Conflict sociologists view tracking as the means by which the wealthy and powerful maintain their position in society. Interactionists see tracking as a self-fulfilling prophecy.

b. charter schools, vouchers, and homeschooling

4. Paragraphs will vary, but students should exhibit an understanding of the issues related to school violence and some of the methods being used to reduce such violence.

📻 *LET'S GET STARTED!*

Before class, write on the chalkboard the definition of the term *religion (a system of roles and norms that is organized around the sacred realm and that binds people together in social groups)*. As students enter the classroom, have them read the definition and then write down some of the basic societal needs that they believe religion serves. *(Students might mention spiritual comfort, emotional support, inspiration, cultural unity, and moral guidance.)* Have volunteers share some of their responses with the class. Then tell students that in Section 2 they will learn about the social functions of religion and about religion in American society.

SECTION ② RESOURCES

REPRODUCIBLE & REVIEW

- Graphic Organizer 14
- Mastering Critical Thinking Skills 14
- Study Skills and Writing Guide
- Section 2 Review, p. 371

TECHNOLOGY

- One-Stop Planner, Lesson 14.2
- Homework Practice Online
- HRW Go site

Visual Answer

Students might mention the crucifix that the priest is wearing or the menorah on the temple wall.

② THE SOCIOLOGY OF RELIGION

● Read to Discover
1. What basic societal needs does religion serve?
2. What are the distinctive features of religion in American society?

● Define
sacred, profane, religion, ritual, animism, shamanism, totemism, theism, monotheism, polytheism, ethicalism, ecclesia, denomination, sect, cult, religiosity, secular

Throughout every time period and in every place humankind has lived, human beings have searched for answers to two basic questions— why do we live, and why do we die? Societies have struggled with the need to give meaning to human existence and to provide people with the motivation for survival. According to sociologist Émile Durkheim, all societies have attempted to satisfy these needs by making a sharp distinction between the sacred and the profane. The **sacred** is anything that is considered to be part of the supernatural world and that inspires awe,

respect, and reverence. The **profane**, on the other hand, is anything considered to be part of the ordinary world and, thus, commonplace and familiar.

This distinction between the sacred and the profane is at the heart of all religions. **Religion** may be defined as a system of roles and norms that is organized around the sacred realm and that binds people together in social groups. As with all basic institutions, religion is a universal phenomenon. However, the form that religion takes may vary from society to society and may change within a single society over time. Religion exists in many different forms because different societies give sacred meaning to a wide variety of objects, events, and experiences. No one thing is considered to be sacred by everyone.

Religion—A Sociological Definition

According to sociologists, religion is a social creation. Things take on sacred meaning only when they are socially defined as such by a group of believers. Things that are sacred in one society may be profane in another society. For example, in Hindu society the cow is revered as holy. To most Christians a cow is regarded as a mere animal. Similarly, many Christians believe that a wafer given in a religious ritual is a sacred symbol, but Hindus would regard this wafer as nothing more than something to eat. Some religions worship their ancestors; other religions honor animals and trees.

INTERPRETING VISUALS Sacred objects and ritual vary greatly between religions. They may include a Buddhist prayer wheel, a church choir singing, a Catholic communion service, or reading from the Torah. *What other sacred object can you identify below?*

TEACH OBJECTIVE 1

SUGGESTION 1: Call on volunteers to identify the three most important societal functions of religion *(social cohesion, social control, and emotional support).* Then have each student create a concept web that identifies and describes the functions of religion, including the different viewpoints on each function provided in this section. Have volunteers present their concept webs to the class. Finally, have students share with the class any examples of these religious functions that they know, other than those mentioned in the section. (You might want to prepare a list of several examples before class to help students.)

SUGGESTION 2: Lead a class discussion on the three most important societal functions of religion *(listed in the previous activity).* Then have each student create an artistic representation of one or more of these functions. Artwork might include drawings, paintings, sculptures, or other types of art. Each student should provide a label giving the title of the artwork and a brief explanation of the piece. Display students' artwork in the classroom.

HOMEWORK: Have each student write a short story about a society in which there is no religion. Students should consider the three basic societal functions of religion when writing their stories. Then select the best short story and have the author read it to the class. Encourage student feedback and discussion.

INTERPRETING VISUALS During the Inquisition of the 1200s, religious leaders had the power to torture disbelievers or those who violated church rules. *How might this be seen as an extreme form of social control?*

Applying Sociology

Jerusalem. The city of Jerusalem in Israel is considered a sacred site in three major world religions—Christianity, Islam, and Judaism.

CRITICAL THINKING
According to conflict theorists, what problems might result from three major religions sharing a sacred site?

ANSWER: It might lead to tensions and conflict among the different religious groups, which has indeed been the case in Jerusalem.

Visual Answer

Students might suggest that those people faced with torture had little choice but to obey church rules.

Religion focuses on the supernatural world, and thus belief in a particular religion is based on faith rather than on science. Sociologists are not concerned with the truth or falseness of any religion. Rather, they focus on the social characteristics of religion and the consequences that religion has for society. One of the topics of interest to sociologists is the functions of religion.

The Functions of Religion

Since religion is a universal phenomenon, sociologists assume that it serves certain essential functions in all societies. The most important functions of religion that are recognized by sociologists include social cohesion, social control, and emotional support.

Social Cohesion One of the most important functions of religion is that it encourages social cohesion— the strengthening of bonds among people. For individuals, both participating in religious ceremonies and sharing beliefs create a sense of belonging, which makes them feel less alone in the world. In his study of suicide, Durkheim found that suicide rates were lowest among those people who had strong attachments to religious groups. These attachments served to anchor people to society, providing them with support and purpose.

However, conflict theorists suggest that social cohesion based on religion may create problems in societies where more than one religion is practiced. Indeed, some societies have been plagued with hostile and continuous conflict. Tensions between Muslims and Hindus, for example, led to the creation of Pakistan from portions of India in 1947. The Middle East has been the scene of great strife between Muslims and Jews.

Social Control Religion also serves as a powerful agent of social control, encouraging conformity to the norms of society. In some societies, norms and values may not only be formalized in laws but may also be supported by religious doctrine. Religious followers' belief in the sacredness of writings such as the Bible, the Torah, and the Qur'an give a divine purpose to social conformity. In addition, religion may function to maintain the traditional social order by presenting this order as one commanded by a supreme being.

Some religions also provide formalized means through which individuals may rid themselves of the guilt associated with straying from their societies' acceptable norms and values. Rituals such as confession and communion serve as emotional releases for individuals while contributing to the unity of the group. Religion thus maintains a control over behavior by providing a standard by which individuals may judge themselves and be judged by other people.

ANIMISM: *Spirits active in influencing human life but not worshiped. Rituals thank or win spirits' good will.*

Shamanism *Spirits communicate with one person (shaman). Shamans can heal sick, predict future.*

Totemism *Kinship between humans and animals/natural objects—totems*

THEISM: *Belief in god or gods. God is divine power worthy of worship.*

Monotheism *Belief in one god; Examples: Judaism, Islam, Christianity; organized structure, priesthood, rituals*

Polytheism *Multiple gods; Example: Hinduism; usually one powerful god and lesser gods*

ETHICALISM: *Based on set of moral principles with sacred quality.*

Involve meditation and purity of thought and action; Examples: Buddhism, Shintoism, Confucianism

INTERPRETING VISUALS Religion serves many functions including offering emotional support and social control. *How might a Hindu wedding, a Christian christening, or a Muslim call to prayer serve as a social function?*

Some conflict sociologists suggest that a religion's emphasis on conformity to an existing social order may inhibit innovation, freedom of thought, and social reform. When a society gives sacred meaning to its norms and values, it may deny individuals the freedom to question or change unjust practices that support inequality. Obedience to religious doctrine may leave little room for ideas and beliefs contrary to that doctrine.

Emotional Support A third function of religion is to provide emotional support for people during difficult times. Religion helps people endure disappointment and suffering by providing a comfort in believing that harsh circumstances have a special purpose. This belief motivates people to survive even when happiness appears out of reach and life seems hopeless.

Religion also attempts to provide answers to the ultimate questions concerning life and death, answers that cannot be provided by science or common sense. These answers lend strength and calm to people as they approach the unknown and the unexpected.

Conflict sociologists argue that the emotional support lent by religion may block social and political change. Religion often encourages people to accept their social conditions because rewards await them in the spiritual life, which will repay them for their pain on Earth. In this way, Karl Marx suggested, religion acts as "the opium of the people." To forget the hardships of

their daily lives, Marx said, people turn to religion and its promise of rewards in the afterlife. When people focus on the afterlife, they are less likely to seek out the source of their troubles and make changes.

The Nature of Religion

Religion exists in varied forms around the world. However, all religions contain certain basic elements. Among these elements are rituals and symbols, belief systems, and organizational structures.

Rituals and Symbols In terms of religion, a **ritual** may be defined as an established pattern of behavior through which a group of believers experiences the sacred. The variety of religious rituals found around the world is enormous, but ritualistic behavior is a part of every religion.

Religious rituals are often used to mark changes in status, such as those surrounding birth, marriage, and death. For example, baptisms, weddings, and funerals are usually conducted in sacred places by persons acknowledged as religious leaders. Rituals are also used to unite believers and reinforce faith. Prayer meetings, worship services, and religious feasts allow believers to express their devotion to their religion while contributing to the unity of the group.

Some rituals involve asking for divine intervention in human affairs. Other rituals focus on giving thanks to divine beings for benefits that believers have received. These rituals generally include the sacred symbols of the specific religion. Particular clothing, herbs, chalices, crosses, books, and other religious symbols are often used only in special places on special days to emphasize their sacred character.

Belief Systems Religions found around the world vary considerably in the content of their belief systems. In general, belief systems can be organized into three basic types: animism, theism, and ethicalism.

Animism is a belief that spirits actively influence human life. Animals, plants, rivers, mountains, and even the wind are believed to contain spirits. Societies with animistic religions do not worship these spirits as gods. Rather, they see these spirits as supernatural forces that can be used to human advantage. Rituals such as fasting, dancing, and purification of the body are often used to win the good will of the spirits or to thank them for gifts.

In one type of animism—called **shamanism**—it is believed that spirits communicate only with one person in the group. This person, called the shaman, is believed to communicate with the spirits either by speaking to them directly or by making his or her soul leave the body and enter the spirit world. Followers not only believe that shamans can communicate with spirits but that they can also heal the sick, predict the future, and see events happening far away. Shamanism is practiced in small preindustrial societies in northern Asia and North and South America.

Another type of animism, called totemism, is most commonly found in Australia and some Pacific islands. **Totemism** involves a belief in kinship between humans and animals or natural objects. The animal or object, called a totem, is considered sacred and is thought to represent a family or clan and their ancestors. Because of its supposed supernatural quality, the totem is treated with awe and respect. No one is allowed to hurt, eat, kill, or even touch it. Totems are seen as helpful protectors who watch over the group.

Some shamans use rattles in ceremonies. This rattle is decorated with a carved hawk face.

A second belief system found around the world is **theism**—the belief in a god or gods. In theism, the god is considered a divine power worthy of worship. There are two types of theism: monotheism and polytheism.

Monotheism is the belief in one god. Judaism, Christianity, and Islam are examples of monotheistic religions. All monotheistic religions contain an organizational structure, sacred writings, worship rituals, and an organized priesthood or ministry. **Polytheism** refers to the belief in a number of gods. The best-known polytheistic religion is probably Hinduism. Polytheistic religions usually center on one powerful god who has control over a number of lesser gods. The lesser gods are thought to have their own separate spheres of influence, controlling such things as harvests, childbirth, and earthquakes.

The third religious belief system, **ethicalism**, is based on the idea that moral principles have a sacred quality. Ethical religions are based on a set of principles such as truth, honor, and tolerance that serve as a guide to living a righteous life. Some examples of ethical religions, which are found mainly in Asia, are Buddhism, Confucianism, and Shintoism. Ethicalism involves meditation and purity of thought and action. The goal for followers of ethical religions is to reach their highest human potential.

Organizational Structures

The organizational structure of religion can be categorized into four types: ecclesia, denominations, sects, and cults. These categories are ideal types of organizational structures that apply mainly to religions found in the West.

An **ecclesia** is a type of religious organization in which most people in the society are members by virtue of their birth. Essentially, an ecclesia is the state church, and it is closely allied with the government. It is a structured bureaucratic organization, and its officials are highly trained and wield considerable power. Worship ceremonies tend to be very formal and follow well-established procedures. Ecclesia do not tolerate religious differences, and they often make membership a matter of law. Fundamentalist Islam in Iran resembles this type of organization.

A **denomination** is a well-established religious organization in which a substantial number of the

Sarah Quinlin-Sheridan of Clarks Summit, Pennsylvania, suggested the following activity: Create a large map of your school district or of one part of it. Organize students into small groups and assign each group a portion of the map. Have each group locate each church in its portion of the map and identify the locations on the map. In addition, groups should prepare a fact sheet for each church that provides the date when it was founded, the size of its congregation, the names of its head clergy, descriptions of its religious services or meetings, descriptions of any youth programs available, and descriptions of any community services the church provides. **COOPERATIVE LEARNING , BLOCK SCHEDULING**

SPOTLIGHT *on New Religious Movements*

Tell students that the world's religions include not only the major belief systems that have been around for thousands of years but also movements that have arisen more recently. Among these relatively new religions are the Muslim Ahmadi sect (8 million members); the Cao Dai, a mixture of many diverse religions in Vietnam (3 million members); the Toronto Blessing, a Christian charismatic movement (300,000 members); and Umbanda, a spirit-healing and spirit-worship movement in Brazil (20 million members). Have each student conduct research on one of these religious movements or on another new religion and then create a fact sheet about it. **BLOCK SCHEDULING**

Exploring Cultural Diversity

Falun Gong. One of the newer religious movements is Falun Gong. Founded in 1992 in China, the movement derived from the tradition of Qi Gong (pronounced *chee-gong*), which involves practicing slow physical movements and meditation. The teachings of Falun Gong are based on virtues related to Buddhism, Confucianism, and Taoism.

Some Falun Gong views are considered radical, however, and are not related to traditional Chinese religion. For example, Falun Gong's leader, who lives in exile in New York, believes extraterrestrials are interfering with Earth and corrupting humanity by influencing the expansion of technology. The Chinese government maintains that Falun Gong is a cult, which promotes superstition and harms Chinese society. As a result, government officials have persecuted many Falun Gong members.

RESEARCH ACTIVITY: Have students conduct research on the controversy surrounding the Falun Gong movement.

Visual Answer

Students might contrast the size and elaborate architecture of the first two buildings with the simplicity of the third.

366

---

population are members. Examples of denominations include the Presbyterian Church and the Baptist Church. Like ecclesia, denominations are formal bureaucratic structures with trained officials. Denominations hold strongly to their own beliefs. However, they tend to be tolerant, acknowledging the rights of others to hold beliefs that differ from their own. Although many members are born into denominations, these organizations also welcome converts.

A **sect** is a relatively small religious organization that typically has split off from a denomination because of differences concerning beliefs. Examples of sects include Jehovah's Witnesses and Hassidic Jews. Sects tend to claim exclusive access to religious truth and often are intolerant of other faiths. These organizations also tend to be hostile toward the existing power structure, seeing it as corrupt and worldly.

The worship ceremonies of sects often encourage displays of emotion and spontaneity such as clapping, dancing, singing, and shouting. Sects also encourage active recruitment of new members. Despite this, many sects are short-lived. Yet some, like the Methodist Church, become denominations over time.

A **cult** is a new religion whose beliefs and practices differ markedly from those of the society's major religions. Often, these beliefs are based on the revelations or visions of the cult leader. Cults are typically led by charismatic figures who appear to have extraordinary—even supernatural—qualities. More often than not, followers are initially attracted to the leader as much as they are to his or her message. These followers are usually disillusioned by traditional religion and by life in general. After accepting the leader's message, they may totally give themselves to the cult and reject the rest of society, including family and friends.

Most cults are short-lived. For the most part, their beliefs are too different for the majority of people in a society to accept. In 1997, 39 members of the Heaven's Gate cult committed mass suicide in California. In videotapes they left behind, they explained that they were "shedding their containers" and "leaving this planet." They believed they would be transported to a higher existence by a spacecraft that was trailing the Hale-Bopp Comet. Such incidents cause many people to view cults as odd groups with strange ideas.

INTERPRETING VISUALS Church denominations can vary greatly. These variations can be seen in the various styles of Protestant houses of worship. *What differences can you find in these houses of worship?*

SUGGESTION 1: Ask students to imagine that they are creating a chart for a magazine feature titled Religion in American Society Today. Have each student create a highly visual chart that illustrates the distinctive features of religion in American society. *(free from persecution; culturally diverse; highly valued but may be losing influence; separation of church and state; many believe in God, but fewer are affiliated with religious organizations, and even fewer regularly attend services; most Americans are monotheistic; Protestants are most numerous, but the Roman Catholic Church is the largest single organization; rising participation in fundamentalist and evangelical Christian groups)*

SUGGESTION 2: Display the back of a $1 bill on an overhead projector and ask students to identify any religious aspects of it. *(Students might point out the motto "In God We Trust" or the eye in the pyramid, which is from the reverse side of the Great Seal of the United States. Tell students that this eye is called the Eye of Providence and that the Latin motto 'Annuit Coeptis' means "He [God] has favored our undertakings.")* Next, ask students what they might conclude from these religious elements on U.S. currency *(that American society is predominantly and historically Christian.)* Use this activity as the basis of a class discussion on the distinctive features of religion in American society *(listed in the previous activity).*

Honoring those who lost their lives in the attacks of September 11, 2001, religious leaders from several major religions joined in services on a national day of mourning. The religious leaders represented the major faiths of the country.

Religion in American Society

The United States has long been a haven for religious freedom. For centuries, immigrant groups have come to America to gain sanctuary from religious persecution. As a result, the United States is now home to hundreds of different religious denominations, sects, and cults. Changing immigration patterns have added to this variety of religions. For example, the growth in immigration from Asia in the 1990s increased the numbers of Buddhists, Muslims, and Hindus living in the United States.

Another feature of religion in the United States is that the majority of Americans hold it in high regard. There is a general opinion in the United States that all people should hold some religious beliefs. According to a survey of public opinion polls taken between 1997 and 1999, between 86 and 94 percent of Americans believe in God. Polls taken by the Gallup Organization in 2001 found that 60 percent of Americans feel that religion is very important in their lives. Some 61 percent believe that religion can answer all or most of today's problems.

Another feature of religions in the United States is the separation of church and state. This separation is a concept that has been derived by courts from the U.S. Constitution. For the protection of the freedom of religions in the United States, the government lacks the official power to either support or deny any religious beliefs. Hence, the United States, unlike many other countries, has no national religion.

Sociologists who study religion in the United States generally focus on people's religious affiliations and religious participation. An additional topic that has gained the attention of sociologists in recent years is the rise of fundamentalist Christianity.

Religious Affiliation Although 90 percent of Americans say that they believe in God, only about 66 percent are affiliated with some religious organization. This figure has remained relatively stable over the past few decades. Even though the United States has many religions, most people with a religious affiliation are members of the major faiths—Christianity, Islam, and Judaism.

If you examine religious affiliation by looking at the major faiths, you will find that Christians who belong to Protestant churches are the most numerous in the United States. However, breaking down the faiths into denominations yields different findings. In the table on page 370, you can see that the Roman Catholic Church is the largest religious organization in the United States. Moreover, the Roman Catholic Church tends to be a unified organization, unlike most of the other denominations. For example, Methodists may claim affiliation to any one of nine different denominations. These include the African Methodist Episcopal Church, the Southern Methodist Church, and the United Methodist Church.

Studies have found a number of demographic differences among religious groups. For example, Jews

Interdisciplinary Connection

THE ARTS

Christian Church Architecture. Christian churches vary greatly in architectural style, size, ornateness, and other factors. For example, Europe's gothic cathedrals are typically huge stone structures with vaulted ceilings, stained glass windows, flying buttresses, gargoyles, and other decorations. In contrast, some Protestant churches in the United States are simple in design and decoration.

CRITICAL THINKING

What might variations in the architecture of a religious group's house of worship reveal about the religion?

ANSWER: how the group views the role of its house of worship within its religion

Exploring Cultural Diversity

■ TEACH

Have students read the feature Religious Diversity in America and answer the first item under Think About It. Next, ask students where in the United States they might expect to find the greatest religious diversity. *(Students might respond that larger cities and coastal regions might have the most religious diversity because many immigrants settled in large cities, particularly along the East and West Coasts.)* Assign students the second item under Think About It to complete as homework.

■ EXTEND

Have students examine the clauses related to religious freedom in the First Amendment of the Constitution of the United States. Then have each student write a paragraph summarizing the guarantees of religious freedom and the separation of church and state in the United States and how these features have influenced American society (such as by promoting increased religious diversity). Have volunteers read their paragraphs to the class.

BLOCK SCHEDULING

Interdisciplinary Connection

LITERATURE

Sacred Religious Texts. Although the major religions in the United States differ in many ways, each has a text it considers to be sacred. The Bible, consisting of the Old and New Testaments, is the sacred text of Christianity. The Old Testament's first five books also form the Torah, the sacred text of Judaism. Every Jewish synagogue keeps a copy of the Torah on parchment scrolls. In Islam, the sacred text is the Qur'an. Christians, Jews, and Muslims each consider their sacred text to be the word of God, as given through various selected people. In Buddhism, the Pali Canon is the sacred text, and in Hinduism most followers believe in the sanctity of the ancient religious writings known as the Vedas.

ACTIVITY: Have students share other information that they might know about each of the major religions in the United States. Then have students discuss how these major religions influence American society.

EXPLORING
Cultural Diversity

RELIGIOUS DIVERSITY IN AMERICA

Since colonial times, people have come to America to enjoy the freedom to worship how they please. Immigrants, particularly those who arrived in the last 30 years, have helped to transform the United States into the world's most religiously diverse country. A brief review of the major religions in the United States illustrates this diversity.

Christianity

During the 1600s, Puritans came to America so they could freely practice their form of Protestantism. To this day, the United States remains a predominantly Christian and Protestant country. Some 77 percent of Americans are Christians and about 50 percent of all Christians are Protestant. However, Roman Catholicism is the largest Christian denomination in the United States.

Judaism

There has been a Jewish presence in North America since the 1600s. However, Jewish immigrants did not begin to arrive in large numbers until the late 1800s. Today more than 5 million Americans are Jewish—more than the Jewish population in all of Israel. New York City and Miami both have larger Jewish populations than Jerusalem, the largest city in Israel.

Islam

Some of the earliest Muslim arrivals in North America came against their will—they were slaves from West Africa. A good number of their descendants among the African American population returned to the Islamic faith during the 1900s. Today the greater number of Muslims in the United States are immigrants from Asia. With a population of about 6 million, American Muslims outnumber American Episcopalians and American Quakers.

Buddhism

The first wave of Japanese immigration in the 1870s brought Buddhism to the United States. Subsequent immigration from Asia, particularly in the last several decades, has brought followers of every major Buddhist school of thought from many Asian countries. A U.S. city, Los

368

CONNECTING to Literature

Tell students that fantasy and science fiction authors often create new cultures and universes. Have students read one of the following fantasy or science fiction novels (or an appropriate novel of the student's choosing) and then write an essay analyzing the role of religion in the story: *Dune* by Frank Herbert, the *Foundation* novels by Isaac Asimov, *The Chronicles of Narnia* by C. S. Lewis, or *The Dark Is Rising* by Susan Cooper. Call on volunteers to read their essays to the class. Follow up with a brief discussion.

BLOCK SCHEDULING

SPOTLIGHT on American Indian Religions

Although many religions practiced in the United States originated elsewhere in the world, some religions are distinctively American, such as those practiced by American Indians. Have students, working individually or in small groups, conduct research on one American Indian religion. Next, have each student or group find an American Indian legend that describes some aspect of the religion and its role in the group's society. Have volunteers read their legends to the class. Then have students discuss how various American Indian religions compare to other religions.

COOPERATIVE LEARNING, BLOCK SCHEDULING

Angeles, ranks as one of the most diverse Buddhist communities in the world.

Hinduism

The Hindu population of the United States was relatively small until quite recently. However, immigration from Asia over the last 20 to 30 years has increased the Hindu American population to more than 1 million. Although Hindus are a fairly recent arrival in the United States, Americans have long been aware of some Hindu beliefs through the writings of Henry David Thoreau and other transcendentalists.

Other Religions

Many other religions are practiced in the United States. These include Baha'i, Taoism, Spiritualism, and diverse Native American and New Age faiths. Just as Americans have the freedom to follow the religion of their choice, they are also free not to worship. More than 13 million Americans state that they follow no religion.

The diversity of America's religious life can be seen in the rituals of religious life in the United States. These include Muslim prayer services, Buddhists using a sand mandala, Protestants raising a cross, a Baptist choir singing hymns, and a young Jewish student studying religious writings.

Think About It

1. **Sociology and Culture** What effect has immigration had on religious diversity in the United States?

2. **Sociology and You** Conduct research on the major religions in your community. Use your findings to write a brief illustrated report.

Think About It Answers

1. Immigration has helped transform the United States into the world's most religiously diverse country.

2. Reports may vary but should provide information on each of the major religions found in your community. Information that students may provide for each religion may be the number of houses of worship and followers in the community, a description of the belief system, and information about the religion's establishment in the community.

CLOSE

Have students discuss whether they think American society is becoming more secular. Give all students a chance to express and defend their opinions.

REVIEW AND ASSESS

Have students complete the **Section 2 Review** on p. 371. As **Alternative Assessment**, you may want to use the functions of religion art piece or the Religion in American Society Today chart in this section's lessons.

RETEACH

Pair students and have each partner create a detailed outline in answer to one of the section's Read to Discover questions. *(What basic societal needs does religion serve? What are the distinctive features of religion in American society?)* Partners should select different questions. After creating their outlines, have partners exchange them and correct, revise, or expand upon each other's outlines as necessary. Then have partners discuss the changes they made. Finally, have the class help you create master outlines for each question.
ENGLISH LANGUAGE LEARNERS , COOPERATIVE LEARNING

Religious Membership in the United States*

Group	Members	Group	Members
Roman Catholic Church	62,391,484	Episcopal Church	2,331,794
Baptist Churches	30,288,639	Reformed Churches	1,975,406
Methodist Churches	12,359,827	Churches of Christ	1,500,000
Pentecostal Churches	11,148,256	Hindu	1,285,000
Lutheran Churches	8,565,925	Jehovah's Witnesses	990,340
Presbyterian Churches	6,115,624	Adventist Churches	887,652
Islam	5,780,000	Christian Churches (Disciples of Christ)	831,125
Eastern Orthodox Churches	4,203,900	Church of the Nazarene	627,054
Jewish	4,140,000		

*Membership of 500,000 or more
Source: The World Almanac and Book of Facts, 2002

INTERPRETING TABLES Immigration and many other factors have led to a great diversity of religious institutions in the United States. *Which faiths have the largest number of members in the United States?*

and Episcopalians tend to have higher educations and to have higher incomes than other religious groups. In terms of region, Baptists and Methodists reside mainly in the South and Midwest. The largest numbers of Catholics and Jews are found in the large cities. Catholics are also numerous in the West. Political differences also appear among the major faiths. Generally, Protestants have traditionally backed the Republican Party, while Catholics and Jews have given their support to the Democrats.

Religious Participation Although the majority of Americans express religious preferences, only about 34 percent of people attend religious services on a regular

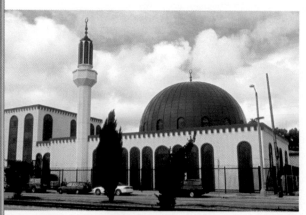

The rising number of immigrants to the United States has contributed to the growth of the Muslim faith in America in recent decades. Muslims have opened mosques in many major U.S. cities.

basis. The proportion of people who attend services regularly has remained fairly stable over the past few decades. Women, African Americans, and older citizens are more likely to participate regularly in services. Among the major faiths, Catholics go to services more often than do Protestants or Jews.

However, regular attendance at a church or synagogue is a poor indicator of religious involvement. Sociologists generally find it difficult to measure **religiosity**, or the depth of people's religious feelings and how they translate these feelings into behavior. Participation in religious services gives little information about religiosity because people attend services for a variety of reasons, including socializing and making business contacts. However, people's attitudes about their own religious feelings and behaviors may provide some insight into religiosity. Only a little more than half of all Americans define themselves as "religious." When deciding how to conduct their lives, Americans are about equally split between paying attention to religious teachings and paying attention to their own views or the views of others. To some sociologists, such statistics indicate that American society is becoming more **secular**. In other words, religion is losing its influence in everyday life in the United States. Interestingly enough, 71 percent of Americans think that religion as a whole is increasingly influential in American life while 24 percent think it is becoming less influential.

Fundamentalist Christianity Membership in several mainstream denominations has been declining in recent years. In contrast, participation in fundamentalist

1. Have students conduct research on religious holidays celebrated by various religious groups around the world. Ask students to research the origins of the holidays, how they are celebrated, and what they mean today. **BLOCK SCHEDULING**

2. Organize students into small groups and give each group a blank outline map of the world. Have groups conduct research on the distribution of the world's major religions and indicate the results on the map. **COOPERATIVE LEARNING, BLOCK SCHEDULING**

3. Have each student write a poem that reflects the three main functions of religion *(social cohesion, social control, emotional support)*. Students might write their poems from a personal perspective or from the perspective of an observer of life and society. Encourage students to employ a spiritual or mystical tone in their poems. When the class next meets, have volunteers share their poems with the class. After each poem, you might want to see if students can identify how the poem reflects each function of religion.
BLOCK SCHEDULING

---

and in evangelical Christian groups has been on the rise. A variety of fundamentalist Christian groups exist in the United States, but they share similar features. They believe in the complete accuracy of the Bible and interpret the Scripture literally. In addition, they view their beliefs as the one true religion. They also believe in personal salvation through conversion——the "born again" experience. They also share a commitment to bringing Jesus Christ into the lives of all nonbelievers. Some 42 percent of Americans describe themselves as "born again" or evangelical Christians.

In recent years, fundamentalist Christians have organized to exert political influence in the United States. Religious conservative activists donate money to political causes, attend political meetings, and campaign for politicians who share their beliefs. These beliefs generally include opposition to abortion, homosexuality, gun control, and sexual permissiveness, and support for prayer in schools and for what they believe to be traditional family values. However, polls show that only about one quarter of Americans support the political views of religious conservatives. Social analysts also point out that voter turnout—and, therefore, voting power——has been falling among religious conservatives.

Some fundamentalist Christian leaders have questioned the wisdom of involvement in the political system. They have urged fundamentalists to adopt a "strategy of separation" from the mainstream culture so that they may follow a Christian lifestyle. Some fundamentalists have

Homeschooling is popular among some Americans who believe that religion should play a larger part in education than public schools allow.

followed this advice by becoming "selective separatists." They remain a part of the mainstream society by voting, working regular jobs, and paying taxes. However, they homeschool their children and avoid all elements of popular culture, such as television, pop music, and movies. They also reject the notion that material possessions are necessary for a happy life. In essence, they have created a counterculture. However, rather than being based on a new set of cultural patterns, this counterculture is based on what they believe to be a return to traditional values.

SECTION 2 REVIEW

1. Define and explain
sacred
profane
religion
ritual
animism
shamanism
totemism
theism
monotheism
polytheism
ethicalism
ecclesia
denomination
sect
cult
religiosity
secular

2. Contrasting Copy the graphic organizer below. Use it to show the difference between the sacred and the profane.

Sacred		Profane
	← →	

3. Finding the Main Idea

a. What basic human needs does religion fulfill?

b. What three basic elements do all religions have in common?

4. Writing and Critical Thinking

Supporting a Point of View Write one or two paragraphs explaining why you agree or disagree with the view that the United States is becoming more secularized. Consider:

• Americans' statements on their faith
• attendance at religious services
• measures of religiosity

Homework Practice Online
keyword: SL3 HP14

CHAPTER *14* REVIEW

ANSWERS

WRITING A SUMMARY
See the section subtitles for the main topics in this chapter.

IDENTIFYING PEOPLE AND IDEAS

1. the roles and norms that ensure the transmission of knowledge, values, and patterns of behavior from one generation to the next

2. formal education by specially trained teachers who follow officially recognized policies

3. term used by sociologists to describe schools' transmission of cultural goals that are not openly acknowledged

4. system by which parents receive a voucher equal to the amount their state spends on education for each student to use to pay tuition at the school of the parents' choice

5. a system in which non-English-speaking students are taught in their native languages until they are proficient enough in English to attend regular classes

6. a system of roles and norms organized around the sacred realm that bind people together in social groups

7. the belief in one god

8. the belief in a number of gods

9. the depth of people's religious feelings and how they translate these feelings into behavior

10. not of a religious nature

CHAPTER

14

Review and Assessment Resources

- Chapter 14 Review, pp. 372–73
- Chapter Review Activities with Answer Key
- Global Skill Builder CD–ROM
- Chapter 14 Test Generator (on the One-Stop Planner)
- Chapter 14 Test (Form A or B)
- Alternative Assessment Handbook
- HRW Go site

 REVIEW

Have students complete the **Chapter 14 Review** on pp. 372–73.

ASSESS

Use one of the chapter tests to assess students' understanding of the content. For **Alternative Assessment**, see the **Alternative Assessment Handbook**.

UNDERSTANDING MAIN IDEAS

1. functionalist—schools work to maintain the stability and smooth operation of society; conflict—schools serve to limit the access of individuals and groups to power and social rewards; interactionist—educational achievement is explained by teacher-student interactions

2. Schools have taken security measures, adopted zero tolerance policies, and begun teaching students how to resolve disputes.

3. Religion is a social creation, and different cultures define the sacred differently.

4. The United States is a haven for those seeking religious freedom and, as a result, is religiously diverse. Americans have a respect for religion, and the separation of church and state is provided for in the U.S. Constitution.

THINKING CRITICALLY

1. Schools stimulate intellectual inquiry and develop the critical thinking skills needed to pursue and gain knowledge.

2. Conflict theorists think that tracking exists to help keep the power in society in the hands of an established elite.

3. Answers will vary, but students might address issues such as educational reform, charter schools, school choice, homeschooling, violence in the schools, or bilingual education.

CHAPTER

 14 Review

 Writing a Summary

Using standard grammar, spelling, sentence structure, and punctuation, summarize the information in this chapter.
Consider:
- the current issues in American education
- the basic social needs served by religion
- the features of American religious life

Identifying People and Ideas

Identify the following people or terms and use them in appropriate sentences.

1. education
2. schooling
3. hidden curriculum
4. school choice
5. bilingual education
6. religion
7. monotheism
8. polytheism
9. religiosity
10. secular

Understanding Main ideas

Section 1 (pp. 350–61)

1. Compare and contrast the functionalist, conflict, and interactionist views of educational issues such as tracking and the transmission of culture.

2. What steps have educational authorities taken to curb violence and other criminal activities in schools?

Section 2 (pp. 362–71)

3. Why do you think religions differ from society to society?

4. What are the major features of religion in the United States?

Thinking Critically

1. **Identifying Cause and Effect** How do schools foster the creation of new knowledge?

2. **Identifying Points of View** What, according to conflict theory, is the relationship between tracking and socioeconomic status?

3. **Making Generalizations and Predictions** What do you think is the most important issue facing American schools today? Explain your answer.

4. **Analyzing Information** What purpose does the separation of church and state serve in the United States?

5. **Drawing Inferences and Conclusions** Compare the percentage of people in the United States who claim a religious preference with the percentage who are formally affiliated with a religious organization. What can you conclude from this comparison?

 Writing About Sociology

1. **Evaluating** Education has changed greatly in the last 50 years. Interview a parent or older person in your community about the differences between education now and education in the past. Write a summary of the changes in education. How has the institution changed? What factors have caused these changes?

2. **Drawing Inferences and Conclusions** Throughout the history of the United States, religious life has changed with the arrival of immigrants, the movement of people from the country to the city, and many other social changes. Use the graphic organizer below to explain in a paragraph how some of these changes affected religious life.

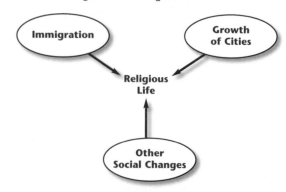

Before class, prepare 20 questions that relate to the chapter material. Then on the chalkboard or a piece of butcher paper, draw a gameboard that consists of a series of 20 squares. Organize students into teams and assign each team a symbol. Start each team's symbol at the beginning of the gameboard. As you ask each question, have the current player on each team write down an answer. Then have teams show their answers. Move each team forward one square for each correct answer. You might also include bonus questions that move teams forward two or three squares. Change team players for each question. The first team to reach the end wins.

ENGLISH LANGUAGE LEARNERS , COOPERATIVE LEARNING

SOCIOLOGY PROJECTS

1. Using Observation Skills Have students visit a preschool or elementary classroom and observe. During the visit, students should write down as many details as possible about teacher-student interactions. Students may also want to note the classroom arrangement. Then have students analyze their observations from an interactionist perspective of education.

2. Connecting to History Have each student conduct research on the history and religious origins of one of the following sacred sites: Bethlehem (Christianity), Bodh Gaya (Buddhism), the Ganges River (Hinduism), Jerusalem (Christianity, Islam, and Judaism), or Mecca (Islam).

BUILDING SOCIAL STUDIES SKILLS

Interpreting Graphs

Study the bar graphs below. Use them to answer the following questions.

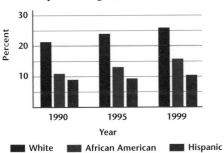

Americans Completing Four or More Years of College, by Race and Hispanic Origin, 1990 to 1999*

Legend: White, African American, Hispanic

*Percentage of population 25 years of age and older
Source: U.S. Census Bureau

1. The graphs show that college graduation rates are

  a. rising for white Americans, African Americans, and Hispanics.

  b. rising for white Americans and African Americans, but falling for Hispanics.

  c. falling for white Americans and African Americans, but rising for Hispanics.

  d. falling for white Americans, African Americans, and Hispanics.

2. How might conflict sociologists use the graphs to support their ideas about educational achievement?

Analyzing Primary Sources

In this excerpt Allen D. Hertzke discusses the two major religious lobbying groups. Read the excerpt, and then answer the questions that follow.

"*Anchored in [Washington] is the left-leaning 'peace and justice' cluster, comprising the liberal mainline Protestants . . . , the peace churches (Mennonites, Friends, Brethren), the black churches, and some Catholic groups. . . . At the other end of the spectrum are those emphasizing traditional values—Christian fundamentalists . . . , some evangelical groups, and Catholic anti-abortion lobbies. . . .*

Christian fundamentalists have been most effective in shaping the congressional agenda on issues that resonate with the cultural conservatism of their constituents, such as support for school prayer and opposition to abortion and pornography. Most of this influence comes from the ability to mobilize their sympathizers to flood Washington with letters and calls. . . .

For the 'peace and justice' cluster the picture is similarly mixed. While these groups have been less successful at mobilization than the fundamentalists, they have access to information gained through church networks . . . that makes up for this deficiency. The mainline churches run a multitude of domestic social service agencies . . . and are also connected to international relief agencies, development programs, and members scattered across the globe. On the basis of these networks, church lobbyists routinely testify on the Hill about the effects of domestic and foreign policies. . . ."

3. Fundamentalists have been successful in shaping the congressional agenda on such issues as

  a. arms control.

  b. foreign aid.

  c. health care.

  d. school prayer.

4. How do the two major ideological camps differ in their approaches to lobbying?

4. protects religious freedom by preventing the government from supporting or obstructing religious practice

5. The majority of Americans express religious preferences, but only 66 percent are formally affiliated with a religious organization. Students may conclude that the United States is becoming more secularized or that many Americans consider religion to be more personal.

WRITING ABOUT SOCIOLOGY

1. Students' summaries should describe some changes that have occurred and attempt to explain them.

2. Paragraphs will vary, but students should note that immigration has led to a wide diversity of religions in the United States, that urban growth has promoted secularization, and that other social changes include a growth in fundamentalist Christianity.

BUILDING SOCIAL STUDIES SKILLS

1. a

2. Conflict sociologists might argue that although college attendance rates are rising for each group, white Americans continue to account for the highest percentage by far.

3. d

4. Christian fundamentalists are able to flood Washington with letters and calls, while the "peace and justice" cluster use church networks of agencies as the basis for lobbying.

SOCIOLOGY PROJECTS

Linking to Community

Using Your Observation Skills Working in a group with two or three students, identify the various religions practiced in your community. Then conduct research on how such religious rituals as baptisms, weddings, and funerals are performed in these religions. Use your findings to write an illustrated report titled "Comparing and Contrasting Religious Rituals in Our Community."

internet connect

Internet Activity: go.hrw.com
KEYWORD: SL3 SC14
Choose an activity on education and religion to:
- create a pamphlet on contemporary issues in public education.
- make a 3-D model of education from either the functionalist or conflict perspective.
- write a profile of a religious group's beliefs and organizational structure.

go.hrw.com

Science and the Mass Media

CHAPTER RESOURCE MANAGER

Objectives	Pacing Guide		Resources

SECTION 1:
Science as
a Social
Institution
(pp. 376–85)

REV Section 1
Review, p. 385

- Identify factors that have contributed to the institutionalization of science.
- Explain how the norms of scientific research differ from the realities of scientific research.

Regular 2 days	**Block** **Scheduling** 1 day

Block Scheduling Handbook with Team Teaching Strategies, Chapter 15

 CNN Presents Sociology: Changing Technology and the Family

RS Graphic Organizer 15

HRW Go site

SM Mastering Critical Thinking Skills 15

PS Readings and Case Studies in Sociology 15

E Research Projects and Activities for Teaching Sociology 15

SM Study Skills and Writing Guide

SECTION 2:
Mass Media
as a Social
Institution
(pp. 386–97)

REV Section 2
Review, p. 397

- Trace the major developments in the history of mass media, and identify the types of mass media in the United States.
- Explain how the sociological perspectives of mass media differ.
- Discuss some contemporary mass-media issues.

Regular 2 days	**Block** **Scheduling** 1 day

Block Scheduling Handbook with Team Teaching Strategies, Chapter 15

Chapter Review And Assessment

REV Chapter 15 Review, pp. 398–99

REV Chapter Review Activities with Answer Key

Global Skill Builder CD–ROM

Chapter 15 Test Generator
(on the One-Stop Planner)

A Chapter 15 Test (Form A or B)

A Alternative Assessment Handbook

HRW Go site

Chapter Resource Key

PS Primary Sources	**A** Assessment	Video
RS Reading Support	**REV** Review	Internet
E Enrichment	Transparencies	Holt Presentation Maker Using Microsoft® PowerPoint®
SM Skills Mastery	CD–ROM	

One-Stop Planner CD–ROM

See the *One-Stop Planner* for a complete list of additional resources for students and teachers.

One-Stop Planner CD–ROM

It's easy to plan lessons, select resources, and print out materials for your students when you use the *One-Stop Planner CD–ROM with Test Generator.*

Chapter Project Preview

The following activities are included in the Chapter Review. You may want to make the suggested preparations.

CHAPTER REVIEW ACTIVITY

Research in Sociology Students will work together in groups to conduct research on an incident of fraud or a hoax in science and then create an illustrated report describing the impact of frauds and hoaxes on the institution of science. In preparation, have each group create an outline of its report for you to approve. You might also want to reserve computer time for students to create their reports.

INTERNET ACTIVITIES

Science and Ethics Students will use provided Internet links to conduct research on recent ethical issues in science and scientific research and then write a report on one case. In preparation, review the Web links provided on the specific HRW Go page to familiarize yourself with the various issues students will be researching. Then provide students with a handout outlining how they should structure and organize their reports and providing other project guidelines.

Technology and Subcultures Students will use provided Internet links to conduct research on the impact of technology on different subcultures within the United States and then work in small groups to create Web pages on the topic. If necessary, provide students with a training class for creating Web pages. In addition, create or provide written instructions for creating Web pages as well as guidelines listing the information that students should include.

Additional Resources

PRINT RESOURCES FOR TEACHERS

Fuller, Steve. *Thomas Kuhn: A Philosophical History for Our Times.* Chicago: University of Chicago Press, 2000. Examines Thomas S. Kuhn's seminal 1962 work, *The Structure of Scientific Revolutions,* in which he introduced the term *paradigm shift.*

Marcus, George E., ed. *Connected: Engagements with Media.* Chicago: University of Chicago Press, 1996. Examines social and political aspects of mass media and information technology.

Mulkay, Michael. *Sociology of Science: A Sociological Pilgrimage.* Bloomington, IN: Indiana University Press, 1991. An insightful exploration of theory and research into the sociology of science.

PRINT RESOURCES FOR STUDENTS

Kohn, Alexander. *False Prophets: Fraud, Error, and Misdemeanor in Science and Medicine.* New York, NY: B. Blackwell, 1986. Discusses frauds and hoaxes in the field of science.

Enables students to examine the realities of science.

Putnam, Robert D. *Bowling Alone: The Collapse and Revival of American Community.* New York: Simon & Schuster, 2000. Examines social conditions in the United States since the 1960s and argues that since that time Americans have become increasingly disconnected from civic and social life.

MULTIMEDIA RESOURCES

Time Tables of History: Science & Innovation (software) Society for Visual Education. Presents a time table of major scientific developments consisting of more than 6,000 stories on a variety of scientific and technological subjects.

Discovering the Scientific Method: Snigs . . . Flirks . . . Blorgs (software) Focus Media. Software that helps students develop an appreciation for the scientific method through numerous problem-solving exercises.

CHAPTER

15

Science and
the Mass Media

SECTION 1
Science as a Social Institution

SECTION 2
Mass Media as a Social Institution

CHAPTER REVIEW

Build on What You Know

Ask students to answer the
following questions:

**How might scientific advances
affect a society?**

Consider:

• economic factors

• the effects on individuals

• scientists' motivations

**What role(s) might mass
media play in a society?**

Consider:

• the availability of information

• the influence on people's
interests and feelings

• technology and the Internet

Internet Activity

Have students access the
Internet through the HRW Go
site to conduct research on
the impact of scientific theory
and discovery on society.
Then have each student
create a theoretical profile
of the effect of one historic
scientist on belief systems,
social norms, and social
institutions. Students' profiles
should include a summary of
the scientist's work as well
as clearly explain how this
work affected or changed
the social structure.

CHAPTER

15

Science and the Mass Media

Build on What You Know

Education and reli-
gion are a central
part of American
society. In this chap-
ter you will explore
two other institutions
that play a key role in
society: science and
mass media. You will
study the rise of
modern science and
its current charac-
teristics. Then you
will turn your atten-
tion to the role mass
media play in Ameri-
can culture.

Sociologists are interested in how
advances in science and technology
such as the research at NASA's transonic
wind tunnel might affect society.

Life in Society

Society is constantly changing. Consequently, the institutional structure of society also changes. Not only do old institutions take on new characteristics, but new institutions develop. Two institutions that have gained increasing importance over the past 150 years are science and mass media.

Our lives are touched on a daily basis by the effects of science. Our health; our immediate environment; the way we learn, communicate, and travel; what goods and services we produce and how we produce them; and our vision of the future are all influenced by science. So great is the influence of science on society that the level of scientific literacy of adults and children has become an issue of public debate.

Mass media have also become part of our daily lives. With modern mass media, Americans can obtain news and sports coverage, music, movies, and other forms of entertainment 24-hours-a-day, 7-days-a-week. Annually, people and businesses in the United States spend billions of dollars on mass media, whether it is spent in advertising, production, or using various media elements. Technological changes allow more people to access more information faster than ever before. As mass media changes, it greatly affects our society. Given the vast influence of science and mass media on modern society, it is not surprising that sociologists have turned their attention to the analysis of these institutions.

> ### ► WHY SOCIOLOGY MATTERS
>
> Sociologists are interested in how mass media affect American society. Use **CNN fyi.com** or other current events sources to learn more about an issue related to mass media's effect on American culture. Present an oral report to the class.
>
> **CNN fyi.com**

TRUTH OR FICTION

What's Your Opinion?

Read the following statements about sociology. Do you think they are true or false? You will learn whether each statement is true or false as you read the chapter.

- Science is always a pure and unbiased field.
- Technological developments have not affected mass media.
- All social groups use mass media in the same way.

◆ Applying Sociology

Science and Mass Media. The social institutions of science and mass media affect Americans' lives everyday in many ways. From the food people eat, to the products they use, to the ways they work and spend their leisure time, people are affected by science, technology, and mass media. At the same time, the social institutions of science and mass media increasingly influence each other as well as other social institutions, such as the economy and politics.

ACTIVITY: Have each student write a paragraph or two describing some of the issues related to science and mass media that he or she thinks sociologists would be interested in studying. Have volunteers share their paragraphs with the class.

OBJECTIVES

1. *Identify factors that have contributed to the institutionalization of science.*

2. *Explain how the norms of scientific research differ from the realities of scientific research.*

LET'S GET STARTED!

Write the following question on the chalkboard: *Why do you think that many scientists, regardless of nationality, share and cooperate with each other rather than compete against each other?* As students enter the classroom, ask them to freewrite a sentence or two speculating on the answer to this question. Call on a few volunteers to share their answers with the class. Encourage other students to provide feedback and discussion. Then tell students that in Section 1 they will learn about the scientific community and about science as a social institution.

SECTION **1** RESOURCES

REPRODUCIBLE & REVIEW
- Graphic Organizer 15
- Research Projects and Activities for Teaching Sociology 15
- Section 1 Review, p. 385

TECHNOLOGY
- One-Stop Planner, Lesson 15.1
- Homework Practice Online
- HRW Go site

Visual Answer

They might have helped him chart and track the movement of the planets around the Sun.

1 SCIENCE AS A SOCIAL INSTITUTION

Read to Discover
1. What factors have contributed to the institutionalization of science?
2. How do the norms of scientific research differ from the realities of scientific research?

Define
science, sociology of science, scientific method, universalism, organized skepticism, communalism, disinterestedness, Matthew effect, paradigm

INTERPRETING VISUALS Nicolaus Copernicus was born in the late 1400s. Copernicus made important discoveries in the field of astronomy and was one of the first scientists to argue that Earth traveled around the Sun, which was a radical idea at the time. *How do you think these tools might have helped Copernicus?*

Although **science**—the pursuit of knowledge through systematic methods—is a central feature of all industrialized countries, its status as an institution is relatively recent. For much of human history, explanations for natural phenomena were sought in the supernatural. Science gained prominence over religious beliefs as the principal method by which to understand nature in the 1600 and 1700s.

The question of how modern science took root can be approached from many angles. For example, some historians of science have focused on the role of the genius. From this perspective, the growth of science results from the creative energies of individuals. Sociologists do not deny the role of the genius in the development of scientific knowledge. However, most sociologists are more interested in how the structure of society and the organization of science itself have affected scientific development. The sociological investigation of how scientific knowledge develops is the **sociology of science.** In this section, you will examine science as a social institution from this sociological perspective.

The Institutionalization of Science in the West

Scientific geniuses have existed since ancient times. Great thinkers in early Babylon, China, Egypt, Greece, India, and Mesoamerica developed elaborate systems of mathematics and astronomy in an attempt to understand the world around them. These early thinkers were among the social elite, and they often pursued such knowledge as a pastime.

The Birth of Science Science emerged as a recognizable system of study in the 300s B.C. In Greece great thinkers such as Plato and Aristotle explored the fields of mathematics, astronomy, the biological sciences, physics, and medicine. During the Hellenistic Age, roughly the 300s to the 100s B.C., Greek culture spread to other countries. In Egypt great libraries and centers of learning were established in large cities. Although the Romans themselves did not produce many notable scientists, Greek scientists living in the Roman Empire continued to make significant contributions.

With the decline of the Roman Empire, the quest in Europe for scientific knowledge slowed. Trade and the exchange of ideas between regions of the world diminished during the Middle Ages. At the same time, the Catholic Church grew in power and influence. Over time, people turned away from science and toward philosophy and religion for explanations of the workings of the natural world. Scientific scholarship did continue after the fall of the Roman Empire. However, the topics of research and the interpretations of findings were strongly influenced by the Catholic Church. As a result, many lines of scientific inquiry were no longer pursued. In addition, most of the scientific research that continued was recast in terms that supported religious teachings. Almost a thousand years passed before science experienced a rebirth in Europe although advances in science continued in other regions of the world.

TEACH OBJECTIVE 1

SUGGESTION 1: Organize the class into small groups and have each group create a large wall chart that uses visuals and other elements to illustrate the factors that contributed to the institutionalization of science. In addition, students' charts should illustrate the cause-and-effect relationships among the various factors. *(See the answers to Question 2 and Question 3a in the Section 1 Review for the information that students' wall charts should include.)* Encourage groups to make their charts clear, colorful, and informative. Display each of the wall charts in the classroom. **COOPERATIVE LEARNING**

SUGGESTION 2: Lead a class discussion on the factors that have contributed to the institutionalization of science. *(See the answers to Question 2 and Question 3a in the Section 1 Review.)* Then hang a large piece of butcher paper along one wall of the classroom. Have students work together to create a time line of the main events and advances that have led to the institutionalization of science. As students continue their study of the section, have them add to the time line. Encourage students to continue to refer to the time line as a study aid. **COOPERATIVE LEARNING**

The Rebirth of Science Four main factors contributed to this rebirth of science in Europe. The first factor was the Renaissance, which began in Italy in the A.D. 1300s. The Renaissance was, in part, a by-product of trade with the East. This trade produced enormous wealth for Italian merchants, bankers, and nobles. Many of them used their fortunes to patronize, or support, the arts and learning.

The development of movable metal type and a practical printing press also played a part in the rebirth of science. These developments made the production of books relatively inexpensive, which greatly facilitated the spread of scientific knowledge. The wide distribution of information, in turn, helped to stimulate the desire for learning.

A third factor in the rebirth of science was the Age of Exploration. From the 1400s to the 1600s, the countries of Europe sailed the world in search of all-water routes to the East. Exploration encouraged the development of science in two ways. First, advances in astronomy and mathematics were needed to assist in navigation. Second, explorers brought back strange plants, animals, and diseases from distant lands that sparked scientific curiosity.

The final factor contributing to the rebirth of science in Europe was the Protestant Reformation. Early Protestants questioned the idea that the power of religious salvation rested in the hands of priests. Instead, they argued that people could find salvation through their own efforts. This emphasis on individualism lessened public resistance to scientific inquiry. Religious officials were not necessarily seen as the final authority on all matters.

The rebirth of science produced a revolution in scientific thought in the 1500s. This scientific revolution redefined the nature of the universe, the methods of scientific research, and the functions of science. In place of a world controlled by divine spirits, scientists envisioned a universe that operated according to a system of natural laws. Rather than employing philosophical speculation, scientists used the **scientific method**—an objective and systematic way of collecting information and arriving at conclusions. Scientists no longer viewed science simply as an intellectual exercise. Instead, they saw that scientific knowledge could be merged with technology to solve problems.

INTERPRETING VISUALS Renaissance scientists such as Johannes Kepler (above), Galileo Galilei (top right), and Isaac Newton (bottom right) made important advances in astronomy, math, and physics. *Why do you think Renaissance artists chose to paint these scientists?*

Interdisciplinary Connection

HISTORY
Mathematical Advances. Many technological advances in the 1600s were made possible because of advances in mathematics. For example, the development of logarithms and calculus led to more accurate timekeeping and aided in the improvement of optical tools such as the telescope and the microscope.

CRITICAL THINKING
How do you think that these technological innovations helped advance science?

ANSWER: Students might note that such advances would have helped scientists in their research.

Visual Answer

because these men were some of the leading thinkers of the day and because the artists' patrons may have requested these portraits be made

Write the steps of the scientific method on the chalkboard. *(See the text on pp. S19–S21 and the chart on p. S20.)* Discuss each of the steps with the class. Next, pair students and have each pair list one or two everyday observations that can be explained or debunked using the scientific method (such as "If the chalkboard eraser is clean, it will erase marks more effectively."). Then instruct students to use the steps of the scientific method to test each observation. **COOPERATIVE LEARNING , BLOCK SCHEDULING**

SPOTLIGHT *on Scientific Specialization*

Provide students with course catalogs from various colleges and universities. Ask students to examine and take notes on the science classes offered. Then on the chalkboard draw several columns with headings representing different scientific disciplines (such as *astronomy, biology, chemistry,* and so on). Have students use their notes to list some subdisciplines for each major scientific discipline. Use the activity as the basis of a class review about the specialization and professionalization of scientific study.

BLOCK SCHEDULING

Sociology in the World Today

Academic Hijinks.

Academic specialization in the sciences and social sciences can be both good and bad. On one hand, specialization has contributed to the expansion of knowledge in a variety of fields. On the other hand, specialization means that people often have little knowledge of fields outside their specialty.

In 1996 a physicist named Alan Sokal submitted an article to a prestigious journal of literary criticism. The article argued that the laws of physics were relative. For example, Sokal suggested that the law of gravity would cease to exist if a person stopped believing in it. His intention was to test whether the journal's editors would publish an article that a physicist or mathematician would immediately recognize as a spoof. The journal's editors failed to consult anyone with such a background, however, and published the article.

ACTIVITY: Lead a brief class discussion on the pros and cons of scientific specialization. For example, have students consider how the sharing of ideas across scientific disciplines might further scientific knowledge.

Modern science has been aided by continuing advances in scientific knowledge, such as the understanding of DNA, and advances in technology, such as more-powerful computers and more-accurate lasers.

The scientific revolution became part of a larger revolution in social thought called the Enlightenment. The Enlightenment supported reason over religious beliefs, and its main tools were the scientific method and scientific facts. One of the consequences of the Enlightenment was the spread of democracy. In turn the emergence of democracy contributed to the development of state-supported systems of education. In addition to spreading scientific knowledge, these systems created new jobs in teaching and research.

Modern Science In spite of the Enlightenment, science remained of interest only to a small segment of society during the 1700s. Science did not become widely significant until the late 1800s and early 1900s. This transformation was brought about by industrialization, which was the result of earlier scientific and technological developments. The central ideal of industrialization was progress, and most people saw science as a tool of progress. In addition to pure research, scientists increasingly saw their task as the development of new technologies that could improve the human condition.

By the early 1900s the modern organization of science was in place. Specialization replaced general interest in the scientific world. The number of disciplines and subdisciplines in science multiplied, and most scientists narrowed their areas of interest to specific fields of research. This tendency toward specialization was reinforced by the university system. Most universities encouraged students to concentrate their studies on a single area or subarea of science.

Specialization of science also reinforced the professionalization of science. Private sponsorship of science gave way to employment in universities, research institutes, private industry, and the government. The availability of funding, the goals of scientific organizations, and the needs of business and government increasingly replaced general curiosity as the springboard for scientific research.

TEACH OBJECTIVE 2

SUGGESTION 1: To help students explain how the norms of scientific research differ from the realities, copy the graphic organizer at the right onto the chalkboard, omitting the italicized answers. Have students copy and complete the organizer. Discuss the answers with the class. **ENGLISH LANGUAGE LEARNERS**

HOMEWORK: Ask students to imagine that all scientists must take a scientific oath of ethics. Have each student write an oath that explains the ideals that ethical scientists should try to maintain and the practices they should avoid. Encourage students to create a poster providing the text of their oath.

Norms of Scientific Research

- *universalism*
- *organized skepticism*
- *communalism*
- *disinterestedness*
- *counter-norms*

Although many scientists try to or would like to follow Merton's norms, reality often falls short of this ideal.

Realities of Scientific Research

- *fraud*
- *competition*
- *Matthew effect*
- *conflicting views of reality*

The Norms of Scientific Research

As the discussion in the previous paragraphs indicates, science is pursued within a social context. Thus, the existing values and norms of a society influence the quest for scientific knowledge. According to Robert K. Merton, the modern scientific community is guided by four basic norms. These norms are universalism, organized skepticism, communalism, and disinterestedness.

Universalism The norm of **universalism** holds that scientific research should be judged solely on the basis of quality. A scientist's social class, race, gender, nationality, or religion should have no bearing on how his or her research findings are evaluated. The norm of universalism helps ensure that the pursuit of scientific research is open to everyone, regardless of his or her social characteristics.

Organized Skepticism According to the norm of **organized skepticism**, no scientific finding or theory is exempt from questioning. Even after a theory or finding has gained wide acceptance, scientists should be willing to continue to question its accuracy. This skepticism is built into the system as part of the scientific method, hence the label "organized." Furthermore, scientists are supposed to suspend judgment until sufficient facts have been collected. The norm of organized skepticism helps to ensure that scientific knowledge does not stagnate and that facts and theories are not blindly accepted.

Communalism The belief that all scientific knowledge should be made available to everyone in the scientific community forms the basis of the norm of **communalism**. This norm also serves to reinforce the idea that findings belong to the entire community, not to individual scientists. This norm holds despite the fact that scientific findings and

phenomena are sometimes named for their discoverers. The sharing of scientific knowledge is important because science is additive—new discoveries generally build on existing knowledge. The norm of communalism helps to ensure that scientists have access to existing knowledge.

Disinterestedness According to the norm of **disinterestedness**, scientists should seek truth, not personal gain. Thus, research topics should be chosen without reference to possible awards, political or religious criteria, or currently popular views. Similarly, scientists should not alter their data in an effort to gain acceptance. Nor should they unfairly criticize the work of others who hold positions contrary to their own.

Counter-norms The vast majority of scientists accept the norms of universalism, organized skepticism, communalism, and disinterestedness in principle. Research suggests that scientists generally follow these norms when the issues of their research are clearly defined. However, if the issues are not well-defined or are controversial, such as cloning or genetic manipulation, scientists often adopt a set of counter-norms.

In such cases, scientists follow the norm of particularism instead of universalism. They base their evaluation of the work of others not on the quality of the research but on the researchers' personal characteristics. Such scientists abandon organized skepticism in favor of organized dogmatism. In other words, they have absolutely no doubts about their own findings, but they completely doubt the findings of others. Rejecting communalism, they follow the norm of solitariness. They consider their findings their own personal property. Finally, scientists take an interested, rather than a disinterested, approach to their work. Their decisions are often influenced by special interests, such as the organizations to which they belong.

The Realities of Scientific Research

Merton's norms of science provide an ideal type for scientific behavior. The realities of scientific inquiry often fall far short of this ideal. The most problematic issues affecting scientific research include fraud, the negative effects of competition, the Matthew effect, and conflicting views of reality.

Fraud The Piltdown hoax is a classic example of fraud in science. In 1912 a group of professional and amateur scientists announced the discovery of several skull fragments and the lower jaw of what appeared to be the

Recent scientific advances in the study of DNA led to advances in medical treatment.

Connecting to Literature

■ TEACH

Have students read the two excerpts in the feature Science Fiction and answer the questions under Think About It. In a class discussion, ask students if any of them like to read or watch science fiction. Next, ask those students who do to give the class some additional examples of how such stories focus on the social implications of science and technology. Then have each student write a similar science fiction "excerpt" that addresses the social implications of some current or future form of science or technology.

✦ CONNECTING *to Science and Technology*

Explain that some science fiction authors attempt to predict the future by examining the cutting edge of science and technology today and extrapolating how society might make use of it tomorrow. Examples include Jules Verne's conjecture of a lunar landing in *From the Earth to the Moon* and Arthur C. Clarke's realistic design of a space station and space shuttle in *2001: A Space Odyssey*. Then have each student read a science fiction novel or short story and summarize some of the author's predictions for the future. **BLOCK SCHEDULING**

◆ Applying Sociology

Science Fiction and Science Fact. Science and science fiction can influence each other in novel ways. For example, the first U.S. space shuttle was named *Enterprise* in honor of the starship of the same name on the *Star Trek* TV series. Conversely, the science-fiction TV series *Babylon 5* made use of actual images of space taken by NASA's Hubble telescope.

ACTIVITY: Have students consider how the institutions of science and mass media can influence each other as well as other aspects of society.

Think About It Answers

1. In *The Martian Chronicles*, space colonists on Mars watch as their home planet, Earth, is destroyed by nuclear war. In "The Martian Way," a space crew discusses Earth during the long journey to Mars.

2. In both stories, the characters feel that Earth is cold and distant. However, in "The Martian Way," the characters have never been to Earth. In *The Martian Chronicles*, the characters have only been away from Earth for a few years and still have family and friends there.

CONNECTING TO
Literature

SCIENCE FICTION

Writers of science fiction focus on how science—real or imagined—affects individuals and society. Ray Bradbury and Isaac Asimov are among the most celebrated American science fiction writers. In the following excerpt from Bradbury's 1950 novel The Martian Chronicles, *space colonists from Earth watch from Mars as their home planet is destroyed by nuclear war. In the excerpt from Asimov's 1952 short story "The Martian Way," a space crew discusses Earth on the long journey to Mars. Both works consider the social implications of scientific and technological advances.*

The Martian Chronicles
by Ray Bradbury

They all came out and looked at the sky that night. They left their suppers or their washing up or their dressing for the show and they came out upon their now-not-quite-so-new porches and watched the green star of Earth there. It was a move without conscious effort; they all did it, to help them understand the news they had heard on the radio a moment before. There was Earth and there the coming war, and there hundreds of thousands of mothers or grandmothers or fathers or brothers or aunts or uncles or cousins. They stood on the porches and tried to believe in the existence of Earth, much as they had once tried to believe in the existence of Mars; it was a problem reversed. To all intents and purposes, Earth was now dead; they had been away from it for three or four years. Space was an anesthetic; seventy million miles of space numbed you, put memory to sleep, depopulated Earth, erased the past, and allowed these people here to go on with their work. But now, tonight, the dead were risen, Earth was reinhabited, memory awoke, a million names were spoken: What was so-and-so doing tonight on Earth? What about this one and that one? The people on the porches glanced sideways at each other's faces.

At nine o'clock Earth seemed to explode, catch fire, and burn.

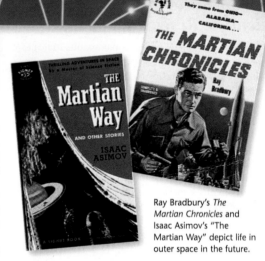

Ray Bradbury's *The Martian Chronicles* and Isaac Asimov's "The Martian Way" depict life in outer space in the future.

"The Martian Way"
by Isaac Asimov

At first . . . the weeks flew past . . . except for the gnawing feeling that every minute meant an additional number of thousands of miles away from all humanity. That made it worse. . . .

The days were long and many, space was empty. . . .

"Mario?" The voice that broke upon his ear-phones was questioning. . . .

"Speaking," he said. . . .

"You know, I've read Earth books—"

"Grounder books, you mean." Rioz yawned. . . .

"—and sometimes I read descriptions of people lying on grass," continued Long. "You know, that green stuff like thin, long pieces of paper they have all over the ground down there, and they look up at the blue sky with clouds in it. Did you ever see any films of that?"

"Sure. It didn't attract me. It looked cold."

Think About It

1. **Summarize** *What is the subject of each of these excerpts?*
2. **Compare and Contrast** *How do the characters' attitudes about Earth differ in each excerpt? How are they similar?*

SUGGESTION 2: Call on students to identify and explain the norms and realities of scientific research and how they differ. *(See the graphic organizer on p. 379 for the answers.)* Then ask students to consider the situation of scientists who conduct research for the government or for private industry. Such scientists are often discouraged from sharing their methods or findings with other scientists for national security reasons or for fear of losing potential profits or giving a competitor a market advantage. Have each student write a newspaper editorial either supporting or opposing the open sharing of scientific research in such situations. Have volunteers read their editorials to the class.

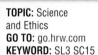

SPOTLIGHT *on Medical Sociology*

Organize the class into groups and ask them to imagine that they are the hosts of a television talk show focusing on science and medicine. Have each group interview a medical sociologist and then use the interview to create a fictional transcript of a television show interview. Students should ask questions about what a medical sociologist does, what the interviewee's particular focus is, how an understanding of sociology helps in his or her job, and what a typical day at work is like. Have a volunteer group act out its interview for the class. **COOPERATIVE LEARNING** , **BLOCK SCHEDULING**

The Piltdown man was presented to the world as the "missing link" between apes and humans. However, later discoveries proved the Piltdown man was a fraud.

"missing link" between apes and humans. The bones were found in a gravel pit near Piltdown Common in Sussex, England. As a result, the discovery came to be known as Piltdown man.

Doubts over the Piltdown man's authenticity surfaced immediately. Critics claimed that the skull fragments and jawbone did not appear to belong together. However, most critics were quieted by the announcement in 1917 that another Piltdown man had been discovered several years earlier. Over time, interest in the discovery faded. Then in 1953 scientist J. S. Weiner once again fueled public debate when he expressed doubts about the finds. Troubled by news that the location of the second Pilt-

down discovery was unknown, Weiner launched his own investigation. His findings proved that Piltdown man was a fraud.

Although outright fraud is rare in science, it does occur. For example, in the early 1980s John Darsee, a Harvard Medical School researcher, falsified data that formed the basis for at least 70 scientific articles on heart disease. Darsee's laboratory chief, Robert Kloner, discovered the fraud. In the late 1980s and early 1990s, the scientific community focused their attention on a bitter dispute between American scientist Robert Gallo and French scientist Luc Montagnier. Both claimed to have been the first to isolate a form of HIV—the virus that causes AIDS. An investigation conducted by the Federal Office of Research Integrity found that the virus grown by Gallo was genetically related to a virus that Montagnier had sent him several years earlier. Gallo, the Office of Research Integrity said, had committed "scientific misconduct" by failing to acknowledge the source of his work.

Competition Many scientists and sociologists of science propose that competition is one of the principal causes of norm violations among scientists. The fear of being "beaten to the punch" on an important discovery can cause scientists to refuse to share unpublished information with their colleagues. The potential for economic profit from

TOPIC: Science and Ethics
GO TO: go.hrw.com
KEYWORD: SL3 SC15

Have students access the Internet through the HRW Go site to conduct research on recent ethical issues in science and scientific research. Then have each student write a short report summarizing a recent fraud or hoax related to unethical scientific research. In addition, each student should speculate on some possible future ethical issues in the field of science. Remind students to use standard grammar, spelling, sentence structure, and punctuation in their reports. Call on volunteers to read their reports to the class. Then use the topics of the reports as the basis of a brief class discussion on the issue of scientific ethics.

Careers
IN SOCIOLOGY

MEDICAL SOCIOLOGIST

Medical sociologists investigate the social factors that affect health care. They concentrate on patient and practitioner behavior, the delivery of health care, and the rate and control of disease. Medical sociologists work in hospitals, health care businesses, social-service organizations, governmental agencies, and medical schools. They hold such jobs as teacher, researcher, administrator, social worker, patient advocate, technical writer, health planner, and policy analyst. How might an understanding of sociology help when analyzing issues such as the delivery of health care and the incidence of disease?

Many medical sociologists study the needs for and social implications of medical treatments. New scientific discoveries and technology in the medical field can influence their work.

Connecting to Science

CONNECTING TO
Science

PREDICTING THE FUTURE

Making predictions about the future is usually the realm of science fiction writers. However, at times scientists make educated guesses about things to come. Educated or not, they are no more than guesses, as the predictions made in 1950 by the magazine *Popular Mechanics* illustrate.

In the years to come, robotic tools and remote-control technology may be more commonplace in the fields of medicine.

2000—from 1950

The houses of 2000, *Popular Mechanics* said, would be made of plastic and light metals like aluminum. Using such materials would make houses cheap to build—as little as $5,000 each. Because of this, houses would not be built to last. Most would stand for only 25 years. The typical house would not have many labor-saving appliances—because they would not be needed. Dishes made of a special kind of plastic would simply dissolve in the sink when immersed in water heated to 250°F. Cleaning the house would be simple as well. Since furniture would be made of plastic or some other synthetic material, cleaning it would require nothing more than a blast of water and detergent from a hose. Meal preparation would not involve much time, either. Most food would be frozen, and electronic ovens would thaw and cook it in a matter of minutes.

Electronic media—telephones, radios, and televisions—would be integrated in 2000, the magazine suggested. Thus, when people talked to each other on the telephone, they would also be able to see each other. Many people would do their shopping in this fashion. When people wanted to send letters to each other, they would sometimes use a facsimile-transmission system that could send or receive a five-page document in no more than a minute. People would travel short distances in alcohol-powered cars. For longer distances, they would use helicopters—which practically every family would own. Countrywide and intercontinental journeys would be made by supersonic airplanes that would travel at 1,000 miles an hour.

Some of the magazine's predictions proved remarkably accurate. Fax machines, online shopping, and microwave ovens are familiar features of life today. However, many more are as far from reality today as they were in 1950. Some predictions may even seem a little silly today.

2050—from Today

In 2000, *Popular Mechanics* once again looked 50 years into the future and predicted what life would be like in the mid-2000s. Here are some of the major forecasts:

- Pilotless passenger airplanes will be common in 2050.
- Minute "robot doctors" inserted into the body will flow through the bloodstream looking for and destroying germs.
- Information resulting from the Human Genome Project will make it possible to tailor drugs to treat individual patients.
- Body parts cloned from a patient's DNA will replace severed limbs or damaged organs.
- New kinds of food called nutraceuticals will make people healthier as they eat them.
- Computerized refrigerators will monitor food stocks and order new supplies from the grocery store.
- Windows will be made of "smart glass" that adjusts its tint to the intensity of sunlight. Windows will also double as flat-screened televisions.
- Doors will have eye- or face-recognition locks.

Think About It

1. **Analyzing Information** *What 1950 predictions had become reality in 2000?*
2. **Making Generalizations and Predictions** *Which of the predictions for 2050 do you think will come true? How will these innovations lead to societal changes? Explain your answer.*

SPOTLIGHT *on Merton's Scientific Norms*

Write on the chalkboard Robert K. Merton's four scientific norms: *universalism, organized skepticism, communalism,* and *disinterestedness.* Briefly discuss the role of each norm in scientific study, then challenge students to apply these norms to nonscientific careers *(such as entertainment, journalism, law enforcement, politics, and religion).* Ask the class to discuss if and how Merton's norms can apply to fields outside of science. For example, disinterestedness (the pursuit of the truth) is an important goal in journalism but not nearly as important in entertainment. **BLOCK SCHEDULING**

SPOTLIGHT *on Paradigm Shifts in Science*

Have students use the library and other resources to conduct research on major paradigm shifts in scientific thought throughout history. Examples of outdated paradigms include the "four elements" (earth, air, fire, and water), alchemy, the flat Earth, Earth as the center of the universe, and the sound barrier. Have each student use the research to create a time line indicating at least four major paradigm shifts. Encourage students to decorate or illustrate their time lines. **BLOCK SCHEDULING**

INTERPRETING VISUALS The giant drawing of the Nazca plain in Peru and of the Navajo land carving in the United States were created by ancient cultures. Their origins are a matter of speculation by scientists. Belief in the existence of life on other planets has influenced people's interpretations of these carvings. *How do different views of reality affect people's interpretation of the carvings?*

scientific discoveries has amplified scientific competition in the past few decades. This pursuit of profit can even cause scientists to publish data that contains a few intentional inaccuracies designed to throw off the competition.

More often, competition results in scientists rushing to publish their data. Publishing data prematurely can result in misinformation, thereby slowing down scientific progress. The rush to publish stems from the fact that scientific achievement is measured in terms of peer recognition. To gain recognition, scientists must share their data with fellow scientists either by publishing in professional journals or by presenting papers at conferences. The pressure to publish is particularly severe for scientists working in university or research settings. Job security in those settings is often tied directly to the quantity of materials published.

The Matthew Effect In 1968 Robert K. Merton noted that honors and recognition tend to go to those scientists who have already achieved recognition. On the other hand, they tend to be withheld from scientists who have not yet made their mark. Merton named this phenomenon the **Matthew effect**, from a Bible verse in the Gospel of Matthew: "For to every one who has will more be given, and he will have abundance; but from him who has not, even what he has will be taken away."

According to Merton, if two scientists independently make the same discovery at about the same time, most or all of the credit will go to the more famous of the two scientists. Similarly, if a group of scientists work together on a project, most of the credit will go to the scientist with the greatest name recognition, regardless of how the work was actually divided.

Sociologists of science have noted that the consequences of the Matthew effect are mixed. On one hand, the Matthew effect can hamper the careers of young scientists by preventing them from gaining recognition. On the other hand, because the views of famous scientists are more readily accepted, the Matthew effect can speed the rate at which new findings are incorporated into the existing body of scientific knowledge.

Conflicting Views of Reality In 1928 sociologist W. I. Thomas noted that "if people define situations as real, they are real in their consequences." For example, when the bubonic plague wiped out one third of the population of Europe during the Middle Ages, many people attributed the epidemic to the anger of God. In response, some people joined a fundamentalist sect called the Brotherhood of Flagellants. Members of the brotherhood publicly whipped themselves in hopes of appeasing God. Others looked for a scapegoat—and found one in the Jewish population. Across Europe, Jews were persecuted unmercifully. In some cities, Jews were driven from their homes and burned to death. In others, thousands of Jews were executed in mass hangings. The fact that flea-infested rats actually spread the epidemic had no bearing on the

Over time, people's view and acceptance of an idea can change dramatically. Most people viewed Charles Darwin's theory of evolution as an absurd idea.

Sociology in the World Today

TEACH

Ask students to read aloud the feature The Ethics of Biotechnology and answer the questions under Think About It. Discuss the feature and the questions' answers as a class. Then have each student write a letter to a fictional state congressperson giving his or her point of view on a current ethical debate in biotechnology (such as genetic engineering) and urging the congressperson to support that position.

EXTEND

Have students conduct library research on cloning or another ethical issue related to biotechnology. Students should examine the scientific, legal, medical, and ethical positions on the issue. In addition, have students form their own opinions and extrapolate the issue's possible implications for future generations. Instruct students to convey their opinions through position papers, political cartoons, persuasive speeches, or other appropriate means of expressing an opinion. **BLOCK SCHEDULING**

Think About It Answers

1. the coming ability to control genetic inheritance

2. Answers will vary. Some students may suggest the use of legal and regulatory protections to ensure the ethical use of biotechnical developments. Other students might suggest a global governing board to oversee biotechnical research around the world.

SOCIOLOGY IN THE
World Today

THE ETHICS OF BIOTECHNOLOGY

New scientific developments are often accompanied by vigorous discussions about how—and if—they should be used. For example, the scientists who built the first atomic bomb during World War II argued over whether this devastating weapon should be used on human populations. Today such biotechnical developments as cloning and human genetic engineering have generated similar debates. In the following excerpt, science writer Ralph Brave outlines the major issues in this debate on biotechnology.

"The . . . science story here (and it's not a small one) is that we are nearing the point where we will unravel one of the great mysteries: How does a single fertilized egg cell become a human being? How does the genome of that first single cell and all the cells that follow 'know' precisely how and when to turn on and off the genetic code so that a baby is formed and develops into adulthood? The molecular and cellular answers are beginning to come into view.

But along with that view comes a sense of the changes it might demand in our conceptions of who we are and, more daunting, the opportunities it might present to alter who we are. Deepening the anxieties generated by these advances is the reality that no one, not even the most advanced scientist, knows at this point how far-reaching or how limited the potential for genetic engineering of the human will turn out to be.

'Biology will become an engine of transformation of our society,' writes [Nobel prize winner] David Baltimore. . . . 'Instead of guessing about how we differ one from another, we will understand and be able to tailor our life experiences to our inheritance. We will also be able, to some extent, to control that inheritance.' In these three sentences, Baltimore expresses why genomic knowledge threatens to take us to the brink of social chaos. The detailed knowledge of our genomes—all 3 billion bits of DNA, which include all our genetic material with its genetic certainties, numerous genetic probabilities and its predicted 'load' of five to ten potentially lethal genes carried by each of us—means that a genetic reordering of our individual lives and our society is coming. . . . While the transition will be at times tumultuous, most scientists believe it ultimately should prove manageable, just as we have socially accommodated other biomedical knowledge through legal and regulatory protections.

But when it comes to the ability to control that inheritance, there is little historical or ethical precedent to serve as a guide—just science-fiction stories. Will human beings become simply another GMO (genetically modified organism)? . . . Or will the genetic revolution realize the dream of addressing enormous swaths of human suffering? Will it even be able, as some hope and others dread, to extend its reach into the suffering that some believe lies embedded in that vague tissue called human nature? Will we treat modifying genes that contribute to disease differently from those that contribute to cognitive features that we label intelligence? Will we monitor athletes for genetic additions that improve performance? (The International Olympic Committee has already called a meeting to address this issue.) How will government intervene between prospective parents and their decisions about the genetic makeup of their children? Will access to genetic enhancements create entirely new and wider social divisions, including, as some have suggested, 'the creation of a master race'?

These questions are the central concerns of a growing number of geneticists, sociologists, bioethicists and legal scholars."

Think About It

1. **Finding the Main Idea** *What, according to Brave, is the greatest ethical challenge of biotechnology?*
2. **Evaluating** *What steps would you take to ensure the ethical use of biotechnical developments?*

![CLOSE icon] **CLOSE**

In a closing discussion, ask students to give their opinions about the role of the institution of science in society and to provide examples from the section that support their comments.

![REVIEW icon] **REVIEW AND ASSESS**

Have students complete the **Section 1 Review** on p. 385. As **Alternative Assessment**, you may want to use the institutionalization of science wall chart or the competition in science editorial in this section's lessons.

RETEACH

Have students create 10-question quizzes covering the information in this section. Then pair students and have partners answer each other's quizzes. **ENGLISH LANGUAGE LEARNERS , COOPERATIVE LEARNING**

EXTEND

Have students conduct research on several new innovations in science and technology and then write a few paragraphs predicting how one or two of the innovations might affect American society. Have volunteers share their findings and predictions with the class. **BLOCK SCHEDULING**

people's actions. People had defined reality in a certain way and acted accordingly.

Contrary to the norm of organized skepticism, science is affected by views of reality. Thomas S. Kuhn, a historian of science, coined the term **paradigm** to describe the set of shared concepts, methods, and assumptions that make up scientific reality at any point in time. Paradigms determine what topics are appropriate for scientific inquiry. They not only establish the methods that can be used to collect and analyze data, but they also identify the interpretations of data that are considered acceptable.

During periods of what Kuhn called "normal science," the scientific community shares a common paradigm. However, many scientists eventually come to believe that the established paradigm cannot explain all existing scientific phenomena. As a result, a new paradigm emerges. This transition to a new paradigm seldom takes place quietly. Views that run counter to the long-established paradigm often meet with resistance. For example, in the 1600s Galileo proclaimed that Earth was not the center of the universe, contrary to the view accepted by science and the Catholic Church. Galileo's ideas were so at odds with established teachings that he was charged with heresy and forced to declare that he was wrong. Galileo's views gained acceptance only after several decades of controversy.

The perceptions of the general public or of the government can also affect science. For example, political ideology

Soviet scientists who disagreed with Trofim Lysenko faced threats of punishment and imprisonment for expressing views that were not accepted by the Soviet government.

and a reluctance to accept Western ideas greatly slowed scientific progress in the former Soviet Union. Trofim Lysenko, the leading Soviet scientist during the 1930s and 1940s, rejected Western ideas regarding genetics because they were at odds with Marxist ideology. Those scientists who disagreed with him were labeled "enemies of the people" and were thrown in prison. Some were even executed. Lysenko fell from favor in the early 1950s, but Soviet science struggled to recover from his influence for decades.

SECTION 1 REVIEW

1. Define and explain
science
sociology of science
scientific method
universalism
organized skepticism
communalism
disinterestedness
Matthew effect
paradigm

2. Sequencing Copy the graphic organizer below. Use it to sequence the discoveries and changes in Western science since ancient times. Explain how advances in science and technology have changed individual and societal behavior.

3. Finding the Main Idea
a. Describe the development of science as a social institution.
b. Compare and contrast the norms and realities of science.

4. Writing and Critical Thinking
Making Generalizations and Predictions Write a brief essay describing how you think scientific discoveries and technological innovations will change society in the future.
Consider:
• the history of science as an institution
• how individual and social behavior may have changed because of these discoveries
• the cooperation and competition in scientific research

300 B.C. Ancient Greeks share scientific knowledge of math, astronomy, and other fields.	**The development A.D. 2000** of computer technology leads to advances in science and medicine.

Homework Practice Online
keyword: SL3 HP15

SECTION 1 REVIEW ANSWERS

1. Define:
• science, p. 376
• sociology of science, p. 376
• scientific method, p. 377
• universalism, p. 379
• organized skepticism, p. 379
• communalism, p. 379
• disinterestedness, p. 379
• Matthew effect, p. 383
• paradigm, p. 385

2. Entries might include: 1300s to 1600s—Renaissance, printing press, Age of Exploration, Protestant Reformation, scientific revolution; late 1800s to early 1900s—industrialization, specialization and professionalization of science

3a. Science emerged as a recognizable system of study in Greece during the 300s B.C. Beginning in the 1300s, science was reborn in Europe as a result of several factors. In the 1500s, a scientific revolution emerged. Industrialization led to the emergence of modern science in the late 1800s and early 1900s.

b. norms—universalism, organized skepticism, communalism, disinterestedness; realities—fraud, competition, Matthew effect, conflicting views of reality

4. Essays will vary, but students should exhibit an understanding of how past advances have affected society.

SECTION 2

OBJECTIVES

1. *Trace the major developments in the history of mass media, and identify the types of mass media in the United States.*

2. *Explain how the sociological perspectives of mass media differ.*

3. *Discuss some contemporary mass-media issues.*

LET'S GET STARTED!

Before class, write the definition of mass media on the chalkboard *(instruments of communication that reach large audiences with no personal contact between those sending the information and those receiving it).* As students enter the classroom, have them examine the definition and then quickly list several types of mass media. Call on students to share some of the items that they listed with the class. Then tell students that in Section 2 they will learn about mass media as a social institution, about some sociological perspectives of mass media, and about how some social issues relate to mass media.

2

MASS MEDIA AS A SOCIAL INSTITUTION

Read to Discover

1. What are the major developments in the history of mass media, and what are the types of mass media in the United States?

2. How do the sociological perspectives of mass media differ?

3. What are some contemporary mass-media issues?

Define

mass media, information society, media convergence, knowledge-gap hypothesis, digital divide, social capital, spiral of silence, agenda setting, gatekeepers, opinion leaders

---

D o mass media play a big part in your life? Look at the list of activities below and identify which you have done in the last few days.

- Read a book, magazine, or newspaper
- Listened to the radio
- Listened to a CD
- Watched a movie at a theater
- Watched television
- Watched a video or DVD
- Surfed the Internet

How much time do you think you spend on these activities? If they take up a lot of your time, you are not alone. The average American spends more than 3,000 hours a year using mass media—that is equivalent to just less than 4 months. **Mass media** are instruments of communication that reach large audiences with no personal contact between those sending the information and those receiving it. For many teenagers, sleeping is the only activity that individuals do more of than watching television. Today life without mass media is almost unthinkable.

The Institutionalization of Mass Media

The emergence of mass media as a social institution is a fairly recent event. The institutionalization of mass media has been driven by a series of intellectual and technological innovations. The first major breakthrough came with the development of writing and paper. Hundreds of years passed before the next major step—the creation of the printing press. Developments during the Industrial Age transformed media into a central force in society. The computer—the most recent and, perhaps, far-reaching development—has also helped to create an information society.

Writing and Paper People in the earliest nomadic societies had little need for any form of media. They lived in small groups, constantly on the move in search of food. To convey information to one another, they often relied on the spoken word. With the development of agriculture, societies became more complex. Individuals began to specialize in specific economic activities. For example, some people became craftworkers, producing tools and jewelry. This production of goods encouraged the development of trade. People soon became aware that they needed some form of written language to record business and other transactions.

The Sumerians, who flourished more than 5,000 years ago in what today is Iraq, produced one of the first forms of writing. Called cuneiform, it involved the use of pictograms—symbols that represent objects. The Sumerians scratched the pictograms into clay tablets. Over time, writing became more elaborate, and in about 1800 B.C. people in the Middle East developed something like an alphabet. Rather than using pictograms to represent objects, this alphabet used a small number of symbols that represented sounds. These symbols could be combined to form thousands of words representing objects and ideas. Traders spread this alphabet around the Mediterranean, and it became the model for later Western alphabets.

Ancient Egyptians used a form of pictograms called hieroglyphics to communicate.

During this time the materials on which people wrote changed too. Some time between 3100 and 2500 B.C. the Egyptians developed papyrus, a type of paper made from reeds. In the 200s B.C. the Greeks began to use parchment, which was made from the skins of goats, sheep, and calves. Parchment was primarily used until the 1400s when the printing press was developed and paper became more commonly used. The Chinese had developed the skill of papermaking as early as the A.D. 100s. However, more than 1,000 years passed before this skill reached Europe.

The Printing Press Until the A.D. 1400s the principal mass medium in Europe was the hand-written book. Hand copying was a long, laborious, and costly process. As a result, the audience for this medium was mostly limited to society's wealthy and powerful elite.

During the 1450s Johannes Gutenberg, a German goldsmith, developed movable metal type. He also built a mechanical press that pushed and held paper against the blocks of type, creating readable text. The combination of movable type and a reliable printing press revolutionized communication. The production of books became relatively inexpensive, which made the widespread distribution of information possible.

The Industrial Age The printing press made the widespread accessibility of information a possibility, not a reality. For centuries, the audience for media was limited to the rich and powerful. However, by the late 1800s and early 1900s the media had begun to play a greater role in most people's lives. Industrialization, for the most part, was responsible for this change.

During the Industrial Revolution, the factory became the chief setting for the production of goods. This shift encouraged a great movement of population to the cities, where most factories were located. With a rising standard of education and increasing requirements for factory work and life in the city, more and more people learned to read and write. As these people earned higher wages, they had more disposable income. To ensure that some of this disposable income was spent on their products, many businesses started advertising. The forces of urbanization, rising literacy, and advertising contributed to the development of what many consider the first true mass medium—the urban newspaper.

For hundreds of years the transfer of information had depended mainly on one medium—the printed word. This changed with the Industrial Age and the development of electronic media, which used electric signals to transmit information. The telegraph and the telephone enabled people to communicate over long distances. Movies, first silent and then with sound, provided a new form of mass entertainment. In time the phonograph, radio, and television brought entertainment into people's homes.

The Computer and the Information Society The digital computer completely transformed the way people store and access information. The information contained in thousands of books can be stored on a handful of computer disks. Different kinds of software, the programs that instruct computers on what to do, allow people to manipulate information in many different ways. Furthermore, the Internet, a global network that links millions of computers, revolutionized the way people communicate and access information. With a few clicks of a mouse, people can send documents, pictures, sound recordings, and movies to locations around the

INTERPRETING VISUALS Technological advances such as Johannes Gutenberg's printing press helped to expand media's availability. *How do you think other technologies such as high-speed printers affect mass media today?*

Applying Sociology

Top Consumer Magazines. In 2000 the top-10 consumer magazines in the United States, based on the Audit Bureau of Circulations, were:

1. *NRTA/AARP Bulletin*
2. *Modern Maturity*
3. *Reader's Digest*
4. *TV Guide*
5. *National Geographic Magazine*
6. *Better Homes and Gardens*
7. *Family Circle*
8. *Good Housekeeping*
9. *Woman's Day*
10. *Ladies' Home Journal*

CRITICAL THINKING
What do you think that the popularity of these magazines reveals about American society?

ANSWER: Students might note that many Americans are interested in issues related to aging, television, travel and geography, the home, and women's issues. In addition, the list suggests that many magazine readers are either older Americans or women.

Chart Answer

1,649 – 337 (88 + 103 + 146)
= 1,312 hours

Many Americans use computers for news and entertainment.

world. Similarly, people can access information stored in computers thousands of miles away.

Today in the United States, almost 50 percent of all workers are employed in information-related fields, such as computer programming, journalism, television-camera operation, and advertising copywriting. This figure will increase because the top seven occupations expected to experience the fastest growth in the early years of the 2000s are computer related. The number of Internet-related jobs is also expected to increase rapidly during that

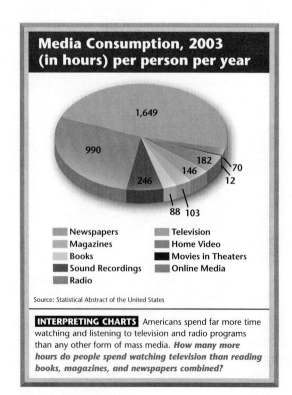

Media Consumption, 2003 (in hours) per person per year

1,649
990
246
182
146
70
12
88 103

- Newspapers
- Magazines
- Books
- Sound Recordings
- Radio
- Television
- Home Video
- Movies in Theaters
- Online Media

Source: Statistical Abstract of the United States

INTERPRETING CHARTS Americans spend far more time watching and listening to television and radio programs than any other form of mass media. *How many more hours do people spend watching television than reading books, magazines, and newspapers combined?*

time. According to many media specialists, such trends show that the United States is an **information society**, or a community in which the exchange of information is the main social and economic activity.

Mass Media in the United States

Americans are able to obtain information from a wide variety of media. These media can be grouped into four categories: print, audio, visual, and online. In recent years some media specialists have argued that separating the media in this fashion is artificial. They believe that various forces have caused the different media to converge.

Print Media The print media include newspapers, magazines, and books. The United States has about 1,500 daily newspapers—those published at least five times a week—which sell a total of about 56 million copies a day. The majority of American adults, nearly 57 percent, read a newspaper every day. Magazines are published periodically—such as once a week or once a month. Almost 18,000 magazines are published in the United States. Covering a huge variety of subjects, these magazines had a total circulation per issue of about 379 million in 2000. More than 80 percent of American households subscribe to at least one magazine. The statistics on books in the United States are similarly impressive. Some 50,000 book publishers put out approximately 70,000 titles a year, and Americans spend about $30 billion annually on book purchases. Reading is a popular pastime for many Americans. Nearly 40 percent of Americans read more than 10 books a year.

The print media have a substantial audience, but that audience is declining. The amount of daily newspapers, newspaper circulation, and newspaper readership have fallen steadily over the last few years. Those people who do read newspapers are spending less time on this activity than they did in the past. While magazine circulation is on the increase, people appear to be spending less time reading magazines. Falling readership has affected books too. The percentage of Americans who read no books at all has risen over the past 20 years. Today it stands at about 13 percent.

Audio Media Sound recordings and radio are the two major categories of audio media. The sound recording business is one of the country's major industries, with a dollar value of about $14.3 billion dollars in 2000. Sound recordings come in several different formats—compact

TEACH

Have students read the feature American Movies and Foreign Markets and answer the questions under Think About It. Then have each student make a list of five recent movies and predict whether each movie might do well in foreign markets. Ask students to make charts showing the names of the movies, the students' predictions of success in various countries or regions of the world, and students' reasoning behind their predictions. Call on students to share some of their predictions with the class.

EXTEND

Ask students to imagine that they are immigrants coming to the United States, with their only exposure to American culture having been through viewing American movies and television. Challenge students to speculate what their expectations of America would be. For example, based on popular westerns, what might be immigrants' impressions of the American West? Based on beach movies, what might be immigrants' impressions of California?

BLOCK SCHEDULING

SOCIOLOGY IN THE
World Today

AMERICAN MOVIES AND FOREIGN MARKETS

Sociologists have long been interested in movies. They are particularly concerned with the social, economic, and political factors that influence movie production and the influence of movies on American and world culture. One issue that has recently caught the attention of sociologists is the globalization of American culture through the export of Hollywood movies. These movies have an immense effect on the cultures of other countries. Conversely, foreign demand for American entertainment may be influencing American culture by affecting the decisions of Hollywood executives.

The Foreign Market

Why would foreign markets affect Hollywood executives? The answer is that foreign box office returns are huge. For example, in the late 1990s foreign box office receipts for American-made movies were between $5 and $6 billion—about the same as the returns from American movie theaters. Furthermore, the world market for American movies is expected to grow at an annual rate of more than 5 percent over the next few years. This rate may increase as more multiscreen theaters are built in Russia, China, and the countries of Eastern Europe. Thus, Hollywood executives fully expect that in the future many movies will make more in foreign markets than they do in the United States.

Effect on Decision-Making

Studies suggest that the power of the foreign box office has begun to influence the kinds of movies that Hollywood makes. The most profitable movies in the foreign market are those that have limited dialogue and lots of action and special affects. These movies are relatively easy for people of all nationalities to understand, and the cost of dubbing or translating them into multiple foreign languages is limited. Casting such movies may be influenced by the foreign box office as well. One or more of the stars must have a proven record in foreign markets. Making accommodations for such stars may require plot or story adjustments—such as the race or sex of a main character might be changed.

Foreign box office concerns also influence the movies that are less likely to be made. Movies with complicated plot lines or those concerned with particular aspects of American political, social, or cultural life often fail to get Hollywood backing. Such movies, Hollywood executives suggest, would be too difficult to understand or of no interest to foreign audiences. Hollywood executives also assert that movies about African Americans do not do well in the foreign market. They charge that foreign audiences cannot relate to African American life experiences and that there are no African American actors of sufficient stature to carry a movie in the foreign market.

These decisions, some sociologists feel, have far-reaching effects. To begin with, they limit the opportunities of minorities, who are already underrepresented in the entertainment media. Other sociologists worry that this favoring of formulaic action movies "dumbs down" and cheapens American culture.

Rush Hour, starring Jackie Chan and Chris Tucker, was one movie that touched on African American life and had large foreign box office returns.

Think About It

1. **Analyzing Information** Why are Hollywood executives susceptible to the demands of foreign markets?
2. **Evaluating** How would the functionalist interpretation of Hollywood decision-making differ from the conflict interpretation?

Exporting American Movies. American movies account for 80 to 95 percent of the foreign markets for films, except in France and Hong Kong, where the percentage drops to about 60. At the same time, foreign films account for only about a 2 percent share of the American film market. In addition, the spread of technology is increasing the number of foreign markets for American movies.

ACTIVITY: Have students discuss how the growing export of American films may be affecting other cultures.

Think About It Answers

1. Foreign box office receipts for American-made movies are large and expected to keep growing.

2. Functionalists might argue that making decisions based upon both the foreign and domestic markets may help to strengthen international ties. Conflict theorists, on the other hand, might argue that changing domestic movies to suit foreign markets hurts American minorities who are already underrepresented in the entertainment media.

390

Percentage of Households with Access to Media	
Type of Media	**Percent**
Radio	99%
Television	98%
Cable Television	68%
Videocassette Recorder	85%
Computer	56.5%
Internet	50.5%

Source: *Statistical Abstract of the United States, 2002,* Nielsen Media Research, National Telecommunications and Information Administration

INTERPRETING TABLES Almost every American has access to a radio and television in their household. However, because of the costs, less than half the population has access to the Internet. *How do you think that lack of access might affect society?*

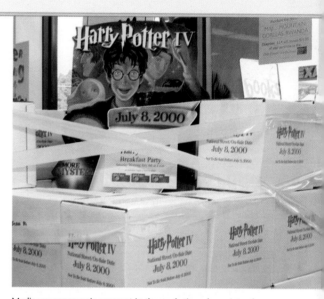

Media convergence is apparent in the marketing of a variety of mass-media products such as books, movies, music, and Internet sites that are all tied together.

discs (CDs), cassette tapes, vinyl records, and music videos. CDs dominate the sound-recording industry, accounting for nearly 90 percent of the market, other new technologies such as MP3s and satellite radio receivers have also grown in popularity.

As of 2001 there were about 10,700 commercial and some 2,200 noncommercial radio stations in the United States. These stations broadcast a variety of formats—everything from news and talk to classic rock to religion. Radio broadcasts have a large audience. Some 99 percent of the homes in the United States have a radio, with an average of six radios per home. Americans older than the age of 12 listen to close to 21 hours a week of radio on average. Every day at least 75 percent of Americans aged 12 or older tune into radio.

Visual Media Movies, television, videocassettes, and DVDs make up the visual media. American movie studios release between 400 and 500 movies a year. These movies fall into a number of genres, or artistic categories, including action, comedy, horror, romance, science fiction and fantasy, and westerns. They attracted an audience of about 1 billion people to the more than 37,000 movie screens at 7,421 theaters across the country, generating a box office take of more than $7 billion in 2000.

Of all media, television reaches one of the largest audiences in the United States. Some 98 percent of American homes have television sets, with an average of two sets per home. About 68 percent of these homes are wired for cable television, which provides a wide variety of channels for viewing. The majority of cable households receive 54 or more channels. The average

American household spends considerable time watching television—about seven and one-half hours a day.

In the past, the major broadcast networks dominated television in the United States. The networks offer a variety of programming, including comedies, dramas, quiz shows, "reality" shows, sports, children's programs, and news. Although some cable TV channels offer a mix of programming, many more focus on a particular genre, such as news, sports, cartoons, religion, music, or movies. Recently, cable TV channels have given the broadcast networks stiff competition, and the network-viewing audience has declined significantly.

About 85 percent of American households that have television also have videocassette recorders (VCRs). People use VCRs to record television shows for replay later or to view movies rented or purchased from video stores. Home video has greatly affected the movie industry. Revenues from the rental and sale of movies on video are about twice the revenues from ticket sales at movie theaters. The sale of DVDs has also led to an increase in visual-media use. In 2000, Americans bought more than $80 million worth of DVDs.

Online Media The most recent media development is the Internet. The Internet and the World Wide Web offer many services, including e-mail, online chat and discussion groups, and online shopping. The billions of sites on the Web deal with practically every imaginable subject.

A recent study found that about 50 percent of American households, or more than 100 million people, have access to the Internet. Of those households with Internet

Teacher to Teacher

Sarah Quinlin-Sheridan of Clarks Summit, Pennsylvania, suggested the following activity: Have students work in groups to conduct research on 24-hour cable news channels such as CNN. Students should examine how popular such channels are, reasons why people watch these channels, the quality of news coverage provided on these channels, and the effects of these channels on different institutions in society, such as politics and the economy. Then have each group create a report or multimedia presentation about its findings.

COOPERATIVE LEARNING , BLOCK SCHEDULING

CONNECTING to Economics

Have students conduct research on the various holdings of some of the large media companies, such as AOL Time Warner. Then ask students to imagine that they work for the company and are creating a brochure for potential stockholders interested in investing in mass media. The brochure should list the various media companies that the parent corporation holds, provide a brief description of each of these companies, and explain why investing in mass media and in this corporation in particular will be profitable now and in the future. **BLOCK SCHEDULING**

---

access, about 60 percent—some 60 million people—are considered active users. On average, they log on about 16 times a month, spending close to 30 minutes on the Internet during each session. Another study found that the majority of people accessing the Internet use it to e-mail friends and family. People are also increasingly using the Internet to shop, as a source of information for work, for entertainment-related activities, and as a source for news.

Convergence Some media specialists believe that the mass media are merging and are no longer separate entities. This **media convergence** is the result, in part, of the integration of the different media technologies. For example, the print media have adopted computer technology. Newspapers are now typeset and laid out by computers. In addition, many daily newspapers have Web sites. Book

publishers are also using computers for typesetting. Furthermore, CD-ROM and online versions of books, called e-books, are becoming more popular. Many radio stations use online technology to make their broadcasts available on the Internet, and some cable companies offer Internet access as part of their television packages.

The merging of media companies has also contributed to this convergence. Movie companies have purchased book publishers, telephone companies have taken over cable television operations, and newspapers have bought Web search engines. Perhaps the most notable of these mergers came in 2000, when the Internet service provider America Online merged with Time Warner, a company with holdings in print, audio, and visual media.

Some scholars think that this convergence may lead to the development of a single communications medium based on computer technology. However, others think

Sociology in the World Today

E-books and Copy Protection. Electronic books, or e-books, often employ a form of electronic copy prevention. Under the Digital Millennium Copyright Act (DMCA), it is illegal in the United States to circumvent copy prevention devices. In 2001, Russian programmer Dmitry Sklyarov wrote a program that circumvents the copy prevention on one type of e-book reader. Because Sklyarov resides in Russia, he was not subject to U.S. law. However, when Sklyarov came to the United States for a programming conference, he was arrested for violating the DMCA. The charges were later dropped in exchange for Sklyarov's testimony against his employer.

CRITICAL THINKING

How does this case illustrate some of the societal issues that technological advances in mass media can create?

ANSWER: Students might note that new forms of mass media can create problems related to copyright protection, international relations, and law.

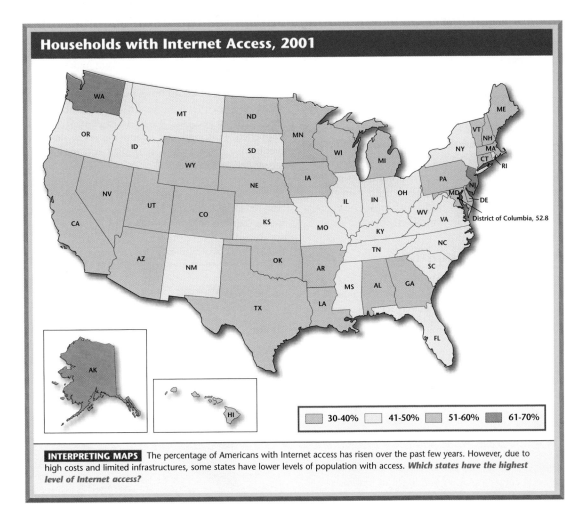

Households with Internet Access, 2001

District of Columbia, 52.8

Legend: 30-40% | 41-50% | 51-60% | 61-70%

INTERPRETING MAPS The percentage of Americans with Internet access has risen over the past few years. However, due to high costs and limited infrastructures, some states have lower levels of population with access. *Which states have the highest level of Internet access?*

Map Answer

the states that appear in purple and green

SUGGESTION 1: Have each student create a chart or visual diagram that describes the functionalist perspective and the conflict perspective of mass media and provides five supporting examples for each perspective. Call on volunteers to share their examples with the class as you write them on the chalkboard. Then have each student write a one-page essay contrasting the two perspectives of mass media and expressing which he or she supports or if he or she supports a blending of the two approaches. Remind students to provide reasons and examples to support their positions.

SUGGESTION 2: Discuss the functionalist perspective and the conflict perspective of mass media with the class. Then draw a horizontal line on the chalkboard, labeling the far left side of the line *Functionalist* and the far right side of the line *Conflict*. Ask students to suggest viewpoints or examples that support the functionalist perspective, the conflict perspective, and perspectives that fall somewhere in between. Record students' responses on the continuum on the chalkboard. Challenge students to defend the functionalist perspective, the conflict perspective, or a view of their own.

Did You Know?

The World Wide Web was developed in 1989 by Tim Berners-Lee and his coworkers at CERN, a scientific organization in Geneva, Switzerland. The first graphical-based Web browser was created in 1993 by Marc Andreesen and others at the National Center for Supercomputing Applications in Illinois.

Chart Answer

64 percent (100 – 36 percent of Americans who infrequently or never watch movies)

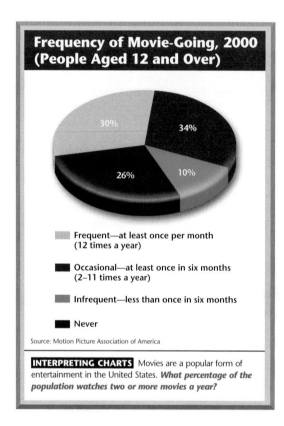

Frequency of Movie-Going, 2000 (People Aged 12 and Over)

- 34%
- 30%
- 26%
- 10%

■ Frequent—at least once per month (12 times a year)

■ Occasional—at least once in six months (2–11 times a year)

■ Infrequent—less than once in six months

■ Never

Source: Motion Picture Association of America

INTERPRETING CHARTS Movies are a popular form of entertainment in the United States. *What percentage of the population watches two or more movies a year?*

that convergence will have the opposite result. The merging of computer technology with elements of print, audio, and visual media may create new media forms and broaden communications choices.

Media Consumption

Americans spend a lot of time using media. If you look at the pie chart on page 388, you will see how many Americans use those media hours. Television is by far the most popular medium. Most Americans spend nearly as much time watching television as they do using all other media.

Individual media usage varies and is strongly influenced by such social factors as age, education, and income. For example, young people are more likely to go to the movies. In 2000, people younger than 30 accounted for some 40 percent of all movie admissions in the United States. However, they are less likely to read newspapers than are older people. Newspaper and book readership increases with education. People with higher incomes are also more likely to have access to cable television and the Internet.

Mass Media— Differing Perspectives

What purpose do mass media fulfill? Different sociological perspectives have contrasting views on this question. The functionalist perspective focuses on the ways in which mass media help to preserve social stability. The conflict perspective, on the other hand, focuses on how mass media serve to maintain the existing social order.

The Functionalist Perspective Functionalist sociologists believe that the mass media perform functions that support the stability and smooth operation of society. These functions include keeping track of what is happening in the world, interpreting information, transmitting cultural values, and entertaining people.

To be productive members of society, people need to know what is going on around them. Through e-mail, family members and friends can let each other know what is happening in their lives. Newspapers, magazines, and news programs on television, radio, and the Internet keep people informed of local, national, and world events. In addition to providing information, media also interpret it. Movies, television, and books—both fictional and factual—try to explain why events happened. Editorials and commentaries in the news media also discuss the importance and meaning of recent developments.

Mass media influence socialization. Some media—such as school textbooks—make a conscious effort to pass on society's basic skills, values, and beliefs. Other media transmit culture inadvertently. For example, the

Electronic media can serve many functional purposes, such as providing a means to communicate, a source of news, and an educational tool.

Case Studies and Other True Stories

� TEACH

Have students read the feature Mass Media and Presidential Politics and answer the questions under Think About It. Then review with students the names of several U.S. presidents who served before presidential debates began to be televised. (You might want to prepare such a list in advance.) Have students discuss which of these presidents might or might not have been elected in the television age and why. (For example, do students think that Franklin D. Roosevelt would be elected today?)

◧ EXTEND

Organize the class into groups and assign each one a different U.S. president, starting with John F. Kennedy. Have each group conduct research into the role that television played in the assigned presidency. Examples include the Nixon/Kennedy debates, Reagan's "Morning in America" campaign, and Clinton's musical appearances on late night television. **COOPERATIVE LEARNING**, **BLOCK SCHEDULING**

Case Studies
AND OTHER TRUE STORIES

MASS MEDIA AND PRESIDENTIAL POLITICS

Mass media—particularly television—have changed the nature of American presidential politics. According to political scientist Doris A. Graber, politics in the age of television is characterized by a decline in the influence of political parties, an increase in the role played by the media in candidate selection, an attraction for candidates who "televise well," and an emphasis on made-for-media campaigning.

Declining Party Influence

In the 1940s, when social scientists first began to examine the effects of the media on presidential campaigns, party affiliation was the most important factor that voters used to determine whether they would vote for a candidate. A candidate's personality and his or her stand on the issues ranked third and fourth on the list of factors of interest to voters. Today personality has replaced political affiliation as the most important determinant of voter appeal.

One reason that party affiliation has dropped in importance is the ability of candidates to speak directly to the public. Today candidates can reach voters in their homes through television advertising and through news coverage. Consequently, candidates are no longer dependent on their political parties to express their views.

The Media as "King Makers"

As candidate personality has come to play a stronger role in influencing voter opinions, the power of the media to influence which candidates are successful has also increased. Early in the primaries, members of the media state which candidates have a chance of winning and which issues will be of importance in the campaign. The media's efforts are assisted by the use of public-opinion polls. Candidates who perform better than early polls predicted they would be perceived as winners and thus receive added news coverage. On the other hand, candidates who perform below expectations often receive little media attention.

Because of the need to attract media support, the skill with which a candidate can play to the cameras is an important consideration when recruiting candidates to run for president. It has often been noted that Abraham Lincoln—with his rough facial features and lanky appearance—would have had considerable difficulty getting elected in the age of television. Image is so important that candidates hire full-time media advisers and acting coaches to help them develop effective television personalities.

The importance of media coverage has also changed the way candidates campaign. Candidates now plan campaign appearances with media exposure in mind. Thus, they tend to favor press conferences, talk show appearances, and trips to interesting places—events that will play well to wide audiences.

The Media and Election 2000

The 2000 presidential-election campaign illustrates the enormous influence of the media on American politics. With candidates George W. Bush and Al Gore running neck-and-neck in opinion polls for much of the campaign, getting the message out to the voters became very important. The two campaigns responded by airing some 2,000 hours of television advertising from June 1 to election day. Much of this advertising was aimed at "toss-up" states—states that both candidates had a chance to win. The campaigns further focused their efforts on large media outlets in these states. For example, the cities of Albuquerque, Detroit, Philadelphia, Portland, and Seattle were hit with more than 40,000 ads at a combined cost of $40 million to the campaigns. This sum amounted to nearly 20 percent of the two campaigns' total spending on advertising. Both candidates hoped that such huge spending and intense media exposure would prove to be a winning strategy for them.

Think About It

1. **Evaluating** How has television coverage affected the way that presidential candidates campaign?

2. **Supporting a Point of View** Do you think the media has too great an influence on presidential elections? Why or why not?

Interdisciplinary Connection

HISTORY

The Kennedy-Nixon Debates. The first televised presidential debate in the United States took place in 1960. Democratic candidate John F. Kennedy debated Republican candidate, Richard Nixon. In the debate, Kennedy appeared fit, tan, and healthy. Nixon, who had recently been in the hospital for a knee injury, appeared underweight and sickly. He wore an ill-fitting shirt and no make-up. The majority of Americans who listened to the debate on the radio declared Nixon the winner. However, the majority of Americans who watched the debate on television chose Kennedy. Many experts attribute Kennedy's later victory in the election to the televised debate.

ACTIVITY: Have students discuss how politicians' skills at using mass media affect their ability to win campaigns.

Think About It Answers

1. Television has led to an emphasis on made-for-media campaigning.

2. Answers will vary, but students should support their positions with examples from the text.

SUGGESTION 3: Organize students into pairs and have each pair write a script for a dialogue in which two sociologists describe and debate the functionalist perspective and the conflict perspective of mass media. Dialogues should address the main points of each perspective and provide several arguments and examples in support of each one. The dialogue should go back and forth between speakers several times. Then select the one or two best dialogues and have the authors perform them for the class.

COOPERATIVE LEARNING

SPOTLIGHT *on News Media*

Have students conduct a survey outside of class to determine what types of media the people in their local community use most often to stay informed of the latest news. Have the class work together to create the survey questions. Then produce photocopies of the surveys for students and have each student survey at least five adults. The survey should ask respondents to report how many hours per day they spend examining the news and where they get their news, such as radio, television, or newspapers. Once the results are tallied, lead a class discussion analyzing them. Challenge students to speculate how the results might be different in 10 years.

BLOCK SCHEDULING

Case Study

Television and Public Opinion. Shanto Iyengar and Donald Kinder conducted experiments to examine how television shapes public opinion in the United States. The researchers controlled which news programs subjects viewed to evaluate the effects of television viewing. Iyengar and Kinder found that television's power to influence viewers is strongest for complex and unfamiliar issues. In other words, the more familiar viewers were with an issue, the less likely they were to be influenced by television reports about it.

CRITICAL THINKING

According to this study, for what types of issues is television most influential?

ANSWER: for complex and unfamiliar issues

Table Answers

white men; underrepresents women and other minority groups

Technology Resources

 CNN Presents Sociology: Changing Technology and the Family

Demography of All Characters in Prime-Time Drama Programs (In Percent)		
Sex	Males	63.1
	Females	36.7
Race and Ethnicity	White	81.7
	African American	12.3
	Hispanic	2.6
	Asian American	1.4
	Other Race	2.0
Age	Older person	0.6
Disability	Mentally Disabled	1.2
	Physically Disabled	0.7

Source: Screen Actors Guild

INTERPRETING TABLES Television producers have been challenged by media critics for not including minorities in their programs. *What groups of people are most represented on television shows? How do you think this compares with current population figures?*

Functionalist sociologists might consider family television viewing a form of interaction and bonding.

stated purpose of a television police drama may be to entertain. However, it also reminds viewers that the United States is a society of laws.

Entertainment is probably the most obvious function of mass media. The majority of TV channels and radio formats are designed to entertain rather than to inform. The same is true of movies. Most people go to the movies and listen to sound recordings for entertainment, not for information.

The Conflict Perspective Conflict sociologists believe that the purpose of social institutions is to maintain the present social order. Some sociologists believe that the role of mass media is to persuade people to accept the existing power structure. Some conflict sociologists assert that media can accomplish this because they are able to control the flow and interpretation of information. In other words, media can decide what information is provided and how it is presented. Because the media are owned by members of the power elite, conflict sociologists argue, this information and its presentation represents the power elite's point of view.

Other conflict sociologists believe that mass media in the United States encourage the acceptance of the power structure by encouraging a culture of consumerism. According to this theory, if people are busy increasing their collection of material possessions, they have no time to think about society's inequalities.

Certain conflict sociologists suggest that the knowledge gap provides an example of how media maintain social inequality. The **knowledge-gap hypothesis**, first advanced by Phillip Tichenor, George Donohue, and Clarice Olien, states that as new information enters society, wealthy and better-educated members acquire it at a faster rate than poor and less-educated people. Therefore, a gap in knowledge widens between these two segments of society. This gap develops even if access to information is equal.

Studies show that a **digital divide**—the gap between those with access to new technologies and those without—exists and may be widening. Access to computers and online media is of particular concern. The groups that lack access include minorities, the children of single mothers, and people with lower incomes and less education. Steps are being taken to close this digital divide, most notably by providing schools with computers and Internet connections. However, such actions may not help to narrow the knowledge gap. Some studies indicate that the "information rich"—those who have better information skills and more resources—are likely to benefit more from greater access to the new technology than are the "information poor."

Some conflict theorists suggest that the misrepresentation and nonrepresentation of minorities in the media

TEACH OBJECTIVE 3

To help students identify some contemporary mass media issues, copy the graphic organizer at the right onto the chalkboard, omitting the italicized answers. Have students copy and complete the organizer. Discuss the answers with the class. Next, organize students into groups and assign each group one of the issues. Have the groups discuss their issues and make notes of students' various points of view. Then call on a spokesperson from each group to summarize the group's discussion for the class.

ENGLISH LANGUAGE LEARNERS , COOPERATIVE LEARNING

Contemporary Mass-Media Issues

- *children watching too much television*
- *violence on television*
- *ratings systems and parental controls*
- *advertising targeting children*
- *disengagement from direct social contact*
- *decline in social capital*
- *Internet causing decline in face-to-face relationships*
- *the power of the media; agenda-setting*

INTERPRETING VISUALS Many conflict sociologists who study mass media have expressed concern over the influence of advertising on children. *How does this cartoon illustrate the concern held by conflict sociologists?*

reinforces social inequality. Several studies of the print media have found that coverage of minorities is limited. One found that in day-to-day coverage, the mainstream media have few stories on minorities, except for those that involve crime, sports, or entertainment. Some of these stories contained stereotypes and biased reporting.

Studies of the entertainment media have made similar findings. A review of prime-time television in the mid-1990s found that only 2 percent of the characters were Hispanic, and most of these played minor roles. A survey of women and minorities on television noted that women, Hispanics, Asian Americans, low-income wage earners, senior citizens, and people with disabilities are all under-represented. Some sociologists are concerned that the absence of minorities from the media may encourage minority children to be less ambitious and expect less from life. Others argue that stereotypical coverage of minorities may encourage white Americans to view minorities negatively. As more attention has been focused on the depiction of minorities in mass media, some effort has been made to increase the presence of minorities in positive roles.

Some Contemporary Mass-Media Issues

One of the major topics covered by mass media is the media themselves. Stories abound on the relationships between the media and a host of social issues—everything from teen suicide to the perceived breakup of the family. Media critics have focused on the effect that media have on children, how the media affect civic life, and the power that media wield.

Mass Media and Children Most children spend an average of about 28 hours each week watching television. It is the primary after-school activity for most students. Many social scientists and the general public express a strong interest in how television affects children. One area of concern is the connection between television violence and aggressive behavior among young people. Dozens of studies have been conducted on this subject over the years. The findings of these studies include the following:

- Television depicts a great deal of violence.
- Television violence encourages viewers to act in aggressive ways and to see aggression as a valid way to solve problems.
- Television violence encourages viewers to be less sensitive to the suffering of others.
- Television violence appears to make viewers fearful of the world around them and less trustful of others.

By the 1990s the U.S. government and the American public began to pressure the television industry to do something

Television Rating System

Rating	Description
TV Y	Programs appropriate for all children.
TV Y7	Programs suitable for children aged seven and over.
TV G	Programs suitable for all ages.
TV PG	Programs that may be unsuitable for younger children. Parental guidance suggested.
TV 14	Programs contain material that may be unsuitable for children under the age of 14.
TV MA	Programs specifically designed for viewing by adults.

INTERPRETING TABLES Television programs are required to label their shows according to content ratings. *How do you think these ratings might help parents limit the negative effects of mass media on children?*

396

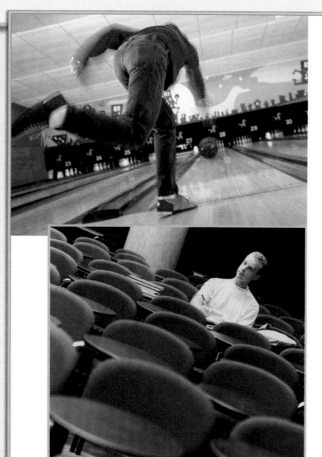

INTERPRETING VISUALS In his book *Bowling Alone*, Robert Putnam argued that Americans have become more disconnected from social life and civic duty. *How do you think mass media has influenced this trend?*

about violent programming. In response, television companies established a rating system in 1997. The ratings provide parents with information about the content and age-appropriateness of programs. In addition, the Telecommunications Act, passed by Congress in 1996, requires all new televisions to have a V-chip. This V-chip allows the viewer to block reception of unwanted programming.

Another area of concern is the relationship between television and performance at school. A study of fourth, eighth, and eleventh graders found a link between the amount of time spent watching television and test scores. Students who watched five or more hours of television scored lower than students who watched very little. Exactly what this link means is unclear. It may indicate that heavy television watching contributes to poor performance at school. Or it may simply show that students who perform poorly in school watch a lot of television.

Regardless of the medium they use—magazines, radio, television, or the Internet—children are bombarded by advertisements. The average child sees between 20,000 and 40,000 commercials each year on television alone. Businesses spend more than $2 billion on advertising directly targeted at children. This figure is of great concern to many people because they believe that children are a vulnerable audience. In other words, children do not have the information or skills to make objective decisions about advertisements. This is particularly true of children who watch a lot of television because they accept advertising claims more readily. In addition, many younger children cannot distinguish between advertisements and regular programming. There have been calls for advertisers to take more care when developing commercials targeted at children. For example, the Telecommunications Act of 1996 encourages advertisers to use a rating system similar to that used by the television companies.

Mass Media's Effect on Civic and Social Life In his book *Bowling Alone* political scientist Robert Putnam argues that since the 1960s Americans have become more and more disconnected from civic and social life. To illustrate this disengagement, Putnam offers an array of statistics. Voting and participation in political activities have fallen over the years. Membership in civic organizations such as the PTA has shown a decline. So, too, has church attendance. In addition, people are entertaining family and friends less often than in the past. Putnam argues that this disengagement has resulted in a decline in the country's social capital. **Social capital** refers to social networks and the reciprocal norms associated with these networks that encourage people to do things for each other. Social capital includes everything from the civic, social, and religious organizations to which people belong to the friendship networks people develop in their neighborhoods, schools, and sports teams.

Putnam attributes a good part of the decline in social capital—perhaps as much as 25 percent—to television. He points out that television is everywhere. Practically every household in the country has a television set, and most have at least two. Americans spend a lot of time in front of these sets, perhaps as much as 40 percent of their free time. Watching television is the primary nighttime activity of the vast majority of adult Americans—often at the expense of most social activities outside the home. As a consequence, television privatizes people's leisure time. Putnam suggests that television watchers tend to be loners, not joiners. The more TV people watch, the less likely they are to participate in civic and social activities.

According to recent studies, the Internet may also encourage disengagement from civil and social life. A two-year study of 169 Internet users found that the more

CLOSE

In a round-robin discussion, ask each student to name a form of mass media or communication technology and state how that form has influenced or affected individuals or society. Continue until students have touched on all of the main points in the section.

REVIEW AND ASSESS

Have students complete the **Section 2 Review** on p. 397. As **Alternative Assessment**, you may want to use the mass-media illustrated time line or the perspectives of mass media article in this section's lessons.

RETEACH

Organize students into groups and have each group create a game that covers the key concepts in this section. Each group should create brief instructions for its game. Then have each group play its game to review this section.

ENGLISH LANGUAGE LEARNERS , COOPERATIVE LEARNING

EXTEND

Have students work in small groups to create and present a mock news presentation in the style of one of the following forms of mass media: 24-hour cable news channels, local or network news programs, an entertainment news show, or a radio news broadcast.

COOPERATIVE LEARNING , BLOCK SCHEDULING

time people spent online, the less interaction they had with family members and friends. A 1999 survey of more than 4,000 Internet users drew similar conclusions. Some people have challenged the findings in these reports. They point out that social networks consist of more than people's face-to-face relationships and that the Internet provides a different form of social life.

The Power of the Media One major criticism of the news media is that they wield too much power. A poll taken in 2000 found that more than 75 percent of the American population believes that the news media have too much power and influence in politics. Observers of the media who agree often cite two examples of news media power—the spiral of silence and agenda setting.

Sociologist Elisabeth Noelle-Neumann suggests that the media are incredibly powerful sources of information that can shape public opinion. She points out that the different forms of news media tend to cover the same stories, often bombarding the public with the same information and the same opinions on these stories. As more and more people accept these opinions, people who disagree are less likely to voice their views. Noelle-Neumann believes that this **spiral of silence** gives the media even more power to influence the way people think.

Some people propose that the news media do not tell the public what to think but what to think about. They argue that the media sets the boundaries of public debate by deciding which issues will receive coverage and which will not, a process known as **agenda setting**. Agenda setting is undertaken by **gatekeepers**—media executives, editors, or reporters who can open or close the "gate" on a particular news story.

However, many people believe that the power of the media to influence opinions and debate is greatly overstated. Some people point out that there are simply too many news outlets for the media to effectively control the flow of information. The public will always be able to find alternative views of news and events. Others suggest that messages from the media do not directly influence behavior or opinions. Rather, this takes place through a multi-step flow of communication. The messages are first reviewed and evaluated by **opinion leaders**—respected individuals in the community—who then pass on the information to friends and acquaintances. Still other media watchers point out that the power of the media is limited by the public's selective reception because people tend to avoid news stories that challenge their beliefs. Nonetheless, mass media, whatever their real power is, play a large role in American society.

SECTION 2 REVIEW

1. Define and explain
mass media
information society
media convergence
knowledge-gap hypothesis
digital divide
social capital
spiral of silence
agenda setting
gatekeepers
opinion leaders

2. Categorizing Copy the graphic organizer below. Use it to evaluate how different communication techniques in mass media have influenced the perceptions, attitudes, and behaviors of people and groups.

	Types of Media Used	Influence on People and Groups
News		
Opinion Pieces and Editorials		
Advertising		

Homework Practice Online
keyword: SL3 HP15

3. Finding the Main Idea
   a. List in chronological order the intellectual and technological innovations that marked the institutionalization of mass media.
   b. Describe and give examples of some recent issues concerning mass media.

4. Writing and Critical Thinking
   Supporting a Point of View How do you think new communication technologies have changed the norms and behaviors of certain groups in the United States? How has individual and societal behavior changed because of these new technologies? Explain your answer in one or two paragraphs.
   Consider:
   • the characteristics of new communication technologies
   • social and behavioral changes caused by new communication technologies
   • the digital divide that limits access to new communication technologies

CHAPTER 15 REVIEW

ANSWERS

WRITING A SUMMARY
See the section subtitles for the main topics in this chapter.

IDENTIFYING PEOPLE AND IDEAS

1. an objective and systematic way of collecting information and arriving at conclusions

2. the norm that scientific research should be judged solely on the basis of quality

3. the norm that no scientific finding or theory is exempt from questioning

4. the norm that all scientific knowledge should be made available to everyone in the scientific community

5. the set of shared concepts, methods, and assumptions that make up scientific reality at any point in time

6. instruments of communication that reach large audiences with no personal contact between those sending the information and those receiving it

7. the merging of mass media

8. the gap between those with access to new technologies and those without

9. a dynamic whereby people who disagree with opinions in the mass media are less likely to voice their views

10. a process whereby the media sets the boundaries of public debate by deciding which issues to cover

CHAPTER 15

Review and Assessment Resources

- Chapter 15 Review, pp. 398–99
- Chapter Review Activities with Answer Key
- Global Skill Builder CD–ROM
- Chapter 15 Test Generator (on the One-Stop Planner)
- Chapter 15 Test (Form A or B)
- Alternative Assessment Handbook
- HRW Go site

 REVIEW

Have students complete the **Chapter 15 Review** on pp. 398–99.

ASSESS

Use one of the chapter tests to assess students' understanding of the content. For **Alternative Assessment**, see the **Alternative Assessment Handbook**.

UNDERSTANDING MAIN IDEAS

1. Renaissance, printing press, Age of Exploration, Protestant Reformation

2. First, advances in astronomy and mathematics were needed to assist navigation. Second, explorers brought back strange plants, animals, and diseases that sparked scientific curiosity.

3. urbanization, rising literacy, and advertising

4. Students might note that young people are more likely to go to the movies but less likely to read newspapers. Newspaper and book readership increase with age, education, and income. People with higher incomes are more likely to have cable and Internet access. New technologies have broadened communications choices.

5. keeping track of what is happening in the world, interpreting information, transmitting cultural values, and entertaining people

6. As new information enters society, wealthy and better-educated members acquire it at a faster rate than poor and less-educated people.

7. It has led to less participation in civic and social activities.

THINKING CRITICALLY

1. The Enlightenment supported reason over religion, and its main tool was the scientific method. The central purpose of industrialization was progress, and science was seen as a tool of progress.

398

CHAPTER

 15 Review

 Writing a Summary

Using standard grammar, spelling, sentence structure, and punctuation, summarize the information in this chapter.
Consider:
- the role of science in American society
- the effect of mass media on Americans

 Identifying People and Ideas

Identify the following people or terms and use them in appropriate sentences.

1. scientific method
2. universalism
3. organized skepticism
4. communalism
5. paradigm
6. mass media
7. media convergence
8. digital divide
9. spiral of silence
10. agenda setting

Understanding Main ideas

Section 1 (pp. 376–85)

1. What four factors contributed to the rebirth of science in Europe?

2. How did world exploration influence societal behavior and the growth of scientific learning?

Section 2 (pp. 386–97)

3. What forces combined to encourage the development of the urban newspaper?

4. How do age, education, and income affect media consumption? How have new technologies affected this trend?

5. What functions do the media serve?

6. According to conflict sociologists, how does the knowledge gap help maintain social inequality?

7. According to Robert Putnam, how has television led to a decline in the social capital?

 Thinking Critically

1. **Identifying Cause and Effect** What effect did the Enlightenment and the Industrial Revolution have on the development of modern science?

2. **Analyzing Information** Why might Robert K. Merton's norms of science be described as an ideal type for scientific behavior?

3. **Drawing Inferences and Conclusions** How might conflicting views of reality influence the pursuit of science?

4. **Supporting a Point of View** Do you think the media wield too much power and influence? Why or why not?

5. **Evaluating** What steps might you take to ensure that advertising directly targeting children is ethical and age-appropriate? Explain your answer.

6. **Drawing Inferences and Conclusions** How have norms and behaviors of subculture groups changed because of advances in science and technology?

 Writing About Sociology

1. **Evaluating** Monitor several newspapers, current events magazines, or television news shows for a week or two to see how many news items concern current ethical issues resulting from scientific discoveries. Note the issues that news items cover. Write a brief report on your findings, illustrating it with quotations and visual materials from the news items.

2. **Summarizing** Consider the changes that American society has faced concerning the development of new communications technologies such as cellular phones and the Internet. Use the graphic organizer below to help explain how these devices have influenced individual behavior and societal behavior as a whole and how they have influenced the norms and behavior of select subgroups.

RETEACH

Select students with a solid grasp of the material presented in the chapter to act as a panel of "experts" to answer other students' questions about science and mass media. Have the other students prepare questions based on key concepts in the chapter, gaps in their notes, or topics they do not understand. Then have students ask the expert panel their questions. During the question-and-answer session, encourage students to take notes. Expand upon or correct panelists' answers as necessary.

ENGLISH LANGUAGE LEARNERS , COOPERATIVE LEARNING

SOCIOLOGY PROJECTS

1. Using Sociological Imagination Pair students and ask them to imagine that they are scientists working on similar research. Have one student play the role of a scientist who tries to follow Merton's norms, and the other play the role of a competitive and secretive scientist. Students should play out a discussion between the two scientists.

2. Connecting to the Arts Have students conduct research on the effects of mass media on the arts. Has media exposure increased public awareness and appreciation of the arts? If so, how? Instruct students to create collages that show the impact of mass media on the visual arts, dance, theater, music, and other aspects of the art world.

BUILDING SOCIAL STUDIES SKILLS

Interpreting Tables

Study the table below. Use it to answer the following questions.

To Report or Not to Report
Reasons Journalists Avoid a Story

Reasons	Print Journalists	Broadcast Journalists
Too Complicated for Audience	47	75
Made Fun of by Other Journalists	40	29
Damaging to the Financial Interests of the News Organization	23	35

Source: Pew Research Center for the People & the Press

1. Journalists may have many different reasons to not report a story. The reason that print and broadcast journalists most often cited for not reporting a story was that
   a. they would be made fun of by other journalists.
   b. it was too complicated for the audience.
   c. the story was too financially damaging.
   d. the story was too damaging and too complicated.

2. How does the information on the table relate to the argument that the media serve as a gatekeeper of information?

Analyzing Primary Sources

The following excerpt explores the portrayal of class in American mass media. Read the excerpt and then answer the questions that follow.

❝Of the various social and cultural forces in our society, the mass media is arguably the most influential in molding public consciousness. Americans spend an average of twenty-eight hours per week watching television. They also spend an undetermined number of hours reading periodicals, listening to the radio, and going to the movies. Unlike other cultural and socializing institutions, ownership and control of the mass media is highly concentrated. Twenty-three corporations own more than one-half of all the daily newspapers, magazines, movie studios, and radio and televisions outlets in the U.S. . . . This media plays a key role in defining our cultural tastes, helping us locate ourselves in history, establishing our national identity, and ascertaining the range of national and social possibilities. . . . The United States is the most highly stratified society in the industrialized world. Class distinctions operate in virtually every aspect of our lives, determining the nature of our work, the quality of our schooling, and the health and safety of our loved ones. Yet remarkably, we, as a nation, retain illusions about living in an egalitarian society. We maintain these illusions, in large part, because the media hides gross inequities from public view.❞

3. According to the author, why do many Americans think the United States has a society without classes?
   a. The media shows too many different classes.
   b. People choose not to watch shows on class.
   c. Americans are not interested in class.
   d. The media hides class inequities.

4. How might the shrinking of the number of media companies affect society?

SOCIOLOGY PROJECTS

Cooperative Learning

Research in Sociology Working in a group with two or three other students, research an incident of fraud or a hoax in science. A starting point for research might be Alexander Kohn's study *False Prophets*. Present your findings to the class in an illustrated report. In the concluding paragraph to your report, note the effect of fraud and hoaxes on the institution of science.

internet connect

Internet Activity: go.hrw.com
KEYWORD: SL3 SC15
Choose an activity on science or mass media to:
- write a theoretical profile of an historic scientist.
- research recent ethical issues in science and make predictions on the future of the field.
- create a Web page about the influence of technology on subculture groups.

---

2. because they embody the idea of perfect scientific behavior, often not met in reality

3. Views that run counter to the long-established paradigm often meet with resistance.

4. Responses will vary, but students should support their positions with examples from the text and real life.

5. Students might suggest requiring advertisers to adopt a rating system.

6. Answers will vary, but students should support their answers with examples from the text.

WRITING ABOUT SOCIOLOGY

1. Reports should discuss the ethical implications of scientific discoveries and reveal an understanding of the effects of science on society.

2. Students should exhibit an understanding of the effects of new communications technologies on society, groups, and individuals.

BUILDING SOCIAL STUDIES SKILLS

1. b

2. It shows that the media do not cover all stories but decide which ones to cover based on various factors.

3. d

4. might lead to fewer differing voices and perspectives being presented

Science and the Mass Media   **399**

399

Across Space and Time

Across Space and Time

Nazi Holocaust

The emergence of the Nazi Holocaust had its beginnings before World War II. During the 1920s Germany was reeling from the humiliating defeat it had suffered during World War I. A depression that began in 1929 further dampened the spirits of the German people, leaving them hungry for change.

Adolf Hitler, a hypnotic speaker and the charismatic leader of the Nazi Party, filled many Germans with new hope, promising them that they would once again take pride in their country. Hitler blamed the problems of Germany on Jews and communists, providing the rest of the population with scapegoats for their anger and frustration. Hitler also told the Germans that they, the "Aryans," were the master race meant to conquer the world and that all other groups of people were inferior.

Hitler's emotional speeches stirred the support of many Germans. In the German election of 1930, the Nazi Party won many seats in the parliament, but not enough to control the entire government by themselves. In 1932 Hitler's Party won two thirds of the vote. German president Paul von Hindenburg, conceding to pressure, appointed Hitler as chancellor.

Hitler then staged an elaborate scheme to achieve the popular support he needed to gain complete control. Under mysterious conditions, the parliament building was set ablaze, and the fire was blamed on a communist uprising. In the chaos that followed the blaze, Hitler was immediately granted emergency powers to deal with the communist threat. He seized this opportunity to make himself dictator and to bring the Nazi Party to power.

Germany was transformed into a police state. Opposition parties and labor unions were disbanded, and the formation of new organizations opposing the Nazi program was outlawed. Newspapers and radio stations were taken over or closed down. The Gestapo, a secret-police force, entered the homes of citizens at will, beating and silencing those who opposed the Nazi Party.

Communists, socialists, and liberals were arrested by the Nazis and forced into large prisons. These prisons were called concentration camps. Hitler, motivated by hate and prejudice against Jews, established policies designed to deprive Jewish citizens of their civil rights. Persecution against the Jews was formalized in 1935 by the passage of the Nuremberg Laws. These laws

During the final days of World War II, U.S. and Soviet troops freed many people confined in concentration camps.

outlawed marriage between Jews and other Germans and paved the way for Hitler to strip the Jews of their last remaining civil rights. Other groups, such as Roma (Gypsies), homosexuals, Jehovah's Witnesses, and Seventh-Day Adventists, became victims of Nazi persecution as well. Anyone who opposed the Nazis was suspect.

What followed was a carefully organized plan for the genocide of an entire group of people. Hitler referred to this plan as the "Final Solution" for the "Jewish problem." Millions of people were killed in the concentration camps created by the Nazis. The principles of democracy and human rights were not upheld in Nazi Germany. Many Germans accepted anti-Jewish policies of the Nazi era for the sake of national interest and self-preservation. Since the Holocaust, efforts have been made to prevent similar events from occurring. Organizations such as the United Nations have established a global justice system to prosecute officials accused of war crimes. Other groups have worked to honor the memory of those killed in the Holocaust in order to bring awareness of the atrocities that have occurred in the past and to prevent them from occurring again.

Think About It

1. **Evaluate** *How did the Nazis' abuse of power grow between 1929 and 1935?*

2. **Making Generalizations and Predictions** *What could be done to prevent future abuses of power like those conducted by the Nazis?*

Sociology in Action

TEACH

Have students read the Sociology in Action feature and then work in small groups to perform the simulation activity. To help students, you might want to provide additional questions for them to consider or a list of some possible actions to take. Then, after each group presents its document, encourage other students to speculate on what consequences the suggested actions would have actually had in Nazi Germany. Challenge students to seriously consider how they might oppose a group such as the Nazis if it came to power today. **COOPERATIVE LEARNING**

EXTEND

Have students work in groups to create museum exhibits about Holocaust "bystanders," individuals who disagreed with Nazi policies but chose not to speak out against them. Reports should focus on accounts of specific bystanders, their motivations and viewpoints, and whether their views changed over time. You might begin the activity by reading aloud the quote by Reverend Martin Niemöller, available online at "A Teacher's Guide to the Holocaust," produced by the Florida Center for Instructional Technology (http://fcit.coedu.usf.edu/holocaust/people/bystand.htm). **COOPERATIVE LEARNING, BLOCK SCHEDULING**

Sociology in Action

UNIT 4 SIMULATION

You Make the Decision . . .

Should you as a German sociologist speak out against the Holocaust?

Complete the following activity in small groups. Imagine that you are a member of a group of German sociologists in the late 1930s. Should your group speak out against the events in Nazi Germany? Work together to prepare a document declaring your position on the events in Europe.

1 Gather Information.
Use your textbook and other resources to find information about the events that occurred in Germany.

- What events might have been a cause of concern for sociologists?

- What did other sociologists say about the events?

You may want to divide different parts of the research among group members.

2 Identify Options.
After reviewing the information that you have gathered, consider what actions you might recommend. Your final decision may be easier to reach if you consider as many options as possible. Be sure to record your options for your document.

3 Predict Consequences.
Now take each option you and the members of your group came up with and consider how each decision might lead to other consequences. Ask yourself questions such as the following:

- Is it important for sociologists to be involved in political events?

- What might be the consequences of your group speaking out in Nazi Germany?

Once you have predicted the consequences, record them as notes for your document.

4 Take Action to Implement Your Decision.
After you have considered your options, you should create your document. Be sure that your document makes your decision about whether to make a statement against events in Germany. You will need to support your decision by including the information you gathered and by explaining why you rejected other options. You may want to create charts, graphs, or maps to support your decision. When you are ready, decide who in your group will present the document. Then make your presentation to the class. Good luck!

CHAPTER 16

Population and Urbanization

More than 5 billion people live in the world today, and even more growth is expected in the future. The impact of population growth is felt most strongly in cities. Population growth and urbanization have changed the face of the world, and sociologists have devoted considerable time to studying the ways in which population and urbanization have affected the social world and the nature of human interaction.

CHAPTER 17

Collective Behavior and Social Movements

In general, social behavior is patterned and predictable. People expect others to act in accord with established norms, and in most instances people do. Sometimes, however, situations occur in which the norms of behavior are unclear. Sociologists refer to the spontaneous social behavior that occurs in such situations as collective behavior. Chapter 17 examines collective behavior and the sociological theories that have been developed to explain it.

Internet Activity

Sociology developed in response to the social turmoil of the 1600s and 1700s. Thus, it is not surprising that sociologists have devoted considerable attention to the study of social change. Sociologists define social change as alterations in various aspects of a society over time. Chapter 18 examines the theories that sociologists have developed to explain how and why societies change and then examines the causes and consequences of modernization for social life and for the natural environment.

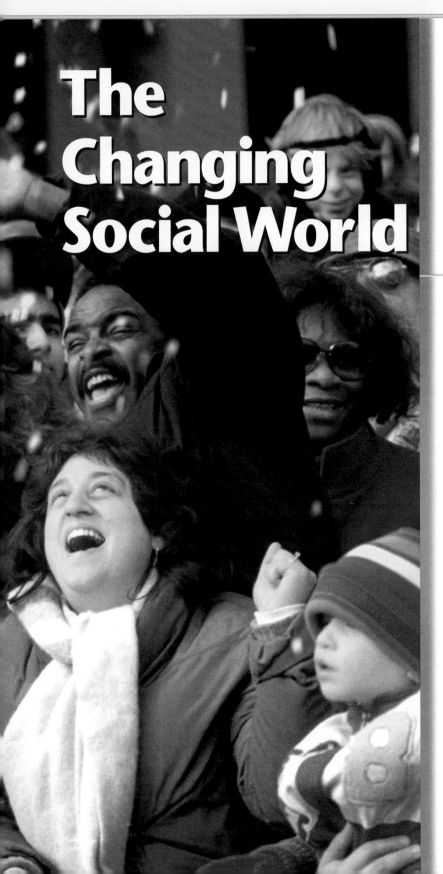

The Changing Social World

UNIT 5

CHAPTER

16 Population and Urbanization

17 Collective Behavior and Social Movements

18 Social Change and Modernization

Sociologists focus on the changes in and characteristics of the social world in which we live. Sociologists study the influence of population change, collective behavior, and social change.

403

Population and Urbanization

CHAPTER RESOURCE MANAGER

Objectives	Pacing Guide	Resources

SECTION 1:
Population Change
(pp. 406–20)

REV Section 1
Review, p. 419

- Identify factors that affect the size and structure of populations and explain how sociologists measure these factors.
- Summarize how sociologists explain population change and describe the programs that have been instituted to control population growth.

Regular
3 days

Block Scheduling
1.5 days

Block Scheduling Handbook with Team Teaching Strategies, Chapter 16

 CNN Presents Sociology: Population Change in Italy

RS Graphic Organizer 16

HRW Go site

SM Mastering Critical Thinking Skills 16

PS Readings and Case Studies in Sociology 16

E Research Projects and Activities for Teaching Sociology 16

SM Study Skills and Writing Guide

Teaching Transparency: World Population Clock

Teaching Transparency: Growth Rates and Doubling Times for Selected Nations, 2001

Teaching Transparency: Age-Sex Population Pyramid for the United States, 2000

Teaching Transparency: Models of City Structure

SECTION 2:
Urban Life
(pp. 421–31)

REV Section 2
Review, p. 431

- Explain how cities evolved and why urbanization is such a recent event.
- Identify the models that have been proposed to explain the structure of cities and summarize the theories that have been put forth to explain city life.

Regular
3 days

Block Scheduling
1.5 days

Block Scheduling Handbook with Team Teaching Strategies, Chapter 16

Chapter Review And Assessment

REV Chapter 16 Review, pp. 432–33

REV Chapter Review Activities with Answer Key

Global Skill Builder CD–ROM

Chapter 16 Test Generator (on the One-Stop Planner)

A Chapter 16 Test (Form A or B)

A Alternative Assessment Handbook

HRW Go site

Chapter Resource Key

PS Primary Sources	**A** Assessment	Video
RS Reading Support	**REV** Review	Internet
E Enrichment	Transparencies	Holt Presentation Maker Using Microsoft® PowerPoint®
SM Skills Mastery	CD–ROM	

One-Stop Planner CD–ROM

See the *One-Stop Planner* for a complete list of additional resources for students and teachers.

One-Stop Planner CD–ROM

It's easy to plan lessons, select resources, and print out materials for your students when you use the *One-Stop Planner CD–ROM with Test Generator.*

Chapter Project Preview

The following activities are included in the Chapter Review. You may want to make the suggested preparations.

CHAPTER REVIEW ACTIVITY

Linking to Community Students will work in small groups to conduct research on the pattern of urban growth for a large city in their state. Then using current and historic maps, students will create a model of urban growth that employs one or more of the three models of city structure and urban growth. Before starting the project, gather a variety of art supplies to help students create their models.

LESSON ACTIVITY

Applying Sociology Students who live in cities will correspond with sociology students in another city about topics dealing with urbanization and city life. Before starting the project, find a fellow sociology teacher in another city willing to conduct the project with you. Then work with your fellow teacher to create one set of project guidelines for students.

INTERNET ACTIVITIES

Effect of Urbanization on U.S. Institutions Students will use provided Internet links to conduct research on the effects of urbanization on American institutions and write a report based upon the research. You might want to examine the activity Web sites in advance and decide what specific information students should provide in their reports. Then, to guide students during their research, provide a skeletal report outline.

Mapping Urban Growth Students will use provided Internet links to conduct research on urban growth in several cities and then create a map illustrating the growth of one of the cities. Before starting the project, complete your coverage of urban ecology and models of city structure, on pp. 425–28 of Section 2.

Additional Resources

PRINT RESOURCES FOR TEACHERS

Aaseng, Nathan. *Overpopulation: Crisis or Challenge?* New York: Franklin Watts, 1991. Provides a historical overview of population growth and explores the problems associated with overpopulation.

Menard, Scott W., and Elizabeth Moen. *Perspectives on Population: An Introduction to Concepts and Issues.* New York: Oxford University Press, 1987. Collection of scholarly essays on basic demographic principles and concepts.

Schwab, William R. *The Sociology of Cities,* 2nd ed. Englewood Cliffs, NJ: Prentice-Hall, 1992. Overview of theory and research on urban sociology.

PRINT RESOURCES FOR STUDENTS

Cities Through Time Series. Runestone Press/Lerner Publications Company, 1999. The series includes two titles, *Daily Life in Ancient and Modern Beijing* and *Daily Life in Ancient and Modern Mexico City.* Each title explores the development of the city from prehistoric to modern times.

Palen, J. John. *The Urban World.* New York: McGraw-Hill Higher Education, 2001. The leading text in urban sociology. Provides a balanced, up-to-date, cross-cultural look at cities and suburbs around the world.

MULTIMEDIA RESOURCES

A Population Story: Collision with the Future? (vhs; 24 min.) Encyclopaedia Britannica Educational Corporation. Animated sequences and live footage combine to tell the story of a future world where overpopulation has reached a critical level.

The Rise of the American City (vhs; 32 min.) Encyclopaedia Britannica Educational Corporation. Discusses how the rise of cities has transformed the American nation and how these cities are now dealing with a host of social issues and challenges.

internet connect

HRW ONLINE RESOURCES

GO TO: go.hrw.com
Then type in a keyword.

TEACHER HOME PAGE
KEYWORD: SL3 Teacher

CHAPTER INTERNET ACTIVITIES
KEYWORD: SL3 SC16
Choose an activity to have students:
• write a report on the effect of urbanization on American institutions.
• create a quiz and answer key based on maps, graphs, charts, databases, and models about the distribution of the American population.
• create a map of the urban growth of a city.

CHAPTER ENRICHMENT LINKS
KEYWORD: SL3 CH16

ONLINE ASSESSMENT
Homework Practice
KEYWORD: SL3 HP16
Standardized Test Prep
KEYWORD: SL3 STP16
Rubrics
KEYWORD: SS Rubrics

CONTENT UPDATES
KEYWORD: SS Content Updates

HOLT PRESENTATION MAKER
KEYWORD: SL3 PPT16

ONLINE READING SUPPORT
KEYWORD: SS Strategies

CURRENT EVENTS
KEYWORD: S3 Current Events

CHAPTER

16

Population and
Urbanization

SECTION 1
Population Change

SECTION 2
Urban Life

CHAPTER REVIEW

Build on What You Know

Ask students to answer the
following questions:

**How might population growth
affect a society?**

Consider:

• urbanization
• housing and transportation
• jobs and production

**Why might the populations
of cities grow faster than
other areas?**

Consider:

• employment opportunities
• migration and immigration
• relative numbers of births
  and deaths

Internet Activity

☑ **internet** connect ≡

TOPIC: Effect of
Urbanization on U.S.
Institutions
GO TO: go.hrw.com
KEYWORD: SC3 SL16

Have students access the
Internet through the HRW Go
site to conduct research on
the effects of urbanization
on American institutions.
Then have each student
write a report based upon
the research. Students
should cite the sources
of their research in their
reports.

CHAPTER

16

Population and Urbanization

WALK

Build on What You Know

Science and mass
media have under-
gone many changes.
Changes in popula-
tion and urbanization
are equally dramatic.
In this chapter you
will study the factors
that affect population
size. Then you will
turn your attention to
urbanization, focus-
ing on the evolution
of cities, models of
city structure, and
theories of city life.

**Many sociologists are interested
in the effects of population
changes on social life. Sociologists are also interested in
the factors that influence how
and where people live.**

To help introduce the chapter, have students discuss the Truth or Fiction statements that appear on this page. You might want to help students by reading the following **true/false** responses to the class.

True Populations grow and even shrink at different rates in various countries of the world.

False The population growth rate is steady and applies to all the countries of the world.

True Historically, people have always desired to live in urban centers, which provide more job opportunities and richer social and cultural lifestyles.

False For much of history, most people have lived in rural areas. The growth of cities is a relatively recent phenomenon that occurred because of factors such as increasing industrialization.

True All U.S. cities grow at basically the same rate and in the same fashion.

False U.S. cities develop in different ways, depending on a variety of social and geographic factors.

Life in Society

Throughout most of human history, the world was chiefly populated by small groups of people who lived nomadic lifestyles or by those who lived in small villages. Large settlements were rare. Today more than 6 billion people live in the world, and even more growth is expected in the near future. The growth of the population in recent years has resulted in tremendous change to many aspects of our social world.

Nowhere is the effect of population growth more evident than in the cities. The movement of large numbers of people from the countrysides to the cities is a relatively recent phenomenon. The effect on social life has been tremendous. In 2001 about 46 percent of the world's population lived in urban areas. It is estimated that 58 percent of the world's population will live in urbanized areas by 2025.

These two major forces, population growth and urbanization, have changed the face of the world in a relatively short amount of time. Thus, it is not surprising that sociologists have devoted considerable time to studying the ways in which population and urbanization have affected the social world and the nature of human interaction.

> ### WHY SOCIOLOGY MATTERS
>
> Sociologists are studying urbanization throughout the world. Use **CNNfyi.com** or other current events sources to learn more about an issue related to urban growth. Write a summary of your findings, including any visuals such as charts or graphs that will help explain your research.
>
> **CNNfyi.com**

• The population growth rate is not the same in every country.

• People have always gravitated toward cities.

• Cities throughout the United States follow one pattern of growth.

◆ Applying Sociology

Global Population Growth and Urbanization. Population growth and urbanization are closely linked. For example, much of today's global population growth occurs in urban areas. The number of cities with more than 1 million residents rose from 12 in 1900 to more than 410 in 2000. In 1950 the world had just eight megacities, or cities with more than 5 million inhabitants. By 2000 there were 41 megacities around the world.

ACTIVITY: Prior to having students read Chapter 16, ask each student to make a list of some possible social consequences of an ever-increasing world population and of growing city populations. Use students' lists as the basis of a brief introductory discussion on the social significance of the study of population change and urbanization.

405

SECTION 1

OBJECTIVES

1. *Identify factors that affect the size and structure of populations and explain how sociologists measure these factors.*

2. *Summarize how sociologists explain population change and describe the programs that have been instituted to control population growth.*

POPULATION CHANGE

Read to Discover

1. What factors affect the size and structure of populations, and how do sociologists measure these factors?
2. How do sociologists explain population change, and what programs have been instituted to control population growth?

Define

population, demography, birthrate, fertility, fecundity, mortality, death rate, infant mortality rate, life expectancy, migration, migration rate, growth rate, doubling time, Malthusian theory, demographic transition theory, zero population growth, family planning

Until relatively recent human history, the world was populated by small bands of people who lived and roamed in primary groups. It took thousands of years for the world population to reach 1 billion. However, in only 150 years it grew to more than 6 billion. Estimates suggest that this figure may exceed 9 billion by 2050.

The rapid population growth of recent years has had a tremendous effect on social life. The study of populations is therefore of great interest to sociologists. A **population** is the number of people living in an area at a particular time. **Demography** is the area of sociology devoted to the study of human populations. One of the major areas of interest to demographers is the measurement of population change.

Measuring Population Change

Three factors affect the growth or decline of a region's population—the birthrate, the death rate, and the rate of migration. These demographic variables determine the size of a population and the population's composition and distribution. They also determine how a population changes over time.

Birthrate The measure most often used by demographers to describe the births within a population is the **birthrate**. This term is the annual number of live births per 1,000 members of a population. Demographers calculate the birthrate by dividing the number of live births in a particular year by the total population for that year. This figure is then multiplied by 1,000. Mathematically, the formula is presented as

$$\text{Birthrate} = \frac{\text{Live births}}{\text{Total population}} \times 1{,}000$$

For example, in the United States about 4 million live births occurred in 2000 within a total population of about 281 million people. Dividing the number of live births by the total population and then multiplying that figure by 1,000 produces a birthrate of 14.6. This figure tells us that there were 14.6 live births for every 1,000 members of the U.S. population in 2000. Demographers often refer to the birthrate as the *crude birthrate*. This measure is considered crude because it is based on the total population, including men, children, and women who are past the age of childbearing. Thus, it is somewhat misleading to compare the birthrates of various societies because societies differ a great deal in the numbers of childbearing-age women they contain. Childbearing-age women range between the ages of 15 and 44. The crude birthrate also does not take into account the fact that various groups within a society may have different birthrates.

Nevertheless, the birthrate gives a relatively clear picture of the fertility of women in any given society. **Fertility** refers to the actual number of births occurring to women of childbearing age. Demographers distinguish fertility from **fecundity**, the biological capability to bear children. In the approximately 30 years between the onset and end of menstruation, women have the biological capacity to bear between 15 and 30 children. But because of various social, economic, and health factors, most women reproduce far below their biological potential.

| World Population Clock, 2002 ||
Time Span	Number of People Born
1 second	4.2 people
1 minute	251 people
1 hour	15,058 people
1 day	361,381 people
1 month	10,991,998 people
1 year	131,903,973 people

Source: Population Reference Bureau

INTERPRETING CHARTS The population of the world is constantly increasing. By studying this table you can see how much the population grows in each time interval. *By how much has the world's population grown in 48 hours?*

TEACH OBJECTIVE 1

SUGGESTION 1: Lead a class discussion on the factors that affect the size and structure of populations *(birthrate, death rate, migration rate, growth rate, and composition factors such as age and sex)* and how sociologists measure these factors. As you lead the discussion, make an outline of the information on the chalkboard and have students copy the outline in their notes. Then, to help students practice measuring rates of population change, copy the graphic organizer at the right onto the chalkboard, omitting the italicized answers. Ask students to copy the organizer and to complete it by calculating the average birthrate, death rate, and growth rate for each fictional region, based on the data provided. Tell students to round their Birthrate and Death Rate answers to the nearest whole number and their Growth Rate answers to the nearest tenth.

Remind students that growth rate is expressed as a percentage. Discuss the answers with the class. **ENGLISH LANGUAGE LEARNERS**

RATES OF POPULATION CHANGE

Region	Total Pop.	Live Births	Deaths	Birthrate	Death Rate	Growth Rate (%)
North	443,592	10,983	5,940	*25*	*13*	*1.2*
South	373,022	5,842	2,957	*16*	*8*	*0.8*
East	672,184	13,401	8,022	*20*	*12*	*0.8*
West	801,835	27,477	10,026	*34*	*13*	*2.1*

Birth and Death Rates for Selected Nations, 2001

	Nation	Birthrate	Death Rate	Infant Mortality Rate	Life Expectancy (Male/Female)
Africa	Ethiopia	44	15	97	51/53
	Gambia	43	14	82	51/54
	Kenya	34	14	74	48/49
	Mauritius	17	7	15.6	67/74
	South Africa	25	14	57	52/54
	Tunisia	19	16	28	70/74
	Congo, Dem. Rep. of	47	16	106	45/50
Asia	Afghanistan	43	19	154	46/44
	Armenia	9	6	16	71/76
	Bangladesh	28	8	66	59/59
	Cambodia	28	11	95	54/58
	China	15	6	31	69/73
	Israel	22	6	5.3	76/80
	Japan	9	8	3.4	77/84
	Singapore	14	5	2.5	76/80
	Tajikistan	19	4	23	66/71
	Yemen	44	11	75	57/61
Europe	France	13	9	4.4	75/83
	Germany	9	10	4.4	74/81
	Hungary	10	14	9.2	66/75
	Italy	9	10	5.2	76/82
	Russia	9	15	16	59/72
	Sweden	10	11	3.4	77/82
Latin America	Argentina	19	8	19.1	70/77
	Bolivia	32	9	63	60/64
	Guatemala	36	7	50	63/68
	Haiti	33	15	80	47/51
	Puerto Rico	15	7	10.5	71/80
North America	Canada	11	8	5.5	76/81
	United States	15	9	7.1	74/80
Oceania	Australia	13	7	5.7	76/82
	Papua-New Guinea	34	11	6.9	56/55
	Solomon Islands	41	7	25	67/68

Source: Population Reference Bureau

INTERPRETING CHARTS Birth and death rates vary between countries because of the different levels of health care, diet, and other cultural factors. *Which continents had the highest birthrate, death rate, and life expectancy?*

Case Study

Nigeria. The African nation of Nigeria is an example of a country with a high birthrate—about 40 births occur per 1,000 persons each year. This high birthrate, combined with a much lower death rate than in the past, has resulted in a young, rapidly growing population. About 44 percent of Nigerians are under the age of 15.

ACTIVITY: Have students discuss some of the social consequences of a country with a large population of young people.

Between 1950 and 1998 the average life expectancy in the developing world rose from 40 to 63 years.

Chart Answers

highest birthrate—Africa; highest death rate—Africa; highest life expectancy—North America

SPOTLIGHT *on World Population Statistics*

Organize the class into six groups and assign each group one of the following regions in the charts on pp. 407 and 412: Africa, Asia: Afghanistan through China, Asia: Israel through Yemen, Europe, Latin America, or North America/Oceania. Have each group use the data in the two charts to create three bar graphs: one showing the infant mortality rate for each country in their group, one showing the life expectancy for males and females for each country, and one showing the growth rate for each country. Have each group mount its three graphs on a posterboard.

COOPERATIVE LEARNING, BLOCK SCHEDULING

Applying Sociology

Income Inequality and Infant Mortality.
One predictor of infant mortality is income inequality. In general, the greater the income gap between a nations' wealthiest and poorest households, the higher the nation's rate of infant mortality. In the mid-1990s, countries with a high income inequality had an infant mortality rate of 45 deaths, compared to 36 deaths for nations with a low income inequality. In addition, countries with high income inequality often have higher percentages of households that lack electricity and access to safe drinking water than do countries with low income inequality.

CRITICAL THINKING

Why might a country's level of income inequality affect its infant mortality rate?

ANSWER: In countries with high income inequality, poor people often do not have access to adequate health care, electricity, or safe drinking water.

Visual Answer

increases the size of the population and the speed at which it is growing

Death Rate Another factor that affects population is **mortality**, or the number of deaths within a society. The measure most often used by demographers to describe the deaths in a population is the **death rate**. This term refers to the annual number of deaths per 1,000 members of a population. Demographers calculate the death rate in much the same way as the birthrate. The number of deaths in a particular year is divided by the total population for that year. This figure then is multiplied by 1,000. Mathematically, the formula is presented as

$$\text{Death rate} = \frac{\text{Deaths}}{\text{Total population}} \times 1,000$$

In the United States there were approximately 2.4 million deaths in 2000 within a total population of about 281 million people. Dividing the number of deaths by the total population and then multiplying that figure by 1,000 gives a death rate of 8.5. This figure tells us that there were 8.5 deaths for every 1,000 members of the United States population in 2000.

Demographers often refer to the death rate as the *crude death rate* because it does not take into account the varying death rates among subgroups in the population. Therefore, it is somewhat misleading to compare the death rates of various countries. To get a clearer picture of the health and life conditions in different countries, demographers also examine infant mortality rates and life expectancies. Turn to the table on page 407 to view infant mortality rates and life expectancies for selected countries around the world.

The **infant mortality rate** is the annual number of deaths among infants under one year of age per 1,000 live births in a population. Demographers calculate the infant mortality rate by dividing the number of deaths of infants under one year of age in a particular year by the number of live births in that same year. This figure then is multiplied by 1,000. The formula can be shown as

$$\begin{array}{c}\text{Infant}\\\text{mortality}\\\text{rate}\end{array} = \frac{\text{Deaths among infants}}{\text{Total live births}} \times 1,000$$

The infant mortality rate provides a general measure of the overall health and quality of life in a society. Infants are particularly open to disease and malnutrition. Thus, the probability of surviving the first year of life is greater in societies that are able to provide adequate medical attention and proper nutrition.

As you can see in the table on page 407, more-developed nations, such as Japan, Singapore, and Sweden, have relatively low rates of infant mortality. More-developed nations have high levels of per capita income, industrialization, and modernization. On the other hand, less-developed nations have low levels of per capita income, industrialization, and modernization. Less-developed nations, such as Ethiopia, Gambia, and Afghanistan, tend to have relatively high rates of infant mortality. For example, in Afghanistan an estimated 154 infants died for every 1,000 children born in 2001.

Examining life expectancies also helps demographers compare the health and life conditions in different countries. **Life expectancy** refers to the average number of years that a person born in a particular year can expect to live. As you can see from the table on

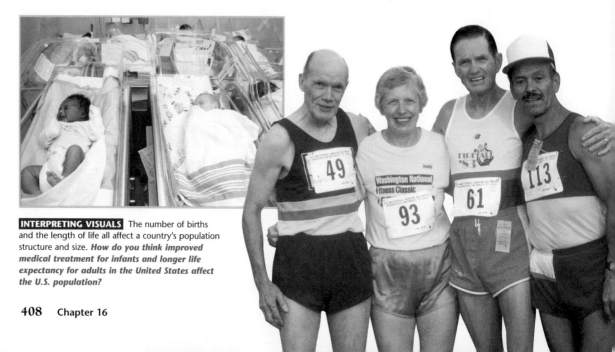

INTERPRETING VISUALS The number of births and the length of life all affect a country's population structure and size. *How do you think improved medical treatment for infants and longer life expectancy for adults in the United States affect the U.S. population?*

Pair students and have each pair conduct research to calculate the birthrate and death rate of your community or of a nearby city, based on the most current data available and the formulas on pp. 406 and 408. Then have each pair use the formula on p. 410 to calculate the overall growth rate of the community or city. Have each pair create a table to present the information. Then call on volunteer pairs to share their tables with the class. Discuss any variations in students' data or calculations. **COOPERATIVE LEARNING**,

BLOCK SCHEDULING

SPOTLIGHT *on Infant Mortality Rates*

Organize students into small groups and have each group conduct research on the infant mortality rate in the United States and in several other countries. Students should include at least one country from each region in the chart on p. 407. Have each group use its findings to prepare and present an oral report supplemented with visual aids. Reports should include factors that lead to infant mortality and advances that have reduced the infant mortality rate in the United States and elsewhere. Students' visual aids might include images, graphic organizers, or transparencies.

COOPERATIVE LEARNING, **BLOCK SCHEDULING**

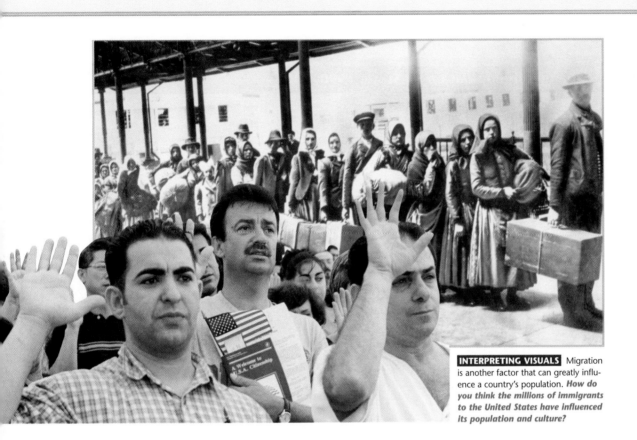

INTERPRETING VISUALS Migration is another factor that can greatly influence a country's population. *How do you think the millions of immigrants to the United States have influenced its population and culture?*

Sociology in the World Today

Migration and Refugees. War and other conflicts often serve as a push factor for migration. The people who flee war-torn regions are called refugees. In the early 2000s, there were about 39 million refugees throughout the world. Some 14 million of these refugees had crossed international borders, and some 25 million were displaced within their own countries.

Most refugees reside in tent cities in the developing world. The Middle East and Africa host the largest numbers of refugee camps. In such camps, water and food supplies are often limited, and electricity is rarely available. In addition, overcrowding and lack of sanitation can lead to the rapid spread of diseases.

RESEARCH ACTIVITY: Have students conduct research on social issues related to refugee camps or on the locations and reasons for some current refugee camps. Ask students to share their findings with the class.

Visual Answer

Immigrants have greatly increased the U.S. population and made the American culture more diverse.

---

page 407, life expectancy is related to the rate of infant mortality. Notice that life expectancies in more-developed nations are much higher than life expectancies in less-developed nations. For example, in Japan fewer than 4 infants died for every 1,000 born, and life expectancy is 77 years for men and 84 years for women. In Ethiopia, where 97 infants died for every 1,000 born, life expectancy is only 51 years for men and 53 years for women. Within a single society, life expectancies can differ according to sex, race, ethnicity, and other social factors.

Demographers distinguish between life expectancy and life span—the maximum length of life that is biologically possible. The life span of humans is generally considered to be about 100 years. Although the expectancies in many countries around the world have increased dramatically during the 1900s, life span has not. The increases in life expectancy have largely come about through reductions in infant mortality. It has proved easier to combat the diseases of childhood than it has been to fight the aging process and the diseases common to old age. As a result, the life span of humans has remained practically unchanged for centuries.

Migration Rate The third demographic variable is **migration**, or the movement of people from one specified area to another. When measuring migration, demographers examine both movement into and out of a specified area.

The annual number of people who move into a specified area per 1,000 members of that area's population is called the in-migration rate. The out-migration rate, on the other hand, refers to the annual number of people who move out of a specified area per 1,000 members of a population. Both these processes are often occurring in a specified area at the same time. Because of this, demographers calculate the **migration rate** as the annual difference between in-migration and out-migration. The effects of the migration rate on population are ordinarily not as significant as the effects of the birthrate and the death rate. One reason for this is that the movement of people does not add to or detract from the global population.

Migration occurs as a result of what demographers call push and pull factors. A push factor is something that encourages people to move out of a certain area. Push factors include religious or political persecution, famine, racial discrimination, and overpopulation. A pull factor is

SUGGESTION 1: Lead a class discussion on the theories that sociologists use to explain population change (*Malthusian theory and the demographic transition theory*) and on the programs that have been instituted to control population growth (*family planning, antinatalism, and economic development of less-developed nations*). Then assign half the class the Malthusian theory and half the demographic transition theory. Ask students to imagine that they belong to an organization that supports their assigned theory. Have each student create a one-page pamphlet for the organization to distribute that describes current population issues according to the assigned theory.

SUGGESTION 2: Call on students to summarize the theories that sociologists use to explain population change and the programs that have been instituted to control population growth (*listed in the Section 1 activity to the left*). Encourage students to express their opinions of each theory and of each program. Then have students, working individually or in pairs, write a futuristic short story about a society in which overpopulation has reached a critical level. Stories should address the reasons for this population growth and how the people are trying to control it. Ask volunteers to read their stories aloud to the class. **COOPERATIVE LEARNING**

Did You Know?

According to the United Nations, six countries—Bangladesh, China, India, Indonesia, Nigeria, and Pakistan—are responsible for half of Earth's annual population growth.

Map Answers

1. California, Nevada, Arizona, and Colorado

2. Questions will vary but may focus on the reasons different states or regions have gained or lost population.

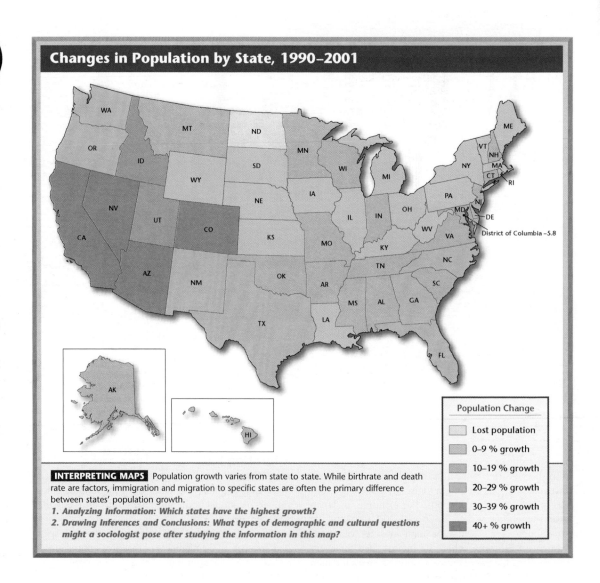

Changes in Population by State, 1990–2001

District of Columbia –5.8

Population Change

- Lost population
- 0–9 % growth
- 10–19 % growth
- 20–29 % growth
- 30–39 % growth
- 40+ % growth

INTERPRETING MAPS Population growth varies from state to state. While birthrate and death rate are factors, immigration and migration to specific states are often the primary difference between states' population growth.

1. Analyzing Information: Which states have the highest growth?

2. Drawing Inferences and Conclusions: What types of demographic and cultural questions might a sociologist pose after studying the information in this map?

something that encourages people to move into a certain area. Religious and political freedom, economic opportunities, and a high standard of living are considered migration pull factors.

Growth Rate The three demographic variables—birthrate, death rate, and migration rate—all affect the size of a population. However, demographers tend to focus on birthrates and death rates when considering a population's **growth rate**, or the rate at which a country's population is increasing. Growth rates are calculated by subtracting the death rate from the birthrate and are usually expressed as percentages. As you recall, the United States had a birthrate of 14.6 per 1,000 and a death rate

of 8.5 per 1,000 in 2000. Subtracting the death rate from the birthrate leaves 6.1 per 1,000 people. Thus, the United States had a growth rate of 0.6 percent, meaning that about 6 people were added to the population for every 1,000 members. You can see the growth rates for selected countries in the table on page 412.

The growth rates in more-developed countries are typically much lower than the growth rates in less-developed nations because modern industrialized countries generally have low birthrates. Countries with lower levels of technology, on the other hand, usually have birthrates that far exceed their death rates. In Afghanistan, for example, the estimated birthrate for 2001 was 43, while the death rate was nearly 19. Thus,

Connecting to Math

TEACH

Have students read the feature Population Statistics and complete the assignments under Think About It. (You might need to provide students with guidance for locating and using U.S. census data. If Internet access is available, you might have students practice accessing U.S. census data online.) Call on volunteers to present their completed charts and graphs to the class. Then have students analyze and discuss the changes and trends that the charts and graphs indicate.

SPOTLIGHT on the U.S. Census Bureau

Organize students into groups and have them conduct research on the U.S. Census Bureau—its origins in the U.S. Constitution, its history, how the census is taken today, the types of jobs at the Census Bureau, and the role that census data plays in government, social programs, and business. Have each group create either a brochure or a series of mock or real Web pages to present its findings. **COOPERATIVE LEARNING**,

BLOCK SCHEDULING

CONNECTING TO
Math

POPULATION STATISTICS

The U.S. Bureau of the Census is the government agency authorized to collect, tabulate, and publish statistical information about the people of the United States. The Census Bureau conducts a nationwide survey of the population every 10 years. In the intervening years the bureau performs several smaller surveys and estimates the total based on all the results.

The bureau also makes projections, or estimates of the population for future dates. These projections show the possible changes in population over time based on assumptions about future births, deaths, in-migration, and out-migration. The Census Bureau produces projections that break down the predicted population by age, sex, race, and Hispanic origin. The chart below shows the changes in the total population and in the Hispanic population between 1980 and 2000.

By applying your math skills to information in the chart, you can create a series of charts and graphs on the population of the United States. Look at the figures in the chart below. You can then use the total population figure and the Hispanic origin figure to calculate the percentage of the Hispanic population for that year. A chart with this information for the years 1980, 1990, and 2000 might look like this:

Year	Total Population	Hispanic Population	Percentage of Population Hispanic
1980	226,546,000	14,609,000	6.4
1990	248,791,000	22,379,000	9.0
2000	275,306,000	32,479,000	11.8

You might present this information in the form of a bar graph:

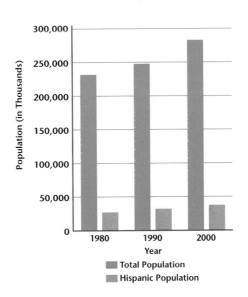

Total Population
Hispanic Population

You might also present the information in a series of pie graphs. Both presentations clearly show that the Hispanic population grew steadily over the last 20 years of the 1900s.

Think About It

1. **Analyzing Information** *Construct a chart showing the racial makeup of the population, for 1980, 1990, and 2000. Then use the information to create a series of three pie graphs. What changes do the pie graphs show?*

2. **Evaluating** *Construct a multiple-line graph showing the projected growth of the total, male, and female populations for the years 2010 to 2025. Write an essay describing the trends in the statistics.*

Interdisciplinary Connection

GOVERNMENT

The 2000 Census. The following are some facts about the 2000 U.S. census form:

• For the first time, the census asked about grandparent caregivers.

• For the first time, people could mark more than one racial category.

• The form was printed in English, Spanish, Chinese, Korean, Tagalog, and Vietnamese. Assistance guides were available in 49 other languages.

• Census workers made an effort to count homeless people at camping sites, shelters, and elsewhere.

ACTIVITY: Lead a short discussion on what these facts about the census indicate about changes in American society.

Think About It Answers

1. Pie graphs should show the populations of racial minorities growing over time.

2. Essays should accurately reflect the data presented in the line graphs.

SUGGESTION 3: Have each student write an essay summarizing the Malthusian theory and the demographic transition theory and the criticisms of each one. Then have students express which theory they most agree with and provide examples and reasons to defend their choice. Call on volunteers to read their essays to the class. Use the essays as the basis of a class discussion on programs that have been instituted to control population growth. Have students discuss if they think such programs are needed and, if so, why.

HOMEWORK: Have each student create a chart that describes each of the three forms of population control and the positive and negative aspects of each method. Students should also write a short caption summarizing the information in the chart.

CONNECTING *to Math*

Have interested students conduct research on how demographers calculate doubling time. Students should then create a chart that explains how to calculate doubling time and then uses 2001 country data to illustrate how some of the doubling-time rates in the chart on this page were calculated. Ask one volunteer to present his or her information to the class and then to use it to teach the other students how to calculate doubling time.

BLOCK SCHEDULING

Applying Sociology

Population Projections.
Projecting future population growth is a difficult task. Population projections are based on future birthrates, and these numbers may be inaccurate. To account for uncertainties, demographers often make several different projections, such as low, medium, and high projections. Regardless of the size of future populations, all countries face population-related challenges.

CRITICAL THINKING

Why is it difficult to predict population growth?

ANSWER: because future birthrates are not known

Chart Answers

highest—Solomon Islands, Yemen; most quickly—Democratic Republic of Congo, Solomon Islands

Technology Resources

 Teaching Transparency: Growth Rates and Doubling Times for Selected Nations, 2001

Growth Rates and Doubling Times for Selected Nations, 2001

	Nation	Growth Rate (in percent)	Doubling Time (in years)
Africa	Ethiopia	2.9	29
	Gambia	3	29
	Kenya	2	33
	Mauritius	1	66
	South Africa	1.2	55
	Tunisia	1.3	44
	Congo, Dem. Rep. of	3.1	22
Asia	Afghanistan	2.4	28
	Armenia	0.3	161
	Bangladesh	2	38
	Cambodia	1.7	27
	China	0.9	79
	Israel	1.6	45
	Japan	0.2	462
	Singapore	0.9	84
	Tajikistan	1.4	44
	Yemen	3.3	25
Europe	France	0.4	204
	Germany	−0.1*	(−)
	Hungary	−0.4*	(−)
	Italy	−0.1*	(−)
	Russia	−0.7*	(−)
	Sweden	−0.1*	(−)
Latin America	Argentina	1.1	62
	Bolivia	2.4	34
	Guatemala	2.9	24
	Haiti	1.7	40
	Puerto Rico	0.8	75
North America	Canada	0.3	179
	United States	0.6	120
Oceania	Australia	0.6	110
	Papua-New Guinea	2.3	29
	Solomon Islands	3.4	23

*A negative number indicates that this nation has a death rate higher than its birth rate; thus the population is shrinking rather than growing.
Source: Population Reference Bureau

INTERPRETING CHARTS By studying the population size and growth rate, demographers can calculate the time it would take for a country's population to double in size. *Which countries had the highest growth rate? Which countries will double in size most quickly?*

the growth rate in this less-developed nation was estimated at 2.4 percent, meaning that 24 people were added to Afghanistan's population for every 1,000 members.

Because growth rates are expressed as percentages, a growth rate of 2.4 appears quite small. In reality, the long-term effect of such a growth rate on population size is enormous because the growth rate is related to a population's **doubling time**. This period of time is the number of years necessary for a population to double in size, given its current rate of growth.

A population growth rate of only 1 percent will cause that population to double its size in about 70 years. A growth rate of 2 percent doubles the population in about 35 years, and it takes a population with a growth rate of 3 percent only 23 years to double in size. Look again at the table on this page. Note that the United States has a growth rate of 0.6 percent and will double its population in just under 120 years. In contrast, Afghanistan, at its current growth rate of 2.4 percent, will double its population in less than 30 years.

To illustrate the significance of doubling time, consider the fact that the population of the world doubled from half a billion to 1 billion between 1650 and 1850, a span of 200 years. The population doubled again between 1850 and 1930, reaching 2 billion in only 80 years. Less than 50 years later, in 1975, it doubled to 4 billion. Demographers estimate that at its current rate of growth of 1.4 percent, the world's population will hit the 8 billion mark shortly after 2025.

Population Composition In addition to changes in population size, demographers also study population composition, or the population's structure. Age and sex are the factors most often used to show the composition of a population.

To study population composition, demographers use a population pyramid. A population pyramid is a graphic representation of the age and sex distribution of a population. It is a two-sided graph showing the percentages of men and women falling into various age groups. The graph is usually shaped like a pyramid because it ranges from the youngest age group at the bottom to the oldest age group at the top, and because the chances of death increase with age.

Have students read the short story "Billenium" by J. G. Ballard (in *The Oxford Book of Science Fiction Stories,* edited by Tom Shippey, Oxford University Press, 1992). In the story, overpopulation has reached a point that individuals must live in cubicles just four square meters in area. The main character finds a secret room to live in and feels that he is living in luxury. Soon, however, he is living with seven people packed in this space. After students read the story, have them discuss their reactions. Then lead a class discussion on how the size of a society's population can affect an individual's feeling of personal freedom. **BLOCK SCHEDULING**

SPOTLIGHT *on Population Pyramids*

Have students locate U.S. Census Bureau data on male and female population projections for 2025 and 2050 and create a population pyramid for each year. Lead a class discussion comparing the population pyramid for the United States in 2000 on p. 413 to the projected population pyramids for 2025 and 2050. Then ask students to draw conclusions about how life in the United States might be different in 2025 and 2050, based on the projected population changes. **BLOCK SCHEDULING**

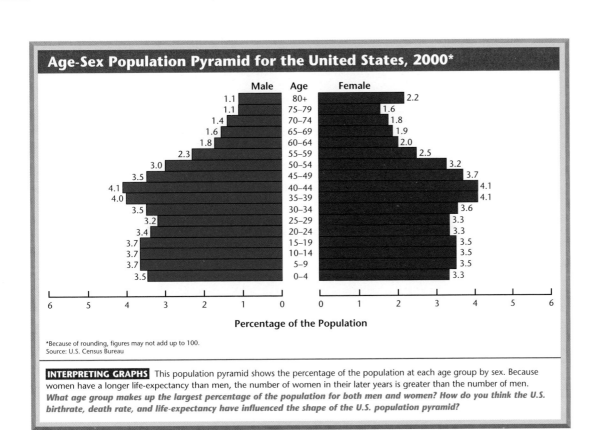

Age-Sex Population Pyramid for the United States, 2000*

Percentage of the Population

*Because of rounding, figures may not add up to 100.
Source: U.S. Census Bureau

INTERPRETING GRAPHS This population pyramid shows the percentage of the population at each age group by sex. Because women have a longer life-expectancy than men, the number of women in their later years is greater than the number of men. *What age group makes up the largest percentage of the population for both men and women? How do you think the U.S. birthrate, death rate, and life-expectancy have influenced the shape of the U.S. population pyramid?*

Sociology in the World Today

Gender Differences in Population Growth.
Women make up more than 50 percent of the U.S. population. Recently, however, the gap between the size of the male and female American population has been shrinking. According to the U.S. Census Bureau, the country's male population is now growing at a faster rate than its female population. In 1990, men made up 48.7 percent of the U.S. population. In 2000 this percentage had increased to 49.1.

CRITICAL THINKING
What might explain the growth of the male population in the United States?

ANSWER: perhaps a rise in the male birthrate or a drop in the male death rate

Graph Answers

largest percentage—ages 40–44 (men), ages 35–44 (women); influence—determine the number of people found at each age level of the pyramid

Demographers gain a great deal of information from population pyramids. For example, the graphs indicate the percentage of older adults within the population who may need care or support. They also show the percentage of childbearing-age women and the percentage of people available for employment. Perhaps most importantly, population pyramids indicate a population's potential for growth. A country with a large percentage of children has an enormous potential for growth. These children will soon grow and have children of their own. A country with a small percentage of children, on the other hand, will have fewer people entering their childbearing years in the future. Therefore, future population growth will be slow.

Look at the population pyramid for the United States on this page. The bulge in the pyramid represents people aged between their late thirties and late forties. This bulge reflects the sharp rise in the birthrate from the late 1940s through the early 1960s as family life resumed following World War II. The pyramid also shows that this baby boom was followed by a "baby bust"—a decline in the birthrate. U.S. birthrates have remained relatively low ever since, making the baby-boom generation the largest percentage of the population. Because the United States has a relatively low birthrate, population growth is likely to be slow.

Turn to page 414 and study the population pyramids for Sweden and Mexico. Notice that the base of Sweden's pyramid indicates that the birthrate has been relatively low for a number of years and that children make up a small percentage of the population. Sweden is producing fewer young people who will grow up and have children themselves. Therefore, Sweden's future population growth will be slow, slower even than that of the United States. This trend is similar to those in other more-developed nations such as Japan and other countries in Northern Europe.

The population pyramid for Mexico stands in sharp contrast to those of the United States and Sweden. Mexico's graph is almost a perfect pyramid shape. This indicates that large numbers of children are being born but that few people in the population are living to old age. When today's children reach their childbearing years, the population of Mexico will grow enormously unless the birthrate slows. Mexico's population pyramid is typical of many less-developed nations around the world.

Technology Resources

Teaching Transparency: Age-Sex Population Pyramid for the United States, 2000

Teacher to Teacher

Glenn Mechem of Union, Missouri, suggested the following activity: Provide students with a list of five or more countries and have students conduct research to create an age-sex population pyramid and a chart of the birthrate, death rate, and growth rate for each country. When students finish the assignment, call on them to answer questions such as the following: Which countries have large percentages of school-age children? Which country has the largest percentage of people over age 65? How does a country's birthrate, death rate, and growth rate influence its age-sex population pyramid?

BLOCK SCHEDULING

CONNECTING to Geography

Have students work in small groups to conduct research on Sweden and Mexico. Each group should create a fact sheet for each country, that provides information on the country's population, language, government, economy, and culture. Students might use sources such as the CIA World Factbook to find information. Ask volunteers to share some of the information on their fact sheets with the class. Then have students use their fact sheets to discuss possible explanations as to why Sweden's and Mexico's populations are so different and are changing in such different ways.

COOPERATIVE LEARNING , BLOCK SCHEDULING

Did You Know?

For the first time in history, the global population has both the largest number of young people (below age 25) and elderly people (above age 64).

Graph Answers

Swedes aged 0–4 years old are one of the smallest age groups, which means that Sweden will probably experience a decreasing population and a shortage of workers in the future.

Mexico's high birthrate could mean a future population boom as its young people reach childbearing age, politically putting a strain on the country's food production, housing, and social services.

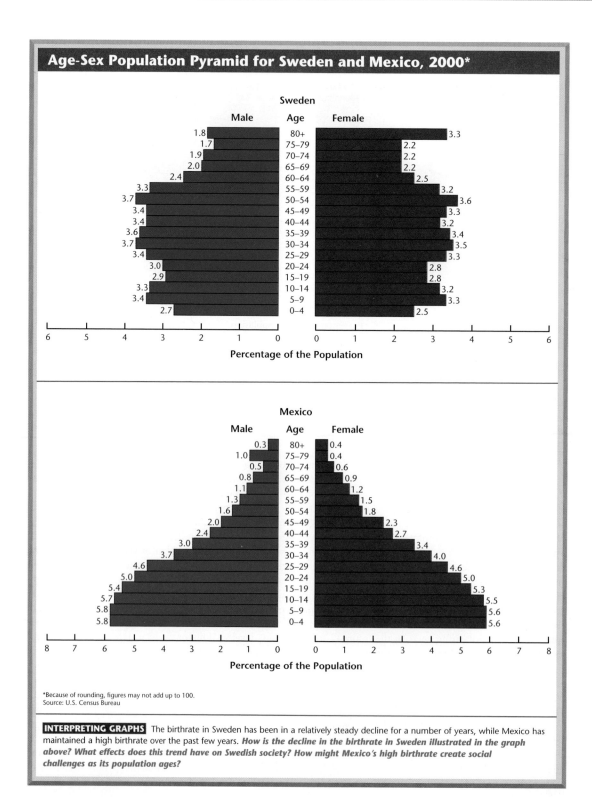

Age-Sex Population Pyramid for Sweden and Mexico, 2000*

*Because of rounding, figures may not add up to 100.
Source: U.S. Census Bureau

INTERPRETING GRAPHS The birthrate in Sweden has been in a relatively steady decline for a number of years, while Mexico has maintained a high birthrate over the past few years. *How is the decline in the birthrate in Sweden illustrated in the graph above? What effects does this trend have on Swedish society? How might Mexico's high birthrate create social challenges as its population ages?*

SPOTLIGHT *on Thomas Robert Malthus*

Organize the class into small groups and have them prepare multimedia exhibits on Thomas Robert Malthus—perhaps in the style of a cable television channel's biography series. Presentations should detail Malthus's early life in England, his education at Jesus College, the publication of *Essay on Population*, his sudden transformation into an intellectual celebrity, his becoming England's first academic economist, his later writings on economics, and his views on the "perfect society." Have each group set up its exhibit in the classroom. **COOPERATIVE LEARNING, BLOCK SCHEDULING**

SPOTLIGHT
on the Demographic Transition Theory

Organize the class into three groups representing the three stages of the demographic transition theory. Ask students to imagine that they live in a country in their group's assigned stage. In a round-robin discussion, ask students to characterize their assigned stages of development. Discussion prompts might include: *What is the birthrate and death rate in your country? What is the state of medical technology? How does the standard of living in your country compare to that in other countries? Is overpopulation a concern in your country?*
COOPERATIVE LEARNING, BLOCK SCHEDULING

Explaining Population Change

A number of theories have been proposed over the years to explain population and population change. Among the theories most often discussed by demographers are Malthusian theory and demographic transition theory.

Malthusian Theory Thomas Robert Malthus (1766–1834), an English economist, outlined a rather gloomy picture of population growth in his *An Essay on the Principle of Population*. Malthus argued that the already rapidly growing population of the 1700s would continue to grow at ever-faster rates. He based this prediction on the fact that population grows through multiplication. In most instances, this multiplication progresses geometrically. A geometric progression is represented by the series of numbers 2, 4, 8, 16, 32, 64, and so on. Following the progression to its logical conclusion, **Malthusian theory** predicted that the population would soon reach astronomical numbers.

According to Malthusian theory, the geometric progression of population has serious social consequences because food production progresses arithmetically. An arithmetic progression is represented by the series of numbers 2, 3, 4, 5, 6, and so on. Food production is arithmetic because the amount of land available for cultivation is limited. Thus, a rapidly growing population could eventually outpace food production and could result in worldwide starvation.

Malthus suggested that two forces could check, or slow, population growth. First, the number of births could be reduced through preventive checks, including birth control, sexual self-control, and delayed marriage and childbearing. Second, the overall population could be reduced through positive checks, including war, disease, and famine.

Malthus did not think that people would use preventive checks to control what he believed to be a coming disaster. In addition to being an economist, Malthus was also a clergyman, and he rejected the use of artificial birth control. Furthermore, he thought that people would halt their sexual activity only when faced with actual famine conditions. Consequently, Malthus predicted that natural factors, such as disease and famine, would bring the population in line with the available food supply.

Malthus failed to foresee two important developments, however. First, he did not

English economist Thomas Robert Malthus predicted that problems might result from population growth.

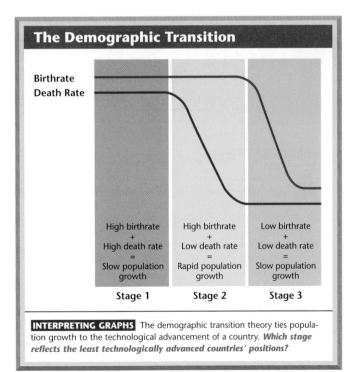

The Demographic Transition

Birthrate
Death Rate

| High birthrate + High death rate = Slow population growth | High birthrate + Low death rate = Rapid population growth | Low birthrate + Low death rate = Slow population growth |
| Stage 1 | Stage 2 | Stage 3 |

INTERPRETING GRAPHS The demographic transition theory ties population growth to the technological advancement of a country. *Which stage reflects the least technologically advanced countries' positions?*

CONNECTING *to the Arts*

Show students the film *Soylent Green* (Metro-Goldwyn-Mayer, 1973, rated PG). Based on Harry Harrison's novel *Make Room! Make Room!*, the story is set in New York City in the year 2022 and depicts a dystopian world dealing with overpopulation. (This film contains some language and scenes that might be inappropriate. You should preview the movie if you have not yet seen it to decide if it is appropriate for your students to view.) After watching the film, have each student write a short essay discussing the film's presentation of issues concerning the environment, government, social classes, economics, technology, morality, and daily life in a large urban center affected by overpopulation. Have volunteers read their essays to the class. **BLOCK SCHEDULING**

SPOTLIGHT *on Demography in the Media*

Lead a class discussion on the role of demographics in the media today—particularly in marketing and advertising. Many companies create media designed to target certain demographics that are of interest to advertisers. Topics for discussion might include the television Nielsen ratings and interactive Web sites that use demographic information to better understand and predict users' behaviors and interests. Challenge students to place a value on the role of demographers in media companies.
BLOCK SCHEDULING

Sociology in the World Today

A Graying World. In Stage 3 of the demographic transition theory, the average age of the population rises as birthrates decline and life expectancies increase. Today people over the age of 60 form the fastest-growing segment of the world population, particularly in industrialized nations. In 1997 Italy became the first country in recorded history where people over age 60 outnumbered those under age 20. In addition, projections estimate that Italy's over-60 age group will outnumber its entire working population by 2035. If this world trend continues, it could strain many countries' social services, health care systems, and state-funded pension programs.

CRITICAL THINKING

What might be some ways that aging countries can address the potential future social problems of this trend?

ANSWER: Answers will vary, but students might mention that governments can begin providing more services for elderly people, offer tax relief to households caring for elderly family members, or reassess public and private health care.

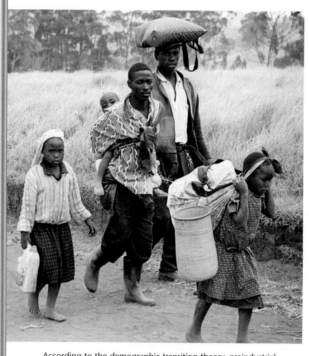

According to the demographic transition theory, preindustrial societies have both a high birthrate and a high death rate because of their level of technological development.

anticipate that advances in agricultural technology would allow farmers to produce more crops on the same amount of land. Second, Malthus foresaw neither the development of effective birth control methods nor their widespread acceptance and use. Modern birth control methods have been particularly effective in reducing the birthrates in more developed nations since the 1960s. Thus, Malthus's predictions have not yet come to pass.

However, some demographers warn that the Malthusian theory is still a possibility, particularly if countries fail to lower population growth rates. They point out that the last documented doubling of the world's population—from 3 billion to 6 billion—took just 39 years. If the population continues to grow at this pace, they argue, there will simply be too many people in need of the world's limited resources.

Demographic Transition Theory Malthusian theory has contributed much to our understanding of population change. However, most demographers favor the explanation provided by the **demographic transition theory**. This theory holds that population patterns are tied to a society's level of technological development. According to this theory, which is based on the population changes in Western Europe over the past 300 years, a society's population moves through three stages.

In Stage 1, which is typical of preindustrial agricultural societies, both the birthrate and the death rate are

Careers
IN SOCIOLOGY

DEMOGRAPHER

A demographer is a specialist who studies the size, composition, and distribution of a population. Demographers collect and analyze statistics related to population size and population change, such as births, deaths, and marriages. Demography often involves predicting future trends and population growth. Some demographers help businesses plan their marketing and advertising programs. Others help countries assess population issues and set population policies. Demographers often spend many years studying statistics and using the latest computer programs to process large volumes of data to obtain the most accurate population figures.

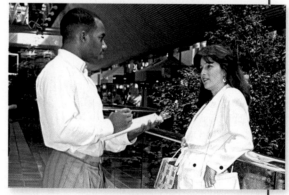

Demographers study the characteristics and structure of a society. They use many tools including population surveys.

high. The birthrate is high in these societies because children are valued as sources of labor and because no effective means of birth control are available. The death rate is high because of the relatively low standard of living and the lack of medical technology to control the spread of disease. The high birthrate and high death rate result in a fairly stable population with little growth and little decline. Western Europe was in Stage 1 prior to the Industrial Revolution. Modern-day examples of Stage 1 societies can be found in some areas of central Africa.

As societies enter the industrial phase, Stage 2, improved medical techniques, sanitation, and increased food production result in a reduction in the death rate. Children are still highly desired, however, so the birthrate remains high. High birthrates and low death rates combine to produce a rapid growth in population. This is the present situation in many developing countries around the world, such as the Democratic Republic of the Congo and Guatemala.

Stage 3 societies have a fully developed industrial economy. During this stage, the birthrate falls due to the increased use of effective birth control methods. Birthrates also decrease because there is a relatively high standard of living and children are no longer needed as workers. The death rate remains low during this stage. The low birthrate and low death rate produce a fairly

stable population. Growth occurs very slowly. Only the most technologically advanced countries of the world, such as those found in North America and Europe, are in Stage 3 of the demographic transition.

Some Stage 3 societies may even approach **zero population growth**, the point at which nearly equal birthrates and death rates produce a growth rate of zero. In some cases, countries have fallen below zero growth, with birthrates lower than their death rates. Thus, the populations in these countries are shrinking. Turn to the chart showing population growth rates on page 412. Note the countries that have shrinking populations.

Some demographers believe that Stage 2 countries currently experiencing rapid population growth will stabilize as they become more industrially advanced. Critics of the demographic transition theory are less optimistic. These critics believe it is unlikely that all countries will follow the stages of technological development found in Europe and North America. As today's preindustrial countries begin to industrialize, the introduction of modern medicine causes their death rates to drop much more quickly than was the case in Western Europe. This difference leads to an increase in population and may hamper modernization in these countries. Any economic gains brought about by industrialization must be used to maintain the same level of subsistence for the rapidly growing population.

INTERPRETING VISUALS According to the demographic transition theory, Stage 3 countries such as Sweden have low birthrates and low death rates. *How do you think industrial development affects these population factors?*

![director icon] **SPOTLIGHT** *on China's One-Child Policy*

Ask students to comment on the image on p. 418 and to answer the Interpreting Visuals question. Then tell students that although China has benefited from its one-child policy, the policy has produced some negative consequences as well. For example, many Chinese place a higher value on male children. As a result, some Chinese parents abandon female infants so that they can try to have a boy without violating the one-child policy. Then have each student write one or two paragraphs predicting the future societal consequences of China's one-child policy.

BLOCK SCHEDULING

CLOSE

Have students retrieve the lists of things they expected to learn in Section 1 in the *Let's Get Started!* activity. Ask volunteers to read their lists and have the class discuss how their expectations for learning the section material have been fulfilled.

REVIEW AND ASSESS

Have students complete the **Section 1 Review** on p. 419. As **Alternative Assessment**, you may want to use the population change poster or the overpopulation short story in this section's lessons.

◆ Applying Sociology

China's One-Child Policy. Although China's one-child policy has helped slow that country's population growth, it has also created some social problems. Because males are more valued than females in Chinese society, some parents abandon female infants at orphanages. As a result of such problems, many regions of China have relaxed the enforcement of the one-child policy. In exchange, the United Nations has pledged to support family planning programs in China.

ACTIVITY: Have students discuss their viewpoints of China's one-child policy as a means of population control.

Visual Answer

The billboard portrays a happy one-child Chinese family in a land of progress, which might influence Chinese citizens to follow the one-child program in hopes of improving their lives and the state of their country.

为四化一对夫妇只生一个孩

INTERPRETING VISUALS Some countries such as China have developed population-control policies to reduce population growth. *How do you think this billboard advertising the one-child program might influence Chinese citizens?*

Controlling Population Growth

The world now contains nearly 6.2 billion people. Although the current growth rate is down to 1.3 percent from a high of 2 percent in the late 1960s, the population of the world continues to grow. More than 99 percent of this growth is occurring in the less-developed nations. These countries are home to about 80 percent of the world's population.

Concerns about growth and the desire for economic development have led many countries to adopt strategies aimed at controlling their populations. Two types of basic strategies are being used. One type includes those strategies designed to lower the birthrate. The other includes those strategies designed to improve economic conditions.

Family Planning One strategy that has been used to lower the birthrate in some countries is **family planning**. This strategy is the conscious decision by couples to have a certain number of children. The goal of family-planning programs is to reduce the number of unplanned pregnancies. Family planning involves the careful use of effective birth-control techniques.

According to demographers, family-planning programs alone have been insufficient to reduce the birthrate in many countries. One reason for the program's lack of success is that these programs are poorly financed. As a result, only a limited number of people are able to use the program services. More importantly, family-planning programs allow parents to decide the number of children that they will have. Often the number of children parents choose to have exceeds the number that will help to slow the population growth. For example, in many less-developed nations children are considered economic assets. Thus, the norm is to have several children. In these countries, many people use family-planning programs only after they have already produced large families.

Some countries have turned to antinatalism to reduce population growth. Antinatalism involves official policies designed to discourage people from having children. Such policies attempt to resocialize the population to value small rather than large families. Antinatalism usually involves rewards and punishments that urge people to have fewer children. For example, China has been involved since the early 1980s in an intensive campaign to reduce the number of births to one child per family. This campaign is based on incentives and sanctions. Birth-control devices are freely available, and couples are counseled as to their use. Couples who follow the one-child program receive special housing,

![RETEACH]

RETEACH
Pair students and have each pair work together to summarize each main part of this section. Then go through the section and ask volunteers to read their summaries for each part of the section in turn. Provide corrections or comments where needed. Review any main points or concepts with which students seem to be having trouble. Finally, ask volunteers to summarize the section's main ideas in a few sentences. **ENGLISH LANGUAGE LEARNERS**, **COOPERATIVE LEARNING**

EXTEND
1. In a class discussion, challenge students to use the chart on p. 406 to estimate how long it would take to fill the classroom, a football field, their state, and the continental United States with people. Tell students to assume that one person would take up about two square feet of space. Then use the activity as the basis of a class discussion on how population change can affect society. **BLOCK SCHEDULING**

2. Have each student make predictions about local, national, and global population changes over the next 10, 50, and 100 years. Students might submit their predictions as oral, written, or visual products. **BLOCK SCHEDULING**

employment, and financial benefits from the government. Those couples who do not conform to the policy face large fines and other penalties. China's policy has produced a significant reduction in the fertility rate. In 2001 the rate was 1.8—just below the level that will keep population growth stable.

Economic Improvements Some critics of family-planning policies believe that economic development must proceed before people in less-developed nations will voluntarily limit their family size. Supporters of economic development believe that better health, higher levels of income, and education will lead to lower birthrates.

However, most less-developed nations do not have the resources to achieve the economic development necessary to raise living standards. Economic assistance packages that are designed to help less-developed nations improve their living conditions often benefit only a very small portion of the population. As a result, the majority of the population remains in poverty, and birthrates remain high.

As a result, some demographers suggest that less-developed nations would be better served by evenly redistributing resources among all members of society. They believe this process would reduce poverty. Once people no longer lack the basic necessities of life, they may voluntarily limit the size of their families.

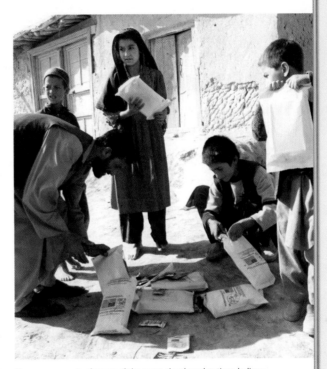

The governments of many of the more-developed nations believe that economic assistance can help less-developed nations such as Afghanistan to slow their population growth.

SECTION 1 REVIEW

1. Define and explain
population
demography
birthrate
fertility
fecundity
mortality
death rate
infant mortality rate
life expectancy
migration
migration rate
growth rate
doubling time
Malthusian theory
demographic transition
  theory
zero population growth
family planning

2. Comparing and Contrasting
Copy the graphic organizer below. Use it to explain the similarities and differences between the two theories on population change.

Malthusian theory	Demographic transistion theory

3. Finding the Main Idea
a. Identify and describe the three factors that affect the size and structure of populations.
b. What are some of the programs that have been created to help control population growth?

4. Writing and Critical Thinking
Drawing Inferences and Conclusions Write a paragraph describing how population growth and geographic factors might influence a country's policies, norms, and cultural values.
Consider:
• the population issues of countries that are attempting to industrialize
• government policies such as China's one-child program

Homework Practice Online
keyword: SL3 HP16

SECTION 1 REVIEW ANSWERS

1. Define:
• population, p. 406
• demography, p. 406
• birthrate, p. 406
• fertility, p. 406
• fecundity, p. 406
• mortality, p. 408
• death rate, p. 408
• infant mortality rate, p. 408
• life expectancy, p. 408
• migration, p. 409
• migration rate, p. 409
• growth rate, p. 410
• doubling time, p. 412
• Malthusian theory, p. 415
• demographic transition theory, p. 416
• zero population growth, p. 417
• family planning, p. 418

2. Malthusian theory— geometric population growth but arithmetic food production, population growth could outpace food production; demographic transition theory—lower birthrate and lower death rate as a result of a higher stage of technological development

3a. birthrate, death rate, and migration rate

b. family planning and economic improvements

4. Paragraphs will vary, but students should support their arguments with examples from the text. Some students may compare and contrast less-developed countries with more-developed countries.

Building Social Studies Skills

■ TEACH

Have students read the Social Studies Skills feature Posing and Answering Questions on this page. Then have each student complete the assignment under Practicing the Skill. You may wish to extend the activity by providing students with other statistical information so that students can practice posing and answering questions about a variety of data.

■ EXTEND

In a class discussion, ask students what types of employees might find themselves posing and answering questions about demographic statistics during the course of their jobs. *(Answers might include network executives, politicians, advertisers, and city planners.)* Then invite several adults who hold such jobs to visit your class and serve as a panel of experts on jobs that use demographic information. Have students ask the panelists what types of questions they pose about demographic information and how they go about answering such questions. **BLOCK SCHEDULING**

POSING AND ANSWERING QUESTIONS

To help students practice their skills for posing and answering questions, organize students into groups of four. Next, assign each group a different chart, graph, or map in the chapter to examine, and assign each group member one of the four steps in the skills feature. Have each student pose and answer questions related to his or her assigned visual and assigned step. Group members should then discuss and expand upon other members' questions. Conclude by having group members share some of their questions and answers with the class.

Practicing the Skill

Questions and answers will vary but should exhibit an understanding of how the chart relates to the text.

BUILDING

Social Studies Skills

POSING AND ANSWERING QUESTIONS

Awareness of the factors that affect the size and structure of populations is key to an understanding of the process of social change. Many sociologists increase their awareness of these and other factors by posing and answering questions.

Posing and answering questions involves formulating questions and knowing how to respond to them. This approach will help you understand information that is presented to you in various forms, such as text, maps, or charts and graphs. Listed below are guidelines that will help you with posing and answering questions.

1. **Determine the kind of information that is presented in the source.** For example, if you are looking at a chart on immigration to the United States, pose questions such as the following: What exact information on immigration does the chart show? How is the information in the chart organized? What kind of immigration statistics are included in the chart?

2. **Find out what can be learned from the information presented.** Ask yourself why the information has been broken into particular classifications or categories. Also, look for relationships among the various kinds of information included in the chart. Pose questions such as the following: Why are these kinds of information linked together in the chart? What is the overall picture presented by these various categories of information?

3. **Decide how the visual information relates to the text.** Ask yourself how the material on immigration presented in the text relates to what is shown in the chart. Think about how the information given in the chart adds to what you have learned about immigration from reading the text.

4. **Learn what patterns and distributions are present.** Take an overall look at the chart. Pose questions about geographic distribution, cultural patterns, and demographic patterns such as the following: What is the total immigration for the time period shown? Did the major sources of immigration change over the time frame covered by the chart?

Applying the Skill

Sociologists pose and answer questions about demographic variables to better understand the effects of population change on societies. You, too, can undertake this task by applying the posing and answering questions guidelines to the chart titled "Birth and Death Rates for Selected Nations" on page 407.

1. **Determine what information is presented.** Study the chart and ask: What regions and countries are included in the chart? What demographic information on these regions and countries is shown in the chart?

2. **Discover what can be learned from the information presented.** Consider why the information is organized by regions. Also, ask yourself what overall picture is presented by including information on birthrates, death rates, infant mortality rates, and life expectancy.

3. **Decide how the information in the chart relates to the text.** Ask yourself how the material on demographic variables presented in the text relates to what is shown on the chart. Think about why the chart adds to what you have read about birthrates, death rates, infant mortality rates, and life expectancy.

4. **Find out what the chart reveals about demographic patterns and distributions.** Consider what the information in the chart can tell you. Pose questions such as the following: In which regions are birthrates, death rates, and infant mortality rates the highest? In which regions is life expectancy the highest? What does this say about these regions?

Practicing the Skill

Turn to the chart titled "Growth Rates and Doubling Times for Selected Nations" on page 412. Pose and answer questions about this chart by applying the guidelines discussed above.

SECTION 2

OBJECTIVES

1. *Explain how cities evolved and why urbanization is such a recent event.*

2. *Identify the models that have been proposed to explain the structure of cities and summarize the theories that have been put forth to explain city life.*

2 URBAN LIFE

Read to Discover

1. How did cities evolve, and why is urbanization such a recent event?
2. What models have been proposed to explain the structure of cities, and what theories have been put forth to explain city life?

Define

urbanization, city, overurbanization, urban ecology, concentric zone model, sector model, multiple nuclei model, urban sprawl, urban anomie theory, compositional theory, subcultural theory

Identify

Ernest W. Burgess, Homer Hoyt, Louis Wirth, Herbert J. Gans, Claude S. Fischer

Some sociologists are particularly interested in the ways that the movement of populations affects the social world. In fact, sociology initially developed from the effort to understand the changes accompanying a particular kind of movement—**urbanization**. This movement involves the concentration of the population in cities. A **city** is a permanent concentration of a relatively large number of people who are engaged mainly in nonfarming activities. Urbanization is a relatively recent event in the history of the world. However, it has profoundly changed the way that most people live their lives.

The Evolution of the City

The first recognizable cities appeared between about 5,500 and 7,000 years ago. Yet until very recently, only a small proportion of the population lived in urban areas. As late as 1800 only about 3 percent of the world's population lived in cities of more than 100,000 inhabitants. As of 2001 approximately 46 percent of the world's people live in urban areas, and the world's urban population is growing by almost 60 million a year. Demographers estimate that by 2030, urban dwellers will make up about 60 percent of the world's population.

Why did it take so long for urbanization to become commonplace? According to sociologists, the rise of cities appears to be tied to two important developments—the Agricultural Revolution and the Industrial Revolution.

The Agricultural Revolution involved the cultivation of grain, the domestication of animals, and the development of a basic agricultural technology. These developments allowed people to produce a surplus of food for the first time. Food surpluses freed large numbers of people from agricultural activities. In time, these people took up more specialized types of work, such as craftwork and trading. These types of activities are most conveniently pursued where there are large permanent concentrations of people. Thus, cities initially arose when people in specialized roles came together in centralized locations.

The further development and spread of cities did not occur for centuries, until the Industrial Revolution replaced hand tools with machines. The Industrial Revolution also replaced traditional sources of energy such as animal labor with new sources such as coal, water, and steam. These new sources of energy dramatically increased productivity and led to the rise of the factory as a system of production. Factories, which were generally located in or near cities, required large pools of labor. Thus, thousands of people left the countryside in search of employment opportunities in the cities.

The Industrial Revolution also produced more-advanced technologies for the transportation and storage of food. These changes allowed cities to support ever-increasing numbers of people who could fill the labor demands generated by further industrial development.

The Preindustrial City Cities first arose about 6,000 years ago on the fertile banks of rivers such as the Nile in Egypt, the Tigris and Euphrates in what is now Iraq, the Indus in what is now Pakistan, and the Huang in China. Similar urban settlements appeared centuries later in other parts of the world.

Compared with the cities of today, early urban settlements were very small. Most preindustrial cities contained a few thousand people while some were considerably larger. Population size was limited by the use of inefficient agricultural techniques that could not

INTERPRETING VISUALS Many European cities built in the Middle Ages were designed to protect their citizens from raiders. *How do you think this town's location and wall might have protected its citizens?*

SECTION 2 RESOURCES

REPRODUCIBLE & REVIEW

- Mastering Critical Thinking Skills 16
- Readings and Case Studies in Sociology 16
- Study Skills and Writing Guide
- Section 2 Review, p. 431

TECHNOLOGY

- One-Stop Planner, Lesson 16.2
- Teaching Transparency: Models of City Structure
- Homework Practice Online
- HRW Go site

Visual Answer

The town's location on a waterfront and its wall would have helped protect it from outside attacks.

SUGGESTION 1: Organize students into groups and give each group a piece of butcher paper. Have each group create a large annotated time line or visual diagram that traces how cities evolved as well as the growth of urbanization. Groups should address the importance of the Agricultural Revolution and the Industrial Revolution to urbanization, and they should describe some of the characteristics of cities at different periods in time. Then have each group display its work in the classroom. Use the time lines and diagrams as visual aids for a class discussion about how cities evolved and why urbanization is such a recent event.

COOPERATIVE LEARNING

SUGGESTION 2: Pair students and have each pair create a series of cause-and-effect chains related to the evolution of cities and the development of urbanization. *(For example: Agricultural Revolution; enabled the production of surplus food; freed many agricultural laborers to do more specialized types of work; these types of occupations were better suited to cities; led more people to settle in cities.)* Each pair should create at least three cause-and-effect chains. Then call on volunteers to share some of their chains with the class. Use the activity as the basis of a discussion on the development of cities, the causes of urbanization, and why urbanization is such a recent event.

COOPERATIVE LEARNING

Interdisciplinary Connection

HISTORY

City Waste Management. Public garbage collection is a relatively recent phenomenon in the United States. For example, in San Francisco laws against public dumping were not passed until 1896, when the city built its first waste incinerator. The rapid growth of the city quickly exceeded the capacity of the incinerator, which led to the city's first landfill in 1935. By 1977 all of San Francisco's landfills were filled to capacity, and the city began shipping its waste to neighboring counties.

ACTIVITY: Use the information about waste management as the basis of a class discussion about the social issues connected with rapid city growth.

Visual Answer

Answers will vary, but students might mention that cities of the past and present differ in architecture, technology, environment, and size in area and population.

INTERPRETING VISUALS Industrialization greatly affected many cities. London was a crowded busy city during the late 1800s. Today, about 75 percent of Americans live in urban areas. *How do you think cities today differ from industrialized cities in the 1800s?*

produce enough food to support more people. In addition, communication and transportation methods were primitive by modern standards. Food had to be carried into the cities from farming areas either by animals or by humans on roads that were typically little more than dirt tracks.

Life in the early cities was quite different from what we know today. Most cities were very crowded and lacked any kind of sanitation system. As a result, death rates in cities were higher than those in rural areas. Ineffective medical techniques also contributed to the high death rates. Because of these conditions, epidemics could drastically reduce the population of a city in a very short time. For example, the Black Death, or bubonic plague, killed about one third of Europe's population between 1347 and 1350.

There was no designated downtown area in preindustrial cities. Traders usually worked out of their homes, which they used as shops. Most people who performed particular crafts or trades lived and worked in distinct sectors of the city. Generally, each occupational grouping had its own quarter. People were also segregated into classes or castes. Poor people usually lived on the outskirts of the city while those who were wealthy lived in the center.

Finally, day-to-day life in preindustrial cities was built around kinship relations and the extended family. With rare exceptions, city governments were organized as monarchies or oligarchies.

The Industrial City The nature of life in preindustrial cities changed little for almost 5,000 years. Then the Industrial Revolution produced an explosive growth in both the size and number of cities. Mechanization allowed farmers to produce a surplus of food. It also reduced the number of workers needed to work the farms. People no longer needed on the farms moved to the cities, where they filled the need for factory workers. Increased food surpluses and improved communication and transportation allowed cities to support ever-increasing numbers of people.

The industrial city differed greatly from the preindustrial city. It covered a greater area and had a much larger population. Commerce became the focal point of life in the industrial city. Central business districts including stores, offices, and banks replaced the segregated trade quarters common in preindustrial cities.

Social life in the industrial city was also transformed. People began to leave their homes to travel to work in offices or factories. The power of the family over the individual lessened as many single people gained their independence in the city. According to sociologists, urbanization also contributed to the rise of a number of social problems. Crime, overcrowding, and pollution all increased as cities grew larger.

The history of the United States illustrates the rapid urbanization that accompanied the Industrial Revolution. In 1790 only 5 percent of the U.S. population lived in cities. By 1860 about one fifth of the population

Mapping Social Forces

◼ TEACH

Have students read the feature Measuring Changes in Urban Life and examine the four maps of Chicago. Next, use the activity under Think About It to prompt a class discussion. Then have students discuss other types of sociological questions that they might pose about the four maps of Chicago.

◼ EXTEND

1. Have students request from the U.S. Census Bureau a Chicago-area map that shows highways and median family income for the most recent year available. Then have each student write a paragraph analyzing whether Chicago still follows the pattern that Hoyt had noted. **BLOCK SCHEDULING**

2. Invite an experienced real estate agent to speak to the class about the residential patterns of your city or of the nearest large city. Ask the speaker to refer to a map and indicate the three grades of residential areas. **BLOCK SCHEDULING**

Mapping
SOCIAL FORCES

MEASURING CHANGES IN URBAN LIFE

In his 1939 study *The Structure and Growth of Residential Neighborhoods in American Cities*, urban sociologist Homer Hoyt attempted to identify patterns in the location of a city's high-, middle-, and low-income residential areas. Hoyt referred to these areas as high-grade, intermediate-grade, and low-grade residential areas. Hoyt noted that as a city grew, high-income areas tended to move from the center along major transportation routes toward open spaces on the city's outer edge. Hoyt used the city of Chicago to illustrate this pattern.

The Evolution of Socioeconomic Areas in Chicago, 1857–1930

1857   1873   1899   1930

▨ Low-Grade Residential Area
▨ Intermediate-Grade Residential Area
▨ High-Grade Residential Area

Chicago

internet connect

TOPIC: Mapping Urban Growth
GO TO: go.hrw.com
KEYWORD: SC3 SL16

Have students access the internet through the HRW Go site to conduct research on urban growth. Then have students working individually or in small groups create a map that illustrates the growth of one of the cities. Display students' completed maps in the classroom.

Think About It

Study Hoyt's four maps of Chicago carefully. Pose and answer a question about the changing residential patterns in Chicago between 1857 and 1930. Then pose and answer a question on what residential patterns in a large city like Chicago might look like today.

Think About It Answers

first sample question—How did the high-grade residential areas of Chicago change over time? sample answer—High-grade residential areas tended to keep to the city's outer edge.

second sample question—Where would low-grade residential areas in today's large cities most likely be located? sample answer—toward the center of the city

SUGGESTION 3: Ask students to imagine that they are time travelers who are studying the history of the development of cities. Have each student write a series of short journal entries describing the various stages of city development that they witness during their travels. Students' journals should mention the importance of the Agricultural and Industrial Revolutions to the growth of urbanization and discuss some of the changes that cities went through over time. When students have finished the assignment, briefly trace the evolution of cities. As you do, call on volunteers to read journal entries appropriate to the stage where the class is in the discussion. Finally, have students discuss why urbanization is such a recent event.

SUGGESTION 4: Organize students into groups and have each group create a board game that is related to how cities evolved and why urbanization is such a recent event. Each group should create a gameboard that has players move along a path tracing the evolution of cities. In addition, groups should create all necessary game pieces and instructions for playing and winning the game. Then have groups exchange games and play the ones they receive. Follow up with a class discussion reviewing the main points in the evolution of cities and urbanization. **COOPERATIVE LEARNING**

◆ Sociology in the World Today

Overurbanization and Underemployment.

One of the most serious consequences of overurbanization is underemployment. Underemployment occurs when people work fewer hours than they would prefer (such as working part-time when a person would prefer to work full-time) or when people must take jobs for which they are overqualified. In cities undergoing rapid urbanization, the population often grows faster than the number of available jobs. Consequently, workers tend to take any job available, no matter how low the pay or how limited the work.

CRITICAL THINKING

What might be strategies for reducing underemployment in rapidly growing cities?

ANSWER: Students might mention that a city could provide tax incentives to draw businesses to the area or create city-funded programs to help expand the economy and create jobs.

Map Answers

1. Students might suggest that the area has continued to grow.

2. The map shows that East Coast cities have grown so large as to form an entire urbanized corridor.

424

Megalopolis, 1960

NEW YORK · NEW HAMPSHIRE · Boston · MASSACHUSETTS · CONNECTICUT · RHODE ISLAND · PENNSYLVANIA · New York City · Atlantic Ocean · NEW JERSEY · MARYLAND · WEST VIRGINIA · DELAWARE · VIRGINIA · Washington, D.C.

N · W · E · S

60 km
0   60 Miles

■ Metropolitan Statistical Area in 1950
■ Counties added by 1960

INTERPRETING MAPS In his book, *Megalopolis*, Jean Gottman described the growth of an urbanized corridor that ran the entire length of the East Coast from Virginia to New Hampshire.
1. **Drawing Inferences and Conclusions:** How do you think this area has changed since 1960?
2. **Analyzing Information:** How do you think this map reflects the fact that about 75 percent of Americans live in urban areas?

lived in urban areas. However, urbanization was largely confined to the Northeast. Today about 75 percent of Americans live in urban areas, and almost every region of the country is heavily urbanized.

Urbanization in more-developed nations has generally followed an ordered progression. In addition, it has usually resulted in increased rates of literacy, greater economic opportunities, and improved health care. Although problems do exist in the cities of the modern world, urbanization and industrialization have led to a higher standard of living than has ever been known before.

Urbanization in the less-developed nations has been less orderly and more rapid. For example, the population

of Mexico City rose from 5 million people in 1960 to more than 18 million in 2000. This figure is expected to exceed 20 million in the early 2000s. In many of the less-developed nations, the rapid growth of cities has led to **overurbanization**—a situation in which more people live in a city than can be supported in terms of jobs and facilities. Thus, people in overurbanized cities do not have adequate housing, food, sewage disposal, or medical services. The crowded and unsanitary living conditions contribute to high rates of illness and death. Overurbanization and the social problems that accompany it have become a major challenge throughout Latin America, Asia, and Africa.

TEACH OBJECTIVE 2

To help students summarize the models that have been proposed to explain the structure of cities and the theories that have been put forth to explain city life, copy the graphic organizer at the right onto the chalkboard, omitting the italicized answers. Have students copy and complete the organizer. Discuss the answers with the class. Then organize the class into small groups and have each group write and perform a short skit about urban life from the perspective of one of the three theories of city life in the graphic organizer. Then have students discuss which theory of city life they support and why. **ENGLISH LANGUAGE LEARNERS** , **COOPERATIVE LEARNING**

MODELS

Concentric Zone Model
City spreads outward from center, resulting in a series of circles, or zones.

Sector Model
City grows in wedge-shaped sectors outward from center to edges of city.

Multiple-Nuclei Model
City develops around several centers of activity, or "nuclei," devoted to specialized land use.

THEORIES

Anomie Theory
City is anonymous and unfriendly and carries negative consequences for residents.

Compositional Theory
Greater diversity of city residents leads to greater variety of lifestyles.

Subcultural Theory
People can find others with similar interests in diverse cities; some people form close ties.

Urban Ecology

During the 1920s and 1930s, sociologists interested in urban life developed an approach to the study of cities called **urban ecology**. This approach examines the relationship between people and the urban environment. In essence, urban ecologists argue that human behavior determines the overall layout of the urban environment. In turn, the urban environment affects human behavior.

According to sociological studies, urban areas do not develop in random patterns. Rather, different areas of a city tend to be used for different, set purposes. As a result, people, buildings, and activities in a city are distributed in certain patterns. Sociologists have developed three models to describe this pattern: the concentric zone model, the sector model, and the multiple nuclei model.

THE WAY WE'RE GOING, THIRTY YEARS FROM NOW THIS WILL BE A DOWNTOWN PARK...

APOLLO 11

INTERPRETING VISUALS Urban growth has led some sociologists to express concern. *How do you think this cartoon illustrates this concern?*

Models of City Structure

Concentric Zone Model

Sector Model

Multiple Nuclei Model

District
1. Central business district
2. Wholesale light manufacturing
3. Low-class residential
4. Middle-class residential
5. Upper-class residential
6. Heavy manufacturing
7. Outlying business district
8. Residential suburb
9. Industrial suburb
10. Commuters' zone

Source: Adapted from "The Nature of Cities," by Chauncy D. Harris and Edward L. Ullman.

INTERPRETING CHARTS These models show different perspectives on urban growth. *What aspects of each model can you recognize in the town nearest to you?*

Case Study

Studying Urban Ecology.
In 1997 the National Science Foundation awarded grants for two long-term studies of urban ecology. The studies are following the urban ecologies of Baltimore, Maryland, and Phoenix, Arizona. These two cities were selected because they greatly differ. Phoenix is a relatively young city that is changing quickly. In contrast, Baltimore is one of the country's oldest cities.

CRITICAL THINKING
Name an advantage of studying a young, rapidly changing city.

ANSWER: Sociologists can compare current changes to the past development of other cities.

Visual Answer

shows an astronaut worrying that urban growth will soon reach the Moon

Chart Answer

Answers will vary, but students should exhibit an understanding of the three models.

Technology Resources

Teaching Transparency: Models of City Structure

HOMEWORK: Have each student collect two to three current news articles that describe either problems or benefits related to city life. Students should write a few sentences summarizing each article. When the class next meets, have volunteers share with the other students some of the articles that they found. Promote student discussion and feedback. Then use the articles to create a bulletin board on urbanization and city life. Encourage students to examine the bulletin board during their free moments in class.

CONNECTING *to History*

Instruct students to read David Macaulay's *City: A Story of Roman Planning and Construction,* in which the author illustrates through detailed drawings and descriptive text how the Romans built preindustrial cities through careful planning. Then have each student create a poster about Roman cities. In their posters, students might highlight the characteristics of a Roman city, describe methods that the Romans used to plan and build cities, or consider how and if Roman methods might be used today.

BLOCK SCHEDULING

Interdisciplinary Connection

ECONOMICS

Economic Urban Renewal. One way cities work to rebuild the economies of low-income urban areas is through Community Development Corporations (CDCs). These corporations partner with local governments, property developers, and private retailers to revitalize low-income, urban neighborhoods. CDCs work to strengthen urban communities by creating affordable housing, providing social services, conducting job training and placement, and initiating enterprise development. According to a recent review of 50 CDCs, the organizations had invested more than $275 million in commercial development and created or retained more than 10,700 jobs.

CRITICAL THINKING

Why might job training be an important part of urban renewal?

ANSWER: Job training increases residents' skills, which encourages existing businesses to hire from within the community and other business to locate in the area.

Visual Answer

Commuter-zone residents traveled to their jobs, which were in the city.

426

INTERPRETING VISUALS According to the concentric zone model, the last ring of city growth was composed of a commuters zone. *What characteristics marked the lives of residents in the commuter zone during the mid-1900s?*

The chart on page 425 provides a visual representation of each of these models.

Concentric Zone Model In 1925 sociologist Ernest W. Burgess proposed the **concentric zone model** to describe urban structure. According to this model, a typical industrial city spreads outward from the center, resulting in a series of circles, or zones.

Each of these zones differs in terms of land use. The central business district, an area used for hotels, banking, commerce, offices, and entertainment, lies at the center. A wholesale-light-manufacturing zone, also called the transition zone, surrounds the central business district. Run-down buildings, poverty, disease, and crime characterize this zone. A series of increasingly expensive residential areas lie beyond the transition zone. The most distant of these areas is the commuters' zone. The city's wealthiest people live in the commuter zone in large, single-family houses away from the noise and bustle of the city. Commuter zone residents travel to their jobs in the city by car or public transportation.

Burgess noted that the city's residential areas are constantly changing. People tend to move to more expensive homes as their socioeconomic status improves. Therefore, the boundaries of the residential zones change over time. He also pointed out that few, if any, cities exactly follow the concentric zone model. Geographic features, such as rivers or lakes and railroad lines, Burgess suggested, might prevent the development of concentric circular zones.

Sector Model Not all sociologists agreed with Burgess's portrayal of city structure. They pointed out that while it did describe some cities, such as Chicago in the early

1900s, it failed to consider important factors, such as available forms of transportation. Sociologist Homer Hoyt addressed this issue in the sector model. Like Burgess, Hoyt proposed that cities grow outward from the center and that the central business district is the core of the city. However, in the **sector model** Hoyt argued that growth occurs in wedge-shaped sectors—not concentric circles—outward from the center to the edge of the city.

According to Hoyt, transportation systems determine land use in the city. For example, warehouses are usually located along railroads that extend from the inner city. Poor people tend to live next to transportation routes that run close to factories. Wealthy people, on the other hand, live near the fastest lines of transportation in attractive areas of the city. Hoyt argued that each sector of land use extends along transportation routes to the edge of the city.

Multiple Nuclei Model Hoyt's sector model painted a fairly accurate picture of the structure of some U.S. cities such as San Francisco. However, it focused on transportation systems available before the widespread use of the automobile. Geographers Chauncy Harris and Edward Ullman developed a model that addressed the influence of the automobile on urban ecology.

In their **multiple nuclei model**, Harris and Ullman suggested that a city does not develop around one central core but around several centers of activity, or "nuclei." Each one of these nuclei is devoted to a specialized type of land use. For example, automobile dealerships often cluster together in one or two areas of the city while light-manufacturing industries are often found in industrial parks on the city's edge. For the most part, clustering occurs because it is beneficial. Several stores grouped together will attract more customers than one single store.

Case Studies and Other True Stories

■ TEACH

Have students read the feature Urban Issues Today and answer the questions that follow it. Then have each student write a news editorial that supports one method for revitalizing central-city areas—either a method mentioned in the feature or another idea. Students' plans should address issues such as economic accessibility for all social classes, city tax revenues, and urban community and green spaces.

■ EXTEND

Organize the class into small groups and ask them to imagine that they are urban renewal planners. Have each group design a plan to revitalize a fictional city's downtown center. The plan should list the city problems that need to be addressed, such as low tax revenues, and then summarize suggestions for addressing some of these problems and revitalizing the downtown area. Have each group present some of its ideas to the city officials (the rest of the class.) **COOPERATIVE LEARNING**, **BLOCK SCHEDULING**

Case Studies
AND OTHER TRUE STORIES

URBAN ISSUES TODAY

One of the major trends in urbanization during the 1900s was the movement from the central cities to the suburbs. Estimates suggest that today more than half of all Americans live in suburbs. As more and more members of the middle and upper classes have flocked to suburbs, low-income minority residents have made up an increasingly higher percentage of the population of central cities. Many large cities—such as St. Louis, Detroit, Newark, Washington, D.C., and Baltimore—now have predominantly minority populations.

Falling Tax Revenues

With the migration of a city's middle- and upper-income residents to the suburbs, the burden of providing city services falls to the poorer members of the community. City services—such as roads, schools, police and fire protection, sanitation, and public parks—are funded in large part through property taxes.

Property taxes are based on property values. Because poor people tend to live in housing with low property values, the tax base declines when they are responsible for generating the bulk of tax revenues. A decline in tax revenues, in turn, generally leads to a decline in city services. Once city services begin to decline, many of the remaining wealthier residents leave the city.

Urban Renewal and Gentrification

During the 1960s and 1970s, state and federal governments attempted to restore many central cities through urban renewal. Urban-renewal programs were designed to provide adequate housing for low-income families and to rebuild the economies of the central cities. In many instances, renewal efforts resulted in single-family homes being bulldozed to make room for high-rise buildings designed to house poor people. Many of these buildings were not well constructed and soon developed problems. In addition, many of the buildings became breeding grounds for crime and violence.

In response to the failure of previous urban-renewal efforts, the federal government

New housing developments in urban centers have replaced older buildings and brought wealthier residents into older neighborhoods.

attempted to ease the housing problems in the central cities by increasing the availability of low-income, single-family housing. In addition, many city governments tried to increase tax revenues through gentrification—the upgrading of specific neighborhoods in an attempt to encourage the middle and upper classes to relocate to the cities. Gentrification appears to have achieved its goals in some cities. A 1999 survey found that many major cities expected their downtown populations to grow by 2010.

Supporters of gentrification argue that it brings considerable benefits to cities. First, property values rise. This, in turn, results in higher property taxes and greater tax revenues. Over time, new stores and restaurants move into the gentrified neighborhoods. However, critics charge that these benefits come at a price. High housing costs and rents, they argue, will drive out long-time residents of gentrified neighborhoods. Small businesses that have been fixtures in these neighborhoods will also leave because of high rents. Rising property values will eventually push the middle class out of the housing market in gentrified areas. As a result, only the wealthy will be able to afford to live in central cities. While these critics agree that central cities need to be revitalized, they feel that government should develop gentrification policies that encourage social and economic diversity by providing affordable housing for low-income and middle-class families.

Think About It
1. **Analyzing Information** *What is gentrification, and what are its advantages and disadvantages?*
2. **Supporting a Point of View** *What steps do you think government might take to revitalize central-city areas while also providing adequate housing for low-income and middle-class families?*

Think About It Answers

1. Gentrification is the upgrading of specific neighborhoods in an attempt to encourage the middle- and upper-classes to relocate to them. Advantages include a rise in property values, which results in greater tax revenues. Disadvantages include the displacement of low-income residents and small local businesses.

2. The government could encourage gentrification while providing financial assistance for low-income residents looking to purchase a home in the neighborhood.

SPOTLIGHT *on Overurbanization*

Have students prepare reports on overurbanization in Asia, Africa, or Latin America by selecting a fast-growing large city in one of these areas and comparing it to a large city in the United States. The report should compare the cities' total population, population growth rate, size in area, technological development, economy, residential patterns, transportation systems, housing, and urban problems. Then have each student conclude the report with suggestions for ways to slow or cope with overurbanization in the researched city. Encourage students to include visuals, such as images or charts, in their reports. **BLOCK SCHEDULING**

CONNECTING *to the Arts*

Have each student conduct research to find three examples of art showing urbanization and city life at various points in time. Art pieces might include paintings, engravings, illustrations, collages, mixed media, or sculptures. Have students write a short caption for each piece of art providing information about the art, such as its creator, title, date, and general subject matter. Then call on volunteers to present some of their art examples to the class for analysis and discussion. Remind students to consider some of the sociological issues and theories related to urbanization and city life when examining the artworks. **BLOCK SCHEDULING**

Sociology in the World Today

Addressing Urban Sprawl. Some groups are working to contain urban sprawl by promoting various environment-friendly development policies. Such policies include setting restrictions and boundaries on growth, so that it might occur without creating sprawl; planning pedestrian-friendly development; and revitalizing existing developed areas before developing new areas.

CRITICAL THINKING

What opposing concerns need to be balanced when addressing urban sprawl?

ANSWER: the need to promote economic growth and commercial and residential development while considering environmental implications

Careers
IN SOCIOLOGY

URBAN AND RURAL SOCIOLOGISTS

Urban sociologists investigate the origin, growth, structure, composition, and population of cities. These sociologists specialize in studying the social and economic patterns of living that are common in the city environment. Many urban sociologists work as urban planners, helping cities plan for the needs of urban populations in areas such as housing, commerce, parks, and transportation. Urban sociology is also related to rural sociology. Rural sociologists study the way of life in rural communities and the contrasts between rural and urban living.

Many urban sociologists are interested in how people interact in urban spaces.

Growth, Harris and Ullman argued, affects not only the size of nuclei but also the number and types of nuclei. Multiple nuclei can develop because of the widespread use of automobiles and highways.

Urban Ecology Models—A Critique These three models describe ideal types of cities. Thus, the models are not expected to be exact reflections of any one or all urban areas in the United States. In combination, however, they reveal the general pattern of land use in cities. For example, they reflect one of the major trends in urbanization of the 1900s—the movement of populations from the central cities to the suburbs. However, they do not reflect several recent developments such as urban sprawl and reverse migration from the suburbs to city downtown areas.

Urban sprawl is characterized by poorly planned development on the edge of cities and towns. Designed with little thought for the surrounding environment, sprawl consumes huge amounts of land. This haphazard development does not fit the rather orderly picture of urban ecology that is presented by the models. Further, these models characterize downtown areas as places for mostly business and industry. All residential areas located downtown in the urban ecology models tend to be home to low-income residents. However, in recent years there has been a well-established trend of reverse migration from the suburbs into the central cities. A 1999 survey of

26 major cities found that they all expected their downtown populations to grow by 2010.

In addition, these models fail to take full account of how cultural factors affect urban ecology. Walter Firey suggested that culture and sentiment may have an important influence on urban development. Firey cited the Italian American community of Boston's North End neighborhood as an example. Some Italian American families, Firey noted, are wealthy enough to move to more expensive neighborhoods. However, they tend to stay in North End because of their cultural attachment to the community.

Explaining City Life

Sociologists are interested not only in the structure of cities but also in the nature of life in cities. Over the years, a number of theories have been proposed to explain city life. Among the most influential theories are urban anomie theory, compositional theory, and subcultural theory.

Urban Anomie Theory In a groundbreaking study titled "Urbanism as a Way of Life," sociologist Louis Wirth put forward an **urban anomie theory**. According to this theory, the city is an anonymous and unfriendly place, and living there carries serious negative consequences for residents. Wirth argued that the size, density, and diversity of urban life discourage the formation of primary group relationships. This argument is

CONNECTING *to the Arts*

In the "Rhapsody in Blue" segment of the Disney animated feature *Fantasia 2000*, animator Eric Goldberg borrows the style of the legendary caricaturist Al Hirshfeld to spin a whimsical tale of the daily lives of several distinctive and diverse characters inhabiting Manhattan during the Jazz Age. The short segment illustrates the American urban experience of that period. Have students view the segment and then lead a class discussion of which theory (or theories) of city life are represented in or contradicted by the story.

BLOCK SCHEDULING

SPOTLIGHT *on Urban Simulation Games*

Have students conduct a study of urban-simulation computer and video games. These games challenge players to build effective communities (such as amusement parks, cities, civilizations, and families), manage growth, and respond to problems. Students should conduct research on the history of urban simulation games, the different categories and types of urban simulation games, the games' relative popularity, reasons that people play these games, and what sociologists might learn from these games. Have each student write an article for a fictional sociology journal reporting his or her findings. **BLOCK SCHEDULING**

particularly true, Wirth said, of those relationships based on kinship ties and the neighborhood. Consequently, life in the city is characterized by relationships only within impersonal secondary groups. The lack of primary group relationships results in anomie, or normlessness.

Why does city life produce anomie? According to Wirth, city dwellers come into contact with many people on a daily basis. Because most of these people are strangers, interaction tends to be short-lived, formal, and shallow. To keep themselves from having to become personally involved with everyone with whom they come into contact, city dwellers often take on an unfriendly impersonal attitude. This attitude discourages interaction and communication, leading individuals to withdraw further from each other. The result is a lack of involvement with others and thus a feeling of detachment.

According to urban anomie theory, the impersonal nature of city life extends to situations that call for social involvement and responsibility. One specific example of city dwellers' withdrawal from social responsibility is the 1964 murder of Kitty Genovese. Returning home from work, Genovese was stabbed repeatedly by an assailant in front of her New York City apartment building. Although the attack lasted for an extended period of time, no one came to her aid. Police investigations later discovered that 38 people had either heard Genovese screaming or had actually witnessed the murder. Most of these people said that they did not intervene because they did not want to get involved.

The Genovese incident caused many sociologists to review Wirth's ideas on city life. In a 1970 study of group behavior, Bibb Latané and John Darley found that the larger the group, the less likely people are to become involved. Latané and Darley proposed that there is a diffusion of responsibility that each group member presumes that someone else will take action. In *Being Urban*, David Karp, Gregory Stone, and William Yoels suggested that this reluctance to get involved is not a result of normlessness. Rather, people are following the norm of noninvolvement. The authors of *Being Urban* argued that the city dwellers' behavior, as described by Wirth, is simply an effective method of handling impersonal city life.

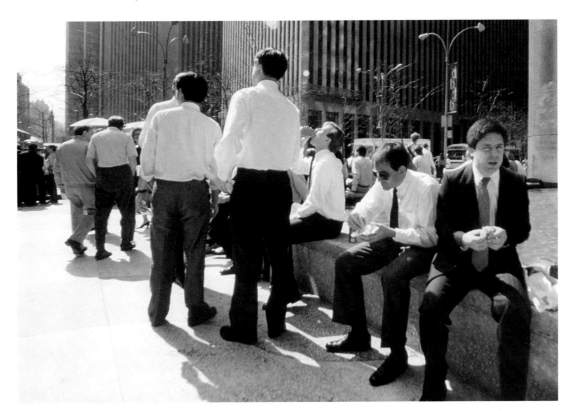

INTERPRETING VISUALS According to the urban anomie theory, urban life is filled with anonymous impersonal relationships. *How does this image of a lunchtime crowd in a city plaza give evidence for or against this theory?*

Sociology Then and Now

Urban Values? In the 1960s sociologist Alex Inkeles and his colleagues interviewed 6,000 men from six developing countries—Argentina, Chile, East Pakistan, India, Israel, and Nigeria—in an attempt to determine the effects of urbanization on people's attitudes and values. The study found four values common to people living in urban areas. The values were openness to new experiences and new ways of doing things, a shift from traditional authority figures to government and occupational authority, belief in the efficacy of science over religion, and ambition for oneself and one's children.

ACTIVITY: Have each student write a short essay expressing his or her opinion of whether these four values accurately characterize urban attitudes in U.S. cities today.

Visual Answer

Some students might suggest that the photo discounts urban anomie theory because it shows many people sharing a public space. Other students might suggest that the photo supports urban anomie theory because few of the people seem to be interacting.

CLOSE

In a class discussion, call on volunteers to identify some major urban issues today. List students' responses on the chalkboard. Then ask students to brainstorm actions that might be taken to combat urban challenges. Have the class evaluate each suggestion.

REVIEW AND ASSESS

Have students complete the **Section 2 Review** on p. 431. As **Alternative Assessment**, you may want to use the evolution of the city time line or visual diagram or the city life skit in this section's lessons.

RETEACH

Have each student write one or two paragraphs about city development, urbanization, and city life. Students should use at least 10 of the section's Define and Identify terms in their paragraphs. Next, tell students to erase each section term and replace it with a numbered blank. Students should list the term that belongs in each numbered blank on the backs of their papers. Then pair students and have partners complete each other's paragraphs and check their answers against the provided answer keys. Finally, quickly review the section's main ideas with students.

ENGLISH LANGUAGE LEARNERS , COOPERATIVE LEARNING

SECTION ② REVIEW ANSWERS

1. Define:
- urbanization, p. 421
- city, p. 421
- overurbanization, p. 424
- urban ecology, p. 425
- concentric zone model, p. 426
- sector model, p. 426
- multiple nuclei model, p. 426
- urban sprawl, p. 428
- urban anomie theory, p. 428
- compositional theory, p. 430
- subcultural theory, p. 431

2. Identify:
- Ernest W. Burgess, p. 426
- Homer Hoyt, p. 426
- Louis Wirth, p. 428
- Herbert J. Gans, p. 430
- Claude S. Fischer, p. 431

3. See the graphic organizer on p. 425 for a summary of each theory.

4a. Cities arose with the Agricultural Revolution, and preindustrial cities were small. Different occupations were located in distinct sectors, and people were segregated into classes or castes. Unsanitary conditions led to high death rates. During the Industrial Revolution people came to the cities in search of jobs. Industrial cities tend to be large, have central business districts, and life is no longer built around the family.

b. Burgess suggests that the typical industrial city spreads outward in a series of zones.

Compositional Theory A number of sociologists have criticized Wirth's theory, saying it portrayed urban life too negatively. They offered several theories that presented a more balanced view of life in the city. One, **compositional theory**, examined the ways in which the composition of a city's population influences life in the city. Factors that affect the composition of a city include age, race, ethnicity, education, income, and occupation. Compositional theory argues that the great diversity of people who live in the city leads to a greater variety of lifestyles than is common in most small towns in the United States.

According to sociologist Herbert J. Gans, five identifiable lifestyles can be found among urban dwellers:

- *The cosmopolites* The cosmopolites are the professionals or intellectuals of the city. They are attracted to life in the city because of its culture, entertainment, and excitement. They also tend to have the financial resources that allow them to take full advantage of the city's diverse attractions.
- *The unmarried or childless* These people work in the city and enjoy the attraction of cultural events and the company of urban friends. Those who marry and decide to have children often move to the suburbs. However, some spend their entire lives in the city.

- *The ethnic villagers* Ethnic villagers are those people who are attracted to the small ethnic areas typical of big cities, such as "Little Havana" or "Little Italy." For ethnic villagers, living among others of the same cultural heritage works to preserve traditions and provides a sense of unity.
- *The deprived* The deprived are those city dwellers who live in disadvantaged or unfavorable circumstances because of poverty. According to Gans, the deprived live in the city because it provides low-skilled jobs, relatively low rent, and public-assistance programs.
- *The trapped* The trapped stay in the city because they cannot afford to leave. Often these are elderly people who are living on fixed incomes.

According to Gans, most individuals who live in cities form communities with others who share the same lifestyle, neighborhood or interests. The city may seem to be an unfriendly, anonymous place to some people. However, it is actually a mosaic composed of a number of groups, each providing a sense of unity and community to its members. In essence, most individuals are able to protect themselves from the unpleasant aspects of city life by forming primary groups with others who are like themselves.

Compositional theory suggests that cities offer a great diversity of lifestyles. According to this theory, city dwellers tend to form relationships and small communities with people who have similar interests or lifestyles.

1. Have half the class work together to build a scale model of a preindustrial city, either real or imagined, and the other half of the class work together to build a scale model of an industrial city, either real or imagined. The models need not be overly elaborate but should demonstrate how technology and business influenced city layout, where different parts of the city were located, available transportation methods, and other applicable features. Then have the class compare and contrast the two models and discuss the ways in which cities have changed. **COOPERATIVE LEARNING**, **BLOCK SCHEDULING**

2. Organize students into small groups and have each group assemble a scrapbook about the development and evolution of your city or of the nearest large city. Scrapbooks might include a copy of the city charter, newspaper articles, maps, photographs, real-estate listings, and tourist brochures. Groups might want to organize their scrapbooks by time period (such as the late 1800s, the early 1900s, the mid-1900s, the late 1900s, and the early 2000s) or by topic (such as the "History of Downtown," "Transportation Through the Years," "Changing Residential Patterns," and "Economic Development").
COOPERATIVE LEARNING, **BLOCK SCHEDULING**

Subcultural Theory In *To Dwell Among Friends*, sociologist Claude S. Fischer employed **subcultural theory** to explain the nature of city life. According to Fischer, the characteristics of the city encourage rather than discourage the formation of primary group relationships. Because of the size and diversity of urban populations, it is possible for people to find others who share the same interests and lifestyles. This opportunity leads to the development of many different subcultures within which close ties may form.

For example, a person living in a small town who is interested in photography might find only a handful of others with the same interest. In a city, on the other hand, there might be thousands of people who are interested in photography. The sheer numbers of people who share this interest can encourage the development of a wide range of clubs, activities, and friendships based on photography. This subculture can continually attract new people as group members meet others who share their interest.

According to subcultural theory, cities provide a place where people develop close ties with others based on their associations in a number of different groups. These groups may be based on such diverse factors as occupation, hobbies, friendships, ethnicity, or even age. Subcultural theory argues that city dwellers are not separated from others. Rather, they are involved in a rich and diverse social life that includes close relationships with family members, friends, neighbors, and associates.

The subculture theory suggests that cities offer a wide range of primary group relationships based on subcultures such as bicycle riders.

Hoyt argues that growth occurs outward in wedge-shaped sectors. Harris and Ullman suggest that cities develop around several distinct nuclei, each devoted to specialized land uses.

5. Essays will vary, but students should exhibit an understanding of the effect of urbanization on societal institutions.

CHAPTER 16 REVIEW
ANSWERS

WRITING A SUMMARY
See the section subtitles for the main topics in this chapter.

IDENTIFYING PEOPLE AND IDEAS

1. number of people living in an area at a particular time

2. annual number of live births per 1,000 members of a population

3. annual number of deaths per 1,000 members of a population

4. average number of years a person born in a particular year can expect to live

5. rate at which a country's population is increasing

6. concentration of relatively large numbers of people who are engaged mainly in non-farming activities

7. study of the relationship between people and the urban environment

8. sociologist who proposed the concentric zone model

SECTION 2 REVIEW

1. Define and explain
urbanization
city
overurbanization
urban ecology
concentric zone model
sector model
multiple nuclei model
urban sprawl
urban anomie theory
compositional theory
subcultural theory

2. Identify and explain
Ernest W. Burgess
Homer Hoyt
Louis Wirth

Herbert J. Gans
Claude S. Fischer

3. Categorizing Copy the graphic organizer below. Use it to explain how each theory describes urban life and the social problems that affect urban subcultures.

```
   Anomie          Compositional
   Theory             Theory
        \            /
         Urban Life
              ↑
        Subcultural
          Theory
```

4. **Finding the Main Idea**
a. Summarize the evolution of cities, focusing on the differences between life in preindustrial cities and life in industrial cities.
b. Compare the views of urban ecology presented by Burgess, Hoyt, and Harris and Ullman. How do they explain urban growth?

5. **Writing and Critical Thinking**
Evaluating Imagine that you are a sociologist studying changes in society caused by urban growth. How do you think urbanization has affected such institutions as family life, education, and social life? Explain your answer in a short essay.
Consider:
• the evolution of cities
• social problems in urban areas
• advantages and disadvantages to urban life

Homework Practice Online
keyword: SL3 HP16

Review and Assessment Resources

- Chapter 16 Review, pp. 432–33
- Chapter Review Activities with Answer Key
- Global Skill Builder CD–ROM
- Chapter 16 Test Generator (on the One-Stop Planner)
- Chapter 16 Test (Form A or B)
- Alternative Assessment Handbook
- HRW Go site

 REVIEW

Have students complete the **Chapter 16 Review** on pp. 432–33.

 ASSESS

Use one of the chapter tests to assess students' understanding of the content. For **Alternative Assessment**, see the **Alternative Assessment Handbook**.

---

9. poorly planned development on the edge of cities and towns

10. sociologist who proposed the urban anomie theory

UNDERSTANDING MAIN IDEAS

1. birthrate, death rate, and migration rate

2. family planning, economic programs, and antinatalism

3. Cities evolved as the Agricultural Revolution produced a surplus of food and freed large numbers of people from agricultural activities. Urbanization is a recent event because it did not occur until the Industrial Revolution enabled cities to grow at a significant rate.

4. concentric zone, sector, and multiple nuclei models

5. crime, overcrowding, and pollution

THINKING CRITICALLY

1. because they do not take into account varying rates among population subgroups

2. push factors—encourage movement out of an area, include religious or political persecution, racial discrimination, overpopulation; pull factors—encourage movement into an area, include religious and political freedom, economic opportunities

3. Malthusian—population growth progresses geometrically and is controlled by preventive and positive checks, fails to account for advances in agricultural technology and birth control; demographic transition—connects population patterns

---

16 Review

Writing a Summary

Using standard grammar, spelling, sentence structure, and punctuation, summarize the information in this chapter.
Consider:
- the growing world population and the different population theories
- the various theories on urbanization
- the social effects of urbanization

 ### Identifying People and Ideas

Identify the following people or terms and use them in appropriate sentences.

1. population
2. birthrate
3. death rate
4. life expectancy
5. growth rate
6. urbanization
7. urban ecology
8. Ernest W. Burgess
9. urban sprawl
10. Louis Wirth

Understanding Main ideas

Section 1 (pp. 406–19)

1. Describe the three demographic variables that determine the size of a population and the population's composition and distribution.

2. What are some of the programs that have been used to control population growth?

Section 2 (pp. 421–31)

3. Describe how cities evolved throughout history and explain why urbanization is such a recent event.

4. What models do sociologists use to explain the structure of cities?

5. What social problems has urbanization helped to create?

Thinking Critically

1. **Analyzing Information** Explain why birthrates and death rates are considered to be crude measures.

2. **Contrasting** How do the push and pull factors of migration differ? Give an example of each factor.

3. **Summarizing** Describe Malthusian theory and demographic transition theory in terms of how each one views population change. What criticisms have been directed at each of these theories?

4. **Evaluating** How have geographic factors influenced the development of cities?

5. **Making Generalizations and Predictions** Do you think urbanization will be a continuing trend in the 2000s? How will this affect American institutions? Explain your answer.

6. **Drawing Inferences and Conclusions** Study the maps and population figures in this chapter. How do you think urbanization and population trends in different regions of the United States might affect socialization in those regions?

 ### Writing About Sociology

1. **Summarizing** Study the compositional theory and subcultural theory of urban life. How have urban problems affected different subcultures in U.S. cities?

2. **Evaluating** Industrialization brought many changes that led to an increase in both population and urbanization. Using a town or city near your school, describe the factors of industrialization that may have encouraged population growth and urbanization in that area, such as the arrival of the railroad or the building of a factory. List the social institutions that may have been affected by this change. Use the graphic organizer below to help you describe the changes in the town you selected.

Industrial Element of Change	Effect on Population and Urbanization	Effect on Institutions

RETEACH

Organize students into small groups and assign each group one of the sections or subsections in this chapter. Have each group develop a detailed outline of its assigned material. Next, instruct each group to exchange its outline with another group. Then have each group write five questions and accompanying answers on the other group's outline. Finally, collect the questions and answers and use them to quiz the class. **ENGLISH LANGUAGE LEARNERS**, **COOPERATIVE LEARNING**

SOCIOLOGY PROJECTS

1. Cooperative Learning Organize students into small groups and have each group create a fictional U.S. city. Groups should briefly summarize the city's history, draw maps of the city at various points in its development, name its chief industries, describe its demographics, and so on.

2. Applying Sociology If your students live in a city, have them correspond with sociology students in another city about topics dealing with urbanization. Students might exchange data, maps, opinions, and personal observations. Have students use the activity to compare and contrast their city with their "sister city."

BUILDING SOCIAL STUDIES SKILLS

Interpreting Tables

Study the table below. Use it to answer the following questions.

U.S. Life Expectancy at Birth, 1900 to 2000			
Year	All	Male	Female
1900	47.3	46.3	48.3
1920	54.1	53.6	54.6
1940	62.9	60.8	65.2
1960	69.7	66.6	73.1
1980	73.7	70.0	77.4
2000	76.9	74.1	79.5

Source: U.S. Census Bureau

1. Advances in science and medicine have contributed to a rising life expectancy for Americans. How much has life expectancy for women increased between 1920 and 1980?

  a. 22.8 years

  b. 28.2 years

  c. 29.1 years

  d. 21.9 years

2. How do you think the demographic trends shown in the graph have affected social life in the United States? What factors have caused these trends?

Analyzing Primary Sources

The following excerpt explores the growing trend toward urbanization in some of the world's most populated cities. Read the excerpt and then answer the questions that follow.

"*Explosive population growth and a torrent of migration from the countryside are creating cities that dwarf the great capitals of the past. By the turn of the century, there will be 21 'megacities' with populations of 10 million or more. Of these, 18 will be in developing countries, including some of the poorest nations in the world. Mexico City already has 20 million people and Calcutta [India] 12 million. According to the World Bank, some of Africa's cities are growing by 10% a year. . . .*

  Is the trend good or bad? Can the cities cope? No one knows for sure. Without question, urbanization has produced miseries so ghastly that they are difficult to comprehend. In Cairo [Egypt] children who elsewhere might be in kindergarten can be found digging through clots of ox dung, looking for undigested kernels of corn to eat. . . . The threat of disease is heightened by urban pollution. . . .

  The megacities will have to defy gravity and invent a sustainable future for themselves. Since the fate of the world is entwined with the fate of its cities, humanity has no other choice."

3. According to the author what will megacities have to do to in the future?

  a. stop growing

  b. become sustainable

  c. encourage people to move to the country

  d. become more organized

4. What problems do megacities face, and why is it important to solve them?

---

to technological development, fails to address how rapid population increases might hamper the modernization of developing nations

4. Cities first arose on the fertile banks of rivers.

5. Answers will vary, but students should exhibit an understanding of how urbanization affects social institutions.

6. Answers will vary, but students should apply the urban anomie, compositional, or subcultural theory to the topic.

WRITING ABOUT SOCIOLOGY

1. Responses will vary, but students should exhibit an understanding of each theory.

2. Answers will vary, but students should exhibit an understanding of the effects of industrialization on population growth and urbanization.

BUILDING SOCIAL STUDIES SKILLS

1. a

2. Answers will vary, but students should analyze the trend of increasing life expectancy for all Americans.

3. b

4. Megacities face problems such as disease, famine, pollution, and poverty, which the author argues must be solved because the future depends upon healthy cities.

SOCIOLOGY PROJECTS

Linking to Community

Research in Sociology Working with a group of two or three other students, research the pattern of urban growth for a large city in your state. Study the theories of urban growth included in this chapter. Using current and historical maps, create a model of urban growth that employs one, two, or all three theories of urban growth.

---

internet connect

Internet Activity: go.hrw.com
KEYWORD: SL3 SC16

Choose an activity on population growth and urbanization to:

• write a report on the effect of urbanization on U.S. institutions.

• create a map of the urban growth of a city.

• create a quiz and answer key based on maps, graphs, charts, databases, and models about the distribution of the U.S. population.

go.hrw.com

Collective Behavior and Social Movements

CHAPTER RESOURCE MANAGER

Objectives	Pacing Guide		Resources

SECTION 1:
Collective
Behavior
(pp. 436–48)

REV Section 1
Review, p. 448

• Contrast the various types of collectivities and describe the explanations for collective behavior that have been proposed.

• Identify the preconditions necessary for collective behavior to occur and explain how they build on one another.

Regular 4 days	**Block** **Scheduling** 2 days

Block Scheduling Handbook with Team Teaching Strategies, Chapter 17

Resources

📼 **CNN.** Presents Sociology: Internet Rumors

📼 **CNN.** Presents Sociology: September 11, 2001: A Turning Point in History

RS Graphic Organizer 17

🔗 HRW Go site

SM Mastering Critical Thinking Skills 17

PS Readings and Case Studies in Sociology 17

E Research Projects and Activities for Teaching Sociology 17

SM Study Skills and Writing Guide

SECTION 2:
Social
Movements
(pp. 449–57)

REV Section 2
Review, p. 455

• Describe the types of social movements that exist and explain how they differ.

• Identify the stages present in the life cycle of social movements and describe ways in which the existence of social movements can be explained.

Regular 4 days	**Block** **Scheduling** 2 days

Block Scheduling Handbook with Team Teaching Strategies, Chapter 17

Chapter Review And Assessment

REV Chapter 17 Review, pp. 458–59

REV Chapter Review Activities with Answer Key

💿 Global Skill Builder CD–ROM

💿 Chapter 17 Test Generator (on the One-Stop Planner)

A Chapter 17 Test (Form A or B)

A Alternative Assessment Handbook

🔗 HRW Go site

Chapter Resource Key

PS Primary Sources	**A** Assessment	📼 Video
RS Reading Support	**REV** Review	🔗 Internet
E Enrichment	🖥 Transparencies	💻 Holt Presentation Maker Using Microsoft® PowerPoint®
SM Skills Mastery	💿 CD–ROM	

One-Stop Planner CD–ROM

See the *One-Stop Planner* for a complete list of additional resources for students and teachers.

One-Stop Planner CD–ROM

It's easy to plan lessons, select resources, and print out materials for your students when you use the **One-Stop Planner CD–ROM with Test Generator.**

Chapter Project Preview

The following activities are included in the Chapter Review. You may want to make the suggested preparations.

CHAPTER REVIEW ACTIVITY

Using Observation Skills Students will analyze propaganda techniques used in television commercials. Students will then write reports documenting their findings. In preparation, create a chart or graphic organizer to help students track and organize their observation notes. (For an example, see the graphic organizer provided for the second Writing About Sociology activity on p. 458.)

LESSON ACTIVITY

Applying Sociology Students will work in groups to interview employees of a local radio station about the station's market and how market information influences advertising. In preparation, contact local radio stations to see if they are willing to

participate in the project and, if so, find out whom students should contact. Then provide each group with information on its contact person.

INTERNET ACTIVITIES

Measuring Public Opinion Students will use provided Internet links to research the ways in which public opinion is measured, analyzed, and manipulated and then create brochures presenting their research. In preparation, provide sample brochures for students to examine and a brochure template for students to use.

Urban Legends Students will use provided Internet links to research collective behavior in the form of urban legends and then write urban legends of their own. You might prepare a sample urban legend as a model for students to use in writing their own legends. In addition, remind students that their legends must be original.

Additional Resources

PRINT RESOURCES FOR TEACHERS
Boorstin, Daniel J. *The Image: A Guide to Pseudo-Events in America.* New York: Vintage Books, 1992. Examines the ways in which the media manipulates information and events to sway public opinion.

Tarrow, Sidney G. *Power in Movement: Social Movements and Contentious Politics.* Cambridge: Cambridge University Press, 1998. Overview of social movements and collective behavior.

PRINT RESOURCES FOR STUDENTS
Brunvand, Jan Harold. *The Baby Train and Other Urban Legends.* New York: W. W. Norton, 1993. Collection of urban legends from around the world. Helps students analyze collective communication.

Gay, Kathleen. *Caution! This May Be an Advertisement: A Teen Guide to Advertising.* New York: Franklin

Watts, 1992. Describes the techniques used by advertisers to persuade consumers to buy their products. Helps students to recognize propaganda techniques and to become wise consumers.

MULTIMEDIA RESOURCES
The Growth of the Labor Movement (filmstrip on vhs; 37 min.) Guidance Associates. Presents the historical development and the current status of the American labor movement.

30-Second Seduction (vhs; 25 min.) Films Incorporated Video. Advertisers and a sociologist explain how television commercials are designed to manipulate human emotions.

The Women's Movement in the United States (Interactive Encyclopedias Series) (software) ABC-CLIO Interactive. Examines some 700 topics related to the women's movement between 1600 and the present.

CHAPTER

Collective Behavior and Social Movements

SECTION 1
Collective Behavior

SECTION 2
Social Movements

CHAPTER REVIEW

Build on What You Know

Ask students to answer the following questions:

How might population density shape collective behavior?

Consider:

- population concentrations and increasing urbanization
- different groups' cultural values and beliefs
- the relationship of individuals to social institutions

How might mass media play a role in social movements?

Consider:

- the development of cable and satellite television technology
- increasing access to the Internet
- increasing popularity of virtual communities

Internet Activity

internet connect

TOPIC: Measuring Public Opinion
GO TO: go.hrw.com
KEYWORD: SL3 SC17

Have students access the Internet through the HRW Go site to conduct research on the ways in which public opinion is measured, analyzed, and manipulated. Then have students, working individually or in small groups, create a brochure about these topics.

434

CHAPTER

17 Collective Behavior and Social Movements

Build on What You Know

Society is rapidly changing as the population grows and becomes urbanized. As society changes, collective behavior may alter and social movements may develop. In this chapter you will explore various types of collectivities and the theories developed to explain collective behavior. You will also study social movements.

Sociologists are interested in how people interact as a collective group.

Life in Society

What is the latest fashion or fad in your school? Have you ever wondered how it suddenly became the "in" thing? Many examples of collective behavior and social movements can be found in communities, news reports, and history books throughout the world.

- In the 1630s a frenzied passion for tulips swept over the Dutch in Holland. Tulips became so desirable and were bought at such a dizzying pace that one bulb soon became as expensive as a house. The Dutch were sure that the world would share their love for tulips, making the sellers wealthy beyond belief. However, thousands of people went bankrupt when the price of tulips plunged.

- The 1963 publication of Betty Friedan's book *The Feminine Mystique* signaled the start of a new social movement that would change the way people viewed gender roles. Since that time, millions of men and women in the United States have actively sought gender equality in all spheres of life.

- In 1965 a California policeman made a routine arrest of an intoxicated driver in a poor section of Los Angeles known as Watts. As the crowd grew, word began to spread that the arrest was racially motivated. Rioting soon broke out in Watts. When the riots ended several days later, 34 people were dead, more than 1,000 people were injured, and 200 buildings had been burned to the ground.

TRUTH OR FICTION *What's Your Opinion?*

Read the following statements about sociology. Do you think they are true or false? You will learn whether each statement is true or false as you read the chapter.

- Collective behavior is fairly easy for sociologists to study.
- Fads and fashions are of little interest to sociologists.
- Social movements are a recent phenomenon.

> ► **WHY SOCIOLOGY MATTERS**
>
> The many social movements of the late 1900s have fascinated sociologists. Use **CNNfyi.com** or other current events sources to learn more about a social movement in the world today. Create a poster of what you learned about the movement.
>
> **CNNfyi.com**

435

SECTION **1**

OBJECTIVES

1. *Contrast the various types of collectivities and describe the explanations for collective behavior that have been proposed.*

2. *Identify the preconditions necessary for collective behavior to occur and explain how they build on one another.*

Before class, write the following scenario on the chalkboard: *You are sitting in a movie theater watching a film, and the film breaks. How does the audience respond?* As students enter the classroom, ask them to respond to the scenario. Most likely, students will say that the audience starts stamping its feet, clapping, or booing. Then ask students why an audience might respond in this way, as none of these actions does anything to fix the film. Guide students to the realization that these actions are a spontaneous response to a situation in which there are no clear standards for behavior. Tell students that such actions are a type of collective behavior, which is the focus of Section 1.

Visual Answer

Students might suggest that commuters on a subway might lack a sense of unity and could possibly have unclear norms for behavior in certain situations.

1

COLLECTIVE BEHAVIOR

Read to Discover

1. How do the various types of collectivities differ, and what explanations for collective behavior have been proposed?

2. What preconditions are necessary for collective behavior to occur, and how do they build on one another?

Define

collective behavior, collectivity, crowd, mob, riot, panic, moral panic, mass hysteria, fashions, fad, rumor, urban legends, public, public opinion, propaganda, contagion theory, emergent-norm theory, value-added theory

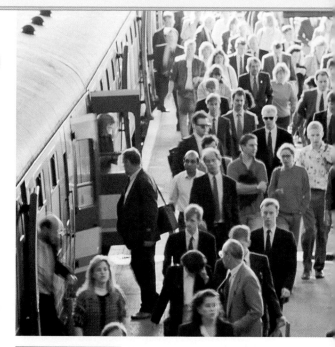

INTERPRETING VISUALS One characteristic of collectivities is that interaction between members is limited. *What other characteristics might commuters on a subway have that would lead a sociologist to consider them to be a collectivity?*

I n general, social behavior is patterned and predictable. People expect others to act in accord with established norms, and usually they do. Without this predictability and cooperative spirit, social interaction would be impossible.

However, sometimes situations occur in which the norms of behavior are unclear. Often in these situations, it appears as though people are making up new norms as they go along. Sociologists refer to this action as **collective behavior**—the relatively spontaneous social behavior that occurs when people try to develop common solutions to unclear situations.

Social scientists have generally found collective behavior to be a difficult topic to study. For one thing, the range of material covered under collective behavior is enormous, including such varied phenomena as lynch mobs, fads, panics, and rumors. Each of these types of collective behavior takes a different form and has different consequences. Collective behavior is also difficult to study because it is relatively short-lived, spontaneous, and emotional. These characteristics sometimes make it difficult to understand how the behavior arises and difficult to measure people's reactions to the situations that spark the behavior. Adding to the problem is the fact that collective behavior usually involves large numbers of people who do not know one another. Because episodes of collective behavior are not enduring aspects of society, it is difficult to subject them to systematic scientific study.

Although collective behavior has always been a fundamental fact of human existence, sociologists in the United States have been systematically studying this type of behavior for little more than a couple of decades. The knowledge they have amassed adds an important dimension to the overall analysis of society and the patterns of social life.

Characteristics of Collectivities

Sociologists refer to groups that exhibit collective behavior as collectivities. Generally, three factors distinguish collectivities from the social groups you read about in Chapter 4. These three factors are limited interaction, unclear norms, and limited unity.

- *Limited interaction* Members of social groups generally interact with one another directly, often for long periods of time. However, interaction among members of collectivities is limited and sometimes nonexistent.
- *Unclear norms* The norms that guide behavior in social groups are clearly defined and widely understood. However, in collectivities, norms for behavior are either unclear or unconventional.
- *Limited unity* The people who form social groups are generally united by an awareness that they are members of these groups. Members of collectivities, on the other hand, seldom share a sense of group unity.

A **collectivity** is a gathering of people who have limited interaction with one another and do not share clearly defined, conventional norms or a sense of group unity.

SUGGESTION 1: To help students compare the various types of collectivities, copy the graphic organizer at the right onto the chalkboard, omitting the italicized answers. Have students copy and complete the organizer. Then call on students to describe the different types of collectivities and provide examples of them. Finally, ask students to describe the three explanations for collective behavior *(contagion theory—the hypnotic power of the crowd encourages people to give up their individuality to the stronger pull of the group; emergent-norm theory—in situations with unclear norms, leaders develop new norms, which the crowd follows; value-added theory—a number of preconditions are necessary for collective behavior to occur).*

ENGLISH LANGUAGE LEARNERS

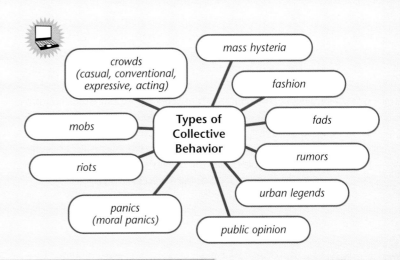

crowds (casual, conventional, expressive, acting)

mass hysteria

fashion

fads

rumors

urban legends

public opinion

mobs

riots

panics (moral panics)

Types of Collective Behavior

Types of Collective Behavior

Collective behavior and the collectivities in which it occurs take many forms. Sociologists identify a wide range of collective behaviors, including crowds, mobs, riots, panics, mass hysteria, crazes, fashions, fads, rumors, urban legends, and public opinion.

Crowds A **crowd** is a temporary gathering of people who are in close enough proximity to interact. Sociologist Herbert Blumer separates crowds into four classifications: casual, conventional, expressive, and acting.

A *casual crowd* is the least organized and most temporary type of crowd. The people in a casual crowd interact little, if at all. Examples of casual crowds include people waiting in line to buy movie tickets and people gathered at a beach.

Behavior in a *conventional crowd* is much more structured than in a casual crowd. People may not interact with one another very much, but they act according to established rules of behavior. Usually they have gathered for a common purpose, such as a funeral, a public lecture, or a baseball game.

An *expressive crowd* has no apparent goal or purpose. This type of crowd forms around emotionally charged activities such as rock concerts. Laughing, shouting, crying, dancing, cheering, and other behaviors that are common in expressive crowds would be considered inappropriate in many other social situations.

INTERPRETING VISUALS An expressive crowd is one that forms around emotionally charged activities such as concerts or sporting events. *What makes these types of crowds different from acting crowds?*

SUGGESTION 2: Organize students into pairs or groups of three and have each group create a visual diagram that provides simple graphics illustrating each type of collective behavior described in this section. The diagram should organize the collectivities by similar types. In addition, students should label and summarize each type of behavior. Then call on volunteers to present their diagrams to the class. Next, ask students to describe examples of each type of collective behavior. Write the examples on the chalkboard. Finally, ask students to apply each of the explanations for collective behavior to the examples. *(See the activity and graphic organizer on p. 437 for this information.)* **COOPERATIVE LEARNING**

SUGGESTION 3: Lead a class discussion comparing the various types of collectivities and describing the three explanations for collective behavior. *(See the activity and graphic organizer on p. 437.)* Then tell students that they are going to play a game of collective charades. Before class, write each of the types of collectivities described in this section on cards. Then organize students into several groups and give each group one card. Provide the groups with a few minutes to prepare a role-play of an example of its assigned type of collective behavior. Then have each group perform its collective charade while other teams try to identify the type of collective behavior being presented. When the groups are finished with the first set of cards, distribute a second set until the class has gone through all the cards. **COOPERATIVE LEARNING**

Visual Answer

A protest movement is well organized and usually nonviolent. Riots occur suddenly, triggered by a single event. Student answers will vary.

Interdisciplinary Connection

HISTORY
The Boston Massacre.
In 1768, tensions were high between British officials and American colonists in Boston. On March 5, 1770, a British soldier got into a fight with a colonist. A crowd began throwing snowballs and shouting insults at the soldier. Soon a small group of troops arrived. The mob grew louder and angrier, and the soldiers fired into the crowd. Five colonists died in what became known as the Boston Massacre.

ACTIVITY: Discuss how this event illustrates mob behavior.

☐ internet connect

TOPIC: Causes and Effects of Riots
GO TO: go.hrw.com
KEYWORD: SL3 SC17

Have students access the Internet through the HRW Go site to conduct research on riots throughout history. Have students create multimedia presentations on the causes and effects of riots.

INTERPRETING VISUALS Mobs and riots are the most violent forms of crowds. Riots have historically erupted when a group believes an injustice has been done. However, recent riots have erupted at soccer games in Europe. *How does a riot differ from a protest movement? What are their impacts on society?*

An *acting crowd* is a violent crowd. The emotions that typify an acting crowd are much more intense than those found in an expressive crowd. The emotions are usually hostile and destructive and generally focus on one particular target. An acting crowd is often formed by a dramatic event and results in the violations of established norms.

For example, during the Euro 2000 soccer championships a game between Germany and England drew thousands of German and English fans to the Belgian city of Charleroi. Before the game, the two sets of fans jammed the city center, taunting each other. Emotions became increasingly heated until fighting broke out. The two sides fought with each other and the police. Fighting continued, on and off, during and after the game. More than 50 people were injured, some 850 unruly fans were placed in jail, and the city center was trashed.

Mobs and Riots The most violent form of an acting crowd is a **mob**. A mob is an emotionally charged collectivity whose members are united by a specific destructive or violent goal. This type of collectivity usually has leaders who urge the group toward the common action and who enforce conformity among the group's members. Although mobs are generally unstable and limited in duration, their actions represent a threat to social order and a challenge to official authority.

One example of mob behavior, the lynch mob, was common in the southern and western United States during the late 1800s and early 1900s. Lynch mobs were formed by vigilantes who, without due process of law, administered supposed justice to people they considered to be criminals. Most lynch mobs were composed of white Americans who believed that violence could be used to maintain a dominance over African Americans and other minority groups. More than 4,700 people in the United States, most of whom were African Americans and members of other minority groups, have been killed by lynch mobs since the 1880s.

Another violent type of acting crowd is a **riot**. A riot is a collection of people who erupt into generalized destructive behavior, the result of which is social disorder. Riots are less unified and less focused than are mobs. People who participate in riots typically lack access to power and so vent their frustrations through destructive actions. A riot often begins when long-standing tensions are triggered by a single event. For example, in 1989 a policeman killed an African American youth in Liberty City, a section of Miami. In response, protestors rioted for several days, attacking the police, looting stores, and setting cars on fire. Unlike mobs, riots end only when the participants exhaust themselves or when officials regain social control.

CONNECTING *to Economics*

Ask a volunteer to use a dictionary to locate and then read aloud the financial meaning of *panic. (Dictionary definitions generally include statements such as a sudden, widespread fear concerning a financial slump or similar event.)* Then have each student conduct research and prepare notes on an American financial panic. Students should consider the causes of the panic, the responses of investors, the responses of the government, and the role mass media played. Ask volunteers to make oral presentations of their research to the class. **BLOCK SCHEDULING**

CONNECTING *to History*

Organize students into groups and have each group conduct research on Orson Welles's live radio broadcast of *The War of the Worlds* on October 30, 1938. (If possible, have the class listen to a copy of the program before starting the project.) Have students examine the techniques Welles used and listeners' responses as well as the reasons for these responses. Then have each group create a series of "live" radio news broadcasts describing the events occurring in response to Welles's radio program. The news broadcasters may initially not be aware that the alien invasion is fictional, but should become aware of this information in time, based on students' research. **COOPERATIVE LEARNING**, **BLOCK SCHEDULING**

Protest movements, however, are better organized, are longer lasting, and the participants continue to work together toward a goal.

Panics Some collective behavior is triggered not by violence but by fear. A **panic** is a spontaneous and unco-ordinated group action to escape some perceived threat. Panics generally occur when people believe that their means of escape are limited or soon to be closed off. The fear of being trapped often results in faulty communication about the threat, which fuels the fear and keeps people from forming logical escape plans.

In a panic, mutual cooperation breaks down, and the norms that govern conventional behavior are lost. The panicky reactions of a group sometimes result in more damage than the damage produced by the threat itself. For example, in 1903 a fire broke out in Chicago's Iroquois Theater. Although the fire was quickly put out and actually did little damage to the building, more than 600 people were killed in their panic to reach the exits. Most of these people were smothered or trampled to death in the stampede.

Panics are most likely to occur in situations that are outside the realm of everyday experience, such as fires, floods, and earthquakes. Because few norms of behavior exist for such situations, the response is sometimes irrational and emotional. Occasionally, a panic is avoided when a leader emerges who can channel the behavior of the individuals involved and direct them toward logical action.

A **moral panic** occurs when people become fearful—often without reason—about behavior that appears to threaten society's core values. Mass media usually identify this behavior and cast it as a major social or moral crisis. Alarmed by the media warnings, the public and various institutions demand action to stamp out the behavior. In the early 1960s the British media launched a moral panic against two youth groups, the "mods" and the "rockers." The often exaggerated and distorted coverage of the groups' lifestyles and occasional violent clashes with each other resulted in public calls for swift action. The police and the courts responded with many arrests and stiff sentences. Moral panics rarely last long. They are often replaced by another more current public concern.

Mass Hysteria Another form of collective behavior formed by fear is **mass hysteria**. Mass hysteria is an unfounded anxiety shared by people who can be scattered over a wide geographic area. This anxiety involves irrational beliefs and behaviors that spread among the population, sometimes unwittingly fueled by the media.

Episodes of mass hysteria are usually short-lived, vanishing as people come to realize that their anxieties have no basis in fact.

One incidence of mass hysteria that had dramatic consequences occurred in 1692 in the Puritan community of Salem, Massachusetts. Tituba, a West Indian slave who lived in Salem, was thought to be skilled in black magic. A group of young girls from the community met regularly with Tituba to listen to her tell exciting and fantastic stories. A few girls in the group began to have strange and unexplainable convulsions, rolling and twisting on the ground as if possessed. Soon, many of the girls in the community were behaving in the same way. Hysteria spread quickly among the villagers, who feared that the girls had been bewitched.

Seeking the source of the bewitchment, Salem's clergy forced the girls to name the people responsible. At first, the girls named only Tituba and two other women as witches. Later, however, few people were safe from their false accusations. The hysteria grew so fevered that people refused to help the accused for fear that they themselves would be branded as witches. Eventually, the girls' accusations were called into question. By that time, the Salem witch trials had resulted in the conviction and execution of 19 innocent people.

INTERPRETING VISUALS Fear of Y2K computer crashes led some Americans to stockpile goods. This fear was felt by people in many parts of the United States. *Why might a sociologist consider this an example of mass hysteria?*

SUGGESTION 4: Organize students into groups and ask them to imagine that they are sociologists hired to train police officers in recognizing and understanding different types of collective behavior. Each group should create a training manual that identifies and describes each of the types of collective behavior as well as the three explanations of collective behavior covered in this section. *(See the activity and graphic organizer on p. 437 for this information.)* Encourage groups to use images to provide visual examples of the different types of collective behavior. Students should design the material to help police quickly identify types of collective behavior that might pose risks to public safety and require intervention.

COOPERATIVE LEARNING

SPOTLIGHT *on Fashion and Fads*

Write the words *fashion* and *fads* on the chalkboard. Ask students to take several minutes to write down a few examples of current fashions and fads in their school. Have volunteers share their lists with the class and have students discuss the similarities of these two types of collective behavior. Then have each student gather as many examples of current trendy fashions and fads as they can and wear or bring the items to school. *(Stress to students that they cannot violate school dress codes or other school rules concerning what items students might bring to school.)* Then have students hold an "Item-of-the-Moment" fashion show.

Sociology Then and Now

Fads and Fashions of the 1920s. A variety of fads spread among American youth during the 1920s. Many young people participated in dance marathons. Couples would dance for days, competing for prize money awarded to the last couple to collapse or drop out. Novelty events such as flagpole sitting also attracted media attention and drew crowds. On the fashion front, collegiate sweaters and straw hats were popular among young men, and women called flappers bobbed their hair and wore short skirts.

ACTIVITY: Have students compare and contrast fads and fashions of the 1920s with those of today. Help students to see how fashions may come and go and how all fads and fashions can be short-lived.

Visual Answer

Answers will vary, but students might discuss celebrity trendsetters, fads, the influence of the fashion industry, and the desire of upper and upper-middle social classes to distinguish themselves through fashion from other social classes.

Fashions and Fads Not all types of collective behavior that spread among large populations involve fear. For example, **fashions** refer to enthusiastic attachments among large numbers of people for particular styles of appearance or behavior. Most fashions are related to clothing, but any cultural artifact that gains widespread acceptance can be a fashion. Typically, fashions are short-lived and are subject to continual change.

Fashions are generally identified with modern industrialized societies. In most preindustrial societies, nearly everyone of the same sex and age dresses alike. Styles of clothing in those societies change little over the years. In industrialized societies, on the other hand, fashions change rapidly. Fashions are prominent in industrialized societies for two reasons. First, change is valued and associated with progress in such societies. For example, in the United States the term *old-fashioned* generally carries a negative meaning. However, the terms *new* and *improved* often bring approval. Second, industrialized societies typically emphasize social mobility. Thus, they give people more opportunities to take on new social statuses and the symbols of these statuses, such as automobiles, clothing, homes, adornments, and points of view.

Fads are somewhat similar to fashions. A fad is an unconventional object, action, or idea that a large number of people are attached to for a very short period of time.

Fads differ from fashions in that they are less predictable and less enduring. People who embrace fads are sometimes seen as frivolous by the majority of the population. Sociologist John Lofland divided fads into four groups: objects, activities, ideas, and personalities. Object fads include such items as hula hoops, Pet Rocks, mood rings, Beanie Babies, and Pokémon cards. Activity fads are often bizarre—such as swallowing live goldfish, crowding into telephone booths, and eating lightbulbs. Attempting to see the future through horoscopes is an idea fad whose popularity comes and goes. Elvis Presley, Michael Jackson, and Princess Diana have all been the subject of personality fads.

Fads appeal primarily to young people, who participate in them mainly as a way to assert their personal identities. Fads often die out when they become uninteresting to the general public or so widespread that they cease to bring special notice to the participants.

INTERPRETING VISUALS Women's fashions have changed greatly over the last century. *What factors do you think have influenced the changes in women's fashion?*

HOMEWORK: Have each student observe a line of people or a place where people wait in line. Places of observation might include a bank lobby, drive-through lanes, fast-food restaurants, the school cafeteria, a movie theater, a concert ticket line, an ATM line, or a bus stop. Tell students to consider the following questions: What behavioral norms are people waiting in line following? What crowd or line-control techniques are being used, if any? What sorts of disruptive behaviors are occurring, if any, and what is causing them? When the class next meets, have students share and compare their observations. Encourage students to consider their observations in light of the three explanations for collective behavior discussed in this section.

SPOTLIGHT *on Gossip and Rumors*

Have students form a circle and play the game Gossip. Begin by writing down a rather complicated rumor. Whisper the statement to the first student. Next, instruct students to whisper the rumor to the next student in line, continuing around the entire circle. Each student may say the statement only once. Then have the final student state aloud whatever he or she heard. Did the final version of the rumor match the original? Ask students to discuss what this game illustrates about the spread of gossip and rumors. *(People often pass on incomplete or incorrect information or interpret rumors and gossip incorrectly or out of context).* **COOPERATIVE LEARNING**,

BLOCK SCHEDULING

Rumors and Urban Legends All collectivities rely on communication among the participants. Some forms of collective behavior consist solely of communication. For example, a **rumor** is an unverified piece of information that is spread rapidly from one person to another. Rumors, which may be true or false, thrive when large numbers of people lack definite information about a subject of interest to them.

The content of a rumor is likely to change over time as it passes from person to person. Each person evaluates the truth of the rumor and, when transmitting it, may emphasize some aspects of the rumor and eliminate others. The changes that the rumor goes through as it circulates among people reflect each person's hopes, fears, and biases about the information. Rumors are generally difficult to control, and some may persist for years. Once a rumor begins, the number of people who are aware of it increases dramatically as each individual spreads the rumor to several others. Rumors typically end only when substantiated evidence is widely provided. Even then, some people continue to believe the rumor.

One of the stranger rumors in recent history involves Paul McCartney of the Beatles. In the late 1960s several college newspapers reported that McCartney had been killed in an automobile accident and that the band had replaced him with a look-alike. As the story spread, supporting evidence was added.

Album-cover photographs supposedly provided clues. In one, McCartney is shown wearing a patch with the initials *O.P.D.*, which supposedly stands for "officially pronounced dead." In another, McCartney is shown barefoot—imagined to be the sign of a corpse. Some rumors suggested that a few of the Beatles' songs contained hidden messages when played backwards. Various members of the band can supposedly be heard singing such things as "Turn me on, Dead Man," and "Paul is dead, miss him." Despite strong denials from McCartney and other band members, people continued to repeat the story. Even today, more than 30 years after the rumor started, the story that McCartney is actually a talented look-alike named William Campbell is still being spread.

In recent years, sociologists and urban anthropologists have become interested in a form of collective communication known as **urban legends**. Urban legends are stories that teach a lesson and seem realistic but are untrue. Like rumors, urban legends arise and spread because of unclear situations. These stories seem realistic because they are usually attributed to specific times and places and are sometimes said to have happened to someone known to the storyteller. The stories quickly become a sort of urban folklore, the purpose of which is to clarify situations by teaching moral lessons.

One typical urban legend called "The Boyfriend's Death" tells the story of a boy and his date who park their car off a particular road by a motel. After spending some time there, the girl tells the boy that she needs to go home. However, the car will not start. After telling the girl to lock herself in the car, the boy starts out on foot for the motel, where he plans to call for help. Much time goes by, but the boy does not return. Eventually, the girl hears a scratching noise on the roof of the car. Too afraid to investigate the sound, she stays in the car all night long. At daylight, some people come by and help the girl out of the car. She looks up to find that her boyfriend is hanging from the tree and that his shoes have been scraping the roof of the car. This story is the origin of the road's name—"Hangman's Road."

This same story appears in many versions in many places, but the moral of the tale is always that teenagers should not park in secluded places. This story also represents the uneasiness parents feel about the freedom that automobiles give to teenagers. Other unclear situations, such as hitchhiking, changing gender roles, and teenage sexuality, also provoke the growth and spread of urban legends.

INTERPRETING VISUALS Rumors about the secret death of Paul McCartney led many people to search album covers for hidden messages. *How do you think rumors like this are spread?*

internet connect

TOPIC: Urban Legends
GO TO: go.hrw.com
KEYWORD: SL3 SC17

Have students access the Internet through the HRW Go site to conduct research on collective behavior in the form of urban legends. Then have each student write an urban legend of his or her own. In addition, students should write explanations that analyze and interpret their legends.

Visual Answer

Answers will vary, but students might suggest that many rumors are spread by word of mouth or by mass media.

Technology Resources

CNN. Presents Sociology: Internet Rumors

Teacher to Teacher

Jennifer Matasovsky of Indianapolis, Indiana, suggested the following activity: During the course of the chapter, have each student keep a journal documenting examples of any types of collective behavior (crowds, mobs, riots, panics, mass hysteria, fashions, fads, rumors, urban legends, and public opinion) that they observe around them or in the local, state, or world news. In addition, provide students with one day to conduct research to find examples of any types of collective behavior that they did not observe. Then have students share some of their examples with the class.

BLOCK SCHEDULING

SPOTLIGHT on Advertising Techniques

Call on students to identify the techniques employed to influence public opinion in advertisements and propaganda (*testimonial, transfer, bandwagon, name calling, plain-folks appeal, glittering generalities, and card stacking*). Next, have students find examples in newspapers and magazines of each technique (or you might bring examples to class to show students). Then organize students into seven groups and assign each group one of the techniques. On the chalkboard, describe a product for students to advertise. Then have each group use its assigned technique to create a print advertisement for the product. Have each group present its advertisement to the class. **COOPERATIVE LEARNING, BLOCK SCHEDULING**

Public Opinion Another form of collective behavior that depends mainly on communication is public opinion. Although it is common to refer to everyone in a society as the public, social scientists reserve the term **public** for a group of geographically scattered people who are concerned with or engaged in a particular issue. Therefore, societies actually contain many publics because there is a different public for each social issue. The public for each single issue changes as people gain or lose interest in it. The interest that a public has in an issue takes the form of attitudes, or opinions, concerning the issue.

Public opinion, then, refers to the collection of differing attitudes that members of a public have about a particular issue. Public opinion is subject to rapid change because members of a public very often change their views on issues. Nevertheless, democratic capitalist countries such as the United States pay an enormous amount of attention to public opinion. People seeking elected office depend on public-opinion polls to identify important social and political issues. Businesses use market research and analysis to identify consumer demands.

Public opinion has such an important place in American society that politicians, interest groups, and businesses spend billions of dollars each year to influence it. **Propaganda**, an organized and deliberate attempt to shape public opinion, is the most effective way to influence what people think. Although this term is usually thought of in a negative way, propaganda does not necessarily contain only false information. Like rumors, propaganda may be true, partly true, or false. However, the intent of propaganda is always the same—to shape the opinions of a public toward some specific conclusion.

A democratic country, such as the United States, depends on citizens who can make wise decisions both when they cast their votes and when they make their purchases. Thus, it is important for people to be alert to the techniques that propagandists use to sway public opinion. Social scientists have identified seven such techniques: testimonials, transfer, bandwagon, name calling, plain-folks appeal, glittering generalities, and card stacking.

The testimonials technique refers to the use of endorsements by famous people to sell products or secure votes. For example, advertisers often use sports heroes to promote sports equipment or clothing. Famous actors are often enlisted to make speeches on behalf of politicians. The goal is to persuade people to transfer their admiration for a celebrity to the products or candidates endorsed by the celebrity.

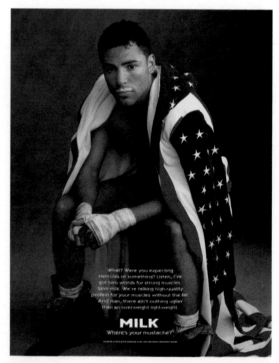

INTERPRETING VISUALS Advertising campaigns often use testimonials of famous people like track star Marion Jones and boxer Oscar de la Hoya to promote their cause or sell their products. *How do you think that using sports figures in ads might help to sell milk?*

Applying Sociology

◼ TEACH

Before having students begin the project outlined in the Propaganda and Advertising feature, ask them to write down two to three television or radio advertisements that come to mind. Ask volunteers to share their lists and describe what made the advertisements memorable: Was it the music? The graphics or images? A personal interest in the product? Note or tally on the chalkboard the products or services students list and have students discuss any similarities among the advertisements or the products.

◼ EXTEND

Explain to students that half-hour or longer infomercials have become increasingly common in recent years. Often, television schedules indicate the times that such infomercials will be aired. Have students view or videotape an infomercial of their choice and compare the techniques used in it to those used in the regular shorter television ads. Students might use a chart similar to the one in the feature to help organize their notes. Then have students discuss their findings as a class. **BLOCK SCHEDULING**

APPLYING
Sociology

PROPAGANDA AND ADVERTISING

How much attention do you pay to television commercials? Perhaps you leave the room, stretch your legs, or fix yourself a snack whenever a commercial appears. Yet advertising is an important part of television broadcasting. Advertisements enable you to watch network television free of charge because the advertisers pay the cost of programming. Advertisers spend billions of dollars each year attempting to persuade viewers that their products are the best and most desirable ones available.

Advertising is actually a form of propaganda. Advertisers try to persuade the public to buy their products by presenting them in a favorable light. To do this, advertisers use such propaganda methods as testimonials, transfer, bandwagon, name calling, plain-folks appeal, glittering generalities, and card stacking. These techniques are explained on page 442 and 444. What kinds of products are advertised on television most often? What propaganda techniques are used to advertise these products? Are there particular kinds of propaganda techniques associated with particular products? Are different kinds of propaganda techniques used at different times of the day? You can apply your sociological skills to answer these questions and to gain a better understanding of how advertisers attempt to sway public opinion. Follow these steps:

Choosing the Programs. In small groups or as a class, look at a local television guide and decide which channel each student will watch. Next, each student should choose a block of time for which he or she will be responsible. The choices should be somewhat evenly divided between hours before 6:00 P.M. and hours after 6:00 P.M. Ensure that Saturday morning, a time when programming and advertising is aimed at children, is covered. In addition, make sure that a wide variety of programming—comedy, drama, cartoons, documentaries, news magazines, sports, and so on—is covered in the selected time periods.

Making the Tally Sheet. Each student should then make a tally sheet similar to the one below. Make sure to leave enough room to record your data.

Product	Advertising Technique

Watching the Programs. Students are now ready to watch the selected programs and to record the data about the television commercials on their sheets. Be sure to record every advertisement that appears during the block of time for which you are responsible.

Combining the Data. Once you and the rest of the class have completed your observations, work in small groups to tally group members' results. Next, combine these results into one class report. Then as a class, analyze the data by looking for answers to the following questions:

1. Which type of product was advertised most frequently?
2. Which advertising technique was used most often?
3. Which products were advertised most often before 6:00 P.M.? Least often?
4. Which types of commercials appeared most frequently after 6:00 P.M.? Least frequently?
5. Were any advertising techniques associated with certain products or times of day?

Think About It

1. **Evaluating** *Did anything in your results surprise you? Explain your answer.*
2. **Drawing Inferences and Conclusions** *Why do you think advertisers might adjust the kinds of products they advertise and the advertising techniques they use for different times of the day?*

Did You Know?

The average 30-second television commercial has fewer than 65 words. Even so, an advertising campaign can take months for a creative team to develop.

Think About It Answers

1. Answers will vary, but students should explain how their results differed from their expectations.

2. Answers will vary, but students should support their explanations with examples from their study. Students might mention that advertisers adjust the kinds of products they advertise and the techniques they use based on the average characteristics of viewers at different times of day or for different types of shows. For example, advertisers would promote different products during shows aimed at children than during shows aimed at adults in their thirties and forties.

TEACH OBJECTIVE 2

SUGGESTION 1: Call on students to identify and summarize the three theories that have been proposed to explain collective behavior *(contagion, emergent-norm, and value-added)*. As students describe the theories, create outlines for each theory on the chalkboard. Students should copy the outlines in their notes. Then have each student use the preconditions for collective behavior outlined in the value-added theory to create a "recipe" for a riot. Students' recipes should provide a list of ingredients and their amounts, cooking or preparation instructions, and a description of what the final "dish" should look like. Have volunteers share their recipes with the class.

SUGGESTION 2: On the chalkboard, list the six preconditions necessary for collective behavior, according to Neil Smelser's value-added theory. Ask students to reread the description of the 1991 Los Angeles riots on pp. 445 and 448. Then ask each student to create a cause-and-effect chart showing the preconditions necessary for collective behavior and to use the 1991 riot to provide a real-life example of each precondition in the chart *(structural conduciveness—authority and power of police in society; structural strain—poverty, powerlessness of people in area; growth and spread of a generalized belief—police and jury prejudiced; precipitating factors—police acquitted in trial; mobilization for action—rioting; social control—police, military controls, curfews).*

The transfer technique is similar to testimonials in that it attempts to associate a product or candidate with something that the public approves of or respects. For example, advertisers might display their product with national symbols, such as the flag and historic monuments, suggesting that buying the product is patriotic. The transfer technique can also be used negatively by linking a competitor's product or an opposing candidate to something the public dislikes.

The bandwagon technique appeals to a public's desire to conform. For example, a politician or product may be promoted as the one already most popular with the public. This technique assumes that people want to be on the winning side of an election or to own what appear to be highly desirable products.

The name-calling technique refers to the use of negative labels or images in order to make competitors appear in an unfavorable light. For example, politicians may accuse their opponents of being reckless spenders or uncaring about the needs of the public. The aim of this technique is to persuade the public to associate the politician or the product with the unfavorable label.

The plain-folks appeal attempts to sway public opinion by appealing to the average American. Thus, a politician may be portrayed as a plain, hard-working American who just wants to do good things for the country. Similarly, average Americans with whom everyone can identify may be shown endorsing a product or candidate.

The glittering generalities technique refers to the use of words that sound positive but have little real meaning. For example, to say that a politician believes in freedom, democracy, and the American way sounds positive. However, it provides little information about the politician's views on the issues.

Card stacking is the practice of presenting facts in a way that places politicians or products in a favorable light. For example, newspapers may give a great deal of attention to politicians they favor and little attention to those they do not. Similarly, advertisers may present statistics or survey results in a way that favors their products over those of their competitors.

INTERPRETING VISUALS Politicians, such as Franklin D. Roosevelt, often use plain-folks appeal and glittering generalities to appeal to a wide base of voters. *How does this slogan reflect these approaches?*

Explaining Collective Behavior

A number of theories have been proposed over the past century to explain collective behavior. These theories are most useful for explaining types of collective behavior in which people are in close proximity with one another, such as crowds, mobs, riots, and panics. Foremost among the theories of collective behavior are contagion theory, the emergent-norm theory, and the value-added theory.

Contagion Theory Gustave LeBon developed the first systematic theory of collective behavior. According to his **contagion theory**, the hypnotic power of a crowd encourages people to give up their individuality to the stronger pull of the group. Individuals become anonymous, with no willpower or sense of responsibility. The crowd, in effect, becomes a single organism operating under one collective mind. In this situation, conventional social norms lose their meaning and, as emotion sweeps through the crowd, behavior becomes unrestrained.

According to LeBon, three factors give crowds power over individuals. First, because of the sheer numbers of people in a crowd, individuals gain an anonymity that makes them feel unconquerable. Second, the spread of emotion is so rapid and contagious that it overtakes the members of a crowd like an epidemic. Third, members of a crowd rapidly enter a state of suggestibility, during which time they are not conscious of their actions. This suggestibility makes them particularly receptive to the manipulations of charismatic leaders.

Contagion theory has its limitations, however. Studies have shown no indication that a collective mind exists in crowds. Any number of motivations for behavior can be found among crowd participants. In addition, behavior in crowds is usually not as uniform as LeBon suggested. Nonetheless, contagion theory is helpful in explaining how behavior spreads among the members of a crowd, freeing them from the restraints of conventional social norms. This theory also provides insight into how emotions work to encourage people toward collective action.

CONNECTING *to History*

Have each student conduct research to discover the steps leading to the 1965 Watts riot in Los Angeles. Instruct students to use the research to create a chart or diagram that illustrates how the events leading to the riot progressed through the six preconditions for collective behavior detailed in the value-added theory. Remind students to include all six preconditions and to provide specific examples for each one. Call on volunteers to share their charts or diagrams with the class. **BLOCK SCHEDULING**

INTERPRETING VISUALS During sporting events, crowds may establish norms that would not have been established in a smaller group. *How might a crowd doing the wave be viewed according to the emergent-norm theory?*

Interdisciplinary Connection

SCIENCE AND TECHNOLOGY

Simulating Panic.
Engineer and physicist Dirk Helbing of Germany and physicists Tamas Vicsek and Illes Farkas of Budapest designed a computer model to simulate collective behavior. The model revealed that people in panics tend to move quickly and randomly. The result is that people run into each other and create bottlenecks in small spaces. Using their computer model to analyze how to lessen such problems, the scientists developed the idea of placing small concrete columns near exits in areas where panicking crowds might create bottlenecks. As a crowd pushes toward the exits, the columns help absorb the pressure. Bottlenecks and injuries are reduced significantly.

ACTIVITY: Have students brainstorm other methods of trying to control crowds and reduce injuries in panics, mobs, and riots.

Visual Answer

Students might suggest that according to the emergent-norm theory, a crowd doing the wave could be seen as the result of a new norm developing through the initiation of a few people.

Emergent-Norm Theory Sociologists Ralph Turner and Lewis Killian, rather than seeing crowd members as acting with one collective mind, acknowledged that the individuals in a crowd have different attitudes, behaviors, and motivations. They sought an explanation of crowd behavior in the social-control function of social norms.

According to their **emergent-norm theory**, the people in a crowd are often faced with a situation in which traditional norms of behavior do not apply. In effect, they find themselves with no clear standards for behavior. Through interaction, new norms gradually emerge when one or more leaders initiate new behaviors. These new norms then provide a common motivation for group action where none existed before. For example, when a film being shown in a movie theater breaks, one person may start stamping his or her feet. Even though this behavior does nothing to help fix the film, the action quickly spreads among the people in the theater. Even if individuals inwardly disagree with the action, they often feel obliged to conform to this new group norm. Crowd behavior therefore appears to be unanimous when, in fact, it may not be.

Value-Added Theory With his **value-added theory**, sociologist Neil Smelser attempted to predict if collective behavior would occur and the direction it might take. Smelser borrowed the value-added concept from economics. In the production process, which transforms raw materials into finished products, each step adds value. Each step is necessary for the addition of value in the next step. As the process moves forward, the range of possibilities narrows, limiting what the finished product might become.

Smelser suggested that this value-added idea also applies to collective behavior. There are six basic preconditions for collective behavior, Smelser said. They are structural conduciveness, structural strain, growth and spread of a generalized belief, precipitating factors, mobilization for action, and social control. These preconditions build on one another, and each one is necessary for the next to occur. The more preconditions that are present, the greater the likelihood of a particular type of collective behavior. Applying the six preconditions to the Los Angeles riots of 1992 offers a real-life illustration of Smelser's theory.

Structural conduciveness refers to the surrounding social structure that makes it possible for a particular type of collective behavior to occur. For example, in 1991 a bystander videotaped the beating of African American motorist Rodney King by four white Los Angeles police officers. The four officers faced charges in a well-publicized trial. The acquittal of the police officers ignited three days of rioting in South Central Los Angeles, leaving more than 50 people dead and more than 2,300 injured. The repeated nationwide broadcast of the videotape and the intense media coverage of the trial fueled the conditions for this collective behavior.

Case Studies and Other True Stories

◼ TEACH

Have students read the feature Responding to Terrorism and answer the questions that follow it. Next, ask students to discuss why such horrific events might have a unifying effect on a society. *(Students might reply that threats to physical and national security draw people together in their fear, concern, and action and encourage people to see themselves more as members of their country and less as individuals.)* Then have students apply one or more of the theories of collective behavior to these events.

◼ EXTEND

Have students work in pairs to interview officials and others about steps taken in the local community following the terrorist attacks of September 11. For example, was security increased at any public buildings? Were evacuation or disaster relief plans reviewed or updated? Were budgets altered? You might assign different pairs different types of people to interview to limit the participation time required for local officials and others. Have each pair write a summary of its interview. **COOPERATIVE LEARNING ,**

BLOCK SCHEDULING

A Generous Country.
After the terrorist attacks of September 11, Americans donated so many supplies that multiple warehouses were required to store them. Supplies ranged from bottled water to food, socks, flashlights, and even $250,000 worth of dog food for the rescue dogs. Many of the items were not needed and were donated to homeless shelters and to similar organizations. Unused medical supplies were given to local EMS drivers and free clinics. The dog food ended up feeding homeless animals at animal shelters across the East Coast.

CRITICAL THINKING

How does Americans' wealth of giving following the tragedy of September 11 reflect the effect of the attack on the country?

ANSWER: The attack unified Americans and gave many people the feeling of a group effort in the face of disaster.

Technology Resources

 CNN Presents Sociology: September 11, 2001: A Turning Point in History

Case Studies

AND OTHER TRUE STORIES

RESPONDING TO TERRORISM

O n the morning of September 11, 2001, the worst terrorist attack on American soil shocked the country. However, almost immediately, Americans came together. Americans made a collective response. In the week after the attacks, 94 percent of the American people took some kind of action.

Actions

Americans who were trained for emergencies—such as doctors, nurses, counselors, fire fighters, demolition workers, and disaster relief specialists—rushed to New York City and the Washington, D.C., area to offer help. Others also looked for ways to offer assistance.

In the hours after the attacks, the emergency medical services warned that blood supplies would quickly be depleted. In response, thousands of people went to hospitals and Red Cross centers to donate blood. In many cities, blood-donation rates ran at two or three times the normal level even though donors had to wait for several hours. Response was so great that many would-be donors had to be turned away because blood-storage facilities were full.

Many Americans were also inspired to display their patriotism. In the nine days immediately following the attacks, some 78 percent of Americans flew flags outside their homes, at work, or on their cars. The demand for American flags was so great that stores rapidly ran out of supplies.

Some Americans took action through their faith. More than 80 percent of Americans offered prayers for

In an act of patriotism, firefighters raised an American flag over the rubble of the World Trade Center.

those who had been personally touched by the tragedy. More than 40 percent attended religious services for the same purpose. On Friday, September 14—a national day of mourning—millions of Americans remembered the dead through silent prayer or quiet reflection.

In addition to emotional support, charitable groups across the country moved swiftly to raise funds for relief efforts. About 60 percent of Americans responded by making donations. Other citizens organized special events to raise funds. For example, actors and musicians held a telethon, "America: A Tribute to Heroes," on September 21. The telethon raised some $110 million to benefit the families who had lost loved ones in the attacks. American children got involved with events of their own. Some raised money by selling lemonade or by washing cars. Other children held drives to gather supplies for the rescue and clean-up workers at the disaster sites. In addition, young people held "write-ins," where people wrote letters of condolence and support to the people of New York City and Washington, D.C.

Attitudes

In addition to showing commonality of action, Americans showed considerable commonality in their attitudes about September 11. For most Americans, the initial response to the attacks was anger. After a short time, many—about 75 percent—began to express anxiety over further attacks. More than half stated that their personal sense of safety and security had been shaken. Furthermore, nearly three quarters said that they felt depressed about the terrorist attacks, half said that they had

SPOTLIGHT
on National Security and Civil Liberties

Have students conduct research on the main provisions of the anti-terrorism legislation passed in the wake of September 11. Instruct students to use the research to write a brief essay discussing the need to balance national security and civil liberties. Ask students to express and defend their own points of view on the topic. Have volunteers share their essays with the class. **BLOCK SCHEDULING**

CONNECTING *to History*

Some people have compared the events of September 11 to the bombing of Pearl Harbor, which precipitated the entry of the United States into World War II. Have students work in pairs to conduct research on the two events. One student in each pair should look for similarities between the events, and the other student should focus on differences. Each pair should then prepare a poster comparing and contrasting the two events.

COOPERATIVE LEARNING, **BLOCK SCHEDULING**

Did You Know?

By December 2001, Americans had donated a total of $1.2 billion to relief funds related to the terrorist events of September 11.

trouble concentrating on their work, and a third admitted that they had difficulty sleeping. Over time, these feelings of anxiety began to decline.

A vast majority of Americans also felt that the events of September 11 had changed the country in a lasting way. During this tragedy many Americans found hope in how the country showed a spirit of unity in its response to the attacks. More than 60 percent said this unity made the country stronger than before. Moreover, nearly 40 percent said that what they had gone through since the attacks had changed them personally and made them better Americans.

American attitudes about how the country should respond to terrorism also showed considerable unity. A large majority favored giving the police

and security services greater powers, even though these powers might adversely affect civil liberties.

A vast majority of Americans strongly supported taking military action against the ruling regime of Afghanistan, which had sheltered and aided those suspected of carrying out the attacks. Most Americans stated a belief that the war on terrorism would be a long one and would take resources away from other important programs. However, about half said that stamping out terrorism was worth this expense. Many Americans also expressed a greater trust in the U.S. government after the tragic events of September 11, 2001. Sociologists will continue to study the lasting effects of this event on Americans and the country.

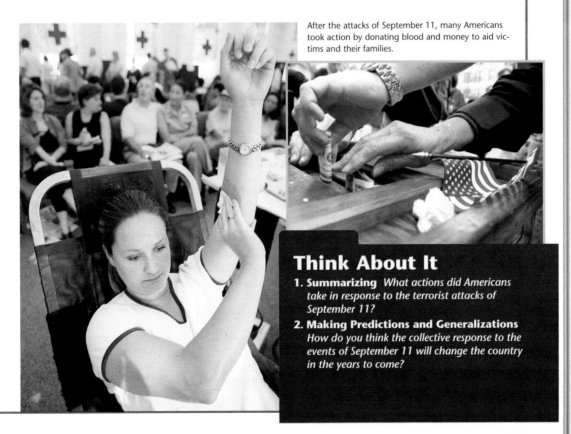

After the attacks of September 11, many Americans took action by donating blood and money to aid victims and their families.

Think About It Answers

1. Trained professionals rushed to New York City and Washington, D.C., to provide assistance. Other Americans gave blood, created patriotic displays, offered prayers, and gave money and supplies to charitable organizations.

2. Answers will vary, but students should provide reasons or examples that support their opinions. Some students might answer that the collective response will increase the sense of national unity and patriotism among Americans but that the effects will decrease as time passes.

Think About It

1. **Summarizing** *What actions did Americans take in response to the terrorist attacks of September 11?*

2. **Making Predictions and Generalizations** *How do you think the collective response to the events of September 11 will change the country in the years to come?*

CLOSE

Have the class debate the role or influence of mass media in shaping collective behavior. Do students think mass media's role is generally positive, negative, or neutral? Do students' opinions vary depending on the type of collective behavior? Students should consider news coverage, advertising, and other mass media.

REVIEW AND ASSESS

Have students complete the **Section 1 Review** on p. 448. As **Alternative Assessment**, you may want to use the collective behavior training manual or the value-added theory cause-and-effect chart in this section's lessons.

RETEACH

Have students work in pairs to create a 10-item, fill-in-the-blank quiz using the section's Define terms. Then have pairs exchange their quizzes, complete the ones they receive, and return them to be corrected. **ENGLISH LANGUAGE LEARNERS , COOPERATIVE LEARNING**

EXTEND

Have students interview police officers or other officials to determine requirements for holding a public parade, rally, or other type of public assembly in your area. Students should present their findings to the class. **BLOCK SCHEDULING**

SECTION 1 REVIEW ANSWERS

1. Define:
- collective behavior, p. 436
- collectivity, p. 436
- crowd, p. 437
- mob, p. 438
- riot, p. 438
- panic, p. 439
- moral panic, p. 439
- mass hysteria, p. 439
- fashions, p. 440
- fads, p. 440
- rumor, p. 441
- urban legends, p. 441
- public, p. 442
- public opinion, p. 442
- propaganda, p. 442
- contagion theory, p. 444
- emergent-norm theory, p. 445
- value-added theory, p. 445

2. Students should explain each propaganda technique shown.

3a. Students should describe how the following are formed: crowds, mobs and riots, panic, mass hysteria, fashions and fads, rumors and urban legends, and public opinion.

b. structural conduciveness, structural strain, growth and spread of a generalized belief, precipitating factors, mobilization for action, and social control; Explanations will vary.

4. Responses will vary, but students should exhibit an understanding of each of the theories of collective behavior.

Structural strain refers to social conditions that put strain on people and thus encourage them to seek some collective means of relief. Structural strain can be produced by conditions such as poverty, overcrowding, discrimination, and conflict. At the time of the trial, these conditions were present in the predominantly African American area of South Central Los Angeles. The growth of a generalized belief makes the structural strain personally meaningful for people. Individuals begin to identify the problem, form opinions about it, and share ways of dealing with it. For example, in South Central Los Angeles, many residents shared a strong resentment of the police and hoped that the four officers would be found guilty of beating Rodney King. At the same time, many residents doubted that an all-white jury would return a fair verdict in the case.

Precipitating factors, the fourth precondition for collective behavior, refer to triggering mechanisms that set off the behavior. These factors are usually quite dramatic and confirm the generalized belief. The confirming evidence then adds to the structural strain felt by people. In the case of the Los Angeles riots, the news that the jury had found the white officers not guilty provided this triggering mechanism.

The first four preconditions in the sequence of collective behavior set the stage for people to act. When the Los Angeles residents realized that community leaders could

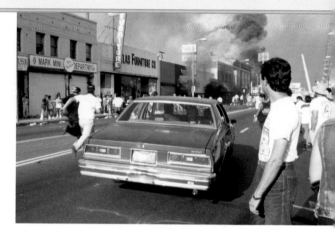

The videotaped beating of Rodney King set off a chain of events that ended in three days of rioting in South Central Los Angeles.

do nothing to change the verdict, many mobilized to express their collective anger and frustration through looting and random acts of destruction. By the time community leaders attempted to intervene, the rioting was out of control. At this point in the sequence, collective behavior can be controlled if mechanisms exist to prevent or minimize the situation. In the case of the Los Angeles riots, the governor of California called in the National Guard and the mayor imposed a curfew on the residents. In addition, President George Bush sent in federal troops. These actions helped put an end to the riots.

SECTION 1 REVIEW

1. Define and explain
collective behavior
collectivity
crowd
mob
riot
panic
moral panic
mass hysteria
fashions
fad
rumor
urban legends
public
public opinion
propaganda
contagion theory
emergent-norm theory
value-added theory

2. Categorizing Copy the graphic organizer below. Use it to evaluate how the communication techniques of government propaganda and advertising influence the perceptions, attitudes, and behaviors of people and groups.

	Government Propaganda	Advertising
Testimonials		
Transfer		
Bandwagon		
Name Calling		
Plain-Folks Appeal		
Glittering Generalities		
Card Stacking		

3. Finding the Main Idea

a. What are the different types of collectivities and how are they formed?

b. Identify the preconditions needed for collective behavior to occur and explain how these preconditions build on one another.

4. Writing and Critical Thinking

Supporting a Point of View Think of a specific instance of a fad, fashion, panic, mass hysteria, or another collectivity. Write a paragraph noting which one of the theories discussed in this section best explains the collective behavior. Give reasons for your answer.
Consider:
- the characteristics of the collectivity
- how theories of collective behavior differ

Homework Practice Online
keyword: SL3 HP17

SECTION 2

OBJECTIVES

1. *Describe the types of social movements that exist and explain how they differ.*

2. *Identify the stages present in the life cycle of social movements and describe ways in which the existence of social movements can be explained.*

LET'S GET STARTED!

Before class, write the following words on the chalkboard: *react, conserve, revise,* and *revolt.* As students enter the classroom, ask them to jot down a definition of each verb, without using a dictionary. When students finish, ask volunteers to share their definitions with the class. Correct students as necessary. Next, ask students which of these verbs imply change *(react, revise, revolt).* Tell students that in Section 2 they will learn about social movements—a more deliberate form of collective behavior that may be defined as a long-term conscious effort to promote or prevent social change.

2 SOCIAL MOVEMENTS

● Read to Discover

1. What types of social movements exist, and how do they differ?

2. What stages are present in the life cycle of social movements, and how can the existence of social movements be explained?

● Define

social movements, reactionary movements, conservative movements, revisionary movements, revolutionary movements, relative deprivation theory, resource mobilization, resource-mobilization theory

The types of collectivities discussed in the previous section are generally short-lived and rarely have a serious effect on society as a whole. **Social movements** are much more deliberate and long-lasting forms of collective behavior. A social movement may be defined as a long-term conscious effort to promote or prevent social change. Social movements may develop around any issue of public concern.

Three factors distinguish social movements from other forms of collective behavior. First, social movements are long-lasting. Second, they possess a highly structured organization with formally recognized leaders. Finally, social movements make a deliberate attempt to institute or block societal change. Those factors combine to give social movements the potential to attract memberships that number in the millions.

Types of Social Movements

The goal of most social movements is to change society. However, social movements differ in the amount of change they seek. Sociologist William Bruce Cameron identified four types of social movements based on the level of change sought. These types are reactionary movements, conservative movements, revisionary movements, and revolutionary movements.

INTERPRETING VISUALS The temperance movement of the late 1800s and early 1900s, led by activists such as Carry Nation, encouraged people to quit drinking and pushed for laws banning the sale and consumption of alcohol. *What type of social movement do you think the temperance movement was?*

Reactionary Movements The main goal of **reactionary movements** is to reverse current social trends—to "turn back the clock." The members of reactionary movements are suspicious of and hostile toward social change. They want to return society to the way they believe it existed in the past. For example, the Ku Klux Klan is a reactionary movement that wants to reimpose the system of racial segregation that existed before the passage of civil rights laws in the mid-1900s. The Ku Klux Klan, like other reactionary movements, has often used fear and violence in support of its cause.

Conservative Movements Most **conservative movements** try to protect what they see as society's prevailing values from change that they consider to be a threat to those values. For example, the religious right seeks to uphold what it views as traditional family and social values. To do that, the religious right has launched political campaigns to elect candidates who support its views and to defeat candidates who oppose them. The religious right has also organized boycotts of television networks that broadcast "antifamily-values" programs and of companies that support such programming through advertising.

SECTION 2 RESOURCES

REPRODUCIBLE & REVIEW

- Readings and Case Studies in Sociology 17
- Research Projects and Activities for Teaching Sociology 17
- Study Skills and Writing Guide
- Section 2 Review, p. 455

TECHNOLOGY

- One-Stop Planner, Lesson 17.2
- Homework Practice Online

Visual Answer

Answers will vary, but students might suggest a conservative movement.

SUGGESTION 1: Call on students to identify the characteristics of social movements that distinguish them from the collective behaviors described in Section 1 *(are longer lasting, have a highly structured organization with formally recognized leaders, make a deliberate attempt to institute or block societal change).* Then, to help students describe the types of social movements that exist, copy the graphic organizer at the right onto the chalkboard, omitting the italicized answers. Have students copy the organizer and complete it by identifying, describing, and providing an example of each type of social movement. Discuss the answers with the class and call on students to explain how the four types of social movements differ.

ENGLISH LANGUAGE LEARNERS

SOCIAL MOVEMENTS

Type	Description and Example
Reactionary	*try to prevent a type of social change and return society to a past way of being; often use fear and violence; example: Ku Klux Klan*
Conservative	*try to protect prevailing values from what are seen as threats to those values; example: the religious right*
Revisionary	*try to improve some part of society through social change; usually use legal methods and focus on a single issue; example: women's suffrage movement*
Revolutionary	*seek a total radical change of existing social structure, overthrow existing government and replace it with their own version; often involve violent or illegal methods; example: the American Revolution*

INTERPRETING VISUALS E.G. Leutze's painting of George Washington crossing the Delaware River shows the spirit of the American Revolution. *How does this image portray some of the characteristics of a revolutionary movement?*

Revisionary Movements The goal of **revisionary movements** is to improve, or revise, some part of society through social change. Revisionary movements usually use legal channels to seek change because they generally support the existing social system as a whole. This type of movement typically focuses on a single issue. For example, the women's suffrage movement of the early 1900s attempted to reform laws that prevented women from voting. The members of the women's suffrage movement used political campaigns, political lobbyists, and the courts to seek reform.

Revolutionary Movements The main goal of **revolutionary movements** is a total and radical change of the existing social structure. Their ultimate aim is to overthrow the existing government and to replace it with their own version of how a government should work. Revolutionary movements typically involve violent or illegal actions and can sometimes result in drastic and widespread social change. This type of movement usually arises when people see no chance for reform to occur. Examples of revolutionary movements include the American Revolution, the Bolshevik Revolution in Russia, and Fidel Castro's revolution in Cuba.

Life Cycle of Social Movements

Although social movements differ in the goals they hope to attain, successful movements appear to have certain characteristics in common. Many of these movements proceed through a series of stages that eventually lead to their acceptance by society. Sociologists Malcolm Spector and John Kitsuse identified four stages in the life cycle of social movements: agitation, legitimation, bureaucratization, and institutionalization.

Agitation Social movements typically emerge out of the belief that a problem exists. In the early stage of the life cycle, a small group of people attempts to stir up public awareness of the issue, often with the intention of gaining widespread support for the social movement. More often than not, potential social movements die out at this point, due either to lack of support or to lack of resources.

Legitimation Movements that find support for their concerns enter the legitimation stage of the life cycle. In this stage, the social movement becomes more respectable as it gains increasing acceptance among the population. The leaders of the movement, who were previously dismissed as cranks, are now seen as legitimate spokespeople of a just cause. Governmental or other authorities also begin to recognize the movement's concerns as legitimate. At this point, the movement often attracts media attention, which in turn serves to bring the movement's goals to the attention of increasing numbers of people. Demonstrations and rallies add to the visibility of the movement.

Bureaucratization As the organizational structure of the movement becomes more formal, it enters the third stage of the life cycle—bureaucratization. At this point, the movement has developed a ranked structure of authority, official policies, and efficient strategies for the future. The original goals of the movement are sometimes swept aside during this stage because increasing amounts of time and energy are needed to handle the day-to-day running of the organization.

Institutionalization In the final, or institutional stage, the movement has become an established part of society. Bureaucrats who oversee daily operations replace the idealistic leaders who helped found the movement. Often these leaders care more about their position in the organization than about the goals of the movement. As a result, the movement frequently resists proposals for change.

The life cycle of a social movement can clearly be seen in the American labor-union movement, which had its beginnings in the late 1800s.

- *Agitation* Low pay and harsh working conditions led many workers to seek support for unions that would protect employee interests.

- *Legitimation* After many years of often violent confrontations between workers and management and after years of resistance from many segments of the population, labor unions finally received official governmental recognition.
- *Bureaucratization* Over the years, labor unions grew in size and number. Today they are firmly established and powerful organizations.
- *Institutionalization* Labor unions are now so well established in society that they resist attempts to change their operating procedures, even though many of these procedures may not benefit their members.

INTERPRETING VISUALS The labor movement offers an example of a social movement that has experienced each of the life-cycle stages. *How do the images of a child laborer, the factory conditions, and a union song book reflect the early stages of agitation and legitimation? How does this contemporary image represent the institutionalization stage?*

SUGGESTION 1: Call on students to identify and describe the four stages present in the life cycle of social movements *(agitation, legitimation, bureaucratization, and institutionalization)* and the theories explaining social movements *(relative deprivation and resource mobilization)*. Then have each student apply each of the theories to three social movements identified in the section (such as the Ku Klux Klan, the religious right, or the women's suffrage movement). *(For example, Ku Klux Klan: relative deprivation—members feel deprived of their "rightful" place in society; resource mobilization—members have access to money, communication, and an existing power structure.)* Have volunteers share their analyses with the class. Use the analyses to contrast the theories of social movements and to illustrate the weaknesses of each one.

HOMEWORK: Have each student write an essay analyzing the two theories of social movements and identifying which of the two theories he or she thinks best explains the existence of social movements. Students should explain and defend their positions and use standard grammar, spelling, sentence structure, and punctuation in their essays. When the class next meets, call on volunteers to read their essays to the class.

INTERPRETING VISUALS The civil rights movement of the 1960s eventually gained wide support among Americans. This 1964 rally in Washington, D.C., featured Martin Luther King Jr. and other civil-rights leaders. *How do you think relative deprivation theory might explain the civil rights movement?*

Explaining Social Movements

Social scientists have proposed a number of theories to explain the existence of social movements. Psychological explanations were popular until about the 1960s. Gustave LeBon offered one such explanation. He believed that only psychologically disturbed people would question the existing social order. LeBon therefore viewed social movements as little more than irrational, moblike collectivities. Similar psychological theories hold that social movements are made up of people who have some kind of personality defect. According to these theories, people join movements as a way to hide from their personal problems and to satisfy their psychological needs for purpose and meaning.

Sociologists tend to reject the notion that people join social movements because something is wrong with them as individuals. These sociologists look to problems in the social structure to explain the existence of social movements. The leading sociological explanations of the emergence of social movements are relative deprivation theory and resource-mobilization theory.

Relative Deprivation Theory One school of sociological thought suggests that social movements arise when large numbers of people feel economically or socially deprived of what they think they deserve. This deprivation is not measured in absolute terms but in comparison to the conditions of others. From the perspective of **relative deprivation theory**, people join social movements because they feel deprived relative to other people or groups with whom they identify. Through these social movements, people seek to gain access to things they lack but others have—such as higher incomes, better working and living conditions, and voting rights.

Relative deprivation theory is often used to explain revolutionary social movements. Interestingly, Karl Marx used a similar argument to explain one of the causes of revolution. In *Wage-Labor and Capital*, Marx noted that capitalism might well give workers higher incomes and better living conditions. However, the workers' dissatisfaction will rise because the wealth of the capitalists will grow at an even greater rate. Marx used the example of houses to illustrate this point. A worker may live in a small house, Marx said. As long as all his neighbors live in small houses, he is con-

Case Studies and Other True Stories

Case Studies
AND OTHER TRUE STORIES

SOCIAL MOVEMENTS AND NEW TECHNOLOGY

The computer-related technology that has developed in recent years has brought great changes to the way we live. Some sociologists suggest that these changes have affected the organization and tactics of social movements. As an example of this, sociologists point to the organic-farming movement. This social movement came to prominence in the United States during the 1990s, when many grocery stores began to carry organically grown foods. However, it started gaining attention some years earlier.

The Movement

People are drawn to social movements because of particular ideas or interests that they hold in common. In the past, the barrier of geography often obstructed the growth of a social movement. Because of distance, people with common interests or ideologies were unable to coalesce and take collective action. However, the Internet has enabled people to overcome the barrier of geography. People on different continents can communicate—and take action—instantaneously. The organic-farming movement used Web sites and e-mail to communicate and grow in popularity.

The organic-farming movement began as an alternative farming method that attempted to avoid the use of chemical fertilizers, genetically altered seeds, and pesticides. Organic farmers generally believe that food raised organically is healthier for human consumption. Many organic farmers point to the possibility of unknown dangers from genetically altered foods and chemicals used on crops. Scientists and others in the food industry have argued against these concerns. Nevertheless, the organic-farming movement has grown. In 1998, sales of organic foods were worth more than $8 billion, which represents an 8 percent growth from the 1997 numbers.

The use of the Internet helped spread the popularity of the organic-farming movement.

Movement Tactics

The organic-farming movement has used new technology to extend the popularity of organic foods. Organic-food supporters have established Web sites to publish reports on the benefits they see in the consumption of organic foods. In addition, organizers use electronic message boards and mass e-mailings to inform people about news of organic farming. Organizers also use e-mail and chat rooms to offer support and information that can help organic farmers and organic-food consumers. Organic farmers share information on farming techniques, business practices, organic-food markets, and many other issues related to organic farming. The instantaneous and mass-media nature of this communication has influenced the growth of the movement.

The growing popularity of organic foods and the demand for regulation of what qualifies as an organic food led the U.S. Department of Agriculture (USDA) to take action. In 2001 the USDA standards for organic foods went into effect, requiring organic farmers to certify with the agency before they can label their produce as organic. The U.S. government has also established penalties for farmers who illegally use the term *organic* for non-organic foods.

Using new technology, the organic-farming movement has continued to grow. American organic farmers use the Internet and e-mail to share news and information with organic farmers in Europe and many other parts of the world.

Think About It

1. **Identifying Cause and Effect** *How has the new communications technology affected the way social movements are organized?*
2. **Evaluating** *How does the organic-farming movement employ the new technology?*

Did You Know?

According to the USDA, organic beef is certified to have come from cattle raised without the use of growth hormones, antibiotics, or any other prohibited drugs. In addition, the cattle must have been fed only organic feed and cannot have been confined more than a specific amount of time. Organic beef costs about twice as much as conventional beef.

Think About It Answers

1. New technology enables members of social movements to communicate and take action without regard to geography.

2. The organic-farming movement has used new technology, including the Internet, e-mail, and Web sites, to share information between the movement and the public.

SUGGESTION 2: Lead a class discussion on the four stages present in the life cycle of social movements and on the explanations of the existence of social movements. *(See the Suggestion 1 activity on p. 452.)* Then organize students into four groups and assign each group one of the four stages in the life cycle of social movements. On the chalkboard, write a brief scenario for a social movement. Ask students to imagine that they work for a television news show. Then have each group create a script and visual aids for a news report about the fictional social movement at a point during the group's assigned stage. Have each group present its news report to the class. Then have students discuss which of the theories explaining the existence of social movements best applies to the movement in the scenario. **COOPERATIVE LEARNING**

CONNECTING *to History*

Organize students into groups and have each group conduct research on the events and accomplishments of a successful social movement in American history, such as the civil rights movement, the women's suffrage movement, or the temperance movement. Instruct the groups to organize their information in the form of a large annotated and illustrated time line. Have each group display its time line in the classroom. Then have students discuss each of the social movements and analyze how the four stages of the life cycles of social movements and the two theories of social movements apply to each one. **COOPERATIVE LEARNING**, **BLOCK SCHEDULING**

(See the Suggestion 1 activity on p. 452.)

◆ Applying Sociology

Touraine's Fields of Action. Sociologist Alain Touraine examines social movements in the context of what he calls their fields of action. The term refers to the complex interactions between a social movement and the social forces it opposes. These interactions might involve how an opposition movement influences a social movement. In addition, as society changes or as a social movement achieves some of its aims, the movement's objectives and methods of action may change or evolve into new movements. For example, the women's movement of the 1970s led to a movement for an Equal Rights Amendment, which in turn gave rise to an opposition movement.

RESEARCH ACTIVITY: Have interested students conduct research on the emergence of the Black Power movement out of the civil rights movement and share their findings with the class.

Map Answers

1. Alaska and Minnesota

2. Answers will vary, but students might suggest that sociologists would be interested in how the movement is affecting state election laws and perceptions of them in American society.

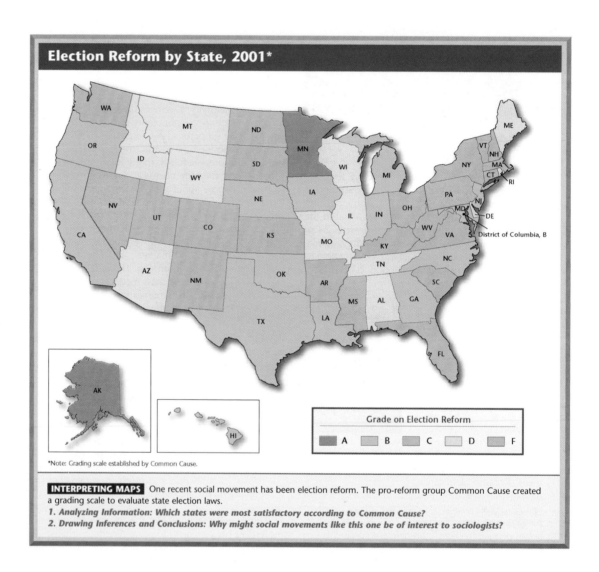

Election Reform by State, 2001*

Grade on Election Reform: A | B | C | D | F

*Note: Grading scale established by Common Cause.

INTERPRETING MAPS One recent social movement has been election reform. The pro-reform group Common Cause created a grading scale to evaluate state election laws.
1. *Analyzing Information: Which states were most satisfactory according to Common Cause?*
2. *Drawing Inferences and Conclusions: Why might social movements like this one be of interest to sociologists?*

tent. However, if a palace arises in the neighborhood, the worker will feel "more uncomfortable, more dissatisfied, more cramped within his four walls."

Resource-Mobilization Theory Today few sociologists agree that feelings of deprivation alone are sufficient to trigger social movements. Some level of deprivation is common among groups in all societies. Yet not all situations of deprivation lead people to organize into social movements.

Most contemporary sociologists believe that social movements can occur only if people are successful in **resource mobilization**. Resource mobilization is the organization and effective use of resources.

According to **resource-mobilization theory**, not even the most ill-treated group with the most just cause will be able to bring about change without resources. The resources necessary to generate a social movement include a body of supporters, financial resources, and access to the media.

The body of supporters must include talented people who have the time and skills necessary to work toward change. College students are particularly likely to support efforts for change because they have time and are well educated. College students were very active in the civil rights movement, organizing sit-ins and participating in demonstrations, marches, and voter registrations in the South. Leadership ability and

CLOSE

Have the class discuss possible reasons for the failure or collapse of social movements. *(For example, a movement may not attract enough followers, its causes may be adopted or accommodated by the existing power structure, internal struggles or divisions may weaken the movement, it may lose sight of its goals, or it may be officially suppressed.)*

REVIEW AND ASSESS

Have students complete the **Section 2 Review** on p. 455. As **Alternative Assessment**, you may want to use the types of social movements newspaper article or the theories of social movements essay in this section's lessons.

RETEACH

Have students work in pairs to create a detailed outline of the section. Pairs should use the headings of the subsections as the main points in their outlines. Have students save their outlines for study aids. **ENGLISH LANGUAGE LEARNERS , COOPERATIVE LEARNING**

EXTEND

Have each student create a wall chart entitled The Life Cycle of a Social Movement. Students should conduct research to provide an example of each stage in a real-life social movement (other than the American labor-union movement). **BLOCK SCHEDULING**

organizational skills are crucial to the ongoing success of a movement. In addition, leaders must be charismatic and well-spoken so that others will be encouraged to join the movement.

In addition, social movements must be able to mobilize financial resources. Money is needed to print leaflets and posters, travel to demonstrations and rallies, rent meeting places, and hire press agents and lawyers. Legal defense is often needed to protect the legal rights of demonstrators who are arrested. Legal actions are also particularly helpful in bringing the concerns of the movement to the attention of the public. Some social movements spend a great deal of energy encouraging people to contribute financial resources to support their causes.

Resource-mobilization theory emphasizes that successful social movements need to gain access to the media. Wide media coverage is the surest way to bring the movement to the attention of the most people possible. Media coverage, which in effect is free publicity, also serves to help movements reserve some of the finances they would normally spend on publicizing the movement.

While resource-mobilization theory helps explain how social movements get started and become successful, it has been criticized for minimizing the importance of deprivation and dissatisfaction. Some sociologists suggest that both deprivation and resource mobilization are necessary for the creation of social movements. People will not mobilize resources unless the perception arises that change is needed. Moreover, the move to make changes will not be successful unless the needed resources can be mobilized.

Social movements, such as the movement to raise awareness about breast cancer, mobilize their resources to rally support and spread their messages.

SECTION 2 REVIEW

1. **Define and explain**
   social movements
   reactionary movements
   conservative movements
   revisionary movements
   revolutionary movements
   relative deprivation theory
   resource mobilization
   resource-mobilization theory

2. **Categorizing**
   Copy the graphic organizer below. Use it to describe the life cycle of a social movement.

   Institutionalization

   Agitation

3. **Finding the Main Idea**
   a. How do the various types of social movements differ?
   b. How do relative deprivation theory and resource-mobilization theory explain social change resulting from social problems within and across groups?

4. **Writing and Critical Thinking**
   Drawing Inferences and Conclusions Using the civil rights movement as an example, describe how each of the theories of social movements would explain the causes of this social movement. Consider:
   • Relative deprivation theory
   • Resource-mobilization theory

Homework Practice Online
keyword: SL3 HP17

SECTION 2 REVIEW ANSWERS

1. **Define:**
   • social movements, p. 449
   • reactionary movements, p. 449
   • conservative movements, p. 449
   • revisionary movements, p. 450
   • revolutionary movements, p. 450
   • relative deprivation theory, p. 452
   • resource mobilization, p. 454
   • resource-mobilization theory, p. 454

2. agitation—initial stirrings of a movement; legitimation—movement viewed as more respectable; bureaucratization—structure of movement more formal; institutionalization—movement an established part of society

3a. See the graphic organizer on p. 450.

b. relative deprivation—people join social movements because they feel deprived relative to other groups; resource-mobilization—only groups with resources will be able to generate social change

4. Responses will vary, but students should demonstrate an understanding of both of the theories of social movement described in the previous answer.

Building Social Studies Skills

◼ TEACH

Have students read the feature Using the Internet. Next, ask students how they determine whether an Internet site or the information on it is credible or current. Then have students work in pairs to perform the Applying the Skill activity. Each pair should search the Internet to find three to five Web sites. Students should then use the points in the feature to rate each Web site's overall reliability on a scale of *1* to *5*, with *1* being the most reliable. Finally, assign the Practicing the Skill activity as homework. **COOPERATIVE LEARNING**

◼ EXTEND

1. Provide students with a format for listing Web sites in a bibliography. Each entry should provide the name of the specific page or article on the Web site being cited, the name of the Web site, the name of the organization that produces the Web site, the date that the cited material was last updated, the URL for the Web site's home page, and the URL for the cited Web page (if different). Then have each pair of students create a bibliography for the Web sites that they used in the previous Applying the Skill activity.

COOPERATIVE LEARNING , BLOCK SCHEDULING

USING THE INTERNET

Have students share with the class some of their favorite Web sites for information. Then select five of the sites, access and print them, and make a photocopy of the printouts for each student. Then have students work as a class or in small groups to evaluate each of the Web sites based on the guidelines in the feature.

Practicing the Skill

(see p. 457)

As an extension to the activity, ask volunteers to identify some of the Web sites they used in their research on rumors. Have the class use the guidelines in the feature to evaluate each site and determine if it was a reliable source of information.

BUILDING

Social Studies Skills

USING THE INTERNET

Are you one of the more than 174 million Internet users in the United States? The Internet is a global network that links millions of computers. It offers many services, including electronic mailing, or e-mail; online chat and discussion groups; online shopping; and the World Wide Web (WWW).

The Web is a set of computer programs that make multimedia presentations—combinations of text, sound, pictures, animation, and video—possible on the Internet. These presentations are known as Web sites. Each site has its own unique address—or URL (uniform resource locator)—that indicates the computer or network where the information is stored. URLs in the United States end with a two or more letter designation that specifies the kind of institution sponsoring the Web site. For example, *com* indicates a commercial organization, *edu* indicates an educational institution, *gov* indicates a nonmilitary government organization, *mil* indicates a military institution, *net* indicates a network service provider, and *org* indicates a nonprofit organization.

Surfing, or browsing, the Web can be a very productive method of research. Because there are more than 50 million Web sites, the Web offers a host of resources that are probably not available in the books or periodicals at your school or public libraries. Many Web sites are also regularly updated. Thus, information on the Web may be more recent than that available in other sources.

The Internet offers many sources for research. Many of the world's libraries and archives can be searched from any computer with online access. There are many types of search tools available. Directories, search engines, and subject guides are three of the major types of search tools. Each search tool is constantly changing. Get to know the strengths and weaknesses of your search-tool choice. Many search engines use keywords to improve search speed and accuracy. Be sure to examine the "Help" files of any search tool to get the full details on search information. Some large Web sites—such as America Online, CNN, MSN, Netscape, and Yahoo!—offer links to a broad range of information. In addition, there are many government sites that provide information on public policy and government organizations. Sites such as CNNfyi.com allow you to access current news and information.

To determine whether a Web site contains reliable information, ask yourself the following questions:

- Is the information clear and easy to read?
- Is a well-respected organization sponsoring the site?
- Does the text contain any obvious mistakes?
- Is the Web site easy to navigate, and are most of the page links active?
- Does the Web site indicate updates, and are they recent?
- Is the information biased?

Internet technology provides a wide range of resources for research projects.

2. Have each student write an essay analyzing and critiquing one of the Web sites from either the Applying the Skill or the Practicing the Skill activity. Students' essays should address each of the bulleted questions on p. 456. Remind students to provide reasons and examples that support their points and to use standard grammar, spelling, sentence structure, and punctuation in their essays. Students should also provide printouts of their Web sites. **BLOCK SCHEDULING**

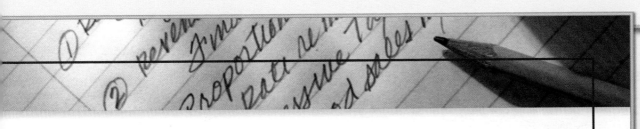

CONNECTING *to History*

Have students conduct an Internet search to find Web sites about either the American Revolution, the women's suffrage movement, or the American civil rights movement of the 1960s. Have students use the sites to create a time line illustrating some of the main events in the social movement being researched. In addition, students should provide a bibliography and printouts of the Internet sites they used. Remind students to use only credible Internet sites, based on the information in the feature. **BLOCK SCHEDULING**

The Internet contains many resources, making it an excellent tool for research. However, there is a lot of inappropriate material on the Web. Many well-respected sites have developed safe areas for young people, known as child-safe zones. Even at these sites you must be careful.

- Never chat with or meet with strangers.
- Never give out any personal information.
- If you get into an unsecured area, get out immediately and tell a parent or teacher.
- Only use well-respected search engines.

You can use the Internet as a research tool by following the guidelines listed below.
1. **Access a search engine.** Log on to the Internet and access one of the Web search engines—such as AltaVista, Excite, Google, Hotbot, Infoseek, Lycos, or Yahoo!
2. **Conduct a search.** Use either a category search or a keyword search. For a category search, find the site's directory and click on the category that would be the most useful source of information for your research topic. For a keyword search, type in one or more words related to your research topic and click on "Search" or "Go."
3. **Review Web sites.** Scroll down the list of Web sites displayed as a result of the search. Access a site and review the information. Repeat steps 2 and 3 until you have sufficient information.

Applying the Skill

To use the Internet to find more information about social movements, you might follow this procedure.
1. **Access a search engine.** Log on to the Internet and access a Web search engine of your choice.
2. **Conduct a search.** For a category search, find the site's directory and click on the "Society and Culture" link. Then scroll down the Topics list and click on the "Sociology" link. For a keyword search, type in "social movement" or some other related terms—"reform

Early computers were large machines. Current personal computers have much more memory and power than these early computers.

movement," "revolutionary movement," "utopian movement," "deprivation theory," "resource-mobilization theory," and so on—and click on "Search."
3. **Review Web sites.** Scroll down the list of Web sites displayed as a result of the search. Study the descriptions of the content of each Web site. Reject those that do not have the type of information that you are looking for. Access those sites that appear to be useful. Repeat steps 2 and 3 until you have enough information to write a sociology encyclopedia entry titled Social Movement.

Practicing the Skill

Use the guidelines to search the Internet for information on a type of collective behavior that consists solely of communication—rumors. Use the materials you find to write a brief magazine article on rumors. Remember to use examples of specific rumors in your article.

Review and Assessment Resources

- Chapter 17 Review, pp. 458–59
- Chapter Review Activities with Answer Key
- Global Skill Builder CD–ROM
- Chapter 17 Test Generator (on the One-Stop Planner)
- Chapter 17 Test (Form A or B)
- Alternative Assessment Handbook
- HRW Go site

REVIEW

Have students complete the **Chapter 17 Review** on pp. 458–59.

ASSESS

Use one of the chapter tests to assess students' understanding of the content. For **Alternative Assessment**, see the **Alternative Assessment Handbook**.

---

2. casual—unorganized, temporary, little interaction; conventional—little interaction but structured; expressive—forms around an activity; acting—violent and destructive

3. Fashions are attachments among people for particular behaviors. Fads are unconventional objects, ideas, or actions popular for a short period of time. Fads are less enduring and less predictable than fashions.

4. reactionary—Ku Klux Klan; conservative—religious right; revisionary—women's suffrage movement; revolutionary—American Revolution

5. Goals are sometimes swept aside because more attention is paid to the day-to-day running of the organization.

6. *Relative deprivation* refers to how economically or socially deprived people feel compared to other groups in society.

7. The resources needed include supporters, financial resources, and media access.

THINKING CRITICALLY

1. Collective behavior is difficult to study because the range of behaviors is enormous, and the behavior is short-lived and difficult to study systematically.

2. structural conduciveness—social structure that makes collective behavior possible; structural strain—conditions that encourage collective action; growth of a generalized belief—makes strain meaningful; precipitating factors—trigger mechanisms that set off collective

---

CHAPTER

 17 Review

Writing a Summary

Using standard grammar, spelling, sentence structure, and punctuation, summarize the information in this chapter.
Consider:
- the different types of collective behavior
- the theories that explain collective behavior
- the definition of a social movement
- how the development of social movements is explained

Identifying People and Ideas

Identify the following people or terms and use them in appropriate sentences.

1. collective behavior
2. crowd
3. fad
4. public opinion
5. emergent-norm theory
6. social movements
7. conservative movements
8. revisionary movements
9. relative deprivation theory
10. resource-mobilization theory

Understanding Main ideas

Section 1 (pp. 436–48)

1. How do collectivities differ from social groups?
2. List and describe the four types of crowds identified by Herbert Blumer.
3. What is the difference between fads and fashions?

Section 2 (pp. 449–55)

4. List and give examples of the four types of social movements identified by William Bruce Cameron.
5. Why are the original goals of a social movement sometimes swept aside during the bureaucratization stage of the social-movement life cycle?
6. What do sociologists mean by the term *relative deprivation*?
7. According to resource-mobilization theory, what kinds of resources are needed for a social movement to be successful?

Thinking Critically

1. **Analyzing Information** Why do you think sociologists have difficulty studying collective behavior?
2. **Making Generalizations and Predictions** Describe the six basic preconditions for collective behavior that Neil Smelser identified. Then develop a hypothetical riot or mob situation in which these six preconditions are present.
3. **Sequencing** Trace the four-stage life cycle of a social movement, using an actual example from history. Choose an example other than labor unions.
4. **Contrasting** How is relative deprivation theory similar to Karl Marx's explanation of one of the causes of revolution?
5. **Evaluating** Discuss the development of the civil rights movement in the United States from the perspective of the resource-mobilization theory.

Writing About Sociology

1. **Summarizing** Imagine that you are running a political campaign or advertising a product. Create several scripts for commercials that advertise your product or candidate. Write a short summary of each type of propaganda strategy that you use to influence the perceptions, attitudes, and behaviors of people and groups.
2. **Drawing Inferences and Conclusions** Use the library or the Internet to research urban legends. Possible sources of urban legends are the features section of your local newspaper and magazine advice columns. You might also interview friends and relatives about any urban legends they may know. For each legend that you collect, write a brief introduction identifying the moral lesson taught. Use the graphic organizer below to help you organize your work.

| Urban Legend | → | Source | → | Summary of Legend | → | Moral Lesson |

RETEACH

Have students work in pairs or small groups to create a 20-item, true-false quiz using the key terms, concepts, and names in this chapter. Each pair or group should also create an answer key for its quiz. Then have pairs or groups exchange quizzes, complete the ones they receive, and then use the answer keys to check their answers.

ENGLISH LANGUAGE LEARNERS , COOPERATIVE LEARNING

SOCIOLOGY PROJECTS

1. Applying Sociology Organize students into groups and assign each group a local radio station. Have each group contact a marketing or advertising person at its assigned station to learn about the station's market. Who listens to the station? How does the station know? How does the station use this information in its advertising? Have the groups share their findings with the class.

2. Connecting to Literature Have each student write a short story involving one or more of the following types of collective behavior: a mob, riot, panic, moral panic, or mass hysteria. Select the best story and have its author read it to the class.

BUILDING SOCIAL STUDIES SKILLS

Interpreting Graphs

Study the graph below. Use it to answer the following questions.

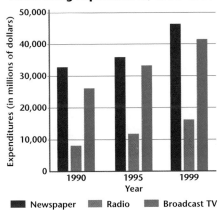

Advertising Expenditures, 1990–1999

Source: *U.S. Statistical Abstract*

1. According to this graph, approximately how much more did advertising expenditures increase for newspapers than for radio?
   a. $15,000
   b. $8,000
   c. $7,000
   d. $14,000
2. What general conclusions about the importance of advertising in American society could you draw from this graph?

Analyzing Primary Sources

The following excerpt describes the mass hysteria that occurred during actor Orson Welles's 1938 radio broadcast of a fictional invasion by Martians. Read the excerpt and then answer the questions that follow.

"*It was not as though listeners hadn't been warned. Most simply didn't pay close attention to the program's opening signature (or tuned in a few seconds late and missed it all together). . . .*

Millions of listeners, conditioned by recent news reports of world-wide political turmoil—and by their inherent trust in the medium of radio—believed what they heard. . . .

A current of fear flowed outward across the nation. Real-life police switchboards, first in New Jersey, then, steadily, throughout the whole Northeast, began to light up . . .

Thousands of telephone calls cascaded into radio stations, newspaper offices, power companies, fire houses, and military posts throughout the country. People wanted to know what to do. . .where to go. . .whether they were safer in the cellar or the attic.

Word spread in Atlanta that a 'planet' had struck New Jersey. In Philadelphia, all the guests in one hotel checked out. Students at a college in North Carolina lined up at telephones to call their parents for the last time. When a caller reached the CBS switchboard, the puzzled operator, asked about the end of the world, said: 'I'm sorry, we don't have that information."

3. What factor led people to believe that the fictional Mars invasion was real?
   a. There had been warnings of an invasion.
   b. The broadcaster failed to tell listeners that it was a fictional account.
   c. Americans trusted radio as a reliable medium.
   d. It was the first broadcast heard by many people.
4. How could this event lead to an understanding of real-life national crises?

behavior; mobilization—action begins; social control—behavior is stopped; examples will vary.

3. agitation, legitimation, bureaucratization, and institutionalization; examples will vary.

4. Relative deprivation theory, like Marx's explanation of revolution, argues that people seek social change because they feel dissatisfaction with their situation compared to other groups in society.

5. The civil rights movement had a large body of college-educated activists, financial support, and wide media coverage.

WRITING ABOUT SOCIOLOGY

1. Scripts and summaries will vary, but students should demonstrate an understanding of propaganda techniques and effects.

2. Introductions will vary, but students should connect urban legends with specific moral lessons.

BUILDING SOCIAL STUDIES SKILLS

1. c

2. Answers will vary, but students might suggest that because of the large amounts of money spent, advertising is a very important activity in society.

3. c

4. Answers will vary, but students might suggest that this event could be studied as how people might act in a real-life situation.

SOCIOLOGY PROJECTS

Linking to Community

Using Your Observation Skills For one week, watch television during prime-time hours to record the commercials shown. For each commercial, make note of the propaganda technique being used and the way that technique is used. At the end of the week, write a brief report on your findings, noting which propaganda technique is used most often.

internet connect

Internet Activity: go.hrw.com
KEYWORD: SL3 SC17
Choose an activity on collective behavior and social movements to:
- create a multimedia presentation on the causes and effects of riots throughout history.
- write and interpret an urban legend of your own.
- create a brochure on measuring, analyzing, and manipulating public opinion in American history.

go.hrw.com

Social Change and Modernization

CHAPTER RESOURCE MANAGER

Objectives	Pacing Guide		Resources

SECTION 1: Explaining Social Change
(pp. 462–70)

REV Section 1 Review, p. 470

- Summarize the theories that social scientists have offered to explain the process of social change.
- Explain how the theories on social change have evolved.

Regular 4 days

Block Scheduling 2 days

Block Scheduling Handbook with Team Teaching Strategies, Chapter 18

- 📼 **CNN** Presents Sociology: Doing Business with Different Cultures
- **RS** Graphic Organizer 18
- 🌐 HRW Go site
- **SM** Mastering Critical Thinking Skills 18
- **PS** Readings and Case Studies in Sociology 18
- **E** Research Projects and Activities for Teaching Sociology 18
- **SM** Study Skills and Writing Guide
- 📽 Teaching Transparency: Characteristics of Modernized and Non-modernized Societies

SECTION 2: Modernization
(pp. 471–79)

REV Section 2 Review, p. 479

- Contrast the views of modernization theory and world-system theory on modernization in less-developed nations.
- Identify some of the positive and negative effects of modernization on social life and the natural environment.

Regular 3 days

Block Scheduling 1.5 days

Block Scheduling Handbook with Team Teaching Strategies, Chapter 18

Chapter Review And Assessment

- **REV** Chapter 18 Review, pp. 480–81
- **REV** Chapter Review Activities with Answer Key
- 💿 Global Skill Builder CD–ROM
- 💿 Chapter 18 Test Generator (on the One-Stop Planner)
- **A** Chapter 18 Test (Form A or B)
- **A** Alternative Assessment Handbook
- 🌐 HRW Go site

Chapter Resource Key

PS	Primary Sources	**A**	Assessment	📼	Video
RS	Reading Support	**REV**	Review	🌐	Internet
E	Enrichment	📽	Transparencies	💻	Holt Presentation Maker Using Microsoft® PowerPoint®
SM	Skills Mastery	💿	CD–ROM		

One-Stop Planner CD–ROM

See the *One-Stop Planner* for a complete list of additional resources for students and teachers.

One-Stop Planner CD–ROM

It's easy to plan lessons, select resources, and print out materials for your students when you use the **One-Stop Planner CD-ROM with Test Generator.**

Chapter Project Preview

The following activities are included in the Chapter Review. You may want to make the suggested preparations.

CHAPTER REVIEW ACTIVITY

Using Observation Skills Students will work in groups to research the process of modernization in various countries and write paragraphs describing their findings. In preparation, you may want to identify for students a number of core, peripheral, and semiperipheral countries on a world map.

LESSON ACTIVITY

Using Sociological Imagination Students will work in groups to create fictional countries and to write brief "histories" describing the causes, process, and effects of modernization on the countries over a period of centuries. Students will supplement their written histories with annotated time lines. In preparation, create a structure for students to follow when creating their histories. You might also specify exactly how

many centuries students' histories and time lines should cover. To increase uniformity, you might provide all students with a fictional description of a country to use for the project.

INTERNET ACTIVITIES

Understanding Social Change Students will use provided Internet links to conduct research on different theories of social change. Each student will then create a pamphlet that outlines the causes, effects, and theories of social change. To help students with the project, provide several sample pamphlets and a template for creating a pamphlet.

Dealing with Modernization Students will use provided Internet links to conduct research on the ways in which different organizations are managing the effects of modernization and then write a profile of one specific organization. To help guide students, provide them with a sample profile of an organization of your choice to use as a template.

Additional Resources

PRINT RESOURCES FOR TEACHERS

Micklethwait, John, and Adrian Wooldridge. *A Future Perfect: The Challenge and Hidden Promise of Globalization.* Times Books, 2000. Primer on globalization's economic, political, and social aspects.

Roberts, J., and Amy Hite, eds. *Modernization to Globalization: Perspectives on Development and Social Change.* Blackwell Publishers, 2000. Classic and modern essays on the processes of social change in less-developed nations.

Volti, Rudi. *Society and Technological Change,* 4th ed. New York: Worth Publishers, 2000. Examines the influence of technology on social change.

PRINT RESOURCES FOR STUDENTS

Frank, Pat. *Alas, Babylon* (Perrenial Classics). New York: HarperCollins, 1999. A small group of people rebuild

after a global disaster. Explores the effects of drastic social change.

The Roman Record (Newspaper History Series). Usborne Books, 1997. Uses a newspaper format to present an overview of Roman history.

MULTIMEDIA RESOURCES

Modern Times (b&w, vhs or dvd; 87 min.) Satire of modern society, directed by Charlie Chaplin in 1936.

Technology's Price (vhs, color; 25 min.) Encyclopaedia Britannica Educational Corporation. Explores the environmental and human costs of our dependence on technology.

Who'll Save Abacaxi? A Third-World Government Simulation (simulation, software) Focus Media, Inc. Simulation in which students act out the roles of officials of a developing country and make decisions that have internal and global implications.

internet connect

HRW ONLINE RESOURCES

GO TO: go.hrw.com
Then type in a keyword.

TEACHER HOME PAGE
KEYWORD: SL3 Teacher

CHAPTER INTERNET ACTIVITIES
KEYWORD: SL3 SC18
Choose an activity to have students:
- create a pamphlet explaining different theories of social change.
- write a profile on an organization dealing with the effects of modernization.
- create a graph or chart illustrating statistics related to the International Monetary Fund.

CHAPTER ENRICHMENT LINKS
KEYWORD: SL3 CH18

ONLINE ASSESSMENT
Homework Practice
KEYWORD: SL3 HP18
Standardized Test Prep
KEYWORD: SL3 STP18
Rubrics
KEYWORD: SS Rubrics

CONTENT UPDATES
KEYWORD: SS Content Updates

HOLT PRESENTATION MAKER
KEYWORD: SL3 PPT18

ONLINE READING SUPPORT
KEYWORD: SS Strategies

CURRENT EVENTS
KEYWORD: S3 Current Events

CHAPTER

18

Social Change and Modernization

SECTION 1
Explaining Social Change

SECTION 2
Modernization

CHAPTER REVIEW

Internet Activity

internet connect

TOPIC: Understanding Social Change
GO TO: go.hrw.com
KEYWORD: SL3 SC18

Have students access the Internet through the HRW Go site to conduct research on different theories of social change. Then have each student create a short pamphlet that outlines the causes, effects, and theories related to social change. Students should correctly use sociology-related terminology in their pamphlets.

CHAPTER

18

Social Change and Modernization

Build on What You Know

Collective behavior, particularly social movements, can have a great effect on society. In this chapter you will explore the process of social change and the effects of modernization on society. You will study not only the theories of social change but also the process of modernization.

Many sociologists are interested in the processes of modernization and social change. Technology is an important part of these changes.

Life in Society

Social change became a defining characteristic of American society in the late 1900s and early 2000s. Arturo Madrid points out this fact in an article titled "Being 'The Other': Ethnic Identity in a Changing Society."

"Over the past four decades America's demography has undergone significant changes. Since 1965 the principal demographic growth we have experienced in the United States has been of peoples whose national origins are non-European. This population growth has occurred both through birth and through immigration. . . . African Americans are now to be found in significant numbers in every major urban center in the nation. Hispanic Americans now number over [23] million people, and although they are a regionally concentrated (and highly urbanized) population, there is a Hispanic community in almost every major urban center of the United States. . . . The Asian American population, which has historically consisted of small and concentrated communities of Chinese, Filipino, and Japanese Americans, has doubled over the past decade, its complexion changed by the addition of Cambodians, Koreans, Hmongs, Vietnamese, et al. . . . To sum up, we now live in one of the most demographically diverse nations in the world, and one that is increasingly more so. During the same period, social and economic change seems to have accelerated. . . . We live in an age of continuous and intense change, a world in which what held true yesterday does not today, and certainly will not tomorrow. What change does, moreover, is bring about even more change. The only constant we have at this point in our national development is change."

TRUTH OR FICTION

What's Your Opinion?

Read the following statements about sociology. Do you think they are true or false? You will learn whether each statement is true or false as you read the chapter.

- Theories on social change have not changed over time.
- Most sociologists combine several theories to explain social change.
- Modernization has been a relatively straight-forward process in all parts of the world.

▶ **WHY SOCIOLOGY MATTERS**

Sociologists have several theories to explain the process of moderization. Use **CNNfyi.com** or other current events sources to learn more about a country experiencing modernization. Create an annotated map of your findings on that country.

CNNfyi.com

461

SECTION 1

OBJECTIVES

1. *Summarize the theories that social scientists have offered to explain the process of social change.*

2. *Explain how the theories on social change have evolved.*

SECTION 1 RESOURCES

REPRODUCIBLE & REVIEW

- Graphic Organizer 18
- Mastering Critical Thinking Skills 18
- Readings and Case Studies in Sociology 18
- Section 1 Review, p. 470

TECHNOLOGY

- One-Stop Planner, Lesson 18.1
- Homework Practice Online

Visual Answer

Answers will vary, but students might suggest that cyclical theory would explain the decline of Maya culture as a result of the natural tendency for societies to pass through stages of development.

🔔 LET'S GET STARTED!

Write the heading *Factors of Social Change* on the chalkboard and draw lines from it to six blanks to be completed. As students enter the classroom, ask them to quickly review Chapter 3, Section 3 and to identify the six factors of social change discussed in that section (*values and beliefs, technology, population, diffusion, the physical environment, and wars and conquests*). Call on volunteers to identify and summarize the factors. As they do, write the factors on the chalkboard. Remind students of some of the issues that they learned about in Chapter 3 regarding social change. Then tell students that in Section 1 they will learn about some sociological theories of social change and about ways in which some of these theories have evolved.

①

EXPLAINING SOCIAL CHANGE

● Read to Discover
1. What theories have social scientists offered to explain the process of social change?
2. How have the theories on social change evolved?

● Define
social change, cyclical theory of social change, ideational culture, sensate culture, idealistic culture, principle of immanent change, evolutionary theory of social change, equilibrium theory of social change, conflict theory of social change

● Identify
Oswald Spengler, Pitirim Sorokin, Talcott Parsons, Ralf Dahrendorf

Sociology grew out of the social turmoil of the 1700s and 1800s. Thus, it is not surprising that sociologists devote considerable attention to the study of social change. Sociologists define **social change** as alterations in various aspects of a society over time. Through the years, sociologists have provided many descriptions of how social change takes place. Sociologists have also suggested numerous theories to explain the process of social change. The most significant of these theories can be grouped into four broad categories: cyclical theory, evolutionary theory, equilibrium theory, and conflict theory.

Cyclical Theory

As you read in Chapter 15, scientists are influenced by their views of reality. Social scientists are no less subject to that tendency than are other scientists. Therefore, it is not surprising that during periods of extreme social turmoil, cyclical theories of social change sometimes appear.

A **cyclical theory of social change** views change from a historical perspective. Societies arise, go through various stages of development, and then decline. Social change is the result of this natural tendency for societies to pass through stages of development. Cyclical theories are likely to gain popularity during periods of extreme social upheaval because people often view events as beyond their control. Cyclical theories are reassuring because they see change as part of a continuing process.

In some cyclical theories, societies are seen as passing through stages of development that mirror the human life cycle. According to this view, societies are born, grow to maturity, decline in old age, and eventually die. From the remains of dead societies emerge new societies that repeat the developmental process. Other cyclical theories hold that societies develop to a certain point and then reverse their development, only to advance once again in the future. Oswald Spengler and Pitirim Sorokin are, perhaps, the most notable proponents of the cyclical theory of social change.

INTERPRETING VISUALS Ancient civilizations such as the Maya have left large-scale ruins as a testament to their past power. *How might a cyclical theory of social change explain the decline of Maya culture?*

Teacher to Teacher

Keith A. Moser of Seguin, Texas, suggested the following activity: Have each student conduct research on one of the sociologists mentioned in this section and then write a one-page biography about the selected individual's life, career, and main contributions to the study of sociology. In addition, students should create time lines that show some of the major world events occurring during the sociologist's life or career, to provide context for the individual's work and theories.

BLOCK SCHEDULING

■ TEACH OBJECTIVE 1

To help students summarize the theories of social change described in this section, copy the graphic organizer on the next page onto the chalkboard, omitting the italicized answers. Have students copy and complete the organizer. Discuss the answers with the class. Then challenge students to come up with examples of the strengths and weaknesses of each theory of social change. *(for example, cyclical: strength—supported by many historical examples of societies that fit the model; cyclical: weakness—does not explain why social change occurs)* **ENGLISH LANGUAGE LEARNERS**

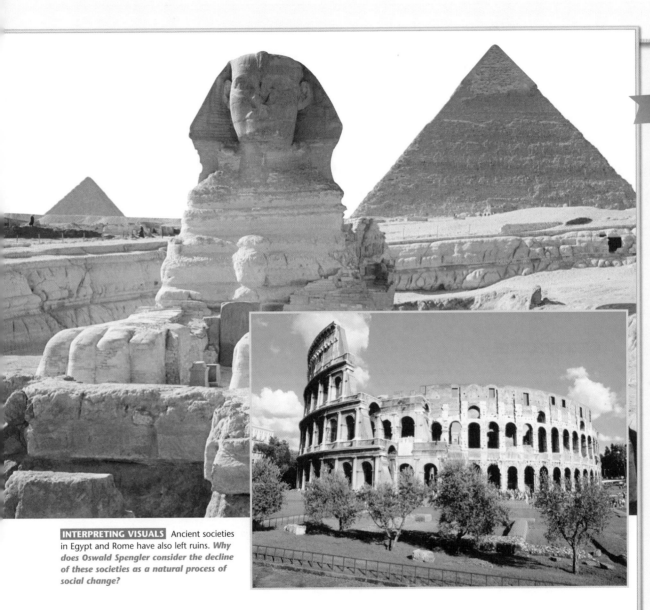

INTERPRETING VISUALS Ancient societies in Egypt and Rome have also left ruins. *Why does Oswald Spengler consider the decline of these societies as a natural process of social change?*

Interdisciplinary Connection

HISTORY

The Olmec and Maya Civilizations. Several early civilizations rose and fell in Mesoamerica—what is now southern Mexico and Central America. The first great Mesoamerican culture was the Olmec. The Olmec people lived on the fertile coastal lowlands along the Gulf of Mexico. Olmec culture reached its peak between 1200 and 100 B.C.

The Maya, who inherited much from the Olmec culture, arose about A.D. 300. The Maya civilization flourished for more than 500 years, primarily in what is now Mexico and Guatemala. The Maya civilization began to decline after A.D. 800. Archaeologists are unsure why the Olmec and Maya civilizations declined.

RESEARCH ACTIVITY: Have each student conduct research on one of these civilizations and create a time line of its history. Then have students discuss their time lines in light of Spengler's theory.

Visual Answer

because Spengler theorized that all societies pass through four stages, the last of which is old age, during which societies crumble and decline

Oswald Spengler German historian Oswald Spengler was deeply troubled by World War I. The brutality of the war led Spengler to question whether social change always results in progress. In his two-volume work, *The Decline of the West*, Spengler suggested that all societies pass through four stages—childhood, youth, adulthood, and old age. Western society, Spengler argued, had reached the prime of adulthood during the 1700s with the Enlightenment. In the early years of the 1900s, it was well into the decline associated with old age. This process, he added, was inevitable. Like other great civilizations of the past, Western civilization was bound to decline and disappear.

Pitirim Sorokin Russian American sociologist Pitirim Sorokin presented a different theory of social change. According to Sorokin's view, all societies fluctuate between two extreme forms of culture. At one extreme are ideational cultures. In an **ideational culture**, truth and knowledge are sought through faith or religion. At the other extreme are sensate cultures. In a **sensate culture**, people seek knowledge through science. Ideational cultures are likely to be devoted to spiritual pursuits, and sensate cultures are likely to be practical and materialistic. Sometimes, societies reach a middle point between those extremes, which he called the **idealistic culture**. Here, Sorokin suggested, ideational and sensate characteristics are combined.

Theory	Description	Criticisms
Cyclical	• Spengler—four stages: childhood, youth, adulthood, old age • Sorokin—fluctuation between ideational culture (spiritual) and sensate culture (scientific), with idealistic culture in the middle	• focused on describing what is, instead of why things happen
Evolutionary	• early—the progress through distinct stages toward complexity • modern—tendency to go along many paths toward increasing complexity	• biased toward the West; does not explain why change occurs • does not explain short-term changes or wars
Equilibrium	• Parsons—occurs as society adapts to maintain stability after a change in one area; involves differentiation and integration	• does not explain widespread social change within or between societies
Conflict	• Marx—results from class conflict and revolution • Dahrendorf—results from social conflicts of all forms	• does not always lead to revolution • does not explain change without conflict

People in Sociology

Pitirim Sorokin. Born in Turya, Russia, Pitirim Sorokin (1889–1968) moved to the United States in 1923. He went on to found the department of sociology at Harvard University in 1930 and to gain international recognition. His books include the *Sociology of Revolution* (1925), *Man and Society in Calamity* (1942), and *A Long Journey* (1963).

ACTIVITY: Have each student conduct research on Sorokin's life, career, and accomplishments. Then have each student create a plaque for him to go in a fictional Sociology Hall of Fame.

Visual Answer

Students might suggest that European society was in a sensate culture at the time, although when Galileo proposed his theory he was initially accused of heresy, which might indicate that Europe was still somewhat in an ideational culture.

According to Sorokin, external factors—such as war or contact with other societies—can hasten a society's shift from one culture to another. However, these external factors do not cause the shift. Sorokin believed that the tendency toward change is present at a society's birth. Something in the society's structure causes it to swing back and forth between an ideational and a sensate culture. Sorokin referred to this natural tendency toward social change as the **principle of immanent change**.

Critics of cyclical theories point out that such explanations often describe what *is*, rather than attempt to determine *why* things happen. From a sociological perspective, the interesting point is not that societies have a life cycle. The real point of interest is why some societies decline or disappear while others continue to grow and adapt to changing conditions. Studying the history of past civilizations might help today's societies.

Evolutionary Theory

In contrast to cyclical theories, the **evolutionary theory of social change** views change as a process that moves in one direction—toward increasing complexity. As members of society attempt to adapt to social and physical conditions in their environment, they push the society forward in development. Each new adaptation serves as the basis for future adaptations. Thus, change is seen as an additive process.

All evolutionary theories hold that societies develop toward increasing complexity. Evolutionary theory was popular among some early sociologists. However, views on how that development takes place have changed over the years. Therefore, it is important to distinguish between the views of early evolutionary theorists and those of modern social evolutionists.

INTERPRETING VISUALS Pitirim Sorokin argued that societies fluctuate between a culture based on the pursuit of religious knowledge and a culture based on scientific knowledge. Sorokin suggested that an idealistic culture contains both characteristics. *What stage of Sorokin's cycle do you think European society was in during the time Galileo presented the theory that Earth revolved around the Sun?*

Write the following terms on the chalkboard: *cyclical, evolutionary, equilibrium,* and *conflict.* Have students work in pairs to write definitions of each term and to provide examples of processes that each term might describe *(for example: cyclical—moon phases; evolutionary—technical innovations; equilibrium—balancing a scale; conflict—labor strikes).* Ask volunteers to share their definitions and responses with the class. Make certain that students understand the meaning of each word. Use the activity as the basis of a class discussion about the theories of social change discussed in the section *(and in the graphic organizer on p. 464)* and how they have evolved. Then have each pair create one or more small images that illustrate the main idea of each theory and the subcategories within it. For example, students might create an image of a pendulum to illustrate Sorokin's cyclical theory that societies fluctuate between ideational culture *(spiritual)* and sensate culture *(scientific),* with an idealistic culture in the middle. Ask volunteers to share some of their images with the class. **COOPERATIVE LEARNING**

HOMEWORK: Have students use what they consider to be the best elements of each social theory (and any elements of their own) to create "recipes" for Social Change Casserole. Students should treat the elements as "ingredients" and provide amounts and preparation instructions.

INTERPRETING VISUALS According to evolutionary theory, social change occurs as a progression toward more complexity. *How do you think these images of shopping areas in Europe during the Renaissance, the 1800s, and contemporary society provide an example of the evolutionary theory?*

Early Evolutionary Theories Evolutionary theorists of the 1800s believed that all societies progress through the same distinct stages of social development. Each stage is supposed to bring with it improved social conditions and increased societal complexity. These early theorists viewed Western civilization as the height of social development.

Auguste Comte, one of the earliest social evolutionists, suggested a three-stage theory of development. According to Comte, in the first stage of development, people in society seek explanations for events by turning to the supernatural. In the next stage, answers are sought in religion or philosophy. In the highest stage of development, members of society turn to science to understand why events happen.

Later, Herbert Spencer carried this idea of social evolution a step further. Influenced by Charles Darwin's *On the Origin of Species,* Spencer argued that societies, like living organisms, evolve from simple to complex. According to Spencer, the process of natural selection guides that evolution. Societies with members able to adjust to changes in the social and natural environments progress to higher stages of development. Societies die out, on the other hand, when members cannot adapt. Spencer referred to this idea as "the survival of the fittest."

Evolutionary theories were popular during the late 1800s and early 1900s because they justified the social and political conditions in Europe and the United States. Spencer's idea that only the strongest societies are meant to survive proved particularly popular. It transformed the domination of the weak by the strong into a natural part of social development. Thus, proponents of Spencer's theory believed it was justifiable for Europe and the United States—the industrial giants of the world—to exploit weaker countries militarily and economically. Spencer also suggested that class differences within

TEACH OBJECTIVE 2

Organize the class into four groups and assign each group one of the following theories of social change: cyclical, evolutionary, equilibrium, or conflict. *(See the graphic organizer on p. 464.)* Have each group determine if and how its assigned theory evolved over time and how the theory is regarded today. Then have each group give a short oral presentation to the class explaining either how sociologists have modified the assigned theory or, if the theory did not evolve much or at all, explain why this is so.

COOPERATIVE LEARNING

CONNECTING *to the Arts*

Tell students that most music and stories have an underlying structure. For example, classical symphonies are normally composed of four movements. Similarly, most movies and television shows have three or four acts. Have each student analyze a symphony, movie, or television show and write a short essay about its structure. Students should relate the performance to one or more of the four theories of social change *(cyclical, evolutionary, equilibrium, or conflict)*, explaining how the structure of the performance fits the pattern(s) and why. For example, a movie may explore the theme of conflict *(two characters with opposing agendas)* in a cyclical story structure *(introduction, discovery, confrontation, and resolution)*.

BLOCK SCHEDULING

Applying Sociology

Evolutionary Universals.
Functionalist theorist Talcott Parsons argues that as societies evolve and become more complex, they develop some common features, which he calls evolutionary universals. These features enable a society to function and maintain stability. Some of the first evolutionary universals societies develop are language, religion, kinship, and technology. In more complex industrialized societies, evolutionary universals include features such as bureaucratic organization, economic markets, and social stratification.

CRITICAL THINKING

Do you agree that all societies will evolve to develop bureaucratic organization, economic markets, and social stratification?

ANSWER: Answers will vary, but students should exhibit an understanding of the criticisms of the equilibrium theory of social change.

Visual Answer

Students might suggest that according to the equilibrium theory, renovations in a city might spur social and economic improvements, which in turn will result in social change.

countries were a natural phenomenon. According to the evolutionary view, individuals who could and should rise to the top would naturally do so.

Critics of early evolutionary theory note that in addition to possessing an ideological bias, it did not attempt to explain *why* social change takes place. Instead, evolutionary theorists merely provided scattered data to support their view that all societies were traveling along the path toward industrialization. When social scientists began to collect extensive data from around the world, they found that social change is not an orderly process. By the early 1920s, most social scientists had rejected evolutionary theory.

Modern Evolutionary Theories Evolutionary theory did not remain out of favor for long. However, when it reappeared, evolutionary theory had abandoned many of the ideas that its critics had challenged. For example, modern evolutionary theorists do not claim that all societies pass through a single set of distinct stages of development on their way toward some ideal of Western society. Rather, they hold that societies have a *tendency* to become more complex over time. Change can result from many sources and can take many paths. Modern social evolutionists do not assume that change always produces progress nor that progress means the same thing in all societies.

An equally important difference between modern and early evolutionary theory is that modern theorists attempt to explain *why* societies change. According to social scientists Gerhard Lenski and Jean Lenski, social evolution takes place because of changes in a society's economic base and its level of technology. New technologies and improvements in old technologies enable societies to change their subsistence patterns. As a society changes its form of subsistence—such as from hunting and gathering to simple horticulture—that society's other social institutions are changed to some degree. Each new level of development provides the basis for future changes.

Critics of modern evolutionary theory agree that it has avoided many of the problems that plagued earlier evolutionary theories; modern theories do provide a limited explanation of social change. However, they do not attempt to explain events such as wars or short-term changes within individual societies.

Equilibrium Theory

As you know, functionalist theory focuses on the ways in which societies maintain order. However, it is impossible to ignore the fact that societies do change. Recognizing this fact, functionalist theorist Talcott Parsons offered the **equilibrium theory of social change**.

Building on the functionalist idea that society resembles a living organism, Parsons argued that a change in one part of the system produces changes in all of the other parts

INTERPRETING VISUALS The equilibrium theory argues that a change in one part of a social system affects other parts of the system. The renovation of historic areas of U.S. cities such as Chicago's Loop has generated growth and economic development in these areas. *How might the equilibrium theory describe the social changes of this historic renovation in Chicago?*

Case Studies and Other True Stories

TEACH

Have students read the feature Virtual Communities and answer the questions that follow it. Organize students into pairs or groups of three, and give students a topic to discuss, such as their favorite movies, television shows, or hobbies. Have each pair or group verbally discuss the topic with their eyes closed. Next, have students discuss the same or another topic by writing notes to each other. Then, have students verbally discuss a topic with their eyes open. Finally, have students use the activity to analyze the issues related to virtual communication. **COOPERATIVE LEARNING**

EXTEND

Pair students and have each pair list some of the short-comings of virtual communities. Then have each pair brainstorm possible solutions to these problems *(for example, the use of icons or graphics to communicate emotions, such as using ":-)" to show happiness; the creation of virtual actors who visually represent individuals in a discussion; the widespread use of web cameras; identification and authentication techniques)*. Call on volunteers to share some of their solutions with the class. **COOPERATIVE LEARNING ,
BLOCK SCHEDULING**

Case Studies
AND OTHER TRUE STORIES

VIRTUAL COMMUNITIES

New technology often drives social change. For example, the development of the personal computer and the Internet has changed the way people interact with one another. Many e-communities are little more than Web sites where members discuss issues of common interest. However, some seem very much like communities in the "real world." Since interaction takes place through a computer screen, technology writer Howard Rheingold notes, they are "virtual communities." In the following excerpt, Rheingold points out that the anonymity that the computer screen provides can be both an advantage and a disadvantage in virtual communication.

"Virtual communities have several advantages over the old-fashioned communities of place. . . . Because we cannot see one another, we are unable to form prejudices about others before we read what they have to say. Race, gender, age, national origin, and physical appearance are not apparent unless a person wants to make such characteristics public. People whose physical handicaps make it difficult to form new friendships find that virtual communities treat them as they always wanted to be treated—as transmitters of ideas and feeling beings, not carnal vessels with a certain appearance and way of walking and talking (or not walking and not talking). Don't mistake this filtration of appearances for dehumanization; words on a screen are quite capable of moving one to laughter or tears, of evoking anger or compassion, of creating a community from a collection of strangers. . . .

Virtual communities have several drawbacks in comparison to face-to-face communication. . . . The filtration factor that prevents one person from knowing the race or age of another participant also prevents them from communicating the facial expressions, body language, and tone of voice that constitute the invisible but vital component of most face-to-face communication. Irony, sarcasm, compassion, and other subtle but all-important nuances that aren't conveyed in words alone are lost when all you can see of a person is a set of words on a screen. This lack of communication bandwidth can lead to misunderstandings, and it is one of the reasons that "flames," or heated diatribes that wouldn't crop up often in normal discourse, seem to appear with relative frequency in computer conferences. On-line communication seems to disinhibit people. Those who would be shy in face-to-face discourse can enter the conversation. And those who are polite in face-to-face discourse are tempted to be ruder than they would be to someone in the flesh.

It is easy to deceive people on-line: for nasty people to wear a polite mask and for nice people to pretend to be nasty. We all wear masks in our lives. We all play many roles at home and at work and in public. But on-line discourse is nothing but masks. We can never be sure about our knowledge of another person when that knowledge is based solely on words on a computer screen."

Sociologists are interested in e-communities and the ways they have influenced social life.

Think About It

1. **Evaluating** *What are the advantages and disadvantages of virtual communities as opposed to traditional communities?*

2. **Supporting a Point of View** *Do you think that social interaction truly takes place when individuals have no face-to-face contact? Why or why not?*

Think About It Answers

1. In virtual communities, people are not inhibited or prejudiced by shyness, race, ethnicity, gender, age, or physical appearance. On the other hand, such communities prevent the exchange of subtle forms of face-to-face communication, which can lead to misunderstandings or the use of deception.

2. Some students may support their point of view with personal examples. Other students may note the use of "emoticons" and acronyms in online messages as methods of communicating facial expressions and tone of voice.

SPOTLIGHT *on Equilibrium Theory*
Have each student write a short story in which a society (real or fictional) is undergoing a significant social change and the theory of equilibrium is guiding the change. *(equilibrium theory— Change in one part of a social system produces changes in all other parts of the system as the social system attempts to maintain stability. The new system is then slightly different from the old one.)* Students' stories might also explore differentiation and integration as explained in the text. **BLOCK SCHEDULING**

SPOTLIGHT *on Conflict Theory*
Have students, working either individually or in small groups, conduct research on the theories of Karl Marx, Ralf Dahrendorf, and other conflict theorists regarding social change. *(See the graphic organizer on p. 464.)* Then have each student or group of students write a dialogue in which two or more of the theorists debate their theories. Students' dialogues should address Marx's vision of class conflict, Dahrendorf's views on racial and ethnic conflict, and relevant examples of conflict shaping society.
COOPERATIVE LEARNING , BLOCK SCHEDULING

◆ Applying Sociology

Critiques of Theories of Social Change.
Sociologist Max Weber argued that theories of social change that rely on one main factor—such as economics, technology, or conflict—cannot account for the variety of change and development that occurs in societies. Based on Weber's argument, sociologist Anthony Giddens argues that no one theory can describe all forms of social change. Giddens suggests that sociologists should instead focus on the influences on social change and on analyzing certain phases that many societies go through as they change.

CRITICAL THINKING
Do you agree with Giddens that no one theory can be developed to account for all types of social change?

ANSWER: Answers will vary, but students should exhibit an understanding of the various critiques of each theory of social change.

Visual Answer

Students might suggest that a conflict theorist would contrast the military power of the state represented by the tanks with the lone individual seeking social change.

468

of the system. This phenomenon occurs because a social system, like a living organism, attempts to maintain stability. When stability is disrupted by change in one part of the system, the other parts of the system adjust to the degree needed to bring the system back into balance, or equilibrium. Although order has been restored, the new system is slightly different from the old system. Thus, social change takes place.

Parsons also offered an explanation of how social equilibrium is maintained through evolutionary change. According to Parsons, evolutionary change takes place through a two-step process of *differentiation* and *integration*. As a society becomes more complex, its social institutions become more numerous and more distinct. The new institutions must work effectively with other parts of the system if social stability is to be maintained. To ensure that this integration takes place, new values and norms are developed to resolve conflicts between new and existing institutions. Thus, equilibrium is maintained even in the face of evolutionary change. Critics of equilibrium theory note that it suffers from the same problems that face all functionalist theories. The emphasis on social order makes it difficult for equilibrium theory to explain widespread social change within or between societies.

Conflict Theory

According to the **conflict theory of social change**, change results from conflicts between groups with opposing interests. In most cases, conflicts arise from disputes over access to power and wealth. Because conflict theorists view conflict as a natural condition in all societies, they see social change as inevitable. Thus, they hold that societies are in a constant state of change or potential change.

Conflict theory is rooted in Karl Marx's theory of class conflict, which he developed in the mid-1800s. Over the years, most conflict theorists have moved away from the emphasis on class. Modern conflict theorists take a much broader view, focusing on social conflict in general.

Karl Marx and Class Conflict Karl Marx held that all of human history is the history of class conflict. By that he meant that all societies throughout history have been subject to conflicts between the people who have power and those who lack power. According to Marx, social change results from the efforts of the powerless to gain power. Usually, those efforts involve the violent overthrow of the people in power. Thus, Marx saw violence as a necessary part of social change.

As you read in Chapter 13, Marx was most interested in how this process would occur in industrial societies. Marx believed that the sharp class divisions and social inequality that were characteristic of early industrial societies eventually would lead the proletariat to overthrow the bourgeoisie. After a revolution, a dictatorship of the proletariat would be established to assist in the transformation to communism—the classless society that Marx considered the ultimate goal of all social evolution.

Class conflict has not resulted in revolution in most modern industrial societies. As a result, most conflict theorists have abandoned Marx's emphasis on class conflict. Instead, they focus on a broad range of social factors that can produce conflict in societies. Ralf Dahrendorf's work is representative of many modern conflict theorists.

INTERPRETING VISUALS In 1989, student protesters occupied Tiananmen Square to challenge the policies of the communist Chinese government. *How would a conflict theorist describe the circumstances portrayed in this image?*

Connecting to History

◼ TEACH

Have students read the feature The American Civil Rights Movement and discuss the questions that follow it. Then ask students which theory of social change they think best explains the occurrence and philosophy of the American civil rights movement and the social changes that resulted from it. *(Many students may suggest the conflict theory, although arguments can also be made for the evolutionary or equilibrium theories.)*

✳ CONNECTING to History

Have students conduct research on one or more events in the history of the American civil rights movement. Then have each student create a cause-and-effect flowchart that illustrates the factors that brought about the event and how the event affected the civil rights movement and American society at large. Ask volunteers to present their flowcharts to the class and to explain the significance of their chosen event(s). **BLOCK SCHEDULING**

CONNECTING TO
History

THE AMERICAN CIVIL RIGHTS MOVEMENT

As recently as 50 years ago, African Americans were treated as second-class citizens throughout much of the southern United States. De jure and de facto segregation limited where African Americans could live, go to school, sit on buses, and eat lunch. Furthermore, African Americans were denied the right to vote.

In the 1940s and 1950s a civil rights movement grew in response to this situation. Civil rights lawyers took the fight to the courtroom, challenging the constitutionality of segregation laws. Movement members—both black and white—staged boycotts, marches, and demonstrations to publicize the plight of African Americans. Authorities, particularly those in such Lower South states as Alabama and Mississippi, sometimes reacted violently to these actions, beating and imprisoning the marchers and demonstrators. After pictures of such police responses were broadcast on television, a groundswell of support for the civil rights movement soon developed. Responding to public pressure, Congress began to chip away at the foundations of segregation by passing a number of civil rights laws. But how successful was the civil rights movement in attaining its goals? In the following excerpt, historian Robert Weisbrot reviews the movement's record.

"Like other reform movements the crusade for racial justice inevitably fell short of the utopian goals that sustained it. Still, if America's civil rights movement is to be judged by the distance it traveled rather than by the barriers yet to be crossed, a record of substantial achievement unfolds. In communities throughout the South, 'whites only' signs that had stood for generations suddenly came down from hotels, rest rooms, theaters, and other facilities. Blacks and whites seldom mingle socially at home, but they are apt to lunch together at fast-food shops that once drew blacks only for sit-ins. Integration extends equally to Southern workers, whether at diner counters or in the high-rise office buildings that now afford every Southern city a skyline.

School desegregation also quickened its pace and by the mid-1970s had become fact as well as law in

By participating in sit-ins, many students became involved in the civil rights movement.

over 80 percent of all Southern public schools. Swelling private school enrollments have tarnished but not substantially reversed this achievement. . . .

Protection of voting rights represents the movement's most unalloyed success, more than doubling the black voter registration . . . in the seven states covered by the 1965 [Voting Rights] Act. Winning the vote literally changed the complexion of government service in the South. When Congress passed the Voting Rights Act, barely 100 blacks held elective office in the country; by 1989 there were more than 6,800, including 24 congressmen and some 300 mayors. Over 4,400 of these officials served in the South, and nearly every [predominantly African American] county in Alabama had a black sheriff. Mississippi experienced the most radical change, registering 74 percent of its voting-age blacks and leading the nation in the number of elected black officials."

Think About It

1. Analyzing Information *What achievements of the civil rights movement does Weisbrot note?*

2. Supporting a Point of View *Do you think that the civil rights movement has a "record of substantial achievement"? Why or why not?*

Did You Know?

During much of the period of the civil rights movement, many U.S. states had laws banning interracial marriage. The U.S. Supreme Court declared such laws unconstitutional in 1967.

Think About It Answers

1. Weisbrot mentions integration in public places, school desegregation, and the protection of voting rights.

2. Answers will vary, but students should compare what they think are the movement's achievements and how far it has come with the obstacles the movement has yet to overcome. For example, some students may note the progress made in school desegregation, while other students may note how the rise in private-school enrollment among white students has limited the success of school desegregation in providing all students with equal educational opportunities.

CLOSE

In a closing discussion, ask each student to select and defend one of the four theories of social change as the best theory. Then have the class work together to combine the most reasonable parts of the four theories to come up with a hybrid theory that students generally agree is a good one.

REVIEW AND ASSESS

Have students complete the **Section 1 Review** on p. 470. As **Alternative Assessment**, you may want to use the social change graphic organizer or recipe in this section's lessons.

RETEACH

Have each student create a detailed outline of the section. Instruct students to use the four theories of social change as the main topics in their outlines. Then have students use their outlines to help you create a master outline on the chalkboard.
ENGLISH LANGUAGE LEARNERS

EXTEND

Have students analyze their school as a microcosm of society and write theories about how it has changed during the past four years and why. Newer students might interview other students and teachers to find out how the school has changed during this period.
BLOCK SCHEDULING

SECTION 1 REVIEW ANSWERS

1. Define:
- social change, p. 462
- cyclical theory of social change, p. 462
- ideational culture, p. 463
- sensate culture, p. 463
- idealistic culture, p. 463
- principle of immanent change, p. 464
- evolutionary theory of social change, p. 464
- equilibrium theory of social change, p. 466
- conflict theory of social change, p. 468

2. Identify:
- Oswald Spengler, p. 463
- Pitirim Sorokin, p. 463
- Talcott Parsons, p. 466
- Ralf Dahrendorf, p. 468

3. See the graphic organizer on p. 464.

4a. because sociologists have based their theories on different events and theoretical perspectives

b. Older theories focused more on describing social change and suggested that all societies follow similar patterns of development. Modern theories provide for different patterns of development and focus more on why societies change.

5. Paragraphs will vary, but students should exhibit an understanding of each of the four theories of social change and the criticisms of each theory.

Ralf Dahrendorf and Social Conflict Ralf Dahrendorf, like all conflict theorists, agrees with Marx's belief that conflict is a central feature of all societies. However, he disagrees with Marx's idea that class conflict is the moving force in human history. Instead, Dahrendorf holds that social conflict can take many forms. Conflict between racial or ethnic groups, religious or political groups, management and labor, men and women, and the young and the old all can lead to social change. Nor does Dahrendorf believe that revolution is the principal way in which conflicts are resolved in modern industrial society. In many instances, interest groups are able to institute social change through compromise and adaptation.

Critics of modern conflict theory note that it suffers from the same problem that troubles equilibrium theory. It has too narrow an emphasis. By concentrating on conflict as the principal cause of social change, conflict theorists ignore changes that occur in the absence of conflict. For example, technological innovations generally do not arise in response to conflict. Nevertheless, they have a profound effect on society. In addition, conflict theory ignores those elements in society that serve to maintain the social order.

No single theory provides a full explanation of all aspects of social change. Given the complex nature of social change, it is very likely that no single theory could ever prove adequate. Therefore, many social scientists combine elements of the various theories in an attempt to gain a better understanding of the nature of social change.

Ralf Dahrendorf suggests that conflict can occur in many ways. Social change can occur through petitions and rallying support behind a cause.

SECTION 1 REVIEW

1. Define and explain
social change
cyclical theory of social change
ideational culture
sensate culture
idealistic culture
principle of immanent change
evolutionary theory of social change
equilibrium theory of social change
conflict theory of social change

2. Identify and explain
Oswald Spengler
Pitirim Sorokin
Talcott Parsons
Ralf Dahrendorf

3. Categorizing Copy the graphic organizer below. Use it to list the four main theories of social change and the subcategories of each theory.

Cyclical Theory	Evolutionary Theory

Equilibrium Theory	Conflict Theory

4. Finding the Main Idea
a. Why have social scientists offered different theories to explain the process of social change?
b. In what ways have theories of social change evolved?

5. Writing and Critical Thinking
Supporting a Point of View Write a paragraph explaining which of the four theories you think provides the best explanation of social change. To support your opinion, include an example of an aspect of society that has changed in recent years because of influences such as technology, political change, or other factors. Consider:
- cyclical theory
- evolutionary theory
- equilibrium theory
- conflict theory

 Homework Practice Online
keyword: SL3 HP18

SECTION 2

OBJECTIVES

1. *Contrast the views of modernization theory and world-system theory on modernization in less-developed nations.*

2. *Identify some of the positive and negative effects of modernization on social life and the natural environment.*

LET'S GET STARTED!

As students enter the classroom, ask them to imagine what the land their school is on might have looked like 200 years ago. Instruct each student to write a one-paragraph description of the land as it might have been and another paragraph describing the land as it is today. Discuss responses with the class, emphasizing the effects human beings and modernization have on the environment. Tell students that in Section 2 they will learn about the sociological theories of modernization.

2 MODERNIZATION

Read to Discover

1. How do modernization theory and world-system theory differ in their views on modernization in less-developed nations?
2. What are some of the positive and negative effects of modernization on social life and the natural environment?

Define

modernization, modernization theory, world-system theory, core nations, peripheral nations, semiperipheral nations, external debt

Many sociologists interested in social change focus on **modernization**. Modernization is the process by which a society's social institutions become increasingly complex as the society moves toward industrialization. Some sociologists interested in modernization concentrate on social change in less-developed nations. Others turn their attention to analyzing the effects of modernization on social life and the natural environment in more-developed nations. This section focuses on these two areas of study.

The Process of Modernization

Social scientists usually divide the countries of the world into two groups—more developed and less developed. The more-developed nations include the United States, Canada, Japan, Australia, and the countries of Western Europe. Most of the less-developed nations are found in Latin America, Africa, and Asia. The more-developed nations have modernized much more rapidly than the less-developed nations. But why is this so? Modernization theory and world-system theory offer two different explanations.

Modernization Theory According to sociologists' view of **modernization theory**, the more-developed nations modernized because they were the first to industrialize. Once less-developed nations begin to industrialize, they too will undergo modernization. Therefore, modernized countries serve as a model and a source for technology and information for those undergoing the modernization process. In addition, modernizing countries will go through the same development stages as those that have undergone modernization. In time, less-developed nations will resemble the more-developed nations in terms of economic and social structure, norms, and values.

SECTION 2 RESOURCES

REPRODUCIBLE & REVIEW

- Research Projects and Activities for Teaching Sociology 18
- Study Skills and Writing Guide
- Section 2 Review, p. 479

TECHNOLOGY

- One-Stop Planner, Lesson 18.2
- CNN. Presents Sociology: Doing Business with Different Cultures
- Teaching Transparency: Characteristics of Modernized and Non-modernized Societies
- Homework Practice Online
- HRW Go site

Visual Answer

Students might mention the modern architecture of the skyscrapers and the busy harbor.

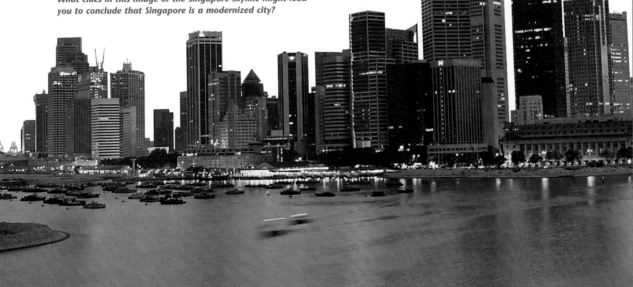

INTERPRETING VISUALS Cities in modernized countries have highly developed infrastructures and often have dramatic skylines. *What clues in this image of the Singapore skyline might lead you to conclude that Singapore is a modernized city?*

TEACH OBJECTIVE 1

After leading a class discussion on the views of the modernization theory and the world-system theory on modernization in less-developed nations, organize the class into three groups. One group will argue in support of modernization theory. Another group will argue in support of world-system theory, and the third group will act as journalists who will ask questions. Give students time to prepare either arguments in support of their assigned position or questions to ask the members of each side of the debate. Then have students conduct an informal debate and panel discussion about the two theories. **COOPERATIVE LEARNING**

HOMEWORK: Have students write one-page position papers supporting either modernization theory or world-system theory. Tell students to support their positions with facts and examples. Students might also suggest modifications to either theory to suit their own points of view, as long as they justify any changes with sound reasoning. Remind students to use standard grammar, spelling, sentence structure, and punctuation in their essays. Then when the class next meets, poll students to determine which theory received the most support. Have the class briefly discuss the results.

Applying Sociology

Modern Attitudes.

Harvard sociologist Alex Inkeles studied the effect of modernization on people's behaviors and attitudes. Inkeles found that people in more-developed countries shared certain characteristics. For example, people in such countries are more likely than those in less-developed countries to join voluntary organizations, read newspapers daily, write public officials, and discuss political issues with their spouses.

CRITICAL THINKING

Why might people in more-developed countries be more politically active than people in less-developed countries?

ANSWER: because they are likely to be better educated, to have better access to political information, and may have a more open political system

Chart Answer

Students might suggest that each characteristic listed would be of interest to many types of sociologists.

Technology Resources

Teaching Transparency: Characteristics of Modernized and Non-modernized Societies

The view that modernization will produce the same social changes in less-developed nations that it produced in more-developed nations forms the basis of modernization theory. According to this view, extended family structures will be replaced by the nuclear family as less-developed nations modernize. Similarly, the role of religion in guiding social interaction will decrease, modern systems of medicine and mass education will arise, and the majority of the population will move to the cities.

Modernization theory had a large following during the 1950s and 1960s. Sociologists of this era believed that modernization was a cure for the various social and economic problems that plagued many less-developed nations. Modernization theorists assumed that through modernization less-developed nations would be able to raise their standard of living and become full partners in the world economy. To speed up the process, many industrialized nations established assistance programs. Money, technology, and economic advisers flooded into the less-developed nations. Yet, these assistance programs had little effect. Many less-developed countries still face major economic and social challenges. As a result, support for modernization theory has weakened over the years.

Why have the predictions of modernization theorists not come true? Critics of modernization theory argue that the theory was doomed to failure because it did not take into account that less-developed nations face conditions that are very different from those faced by the more-developed nations. When the more-developed nations began to modernize, they had large amounts of land and resources and relatively self-sufficient economies. The less-developed nations, on the other hand, have a long history of economic dependence on the West. This economic dependence has many causes, but some sociologists point out that many less-developed nations were once colonies of the world's major industrial powers. These sociologists suggest that the colonial powers used their colonies as sources of raw materials and cheap labor. While this arrangement helped the colonial powers to industrialize, it greatly slowed economic development in the colonies.

In addition, the population pressures faced by less-developed nations are very different from those faced by more-developed nations. For example, during its modernization period the United States had a relatively small population and a great deal of land. Thus, population growth did not present a serious problem. Other countries, such as Great Britain and France, were able to ease their population pressures by sending people to various colonies. Less-developed nations, on the other hand, begin the modernization process with already large populations. The population pressure is made worse when they industrialize. As you read in Chapter 16, as less-developed nations begin to industrialize, the introduction of modern medicine causes their death rates to drop markedly. Because birthrates remain high while death rates decline, the population grows at a very fast rate. Most of the economic gains produced by industrialization must be used to maintain the existing standard of living for an expanding population. As a result, the modernization process in such countries slows. The chart on this page shows how modernized societies and non-modernized societies differ.

Modernization is also slowed in many less-developed nations by antimodernization sentiments. For example, in many Islamic countries, modernization is seen as a threat to traditional social and religious values. The revolution that overthrew the shah of Iran in 1979 was, in part, a reaction to the shah's support of modernization based on a Western model.

Characteristics of Modernized and Non-modernized Societies

Characteristics	Non-modernized Societies	Modernized Societies
Family	Extended	Nuclear
Family Size	Larger	Smaller
Population	Rural	Urban
Life Expectancy	Lower	Higher
Infant Mortality	Higher	Lower
Religious Orientation	More	Less
Formal Education	Little	Widespread
Technology	Simple	Complex
Division of Labor	Simple	Complex
Statuses	Mostly ascribed	Mostly achieved
Social Stratification	Rigid	More open
Social Change	Gradual	Rapid

INTERPRETING CHARTS Modernized and non-modernized societies maintain very different characteristics. *Which characteristics do you think are most significant to sociologists?*

SUGGESTION 1: To help students identify some of the positive and negative consequences of modernization on social life and the natural environment, copy the graphic organizer at the right onto the chalkboard, omitting the italicized answers. Have students copy and complete the organizer. Discuss the answers with the class. Then have each student create a poster illustrating the positive and negative consequences of modernization. Students might focus their posters on just one viewpoint, if they wish. Encourage students to be creative and to organize their posters in a visually pleasing way. Have volunteers present and explain their posters to the class. **ENGLISH LANGUAGE LEARNERS**

EFFECTS OF MODERNIZATION

Positive	Negative
• *increase in standard of living* • *longer life expectancies* • *lower birthrates* • *higher rates of literacy* • *decrease in economic and social inequality* • *more personal comforts* • *improved infrastructure* • *electricity and communication technology* • *establishment of educational institutions*	• *loss of some traditional authority for the family and religion* • *weaker social relationships and increased feelings of social isolation* • *moral and ethical questions* • *some environmental problems* • *some health problems*

The most powerful core nations form the G8, a group of industrialized democratic countries that help establish trade policies. Leaders of semiperipheral nations such as Taiwan and South Korea have hosted their own economic conferences to deal with trade issues concerning their countries.

ECONOMICS

Human Poverty Index. The Human Poverty Index rates countries based on five factors: access to health care and safe water, life expectancy, literacy, and the country's percentage of malnourished children. Blending these five factors provides a rough estimate of a country's overall level of poverty and development.

RESEARCH ACTIVITY: Have students conduct research on the human poverty index rates for various core, semiperipheral, and peripheral countries and then discuss their findings.

World-System Theory The world-system theory offers a different explanation for why societies modernize at different rates. Proposed by the sociologist and historian Immanuel Wallerstein, **world-system theory** views modernization in terms of the world economy.

According to the world-system theory, the world system comprises three types of nations—core, peripheral, and semiperipheral. **Core nations** are the most powerful developed nations—the United States, Canada, Japan, and the countries of Western Europe—that form the center, or core, of the world economy. They control most of the world's productive, technological, and financial resources. Core nations have diversified economies with strong manufacturing and service sectors.

Peripheral nations are the poor countries in Latin America, Africa, and Asia. They control few productive resources, and they depend on the core nations for financial aid, technology, and manufactured goods. They also depend on the core nations to buy their main products—mostly raw materials and farm goods, such as coffee, cocoa, and sugar. Unlike core nations, many peripheral nations have economies that rely heavily on the exportation of a single product.

Semiperipheral nations are somewhere in between core and peripheral nations. They may be industrialized but may not play a central role in the world economy. Or they may be only somewhat diversified in terms of their economy or exports. Semiperipheral nations include smaller Western European countries, such as Spain and Portugal, and the newly developed nations of Asia, such as South Korea and Taiwan.

On the surface, the economic relationships among these various types of nations appear to be a positive arrangement. For example, by locating production facilities in peripheral nations or by purchasing raw materials from them, businesses in core nations are able to lower their production costs. In return for such cooperation, peripheral nations receive technological and economic assistance from the core nations. World-system theorists argue that, despite such apparent benefits, peripheral nations actually gain little from this arrangement. They note that the arrangement creates a lack of economic diversity, a dependence on exports and foreign assistance, and increased economic inequality among the people in peripheral nations.

The lack of economic diversity in peripheral nations is a serious problem because it slows economic growth.

Exploring Cultural Diversity

▣ TEACH

Have students read the feature Globalization and Social Change and answer the questions and complete the activity under Think About It. Then organize students into four groups and assign each group one of the subhead topics from the feature: economic globalization, globalization and transportation, tourism, or diversity in America. Instruct the groups to create collages showing how their assigned forces have encouraged globalization and changed American society. **COOPERATIVE LEARNING**

▣ SPOTLIGHT *on Tourism vs. Modernization*

Tell students that many people think that one of the negative consequences of modernization is the impersonalization of society. However, the increase in tourist travel due to globalization brings people of widely different cultural backgrounds into contact. Have students present short speeches giving specific examples of how tourism affects some of the consequences of globalization.

BLOCK SCHEDULING

▣ **internet** connect ▤

TOPIC: Dealing with Modernization
GO TO: go.hrw.com
KEYWORD: SL3 SC18

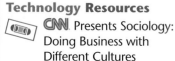

Have students access the Internet through the HRW Go site to conduct research on the ways in which different organizations are managing the effects of modernization. Then have each student choose one of the organizations he or she researched and write a profile of the organization's aims and programs. Remind students to use standard grammar, spelling, and punctuation when writing their profiles.

Technology Resources

📼 **CNN.** Presents Sociology: Doing Business with Different Cultures

---

EXPLORING
Cultural Diversity

GLOBALIZATION AND SOCIAL CHANGE

One of the most powerful forces influencing life today is globalization, the process by which societies around the world become increasingly interconnected and interdependent. Globalization increases interaction among societies, which leads to an almost constant exchange of material objects and ideas. This process of cultural exchange, or diffusion, is one of the major sources of social change that is connected to the process of modernization.

Economic Globalization

The most prominent feature of economic globalization is the multinational corporation—a company that has factories and offices in several countries. Many of the largest and most powerful multinationals have originated in the United States. Foreign markets have become the major focus for many American multinationals. Some companies now receive 50 percent or more of their profits from overseas operations, and their expansion plans are concentrated more on overseas countries than on the United States. American multinationals have spread not only products to other countries but also business ideas. For example, many different kinds of foreign companies have adopted the business approach used by the American fast-food industry.

The exchange of products and ideas is not one way, however. For example, American consumers are able to buy South Korean cars, Japanese audio equipment, Mexican food products, and a variety of other items from a host of countries. Many American corporations have adopted management techniques long practiced by Japanese companies.

Globalization and Transportation

Globalization has also helped transform the world's transportation systems. Multinational corporations have their operations dispersed across the globe. Transportation systems have been improved to ensure that raw materials reach their factories and that finished products reach their markets. As a result, the volume of international transportation has grown markedly in recent years. Air transportation offers a vivid illustration of this. Between 1990 and 1998, passenger kilometers flown increased by almost 40 percent, and freight kilometers flown rose by close to 70 percent.

Tourism

This rise in international transportation is reflected in the increase in travel and tourism. In 1999 nearly 51 million tourists—representing practically every country in the world—visited the United States. Some 24.5 million Americans traveled overseas, with more than 20 percent of them visiting several countries. Increased international tourism tends to promote face-to-face interactions among people of differing cultural backgrounds. This interaction, in turn, increases the chance of cultural diffusion and social change.

CONNECTING *to Economics*

Invite a representative from a company that either does business with other countries or has locations worldwide to speak to the class. Topics the speaker may address include the following: where the company's branches are located, the type of work the company does, why it makes sense to be global, the effects of cultural differences on the company's foreign business or locations, and how the company's foreign business or locations affect other countries. Have students prepare a series of questions to ask the speaker as well. **BLOCK SCHEDULING**

SPOTLIGHT *on Globalization in the News*

Have each student follow the news for several days and collect examples of articles or television news stories related to globalization and other issues covered in this feature. Instruct students to write a short summary of each news story and to provide a clipping of any print articles, if possible. Then call on volunteers to share some of their news stories with the class for discussion. Finally, collect the clippings and use them to create a bulletin board on globalization. **BLOCK SCHEDULING**

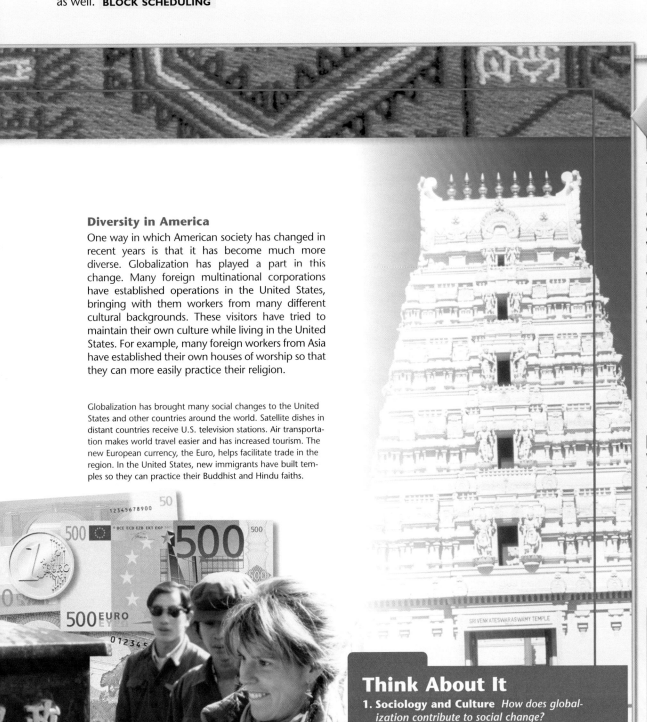

Diversity in America

One way in which American society has changed in recent years is that it has become much more diverse. Globalization has played a part in this change. Many foreign multinational corporations have established operations in the United States, bringing with them workers from many different cultural backgrounds. These visitors have tried to maintain their own culture while living in the United States. For example, many foreign workers from Asia have established their own houses of worship so that they can more easily practice their religion.

Globalization has brought many social changes to the United States and other countries around the world. Satellite dishes in distant countries receive U.S. television stations. Air transportation makes world travel easier and has increased tourism. The new European currency, the Euro, helps facilitate trade in the region. In the United States, new immigrants have built temples so they can practice their Buddhist and Hindu faiths.

Think About It

1. **Sociology and Culture** *How does globalization contribute to social change?*
2. **Sociology and You** *How has globalization affected your community? Write a paragraph explaining the changes that globalization has brought to your life.*

Sociology in the World Today

Technology Professionals in India. Many high-tech American companies have begun to outsource work to India, which has a large number of English-speaking high-tech workers. Because India is a peripheral nation, wages are low. For example, an experienced programmer in India might make less than $1,500 per month. In comparison, salaries for experienced programmers in the United States start at about $4,000 per month.

CRITICAL THINKING
What might be some disadvantages of outsourcing work to peripheral nations?

ANSWER: Answers will vary, but students might mention that companies can cut production costs.

Think About It Answers

1. Globalization increases interaction among societies, which leads to cultural exchange and diffusion.

2. Paragraphs will vary, but students should exhibit an understanding of globalization and some of the social changes that result from it. For example, students may note that many of the products they use are made in foreign countries.

SUGGESTION 2: Lead a class discussion on the positive and negative effects of modernization on social life and the natural environment, as discussed in this section. *(See the graphic organizer on p. 473.)* Then have each student write an editorial expressing whether he or she thinks the positive consequences of modernization outweigh the negative consequences. Remind students to provide support for their positions and to use standard grammar, spelling, sentence structure, and punctuation in their editorials. Ask volunteers to read their editorials to the class.

SUGGESTION 3: Organize students into small groups and assign half the groups the positive effects and half the groups the negative effects of modernization on social life and the natural environment, as discussed in this section. *(See the graphic organizer on p. 473.)* Ask the groups to imagine that they are a nonprofit organization interested in either increasing or decreasing economic funding and other support to help developing countries modernize. Instruct the groups to create print advertisements in support of their assigned position on this issue. Groups assigned positive effects should focus on increasing support. Groups assigned negative effects should work on decreasing support. Then have each group present its advertisement to the class. **COOPERATIVE LEARNING**

Sociology in the World Today

Mexico's Border Industrialization Program. In 1969 the Mexican government established a tax-free and tariff-free zone along the country's northern border. The goal was to encourage multinational corporations to relocate in the zone. Within five years, more than 650 American companies had established factories in the region. By the end of the 1990s this number had more than tripled.

RESEARCH ACTIVITY: Have interested students conduct research on the North American Free Trade Agreement and its effects and then share their findings with the class.

Visual Answer

Students might suggest that the forge shows the high level of industrialization in Taiwan, which is a semiperipheral country.

For economic growth to occur, the number and variety of goods and services a nation produces must increase. This increase, in turn, is dependent on the nation's workforce having a wide variety of skills. However, some sociologists and economists have observed that when core nations are heavily involved in the economy of a peripheral nation, economic activity concentrates in those areas that meet the needs of the core nations. In most cases, the result is that the majority of a peripheral nation's workforce ends up working in a narrow range of unskilled or semiskilled positions.

Export dependency and reliance on foreign financial aid result from this concentration of economic activity in peripheral nations. Because most economic activity in a peripheral nation is tied to meeting the needs of core nations, it seldom produces enough goods and services to have a self-sufficient economy. Thus, the nation's economic survival is dependent on exporting goods or raw materials to the core nations. If world demand for these goods declines, the peripheral nation's economy suffers greatly, and the peripheral nation often turns to the core nations for loans and other types of financial aid. Because of a lack of economic growth, the peripheral nation may find it difficult to repay its loans. Therefore, it remains in debt to the core nations. The graph on page 477 lists the countries in Africa, Asia, Latin America, and Europe with the highest external debt. A country's **external debt** is the amount it owes to foreign individuals, organizations, companies, and governments.

World-system theorists argue that this economic dependence and the lack of economic diversification work together to increase social stratification in peripheral nations. Money likely becomes concentrated in the hands of a few people who have close ties to the core nations. These people, therefore, have a vested interest in

INTERPRETING VISUALS Semiperipheral nations are industrialized nations that are somewhat dependent on core nations. *How does this forge in Taiwan reflect the industrialized nature of a semiperipheral country?*

maintaining the system. As a result, most peripheral nations remain at a low level of modernization.

Many critics of world-system theory admit that it is useful in explaining why many of the less-developed nations have low levels of economic growth. However, they point out that the theory does not explain why certain core nations emerged as industrial powers. In addition, critics note that the theory does not explain why some semiperipheral nations, such as South Korea and Taiwan, have modernized to the point that they are able to challenge the core nations economically.

Modernization and world-system theories share certain characteristics. They both define modernization in terms of economic development. They also use development in the West as the model for modernization. Some sociologists have suggested that modernization be looked at differently. For example, one view stresses the role that *place* plays in modernization. This theory takes into consideration how a nation's culture, economic practices, and regional diversity influence its development and its role in the world system.

World-system theorists look at the relationships between core nations and peripheral nations. American businesses have located factories in Mexico because of the lower cost of labor there.

External Debt for Selected Countries, 2000

Countries	External Debt (in millions of dollars)
Africa	
Egypt	~28,000
Ethiopia	~5,000
Kenya	~6,000
Zimbabwe	~4,000
Morocco	~17,000
Asia	
China	~150,000
Indonesia	~140,000
Pakistan	~30,000
Turkey	~115,000
India	~100,000
Latin America	
Brazil	~235,000
Mexico	~150,000
Argentina	~145,000
Venezuela	~38,000
Chile	~37,000
Europe	
Russia	~160,000
Poland	~63,000
Hungary	~30,000
Romania	~10,000
Former Yugoslavia (Serbia, Montenegro)	~14,000

Source: U.S. Statistical Abstract, 2002

INTERPRETING GRAPHS Economic debt prevents many less-developed countries from modernizing. Some activists have called for forgiveness of debts to aid these countries. *Which continent holds the largest debt?*

SPOTLIGHT *on Modernization and Humor*

Have students examine and discuss the cartoon on p. 479. Next, organize the class into groups of three and instruct the groups to create one-panel cartoons or multi-panel comic strips that address one or more of the main topics covered in this section. You might want to provide students with a list of topics or approve students' selected topics. Display the groups' completed cartoons on the wall or on a table and have students examine them. Then have the class vote on which is the funniest cartoon and which cartoon best addresses its topic. **COOPERATIVE LEARNING** ,

BLOCK SCHEDULING

■ CLOSE

Ask students to discuss how modernization theory and world-system theory might be different if they had been created by sociologists in less-developed countries or in countries located in the Eastern Hemisphere.

■ REVIEW AND ASSESS

Have students complete the **Section 2 Review** on p. 479. As **Alternative Assessment**, you may want to use the modernization position paper or editorial in this section's lessons.

Visual Answer

Students might suggest improvements in industry, technology, and education.

SECTION ❷ REVIEW ANSWERS

1. Define
- modernization, p. 471
- modernization theory, p. 471
- world-system theory, p. 473
- core nations, p. 473
- peripheral nations, p. 473
- semiperipheral nations, p. 473
- external debt, p. 476

2. education—improves; work—social and economic inequality decrease; religion and family—lose traditional authority; Examples will vary.

3a. Modernization theory argues that less-developed countries will eventually modernize. World-system theory argues that the concentration of wealth and power in core nations slows modernization in less-developed countries.

b. See the graphic organizer on p. 473.

4. Essays will vary, but students should note how both theories use development in the West as the model for modernization.

The Consequences of Modernization

Regardless of the reasons why a society modernizes or at what rate, modernization has both positive and negative consequences for social life and the natural environment. The most notable positive consequence of modernization is an increase in a country's standard of living. Modernization brings with it longer life expectancies, lower birthrates, higher rates of literacy, a decrease in economic and social inequality, and more personal comforts.

Modernization offers many benefits to developing countries. The growth of industry and expansion of technology in a developing country can greatly improve the infrastructure of the region. An infrastructure is a system of roads, ports, and other facilities needed by a modern economy.

Modernization is often accompanied by the arrival of electricity and communication technology such as telephones. These services raise the quality of life for residents. However, these services are often limited to wealthier citizens of developing countries. Modernizing countries also benefit from the establishment of education institutions such as colleges and universities. These institutions train professionals and improve the quality of life in developing nations.

Modernization also has some costs. The very same technological innovations that improve the standard of living and prolong life in modern societies also give rise to problems. For example, the family and religion lose some of their traditional authority in modern society. The government, on the other hand, takes on a larger role in directing people's lives. Because people move more frequently in modern societies, social relationships are

INTERPRETING VISUALS Modernization can bring many changes to the daily lives of a country's citizens. The changes in kitchen products and communication are an example of how new technology can affect daily life. *What benefits do you believe modernization brings to people's daily lives?*

Pair students and have the pairs review all the key terms, people, and theories in this section. Then have partners take turns asking each other questions based on their review of the text.
ENGLISH LANGUAGE LEARNERS , COOPERATIVE LEARNING

EXTEND

1. Ask students why they think theories of modernization are limited in their efforts to explain the complexities of the social processes involved in modernization. Have students present their thoughts in the form of oral reports. **BLOCK SCHEDULING**

2. Invite several generations of a local family to speak to the class as a living time line. For example, the family might consist of a great-grandmother, a grandfather, a mother, and a child. The guests should talk about the changes they have witnessed in society (or specifically in their communities) during their lifetimes. Conclude by having students ask the guests questions and take notes on the similarities and differences in the guests' responses.
BLOCK SCHEDULING

likely to be weaker than they are in traditional societies. Thus, feelings of social isolation are more common. In addition, people often find themselves faced with conflicting norms and role expectations.

Modern technology also gives rise to moral and ethical questions. For example, at what point should doctors give up the fight to keep terminally ill patients alive through the use of modern medical technology? Or, now that humans have the ability to destroy the world through nuclear warfare, what steps should be taken to prevent such warfare? These questions and many others like them arise in modern society.

The effects of modernization on the natural environment also cannot be ignored. Modernization has brought with it the problems of soil, water, and air pollution. The use of pesticides in agriculture and chemicals in manufacturing have created serious environmental and health problems—most of them unanticipated. For example, each year modern societies are faced with finding safe ways to dispose of huge amounts of hazardous waste—the by-products of

Walt Handelsman © Tribune Media Services, Inc. All rights reserved. Reprinted with permission.

Some consequences of modernization are changes in the means of communication. As more people rely on technology to communicate, personal contact may diminish.

industry. Although many advanced countries have been able to set high environmental standards, less-developed nations often face many environmental challenges as they attempt to modernize.

SECTION 2 REVIEW

1. Define and explain
modernization
modernization theory
world-system theory
core nations
peripheral nations
semiperipheral nations
external debt

2. Identifying Cause and Effect
Copy the graphic organizer below. Use it to explain how modernization affects different social institutions within a society. Choose one country to use as an example in your explanation of the effects of modernization.

Education — Work

Modernization

Religion — Family

Homework Practice Online
keyword: SL3 HP18

3. Finding the Main Idea

a. How do modernization theory and world-system theory differ in the way they view the modernization process in less-developed nations?

b. What are some of the positive and negative consequences of modernization?

4. Writing and Critical Thinking

Identifying a Point of View Write a brief essay exploring why some sociologists suggest that the modernization and world-system theories are ethnocentric because they view modernization in Western terms.
Consider:
• modernization theory and its focus
• world-system theory and its focus

Review and Assessment Resources

- Chapter 18 Review, pp. 480–81
- Chapter Review Activities with Answer Key
- Global Skill Builder CD–ROM
- Chapter 18 Test Generator (on the One-Stop Planner)
- Chapter 18 Test (Form A or B)
- Alternative Assessment Handbook
- HRW Go site

REVIEW
Have students complete the **Chapter 18 Review** on pp. 480–81.

ASSESS
Use one of the chapter tests to assess students' understanding of the content. For **Alternative Assessment**, see the **Alternative Assessment Handbook**.

---

9. nations that may be industrialized but may not play a central role in the world economy or that may be somewhat diversified in terms of their economy or exports

10. amount a country owes to foreign individuals, organizations, companies, and governments

UNDERSTANDING MAIN IDEAS

1. ideational—truth and knowledge are sought through faith or religion; sensate—people seek knowledge through science

2. Evolutionary theories of social change view change as a process toward increasing complexity.

3. Equilibrium theory argues that a change in one part of the social system produces changes in all other parts of the system. Some sociologists prefer this theory because it explains how societies are able to change yet maintain order.

4. because they view conflict as a natural condition in all societies

5. because people believed that modernization was a cure for the various social and economic problems found in many less-developed nations

6. issues such as the use of technology to keep terminally ill people alive and working to prevent nuclear warfare

THINKING CRITICALLY

1. because people often view events as being beyond their control during such periods

---

CHAPTER

 18 Review

Writing a Summary

Using standard grammar, spelling, sentence structure, and punctuation, summarize the information in this chapter. Consider:
- theories of social change
- theories of modernization
- positive and negative effects of modernization

Identifying People and Ideas

Identify the following people or terms and use them in appropriate sentences.

1. social change
2. cyclical theory of social change
3. evolutionary theory of social change
4. equilibrium theory of social change
5. Ralf Dahrendorf
6. modernization theory
7. world-system theory
8. core nations
9. semiperipheral nations
10. external debt

Understanding Main ideas

Section 1 (pp. 462–70)

1. According to Pitirim Sorokin, how do ideational and sensate cultures differ?
2. What are the major features of the evolutionary theory of social change?
3. Briefly describe the equilibrium theory of social change. Why does this theory appeal to some sociologists?
4. Why do conflict theorists view social change as inevitable?

Section 2 (pp. 471–79)

5. Why did modernization theory have a strong following in the 1950s and 1960s?
6. What moral and ethical issues does modern technology pose?

Thinking Critically

1. **Analyzing Information** Why do you think cyclical theories of social change are appealing during periods of extreme social turmoil?
2. **Summarizing** How do modern evolutionary theories attempt to avoid the criticisms leveled against early evolutionary theories of social change?
3. **Comparing and Contrasting** How are the functionalist and conflict perspectives of social change similar and different?
4. **Drawing Inferences and Conclusions** Why do you think that in the world-system theory, the relationship between core nations and peripheral nations is sometimes defined as an international division of labor?
5. **Evaluating** Do you think the benefits of modernization outweigh the disadvantages? Explain your answer.

Writing About Sociology

1. **Identifying Points of View** Some sociologists criticized the modernization theory that was popular in the 1950s and 1960s. Write two paragraphs explaining why they criticized the theory and what events since 1960 may have influenced the view of these sociologists.
2. **Drawing Inferences and Conclusions** Consider the four theories of social change addressed in this chapter. Write a short essay explaining how each of these theories might describe the events of the 1960s civil rights movement in the United States. You may want to reread Section 3 of Chapter 3 for a reminder of the events of the movement. Use the graphic organizer below to help explain your answer.

◼ RETEACH

Have students work in pairs or groups of three to create worksheets with answer keys that cover the main points of Chapter 18. Then have pairs trade their worksheets with other pairs and complete each other's assignments. Finally, have pairs return their completed worksheets to be checked for accuracy.

ENGLISH LANGUAGE LEARNERS , COOPERATIVE LEARNING

◼ SOCIOLOGY PROJECTS

1. Using Sociological Imagination Have students work in small groups to create fictional countries and write brief "histories" that describe the causes, process, and effects of modernization on those countries over a period of centuries. Students should supplement their written histories with annotated time lines.

2. Connecting to Economics Have students conduct research on ways in which the United States funds or supports modernization in developing countries. Each student should present his or her findings in the form of a news article.

✏ BUILDING SOCIAL STUDIES SKILLS

Interpreting Graphs

Study the bar graph below. Use it to answer the following questions.

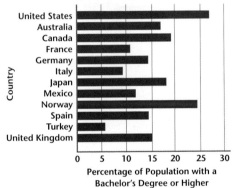

University Educational Attainment by Country, 1998

Country (United States, Australia, Canada, France, Germany, Italy, Japan, Mexico, Norway, Spain, Turkey, United Kingdom)

Percentage of Population with a Bachelor's Degree or Higher (0, 5, 10, 15, 20, 25, 30)

Source: *U.S. Statistical Abstract, 2000*

1. How much greater of a percentage of the U.S. population has earned a bachelor's degree or higher than the United Kingdom?
   a. 12 percent
   b. 22 percent
   c. 8 percent
   d. 10 percent

2. The process of modernization and the percentage of educational attainment are related. Based on this, what countries in this graph are the most developed? Which are the least?

Analyzing Primary Sources

Modernization has not only affected cultures around the world but also subcultures inside the United States. In the following excerpt Jerry Savells studied the influence of modernization on the Amish.

❝*The Amish in this sample show some gradual change in their religious practices. Over ten percent of the respondents had changed their religious preference from Old Order to New Order within the context of one generation. . . .*

The Old Order Amish prohibit ownership of automobiles, telephones, and electricity in the home. However, farm tractors are now being used by the New Order Amish in some areas; in Kalona, tractors were acceptable if they had steel wheels, not rubber tires. The adoption of the latter would create too much mobility.

In both Plain City and Intercourse, diesel generators are now considered an acceptable innovation to supply the barn (not the house) with electricity. The Amish dairy farmer—like all other dairy farmers—must meet state health standards regarding proper refrigeration of milk which is sold commercially. . . .

A few of the Amish in Berne are now beginning to use cameras, especially to photograph their children, a practice that would have brought immediate censure a few years ago. Even when this practice is known to other family members, it is regarded as a taboo topic for everyday conversations. Most of the Old Order Amish interviewed in Berne still believe that the Bible forbids taking 'graven images' of persons.❞

3. According to Savells, how have the New Order Amish been affected by modernization?
   a. They have electricity in their houses.
   b. They use rubber-tired tractors.
   c. They use telephones.
   d. They use electricity in barns only.

4. How important do you think economic factors are in the choice of some Amish to modernize?

SOCIOLOGY PROJECTS

Cooperative Learning

Using Your Observation Skills Work with a group of classmates to research the process of modernization around the world. Each member of the group should select one country. Determine if the country is a core, peripheral, or semiperipheral country. Write a short paragraph explaining why it fits in the category. As a group create a map to show the location of the countries.

▣ internet connect

Internet Activity: go.hrw.com
KEYWORD: SL3 SC18
Choose an activity on social change and modernization to:
- create a pamphlet explaining different theories of social change.
- create a graph or chart illustrating statistics related to the International Monetary Fund.
- write a profile on an organization dealing with the effects of modernization.

go.hrw.com

2. Modern theories do not claim that all societies pass through a single set of distinct stages of development but instead hold that societies have a tendency to become more complex.

3. functionalists—focus on how societies maintain order; conflict theorists—focus on conflicts between social groups; both—view social change as resulting from social disruption

4. because economic activity in peripheral nations is largely tied to meeting the economic needs of core nations

5. Answers will vary, but students should exhibit an understanding of the effects of modernization.

WRITING ABOUT SOCIOLOGY

1. Paragraphs will vary, but students should mention that the theory was criticized because assistance programs to help less-developed nations industrialize had little effect.

2. Essays will vary, but students should exhibit an understanding of each theory of social change.

BUILDING SOCIAL STUDIES SKILLS

1. a

2. most—United States, Norway; least—Turkey, Italy

3. d

4. important; decision to use diesel generators is tied to being able to sell milk commercially

Across Space and Time

Across Space and Time

Democracy in Eastern Europe

During the late 1960s Leonid Brezhnev became the leader of the Soviet Union. In reaction to protests that had occurred in the communist countries of Eastern Europe, he issued the Brezhnev Doctrine. This document stated that the Soviet Union would intervene in any satellite nation that seemed to be moving away from communism. As a result of the document and the actions of the Soviet Union, much dissent in countries under Soviet control was squelched during the 1970s.

The announcement of the Helsinki Accords in the late 1970s improved the climate for many dissidents in Eastern European countries. Those who opposed totalitarian rule called on their governments to abide by the human rights articles of the accords. In Poland economic troubles also fueled the growth of dissent. Huge price increases in 1980 sparked massive labor strikes. The strikers demanded political and economic reforms. They formed an independent trade union called Solidarity. However, Polish dissidents faced several more years of restrictions and martial law.

In 1985 Mikhail Gorbachev became the new leader of the Soviet Union. Gorbachev soon began to overhaul the country's political and economic systems. Gorbachev began a series of reforms known as glasnost (GLAZ-hohst), which means openness. Glasnost relaxed restrictions on dissent, allowing people to speak freely and read whatever they liked. However, Americans and Western European leaders called for more government reforms. Standing at the Brandenburg Gate of the Berlin Wall in 1987, President Reagan asked Gorbachev to show his commitment to democratizing efforts in Eastern Europe. Reagan shouted, "If you seek liberalization, come here to this gate. Mr. Gorbachev, open this gate! Mr. Gorbachev, tear down this wall!"

In 1989 Poland became the first Eastern European country to throw off communist rule. In April of that year, the government legalized Solidarity. Poland's first non-communist prime minister in 40 years was elected. In the 1990s the Communist Party in Poland was dissolved and replaced by two social democratic parties.

Other countries joined Poland in throwing off communist control. In Czechoslovakia, protesters took to the streets to demand reform. When the protesters gained the support of the workers, who went on a national strike, the government quickly gave in. Shortly thereafter the national legislature selected Vaclav Havel,

Protesters gathered at the Berlin Wall in 1989 to celebrate the collapse of communism in East Germany.

a writer and former dissident leader, as the country's new president. The transition to democracy was so smooth in Czechoslovakia that people called it the Velvet Revolution.

In East Germany the government came under increasing pressure to open its borders. Many East Germans had been traveling to Czechoslovakia or Hungary and from there escaping to West Germany. As protests grew, the East German government agreed to open the country's borders at midnight on November 9, 1989. That night thousands of Berliners from both East and West Germany gathered at the infamous Berlin Wall. On the stroke of midnight, they raced to break holes in the wall or to climb over it. The fall of the Berlin Wall became the most powerful symbol of the collapse of communism.

Think About It

1. **Summarizing** How did glasnost and changes in Soviet policies affect satellite countries such as Poland, Czechoslovakia, and Germany?

2. **Drawing Inferences and Conclusions** Why might a sociologist consider the democratic reforms in Eastern Europe a multinational social movement?

Sociology in Action

Sociology in Action

UNIT 5 SIMULATION

You Resolve the Conflict . . .

How could a group of people resolve a conflict over what types of reforms should be enacted?

Complete the following activity in small groups. Imagine that two leaders from opposing political groups are having a disagreement over what types of reforms to enact. Prepare a presentation outlining ways to help the two political factions resolve their differences.

1 Consider Persuasion.

Encourage the two leaders to try to persuade one another to come around to the other's point of view. To help the two leaders come up with persuasive arguments for their side, list reasons why they feel the way that they do.

- What reasons do each of the leaders have for supporting their cause?

- Why does he or she oppose the other leader's positions?

Then rank each reason in order of persuasiveness. Finally, urge the leaders to present their most persuasive reasons to one another in an effort to sway the other to his or her point of view.

2 Compromise.

Explain to the two leaders that sometimes compromise is necessary to resolve a conflict. Tell them that they may both have to give up something to reach an agreement. Ask them to consider what they would be willing to give up to reach a compromise and resolve their disagreement. Then encourage the leaders to meet to discuss a compromise that they could both agree to.

- What are the areas or the positions in which the two leaders might agree?

- What might each leader be willing to give up in order to reach an agreement?

- What would each leader refuse to give up in a compromise?

3 Debate the Issue.

Suggest to the leaders that they hold a debate. Gather information about the advantages and disadvantages of each side of their disagreement.

- What advantages and disadvantages might each leader have for supporting his or her point of view?

- What are the leaders' most convincing arguments for their reforms?

Then consider having the leaders prepare flash cards outlining the best arguments they can come up with in support of their side. Finally, recommend that the two leaders debate their disagreement. They might want to include charts and graphs to better demonstrate their positions.

4 Consider Negotiation.

Urge the two leaders to negotiate their conflict. Have them meet to discuss their positions and what they would be willing to agree to. Tell them that perhaps by working together to resolve the conflict, they will arrive at a solution that neither had considered before. Have your group decide who will prepare which part of the presentation. Then make your presentation to the class. Good luck!

HOLT
Sociology
The Study of Human Relationships

Reference

Time Line of Early Sociology

1776 The American Revolution begins.

1789 The French Revolution begins.

1798 Eli Whitney develops interchangeable parts for manufacturing, helping to spur the growth of the Industrial Revolution.

1837 Harriet Martineau publishes *Theory and Practice of Society in America.*

1897 Émile Durkheim publishes his study *Suicide.*

1889 Jane Addams opens Hull House settlement home.

1931 Jane Addams receives the Nobel Peace Prize.

1907 The Ford Motor Company produces the first Model T automobile.

1800

1850

1900

1838 Auguste Comte gives the social science of sociology its name.

1848 Karl Marx and Friedrich Engels issue the "Communist Manifesto."

1850 Herbert Spencer publishes his study *Social Statics.*

1892 The University of Chicago establishes the first department of sociology.

1904 Max Weber publishes *The Protestant Ethic and the Spirit of Capitalism.*

The ASA
Code of Ethics

Introduction

American Sociological Association's
Code of Ethics
The American Sociological Association's (ASA's) Code of Ethics sets forth the principles and ethical standards that underlie sociologists' professional responsibilities and conduct. These principles and standards should be used as guidelines when examining everyday professional activities. They constitute normative statements for sociologists and provide guidance on issues that sociologists may encounter in their professional work.

ASA's Code of Ethics consists of an Introduction, a Preamble, five General Principles, and specific Ethical Standards. This Code is also accompanied by the Rules and Procedures of the ASA Committee on Professional Ethics which describe the procedures for filing, investigating, and resolving complaints of unethical conduct.

The Preamble and General Principles of the Code are aspirational goals to guide sociologists toward the highest ideals of sociology. Although the Preamble and General Principles are not enforceable rules, they should be considered by sociologists in arriving at an ethical course of action and may be considered by ethics bodies in interpreting the Ethical Standards.

The Ethical Standards set forth enforceable rules for conduct by sociologists. Most of the Ethical Standards are written broadly in order to apply to sociologists in varied roles, and the application of an Ethical Standard may vary depending on the context. The Ethical Standards are not exhaustive. Any conduct that is not specifically addressed by this Code of Ethics is not necessarily ethical or unethical.

Membership in the ASA commits members to adhere to the ASA Code of Ethics and to the Policies and Procedures of the ASA Committee on Professional Ethics. Members are advised of this obligation upon joining the Association and that violations of the Code may lead to the imposition of sanctions, including termination of membership. ASA members subject to the Code of Ethics may be reviewed under these Ethical Standards only if the activity is part of or affects their work-related functions, or if the activity is sociological in nature. Personal activities having no connection to or effect on sociologists' performance of their professional roles are not subject to the Code of Ethics.

Preamble

This Code of Ethics articulates a common set of values upon which sociologists build their professional and scientific work. The Code is intended to provide both the general principles and the rules to cover professional situations encountered by sociologists. It has as its primary goal the welfare and protection of the individuals and groups with whom sociologists work. It is the individual responsibility of each sociologist to aspire to the highest possible standards of conduct in research, teaching, practice, and service.

The development of a dynamic set of ethical standards for a sociologist's work-related conduct requires a personal commitment to a life-long effort to act ethically; to encourage ethical behavior by students, supervisors, supervisees, employers, employees, and colleagues; and to consult with others as needed concerning ethical problems. Each sociologist supplements, but does not violate, the values and rules specified in the Code of Ethics based on guidance drawn from personal values, culture, and experience.

General Principles

The following General Principles are aspirational and serve as a guide for sociologists in determining ethical courses of action in various contexts. They exemplify the highest ideals of professional conduct.

Principle A: Professional Competence
Sociologists strive to maintain the highest levels of competence in their work; they recognize the limitations of their expertise; and they undertake only those tasks for which they are qualified by education, training, or experience. They recognize the need for ongoing education in order to remain professionally competent; and they utilize the appropriate scientific, professional, technical, and administrative resources needed to ensure competence in their professional activities. They consult with other professionals when necessary for the benefit of their students, research participants, and clients.

Principle B: Integrity
Sociologists are honest, fair, and respectful of others in their professional activities—in research, teaching, practice, and service. Sociologists do not knowingly act in ways that jeopardize either their own or others' professional welfare. Sociologists conduct their affairs in ways that inspire trust and confidence; they do not knowingly make statements that are false, misleading, or deceptive.

Principle C: Professional and Scientific Responsibility
Sociologists adhere to the highest scientific and professional standards and accept responsibility for their work. Sociologists understand that they form a community and show respect for other sociologists even when they disagree on theoretical, methodological, or personal approaches to professional activities. Sociologists value the public trust in sociology and are concerned about their ethical behavior and that of other sociologists that might compromise that trust. While endeavoring always to be collegial, sociologists must never let the desire to be collegial outweigh their shared responsibility for ethical behavior. When appropriate, they consult with colleagues in order to prevent or avoid unethical conduct.

Principle D: Respect for People's Rights, Dignity, and Diversity
Sociologists respect the rights, dignity, and worth of all people. They strive to eliminate bias in their professional activities, and they do not tolerate any forms of discrimination based on age; gender; race; ethnicity; national origin; religion; sexual orientation; disability; health conditions; or marital, domestic, or parental status. They are sensitive to

cultural, individual, and role differences in serving, teaching, and studying groups of people with distinctive characteristics. In all of their work-related activities, sociologists acknowledge the rights of others to hold values, attitudes, and opinions that differ from their own.

Principle E: Social Responsibility

Sociologists are aware of their professional and scientific responsibility to the communities and societies in which they live and work. They apply and make public their knowledge in order to contribute to the public good. When undertaking research, they strive to advance the science of sociology and to serve the public good.

Ethical Standards

1. Professional and Scientific Standards

Sociologists adhere to the highest possible technical standards that are reasonable and responsible in their research, teaching, practice, and service activities. They rely on scientifically and professionally derived knowledge; act with honesty and integrity; and avoid untrue, deceptive, or undocumented statements in undertaking work-related functions or activities.

2. Competence

(a) Sociologists conduct research, teach, practice, and provide service only within the boundaries of their competence, based on their education, training, supervised experience, or appropriate professional experience.

(b) Sociologists conduct research, teach, practice, and provide service in new areas or involving new techniques only after they have taken reasonable steps to ensure the competence of their work in these areas.

(c) Sociologists who engage in research, teaching, practice, or service maintain awareness of current scientific and professional information in their fields of activity, and undertake continuing efforts to maintain competence in the skills they use.

(d) Sociologists refrain from undertaking an activity when their personal circumstances may interfere with their professional work or lead to harm for a student, supervisee, human subject, client, colleague, or other person to whom they have a scientific, teaching, consulting, or other professional obligation.

3. Representation and Misuse of Expertise

(a) In research, teaching, practice, service, or other situations where sociologists render professional judgments or present their expertise, they accurately and fairly represent their areas and degrees of expertise.

(b) Sociologists do not accept grants, contracts, consultation, or work assignments from individual or organizational clients or sponsors that appear likely to require violation of the standards in this Code of Ethics. Sociologists dissociate themselves from such activities when they discover a violation and are unable to achieve its correction.

(c) Because sociologists' scientific and professional judgments and actions may affect the lives of others, they are alert to and guard against personal, financial, social, organizational, or political factors that might lead to misuse of their knowledge, expertise, or influence.

(d) If sociologists learn of misuse or misrepresentation of their work, they take reasonable steps to correct or minimize the misuse or misrepresentation.

4. Delegation and Supervision

(a) Sociologists provide proper training and supervision to their students, supervisees, or employees and take reasonable steps to see that such persons perform services responsibly, competently, and ethically.

(b) Sociologists delegate to their students, supervisees, or employees only those responsibilities that such persons, based on their education, training, or experience, can reasonably be expected to perform either independently or with the level of supervision provided.

5. Nondiscrimination

Sociologists do not engage in discrimination in their work based on age; gender; race; ethnicity; national origin; religion; sexual orientation; disability; health conditions; marital, domestic, or parental status; or any other applicable basis proscribed by law.

6. Non-exploitation

(a) Whether for personal, economic, or professional advantage, sociologists do not exploit persons over whom they have direct or indirect supervisory, evaluative, or other authority such as students, supervisees, employees, or research participants.

(b) Sociologists do not directly supervise or exercise evaluative authority over any person with whom they have a sexual relationship, including students, supervisees, employees, or research participants.

7. Harassment

Sociologists do not engage in harassment of any person, including students, supervisees, employees, or research participants. Harassment consists of a single intense and severe act or of multiple persistent or pervasive acts which are demeaning, abusive, offensive, or create a hostile professional or workplace environment. Sexual harassment may include sexual solicitation, physical advance, or verbal or non-verbal conduct that is sexual in nature. Racial harassment may include unnecessary, exaggerated, or unwarranted attention or attack, whether verbal or non-verbal, because of a person's race or ethnicity.

8. Employment Decisions

Sociologists have an obligation to adhere to the highest ethical standards when participating in employment related decisions, when seeking employment, or when planning to resign from a position.

8.01 Fair Employment Practices

(a) When participating in employment-related decisions, sociologists make every effort to ensure equal opportunity and fair treatment to all full- and part-time employees. They do not discriminate in hiring, promotion, salary, treatment, or any other conditions of employment or career development on the basis of age; gender; race; ethnicity; national origin; religion; sexual orientation; disability; health conditions; marital, domestic, or parental status; or any other applicable basis proscribed by law.

(b) When participating in employment-related decisions, sociologists specify the requirements for hiring, promotion, tenure, and termination and communicate these requirements thoroughly to full- and part-time employees and prospective employees.

(c) When participating in employment-related decisions, sociologists have the responsibility to be informed of fair employment codes, to communicate this information to employees, and to help create an atmosphere upholding fair employment practices for full- and part-time employees.

(d) When participating in employment-related decisions, sociologists inform prospective full- and part-time employees of any constraints on research and publication and negotiate clear understandings about any conditions that may limit research and scholarly activity.

8.02 Responsibilities of Employees

(a) When seeking employment, sociologists provide prospective employers with accurate and complete information on their professional qualifications and experiences.

(b) When leaving a position, permanently or temporarily, sociologists provide their employers with adequate notice and take reasonable steps to reduce negative effects of leaving.

9. Conflicts of Interest

Sociologists maintain the highest degree of integrity in their professional work and avoid conflicts of interest and the appearance of conflict. Conflicts of interest arise when sociologists' personal or financial interests prevent them from performing their professional work in an unbiased manner. In research, teaching, practice, and service, sociologists are alert to situations that might cause a conflict of interest and take appropriate action to prevent conflict or disclose it to appropriate parties.

9.01 Adherence to Professional Standards

Irrespective of their personal or financial interests or those of their employers or clients, sociologists adhere to professional and scientific standards in (1) the collection, analysis, or interpretation of data; (2) the reporting of research; (3) the teaching, professional presentation, or public dissemination of sociological knowledge; and (4) the identification or implementation of appropriate contractual, consulting, or service activities.

9.02 Disclosure

Sociologists disclose relevant sources of financial support and relevant personal or professional relationships that may have the appearance of or potential for a conflict of interest to an employer or client, to the sponsors of their professional work, or in public speeches and writing.

9.03 Avoidance of Personal Gain

(a) Under all circumstances, sociologists do not use or otherwise seek to gain from information or material received in a confidential context (e.g., knowledge obtained from reviewing a manuscript or serving on a proposal review panel), unless they have authorization to do so or until that information is otherwise made publicly available.

(b) Under all circumstances, sociologists do not seek to gain from information or material in an employment or client relationship without permission of the employer or client.

9.04 Decisionmaking in the Workplace

In their workplace, sociologists take appropriate steps to avoid conflicts of interest or the appearance of conflicts, and carefully scrutinize potentially biasing affiliations or relationships. In research, teaching, practice, or service, such potentially biasing affiliations or relationships include, but are not limited to, situations involving family, business, or close personal friendships or those with whom sociologists have had strong conflict or disagreement.

9.05 Decisionmaking Outside of the Workplace

In professional activities outside of their workplace, sociologists in all circumstances abstain from engaging in deliberations and decisions that allocate or withhold benefits or rewards from individuals or institutions if they have biasing affiliations or relationships. These biasing affiliations or relationships are: 1) current employment or being considered for employment at an organization or institution that could be construed as benefiting from the decision; 2) current officer or board member of an organization or institution that could be construed as benefiting from the decision; 3) current employment or being considered for employment at the same organization or institution where an individual could benefit from the decision; 4) a spouse, domestic partner, or known relative who as an individual could benefit from the decision; or 5) a current business or professional partner, research collaborator, employee, supervisee, or student who as an individual could benefit from the decision.

10. Public Communication

Sociologists adhere to the highest professional standards in public communications about their professional services, credentials and expertise, work products, or publications, whether these communications are from themselves or from others.

10.01 Public Communications

(a) Sociologists take steps to ensure the accuracy of all public communications. Such public communications include, but are not limited to, directory listings; personal resumes or curriculum vitae; advertising; brochures or printed matter; interviews or comments to the media; statements in legal proceedings; lectures and public oral presentations; or other published materials.

(b) Sociologists do not make public statements that are false, deceptive, misleading, or fraudulent, either because of what they state, convey, or suggest or because of what they omit, concerning their research, practice, or other work activities or those of persons or organizations with which they are affiliated. Such activities include, but are not limited to, false or deceptive statements concerning sociologists' (1) training, experience, or competence; (2) academic degrees; (3) credentials; (4) institutional or association affiliations; (5) services; (6) fees; or (7) publications or research findings. Sociologists do not make false or deceptive statements concerning the scientific basis for, results of, or degree of success from their professional services. (c) When sociologists provide professional advice or comment by means of public lectures, demonstrations, radio or television programs, prerecorded tapes, printed articles, mailed material, or other media, they take reasonable precautions to ensure that (1) the statements are based on appropriate research, literature, and practice; and (2) the statements are otherwise consistent with this Code of Ethics.

10.02 Statements by Others

(a) Sociologists who engage or employ others to create or place public statements that promote their work products, professional services, or other activities retain responsibility for such statements.

(b) Sociologists make reasonable efforts to prevent others whom they do not directly engage, employ, or supervise (such as employers, publishers, sponsors, organizational clients, members of the media) from making deceptive statements concerning their professional research, teaching, or practice activities.

(c) In working with the press, radio, television, or other communications media or in advertising in the media, sociologists are cognizant of potential conflicts of interest or appearances of such conflicts (e.g., they do not provide compensation to employees of the media), and they adhere to the highest standards of professional honesty (e.g., they acknowledge paid advertising).

11. Confidentiality

Sociologists have an obligation to ensure that confidential information is protected. They do so to ensure the integrity of research and the open communication with research participants and to protect sensitive information obtained in research, teaching, practice, and service. When gathering confidential information, sociologists should take into account the long-term uses of the information, including its potential placement in public archives or the examination of the information by other researchers or practitioners.

11.01 Maintaining Confidentiality

(a) Sociologists take reasonable precautions to protect the confidentiality rights of research participants, students, employees, clients, or others.

(b) Confidential information provided by research participants, students, employees, clients, or others is treated as such by sociologists even if there is no legal protection or privilege to do so. Sociologists have an obligation to protect confidential information, and not allow information gained in confidence from being used in ways that would unfairly compromise research participants, students, employees, clients, or others.

(c) Information provided under an understanding of confidentiality is treated as such even after the death of those providing that information.

(d) Sociologists maintain the integrity of confidential deliberations, activities, or roles, including, where applicable, that of professional committees, review panels, or advisory groups (e.g., the ASA Committee on Professional Ethics).

(e) Sociologists, to the extent possible, protect the confidentiality of student records, performance data, and personal information, whether verbal or written, given in the context of academic consultation, supervision, or advising.

(f) The obligation to maintain confidentiality extends to members of research or training teams and collaborating organizations who have access to the information. To ensure that access to confidential information is restricted, it is the responsibility of researchers, administrators, and principal investigators to instruct staff to take the steps necessary to protect confidentiality.

(g) When using private information about individuals collected by other persons or institutions, sociologists protect the confidentiality of individually identifiable information. Information is private when an individual can reasonably expect that the information will not be made public with personal identifiers (e.g., medical or employment records).

11.02 Limits of Confidentiality

(a) Sociologists inform themselves fully about all laws and rules which may limit or alter guarantees of confidentiality. They determine their ability to guarantee absolute confidentiality and, as appropriate, inform research participants, students, employees, clients, or others of any limitations to this guarantee at the outset consistent with ethical standards set forth in 11.02(b).

(b) Sociologists may confront unanticipated circumstances where they become aware of information that is clearly health- or life-threatening to research participants, students, employees, clients, or others. In these cases, sociologists balance the importance of guarantees of confidentiality with other principles in this Code of Ethics, standards of conduct, and applicable law.

(c) Confidentiality is not required with respect to observations in public places, activities conducted in public, or other settings where no rules of privacy are provided by law or custom. Similarly, confidentiality is not required in the case of information available from public records.

11.03 Discussing Confidentiality and Its Limits

(a) When sociologists establish a scientific or professional relationship with persons, they discuss (1) the relevant limitations on confidentiality, and (2) the foreseeable uses of the information generated through their professional work.

(b) Unless it is not feasible or is counter-productive, the discussion of confidentiality occurs at the outset of the relationship and thereafter as new circumstances may warrant.

11.04 Anticipation of Possible Uses of Information

(a) When research requires maintaining personal identifiers in data bases or systems of records, sociologists delete such identifiers before the information is made publicly available.

(b) When confidential information concerning research participants, clients, or other recipients of service is entered into databases or systems of records available to persons without the prior consent of the relevant parties, sociologists protect anonymity by not including personal identifiers or by employing other techniques that mask or control disclosure of individual identities.

(c) When deletion of personal identifiers is not feasible, sociologists take reasonable steps to determine that appropriate consent of personally-identifiable individuals has been obtained before they transfer such data to others or review such data collected by others.

11.05 Electronic Transmission of Confidential Information

Sociologists use extreme care in delivering or transferring any confidential data, information, or communication over public computer networks. Sociologists are attentive to the problems of maintaining confidentiality and control over sensitive material and data when use of technological innovations, such as public computer networks, may open their professional and scientific communication to unauthorized persons.

11.06 Anonymity of Sources

(a) Sociologists do not disclose in their writings, lectures, or other public media confidential, personally identifiable information concerning their research participants, students, individual or organizational clients, or other recipients of their service which is obtained during the course of their work, unless consent from individuals or their legal representatives has been obtained.

(b) When confidential information is used in scientific and professional presentations, sociologists disguise the identity of research participants, students, individual or organizational clients, or other recipients of their service.

11.07 Minimizing Intrusions on Privacy

(a) To minimize intrusions on privacy, sociologists include in written and oral reports, consultations, and public communications only information germane to the purpose for which the communication is made.

(b) Sociologists discuss confidential information or evaluative data concerning research participants, students, supervisees, employees, and individual or organizational clients only for appropriate scientific or professional purposes and only with persons clearly concerned with such matters.

11.08 Preservation of Confidential Information

(a) Sociologists take reasonable steps to ensure that records, data, or information are preserved in a confidential manner consistent with the requirements of this Code of Ethics, recognizing that ownership of records, data, or information may also be governed by law or institutional principles.

(b) Sociologists plan so that confidentiality of records, data, or information is protected in the event of the sociologist's death, incapacity, or withdrawal from the position or practice.

(c) When sociologists transfer confidential records, data, or information to other persons or organizations, they obtain assurances that the recipients of the records, data, or information will employ measures to protect confidentiality at least equal to those originally pledged.

12. Informed Consent

Informed consent is a basic ethical tenet of scientific research on human populations. Sociologists do not involve a human being as a subject in research without the informed consent of the subject or the subject's legally authorized representative, except as otherwise specified in this Code. Sociologists recognize the possibility of undue influence or subtle pressures on subjects that may derive from researchers' expertise or authority, and they take this into account in designing informed consent procedures.

12.01 Scope of Informed Consent

(a) Sociologists conducting research obtain consent from research participants or their legally authorized representatives (1) when data are collected from research participants through any form of communication, interaction, or intervention; or (2) when behavior of research participants occurs in a private context where an individual can reasonably expect that no observation or reporting is taking place.

(b) Despite the paramount importance of consent, sociologists may seek waivers of this standard when (1) the research involves no more than minimal risk for research participants, and (2) the research could not practicably be carried out were informed consent to be required. Sociologists recognize that waivers of consent require approval from institutional review boards or, in the absence of such boards, from another authoritative body with expertise on the ethics of research. Under such circumstances, the confidentiality of any personally identifiable information must be maintained unless otherwise set forth in 11.02(b).

(c) Sociologists may conduct research in public places or use publicly available information about individuals (e.g., naturalistic observations in public places, analysis of public records, or archival research) without obtaining consent. If, under such circumstances, sociologists have any doubt whatsoever about the need for informed consent, they consult with institutional review boards or, in the absence of such boards, with another authoritative body with expertise on the ethics of research before proceeding with such research.

(d) In undertaking research with vulnerable populations (e.g., youth, recent immigrant populations, the mentally ill), sociologists take special care to ensure that the voluntary nature of the research is understood and that consent is not coerced. In all other respects, sociologists adhere to the principles set forth in 12.01(a)-(c).

(e) Sociologists are familiar with and conform to applicable state and federal regulations and, where applicable, institutional review board requirements for obtaining informed consent for research.

12.02 Informed Consent Process

(a) When informed consent is required, sociologists enter into an agreement with research participants or their legal representatives that clarifies the nature of the research and the responsibilities of the investigator prior to conducting the research.

(b) When informed consent is required, sociologists use language that is understandable to and respectful of research participants or their legal representatives.

(c) When informed consent is required, sociologists provide research participants or their legal representatives with the opportunity to ask questions about any aspect of the research, at any time during or after their participation in the research.

(d) When informed consent is required, sociologists inform research participants or their legal representatives of the nature of the research; they indicate to participants that their participation or continued participation is voluntary; they inform participants of significant factors that may be expected to influence their willingness to participate (e.g., possible risks and benefits of their participation); and they explain other aspects of the research and respond to questions from prospective participants. Also, if relevant, sociologists explain that refusal to participate or withdrawal from participation in the research involves no penalty, and they explain any foreseeable consequences of declining or withdrawing. Sociologists explicitly discuss confidentiality and, if applicable, the extent to which confidentiality may be limited as set forth in 11.02(b).

(e) When informed consent is required, sociologists keep records regarding said consent. They recognize that consent is a process that involves oral and/or written consent.

(f) Sociologists honor all commitments they have made to research participants as part of the informed consent process except where unanticipated circumstances demand otherwise as set forth in 11.02(b).

12.03 Informed Consent of Students and Subordinates

When undertaking research at their own institutions or organizations with research participants who are students or subordinates, sociologists take special care to protect the prospective subjects from adverse consequences of declining or withdrawing from participation.

12.04 Informed Consent with Children

(a) In undertaking research with children, sociologists obtain the consent of children to participate, to the extent that they are capable of providing such consent, except under circumstances where consent may not be required as set forth in 12.01(b).

(b) In undertaking research with children, sociologists obtain the consent of a parent or a legally authorized guardian. Sociologists may seek waivers of parental or guardian consent when (1) the research involves no more than minimal risk for the research participants, and (2) the research could not practically be carried out were consent to be required, or (3) the consent of a parent or guardian is not a reasonable requirement to protect the child (e.g., neglected or abused children).

(c) Sociologists recognize that waivers of consent from a child and a parent or guardian require approval from institutional review boards or, in the absence of such boards, from another authoritative body with expertise on the ethics of research. Under such circumstances, the confidentiality of any personally identifiable information must be maintained unless otherwise set forth in 11.02(b).

12.05 Use of Deception in Research

(a) Sociologists do not use deceptive techniques (1) unless they have determined that their use will not be harmful to research participants; is justified by the study's prospective scientific, educational, or applied value; and that equally effective alternative procedures that do not use deception are not feasible, and (2) unless they have obtained the approval of institutional review boards or, in the absence of such boards, with another authoritative body with expertise on the ethics of research.

(b) Sociologists never deceive research participants about significant aspects of the research that would affect their willingness to participate, such as physical risks, discomfort, or unpleasant emotional experiences.

(c) When deception is an integral feature of the design and conduct of research, sociologists attempt to correct any misconception that research participants may have no later than at the conclusion of the research.

(d) On rare occasions, sociologists may need to conceal their identity in order to undertake research that could not practicably be carried out were they to be known as researchers. Under such circumstances, sociologists undertake the research if it involves no more than minimal risk for the research participants and if they have obtained approval to proceed in this manner from an institutional review board or, in the absence of such boards, from another authoritative body with expertise on the ethics of research. Under such circumstances, confidentiality must be maintained unless otherwise set forth in 11.02(b).

12.06 Use of Recording Technology

Sociologists obtain informed consent from research participants, students, employees, clients, or others prior to videotaping, filming, or recording them in any form, unless these activities involve simply naturalistic observations in public places and it is not anticipated that the recording will be used in a manner that could cause personal identification or harm.

13. Research Planning, Implementation, and Dissemination

Sociologists have an obligation to promote the integrity of research and to ensure that they comply with the ethical tenets of science in the planning, implementation, and dissemination of research. They do so in order to advance knowledge, to minimize the possibility that results will be misleading, and to protect the rights of research participants.

13.01 Planning and Implementation

(a) In planning and implementing research, sociologists minimize the possibility that results will be misleading.

(b) Sociologists take steps to implement protections for the rights and welfare of research participants and other persons affected by the research.

(c) In their research, sociologists do not encourage activities or themselves behave in ways that are health- or life-threatening to research participants or others.

(d) In planning and implementing research, sociologists consult those with expertise concerning any special population under investigation or likely to be affected.

(e) In planning and implementing research, sociologists consider its ethical acceptability as set forth in the Code of Ethics. If the best ethical practice is unclear, sociologists consult with institutional review boards or, in the absence of such review processes, with another authoritative body with expertise on the ethics of research.

(f) Sociologists are responsible for the ethical conduct of research conducted by them or by others under their supervision or authority.

13.02 Unanticipated Research Opportunities

If during the course of teaching, practice, service, or non-professional activities, sociologists determine that they wish to undertake research that was not previously anticipated, they make known their intentions and take steps to ensure that the research can be undertaken consonant with ethical principles, especially those relating to confidentiality and informed consent. Under such circumstances, sociologists seek the approval of institutional review boards or, in the absence of such review processes, another authoritative body with expertise on the ethics of research.

13.03 Offering Inducements for Research Participants

Sociologists do not offer excessive or inappropriate financial or other inducements to obtain the participation of research participants, particularly when it might coerce participation. Sociologists may provide incentives to the extent that resources are available and appropriate.

13.04 Reporting on Research

(a) Sociologists disseminate their research findings except where unanticipated circumstances (e.g., the health of the researcher) or proprietary agreements with employers, contractors, or clients preclude such dissemination.

(b) Sociologists do not fabricate data or falsify results in their publications or presentations.

(c) In presenting their work, sociologists report their findings fully and do not omit relevant data. They report results whether they support or contradict the expected outcomes.

(d) Sociologists take particular care to state all relevant qualifications on the findings and interpretation of their research. Sociologists also disclose underlying assumptions, theories, methods, measures, and research designs that might bear upon findings and interpretations of their work.

(e) Consistent with the spirit of full disclosure of methods and analyses, once findings are publicly disseminated, sociologists permit their open assessment and verification by other responsible researchers with appropriate safeguards, where applicable, to protect the anonymity of research participants.

(f) If sociologists discover significant errors in their publication or presentation of data, they take reasonable steps to correct such errors in a correction, a retraction, published errata, or other public fora as appropriate.

(g) Sociologists report sources of financial support in their written papers and note any special relations to any sponsor. In special circumstances, sociologists may withhold the names of specific sponsors if they provide an adequate and full description of the nature and interest of the sponsor.

(h) Sociologists take special care to report accurately the results of others' scholarship by using correct information and citations when presenting the work of others in publications, teaching, practice, and service settings.

13.05 Data Sharing
(a) Sociologists share data and pertinent documentation as a regular practice. Sociologists make their data available after completion of the project or its major publications, except where proprietary agreements with employers, contractors, or clients preclude such accessibility or when it is impossible to share data and protect the confidentiality of the data or the anonymity of research participants (e.g., raw field notes or detailed information from ethnographic interviews).

(b) Sociologists anticipate data sharing as an integral part of a research plan whenever data sharing is feasible.

(c) Sociologists share data in a form that is consonant with research participants' interests and protect the confidentiality of the information they have been given. They maintain the confidentiality of data, whether legally required or not; remove personal identifiers before data are shared; and if necessary use other disclosure avoidance techniques.

(d) Sociologists who do not otherwise place data in public archives keep data available and retain documentation relating to the research for a reasonable period of time after publication or dissemination of results.

(e) Sociologists may ask persons who request their data for further analysis to bear the associated incremental costs, if necessary.

(f) Sociologists who use data from others for further analyses explicitly acknowledge the contribution of the initial researchers.

14. Plagiarism
(a) In publications, presentations, teaching, practice, and service, sociologists explicitly identify, credit, and reference the author when they take data or material verbatim from another person's written work, whether it is published, unpublished, or electronically available.

(b) In their publications, presentations, teaching, practice, and service, sociologists provide acknowledgment of and reference to the use of others' work, even if the work is not quoted verbatim or paraphrased, and they do not present others' work as their own whether it is published, unpublished, or electronically available.

15. Authorship Credit
(a) Sociologists take responsibility and credit, including authorship credit, only for work they have actually performed or to which they have contributed.

(b) Sociologists ensure that principal authorship and other publication credits are based on the relative scientific or professional contributions of the individuals involved, regardless of their status. In claiming or determining the ordering of authorship, sociologists seek to reflect accurately the contributions of main participants in the research and writing process.

(c) A student is usually listed as principal author on any multiple authored publication that substantially derives from the student's dissertation or thesis.

16. Publication Process
Sociologists adhere to the highest ethical standards when participating in publication and review processes when they are authors or editors.

16.01 Submission of Manuscripts for Publication
(a) In cases of multiple authorship, sociologists confer with all other authors prior to submitting work for publication and establish mutually acceptable agreements regarding submission.

(b) In submitting a manuscript to a professional journal, book series, or edited book, sociologists grant that publication first claim to publication except where explicit policies allow multiple submissions. Sociologists do not submit a manuscript to a second publication until after an official decision has been received from the first publication or until the manuscript is withdrawn. Sociologists submitting a manuscript for publication in a journal, book series, or edited book can withdraw a manuscript from consideration up until an official acceptance is made.

(c) Sociologists may submit a book manuscript to multiple publishers. However, once sociologists have signed a contract, they cannot withdraw a manuscript from publication unless there is reasonable cause to do so.

16.02 Duplicate Publication of Data
When sociologists publish data or findings that they have previously published elsewhere, they accompany these publications by proper acknowledgment.

16.03 Responsibilities of Editors
(a) When serving as editors of journals or book series, sociologists are fair in the application of standards and operate without personal or ideological favoritism or malice. As editors, sociologists are cognizant of any potential conflicts of interest.

(b) When serving as editors of journals or book series, sociologists ensure the confidential nature of the review process and supervise editorial office staff, including students, in accordance with practices that maintain confidentiality.

(c) When serving as editors of journals or book series, sociologists are bound to publish all manuscripts accepted for publication unless major errors or ethical violations are discovered after acceptance (e.g., plagiarism or scientific misconduct).

(d) When serving as editors of journals or book series, sociologists ensure the anonymity of reviewers unless they otherwise receive permission from reviewers to reveal their identity. Editors ensure that their staff conform to this practice.

(e) When serving as journal editors, sociologists ensure the anonymity of authors unless and until a manuscript is accepted for publication or unless the established practices of the journal are known to be otherwise.

(f) When serving as journal editors, sociologists take steps to provide for the timely review of all manuscripts and respond promptly to inquiries about the status of the review.

17. Responsibilities of Reviewers
(a) In reviewing material submitted for publication, grant support, or other evaluation purposes, sociologists respect the confidentiality of the process and the proprietary rights in such information of those who submitted it.

(b) Sociologists disclose conflicts of interest or decline requests for reviews of the work of others where conflicts of interest are involved.

(c) Sociologists decline requests for reviews of the work of others when they believe that the review process may be biased or when they have questions about the integrity of the process.

(d) If asked to review a manuscript, book, or proposal they have previously reviewed, sociologists make it known to the person making the request (e.g., editor, program officer) unless it is clear that they are being asked to provide a reappraisal.

18. Education, Teaching, and Training

As teachers, supervisors, and trainers, sociologists follow the highest ethical standards in order to ensure the quality of sociological education and the integrity of the teacher-student relationship.

18.01 Administration of Education Programs

(a) Sociologists who are responsible for education and training programs seek to ensure that the programs are competently designed, provide the proper experiences, and meet all goals for which claims are made by the program.

(b) Sociologists responsible for education and training programs seek to ensure that there is an accurate description of the program content, training goals and objectives, and requirements that must be met for satisfactory completion of the program.

(c) Sociologists responsible for education and training programs take steps to ensure that graduate assistants and temporary instructors have the substantive knowledge required to teach courses and the teaching skills needed to facilitate student learning.

(d) Sociologists responsible for education and training programs have an obligation to ensure that ethics are taught to their graduate students as part of their professional preparation.

18.02 Teaching and Training

(a) Sociologists conscientiously perform their teaching responsibilities. They have appropriate skills and knowledge or are receiving appropriate training.

(b) Sociologists provide accurate information at the outset about their courses, particularly regarding the subject matter to be covered, bases for evaluation, and the nature of course experiences.

(c) Sociologists make decisions concerning textbooks, course content, course requirements, and grading solely on the basis of educational criteria without regard for financial or other incentives.

(d) Sociologists provide proper training and supervision to their teaching assistants and other teaching trainees and take reasonable steps to ensure that such persons perform these teaching responsibilities responsibly, competently, and ethically.

(e) Sociologists do not permit personal animosities or intellectual differences with colleagues to foreclose students' or supervisees' access to these colleagues or to interfere with student or supervisee learning, academic progress, or professional development.

19. Contractual and Consulting Services

(a) Sociologists undertake grants, contracts, or consultation only when they are knowledgeable about the substance, methods, and techniques they plan to use or have a plan for incorporating appropriate expertise.

(b) In undertaking grants, contracts, or consultation, sociologists base the results of their professional work on appropriate information and techniques.

(c) When financial support for a project has been accepted under a grant, contract, or consultation, sociologists make reasonable efforts to complete the proposed work on schedule.

(d) In undertaking grants, contracts, or consultation, sociologists accurately document and appropriately retain their professional and scientific work.

(e) In establishing a contractual arrangement for research, consultation, or other services, sociologists clarify, to the extent feasible at the outset, the nature of the relationship with the individual, organizational, or institutional client. This clarification includes, as appropriate, the nature of the services to be performed, the probable uses of the services provided, possibilities for the sociologist's future use of the work for scholarly or publication purposes, the timetable for delivery of those services, and compensation and billing arrangements.

20. Adherence to the Code of Ethics

Sociologists have an obligation to confront, address, and attempt to resolve ethical issues according to this Code of Ethics.

20.01 Familiarity with the Code of Ethics

Sociologists have an obligation to be familiar with this Code of Ethics, other applicable ethics codes, and their application to sociologists' work. Lack of awareness or misunderstanding of an ethical standard is not, in itself, a defense to a charge of unethical conduct.

20.02 Confronting Ethical Issues

(a) When sociologists are uncertain whether a particular situation or course of action would violate the Code of Ethics, they consult with other sociologists knowledgeable about ethical issues, with ASA's Committee on Professional Ethics, or with other organizational entities such as institutional review boards.

(b) When sociologists take actions or are confronted with choices where there is a conflict between ethical standards enunciated in the Code of Ethics and laws or legal requirements, they make known their commitment to the Code and take steps to resolve the conflict in a responsible manner by consulting with colleagues, professional organizations, or the ASA's Committee on Professional Ethics.

20.03 Fair Treatment of Parties in Ethical Disputes

(a) Sociologists do not discriminate against a person on the basis of his or her having made an ethical complaint.

(b) Sociologists do not discriminate against a person based on his or her having been the subject of an ethical complaint. This does not preclude taking action based upon the outcome of an ethical complaint.

20.04 Reporting Ethical Violations of Others

When sociologists have substantial reason to believe that there may have been an ethical violation by another sociologist, they attempt to resolve the issue by bringing it to the attention of that individual if an informal resolution appears appropriate or possible, or they seek advice about whether or how to proceed based on this belief, assuming that such activity does not violate any confidentiality rights. Such action might include referral to ASA's Committee on Professional Ethics.

20.05 Cooperating with Ethics Committees

Sociologists cooperate in ethics investigations, proceedings, and resulting requirements of the American Sociological Association. In doing so, they make reasonable efforts to resolve any issues of confidentiality. Failure to cooperate may be an ethics violation.

20.06 Improper Complaints

Sociologists do not file or encourage the filing of ethics complaints that are frivolous and are intended to harm the alleged violator rather than to protect the integrity of the discipline and the public.

Note: This revised edition of the ASA Code of Ethics builds on the 1989 edition of the Code and the 1992 version of the American Psychological Association's Ethical Principles of Psychologists and Code of Conduct.

Glossary

This Glossary contains terms you need to understand as you study sociology. After each key term there is a brief definition or explanation of the meaning of the term as it is used in *Holt Sociology*. The page number refers to the page on which the term is introduced in the textbook.

Phonetic Respelling and Pronunciation Guide

Many of the key terms in this textbook have been respelled to help you pronounce them. The letter combinations used in the respelling throughout the narrative are explained in the following phonetic respelling and pronunciation guide. The guide is adapted from Webster's Tenth New Collegiate Dictionary, Merriam-Webster's New Geographical Dictionary, and Merriam-Webster's New Biographical Dictionary.

Mark	As In	Respelling	Example
a	alphabet	a	*AL-fuh-bet
ā	Asia	ay	AY-zhuh
ä	cart, top	ah	KAHRT, TAHP
e	let, ten	e	LET, TEN
ē	even, leaf	ee	EE-vuhn, LEEF
i	it, tip, British	i	IT, TIP, BRIT-ish
ī	site, buy, Ohio	y	SYT, BY, oh-HY-oh
	iris	eye	EYE-ris
k	card	k	KAHRD
ō	over, rainbow	oh	OH-vuhr, RAYN-boh
ū	book, wood	ooh	BOOHK, WOOHD
ö	all, orchid	aw	AWL, AWR-kid
öi	foil, coin	oy	FOYL, KOYN
aù	out	ow	OWT
ə	cup, butter	uh	KUHP, BUHT-uhr
ü	rule, food	oo	ROOL, FOOD
yü	few	yoo	FYOO
zh	vision	zh	VIZH-uhn

*A syllable printed in small capital letters receives heavier emphasis than the other syllable(s) in a word.

A

absolute monarchy authoritarian type of government in which the hereditary ruler holds absolute power. **338**

accommodation state of balance between cooperation and conflict. **72**

achieved status status acquired by an individual on the basis of some special skill, knowledge, or ability. **66**

acquired immune deficiency syndrome (AIDS) fatal disease caused by a virus that attacks an individual's immune system, leaving the person vulnerable to a host of deadly infections. **286**

adolescence period between the normal onset of puberty and the beginning of adulthood. **120**

ageism belief that one age category is by nature superior to another age category. **272**

agenda setting the argument that the media sets the boundaries of public debate by deciding which issues will receive coverage and which will not. **397**

agents of socialization specific individuals, groups, and institutions that provide the situations in which socialization can occur. **112** *See also* socialization.

aggregate group of people gathered in the same place at the same time who lack organization or lasting patterns of interaction. **78**

agricultural society type of society characterized by the use of draft animals and plows in the tilling of fields. **74**

alternative medicine treating illnesses with unconventional methods such as acupuncture, biofeedback, massage, meditation, yoga, herbal remedies, and relaxation techniques. **285**

Alzheimer's disease organic condition that results in the progressive destruction of brain cells. **168**

animism belief system in which spirits are active in influencing human life. **365**

anomie situation that arises when the norms of society are unclear or are no longer applicable. **180**

anthropology comparative study of various aspects of past and present cultures. **7**

anticipatory socialization learning of the rights, obligations, and expectations of a role in preparation for assuming that role at a future date. **126**

antinatalism official policies designed to discourage births. **418**

aptitude capacity to learn a particular skill or acquire a particular body of knowledge. **99**

ascribed status status assigned according to standards that are beyond a person's control. Age, sex, family heritage, and race are examples of ascribed statuses. **66**

assimilation blending of culturally distinct groups into a single group with a common culture and identity. **243**

authoritarianism type of government in which power rests firmly with the state. **338**

authority legitimate power. **334**

baby-boom generation collective term for the approximately 76 million children born in the United States from 1946 through 1964. **274**

barter practice of exchanging one good for another. **74**

bilateral descent descent system in which kinship is traced through both parents. **301**

bilingual education system of education in which non-English-speaking students are taught in their native languages until they are prepared to attend classes taught in English. **361**

bilocality residential pattern in which a newly married couple is allowed to choose whether they will live with the husband's parents or the wife's parents. **300**

birthrate annual number of live births per 1,000 members of a population. **406**

bourgeoisie (boor-ZHWAH-zee) owners of the means of production in a capitalist society. **208**

bureaucracy ranked authority structure that operates according to specific rules and procedures. **83**

capitalism economic model in which the factors of production are owned by individuals and that is regulated by the forces of profit and competition. **325**

caste system system in which scarce resources and rewards are distributed on the basis of ascribed statuses. **206** *See also* class system.

charismatic authority power that is legitimated on the basis of the personal characteristics of the individual exercising the power. **335**

charter schools alternative schools which are funded by public money but are privately operated. **358**

city permanent concentration of relatively large numbers of people who are engaged mainly in nonagricultural pursuits. **421**

class system system in which scarce resources and rewards are determined on the basis of achieved statuses. **208** *See also* caste system.

coercion power that is exercised through force or the threat of force. **335**

collective behavior relatively spontaneous social behavior that occurs when people try to develop common solutions to unclear situations. **436**

collectivity collection of people who have limited interaction with each other and who do not share clearly defined, conventional norms. **436**

communalism a belief held among some scientists that all scientific knowledge should be made available to everyone in the scientific community. **379**

communism political and economic system in which property is communally owned. **326**

competition interaction that occurs when two or more persons or groups oppose each other to achieve a goal that only one can attain. **69**

compositional theory theory of city life that examines the ways in which the composition of a city's population influences life in the city. According to this theory, individuals are able to protect themselves from the anonymity of the city by forming primary groups with others who are like themselves. **430**

concentric zone model model of urban structure proposed by Ernest W. Burgess in which the typical industrial city is said to spread outward from the center in a series of circles within circles. **426**

conflict deliberate attempt to oppose, harm, control by force, or resist the will of another person or persons. **71**

conflict perspective theoretical perspective that focuses on those forces in society that promote competition and change. **16**

conflict theory of social change theory that views social change as the result of conflicts between groups with opposing interests. **468**

conservative movements social movements that try to protect from change what they see as society's prevailing values. **449**

constitutional monarchy type of government in which the ruler, or monarch, is nothing more than the symbolic head of state. Constitutional monarchies are considered democratic because the ultimate power rests with elected officials. **337**

contagion theory theory of collective behavior proposed by Gustave LeBon in which the hypnotic power of a crowd is said to encourage people to give up their individuality to the stronger pull of the group. Individuals then become anonymous, with no will power or sense of responsibility. **446**

control theory theory of deviant behavior in which deviance is seen as a natural occurrence and conformity is seen as the result of social control. **182**

cooperation interaction that occurs when two or more persons or groups work together to achieve a goal that will benefit many people. **71**

core nations according to the world-system theory of modernization, those more developed nations that are at the center of the world economy and upon which less developed nations are economically dependent. **473** *See also* peripheral nations.

corporation business organization that is owned by stockholders and is treated by law as if it were an individual person. **328**

corrections sanctions—such as imprisonment, parole, and probation—used to punish criminals. **195**

counterculture group that rejects the values, norms, and practices of the larger society and replaces them with a new set of cultural patterns. **39**

courting buggy a horse-drawn carriage received by Amish men during their teenage years. **134**

courtship a social interaction similar to dating but with the sole purpose of eventual marriage. **127**

crime any act that is labeled as such by those in authority, is prohibited by law, and is punishable by the government. **187**

crime syndicate large-scale organization of professional criminals that controls some vice or business through violence or the threat of violence. **193**

criminal-justice system the system of police, courts, and corrections. **193**

criminologists social scientists who study criminal behavior. **179**

crowd temporary collection of people who are in close enough proximity to interact. **437**

cult religious group founded on the revelations of a person believed to have special knowledge. **366**

cultural lag situation in which some aspects of the culture change less rapidly, or lag behind, other aspects of the same culture. **60**

cultural pluralism policy that allows each group within society to keep its unique cultural identity. **242**

cultural relativism belief that cultures should be judged by their own standards. **36**

cultural-transmission theory theory that views deviance as a learned behavior transmitted through interaction with others. **184**

cultural universals common features that are found in all human cultures. **31**

culture shared products of human groups. These products include both physical objects and the beliefs, values, and behaviors shared by the group. **24** *See also* material culture; nonmaterial culture.

culture complexes clusters of interrelated culture traits. **29**

culture patterns combination of a number of culture complexes into an interrelated whole. **29**

culture trait individual tool, act, or belief that is related to a particular situation or need. **27**

cyclical theory of social change historical view of social change in which societies are seen as rising and then falling or as continuously moving back and forth between stages of development. **462**

D

dating a social behavior that allows individuals to choose their own marriage partners. **127**

death rate annual number of deaths per 1,000 members of a population. **408**

de facto segregation segregation based on informal norms. **243**

degradation ceremony the process of labeling an individual as deviant. **185**

de jure segregation segregation based on laws. **243**

democracy type of government in which power is exercised through the people. **337**

democratic socialism combination of a democratic government and a socialist economy. **338**

demographic transition theory theory of population in which population patterns are said to be tied to a society's level of technological development. Theoretically, a society's population progresses through three distinct stages. **416**

demography scientific study of human populations. **406**

denomination well-established religious organization in which a substantial portion of the population are members. **365**

dependency shift from being an independent adult to being dependent on others for physical or financial assistance. **170**

dependency ratio the number of workers for each person receiving Social Security benefits. **274**

deviance behavior that violates significant social norms. **176**

dictatorship authoritarian type of government in which power is in the hands of a single individual. **338**

differential association proportion of associations a person has with deviant versus non-deviant individuals. **184**

diffusion spread of culture traits—ideas, acts, beliefs, and material objects—from one society to another. **57**

digital divide the gap between those with access to new technologies and those without. **394**

discrimination denial of equal treatment to individuals based on their group membership. **238**

disinterestedness norm in scientific research in which scientists should seek truth, not personal gain. **379**

division of labor specialization by individuals or groups in the performance of specific economic activities. **73**

doubling time number of years necessary for a population to double in size, given its current rate of growth. **412**

drug any substance that changes mood, behavior, or consciousness. **137**

dual-earner families families in which both husband and wife have jobs. **310**

dyad group with two members. **78**

dysfunction negative consequence an element has for the stability of the social system. **14**

early adulthood first era of adulthood, spanning ages 17 through 39. **150**

ecclesia type of religious organization in which all people in the society are members by virtue of their birth. **365**

e-commerce economic transactions that occur over the Internet or other electronic communication systems. **331**

e-community a community of people who interact through the Internet or other electronic communication. **80**

economic institution system of roles and norms that governs the production, distribution, and consumption of goods and services. **322**

economics study of the choices people make in an effort to satisfy their wants and needs. **8**

education system of roles and norms that ensures the transmission of knowledge, values, and patterns of behavior from one generation to the next. **350**

egalitarian a family in which the mother and father share power. **302**

emergent-norm theory theory of collective behavior proposed by Ralph Turner and Lewis Killian. According to this theory, the people in a crowd are often faced with a situation in which traditional norms do not apply. Gradually, new norms emerge when a leader initiates new behavior. **447**

endogamy marriage within one's own social category. **207**

equilibrium theory of social change Talcott Parsons's view of social change in which society is likened to a living organism. Change in one part of the social system produces change in all other parts as the system attempts to regain balance, or equilibrium. **466**

ethicalism belief system in which moral principles have a sacred quality. **365**

ethnic cleansing the process of removing a group from a particular area through terror, expulsion, and mass murder. **246**

ethnic group individuals who share a common cultural background and a common sense of identity. **233**

ethnicity set of cultural characteristics that distinguishes one group from another group. **233**

ethnocentrism tendency to view one's own culture and group as superior to all other cultures and groups. **35**

evolutionary theory of social change view of social change in which change is seen as a process that moves toward increasing complexity. **464**

exchange individual, group, or societal interaction undertaken in an effort to receive a reward in return for actions. **69**

exchange theory theory that holds that people are motivated by self-interests in their interactions with other people. **69**

exogamy marriage outside of one's own social category. **207**

expressive leaders leaders who are emotion-oriented. **81**
See also leaders; instrumental leaders.

extended family family form that consists of three or more generations of a family sharing the same residence. **296**

external debt the amount owed to foreign individuals, organizations, companies, and governments. **476**

factors of production resources that can be used to produce and distribute goods and services. **322**

fad unconventional thought or action that a large number of people are interested in for a very short period of time. **440**

family group of people who are related by marriage, blood, or adoption and who live together and share economic resources. **296**

family of orientation nuclear family into which a person is born. **296**

family of procreation nuclear family consisting of an individual, his or her spouse, and their children. **296**

family planning conscious decision by married couples to have only a certain number of children. **418**

fashion enthusiastic attachment among large numbers of people for a particular style of appearance or behavior. **440**

fecundity biological potential for reproduction. **406**

feral children wild or untamed children. **102**

fertility actual number of births per 1,000 women of childbearing age in a population. **406**

folkways norms that do not have great moral significance attached to them—the common customs of everyday life. **27**

formal group a group in which the structure, goals, and activities of the group are clearly defined. **79**

formal organization large, complex secondary group that has been established to achieve specific goals. **83**

formal sanction reward or punishment that is given by some formal organization or regulatory body, such as the government, the police, a corporation, or a school. **51**

free enterprise system an economic system with limited government control of business operations. **326**

free trade trade between nations that is unrestricted by trade barriers. **330**

function positive consequence an element of society has for the maintenance of the social system. **13** *See also* dysfunction; latent function; manifest function.

functionalist perspective theoretical perspective that views society as a set of interrelated parts that work together to produce a stable social system. **14**

gatekeepers media executives, editors, or reporters who can open or close the "gate" on a particular news story. **397**

Gemeinshaft (guh-MYN-shahft) societies in which most members know one another, relationships are close, and activities center on the family and the community. **77**

gender behavioral and psychological traits considered appropriate for men and women. **262**

gender identity the awareness of being masculine or feminine as those traits are defined by culture. **263**

gender roles specific behaviors and attitudes that a society establishes for men and women. **262**

generalized other internalized attitudes, expectations, and viewpoints of society that we use to guide our behavior and reinforce our sense of self. **108**

genocide extermination aimed at intentionally destroying an entire targeted population. **244**

gerontology scientific study of the processes and phenomena of aging. **164**

Gesellshaft (guh-ZEL-shahft) societies in which social relationships are based on need rather than on emotion, relationships are impersonal and temporary, and individual goals are more important than group goals. **77**

glass ceiling the invisible barrier that prevents women from gaining upper-level positions in business. **269**

graying of America the phenomenon of the growing percentage of elderly Americans as part of the total U.S. population. **273**

group set of two or more people who interact on the basis of shared expectations and who possess some degree of common identity. **73**

growth rate birthrate minus the death rate. **410**

heredity transmission of genetic characteristics from parents to children. **98**

heterogamy tendency for individuals to marry people who have social characteristics different from their own. **306**

hidden curriculum transmission by schools of cultural goals that are not openly acknowledged. **353**

history study of past events. **8**

homeschooling education system in which a child's main education is undertaken by parents at home. **360**

homogamy tendency for individuals to marry people who have social characteristics similar to their own. **129, 305**

horizontal mobility type of social mobility in which the individual moves from one position in a social-class level to another position in that same social-class level. **217**

horticultural society type of society characterized by a reliance on vegetables grown in garden plots as the main form of subsistence. **74**

hunting and gathering society type of society characterized by the daily collection of wild plants and the hunting of wild animals as the main form of subsistence. **73**

I unsocialized, spontaneous, self-interested component of the personality and self-identity. **109**

idealistic culture type of culture in Pitirim Sorokin's cyclical theory of social change that combines both ideational and sensate characteristics. **463** *See also* ideational culture; sensate culture.

ideal type description of the essential characteristics of some aspect of society. **14**

ideational culture type of culture in Pitirim Sorokin's cyclical theory of social change in which people seek truth and knowledge through faith or religion. **463**

ideology system of beliefs or ideas that justifies some social, moral, religious, political, or economic interests held by a social group or by society. **54**

incest taboo norm forbidding sexual relations or marriage between certain relatives. **302**

industrial societies type of society in which the mechanized production of goods is the main economic activity. **74**

infant mortality rate annual number of deaths among infants under one year of age per 1,000 live births in a population. **408**

informal group a group in which there is no official structure or established rules of conduct. **79**

informal sanction spontaneous expression of approval or disapproval given by an individual or individuals. **53**

information society a society in which the exchange of information is the main social and economic activity. **388**

in-group group that an individual belongs to and identifies with. **80** *See also* out-group.

instinct unchanging, biologically inherited behavior pattern. **98**

institutionalized discrimination discrimination that is an outgrowth of the structure of society. **239**

instrumental leaders leaders who are task-oriented. **81** *See also* leaders; expressive leaders.

interactionist perspective theoretical perspective that focuses on how individuals interact with one another in society. **17**

interest group organization that attempts to influence the political decision-making process. **342**

intergenerational mobility form of vertical mobility in which status differs between generations in the same family. **218**

internalization process by which a norm becomes a part of an individual's personality, thereby conditioning the individual to conform to society's expectations. **50**

iron law of oligarchy tendency of organizations to become increasingly dominated by small groups of people. **87**

junta authoritarian type of government in which political power has been seized from the previous government by force. **338**

kinship network of people who are related by marriage, birth, or adoption. **296**

knowledge gap hypothesis as new information enters society, wealthy and better-educated members acquire it at a faster rate than poor and less-educated people. **394**

labeling theory theory that focuses on how individuals come to be labeled as deviant. **185**

labor force all individuals 16 and older who are employed in paid positions or who are seeking paid employment. **157**

laissez-faire capitalism pure form of capitalism in which the government does not interfere in the economy. **326**

language organization of written and spoken symbols into a standardized system. **25**

late adulthood third and last era of adulthood, spanning ages 65 and over. **150**

latent function unintended and unrecognized consequence of some element of society. **16**

law of demand principle that states that the demand for a product increases as the price of the product decreases and demand decreases as price increases. **325**

law of supply principle that states that producers will supply more products when they can charge higher prices and fewer products when they must charge lower prices. **325**

laws written rules of conduct that are enacted and enforced by the government. By definition, the violation of these norms is considered a criminal act. **27**

leaders people who influence the attitudes and opinions of others. **81** *See also* expressive leaders; instrumental leaders.

legal discrimination discrimination that is upheld by law. **239**

legitimacy right of those people in power to control, or govern, others. **334**

life chances likelihood individuals have of sharing in the opportunities and benefits of society. **223**

life expectancy average number of years a person born in a particular year can be expected to live. **223, 408**

life structure combination of statuses, roles, activities, goals, values, beliefs, and life circumstances that characterize an individual. **150**

looking-glass self interactive process by which we develop an image of ourselves based on how we imagine we appear to others. **107**

Malthusian theory theory of population proposed by Thomas Malthus, in which population increases geometrically and the food supply increases arithmetically. Because the food supply cannot keep up with the expanding population, Malthus predicted widespread starvation would result. **415**

managed-care the use of health-insurance plans to help control health care costs. **281**

manifest function intended and recognized consequence of some element of society. **14**

marriage set of norms that specify the ways in which family structure should be organized. **297**

mass hysteria unfounded anxiety shared by people who are scattered over a wide geographic area. **439**

mass media newspapers, magazines, books, television, radio, films, and other forms of communication that reach large audiences without personal contact between the individuals sending the information and those receiving it. **113, 386**

master status status that plays the greatest role in shaping a person's life and determining his or her social identity. **66**

material culture physical objects created by human groups. Sociologists and anthropologists use the term *artifacts* to refer to the physical objects of material culture. **24**

matriarchy a family in which the mother holds most of the authority. **302**

matrilineal descent descent system in which kinship is traced through the mother's family. **301**

matrilocality residential pattern in which a newly married couple are expected to live near or with the wife's parents. **300**

Matthew effect tendency for honors and recognition to go to those scientists who have already achieved recognition. On the other hand, they tend to be withheld from scientists who have not yet made their mark. **383**

me part of the identity that is aware of the expectations and attitudes of society; the socialized self. **109**

mechanical solidarity close-knit social relationships common in preindustrial societies that result when a small group of people share the same values and perform the same tasks. **77** *See also* organic solidarity.

media convergence the idea that mass media are merging and are no longer separate entities. **391**

Medicaid state and federally funded health-insurance program for people with little or no money. **275**

Medicare government-sponsored insurance plan for elderly or disabled persons. **275**

mentor someone who fosters an individual's development by believing in the person, sharing the person's dreams, and helping the person achieve those dreams. **152**

middle adulthood second era of adulthood, spanning the ages 40 through 59. **150**

middle-old people aged 75 to 84. **165**

migration movement of people from one specified area to another. **409**

migration rate annual difference between in-migration and out-migration. **409**

minority group category of people who share physical characteristics or cultural practices that result in the group being denied equal treatment. **235**

mob emotionally charged collectivity whose members are united by a specific, and often violent, goal. **438**

modernization process by which a society's social institutions become increasingly complex as the society moves toward industrialization. **471**

modernization theory theory of modernization that argues that the more-developed nations of the world were the first to modernize because they were the first to industrialize. **471**

monarchy type of government in which one person rules. In a monarchy, the ruler comes to power through inheritance. **337**

monogamy marriage of one man to one woman. **297**

monotheism belief in one god. **365**

moral panic phenomenon that occurs when people become fearful about behavior that appears to threaten society's core values. **439**

mores (MORE-ayz) norms that have great moral significance attached to them. **27**

mortality number of deaths in a society. **408**

multinational a corporation that has factories and offices in several countries. **330**

multiple-nuclei model model of urban structure proposed by Chauncey Harris and Edward Ullman in which the city is said to have a number of specialized centers devoted to different types of land use. **426**

narcissism extreme self-centeredness. **48**

negative sanction sanction in the form of a punishment or the threat of punishment. **51** *See also* sanction; positive sanction.

neolocality residential pattern in which a newly married couple is free to set up their residence apart from both sets of parents. **301**

nonmaterial culture abstract human creations, such as language, ideas, beliefs, rules, skills, family patterns, work practices, and political and economic systems. **24**

norms shared rules of conduct that tell people how to act in specific situations. **26**

novice phase term proposed by Daniel Levinson and his colleagues for the first three stages of the early adulthood era. **151**

nuclear family family form that consists of one or both parents and their children. **296**

objective method technique used to rank individuals according to social class in which sociologists define social class in terms of factors such as income, occupation, and education. **215**

old-old people aged 85 and older. **165**

oligopoly situation that exists when a few people control an industry. **328**

opinion leaders respected individuals in the community. **397**

organic solidarity impersonal social relationships, common in industrial societies, that arise with increased job specialization. **77** *See also* mechanical solidarity.

organized skepticism a norm in scientific research in which no scientific finding or theory is exempt from questioning. **379**

out-group any group that an individual does not belong to or identify with. **80** *See also* in-group.

overurbanization situation in which more people live in the city than the city can support in terms of jobs and facilities. **424**

panic spontaneous and uncoordinated group action to escape some perceived threat. **439**

paradigm set of shared concepts, methods, and assumptions that make up the scientific reality at any point in time. **385**

pastoral society type of society characterized by a reliance on domesticated herd animals as the main form of subsistence. **73**

patriarchy system in which men are dominant over women. **265, 302**

patrilineal descent descent pattern in which kinship is traced through the father's family. **301**

patrilocality residential pattern in which a newly married couple is expected to live with or near the husband's parents. **300**

peer group primary group composed of individuals of roughly equal age and social characteristics. **112**

peripheral nations according to the world-system theory of modernization, those less developed nations that are economically dependent on the core, or more developed, societies. **473** *See also* core nations.

personality sum total of behaviors, attitudes, beliefs, and values that are characteristic of an individual. **98**

plea bargaining process of legal negotiation that allows an accused person to plead guilty to a lesser charge in return for a lighter sentence. **195**

pluralist model model in which the political process in the United States is said to be controlled by interest groups that compete with one another for power. **345**

police discretion the power held by police officers to decide who is actually arrested. **194**

political institution system of roles and norms that governs the distribution and exercise of power in society. **334**

political party organization that seeks to gain power in the government through legitimate means. **339**

political science study of the organization and operation of governments. **8**

polyandry form of polygamy in which a woman is permitted to marry more than one man at a time. **300**

polygamy marriage with multiple partners. **297**

polygyny form of polygamy in which a man is permitted to marry more than one woman at a time. **300**

polytheism belief in a number of gods. **365**

population number of people living in an area at a particular time. **406**

population pyramid graphic representation of the age and sex distribution of a population. **412**

positive sanction sanction in the form of a reward. **50** *See also* negative sanction; sanction.

postindustrial society type of society in which economic activity centers on the production of information and the provision of services. **77**

poverty standard of living that is below the minimum level considered decent and reasonable by society. **221**

poverty level minimum annual income needed by a family to survive. **221**

power ability to control the behavior of others, with or without their consent. **209, 334**

power-elite model model in which political power in the United States is said to be exercised by and for the privileged few in society. **345**

preindustrial society type of society in which food production—carried out through the use of human and animal labor—is the main economic activity. **73**

prejudice unsupported generalization about a category of people. **238**

prestige respect, honor, recognition, or courtesy an individual receives from other members of society. **209**

primary deviance nonconformity undetected by authority in which the individuals who commit deviant acts do not consider themselves to be deviant, and neither does society. **185** *See also* deviance; secondary deviance.

primary group small group of people who interact over a relatively long period of time on a direct and personal basis. **79** *See also* secondary group.

primary sector sector of the economy that deals with the extraction of raw materials from the environment. **323** *See also* secondary sector; tertiary sector.

principle of immanent change according to Pitirim Sorokin's cyclical theory of social change, the natural tendency of a society's structure to swing back and forth between and ideational and sensate culture. **464** *See also* ideational culture; sensate culture.

profane anything considered to be part of the ordinary world and thus commonplace and familiar. **362**

profession high-status occupation that requires specialized skills obtained through formal education. **157**

proletariat workers in a capitalist society who sell their labor in exchange for wages. **208**

propaganda organized and deliberate attempt to shape public opinion. **442**

proportional representation system in which a party receives a number of seats in government related to the popular votes they receive. **341**

protectionism use of trade barriers to protect domestic manufacturers from foreign competition. **330**

psychology science that deals with the behavior and thinking of organisms. **7**

puberty physical maturing that makes an individual capable of sexual reproduction. **120**

public group of geographically scattered people who are interested in and divided by some issue. **442**

public opinion collection of differing attitudes that members of a public have about a particular issue. **442** *See also* public.

race category of people who share inherited physical characteristics and who are perceived by others as being a distinct group. **232**

racial profiling the practice of assuming nonwhite Americans are more likely to commit crimes than white Americans. **195**

racism belief that one's own race or ethnic group is naturally superior to other races or ethnic groups. **240**

rationality the process of subjecting every feature of human behavior to calculation, measurement, and control. **83**

rational-legal authority power that is legitimated by formal rules and regulations. **335**

reactionary movements social movement with a goal to reverse current social trends. **449**

recidivism repeated criminal behavior. **195**

reciprocal roles corresponding roles that define the patterns of interaction between related statuses. **67**

reciprocity idea that if you do something for someone, they owe you something in return. **69**

reference group any group with whom individuals identify and whose attitudes and values they often adopt. **80**

reformulation the process of adapting borrowed cultural traits. **57**

relative deprivation theory theory that states that certain people have a lesser portion of social rewards compared to other people or groups. **452**

religion system of roles and norms organized around the sacred realm that binds people together in social groups. **362**

religiosity importance of religion in a person's life. **370**

reputational method technique used to rank individuals according to social class. This is done by asking individuals in the community to rank other community members based on what they know of their characters and life-styles. **214**

resocialization break with past experiences and the learning of new values and norms. **115**

resource mobilization the organization and effective use of resources as essential to social movements. **454**

resource-mobilization theory theory of social movements that states that even the most ill-treated group with the most just cause will not be able to bring about change without resources. **454**

revisionary movements social movements that try to improve or revise some part of society through social change. **450**

revolutionary movements type of social movement, the goal of which is a total and radical change of the existing social structure. **450**

riot crowd that erupts in generalized destructive behavior, the purpose of which is social disorder. **438**

ritual established pattern of behavior through which a group of believers experience the sacred. **364**

role behavior—the rights and obligations—expected of someone occupying a particular status. **66**

role conflict situation that occurs when fulfilling the expectations of one role makes it difficult to fulfill the expectations of another role. **68**

role expectations socially determined behaviors expected of a person performing a role. **67**

role performance actual behavior of a person performing a role. **67**

role set different roles attached to a single status. **68**

role strain situation that occurs when a person has difficulty meeting the expectations of a single role. **68**

role-taking taking or pretending to take the role of others. **108**

rumor unverified piece of information that is spread rapidly from one person to another. **441**

S

sacred anything that is considered to be part of the supernatural world and that inspires awe, respect, and reverence. **362**

sanctions rewards or punishments used to enforce conformity to norms. **50** *See also* formal sanction; informal sanction; negative sanction; positive sanction.

sandwich generation Americans caught between the needs of their children and their aging parents. **313**

scapegoating practice of placing blame for one's troubles on an innocent individual or group. **240**

school choice a broad movement to provide alternatives to public school systems to which parents can choose to send their children. **358**

schooling instruction by specially trained teachers who follow officially recognized policies. **350**

science pursuit of knowledge through systematic methods. **376**

scientific method objective, logical, and systematic way of collecting empirical data and arriving at conclusions. **377**

secondary deviance nonconformity that results in the individuals who commit acts of secondary deviance being labeled as deviant and accepting that label as true. **185** *See also* deviance; primary deviance.

secondary group group in which interaction is impersonal and temporary in nature. **79** *See also* primary group.

secondary sector sector of the economy that concentrates on the use of raw materials to manufacture goods. **323** *See also* primary sector; tertiary sector.

second shift the phenomenon of individuals having to complete household duties after working away from home. **270**

sect relatively small religious organization that typically has split off from a denomination because of doctrinal differences. **366**

sector model model of urban structure proposed by Homer Hoyt in which the growth of a city is said to occur in wedge-shaped sectors that extend outward from the center to the edge of the city. **426**

secular non-religious. **370**

segregation physical separation of a minority group from the dominant group. **243**

self conscious awareness of possessing a distinct identity that separates us from other members of society. **107**

self-fulfilling prophecy prediction that results in behavior that makes the prediction come true. **239**

self-fulfillment commitment to the full development of one's personality, talents, and potential. **46**

semiperipheral nations according to the world-system theory of modernization, nations which are between core nations and peripheral nations in terms of industrialization and level of exports. **473**

sensate culture type of culture in Pitirim Sorokin's cyclical theory of social change in which people seek knowledge through science. **463** *See also* idealistic culture; ideational culture.

sexism belief that one sex is by nature superior to the other. **265**

shamanism belief system in which spirits communicate only with one person acknowledged as a specialist. **365**

significant others specific people, such as parents, brothers, sisters, other relatives, and friends, who have a direct influence on our socialization. **108**

slavery ownership of one group of people by another group. **244**

small group group with few enough numbers that everyone is able to interact on a face-to-face basis. **78**

social capital social networks and the reciprocal norms associated with these networks that encourage people to do things for each other. **396**

social category group of people who share a common trait or status. **78**

social change alterations in various aspects of a society over time. **462**

social class grouping of people with similar levels of wealth, power, and prestige. **208**

social control enforcing of norms through either internalization or sanctions. **53**

social Darwinism perspective that holds that societies evolve toward stability and perfection. **11**

social gerontology subfield of gerontology that studies the nonphysical aspects of aging. **164**

social inequality unequal sharing of social rewards and resources. **206**

social institution system of statuses, roles, values, and norms that is organized to satisfy one or more of the basic needs of society. **68**

social integration degree of attachments people have to social groups or to society. **141**

social interaction how people relate to one another and influence each other's behavior. **4**

socialism economic model in which the factors of production are owned by the government, which regulates all economic activity. **325**

socialization interactive process through which individuals learn the basic skills, values, beliefs, and behavior patterns of society. **107**

social mobility movement between or within social classes or strata. **217**

social movement long-term conscious effort to promote or prevent social change. **54, 449**

social network web of relationships that is formed by the sum total of an individual's interactions with other people. **80**

social phenomena an observable fact or event that involves the human society. **4**

social psychology study of how an individual's behavior and personality are affected by the social environment. **8**

social sciences related disciplines that study various aspects of human social behavior. **7**

social stratification ranking of individuals or categories of people on the basis of unequal access to scarce resources and social rewards. **206**

social structure network of interrelated statuses and roles that guides human interaction. **66**

society group of mutually interdependent people who have organized in such a way as to share a common culture and have a feeling of unity. **24**

sociobiology systematic study of the biological basis of all social behavior. **98**

socioeconomic status (SES) rating that combines social factors such as level of education, occupational prestige, and place of residence with the economic factor of income in order to determine an individual's relative position in the stratification system. **211**

sociological imagination ability to see the connection between the larger world and our personal lives. **5**

sociological perspective a viewing of the behavior of groups in a systematic way. **4**

sociology social science that studies human society and social behavior. **4**

sociology of science sociological perspective that examines how scientific knowledge develops. **376**

spiral of silence belief that as more people accept common opinions the people who disagree are less likely to voice their views. **397**

state primary political authority in society. **334**

status socially defined position in a group or in a society. **66** *See also* achieved status; ascribed status; master status.

stereotype oversimplified, exaggerated, or unfavorable generalization about a category of people. **239**

stigma mark of social disgrace that sets the deviant apart from the rest of society. **177**

strain theory theory of deviant behavior that views deviance as the natural outgrowth of the values, norms, and structure of society. **180**

subcultural theory theory of city life in which the characteristics of the city are said to encourage rather than discourage the formation of primary group relationships. **431**

subculture group with its own unique values, norms, and behaviors that exists within a larger culture. **38**

subjective method technique used to rank individuals according to social class in which the individuals themselves are asked to determine their own social rank. **215**

subjugation maintaining of control over a group through force. **244**

subsistence strategies ways in which a society uses technology to provide for the needs of its members. **73**

suffrage the right to vote. **268**

symbol anything that stands for something else and has a shared meaning attached to it. Language, gestures, images, sounds, physical objects, events, and elements of the natural world can serve as symbols as long as people recognize that they convey a particular meaning. **17**

symbolic interaction interaction between people that takes place through the use of symbols. **17**

techniques of neutralization suspending moral beliefs to commit deviant acts. **185**

technology knowledge and tools people use for practical purposes. **24, 56**

terrorism use of threatened or actual violence in the pursuit of political goals. **191**

tertiary sector sector of the economy that concentrates on the provision of services. **323** *See also* primary sector; secondary sector.

theism belief in a god or gods. **365**

theoretical perspective general set of assumptions about the nature of phenomena. In the case of sociology, a theoretical perspective outlines certain assumptions about the nature of social life. **14**

theory systematic explanation of the relationship among phenomena. **14**

total institution setting in which people are isolated from the rest of society for a set period of time and subjected to the control of officials of varied ranks. **115**

totalitarianism most extreme form of authoritarian government. Under totalitarianism, government leaders accept few limits on their authority. **327**

totemism belief in a kinship between humans and animals or natural objects. **365**

tracking assignment of students to different types of educational programs. **353**

traditional authority power that is legitimated by long-standing customs. **334**

transfer payments principal way in which the government attempts to reduce social inequality by redistributing money among various segments of society. **226**

triad three-person group. **78**

unemployment situation that occurs when people do not have jobs but are actively seeking employment. **157**

unemployment rate percentage of the civilian labor force that is unemployed but actively seeking employment. **157**

universalism a norm in scientific research that holds that research should be judged solely on the basis of quality. **379**

urban anomie theory theory of city life in which the city is seen to be an anonymous and unfriendly place that carries serious negative consequences for those who live there. **428**

urban ecology approach that examines the relationship between people and the urban environment. **425**

urban legends stories that are untrue but that seem realistic and teach a lesson. **441**

urban sprawl phenomenon characterized by poorly planned development on the edge of cities and towns. **428**

urbanization concentration of the population in cities. **76, 421**

Value-added theory theory that explains crowd behavior as a process that moves from step to step. **447**

values shared beliefs about what is good or bad, right or wrong, desirable or undesirable. **25**

vertical mobility movement between social classes or strata in which the individual moves from one social-class level to another. **217**

Vestehen empathetic understanding of the meanings others attach to their actions. **14**

voluntary association nonprofit association formed to pursue some common interest. **83**

voluntary childlessness conscious choice to remain childless. **313**

wage gap the level of women's income relative to that of men. **269**

wealth most obvious dimension of social stratification because it is made up of the value of everything the person owns and money earned through salaries and wages. **208**

white-collar crime crime that is committed by an individual or individuals of high social status in the course of their professional lives. **192**

white ethnics collective reference to immigrants from the predominantly Catholic countries of Ireland, Italy, France, Poland, and Greece. **256**

women's movement social movement that supported the idea that the sexes are socially, politically, and economically equal. **268**

world-system theory theory of modernization, by Immanuel Wallerstein, in which the spread of capitalism is seen as producing an international division of labor between more-developed and less-developed nations. According to this view, the more-developed nations control the factors of production and the less-developed nations serve as sources of cheap labor and raw materials. **473**

young-old people aged 65 to 74. **165**

zero population growth point at which nearly equal birthrates and death rates produce a growth rate of zero. **417**

zero tolerance a set of policies created to prevent school violence. **361**

Index

G

Galileo, 385
Gambia, 408
gambling, 192
games: in childhood, 109
Gandhi, Mohandas, 335
gangs: and drug-related crime, 137; and violence, *f178*; in the United States, *f178*; why young people join, 178
Garfinkel, Harold, 185
gatekeepers, 397;
gay rights movement, 56
Gemeinschaft, 77
gender, 262–67; definition of, 262; expectations, 262–65; inequality, 265; roles, 262–65; and sports, *p264*
gender identity, 263
gender roles: cross-cultural variations, 263; definition of, 262; socialization, 263–65
generalized other, 108
Generation 2001, *f47*
Genie, 103, 106, 117
genocide, 244
Genovese, Kitty, 429
gentrification. *See* urbanization.
German Americans, 247
Germany, 247
gerontologist, 275
gerontology, 164; *See also* social gerontology.
Gesellschaft, 77
Gilbert, James, 139
Glenn, John, *p272*
globalization. *See* economy.
Goals 2000, 358
Goffman, Erving, 177
gonorrhea, 137
Gore, Al, 343
Gottfredson, Michael, 184
Gottman, Jean, *m424*
government: absolute monarchy, 338; authoritarianism, 338, authoritarian systems, 338–39; constitutional monarchy, 337; democracy, 337; democratic socialism, 338; democratic systems, 337; dictatorship, 338; junta, 338; monarchy, 337; totalitarianism, 338; types of, 335, 337–39, versus state, 335
Graber, Doris, 393
"graying of America," 273–74, *c274*
Gray Panthers, 171
Great Britain: constitutional monarchy, 337; race relations in, *f241*
Great Depression, *p8*
Greece, 376
Greeks: ancient, 387
group relationships: as continuum, 78–81, *c79*; in formal organizations, 83

groups, 73, *p78*, 78–81; in contrast to aggregates, 78; in contrast to social category, 78; definition of, 73; dyad, 78; features of group structure, 78; formal, 79; informal, 79; in-group, 80, *p80*; organization as feature of, 79; out-group, 80; as part of social network, 80; primary, 79; reference, 83; requirements for, 79; secondary, 79–80; size as feature of, 78; small, 78; time as feature of, 79; triad, 78; types of, 78–81
growth rate, 410, 412, *c412*; definition of, 410; and doubling time, 412, *c412*
Guatemala, 417
Gutenburg, Johannes, 87
Gypsies: and the Nazi Holocaust, 246

H

hallucinogens, 137, *c138*
handguns, 190
Harijans, 207
Harris, Chauncy, 426
Harris, Marvin, 36
hashish, 137–138, *c138*, 140
Hawthorne study, 86
health, health care, 280–87; access to, 283; cost of, 280–81, *c281*; for the elderly, 283; government-sponsored, 285; insurance, 283, *m284*, 285; online, *f282*; politics, 285; of the poor, 223, 283–84; in the United States, 223
Heaven's Gate, 366
Henslin, James, 46
hereditary chieftainship, 74
hereditary monarchy, 74
heredity, 98–100; definition of, 98; nature versus nurture debate, 98–99;
heroin, 137–138, *c138*, 141
hidden curriculum, 353; definition of, 353
Hinduism, Hindus, *p35*, 36, 246, 362, 363, 367, 369
hippie movement, 39
Hirschi, Travis, 182, 184
Hispanics: and bilingual education, 361; breakdown by area of origin, 248, *c248*; characteristics of, 249; and divorce, 309; and educational attainment, 248, 354; illegal immigrants among, 159, 248; occupations among, *c249*; political power among, 248; poverty among, 222, *c223*, 224; unemployment among, 248; voter participation of, 344
history, 8
Hitler, Adolf, 338, 339
HIV. *See* acquired immune deficiency syndrome.
Holocaust, 246
homeschooling, 360
homogamy, 129; definition of, 129
Hopkins, Rodney W., 143
horizontal mobility, 217
Horowitz, Irving Lewis, 211
horticultural societies: characteristics of, 74; definition of, 74
housing: for the poor, 226

international terrorism, 191; responding to, *f446*, September 11, 2001, attacks, 58, 191, 446

tertiary sector, 323-25; definition of, 323

testimonials technique: in propaganda, 442

theism, 365

theoretical perspective, 14, 16–17; definition of, 14; *See also* conflict perspective; functionalist perspective; interactionist perspective.

theory, 14; compositional, 430; conflict, 16, 468–69; contagion, 446; cultural-transmission, 184; cyclical, 462; definition of, 14; demographic transition, 416; emergent-norm, 447; equilibrium, 466; evolutionary, 464; exchange, 69, *p69*; labeling, 185; Malthusian, 415; modernization, 471–73; resource-mobilization, 454–55; social learning, 110–11; structural-strain, 448; urban anomie, 428; world-system, 473

Thomas, W. I., 239, 383

Thoreau, David, 369

Tibet, 104

Tichner, Phillip, 394

Tiger, Lionel, 65, 110

"timid bigot," 240

To Dwell Among Friends, 431

total institution: as agent of socialization, 115; definition of, 115; resocialization and, 115

totalitarianism, 7, 338

toxic pollution, 192

tracking: in schools, 353–54

trade barriers, 330

traditional authority, 334–35; definition of, 334

tranquilizers, *c138*

transfer payments: definition of, 226

transfer technique: in propaganda, 446

triad, 78

Trobriand Islanders, 135

Turkey, 243

Turks, 243, 246

Turner, Ralph, 447

Tydings-McDuffie Act, 251

Uganda, 101, 244

Ullman, Edward, 426

underclass, 217

unemployment: among African Americans, *c157*; definition of, 157; among Hispanics, *c157*; among men, *c157*; among women, *c157*; *See also* unemployment rate.

unemployment rate, 157, *c157*; definition of, 157

Uniform Crime Reports, 187

United Kingdom. *See* Great Britain.

United States: aging of population, 273; AIDS, 286–87; birthrate in, *c407*, 410; cities in, 422, 424; crime in, 137; cultural pluralism in, 242; death rate in, *c407*; disabled person in, 276–77; discrimination in, 272; distribution of wealth in, 208–09; divorce in, 309; economy of , 327–33; educational

reform in, 356, 358; energy policy, 58, 61; equality under the law, 45; family life in, 215–17, 310–17; food consumption in, 59; gangs in, *f178*; growth rate in, 410; health in, 280–84; health care in, 280–84; immigration policies, 250–51; infant mortality rate in, *c407*; interest groups in, 342, 344; issues in education, 356–61; marital status in, *c311*; marriage and courtship in, 310–17; as a "melting pot", 352; minority groups in, 247–57; policies toward Native Americans, 37; political system, 339–45; population distribution, *c410*; population pyramid, *c413*; as postindustrial society, 77; poverty in, 221–22; production of goods in, 77; religion in, 367–71; social class in, 214–20, *c214*; social mobility in, 217–18; voter participation in, 344, *c344*

United States Bureau of Labor Statistics, 161

United States Department of Agriculture, 221, 453

universalism, 379

upper class: in the United States, 214, *c214*, 216

upper-middle class: in the United States, 214, *c214*, 216

urban anomie theory: of city life, 428

urban ecology, 425–26, 428; concentric zone model, 425–26, *c425*; definition of, 425; multiple-nuclei model, 426; overurbanization, 424; sector model, 426; *See also* cities.

urbanization, 9, 76, 421; urban issues, *f427*

urban legends, 441

urban renewal, 427

urban sociology, 428

urban sprawl, 428

Uses of Enchantment: The Meaning and Importance of Fairy Tales, 114

Utes, 37

vagrancy, 192

Vaishyas, 207

value-added theory, 447

values, 25–26; American, 44–46, 48; as component of culture, 25; definition of, 25; as source of social change, 4, 56

V-chip. *See* mass media.

Veblen, Thorstein, 216, 219

Verstehen, 14

vertical mobility, 217

vested interests: as source of resistance to social change, 61

victimless crime, 192

Vietnamese Americans, 250; *See also* Asian Americans.

violent crime, 3, 190, 360–61

virtual communities, *f467*

voluntary association, 83

voluntary childlessness, 313

volunteers, 171

vote, voting, 56, 339, *c342*, *c344*, 344

Voting Rights Act, 56, 243, 469

vouchers, 358, 359

Acknowledgments

For permission to reprint copyrighted material, grateful acknowledgment is made to the following sources:

Academic Press, Inc., a division of Harcourt, Inc.: From *Genie: A Psycholinguistic Study of a Modern-Day "Wild Child"* by Susan Curtiss. Copyright © 1977 by Academic Press, Inc.

American Sociological Association: "The American Sociological Association Code of Ethics." Copyright © 1999 by American Sociological Association.

The Associated Press: From "Study Finds Rise in Signs of Eating Disorders after TV Comes to Fiji" by Alexis Chiu from *AP Online*, May 19, 1999. Copyright © 1999 by The Associated Press. From "Serious Crimes Fall for the 8th Consecutive Year" from *The New York Times*, May 8, 2000. Copyright © 2000 by The Associated Press. From "Booming 1990s Still Left Large Pockets of Poverty in South, Midwest, Despite Overall Improvements" by Genaro C. Armas from *AP Online*, December 19, 2001. Copyright © 2001 by The Associated Press.

Brooks/Cole, an imprint of the Wadsworth Group, a division of Thomson Learning: From "Social Classes in the United States" from *The American Class Structure in an Age of Growing Inequality: A New Synthesis*, 5th edition, by Dennis Gilbert. Copyright © 1998 by Dennis Gilbert.

Carnegie Endowment for International Peace, Washington, DC (http://www.ceip.org/pubs): From "Aiding Democracy Abroad: The Learning Curve" (page 6) by Thomas Carothers. Copyright © 1999 by Carnegie Endowment for International Peace.

Chicago Tribune Company: From "Report Finds Girls Shun Computers" by Lisa Anderson from *Chicago Tribune*, April 12, 2000. Copyright © 2000 by Chicago Tribune Company. From "Backers Seek End to Government Gathering of Data" by V. Dion Haynes from *Chicago Tribune*, December 26, 2001. Copyright © 2001 by Chicago Tribune Company.

Common Cause: From summary table on *Common Cause* website, accessed December 14, 2001, at http://www.commoncause.org/publications/erefor/summary.htm. Copyright © 2001 by Common Cause.

Don Congdon Associates, Inc.: From *The Martian Chronicles* by Ray Bradbury. Copyright 1950, renewed © 1977 by Ray Bradbury.

CQ Press, a division of Congressional Quarterly Inc.: From "The Role of Religious Lobbies" by Allen D. Hertzke from *Religion in American Politics*, edited by Charles W. Dunn. Copyright © 1989 by Congressional Quarterly Inc.

Dutton, A Member of Penguin Group (USA) Inc.: From *Passages: Predictable Crises of Adult Life* by Gail Sheehy. Copyright © 1974, 1976 by Gail Sheehy.

The Feminist Press at The City University of New York, www.feministpress.org: From *Families As We Are: Conversations from Around the World* by Perdita Huston. Copyright © 2001 by Perdita Huston.

Robert L. Fizzell: From "What Do We Mean by 'Alternative Education?'" by Robert L. Fizzell from *OAAE Newsletter*, Fall 1999. Copyright © 1999 by Oregon Association for Alternatives in Education.

The Free Press, a division of Simon & Schuster: Adapted from "Structural Strain Theory of Deviance" from *Social Theory and Social Structure* by Robert K. Merton. Copyright 1957 by The Free Press; renewed © 1985 by Robert K. Merton.

The Gallup Organization, Inc.: "Job Satisfaction Polls 1989 and 1999" and "Public Opinion on the Environment Polls 1990, 1995 and 1999" by The Gallup Organization. Copyright © 2000 by The Gallup Organization, Inc.

Harcourt, Inc.: From *Middletown: A Study in Contemporary American Culture* by Robert S. Lynd and Helen Merrell Lynd. Copyright 1929 by Harcourt, Inc. and renewed © 1957 by Robert S. and Helen M. Lynd.

Henry Holt and Company, LLC: From "The Authoritarian Character" from *Escape from Freedom* by Erich Fromm. Copyright 1941 and renewed © 1969 by Erich Fromm.

Inter-University Consortium for Political and Social Research: From survey "Prestige Ratings for Selected Occupations in the United States" from *General Social Survey Cumulative File*, 1972–1986, James A. Davis and Tom W. Smith, Chief Investigators. Copyright © 1986 by National Opinion Research Center.

Lancaster Mennonite Historical Society, 2215 Millstream Road, Lancaster, PA 17602-1499, www.lmhs.org: From "Social Change Among the Amish in Eight Communities" by Jerry Savells from *Pennsylvania Mennonite Heritage*, vol. 13, no. 3, July 1990. Copyright © 1990 by Lancaster Mennonite Historical Society.

Arturo Madrid: From "Being 'The Other': Ethnic Diversity in a Changing Society" by Arturo Madrid from *Academe*, Bulletin of the American Association of University Professors, vol. 76, no. 6, November-December 1990, page 17. Copyright © 1988 by Arturo Madrid.

Gregory Mantsios: From "Media Magic: Making Class Invisible" by Gregory Mantsios from *Race, Class, and Gender in the United States*, Third Edition, edited by Paula S. Rothenberg. Copyright © 1995 by Gregory Mantsios.

Motion Picture Association: From survey "Frequency of Movie-Going Among Total Public Age 12 & Over" from *Motion Picture Association* website, accessed February 19, 2002, at http://www.mpaa.org/useconomicreview/2000AttendanceStudy/sld003.htm. Copyright © 2002 by Motion Picture Association.

The Nation Company, L.P.: From "Governing the Genome" by Ralph Brave from *The Nation*, December 10, 2001. Copyright © 2001 by the Nation Company, L.P.

The New York Times Company: From "Problems Seen For Teenagers Who Hold Jobs" by Stephen Greenhouse from *The New York Times*, January 29, 2001. Copyright © 2001 by The New York Times Company.

W. W. Norton & Company, Inc.: From *Freedom Bound: A History of America's Civil Rights Movement* by Robert Weisbrot. Copyright © 1990 by Robert Weisbrot.

Oxford University Press, Inc.: From *The Sociological Imagination* by C. Wright Mills. Copyright © 2000 by Oxford University Press, Inc.

Pearson Education: From "The 100 Percent American" from *The Study of Man: An Introduction* by Ralph Linton. Copyright 1936 and renewed © 1964 by Prentice-Hall, Inc.

Perseus Books Publishers, a member of Perseus Books, L.L.C.: From *Corporate Cultures: The Rites and Rituals of Corporate Life* by Terrence Deal and Allan Kennedy. Copyright © 1982 by Addison-Wesley Publishing Company, Inc.

Population Reference Bureau: "Children Living with Their Grandparents" and "Intergroup Couples, 1998" from *Population Reference Bureau Reports on America*. Copyright © 1999 by Population Reference Bureau.

Primedia Special Interest Publications–History Group: From "Night of the Martians" by Edward Oxford from *American History Illustrated*, October 1988. Copyright © 1988 by American History Illustrated.

Time Inc.: From "Megacities" by Eugene Linden from *Time*, January 11, 1993. Copyright © 1993 by Time Inc. From "The Global Village Finally Arrives" by Pico Iyer from *Time*, December 12, 1993. Copyright © 1993 by Time Inc.

U.S. Army and Army Reserve: Trademarked recruiting slogan "Be All You Can Be."® for the United States Army.

Veronis Suhler Stevenson: From "Forecast of Media Consumption, 2000" from *Veronis Suhler Communications Industry Forecast*, 15th edition, 2001. Copyright © 2001 by Veronis Suhler Stevenson.

McKenzie Wark: From "Cyberpunk: From Subculture to Mainstream" by McKenzie Wark. Copyright © 1992 by McKenzie Wark.

The Washington Post: From "Aging Americans Are Staying Healthier, Study Finds" by Ceci Connolly from *The Washington Post*, May 9, 2000. Copyright © 2000 by The Washington Post. From "Married-With-Children Still Fading" by D'Vera Cohn from *The Washington Post*, May 15, 2001. Copyright © 2001 by The Washington Post.

Waveland Press, Inc.: From "Holy Beef, U.S.A." from *Good to Eat: Riddles of Food and Culture* by Marvin Harris. Copyright © 1985 by Marvin Harris. Published by Waveland Press, Inc., Prospect Heights, IL, 1985; reissued 1998. All rights reserved.

John Wiley & Sons, Inc.: From "Virtual Communities" by Howard Rheingold from *The Community of the Future*, edited by Frances Hesselbein, Marshall Goldsmith, Richard Bechard, and Richard F. Schubert. Copyright © 1998 by The Peter F. Drucker Foundation for Nonprofit Management.

World Health Organization, Geneva, Switzerland: From "Regional HIV/AIDS Statistics and Features, End of 1999" from *World Health Organization* website, accessed February 19, 2002, at http://www.who.int/HIV_AIDS/Overheads/wad00stats-E-13/sld010.htm. Copyright © 2002 by World Health Organization.

Sources Cited:

"Merton's Patterns of Prejudice and Discrimination" from *Discrimination and National Welfare*, edited by R. M. MacIver. Published by HarperCollins, New York, 1948.

From *Community Cohesion: A Report of the Independent Review Team*, commissioned by Her Majesty's Home Office (UK), accessed December, 2001, at http://www.nexuspub.com/july97/recycle.htm.

From Table 1 "Personality Type in Relation to Activity and Life Satisfaction (Age 70-79)" from "Personality and Patterns of Aging" by Bernice L. Neugarten, Robert J. Havighurst, and Sheldon S. Tobin from *Journal of Gerontology*, 1965.

From *The Peter Principle* by Laurence J. Peter. Published by William Morrow & Company, Inc., a division of HarperCollins Publishers, Inc., New York, 1969.

Quote by Jeffrey Passell from "As Labor Pool Shrinks, A New Supply is Tapped" by Louis Uchitelle from *The New York Times*, December 20, 1999.

Photo Credits

FRONTMATTER: TOC—Page iv (t), Sam Dudgeon/HRW Photo; iv (b), Galen Rowell/Corbis; v (t), Leif Skoogfors/Corbis; v (b), Christie's Images/Corbis; vi (t), Will Hart/PhotoEdit; vi (b), Ron Chapple/FPG International/Getty Images; vii (t), Jeff Greenberg/PhotoEdit; vii (b), Paul A. Souders/Corbis; viii (t), Morrison Photography; viii (b), Owen Franken/Corbis; ix (t), Branson Reynolds/Index Stock; ix (bl), Sam Dudgeon/HRW Photo; ix (br), The White House Collection, copyright White House Historical Association and The National Archives and Records Administration; x, Richard Stockton/Index Stock; xi (t), Elis Years/Getty Images/FPG International; xi (b), Inge Yspeert/Corbis; xii (t), Myrleen Ferguson Cate/PhotoEdit; xii (b), Morrison Photography; xiii (t), Spencer Grant/PhotoEdit; xiii (b), Jack Fields/Corbis; xiv, Kevin Fleming/CORBIS; xvi, CNN; xvii (c), Michael Newman/PhotoEdit; xvii (t), Walter Bibikow/Index Stock; xvii (b), Sam Dudgeon/HRW Photo; xviii, Sam Dudgeon/HRW Photo; HOW TO—xxiii, Sam Dudgeon/HRW Photo; xxvii, Sam Dudgeon/HRW Photo; SKILL HANDBOOK—S0 (t), EyeWire; S0 (b), Corbis Images; S1 (l), Charles & Josette Lenars/Corbis; S1 (tr), Earl & Nazima Kowall/Corbis; S1 (bl), Rodney White/AP Photo; S2 (tl), Corbis-Bettmann; S2 (bl), AFP/Corbis; S2 (br), Ted Spiegel/Corbis; S3 (tl), Catherine Karnow/Corbis; S3 (br), Sam Dudgeon/HRW Photo; S3 (tr) AFP/Corbis; S4 (t), Sam Dudgeon/HRW Photo; S4 (b), PhotoDisc; S5 (tl), David Young-Wolff/PhotoEdit; S5 (b), The Granger Collection, New York; S6, Victoria Smith/HRW Photo; S7, Sam Dudgeon/HRW Photo; S8 (t), Corbis Images; S8 (c), Sam Dudgeon/HRW Photo; S10 (t), Corbis Images; S10 (b), Myrleen Ferguson Cate/PhotoEdit; S10 (c), Victoria Smith/HRW Photo; S11, PhotoDisc; S14, Sam Dudgeon/HRW Photo; S16, Victoria Smith/HRW Photo; S18, Sandy Felsenthal/Corbis; S19, Joseph Sohm; ChromoSohm Inc./Corbis; S20, Bettmann/Corbis; S22, Rhoda Sidney/PhotoEdit; S23, David Young-Wolff/PhotoEdit.

UNIT 1: Page 1, Mark Gibson Photography; 92, David Rubinger/Corbis; 93 (b), Sam Dudgeon/HRW Photo.

CHAPTER 1: Page 2, Pablo Corral V/Corbis; 3, Sam Dudgeon/HRW Photo; 4, Gail Mooney/Corbis; 5 (t), David H. Wells/Corbis; 5 (cl), Bob Krist/Corbis; 7, Charles & Josette Lenars/Corbis; 8, Corbis; 9, Leonard de Selva/Corbis; 10, Hulton Archive/Getty Images; 11 (b), Hulton-Deutsch Collection/Corbis; 11 (t), Bettmann/Corbis; 12 (t), Archivo Iconografico, S.A./Corbis; 13 (c), Bettmann/Corbis; 14, The Granger Collection, New York; 15, Wallace Seawell/MPTV; 16, Leif Skoogfors/Corbis; 17, Staffan Widstrand/Corbis; 18 (c,r), Bettmann/Corbis; 18 (bl) UIC Photographic Services; 19 (0), Bettmann/Corbis.

CHAPTER 2: Page 22, Michael Newman/PhotoEdit; 23, PhotoDisc; 24, Christie's Images/Corbis; 25(t), Christie's Images/Corbis; 25 (b), Joe McDonald/Corbis; 26 (tl), © Lonnie Duka/Index Stock Imagery, Inc.; 26 (tr), Corbis; 28, Annie Griffiths Belt/Corbis; 29, Bob Mitchell/Corbis; 30, Michael S. Yamashita/Corbis; 31, David & Peter Turnley/Corbis; 32, Wolfgang Kaehler/Corbis; 33 (t), Wolfgang Kaehler; 33 (c), Bettmann/Corbis; 34, Galen Rowell/Corbis; 35 (br), Fotos and Photos/Index Stock Imagery, Inc.; 35 (bl), Michael Schmelling/AP Photo; 36, Kevin Fleming/Corbis; 37, Mary Kate Denny/PhotoEdit; 39, John Dominis/Index Stock.

CHAPTER 3: Page 42, Michael Krasowitz/Getty Images; 43, Sam Dudgeon/HRW Photo; 44, AFP/Corbis; 45 (b), Michael Conroy/AP Photo; 45 (t), James P. Blair/Corbis; 46, Mark Richards/PhotoEdit; 47, Myrleen Ferguson Cate/PhotoEdit; 48, PhotoDisc; 50, Chris Trotman/Duomo/Corbis; 51, Michael Newman/PhotoEdit; 53, Michael S. Yamashita/Corbis; 54, Bettmann/Corbis; 55, Morrison Photography; 56 (bl), Bettmann/Corbis; 56 (br), Todd A. Gipstein/Corbis; 57, Bill Keane, Inc. Reprinted with special permission of King Features Syndicate; 58, LM Otero/AP Photo; 59, Burke/Triolo Productions/Getty Images; 61, Dennis Cook/AP Photo.

CHAPTER 4: Page 64, Bill Ross/Corbis; 65, Sam Dudgeon/HRW Photo; 66, Michael Newman/PhotoEdit; 67, Duomo/Corbis; 68, James Levin/Getty Images; 69, Gary W. Nolton/Getty Images; 70, 1998 Jan Eliot. Reprinted with permission of Universal Press Syndicate. All rights reserved.; 71 (l), Mary Kate Denny/PhotoEdit; 71 (br), Chip Henderson/Index Stock; 72, Henryk Kaiser/Index Stock; 73, Daniel Morrison/Index Stock; 74, Pablo Corral V/Corbis; 75, Lawrence Manning/Corbis; 78, Leif Skoogfors/Corbis; 79, Todd Gipstein/Corbis; 80, Mary Ann Chastain/AP Photo; 83, Jim McGuire/Index Stock, 84, Bill Melton/IndexStock; 85 (bl), Anna Clopet/Corbis; 85 (cr), Steven Peters/Getty Images; 85 (tr), Eye Ubiquitous/Corbis; 87, David Young-Wolff/PhotoEdit; 88, DILBERT reprinted by permission of United Feature Syndicate, Inc.; 89, Peter Byron/PhotoEdit; 91, The New Yorker Collection 1983, Jack Ziegler, from cartoonbank.com. All rights reserved.

UNIT 2: Page 94–5, Tony Freeman/PhotoEdit; 200, Dean Conger/Corbis; 201, Sam Dudgeon/HRW Photo.

CHAPTER 5: Page 96, Wolfgang Kaehler/Corbis; 97, Sam Dudgeon/HRW Photo; 99 (tl), AFP/Corbis; 99 (cl), Dennis Degnan/Corbis; 99 (bl), Henry Diltz/Corbis; 99 (r), AFP/Corbis; 100 (t), Archivo Iconografico, S.A./Corbis; 100 (b), O'Brien Productions/Corbis; 101, Paul Almasy/Corbis; 102, Hulton-Deutsch Collection/Corbis; 104, Tom Nebbia/Corbis; 105 (t), AFP/Corbis; 105 (cr), Galen Rowell/Corbis; 105 (bc), Charles & Josette Lenars/Corbis; 105 (b), Galen Rowell/Corbis; 106, Ted Spiegel/Corbis; 107, Michael Newman/PhotoEdit; 108, David Young-Wolff/PhotoEdit; 109, Myrleen Ferguson Cate/PhotoEdit; 110, PhotoDisc; 112, David Young-Wolff/PhotoEdit; 113 (t), Will Hart/PhotoEdit; 113 (b), Mary Kate Denny/PhotoEdit; 114, Bettmann/Corbis; 115, A. Ramey/PhotoEdit.

CHAPTER 6: Page 118, Chuck Savage/Corbis; 119, Sam Dudgeon/HRW Photo; 120, Vince Streano/Corbis; 121, Corbis; 122, Paul A. Souders/Corbis; 123 (t,b), David Young-Wolff/PhotoEdit; 125 (t), Bonnie Kamin/PhotoEdit; 125 (b), David Young-Wolff/PhotoEdit; 126, NOVASTOCK/PhotoEdit; 127, Bettmann/Corbis; 128, PhotoDisc; 129 (t), Minnesota Historical Society/Corbis; 129 (b), Ron Chapple/FPG International/Getty Images; 130, Sam Dudgeon/HRW Photo; 131, V.C.L/Getty Images/FPG International; 132 (br), David Davis/Index Stock; 133 (bl), Sam Dudgeon/HRW Photo; 133, Jim-Marshall Mantel/Corbis; 134, Joe McDonald/Corbis; 135, Reuters NewMedia Inc./Corbis; 136, Richard Hutchings/PhotoEdit; 137, Bettmann/Corbis; 139, Stringer/AP Photo; 140, Tony Freeman/PhotoEdit; 142 (tr), Mary Kate Denny/PhotoEdit; 144, Jack Fields/Corbis; 145 (t,b), Jack Fields/Corbis; 145 (bc), Douglas Peebles/Corbis.

CHAPTER 7: Page 148, Ronnen Eshel/Corbis; 149, Sam Dudgeon/HRW Photo; 150, Ronnie Kaufman/Corbis; 152 (b), 1982 by Nicole Hollander; 152 (t), Randy Miller/Corbis; 153, PhotoDisc; 154, Tim Brown/Index Stock; 155 (l), Robert Brenner/PhotoEdit; 155 (tr), Elena Rooraid/PhotoEdit; 155 (br), Tony Freeman/PhotoEdit; 158, Steve Kahn/Getty Images/FPG International; 159, Juan Silva Productions/Getty Images/The Image Bank; 160 (cl), Mary Kate Denny/PhotoEdit; 160 (bl), John Lamb/Getty Images/Stone; 160 (tr), Wides + Holl/Getty Images/FPG International; 160 (br), Ron Chapple/Getty Images/FPG International; 162, Sam Dudgeon/HRW Photo; 164 (l), Walter Hodges/Corbis; 164 (tc), Gary Braasch/Corbis; 164 (bc), Pat O'Hara/Corbis; 164 (c), Dean Conger/Corbis; 165, Jay Syverson/Corbis; 167, Ed Young/Corbis; 168 (b), Todd Gipstein/Corbis; 168 (tr), Annie Griffiths Belt/Corbis; 170 (bl), Bob Krist/Corbis; 170 (t), Charles E. Rotkin/Corbis; 171, Morrison Photography.

CHAPTER 8: Page 174, Patricia McDonnell/AP Photo; 175, Sam Dudgeon/HRW Photo; 176, David Lees/Getty Images/FPG International; 177, Joseph Sohm; ChromoSohm Inc./Corbis; 178, Bettmann/Corbis; 179 (b), Zits Partnership. Reprinted with special permission of King Features Syndicate.; 179 (t), Raymond Gehman/Corbis; 180, Leif Skoogfors/Corbis; 181 (tl), David & Peter Turnley/Corbis; 181 (tr), AFP/Corbis; 182, Annie Griffiths Belt/Corbis; 184, Bettmann/Corbis; 190, Jeff Greenberg/PhotoEdit; 191, Doug Mills/AP Photo; 193 (t), Bettmann/Corbis; 193 (b), Scott Audette/AP Photo; 194, Tony Gutierrez/AP Photo; 195, Ed Kashi/AP Photo; 197, Spencer Grant/PhotoEdit.

UNIT 3: Page 202–3, Spencer Grant/PhotoEdit; 290, Archive Photos; 291, Sam Dudgeon/HRW Photo.

CHAPTER 9: Page 204, Sandro Vannini/Corbis; 205, Sam Dudgeon/HRW Photo; 206, Michael S. Lewis/Corbis; 207 (tl), Earl & Nazima Kowall/Corbis; 207 (tr), Sheldan Collins/Corbis; 208 (bc), Mitchell Gerber/Corbis; 208 (bl), Roger Ressmeyer/Corbis; 208 (br), Tony Freeman/Corbis; 211, Amy E. Conn/AP Photo; 212, Jacques M. Chenet/Corbis; 215 (br), Dave G. Houser/Hearst Castle/CA Park Service/Corbis; 215 (bc), Paul A. Souders/Corbis; 215 (bl), Lynn Goldsmith/Corbis; 216 (b), Roger Ressmeyer/Corbis; 216 (br), Joel W. Rogers/Corbis; 217, Morton Beebe, S.F/Corbis; 218, Ryan McVay/Getty Images/PhotoDisc; 219, Ben Margot/AP Photo; 220, David J. Phillip/AP Photo; 223, Owen Franken/Corbis; 224, Ric Feld/AP Photo; 225 (tl), Eric Draper/AP Photo; 225 (tr), Corbis; 225 (b), Owen Franken/Corbis; 226 (t), Danny Johnston/AP Photo; 226 (b), Charles Gupton/Getty Images/Stone.

CHAPTER 10: Page 227, Michael S. Green/AP Photo; 231, ImageState; 232 (b), Mug Shots/Corbis Stock Market; 232 (b), Sam Dudgeon/HRW Photo; 233 (tr), David Young-Wolff/PhotoEdit; 233 (tl), A. Ramey/PhotoEdit; 233 (cr), Gunter Marx Photography/Corbis; 233 (cl), Lawrence Migdale/Getty Images/Stone; 234, Jeff Greenberg/PhotoEdit; 235, Robert Garvey/Corbis; 236, Mary Kate Denny/PhotoEdit; 237, Dave Martin/AP Photo; 238 (b), Bettmann/Corbis; 239, Bettmann/Corbis; 241, Max Nash/AP Photo; 242 (t), The Granger Collection, New York; 242 (c), Corbis; 243 (t), Carl & Ann Purcell/Corbis; 243 (b), Rudi Von Briel/PhotoEdit; 244 (t), Robert Maass/Corbis; 244 (cl), James A. Sugar/Corbis; 245, Bettmann/Corbis; 246, Michael St. Maur Sheil/Corbis; 247, Rodney White/AP Photo; 250 (tr), Jonathan Nourok/PhotoEdit; 250 (tl), Doug Mills/AP Photo; 251, David Young-Wolff/PhotoEdit; 253, Gary Conner/PhotoEdit; 254 (b), Tony Freeman/PhotoEdit; 254 (bl), Bonnie Kamin/PhotoEdit; 255 (b), Mark Gibson/Corbis; 256, Joseph Sohm; ChromoSohm/Corbis; 257, Rudi Von Briel/PhotoEdit.

CHAPTER 11: Page 260, Anne Powell/Index Stock; 262, Archive Photos/PictureQuest; 262, Sam Dudgeon/HRW Photo; 263, Tiziana and Gianni Baldizzone/Corbis; 264 (br), Joseph Sohm; ChromoSohm Inc./Corbis; 264 (bl), David Young-Wolff/PhotoEdit; 265, Richard Hutchings/PhotoEdit; 266, Roger Ressmeyer/Corbis; 267 (c), Robert Caputo/Aurora; 267 (tr), Duomo/Corbis; 267 (bl), Lonnie Duka/Index Stock; 268, The Granger Collection, New York; 270 (bl), Reuters NewMedia Inc./Corbis; 270 (br), Gary Conner/Index Stock; 271 (t), Dennis Cook/AP Photo; 272, Donna Day/Getty Images/Stone; 274, Owen Franken/Corbis; 275 (t), Gail Oskin/AP Photo; 275 (b), Spencer Grant/PhotoEdit; 276, Jose Carillo/PhotoEdit; 277, Jonathan Nourok/PhotoEdit; 280 (bl), Terry Vine/Getty Images/Stone; 280 (br), Richard T. Nowitz/Corbis; 282 (t), Matthew Borkoski/Index stock; 283 (bl), Walter Hodges/Corbis; 285, Tom McCarthy/PhotoEdit; 287, Wally McNamee/Corbis; 289, 2000, The Washington Post Writers Group. Reprinted with permission.

UNIT 4: Page 292–3, Paul Conklin/PhotoEdit; 400, U.S. Army Photograph; 401, Sam Dudgeon/HRW Photo.

CHAPTER 12: Page 293 (br), News & Observer, Jim Bounds/AP Photo; 294, Lawrence Sawyer/Index Stock; 295, Sam Dudgeon/HRW Photo; 296, Tom McCarthy/PhotoEdit; 297 (tr), David Young-Wolff /PhotoEdit; 297 (tl), Catherine Karnow/Corbis; 298–9 (b), Richard T. Nowitz/Corbis; 298, Marc Garanger/Corbis; 299 (t), Roger Wood/Corbis; 299 (cr), Christine Osborne/Corbis; 300, Earl & Nazima Kowall/Corbis; 301, Branson Reynolds/Index Stock; 302 (bl), Bill Aron/PhotoEdit; 302 (br), Myrleen Ferguson Cate/PhotoEdit; 303, Paul Barton/Corbis StockMarket; 304 (t), Alison Wright/Corbis; 305, Ewing Galloway/Index Stock; 306 (tl), Owen Franken/Corbis; 306(tr), Charles Rex Arbogast/AP Photo; 306 (c), Robert Brenner/PhotoEdit; 307, Michael Newman/PhotoEdit; 309, Michael Newman/PhotoEdit; 310, STAHLER reprinted by permission of United Feature Syndicate, Inc., and Newspaper Enterprise Association, Inc.; 313, David Young-Wolff/PhotoEdit; 314, Ryan McVay/Getty Images; 316, Tony Freeman/PhotoEdit; 317, Paul Conklin/PhotoEdit.

CHAPTER 13: Page 320, Charles O'Rear/Corbis; 321, Sam Dudgeon/HRW Photo; 322, David Harry Stewart/Getty Images/Stone; 323, (tr), Ecoscene/Corbis; 323 (cr), Paul A. Souders/Corbis; 323 (tl), Jan Butchofsky-Houser/Corbis; 324 (tl), Ron Watts/Corbis; 324 (tr), Macduff Everton/Corbis; 324 (cr), Chuck Fishman/Getty Images; 325, Bettmann/Corbis; 326 (tl), Rudi Von Briel/PhotoEdit; 326 (tr), Bettmann/Corbis; 327, Brett Coomer/AP Photo; 328 (bl), Dallas and John Heaton/Corbis; 328 (c), Reuters NewMedia Inc./Corbis; 328 (br), Bettmann/Corbis; 329, Monika Graff/AP Photo; 330, John Slater/Corbis; 332, Nati Harnik/AP Photo; 333, FPG International/Getty Images; 334, Bettmann/Corbis; 335 (tl), Murad Sezer/AP Photo; 335 (tr), AFP/Corbis; 336, Hulton-Deutsch Collection/Corbis; 337, Hulton Archive by Getty Images; 338 (tl,tr), Wally McNamee/Corbis; 339, Bettmann/Corbis; 340, Achmad Ibrahim/AP Photo; 341 (tl), Sam Dudgeon/HRW Photo; 341 (tr), The White House Collection, © White House Historical Association and The National Archives and Records Administration; 344, TK; 345, Ric Feld/AP Photo; 347, 1991, Jeff Koterba, Omaha World Herald. Reprinted by permission.

CHAPTER 14: Page 348, Spencer Platt/Getty Images; 349, Sam Dudgeon/HRW Photo; 350, Jonathan Blair/Corbis; 351 (bl), Chip Henderson/Index Stock; 351 (br), PhotoDisc; 352, Itsuo Inouye/AP Photo; 353 (tl), Zephyr Picture/Index Stock; 353 (tr), Steve Wanke/Index Stock; 354, Robert Garvey/Corbis; 357, THE BUCKETS reprinted by permission of United Feature Syndicate, Inc.; 358, Reprinted by permission of Milt Priggee.; 359, Mark Foley/AP Photo; 360 (tr), Tim Martin/AP Photo; 360 (tl), Michael Newman/PhotoEdit; 361, Cleve Bryant/PhotoEdit; 362 (c), AFP/Corbis; 362 (br), Ted Spiegel/Corbis; 362 (bl), Nathan Benn/Corbis; 362 (cl), SuperStock; 363, Bettmann/Corbis; 364 (tr), Christine Osborne/Corbis; 364 (tc), Tim Wright/Corbis; 364 (tl), Nik Wheeler/Corbis; 365, Canadian Museum of Civilization/Corbis; 366 (br), Lee Snider; Lee Snider/Corbis; 366 (bl), Index Stock/Scott Berner; 366 (cr), Index Stock/Rick Strange; 367, Joe Raedle/Getty Images; 368 (bl), Adam M. Bettcher/AP Photo; 368 (br), Elise Amendola/AP Photo; 368 (c), Kelly-Mooney Photography/AP Photo; 369 (bl), Stephanie Maze/Corbis; 369 (br), Jules T. Allen/AP Photo; 369 (tr), Richard T. Nowitz/AP Photo; 370, Michael Newman/PhotoEdit; 371, Laura Dwight/Corbis.

CHAPTER 15: Page 374, Corbis; 375, Sam Dudgeon/HRW Photo; 376, Bettmann/Corbis; 377 (bl), Bettmann/Corbis; 377 (cr), SuperStock; 377 (br), The Art Archive/Egyptian Museum Cairo/Dagli Orti; 378 (tl), Richard T. Nowitz/Corbis; 378 (cr), Doug Martin/Photo Resources; 378 (tr), Richard T. Nowitz/Corbis; 379, PhotoDisc; 380 (tr), From THE MARTIAN CHRONICLES (Bantam Ed: Jacket cover) by RayBradbury, copyright 1946, 1948, 1950, 1958 by Ray Bradbury. Copyright renewed 1977 by Ray Bradbury. Used by permission of Bantam Books, a division of Random House, Inc. The Michael Barson Collection / PastPerfect/ PRC Archive. Photo by Rob Huntley/Lightstreamsource: PRC Archive; 380 (tl), The Martian Way by Isaac Asimov, 1955, Signet Books; 381 (t), Hulton Archive by Getty Images; 381 (b), Michael Newman/PhotoEdit; 382 (t), H. Morgan/Photo Researchers, Inc.; 383 (tc), Jacob Halaska/Index Stock; 383 (tl), Yann Arthus-Bertrand/Corbis; 383 (b), Corbis; 385, Hulton-Deutsch Collection/Corbis; 386, The Art Archive/Egyptian Museum Cairo /Dagli Orti; 387 (cr), Bettmann/Corbis; 387 (br), B.C. Moller/Getty Images/FPG International; 388, Smith Richard Frank/Corbis Sygma; 389, Mitchell Gerber/Corbis; 390, Noel Laura/Corbis Sygma; 392, David Young-Wolff/PhotoEdit; 394, Raoul Minsart/Corbis; 395, HI & LOIS reprinted with special permission of King Features Syndicate.; 396 (t), Stewart Cohen/Getty Images/Stone; 396 (cl), The Image Bank/Getty Images/David Paul Productions.

UNIT 5: Page 402–03, Joseph Sohm; ChromoSohm Inc./CORBIS; 482, Woodfin Camp & Associates, Inc.; 483, Sam Dudgeon/HRW Photo.

CHAPTER 16: Page 404, Reuters NewMedia Inc./Corbis; 405, Sam Dudgeon/HRW Photo; 408 (bl), Richard T. Nowitz/Corbis; 408 (br), Joseph Sohm; ChromoSohm Inc./Corbis; 409 (tl), AFP/Corbis; 409 (tr), Bettmann/Corbis; 415, Bettmann/Corbis; 416 (t), Reuters NewMedia Inc./Corbis; 416 (b), Rhoda Sidney/PhotoEdit; 417 (br), Ted Spiegel/Corbis; 417 (b), Walter Bibikow/FPG International LLC; 418, Alain Le Garsmeur/Corbis; 419, Reuters NewMedia Inc./Corbis; 421, Charles & Josette Lenars/Corbis; 422 (tr), Corbis Images; 422 (tl), Geoffrey Clements/Corbis; 425, TK; 426, Bettmann/Corbis; 427, James A. Sugar/Corbis; 428, A. Ramey/PhotoEdit; 429, Kit Kittle/Corbis; 430, Sandy Felsenthal/Corbis; 431, Karen Vibert-Kennedy, San Francisco Examiner/AP Photo.

CHAPTER 17: Page 434, Darren Robb/Getty Images/FPG Interantional; 435, Sam Dudgeon/HRW Photo; 436, Elis Years/Getty Images/FPG International; 437 (b), Judy Griesedieck/Corbis; 437 (cr), Rick Stewart/Getty Images/Allsport Concepts; 438 (tl), Bettmann/Corbis; 438 (tr), Florida Times-Union, Stuart Tannehill/AP Photo; 439, Branson Reynolds/Index Stock; 440 (br), Hulton-Deutsch Collection/Corbis; 440 (bl), TIME Inc./Courtesy of the general libraries, The University of Texas at Austin/HRW photo by Victoria Smith.; 440 (bc), PhotoDisc; 441, The Advertising Archive Ltd.; 442 (bl,br), Courtesy of National Fluid Milk Processor Promotion Board; 445, Jeff Bray/Index Stock; 446, David J. & Janice L. Frent Collection/Corbis; 446, Thomas E. Franklin/The Record (Bergen County, NJ)/Corbis/SABA; 447 (bl), AFP/Corbis; 447 (br), Carl D. Walsh/Aurora Photo; 448, Michael Newman/PhotoEdit; 449, Corbis-Bettmann; 450, Art Resource, NY; 451 (bl), Rick Bowmer/AP Photo; 451 (c), The Granger Collection, New York; 451 (br), Corbis-Bettmann; 451 (cr), UPI/Corbis-Bettmann; 452, UPI/Corbis-Bettmann; 453, Darren McCollester/Getty Images; 455, AFP/Corbis; 456, Antonio Mo/Getty Images/FPG International; 457, Bettmann/Corbis.

CHAPTER 18: Page 460, Richard T. Nowitz/Corbis; 461, Sam Dudgeon/HRW Photo; 462, Carl & Ann Purcell/Corbis; 463 (t), Roger Wood/Corbis; 463 (cr), Dallas and John Heaton/Corbis; 464, Archivo Iconografico, S.A./Corbis; 465 (tl), The Art Archive; 465 (cl), Historical Picture Archive/Corbis; 465 (tr), Cordaiy Photo Library Ltd./Corbis; 466 (b), Richard Cummins/Corbis; 467, Inge Yspeert/Corbis; 468, Jeff Widener/AP Photo; 469, Bettmann/Corbis; 470, A. Ramey/PhotoEdit; 471, Richard Stockton/Index Stock; 473 (t), Tom Hanson/AP Photo; 473 (c), Luis Romero/AP Photo; 474 (br), George Hall/Corbis; 474 (bl), Adrian Arbib/Corbis; 474–5 (b), Owen Franken/Corbis; 475 (r), Joseph Sohm; ChromoSohm Inc./Corbis; 475 (c), Int. Monetaire Europeen/Corbis Sygma; 476, Paul Almasy/Corbis; 477, Annie Griffiths Belt/Corbis; 478 (bl), Richard Cummins/Corbis; 478 (t), Elizabeth Whiting & Associates/Corbis; 478 (br), Hulton-Deutsch Collection/Corbis; 478 (bc), Corbis; 479, TK.

BACKMATTER: TIMELINE—Page R1 (bc), Hulton-Deutsch Collection/Corbis; R1 (tc), Bettmann/Corbis; R1 (br), The Granger Collection, New York; R1 (cl), UIC Photographic Services; R1 (bl), Hulton Archive/Getty Images; R1 (t), Art Resource, NY; R1 (cl), Bettmann/Corbis; R1 (tr), Bettmann/Corbis; APPENDIX—484, Jeff Bray/Index Stock.

Illustrations
Organizational charts, flowcharts, graphs, and icons created by Preface, Inc.